NOV 0 8 2000

NOV 0 8 2000

D0211893

NOV 0 8 2000

NOV 0 8 2000

Encyclopedia of

GERMAN LITERATURE

Volume 2
J–Z

Encyclopedia of

GERMAN LITERATURE

Volume 2
J–Z

MATTHIAS KONZETT

Editor

Fitzroy Dearborn Publishers
Chicago and London

Copyright © 2000 by
FITZROY DEARBORN PUBLISHERS

All rights reserved including the right of reproduction in whole or in part in any form.
For information write to:

FITZROY DEARBORN PUBLISHERS
919 N. Michigan Avenue, Suite 760
Chicago, Illinois 60611
USA

or

FITZROY DEARBORN PUBLISHERS
310 Regent Street
London W1R 5AJ
England

British Library and Library of Congress Cataloging in Publication Data are available.

ISBN 1-57958-138-2

First published in the USA and UK 2000

Index prepared by AEIOU Inc., Pleasantville, New York
Typeset by Sheridan Books Inc., Ann Arbor, Michigan
Printed by Sheridan Books Inc., Ann Arbor, Michigan
Cover design by Chicago Advertising and Design, Chicago, Illinois

Cover illustration: Gabriele Münter, *Zuhören*, 1909 © 1999 Artists Rights Society (ARS),
New York/VG Bild-Kunst, Bonn

CONTENTS

ALPHABETICAL LIST OF ENTRIES

ALPHABETICAL
LIST OF WORKS

J

Urs Jaeggi 1931–

Urs Jaeggi gained prominence simultaneously as a literary and a scholarly writer during the 1960s. Then a young professor of sociology, he was an important voice of the 1960s movement and a mentor of student leader-activist Rudi Dutschke. By 1969, Jaeggi was well known for a volume of short stories, two novels, and an influential sociological study, *Macht und Herrschaft in der Bundesrepublik* (1969). West Germany was to remain the country of his life and career. Jaeggi was close to the Dortmund "Group 61" (literature of the worker's world) and became a prominent theorist of *Literatursoziologie* (the sociology of literature). With this background, Jaeggi's literary themes were anti-establishment and highly critical of bourgeois society and politics, and they evolved into an opus seeking alternative thought and lifestyles and the emancipation of the individual from societal, political, and aesthetic constraints.

Adding a third area to literary and scholarly writing, Jaeggi early on branched out into the world of visual arts, with a first museum exhibition of paintings and object art in 1985 and regular ones since then. Diversification of his talents did not aid a smooth reception, particularly since this writer-artist is avant-garde in all three fields. Breaking out of conventions and prescribed or stereotypical social roles has been Jaeggi's direction in theory and in practice, and critics have not always been willing to follow this artist to the forefront of experimentation. Jaeggi's prose works have been well received, however, and most of them have been republished.

The protagonist in *Die Komplicen* (1964; Accomplices) leaves his family and profession and becomes an outsider to experience alternative living. The ensuing life's journey in book form develops as a modern-day picaresque novel, setting the pattern for subsequent ones. Most of Jaeggi's protagonists oscillate between established and alternate lifestyles: they are at one time engaged in contemporary happenings and yet distanced; they "belong" and yet they are strangers. These literary figures are truly undecided—for them, there are always various positions from which to view the world, points and counterpoints to consider, and reasons and counterarguments for everything; unequivocal solutions cannot be found. Thus, Jaeggi has been portraying man in his postmodern condition long before this trend became defined and fashionable. While it is a sign of their questing and questioning, the very wavering and even questionableness of his characters have sometimes been mistaken and criticized as a lit-erary shortcoming. The possibility of otherness, of being contrary to expectations, or being of hard to define character, emerged as surrealistic and sometimes scurrile or farcical, especially in the short stories (*Die Wohltaten des Mondes* [1963; The Good Deeds of the Moon]). In the later work, the surrealist tendency is gradually replaced by realistic components that strengthen the portrayal of the protagonist's suffering. In *Ein Mann geht vorbei* (1968; A Man Passes By), *Brandeis* (1978; Brandeis), and *Grundrisse* (1981; Ground-Plans), the main figure meets with a major life crisis, which increasingly conveys the message that society, not the individual, is out of joint, and that the two clash because of incompatible differences.

In *Brandeis*, the protagonist is extremely exposed and vulnerable. Only after a complete mental and physical breakdown can Brandeis begin anew and overcome the personal crisis, which has resulted from societal and political ills. This work has often been called the most important novel of the student movement. Partly autobiographical, it is set in Germany and New York, where the author taught at the New School for Social Research. Brandeis, a sociology professor (married, one child) had previously taught at Berne, Bochum, and Berlin, where he found himself caught between representing student interests and alienating his colleagues and the administration, while at the same time maintaining a critical stand opposite student demands and stereotypical thought. For some, he is an outsider, for others a *Scheißliberaler* ("liberal at all cost"). He suffers a breakdown in New York, which is triggered but not caused by additional tension over the Vietnam War and his firsthand experience of the violence and destitution of the big city. A character such as Brandeis cannot but go into crisis: intellectually and emotionally he is deeply sympathetic to a justified social revolution, but he cannot bring theory and practice together; he cannot effect change, and therefore becomes ill.

Grundrisse follows as a reckoning with the social and environmental politics of the 1970s in Germany and their international repercussions, and it opens out to a utopian vision via the emergence of several strong female characters. The new women's movement of the 1970s is visible in this novel as a literary expression of the force of women in society, a subject Jaeggi had researched in scholarly, sociological papers as early as 1963. Some of these findings appear in his essay collection *Versuch über den Verrat* (1984; The Shadow of Betrayal). In the passages on feminism, the author mentally converses with famed women of literature, film, and cultural theory, discussing gender division and the possibilities for a more just society. Two more novels followed after a time of more theoretical work and the finishing up of an academic career in the mid–1980s. The title figure of *Rimpler* (1987) represents yet another *Aussteiger* (drop out), this time at the end of his career from the start of the novel. In this novel, leaving is neither voluntary nor reversible; Rimpler has become ill and finds himself in psychiatric treatment. As a policeman he had stood on the opposite side of rioting youths—his own daughter among them. The narrative consists of therapeutic talks between patient and doctor, constituting yet another literary treatment of intolerable societal conditions within the conventional system.

Soulthorn (1990) is a journey home, from Berlin to the author's birthplace Solothurn in Switzerland, and it is a rapprochement between different aspects of self. After the professional leaves the academy, many *Aussteiger*-stories later, he approaches his true calling: the artist as a free agent. The I of the first person narrative blends more than ever with the author. Painter Kocher visits "Soulthorn," his love-hate and the site of pain and joy. Talking to his woman friend, he shows her the town as his place of origin, of his intellectual and artistic beginnings and returns. At the same time it is a story of the end of the relationship, as the artist frees himself more and more from all ties. It is the time in which, in real life, the author increasingly moved from the written word to the visual arts, without, however, abandoning letters altogether. At this time, aesthetic essays and treatises as well as lyrical texts for performance with sound all appear. In discussing his own work, Jaeggi has explained that it seems sensible not to ask, "is it art?" but to see to it that experience is transformed in rich and convincing ways.

Newspapers and magazines routinely review critically Jaeggi's literary output, his public readings and performances, and his art exhibitions. Some critics see a weakness of expression in Jaeggi's style of imperfection, which resists the definition of a direction; others see this as intentional. If his language appears spontaneous, unrefined, and without careful polishing, it also seems like a rebellion against the assumption that art should achieve perfection, like an attempt at exploding plan and form from within by way of a flood of perceptions, thoughts, and emotions. This realization about the work of Urs Jaeggi was evident in the presentations given at the Jaeggi Symposium (Universität Bern, 1996). In *Das Heiße und das Kalte: Kunst und Gesellschaft* (1997; The Hot and the Cold: Art and Society), contributors speaking on diverse yet intertwined subjects such as sociology, literature, feminism, and art agreed that Jaeggi the artist produces pure art about our impure existence.

IRMGARD HUNT

Biography

Born in Solothurn, Switzerland, 23 June 1931. Studied at the University of Bern; Ph.D. in sociology, 1959; in the writer's union from 1965; involved in the 1960s movement; researcher at Dortmund, 1960; teacher, from 1961, at the universities of Bern, Bochum, Berlin, and (1970–71) the New School for Social Research, New York; lecture tour in Ivory Coast, Ghana, Nigeria, and Cameroon, 1989; freelance writer and artist in Berlin since 1993. Literature Prize, City of Bern, 1963; Literature Prize, City of Berlin, 1964; Literary Prize, Canton of Bern, 1978; Ingeborg Bachmann Prize, Klagenfurt, 1981; Art Prize, Canton of Solothurn, 1987; German writers' (VS) representation in Australia, 1995; Swiss Literary Archives establish Jaeggi archive of his literary and scholarly manuscripts, 1996; Art Prize Vienna, 1997. Currently lives in Berlin.

Selected Works

Collections
Was auf den Tisch kommt, wird gegessen (essays), 1981
Versuch über den Verrat (essays), 1984; translated in excerpts as *The Shadow of Betrayal,* 1987
Fazil und Johanna (short stories), 1985

Poetry
Heicho, with graphics by Schang Hutter, 1985
SchiZaro (poem on wood), 1987
Pulsion, 1995
D&G, with John Kinsella, 1996

Fiction
Die Wohltaten des Mondes, 1963
Die Komplicen, 1964
Ein Mann geht vorbei, 1968
Geschichten über uns, 1973
Brandeis, 1978
Grundrisse, 1981
Rimpler (RIAS radio play, 1986), 1987
Soulthorn, 1990

Other
Die gesellschaftliche Elite, 1960
Der Soziologe, 1966
Der Vietnamkrieg und die Presse, 1967
Ordnung und Chaos: Strukturalismus als Methode und Mode, 1968
Macht und Herrschaft in der Bundesrepublik, 1969
Für und wider die revolutionäre Ungeduld, 1972
Literatur und Politik, 1972
Kopf und Hand: Das Verhältnis von Gesellschaft und Bewußtsein (with Manfred Faßler), 1982

Edited Work
Geist und Katastrophe: Studien zur Soziologie im Nationalsozialismus, 1983

Further Reading

Althaus, Gabriele, et al., editors, *Avanti Dilettanti: Über die Kunst, Experten zu widersprechen,* Berlin: Metropol, 1992
Hiekisch-Picard, Sepp, and Peter Spielmann, editors, *Urs Jaeggi: Figuren,* Zurich: Arche, 1991
Hunt, Irmgard E., *Urs Jaeggi: Eine Werkbiographie,* New York: Lang, 1993
Trübner, Peter, editor, *Das Heiße und das Kalte: Kunst und Gesellschaft,* Bern: Lang, 1997

Ernst Jandl 1925–

Ernst Jandl is the most celebrated and the most enduring exponent of a form of experimental poetry based upon language manipulation, usually termed concrete poetry, which emerged in the
1950s, initially through the work of the Swiss author Eugen
Gomringer, and later through the work of the Wiener Gruppe
(Viennese Group), which was formed by authors such as H.C.
Artmann, Gerhard Rühm, Konrad Bayer, Oswald Wiener, and
Friedrich Achleitner. Disillusioned with the literary atmosphere
in Austria and heirs to that language skepticism that characterizes the modern Austrian tradition, these writers rejected conventional forms and sought to establish a new cultural tradition
by looking back to those artists who had previously been dismissed as "degenerate"—the Expressionists, the Dadaists, and
the surrealists—to try to establish a continuity that went beyond
the immediate fascist past and the conservative contemporary
social atmosphere, and to generate a new literary avant-garde.

Although never formally a member of the Wiener Gruppe,
Jandl drew much inspiration from their activities and the historical models they emulated—poets such as the Expressionist August Stramm, the Dadaists Hans Arp and Kurt Schwitters, or
Gertrude Stein—and he refined these models in order to develop
his own distinctive style of experimental poetry. His work lacks
the abstract theoretical approach that forms the basis of the
Wiener Gruppe (much of which is only accessible through their
theory) and is far more pragmatic, but it shares essential features
with their work. Jandl stressed the principle of language as "raw
material" rather than as a descriptive tool: the poems are themselves objects and not statements about objects. For Jandl, this
new poetry was "concrete" because it realizes possibilities within language and makes objects out of language. Form is, then,
not a means of expressing content but is itself content since the
individual poem does not describe but shows or demonstrates.
In this, Jandl's work reflects the crisis of language and the language skepticism that have become pervasive features of 20th-
century Austrian literature and thought, not least through the
influence of Ludwig Wittgenstein. This poetry is self-referential
in the sense that its subject matter is its own medium, yet with
Jandl's poems one has more than autotelic linguistic structures.
Certainly, some of the poems are simply a humorous manipulation or destruction of linguistic material that seem ends in themselves, but the majority use linguistic manipulation to make a
statement that is more than self-referential.

Although committed to experimental poetry from the first,
Jandl could initially only find a publisher for the more conventional verse of the collection *Andere Augen* (1956; Other Eyes),
which, even though characterized by the avoidance of metaphor
or simile and the marked influence of William Carlos Williams's
poetry in its linguistic reductionism, does not employ the linguistic manipulation that is the key feature of Jandl's concrete
poetry. Thematically, the poems are a skeptically distanced observation of life through the everyday, dwelling on hunger, cold,
poverty, illness, and the self, with a tendency to the macabre;
these are also the recurrent motifs in all Jandl's poetry.

Subsequently, he turned to radical experimentation and published the first major collection in 1966 under the title *Laut und
Luise*. This and the two later collections, *sprechblasen* (1970;
speech bubbles) and *der künstliche baum* (1970; the artificial

tree), indicate the variety of methods that Jandl was to employ in
his verse: visual poems, puns and word games, collages, permu-
tations, sound shifts, speaking texts, foreign language gags, and
notes for acoustic experiments. Some poems explore the exuber-
ant richness of dialect, some are pure sound poems of the
Schwitters variety, others are grotesque linguistic inventions on
the Christian Morgenstern model, and others are in the style of
the Baroque figure poem. In such verse Jandl conducts an exploration of language that exemplifies the full range of techniques
employed in concrete poetry, in that the poems embrace the semantic, the phonetic, and the visual.

Above all, Jandl is best known for his *Sprechgedichte* (spoken
poems), which require an oral delivery to realize their full potential, and which Jandl has popularized through recorded performances of his work. The most famous is "schtzngrmm," a
reduced form of "Schützengraben" (trench); the vowels have
been removed because, as Jandl observed, the war does not sing.
The poem takes the basic phonological elements of the word and
uses them to create a sound picture of the battlefield, ending
with "t-tt" to suggest "tot" (dead).

Such *Sprechgedichte* also form the core of *sprechblasen*, which
again demonstrates a variety of techniques and a complex relationship between the semantic level and the text structure. These
poems often make parodic reference to the classical poetic canon
and frequently allude to the Nazi period and the suffering of
war.

Although famous for the humor of his verse and his playful
destruction of language, Jandl is not only a linguist clown or jug-
gler; he also produced the more traditional poems of *dingfest*
(1973; *thingsure*), which contains a wide variety of poems written between 1952 and 1968. The title is itself the thematic core
of the poems: *Dinge* (objects or situations) become "fixed" (*fest*)
through language. The verbal sign attached to the object is not
the object, and the syntactical relationship between signs is not
the world. Some poems simply state this proposition; by disrupting or dissolving the linguistic form, others demonstrate the
chimerical nature of language. Throughout the collection there is
the recurrent reflection of, and on, the immobility of the linguistic form that creates social stasis, and this is juxtaposed with
simple statements of the transience of individual human existence. This theme of cultural and existential pessimism is one
that marks the whole of Jandl's work, with the latter dominating
in the later verse.

In these later poems, such as the collections *die bearbeitung
der mütze* (1978; Processing the Cap) and *der gelbe hund* (1980;
The Yellow Dog), more extreme experimentation is replaced by
a form of simplified and grammatically incorrect German, referred to as *Gastarbeiterdeutsch* (language of the immigrant
workers), which in its ungrammaticality makes the language
rather than its users alien and places the linguistic barrier between word and world to illuminate the relative validity of language structures.

For Jandl, linguistic poetry is more than anarchic individualism and is intended as an emancipation from the historical and
social determinism of linguistic convention. Experimentation
with language is, for Jandl, a statement of freedom in its deviation from the standardized and manipulated social norms of the

contemporary world. While much so-called concrete poetry is often considered trivial ephemera, Jandl's innovative work has a lasting quality that is intellectually challenging and rewards continued study.

MALCOLM READ

Biography

Born in Vienna, Austria, 1925. Studied German and English literature; worked for many years as a teacher at a gymnasium in Vienna; in the United States as a guest professor at the University of Texas, Austin, 1971. Received numerous awards, including the Heinrich Kleist Prize (Berlin) and the Friedrich Hölderlin Prize (Homburg). Married to the Austrian poet Friederike Mayröcker.

Selected Works

Collections
Gesammelte Werke, 1985
Poetische Werke, edited by Klaus Siblewski, 1997

Poetry
Andere Auge, 1956
Laut und Luise, 1966
der künstliche baum: gedichte, 1970
sprechblasen: gedichte, 1970
die männer, 1973
dingfest: gedichte, 1973; as *thingsure*, translated by Michael Hamburger, 1997
serienfuss, 1974
Die schöne Kunst des Schreibens, 1976
die bearbeitung der mütze: gedichte, 1978
Aus der Fremde: Sprechoper in 7 Szenen, 1980
der gelbe hund: gedichte, 1980
selbstportrait des schachspielers als trinkende uhr: gedichte, 1983
Das Öffnen und Schließen des Mundes. Frankfurter Poetik-Vorlesung, 1985
idyllen: gedichte, 1989
das röcheln der mona lisa: gedichte szene prosa, 1990
stanzen, 1992
lechts und rinks: gedichte, statements, peppermints, 1995
peter und die kuh: gedichte, 1996

Further Reading

Abraham, Werner, "Das Konzept der 'projektiven Sprache' bei Ernst Jandl," *Deutsche Vierteljahrsschrift für Literaturwissenschaft und Geistesgeschichte* 56 (1982)
Berger, Albert, "Ernst Jandl," in *Die deutsche Lyrik von 1945 bis 1975*, edited by Klaus Weissenberger, Düsseldorf: Bagel, 1981
Butler, Michael, "From the 'Wiener Gruppe' to Ernst Jandl," in *Modern Austrian Writing*, edited by Alan Best and Hans Wolfschütz, London: Wolff, and Totowa, New Jersey: Barnes and Noble, 1980
Hage, Volker, "Rückblick auf die konkrete Poesie: Ernst Jandl and Gerhard Rühm," in *Die Wiederkehr des Erzählers: Neue deutsche Literatur der siebziger Jahre*, Frankfurt: Ullstein, 1982
Kaukoreit, Volker, and Kristin Pfoder-Schewig, editors, *Ernst Jandl*, Munich: Text und Kritik, 1996
König, Fritz, "Ernst Jandl and Concrete Poetry," in *Major Figures of Contemporary Austrian Literature*, edited by Donald G. Daviau, New York: Lang, 1987
Murdoch, Brian, and Malcolm Read, "An Approach to the Poetry of Ernst Jandl," *New German Studies* 5, no. 3 (1977)

Jean Paul (Johann Paul Friedrich Richter) 1763–1825

Johann Paul Friedrich Richter burst upon the literary scene in 1795 with the publication of the novel *Hesperus; oder, 45 Hundsposttage: Eine Biographie* (*Hesperus; or, Forty-five Dog-Post-Days: A Biography*). He was then 32 years old and had published collections of satires and another novel, *Die unsichtbare Loge* (1793; *The Invisible Lodge*). *Hesperus* marked him as a humorous narrator in the manner of Laurence Sterne, who alternated between humorous and satirical scenes on the one hand and sublime and sentimental scenes of friendship and love on the other. For his first novel, *The Invisible Lodge*, Richter had created the narrator figure of "Jean Paul," translating his first names "Johann Paul" into French out of admiration for "Jean Jacques" (Rousseau). A large audience of enthusiastic fans, especially women, immediately identified this "Jean Paul" with the author Richter, which contributed to his typical play with reality and fictionality.

Jean Paul, like Schiller and Fichte, was born between the Goethe generation of the Sturm und Drang and that of the early Romantics. Nevertheless, Jean Paul remained aloof from all literary groups or "schools." Histories of German literature treat Jean Paul as a special case "between *Klassik* and Romanticism," together with Hölderlin and Heinrich von Kleist.

There are four periods of writing discernible in Jean Paul's life, the second and third of which had the most impact on audiences during his and subsequent ages. The first period of the 1780s is characterized by unsuccessful satires in the Enlightenment tradition; many of them remained unpublished. His first collection of works had the title *Grönländische Prozesse; oder, Satirische Skizzen* (1783; Trials in Greenland, or Satirical Sketches); the second collection, much delayed, appeared as *Auswahl aus des Teufels Papieren* (1789; Selections from the Devil's Papers). Both were published anonymously.

The narrative voice of Jean Paul, which Richter created for *The Invisible Lodge*, was characterized by its personal appeal. The first-person narrator "Jean Paul" told stories about "real" people whom he knew or wanted to meet; he wrote biographies, not mere novels, and he worked either from personal experience or from documents (supplied to him in *Hesperus* by a "mail dog"). In *The Invisible Lodge*, he was a participant in the events, the private tutor of the protagonist; in *Hesperus*, he would discover in the end that he belonged to the family of the main characters. Throughout his writing career, Richter found a way for Jean Paul to meet the protagonists either in the text itself or in a follow-up story.

Jean Paul inserted digressions, originally called *Extrablätter*, essays, aphorisms, and satires within his narrations, talking "personally" to the reader. His stories were of three kinds, generating three "genres," which he later defined, in the second edition of the *Vorschule der Ästhetik* (1804, second edition 1813; *Horn of Oberon: Jean Paul Richter's School for Aesthetics*), as Italian, German, and Dutch "schools." The Italian school, represented by *The Invisible Lodge, Hesperus*, and, later, *Titan* (1800–1804), takes place at a small court in Germany (Richter created his own fictitious, but realistically described, *Kleindeutschland*) and is centered on the educational experiences of a young man, the "hidden prince," the successor to the throne. The young man is not aware of his true identity and experiences the decadence, immorality, and intrigues of the court from outside, so that he can be the "philosopher king" upon his succession to the throne. In fact, his indignation about the condition of the ruling class turns the protagonist into a revolutionary, inspired by the French Revolution, only to learn at the end that his revolution must come from above. These stories could be described as a combination of the older *Staatsroman* with the emerging bildungsroman.

Contrary to the opinion of many scholars, this plot has significance, although it is overshadowed by scenes of friendship and love, by mysteries reminiscent of the Gothic novel, especially in *Titan,* and by enthusiastic and uplifting immersions in nature and communions with the divine. The works' elevated style and sublime nature, although contrasting with their social satire and self-deprecating humor, make these stories akin to sublime Italian paintings of Raphael, Tiepolo, or Guido Reni.

As an appendix to *The Invisible Lodge*, Richter published the prototype for his "Dutch," or idyllic, stories, *Das Leben des vergnügten Schulmeisterlein Maria Wutz in Auenthal* (1793; The Life of the Cheerful Schoolmaster Maria Wutz). This is the story of a *Kauz*, an odd fellow on the margin of society and a prototype for many *Käuze* in the German literature of the 19th century. The Dutch stories are also biographies, as indicated by titles such as *Leben des Quintus Fixlein, aus fünfzehn Zettelkästen gezogen* (1796; *Life of Quintus Fixlein, Extracted from Fifteen Letter-Boxes*) and *Leben Fibels, des Verfassers der Bienrodischen Fibel* (1812; Life of Fibel, Author of the Bienroda Primer). Their protagonists are teachers or Lutheran ministers, and the extreme poverty of their narrow village life forces them to color reality with a transforming imagination to make life bearable or even happy. For "normal" people, they seem to be on the verge of (non-aggressive) insanity. They are also authors in their odd ways: Fibel authors a "Fibel"—a primer for elementary schools. Wutz is far too poor to buy books; he instead takes titles from the catalog of the Leipzig book fair and writes them himself. The narrator Jean Paul becomes part of the story; in *Quintus Fixlein*, he is even instrumental in achieving a happy end.

Later in his career, Richter tried to achieve a middle ground between these two extremes: he depicted life in German small towns, as he himself knew them; his representations were realistic but still transformed by the Romantic imagination. This middle ground is what he called the "German school," with the novels *Siebenkäs* (1796–97) and *Flegeljahre* as its two outstanding examples. The full title of *Siebenkäs* (usually known in the second, enlarged, and more realistic edition of 1818) is the most baroque of Richter's many fanciful titles: *Blumen-, Frucht- und Dornenstücke; oder, Ehestand, Tod, und Hochzeit des Armenad-*

vokaten F. St. Siebenkäs im Reichsmarktflecken Kuhschnappel (translated as *Flower, Fruit, and Thorn Pieces; or, The Married Life, Death, and Wedding of the Advocate of the Poor, Firmian Stanislaus Siebenkäs,* which omits the last part of the original title, "in the Imperial small market town of Kuhschnappel"). Siebenkäs and his look-alike friend Leibgeber are humorists trying to keep their inner distance from bourgeois pettiness through their satirical speeches and shocking behavior. Siebenkäs, imprisoned in poverty, writes (Richter's) *Auswahl aus des Teufels Papieren* to earn money, but his rescue occurs through a feigned death (*Scheintod*). His married life consists of true "thorn pieces." As appendices, Richter added two "flower pieces" and one philosophical "fruit piece." The first flower piece, Richter's most anthologized text, is the "Rede des toten Christus vom Weltgebäude herab, daß kein Gott sei" (Speech of the Dead Christ from the Universe That There Is No God"). He himself framed this dream vision carefully as a warning against atheism, but beginning with the French translation in Germaine de Staël's book on Germany (1813), which made the text famous, its message was usually understood as: "there is no God."

In *Flegeljahre* (1804–5; *Walt and Vult; or, The Twins*), the protagonist Walt, a poet unaware of the tricks and pitfalls of bourgeois intrigues, is lured by the futile hopes of an inheritance (like Siebenkäs) into unpleasant encounters with society. He would prefer, however, to stay within the magic realm of nature, friendship, and love and to write his Romantic novel (in the manner of Jean Paul!) together with his twin brother Vult, author of *Grönländische Prozesse*, Vult being responsible for the novel's digressions. Their life and work together, however, ends in one of Walt's dreams (one of many of Richter's grandiose dream visions), during which Vult, jealous because of his rejection in love, is preparing to leave.

Flegeljahre, together with *Titan,* is considered the greatest achievement of Richter's third period of writing. *Titan,* together with the theme of the hidden prince, also offers Richter's critique of his age. In this critique, one aspect of immorality, aestheticism, is personified by the evil character of Roquairol, Jean Paul's devil figure. As a "comic" appendix to *Titan,* the wild humorist Giannozzo, the balloonist, retells his flights and encounters; and in a satirical yet very serious manner, Leibgeber takes issue with Fichte's philosophy in *Clavis Fichtiana seu Leibgeberiana* (1800). One of the first echoes of these appendices was the *Nachtwachen* by Bonaventura of 1805.

At this point in his life, at the climax of his reputation, Richter considered that the time had come to summarize his decades of reflections on two subjects dear to his heart: poetics and education. The *Vorschule der Ästhetik,* written at the time of *Titan* and *Flegeljahre,* defines his ideas on poetry; genius; the "romantic" age, meaning Europe after classical antiquity; the comic; humor; wit and metaphors; the German language; and, last but not least, the German literature of his own age. It ends with a moving tribute to Johann Gottfried Herder, Richter's great mentor, who had passed away in December 1803.

The *Vorschule* was followed by *Levana; oder, Erziehungslehre* (1807; *Levana; or, The Doctrine of Education*), Richter's seemingly fragmentary ideas on education. Primarily addressing parents and private tutors and responding to Rousseau's *Emile,* Richter progresses from practical hints for the care of babies to principles of *Bildung* and character formation. *Levana* was well received, especially in its practical aspects.

Can a Romantic poet like Walt in *Flegeljahre* live in a bourgeois society? It seems unlikely, and the texts of Richter's fourth and last period seem to confirm this incompatibility. While texts like *Dr. Katzenbergers Badereise* (1809; Dr. Katzenberger's Journey to a Spa) and the novel *Der Komet* (1820–22; The Comet) question or even satirize the figure of the poet and ask whether poetic imagination can falsify reality, they also paint a rather unfriendly picture of bourgeois society. Richter did not feel at home in the new world of materialistic capitalism and nationalism. During the years after the disastrous Prussian defeat of 1806–7, which he considered a moral defeat for the Germans (as did so many others), Richter had tried to address his audience with *Friedens-Predigt an Deutschland* (1808; Peace Sermon for Germany) and *Dämmerungen für Deutschland* (1809; Twilights for Germany); but his balanced, non-partisan, sometimes vague approach to the Napoleonic conflicts did not find a receptive audience. It was only in the 20th century that his *Kriegserklärung gegen den Krieg* (Declaration of War against War) has found acceptance among pacifists.

Richter's early vision of his own death, his intense skepticism reinforced by Kant, and his need for hope and harmony led to a lifelong preoccupation with the immortality of the soul. This preoccupation found its first book-length expression in the dialogues of *Das Kampaner Thal; oder, Über die Unsterblichkeit der Seele* (1797; The Campaner Thal; or, Discourses on the Immortality of the Soul), in which the narrator Jean Paul recounts debates on immortality among a group of young persons sojourning in the Pyrenees. The memorable end of the poetic dialogues is an ascent into the evening sky in a balloon, which translates the dream of flying into a metaphorical reality.

Late in life, Richter returned to the subject, updating his arguments and his characters, in *Selina; oder, Über die Unsterblichkeit* (1827; Selina; or, On Immortality), which was left two-thirds finished at the time of his death. The book contains lively debates on then current philosophical ideas and controversies.

Jean Paul's image and legacy were never simple and uniform: Young Germany saw him as a social critic and political progressive, but young writers of all ages have admired his high-flying poetic imagination, his mastery of metaphorical language, his complex, humorous worldview, and the perspective of a "planetary traveler." The French remembered his nightmare that God is dead, while in England and the United States, following Thomas Carlyle, his image remained that of a humorist. In Germany, the view of the "idyllic" Jean Paul prevailed, until Stefan George's circle and the Expressionists rediscovered his "sublime" flights into infinity.

WULF KOEPKE

See also Aesthetics

Biography

Born in Wunsiedel (Fichtelgebirge, now Bavaria), 21 March 1763. Studied at the University of Leipzig, 1781–84; abandoned the study of theology to become a freelance writer; returned to Hof to live in extreme poverty with his widowed mother and younger brothers; private tutor, 1787, 1790–94; after the death of his mother, moved to Leipzig, 1797–98, Weimar, 1798–1800, and Berlin, 1800–1801; moved to Meiningen, 1801, and Coburg, 1803; moved to Bayreuth, 1804; received a pension from the king of Bavaria after 1815; increasing blindness in his last years. Died in Bayreuth, 14 November 1825.

Selected Works

Collections
Sämmtliche Werke, 65 vols., 1826–38
Jean Pauls Sämtliche Werke: Historische-kritische Ausgabe, edited by Eduard Berend, 1927–
Sämtliche Werke, edited by Norbert Miller and Wilhelm Schmidt-Biggemann, 10 vols., 1959–85

Fiction
Grönländische Prozesse; oder, Satirische Skizzen, 2 vols., 1783; 2nd revised edition, 1822
Auswahl aus des Teufels Papieren, 1789
Die unsichtbare Loge, 2 vols., 1793; 2nd edition, 1822; as *The Invisible Lodge*, translated by Charles T. Brooks, 1883
Hesperus; oder, 45 Hundsposttage: Eine Biographie, 3 vols., 1795; 3rd edition, 4 vols., 1819; as *Hesperus; or, Forty-five Dog-Post-Days: A Biography*, translated by Charles T. Brooks, 2 vols., 1864
Leben des Quintus Fixlein, aus fünfzehn Zettelkästen gezogen, 1796; 2nd edition, 1801; as *Life of Quintus Fixlein, Extracted from Fifteen Letter-Boxes*, in *German Romance*, vol. 3, translated by Thomas Carlyle, 1827; reprinted 1991
Blumen-, Frucht-, und Dornenstücke; oder, Ehestand, Tod, und Hochzeit des Armenadvokaten F. St. Siebenkäs im Reichsmarktflecken Kuhschnappel, 3 vols., 1796–97; 2nd revised and enlarged edition, 4 vols., 1818; as *Flower, Fruit, and Thorn Pieces; or, The Married Life, Death, and Wedding of the Advocate of the Poor, Firmian Stanislaus Siebenkäs*, translated by Edward Henry Noel, 2 vols., 1845
Jean Pauls biographische Belustigungen unter der Gehirnschale einer Riesin, 1796
Der Jubelsenior, 1797
Jean Pauls Briefe und bevorstehender Lebenslauf, 1799
Titan, 4 vols., 1800–1803; as *Titan: A Romance*, translated by Charles T. Brooks, 1862
Das heimliche Klaglied der jezigen Männer, 1801
Flegeljahre, 4 vols., 1804–5; as *Walt and Vult; or, The Twins*, translated by Eliza Buckminster Lee, 2 vols., 1846
Des Feldpredigers Schmelzle Reise nach Flätz mit fortgehenden Noten, 1809; as *Army Chaplain Schmelzle's Journey to Flaetz*, in *German Romance*, vol. 3, translated by Thomas Carlyle, 1827; reprinted 1991
Dr. Katzenbergers Badereise, 2 vols., 1809; 2nd revised and enlarged edition, 1823
Leben Fibels, der Verfassers der Bienrodischen Fibel, 1812
Der Komet; oder, Nikolaus Marggraf, 3 vols., 1820–22

Autobiography
Wahrheit aus Jean Paul's Leben, edited by Christian Otto and Ernst Förster, 8 vols., 1826–33

Treatises
Das Kampaner Thal; oder, Über die Unsterblichkeit der Seele, 1797; as *The Campaner Thal; or, Discourses on the Immortality of the Soul*, translated by Juliette Bauer, 1848
Palingenesien, 2 vols., 1798
Clavis Fichtiana seu Leibgeberiana, 1800
Vorschule der Ästhetik, nebst einigen Vorlesungen in Leipzig über die Parteien der Zeit, 1804; revised and enlarged edition, 3 vols., 1813; as *Horn of Oberon: Jean Paul Richter's School for Aesthetics*, translated by Margaret R. Hale, 1973
Levana; oder, Erziehungslehre, 2 vols., 1807; 2nd revised and enlarged edition, 3 vols., 1814; as *Levana; or, The Doctrine of Education*, translated by A.H., 1848
Friedens-Predigt an Deutschland, 1808
Dämmerungen für Deutschland, 1809

Herbst-Blumine; oder, Gesammelte Werkchen aus Zeitschriften, 3 vols.,
  1810–20
Museum, 1814
Mars und Phöbus Thronwechsel im Jahre 1814, 1814
Politische Fastenpredigten während Deutschlands Marterwoche, 1817
Über die deutschen Doppelwörter, 1820
*Kleine Bücherschau: Gesammelte Vorreden und Rezensionen, nebst
  einer kleinen Nachschule zur ästhetischen Vorschule,* 2 vols., 1825
Selina; oder, Über die Unsterblichkeit, 1827

Further Reading

Arnold, Heinz Ludwig, editor, *Jean Paul: Sonderband Text und Kritik,* revised edition, Munich: Text und Kritik, 1983

Berend, Eduard, editor, *Jean Pauls Persönlichkeit in Berichten der Zeitgenossen,* Berlin: Akademie, 1956

Bruyn, Günter de, *Das Leben des Jean Paul Friedrich Richter,* Halle: Mitteldeutscher Verlag, 1975

Casey, Timothy J., and Casey, Erika, editors and translators, *Jean Paul: A Reader,* Baltimore, Maryland, and London: Johns Hopkins University Press, 1992

Götz, Müller, *Jean Pauls Ästhetik und Naturphilosophie,* Tübingen: Niemeyer, 1983

Harich, Wolfgang, *Jean Pauls Revolutionsdichtung: Versuch einer neuen Deutung seiner heroischen Romane,* Berlin: Akademie, 1974

Jahrbuch der Jean-Paul-Gesellschaft (1966–)

Kommerell, Max, *Jean Paul,* Frankfurt: Klostermann, 5th edition, 1977

Ortheil, Hanns-Josef, *Jean Paul: Mit Selbstzeugnissen und Bilddokumenten,* Reinbek bei Hamburg: Rowohlt, 1984

Schmitz-Emans, Monika, *Schnupftuchsknoten oder Sternbild: Jean Pauls Ansätze zu einer Theorie der Sprache,* Bonn: Bouvier, 1986

Schweikert, Gabriele, et al., editors, *Jean Paul Chronik,* Munich: Hanser, 1975

Schweikert, Uwe, editor, *Jean Paul,* Darmstadt: Wissenschaftliche Buchgesellschaft, 1974

Sprengel, Peter, editor, *Jean Paul im Urteil seiner Kritiker,* Munich: Beck, 1980

Ueding, Gert, *Jean Paul,* Munich: Beck, 1993

Wölfel, Kurt, *Jean-Paul-Studien,* Frankfurt: Suhrkamp, 1989

Vorschule der Ästhetik 1804

Treatise by Jean Paul

The poetological treatise by Jean Paul bears the complete title *Vorschule der Ästhetik, nebst einigen Vorlesungen in Leipzig über die Parteien der Zeit* (literally, Preschool for Aesthetics, plus Some Lectures in Leipzig on the Literary Factions of the Time; translated as *Horn of Oberon: Jean Paul Richter's School for Aesthetics*); the subtitle refers to the third narrative part, which describes three fictional lectures on contemporary literature delivered by the narrator Jean Paul during the Leipzig book fair. The *School for Aesthetics* appeared at the height of Jean Paul's reputation and was written concurrent with his highest narrative achievements, *Titan* (1800–1803) and *Flegeljahre* (1804–5); it was followed by his influential book on education, *Levana* (1807). The favorable response to the *School for Aesthetics* enabled Jean Paul to issue a second, expanded edition in 1813, which is the version used by today's readers. Jean Paul never stopped reflecting on these matters, and his last published book of 1825, *Kleine Bücherschau* (Little Overview of Books),

contains, together with his collected book reviews, a *Kleine Nachschule zur ästhetischen Vorschule* (Little Postschool for the Aesthetic Preschool).

While the *School for Aesthetics* lacks the systematic authority of Kant's third critique, the programmatic self-assured qualities of Schiller's essays, and the fervor of Friedrich Schlegel's early poetology, it has had its long-term impact in very significant areas. Jean Paul's best-known achievement is his new concept of humor, which replaced the then current views on satire and humor, and which is a concept still relevant for today's debates. Other less well-acknowledged debts to the *School for Aesthetics* include definitions of the novel, "wit" and nature of the metaphoric language, and Jean Paul's views on the literary scene of his age, especially aesthetic "nihilism," by which he meant Romantic aestheticism or *l'art pour l'art*. Because of Jean Paul's witty and often self-consciously humoristic style, scholars sometimes miss the important insights and serious theoretical considerations of the *School for Aesthetics*, which, in addition to the previous points, offer a unique view of German literary life at the beginning of the 19th century, a view that often diverges from our academic literary histories.

Jean Paul had begun reflecting on his craft at the very beginning of his writing career; the *School for Aesthetics* was the sum of over 20 years of writing and thinking. For Jean Paul, only an experienced writer could contribute meaningful insights into poetics—he granted exceptions for Aristotle and Kant. The strength of his text is that he focuses squarely on his own concerns and disregards the demands for a "systematic" approach. These concerns are primarily the nature of poetry (*Dichtung*); the degrees of poetic creativity and the requirements for "genius"; the character of "romantic" poetry, by which he means the literature after classical antiquity, which he also calls "modern" (!); the definition of the sublime; the source and expressions of the comic; humor, or the "romantic comic" or "inverted sublime"; the ill-defined genre of the novel and its different forms; the nature of imagery, in particular, metaphors and allegories; style and techniques of writing; and ideas on the German language.

Jean Paul never offers theorems without examples, and his range of familiarity with literature from all ages and cultures is astounding. He is nonpolemical but firm in his value judgments. He never mentions his own works without some friendly irony. The following points merit special attention in view of recent debates. First, Jean Paul proposes the notion of the "passive genius" (*das passive Genie*) who is specially receptive to stimulation but not strong enough creatively to transform it. In an overstimulated age (as Jean Paul considered his own), this type of *Grenzgenie* (border genius) becomes a frequent, albeit problematic phenomenon. Second, "Romantic" poetry in Jean Paul's typology of "Greek versus Romantic" was for him, with regard to Western literature, synonymous with "Christian" literature, namely, literature based on Christian devaluation of the body and this life in comparison with the spiritual, the inward, and the eternal. Third, Jean Paul considered "satire," or social criticism in literary form, as nonpoetic, as opposed to humor. Fourth, in his analysis of humor, the second of four constituent elements, the "annihilating or infinite idea of humor," has generated special interest. Wolfgang Kayser, in his seminal 1957 book, considered it to be the nucleus for a definition of the modern grotesque. Fifth, for Jean Paul, witty similes and metaphors were not only a means to revitalize and repoeticize an abstract language but, more important, a heuristic means to reach truths that were inaccessible to analytical reasoning. Sixth, Jean Paul distinguished three "schools" of novels, or types of narratives, found in his own works: the "Italian" school of high romance and courtly intrigues; the "Dutch" school of the village idylls, where odd characters find happiness in poverty; and the "German" school of the small-town middle class, the form closest to his heart, but dangerously close to a mere "realism" that would preclude a romantic glow over life, which Jean Paul considered indispensable for all poetry.

For Jean Paul, there were two extremes that he considered dangerous for the literature of his day: poetic "materialism" and "nihilism." In the third narrative part of the *School for Aesthetics,* he describes the materialists as *Stilistiker.* They were mere imitators of facts, realists of the Enlightenment such as Friedrich Nicolai. For Jean Paul, they made up the vast majority of the writers of his time; therefore, his "lecture" in Leipzig draws a large audience who leaves highly dissatisfied. The *Poetiker* whom we would call Romantics, were "nihilists" who wrote poetry about poetry without any foundation in real nature. According to Jean Paul, poetry without such nourishment withers away into the sublime artificiality of *l'art pour l'art.* After angering this second group as well, Jean Paul cannot be surprised to have hardly any audience left for his third lecture on "poetic" poetry. The one handsome young man who appears turns out to be Albano, the protagonist of Jean Paul's own novel *Titan.* The lecture ends with a moving eulogy for Johann Gottfried Herder, Jean Paul's great mentor who had just passed away in December 1803.

Jean Paul's independent stand, his criticism of Schiller and the Romantics, and his emphasis on the comic and the modern made his book attractive for the writers of Young Germany and for the earlier poetic realists, who found it inspirational for ideas on humor, the novel, and witty language as an expression of freedom. For the following generations, it remained merely a source book on the definition of humor, until the generation of the Expressionists early in the 20th century rediscovered the poetry and poetics of Jean Paul. He has remained a "writer's writer" for all ever since, even to such unlikely groups as the young generation of GDR writers in the 1970s. Recent theories of the sublime, metaphor, and humor make the *School for Aesthetics* a useful reference book. It is the only major text by Jean Paul available in a recent translation with an excellent commentary.

WULF KOEPKE

Editions

First edition: *Vorschule der Ästhetik, nebst einigen Vorlesungen in Leipzig über die Parteien der Zeit,* Hamburg: Perthes, 1804; revised and enlarged edition, 3 vols., Stuttgart and Tübingen: Cotta, 1813
Critical edition: (based on the text of the revised edition) in *Jean Paul's Sämtliche Werke: Historisch-kritische Ausgabe,* edited by Eduard Berend, vol. 11, Weimar: Böhlau, 1935; a frequently used edition based on the critical edition, with notes, commentary, and an index, is found in *Sämtliche Werke,* edited by Norbert Miller, vol. 5, Munich: Carl Hanser, 1963
Translation: *Horn of Oberon: Jean Paul Richter's School for Aesthetics,* translated by Margaret R. Hale, Detroit, Michigan: Wayne State University Press, 1973

Further Reading

Berend, Eduard, *Jean Pauls Ästhetik,* Berlin: Duncker, 1909
Higonnet, Margaret R., "Jean Paul Richter: Kunstrichter," *Journal for English and German Philology* 76 (1977)
Koepke, Wulf, "Jean Paul Richter's School for Aesthetics: Humor and the Sublime," in *Eighteenth-Century German Authors and Their Aesthetic Theories: Literature and the Other Arts,* edited by Richard Critchfield and Wulf Koepke, Columbia, South Carolina: Camden House, 1988
———, "Die Moreske einer Moreske oder die dunkle Seite des Humors," *Jahrbuch der Jean-Paul-Gesellschaft* 26/27 (1991/92)
Müller, Götz, *Jean Pauls Ästhetik und Naturphilosophie,* Tübingen: Niemeyer, 1983
Wiethölter, Waltraud, *Witzige Illumination: Studien zur Ästhetik Jean Pauls,* Tübingen: Niemeyer, 1979

Elfriede Jelinek 1946–

Elfriede Jelinek is recognized widely as one of the most significant contemporary writers of literature in German and as one of the most controversial authors in Austria. Prolific in a variety of genres, she has written poetry, prose, radio plays, drama, screen plays, essays, and translations. Her pointed criticism of mass culture, class and gender, and Austrian history and bourgeois values has earned her the reputation of possessing a *böser Blick* (contemptuous gaze). Desiring to avoid scandal or intimidated by the overwhelming challenge her densely woven images present, few Austrian theaters produced her plays before the 1990s. Despite the ongoing resistance to her writing (the popular press in Austria continues to be her more ardent critic), Jelinek's work has gained in popularity. Besides making the best-seller list with her novel *Lust* (1989; *Lust*), she has received numerous prestigious literary awards, among which the Büchner Prize is the most recent. The author herself enjoys a nearly unmatched notoriety, which accounts for numerous interviews in various media, including an in-depth exposé of her work on German television (1997). Self-stylized and commanding, Jelinek holds the attention of the public that has come either to admire or to scorn her.

Jelinek made her literary debut in 1967, with her collection of poetry in *Lisas Schatten* (Lisa's Shadow). Strongly influenced by the avant-garde techniques and experimental tendencies of the Wiener Gruppe, which sought to continue the avant-garde projects of the 1920s crushed by the Nazis, Jelinek's early works are characterized by a radical experimentation of language and form. The elimination of punctuation and capital letters for proper nouns, the use of collage and montage, and the semantic overlaying of meaning are some of the techniques she employed to provoke the dominant social order and its "normalization" of oppression and asymmetrical power structures. Her affiliations with the politically engaged faction of the Grazer Gruppe led to involvement in the avant-garde literary journal *manuskripte,* in which many of Jelinek's essays and short texts were first featured.

In her first novel, *wir sind lockvögel baby*! (1970; We Are Decoys Baby), which the renowned publisher Rowohlt immediately accepted, Jelinek disassembles the slick commercial surfaces of the culture industry that manufactures and sells dreams. A compilation of quotes from such popular genres as advertisements, James Bond novels, and television serials structures the novel. The criticism of the media seen in most of Jelinek's writing, which places her in the tradition of the Frankfurt School, is one that is concerned with the relationship between the cultural industry and the subject. Even though Jelinek subscribes to a strong intertextual approach, her work, she insists, should not be mistaken for a postmodern pastiche of citations, which, in her eyes, lacks political commitment.

Rich in irony, extremely provocative in style and perspective, Jelinek sees herself in the tradition of German Jewish writers such as Franz Kafka, Walter Serner, and Karl Kraus, with whom she shares a fine sensibility for satire. Language, as she often states, is a weapon she aggressively uses to deconstruct social practices and discourses that ideology renders commonsensical. Her critique of ideology and its sustaining myths is indebted profoundly to the work of Roland Barthes, particularly his reading of cultural signs, as exemplified in his collection of essays *Mythologies.* For Jelinek, myths are not innocent. They shape perception and conceal or normalize social and economic relations of power. In the essay *Die endlose Unschuldigkeit* (1980; The Endless Innocence), she identifies her theoretical allegiances and defines her literary project. Her anti-illusory style is concerned with denaturalizing ideological systems of thought and perception and their implicit regulation of class, gender, and historical knowledge. She perverts the myths whose formulas have fixed, dehistoricized, and depoliticized identities and reduces them to stereotypes and clichés. Jelinek's project of demystification may best be read as an adaptation of Barthes's assertion that the finest weapon against myth is to exaggerate and "mythify" it. Rather than formulating a utopia, Jelinek, as a *Schriftverstellerin,* engages the epistemologies and social practices she criticizes only simultaneously to deconstruct, displace, and subvert them. Her textual analyses of popular culture, as well as specific literary and philosophical discourses, seek to unmask linguistic and cultural models in order to shed light on the semiotics of violence that define Western thought. This technique may be found to varying degrees in all of her work.

As a self-avowed Marxist who was a member of the Austrian Communist Party (KPÖ) from 1974 to 1991, Jelinek's writing throughout her career exemplifies a feminist and Marxist social critique. She exquisitely portrays consumer society and its production and commodification of consumers, and through her satirical methods of distortions and elucidations, she illustrates the violence and alienation intrinsic to capitalism. Her novel *Michael: Ein Jugendbuch für die Infantilgesellschaft* (1972;

Michael: An Adolescent Novel for the Infantile Society) was her first attempt to translate into literature the theoretical position of her essay *Die endlose Unschuldigkeit.* In *Michael,* she introduces television as the "super-ego of mass communication" that assembles its subjects, delimits identity, and thwarts critical thinking, thus keeping the spectator in a state of infancy. Tellingly, the title is taken from the autobiographical prose *Michael: Ein deutsches Schicksal* (1929; Michael: A German Fate) authored by the Nazi minister of propaganda, Joseph Goebbels. Among other commodities the patriarchal culture industry produces, the image of woman as a projection of male desire and consumable body emerges as a central topic in Jelinek's works.

Jelinek focuses on the exploitation and oppression of women. For instance, in *Die Liebhaberinnen* (1975; *Women as Lovers*), the first of her novels to receive critical acclaim, she draws a parallel between the uneven distribution of power in the private and public spheres. As is often the case in Jelinek's writing, form dominates content, which in turn resonates with Marshall Luhan's insight that "the medium is the message." In *Women as Lovers,* Jelinek self-consciously parodies the romance novel by organizing her novel and the lives of its two female protagonists from different classes according to the properties of the genre. She employs the narrative of romantic love to demythify it. Her women appear as constructs of ideologically crafted mythologies (Barthes) of daily life such as romantic love, motherhood, and bourgeois feminist notions of female autonomy and self-determination. In other words, Jelinek's women, regardless of their class affiliation, are intricately produced by the patriarchal capitalist scripts that they internalize and perform. On stage and in her novels, they represent speaking corpses and a very specific image of the "undead" that Jelinek uses in a number of her works.

Jelinek's first play, *Was geschah, nachdem Nora ihren Mann verlassen hatte* (1980; *What Happened after Nora Left Her Husband*), rewrites two Ibsen plays to speculate critically on whether Nora's emancipation is possible if it is rooted in bourgeois notions of selfhood. So-called self-actualization is paired with Nora playing into the hands of the multinationals and becoming their pawn. In the play *Clara S.* (1984), a reference to German composer Clara Schumann, wife of Robert Schumann, Jelinek mocks the notions of artistic genius that patriarchy reserves for its male prodigy. Resistance to recognizing women as artists, as people who produce in addition to reproducing, is the focal point of Jelinek's polemic. Her characters thus embody psychoanalytical concepts of masculinity and femininity only to pervert psychoanalytical discourse. Since "lack" characterizes woman, it can only be compensated by bearing children, preferably sons. Thus, the figure Clara S. is an elaboration of the cultural script; her complaints and resistance cannot match its power. According to Jelinek, in the war of the sexes, women have no chance against the murderous machine called man, as can be seen in *Krankheit; oder, Moderne Frauen* (1992; Disease; or, Modern Women), in which women appear as vampires. The representation of Emily, the transfiguration of poet Emily Brontë, reverses the trope of woman as nature and turns her into both monstrosity and social disease: vampire, nurse, and lesbian. Emily liberates the childbearing Carmilla by recruiting her to the ranks of the undead. The voice of patriarchy Jelinek introduces to comment on the subversion of biological destiny resonates with the language of fascism. In *Raststätte* (1994; *Services*), two married women who arrange an illicit meeting for sexual adventure with two ravenous animals are duped by their husbands, who borrow the identities of the intended suitors.

As in most of Jelinek's texts, the characters are not psychologically developed; that is, they lack both introspection and inner depth. Instead, her caricatures perform discursive structures, stereotypes, and platitudes that Jelinek in turn satirically deforms. All of her characters are inauthentic instruments of language who vanish when they are done speaking; they embody a polemic, a repertoire of quotes, and represent objectified bodies. In her essay "Ich möchte seicht sein" (1983; I Want to Be Shallow), she describes the anti-identificatory, anti-illusory theater she envisions to go beyond Brecht. In short, she writes, "I want to purge theater of life. I do not want any theater." The "theater of themes" she develops thus also unsettles classical notions of theater. Moreover, Jelinek, as playwright, perceives her dramas as an aggressive attack against the institution of theater, which traditionally has barred women from its stages.

Beginning in 1975, Jelinek's prose turned toward a narrative style that is based on a more linear plot while maintaining the caricature-like nature of her figures, as well as her critical destruction of existing cultural norms. *Die Ausgesperrten* (1980; *Wonderful, Wonderful Times*), for example, reveals an elaborate intertextual narrative modeled on the genre of the bildungsroman. Yet in contrast to the characters in the traditional bildungsroman, Jelinek's characters are not transformed despite their strenuous efforts to escape their social class. They are trapped in a false consciousness of individuality and autonomy, and in an economic system that binds them to their class. In her subsequent autobiographically inflected novel, *Die Klavierspielerin* (1983; *The Piano Teacher*), Jelinek caustically deconstructs classical psychoanalytical interpretations of female development and femininity while sketching the mother-daughter relationship as a fertile ground for the transmission of cultural imperatives. Female sexuality, identity, and Erika's career are controlled by an engulfing mother who persistently thwarts her daughter's independence. Painful scenes of masochistic self-mutilation symbolically represent the daughter's attempts to sever herself from a smothering symbiosis. Similarly, forsaking the radical montage technique of earlier texts, while creating a complex experience of voyeuristic aversion and fascination, Jelinek's raw antipornographic novel *Lust* reduces traditional gender arrangements to attributes of power and sexuality. The literary peep show showcases the repeated instrumentalization and abuse of the female body for male pleasure. As Gerti finds out in her relationship with her husband, for whom she produces a son, and then later in the relationship with her illicit lover, who rapes her, female desire and the longing for romantic love are never fulfilled. The novel also asserts the impossibility of producing a female pornography since the grammar of the genre is embedded in the language of patriarchy. Jelinek's short piece *Begierde und Fahrerlaubnis* (1987; Desire and Permission to Proceed), subtitled *eine Pornographie,* which filmmaker Ulrike Ottinger staged, presents a muted female character who requests permission to be the agent of her desire. Given Jelinek's representation of the sexes as "alien and enemy continents" (*The Piano Teacher*), her affinity for the work of Ingeborg Bachmann does not come as a surprise. Bachmann saw everyday fascism as intrinsic to a patriarchal society and to the relationships between men and women. In 1990, Jelinek's screenplay based on Bachmann's novel *Malina* was produced in collaboration with avantgardist filmmaker Werner Schroeter.

A steadfast confrontation with Austria's fascist history and the nation's pervasive historical amnesia also appears in most of Jelinek's works. Compared to Germany, public discussions of Austria's involvement in the Third Reich and in the Holocaust came much later. Jelinek's texts recall the victims of Nazi crimes who, in her estimation, have been purged from Austria's collective conscience. Owing to her unabashed attack on Austrian culture and tradition, its icons and symbols, and the cultural artifacts that arouse deep national attachments, Jelinek has been charged as a *Nestbeschmutzerin* (one who befouls one's own nest). In particular, the play *Burgtheater: Posse mit Gesang* (1984; Burgtheater: A Farce with Song) drew fierce criticism and has yet to be performed at Austria's national theater in Vienna. The play's relentless satirization of revered actors of the Burgtheater, who supported Austria's *Anschluß* and who expressed an admiration for Germanness and a vicious anti-Semitism, aims at the heart of Austrian national identity. Although the names of Paula Wessely and Attila Hörbinger, two icons of Austrian film and theater of the 1930s and 1940s, are never mentioned, conspicuous parallels are drawn between the stage personae and their historical antecedents. Jelinek, however, is less interested in the historical persons than in probing what they stood for and how they became tools of fascist ideology. As in all of her writing, the characters serve as instruments for prefabricated speech acts.

Beginning with her novel *Oh Wildnis, oh Schutz vor ihr* (1985; Oh Nature, Protect Us against It), Jelinek's linguistic compositions again become dense, radical collages of monologues, intricate chains of association, and brilliantly tooled puns. Her characters, in the works to follow, rehearse monologues riddled with quotes from such diverse sources as Martin Heidegger, Hannah Arendt, popular culture, the yellow press, and correspondences belonging to the Red Army Faction during their incarceration. The frequent topics of homeland (*Heimat*), metaphysics, and the mystical bond to nature, celebrated in various genres, are mocked in *Oh Wildnis*. In addition, Jelinek's provocative confrontation with concepts of nationalism and national identity are also evidenced in *Wolken: Heim* (1990; Clouds: Home). Here, nationalist blood and soil discourses are dramatized. A collective German "we" participates in an identity discourse based on exclusion that appropriates and perverts all sorts of poetic and philosophical texts (Hölderlin, Hegel, Fichte, and Kleist) for its own ends. The collective "we" represents a community that sets itself off against an unwelcome and vilified "other." In Jelinek's drama, the "we" fortifies itself against the "other" through its very Heideggerian "being" and "spirit." Yet the effusive usage of "we" (*wir*), as in "wir aber wir aber wir aber" without punctuation, ridicules the self-indulgent, hysterical concept of the community's self-worth and its sense of superiority. Jelinek derides the metaphysical tradition from which the communal "we" draws its consciousness and identity. Similar to but more radical than in her other works, Jelinek allows language to speak for itself, which helps tease out the ideological and, in this case, protofascist tendencies that reside within its configurations.

Similarly in *Totenauberg* (1991: Mountain of the Dead), central philosophical concepts and political categories such as alienation under capitalism are dissected; in Jelinek's estimation, these categories lay the ground for anti-Semitism and racism.

Once again, she attacks the cherished concept of homeland (*Heimat*), and the romantic, bourgeois phantasms of nature and nation, by focusing on the properties of language that shape these concepts. In *Totenauberg*, Jelinek imagines a meeting in an alpine landscape between the distinguished 20th-century philosopher Martin Heidegger and his colleague and student Hannah Arendt. Diatribes against skiers, mountain climbers, and tourists are included along with discourses on xenophobia, nationalist thought, and Auschwitz.

With her magnum opus *Die Kinder der Toten* (1995; Children of the Dead), Jelinek further thematizes the haunting specter of fascism in contemporary Austrian society, which either implicitly or explicitly influences all of her texts. Her invective display of the discourses of annihilation and "normalization" that the *Urvolk* obsessively reproduces shatters the tenaciously tended narratives of the lack of culpability that have shaped Austrian national identity. Jelinek writes against the repression of historical continuity by linking past and present. Her sweeping prose exposes the violence intrinsic to bourgeois ideological constructs and its institutional foundations that, in her vocabulary, lay the ground for protofascist practices. The theater project *Stecken, Stab und, Stangl* (1997) represents Jelinek's continued preoccupation with Austria's amnesiac response to its fascist past, which became intensely conspicuous in the generally disinterested public reaction to the murder of four Roma in 1995. The play is part of a trilogy of works (*Wolken: Heim* and *Services*) that Jelinek refers to as a theater of themes. In the Benjaminiam sense of remembering the dead whose histories/stories are forgotten, she establishes a literary epitaph for those who are driven into the peripheries, dispossessed, and forced to exist outside the national referents and the "imagined community." The dead are buried symbolically in various speech acts and in an excess of language that deflects the coming to grips with these killings. In an inversion of Wittgenstein's dictum "Wovon man nicht reden kann, darüber soll man schweigen" (One should remain silent concerning those things about which one cannot speak), *Stecken, Stab, und Stangl* speaks the uncensored thoughts of the collective and serves as a mirror in which the specularized national self finds itself exposed. The imagined national community recites its clichés, its familiar turns of phrase, and its ideologically mapped emotional structures, and it displays its chronic inability to mourn the past atrocities committed in the name of nationalism. For Jelinek, sports figures among the social institutions that fuel chauvinist concepts of national pride and anesthetize its constituents.

The events broadcast in *Ein Sportstück* (1998; A Sportpiece) appeal to the masses who are herded together to revel in the heroic athletic achievements and victories of their cultural icons. Again, Jelinek airs her suspicion of the culture industry and its part in shaping a collective memory that all too willingly screens out its fascist past.

BARBARA KOSTA

Biography

Born in Mürzzuschlag, Styria, Austria, 20 October 1946. Studied art history and drama in Vienna; graduated with an organist diploma at the Vienna conservatory, 1971; member of Grazer Autorenversammlung, 1973–92, and Austria's Communist Party, 1974–91; reviewer for Austria's monthly magazine *Extrablatt* and contributor to the Berlin magazine *Die schwarze Botin* and the Austrian literary magazine *Manuskripte;* translated works by Thomas Pynchon and Georges Feydeau. Heinrich Böll Prize, 1986; Peter Weiss Prize, 1994; Walter Hasenclever Prize, 1994; Georg Büchner Prize, 1998. Currently lives in Vienna, where her most recent play, *Ein Sportstück,* premiered.

Selected Works

Prose

Lisas Schatten, 1967
wir sind lockvögel baby! Roman, 1970
Michael: Ein Jugendbuch für die Infantilgesellschaft: Prosa, 1972
Die Liebhaberinnen: Roman, 1975; as *Women as Lovers,* translated by Martin Chalmers, 1994
*bukolit: Hörroman,*1980
Die Ausgesperrten: Roman, 1980; as *Wonderful, Wonderful Times,* translated by Michael Hulse, 1990
Die endlose Unschuldigkeit: Prosa—Hörspiel—Essay, 1980
Die Klavierspielerin, 1983; as *The Piano Teacher,* translated by Joachim Neugroschel, 1988
Oh Wildnis, oh Schutz vor ihr: Prosa, 1985
Lust, 1989; translated by Michael Hulse, 1992
Die Kinder der Toten: Roman, 1995

Plays

Was geschah, nachdem Nora ihren Mann verlassen hatte; oder, Stützen der Gesellschaften (produced 1979), 1980; as *What Happened after Nora Left Her Husband; or, Pillars of Society,* translated by Tinch Minter, in *Plays by Women,* vol. 10, 1994
Clara S.: Musikalische Tragödie (produced 1982), in *Theaterstücke,* 1984
Burgtheater: Posse mit Gesang (produced 1985), in *Theaterstücke,* 1984
Begierde und Fahrerlaubnis (eine Pornographie), in *Blauer Streusand,* edited by Barbara Alms, 1987
Theaterstücke, 1984; expanded edition, 1992
Präsident Abendwind (produced 1987), in *Anthropophagen im Abendwind,* 1988
Die Klavierspielerin: Melodrama in einem Akt: Nach dem gleichnamigen Roman Elfriede Jelineks, 1989
Wolken: Heim (produced 1988), 1990
wir sind lockvögel baby! Theaterexperiment nach dem gleichnamigen Roman Elfriede Jelineks, 1990
Körperliche Veränderungen/Der Wald: Mini-Operas nach Texten von Elfriede Jelinek, 1991
Unruhiges Wohnen: Tanztheater, 1991
Totenauberg (produced 1992), 1991
Krankheit; oder, Moderne Frauen (produced 1987), in *Theaterstücke,* expanded edition, 1992
An den, den's angeht: Zusatztext zu Wolken: Heim, 1993
Raststätte; oder, Sie machen's alle (produced 1994), 1994; as *Services; or, They All Do It,* translated by Nick Grindell, 1996
Stecken, Stab, und Stangl (produced 1996), with *Raststätte* and *Wolken: Heim,* 1997
Ein Sportstück (produced 1998), 1998

Further Reading

Bartens, Daniela, and Paul Pechmann, editors, *Elfriede Jelinek: Die Internationale Rezeption,* Graz: Droschl, 1997
Bartsch, Kurt, and Günther A. Höfler, editors, *Elfriede Jelinek,* Graz: Droschl, 1991
Fiddler, Allyson, *Rewriting Reality: An Introduction to Elfriede Jelinek,* Oxford and Providence, Rhode Island: Berg, 1994
Gürtler, Christa, and Alexander von Bormann, editors, *Gegen den schönen Schein: Texte zu Elfriede Jelinek,* Frankfurt: Neue Kritik, 1990

Janz, Marlies, *Elfriede Jelinek,* Stuttgart: Metzler, 1995

Pflüger, Maja Sibylle, *Vom Dialog zur Dialogizität: Die Theaterästhetik von Elfriede Jelinek,* Tübingen: Francke, 1996

Die Klavierspielerin 1983

Novel by Elfriede Jelinek

Elfriede Jelinek is one of Austria's most controversial contemporary writers, and it could be said that no other woman writer has been so vehemently attacked by journalists and literary critics, at least in Austria. Yet among her many literary tributes, she has been awarded the prestigious Heinrich Böll Prize (1986) and, most recently, the Georg Büchner Prize (1998). Jelinek has made a name for herself by harshly criticizing male domination and violence, often dealing with taboo themes such as pornography, while at the same time attempting to create a feminine language for obscenity. Widely known as a novelist (*Die Klavierspielerin* [*The Piano Teacher*] being her sixth novel of a list of nine to date, spanning the years 1970–95), she has also written poetry, dramas, radio plays, film scripts, and libretti, as well as essays on political and aesthetic themes. In fact, *The Piano Teacher* was transmitted as a radio play in 1988 with a musical score by composer Patricia Jünger; a year later she was also responsible for a musical adaptation on stage, when passages from the novel were selected for a one-hour melodrama that was premiered at the Basel theater in November (director: Barbara Mündel). Noticeably, the male protagonist was omitted from the stage production and, somewhat ironically, the piano was replaced by percussion instruments in order to highlight the violence and indoctrination, while the play focuses on the ritualized self-destruction of the "heroine." In May 1989, the Wuppertal dance theater formation Mind the Gap also performed a dance version of the novel, emphasizing its grotesque and farcical elements. A film adaptation remains under discussion.

With explicit sexual scenes that border on the pornographic, the novel itself has been contentiously debated since its publication in 1983, not least due to the fact that the author willingly "courts" the media and has openly admitted the autobiographical traits of this book. Similar to the novel's protagonist, Jelinek studied music at the conservatory in Vienna; her mother wanted her to become a concert pianist; her father had to be admitted to a psychiatric clinic; and her own upbringing, governed by her mother, was strict and authoritarian. *The Piano Teacher* is in fact the only novel to date in which Jelinek reworks experiences from her childhood. Numerous interviews have resulted in a variety of interpretations, ranging from biographical, psychoanalytical, and feminist to, more recently, socioeconomic and political readings; predominant themes in these accounts are the mother-daughter relationship and the depiction of sexuality as sadomasochistic.

Particular cause for debate has been the extent to which the story of Erika Kohut, a piano teacher in her mid-30s, and her symbiotic relationship with her abusive mother can be considered an individual, pathological "case study." As Jelinek would have us believe, however, the characters are representative in nature; hence, the use of generic terms such as "the daughter," "Mother," and "the Man." In this reading, the characters illustrate common experiences and thereby reflect Jelinek's socialist beliefs (until 1991, she had been a member of the Austrian Communist party [KPÖ] for 20 years). Her desire for such generalization has resulted in a mixed reception among feminist and nonfeminist critics alike, since she presents "the struggle of the sexes as that of the constant degradation, manipulation and humiliation of women at the hands of their masculine sexual counterparts" (Fiddler, 1994). Interestingly, at the time of publication, male journalistic reviewers tended to focus on Jelinek's style of writing and the mixture of irony and black humor with which she depicts the horrific abnormality of the mother-daughter relationship (e.g., Baier). In the 1990s, critics have focused more and more on her use of satirical language and her ability to objectify potentially sentimental scenes (e.g., Höfler).

The theme of the mother-daughter relationship resonates with similar themes in other novels written in German by women writers during the 1970s and 1980s (e.g., Karin Struck's *Die Mutter* [1975; Mother], Gabriele Wohmann's *Ausflug mit der Mutter* [1976; Outing with Mother], and Waltraud Anna Mitgutsch's *Die Züchtigung* [1985; *Punishment*]), and the depiction of conflict between a tyrannized daughter and all-powerful mother is nothing new. Jelinek, however, does not write here in the first person, preferring distance between authorial and fictional subject, nor does she invite reader identification; there is no sentimentality and no analytical reflection whatsoever. Her daughter figure is unable to grow up and develop a sense of self-identity. It is this latter aspect, the absence of any attempt at or development toward independence, that is a contentious issue for feminists.

What makes this mother-daughter portrayal so different from other autobiographically based depictions is the level of violence, physical and sexual, between mother and daughter (suggestive of a lesbian, incestuous relationship), which is then reflected in the second part of the novel in the teacher-pupil relationship of Erika Kohut and Walter Klemmer, who is ten years younger, musically talented, and athletic. The narrative tone of this work is so direct and open that shocking scenes such as the rape of the mother by the daughter and the rape of Erika by Klemmer seem like normal, everyday occurrences. Similarly, Erika's voyeurism in the form of visits to peep shows and using binoculars to watch couples copulating in the Prater park; her self-mutilation with razor blades, needles, and pegs; and in the final scene, a self-inflicted knife wound in her shoulder all demand of the reader a strong disposition. The strength of the novel lies in the author's unflinching description of sex as brutal and violent. On paper, her daughter figure voices sadomasochistic desires to Klemmer and wants to be gagged and bound, tortured until she can no longer stand up; in her mind, she is desperate for true love and hopes that Klemmer will deny her wishes. But masculine pride has been hurt by a series of frustrations and humiliations, culminating in a letter, which reads more like a contract, where the intended victim is stipulating to the proposed persecutor how she is to be punished. As in the acts of self-mutilation, the masochist is determining her own pain threshold; it is one of the rare moments that she attempts to exert authority and control. For Klemmer, the letter proves to be the last straw, bringing out the sadist in him: he mercilessly beats up and rapes the object of his desire. Thus, Erika Kohut proves to be a failed masochist as well as a failed concert pianist.

Piano playing, and music in general, has ominous undertones throughout Jelinek's oeuvre. Her first piano player, Anna Witkowski, appeared in *Die Ausgesperrten* (1980; *Wonderful, Wonderful Times*). Neither Anna nor Erika succeed in emancipating themselves by dint of their musical education. In both works, the mothers want to fulfill their own dreams through their daughters' careers. In her novel *Lust* (1989; *Lust*), it is the father who makes his son learn to play the violin because he, too, wants to parade him at concerts: once again, music serves as a mechanism of control. With her stress on the petty bourgeois aspirations of these mothers and fathers, Jelinek does satirize the pursuit of musical excellence for material ends by illustrating the horrific consequences.

A sense of doom and gloom pervades all of Jelinek's fiction. In *The Piano Teacher*, this is typified by the ambivalent feelings of love for and hatred of the mother by both the fictional and real daughter. Interviewed in 1997 for a television documentary about her double function as an artist, her significance as a writer and as a figure of public discussion, Jelinek reiterated the psychological and physical torture she suffered at the hands of her own disciplinarian mother, claiming that, after the publication of *The Piano Teacher*, many women had thanked her for "killing" the mother on their behalf (i.e., shattering myths of motherhood). Without a doubt, this novel has touched a raw nerve in patriarchal, Austrian society.

PETRA M. BAGLEY

Editions

First edition: *Die Klavierspielerin*, Reinbek bei Hamburg: Rowohlt, 1983
Translation: *The Piano Teacher*, translated by Joachim Neugroschel, New York: Weidenfeld and Nicolson, 1988; London: Serpent's Tail, 1989

Further Reading

Baier, Lothar, "Abgerichtet, sich selbst zu zerstören: Ein Roman, der Gesellschaftskritik in seiner Sprache entfaltet, Elfriede Jelineks *Klavierspielerin*," *Süddeutsche Zeitung*, no. 161, 16–17 July 1983
Fiddler, Allyson, *Rewriting Reality: An Introduction to Elfriede Jelinek*, Oxford and Providence, Rhode Island: Berg, 1994
———, "Reading Elfriede Jelinek," in *Postwar Women's Writing in German: Feminist Critical Approaches*, edited by Chris Weedon, Oxford and Providence, Rhode Island: Berghahn, 1997
Höfler, Günther A., "Vergrösserungsspiegel und objektiv: Zur Fokussierung der Sexualität bei Elfriede Jelinek," in *Elfriede Jelinek*, edited by Kurt Bartsch and Günther A. Höfler, Graz and Vienna: Droschl, 1991
Kecht, Maria-Regina, "In the Name of Obedience, Reason, and Fear: Mother-Daughter Relations in W.A. Mitgutsch and E. Jelinek," *German Quarterly* 62, no. 3 (1989)
Kosta, Barbara, "Muttertrauma: Anerzogener Masochismus, W.A. Mitgutsch, *Die Züchtigung* und E. Jelinek, *Die Klavierspielerin*," in *Mütter, Töchter, Frauen: Weiblichkeitsbilder in der Literatur*, edited by Helga Kraft and Elke Liebs, Stuttgart: Metzler, 1993
Mahler-Bungers, Annegret, "Der Trauer auf der Spur: Zu Elfriede Jelineks *Die Klavierspielerin*," in *Masochismus in der Literatur*, Freiburger literaturpsychologishe Gespräche 7, edited by Johannes Cremerius et al., Würzburg: Königshausen und Neumann, 1988
Meyer, Anja, *Elfriede Jelinek in der Geschlechterpresse: "Die Klavierspielerin" und "Lust" im printmedialen Diskurs*, Hildesheim, Zurich, and New York: Olms-Weidmann, 1994

Totenauberg 1991

Play by Elfriede Jelinek

In the wake of Austria's Waldheim affair, a significant number of writers have confronted Austria's problematic past and its cultural "amnesia" concerning the embarrassing truth of its Nazi complicity. Most notably, Thomas Bernhard's play *Heldenplatz* (1988; Heroes Square) caused a national scandal when it premiered at Austria's elite theater institution, the Burgtheater. The play depicts an unrepenting cultural climate that left Jewish survivors with the oppressive options of acquiescence or suicidal despair. Elfriede Jelinek's earlier play *Burgtheater* (1984), which implicated some of the theater's most cherished actors (the Hörbiger brothers; Paula Wesseley) and their role in Nazi propaganda cinema, was rejected at the time of its premiere at the Burgtheater because of its discomforting content. By the time of *Totenauberg*'s premiere in 1991, the cultural climate had significantly changed and the play was performed at the Burgtheater, finally bestowing upon Jelinek the national recognition given to Austria's most esteemed playwrights.

Jelinek's *Totenauberg* (Mountain of the Dead) stages historical memory not in descriptive but in performative terms of sociocultural negotiation. The central drama of her play evolves around a fictive encounter with Hannah Arendt, the "rootless" Jewish refugee and political philosopher, and Martin Heidegger, the "natively grounded" thinker of the history of Western ontology. Arendt's Jewish identity, as the play shows, cannot be taken for granted but has to be recast and renegotiated in the present cultural landscape in which the epistemic notions of belonging (Heidegger's *Zugehörigkeit*) and displacement (Arendt's uprootedness) once again clash as competing definitions of culture. As Gitta Honegger notes, characters in this play "turn almost literally into 'figures of speech.'" Heidegger, for example, wears a scaffold-like costume personifying his concept of the *Gestell* (scaffold) the framework upon which Western metaphysics is to be rebuilt. In Jelinek's parody, he frequently stumbles on stage with this support structure that imprisons the thinker in a cage of his own making. It is ultimately the conflict of discourses on essentialist and non-essentialist interpretations of culture that provide the dramatic action in the play. This linguistic scenario of competing discourses takes place against the background of an equally disharmonious visual scenario of a thoroughly commodified tourist landscape littered with corpses of mountain climbers who have fallen to their death. This visual landscape evokes even more disturbing associations of mass death through cinematic interludes depicting the deportation of Jews. Jelinek's visual and verbal scenarios offer a sobering perspective on the cultural death that overshadows Austria's economic reconstruction, one built on a persistent historical amnesia.

This amnesia, as the play suggests, has grown even stronger after the fall of communism as the last visible alternative to a pervasive Western capitalism. Cultural identities have now become marketable commodities and the primary privilege of the affluent. Marketing its *Heimat* and *Wintersport* arena as a tourist commodity and guarding its territorial boundaries against the economic refugees of Eastern Europe, Austria's postindustrial leisure society has not only forgotten its past but has managed to resurrect it in a more sanitized and socially acceptable manner. Asylum laws, ecological awareness, and physical health and fitness routines replace the former visible aspects of fascist ideology, stressing dubious constructions of biological native right and organic wholeness of culture. Under such revisionist circumstances, as Jelinek shows, Jewish identity remains one of wholesale expulsion and invisibility that can only indirectly point to the artificiality and pathology of Austria's cultural landscape. In the play, Arendt's voice can barely differentiate itself from and stem against the overwhelming power of other discourses (sport, *Heimat,* genetics, and motherhood) that have equally usurped Heidegger's notions of reflective *Dasein* (Being) and *Zugehörigkeit* (Belonging). Indeed, much of the play parodies Heideggerian rhetoric by undermining its essentialist assumptions through polysemic contamination via other discourses. Serious Heideggerian reflections thus take on an aspect of comical banality, while at the same time unmasking a deeper and persistent cultural narcissism: "By means of sport we become the ornament of our being. . . . Sport has now become our true interpretation (*Auslegung*), our work."

With its polysemic ironies, Jelinek's *Totenauberg* is far from reinstating and reinserting a defined type of identity, much less Jewish ethnicity, into Austria's hegemonic culture. Jelinek's acknowledged debt to Karl Kraus's linguistic scrutiny of cultural icons and identity lends her writing a cosmopolitan irony that belies any facile accommodation of a national or ethnic identity. Following in the tradition of Austria's assimilated Jewish writers, Jelinek articulates ethnic concerns from within a multicontextual perspective that subordinates ethnic concerns to a more complex and hybrid model of cultural identity. Even though her play specifically refers to the traumatic experience of the Holocaust as a potential unifying focus for Jewish identity, it remains thoroughly multilayered and relocates the past always through its present reconfigurations of cultural ideologies such as the marketable discourse on *Heimat,* the asylum debate, and the notions of ecology and organic health. Likewise, Jelinek's characters possess no sharp boundaries, and their discourses are for the most part interchangeable. The author's severe cultural critique of commodified discourse thus constitutes at the same time a constructive refusal to entertain a sentimental Jewish identity in an era of philo-Semitism with its abundant fetishism

of exemplary Jewish victims and what Henryk Broder calls its fascination with "dead and half-dead Jews."

Even Arendt, often seen as the exemplary Jewish philosopher of this century, is more soberly described by Jelinek as "a good essayist in practical thinking" who never had the luxury of exploring pure ontologies in Heideggerian fashion but had to settle for a hybrid set of reflections that arose from her cultural displacement and adjustment. Jelinek's linguistic scenario of competing and overlapping discourses that resonate in Austria's cultural landscape ultimately restores Arendt's displacement as a cultural position indigenous to Germany or Austria rather than making her exile appear as an exceptional anomaly from within a presumably grounded *Heimat.* Locating displacement at the center of Austria's cultural discourses in which notions of belonging mask discontinuity, rupture, and difference, the author highlights the complex subject positions and ideologies that compete with one another in any construction of culture. In so doing, she recovers the diasporic element that had shaped Vienna's cultural identity at the turn of the century and that had subsequently been demonized in Austria as being exclusively Jewish rather than the unique result of cross-cultural encounters.

MATTHIAS KONZETT

Editions
First edition: *Totenauberg,* Reinbek bei Hamburg: Rowohlt, 1991

Further Reading
Becker, Peter von, "Wir leben auf einem Berg von Leichen und Schmerz," *Theater Heute* (1992)

Berka, Sigrid, "Ein Gespräch mit Elfriede Jelinek," *Modern Austrian Literature* 26, no. 2 (1993)

Fiddler, Allyson, *Rewriting Reality: An Introduction to Elfriede Jelinek,* Oxford and Providence, Rhode Island: Berg, 1994

Hoesterey, Ingeborg, "Postmoderner Blick auf österreichische Literatur: Bernhard, Glaser, Handke, Jelinek, Roth," *Modern Austrian Literature* 23, no. 3–4 (1990)

Honegger, Gitta, "This German Language . . . : An Interview with Elfriede Jelinek," *Theater* 25 (1994)

Janz, Marlies, *Elfriede Jelinek,* Stuttgart: Metzler, 1995

Kathrein, Karin, "Heimat ist das Unheimlichste: Elfriede Jelinek zu *Totenauberg,*" *Bühne,* Heft 9 (Wien, 1992)

Konzett, Matthias, "The Politics of Recognition in Contemporary Austrian Jewish Literature," *Monatshefte* 90, no. 1 (1998)

Roos, Theo, "Bei der Stange bleiben: Ein Gespräch mit Elfriede Jelinek über ihr neues Heidegger-Stück," *Symptome, Zeitschrift für epistemologische Baustellen,* Heft 8 (1991)

Winter, Riki, "Gespräch mit Elfriede Jelinek," in *Elfriede Jelinek,* edited by Kurt Bartsch and Günther A. Höfler, Graz: Droschl, 1991

Jesuit Drama

The Jesuit drama of the German-speaking areas of Europe was part of a cultural phenomenon that flourished on both sides of the Atlantic between 1540, when Pope Paul III sanctioned the newly founded Society of Jesus, and 1773, when the society was temporarily suppressed. Written exclusively in Latin, Jesuit drama transcends the linguistic frontiers that demarcate modern literatures; in Germany, the focus of the Lutheran Reformation, Jesuit drama flourished with particular vigor as an effective yet peaceful weapon in a holy war waged against the tenets of the new Protestantism. Because of its intention to strengthen and restore the faith, Jesuit drama may justly claim to have been the principal literary manifestation of the Counter Reformation in Central Europe.

The Society of Jesus aimed to propagate and defend the faith and to provide instruction in it; these were also the objectives of Jesuit drama, which was a direct product of the society's educational program. Jesuit plays were written by educators and teachers for performance by their pupils in the expanding network of schools and colleges set up to champion Roman Catholicism and reconvert those parts of Germany, Austria, and Switzerland that had already lapsed. It is therefore not surprising that Jacobus Pontanus, the educational theorist whose thinking shaped the *Institutio Studiorum* or Jesuit educational program of 1599, turned to writing plays in Augsburg, or that Jacobus Gretser of Ingolstadt made a specialty of "conversion" dramas featuring St. Paul, St. Augustine, and the home-grown Udo of Magdeburg.

Initially, Jesuit drama in Germany was closely related to humanist school drama: both were written and performed at schools and were designed to combine the inculcation of morals with a command of Latin and the ability to speak clearly and move easily in public, attainments that would be useful later in professional life. It also inherited subject matter from modern "classics" from the Netherlands such as *Euripus,* a masterly example of the "progress" play (in which the protagonist makes his progress through the ups and downs of life toward his eternal goal) by Levin Brecht, a Fransciscan based in Antwerp. Jesuit drama also borrowed from *Asotus* (1510) by Macropedius and *Acolastus* (1529) by Gnaphaeus, two effective treatments of the "prodigal son" theme. For the next two centuries, the genre's subject matter was drawn mainly from the lives and legends of saints, martyrs and biblical figures, Church history, and Christian eschatology. Along with the wandering players, the Jesuits (and the Benedictines) provided most people's experience of dramatic entertainment.

Cenodoxus by Jakob Biedermann was the first major Jesuit drama of the 17th century: its first performance in Munich in 1609 was a momentous event comparable with the premieres of Schiller's *Die Räuber* and Hauptmann's *Vor Sonnenaufgang.* Its focus on a saintly scholar who is secretly consumed by pride and hypocrisy touched the raw nerve of a whole era, while its effective treatment of its central character's self-righteous egoism may be regarded as the first successful attempt by a German playwright to create a fully rounded dramatic character. Plays such as Biedermann's *Cenodoxus* and *Theophilus felix* (1621) by the Bavarian Georg Bernhardt posed a leading question: How should the individual human being define himself, set as he is in his own appointed place in the social order and caught as he is between the rival claims of life on earth and the life hereafter, between self-fulfillment and the sacrifice of self for a greater good? Such a question has its analogies in the contemporaneous drama of Elizabethan and Jacobean England, but the Jesuit dramatists posed it from a position of certainty, not doubt. This position, in turn, profoundly affected the Jesuits' relationship to the traditional dramatic genres and encouraged them to adapt the methods of tragedy to Christian ends and experiment with interesting hybrids. Even their most uncompromisingly serious plays tend to contain a strong element of humor in the manner of Plautus,

while from Senecan tragedy they took the chorus, which suited their religious performance venues and didactic purposes, since it addressed audiences directly. Significantly, the Jesuit playwrights also realized that to make ideas into effective drama they could use allegory: indeed, a key feature of their drama is its personification of abstract concepts that often intermingle or alternate with the historical or legendary dramatis personae. In this way, issues raised by the dramatic action and the protagonist's soul or conscience frequently play their part(s) visibly in personified form. These plays are thus the counterparts of the allegorizing religious sculpture and painting of the Baroque period.

During the High Baroque period, Jesuit drama reached its apex in artistic and theatrical terms. In the Vienna of Emperor Leopold I, Nicolaus von Avancini edified and entertained large audiences with performances of his *Pietas victrix* (1659; Piety Victorious), a grandiose drama that glorified the Roman Church and Holy Roman Empire by dramatizing the victory of Constantine. Two years earlier, in Cologne, *Rusticus imperans* (1657; The Peasant as Ruler) by Jacob Masen illustrated another facet of the period's great sociopolitical debate by reworking the theme of the drunken peasant who wakes up to find himself king, if only for a day. Elements of this debate are still apparent in the dramas of Johann Baptist Adolf, although these are arguably more significant as dramatic precursors of the *Zauberstücke* of Viennese popular comedy, a secularized offshoot of Jesuit drama that flourished in and after the decades when the Society of Jesus was suppressed. Indeed, the literary-historical importance of German Jesuit drama has generally been seen to lie in its influence on later playwrights: Zacharias Werner's efforts to dramatize religious ideals, which, like Ferdinand Raimund's ability to amuse, touch and edify by moving between the supernatural sphere and the down-to-earth, certainly owe something to Jesuit drama.

More recently, interest has turned to the Jesuits' creative use of stage effects to thematize abstract arguments and bring ideological issues before a broader public than the one addressed by their vernacular contemporaries. Bilingual programs with synopses (*periochae*), many now collected in Szarota's monumental edition, facilitated audience participation and have recorded for us many a long-vanished play. That Latin remained the Jesuits' sole verbal medium may seem paradoxical, but it shows that drama consists of more than words and that in addressing the spiritual needs of the contemporary world, the Jesuits brought about a rebirth of "classical" tragedy, comedy, and, often, a mixture of both, which had broader immediate appeal than the neoclassical revivals championed by their European and German contemporaries.

PETER SKRINE

See also Religion and Literature

Further Reading

Best, Thomas W., *Jacob Bidermann*, New York: Twayne, 1974

Dyer, Denis, *Jacob Bidermann: Cenodoxus*, Edinburgh: Edinburgh University Press, 1975

Griffin, Nigel, *Jesuit School Drama: A Checklist of Critical Literature*, London: Grant and Cutler, 1976; *Supplement I*, London: Grant and Cutler, 1986

Müller, Johannes, *Das Jesuitendrama in den Ländern deutscher Zunge vom Anfang (1555) bis zum Hochbarock (1663)*, Augsburg: Filser, 1930

Skrine, Peter, "New Light on Jesuit Drama in Germany," *German Life and Letters*, New Series 34, no. 3 (April 1981)

Sprengel, Peter, "Der Spieler-Zuschauer im Jesuitentheater: Beobachtungen an frühen oberdeutschen Ordensdramen," *Daphnis* 16 (1987)

Szarota, Elida Maria, *Das Jesuitendrama im deutschen Sprachgebiet: Eine Periochen-Edition*, 4 vols., Munich: Fink, 1979–87

Valentin, Jean Marie, *Le Théâtre des Jésuites dans les pays de langue allemande: Répertoire chronologique des pièces représentées et des documents conservés (1555–1773)*, Stuttgart: Hiersemann, 1983–84

———, *Theatrum Catholicum*, Nancy: Presses Universitaires, 1990

Wimmer, Ruprecht, *Jesuitentheater: Didaktik und Fest: Das Exemplum des ägyptischen Joseph auf den deutschen Bühnen der Gesellschaft Jesu*, Frankfurt: Klostermann, 1982

Jewish Culture and Literature

The burning of books in 1933 marked the end of 150 years of German-Jewish cultural life, characterized by an almost endless list of Jewish writers, thinkers, and artists. This period, however, was a relatively short episode when considered in the context of more than 1,000 years of Jewish history and culture in Germany. This history is one of exploitation, persecution, and bloodshed, interrupted by periods of remarkable creativity.

In the Middle Ages, for example, centers of Jewish theological and spiritual thinking could be found in German territories. The Yiddish language developed on the basis of German varieties, and early Yiddish literature emerged. It was only in the late 18th century that Jews started to embrace German language and culture—and were allowed to do so. Until the Enlightenment, Jewish life and literature had remained distinct, but from the late 18th century on Jews became part of German culture—although their wholehearted approach to assimilation and acculturation was met with latent suspicion or even hostility. The characterization of the period between 1780 and 1933 as a "German-Jewish dialogue" or even as a "German-Jewish symbiosis" has, however, been challenged by Gershom Scholem (1897–1982). In a genuine dialogue, both partners ideally respect each other for what they are. Since the time of the early Enlightenment, however, Jews were expected to give up their language, their distinct cultural identity, and sometimes their religion as a price for emancipation.

Germany rejected its Jewish writers, artists, and thinkers, and with them the entire German-Jewish heritage in 1933. After 1945, these intellectuals were claimed back as Germans, but the German society remained uneasy about their Jewishness. Jewish, German, or Jewish-German? These attributes can be seen as adequate descriptions of three periods of a 1,000-year history.

The first such period can be described as the Ashkenaz period. Evidence for the existence of Jewish settlements in German territory on the banks of the Rhine can be traced back to the ninth century. These settlements were founded in former Roman cities such as Speyer, Worms, Mainz, Trier, Cologne, and Regensburg and spread northward and eastward during the next centuries. Hebrew sources call this first compact area of Jewish settlement *Ashkenaz*. In the Bible, Ashkenaz is the name of a people and a country bordering on Armenia and the Upper Euphrates (Genesis 10:3 and 1 Chronicles 1:6), but the term became identified with Germany and German Jewry. Until the end of the 11th century, Jews seem to have lived peacefully as a minority among the German majority. In the developing Holy Roman Empire of German Nation, Jewish merchants, with their connections to Italy,

southern France, Spain, and especially the Byzantine Empire, had an important role to play in the economy. They were therefore granted privileged conditions by the emperors. Ashkenaz, especially Mainz and Worms, became spiritual centers for all Jews in Central Europe and attracted students from far away, among them the famous commentator of the Bible and the Talmud, Rashi Solomon ben Isaac (1040–1105) from France.

At the beginning of the 11th century, Gershom ben Juda, the most influential Talmudic scholar of his period, shaped Ashkenazic Jewry by his legal decisions (*takkanot*), which were not only based on the Bible and the Talmud but also influenced by German law. The most well known of these *takkanot* is the ban on bigamy. Until then, Jews had been allowed to have more than one wife.

The first synagogues on German territory—influenced by ecclesiastical architecture—were built in Cologne (1012 or 1040), Trier (1066), Speyer (1090), Worms (1174–75), and Regensburg (1225).

Apart from religion, one of the main differences between the Jewish minority and the German majority in Ashkenaz seems to have been the fact that most Jews, at least most male Jews, could read and write. The spoken language of daily communication at that time is assumed to have been the local variety of German. The written language, however, was Hebrew.

Things started to change dramatically with the First Crusade (1096–99). Stirred up by apocalyptic preaching, the mob heading east for Jerusalem began its fight against the "heathens" by slaughtering the Jewish communities. In this first period of persecution, parts of the established ecclesiastical elites—bishops, even the pope—together with local councils and the emperor tried to prevent acts of violence against Jews. In the centuries that followed, however, Christian theology underwent a fundamental change. Christ was no longer worshipped as *Christus Pantokrator,* the emperor of the world, but as the suffering Messiah whose wounds had been inflicted by the Jews. These ideas, made popular by the Minorites, and the new theological emphasis on the Eucharist formed the basis for a number of anti-Jewish myths that spread all over Europe: Jews were not only held responsible for the death of Christ but also accused of host desecration and ritual murder. In the economically and politically unstable times of the late 13th century, Jews, and especially well-off Jews, were no longer a well-accepted minority but instead became the target of xenophobia and envy. Pogroms occurred regularly between the 12th and the 14th century, culminating in the so-called Plague Pogroms (1347–54).

As a reaction to the First Crusade, a new form of spirituality and piety emerged among Jews, centered around the idea of martyrdom. During the first pogroms in the 11th century, Jews had tried to defend themselves. Now self-sacrifice became a permanent doctrine. Ashkenaz became famous for its mysticism and piety, and contact between Jews and Christians decreased. Although plenty of medieval theological books claim to be dialogues between Jews and Christians, most of them are fictitious and only introduce a Jewish character—whose task it is to ask questions and then be persuaded at the end by a Christian—in order to stress the superiority of the Christian faith.

During the 12th, 13th, and 14th centuries, Jews and the majority of Germans had little in common culturally. Nevertheless, a Jewish minstrel (*Minnesänger*), Suesskind von Trimberg, is known to have lived in the 13th century; he wrote his lyrics, six of which have survived, in Middle High German.

The first evidence of the Yiddish language goes back to the second half of the 13th century. The spoken languages of the Jews in Ashkenaz were the regional varieties of German with a Hebrew vocabulary that reflected religious domains. A Jewish variety of German emerged, and it started to develop independently of German. In times of isolation and persecution, communication became more and more restricted to fellow Jews, some of whom were from other places in which a different German dialect was spoken. Hebrew vocabulary and a mixture of features from different German dialects became the characteristics of this new Judeo-German language. This language was coined as West Yiddish by 20th-century philologists; East Yiddish developed subsequently in Poland, Lithuania, Ukraine, and Russia. The speakers themselves referred to the language as *tajtsh* (German), *leshonenu* (our language), or *loshn Ashkenaz* (the German language). Yiddish became the written language primarily of women, who were not usually educated in Hebrew. It was for them that passages from the Bible, prayer books, devotional literature, and so-called Minhagim-books, which describe Jewish customs and appropriate behavior in different everyday situations, were translated into Yiddish. Private letters were written in Yiddish, as well as legal documents. The beginnings of an early Yiddish literature are marked by the Yiddish adaptations of the Wigalois-story, *Widuwilt* (likely 14th century), and the Gudrun-saga, *Dukus Horant* (1382–83).

The next period spanned from 1420 to 1750. Sixty years after the Plague Pogroms, during which some 350 Jewish communities were destroyed, Jewish life in German territories was declining, a process that would continue for almost another 200 years. A number of surviving communities were expelled, and others were burdened with heavy taxes by the emperor and the German sovereign princes. The Jews had lost their economic power. A fierce anti-Judaism supported by the Church led to the establishment of ghettos in most towns, where Jews continued to live during the 15th century. In the 16th century, the Reformation and the new Protestant church failed to bring about a change in the general attitude toward Jews. In the year 1603, between 8,000 and 10,000 Jews lived in Germany, mostly in the Reichsstädte, the independent towns of the Holy Roman Empire, and in Hildesheim, Paderborn, Trier, Cologne, Mainz, Speyer, Bamberg, and Fulda.

As a consequence of constant persecution and exploitation through the imposition of heavy taxes during the 15th century, most of the influential rabbinical families left, and the traditional centers of Jewish culture and scholarship lost their significance. Despite the general atmosphere of decline, however, some of the most famous West Yiddish literature was written and published in this period. The *Shmu'el-Buch* by Moshe Esrim Vearba, presumably written in the 15th century, tells the biblical story of King David in the style of a medieval heroic epic—complete with gripping fights and erotic passages. Also dating back to the 15th century is *Akedas Jitshak,* an epic poem about the sacrificing of Isaac. Still popular in the 19th century was Elia Levita Bachur's *Bovo-Buch* (1507–8), an adaptation of an English adventure narrative. The most popular Jewish narrative tradition was the *ma'ase,* which combines story, legend, and fairy tale, and which collects religious and secular motifs from Europe, the Middle East, and even the Far East. The most famous collection of *ma'ases,* the *Ma'ase-Buch,* dates back to the early 16th century. Also published about 1600 was the popular *Tsene Urene,* a free adaptation of the Bible for women.

From 1600 onward, the social and economic situation of the Jews in Germany gradually began to improve. Their numbers increased thanks to the arrival of the Sephardim, Jews originating from Spain and Portugal, who had been expelled from these countries in 1492. After the Thirty Years' War, some of the sovereign princes realized that Jews could play an important part in the economic recovery of the provinces and granted them more tolerable conditions. In 1700, approximately 25,000 Jews lived in German territories; in 1750, the number had grown to approximately 60,000.

A Jewish elite emerged, the so-called *Hofjuden,* who were granted individual privileges by the sovereign princes and were no longer subject to inner-Jewish jurisdiction. By contrast, an impoverished group of Jews, who could not afford to pay the high taxes and therefore were not allowed to settle down, moved from town to town, dependent on charity or trying to survive as peddlers. This situation weakened the authority of the traditional Jewish elites and institutions, the rabbis and the councils of elders. Many Jews were too poor to learn Hebrew, and an increasingly large group could not follow the prayers in Hebrew any more. Consequently, more religious literature was translated into Yiddish. A small circle of *Hofjuden* not only knew German but had started to learn other European languages as well. As early as 1700, this group formed the beginning of the Jewish enlightenment, the *Haskalah.* The Haskalah is often mistaken for a movement that, from the very beginning, promoted Jewish assimilation into German society. This is definitely not the case. The *Haskalah* and its famous protagonist, Moses Mendelssohn (1729–86), advocated first of all an inner-Jewish reform. The *Haskalah* targeted socially emancipated Jews who left the ghetto but remained attached to Jewish religion and tradition. These modernizers, the so-called *Maskilim,* fought the Yiddish language as a stigma of the ghetto and tried to reinstate Hebrew as the true Jewish language. Mendelssohn's translation of the Bible into German, written in Hebrew letters and with a Hebrew commentary, was an attempt to lead Jews back to the Bible and to the Hebrew of the Bible, and to lead them away from Yiddish, which he despised as a jargon.

After his famous dispute with the Swiss clergyman Johann Caspar Lavater in 1769–70, Mendelssohn came to realize the dilemma into which the Enlightenment and emancipation would lead the Jews: Jews would never be accepted as equals as long as they kept their traditions, their language, and their religion.

Some of his own children and grandchildren, among them Dorothea Schlegel and the composer Felix Mendelssohn-Bartholdy, abandoned Judaism and were baptized, an act that, as Heinrich Heine put it, was seen as the admission ticket to society.

The third period has been characterized as a German-Jewish symbiosis. It would take a further 85 years following Moses Mendelssohn's death before Jews would formally be granted civil rights in Germany in 1871 (1867 in the Habsburg Empire). The linguistic projects of the *Maskilim* also were partly successful. While knowledge of Hebrew did not improve, almost from one generation to the next, Jews started to adopt the German language. Education and culture became the most popular ways by which Jews, with remarkable success, integrated into the German society. By the end of the 19th century, especially in urban centers such as Berlin or Vienna, most Jews belonged to the middle class or even to the upper middle class, while only a quarter of the Jewish population could be classified as working class. About 1900, approximately one percent of the Prussian population was Jewish, but ten percent of pupils in higher education were Jews. The average level of education, therefore, was distinctly higher among Jews than among Christians. A Jewish professional profile emerged: trade and finance were the traditional economic areas open to Jews, and the professions such as law, medicine, and journalism were now accessible to highly qualified Jewish academics. Even after 1871, however, they still faced entry restrictions to universities, administrative positions, the judiciary, schools, and the army. This is the sociological background that fostered the amazing intensity of Jewish contributions to German literature.

The first Jewish poet who is known to have written in German is Ephraim Moses Kuh (1731–90), whose *Hinterlassene Gedichte* were published in 1792. Kuh is the protagonist in Berthold Auerbach´s novel *Dichter und Kaufmann* (1840). Auerbach (1812–82) himself exemplified the successful emancipation and acculturation of Jews; by contrast, Heinrich Heine was torn all of his life between his Jewish background and assimilation.

From the very beginning, Jewish attempts to participate in German cultural life were met with reservation or even hostility. As a reaction to the famous Jewish *Salons* of Rahel Varnhagen or Henriette Herz, where poets and politicians, scientists and philosophers, men and women, and Jews and Christians met on an equal level, the so-called *christlich-deutsche Teegesellschaften* were established, in which neither women nor Jews were allowed to take part. Heinrich Heine and his contemporary Ludwig Börne, who both founded a new tradition of journalism and criticism, were often attacked as Jews—although both of them had formally abandoned Judaism.

From 1870 on, anti-Semitism began to emerge. Based on almost 2,000 years of Christian anti-Judaism, new stereotypes were added to the images associated with Judaism. Jews became associated with liberalism, capitalism, and socialism—in short, everything that made the late 19th century an uncertain period and that questioned established values and ways of life. Anti-Semitism became a latent and socially acceptable condition in German society of the time. This is reflected in the stereotypical way that German authors such as Wilhelm Raabe or Gustav Freytag portrayed Jewish characters. At the end of his life, even

Auerbach came to admit that his lifelong struggle for emancipation and assimilation might have been in vain. To safeguard Jewish civil and social equality, the *Central-Verein Deutscher Staatsbürger jüdischen Glaubens* (CV) was founded in 1893; this organization opposed apostasy, intermarriage, Zionism, and Internationalism.

The latent rejection of Jewish culture and religion by German society caused Jewish writers, historians, and philosophers to recollect their own cultural, historical, and religious heritage. From the Enlightenment until 1933, authors such as Heinrich Heine, Jakob Wassermann, Arthur Schnitzler, Else Lasker-Schüler, Arnold Zweig, Joseph Roth, and Alfred Döblin, to mention but some of the most famous names, returned to traditional Jewish motifs, portraying Jewish characters in past and present and idealizing the "authentic" way of life of Eastern-European Jewry. Isaac M. Jost and Heinrich Graetz founded a Jewish historiography. The *Wissenschaft des Judentums* emerged, centered around Leopold Zunz, Abraham Geiger, and Samuel Hirsch. It combined a modern intellectual approach with a restatement of Jewish thought, history, and tradition, as well as an inner reform of Judaism.

This special combination of complete assimilation with a reflection of Jewish heritage and the modernization of Jewish traditions in many areas can be seen as one of the main characteristics of German-Jewish culture between 1780 and 1933. As George L. Mosse has pointed out, German Jews developed a lasting attachment to the ideals of the German Enlightenment—including tolerance, rationalism, and optimism—long after German society had abandoned them.

The many facets of German-Jewish life in the Weimar Republic came to an end when Hitler was elected to power and Jews were excluded from German culture. The *Jüdischer Kulturbund* remained the only framework in Germany in which Jewish cultural life could officially take place between 1933 and 1941. The start of the deportations marked the end of over 1,000 years of Jewish life in Germany. German-Jewish writers, thinkers, and artists continued to work in exile, and even after the war and the Holocaust, Jewish writers contributed to German literature: Ilse Aichinger, Hilde Domin, Erich Fried, Wolfgang Hildesheimer, Stephan Hermlin, Stefan Heym, Jurek Becker, Rose Ausländer, Nelly Sachs, Paul Celan, and Sarah Kirsch, to mention but a few. Philosophers such as Theodor Adorno, Max Horkheimer, and Herbert Marcuse deeply influenced the young generation in the late 1960s and early 1970s. Nevertheless, Germany has ceased to be the center of Jewish culture that it was before 1933.

GERTRUD REERSHEMIUS

See also Exile Literature; Holocaust (Shoah) Literature

Further Reading

Breuer, Mordechai, et al., editors, *German-Jewish History in Modern Times. Volume One: Tradition and Enlightenment, 1600–1780,* New York: Columbia University Press, 1997

Grimm, Gunter E., and Hans-Peter Bayerdörfer, *Im Zeichen Hiobs: Jüdische Schriftsteller und deutsche Literatur im 20. Jahrhundert,* Königstein: Athenäum, 1985

Hermand, Jost, *Judentum und deutsche Kultur: Beispiele einer schmerzhaften Symbiose,* Cologne, Weimar, and Vienna: Böhlau, 1996

Herzig, Arno, *Jüdische Geschichte in Deutschland: Von den Anfängen bis zur Gegenwart,* Munich: Beck, 1997

Mosse, George L., *German Jews Beyond Judaism,* Bloomington: Indiana University Press, 1985

Scholem, Gershom, "Wider den Mythos vom deutsch-jüdischen Gespräch," *Bulletin des Leo-Baeck-Instituts* 27 (1964)

Schulte, Christoph, editor, *Deutschtum und Judentum: Ein Disput unter Juden aus Deutschland,* Stuttgart: Reclam, 1993

Uwe Johnson 1934–1984

Unlike any other German author, Uwe Johnson, who lived in both East and West Germany, grappled in almost all of his works with the divided Germany and its ideological and personal ramifications. He therefore has been repeatedly called "Dichter der beiden Deutschland" (author of the two Germanies), a term coined in the early 1960s by the West German critic Günter Blöcker. Johnson himself considered this label inappropriate since, on the one hand, it was linked to an ideological appropriation by West Germany and, on the other hand, because throughout his life his works were unavailable in East Germany.

With the opening of the wall and the unification of Germany, this situation has changed considerably. Since 1989, Johnson's work has received unprecedented attention in East and West Germany, both in the general media and in academia: his works have been reissued by his publisher Suhrkamp, numerous meetings and conferences focusing upon Johnson's work have taken place, a new yearbook and a new international series on Johnson scholarship were established, the Johnson archive in Frankfurt/Main published many of his early texts for the first time, and the archive also put together a Johnson exhibit that toured Germany in 1991.

While there is a growing consensus about Johnson's central role in postwar German literature, there is no agreement on whether Johnson's work is part of East or West German literature. While prior to 1989 most critics presumed that Johnson was part of West German literature, since 1989 Johnson has been discovered as an author of and about East Germany. Prominent intellectuals and scholars including Günter Grass, Hans Mayer, and Manfred Bierwisch have declared Johnson to be the most significant author who came out of the German Democratic Republic (GDR). Instead of trying to classify Johnson as either East or West German author, however, one can read Johnson's texts as challenging standard East/West classifications: his works explore the way in which both German states depended on one another and reacted to each other within the logic of the Cold War. From this vantage point, the term "author of the two Germanies" gains new meaning and validity.

The narratives Johnson wrote in the 1950s and early 1960s all deal with the situation of the individual in a socialist state that betrays the socialist ideals of building a more humane and just society. *Ingrid Babendererde: Reifeprüfung 1953* (1985; Ingrid Babendererde: High School Diploma) and *Mutmaßungen über Jakob* (1959; *Speculations about Jakob*), the two novels he wrote in East Germany, portray increasingly disillusioned individuals in conflict with the state; *Das dritte Buch über Achim* (1961; *The Third Book about Achim*), the first book he wrote in the West, portrays the failing communication between East and West Germans; and *Zwei Ansichten* (1965; *Two Views*) is the allegorical tale of a love relationship that does not survive the building of the wall. Several characters in these narratives decide to leave East Germany, but the Federal Republic of Germany (FRG) appears at no point as a viable alternative to the GDR.

Johnson wrote his first novel *Ingrid Babendererde* at the age of 19. For reasons that say more about the ideological situation in the two German states during the 1950s than about the quality of the novel, Johnson was neither able to publish it in the GDR nor in the FRG. (*Ingrid Babendererde* appeared posthumously in West Germany in 1985.) Johnson's second novel, *Speculations about Jakob,* is probably his best-known work, and its challenging narrative structure—influenced by William Faulkner—puts the text squarely into the modernist tradition. Much like a typical detective story, *Speculations about Jakob* starts out with the unexplained death of Jakob. Adopting a range of narrative techniques and perspectives, among them that of a Stasi (state security) officer, the novel seeks to reconstruct Jakob's life. Yet the circumstances of his death remain unsolved, deliberately leaving the burden of making sense of Jakob's life and death to the reader. Considering that the novel was written in the late 1950s, *Speculations about Jakob* includes surprisingly detailed descriptions of Stasi surveillance and recruitment methods. This aspect alone made the work unacceptable in the East; ironically, Johnson's careful if not sympathetic depiction of the Stasi officer also provoked critical reactions in the West.

Johnson left East Berlin for West Berlin in 1959, just before *Speculations about Jakob* appeared with the West German publisher Suhrkamp. Defying the political realities of the Cold War, Johnson insisted that he did not escape from East Germany but that he had merely moved to West Berlin. This personal assessment did not stop the GDR from calling him a traitor, nor did it prevent the FRG from trying to embrace him as a dissident. His third novel, *The Third Book about Achim,* appeared in 1961, just weeks after the building of the Berlin Wall. Not surprisingly, Johnson's works were dismissed in the GDR for their alleged formalism. Prominent GDR authors such as Peter Hacks and

Hermann Kant attacked Johnson publicly in the early 1960s. Yet a number of other GDR authors were influenced by or responded to Johnson's works in their own writings (e.g., Christa Wolf in *The Quest for Christa T.* [1969] and Fritz Rudolf Fries in *Auf dem Weg nach Oobliadooh* [1966; On the Way to Oobliadooh]). After the smear campaigns of the early 1960s, Johnson's works were entirely ignored in the GDR until 1986, when Jürgen Grambow succeeded in publishing an article on Johnson in the GDR journal *Sinn und Form*. Grambow eventually gained official approval for the publication of an anthology of Johnson's works, a project that did not appear until late in 1989, almost concurrently with the opening of the Berlin Wall.

In West Germany, Johnson became a well-known and controversial author with the publication of his two novels in 1959 and 1961. Johnson received important literary prizes; excerpts of his works were included in high school textbooks; and his works were translated into several different languages, which turned him into an internationally known author. The flip side of his success were attacks from conservatives critics who accused him of supporting communism and justifying the Berlin Wall. The most notorious case was Hermann Kesten's misrepresentation of Johnson, which resulted in a media frenzy and a parliamentary attempt—under the leadership of secretary of state Heinrich von Brentano—to revoke a prestigious grant that Johnson had received. The allegations proved to be wrong, and the resolution was withdrawn, but reactions such as this one contributed to the fact that Johnson never felt at home in West Germany. He spent long periods in New York City and moved permanently to England in 1974, where he died 10 years later at the age of 49.

Johnson's understanding of his role as a writer overlaps with the socialist realist notion of the writerly role, yet his aesthetic principles are entirely incompatible with those propagated by socialist realism: Johnson believed in the important societal role of the author and literature, but he rejected any attempt to instrumentalize art for political ends. His writings are based on minute and detailed descriptions of "reality," yet his writings undercut any one-dimensional notion of reality; he did not experiment with language for its own sake but saw the need for finding new narrative means in order to approximate what he considered the multidimensional "truth." In his Frankfurt lecture series (*Begleitumstände: Frankfurter Vorlesungen* [1980; Related Circumstances: Frankfurt Lectures]), Johnson explains that his own position between two ideologically opposed systems requires a new language and new narrative styles. He also maintains that the German-German border, the symbol for the ideological division of the world, has direct implications for his writings: the border turns into a figure for the difficulties of representation in the postwar world. *Speculations about Jakob* is probably the best example of this dimension of Johnson's aesthetics. The work's multiple narrative perspectives preclude the reader from identifying with any one perspective or ideological stance. Provoking the reader's active participation in the reading process, the novel attempts—both in terms of narrative style and of content—simultaneously to expose and defy the either/or logic of the Cold War.

It took Johnson 15 years to complete his monumental novel *Jahrestage: Aus dem Leben der Gesine Cresspahl* (*Anniversaries: From the Life of Gesine Cresspahl*); the first three parts of this work were published in the early 1970s, and the last part did not appear until 1983, one year before his death. Tracing the lives of three generations under different political systems and in different countries (from the Weimar Republic and National Socialism to the two German states in the 1950s and the United States in the 1960s), the thematic and historical scope of *Anniversaries* extends far beyond that of Johnson's other works. The novel chronicles one year in the life of Gesine Cresspahl (1967–68), a German woman in her mid-30s who lives in New York City and who reconstructs her own past and that of her parents for her daughter Marie. *Anniversaries* can be considered a work of remembrance regarding the history and legacy of fascism and the Holocaust, the early postwar period, and the failed socialist experiments in the GDR and Czechoslovakia (the novel ends on 20 August 1968, the day of the Soviet invasion.) The novel is sustained by an unresolved tension between Gesine's critical distance to the free market economy, crime, racism, and other aspects of U.S. society and her daughter Marie's immersion in U.S. society. Contrary to earlier assessments that considered *Anniversaries* aesthetically conventional, scholarly discussions of the 1990s have explored, among other aspects, the intersection of postmodern and political dimensions in Johnson's novel.

Among the shorter pieces Johnson wrote and published before completing the last part of *Anniversaries* are *Eine Reise nach Klagenfurt* (1974; A Trip to Klagenfurt), his literary reaction to the sudden death of his friend Ingeborg Bachmann, and the controversial story *Skizze eines Verunglückten* (1981; Sketch of an Accident Victim). The story, dealing with the figurative "death of an author" after he kills his unfaithful wife, provoked autobiographical readings that placed the story in the context of Johnson's failed marriage. Considering Johnson's general reluctance to expose the inner life—that of his characters and his own— others have argued that the story should be viewed as a literary response to the work of Max Frisch, especially his *Skizze eines Unglücks* (1972; Sketch of an Accident). Johnson, in fact, wrote the story on the occasion of Frisch's 70th birthday.

Johnson's works and his biography have gained new relevance in the post–Cold War era. Precisely because his work deals with a political period that has become historical since German unification, his writings are of interest to those seeking to understand more fully the most recent German past and its implications for the present. In the immediate postunification period, Johnson's works served as an object of identification for some East German readers. Several referred, for instance, to Johnson's critical portrayal of the Federal Republic (e.g., in the 29 May 1968 chapter from *Anniversaries*, "Wenn Jerichow zum Westen gekommen wäre" [If Jericho Had Become Part of the West]), and in the essay "Versuch eine Mentalität zu erklären" [Attempt to Explain a Mentality]). These texts portray East Germans who feel estranged or not welcome in the West, and they describe negative aspects of consumerism and the mass media—aspects that invite comparisons with a critical assessment of the effects of German unification. Other readers in East and West Germany consider the rediscovery of Johnson's works, decades after they were written, as an opportunity to work through aspects of GDR history that were, prior to 1989, largely inaccessible or taboo.

Thus, Johnson's works serve various roles today: they function as a "literary archaeology" of the GDR (Mecklenburg), but they also challenge an exclusive foregrounding of the "other" Germany (GDR) that tends to erase the role of the old FRG. His works interrogate not only East-West differences and the dynamics between both German states but also the history preceding the division of Germany, namely, the Nazi period and World War II.

FRIEDERIKE EIGLER

Biography
Born in Kammin, Pomerania (now Kamién Pomorski, Poland), 20 July 1934. Studied at the University of Rostock, 1952–54; University of Leipzig, 1954–56, degree in German literature, 1956; worked as a freelance writer; in Güstrow until 1959; in West Berlin, 1959–74; in England from 1974; first trip to the United States, 1961; German language editor, Harcourt Brace, New York, 1966–67; grant, Rockefeller Foundation, New York, 1967–68. Fontane Prize, 1960; International Publishers Prize, 1962; Villa Massino grant, 1962; Büchner Prize, 1971; Raabe Prize, 1975; Thomas Mann Prize, 1979; Literature Prize, Cologne, 1983. Died 23 February 1984.

Selected Works

Fiction
Mutmaßungen über Jakob, 1959; as *Speculations about Jakob,* translated by Ursule Molinaro, 1963
Das dritte Buch über Achim, 1961; as *The Third Book about Achim,* translated by Ursule Molinaro, 1967
Karsch und andere Prosa, 1964; translated in part as *An Absence,* by Richard and Clara Winston, 1969
Zwei Ansichten, 1965; as *Two Views,* translated by Richard and Clara Winston, 1966
Jahrestage: Aus dem Leben von Gesine Cresspahl, 4 vols., 1970–83; as *Anniversaries: From the Life of Gesine Cresspahl,* vols. 1–2 translated by Leila Vennewitz, 1975; vols. 2–4 translated by Vennewitz and Walter Arndt, 1987
Skizze eines Verunglückten, 1981
Ingrid Babendererde: Reifeprüfung 1953, 1985
Versuch, einen Vater zu finden. Marthas Ferien, 1988

Other
Eine Reise nach Klagenfurt, 1974
Berliner Sachen: Aufsätze, 1975
Begleitumstände: Frankfurter Vorlesungen, 1980

Translations
Israel Potter, by Herman Melville, 1960
In diesem Land, by John Knowles, 1963

Edited Works
Bertolt Brecht, *Me-ti: Buch der Wendungen,* 1965
Hans Mayer, *Das Werk von Samuel Beckett—Berliner Colloquium,* 1975
Max Frisch, *Stich-Worte,* 1975
Margret Boveri, *Verzweigungen,* 1977

Further Reading
Berbig, Roland, and Erdmut Wizisla, editors, *"Wo ich her bin . . .": Uwe Johnson in der D.D.R.,* Berlin: Kontext, 1993; 2nd edition, 1994
Fellinger, Raimund, editor, *Über Uwe Johnson,* Frankfurt: Suhrkamp, 1992
Fickert, Kurt J., *Dialogue with the Reader: The Narrative Stance in Uwe Johnson's Fiction,* Columbia, South Carolina: Camden House, 1996
Gansel, Carsten, editor, *Wenigstens in Kenntnis leben: Notate zum Werk Uwe Johnsons,* Neubrandenburg: Literaturzentrum Neubrandenburg, 1991
Gansel, Carsten, and Nicolai Riedel, editors, *Uwe Johnson zwischen Vormoderne und Postmoderne: Internationales Uwe Johnson Symposium 22.–24.9.1994,* Berlin and New York: de Gruyter, 1995
Golisch, Stefanie, *Uwe Johnson zur Einführung,* Hamburg: Junius, 1994
Grambow, Jürgen, "Heimat im Vergangenen," *Sinn und Form* 1 (1986)
Mayer, Hans, "Mutmaßungen über Jakob," in *Johnson: Ansichten, Einsichten, Aussichten,* edited by Manfred Jurgensen, Bern and Stuttgart: Francke, 1989
Mecklenburg, Norbert, *Die Erzählkunst Uwe Johnsons: Jahrestage und andere Prosa,* Frankfurt: Suhrkamp, 1997

Jahrestage: Aus dem Leben von Gesine Cresspahl 1970–1983
Novel by Uwe Johnson

Uwe Johnson lived in New York from 1966 to 1968, working first as a publisher's reader, then living on a stipend from the Rockefeller Foundation, and it was here that he began the novel that would take him until 1983 to complete. The first three volumes of *Jahrestage* were published in quick succession in 1970, 1971, and 1973, but readers then had to wait ten years for the final volume. Johnson's writer's block derived from a number of personal reasons, and he died less than a year after finishing *Jahrestage.* The novel's reception was mixed in the 1970s, with some critics thinking that Johnson had reverted to an outmoded realist aesthetic, revoking the experimental modernism of his early novels. Upon its completion, however, critics were generally of the opinion that this novel of nearly 2,000 pages was one of the best works by a contemporary German writer. Since German reunification, Johnson's reputation has been greatly enhanced, and now it is generally recognized that *Jahrestage* is both a major 20th-century novel and Johnson's most important work.

Living in New York gave Johnson distance from the cold war Germany of the 1960s, and he was fascinated by U.S. life and culture. At the same time, Johnson's perspective on Germany deepened. Whereas in his earlier novels he had concentrated on the German present, he now began to research extensively for a novel that was to narrate the immediate prehistory of the present in the years during the Third Reich and in subsequent years in East Germany until 1953. This could have given his story a straightforward chronology, but instead Johnson decided to set his German history in the present, and in New York, giving it both temporal and spatial frameworks of distance.

Jahrestage: Aus dem Leben von Gesine Cresspahl (Anniversaries: From the Life of Gesine Cresspahl) is the novel's full title, which points to some of the complexities of its form: "Jahrestage" can be translated as "days of the year" and "anniversaries." The novel contains 366 chapters of varying length, dated consecutively from 21 August 1967 to 20 August 1968. Each one is devoted to one day in the life of Gesine Cresspahl in New York, where she works as a foreign-languages secretary for a large commercial bank. Gesine tries to reconstruct the story of her childhood and youth in a small town in Mecklenburg, telling much of this story to her daughter, Marie. The anniversaries that the calendrical structure of the novel evokes are both personal and historical, related to Gesine and her family and to German and world history. The subtitle is also ambiguous: on the one hand, it suggests that Gesine is the novel's narrator; on the other hand, it suggests that another narrator tells her story. Johnson described *Jahrestage* as a story of one person's consciousness, but his narrative is far more complex than this implies. An astounding variety of voices and perspectives, forms of dialogue and monologue, complex allusions, and a range of registers from the factual and documentary, the encyclopedic and the imaginary, to the personal and emotive make this novel a polyphonic tour de force. A compendium of characters and places with several hundred entries was published with the final volume. A line-by-line commentary on the novel has been published (see Helbig et al., below) and a CD-ROM presenting some of the many sources Johnson used in writing it is also in preparation: the scope of this work is evidently inexhaustible.

It is now generally agreed that *Jahrestage*'s thematization of German guilt after the Holocaust is of unequaled intensity. The story manifests this guilt by focusing upon two moments in time: the catastrophic background to Gesine's childhood from 1933 to 1945 and a year in her life in New York in 1967–68. Here, Gesine has contact with Jewish Holocaust survivors, whose presence recalls her own guilt as a German. *Jahrestage* is one of a great many postwar German novels that deals with the Third Reich, but one of very few written from a German perspective in which remembrance for Jewish victims is a central issue.

The treatment of the past in *Jahrestage* is always informed by the present, and thus there is no straightforward narration of the past "as it was." The modernist epistemological concerns of Johnson's fiction from the very beginning are again fundamental to this novel's narrative form. Any similarities to Proust's narrative of a childhood remembered are only superficial; for Johnson, the past and the present are separated by a divide that critics have taken to reflect the collapse after the Holocaust of any positive notion of tradition. The third and fourth volumes of *Jahrestage* show how the GDR, where Gesine lived until 1953, systematically betrayed its socialist ideals, so that some critics have argued that Johnson's novel is entirely pessimistic. There is general agreement that Johnson's chronicle of the early years of the GDR is a major achievement, which contributed to the author's growing popularity since German reunification.

Other critics have paid more attention to the present, seeing it as more than just the location of a narrative about the past. Johnson's novel stands in a long tradition of German writers' interest in the United States, and *Jahrestage* is unique in its colorful portrayal of everyday life in New York. The present has its own plot, too. When Gesine is selected by her bank to go to Prague in order to negotiate a loan for the reform government, she feels that this is her last chance to work for an alternative to both capitalism and totalitarian communism. The novel ends on 20 August 1968, with Gesine on her way to Prague, unable to know that the reform will be crushed that night by a Soviet invasion. Her hopes will be shattered, and critics are generally dismissive of any suggestion that *Jahrestage,* in showing this, still manages to keep alive the sense of an alternative. The fact that *Jahrestage,* like all of Johnson's novels, was not published in the GDR probably prevented any serious critical reception of its thematization of reform socialism.

GREG BOND

Editions

First edition: *Jahrestage: Aus dem Leben von Gesine Cresspahl,* 4 vols., Frankfurt: Suhrkamp, 1970–83

Translation: *Anniversaries: From the Life of Gesine Cresspahl,* vol. 1–2 translated by Leila Vennewitz, vols. 3–4 translated by Vennewitz and Walter Arndt, New York: Harcourt Brace, 1975–87

Further Reading

Auerochs, Bernd, "'Ich bin dreizehn Jahre alt jeden Augenblick': Zum Verhältnis zwischen Deutschen und Juden in Uwe Johnsons *Jahrestagen,*" *Zeitschrift für deutsche Philologie* 112 (1993)

Baker, Gary, "The Influence of Walter Benjamin's Notion of Allegory on Uwe Johnson's *Jahrestage*: Form and Approach to History," *Colloquia Germanica* 66 (1993)

Bengel, Michael, editor, *Johnsons "Jahrestage,"* Frankfurt: Suhrkamp, 1985

Bond, D.G., *German History and German Identity: Uwe Johnson's "Jahrestage,"* Amsterdam and Atlanta, Georgia: Rodopi, 1993

Fries, Ulrich, *Uwe Johnsons "Jahrestage": Erzählstruktur und politische Subjektivität,* Göttingen: Vandenhoeck und Ruprecht, 1990

Helbig, Holger, et al., editors, *Johnsons "Jahrestage": Der Kommentar,* Göttingen: Vandenhoeck und Ruprecht, 1999

Michaelis, Rolf, editor, *Kleines Adreßbuch für Jerichow und New York: Ein Register zu Uwe Johnsons Roman "Jahrestage,"* Frankfurt: Suhrkamp, 1983

Riordan, Colin, *The Ethics of Narration: Uwe Johnson's Novels from "Ingrid Babendererde" to "Jahrestage,"* London: Modern Humanities Research Association for the Institute of Germanic Studies, 1989

Schmidt, Thomas, "'Es ist unser Haus, Marie': Zur Doppelbedeutung des Romantitels *Jahrestage,*" *Johnson-Jahrbuch* 1 (1994)

Mutmaßungen über Jakob 1959

Novel by Uwe Johnson

The appearance of Uwe Johnson's first published novel immediately attracted considerable critical attention, not least because Johnson was one of the very first authors to engage directly in literary form with the theme of a divided Germany. Much of its impact, however, can also be attributed to its complex modernist form, which was perceived by many critics as willfully obscurantist in comparison to the more conventional narrative writing of older contemporaneous authors such as Heinrich Böll.

Mutmaßungen über Jakob (1959; *Speculations about Jakob*) takes the form of a seemingly unshaped montage of various narrative techniques. Dialogues take place between initially unnamed speakers and are intermixed with monologic first-person sections, again from unnamed speakers; interspersed among these are also sections of apparently traditional third-person narration, from a narrative voice of indeterminate location. Thus, it is perhaps unsurprising that early critical reactions followed two quite distinct lines: either "keys" to the sequence of fictional events underlying the text (Popp), which tended to lose sight of the novel's narrative specificity, or stylistic comparisons with William Faulkner—whom Johnson was known to admire—which failed to understand the particular resonance of the novel's historical setting. The work is indeed inseparable from its historical-political context and not merely imitatively modernist; its perhaps idiosyncratic complexity of form generates rather than obscures possibilities of meaning and serves to challenge entrenched thinking about the way in which "identity" is construed, with implications for a context much wider than that of the divided Germany of the 1950s alone.

The story of the East German railway dispatcher Jakob Abs, which gradually emerges as the reader begins to penetrate and locate the various narrative voices, does indeed represent at its simplest level a poignant example of the dilemmas faced by citizens of the GDR living with the aftermath of World War II: divided families, emotions torn between loyalty to a new socialist ideal or to personal bonds of long-standing affection. In seeking to reconcile his desire to serve the state through honest work with his recognition that the state requires absolute loyalty even at the cost of entrapping loved ones, Jakob finds his understanding of the state's role in individual lives profoundly shaken. The suppression of the 1956 Hungarian uprising, in which he plays an unwilling part by virtue of his role as railway functionary, juxtaposed with his visit to the West at the time of the Suez crisis serves only to confuse further his understanding of the private man's role in the modern political world. His death crossing railway lines in the fog on his return has provided the impetus for the speculations of the title, which some early critics, as they sought to incorporate Johnson's work into a Cold War context, read as a reflection on the relative merits of the two German systems. As Hans Magnus Enzensberger pointed out when he called Johnson's novel "the first German novel since the war," however, it is a work that ultimately belongs on neither side of the political divide.

Later critical approaches have made this abundantly clear by elucidating the novel's modernist structure, perhaps most profitably in relation to the Bakhtinian concept of "dialogism" (Bond). What is striking upon a closer examination of the text's narrative strategies is the balance between the various subjectively shaped sections (dialogues, monologues) that struggle to form a coherent picture of Jakob and his motivation and the interspersed third-person diegetic segments, which seem to present a much simpler, consensus view of the reality of the man in his physical presence. There is no overall, organizing, or conventional narrative voice, so that no one perspective is privileged over another, and the reader is encouraged, as it were, to experiment with various perspectives on the central figure, whose ultimate inaccessibility is not necessarily to be read as a statement on the impenetrability of all human existence, nor, indeed, as an indictment of either German state. Instead, this figure can be seen as a focus for the dialogic process of understanding the self through the ceaselessly adjusted relation between self and other, a process in which all the figures are engaged, and which the novel also demands of the reader. Thus, in its refusal of a one-voiced perspective, the novel represents not just a modernist tour de force but also a challenge to all ideological fixation and, most particularly, to the sharp divide represented by the self-understanding and mutual recrimination of the two Germanies in the Cold War period.

The reassessment of the novel's political significance has also been paralleled by a new understanding of its ethical agenda, which some now see as a precursor to the broader sweep of historical investigation in Johnson's tetralogy *Jahrestage* (1970–83; *Anniversaries*). Colin Riordan in particular has stressed Johnson's scrupulousness in his search to understand the past of his two German homelands—that is, his central concern on the one hand to embody in his text a multiplicity of open-ended discourses that resist the reader's desire for easy foreclosure, yet on the other hand to capture and render with respect the integrity and weight of individual lives through minute attention to variations of idiom and the minutiae of everyday existence. More recent criticism (Mecklenburg) has benefited from two factors. First, critics such as Mecklenburg have had access to the full range of Johnson's papers, so that it is now possible to see more clearly how the novel's manner evolved and to appreciate fully its cultivation of intellectual independence both from Western European experimental writing and from socialist realism. Second, the reunification of Germany has enabled a fuller understanding of GDR history and thought, throwing into relief Johnson's extraordinarily sensitive and profound critique of the "Workers' State" even in this early novel. Thus, a text that was initially seen either as a precocious aesthetic experiment or as a Cold War polemic has come to be appreciated as an articulation of a unique critical perspective on the aims and ideals of the GDR by an informed insider and as a moving record of the state and its dilemmas in its early years. It remains, however, a novel whose central figure engages the reader powerfully despite the complexity of presentation; this combination, in turn, heralds very clearly Johnson's supreme balancing act in *Jahrestage* between skeptical distance and profound humanity.

MARY E. STEWART

Editions

First edition: *Mutmaßungen über Jakob*, Frankfurt: Suhrkamp, 1959
Translation: *Speculations about Jakob*, translated by Ursule Molinari, London: Cape, 1963

Further Reading

Bond, D.G., "The Dialogic Form of of Uwe Johnson's *Mutma(ungen über Jakob*," *Modern Language Review* 84 (1989)
Boulby, Mark, *Uwe Johnson*, New York: Ungar, 1974
Fickert, Kurt J., *Dialogue with the Reader: The Narrative Stance in Uwe Johnson's Fiction*, Columbia, South Carolina: Camden House, 1996
Popp, Hansjürgen, *Einführung in Uwe Johnsons Roman "Mutmaßungen über Jakob,"* Stuttgart: Klett, 1967
Riordan, Colin, *The Ethics of Narration: Uwe Johnson's Novels from "Ingrid Babendererde" to "Jahrestage,"* London: Modern Humanities Research Association for the Institute of Germanic Studies, 1989

Journals

Literary journals have, at least since the 17th century, served as a very important public forum for critical discussions of specific issues of scholarly, poetological, pedagogical, and artistic relevance. The German word "Zeitschrift" was first coined in 1645, but at that time it did not differ much from the equally diffusely defined term "Zeitung." The first known journal in Germany, *Monatsgespräche*, was published by Johann Rist between 1663 and 1668, and it was followed by the monthly journal *Schertz- und ernsthaffter, vernünfftiger und einfältiger Gedancken uber allerhand lustige und nützliche Bücher und Fragen*, edited by Christian Thomasius in Leipzig between 1688 and 1689. Under the influence of English journals such as *The Tatler* (1709–11) and *Spectator* (1711–13), both edited by Joseph Addison and Richard Steele, the Hamburg writer Johann Mattheson (1681–1764) founded the journal *Der Vernünfftler* in 1713 and published 100 issues of it until 1714. This journal mostly consisted of German translations of the English contributions to the *Tatler* and the *Spectator*. The Swiss scholars Johann Jacob Bodmer (1698–1783) and Johann Jacob Breitinger (1701–76) created the moralistic weekly, *Discourse der Mahlern*, in 1721 and published it for two years. Many other journals of this kind, such as *Der Patriot* (1724–26; edited by Barthold Hinrich Brockes) and *Die Vernünfftigen Tadlerinnen* (1725–26; edited by Johann Christoph Gottsched), followed suit. But only the *Neue Beyträge zum Vergnügen des Verstandes und Witzes* (1744–48), also known as *Bremer Beiträge,* edited by Karl Christian Gärtner (1714–84), was seriously dedicated to literary analysis and criticism. Many university academies published journals beginning in the early 18th century, of which many are still in existence today, including the *Göttingische Anzeiger von gelehrten Sachen* which was founded in 1759 and then renamed *Göttingische gelehrte Anzeigen* in 1802.

Nevertheless, the history of modern scholarly journals dealing with German language and literature does not begin before the early 19th century, and it is closely linked with the emergence of the academic discipline of philology, which was supported by such scholars as the brothers Jacob and Wilhelm Grimm, Karl Lachmann, Georg Friedrich Benecke, August Wilhelm Schlegel, Friedrich Heinrich von der Hagen, Karl Wilhelm Göttling, and Karl Simrock, who published many of their articles and extremely important book reviews in journals, newspapers, and yearbooks.

The oldest and today still extant academic journal, *Zeitschrift für deutsches Altertum* (ZfdA), was founded by Moriz Haupt in 1841 and expanded in 1876 with the addition of the *Anzeiger für deutsches Altertum und deutsche Literatur.* With volume 19, the journal's title was revised to *Zeitschrift für deutsches Altertum und deutsche Literatur* to reflect a broadened scope, which also covered cultural-historical and literary-linguistic aspects. This journal has been dedicated exclusively to the investigation of the German Middle Ages in all its cultural and literary ramifications. The *Zeitschrift* carries both critical articles and extensive book reviews on medieval German literature. In 1998, Franz Josef Worstbrock passed on the editorship to Joachim Heinzle.

In 1846, Ludwig Herrig and Heinrich Viehoff created the *Archiv für das Studium der neueren Sprachen,* also known as *Herrigs Archiv,* which not only focuses on German literature and linguistics but also includes equally important sections dedicated to other European languages. This journal covers a wide span from the Middle Ages to modern times and has most recently been edited by Horst Brunner, Klaus Heitmann, and Dieter Mehl, who are responsible for their respective specialty language areas. The *Zeitschrift für deutsche Philologie* (ZfdPh), founded in Halle in 1868 by Ernst Höpfner and Julius Zacher, publishes articles on both medieval and modern German literature and also includes many book reviews. It has recently been edited by a team of scholars: Werner Besch, Norbert Oellers, Ursula Peters, Hartmut Steinecke, and Helmut Tervooren. In 1874, Hermann Paul and Wilhelm Braune founded the famous and still highly authoritative *Beiträge zur Geschichte der deutschen Sprache und Literatur,* often simply referred to as *Beiträge* and abbreviated as PBB (Paul, Braune, Beiträge), to provide a forum for research on German medieval philology and literature. In 1955, with volume 76, this journal experienced a split because of the ideological conflicts in the field of Germanics as practiced in West and East Germany. The *Beiträge* continued to appear in both countries, published in Halle (East) until 1991 and in Tübingen (West), until both journals merged again in 1992. The journal has been published in Tübingen only since then. The journal has recently been edited by Klaus Grubmüller, Thomas Klein, and Jan-Dirk Müller. The *Germanisch-Romanische Monatsschrift* (GRM), established in Heidelberg in 1909 by Heinrich Schröder, pursues a similarly broad approach, although its particular emphasis rests on comparative interpretations that build bridges between the Romance languages and the Germanic language areas, including Anglo-Saxon, and, at least in its original intention, pedagogy. Recently, this journal has been edited by Conrad Wiedemann.

Between 1870 and 1887, the *Archiv für Literaturgeschichte* appeared in print (it is also known as *Schnorrs Archiv* after its founder), publishing positivistic studies on contemporary literature. As its successor, Bernhard Sufert, Erich Schmidt, and Bernhard Suphan published the *Vierteljahrsschrift für Litteraturgeschichte* from 1888 to 1893, which concentrated on contemporary German literature. When this journal ceased to exist, August Sauer created a new quarterly journal in 1894, *Euphorion,* which was later edited by the famous Germanists Konrad Burdach and Julius Petersen. Between 1934 and 1944, during the years of the Nazi regime, the journal, then edited by Hermann Pongs, assumed the new title *Dichtung und Volkstum* to demonstrate its political alignment with the Nazi ideology, but it then ceased its publication shortly before the end of the war. Hans Pyritz resurrected the journal in 1950, returning to its original title *Euphorion*; he later handed it over to Richard Alewyn in 1956, who was subsequently replaced by Rainer Gruenter and Arthur Henkel. Recently, it has been edited by Wolfgang Adams and covers the entire history of German literature and its relationship with world literature. In 1903, the *Archiv für Kulturgeschichte* (AfKg) was established as a scholarly journal for studies dealing with the broad range of cultural history, including German. This journal bridges the differences between the fields of literature, history, visual arts, music, and religion. Recently, this *Archiv* has been edited by the historian Egon Boshof.

In 1923, Paul Kluckhohn and Erich Rothacker established the famous *Deutsche Vierteljahresschrift für Literaturwissenschaft und Geistesgeschichte* (DvjS or DVLG) to set up an intellectual platform for individual studies that are strictly opposed to positivism and that instead embrace the movement of "Geistes-geschichte," which attempts to perceive cultural history in its extensive literary, philosophical, art historical, and religious-historical contexts from an interdisciplinary perspective. This journal regularly publishes extensive research reports about particular topics, but it does not include book reviews. The most recent editors—Richard Brinkmann, Gerhart von Graevenitz, and Walter Haug—have been responsible for individual periods in the intellectual and literary history of the German-speaking world.

Several new journals were founded after World War II, and they pursue particular aspects of culture. *Theater der Zeit,* founded in 1946 in East Berlin, is dedicated to the entire field of theater; *Maske und Kothurn* (since 1955) specializes in theater, film, television, and other visual media; *Fabula. Zeitschrift für Erzählforschung* (since 1958) focuses on international narrative and literary research; and *Theater heute,* founded in 1960, concentrates on contemporary theater. Also in 1960, Hermann Kunisch created the *Literaturwissenschaftliches Jahrbuch,* a publication forum set up by the Görres-Gesellschaft, which focuses on medieval, but partly on modern German literature in its European context.

In order to build a transatlantic bridge for Germanist research, Paul Stapf created the *Colloquia Germanica* (CG) in 1967, which is printed by the Francke Verlag in Bern, Switzerland, for the University of Kentucky in Lexington, Kentucky. The *Colloquia,* covering the entire history of German literature, has recently been edited by Theodore Fiedler.

After World War II, many attempts were made to develop new ideas for the didacticization of the history of German literature. *Der Deutschunterricht* (DU), founded in Stuttgart in 1947, focuses more on the pragmatic aspects of teaching German language and literature at the "Gymnasium" (high school) level, offering particularly practical advise, teaching models, interpretive strategies, and analyses of everyday teaching experiences. To parallel this endeavor, the pedagogical journal *Deutschunterricht* was established in East Berlin in 1948. *Wirkendes Wort* (WW), founded in Düsseldorf in 1950, publishes articles of a wider scope, integrating both pedagogical aspects and literary interpretations. Recently, it has been edited by Heinz Rölleke, a specialist in the field of fairy-tale research. Other important journals focusing on pedagogy, linguistics, and applied linguistics are *Mitteilungen des Deutschen Germanistenverbandes,* published in Frankfurt a.M. since 1954; *Diskussion Deutsch* (DD), founded in Frankfurt a.M. in 1970, dealing with the practical aspects of teaching German at the various school levels; *Praxis Deutsch. Arbeitsblätter für die Sekundarstufe I,* published since 1973; *Muttersprache,* originally called *Zeitschrift zur Pflege und Erforschung der deutschen Sprache,* first published between 1886 and 1943 and then rejuvenated in 1949; *Deutsche Sprache. Zeitschrift für Theorie, Praxis, Dokumention,* founded in 1973 and recently edited by Siegfried Grosse and others; *Germanistische Linguistik,* founded in 1969 by Ulrich Knoop, Wolfgang Putschke, Ludwig Erich Schmitt, and Herbert E. Wiegand, recently edited by Gisela Schoenthal; *Deutsch als Fremdsprache,* founded in 1963, recently edited by Gerhard Helbig; *Zeitschrift für Dialektologie und Linguistik,* first edited by Hermann Teichel in 1924 under the title *Teuthonista,* recently edited by Joachim Göschel; *and Jahrbuch Deutsch als Fremdsprache,* which has been edited by Alois Wierlacher since 1975.

To meet the need of the Germanists in East Germany, Luis Fürnberg and Hans-Günther Thalheim created the journal

Weimarer Beiträge (WB) in 1955. Having shed its Marxist orientation, it has recently been edited by an international team of scholars: Peter Engelmann, Wendelin Schmidt-Dengler, and Michael Franz. Most of the East German universities also have published their own journals since 1951–52, including the *Wissenschaftliche Zeitschrift der Humboldt-Universität zu Berlin,* the *Wissenschaftliche Zeitschrift der Ernst-Moritz-Arndt-Universität Greifswald,* the *Wissenschaftliche Zeitschrift der Martin-Luther-Universität Halle-Wittenberg,* the *Wissenschaftliche Zeitschrift der Friedrich-Schiller-Universität Jena,* and others. Each of them ran several subseries, one of which, "Gesellschafts- und sprachwissenschaftliche Reihe," regularly highlights German literature. Since 1980, Germanists in East Germany also could turn to the *Zeitschrift für Germanistik* (ZfG), which addresses all areas in the history of German literature. A Swiss journal dedicated to German literature, edited by Theophil Spoerri and Emil Staiger under the title *Trivium* and subtitled *Schweizerische Vierteljahresschrift für Literaturwissenschaft und Stilkritik,* appeared only between 1942 and 1951.

Although yearbooks do not necessarily fall under the category of journals, in reality they fulfill the same purpose, even though they often are much more limited in their thematic orientation. In 1957, the first volume of the *Jahrbuch der Deutschen Schillergesellschaft* appeared in print; it concentrates on the time of Friedrich Schiller but covers the entire modern history of German literature, and it provides important information on research, archives, and source materials. In contrast, the *Goethe-Jahrbuch,* founded in 1880 and published until 1913, was exclusively dedicated to the work of Johann Wolfgang von Goethe. It was succeeded by the *Jahrbuch der Goethe-Gesellschaft,* which was first published in 1914; it was continued until 1935, when it was renamed as *Goethe. Vierteljahresschrift der Goethe-Gesellschaft.* In 1972, the yearbook returned to its original title, *Goethe Jahrbuch.* Many other literary societies have followed these two models since then and have published their own yearbooks, including the *Grillparzer-Jahrbuch* (founded in 1891); *Jahrbuch der Kleistgesellschaft* (established in 1922); *Aurora. Jahrbuch der Eichendorff-Gesellschaft* (founded in 1929); *Hölderlin-Jahrbuch,* also known as *Iduna* (established in 1944); the *Hebbel-Jahrbuch* (founded in 1951); the *Heine-Jahrbuch* (published since 1951); the *Jahrbuch der Raabe-Gesellschaft* (created in 1960); the *Jahrbuch der Jean-Paul-Gesellschaft* (established in 1966); the *Hoffmannsthal-Blätter* (founded in 1968); the *Lessing-Yearbook* (created in 1969); the *Jahrbuch der Karl-May-Gesellschaft* (published since 1970); the *Jahrbuch der Internationalen Brecht-Gesellschaft* (founded in 1971; since 1974, published as *Brecht-Jahrbuch*); *Wolfram-Studien,* or *Veröffentlichungen der Wolfram von Eschenbach Gesellschaft* (established in 1979); and the *Jahrbuch der Oswald von Wolkenstein Gesellschaft* (in existence since 1980–81).

The academic discipline of Germanistik is practiced all over the world, as the large number of international Germanist journals indicates. Only some of these will be listed here. In 1897, the first volume of the highly respected *Journal of English and Germanic Philology* (JEGP) appeared in print in Urbana, Illinois; it deals with Germanic, English, and Nordic literature and philology. It has recently been edited by Achsah Guibborg, Marianne Kalinke, James M. McGlathery, Jack Stilling, and Charles D. White. Articles are published in both English and German. Two years later the *Monatshefte für deutschen Unterricht, deutsche Sprache und Literatur* was founded in Madison, Wisconsin; this journal primarily addresses Germanists in North America and includes both literary and pedagogical studies, book reviews, and necrologies in German and English. Its most recent editor is Cora Lee Nollendorfs.

Since 1928, the American Association of Teachers of German has published its own journal, *German Quarterly* (GQ), which is dedicated to the wide range of research on the history of German literature from the Middle Ages to the present. The editorship of *GQ* rotates regularly and has recently been in the hands of Dagmar Lorenz. As a companion journal that addresses only pedagogical and didactic issues, the American Association of Teachers of German also founded *Die Unterrichtspraxis* (UP) in 1968; this journal includes articles, reviews, statistical notes, and reports about the teaching of German. Recently, it has been edited by Jürgen Koppensteiner. The *Germanic Review* (GR), published by the Germanic Department of Columbia University, New York, since 1926, has also gained an international reputation. *Modern Language Notes* (MLN), published in Baltimore, Maryland, since 1886, serves as a scholarly forum for all modern languages and literatures—it always offers a particular German section. The Canadian journal *Seminar. A Journal of Germanic Studies,* published since 1965 and most recently edited by Rodney Symington, prints critical articles and reviews on all aspects of German literature. It also serves as the official forum for Germanists in Canada and the Pacific Rim countries. On a more regional level, *Germanic Notes,* edited by Richard F. Krummel since 1970, publishes articles and reviews from all fields of German literature and linguistics. It was renamed *Germanic Notes and Reviews* in 1992 to reflect its expanded range, and it offers both critical articles on specific issues and extensive reviews of new publications in particular areas of interest.

Since 1975, *Michigan Germanic Studies* (MGS) has appeared in print, edited by Roy C. Cowen, offering articles on all aspects of the history of German literature. In 1987, the German Studies Association launched its *German Studies Review* (GSR) in Tempe, Arizona, edited by the political historian Gerald Kleinfeld; this journal provides a unique avenue for interdisciplinary approaches to the study of German literature, history, politics, art, music, and religion. The journal *Tristania,* founded by Lewis A.M. Sumberg in 1975 and most recently edited by Albrecht Classen, exclusively focuses on studies and reviews related to German and other European *Tristan* texts from all periods.

In England, Germanists can publish their articles in the quarterly *German Life and Letters* (GLL; established in 1936–37), which has recently been edited by a team of scholars including G.P.G. Butler, L.W. Forster, and G. Gillespie. This journal covers both literary studies and cultural investigations. From 1886 to 1912, the English Goethe Society published its own journal, which was resumed from 1924 onward. The *Modern Language Review* (MLR), produced by the Cambridge University Press since 1905, covers a wider range of European languages, similar to the North American *Publications of the Modern Language Association* (PMLA, published since 1884). The Finnish journal *Neuphilologische Mitteilungen,* in print since 1899 and most recently edited by Päivi Pahta, is primarily focused on Germanic philology, but it also accepts articles on German medieval literature. The Norwegian journal *Edda. Nordisk tidsskrift for litteraturforskning,* published since 1914, and the Swedish journal *Studia Neophilologica,* founded by R.E. Zachrisius in 1928 and recently edited by Gunnar Sorelius, have a very similar thematic approach. The Belgian journal *Leuvense Bijdragen,* published

since 1974, specializes in general and German philology. Low German Studies make up the focus of the Swedish journal *Niederdeutsche Mitteilungen* (published since 1945) and the German journal *Niederdeutsches Jahrbuch* (published since 1875). The Dutch journal *Neophilologus* (established in 1915) publishes both philological and literary studies that pertain to German language and literature. In 1972, the Dutch publishing house Rodopi created two new journals for the study of German literature: the *Amsterdamer Beiträge zur älteren Germanistik* (ABäG), originally edited by Arend Quak and the late Cola Minis, focuses on premodern German literature and language, and the *Amsterdamer Beiträge zur neueren Germanistik,* edited by Marianne Burkhard and Gerd Labroisse, is limited to the modern period. In the same year, Rodopi also initiated a new journal for German literature written in the period between the Middle Ages and the modern times, *Daphnis. Zeitschrift für mittlere deutsche Literatur.* Recently, this journal has been edited by Barbara Becker-Cantarino, Martin Bircher, and others.

In 1946, one year after World War II, the highly respected French journal *Etudes Germaniques* (EG) began its publication and offered critical and theoretical articles on German literature and a large number of book reviews. Recently, the journal has been edited by Jean Marie Valentin. Also in 1946, the Italian *Rivista di letterature moderne e comparate* was founded; it provides a scholarly forum for literary scholars in Italy. The Danish journal *Orbis litterarum* (published since 1943) covers English, Romance, and Germanic literature. Recently, the German section has been edited by Engt Algot Sørensen.

Reflecting novel trends in German literary scholarship in the late 1960s and 1970s, a number of new journals appeared. *Arcadia,* established by Horst Rüdiger in 1966, publishes articles and book reviews in comparative literary studies. In *Poetica. Zeitschrift für Sprache und Literaturwissenschaft,* founded in 1967, the emphasis rests on poetological and interpretative analysis, whereas theoretical issues in literary studies predominate in *Poetics. International Review for the Theory of Literature,* which has been published since 1972 and has most recently been edited by Ulrich Broich, Renate Lachmann, Eberhard Lämmert, Glenn W. Most, Volker Schupp, and Karlheinz Stierle. The *Jahrbuch für Internationale Germanistik* (JIG; established in 1969) contains articles and short notes about the entire history of German literature; it also includes reports about recent research projects and doctoral dissertations. *Sprachkunst,* published in Vienna, Austria, since 1970 and edited by Hermann Blume, is open to all aspects of literary scholarship; however, it does accentuate German and Austrian literature. In 1971, the *Zeitschrift für Literaturwissenschaft und Linguistik* (LiLi), edited by Helmut Kreuzer, Wolfgang Haubrichs, Wolfgang Klein, and Brigitte Schlieben-Lange, began its publication; it dedicates each of its volumes to specific topics in the history of German literature and linguistics. The left-leaning *Literaturmagazin,* first edited by Hans Christoph Buch in 1973, mostly carries articles by writers, poets, and scholars that address questions pertaining to contemporary German and world literature. It was followed by *Kontext. Literatur und Wirklichkeit* in 1976, which pursues very similar interests. The *Internationales Archiv für Sozialgeschichte der deutschen Literatur* (IASL, founded in 1976), however, edited by Wolfgang Frühwald, Georg Jäger, and Alberto Martino, focuses on the sociohistorical backgrounds and contexts of German literature and theater; it also offers extensive reviews. The journal *Literatur für Leser. Zeitschrift für Interpretationspraxis und geschichtliche Erkenntnis,* published since 1978, combines critical articles on German literature with didactic and pedagogical studies.

General cultural and aesthetic questions are addressed in such journals as the *Frankfurter Hefte* (printed since 1946), *Universitas* (published since 1946), *Merkur* (published since 1947), *Der Monat* (printed since 1948–49), *Neue deutsche Hefte* (printed since 1954), *Das Argument* (published in 1959), *Text und Kritik* (established in 1963), *Kursbuch* (founded in 1965), *Akzente* (created in 1969), *Ästhetik und Kommunikation* (established in 1970), *Die Eule* (founded in 1979), and *Freibeuter* (founded in 1979).

The Austrian journal *Literatur und Kritik,* published since 1966, primarily contains literary texts and critical studies by Austrian writers and scholars. *Modern Austrian Literature,* founded and edited by Donald G. Daviau (published in Riverside, California) in 1977, is now the *Journal of the International Arthur Schnitzler Research Association,* which covers 20th-century Austrian literature.

Since 1983, *Arbitrium,* edited by Wolfgang Frühwald and Wolfgang Harms, has produced book reviews for the entire field of German literary scholarship. Several journals exclusively provide bibliographical information, including the *Bibliographie der deutschen Literaturwissenschaft,* originally edited by Hanns W. Eppelsheimer and Clemens Köttelwesch, published since 1957, and retitled *Bibliographie der deutschen Sprach- und Literaturwissenschaft* in 1969; and *Germanistik. Internationales Referatenorgan mit bibliographischen Hinweisen,* published since 1960. International research in its widest scope is covered by the monumental *Internationale Bibliographie der Zeitschriftenliteratur,* founded by F. Dietrich in 1897.

ALBRECHT CLASSEN

See also Athenäum; Blätter für die Kunst; Die Fackel; Die Horen; Der Ruf

Further Reading

Blinn, Hansjürgen, *Informationshandbuch Deutsche Literaturwissenschaft,* Frankfurt: Fischer Taschenbuch, 1982

Bluhm, Lothar, *Die Brüder Grimm und der Beginn der Deutschen Philologie: Eine Studie zu Kommunikation und Wissenschaftsbildung im frühen 19. Jahrhundert,* Hildesheim: Weidmann, 1997

Bohrmann, Hans, and Peter Schneider, *Zeitschriftenforschung: Ein wissenschaftsgeschichtlicher Versuch,* Berlin: Spiess, 1975

Diesch, Carl, *Bibliographie der germanistischen Zeitschriften,* Leipzig: Hiersemann, 1927; reprint, Stuttgart: Hiersemann, 1970

Eggers, Hans, *Das Frühneuhochdeutsche und das Neuhochdeutsche* (Deutsche Sprachgeschichte, vol. 2), Reinbek bei Hamburg: Rowohlt, 1986

Gerlach, Peter, *Zeitschriftenforschung: Probleme und Lösungsansätze dargestellt am Beispiel Journalism quarterly (1964–1983),* Wiesbaden: Harrassowitz, 1988

Habermas, Jürgen, *The Structural Transformation of the Public Sphere: An Inquiry into a Category of Bourgeois Society,* Cambridge, Massachusetts: MIT Press, and Cambridge: Polity Press, 1989

Kirchner, Joachim, *Das deutsche Zeitschriftenwesen, seine Geschichte und seine Probleme,* Wiesbaden: Harrassowitz, 1942; 2nd, revised edition, 1962

Kirchner, Joachim, editor, *Bibliographie der Zeitschriften des deutschen Sprachgebiets bis 1900,* 4 vols., Stuttgart: Hiersemann, 1966

Kuhles, Doris, *Deutsche literarische Zeitschriften von der Aufklärung bis zur Romantik: Bibliographie der kritischen Literatur von den Anfängen bis 1990,* Munich: Saur, 1994

Laakmann, Dagmar, and Reinhard Tghart, *Literarische Zeitschriften und Jahrbücher, 1880–1970: Verzeichnis der im Deutschen Literaturarchiv erschlossenen Periodica,* Marbach: Deutsches Literaturarchiv, 1972

Pross, Harry, *Literatur und Politik: Geschichte und Programme der politisch-literarischen Zeitschriften im deutschen Sprachgebiet seit 1870,* Olten: Walter, 1963

Raabe, Paul, *Einführung in die Bücherkunde zur deutschen Literaturwissenschaft,* Stuttgart: Metzler, 1961; 10th edition, 1984

Rosenfeld, Hellmut, "Zeitung und Zeitschrift," in *Reallexikon der deutschen Literaturgeschichte,* edited by Klaus Kanzog and Achim Masser, vol. 4, Berlin and New York: de Gruyter, 1984

Zeitschriften-Verzeichnis Germanistik: Bestände der Sondersammelgebietsbibliothek, Frankfurt: Weisbecker, 1978

Jugendstil

Jugendstil is the German name for an international movement in art that began at the turn of the 20th century. Elsewhere it was called art nouveau, modern style, *Stile Modernista, De Stijl, Sezessionsstil,* or *Stile Liberty. Jugendstil* may refer either to the movement as a whole or to its specifically German manifestations. While *Jugendstil* was originally principally associated with painting, drawing, architecture, design, and applied arts and crafts—anything from sofa cushions to town planning, according to Hermann Muthesius—since the 1940s the term *literary Jugendstil* has also been used alongside neo-Romanticism, Impressionism, symbolism, decadence, aestheticism, and vitalism.

The name *Jugendstil* is closely associated with the Munich periodical *Jugend* (1896–1940), although the founder and sole editor, Georg Hirth, denied having invented the term and spoke of his journal's "programmatic lack of programme." The word was coined in 1897 (in an article about the influence of *Jugend* on an exhibition in Leipzig), and it was current by 1899. Nonetheless, some art historians minimize the relationship of the movement and the periodical, maintaining that the name simply reflects the drive for aesthetic rejuvenation pervading Germany in the last years of the 19th century.

Whether primarily influencing or influenced, *Jugend* was certainly part of a general trend that emerged in the 1890s. Other journals were founded: *Pan,* under Otto Julius Bierbaum and Julius Meier-Graefe in Berlin (1895), *Simplicissimus* in Munich (1896), and *Ver Sacrum* in Vienna (1898). Dissatisfaction with the restrictive influence of older, backward-looking artists on exhibitions and galleries led to the founding of secession movements (1892 in Munich, 1897 in Vienna, and 1898 in Berlin). From early on, the participants were conscious of being involved in the deliberate creation of a new style. Otto Wagner wrote that "this is not the Renaissance of the Renaissance; a Naissance is happening." It was inspired by similar developments abroad: the Arts and Crafts movement and its principal organ *The Studio* (1893), as well as *The Dial* (1889) and *La Revue blanche* (1891). William Morris was particularly influential and was seen as the very embodiment of cultural unity: not only did he write the texts of his books, he designed, illustrated, printed, bound, and sold them himself.

From further afield, the influence of Japanese art was keenly felt. The German-born Samuel Bing (whose own Paris gallery was called "L'Art Nouveau") held an exhibition of Japanese drawing and illustrated books in the Ecole des Beaux Arts in 1890. He aimed to show how far the Western artistic tradition had moved away from nature and feeling toward a strait-jacketed, formalized composition. Japanese art, too, was an inspiration for the use of flat planes in *Jugendstil* work.

Jugendstil emerged for a generation alienated by technological and industrial advance, urban anonymity, and the pure functionality of the mechanically produced objects surrounding them. At the same time, it challenged the predominantly historicist approaches of cultural and artistic thought. The painters and graphic artists of the *Jugendstil* period turned their back on the representation of profane social reality and conjured up instead dreamlike idylls (often in spacious parks, dense jungles, or on islands), offering a paradigm for the harmonious commingling of humanity and nature. They were concerned to express the unity of art and life and the eurhythmic relationship of the individual artist to an idealized, utopian society.

For some, utopianism led to art of transcendentalist interiority or a mythologic, escapist, Wagner-inspired longing for death. But *Jugendstil* was perfectly consistent in also manifesting the need felt by many to give coherent aesthetic expression to the business of everyday life. Hence, Charles Rennie Mackintosh's design of fully furnished dwellings such as the Hill House in Helensburgh (1902)—sometimes called a "Scottish *Gesamtkunstwerk*"—Antoni Gaudí's Palacio Güell (1885–90); cutlery, china, furniture and clothes by Henry van de Velde; and, most famously, the tulip-entrances to the Paris underground by Hector Guimard (the movement was for a while known in France simply as *Style Métro*). Despite its antirealist stance, there was a social dimension in the movement's attempts to repolarize contemporary values, to celebrate youth and vitality instead of age and experience, to look to the future rather than taking inspiration from the distant past, and to encourage unfettered eroticism and the breaking of outdated taboos.

Jugendstil art is dominated by a relatively small number of motifs from the natural world. They include sinuous undulating lines and waves; abstract ornamental patterns (often floral or involving single-celled creatures, protozoa or amoebae); insects and serpents; vegetable profusion and the intertwined roots and branches of trees; elegant flowers such as lilies, narcissi, irises, orchids, and poppies; birds, in particular swans and flamingos, or forest birds whose contours melt into the surrounding foliage; female forms, either real women, nymphs, or nixies, with long wavy hair and curvaceous bodies, sometimes naked but often wearing veils or flowing, diaphanous clothing; and the sensuous intertwining of human bodies or their erotic alternation in dance. These are usually highly stylized and depicted so as to give strong suggestions of continuous or continual movement.

The spaces of the picture are not those of traditional three-dimensional realism; instead the emphasis on planes and surfaces gives an impression of "spacelessness."

The deliberate ornamentation and stylization of reality was not an aesthetic end in itself, nor merely an attempt to transpose natural forms into art. The lines and elaborate ornaments were ultimately designed to communicate the emotions of experience: the architect August Endell wrote in 1898, "[R]ising forms awaken different feelings from descending or horizontally extending forms. There is restrained force immanent in the curve, the straight line has sharpness and speed." Moreover, such stylization overtly repudiated the principles on which naturalism was based and expressed the fundamental *Jugendstil* principle of the underlying oneness of all being: "The ornaments are symbols of the unity of life" (Rasch). This is the spirit strongly influenced by Ernst Haeckel's *Kunstformen der Natur* (1899; Artistic Forms in Nature), in which simple life-forms such as coral and seaweed are examined in order to find the simplest physical and aesthetic principles to which life could be reduced.

Jugendstil had a special association with the book. The new journals (such as Stefan George's *Blätter für die Kunst*, since 1892) sought to promote an artistic synthesis of the visual and the written. Influenced by Japanese art, text and graphic illustration were melded together, the lettering often proceeding organically from the imagery and the frame of a picture becoming part of the image itself. While this coordination of different page elements seems self-evident nowadays, its revolutionary impact in the 1900s should not be underestimated. Not only was *Jugend* one of the first German periodicals to change the illustrations on its title page weekly, it was innovative simply by changing the position of the title banner on the cover from issue to issue.

Despite this association, the meaningfulness of the term *Jugendstil* for literature itself is hotly debated. Hermand (1964, 1965) identifies three phases of development in which *Jugendstil* art and literature are linked. An early "carnival" stage concerned with gaiety, dance, and movement can be associated with *Jugend, Simplicissimus,* and Arno Holz and Ernst von Wolzogen's *Überbrettl.* A second "floral" stage is represented by *Pan, Jugend, Die Insel,* and artists such as Otto Eckmann, Hans Christiansen, and "Fidus" (Hugo Höppener) together with authors such as Richard Dehmel, Johannes Schlaf, Alfred Mombert, and Julius Hart. Finally, there is a more abstract, "geometric-symbolic" phase in the works of Peter Behrens and van de Velde in the arts and Stefan George, Hugo von Hofmannsthal, Karl Vollmoeller, and Eduard Stucken among writers.

As is usual with such classifications, the boundaries are fluid rather than rigid, and Hermand's structures have stimulated much debate about which writers to include under the general heading of *Jugendstil.* Jost locates the origins in Nietzsche's *Also sprach Zarathustra* (1883–85; *Thus Spake Zarathustra*); the 1908 luxury Insel edition was bound by van de Velde, who also illustrated the first, posthumous edition of *Ecce Homo* (1908). Rasch suggests as the three most obvious names Cäsar Flaischlen, Felix Dörmann, and Johannes Schlaf, but they are not featured in the important anthologies by Hermand (1964) and Winkler; Rasch specifically excludes Rilke, George, and Hofmannsthal, who are. Winkler includes Hofmannsthal's *Das kleine Welttheater* (1897–1903; *The Little Theater of the World*), but the anthology is dominated by lesser-known works:

Karl Wolfskehl's *Orpheus* (1909), Maximilian Dauthendy's *Glück* (1895; Happiness), and Ernst Hardt's *Ninon von Lenclos* (1905). Nonetheless, poems such as George's "Die Spange," "Die Maske," and "Stimmen im Strom"; Hofmannsthal's "Die Töchter der Gärtnerin"; and Rilke's *Das Stundenbuch* (1905; *The Book of Hours*) show clearly the stylistic or motivic influence of *Jugendstil.*

On one level, the term *Jugendstil* is used for work in which certain themes and motifs are prominent (Hermand's anthology groups the poems thematically, with sections for swans, pools and boats, dusk, flowers, springtime, dance, and "monistic intertwinedness"). There are also certain consistent formal characteristics of *Jugendstil* writing. It tends to be highly stylized, sometimes insistently alliterative and assonant (Emil Rudolf Weiß's "Pedal"), often using the rhetorical device of anaphora, with several lines in a poem beginning "und" (Stadler's "Erfüllung" or George's "Der Teppich"), "wenn" (Dehmel's "Narzissen"), or with an article (Jakobowski's "Das sind die keuschesten Rosen"). The situations depicted are usually plain and uncluttered, the protagonists rarely precisely identified (often merely "du" and "ich"), and their mutual interdependence is stressed. Space is simply structured with strongly established horizontal and vertical planes. Reflection and the action of circling link or emphasize the planes. Black and white or simple bold colors help structure the poems and are frequently symbolically charged. Alternatively, dusk or darkness set a tone of menace.

Such devices are employed to inhibit the operation of logic and causality. They are an equivalent of the reduction of three-dimensionality and the use of the plane in *Jugendstil* drawing. The literature often manifests an indifference to action and ordered chronology, and a preference for language of legato continuity in which verbs are used in the chronologically neutral infinitive, imperative, or present participle (enhancing the importance of *Gebärde*). Grammatical indications of logical progression or causality are removed. The favored themes of dance, ecstasy, and intoxication serve the same purpose. Lyric poetry, the lyrical drama, and the stream-of-consciousness technique in prose are felt to be the forms in which such techniques are most fully developed. Rounded characterization, psychological or social analysis, and a concern for the *events* of a narrative are largely abandoned. Symbolic objects become the bearers of significance.

The women in *Jugendstil* art and literature are equally stylized, and where men appear, they are feminized or even androgyne. Woman was seen as the incarnation of elemental life and, similar to life itself, inspired an ambivalent mixture of desire and trepidation. Common individual figures include the Madonna, Salome, martyrs, and pubertal girls. Two general types dominate, however: the *femme fatale* (or hetaera) and the *femme fragile* (or its associated subtype, the *femme enfant*). Both types ignore the humane and intellectual dimensions of womanhood, again in a deliberately antirealist spirit, and can be seen as another form of social escapism not into utopia but into a kind of sexual paradise. Modern criticism commonly interprets these female figures as projections of male erotomania or sexual anxiety (Wittmann). A typical fictional manifestation of the *femme fragile* will end with her death so that the male lover can celebrate the perfect ideal purity of his emotions. Contemporary women were not slow to expose the gap between the male projections of

literary *Jugendstil* and reality: Frieda von Bülow's *Die stilisierte Frau* (The Stylized Woman) appeared in *Die neue Rundschau* as early as 1899.

This was not the only form of attack. The *Jugendstil* element in Thomas Mann's early work is also satirical, albeit more indulgently so, as in *Tristan* (1903): Detlev Spinell refuses to allow mere facts to hamper his imaginative reconstruction of the scene when Gabriele Klöterjahn's future husband first comes upon her, and she is seen as a sort of *Jugendstil* picture, with a crown in her hair, singing with her friends by a fountain. Christian Morgenstern wrote one of his *Galgenlieder* (1905; *Gallows Songs*) on the *Jugendstil* chair, which he claimed was more suited to the aesthete's "Sitz-Geist" than to the "Sitz-Fleisch" (more to his spiritual side than his backside). The movement as a whole was much mocked by its opponents as "style nouilles" (noodle style) or "Bandwurmstil" (tapeworm style), but criticism and attacks were not only made from outside. Hans von Gumppenberg and others contributed parodies to the very journals that most championed the movement.

It was a combination of such internal skepticism and the maturing of individuals' talents that led to the movement's decline. Many of the Expressionist generation—including Stadler, Heym, Trakl, and Lasker-Schüler—had their roots in *Jugendstil,* but some were later vehemently negative about their early work. If in one sense, most authors writing between 1890 and 1910 partook of *Jugendstil* in some way, no major writer is adequately described with that label (even artists such as van de Velde were later embarrassed by it). For most authors, *Jugendstil* was merely either "an ingredient or a phase" (Jost).

ROBERT VILAIN

See also Decadence

Further Reading

Eschmann, Karl, *Jugendstil: Ursprünge, Parallelen, Folgen,* Kastellaun: Henn, 1976; Göttingen: Muster-Schmidt, 1991

Fahr-Becker, Gabriele, *Jugendstil,* Cologne: Könemann, 1996

Hajek, Edelgard, *Literarischer Jugendstil: Vergleichende Studien zur Dichtung und Malerei um 1900,* Düsseldorf: Bertelsmann, 1971

Hermand, Jost, *Jugendstil: Ein Forschungsbericht, 1918–1964,* Stuttgart: Metzler, 1965

Hermand, Jost, editor, *Lyrik des Jugendstils: Eine Anthologie,* Stuttgart: Reclam, 1964

——, editor, *Jugendstil,* Wege der Forschung, vol. 110, Darmstadt: Wissenschaftliche Buchgesellschaft, 1971

Hofstätter, Hans Hellmut, *Geschichte der europäischen Jugendstilmalerei: Ein Entwurf,* Cologne: DuMont Schauberg, 1963

Jost, Dominik, *Literarischer Jugendstil,* Stuttgart: Metzler, 1969; 2nd edition, 1980

Klotz, Volker, "Jugendstil in der Lyrik,' *Akzente* 4 (1957)

Kluge, Gerhard, "Die Gebärde als Formprinzip in der Lyrik des deutschen Jugendstils," in *Aufsätze zu Literatur und Kunst der Jahrhundertwende,* Amsterdamer Beiträge zur neueren Germanistik, vol. 18, Amsterdam: Rodopi, 1984

Koreska-Hartmann, Linda, *Jugendstil, Stil der "Jugend": Auf den Spuren eines alten, neuen Stil- und Lebensgefühls,* Munich: Deutscher Taschenbuchverlag, 1969

Langer, Alfred, *Jugendstil und Buchkunst,* Leipzig: Edition Leipzig, 1994

Madsen, Stephan Tschudi, *Jugendstil: Europäische Kunst der Jahrhundertwende,* Munich: Kindler, 1967

Rasch, Wolfdietrich, "Fläche, Welle, Ornament," in *Zur deutschen Literatur seit der Jahrhundertwende*, Stuttgart: Metzler, 1967

Scheible, Hartmut, *Literarischer Jugendstil in Wien: Eine Einführung*, Munich: Artemis, 1984

Sembach, Klaus-Jürgen, *Jugendstil: Die Utopie der Versöhnung*, Cologne: Taschen, 1990

Sternberger, Dolf, *Über den Jugendstil und andere Essays*, Hamburg: Claassen, 1956

Wende, Waltraud, "Der Jugendstil der 'Jugend': Eine literarisch-künstlerische Zeitschrift der Jahrhundertwende," *Philobiblon* 37, no. 3 (1993)

Winkler, Michael, editor, *Einakter und kleine Dramen des Jugendstils*, Stuttgart: Reclam, 1974

Wittmann, Livia Z., "Zwischen 'femme fatale' und 'femme fragile'—die Neue Frau?: Kritische Bemerkungen zum Frauenbild des literarischen Jugendstils," *Jahrbuch für internationale Germanistik* 17, no. 2 (1985)

Das Junge Deutschland

The literary movement of the 1830s known as Das Junge Deutschland (Young Germany) existed as a subversive political conspiracy almost entirely in the imagination of the governments of the German Confederation, which might even be credited with having created it by a censorship ban issued on 10 December 1835. There was, however, a stirring among writers and intellectuals after the revolution of July 1830 in France, which caused only minor ripples in the well-carpentered Metternichian system but seemed to promise a Hegelian historical turn after the torpor and stasis following the Congress of Vienna in 1815. What concerned this generation was an opening of public discourse to the new ideas of the age. This meant a struggle with the increasingly tightened censorship regulations of the Confederation and a turn of literature away from what was perceived, fairly or not, as the indifferent aestheticism of Goethe and the Romantics and toward purposes of immediate public relevance. The models were two older writers, Ludwig Börne and Heinrich Heine, both of whom were in exile in France and therefore associated with the transmission of the ideals of liberty and equality deriving from the French Revolution.

Das Junge Deutschland has had a variety of definitions, some of which include Börne and Heine themselves and up to two dozen or more writers of the time. But all definitions must include the four writers named in the decree of 1835: Ludolf Wienbarg, Theodor Mundt, Heinrich Laube, and Karl Gutzkow; Heine's name was added to the ban at Metternich's insistence. Wienbarg, fiercely nationalistic but also politically the most democratic of the group, gave some momentum to the designation *Das Junge Deutschland* by dedicating his *Ästhetische Feldzüge* (1835: Aesthetic Campaigns) "to the young Germany, not the old." This was a series of lectures he had given at the University of Kiel, then a Danish institution, where he had been appointed to teach Danish literature (which, however, he refused to do). Born under Danish sovereignty in Altona, Wienbarg was extremely hostile to Denmark all his life. His lectures drew activist implications from the German aesthetic and literary tradition, especially from Heine. For this he was dismissed from his university position despite student demonstrations in his support.

Mundt was basically of a scholarly temperament and was in later years to have a significant career as a literary historian. But as a Young German he published, along with other experimental works, a novel entitled *Madonna* (1835) narrating a woman's liberation from religious and sexual oppression. As a consequence, on the day he was to give his inaugural lecture for a teaching position at the University of Berlin in April 1835, the doors to the hall were locked by the rector, the Norwegian Romantic Henrich Steffens, and were not to be opened for seven years.

Laube was a former student athlete and fraternity activist who had developed free-thinking views, especially in matters of religion, and was one of Heine's warmest admirers in this generation until political differences during the revolution of 1848 separated them. In 1833, he had taken over the editorship of the *Zeitung für die elegante Welt* (Gazette for the Elegant World), a moribund daily that he rejuvenated and attempted to turn into an organ for dissident views, but he was arrested later that year. According to the Carlsbad Decrees of 1819, fraternity membership was punishable by six years of fortress imprisonment, and leadership by death; in 1830, the king of Prussia, Frederick William III, amnestied all former fraternity members contingent upon future good behavior. For eight months, Laube was held in a Berlin jail, much of it in solitary confinement without light or companionship, while the authorities combed his writings for transgressions that would permit reinstatement of charges against him. He was eventually sentenced to six years in prison, afterward commuted to a year and a half of house arrest. Nevertheless, among his many works he managed to write what may be the best novels of the movement, a trilogy entitled *Das junge Europa* (Young Europe), consisting of *Die Poeten* (1833; The Poets), an epistolary novel attempting to enact modern ideas; *Die Krieger* (1837; The Warriors), a thoughtful and observant depiction of the Polish revolution of 1831; and *Die Bürger* (1837; The Citizens), a novel expressing the sense of failure and frustration that had come to beset his generation. In later years, Laube became prominent as the manager of the renowned Vienna Burgtheater.

Laube's successful subsequent career and the relative lightness of his eventual sentence have contributed to a view that the Young Germans were not so severely persecuted after all. This view does not consider, however, that government threats of terrorist measures can be effective without actually creating martyrs by carrying them out. This tactic was most effectively applied against the most ambitious and energetic of the group,

Gutzkow, who also was to survive to pursue a long and prominent, if not very happy, career in later years. Even more than Mundt, Gutzkow was obsessed with religious and sexual emancipation, which for him were essentially the same issue, as they were for Heine. In the 1830s, he had written a number of challenging works, including a satire on current events, *Briefe eines Narren an eine Närrin* (1832; Letters of a Harlequin to a Columbine), and a novel, *Maha Guru* (1833), a transparent allegory of an attempted reform of Tibetan religion by a liberal lama. Like all of his works at this time and long thereafter, Gutzkow's writings were banned upon publication, but he managed to create a crisis with a novel especially suited to the purposes of the governments entitled *Wally, die Zweiflerin* (1835; *Wally the Skeptic*), in which an elegant young woman becomes disoriented through her ruminations on love, marriage, social propriety, and the literal truth of the Bible. Particularly notorious is an episode in which Wally, in imitation of a scene in a medieval epic, shows herself nude to her admirer on the day she is to marry another. *Wally* is a hard book to like. Not only is it disorganized and ill written—Gutzkow was one of the worst stylists in the history of German letters—but its central female figure is an exasperating ninny. Gutzkow combines his fixation on sexual emancipation with a strong streak of misogyny that can become quite unpleasant. The book enabled the governments, however, to split the middle-class public by avoiding the political ground and charging Gutzkow with blasphemy and prurience. *Wally* was employed to motivate the ban against the Young Germans, "whose efforts openly tend to attack the Christian religion in the most insolent way, to denigrate existing social relations, and to destroy all decency and morality, in literary works accessible to all classes of people."

In this project, the governments were materially assisted by the most prominent literary critic of the time, Wolfgang Menzel, who mounted a violent attack on *Wally* in his Stuttgart newspaper. Menzel, for reasons that have never been entirely clear, was then in transition from a mildly liberal to a radically conservative position. Along the way he developed a pronounced anti-Semitic streak and began to refer to Young Germany as "Young Palestine," even though none of the Young Germans was Jewish; it was a form of guilt by association with the Jewish model figures, Börne and Heine. Then and later, Menzel was regarded as the instigator of the ban; he became notorious as the "denunciator," whom both Gutzkow and Heine tried unsuccessfully to provoke into a duel. Börne savaged him in the last of his fierce polemics, *Menzel der Franzosenfresser* (1837; Menzel the French-Eater). Although even today he is sometimes blamed for the ban, we know that it was in preparation well before Menzel's attacks appeared, but he provided the governments with eminently valuable support from within the literate middle-class public.

Paradoxically, the decree was so draconian that it was difficult to enforce. It was taken to mean that the writers' names could not be mentioned in print at all, with the result that the text of the ban itself could not be published. It was also understood to be a ban on all works, past, present, or future. But the Prussian bureaucracy, in what may have been an act of subversion from within the educated class, ruled that a ban on future works was illegal. This annoyed the king, who instituted a special precensorship for the five writers. In 1842, early in the reign of his successor, Frederick William IV, all but Heine (on the grounds that he lived outside Germany) were allowed to free themselves from the precensorship through a loyalty oath. Wienbarg, an alcoholic who had disappeared into an obscure career of local journalism, did not sign; Laube, whose spirit had been impaired by his solitary confinement, and Mundt, who still wanted his academic position, did sign; Gutzkow stubbornly negotiated a formulation that committed him to nothing.

These outcomes, along with the facts that the Young Germans survived the ordeal, that the chief malefactor, Gutzkow, served only three months in jail, and that they continued publishing, more or less (because their publisher, Julius Campe in Hamburg—also threatened by name in the decree—invented with his customary deviousness all sorts of evasions of the censorship), have sometimes caused observers to underestimate the movement's significance, but it did have an inhibiting effect, not least because in practice it threatened not only publishers but also printers with prosecution. Campe, in fact, was totally shut down in 1841 and got back into business only through an accident, as a beneficiary of one of the charitable gestures after the great fire that devastated Hamburg in 1842. Heine had a most difficult time coping with the ban and its disruption of his career, but its most damaging effect, which may have been intended, was to destroy any remnant of solidarity among the Young Germans themselves.

The Young Germans had never been a tightly knit group and, in fact, had been much inclined to negative criticism of one another. In 1835, Gutzkow and Wienbarg made an effort to bring the oppositional generation together in a periodical on the French model, the *Deutsche Revue* (German Review), but it was banned before it could appear; only the proofs of the first issue have survived. However, the comprehensive ban caused unseemly squabbling: all the Young Germans denied that they were Young Germans, that there was any such thing as Young Germany, or that they had any connection with or admired any of the others. In fact, the ban was a success. By the end of 1838, Young Germany had to all intents and purposes ceased to exist. Nor was it recalled with much affection. More radical observers, among them Marx and Engels, dismissed what they regarded as the group's retained idealism with scorn. Georg Büchner, in a famous letter to Gutzkow of 1836, declared that society could not be reformed by means of the idea or by the educated class. The prose texts were felt to be heavy, overly intellectual, and inaccessible except to the highly educated, so that dissident writers in the following decade turned to popular verse and politicized folk songs. Conservatives and reactionaries, on the other hand, deplored the employment of literature for social and political ends. For a long time, Young Germany came to be cited as an example in literature of how not to create a political movement.

In the 1890s, however, this changed. The resistance to the censorship of modern literature motivated a historical and scholarly interest in Young Germany lasting into the Weimar Republic and producing a series of learned, detailed studies of fundamental importance. Interest was revived again by the socially activist literary scholarship of the 1970s, and although it has declined some since, signs of yet another wave emerged in the 1990s. The Young German episode continues to be an exemplary chapter in literary history of the conflict of freedom of expression with oppressive power.

JEFFREY L. SAMMONS

See also Karl Gutzkow; Heinrich Heine; Vormärz

Further Reading

Butler, E.M., *The Saint-Simonian Religion in Germany: A Study of the Young German Movement*, Cambridge: Cambridge University Press, 1926

Dietze, Walter, *Junges Deutschland und deutsche Klassik: Zur Ästhetik und Literaturtheorie des Vormärz*, Berlin: Rütten und Loening, 1957

Hermand, Jost, editor, *Das Junge Deutschland: Texte und Dokumente*, Stuttgart: Reclam, 1966

Houben, H.H., *Jungdeutscher Sturm und Drang: Ergebnisse und Studien*, Leipzig: Brockhaus, 1911

Koopmann, Helmut, *Das Junge Deutschland: Analyse seines Selbstverständnisses*, Stuttgart: Metzler, 1970

——, *Das Junge Deutschland: Eine Einführung*, Darmstadt: Wissenschaftliche Buchgesellschaft, 1993

Kruse, Joseph A., and Bernd Kortländer, editors, *Das Junge Deutschland: Kolloquium zum 150. Jahrestag des Verbots vom 10. Dezember 1835*, Hamburg: Hoffmann und Campe, 1987

Sammons, Jeffrey L., *Six Essays on the Young German Novel*, Chapel Hill: University of North Carolina Press, 1972

Steinecke, Hartmut, *Literaturkritik des Jungen Deutschland: Entwicklungen, Tendenzen, Texte*, Berlin: E. Schmidt, 1982

Wülfing, Wulf, *Schlagworte des Jungen Deutschland: Mit einer Einführung in die Schlagwortforschung*, Berlin: E. Schmidt, 1982

Wülfing, Wulf, editor, *Junges Deutschland: Texte, Kontexte, Abbildungen, Kommentar*, Munich: Hanser, 1978

Ernst Jünger 1895–1998

No other writer can offer direct testimony of so much German history, and few have cultivated such an exacting style in which to recount what they have witnessed. Yet Ernst Jünger's writing throughout an astonishingly long career has always presented a problem because of his insistence on adding an apocalyptic and mythic interpretation to every phenomenon he encountered. For this reason, controversy persists over his literary significance as well as his ideological standpoint. His early success came with writings adapted from the diaries he kept as a soldier on the western front in World War I. He embraced the agonistic enterprise shared by combatants on all sides, and he reveled in the extremities to which the destructive power of modern military techniques tested the capacities of his senses, so that the values by which he measured the heroic spectacle had almost no connection with the political purposes pursued by particular states and regimes. Although most critics concede that this unwavering eye does record the phenomena of conflict with rare vividness and precision, many also ascribe the core of Jünger's talent—the ability to focus on appalling horrors without flinching—to a deficient sensibility rather than a higher power of vision.

It appears that the authority with which he writes frequently turns paradoxically against the judgments he offers on the things he observes. As a writer on the war, he can insist that his work is that of a soldier who has taken up the pen rather than merely a man of letters touched by battle. He earned the highest decorations won by any young infantry officer and was wounded repeatedly, and although this lets him speak of warfare with an authentic voice, his fascination with this one facet of the human condition might have denied him an understanding of either the personal or the social context within which a larger realm of meaning could become clear. Nonetheless, it is his position as a fascinated observer that conditions those distinctive powers that assert themselves in everything he writes. His travel books frame every scene he witnesses with an aura of magical intensity. His book *Subtile Jagden* (1967; Subtle Hunts) describes a lifetime of entomological observation and collection, a field in which he developed considerable expertise. His speculations concerning the effect of technological power and industrial organization on human sensibilities, notably *Der Arbeiter* (1932; The Worker),

present remarkable dystopian visions of the 20th century and exerted a lasting influence on Martin Heidegger. His *Annäherungen: Drogen und Rausch* (1970; Approaches: Drugs and Intoxication) is a retrospective on his life of experimentation with altered states of consciousness.

Following the logic of his impassioned stand on the value of the war, he involved himself in the ideological debates of the Weimar period as a contributor to and editor of militarist journals. During the late 1920s, he showed some sympathetic interest in the National Socialist movement but had certainly rejected the party before it came to power in 1933. Resolutely resisting overtures made to him by the new regime, he retired to the country and refused any part in the totalitarian public sphere. Yet he also refused to participate in any form of resistance to Hitler's rule at any time. His most famous novel, *Auf den Marmorklippen* (1939; On the Marble Cliffs), did express his disdain for the Nazi barbarism, although this was couched in the vague, timeless terms that made it possible to publish the book under those circumstances. Jünger's protagonist in the narrative opposes the destructive tyrant as a representative of evil yet also reveals a certain admiration for him as an adept of power and looks on the catastrophe wrought by his triumph as part of a necessary cycle in the cosmic order of things.

During World War II, Jünger served in the army once again, and although he did earn another medal for valor, he remained on the margin of the conflict. His situation with the occupation command in Paris was highly privileged, giving him the opportunity to observe both the day-to-day effects of the German military triumph over its neighbors and the process by which the Nazi political authority was exerted over the army. He felt an acute consciousness of this privileged vantage and took pains to discharge the obligation that came with it by meticulous commentary in a series of journals kept through the invasion and occupation of France, a visit to the eastern front, and then the collapse and defeat of Hitler's forces. In these journals, although he necessarily records the suffering he observes, his attention lingers where he is able to find a literary device that will turn horror into a mythic revelation and to reveal himself as the heroic exponent of aesthetic sensation. In *Der Arbeiter,* he develops the term *heroischer Realismus* to describe this posture, but in these journals the reader can see how much contradiction exists between the two ideas of heroism and realism.

His refusal to undergo the denazification process (on the grounds that he had never been a Nazi) caused the British occupation administration to refuse permission for him to publish in Germany. Some of his work came out in special editions for German prisoners of war during this period. In 1949 he published *Heliopolis*, a long allegorical novel set in the future. With this fiction and with his essays and reflections from this period leading up to the novel *Gläserne Bienen* (1957; *The Glass Bees*), he made it clear that he no longer saw any genuine promise in the forms of collective organization based on technology but looked to individual experience as the fullest expression of a human essence and the deepest reflection of the cosmos. These writings established Jünger in the role of a man devoted to esoteric wisdom rather than simply the impassioned visions of a soldier, and in this role he found public recognition from the establishment of the German Federal Republic with a series of major literary prizes culminating in the Goethepreis of Frankfurt in 1982.

He sustained an impressive level of accomplished writing as he approached 100 years of age. The detective novel *Eine gefährliche Begegnung* (1985; *A Dangerous Encounter*) achieved notable success in 1985, and his speculations and journals continued to appear until 1995.

MARCUS BULLOCK

See also Fascism and Literature; War Novels

Biography

Born in Heidelberg, 29 March 1895. Studied biology in Leipzig and Naples, 1923–26; in the French Foreign Legion, 1913; volunteer in the German army during World War I; served at the western front, 1914–18; captain during World War II; discharged from the army, 1944; officer in the Reichswehr, 1919–23; writer for the radical right-wing journals *Standarte, Arminius, Widerstand,* and *Der Vormasch,* 1925–31; in Berlin, 1927; freelance writer from 1927; in Goslar, 1933–36, Überlingen, 1936–39, Kirchhorst, 1939–48, Revensburg, 1948–50, and Wilfingen, from 1950; banned from publishing his work in 1945; ban lifted, 1949; traveled extensively in the 1950s and 1960s; co-editor of *Antaios,* 1959–71. Culture Prize (Goslar), 1956; City of Bremen Prize, 1956; literary prize of the Federal League of German Industry, 1960; Immermann Prize (Düsseldorf), 1965; Humboldt Society gold medal, 1981; Goethe Prize, 1982; Accademia Casentinese, Dante Alighieri International Prize, 1987; Tevere Intern Prize, 1987; honorary doctorate, University of Bilbao, Spain; Great Order of Merit, Federal Republic of Germany, 1959. Died in Wilfingen, 17 February 1998.

Selected Works

Fiction

Afrikanische Spiele, 1936; as *African Diversions,* translated by Stuart Hood, 1954

Auf den Marmorklippen, 1939; as *On the Marble Cliffs,* translated by Stuart Hood, 1947

Heliopolis: Rückblick auf eine Stadt, 1949

Besuch auf Godenholm (stories), 1952

Gläserne Bienen, 1957; revised edition, 1960; as *The Glass Bees,* translated by Louise Bogan and Elizabeth Mayer, 1961

Sturm, 1963

Die Zwille, 1973

Eumeswil, 1977; as *Eumeswil,* translated by Joachim Neugroschel, 1993

Aladins Problem, 1983; as *Aladdin's Problem,* translated by Joachim Neugroschel, 1993

Eine gefährliche Begegnung, 1985; as *A Dangerous Encounter,* translated by Hilary Barr, 1993

Other

In Stahlgewittern: Aus dem Tagebuch eines Stosstruppführers, 1920; as *The Storm of Steel: From the Diary of a German Storm-Troop Officer on the Western Front,* translated by Basil Creighton, 1929

Der Kampf als inneres Erlebnis, 1922

Das Wäldchen 125: Eine Chronik aus den Grabenkämpfen 1918, 1925; as *Copse 125: A Chronicle from the Trench Warfare of 1918,* translated by Basil Creighton, 1930

Feuer und Blut: Ein kleiner Ausschnitt aus einer grossen Schlacht, 1925

Das abenteuerliche Herz: Aufzeichnungen bei Tag und Nacht (essays), 1929; heavily revised version, 1938

Der Arbeiter: Herrschaft und Gestalt, 1932

Blätter und Steine (essays), 1934

Geheimnisse der sprache: Zwei Essays, 1934

Lob der Vokale, 1937

Gärten und Strassen: Aus den Tagebüchern von 1939 und 1940 (diaries), 2 vols., 1942

Myrdun: Briefe aus Norwegen, 1943

Der Friede: Ein Wort an die Jugend Europas, ein Wort an die Jugend der Welt, 1945; as *The Peace,* translated by Stuart Hood, 1948

Atlantische Fahrt (diaries), 1947

Sprache und Körperbau, 1947; revised edition, 1949

Ein Inselfrühling: Ein Tagebuch aus Rhodos, 1948

Strahlungen (diaries), 1949

Über die Linie, 1950

Das Haus der Briefe, 1951

Am Kieselstrand, 1951

Der Waldgang, 1951

Drei Kiesel, 1952

Der gordische Knoten, 1953

Ernst Jünger: Eine Auswahl, edited by Arnim Mohler, 1953

Das Sanduhrbuch, 1954

Geburtstagsbrief: Zum 4. November 1955, 1955

Die Herzmuschel, 1955

Sonnentau: Pflanzenbilder, 1955

Am Sarazenenturm (on Sardinia), 1955

Die Schleife, Dokumente zum Weg, 1955

Rivarol, 1956

Serpentara, 1957

San Pietro, 1957

Jahre der Okkupation (diary), 1958

Mantrana, 1958

An der Zeitmauer, 1959

Der Weltstaat: Organismus und Organisation, 1960

Ein Vormittag in Antibes, 1960

Sgraffiti (essays), 1960

Werke, 10 vols., 1960–65

Das spanische Mondhorn, 1962

Fassungen, 1963

An Friedrich Georg zum 65. Geburtstag, 1963

Typus, Name, Gestalt, 1963

Grenzgänge (essays), 1966

Subtile Jagden (essays), 1967

Im Granit (on Corsica), 1967

Zwei Inseln: Formosa, Ceylon, 1968

Federbälle, 1969

Annäherungen: Drogen und Rausch, 1970

Lettern und Ideogramme (on Japan), 1970

Ad Hoc (essays), 1970

Sinn und Bedeutung: Ein Figurenspiel (essays), 1971

Zahlen und Götter. Philemon und Baucis: Zwei Essays, 1974

Eine Begegnung: Acht Abbildungen nach Zeichnungen und Briefen von Ernst Jünger und Alfred Kubin (correspondence), 1975
Sämtlichte Werke, 18 vols., 1978–83
Siebzig verweht (diary), 2 vols., 1980–81
Flugträume (selections), 1983
Autor und Autorschaft, 1984
Die Schere, 1990

Edited Works
Aufmarsch des Nationalismus, 1926
Die Unvergessenen, 1928
Das Antlitz des Weltkrieges, 1930
Hier spricht der Feind, 1930
Krieg und Krieger, 1930
Luftfahrt ist not! 1930
Franz Schauwecker, *Der feurige Weg*, 1930
Der Kampf um das Reich, 1931

Further Reading

Berman, Russell A., "Written Right across Their Faces: Ernst Jünger's Fascist Modernism," in *Modernity and the Text: Revisions of German Modernism*, edited by Andreas Huyssen and David Bathrick, New York: Columbia University Press, 1989

Bohrer, Karl Heinz, *Die Ästhetik des Schreckens: Die pessimistische Romantik und Ernst Jüngers Frühwerk*, Munich and Vienna: Hanser, 1978

Bullock, Marcus Paul, *The Violent Eye: Ernst Jünger's Visions and Revisions on the European Right*, Detroit, Michigan: Wayne State University Press, 1992

Loose, Gerhard, *Ernst Jünger: Gestalt und Werk*, Frankfurt: Klostermann, 1957

Neaman, Elliot Yale, *A Dubious Past: Ernst Jünger and the Politics of Literature after Nazism*, Berkeley: University of California Press, 1999

Nevin, Thomas, *Ernst Jünger and Germany: Into the Abyss, 1914–1945*, Durham, North Carolina: Duke University Press, 1996; London: Constable, 1997

Sokel, Walter, "The Postmodernism of Ernst Jünger in his Proto-Fascist Stage," *New German Critique* 59 (Spring–Summer 1993)

Stern, J.P., *Ernst Jünger*, Cambridge: Bowes and Bowes, and New Haven, Connecticut: Yale University Press, 1953

Jung Wien

The beginnings of the literary circle Jung Wien, which shaped the cultural and literary modernism of Vienna, was first mentioned in a brief diary entry in the spring of 1890 by Arthur Schnitzler, one of the movement's key proponents. In this same entry of 2 April 1890, Schnitzler indicated that the Jung Wien circle had laid claim to the Café Griensteidl as the group's permanent home. Strategically placed on the Michaelerplatz at the corner of the Herrengasse and the Schauflergasse, nine young, aspiring literary figures congregated daily at the Café Griensteidl to canvass Europe's major newspapers and to engage in heated discussions on topics concerning art, literature, aesthetics, and all aspects of cultural life. Café Griensteidl thus became the center for all artistic and literary development during the closing decade of the 19th century, which catapulted Vienna into the forefront of modern, avant-garde trends in Europe. From 1890 to 1897, the year in which Café Griensteidl was demolished and Karl Kraus's biting satirical work *Die demolierte Literatur* (1896; The Demolished Literature) appeared condemning the Jung Wien movement as superficial and neurotic, the coffeehouse stood as the bastion for literary modernism in Vienna. An article in the daily *Berliner Tageblatt* in 1896 aptly confirmed the role that the Café Griensteidl played in the life of Viennese modernity: it is "both the birthplace and battleground of the whole literary and artistic development of modern Vienna." Among the group's members are represented Vienna's finest modern authors: Arthur Schnitzler, Hermann Bahr, Hugo von Hofmannsthal, Richard Beer-Hofmann, Felix Salten, Felix Dörmann, Leopold von Adrian, and Rudolph Lothar. Karl Kraus, too, was a regular at the coffeehouse meetings between November 1893 and December 1894 before falling into disfavor with the group. Others who were members of the Jung Wien literary circle but who were not Café Griensteidl devotees included Peter Altenberg, Otto Stoessl, Raoul Auernheimer, and Paul Wertheimer, all of whom called Café Central their home.

Although Schnitzler was the first to mention the existence of this new group, it was Hermann Bahr who would assume the self-appointed role of spokesman and theorist of the circle. Having returned from an extended stay in France and Spain, Bahr brought back to Vienna the fervor and zeal for the new mode of literary Impressionism, or, as he called it, "nervous romanticism." Once back in Vienna, Bahr quickly took to writing essays, feuilletons, and plays in which he adopted the latest literary trends, thus bringing new currents to the developing literary and artistic culture of Vienna. Bahr placed great emphasis on the need to develop a keen sensitivity to self and the world. In his essay *Die Überwindung des Naturalismus* (1891; The Conquest of Naturalism), Bahr makes reference to this view by emphasizing the importance of the role played by "nerves" in French decadent literature. He believed that naturalism would be superseded by a "mysticism of nerves," for it is possible to convey the true state of mind only through the account of nervous sensations. Bahr's notion of literary Impressionism was very much rooted in emerging psychoanalytic and philosophical publications and debates of his age. One such work that had a profound influence on his ideas was Ernst Mach's pioneering *Die Analyse der Empfindungen* (1886; Analysis of Sensations). Bahr's unique ability to anticipate the successive changes in postnaturalist movements made him a crucial figure of avant-garde ideas in Vienna. He was also the cofounder of the literary weekly *Die Zeit*, which provided the young artists with a much-needed public forum. Although Bahr's role had a profound political and cultural effect on Viennese society, which contributed significantly in galvanizing the Jung Wien circle, it was the literary talents of both Schnitzler and Hofmannsthal that brought to fruition the literary Impressionism of fin de siècle Vienna. As Alfred von Berger rightly indicated on 16 July 1905 in an article that appeared in Vienna's popular daily *Neue Freie Presse*, "Hofmannsthal, and next to him Schnitzler, are obviously the models for our younger and youngest writers."

One of the main objectives that this young generation of writers sought to achieve in their literary work was to purge the language of its bourgeois constraints and in its place offer a rejuvenated, more "authentic" literary language. Within the circle, no one showed more sensitivity to the revival of language and the genius of form than the young 16-year-old Hofmannsthal. In 1891, when Bahr introduced him to the group, they hailed his lyric poetry as the paradigm of aesthetic perfection. Hofmannsthal excelled at blending in his work a perfect form of expression with an insightful expression to capture the ephemeral. He sought to unify the subjective and the objective worlds at the point at which they intersect: the level of emotions and impressions. Like Hofmannsthal's early work, those of the Jung Wien circle reflected an unusual preoccupation with the idea of death and the pathologies of human sexual behaviors. Among some of the important works that reveal these preoccupation are Hofmannsthal's *Der Tor und der Tod* (1900; The Fool and Death) and *Der Tod des Tizian* (1901; The Death of Titan), Beer-Hofmann's *Der Tod Georgs* (1900; The Death of Georg), and Schnitzler's *Anatol* (1893; Anatol) and *Der Reigen* (1900; The Dance of Death). Schnitzler especially used drama with great skill (mainly one-act plays) to reveal the existing social tensions among the sexes as well as fin de siècle Vienna's frivolous, self-indulging infatuation with human sexuality. In his plays, Schnitzler's protagonists are often represented as well-to-do young bachelors who are caught in an existential ennui, living in a world intermingled with illusion and reality.

The hazy demarcation between fact and fiction pervaded all of Viennese society, even journalism. For all of Vienna's coffee-house literati, the newspaper and especially the feuilleton (cultural essay) section was held in high esteem, as was a journalistic style of writing. Stefan Zweig, in his autobiography *Die Welt von Gestern* (1941; The World of Yesterday), puts it most aptly when he writes that it was indeed the dream of every young author to become a feuilletonist for Vienna's *Neue Freie Presse*, whose feuilleton editor was none other than Theodor Herzl. The feuilleton was a subjective response to an objective reality that most often was conveyed in a language so adjective laden that the real or factual elements were lost in the verbiage. In this manner, objective facts were viewed through the prism-like emotions of the writer. Truth becomes fiction, and reality becomes illusion.

It was in the context of rapid social modernization and the search for a new literary and cultural identity on the threshold of the 20th century that Vienna's young writers embarked on a path to acquire a new way of understanding the subjective and objective worlds, not by knowing but through feeling.

ISTVAN VARKONYI

See also Austria: Late Habsburg Literature in Vienna; Hermann Bahr

Further Reading

Burri, Michael, "Theodor Herzl and Richard von Schaukal: Self-Styled Nobility and the Sources of Bourgeois Belligerence in Prewar Vienna," *Austrian History Yearbook* 28 (1997)

Fischer, Jens Malte, *Fin de Siècle: Kommentar zu einer Epoche*, Munich: Winkler, 1978

Gluck, Mary, "Beyond Vienna 1900: Rethinking Culture in Central Europe," *Austrian History Yearbook* 28 (1997)

Jensen, Robert, "A Matter of Professionalism: Marketing Identity in Fin-de-Siècle Vienna," *Austrian History Yearbook* 28 (1997)

Thompson, Bruce, *Schnitzler's Vienna: Image of a Society*, London and New York: Routledge, 1990

Wunberg, Gotthart, and Johannes J. Braakenburg, editors, *Die Wiener Moderne: Literatur, Kunst, und Musik zwischen 1890 und 1910*, Stuttgart: Reclam, 1981

K

Franz Kafka 1883–1924

Kafka's work first came into prominence after his death, partly through the efforts of his friend and literary executor Max Brod and partly through the influential writings of foreign admirers such as the French existentialist Albert Camus. During his lifetime Kafka only published some of his shorter fiction, leaving the manuscripts of his three major novels unfinished and much of his other work in a form that was evidently not meant for publication. He never was able to support himself with his writing, working for most of his adult life as an executive in the field of workman's compensation insurance. He had qualified himself for such employment by successfully completing university training in law, a field that, although he professed to have little interest in or aptitude for it, informs much of his fiction (e.g., "Vor dem Gesetz" [1915; "Before the Law"] and *Der Prozeß* [1925; *The Trial*]).

Kafka's first important work of fiction, the short story *Das Urteil* (1916; *The Judgment*), was written in one sitting in the fall of 1912. He wrote it directly into his notebook, adding afterward the comment "this is the way it should be done." The story was in large measure a response to his first meeting with the woman who would later become his fiancée, Felice Bauer, but its interest goes far beyond the biographical background. In this story Kafka for the first time found his characteristic voice and style—that striking mixture of realism and outrageous fantasy that is delivered in a cool, matter-of-fact manner—which is now so familiar from his later works and those of his many imitators. Later that same fall he wrote *Die Verwandlung* (1915; *The Metamorphosis*), the world-famous tale of the young salesman Gregor Samsa, who wakes up one morning to find himself transformed into a "monstrous vermin" resembling a giant beetle. The reactions of Gregor and those close to him to this metamorphosis—and not the amazing transformation itself—are the focus of Kafka's attention. The story begins after the incredible event has already taken place and takes it as an indisputable given, examining instead the devastating and entirely plausible aftereffects. In this way Kafka takes the classical German *Novelle*, a form that traditionally chronicled what Goethe called an "unheard-of occurrence," and moves it in a surprising new direction.

Kafka's stories and novels typically narrate events that follow or accompany an "unheard-of" event without paying much attention to the event itself, which is simply assimilated into the background. Thus, *In der Strafkolonie* (1919; *The Penal Colony*) tells of a crisis in a society dominated by an incredibly complex execution machine that is supposed to kill condemned prisoners by writing on their bodies the text of the rule they have broken. The novel *The Trial* follows the life of Josef K. after he awakens one morning to find himself under arrest for an unspecified offense, which neither he nor his accusers ever even attempt to discuss. *Ein Landarzt* (1919; *A Country Doctor*) relates the unseemly and uncanny events surrounding a doctor's otherwise ordinary visit to the home of a patient. *Ein Bericht für eine Akademie* (1917; *A Report to an Academy*) is delivered in sober academic style by an ape who has managed to transform himself into a human being. The tiny story "Der neue Advokat" (1917; "The New Advocate") describes the psychological difficulties experienced by Alexander the Great's warhorse Bucephalus after the great steed has given up carrying men into battle and has turned instead to an apparently successful career as an attorney.

Similar to *A Report to an Academy* and "The New Advocate," a number of Kafka's stories deal with animals possessing human consciousness. *Schakale und Araber* (1917; *Jackals and Arabs*), for example, reports a conversation between a traveler and one of the jackals, which is found in the vicinity of an Arab camp. *Forschungen eines Hundes* (1922; *Investigations of a Dog*) is exactly what the title suggests: the "scientific" findings of a dog who is engaged in research about the lives of dogs. *Der Bau* (1923; *The Burrow*) is told entirely from the point of view of an animal desperately seeking to ensure the security of its burrow from sinister forces that may have already penetrated its interior. All these animal stories were probably written in reaction to Kafka's view of himself as part animal, a view made all the more plausible by the fact that the Czech word *kavka* is an ordinary designation for an animal, the crow or jackdaw.

Even the Kafka novels and stories that do not depend on any incredible event create an atmosphere of anxiety and uncertainty that is very similar to that found in the tales just mentioned. Kafka's first novel, *Der Verschollene* (The Missing Person, published in 1927 by Max Brod as *Amerika* [*America*]), sends its leading character on a dreamlike journey to and through a fantasy America, a journey that is fraught with unexpected dangers and outrageous turns of events. The story *Ein Hungerkünstler* (1924; *A Hunger Artist*) chronicles the last fabulous achievement of a performer who makes his living by fasting in public.

Kafka's last novel, *Das Schloß* (1926; *The Castle*), documents the efforts of the newly arrived Josef K. to establish a place for himself in a village dominated by the inscrutable, arbitrary power of officials living in a nearby castle.

The combination of the ordinary and the amazing in Kafka's fiction has fascinated and troubled generations of readers. The stories seem to demand a special interpretive effort to explain their mysteries, yet they stubbornly resist all attempts to interpret them. The history of Kafka's reception, in the main, is the history of attempts to find a productive strategy for interpretation. These efforts began already with Max Brod, a prominent Zionist as well as a successful writer, who wanted Kafka's work to be understood in a primarily religious context. Brod's view of his friend's fiction was based both on a long personal association and on Brod's own agenda, but it was well rooted in elements that are clearly present in Kafka's writing. Kafka had been fascinated with his Jewish heritage at least since the time of his visits to the Yiddish theater in 1911, and there are countless traces of religious concerns throughout his stories and notebooks. Biblical echoes abound, and there are even stories such as *Das Stadwappen* (1920; *The City Coat of Arms*) that rework Old Testament material. At the time of his death, Kafka was seriously engaged with Zionist activities, working conscientiously at his Hebrew studies, and considering a move to Palestine.

Another strain of Kafka criticism arose early on through the influence of the French existentialists, who saw in Kafka a precursor who shared their own concerns. For them, Kafka was clearly a philosophical writer attempting to deal with the universal human problem of the irrationality of the universe. As a consequence, they saw the novels *The Trial* and *The Castle* as Kafka's defining texts; both tell tales of individuals thrown into a bizarre and ultimately unfathomable world in which they struggle to survive and which they try in vain to comprehend. Kafka's protagonists were seen as existentialist heroes who followed the pattern of the mythic Sisyphus, eternally struggling to roll a stone up a hill and eternally certain that it would roll down again.

Both Brod and Camus understood Kafka as a writer who was concerned with the most important questions of human existence, and this understanding has set the tone of all subsequent discussions of Kafka's work. Although Brod considered his friend to be a sort of "humorist," Kafka's undeniable comic side has never figured very prominently in the mainstream of Kafka scholarship. Readers have always believed that, in spite of his powerful sense of humor, Kafka took an earnest if not downright somber or tragic view of human life. The world may be bizarre and even silly, but it inevitably crushes us. It is that combination of outrageous strangeness with crushing power that has come to define the now popular adjective "Kafkaesque." The Kafkaesque world is goofy, but also lethal.

If readers generally agree on their overall sense of what Kafka's world is like, however, they do not agree at all on the meaning of the individual texts. Various interpretive strategies have been employed, all leading in different directions. The problem is not really that these strategies have failed; rather, the problem seems that too many of them have been at least plausibly successful. Psychoanalytic critics, for example, taking their cue from Kafka's own statement in his notebooks that he had been thinking of Freud when he wrote *The Judgment* have produced Freudian readings of most of the stories and novels and find in them revealing studies of repression, Oedipal conflicts, and other classical psychological conditions. Biographical criticism has found a ready explanation for many difficult elements in the texts by relating them to what we know of Kafka's personal experiences and concerns. Rhetorical and "formalist" criticism has looked to Kafka's complex play with language as the best way to understand the structure of his fictions. An earlier generation of Marxists found class conflict to be centrally important in stories such as *The Penal Colony* and *Jackals and Arabs,* and, more recently, neo-Marxists have seen Kafka's work as a whole as embedded in particular social, political, and economic contexts. Indeed, the historical "embeddedness" of Kafka's stories has been a prominent theme in some of the most recent criticism.

There can be little question that an understanding of Kafka's historical context is crucial to an understanding of his work, and nearly all schools of criticism (with the possible exception of the most extreme adherents of "new critical" formalism) would agree on the need for an effort at appropriate contextualization. What is appropriate may remain a point of contention, but there are a number of features of Kafka's background whose importance are not much in dispute. Among them we may certainly count Kafka's experience as a German-speaking Jew in the predominantly gentile and frequently Czech-speaking society of Austro-Hungarian Prague. Kafka could never ignore his status as the member of a minority, but the meaning of that minority status and its impact on him is not absolutely clear. As a Jew, Kafka was clearly part of an embattled minority that sought at times to assimilate into the majority (as Kafka's father wished to do) and at times to distinguish itself as a separate society (as his friend Max Brod wished to do). As a speaker of German, however, Kafka was associated with the upper social stratum and with the predominant cultural heritage of central Europe. Kafka, for example, had no trouble identifying himself with the Prussian nobleman Heinrich von Kleist, despite the latter's social and religious distance. What counted for Kafka was that both men were writers facing similar personal and philosophical dilemmas.

Kafka grew up in a world that pulled him constantly in different directions. The Austro-Hungarian Empire of the late 19th and early 20th centuries was an experiment in multiculturalism, and similar to many such experiments, it had a distinctly mixed success. Kafka the writer belonged (and saw himself as belonging) to a highly prized German tradition of fiction writing that went back to the age of Goethe. At the same time, however, he could not ignore his participation in an alternative Jewish literary heritage that not only included the Torah and its enormous body of commentary but also folk traditions such as the Yiddish theater, which in turn many, including his own father, thought of as more than a little disreputable. Kafka's family background, too, may have pulled him in opposite directions. His father was a self-made middle-class merchant, a man who had risen from poverty and who valued practicality, physical vigor, and a keen eye on the cash box. On his mother's side, however, were people of a more intellectual bent: rabbis and doctors who valued words higher than coins.

Kafka's linguistic situation was also full of conflict, since he spoke German but lived in a society in which Czech was the predominant local language. Kafka's command of Czech was, in his own opinion, only minimal, but it is clear from the documents he produced at the insurance company that he was quite capable of speaking and even writing this language well when necessary.

Although he relied upon Milena Jesenska to translate his fiction into Czech, he reviewed her translations and at times made suggestions. Two other languages figure importantly in Kafka's background, Yiddish and Hebrew, both of which he studied and valued highly as an essential part of his heritage. Although he never mastered either, his belief in the desirability of doing so remained strong. Traces of Kafka's knowledge of Czech, Yiddish, and Hebrew can be found in his fiction, and these traces at times offer important clues to his literary intentions.

Kafka's place in literary history, although secure, has been difficult to assess properly, in part because his contribution is so unique and in part because he legitimately belongs to so many different traditions. Efforts to align his work with the Expressionist movement, for example, have not been entirely successful. While his work clearly shows some Expressionist traits, including the use of dreamlike plot structures, he does not share the political or social goals that were so prominently portrayed within Expressionist writing. His style also owes something both to the Romantics, especially E.T.A. Hoffmann and his beloved Kleist, and to the realists, particularly Gustave Flaubert, whose use of a first-person point of view within a third-person narrative (*style indirect libre* or *erlebte Rede*) Kafka emulated in many of his novels and stories. Kafka's material, moreover, comes not only from his own imagination, personal experiences, and, occasionally, actual dreams but from a wide variety of literary sources. He drew on the Old Testament, as already mentioned, and he also frequently turned to classical mythology, as in *Das Schweigen der Sirenen* (1917; *The Silence of the Sirens*), *Poseidon* (1920), and a number of other stories. His profession as a lawyer also had a profound influence on his work, providing material for many of the stories and the entire framework for the plot of *The Trial*. Kafka read widely, and the documentable sources for his work range equally widely.

It is perhaps not surprising, given all the variety of his affiliations, that Kafka should be claimed by many different groups, all with some legitimacy. One finds him described as a German writer (although he never lived in Germany), a Jewish writer (although he struggled to find his identity as a Jew), an Austrian writer (although the then present nation of Austria did not include his home city), a Czech writer (although his Czech was not strong and the Czech nation did not exist during his formative years), and more. Although Kafka did not live to see the Holocaust, its aftermath has figured strongly in the vehemence with which these various claims are pressed. Those who state the case for understanding Kafka as part of the German tradition are confronted with the strong likelihood that, had he lived, he would have been taken by German soldiers, as were so many of his friends and relatives, to die in a concentration camp. Those who insist that his Jewish roots are far more important than his participation in the German cultural tradition are confronted with the overwhelming evidence of Kafka's own letters and notebooks, which clearly document his strong sense of affiliation with that tradition. Such apparent contradictions demonstrate the difficulty of categorizing the richly complex phenomenon that Kafka and his work have become.

It would be hard to overestimate the influence Kafka's work has had on literature and culture around the world. Much of the Latin American fiction of the 20th century, for example, has developed out of an impulse that was first delivered by an exposure to Kafka's stories. American writers have also studied his work, some with a nearly scholarly diligence. One need only cite the case of novelist Philip Roth, who not only poured over Kafka's stories, letters, and notebooks but even went so far as to make Kafka into one of his fictional characters. Even the film industry has been influenced not only in the films that explicitly treat Kafka's works (*The Trial* has been the most recent Hollywood effort) but also in the "Kafkaesque" atmosphere and techniques of dozens of others.

CLAYTON KOELB

See also Prague

Biography

Born in Prague, Austro-Hungarian Empire (now the Czech Republic), 3 July 1883. Studied law at Karl Ferdinand University, Prague, 1901–6; qualified in law, 1907; unpaid work in law courts, 1906–7; employed by Assicurazioni Generali insurance company, 1907–8, and Workers Accident Insurance Institute, 1908–22; confined to a sanatorium for tuberculosis, 1920–21. Died 3 June 1924.

Selected Works

Collections

Gesammelte Werke, edited by Max Brod and Heinz Politzer, 6 vols., 1935–37
Gesammelte Werke, edited by Max Brod et al., 11 vols., 1950–74
Sämtliche Erzählungen, edited by Paul Raabe, 1970
The Complete Stories, edited by Nahum N. Glatzer, 1971
Shorter Works, edited and translated by Malcolm Pasley, 1973
The Complete Novels, translated by Edwin and Willa Muir, 1983
Schriften, Tagebücher, Briefe, edited by Jürgen Born et al., 1983–
Collected Stories, edited by Gabriel Josipovici, 1993

Fiction

Betrachtung, 1913
Der Heizer: Ein Fragment, 1913
Die Verwandlung, 1915; edited by Peter Hutchinson and Michael Minden, 1985; as *Metamorphosis*, translated by Eugene Jolas, in *Transition* (Paris), 1936–38; translated by A.L. Lloyd, 1946; as *The Metamorphosis*, translated by Willa and Edwin Muir, in *The Penal Colony: Stories and Short Pieces*, 1948; translated and edited by Stanley Corngold, 1972; translated by Joachim Neugroschel, in *The Metamorphosis and Other Stories*, 1993
Das Urteil, 1916
In der Strafkolonie, 1919; as *In the Penal Settlement: Tales and Short Prose Works*, translated by Ernst Kaiser and Eithne Wilkins, 1949
Ein Landarzt: Kleine Erzählungen, 1919
Ein Hungerkünstler: Vier Geschichten, 1924
Der Prozeß, edited by Max Brod, 1925; as *Der Process*, edited by Malcolm Pasley, 1990; as *The Trial*, translated by Edwin and Willa Muir, 1937 (also published with revisions and additional material translated by E.M. Butler, 1956); translated by Douglas Scott and Chris Waller, 1977; translated by Idris Parry, 1994
Das Schloß, 1926; edited by Malcolm Pasley, 1982; as *The Castle*, translated by Willa and Edwin Muir, 1930 (also published with revisions and additional material translated by Eithne Wilkins and Ernst Kaiser, 1953); translated by Mark Harmon, 1998
Amerika, 1927; original version, as *Der Verschollene*, edited by Jost Schillemeit, 1983; as *America*, translated by Edwin and Willa Muir, 1938
Beim Bau der chinesischen Mauer, edited by Max Brod and Hans Joachim Schoeps, 1931; as *The Great Wall of China, and Other Pieces*, translated by Edwin and Willa Muir, 1933
Parables in German and English, translated by Edwin and Willa Muir, 1947

The Penal Colony: Stories and Short Pieces, translated by Willa and Edwin Muir and C. Greenberg, 1948

Wedding Preparations in the Country, and Other Posthumous Prose Writings, translated by Ernst Kaiser et al., 1954 (also published as *Dearest Father: Stories and Other Writings,* 1954)

Parables and Paradoxes: Parabeln und Paradoxe (bilingual edition), 1958

Metamorphosis and Other Stories, translated by Willa and Edwin Muir, 1961

Description of a Struggle and Other Stories, translated by Willa Muir et al., 1979

Other

Tagebücher 1910–1923, 1951; edited by Hans Gerd Koch, Michael Müller, and Malcolm Pasley, 1990; as *The Diaries of Franz Kafka,* edited by Max Brod, vol. 1, *1910–1913,* translated by Joseph Kresh, 1948, vol. 2, *1914–1923,* translated by Martin Greenberg with Hannah Arendt, 1949

Briefe an Milena, edited by Willy Haas, 1952; as *Letters to Milena,* translated by Tania and James Stern, 1953; translated by Philip Boehm, 1990

Briefe 1902–1924, edited by Max Brod, 1958; as *Letters to Friends, Family, and Editors,* translated by Richard and Clara Winston, 1977

Briefe an Felice, edited by Erich Heller and Jürgen Born, 1967; as *Letters to Felice,* translated by James Stern and Elisabeth Duckworth, 1973

Briefe an Ottla und die Familie, edited by Hartmut Binder and Klaus Wagenbach, 1974; as *Letters to Ottla and the Family,* translated by Richard and Clara Winston, 1982

Max Brod, Franz Kafka: Ein Freundschaft, 2 vols., 1987–89

Briefe an die Eltern aus den Jahren 1922–1924, edited by Josef Cermak and Martin Svatos, 1990

Further Reading

Citati, Pietro, *Kafka,* London: Secker and Warburg, and New York: Knopf, 1990

Deleuze, Gilles, *Kafka: Toward a Minor Literature,* translated by Dana Polan, Minneapolis: University of Minnesota Press, 1986

Gilman, Sander, *Franz Kafka, the Jewish Patient,* New York: Routledge, 1995

Gray, Ronald, *Franz Kafka,* Cambridge: Cambridge University Press, 1973

Heller, Erich, *Kafka,* London: Fontana, 1974, and New York: Viking, 1975

Karl, Frederick, *Franz Kafka, Representative Man,* New York: Ticknor and Fields, 1991

Pawel, Ernst, *The Nightmare of Reason: A Life of Franz Kafka,* London: Harvill, and New York: Farrar Straus, 1984

Robertson, Richie, *Kafka: Judaism, Politics, and Literature,* Oxford: Clarendon Press, and New York: Oxford University Press, 1985

Stern, J.P., editor, *The World of Franz Kafka,* London: Weidenfeld and Nicolson, and New York: Holt, Rinehart, and Winston, 1980

Der Prozeß 1925

Novel by Franz Kafka

More than any other work, this novel of approximately 300 pages has contributed to the coinage of the term *Kafkaesque* for a situation that is both threatening and hopeless. Similar to Kafka's other two novels, *Der Verschollene* (The Missing Person; first published as *Amerika,* 1927; translated as both *Amerika* and *America*) and *Das Schloß* (1926; *The Castle*), *Der Prozeß* (1925; *The Trial*) remained a fragment and was among the works that the author asked to have burned after his death by his friend Max Brod; in contrast to the other two novels, however, it has a clear and decisive ending. It was thanks to this fact that Brod chose *Der Prozeß,* or—as Kafka had tentatively titled it—*Der Process,* as the first of his friend's manuscripts to be published posthumously. Brod was trying to make Kafka, who hitherto had only been known for his shorter works, known as an author of longer fiction. In addition to making numerous small textual changes, Brod first published the work without the existing fragmentary chapters, and he arranged the unnumbered chapters on the basis of his memory of discussions with Kafka. He later expressed doubt about the correct chapter sequence and, in his second edition of the novel, added the unfinished chapters as well as the passages that Kafka had deleted. Due to the historical circumstances, this second edition of 1935 did not reach many readers—in fact, it caused the banning of all of Kafka's works in Germany—but it is in this form that the work became known worldwide—and, after 1945, in Germany—in many reprints as well as translations. As a result, the influence of the recent critical edition, which includes not only all textual variations but also Kafka's original spelling, has so far been restricted to academic circles and scholars.

The immense attraction that *The Trial* has held for both critics and general readers can only be explained by the way in which the novel uses realistic language to invite a literal understanding of the story while challenging those interpretations with the noticeable presence of an abstract meaning. The novel's all-encompassing metaphor is that of a 30-year-old man's sudden and unexplained arrest and his struggle against the invisible powers that have indicted him. They continue to let him go about his personal life and his professional duties until he gives up his resistance and accepts his execution. The protagonist's name, Josef K., as well as his personal circumstances as a bank employee and would-be lover of a neighboring roomer called Fräulein Bürstner (abbreviated in the manuscript as F.B., the initials of Kafka's twice-betrothed Felice Bauer), has led many early critics to favor an autobiographical interpretation.

In an essay written when Kafka was still alive (1921), however, Max Brod called the novel "the standard digest of pangs of conscience" and thus cleared the path for a series of theological interpretations. Furthermore, the uncanny aspects of the invisible "Court" and the dreamlike experiences of the protagonist have invited a string of psychological and psychoanalytic interpretations. Josef K.'s human isolation and loneliness also became the object of many existentialist analyses. From a more historical-philosophical side, K.'s fate has been seen by Walter Benjamin and his school of followers as the human situation in its primeval state, one which we have still not overcome today. A clear shift to more political-historical interpretations occurred during Hitler's reign over Germany, when German and Austrian exiles, among them Hannah Arendt, saw Josef K.'s dilemma as representative of the "fate of the Jewish people" and the author of the novel as a prophet of things to come after his death. Similar political interpretations were also used to criticize communist dictatorships. In some communist countries themselves (including East Germany), however, Josef K.'s weak and ineffective struggle against the "Court" was usually criticized as a sign of the author's yielding to the capitalist state.

Following the reception of French philosophers in Germany during the immediate post-war period, existentialist readings became once more popular and stressed the absurdity of the protagonist's situation. During the 1950s, the ideological interpretations gradually gave way to new looks at the novel from more literary angles, which investigated such phenomena as the narrator's perspective (being both that of the protagonist and that of a separate narrator) and the frequent repetition of the protagonist's acts of assertion and frustration. More recent critics have developed this trend further by denying that the novel has any ideological meaning and by instead relating it to contemporary linguistic theories such as those promoted by Ferdinand de Saussure and Ludwig Wittgenstein.

Today the most common modes of looking at the novel are those concentrating on the poetic reflection of the act of writing, which at every moment both creates and destroys form, or those highlighting a literary representation of modern man's thirst for, and simultaneous lack of, personal responsibility and human interaction. In either case, the critics no longer claim to possess the one and only clue to the novel's meaning, and some even suggest that every reader must find its meaning for him- or herself by relating it to their personal life's "process" and "trial"—both meanings are implied in the German title.

The Trial has left its imprint on many works by other writers and has inspired new works of art in different realms. For example, its traces have been detected in works of fiction originating in Germany, including Peter Weiss's *Fluchtpunkt: Roman* (1962; *Exile: A Novel*) and Walter Jens's *Nein—Die Welt der Angeklagten* (1977; No—The World of the Accused); in France, including Jean-Paul Sartre's *La Nausée* (1938; *Nausea*) and Albert Camus's *La peste* (1947; *The Plague*); in Spain, including Luis Martín-Santos's *Tiempo de silencio* (1962; Time of Silence) and Antonio Martínez-Menchén's *Cinco variaciones* (1963; Five Variations); and in the United States, including Saul Bellow's *The Victim* (1947) and Joseph Heller's *Catch 22* (1961). There have been a number of stage adaptations of the novel, among them in Paris by André Gide and Louis Barrault in 1947, in Prague by Jan Grossman in 1966, in Bremen by Peter Weiss in 1975, and in London by Steven Berkoff in 1976. Two films based on the novel are by Orson Welles (1962) and—with a script by Harold Pinter—by David Jones (1992). Gottfried von Einem's opera *Der Prozeß*, also based on Kafka's work, had its world premiere at the 1953 Salzburg Festival; and pictorial renderings of events in *The Trial*, as well as in other works by Kafka, were shown at an exhibit titled "Kunst zu Kafka" ("Art in Connection with Kafka"), which toured European cities in 1974–75. Thus, the novel that was to be burnt before it was published has now taken on a life of its own, and its resonance keeps growing far beyond the realm of literature.

HELMUT F. PFANNER

Editions

First edition: *Der Prozeß: Roman,* edited by Max Brod, Berlin: Verlag Die Schmiede, 1925; with unfinished chapters and passages deleted by the author, edited by Max Brod, in *Gesammelte Schriften,* vol. 3, Berlin: Schocken, 1935

Critical edition: *Der Process,* edited by Malcolm Pasley, in *Schriften, Tagebücher, Briefe,* edited by Jürgen Born et al., Frankfurt: Fischer, 1990

Translations: *The Trial,* translated by Willa and Edwin Muir, London: Golancz, and New York: Knopf, 1937 (also published with revisions and additional material translated by E.M. Butler, New York: Random House, 1956); translated by Douglas Scott and Chris Waller, London: Picador, 1977; translated by Idris Parry, Harmondsworth, Middlesex: Penguin, 1994

Further Reading

Bloom, Harold, *Franz Kafka's The Trial,* Modern Critical Interpretations, New York: Chelsea House, 1987

Dodd, W.J., *Kafka: Der Prozeß,* Glasgow: University of Glasgow French and German Publications, 1991

Jaffe, Adrian H., *The Process of Kafka's Trial,* East Lansing: Michigan State University Press, 1967

Müller, Michael, *Franz Kafka: Der Prozeß,* Stuttgart: Reclam, 1993

Rolleston, James, *Twentieth Century Interpretations of "The Trial": A Collection of Critical Essays,* Englewood Cliffs, New Jersey: Prentice Hall, 1976

Zimmermann, Hans Dieter, editor, *Nach erneuter Lektüre: Franz Kafkas "Der Process,"* Würzburg: Königshausen und Neumann, 1992

Das Schloß 1926
Novel by Franz Kafka

When Kafka's posthumous novel, *Das Schloß (The Castle),* was about to appear in December 1926, the publisher's advertisement described the work as "Franz Kafka's *Faust.*" This striking, although not entirely accurate, designation stood in stark contrast to the reputation Kafka had built up during his lifetime as the author of numerous carefully polished stories, novellas, and short prose pieces. The executor of his testament, Max Brod, was eager to present Kafka as a major author, and *The Castle* was the work that Brod believed was destined to fulfill this claim. *The Castle* is the third and last of Kafka's unfinished attempts to wrestle with the novel genre; it is also his most ambitious. While most readers and critics prefer his short stories, *The Castle* is the work that has assured Kafka's international fame. Indeed, due to the fact that Kafka's works as a whole were placed, in 1935, on the National Socialists' list of "degenerate writing," Kafka's third novel was at first better known in its English and French translations. Through these translations, *The Castle* exerted an extraordinary influence on mid-century literature outside of Germany. In 1940, the exiled Thomas Mann wrote an "homage" to Kafka centering on *The Castle,* which he called "this very remarkable and brilliant novel." Within German-speaking nations, *The Castle* first began to attain classic status after its republication in 1951.

Kafka's friend and first editor, Max Brod, played a significant role in the early reception of the novel. Appropriating Kafka's writing to his own special interests, Brod saw his friend's writings—notably the three unfinished novels—as representations of a constantly frustrated quest for divine grace. Thomas Mann also saw *The Castle,* with its "puzzling, remote, incomprehensible" central symbol, the Castle itself, in religious terms. At the same time, Mann was keenly aware of Kafka's other face: his talent for inventing absurd episodes akin to slapstick comedy. Mann termed Kafka a "religious humorist."

Other early readings focused more on the novel's social dynamics than its religious ones. Kafka's protagonist, cryptically designated only as "K.," finds himself caught from the outset between two domains: the obscure and uncaring Castle and the primitive and poverty stricken village. Rex Warner's 1941 novel, *The Aerodrome,* inspired by Kafka's *The Castle,* adapts this polar structure for socialist purposes by opposing the elitist and ruthless air force to the unintelligent and oppressed underclass in the village. After the end of World War II, scholars in the early years of the German Democratic Republic similarly emphasized the novel's presentation of a social dystopia.

Another strain of reception saw *The Castle* as a variant of the French existentialist world view promulgated most famously by Sartre and Camus. In these readings, K.'s repeatedly frustrated attempt to establish his identity as a land surveyor who has been summoned by the Castle becomes a metaphor for the crisis of human existence in an absurd world. Much of what today's culture calls the "Kafkaesque" stems from this understanding of K.'s efforts: to win recognition from the Castle is a Sisyphean labor that is doomed to remain unsuccessful.

There are as many different ways of reading *The Castle* as there are critical approaches and theories. Allegorical readings such as those developed in the early phases of the work's reception tend to be excessively reductive. Given the complexity and subtlety of the novel—and of all of Kafka's writing—it is unwise to privilege one allegory over any other.

The Castle was composed using the same narrative technique that distinguishes *Das Urteil* (1912; *The Judgment*), the work Kafka had described as a "breakthrough" ten years earlier. Although written in the third person, these narratives restrict their perceptual field to that of their protagonists, allowing the reader to see, hear, and know nothing that is not present to the mind and senses of this central figure. Kafka had originally intended to write *The Castle* in the first-person form, which he had used in many of his later works (notably his animal tales), but after he had made some headway into the novel, he switched to the third-person and replaced the pronoun "I" with the initial "K." in the opening chapters. Kafka's choice of limited third-person narration is not merely of formalist interest; rather, it underscores his continued adherence to the principles of late-19th-century empiricism, with its belief in the centrality of individual consciousness. The unreliability that seems to characterize the world outside K., whether it be the world of the village or the Castle, is a direct function of this emphasis on subjectivity. This does not mean to say, however, that there is no way for the reader to escape K.'s blinkered vision and imperfect understanding; Kafka's method of presenting K.'s convoluted and often contradictory thoughts and responses draws attention to his protagonist's limitations.

The Castle puts its readers to an exacting test. A modernist adaptation of 19th-century realism's predilection for extensive detail, the novel contains lengthy passages that highlight both its protagonist's inability to comprehend the situations with which he is confronted and his sensation that time has been peculiarly stretched and distorted. The inset narratives of the Barnabas family, in particular the story of Amalia's disgrace, have the same numbing effect on the reader as they do on the bewildered K. In its tendency to almost excessive narrative proliferation, *The Castle* forms a counterpart to Proust's *In Search of Time Lost* and Joyce's *Ulysses.*

Recent Kafka scholarship has paid increasing attention to the cultural contexts of his work. The 1950s insistence on the universality or even otherworldliness of his writing—the idea of Kafka as "timeless and placeless"—has given way to a more historicized vision. Kafka's position among the German-speaking Jewish minority in Prague; his engagement with the political and social issues of his day; his extensive reading of works by writers and thinkers such as Kierkegaard, Schopenhauer, Nietzsche, and Freud; and his deeply ambivalent relationship to history and tradition have all received increasing attention. Unlike many of the shorter works, *The Castle* has been less thoroughly mined for indications of Kafka's various cultural involvements. Nonetheless, it is one of the richest examples of Kafka's aesthetic modernism.

JUDITH RYAN

Editions

First edition: *Das Schloß: Roman,* Munich: Wolff, 1926 (a shortened version Kafka's manuscript)

Critical edition: *Das Schloß: Roman,* in *Gesammelte Werke,* vol. 4, Berlin: Schocken, 1935; *Das Schloß: Roman, in der Fassung der Handschrift,* edited by Malcolm Pasley, Frankfurt: Fischer, 1982

Translations: *The Castle,* translated by Willa and Edwin Muir, New York: Knopf, 1930; *The Castle: A New Translation, Based on the Restored Text,* translated by Mark Harman, New York: Schocken, 1998

Further Reading

Cohn, Dorrit, "K. Enters the Castle: On the Change of Person in Kafka's Manuscript," *Euphorian* 62 (1968)

Emrich, Wilhelm, *Franz Kafka,* Königstein: Athenäum, 1981

Ronnel, Avital, "Doing Kafka in 'The Castle': A Poetics Desire," in *Kafka and the Contemporary Critical Performance: Centenary Readings,* edited by Alan Udoff, Bloomington: Indiana University Press, 1987

Sokel, Walter, *Franz Kafka: Tragik und Ironie: Zur Struktur seiner Kunst,* Munich: Langen, 1964

Sussman, Henry, *Franz Kafka: The Geometrician of Metaphor,* Madison, Wisconsin: Coda Press, 1979

Unseld, Joachim, *Franz Kafka: Ein Schriftstellerleben,* Munich: Hanser, 1982; as *Franz Kafka: A Writer's Life,* translated by Paul F. Dvorak, Riverside, California: Ariadne Press, 1994

Die Verwandlung 1915

Novella by Franz Kafka

Kafka wrote *Die Verwandlung* (*The Metamorphosis*), his most popular work, shortly after he had made his literary breakthrough with the publication of his story *Das Urteil* (1912; *The Judgment*). It was published three years later in an Expressionist journal edited by René Schickele and then in the famous series of

German avant-garde literature published by Kurt Wolff. The story was immediately praised by the critics, who marveled at its relentless suspense and the minute description of detail with which the author drives the fantastic event to its logical conclusion: a traveling salesman wakes up one morning and finds himself transformed into a giant vermin; he loses the trust of his employer and the love of his family members; but while they experience a boost in their lives, he gradually vanishes from their existence. Early readers also saw the story as a symbolic portrayal of the German-speaking Jewish minority in Prague's predominantly Czech population, which in turn was situated in the multi-cultural population of the Austro-Hungarian monarchy; Kafka's personal life in the oppressive atmosphere of a bourgeois family under the dominance of an authoritarian father; or the dissatisfaction that Kafka experienced in his profession as an employee of an insurance company. Although some critics have tried to categorize the work within the framework of German Expressionism, such attempts fall short in explaining the full significance of the story, which has fascinated readers worldwide and has been Kafka's most frequently published and most often translated work.

The dramatic content of *The Metamorphosis* is underscored by its tripartite structure. In each section, the protagonist, Gregor Samsa, loses another connection to his surroundings—first his job, then his place as a family member, and, finally, his physical existence. Each part also ends with a new blow: his flank is wounded by a door slammed closed by his father; then he is hit by an apple thrown at him by his father, which causes a mortal wound; and ultimately he is swept away as a lifeless piece of waste by the family's charwoman. Significantly, the more Gregor—his name recalls the protagonist in Hartmann von der Aue's medieval epic *Gregorius,* who was abandoned as a child in a small boat—falls into oblivion with his family, the more he relishes the memories of his past. Looking through the door into the kitchen, he sees his father reading the newspaper, as he had done when he was the family's only bread earner. Also, the office manager who reminds him of his duties must report to the director of the firm in a similar dependency that Gregor earlier experienced vis-à-vis the office manager. Gregor is also reminded of his present affliction when he sees the facade of a hospital outside of his window. But the most direct reminders of his past are the three roomers taken in by his family in order to make up for the loss of income due to Gregor's transformation: in their bourgeois behavior, with one of them acting as their spokesperson, the three men reflect both the father's position as head of the household and Gregor's standing in the family at the moment when he had chosen their apartment. In their marionette-like reaction to the vermin's appearance, they act similarly to the Samsa family when they first witness Gregor's transformation. As the cryptograph of the name Samsa suggests, Kafka closely identified with the hero's plight.

Despite its autobiographical undertones, *The Metamorphosis* traces a growing distance between the narrator and his protagonist. While in the beginning the reader finds it difficult to distinguish Gregor's fate from that of the narrator, the narrator's separate perspective becomes more evident when he expresses assumptions about Gregor's inner experiences ("Gregor *could* not recall hearing [the music] all this time"), and when he ultimately refers to Gregor's relatives no longer as "father," "mother," and "sister," but as "Mr. and Mrs. Samsa," and "Grete"—the sound of her name also suggests her closeness to Gregor. The noticeable rejuvenation of the Samsa family that results from its riddance of the shameful vermin reflects the irony with which the narrator—who obviously survives Gregor's fate—looks upon the optimistic outlook of the three remaining family members, who with their celebration of a bourgeois lifestyle and materialism enter the same path that resulted in Gregor's transformation, and thus, also leads to death.

As Kafka criticism in general, and here more specifically, has tried to come to grips with both the symbolic and the allegoric meanings of his work, there has been a gradual shift from the earlier rather narrow and often mutually contradictory readings of *The Metamorphosis* to a wider perspective, which allows for more universal interpretations. Not overlooking other viewpoints, today's reader may still see Gregor's fate from a predominantly historical, sociological, philosophical, Marxist, psychoanalytic, autobiographic, or religious perspective; but the major common denominator shared by recent criticism of *The Metamorphosis* is the assumption that the story presents the reader with the metaphor for a human existence in which spiritual reflection and interpersonal communication have been sacrificed for the sake of materialistic efficiency. What makes it difficult to understand the total impact of this situation on Gregor's life is the fact that Kafka has endowed his protagonist and the figures around him with both positive and negative elements, which reflect their ongoing loss of humanity. While Gregor himself suffers from the loss, he also senses a strong nostalgia in his craving to hear his sister play the violin, but he hoards an object of art, the picture of a fur lady in his room, as if it were a material—and, by implication, also sexual—object; conversely, Gregor's sister, who tries to charm the ruthless roomers with her violin play and who cares for Gregor more than their parents, ultimately performs a complete turnabout vis-à-vis her brother and condemns him. It is the mother whose love for Gregor lasts the longest, although she finds it almost impossible to express it due to the constraints put upon her by her husband, whose coldness, however, does mellow in the course of the story. Gregor's state, too, is in transition rather than an absolute status quo. However, most critics agree that the protagonist's yearning for food—different from the food eaten by others—expresses the existential dilemma between his spiritual and bodily needs.

Although Kafka also used the motif of equating men with animals in other works—a man's change into a bug in *Hochzeitsvorbereitungen auf dem Lande* (written 1907; published 1953; *Wedding Preparations in the Country*) and the change of an animal into a human being in *Ein Bericht für eine Akademie* (1917; *A Report to an Academy*)—nowhere has this equation been depicted as convincingly as in this story. While critics have pointed to possible influences by such writers as E.T.A. Hoffmann, Dostoyevsky, Freud, Adler, and Kierkegaard, the literary coinage of *The Metamorphosis* is uniquely Kafka's and has exerted a continuing effect upon readers. Later writers of various ranks and nationalities have declared their indebtedness to this story (or have been related to it by critics), including Jorge Luis Borges, André Breton, Peter Handke, Mario Lancelotti, Alain Robbe-Grillet, Ernesto Sábbato, and Martin Walser. *The Metamorphosis* was adapted for German television (ZDF) by Jean Nemec (1975), and it has inspired several stage adaptations, including those by Steven Berkoff in London (1969), Brad Davis in Los Angeles (1982), Tim Roth in London (1986), Roman Polanski in

Paris (1988), and Mikhail Baryshnikov in New York (1989). Already a classic of modern literature, *The Metamorphosis* will continue to fascinate readers worldwide.

HELMUT F. PFANNER

Editions

First edition: "Die Verwandlung," in *Die Weißen Blätter,* nos. 10–12, 1915; first book edition as *Die Verwandlung,* Leipzig: Kurt Wolff, 1916

Critical editions: in *Schriften, Tagebücher, Briefe,* edited by Jürgen Born et al., Frankfurt: Fischer, 1994–96; a convenient collection is *Sämtliche Erzählungen,* edited by Paul Raabe, Frankfurt: Fischer Bücherei, 1970

Translations: *Metamorphosis,* translated by Eugene Jolas, in *Transition* (Paris), nos. 25-27 (1936–38); translated by A.L. Lloyd, New York: Vanguard Press, 1946; *The Metamorphosis,* translated by Willa and Edwin Muir, in *The Penal Colony: Stories and Short Pieces,* New York: Schocken Books, 1948; translated and edited by Stanley Corngold, New York: Bantam, 1972; translated by Joachim Neugroschel, in *The Metamorphosis and Other Stories,* New York: Scribner, 1993

Further Reading

Bloom, Harold, editor, *Franz Kafka's The Metamorphosis,* New York: Chelsea House, 1988

Corngold, Stanley, *The Commentators' Despair: The Interpretation of Kafka's Metamorphosis,* Port Washington, New York: Kennikat Press, 1973

Hibberd, John, *Kafka: Die Verwandlung,* London: Grant and Cutler, 1985

Schubiger-Cedraschi, Jürg, *Franz Kafka: Die Verwandlung,* Zurich: Atlantis Verlag, 1969

Wiese, Benno von, "Franz Kafka: Die Verwandlung," in *Die deutsche Novelle von Goethe bis Kafka,* Düsseldorf: Bagel, 1956

Georg Kaiser 1878–1945

Kaiser became the most prolific and successful German Expressionist dramatist. His success owed much to the variety in form and setting of his dramas and to their technical mastery. His dramatic career is usually divided into three periods. He wrote social critical works attacking the narrowness of petty bourgeois life and exploring the conflict between mind and body, dramas of renewal in which a "New Man" searches out a new ethical vision, and messianic dramas that aim for a new world theater that can represent a religious faith. This schema, however, does not match the dating of the plays; nor does it include his anti-Nazi statements or the late "Greek" dramas.

Central to all of these works is Kaiser's claim in his essay "Vision und Figur": "The figures who incorporate the vision are manifold. . . . And of what does the vision consist? Only one thing: the renewal of man." This vision is coupled with a deliberately worked-out so-called cubist form, so that Kaiser as a dramatist, similar to the novelist Robert Musil, appears as cool and calculating as a technician and yet as passionate and single-minded as a visionary. "Writing a drama," Kaiser claimed, "is working out a thought to its end." The elements of quest and the complete involvement of his central characters' search for new intensity of existence leads them to obsession. The drama, and often tragedy, comes with the realization that vision and reality do not and even cannot coincide. In the second group of plays, the central figure is more prophetic, and death follows often because his message is not accepted (*Die Bürger von Calais* [1914; *The Burghers of Calais*], *Von morgens bis Mitternachts* [1916; *From Morn to Midnight*], and the *Gas* trilogy). In the third group of plays, the spiritual effects of love are examined; these works often isolate a couple away from reality in a self-centered vision (e.g., *Zweimal Oliver* [1926], *Rosamunde Floris* [1940], and *Alain und Elise* [1940]).

In all the dramas, a breakthrough of a new vision or idea emerges, often as a struggle against the restrictions of traditional language. These works won audience acclaim not least because the text was only one factor in a total theatrical experience. In the *Gas* trilogy for example, Kaiser used abstract, geometric forms in the stage settings, highlighted constellations of characters, paralleled scenes in different parts of the trilogy, dehumanized individuals into robotic numbers, and employed a sliding roof to reveal either the sky or its mechanical reproduction. The double effect of restriction and superhuman symbolism, and the sense of threat to individuals and mankind in general, gave this trilogy an almost science-fiction quality. The timing of the *Gas* trilogy has supported an overall interpretation that Kaiser meant it as a warning not to repeat the catastrophe of World War I and the industrial processes that led to its outbreak. In their place, Kaiser offers the vision of a utopian, environmentally conscious, and economically independent society. This society, however, is defeated by argument and brute force.

Ironically, the ideal of the "New Man" in Kaiser's works is flawed in practice. Even the self-sacrifice of Eustache de St. Pierre in *The Burghers of Calais* has been shown to rest on corrupt motives (Lämmert), and the final scene, a parody of Baroque drama, shows a vision only dimly understood by the select few. Despite this, or the obviously stagy ending of the Cashier in *From Morn to Midnight,* who is electrocuted on a crosslike structure, or the explosion that destroys all in the apocalyptic end of the *Gas* trilogy, the idealism of the central figures made outstanding theater. Such features from Kaiser's second dramatic period emphasized the pathos of Expressionist style, which he used to highlight modern civilization, especially in the big city, as a dehumanizing force. The way in which *The Burghers of Calais* seeks a solution and turns ideas into self-sacrificial action made it one of the few Expressionist dramas to be widely studied in schools and hence generally well known, but *From Morn to Midnight,* with its fast tempo, cinematic overstatement, so-called *Sekundenstil,* overemphatic language, and breathless adaptation of the so-called station drama style of Arnold Strindberg, was more up-to-date in its setting and in its presentation of everyday rather than exceptional people. The *Gas* trilogy, whose influence on Fritz Lang's monumental film *Metropolis* cannot be overemphasized, appealed to a later generation by identifying problems such as racism, trade unionism, facism, nepotism, and the manipulation of labor for economic profit. Kaiser also showed that human nature is fundamentally corrupt (see *Hölle, Weg, Erde* [1919; Hell, The Way, Earth] where the "New Man," for once, is successful). In *Nebeneinander* (1923; Shoulder to Shoulder), heroism is self-defeating and leads eventually to suicide. In *Gats* (1925; Gats), the central figure's wrong-headed attempt to save mankind from mass unemployment by peddling a drug to cause sterility leads to society rejecting and destroying him as a threat to life itself. In *Der Soldat Tanaka* (1940; The Soldier Tanaka), banned after its first performance in Switzerland in 1940, the realization that war itself is a denial of dignity leads to spiritual rebirth, but also to execution. Such double-edged criticism of the individual and society intrigued audiences and inspired later works by Eugene O'Neill and Bertolt Brecht.

Realizing that theatergoers might enjoy lighter fare than emphatic portrayals of societies with individuals destroyed by the machine or the community, Kaiser turned to comedy, where his command of witty language ensured his further and continuous success. During the 1920s, satirical attacks on Hitler and Nazism reveal his basic pacifism, whereas plays of the later period, including *Das Frauenopfer* (1918; Victim of Women), *Der Brand im Opernhaus* (1919; Fire in the Opera House), *Gilles und Jeanne* (1923; Gilles and Jeanne), *Oktobertage* (1928; The Phantom Lover), and *Hellseherei* (1929; Second Sight), explore the consequences of establishing a form of personal truth through a flight from reality. Critical reception veered from adulation to condemnation of the final so-called Greek plays *Zweimal Amphitryon* (1944), *Pygmalion* (1948), and *Bellerophon* (1948), which escaped into the world of myth. With his theories, Kaiser showed the possibilities and limits of Expressionist drama; with his practice, he illuminated the fatal dialectic between modern civilization and humanity. This approach often resulted in simplistic overstatement, as in his early Socrates drama *Der gerettete Alkibiades* (1920; Alkibiades Saved), where Expressionistic fervor is counterbalanced by self-destructive hatred, a trait that can also be seen in the self-criticism of his early central figures.

BRIAN KEITH-SMITH

Biography

Born in Magdeburg, 25 November 1878. Bookshop clerk in Magdeburg, 1895; apprentice in an import/export business, 1896–99; in Buenos Aires, Argentina, where he worked with the local branch of the Berlin AEG (electric company), 1899; contracted malaria and returned to Germany, 1901; nervous breakdown, 1902; in Munich, 1918; imprisoned for six months for embezzlement, Munich; 1920–21; in Berlin, 1921; great popularity of his plays, 1921–33; his works banned by the Nazi regime, from 1933; writing in Berlin, 1934–37; fled to Switzerland, 1938; in Switzerland, 1939–44. Member of the Prussian Academy of Arts, 1926, and the German Academy, 1930; honorary president, Association for German Writers in Exile, 1945. Died 4 June 1945.

Selected Works

Collections
Stücke, Erzählungen, Aufsätze, Gedichte, edited by Walther Huder, 1966
Werke, edited by Walther Huder, 6 vols., 1971–72

Plays
Die jüdische Witwe (produced 1921), 1911
Claudius (produced 1918); in *Hyperion,* 1911
Friedrich und Anna (produced 1918); in *Hyperion,* 1911
König Hahnrei (produced 1931), 1913
Der Fall des Schülers Vehgesack (produced 1915), 1914
Rektor Kleist (produced 1918), 1914
Grossbürger Möller (produced 1915), 1914; revised version, as *David und Goliath* (produced 1922), 1920; as *David and Goliath,* translated by B.J. Kenworthy, in *Plays 2,* 1981
Die Bürger von Calais (produced 1917), 1914; as *The Burghers of Calais,* translated by J.M. Ritchie and Rex Last, in *Five Plays,* 1971
Europa (produced 1920), 1915
Der Zentaur (produced 1917), 1916
Von Morgens bis Mitternachts (produced 1917), 1916; as *From Morn to Midnight,* translated by Ashley Dukes, in *Poet Lore,* vol. 21, 1920; also translated by Ulrich Weisstein, in *Plays for the Theatre: An Anthology of World Drama,* edited by O.G. and L. Brockett, 1967; as *From Morning to Midnight,* translated by J.M. Ritchie, in *Five Plays,* 1971
Die Sorina; oder, Der Kindermord (produced 1917), 1917
Die Versuchung (produced 1917), 1917
Die Koralle (produced 1917), 1917; as *The Coral,* translated by Winifred Katzin, 1963; also translated by B.J. Kenworthy, in *Five Plays,* 1971
Das Frauenopfer (produced 1918), 1918
Juana (produced 1918), 1918
Gas I (produced 1918), 1918; translated by Herman Scheffauer, 1957; also translated by B.J. Kenworthy, in *Five Plays,* 1971
Der Brand im Opernhaus (produced 1918), 1919; as *Fire in the Opera House* translated by Winifred Katzin, in *Eight European Plays,* 1927
Hölle, Weg, Erde (produced 1919), 1919
Gas II (produced 1920), 1920; translated by Winifred Katzin, 1963; translated by B.J. Kenworthy, in *Five Plays,* 1971
Der gerettete Alkibiades (produced 1920), 1920; as *Alkibiades Saved,* translated by Bayard Quincy Morgan in *An Anthology of German Expressionist Drama,* edited by Walter H. Sokel, 1963
Der Protagonist (produced 1922), 1921; as *The Protagonist,* translated by H.F. Garten, in *Tulane Drama Review 5* (1960)
Noli me tangere, 1922
Kanzlist Krehler (produced 1922) 1922
Der Geist der Antike, 1923
Gilles und Jeanne (produced 1923), 1923
Die Flucht nach Venedig (produced 1923), 1923; as *The Flight to Venice,* translated by B.J. Kenworthy, in *Plays 2,* 1981
Nebeneinander (produced 1923), 1923
Kolportage (produced 1924), 1924
Gats (produced 1925), 1925
Der mutige Seefahrer (produced 1925), 1926
Zweimal Oliver (produced 1926), 1926
Papiermühle (produced 1926), 1927
Der Zar lässt sich photographieren, music by Kurt Weill (produced 1928), 1927

Der Präsident (produced 1928), 1927; as *The President*, translated by B.J. Kenworthy, in *Plays 2*, 1981

Oktobertag (produced 1928), 1928; as *The Phantom Lover*, translated by Hermann Bernstein and Adolf E. Meyer, 1928; as *One Day in October*, translated by B.J. Kenworthy, in *Plays 2*, 1981

Die Lederköpfe (produced 1928), 1928

Hellseherei (produced 1929), 1929

Zwei Krawatten (produced 1929), 1929

Mississippi (produced 1930), 1930

Der Silbersee (produced 1933), 1933

Adrienne Ambrosat (produced 1935), 1948?; translated as *Adrienne Ambrosat*, in *Continental Plays 2*, 1935

Das Los des Ossian Balvesen (produced 1939), 1947?

Der Gärtner von Toulouse (produced 1945), 1938

Der Schuss in dei Öffentlichkeit (produced 1949), 1939

Der Soldat Tanaka (produced 1940), 1940

Rosamunde Floris (produced 1953), 1940

Alain und Elise (produced 1954) 1940

Die Spieldose (produced 1943), in *Stücke, Erzählungen, Aufsätze, Gedichte*, 1966

Der englische Sender (radio play), 1947

Zweimal Amphitryon (produced 1944); in *Griechische Dramen*, 1948

Das Floss der Medusa (produced 1945), 1963; as *The Raft of the Medusa*, translated by Ulrich Weisstein, in *First Stage*, vol. 1, 1962; translated by George Wellwarth, in *Postwar German Theater*, edited by Michael Benedikt and George E. Wellwarth; H.F. Garten and Elizabeth Sprigge, in *Plays 2*, 1981

Agnete (produced 1949), 1948

Pygmalion (produced 1953); in *Griechische Dramen*, 1948

Bellerophon (produced 1953); in *Griechische Dramen*, 1948

Klawitter (produced 1949), 1949

Napoleon in New Orleans (produced 1950); in *Stücke, Erzählungen, Aufsätze, Gedichte*, 1966

Schellenkönig; in *Stücke, Erzählungen, Aufsätze, Gedichte*, 1966

Five Plays (includes *From Morn to Midnight; The Burghers of Calais; The Coral; Gas I; Gas II*), translated by B.J. Kenworthy, Rex Last, and J.M. Ritchie, 1971; as *Plays I*, 1985

Plays 2 (includes *The Flight to Venice; One Day in October; The Raft of the Medusa; David and Goliath; The President*), translated by B.J. Kenworthy, H.F. Garten, and Elizabeth Sprigge, 1981

Fiction

Es ist genug, 1932

Villa Aurea, 1940

Leutnant Welzeck (fragment); in *Stücke, Erzählungen, Aufsätze, Gedichte*, 1966

Other

"Vision und Figur," 1918

Georg Kaiser in Sachen Goerg Kaiser: Briefe 1916–1933, edited by Gesa M. Valk, 1989

Further Reading

Adling, W., "Georg Kaisers Drama *Von morgens bis mitternachts* und die Zersetzung des dramatischen Stils," *Weimarer Beiträge 5* (1959)

Arnold, Arnim, editor, *Georg Kaiser*, Stuttgart: Klett, 1980

Benson, Renate, *German Expressionist Drama: Ernst Toller and Georg Kaiser*, London: MacMillan, and New York: Grove Press, 1984

———, "Georg Kaiser," in *International Dictionary of Theatre: 2 Playwrights*, edited by Mark Hawkins-Dady, Detroit, Michigan and London: St. James Press, 1994

Callandra, Dennis, "Georg Kaisers *From Morn to Midnight*: The Nature of Expressionist Performance," *Theatre Quarterly 6* (1976)

Denkler, Horst, *Georg Kaiser: "Die Bürger von Calais,"* Munich: Oldenbourg, 1967

Diebold, Bernhard, *Der Denkspieler Georg Kaiser*, Frankfurt: Frankfurter Verlags-Anstalt, 1924

Durzak, Manfred, *Das Expressionistische Drama: Carl Sternheim, Georg Kaiser*, Munich: Nymphenburger, 1978

Keith-Smith, Brian, "The Gas Trilogy," in *International Dictionary of Theatre*, vol. 1, edited by Mark Hawkins-Dady, Chicago and London: St. James Press, 1992

Kenworthy, Brian J., *Georg Kaiser*, Oxford: Blackwell, 1957

Lämmert, E., "Kaisers *Die Bürger von Calais*," in *Das deutsche Drama*, vol. 2, edited by Benno von Wiese, Düsseldorf: Bagel, 1960

Last, Rex W., "Symbol and Struggle in Georg Kaiser's *Die Bürger von Calais*," *German Life and Letters 19* (1966)

Neis, Edgar, *Erläuterungen zu Georg Kaisers "Die Bürger von Calais,"* 3rd edition, Hollfeld: Bange, 1982

Paulsen, Wolfgang, *Georg Kaiser: Die Perspektiven seines Werkes*, Tübingen: Niemeyer, 1960

Pausch, Holger A., and Ernest Rheinhold, editors, *Georg Kaiser: Eine Aufsatzsammlung nach einem Symposium in Edmonton (Kanada)*, Berlin and Darmstadt: Agora, 1980

Rühle, G., "Georg Kaiser Gas 1.Teil, Gas 2.Teil," in *Zeit und Theater: Vom Kaiserreich zur Republik, 1913–1925*, vol. 1, Berlin: Propyläen, 1972

Schueler, H.J., "The Symbolism of Paradise in Georg Kaiser's *Von morgens bis mitternachts*," *Neophilologus 68* (1984)

Steffens, Wilhelm, *Georg Kaiser*, Velber: Friedrich, 1969

Tyson, Peter K., *The Reception of Georg Kaiser (1915–1945): Texts and Analysis*, 2 vols., Bern, Frankfurt, and New York: Lang, 1984

Kaiserchronik ca. 1150

Sixteen complete manuscripts and 25 fragments attest to the—by medieval standards—phenomenal popularity of the *Kaiserchronik*. Further evidence of its importance is provided by numerous revised versions and continuations. Arranged in rhymed pairs, 17,283 verses relate the history of the emperors of the Roman and Holy Roman Empire from Caesar to Konrad III, who reigned from 1138–52. The manuscript abruptly breaks off at Christmas of 1146, after depicting the crusade preaching of Bernard of Clairvaux (1090–1153). The *Kaiserchronik*, how-ever, is noteworthy for more than its widespread dissemination. It constitutes the first appearance in German of the traditional Latin genre, the historical chronicle, and it provided the model for all other German vernacular chronicles that followed. But even without these distinctions, the *Kaiserchronik* is, without doubt, one of the most impressive literary achievements of the German Middle Ages. Nonetheless, like so many other works from the Early Middle High German period, it leaves many questions about its dating and authorship unanswered. Most scholars are in agreement, for example, that the *Kaiserchronik* as it now exists was completed by a Regensburg cleric around 1147. But since the work appears to end in mid-sentence "the king did not tarry any longer," it is unclear whether the poet intended to carry on with his writing at some later point or whether he considered the chronicle finished for all practical purposes, later continuations notwithstanding. Further, given the current state of research, questions regarding the beginning date of composition—suggestions range from 1126 to the early 1140s—and whether one or more poets were involved in the writing must likewise remain open.

In the Prologue, the poet addresses his audience and says that he is going to impart something of value to attentive listeners. Those who will not pay attention to the exemplary tales that he is about to relate, he claims, are of no value to themselves or society. Just who comprised the audience is not certain, but given the use of the vernacular language, it is highly likely that the target group was composed of members of the feudal nobility and ministerials, possibly even members of a cloister who were not versed in Latin.

Then the poet goes on to explain his work as constituting a chronicle of the Roman Empire from the beginning to the present day, although the balance is somewhat tilted in favor of the Roman emperors. Of the 17,283 verses, verses 43–14,281 deal with 36 Roman emperors, not all of them historically verifiable. Lines 14,282–17,283 deal with 19 German emperors. There is a lengthy span of time between the last Greek emperor mentioned (Constantine VI) and the restoration of the Roman Empire by Charlemagne. Clearly, for the *Kaiserchronik* poet, the Greeks had no claim on the Roman crown. In addition, the poet does not merely depict the Roman emperors, but he also profiles the popes, who played a role in the empire. Further, he presents both good and bad emperors and popes. Thus, it seems clear that the Roman Empire for the *Kaiserchronik* poet must be viewed as a cooperative venture of the church and the world, of pope and emperor. But the main purpose, and thus the usefulness, of the *Kaiserchronik* was to depict rulers, both pagan and Christian, who could be taken as worthy role models by the secular nobility of the poet's time. The section dealing with the emperor Trajan may be taken as an excellent example of this poetic intent. The picture of Trajan that is presented in the *Kaiserchronik* is consonant with the one developed by the historians of late Antiquity, namely, that Trajan is the epitome of the just ruler who respected his nobles, but ruled all levels of society justly and without bias. In fact, according to the *Kaiserchronik*, Trajan was so just that when he died, Pope Gregory interceded on behalf of his soul. As a result, even though a pagan, Trajan's soul was saved from hell and put into St. Gregory's care until the Last Judgment. In order to make sure that the meaning of the Trajan episode is clear, the poet admonishes all secular kings to take Trajan as a model for their own actions. Essentially, the story of Trajan exemplifies the main concerns of the poet very well.

Of course, emperors such as Constantine and Charlemagne, who worked hand-in-glove with their respective popes (coincidentally their brothers, according to the chronicle), are the rulers most worthy of emulation. But it must be emphasized again: paramount in the poet's concept of sovereignty was the obligation of the ruler, whether pagan or Christian, to uphold laws of the empire, which ranged from the administration of the emperor's house to maintaining distinctions among the levels of society.

The *Kaiserchronik,* however, is much more than a dry recounting of the lives of famous men and women. It is, in fact, a mirror of medieval Christian society and its firmly held belief system. Replete with fanciful tales and distortions of history, spurious emperors, and relationships that did not exist in real life, the work is brimming with fascinating episodes—real or imagined—from the lives of the—real or imagined—Roman emperors. While modern historians can claim, and rightly so, that the *Kaiserchronik* is not a reliable historical document, it must be remembered that the modern concept of history as a depiction of discrete points in time does not correspond with the medieval view of history. For the medieval individual there was only one history—the history of salvation that began with the creation. The actions and maneuvering of mere humans were of little importance except insofar as they were part of the divine scheme and furthered the divinely ordained order on earth. Thus, the more important notion for the poet and his audience was not whether the chronology presented in the work was correct, but rather how the secular and ecclesiastical rulers carried out their responsibilities toward society.

The *Kaiserchronik* has no equal before or since in the vernacular, and it is just one more—magnificent—example of the concern of the medieval church for the establishment and preservation of a just society, in which all, high or low, would receive their due.

FRANCIS G. GENTRY

See also Middle High German

Editions

Die Kaiserchronik eines Regensburger Geistlichen, edited by Edward Schröder, Hannover: Weidmann, 1892

Further Reading

Gellinek, Christian, "The German Emperor's Chronicle: An Epic Fiction?," *Colloquia Germanica* 5 (1971)

Gentry, Francis G., "Kaiserchronik," in *German Writers and Works of the Early Middle Ages, 800–1170, Dictionary of Literary Biography,* vol. 148, edited by Will Hasty and James Hardin, Detroit, Michigan: Gale Research, 1995

Myers, H.A., "The Concept of Kingship in the *Kaiserchronik*," *Traditio* 27 (1971)

Immanuel Kant 1724–1804

From our own perspective, Kant is the most important thinker of the Enlightenment period and one of the great philosophical systematizers. He was also immensely influential on the Romantic thinkers, known as "German Idealists," who succeeded him.

In his "precritical period," Kant worked largely within the philosophical framework established by Wolff and Leibniz. Following the second period, the so-called silent decade, during which he published practically nothing, his third—the "critical"—period contains his major works. These include, above all, the three critiques—works in which Kant sought to establish the boundaries of legitimate philosophical inquiry (*Kritik der reinen Vernunft* [1781; *Critique of Pure Reason*]), moral action (*Kritik der praktischen Vernunft* [1788; *Critique of Practical Reason*]), and aesthetic and scientific judgment (*Kritik der Urteilskraft* [1790; *Critique of Judgment*]). The first, Kant's so-called Copernican revolution in philosophy, consists of his radical limitation of human knowledge, which at the same time secures it more firmly, to what can be shown to have its grounds in the constitution not of the world itself but in the human capacity to make sense of the world. In this way, Kant thought that he was able to "protect the Ideas" (God, freedom, and immortality) that underlie Western thought by, as he put it, "denying knowledge to make room for faith." For Kant, these three ideas are the necessary postulates of knowing anything.

Kant himself saw his work as answering three main questions: What can I know? What ought I to do? and What may I hope? Concepts central to Kant's work include the distinction between the "phenomenon" (things as we see them in time and space) and the "noumenon" (*Ding an sich,* or thing-in-itself); the categorical imperative (defined on one occasion as "Act always in such a way as if, through your maxims, you were giving laws to the universal Kingdom of ends"); and the notion of "free beauty" (*pulchritudo vaga*). A more discursive way into his system is offered by his *Prolegomena zu einer jeden künftigen Metaphysik* (1783; *Prolegomena to Any Future Metaphysics*).

Kant was a major figure in late 18th-century intellectual life. According to a contemporary, his works could be found in ladies' boudoirs, while hairdressers used Kantian terminology. Kant was intensively read by his pupil Herder, of whose *Ideen zur Philosophie der Geschichte der Menschheit, Part 1* (1784; *Ideas on the Philosophy of the History of Humanity*) he wrote an important review (1785). Such thinkers as Reinhold and Jacobi debated the problems of Kantian epistemology and, in particular, the concept of the *Ding an sich*. Jacobi remarked that without the *Ding an sich* it was impossible to enter Kant's system but that, with it, it was impossible to stay in it.

Equally, Kant was a major influence on Schiller, who, in *Über die ästhetische Erziehung des Menschen* (1795; *On the Aesthetic Education of Man*) and other essays, sought to mitigate the perceived harshness of Kantian morality, supplementing the Kantian influence on duty with the notion of inclination ("eine Neigung zur Pflicht"). Schiller's ambivalent yet fruitful attitude toward Kant is well summarized in his complaint in one of his *Xenien* that he had spent 20 wasted years on Kant: 10 trying to understand him and another 10 to free himself again ("Zwei Jahrzehnte kostest du mir: zehn Jahre verlor ich, / Dich zu begreifen, und zehn, mich zu befreien von dir"). A similar ambiguity is found in Goethe's reception of Kant. In one of his maxims and reflections, Goethe called for a similar supplement to Kant's intellectualism, writing that, following the critique of reason, "a critique of the senses is required, if art in general, especially German art, is ever somehow to restore itself and progress in a cheerful, vital way."

The concluding section of the second critique was, as the critic Alexander Gode-von Aesch argued, the starting point for a dualistic view that Romanticism sought to overcome: "There are two things that fill the mind and soul [das Gemüt] with ever new and ever increasing admiration and awe: the starry heavens above me and the moral law within me." And with its summative formulation of the principles of aesthetics (founded in Germany in 1750 by Baumgarten), Kant's third critique provided Romantics and classicists alike with what they took to be a definitive account of beauty and art as arousing "disinterested pleasure." An extreme example of Kant's effect was provided by Kleist, who, following his "Kantkrise" of 1801, was plunged into precisely the kind of nihilism that Kant believed he had avoided. As far as philosophy is concerned, both Fichte and Schelling took Kant as their starting point but used him in very different ways, and, without Kant, it is difficult to understand the three main 19th-century German philosophers. Hegel developed the notion of reason as found in Kant, emphasizing the dynamic properties of thought that he called "dialectical." By contrast, Schopenhauer saw himself as the unique successor to Kant, arguing that the unknowable *Ding an sich* could indeed be known, through the body, as the will to life. More radically, Nietzsche called Kant a "cunning Christian" and objected that Kant's morality "reeks of cruelty." In the late 19th century, the neo-Kantian schools in Marburg and Heidelberg tried to rehabilitate him in German intellectual circles ("Es muß auf Kant zurückgegangen werden!"—Otto Liebmann) and to think through the implications of his philosophy ("Kant verstehen heißt über ihn hinausgehen"—Windelband).

Likewise, in the 20th century, Kant's importance has in no way diminished. In *Kant und das Problem der Metaphysik* (1929), Heidegger reinterpreted the first critique as providing a foundation for metaphysics of the kind he explored in *Sein und Zeit* (1927; *Being and Time*). In *La Verité dans le peinture* (1979; *The Truth in Painting*), Derrida offered a "deconstructive" reading of Kant's third critique, uncovering in it the logic of the "parergon" (frame), and Lyotard, whose postmodernist aesthetics draws heavily on Kant's discussion of the category of the sublime, claimed in "The Sign of History" (1982), "The name 'Kant' marks at once the prologue and the epilogue to modernity. And as the epilogue to modernity, it is also a prologue to postmodernity."

PAUL BISHOP

See also Aufklärung

Biography

Born in Königsberg, in East Prussia (now Kaliningrad, Russia), 22 April 1724. Studied at the Univeristy of Königsberg, 1740–46; taught as a private tutor; returned to the University of Königsberg, 1755, where he qualified as a lecturer; appointed professor, 1770; retired in 1796. Died in Königsberg, 12 February 1804.

Selected Works

Collections

Gesammelte Schriften, edited by the Berlin Academy of Sciences, 1902–
Kants Werke, 11 vols., edited by Ernst Cassirer, 1912–23
The Cambridge Edition of the Works of Immanuel Kant, edited by Paul Guyer and Allen W. Wood, 1992–

Philosophical Writing

Der einzig mögliche Beweisgrund zu einer Demonstration das Daseyns Gottes, 1763; as *The One Possible Basis for a Demonstration of the Existence of God*, translated by Gordon Treash, 1979
Versuch, den Begriff der negativen Grössen in die Weltweisheit einzuführen, 1763
Untersuchungen über die Deutlichkeit der Grundsätze der natürlichen Theologie und der Moral, 1764
Träume eines Geistersehers erläutert durch Träume der Metaphysik, 1766; as *Dreams of a Spirit-Seer, Illustrated by Dreams of Metaphysics*, translated by Emmanuel F. Goerwitz, 1900
De Mundi Sensibilis atque Intelligibilis Forma et Principiis: Dissertation, 1770; as *Kant's Inaugural Dissertation of 1770*, translated by William J. Eckoff, 1894
Kritik der reinen Vernunft, 1781; revised edition, 1787; as *Critique of Pure Reason*, translated by J.M.D. Meiklejohn, 1878
Prolegomena zu einer jeden künftigen Metaphysik die als Wissenschaft wird auftreten können, 1783; as *Prolegomena to Future Metaphysic*, translated by John Richardson, 1819
Grundlegung zur Metaphysik der Sitten, 1785; as *Fundamental Principles of the Metaphysics of Ethics*, translated by Thomas Kingsmill Abbott, 1895
Metaphysische Anfangsgründe der Naturwissenschaft, 1786; as *Metaphysical Foundations of Natural Science*, translated by James Ellington, 1970
Kritik der praktischen Vernunft, 1788; as *Kant's Critique of Practical Reason*, translated by Thomas Kingsmill Abbott, 1879
Kritik der Urteilskraft, 1790; 2nd edition, 1793; 3rd edition, 1799; as *Kant's Kritik of Judgment*, translated by J.H. Bernard, 1892; as *The Critique of Judgement*, translated by James Creed Meredith, 1952
Die Religion innerhalb der Grenzen der bloßen Vernunft, 1793; 2nd edition, 1794; as *Religion within the Boundary of Pure Reason*, translated by J.W. Semple, 1838
Die Metaphysik der Sitten, 1797; 2nd edition, 1798–1803; as *The Metaphysic of Morals*, translated by A.F.M. Willich, 1799
Der Streit der Fakultäten, 1798; as *The Conflict of the Faculties*, translated by Mary J. Gregor, 1979

Further Reading

Cassirer, Ernst, *Kant's Life and Thought*, New Haven, Connecticut: Yale University Press, 1981
Caygill, Howard, *A Kant Dictionary*, Oxford and Cambridge, Massachusetts: Blackwell, 1995
Copleston, Frederick, *A History of Philosophy*, vol. 6, *Wolff to Kant*, Westminster, Maryland: Newman Press, 1960
Deleuze, Gilles, *Kant's Critical Philosophy*, translated by H. Tomlinson and B. Habberjam, London: Athlone Press, 1984
Guyer, Paul, editor, *The Cambridge Companion to Kant*, Cambridge and New York: Cambridge University Press, 1992
Körner, Stephan, *Kant*, Harmondsworth: Penguin, 1955; New Haven, Connecticut, and London: Yale University Press, 1982
Roberts, Julian, "Kant," in *German Philosophy: An Introduction*, Cambridge: Polity Press, and Atlantic Highlands, New Jersey: Humanities Press International, 1988
Schaper, Eva, *Studies in Kant's Aesthetics*, Edinburgh: Edinburgh University Press, 1979
Scruton, Roger, *Kant*, Oxford and New York: Oxford University Press, 1982
Walker, Ralph, *Kant*, London: Routledge and Kegan Paul, 1978
Willey, Thomas E., *Back to Kant: The Revival of Kantianism in German Social Thought, 1860–1914*, Detroit, Michigan: Wayne State University Press, 1978

Kritik der Urteilskraft 1790

Philosophical Essay by Immanuel Kant

Kant's third critique, first published in 1790 (2nd edition, 1793; 3rd edition, 1799; *The Critique of Judgement*), consists of two parts: "Critique of Aesthetic Judgment" and "Critique of Teleological Judgment." It occupies an important place in the critical philosophy, as the other two critiques might appear to some to leave humanity divided between the phenomenal realm (determined in time and space) and the noumenal realm (in which alone freedom is possible), as Kant was aware:

> Albeit, then, between the realm of the natural concept, as the sensible, and the realm of the concept of freedom, as the supersensible, there is a great gulf fixed . . . [still] the concept of freedom is meant to actualize in the sensible world the end proposed by its laws. . . . There must, therefore, be a ground of the unity of the supersensible that lies at the basis of nature.

Significantly, the critique deals with both art and science in terms of judgment ("the faculty of thinking the particular as contained in the universal," for "purposefulness," seen subjectively, is an aesthetic and, seen objectively, a teleological judgment).

The first part, "Critique of Aesthetic Judgment," examines judgments of taste. Central to Kant's aesthetics is the notion of "free beauty" (*pulchritudo vaga*), which is the object of a particular kind of judgment. For Kant, when we judge beauty, we do so apart from a concept: "The beautiful is that which, apart from a concept, pleases universally." Such a judgment involves the "free play" of the faculties of the imagination and the understanding. Furthermore, there is purposiveness in beauty but no purpose—"Zweckmäßigkeit ohne Zweck"—and because our judgment does not involve the question of its utility, we judge beauty disinterestedly (a view that can be traced back at least as far as Shaftesbury). In addition, although beauty is not concerned with the realm of action, it is nonetheless, for Kant, a symbol of the morally good. As examples of natural free beauty, Kant cites flowers, birds, and crustacea and, as man-made examples, ornamental designs, framework foliage, or leaf-patterned wallpaper.

The second major category explored by Kant in "Critique of Aesthetic Judgment" is the sublime. Drawing on a tradition including Longinus, Boileau, and Edmund Burke, Kant first investigated the notion in *Beobachtungen über das Gefühl des Schönen und Erhabenen* (1763; *Observations on the Feeling of the Beautiful and Sublime*). Whereas in that work Kant proposes sexual differences and national characteristics as examples of the distinction between beauty (which "charms") and the sublime (which "moves"), in the third critique his approach is more systematic. Furthermore, he subdivides the sublime into the mathematically sublime (e.g., the effect of the pyramids or St. Peter's in Rome), and the dynamically sublime, for example:

> bold, overhanging, and, as it were, threatening rocks, thunderclouds piled up in the vault of heaven, borne along with flashes and peals, volcanoes in all their violence of destruction, hurricanes leaving desolation in their track, the boundless ocean rising with rebellious force, the high waterfall of some mighty river.

As opposed to the beautiful, the sublime offers a "negative pleasure," and whereas the judgment of beauty involves the free play of the imagination and the understanding (the faculty of empirical concepts), that of the sublime involves imagination and reason (the faculty of rational ideas). Finally, Kant emphasizes, in contrast to Boileau and Burke, that "true sublimity must be sought only in the mind of the judging subject, and not in the object of nature that occasions this attitude." Most remarkable in Kant's account, however, is his notion that the sublime involves the "sacrifice" of the imagination to reason and the idea of freedom.

In the second part, "Critique of Teleological Judgment," Kant regards nature itself as, so to speak, a work of art in that it is purposive without purpose. Arguing against intentionality in the natural world, the third critique "does not," as Stephan Körner has rightly emphasized, "develop a teleological metaphysics. On the contrary, it shows that teleological principles are not constitutive of the empirical world, but can only be regulative for our reflection upon the empirical world." Thus, although nature has no discernible purpose, we cannot think of nature except in terms of purpose. Summed up in the form of a maxim, Kant argues that "everything in the world," including war, "is good for something or other; nothing in it is vain; we are entitled . . . to expect nothing from nature and its laws but what is purposive in relation to the whole." Humanity, as "the being upon this earth who is the ultimate purpose of nature," has as an ultimate purpose: not happiness but culture, defined as "the production in a rational being of an aptitude for any purpose (and consequently in his freedom)." Art, too, has a role to play here, for even if it does not make a person morally better, it makes him or her civilized.

Often regarded as the work that unpacks what Kant neatly stores away elsewhere, the style of the third critique differs considerably from the previous two. Goethe annotated his copy of the work extensively, and although he described Kant's treatment of rhetoric as excellent, of poetry as not too bad, and of painting and architecture as inadequate (Eckermann), such essays as "Anschauende Urteilskraft" (1820; "Apperceptive Judgment") reveal the extent of the effect of the second part on Goethe's scientific thinking. Schiller's definition of beauty as "Freiheit in der Erscheinung" (freedom in appearance) reworked Kant's aesthetics within a largely Kantian framework. By conflating "intellectual intuition" (a non-sensory form of cognition whose possibility Kant had denied) with aesthetic intuition (*Philosophie der Kunst* [1802–3; *Philosophy of Art*]), Schelling harnessed Kantian ideas for Romantic ends. Nietzsche rejected Kant's view of beauty as disinterested pleasure with vehemence:

"Without interest! Compare with this definition one framed by a genuine 'spectator' and artist—Stendhal, who once called the beautiful *une promesse de bonheur*" (*Zur Genealogie der Moral* [1887; *On the Genealogy of Morals*]). More recently, French critics such as Deleuze, Derrida, and Lyotard have redirected attention to this rich and complex work.

PAUL BISHOP

See also Aesthetics

Editions
First edition: *Kritik der Urtheilskraft,* Berlin and Libau: Bey Lagarde und Friederich, 1790
Critical edition: in *Gesammelte Schriften,* edited by the Berlin Academy of Sciences, vol. 5, Berlin: Georg Reimer, 1913
Translation: *The Critique of Judgement,* translated by James Creed Meredith, Oxford: Clarendon Press, 1952
Critical edition of a translation: in *The Cambridge Edition of the Works of Immanuel Kant,* edited by Paul Guyer and Allen W. Wood, *Aesthetics and Teleology,* Cambridge: Cambridge University Press, forthcoming

Further Reading
Cassirer, Heinrich Walter, *A Commentary on Kant's "Critique of Judgment,"* London: Methuen, 1938
Caygill, Howard, *Art of Judgement,* Oxford and Cambridge, Massachusetts: Blackwell, 1989
Cohen, Ted, and Paul Guyer, editors, *Essays in Kant's Aesthetics,* Chicago: University of Chicago Press, 1982
Coleman, Francis X.J., *The Harmony of Reason: A Study in Kant's Aesthetics,* Pittsburgh, Pennsylvania: University of Pittsburgh Press, 1974
Crawford, Donald W., *Kant's Aesthetic Theory,* Madison and London: University of Wisconsin Press, 1974
Crowther, Paul, *The Kantian Sublime: From Morality to Art,* Oxford: Clarendon Press, and New York: Oxford University Press, 1989
Derrida, Jacques, *La Vérité en peinture,* Paris: Flammarion, 1978; as *The Truth in Painting,* translated by Geoff Bennington and Ian Mcleod, London and Chicago: University of Chicago Press, 1987
Guyer, Paul, *Kant and the Claims of Taste,* London and Cambridge, Massachusetts: Harvard University Press, 1979
Kemal, Salim, *Kant and Fine Art,* Oxford: Clarendon Press, and New York: Oxford University Press, 1986
Lyotard, Jean-François, *Leçons sur l'analytique du sublime,* Paris: Galilée, 1991; as *Lessons on the Analytic of the Sublime,* translated by Elizabeth Rottenberg, Stanford, California: Stanford University Press, 1994
McCloskey, Mary A., *Kant's Aesthetic,* Albany: State University of New York Press, 1986; Basingstoke: Macmillan, 1987
McFarland, John D., *Kant's Concept of Teleology,* Edinburgh: University of Edinburgh Press, 1971
Molnár, Géza von, *Goethes Kantstudien,* Weimar: Hermann Böhlaus Nachfolger, 1994
Osborne, Harold, *Aesthetics and Criticism,* London: Routledge and Kegan Paul, and New York: Philosophical Library, 1955
Schiller, Friedrich, *Über die ästhetische Erziehung des Menschen in einer Reihe von Briefe,* in *Die Horen,* Tübingen: Cotta, 1795; as *On the Aesthetic Education of Man, in a Series of Letters,* edited and translated by Elizabeth M. Wilkinson and Leonard A. Willoughby, Oxford: Clarendon Press, and New York: Oxford University Press, 1967

Anna Luise Karsch 1722–1791

Anna Luise Karsch was a prominent female poet in the 18th century: her fame was based on her supposed "natural" talent in writing heroic and anacreontic poetry, as well as fables, ballads, and stories in verse. Because of her gender, social standing, and her lack of education, however, she was an outsider (Becker-Cantarino) to the contemporary literary culture, and her work remained relatively marginalized within the German literary canon until the 1990s. Since then, research on her life and work has increased distinctly. A symposium and exhibition of the Staatsbibliothek Preußischer Kulturbesitz in Berlin took place in the fall of 1991 to commemorate the 200th anniversary of her death. Access to archival holdings of her work has been facilitated by German reunification. Today, the main areas of research on Anna Luise Karsch involve her epistolary work and her proximity to the contemporary feminine letter-writing culture, her unique contribution to German literary history, and a newly differentiated assessment of her poetry.

Anna Luise Dürbach was born in the rural village of Hammer in Lower Silesia. Disallowed to read, Anna Luise made up poems in her head for entertainment. She was married at age 16 in 1738 to Michael Hirsekorn, a stingy, abusive, and alcoholic weaver who destroyed her books. She moved with him to the city of Schwiebus and bore him four children. As soon as Friedrich II legalized divorce in Prussia, Hirsekorn divorced Anna Luise in 1749 on the grounds that her dowry was not as large as promised, and he threw her out, pregnant and penniless. Her mother arranged a second marriage to Karsch, a tailor who spent his earnings in the tavern, driving Anna Luise to compose *Gelegenheitsgedichte* (poems for weddings, baptisms, funerals, and other occasions) to support the family. Additionally, she wrote poems heralding Friedrich II's victories in Silesia, which won her the attention of the region's literati.

In the 1750s, a traveling nobleman invited Anne Luise to live and work in Berlin, and this marked the true beginning of her literary career. Soon known as "Karschin," she was applauded in literary salons for her ability to compose and recite original poems on her feet. Many of these were anacreontic: poems on wine, love, and country life. Karschin was also known for her remarkable ugliness, for it contradicted the contemporary ideal of feminine beauty as an inspiration for art. She capitalized on her appearance, cultivating a self-image as "Belloise" (beautiful Louise) in order to emphasize her *schöne Seele* (naive inner beauty), an all-important concept to Empfindsamkeit, the emerging antirationalist movement in literature. A sensation in Berlin, she even enjoyed the audience of Friedrich II in 1763. Karschin was considered a living example of the ideal portrayed in the idyllic *Schäferdichtung* (pastoral) and was called a *Naturwunder*, a *Naturgenie*, and a German Sappho—monikers pointing to the elite's admiration of her ability to compose verse in spite of her background and lack of education.

Nonetheless, her economic situation improved only slightly. Although her husband was drafted into the Prussian army, after which she lived in separation from him, she was still obliged to support not only her children but also her unemployed brothers. She lived entirely from her earnings as an independent author: she received a meager pension of 200 talers per year, and Friedrich II's promise of a small salary and a house was not ful-filled until 1789 by his successor, two years before her death. Hence, while she enjoyed some material comfort in Berlin, she died in poverty while supporting her extended family single-handedly.

A significant aspect of Karschin's literary production, and one largely overlooked until recently, is her epistolary correspondences. A 1996 critical edition of her letters to Johann Ludwig Gleim places her in the company of other women known for their letter writing: Luise Kulmus Gottsched, Meta Klopstock, and Sophie Mereau. One possible explanation for the delayed interest in Karschin's letters is her own guardedness: she considered them to be too private for publication, the very quality that renders them significant to literary historians today. Unburdened by public expectations, they reveal passionate emotion toward her primary addressee (Gleim) and sharp insight into contemporary society and culture.

Nonetheless, her letters were not the only outlets for Karschin's observations: there is a palpable tension between the anacreontic mode of and her social criticism in several of her poems. Her anacreontic poem "Belloisens Lebenslauff," for example, demonstrates a distanced stance vis-à-vis the genre and the role she played in literary society. She was one of few female authors of her time who documented the misery of her marriage:

Ob gleich ein mürrisches Gemüth
Mir an der Seite ging, so wie der Kerkermeister
An des Gefangnen Seitte geht—
Apoll ermunterte schon meine Lebens Geister;
Die kleinstte Freude war erhöht
Durch seine Gegenwart, die ich noch nicht gespührt,
Bis mein Verhängniß auß dem Joch
Mich in ein dreimahl härtres noch
Gewaltiglich geführet.

Even though a grumpy character
Went by my side, like a jailer
With his prisoner—
Apollo cheered my life's spirit;
The smallest joy was heightened
By this presence I did not feel
Until fate led me
Violently
From the yoke
To one three times as hard.

Moreover, her appearances in Berlin may have been a conscious performance on her part: Karschin gave her audience what they sought, a simple country girl. The cliché that survived into the 20th century of Karschin as a naive poet, however, has been refuted by the study of archival material (Bennholdt-Thomsen and Runge): she edited her work, was not purely inspired by the moment, and largely shaped the content of her work to fit the demands of the marketplace. Her self-portrayal as a "natural" talent probably had less to do with reality than with an economically motivated manipulation of class stereotypes.

HEATHER FLEMING

Biography

Born in Züllichau, 1 December 1722. Received little formal education; learned to read and write from great uncle; married at 16, 1738; divorced by husband, 1749; married again, 1749; lived in Poland, began to earn living by writing verses commemorating special occasions; settled in Glogau/Prussia with aid of local pastors and teachers, 1755; first publication of poems during Seven Years' War; separated from husband, brought to Berlin by Baron von Kottwitz, 1761; friendship with Lessing, Moses Mendelssohn, and K.W. Ramler; received by Frederick the Great, promised pension and house, 1763, but promise remained unfulfilled until 1789, by Frederick William II. Died in Berlin, 12 October 1791.

Selected Works

Collections

Das Lied der Karschin: Die Gedichte der Anna Louise Karschin mit einem Bericht ihres Lebens, edited by Herbert Menzel, 1938
Herzgedanken: das Leben der "deutschen Sappho" von ihr selbst erzählt, edited by Barbara Beuys, 1981
O, mir entwischt nicht was die Menschen fühlen: Gedichte und Briefe von Anna Louisa Karschin: Mit zeitgenössischen Illustrationen, edited by Gerhard Wolf, 1982
Gedichte und Lebenszeugnisse, edited by Alfred Anger, 1987

Poetry

Gesänge der Freude und des Lobes bey dem Feyerlichen Dankfest, 1756
Der 13. May 1758 als der Tag des Schreckens in Glogau, 1758
Den 3ten November 1760: Gross durch den Sieg des Königs bey Torgau, 1760
Gesänge bey Gelegenheit der Feierlichkeiten Berlins, 1763
Den Vater des Vaterlandes Friederich den Grossen, bey triumphirender Zurückkunft besungen im Namen Seiner Bürger, 1763
An ihro Königliche Hoheit die Herzogin von Braunschweig [verses addressed to Elizabeth Christina Ulrica of Brunswick on her marriage to Prince Frederick William, later King of Prussia], 1764
Einige Oden über verschiedene hohe Gegenstände, 1764
Poetische Einfälle: Erste Sammlung, 1764
Auserlesene Gedichte, 1764
Auf den Tod der jungen Elise, 1770
Gesang auf die Eheverbindung Kochischen Acteurs Herrn Henkens mit . . . Mademoiselle Schickin, 1772
Auf die Geburtsfeier Ihro Hochfürstlichen Durchlaucht der Gemahlin des Prinzen Friedrichs von Braunschweig-Wolffenbuttel, 1772
Gedichte von Anna Louisa Karschin, 1792
Die Spazier-Gänge von Berlin. [Drei unbekannte Gedichte], 1921

Other

Mein Bruder in Apoll: Briefwechsel zwischen Anna Louisa Karsch und Johann Wilhelm Ludwig Gleim, edited by Nörtemann and Ute Pott, 1996

Further Reading

Bach, Carl Philipp Emanuel, *Die letzten Leiden des Erlösers: Passionskantate nach Texten von Karschin, Ebeling und Eschenburg: Für 5 Soli, Chor, und Orchester,* edited by Hans-Josef Irmen, Vaduz, Lichtenstein: Prisca, 1982
Becker-Cantarino, Barbara, "'Outsiders': Women in German Literary Culture of Absolutism," *Jahrbuch fur Internationale Germanistik* 16, no. 2 (1984)
Bennholdt-Thomsen, Anke, and Anita Runge, editors, *Anna Louisa Karsch (1722–1791): Von schlesischer Kunst und Berliner "Natur": Ergebnisse des Symposions zum 200. Todestag der Dichterin,* Göttingen: Wallstein, 1992
Dawson, Ruth P., "Selbstzahmung und weibliche Misogynie: Verserzahlungen von Frauen im 18. Jahrhundert," *Der Widerspenstigen Zähmung: Studien zur bezwungenen Weiblichkeit in der Literatur vom Mittelalter bis zur Gegenwart,* edited by Sylvia Wallinger and Monika Jonas, Innsbruck: Institut fur Germanistik, Universität, 1986
Hausmann, Elisabeth, *Die Karschin, Friedrichs des Grossen volksdichterin: Ein leben in briefen,* Frankfurt: Societäts, 1933
Knowlton, James, "Inventing an Author: The (Self-)Constructed Authorship of Anna Louisa Karsch as Reflected in an Autobiographical Poem," *Colloquia Germanica* 27, no. 2 (1994)
Modersheim, Sabine, "Igel oder Amor? Zum Briefwechsel zwischen Anna Louisa Karsch und Johann Wilhelm Ludwig Gleim," in *G.A. Bürger und J.W.L. Gleim,* edited by Hans-Joachim Kertscher, Tübingen: Niemeyer, 1996
Molzahn, Ilse, "Die Karschin, eine 'schlesische Nachtigall'," *Schlesien: Arts, Science, Folklore* 10 (1965)
Muncker, Franz, editor, *Anakreontiker und preussisch-patriotische Lyriker,* Stuttgart: Union deutsche Verlagsgesellschaft, 1893–95
Nickisch, Reinhard M.G., "Die Frau als Briefschreiberin im Zeitalter der deutschen Aufklarung," *Wolfenbutteler Studien zur Aufklarung* 3 (1976)
Pott, Ute, "Die Freundschaft und die Musen: Gleim in seinen Briefen an die Dichterin Anna Louisa Karsch und ihre Tochter Luise von Klencke," in *G.A. Bürger und J.W.L Gleim,* edited by Hans-Joachim Kertscher, Tübingen: Niemeyer, 1996
——, *Briefgespräche: Über den Briefwechsel zwischen Anna Louisa Karsch und Johann Wilhelm Ludwig Gleim; mit einem Anhang bislang ungedruckter Briefe aus der Korrespondenz zwischen Gleim und Caroline Luise von Klencke,* Göttingen: Wallstein, 1998
Schaffers, Uta, *Auf überlebtes Elend blick ich nieder: Anna Louisa Karsch in Selbst- und Fremdzeugnissen,* Göttingen: Wallstein, 1997
Schlaffer, Hannelore, "Naturpoesie im Zeitalter der Aufklarung: Anna Luisa Karsch
(1722–1791): Ein Portrait," in *Deutsche Literatur von Frauen,* edited by Gisela Brinker-Gabler, Munich: Beck, 1988
Singer, Heidi Maria, "Leben und Zeit der Dichterin A.L. Karschin," *Dissertation Abstracts International* 44, no. 10 (April 1984)
Staupe, Gisela, editor, *Anna Louisa Karsch (1722–1791): Dichterin für Liebe, Brot und Vaterland: Ausstellung zum 200. Todestag 10. Oktober bis 16. November 1991,* Berlin: Staatsbibliothek Preussischer Kulturbesitz, 1991

Marie Luise Kaschnitz 1901–1974

Marie Luise Kaschnitz is regarded as one of the most prominent German women writers after World War II. She published her numerous public and private poems in several collections, was a brilliant essayist, and wrote radio plays and stories. In 1960 she was a guest lecturer at the Endowed Chair for Poetics in Frankfurt.

Kaschnitz focused on human misery during the Third Reich, the role of women in family and society, Christian values, and human existence. She was influenced more by the tradition of German Enlightenment than by Christian tradition. The speech entitled "Das Besondere der Frauendichtung" (What Characterizes Women's Literature?), given by Kaschnitz, Ilse Langner, and Ode Schaefer at the Deutsche Akademie für Sprache und Dichtung (German Academy for Language and Poetry) in 1957 was still based on traditional notions of femininity. As critic Beth Muellner writes, "Marie Luise Kaschnitz's work is haunted by the demons of Germany's fascist past as she explores the distress and disillusionment of postwar Germany." Although Kaschnitz never saw herself as a feminist, her female protagonists are always in the foreground. For example, her novel *Liebe beginnt* (1933; Love Begins) tells the story of a couple who live together without being married, and her short story "Das dicke Kind" (1951; The Fat Child) shows the significance of the sister relationship for the development of the self, which prefigures narratives based on the sister plot found in later 20th-century women's literature and film.

Kaschnitz used multiple genres to transgress the boundaries set by patriarchy. For example, she transformed the contemplative literary form of the essay into a powerful tool for the simultaneous articulation of personal voice and political conviction. Similarly, she changed the fable and the parable in an effort to counter the seemingly vapid nature of consumer society by giving the quest for meaning in these texts an aesthetic and individualistic turn. Her poem "Die Katze" (1957; The Cat) can be read as a feminist fable. In the 1950s the production of *Hörspiele* (radio plays) increased dramatically in competition with television. These plays tended to be socially critical, reflecting the reality of early postwar Europe. Kaschnitz's *Was sind denn sieben Jahre?* (1953; What Are Seven Years?) is an example of such a tendency. Like many postwar writers, Kaschnitz was preoccupied with thoughts of death and mortality and depicted them powerfully in her work *Totentanz und Gedichte zur Zeit* (1947; Dance of Death and Poems at Present).

Kaschnitz's poetry ranges from the very skeptical to an almost epiphanic spiritualism. Her political poetry is in response to, and critical of, the Third Reich and the Holocaust. Important examples can be found in Hilde Domin's anthology *Nachkrieg und Unfrieden: Gedicht als Index 1945–1970* (1970). Kaschnitz's early unpublished poems already show traits that were to characterize the rest of her oeuvre: questions about suffering and its overcoming, and the responsibility of the individual for the *Gestaltung* of the world, the problem of an existence as a writer after the Nazi period. In the immediate postwar period, her works also show elements of skepticism about language (*Sprachskepsis*) and lyrical abstruseness in image and metaphor. Her poetic language often demonstrates a terseness in expression and veiled or obscure allusions. In *Orte* (1973; Places) she writes: "Frankfurt in the war, and where is it supposed to have existed, our inner immigration? . . . better to survive, better to be there, to continue working, only after the specter has gone away. We are not politicians, we are not heros, we did something else." Kaschnitz also writes what can best be termed prose poetry, as in "Beschreibung eines Dorfes" (1966; Description of a Village), and *Steht noch dahin* (1970; It Remains to Be Seen). Her spiritual poetry looks for some ray of faith and hope to emerge from the disaster of history. There is evidently a strong desire for spiritual guidance, as can be seen in her sonnets "Die Ewigkeit" (Eternity) and "Eines Tages" (One Day). "Die Ewigkeit" evokes the theme of *carpe diem* as it explores the relationships among love, death, and the present. Her poems sometimes orient themselves according to classical models, turning to antique myth as a form of resistance. (In her novel *Elissa* [1933] one finds underneath the myth of Dido veiled references to contemporary problems.) Such a use of the antique stems from a desire to counter the chaos of her time. In her sonnets, Kaschnitz captures the spirit of this form as it has been developed since Petrarch, making it both entirely modern and ageless.

The tension that is created by the instinct for survival versus the knowledge that one has not resisted Nazism is present in all of Kaschnitz's works. She knows that she has to defy Nazism, but she also realizes the limits of her own courage. As a painful compromise, she concentrates on themes such as nature and the relationship between the sexes during the Third Reich. This attempt to compromise changes, however, is found in the novel *Liebe beginnt*. Here her confrontation with Italian fascism signals the problems of opposing a totalitarian state and prefigures her later inner emigration. The protagonist Andreas is modeled after Kaschnitz's husband, Guido von Kaschnitz-Weinberg, a scientist who concentrated on his research as a kind of inner emigration, struggling against an insidious desire to ignore fascist ideology. The other protagonist, Silvia, also struggles with her situation, expressing her wish for the freedom of the individual.

Kaschnitz's volume of essays *Menschen und Dinge 1945* (1946; People and Things) contains a program for her work in the postwar era. In these 12 essays, she is concerned with observing her time from the perspective of its meaning for the individual. In the volume *Totentanz und Gedichte zur Zeit*, she tries to take a coherent look at the destroyed reality of postwar Germany. In the early 1950s Kaschnitz is still prone to pathos, especially in the volumes of poetry entitled *Zukunftsmusik* (1950; Music of the Future) and *Ewige Stadt: Rom-Gedichte* (1951; Eternal City: Rome-Poems). But *Neue Gedichte* (1957; New Poems) already reveals a new compact, non-pathetic language and freer forms. She does not resort to elaborate metaphors and words anymore; everything is precise, compact, transparent.

The 1950s ended in a major tragedy for Kaschnitz: the death of her husband. She grieves this loss in "Dein Schweigen—meine Stimme" (Your Silence—My Voice). Even in some short stories such as *Lange Schatten* (1960; Long Shadows), there are clear autobiographical signs of this period of bereavement. In the poems collected in *Ein Wort weiter* (1965; One More Word), the compactness of language continues. The basic tone is dark, full of pain, but simultaneously very clear. The cycle "Zoon politikon" was published on the occasion of the Auschwitz trial. *Beschreibung eines Dorfes* shows a connecting of nature themes and the perception of contemporary changes. Changes that technology brings are shown through the example of the village Bollschweil in Breisgau, the Kaschnitz's family home. She writes this in rhythmic prose and it functions like the draft of a more complete description that is yet to come. *Ferngespräche* (Long-Distance Calls), also written in 1966, is a collection of short stories. The 1970 work *Steht noch dahin* is even more compact in style and often sharper. Here she creates a portrait of the times in short prose pieces. The style of this prose has its equivalent in the poems of the volume *Kein Zauberspruch* (1972). The first part of this volume contains poems from the years 1962–70. They are like sketches that are reduced to the most necessary signs; the language is very concentrated. An important theme is the confrontation with her own times and with the proximity of death.

In the second part of the volume there are poems from the years 1970–72. Longer than most of her other poetry and incorporating a variety of themes, these poems appear as collages of different insights and memories.

The literary diary occupies a central place in Kaschnitz's writing. In her unpublished diaries she explains why this form of writing is crucial to her presence in the world: "I do not write just to pass the time. I am waiting for the chance to analyze that which has happened. I am on a search." In the reliving of childhood memories (for example, the autobiographical stories in *Das Haus der Kindheit* [1956; The House of My Childhood]); the remembrance of geographical locations (*Engelsbrücke: Römische Betrachtungen* [1955; Engelsbrücke: Roman Observations]), in which she laments her inability to live her own life in Rome; and the discussion of the workings of her own soul after the death of her husband (*Wohin denn ich* [1963; Where Do I Go]), her diaries become increasingly broader in scope and refer less and less to a particular topic. Kaschnitz sees travel as an *Unterwegssein* (Being on the Way); that is, a metaphorical condition relevant to her entire life. Her diaries' strongly visual and acoustic descriptions of landscape and emphasis on seeing and hearing bring the relationship between observer and world to the foreground. The title of her 1968 *Tage, Tage, Jahre* (Days, Days, Years) indicates the almost surrealistic entries, which function as a soft yet clear protest against the too rational and one-dimensional reality of banks and money markets. The last diary entries, *Orte*, written in 1973, are like a mosaic of personal experiences and time-specific constellations, each of which are not more than half a page long. There are no subtitles, numbers, or dates to give a clue as to the context. Kaschnitz seems to string together randomly collected thoughts. All the *Orte* in her life pass before her eyes. Notwithstanding, the "I" does not lose itself in the past but remains stable in the present. This form of poetical work is characterized by Kaschnitz herself as very feminine. She wanted the dialogues in her diaries to be understood as a Socratic dialogue—that is, as a very conscious dialogue style that leads to knowledge. Her diaries thus afford a crucial interpretive background for her works.

Religion is for Kaschnitz not traditional piety, but the tension between doubt and hope. Her words are not just edifying. There is a comprehension of tradition in her works. One might almost call it a religious interpretation of a secular world. The general themes of personal searching, alienation, and existential angst run like a red thread through her writing. She tried to confront the anonymity and technocracy of the modern world with a "Prinzip Hoffnung."

KAMAKSHI P. MURTI

Biography

Born in Karlsruhe as Marie Luise von Holzing-Berstett, 31 January 1901. Grew up in Potsdam and Berlin; after finishing school, worked in Weimar, Munich, and Rome in bookstores; married Viennese archaeologist Guido von Kaschnitz-Weinberg, 1925, whom she accompanied on several foreign study trips; lived again in Germany, 1932–55; wrote prose initially, then poems as well, but published own collection of poetry only after breakdown of Nazi regime; lived for a while in Rome, then, after death of husband in 1958, moved to Frankfurt. Georg Büchner Prize, 1955. An award has now been named after her: the Marie Luise Kaschnitz Prize. Died in Rome, 10 October 1974.

Selected Works

Collections
Gesammelte Werke, edited by Christian Büttrich and Norbert Miller, 7 vols., 1981–89

Poetry
Gedichte, 1947
Totentanz und Gedichte zur Zeit, 1947
Zukunftsmusik, 1950
Ewige Stadt: Rom-Gedichte, 1951
Neue Gedichte, 1957
Dein Schweigen—meine Stimme: Gedichte, 1958–1961, 1962
Ein Wort weiter, 1965
Kein Zauberspruch, 1972
Ein Lesebuch: 1964–1974, ed. by Heinrich Vormweg, 1975
Selected Later Poems of Maria Luise Kaschnitz, translated by Lisel Mueller, 1980

Fiction
Liebe beginnt, 1933
Elissa, 1937
Das dicke Kind und andere Erzählungen, 1952
Das Haus der Kindheit, 1956; as *The House of Childhood*, translated by Anni Whissen, 1990
Lange Schatten, 1960; as *Long Shadows*, translated by Kay Bridgewater, 1966; translated by Anni Whissen, 1995
Ferngespräche, 1966
Beschreibung eines Dorfes, 1966

Diaries
Engelsbrücke: Römische Betrachtungen, 1955
Wohin denn Ich, 1963
Das Tagebuch der Schriftstellers, 1965
Tage, Tage, Jahre, 1968
Orte, 1973

Other
Griechische Mythen, 1943
Menschen und Dinge 1945, 1946
Hörspiele, 1962
Steht noch dahin, 1970; selections as *Whether or Not*, translated by Lisel Mueller, 1984
Der alte Garten, 1975
Florens: Eichendorffs Jugend, 1984

Further Reading

Baus, Anita, *Standortbestimmung als Prozeß: Eine Untersuchung zur Prosa von Marie Luise Kaschnitz*, Bonn: Bouvier, 1974

Eigler, Friederike, and Susanne Kord, *The Feminist Encyclopedia of German Literature*, Westport, Connecticut: Greenwood Press, 1997

Gersdorff, Dagmar von, *Marie Luise Kaschnitz: Eine Biographie*, Frankfurt: Insel, 1992

Östbö, Johannes, *Wirklichkeit als Herausforderung des Wortes: Engagement, poetologische Reflexion und dichterische Kommunikation bei Marie Luise Kaschnitz*, Frankfurt and New York: Lang, 1996

Reichardt, Johanna Christine, *Zeitgenossin: Marie Luise Kaschnitz: Eine Monographie*, Frankfurt and New York: Lang, 1984

Schönau, Walter, "Zum Schwesternmotiv im Werk der Marie Luise Kaschnitz," in *Phantasie und Deutung: Psychologisches Verstehen von Literatur und Film: Frederick Wyatt zum 75. Geburtstag*, edited by Wolfram Mauser, et al., Würzburg: Königshausen and Neumann, 1986

Stephan, Inge, "'Vom Ich in der Fremde'—Fremdheitserfahrung in der Beziehung: Überlegungen zu den beiden Erzählungen 'Der

Spaziergang' und 'Der Pilzsucher' aus dem Nachlaß von Marie Luise Kaschnitz," in *Marie Luise Kaschnitz*, edited by Uwe Schweikert, Frankfurt: Suhrkamp, 1984

Strack-Richter, Adelheid, *Öffentliches und privates Engagement: Die Lyrik von Marie Luise Kaschnitz*, Frankfurt: Lang, 1979

Suhr, Ulrike, *Poesie als Sprache des Glaubens: Eine theologische Untersuchung des literarischen Werkes von Marie Luise Kaschnitz*, Stuttgart: Kohlhammer, 1992

Vetter, Helga, *Ichsuche: Die Tagebuchprosa von Marie Luise Kaschnitz*, Stuttgart: M and P, 1994

Erich Kästner 1899–1974

Erich Kästner is widely known as a children's author, the most famous of his 19 children's books being the much translated *Emil und die Detektive* (1928; *Emil and the Detectives*) while his semi-autobiographical novel *Fabian: Die Geschichte eines Moralisten* (1931; Fabian: The Story of a Moralist) constitutes an important literary account of the Weimar period. However, it is mainly as a satirist of that epoch and a writer of what he liked to call *Gebrauchslyrik* (poems for everyday use) in the volumes *Herz auf Taille* (1928; Tight-Fitting Heart), *Lärm im Spiegel* (1929; Noise in the Mirror), *Ein Mann gibt Auskunft* (1930; A Man Gives Information), and *Gesang zwischen den Stühlen* (1932; Singing between the Stools) that he has carved himself a niche in German literary history. Each of these first four volumes of poetry had edition runs of 15,000 despite the economic crisis of the early 1930s.

Kästner epitomized the dynamic and collaborative art scene of Berlin in the Weimar period, in his own words "then the most interesting metropolis on earth" with more theaters and cabarets than anywhere else in the world and a hundred daily newspapers and magazines. Kästner wrote for several of them but most importantly for the famous pacifist journal *Weltbühne*, edited by Carl von Ossietsky. Every day Kästner met up with writers, publicists, reporters, composers, cabaret artists, cartoonists, stage designers, and filmmakers in the boulevard cafés, preferably the Carlton, Schwannecke, or "Romanisches Café," to discuss the political events of the crisis-ridden Weimar Republic, engage in interdisciplinary artistic projects, and sharpen his wit on the repartee of his largely Jewish circle of friends until around four o'clock each morning. He carried a writing pad with him, constantly jotting down ideas and images in shorthand and producing a poem a day in the cafés and all-night bars, usually under the pressure of some deadline. Here, *producing* is the operative word: Kästner conceived of his work not as the outpourings of a solitary poet-seer but as a handicraft with a purpose, referring to himself together with his typist, Elfriede Mechnig, as "a small verse factory" or "Kästner & Co." The purpose of his verse was to identify and diagnose the prevalent social ills of his day: to lay the ghosts of World War I jingoism to rest, to castigate the revival of the military-industrial complex, to warn against the rise of fascism, and above all to depict "the lonely crowd"—the impoverished human relationships and desolate cityscapes of metropolitan life. His lyrical forms were geared perfectly to the task of critical exposure. Written usually in iambic tetrameter or pentameter, his poems always rhyme as in the cabaret songs of the period. The simple syntax and end-stop lines make his verse easy to learn by heart and thus transportable beyond the printed page. To avoid all pathos or sentimentality, Kästner developed a hard-boiled, streetwise, and lapidary style that made use of the bluff Berlin vernacular and a thoroughly urban imagery that included spittoons, patent-leather handbags, and shaving lather. A contemporary critic described his poetry as "passionately cool word-photography" and said that his stanzas gave the same kind of pleasure as well-placed punches in a boxing match. Kästner wrote,

> The satirist hates sprinkling sugar in the eyes or nappies of adult people. Then preferably pepper! . . . He is plagued by the passion to call what is wrong by its proper name. His method is the exaggerated presentation of negative facts with more or less artistic means for a more or less non-artistic purpose.

Politically nonaligned and yet an advocate of participatory democracy without pyramidal structures (seldom enough in the "Republic without Republicans," as Weimar has been aptly called), he was attacked from the Right as an "intellectual prop for communist polemics" and a "cultural Bolshevist" and from the Left, most famously by Walter Benjamin in 1931, for "negativistic quietism" and "complacent fatalism." One literary historian, Heinz Kindermann, came a little closer to identifying the tightrope walk of Kästner's art when, in 1930, he wrote,

> With icy calm Kästner indicts his epoch in his polemical poems, but never without a forward-looking perspective; always ready to bring down his opponents by means of superlative irony, and yet behind this show of pitilessness and partisanship to offer help; brutal in his over-honesty and yet capable of the most sensitive and inexpressible feelings.

However, the very same professor felt it more opportune after the Nazi takeover of 1933 to write of "Kästner, that Mephistophelian mocker and world-negator who up to now has chosen to seek his salvation in the complete destruction of the globe and its population!" It is no wonder that the Nazis hated Kästner. It was they to whom he referred in the poem "Denn ihr seid dumm" (1932; For You Are Fools):

> It's often easy to conceal puerility
> (for some seem wise whose lips are just shut tight)
> but you prefer to show off your stupidity—
> one hears your brainless yowling day and night!

In another poem, titled "Die andere Möglichkeit" (1930; The Other Possibility), he undermines one of the main platforms of

German fascism: the legend that Germany had in fact won the "Great War" but had been "stabbed in the back" by its own "Jewish" politicians, who treacherously signed the Treaty of Versailles. Kästner turns this argument on its head by painting the dreadful scenario of what might have happened had the Germans actually won World War I:

> If we had really won the war
> with drum-rolls and alarum
> then Germany'd be beyond repair
> and like a lunatic asylum.
> . . .
> If we had really won the war,
> then we'd claim pride as our invention,
> and evenings when we lay in bed
> we'd horizontally stand to attention.

However, his potentially most damaging attack on Nazism was linguistic: his pared-down, laconic, sobering language and the reduction of national myths to the level of the banal was the exact opposite to their pseudomystical, subrational, and thoroughly mendacious rhodomontade, as in the poem "Ganz rechts zu singen" (1933; To Be Sung on the Far Right): "There is no lovelier way to die / than in groups of tens of millions. / Big industry beckons with pies in the sky / and cheap weapons in their billions." But Kästner's most memorable and, uncannily, most prophetic antimilitarist poem was "Kennst Du das Land, wo die Kanonen blühn?" (1928; Knowst Thou the Land Wherein the Cannons Grow?). It is a provocative parody of one of the most sublimely lyrical texts in the German canon: Goethe's exquisite "Mignon" ("Knowst thou the land wherein the lemons grow / And where among dark leaves the golden oranges glow?"), a poem full of imagery of the fecundity and serene warmth of the Mediterranean. Kästner's lampoon is a chilling analysis of the dead hand of militarism and of what went wrong with the Weimar Republic—the fact that most of its citizens had been simultaneously victims and perpetrators of a patriarchal-militaristic socialization that made them entirely unfit for a nascent democracy—combined with an equally chilling prognosis about its impending end:

> There new-born babies come out wearing spurs
> with tidy hair-crease rather than a bob!
> It's not civilians that get born but craven curs.
> He gets promoted who can shut his gob.
> . . .
> There freedom cannot ever reap or sow.
> Barracks are all they ever want to build.
> Knowst thou the land wherein the cannons grow?
> You don't, my friend? Then certainly you will!"

Kästner was made to feel in no uncertain terms what he had prophesied: he was in the crowd at the "Burning of the Books" on 10 May 1933 on the Opera Square opposite Berlin University and heard the following words being raucously called out: "Against decadence and moral decay! For discipline and morality in the family and state! I commit to the flames the works of Heinrich Mann, Ernst Glaeser, and Erich Kästner!" When some actress acquaintance of his shouted out, "That's Kästner standing over there!" he wisely slipped away through the crowd.

Throughout the Third Reich, Kästner's works were banned, and on two occasions he was arrested and interrogated for hours in the Gestapo headquarters. He would never have survived the Hitler period had the regime realized that he was half-Jewish—a fact known only to him and his mother—or had it emerged that his poem "Knowst Thou the Land" was passed secretly from hand to hand in the Warsaw ghetto, translated into French by the Resistance and, in the last stages of the war, exchanged for precious cigarettes by German soldiers on the front.

Kästner initially greeted the new postwar Germany with enormous energy and hope, writing chansons and satires for the Munich cabarets "Die kleine Freiheit" and "Die Schaubude" and a political comedy titled *Die Schule der Diktatoren* (1956; The School of Dictators), but he never really found an artistic métier to suit the changed circumstances, possibly because Munich, where he settled for the rest of his life, was too provincial and smug and lacked the cut and thrust of Berlin or possibly because, in comparison to Weimar, the postwar Federal Republic had become culturally bland because of the loss of the ferment formerly provided by Germany's Jewish culture workers. Kästner continued to speak out, protesting against the restorative tendencies under Adenauer and the reinstallment of former Nazis in high positions, against what Alexander and Margarete Mitscherlich have called the postwar "inability to grieve" about the Holocaust, against the reestablishment of the German army, and against the stationing of atomic missiles on German soil. However, the West German establishment showered him with literary awards rather than listening to him. One group did react to his writings as in predemocratic times: the self-styled Protestant Youth Association for Decisive Christianity once more publicly burned his books in 1965, along with those of Albert Camus, Françoise Sagan, Vladimir Nabokov, and Günter Grass. The action was greeted by the German YMCA and some Christian Democratic parliamentarians. At least this showed that there were still some nappies in which Kästner was successfully sprinkling pepper.

EOIN BOURKE

See also Children's Literature

Biography
Born in Dresden, 24 February 1899. Served in World War I; studied history, German literature, and philosophy in Leipzig and Berlin; received his Ph.D. in German literature, 1927; editor for the *Leipziger Tageblatt*; worked as a freelance writer for *Berliner Tageblatt*, *Frankfurter Zeitung*, and *Weltbühne* in Berlin; his writings were banned by the Nazis and could only be published abroad; moved to Munich in 1945, where he was an editor at the *Neue Zeitung*, 1945-48; editor of *Pinguin*, from 1946; cofounder of the cabaret *Schaubühne*; president of the German Pen-Club, 1951. Büchner Prize, 1957; Hans Christian Andersen Medal, 1960. Died in Munich, 29 July 1974.

Selected Works

Collections
Gesammelte Schriften, 7 vols., 1959
Gesammelte Schriften für Erwachsene, 8 vols., 1969

Poetry
Herz auf Taille, 1928
Lärm im Spiegel, 1929
Gesang zwischen den Stühlen, 1932

Ein Mann gibt Auskunft, 1930
Doktor Erich Kästners lyrische Apotheke, 1936
Die dreizehn Monate, 1955
Let's Face It: Poems, translated by Patrick Bridgwater et al., 1963

Novels
Fabian: Die Geschichte eines Moralisten, 1931
Drei Männer im Schnee, 1934
Die verschwundene Miniatur, 1935
Georg und die Zwischenfälle, 1938
Till Eulenspiegel, 1938
Der gestiefelte Kater, 1950
Münchhausen, 1951
Don Quichotte, 1956
Als ich ein kleiner Junge war, 1957
In Probepackung, 1957
Notabene 45, 1961
Gullivers Reisen, 1961
Unter der Zeitlupe, 1967
. . . was nicht in euren Lesebüchern steht, 1968
Wer nicht hören will, muß lesen, 1971

Children's Literature
Emil und die Detektive, 1928; as Emil and the Detectives, translated by
   May Massee, 1930
Pünktchen und Anton, 1931
Das fliegende Klassenzimmer, 1933
Das doppelte Lottchen, 1949
Als ich ein Junge war, 1957

Edited Works
Gesammelte Schriften, 7 Bände, 1959
Gesammelte Schriften für Erwachsene, 1969
Das Erich Kästner Lesebuch, 1978
Gedichte, 1981

Kästner für Erwachsene. Ausgewählte Schriften. 4 Bände, 1983
Lesestoff, Zündstoff, Brennstoff. Lyrik und Prosa gegen den Krieg,
   1984
Kästner für Kinder, 2 Bände, 1985

Further Reading

Bemmann, Helga, Humor auf Taille: Erich Kästner, Leben und Werk,
   Berlin: Verlag der Nation, 1983
Benjamin, Walter, "Linke Melancholie," in Gesammelte Schriften, vol.
   3, Frankfurt: Suhrkamp, 1972
Benson, Renate, Erich Kästner: Studien zu seinem Werk, Bonn: Bouvier,
   1973
Beutler, Kurt, Erich Kästner: Eine literaturpädagogische Untersuchung,
   Weinheim and Berlin: Beltz, 1967
Drouve, Andreas, Erich Kästner: Moralist mit doppeltem Boden,
   Marburg: Tectum, 1993
Enderle, Luiselotte, Erich Kästner mit Selbstzeugnissen und
   Bilddokumenten, Reinbek bei Hamburg: Rowohlt, 1960; 14th
   edition, 1993
Kiesel, Helmuth, Erich Kästner, Munich: Beck, 1981
Kordon, Klaus, Die Zeit ist kaputt: Die Lebensgeschichte des Erich
   Kästner, Weinheim, Basle: Beltz, 1994
Last, Rex William, Erich Kästner, London: Wolff, 1974
Schneyder, Werner, Erich Kästner: Ein brauchbarer Autor, Munich:
   Kindler, 1982
Wagener, Hans, Erich Kästner, Berlin: Colloquium, 1973
Walter, Dirk, Zeitkritik und Idyllensehnsucht: Erich Kästners Frühwerk
   (1928–1933) als Beispiel linksbürgerlicher Literatur in der Weimarer
   Republik, Heidelberg: Winter, 1977
Winkelman, John, Social Criticism in the Early Works of Erich Kästner,
   Columbia: Curators of the University of Missouri, 1953
Wolff, Rudolf, editor, Erich Kästner: Werk und Wirkung, Bonn:
   Bouvier, 1983

Gottfried Keller 1819–1890

In his critically distanced autobiographical sketch of 1876, Keller stressed the vital inspiration he felt he had derived from the turbulent political events of his time, which, after the years he misspent when he aspired to become a painter, had helped him to find his true vocation as a poet and writer. Dismissing his early political poetry as crude in tone and execution, he continued: "Dennoch beklage ich heute noch nicht, dass der Ruf der lebendigen Zeit es war, der mich weckte und meine Lebensrichtung entschied" (Yet even today I do not regret that it was the call of the lively times which roused me and determined the direction my life was to take).

Keller's life spans the long, drawn-out struggle of the Swiss to establish a new constitution after the upheaval of the French Revolution and the rise and fall of Napoléon. Their hope was to maintain aspects of their traditional federalism while creating a centralized modern state, which would be flexible enough to deal with the rapidly changing economic, sociological, and political pressures, yet would give due consideration to the political, linguistic, confessional, and cultural minorities within their national borders. Keller soon found himself drawn to the radical wing of the Liberal Party. The Liberals, together with several of the German émigré writers who had found refuge in Zurich, supported his poetic efforts and helped him to establish a modest literary career by giving him a grant that allowed him to study first in Heidelberg, and later in Berlin.

In Heidelberg, Keller was decisively influenced by the teaching of the humanistic Young-Hegelian, Ludwig Feuerbach. Feuerbach's definition of humanity as intrinsically divine, and his idea that the supreme principle of philosophy is the unity between man and man, a unity that should find expression in love, found an echo in Keller's own convictions and helped to shape his outlook on life. At the same time, Keller's acute sense of realism and his personal experiences made him aware that the historical, economic, social, and political changes of the age affected everyone. Many of his stories present the uncertainty in public affairs as constricting and hindering every individual, however humble and obscure. As he put it in his long autobiographical novel Der grüne Heinrich (1853–55; revised 1880; Green Henry), the only way to counter these evils was by active resistance, "Leiden, Irrtum und Widerstandskraft erhalten das Leben lebendig, wie mich dünkt" (As it appears to me, it is suffering, error and the power of resistance which sustain the vigor of life).

According to Keller, potent forces coexist in a man's life, some hindering his development, others promoting it. It is this comprehensive and at all times skeptical view of life that early on enabled Keller to do justice to the positive and negative sides of the emerging Swiss democracy. But at no time was he a writer *engagé* in the modern sense of the word. His main concern was the life of the individual within the community. He never shirked facing up to the essential dilemma of the Liberal State, which, while guaranteeing personal freedom, is forced to curb the fullest development of the individual in the very name of that freedom. He therefore put his hopes on the individual's potential ability and willingness to restrict personal excesses. Pessimistically conscious of man's frailty, he nevertheless clung to the 18th-century view of man as a sensible being, endowed with innate qualities of good that could be brought out by education. He saw it as a writer's task to play a definite part in this educative process by affirming and revealing the force of human dignity even in the humblest member of society.

To this end, Keller claimed that a writer had the right, even in the age of frock coats and railways, as he put it, to draw on traditional popular forms of narration such as the fairy tale, legend, or myth or to invoke a proverb, epigram, or literary allusion in the title of his stories. As he saw it, such devices not only elicit definite responses from the reader but also lend the story a certain timelessness. "Wo wird denn das sogenannte Zeitgemässe meistens bleiben, wenn die Zeit oder das Zeitlein vorüber ist?" (What will remain in the end of the so-called relevance to the times when the era or a smaller span of years have passed?), he asked in 1877, rejecting the constraints of historicity in the name of poetic freedom. Yet, his stories take accurate account of changing historical, political, sociological, and cultural developments and their effects on the individual, and, in spite of their simple forms, his stories are never quaint. G.H. Lewes, in a review of contemporary German fiction in an 1858 issue of the *Westminster Review,* sums up his impression of Keller's realism with a reference to "Die drei gerechten Kammacher," one of the stories collected in *Die Leute von Seldwyla* (1856–74; *The People of Seldwyla*). Keller based this story on a remark in Bayle's *Dictionnaire,* which claims that a state consisting exclusively of righteous citizens would inevitably be doomed. Keller ironically transformed the traditional fairy-tale pattern of three men who set forth to seek their fortune into a frightening vision of modern man's predicament—chasing jobs and modest advancement in constant dread of unemployment. Lewes's comments are typical of the responses accorded to Keller's stories by his contemporaries:

> There is but little of what is called "story" in this novelle, little incident and intrigue; but the characters and situations are so presented that we seem to live in this narrow world, and watch every detail with untiring interest. . . . The story itself is fantastic enough, yet one never feels it is not literally true. That unpleasantly virtuous maiden, and those horribly virtuous combmakers, are like the people we have known and avoided.

Lewes's enthusiasm for Keller's realism may strike a modern critic as naive, yet it testifies to the persuasive skill with which Keller translated life into art, and which enabled him to achieve his expressed aim of evoking the general by illustrating the individual.

One significant aspect of this process of transformation is the fact that Keller never talks down to his readers. However much he may ironize, satirize, and generally castigate the weak and misguided among his characters, he never totally withdraws his sympathy for their suffering, and, in spite of his skepticism, he holds that his readers should be capable of similar understanding. Only as an indication of wrong-headedness does one find in Keller's writings a giveaway remark like that of Edith Wharton's narrator in *Ethan Frome,* "my heart tightened at the thought of the hard compulsions of the poor." Wharton was deeply influenced by Keller's "Romeo and Julia auf dem Dorfe" when composing *Ethan Frome,* but her story is written from the point of view of the rich observing the poor. Keller's firsthand experience of material and spiritual deprivation, by contrast, inspired him to find unforgettable images that express these hard compulsions, as, for instance, the horrifying race of the combmakers with which the tale ends and the depiction of which is at times reminiscent of the suffering of the damned in Dante's *Purgatorio.*

Keller saw his style as deeply rooted in his nature—"es liegt mein Stil in meinem persönlichen Wesen." Keller's style, however, is complex and cannot easily be pressed into a mold. He neither shuns poetic diction nor the use of the grotesque. Stories such as "Romeo und Julia auf dem Dorfe" and "Regine" reach the tragic plane. His narrative modality is varied and challenging. He glides easily from a humorous mode to an irony and sarcasm that is expressive of his skeptical mind. He expects his readers to acknowledge the nuances and comprehend their significance within the context of a sentence, a paragraph, and the tale as a whole. The effect on readers is an enrichment of their imaginative understanding and a strengthening of their skeptical consciousness, both of which Keller regarded as essential for the development of individuals and society.

Only in his late novel *Martin Salander* (1886), which treats the greed, corruption, and breakdown of moral standards in the personal, public, and political life in Switzerland, does an analytical reporting style prevail over inventiveness, which is in keeping with the novel's subject matter. As far as his short stories were concerned, Keller shrugged off the heated theoretical debate about the formal requirements of the well-made novella—which he regarded both as irrelevant for the telling of a lively tale as well as largely contrived after the fact. Although capable of writing an aesthetically pleasing, tightly constructed, and rounded story, Keller in many of his tales displays a skeptical refusal to adhere to a single point of view (or a single set of values) or to cast into a unified whole what is essentially disparate and ambivalent.

As has been suggested by critics, this may well be the reason for his predilection for the cycle form, since the cycle is both an integrative and a relativizing organization; the reader is constantly challenged to trace correspondences as well as differences and to readjust interpretations. Keller stated that he invariably conceived of themes and motives in relation to a group of stories that were closely related to each other.

It testifies to the complexity of Keller's writings that critical views are divided. Nineteenth-century critics set the direction future research was to take when they emphasized the wholesomeness of his work, praised the way he measured human endeavor against the foil of reason, and stressed his humor as an important balancing mechanism.

Twentieth-century critics have tended to follow two lines of approach. They accept Lukács's view that it was above all Keller's democratic disposition that gave him a unique position in German literature but also—since the German state developed in a totally different direction—led to his eventual isolation. They also follow Lukács's emphasis on Keller's ability to combine humanist ideals with the realistic depiction of sociocultural phenomena. Others play down Keller's political commitment in favor of his humanist concerns. They regard the most important aspect of his work to be his insistence on man's precarious situation—in his works we are constantly forced to distinguish between illusion and reality, deception and truth, and authenticity and inauthenticity.

There have also been several psychoanalytical studies, exploring Keller's anxiety and anguish, his frustration, his Oedipal relation to his mother, the psychological consequences of his dwarflike stature, his excessive drinking bouts, and his notorious idleness. These tend to present Keller as having lost out in life or as the victim of his environment. In recent years scholars have shifted the emphasis on to the skeptical ambivalence of Keller's writings, and the narrative modality of his shorter prose work has received more attention than the novels.

The centenary of Keller's death in 1990 was a subdued affair. There were the usual articles in Swiss and German papers, and a few university conferences were organized. Zurich mounted an exhibition. Rather than risking an overall assessment of his art, contributors looked at various aspects of his work, especially its educative emphases. While there was general agreement that Keller was a worthwhile author, no attempt was made to elucidate the reasons why Nietzsche, in 1877, at a time when Storm, Meyer, Raabe, and Fontane had reached their zenith, should have called Keller "den einzigen lebenden deustchen Dichter" (The only German poet alive today).

EVE MASON

Biography

Born in Zurich, Switzerland, 19 July 1819. Studied painting with Peter Steiger, 1834, and Rudolf Meyer, 1837; attended the Munich Academy, 1840–42; concentrated on writing, 1842; studied at the University of Heidelberg, 1848–50; studied at the University of Berlin, 1850–55; worked as first secretary to the cantonal authorities of Zurich (Staatsschreiber), 1861–76. Died 15 July 1890.

Selected Works

Collections

Sämtliche Werke, edited by Jonas Fränkel and Carl Helbling, 24 vols., 1926–54
Werke, edited by Clemens Heselhaus, 2 vols., 1982
Sämtliche Werke, edited by Thomas Böning et al., 7 vols., 1989–96

Fiction

Der grüne Heinrich, 1853–55; revised edition, 1879–80; as *Green Henry,* translated by A.M. Holt, 1960
Die Leute von Seldwyla (includes *Frau Regel Amrain und ihr Jüngster; Pankraz, der Schmoller; Romeo und Julia auf dem Dorfe*), 1856; enlarged edition, 2 vols., 1874 (vol. 2 includes *Kleider machen Leute;*

Der Schmied seines Glückes); as *The People of Seldwyla,* translated by Martin Wyness, 1911; translated by M.D. Hottinger, with *Seven Legends,* 1929; *Romeo und Julia auf dem Dorfe,* edited by Erika and Martin Swales, 1996; as *A Village Romeo and Juliet,* translated by Paul Barnard Thomas and Bayard Quincy Morgan, 1955
Sieben Legenden, 1872; edited by K. Reichert, 1965; as *Seven Legends,* translated by Martin Wyness, 1911; translated by C.H. Handschin, 1911; translated by M.D. Hottinger, with *The People of Seldwyla,* 1929
Züricher Novellen (includes *Hadlaub* and *Der Landvogt von Greifensee*), 1877
Das Sinngedicht, 1881
Martin Salander, 1886; translated by Kenneth Halwas, 1963
Clothes Maketh Man and Other Swiss Stories, translated by K. Freiligrath Kroeker, 1894
Stories, various translators, edited by Frank G. Ryder, 1982

Poetry

Gedichte, 1846
Neue Gedichte, 1852
Gesammelte Gedichte, 1883
Gedichte, edited by Albert Köster, 1922

Letters

Briefwechsel, with Theodor Storm, edited by Albert Köster, 1904
Briefwechsel, with Paul Heyse, edited by Max Kalbeck, 1919
Gottfried Keller in seinen Briefen, edited by Heinz Amelung, 1921
Briefwechsel, with J.V. Widmann, edited by Max Widmann, 1922
Briefe an Vieweg, edited by Jonas Fränkel, 1938
Gesammelte Briefe, edited by Carl Helbling, 4 vols., 1950–54
Briefwechsel, with Hermann Hettner, edited by Jürgen Jahn, 1964
Aus Gottfried Kellers glücklicher Zeit: der Dichter im Briefwechsel mit Marie und Adolf Exner, edited by Irmgard Smidt, 1981
Kellers Briefe, edited by Peter Goldammer, 1982
Mein lieber Herr und bester Freund: Gottfried Keller im Briefwechsel mit Wilhelm Petersen, edited by Irmgard Smidt, 1984
Briefwechsel, with Emil Kuh, edited by Irmgard Smidt and Erwin Steitfeld, 1988

Further Reading

Boeschenstein, Hermann, *Gottfried Keller,* Stuttgart: Metzler, 1969; 2nd edition, 1977
Flood, John L., and Martin Swales, editors, *Gottfried Keller, 1819–1890: London Symposium 1990,* Stuttgart: Heinz, 1991
Hart, Gail K., *Readers and Their Fictions in the Novels and Novellas of Gottfried Keller,* Chapel Hill: University of North Carolina Press, 1989
Jackson, David, "'Pankraz, der Schmoller' and Gottfried Keller's Sentimental Education," *German Life and Letters* 30, no. 1 (1979)
Kolb, Waltraud, *Die Rezeption Gottfried Kellers im englischen Sprachraum bis 1920,* Frankfurt and New York: Lang, 1992
Muschg, Adolf, *Gottfried Keller,* Munich: Kindler, 1977
Pizer, John, "Duplication, Fungibility, Dialectics, and the 'Epic Naiveté' of Gottfried Keller's *Martin Salander,*" *Colloquia Germanica* 25 (1992)
Renz, Christine, *Gottfried Kellers "Sieben Legenden": Versuch einer Darstellung seines Erzählens,* Tübingen: Niemeyer, 1993
Ruppel, Richard R., *Gottfried Keller and His Critics: A Case Study in Scholarly Criticism,* Columbia, South Carolina: Camden House, 1996
Steinlin, Laurenz, *Gottfried Kellers materialistische Sinnbildkunst,* Bern and New York: Lang, 1986
Swales, Erika, *The Poetics of Scepticism: Gottfried Keller and Die Leute von Seldwyla,* Oxford and Providence, Rhode Island: Berg, 1994

Wysling, Hans, editor, *Gottfried Keller: Elf Essays zu seinem Werk*, Munich: Fink, 1990

Der grüne Heinrich 1853–1855
Novel by Gottfried Keller

In the political climate that followed the 1830 July revolution in France, Theodore Mundt, one of the leading critics of the day and himself a novelist, reflected in his book *The Art of German Prose* (1837) on what the future of the various literary genres might be. He envisaged the prose novel as combining a panoramic view of social conditions with a description of the protagonist's development and education—a kind of *Wilhelm Meister* fleshed out with social themes. The writers of the Jung Deutschland movement, however, preferred the deliberately formless yet politically slanted novel, one that was shot through with theoretical and ideological reflections. As Karl Gutzkow asserted, the aim and purpose of the time was to portray man as a citizen, not as an individual human being.

It was only after the disappointments of the failed 1848 Revolution that two novels appeared that could be said to fit into Mundt's overall scheme, albeit loosely. Both Adalbert Stifter's *Der Nachsommer* (1857; *Indian Summer*) and Gottfried Keller's *Der grüne Heinrich* (first version 1853–55; *Green Henry*) came close to reviving the educative novel insofar as they portray the individual as being, at least potentially, rational and capable of self-cultivation; these works thereby upheld the values of traditional 18th century enlightened thinking in a progressively industrialized, politicized, and capitalist world.

Significantly, both the Austrian Stifter and Swiss Keller were somewhat distanced from the mainstream political, social, economic, and cultural process as it evolved after 1848 in Germany. But whereas Stifter's novel is characterized by a certain clarified atmosphere and a remoteness from contemporary realities—indeed, Stifter wrote it deliberately "against the times"—Keller's novel immediately leads the reader into the difficulties experienced by a sensitive, imaginative human being in search of a personal identity and purpose in life. The world portrayed in the novel is in flux; nothing can be taken for granted, least of all one's own capacity for distinguishing clearly between right and wrong, reality and illusion, and truth and fabrication. While the young hero of *Der Nachsommer* is led gradually by a benign mentor to affirm the wisdom of a carefully worked out educational program, Keller's Henry has to fight his own battles without guidance.

In a letter of 10 April 1881, after revising the novel, Keller emphasized the main theme of the book as being the educational problems of a fatherless boy. The novel portrays the father as an intelligent, imaginative, and purposeful man, who through force of intellect and hard work has made the transition from farming to middle-class status: he is a skilled artisan and property owner. Motivated by a desire to spread his acquired knowledge among his fellow craftsmen, he plays an important part in the social progress of the community. The loss of this father robs the boy of an exemplar of personal conduct, and thereby a vital link with society. While the father's development was sup-

ported by the strong framework of a guild, the combination of the establishment of freedom of trade in 1831 with the growing pressure of industrialization led to increased competition among craftsmen. Nevertheless, a certain work ethos persisted, especially perhaps in Switzerland, which demanded that you prove yourself through your labors. Having chosen the free vocation of an artist, Henry finds himself constantly thrown into conflict by the competing demands of the imaginative realm and those of dire reality, in which a man's worth only seems to be determined by economic considerations. Henry often ponders the means by which he can prove himself to his fellow men and be of service to them. The romantic notion of artistic isolation and individuation is not for him. However, neither can he affirm the unquestioning contentment that Hulda, the Munich seamstress, finds in her daily work. The novel constantly confronts one of the important issues of the age: how far and how deeply economic conditions affect the morality of the individual and society. It was an issue that was either glossed or sentimentalized in the more trivial novels of lesser authors—to the satisfaction of general readers who did not necessarily want their complacency disturbed.

The society depicted by Keller is unmistakably that of Switzerland in the early part of the 19th century, a period of rapid transition from an Ancien Regime to democracy, and from a mainly agricultural economy to that of industrialized capitalism. Henry spends crucial years in Munich, the capital of the reactionary kingdom of Bavaria, and a notable center for the arts. The novel makes sharp and critical analyses of the differences and similarities between Munich and Switzerland. Henry is disappointed in the Switzerland to which he finally returns. Among isolated remnants of goodwill, there now flourishes corruption. Enthusiastic liberal hopes have given way to state-centered administration.

The first and second versions of the novel are separated by almost 30 years, although Keller had planned a later revision from the start. The differences between the two versions capture the altered tenor of the times. The first version ends on a somber but ultimately conciliatory note. On his way home to ask his mother's forgiveness for his failings and for his callous exploitation of her devotion, Henry encounters her funeral procession. Soon after, he dies of remorse, and luscious green grass sprouts on his grave. His death has the effect of an atonement that, to a certain extent, meets with the expectations of possible reconcilement that characterized the years immediately following the failure of the 1848 Revolution. The second version is starkly realistic in its refusal to allow such harmonizing solutions.

"You only ever do what you can't resist doing . . . You will always avoid what you don't like." So one of Henry's Munich friends tells him in a heated argument about moral conduct. The reproach adroitly describes the path Henry has taken through life up until this point in the novel. The truth of the remark hits home, but it takes many months of irresolution before Henry can bring himself to confront his own shortcomings and to abandon his vain aspirations of becoming a landscape painter.

Keller announced in a letter of 1850 that he did not intend to write a tendentious socialist novel in which society was blamed for all the ills that befall his hero. The cause of Henry's failure is to be sought, rather, in his character. Keller explained that the moral of his book was based on the proverb: "God helps those that help themselves."

To a considerable degree, the finished novel exemplifies this intention. If it were not for the animation of his imaginative prose, the accuracy of his observation, and the breadth and depth of his reflections, Keller might be accused of writing an entirely pessimistic novel. Relying on the facts of Keller's biography, the novel traces Henry's progress through life from fatherless infancy to the disillusionment of manhood. The work both invites and rejects comparisons with that typical German novel form, the bildungsroman (whose central meaning, the formation of character and personality, is only imperfectly rendered in the English translation "educative novel"). To whatever degree his character may be said to develop, Henry attains no harmony of being and no important insights into the greater world; nor does he follow a path to ever-greater inwardness. His final realization is that his talent is too insignificant to sustain his choice of vocation and that some kind of modest contentment can be found through working for the community. Although the second version often is seen as ending on an optimistic and serene note, the tone seems, rather, to be one of resignation.

From the beginning, the novel had a mixed reception. Keller's sister is said to have used the unsold copies of the first version to kindle the fire. The second version fared better, but even today, critics are divided about its merits. Some rate Keller as one of the great masters of 19th-century literature. They see the drama of the novel as arising from the conflict between imaginative potential and the constrictions of practical living, and they value the poetical vigor and inventiveness with which Keller portrays the tensions. Others are irritated by what seems to be a simplistic equation between bad art and moral irresponsibility.

While most critics seem to agree, to a greater or lesser extent, that, in comparison with the French realists, Keller's depiction of social life is narrow, few would go as far as J.P. Stern, who claims: "All comes to him (Henry): the world is hardly more than his world, not exactly unreal, but malleable." Such a verdict not only ignores the great differences in social, political, and cultural conditions in France, Germany, and Switzerland at the time, but also fails to recognize that it is precisely Keller's highly developed sense of realism that leads him to limit Henry's perception of the world. Keller characterizes Henry throughout as a reflection of his circumstances and restricted experience, both of which qualify and limit his understanding. Henry's markedly provincial reaction to the spectacle of the Royal Bavarian cavalry—a subjective mixture of democratic pride and awe of German might—is typical in this respect. Keller uses the incident both to pinpoint a stage in Henry's development and to remind readers of the democratic principles that were betrayed in 1848.

Several critics prefer the first version of the novel, not only for its greater spontaneity and more interesting narrative structure, but because its use of a narrator allows Keller to explore the protagonist's experiences with an imaginative rigor that is not always present in the second. In the revised version, memory becomes the supreme organizing principle—with the result that the biographical detail at times threatens to overshadow artistic demands.

However, Keller's narrative frequently reflects ironically on his younger alter ego and the structure of the novel as a whole. At one point Keller allows his hero to find shelter in a count's country house. When the count and his adopted daughter turn out to be the very people who bought Henry's pictures at Munich, which he had been forced to sell to stave off hunger, there is much talk about adventure, coincidence, chance, fortune, and fate. The improbabilities allow Keller to introduce Henry to a circle of cultivated people of a higher social standing, where he extends his education by reading in the count's library and by discussing Feuerbach's views on God and man. These chapters read like a reflection upon some of the conventional features of the bildungsroman, scaled down to a cozier, bourgeois level. At the same time, they suggest an ironic concession to popular taste, especially when the count's adopted daughter, with whom Henry has fallen in love, is revealed to be the count's rightful niece. There is no fairy-tale ending, however, since Henry, as usual, hesitates too long in declaring himself. It is as if Keller, who in *Clothes Maketh Man* makes cruel fun of the human craving for romance, was raising readers' hopes of an escapist ending in order to dash them.

The conclusion of the novel is open-ended. It raises uneasy questions about the validity of Henry's decision to serve the community and throws a skeptical light over the whole novel. Readers are challenged to make up their own minds and to decide whether they want to underwrite the critical view that "Keller is not the philistine apologist of a banal status quo. As narrator, he highlights what his hero fails to recognize, the richness and poetry immanent in the real" (Swales) as a sufficient explanation for the novel's essential ambiguity.

Keller's friend and correspondent, the North German writer Theodor Storm, criticized the ending of the novel as too biographical—a point that modern critics have taken up, extending it to the whole novel. Others argue that, far from being purely autobiographical, the negative ending reflected the mood of disillusionment prevalent in the later part of the 19th century. Some have underlined the consistency in the portrayal of Henry's divided personality, which is torn between a humanistic and a deterministic view of mankind. Ignoring to some extent the bleak tones of endurance in the final chapter, many critics have preferred an affirmative approach, emphasizing the positive aspects of Henry's desire to serve the community. Recent critics, when preoccupied with the recurrent question of whether or not the novel could be considered a bildungsroman, are inclined to accept the novel's inherent contradictions as a challenging characteristic of Keller's writing, which is aimed at involving readers by forcing them to face reality. Several critics stress the theme of social responsibility that runs through the novel, and they argue that its central concern is Henry's humanity, not his art. As with other works of Keller, the role of humor as a conciliatory force is explored. Keller's contemporary and fellow writer, Paul Heyse, wrote that Keller used humor to bridge over "the gaps and fissures" in the world order. Recent critical trends have interpreted Keller's very act of narration as amounting to an aesthetic transcendence.

EVE MASON

Editions

First edition: *Der grüne Heinrich,* first version, Brunswick: Vieweg, 1853–55; revised edition, Stuttgart: Göschen, 1879–80

Critical edition: in *Sämtliche Werke,* edited by Jonas Fränkel and (from 1944) Carl Helbling, vols. 3–6 and 16–19, Bern and Leipzig: Benteli, 1926; also in *Sämtliche Werke,* edited by Thomas Böning et al., vols. 2, 3, Frankfurt: Deutscher Klassiker Verlag, 1989–96

Translation: *Green Henry,* translated by A.M. Holt, London: Calder, and New York: Grove Press, 1960

Further Reading

Minden, Michael, *The German Bildungsroman: Incest and Inheritance*, Cambridge and New York: Cambridge University Press, 1997

Preisendanz, Wolfgang, "Keller: Der grüne Heinrich," in *Der Deutsche Roman: Vom Barock bis zur Gegenwart: Struktur und Geschichte*, 2 vols., edited by Benno von Wiese, Dusseldorf: Bagel, 1963

Rohe, Wolfgang, *Romane aus Diskursen: Gottfried Kellers "Der grüne Heinrich,"* Munich: Fink, 1993

Sautermeister, Gert, "Erinnerungsarbeit in Kellers Bildungsroman *Der grüne Heinrich*," *Cahiers d'Études Germaniques* 29 (1995)

Selbmann, Rolf, *Der deutsche Bildungsroman*, Stuttgart: Metzler, 1984; 2nd edition, 1994

Stern, J.P., *Idylls and Realities: Studies in Nineteenth-Century German Literature*, London: Methuen, and New York: Ungar, 1971

Swales, Martin, *The German Bildungsroman from Wieland to Hesse*, Princeton, New Jersey: Princeton University Press, 1978

Romeo und Julia auf dem Dorfe 1856

Novella by Gottfried Keller

Romeo und Julia auf dem Dorfe (*A Village Romeo and Juliet*) first appeared in volume 1 of *Die Leute von Seldwyla* (*The People of Seldwyla*), and it is probably the best known of Gottfried Keller's shorter works. In some ways it is uncharacteristic of the author. As a follower of Feuerbach, Keller is essentially positive in outlook, and one of the great themes of his oeuvre is the "salvation" of rather feckless characters, who are then educated to be useful members of society. In *A Village Romeo and Juliet*, by contrast, the sins of the fathers are inexorably visited on the children, for whom there is no escape—except in death—from the chain of events initiated by their parents. It is, however, characteristic of Keller that, in spite of much incidental realistic detail, he does not expose the reader to the full harshness of his theme. Fontane called Keller a *Märchenerzähler* (teller of fairy tales), and here, as elsewhere, the most bitter of fates has something of the dreamlike qualities associated with fairy tales. The idyllic setting, touches of caricature, baroque images, quiet humor, and warm human sympathy further help to draw the sting from the bitter tale the author tells. Keller's charity and understanding embrace the parents as well as their offspring. Nor is the slightly sinister figure of the Black Fiddler an incarnation of absolute evil; rather, he is a jocose and not ungenerous tempter, who is himself a victim and deserving of sympathy. Strikingly, the strongest—albeit indirect—criticism is reserved for those narrow-minded moralists who can only see in the fate of the star-crossed lovers evidence of the "Entsittlichung und Verwilderung der Leidenschaften."

The story of Sali and Vrenchen, who are separated by a family feud over a strip of land that properly belongs to neither party and who commit suicide after a day and night spent together, did not find immediate public acceptance. Despite the moralizing paragraphs (removed from the definitive edition of 1874) that Keller had added by way of conclusion, the story was declared to be unfit for family reading, since it apparently celebrated illicit sex and self-murder. The original printing of 500 volumes had not been sold out when the second edition appeared. Public and critical opinion, however, then began to warm to the work: it rapidly passed into the canon of 19th-century German literature and has subsequently generated a mass of critical commentary, the one unifying theme of which is the general agreement on the novella's status as a masterpiece of German prose fiction.

Fontane hailed *A Village Romeo and Juliet* as a "wundervolle Erzählung" (miraculous tale), but he saw the work as falling into two halves, the first realistic and the second romantic—a view that persisted as late as 1981 (Bernd). More modern critics, however, have pointed to the chain of strict causality that leads from the opening idyll to the final catastrophe and that binds the disparate elements together. Following Berthold Auerbach's celebrated contemporary review, the tendency has been to regard the work as typifying poetic realism in its combination of concrete reality (it draws upon a joint suicide reported in the Zürich *Freitagszeitung* in 1847 and issues associated with peasant life, bankruptcy, and vagrancy) and the conscious evocation of a poeticized idyll. There is little agreement about whether reality or idyll predominates. Some have emphasized the realism (Alker, Silz), even interpreting the novella as an exposure of the rapacity of acquisitive bourgeois society (Holmes, Richter, and, to a lesser extent, Martini). As early as 1907, Köster drew attention to the highly symbolic content of the novella, and much critical effort has been expended on the interpretation of the symbols, although, inevitably, there is little agreement as to what they represent. Thus, the opening idyll, usually conceived as a grandiose celebration of a "heile Welt," where order, stability, and harmony prevail, has also been seen as an illusion that hides a reality where most men will cheat to secure material advantage and where "harmony" is purchased by the dispossession of one's neighbors. Similarly, the domestic idyll represented by the gingerbread house bought at the Sunday fair can be understood as an expression of the lovers' hopes, but also as a symbol of the inevitable internalization of emotions in a schizophrenic society where private life and private enterprise are antithetical (Holmes).

The love between Sali and Vrenchen has equally been regarded as an evocation of "perfect love" (Cooke) and as a demonstration of that which is impossible in bourgeois society (Richter), but also as a "deadly internalization of the concept of private property" (Sautermeister) and as showing "structures of incest" (Holub). The suicide has similarly provoked widely differing interpretations. The prevailing view is that in preferring voluntary death to the licentiousness and vagrancy offered to them by the Black Fiddler, Sali and Vrenchen are in fact reasserting the values of bourgeois society from which they have been excluded by their parents' dishonesty and ruin. Their suicide thus testifies to the strong moral forces operative in Swiss society (Fife). Others have celebrated the suicide as an "epiphany," the action of two souls in perfect harmony (Dickerson), or as a Dionysian reunification and "detoxification" of a divided and poisoned world (Maier). Many see the suicides in negative terms, however—as a strategy for avoiding the compromises required by real life (Lindsay, McCormick). In this sort of reading, the lovers become the victims of their own unconditional ideal precisely because it is incompatible with reality (Kaiser). Yet others see the lovers as the victims of economic pressures that render "normal" existence impossible for them (Sautermeister). Alternatively, the lovers are seen as being hounded to their deaths by the false concept of order upon which society is grounded (Thomas). Elsewhere, they are regarded as the engineers of their own destruction in a social order that was designed to contain mankind's innate aggressiveness and selfishness but which paradoxically generates its own forms of aggression (Mason).

W.A. Coupe

Editions

First edition: *Romeo und Julia auf dem Dorfe*, in *Die Leute von Seldwyla*, Berlin: Vieweg, 1856

Critical edition: *Romeo und Julia auf dem Dorfe*, edited by Erika and Martin Swales, Bristol: Bristol Classical Press, 1996

Translation: *A Village Romeo and Juliet*, translated by Paul Barnard Thomas and Bayard Quincy Morgan, London: John Calder, and New York: Ungar, 1955

Further Reading

Boeschenstein, Hermann, *Gottfried Keller*, Stuttgart: Metzler, 1969; 2nd edition, 1977

Ermatinger, Emil, *Gottfried Kellers Leben*, 8th edition, Zurich: Artemis, 1950

Flood, John L., and Martin Swales, editors, *Gottfried Keller: London Symposium, 1990*, Stuttgart: Heinz, 1991

Hart, Gail K., *Readers and Their Fictions in the Novels and Novellas of Gottfried Keller*, Chapel Hill: University of North Carolina Press, 1989

Kaiser, Gerhard, *Gottfried Keller: Das gedichtete Leben*, Frankfurt: Insel, 1981

Swales, Erika, *The Poetics of Scepticism: Gottfried Keller and Die Leute von Seldwyla*, Oxford and Providence, Rhode Island: Oxford University Press, 1994

Irmgard Keun 1910–1982

In the highly charged cultural and social atmosphere of the Weimar Republic, the figure of the modern woman dominated the cultural scene as both an object of desire and source of anxiety. The writer Irmgard Keun achieved immediate popular success and critical attention by focusing her early work on this icon of modernity. Through her exploration of the possibilities and limits of the image of the New Woman, the social criticism of Keun's work encompassed other major contemporary discourses: urbanization, consumerism, sexuality, mass culture. Both the form and content of Keun's work correspond to the dominant style of the mid- to late-1920s, the Neue Sachlichkeit. For their frank treatment of sexuality, Keun's books were banned by the Nazis in 1933. Unable to publish in Germany, she went into exile in 1936, then returned with false papers to live illegally in Germany after 1940. Although she continued to write and publish, Keun was unsuccessful in reestablishing a literary reputation in the postwar era. Her writing gradually ceased and her earlier works were largely forgotten, until Claassen began republishing her major works in 1979, sparking a rediscovery and reevaluation of Keun as a writer.

Keun's first novel, *Gilgi—eine von uns* (1931; Gilgi—One of Us), featured a protagonist bearing many traits of the New Woman. Employed as a stenographer—the new occupation for women in the 1920s—Gilgi is economically independent, sexually emancipated, and self-reliant. While the novel's success, with a sale of 30,000 copies in its first year, suggested that Gilgi was perhaps a figure of identification for young female readers, Keun's narrative ultimately deconstructs the image of the New Woman, as well as the fantasies of total emancipation that attended it. The novel depicts the economic marginalization of the female white-collar worker in the urban landscape of the 1920s. Neither skill nor diligence can ensure Gilgi economic advancement—or even job security—in the unstable economic climate of the Weimar era. Gilgi embraces the emerging sexual freedoms and resists pressure to conform to bourgeois moral standards. However, Keun's novel also reveals the consequences of exercising this freedom. Here, as in Keun's subsequent novels, love comes at a high cost for the

New Woman, as the heterosexual love relationship requires the woman to surrender her independence. Gilgi not only loses her job as she encounters the incompatibility of the rationalized world of work and the bohemian life she leads with her lover, but she also becomes pregnant. The appearance of this novel coincided with the climax of the debate over Paragraph 218 of the German criminal code, which outlawed abortion. Keun's narrative depicts the precarious economic situation of urban women as a possible justification for abortion. Gilgi chooses, however, to have her baby and raise the child as a single mother. The resolution of the novel thus posits what has been called the New Mother as a replacement for the New Woman (von Ankum). Single motherhood is portrayed here, as in many other works of the period, as potentially emancipating.

Keun's second novel, *Das kunstseidene Mädchen* (1932; *The Artificial Silk Girl*), also focuses on the realities of modern urban life for women, although here, beneath Keun's colorful language and humor, lies a greater sense of disillusionment. She depicts the economic dependence of working women on men; sexual exploitation is revealed as the sole means to the financial security and glamorous life the heroine desires. Doris's pursuit of glamor situates her as a subject of the film and magazine consumer culture of the 1920s and 1930s, suggesting her susceptibility to a fantasy prescribed by the entertainment industry embodying sexual power, economic power through consumption, and escape from the mundane world of work. In Doris's search for an autonomous self, however, she comes to see this model of happiness as illusory.

Although these works may be seen as subtly opposing the ideologies of popular films, they exhibit a filmic quality that was immediately apparent. *Gilgi* was filmed in 1932, *The Artificial Silk Girl* in 1959. Keun's filmic style of narration, marked by rapid changes of scene and abrupt, fragmented language, is best exemplified in *The Artificial Silk Girl*, where Doris acts as cinematographer, director, and star of the production of her own life. Her experience of the city is mediated, as she is aware of always being looked at and seeks control over the gaze directed at her.

Such scenes bring to mind the *flâneur* as described by Walter Benjamin and invite a consideration of the possibility of a *flâneuse*, similarly observing and recording the streets of the city.

In Keun's prose, the problem of language and communication highlights the status of the Other in modern society. Her works examine the relationships among gender, class, and speech. Her characters experience crises of language—a sense of the inadequacy of speech to express their experiences of modern life—that may be seen as reflections on the marginality of the modern woman. In these struggles for self-expression, Keun not only demonstrates her heroines' alienation from the dominant discourse of their society, but also reveals the failure of this discourse to include the experiences of outsiders.

In exile, Keun joined a community of émigré writers on the Belgian coast. This was a difficult but productive period for her in the stimulating environment of colleagues and supportive publishers; she produced four books between 1936 and 1938. These works reflect the same sharp wit and penetrating observation that characterized her initial writing. Her satirical wit and social criticism were redirected from the later Weimar years to the Nazi era, lending to the social analysis of her works an immediacy that may be seen as a distinguishing characteristic of her writing.

In *Nach Mitternacht* (1937; *After Midnight*), Keun mockingly portrays the orchestration of public life by the Nazis and explores the penetration of Nazi domination into the private sphere. She takes aim at the middle classes, revealing the hypocrisy and self-serving motivations underlying allegiance to the Nazis. The determined young woman engaged in a struggle for self-assertion disappears from Keun's work at this juncture. The New Woman of her early work is replaced in *D-Zug dritter Klasse* (1938; D Train Third Class) by a timid woman who accumulates three fiancés through an inability to assert her own wishes. Keun's novels begin to reflect a narrowing of options for women, and the brutality and misogyny of daily life under National Socialism becomes an explicit theme. Female voices gradually give way to those of men and children. In *Das Mädchen mit dem die Kinder nicht verkehren durften* (1936; translated as *The Bad Example* and as *Grown-ups Don't Understand*), the hypocrisy and authoritarian character of the adult world is uncovered by an adolescent girl, and in *Kind aller Länder* (1938; Child of All Nations), the experience of emigration is rendered through the eyes of a child. Both novels employ naïve and clever young protagonists whose naïveté is artfully constructed, making their satirical insight all the more penetrating.

Back in Germany after the war, Keun eventually resumed her writing, producing short satirical pieces for the newspapers and radio in Cologne. These pieces appeared in 1954 as *Wenn wir alle gut wären* (If We All Were Good). In 1950, Keun published *Ferdinand, der Mann mit dem freundlichen Herzen* (Ferdinand, the Man with the Friendly Heart). Here she again adopts a naïve-outsider perspective, satirizing the rash de-Nazification, black-market profiteering, and disjointed relations between men and women in postwar society. *Ferdinand* was to be Keun's last major work. Like many exile writers, she experienced difficulty in finding an audience after the war. Her attempt to regenerate her career was weakened by alcoholism and depression. Keun's disappearance from the postwar German literary scene lasted until the late 1970s. Years of neglect and alienation were brought to an end with the republication of her works, a film

version of *After Midnight,* and critical recognition. Keun received particular attention from feminists, who made the neglect of her work itself a subject of investigation, analyzing the "self-evident forgetting of female cultural achievements" (Krechel). Keun was celebrated not only for her presentation of modernity from a female perspective, but also, as in a speech by playwright Elfriede Jelinek at the city library in Cologne on 5 March 1980, for her anti-fascist stance and the critical, diagnostic character of her depiction of German society in the late 1920s and 1930s.

HILLARY HOPE HERZOG

Biography

Born 6 Feburary 1910, in Berlin. Moved to Cologne and attended drama school in 1926; thereafter, worked as a writer and actress; in 1933 her books were confiscated, and an appeal led to interrogation by the Gestapo; emigrated to Brussels, 1935, friendship with Joseph Roth, 1936–38, during his final exile years; traveled to the United States, Nice, and Amsterdam before she resumed an illegal residence near Bonn and Munich from 1940–45. Died in Cologne, 5 May 1982.

Selected Works

Novels

Gilgi—eine von uns, 1931
Das kunstseidene Mädchen, 1932; as *The Artificial Silk Girl,* translated by Basil Creighton, 1933
Das Mädchen mit dem die Kinder nicht verkehren durften, 1936; as *The Bad Example,* translated by Leila Berg and Ruth Baer, 1955; republished as *Grown-ups Don't Understand,* 1955
Nach Mitternacht, 1937; as *After Midnight,* translated by James Cleugh, 1938
Kind aller Länder, 1938
D-Zug dritter Klasse, 1938
Ferdinand, der Mann mit dem freundlichen Herzen, 1950

Essays

Wenn wir alle gut wären: Kleine Begebenheiten, Erinnerungen und Geschichten, 1954

Letters

Ich lebe in einem wilden Wirbel: Briefe an Arnold Strauß 1933 bis 1947, edited by Gabriele Kreis and Marjory S. Strauss, 1988

Other

Bilder und Gedichte aus der Emigration, 1947
Blühende Neurosen: Flimmerkisten-Blüten, 1962
Als ich Bazillenträger war, 1985

Further Reading

Ankum, Katharina von, "Material Girls: Consumer Culture and the 'New Woman' in Anita Loos' *Gentlemen Prefer Blondes* and Irmgard Keun's *Das kunstseidene Mädchen*," *Colloquia Germanica* 27, no. 2 (1994)

———, "Motherhood and the 'New Woman': Vicki Baum's *Stud. Chem. Helene Willfüer* and Irmgard Keun's *Gilgi—eine von uns*," in *Women in German Yearbook,* vol. 11, edited by Sara Friedrichsmeyer and Patricia Herminghouse, Lincoln: University of Nebraska Press, 1995

———, "Gendered Urban Spaces in Irmgard Keun's *Das kunstseidene Mädchen*," in *Women in the Metropolis: Gender and Modernity in Weimar Culture,* Berkeley: University of California Press, 1997; as "'Ich liebe Berlin mit einer Angst in den Knien': Weibliche Stadterfahrung in Irmgard Keuns *Das kunstseidene Mädchen*," *German Quarterly* 67, no. 3 (1994)

Beutel, Heike, and Anna Barbara Hagin, editors, *Irmgard Keun: Zeitzeugen, Bilder, und Dokumente erzählen,* Cologne: Emons, 1995

Gleber, Anke, *The Art of Taking a Walk: Flânerie, Literature, and Film in Weimar Culture,* Princeton, New Jersey: Princeton University Press, 1999

Horsley, Ritta Jo, "'Warum habe ich keine Worte? . . . . Kein Wort tritt zutiefst hinein': The Problematics of Language in the Early Novels of Irmgard Keun," *Colloquia Germanica* 23, no. 3/4 (1990)

———, "Witness, Critic, Victim: Irmgard Keun and the Years of National Socialism," in *Gender, Patriarchy, and Fascism in the Third Reich: The Response of Women Writers,* edited by Elaine Martin, Detroit, Michigan: Wayne State University Press, 1993

Jelinek, Elfriede, "Über Irmgard Keun," in *Das kunstseidene Mädchen: mit Materialien,* by Irmgard Keun, Stuttgart: Klett, 1981

Kosta, Barbara, "Unruly Daughters and Modernity: Irmgard Keun's *Gilgi—eine von uns,*" *German Quarterly* 68, no. 3 (1995)

Krechel, Ursula, "Irmgard Keun: Über das Vergessen weiblicher Kulturleistungen," in *Das kunstseidene Mädchen: mit Materialien,* by Irmgard Keun, Stuttgart: Klett, 1981

Kreis, Gabriele, *'Was man glaubt, gibt es': Das Leben der Irmgard Keun,* Zurich: Arche, 1991

Lensing, Leo A., "Cinema, Society, and Literature in Irmgard Keun's *Das kunstseidene Mädchen,*" *Germanic Review* 60, no. 4 (1985)

Marchlewitz, Ingrid, *Irmgard Keun: Leben und Werk,* Würzburg: Königshausen und Neumann, 1999

Rosenstein, Doris, "Nebenbei bemerkt: Boheme-Gesten in Romanen Irmgard Keuns," in *Erkundungen: Beiträge zu einem erweiterten Literaturbegriff,* edited by Jens Malte Fischer, et al., Göttingen: Vandenhoeck und Ruprecht, 1987

Sautermeister, Gert, "Irmgard Keuns Exilroman *Nach Mitternacht,*" in *Exilliteratur, 1933–1945,* edited by Wulf Koepke and Michael Winkler, Darmstadt: Wissenschaftliche Buchgesellschaft, 1989

Shafi, Monika, "'Aber das ist es ja eben, ich habe ja keine Meinesgleichen': Identitätsprozeß und Zeitgeschichte in dem Roman *Das kunstseidene Mädchen* von Irmgard Keun," *Colloquia Germanica* 21, no. 4 (1988)

Soltau, Heide, "Die Anstrengungen des Aufbruchs: Romanautorinnen und ihre Heldinnen in der Weimarer Zeit," in *Deutsche Literatur von Frauen,* edited by Gisela Brinker-Gabler, vol. 2, Munich: Beck, 1988

Wittmann, Livia Z., "Irmgard Keun: A German Deviation," in *Faith of a (Woman) Writer,* edited by Alice Kessler-Harris and William McBrien, New York: Greenwood Press, 1988

Sarah Kirsch 1935–

Sarah Kirsch was one of a new generation of young poets of the German Democratic Republic (GDR) in the 1960s who was credited with resuscitating for the East German lyric the primacy of subjective experience. Her literary debut, *Gespräch mit dem Saurier* (1965; Conversation with the Dinosaur), authored jointly with her then-husband Rainer Kirsch, is sometimes marred by a skittish sentimentality but also demonstrates a feisty resistance to collective norms and values and hints at that sensuous restlessness that characterizes Kirsch's mature work. In *Landaufenthalt* (1967; Country Sojourn), she established herself as an original and rebellious poetic voice. The "baby-talk" (Adolf Endler) has gone, rhyme is abandoned, and an adventurous use of elliptical narrative, punctuation, and syntax reflects a self-assertive yearning to escape and experience a world beyond the claustrophobic confines of the GDR.

In the 1970s, Kirsch wrote two collections of stories: *Die ungeheuren bergehohen Wellen auf See* (1973; The Enormous Mountainous Waves at Sea) and *Die Pantherfrau* (1973; The Panther Woman), five lightly edited interviews with women from different stations in GDR life. Both these volumes test the official version of how women lived in the GDR against the reality of their lives and can be seen as a pioneering contribution to East German women's writing. However, this does not mean that Kirsch is a ready ally of feminism. She commented in an interview in 1978 that she would never attend bookshops and readings that were exclusively for women. Yet her love poetry, which grapples so precisely and honestly with what she has felt and experienced as a woman and in which—despite being so often the loser—she seems to emerge stronger and wiser, is eloquent testimony to the toughness and independence of spirit sought by the modern woman.

Notwithstanding the achievement of these two prose volumes, the essence of Kirsch's particular contribution to GDR women's writing is found in her poetry. At her most distinctive in her nature or love poetry, and not infrequently combining the two, Kirsch manages to hold the balance between celebration of the natural world, exploration of feelings and emotions, and also the call of history. For example, the richly erotic celebration of summer as a lover's attentiveness in "Süß langt der Sommer ins Fenster" ("Summer Reaches Sweetly into the Window") is brutally arrested by the sudden intrusion of one of the best-remembered images of the Vietnam War: children fleeing with napalm burns down a country road.

In the often magical and incantatory quality of the poems in *Zaubersprüche* (1973; Conjurations), we find the most intense and poetically precise focus on her emotional life. Love here can be many different things: beckoning siren or sheer physical, erotic pleasure. However, most often we find Kirsch in the role of insecure and vulnerable partner whose capacity to love without reserve is seldom fully reciprocated. However, self-irony and the ability to work through her insecurity and vulnerability ensure that she never languishes in the role of neglected, forsaken lover. Loss or betrayal are invariably made a source of poetic energy.

Kirsch was never at ease with the cultural orthodoxies of the GDR. Despite finding a powerful ally in Franz Fühmann, who, in defense of Kirsch, dismissed the notion that it was the function of the writer to provide good cheer and morale boosters for the social process, *Zaubersprüche* was heavily criticized in the GDR for its dominantly pessimistic note. This precipitated Kirsch's final break with the East German authorities. After refusing to withdraw her signature from the petition in November 1976 against the expatriation of Wolf Biermann, her fall from grace was total. The publication of *Rückenwind* (1976; Tail-wind) met with deafening silence and saw the initiation of a campaign of intimidation by the *Stasi* and harassment by her neighbors. At the end of August 1977, she was granted an exit visa for West Berlin.

Drachensteigen (1979; Kite Flying) consists of poems written between 1976 and 1979 in the GDR, West Berlin, and Italy that draw on her exile but offer no easy statement on the troubling switch to entirely new social and political circumstances. "The Last of November" (the poem has an English title), set in and around the Reichstag wasteland in West Berlin, reserves its last lines for "unsere toten Dichter"—her exiled fellow poets, dead because they have been cut off from the roots of their writing and the natural audience for it. This sense of loss and deracination touches all the Italian poems in *Drachensteigen* but is moderated by the exotic shock of light, weather, and the fauna and flora of the Mediterranean. There is also a mystical feel for landscape—something that recurs in the dense poetic prose that would be her favored form in the 1980s and 1990s—along with a sense that the pleasures grasped and the consolations to be drawn from the intense experience of nature are precarious. The move in 1983 to a remote rural corner of Schleswig-Holstein offers moments of intermittent, intoxicating escape, found mostly—as in *Das simple Leben* (1994; The Simple Life)—in response to the passage of the seasons, wind and sea, or wine-borne evenings with intimates. However, as the news is turned on and the newspapers opened, these moments of idyll prove all too fleeting. The outside world is never far away.

Where does one existence end and another begin? Kirsch's occasional ironic references to "the first half of my country" suggest a deceptively clean break with the GDR. To look at the gentle jab that she takes at former poet-friends in *Erdreich* (1982; Earth) or in *Allerlei-Rauh* (1988; Hotch Potch), with its evocation of Prenzlauer Berg and a magical summer in Mecklenburg that Christa Wolf would also immortalize in *Sommerstück* (1989; Summer Piece), as well as *Das simple Leben* and its forays, real and in the imagination, into the GDR, it is clear that Kirsch's preoccupation with her former home is a continuing one. The country and its legacy, its people and poets, are a stubbornly lingering presence that weaves in and out of much that she has written since 1977.

MARTIN KANE

Biography

Born in Bernstein in Limlingerode, 16 April 1935. Studied at the University of Halle, degree in biology, 1959; studied at the Johannes R. Becher Institute for Literature in Leipzig, 1963–65; member of the Socialist Unity Party and the Writers Union, but expelled from both due to protests over the revocation of the East German citizenship of Wolf Biermann, 1976; in West Germany, 1977; traveled to Italy, France, and the United States; member of the Deutsche Akademie für Sprache und Dichtung, Darmstadt, 1990; appointed to Brothers Grimm professorship, University of Kassel, 1997. Heine Prize, 1973; Petrarca Prize, 1976; Villa Massimo grant; Austrian Critics' Prize, 1981; Gandersheim Prize, 1983; Hölderlin Prize, 1984; Gold Medal, literature prize, 1986; Schleswig-Holstein Art Prize, 1987; City of Mainz Prize, 1988; Konrad Adenauer Foundation Literature Prize, 1993; Peter Huchel Prize, 1993; Büchner Prize, 1996; Annette von Droste Hülshoff Prize, 1997. Currently lives in Schleswig-Holstein.

Selected Works

Poetry

Gespräch mit dem Saurier, with Rainer Kirsch, 1965
Gedichte, 1967
Landaufenthalt, 1967; revised edition, as *Gedichte*, 1969
Zaubersprüche, 1973; translated in *Conjurations*, translated by Wayne Kvam, 1985
Es war dieser merkwürdige Sommer: Gedichte, 1974
Rückenwind, 1976
Musik auf dem Wasser, 1977
Katzenkopfpflaster, 1978
Wintergedichte: Poetische Wandzeitung, 1978
Sommergedichte: Poetische Wandzeitung, 1978
Drachensteigen: Vierzig neue Gedichte, 1979
Papiersterne: 15 Lieder für Mezzosopran und Klavier, music by Wolfgang von Schweinitz, 1981
Erdreich, 1982
Poems, translated by Jack Hirschman, 1983
Der Winter, 1983
Katzenleben, 1984; as *Catlives*, translated by Marina Roscher and Charles Fishman, 1991
Mädchen, pfeif auf den Prinzen! with Günter Grass, 1984
Hundert Gedichte, 1985
Landwege: Eine Auswahl, 1980–1985, 1985
Conjurations: The Poems of Sarah Kirsch, translated by Wayne Kvam, 1985
Three Contemporary German Poets: Wolf Biermann, Sarah Kirsch, Reiner Kunze, edited by Peter J. Graves, 1985
Lyrik, with drawings by A.R. Penck, 1987
Luft und Wasser, with Ingo Kühl, 1988
Die Flut, poems selected by Gerhard Wolf, 1989
Schneewärme, 1989
Tiger im Regen, with Song Hyun-Sook, 1990
The Brontës Hats, translated by Wendy Mulford and Anthony Vivis, 1991
Eisland: Gedichte, 1992
Erlkönigs Tochter: Gedichte, 1992
Wasserbilder: Ein gemischtes Bündel, 1993
Winter Music: Selected Poems, translated by Margitt Lehbert, 1994
Ich Crusoe: Sechzig Gedichte und Sechs Aquarelle, 1995
Bodenlos: Gedichte, 1996
Luftspringerin: Gesammelte Gedichte und Prosa, 1997

Fiction

Die Pantherfrau: 5 unfrisierte Erzählungen aus dem Kassetten-Recorder, 1973; as *Die Panther-frau: 5 Frauen in der DDR*, 1978; as *The Panther Woman*, 1989
Die ungeheuren bergehohen Wellen auf See, 1973
Spreu, 1991
Schwingrasen, 1991

Play

Die betrunkene Sonne, Der Stärkste (radio play), with Rainer Kirsch, 1962

Other

Berlin-Sonnenseite: Deutschlandtreffen der Jugend in der Hauptstadt der DDR Berlin, with Rainer Kirsch, 1964
Hänsel und Gretel: Eine illustrierte Geschichte für kleine und grosse Leute nach der gleichnamigen Märchenoper von Adelheid Wetter und Engelbert Humperdinck, 1972
Caroline im Wassertropfen (for children), 1975
Zwischen Herbst und Winter (for children), 1975
Wiepersdorf, 1977
Erklärung einiger Dinge: Dokumente und Bilder, 1978

Schatten, illustrated by Kota Taniuchi, 1979
Sieben Häute, 1979
Ein Sommerregen, illustrated by Kota Taniuchi, 1979
Wind, illustrated by Kota Taniuchi, 1979
La Pagerie (diary), 1980
Hans mein Igel (adaptation of a story by the Grimm brothers), 1980
Geschlechtertausch: Drei Geschichten über die Umwandlung der Verhältnisse, with Irmtraud Morgner and Christa Wolf, 1980
Landleben, photographs by Olaf Plotz, 1984
Irrstern: Prosa, 1986
Galoschen: Immerwährender Kalender, 1987
Allerlei-Rauh: Eine Chronik, 1988
Das simple Leben, 1994

Edited Works
Elke Erb, *Trost: Gedichte und Prosa,* 1982
Annette von Droste-Hülshoff, 1988

Translations
Anna Akhmatova, *Ein niedagewesener Herbst,* translated with Rainer Kirsch, 1967
Novella Matveeva, *Gedichte.* translated with Eckhard Ulrich, 1967
Lavissa Vasil'eva, *Gedichte,* translated with Ilse Krätzig, 1971
Radka Aleksandrova, *Laiko, Piff und Onkel Wertscho,* 1972
Jordan Drumnikov, *Das fliegende Regenschirmchen,* 1973
Leda Mileva, *Der kleine hellblaue Luftballon und die Puppe mit dem rosa Kleidchen,* 1973

Further Reading
Allkemper, Alo, "Sarah Kirsch," in *Deutsche Dichter des 20 Jahrhunderts,* edited by Hartmut Steinecke, Berlin: E. Schmidt, 1994
Cosentino, Christine, *"Ein Spiegel mit mir drin": Sarah Kirschs Lyrik,* Tübingen: Francke, 1990
———, "'An Affair on Uncertain Ground': Sarah Kirsch's Poetry Volume 'Erking's Daughter' in the Context of Her Prose after the 'Wende'," in *Studies in Twentieth Century Literature* 1 (1997)
Frühwald, Wolfgang, "Die 'Endlichkeit dieser Erde': Laudatio auf Sarah Kirsch," *Sinn und Form* 45 (1993)
Graves, Peter J., "Sarah Kirsch: Some Comments and a Conversation," *German Life and Letters* 44, no. 4 (1990–91)
Heidenreich, Wolfgang, editor, *Sarah Kirsch: Texte, Dokumente, Materialien,* Baden-Baden and Zurich: Elster, 1995
Hopwood, Mererid, and David Basker, editors, *Sarah Kirsch,* Cardiff: University of Wales Press, 1997
Kirsten, Wulf, "'Die Welt ist ein Ghöft im Winter': Rede auf Sarah Kirsch," *Heine-Jahrbuch* 32 (1993)
Lübbe-Grothues, Grete, "'Rote Füchsin'—'Grauer Regen': Liebesgedichte von Sarah Kirsch," *Schweizer Monatshefte* 76, no. 3 (1996)
Mabee, Barbara, "Geschichte, Erinnerung, und Zeit: Sarah Kirschs Lyrik," in *Zwischen gestern und morgen : Schriftstellerinnen der DDR aus amerikanischer Sicht,* edited by Ute Brandes, Berlin: Lang, 1992
Sarah Kirsch, Munich: Edition Text und Kritik, 1989
Wagener, Hans, *Sarah Kirsch,* Berlin: Colloquium, 1989

Egon Erwin Kisch 1885–1948

During a remarkably productive writing career, Kisch developed the concept of reportage and provided definitive examples of it based upon his own experience. Pursuing a sensational and adventurous life, he captured his observations and impressions in a new literary form that was founded in factual reporting. His writing describes the devastating disclosures of a cub reporter in Prague, service with the Austro-Hungarian army in World War I, revolutionary postwar activities in Vienna, and extensive travels throughout the United States, the Soviet Union, and the Orient. Kisch details his arrest by the Nazis, a landing in Australia achieved by leaping from the deck of a ship, the Spanish Civil War, and exile in Mexico.

From an early date Kisch was preoccupied with marginal figures of society such as prostitutes, pimps, and petty criminals and followed with interest court trials. As a cub reporter for the *Prager Tageblatt* and *Bohemia,* he concerned himself with such subjects locally in the collections *Aus Prager Gassen und Nächten* (1912; Out of Prague's Alleys and Nights), *Prager Kinder* (1913; Children of Prague), and *Der Mädchenhirt* (1914; The Pimp), the latter of which served twice as a film scenario.

The desire to be first with the news, to hunt for sensation, and to uncover details led to the revelations of the Redl affair. This constituted a spectacular adventure in investigative journalism that shook the capitals of Europe, and it made Kisch famous overnight. When the star soccer player and locksmith's apprentice failed to appear for an important game, the reason for the absence was brought to light. He had been employed in a break-in at the apartment of an important government official. The forced entry revealed treason involving the betrayal of military secrets to the Russians. This disclosure led to the compulsory suicide of the Chief of the General Staff of the Prague Army Corps in an attempt to conceal the facts. The Austro-Hungarian monarchy was rocked to its foundations and was revealed before the other European powers as seriously undermined in its military operations, as the war would prove the following year.

While serving with the 11th Infantry regiment on the Serbian front, Kisch was wounded; thereafter, he was assigned to the press section of the War Office in Vienna, where he became involved in the revolutionary activities of the Red Guard at war's end. His experiences are collected in what is now entitled *Schreib das auf, Kisch* (1922; Write It Down, Kisch).

His devotion to journalism is documented by the historical anthology *Klassischer Journalismus* (1923; Classical Journalism), and his report of espionage in *Der Fall des Generalstabschefs Redl* (1924; The Case of the Chief of the General Staff Redl) caused him to be acclaimed as the foremost investigative journalist of his time. This scandal lent itself to a film scenario on four occasions, as well as to a play by John Osborne. The year 1924 also saw the appearance of his first collection of reportage, *Der rasende Reporter* (1924; The Raging Reporter), a title that earned him his nickname. Included are sketches as varied in subject and as geographically diverse as the homeless of Whitechapel, a flea market in France, swine slaughter in Denmark, and a homicide robbery in the Hotel Bristol. What Kisch terms his "logical fantasy" is employed to order his factual material and to present it as he will. Similar in conception was *Hetzjagd durch die Zeit* (1925; Pursuit Through Time), which treats a variety of subjects; on the other hand, the collection *Wagnisse in aller Welt* (1927; Worldwide Exploits) distinguishes itself by the continuities among sketches based upon the author's experiences among the peoples of North Africa.

Kisch had become a member of the Austrian Communist Party in its earliest days and the German KPD in 1925. Partly for this reason, he shared with many of his countrymen an avid interest in the transformation of the USSR. He visited Moscow and various parts of Russia, capturing his experiences in *Zaren, Popen, Bolschewiken* (1927; Tsars, Priests, and Bolsheviks), a collection of his reportage that was very successful.

A kind of homage was paid to the country that represented the other dominant economic system in *Paradies Amerika* (1930: Paradise America), which, similar to his Russian collection, appealed to the national curiosity of his readers, was immensely popular, and was translated into many languages. Based on his visit to this country during the two previous years, Kisch depicts Doctor Becker in 40 short sketches that treat all aspects of American society. Becker visits and describes film studios, a mortuary, Sears and Roebuck, the Bureau of Standards, and prominent personalities such as Charlie Chaplin and Upton Sinclair. He expresses awe at the New York Public Library and the Library of Congress. Americans are described as prudish, puritanical, provincial, and hypocritical, but Kisch is most distressed by the homogeneity and conformism that characterizes the country and its citizens. Rephrasing the cliché that the United States is the land of unlimited possibilities, he calls it the land of impossible limitations.

Travel in the Soviet Union, Tashkent, and the Orient is reflected in *Asien gründlich verändert* (1932; Changing Asia), which deals with the way in which Muslim people of that area experience industrialization as they are incorporated into the USSR. *China geheim* (1933; Secret China) is a fascinating study of turmoil, civil war, Japanese occupation, corruption, and intrigue in that country.

Kisch was arrested by the Nazis in 1933 on the day after the Reichstag fire, interred in Spandau, and then deported to Czechoslovakia. These experiences precipitated his years of anti-Nazi activity. In Paris, he participated in the first International Congress of Writers for the Defense of Culture, and in 1934, as a delegate of the World Committee against War and Fascism, he traveled to Australia to attend an antiwar congress. When denied entry to that country, he leapt from the deck of a ship in Melbourne, breaking a leg but achieving celebrity status that caused him to become included in pacifist and antifascist demonstrations in that country. These events are captured in *Landung in Australien* (1937; Australian Landfall).

Kisch served as a professional journalist in Spain during the Civil War in 1937–38, and in late 1939 he left Europe with visas for Chile and the United States. While in the latter country, according to the records of the FBI, he was held as a "well known German Communist and Comintern agent under physical surveillance." In November 1940, he and his wife Gisl crossed at Laredo, Texas, into exile in Mexico, where during the years that followed he felt little of the alienation and isolation that often befell exiles. His Spanish continued to serve him well, and he enjoyed close working relations with the political left, which was represented by Bodo Uhse, Anna Seghers, Theodor Balk, André Simone (Otto Katz), and many others. His exile activities included the establishment of the journal *Freies Deutschland* (Free Germany), which supported a movement heard throughout the hemisphere, and the foundation of the Heinrich Heine Club, a center of cultural activity for the German exile community.

In 1941 *Sensation Fair* appeared in English (the original version was published in 1942 as *Marktplatz der Sensationen*). This work was very widely received and reviewed. Largely autobiographical, it reflects upon the technique of reportage with Kisch's characteristic concreteness and adherence to realistic detail in the vein of *Neue Sachlichkeit* (New Objectivity). In this work, Kisch confesses he "serves up such details and such an association of ideas that reality becomes at least as interesting as any product of the imagination." For example, the description of a squabble among prostitutes projects itself into an extended treatment of the day-to-day operations of the vice squad. This description, however, is not limited to facts; nor does it ignore the "product of the imagination." Indeed, the reader is often unable to distinguish between fact and the imitation of truth. In this work, Kisch concedes that he is able to take advantage of the reader's uncertainty in this regard, especially in reportage concerning a foreign country; distance and the reader's unfamiliarity provide the author a certain license. Kisch also observes, however, that a balance must be achieved between fantasy and fact. Otherwise the reporter will not be believed and discredit himself: "True, you can't let your fancy go tripping off wherever she will; she has to confine herself to the strait [sic] and narrow path that leads from fact to fact, she can range only so far as the rhythmic harmony with these facts will allow."

On 10 May 1942, the ninth anniversary of the Nazi book burning, an exile publishing house was founded, El Libro Libre—Das Freie Buch, the logo of which bore great similarity to that of the journal *Freies Deutschland* and consisted of a book crushing a swastika. The first publication was *Markplatz der Sensationen* in the German original. *Entdeckungen in Mexiko* (1946; Discoveries in Mexico), born of his exile experience, deals with the products and resources of his host country and includes geography, history, fairy tales, and fantasy.

During his Mexican exile years, Kisch became increasingly conscious of his Czech identity, and in response to a bid by the Czech government he returned as a great celebrity to Prague. His last days were spent writing about the visit of Karl Marx to a Bohemian resort site. Not long after the Communists assumed control of Czechoslovakia, Kisch died on 31 March 1948 and was accorded a state funeral.

WARD B. LEWIS

Biography

Born in the German-Jewish community of Prague, Czechoslovakia, 29 April 1885. Attended a school of journalism in Berlin; local reporter with *Bohemia* in Prague, 1906–13, and thereafter associated with the *Berliner Tageblatt* in Berlin; served in World War I; attached to the press of the military staff in Vienna, where at the war's end he was active in the unrest of 1918 as a leader of the Red Guard; resettlement in Berlin and extensive world travels reflected in his writing; as a communist, exiled in Mexico, 1940; returned to Prague, 1946. Died in Prague, 31 March 1948.

Selected Works

Journalistic Writing

Aus Prager Gassen und Nächten, 1912
Prager Kinder, 1913
Der Mädchenhirt, 1914
Schrieb das auf, Kisch, 1922
Klassischer Journalismus, 1923
Der Fall des Generalstabschefs Redl, 1924
Der rasende Reporter, 1924
Hetzjagd durch die Zeit, 1925
Wagnisse in aller Welt, 1927
Zaren, Popen, Bolschewiken, 1927
Paradies Amerika, 1930
Asien gründlich verändert, 1932; as *Changing Asia,* translated by Rita Reil, 1935
China geheim, 1933; as *Secret China,* translated by Michael Davidson, 1935
Geschichten aus sieben Ghettos, 1934; as *Tales from Seven Ghettos,* translated by Edith Bone, 1948
Landung in Australien, 1937; as *Australian Landfall,* translated by John Fisher and Irene and Kevin Fitzgerald, 1969

Sensation Fair, translated by Guy Endore, 1941; original German text published as *Marktplatz der Sensationen,* 1942
Entdeckungen in Mexiko, 1946

Further Reading

Geisler, Michael, *Die literarische Reportage in Deutschland,* Königstein: Scriptor, 1982
Geissler, Rudolf, *Die Entwicklung der Reportage Egon Erwin Kischs in der Weimarer Republik,* Cologne: Pahl-Rugenstein, 1982
Haupt, Klaus, and Harald Wessel, *Kisch war hier,* Berlin: Verlag der Nation, 1985; 2nd edition, 1988
Lewis, Ward B., "Egon Erwin Kisch beehrt sich darzubieten: *Paraides Amerika,*" *German Studies Review* 13, no. 2 (1990)
Patka, Marcus G., *Egon Erwin Kisch: Stationen im Leben eines streitbaren Autors,* Vienna: Böhlau, 1997
Prokosch, Erdmute, *Egon Erwin Kisch: Reporter einer rasenden Zeit,* Bonn: Keil, 1985
Schlenstedt, Dieter, *Egon Erwin Kisch: Leben und Werk,* Berlin: Volk und Wissen, 1985
Segel, Harold B., "Introduction," in *Egon Erwin Kisch, The Raging Reporter: A Bioanthology,* West Lafayette, Indiana: Purdue University Press, 1997
Siegel, Christian Ernst, *Egon Erwin Kisch: Reportage und Politischer Journalismus,* Bremen: Schünemann, 1973
———, "Egon Erwin Kisch: Theorie des Fakten-Genres," in *Die Reportage,* Stuttgart: Metzler, 1978
Utitz, Emil, *Egon Erwin Kisch: Der klassische Journalist,* Berlin: Aufbau-Verlag, 1956

Klabund (Alfred Henschke) 1890–1928

The pseudonym adopted by Alfred Henschke, a conflation of *Klabautermann* (bogeyman) and *Vagabund* (vagabond), is indicative of his schizoid poetic persona. He cast himself initially, not unlike the young Brecht, in the then youthfully fashionable role of a modern François Villon, to whom he paid homage in his lyrical portrait *Der himmlische Vagant* (1919; The Heavenly Vagabond). After casting himself as a restless *poète maudit* and *bête noire* of polite bourgeois society, he would later, in *Irene; oder, Die Gesinnung* (1918; Irene or Conviction), reinterpret Klabund as meaning *Wandlung* (transformation), the central concept of the Expressionist creed of spiritual regeneration.

Klabund's first transformation, referred to in the ecstatically baroque, self-castigating, confessional verse of *Irene,* was one that was typical of his generation. The jingoistic patriot of the bellicose *Klabunds Soldatenlieder* (1914; Klabund's Soldiers' Songs) became the pacifist who in 1917 wrote an open letter to the Kaiser calling for an end to the war, which earned him a charge of *lèse majesté* and a later period of imprisonment as a suspected Spartakist sympathizer. Yet Klabund was never a political activist, and what critical social comment exists in his work shows a democratic liberalism that is tainted with cynical resignation.

His work is fraught with such contradiction. His first collection of poetry, *Morgenrot! Klabund! Die Tage dämmern!* (1912; Dawn! Klabund! The Days Are Dawning!), would suggest the early Expressionist apostrophizing of the spirit of renewal and *Aufbruch* (awakening), but what emerges is a cynicism reminiscent of Heine or Wedekind.

Klabund is remembered not only for the recognized quality of his chansons, *Brettllieder* (cabaret songs), and *Bänkellieder* (street ballads) (see *Die Harfenjule,* 1927; *Chansons,* 1930), which are often coarse and vulgar, and which satirize bourgeois manners and document in resigned tones the urban existence of the poor in a style that places him close to the *Neue Sachlichkeit* (New Obectivity) of Erich Kästner, but also for the esoteric and eccentric religious syncretism, predominantly Taoist, of *Dreiklang* (1919; Triad). Between these poles of cynical observer and poetic visionary, there is a core of personal verse. With few exceptions, however, such verse lacks a sustained quality, is derivative and forced, and becomes an exercise in form.

In the trilogy of novels *Moreau* (1916), *Mohammed* (1917), and *Pjotr* (1923; *Peter the Czar*), it is the rhythmical prose and Expressionist *Telegrammstil* that holds readers' attentions and that has received most critical comment. There is, however, a prescience in their sequence. In each, a representative figure confesses his inner soul. General Moreau, the democrat, is forced to recognize that the people are rabble; in *Mohammed,* the prophet's faith is blown across the desert; in *Pjotr,* violence and ruthless tyranny are shown as the realities of the modern state. Within these, the failure of Weimar democracy and of Expressionist Idealism and a following era of repression are all anticipated.

By contrast, the more successful novel *Bracke* (1918; *Bracke, the Fool*), an anecdotal sequence of picaresque, Eulenspiegel rogue tales, is culled from *Hans Clawert* (1587). There is a much greater ease in this work than in the stylistic mannerism of the serious novels, and an obvious affinity exists between the author and the cynical rogue and irreverent clown. Again, the duality of the serious, concerned individual and the careless vagabond emerges.

Above all, Klabund was known for his free adaptations of Oriental verse, predominantly Chinese. Although he was the most popular among the many who in the interwar years developed an interest in Chinese literature and philosophy, he was not an innovator; he followed the vogue of *chinoiserie* that emerged in Europe in the 1920s. Working from existing French and older German sources, Klabund rendered many verses, some from the Confucian *Schi King* (Book of Songs), but the majority from the poets of the T'ang Dynasty, most notably Li-tai-pe and Tu-Fu. It is Li-tai-pe, the dreamer, the intoxicated visionary, and the vagabond poet, with whom Klabund, and most of his generation, felt the greatest affinity.

Klabund's mediating influence is also visible in his rendition of the canonical Taoist work the *Tao-te-king* (Book of the Way and Its Power) in *Laotse, Sprüche* (1921; Lao-tse, Aphorisms). From the elliptical source, Klabund constructs a poetic work that owes as much to German Expressionist Idealism as to Taoist thought.

Most celebrated of all Klabund's free adaptations of Oriental literature was *Der Kreidekreis* (1925; *The Circle of Chalk*), which he took from the Yüan Dynasty drama *Hui-lan chi*. The play dominated the stage in 1925; it was performed in all major German cities and later throughout Europe. Klabund turns the austere moral parable of the original into a romantic fairy tale that abounds in quasi-Taoist religio-philosophical symbolism. Its only lasting influence was Brecht's *Der kaukasische Kreidekreis* (1945; *The Caucasian Chalk Circle*).

Klabund's eclecticism is symptomatic both of a generation that was seeking political, cultural, and spiritual reorientation in the dissonant and fractured world that emerged from the war and of an individual whose tubercular condition prompted a creative frenzy in which quality was frequently sacrificed to quantity. Much of his literary output served simply as a source of income for an author who possessed a protean literary versatility. For this reason his work has been largely neglected by critics, who view him as a popular yet minor representative of many features of Weimar literature. While it is true that his work seldom exhibits any lasting qualities, Klabund's popularity among his contemporaries serves to illuminate the cultural landscape from which he emerged.

MALCOLM READ

Biography

Born in Crossen an der Oder, 4 November 1890. Diagnosed as tubercular at age of 16; studied German, philosophy, and drama in Munich, Berlin, and Lausanne; from 1912, worked as freelance author in Munich and Berlin; friendship with Gottfried Benn and Bertolt Brecht; married actress Carola Neher, 1925. Died in Davos, Switzerland, 14 August 1928.

Selected Works

Collections
Gesammelte Werke, 1930
Der himmlische Vagant, 1968

Poetry
Morgenrot! Klabund! Die Tage dämmern, 1912
Klabunds Soldatenlieder, 1914
Li-tai-pe, 1916
Die Himmelsleiter, 1916
Irene; oder, Die Gesinnung, 1918
Der himmlische Vagant, 1919
Dreiklang, 1919
Das Blumenschiff, 1921
Laotse, Sprüche, 1921
Das heiße Herz, 1922
Gedichte, 1926
Die Harfenjule, 1927
Chansons, 1930

Plays
Der Kreidekreis, 1925; as *The Circle of Chalk*, translated by James Laver, 1929
XYZ, 1928

Novels
Moreau: Roman eines Soldaten, 1916
Mohammed: Roman eines Propheten, 1917
Bracke, 1918; as *Bracke, the Fool*, translated by Hermann George Scheffauer, 1927
Pjotr: Roman eines Zaren, 1923; as *Peter the Czar*, translated by Hermann George Scheffauer, 1925
Borgia, 1928; as *The Incredible Borgia*, translated by Louise Brink, 1929
Rasputin, 1929

Stories
Klabunds Karussell, 1914
Der Marketenderwagen, 1916
Marietta, 1920
Heiligenlegenden, 1921
Der letzte Kaiser, 1923
Kriegsbuch, 1929

Further Reading

Grothe, Heinz, *Klabund: Leben und Werk eines Dichters*, Berlin: Goldstein, 1933
Gilman, Sander L., *Form und Funktion: Eine strukturelle Untersuchung der Romane Klabunds*, Frankfurt: Athenäum, 1971
Kaulla, Guido von, *Brennendes Herz Klabund: Legende und Wirklichkeit*, Zurich: Classen, 1971
Mittelgöker, Jutta, "Revolutionär der Seele: Zum Gedanken an Klabund," *Der Literat* 30 (1988)
Paulsen, Wolfgang, "Klabund," in *Der Dichter und sein Werk: Von Wieland bis Christa Wolf*, by Paulsen, Frankfurt and New York: Lang, 1993
Read, Malcolm, "Brecht, Klabund, and the Chalk Circle," *Modern Languages* 53, no. 1 (1972)
Reich-Ranicki, Marcel, "Klabunds Wettlauf mit dem Tod," in *Nachprüfung: Aufsätze über deutsche Schriftsteller von gestern*, Munich: Piper, 1961
Giefer, Günter, "Vor 50 Jahren starb Klabund," *Neue deutsche Hefte* 159 (1978)
Wegner, Matthias, *Klabund und Carola Neher: Eine Geschichte von Liebe und Tod*, Berlin: Rowohlt, 1996

Klassik

German Classicism (*Klassik* or *Weimarer Klassik*) dates from the publication of Goethe's drama *Iphigenie* (*Iphigenia*) in 1787 until Schiller's death in 1805. Johann Wolfgang (von) Goethe (1749–1832) and Friedrich (von) Schiller (1759–1805) (the *von* is optional as it indicates the noble title conferred on them in 1782 and 1802, respectively, by the Holy Roman Emperor on the recommendation of Duke Karl August (1757–1828) had already achieved fame throughout Europe during their Sturm und Drang years with works such as *Die Leiden des jungen Werthers* (1774; revised 1787; *The Sorrows of Young Werther*) and *Die Räuber* (1781; *The Robbers*). After more than a ten-year hiatus, they embarked on their second (the so-called classical) phase of creative activity, formulating and giving poetic concretization to a program of aesthetic-ethical humanism in an effort to counteract the "barbaric" state of affairs they perceived all around them. To this end, Goethe rewrote the prose versions of the dramas *Iphigenia* and *Torquato Tasso* (1790), conceived and written some ten years earlier, into rhymeless blank verse, balanced and measured, that expressed high moral values in an elevated style. The structure is classical in its simplicity: five acts, Aristotelian dramatic unity, and five characters symmetrically arranged. In the case of *Iphigenia,* Goethe took up a challenge by Wieland (1733–1813), who had tauntingly asked, "Where is our Corneille, our Racine" and who suggested to Goethe that he emulate the foremost writers of the *tragédie classique* of French classicism. Likewise, an unpublished novel of 1777, *Wilhelm Meisters theatralische Sendung* (*Wilhelm Meister's Theatrical Mission*), was rewritten as *Wilhelm Meisters Lehrjahre* (1795; *Wilhelm Meister's Apprenticeship*) and became the prototype of the bildungsroman. Challenged by Schiller to write a modern idyll, Goethe wrote *Hermann und Dorothea* (1798), an epic in hexameters set against the backdrop of the French Revolution (1789). The year 1797 is known as the "year of the ballad," when Goethe and Schiller tried out an old form that still combined epic, dramatic, and lyrical elements. The poetry they wrote during this period is in the form of odes and hymns—philosophical, reflective, and didactic. Schiller's major dramas fall into this period: the trilogy *Wallenstein* (1798–99), *Maria Stuart* (1801), *Die Jungfrau von Orleans* (1801; *The Maid of Orleans*), and *Wilhelm Tell* (1804), as well as essays on aesthetic topics, notably *Über die ästhetische Erziehung des Menschen in einer Reihe von Briefen* (1795; *On the Aesthetic Education of Man in a Series of Letters*) and *Über naive und sentimentalische Dichtung* (1795–96; *On the Naive and Sentimental in Literature*). Both treatises were published in *Die Horen* (*The Horae*), a journal that Schiller was editing.

The designation *Klassik* was given to this period later by literary historians when the texts of Goethe and Schiller were used as pretexts for constructing a German identity and nation, beginning with Georg G. Gervinus (1805–71), who used the term *Deutsche Klassik* in his *Geschichte der poetischen Nationalliteratur der Deutschen* (1835–42; *History of the Poetic National Literature of the Germans*). This term, as well as the two authors' names, continued to be evoked whenever national unity and German character were at stake: by the liberal-democratic movement in the middle of the 19th century (the 1859 Schiller centennial caused spectacular celebrations across Germany), by the conservative German national movement at the end of the 19th century, at the founding of the Second Reich in 1871, at Germany's first try at democracy during the Weimar Republic (1918–33), and by the propaganda machine of Hitler's Third Reich. However, Schiller's reception in the Third Reich ended with an ironic twist. At first, there was a complete adoption of Schiller. A book by Hans Fabricius, *Schiller als Kampfgenosse Hitlers* (Schiller as Hitler's Comrade-in-Arms), was in its second printing in 1934, the year of the 175th anniversary of Schiller's birth, when cultish celebrations also took place with spectacular and symbolic displays of torches and flags, flames, lights, and colors. Tell, the man of action, was identified with Hitler, the Führer, as Germany's savior. This came to an abrupt end when a Swiss waiter, Maurice Bavaud, tried to assassinate Hitler, which caused any mention of *Tell* to be forbidden and purged from all school textbooks. Bavaud was caught and executed while Tell, who kills the tyrant Geßler, is hailed as the "savior" of the Swiss people at the end of Schiller's play. Such statements as "There is a limit to the power of tyrants," the mention of the murder of the emperor, the shouts of "freedom! freedom!", Bertha renouncing her privileges as a noblewoman and asking the people to be received as an equal (*Bürgerin*), and Rudenz releasing his subjects from bondage into freedom were, as a whole, too much political dynamite to be performed on stage, even in Schiller's time. For the premiere at the court theater in Weimar, Schiller cut out the whole fifth act as well as other *bedenkliche Stellen* (disturbing scenes). When Iffland wanted to stage a performance in Berlin, he also asked for changes, although, as he said, the Berlin rulers permitted "what no other monarchy permitted." Among other changes, Schiller replaced the words "freedom! freedom!" with "rescue and salvation" (*Rettung und Erlösung*). Politically inoffensive and far more popular were the stereotyped, sentimental comedies and melodramas written by Iffland (1759–1814) and Kotzebue (1761–1819), the latter flooding German stages with some 200 plays. This led Goethe to complain that his dramas were performed only once every three to four years and that the public found them boring and adding that, had they been well received, he could have produced a "whole dozen" dramas such as *Iphigenia* and *Tasso*. Thus, Goethe and Schiller managed to alienate both the public and the authorities. Nor did they seem to care much as they deliberately caused a scandal by publishing the *Xenien* (1796), a series of polemic distichs in which they mercilessly attacked mediocrity and held up many well-known names to ridicule, offending both friend and foe. There were the inevitable counterattacks, but none could match the two masters in authoritative voice, urbanity, and wit.

Goethe and Schiller profoundly cared about political and civil freedom and equality, the attainment of which would require drastic social changes that neither the politically impotent public nor the rulers of the ancien régime could or would bring about. Realistically, the only hope for reform in the hierarchical, absolutist, even still feudal political system lay with the progressive, lesser nobility (*Reformadel*) who had the interest, knowledge, and means to begin enacting changes. Goethe and Schiller depict the progressive nobility in their works: Bertha and Rudenz in *Tell* and Therese, Jarno, and Lothario in *Wilhelm Meister,* who resist the temptation to emigrate to the United States and begin to emancipate their own subjects, thereby giving up some of their own privileges as nobles. In Prussia, reforms were initiated by such people as Reichsfreiherr von und zum Stein (1757–1831), von Hardenberg (1750–1822), the generals von Gneisenau (1760–1831) and von Scharnhorst (1755–1813), and Wilhelm von Humboldt (1767–1835), a friend of Schiller's and Goethe's and the founder of the German *Gymnasium* and the university in Berlin that still bears his name. It is this group in society that Goethe and Schiller challenge, appeal to, and address in their works. Schiller's first version of the *Letters on the Aesthetic Education of Man* was literally addressed to Duke Friedrich von Augustenburg, a Danish patron who had given him a generous stipend for three years to "support [*erhalten*] one of mankind's teachers." (Schiller suffered from periodic bouts of severe illness during the last 13 years of his life, and a premature announcement of his death had appeared in an Austrian newspaper.) Goethe, commenting on the alleged difficulty of *Tasso*, said,

> a young man from a good family with sufficient intellect and an education [*Bildung*] acquired through association with graceful and harmonious people [*vollendete Menschen*] of the higher and highest circles [*Stände*] will not find *Tasso* difficult.

Not surprisingly, such a stance came under heavy criticism by the advocates of *literature engagé*, such as the "Young Germans" Börne (1786–1837) and Gutzkow (1811–78), Brecht (1898–1956), most Marxist critics, and the political activists of the 1960s and 1970s who accused Goethe and Schiller of political aloofness, aesthetic snobbery, and intellectual elitism and considered their works irrelevant, antiquated, and "dead." (Brecht: "Die Klassiker sind tot," i.e., in terms of a changed social reality.) However, their lofty style, sententious sayings, idealized language, and subject matter also inspired an endless stream of parodies, with the result that Goethe and Schiller are the most parodied authors in German literature. Thus, reception history shows four discernible strands—the parodistic, the adulatory, dismissal as antiquated, and canonization—as the unsurpassed masters of language and substance pronouncing eternal verities.

The debate about Goethe and Schiller as relics of the past or as still relevant and exemplary continues both academically and in many fictionalized accounts of their lives and works, and their plays are still performed. *Klassik* has become institutionalized as *Stiftung* (endowment) *Weimarer Klassik,* an enormous cultural enterprise administering 22 museums (including one for each), their houses, the Goethe and Schiller Archive, the Herzogin Anna Amalia Bibliothek, and many other buildings and parks. There are many tourist attractions, and scholars from all over the world descend on Weimar to attend conferences and do research. There is a Schiller Society and a Goethe Society, each with a yearbook, and there is a separate Goethe Society of North America and one in England, each with its own yearbook. For the year 1999, the European Union has designated Weimar "Kulturhauptstadt Europas," which is quite appropriate in one sense and somewhat amusing in a historical sense. Goethe and Schiller always considered themselves Europeans, if not citizens of the world (*Weltbürger*). In their view, the artist is privileged and duty bound to be "Zeitgenosse aller Zeiten" (contemporary

to all time periods). Schiller was made an honorary French citizen (1792) and in Germany was forbidden to write by his Duke Karl Eugen and had to flee to Mannheim to escape incarceration (1782). Goethe was received and honored by Napoléon but by none of the four German kings. The subject matter for their "classical" plays is taken not from German history but from that of other European countries: for *Iphigenia,* ancient Greek mythology; for *Tasso,* the life of the Italian Renaissance poet Tasso; for *Wallenstein,* the European theater of war of the Thirty Years' War (1618–48); for *Maria Stuart,* English history (1542–87); for *The Maid of Orleans,* French history (1412–3l); and for *Tell,* the history of the Swiss people in the first decade of the 14th century. Furthermore, the plays are addressed to all humanity (see below), transcending any national boundaries. Being labeled "classical" or "national" would have been meaningless to them.

Weimar being named "Cultural Capital" is amusing in a historical sense because, when the young Duke Karl August invited Goethe to come to Weimar for a visit in 1775, it was a tiny town of 6,000 inhabitants located in the duchy of Saxe-Weimar-Eisenach, which was one of the smallest and economically most backward of the 350 independent and sovereign territories in Germany. What made Goethe, a young lawyer and famous author and the proud son of a patrician family in the free city of Frankfurt, spend the remaining 57 years of his life in Weimar in the service of a duke eight years his junior? One answer is the respect and trust they had for each other. On the strength of his administrative abilities, Goethe rose rapidly through the ranks, and the duke appointed him to the highest offices of privy councilor and minister over the objections of his senior councilors. For ten years he worked tirelessly, improving the living conditions of the inhabitants, providing jobs by building roads and opening a mine, reducing tax levies, and so on, understanding that any gain in human dignity and freedom would come from economic improvement. Many sayings in *Tasso,* spoken by Antonio, reflect these experiences: "It is easy to obey a noble Lord, who *convinces* when he commands"; "What one *is* one learns from other human beings, only life teaches what we are"; and "Only life's labors teach us to appreciate the good things in life." Another reason is that the *Residenzstadt* Weimar was regarded as a *Musenhof* (court of the muses), a safe distance away from the saber-rattling Hohenzollerns in Berlin-Potsdam. It had a respectable Hoftheater where Goethe starred as Orest in *Iphigenia* and whose sole director he was from 1791 to 1817. The duke's mother, Anna Amalia, was a supporter and tireless promoter of the arts. As a tutor for her son, she had hired Christoph Martin Wieland, a well-known translator from several languages (22 dramas of Shakespeare) and author of many works in an elegant, urbane, and witty rococo style. In 1794 he developed a friendship with Schiller, whom he had helped get a position as professor of history at the University of Jena (1789) and who in 1799 settled permanently in Weimar. Similarly, on Goethe's recommendation, the duke appointed Johann Gottfried Herder (1744–1803) superintendent of churches and schools.

Herder had been Goethe's mentor during the Sturm und Drang days in Strasbourg and was very influential in shaping not only his views but also the zeitgeist of the period, the emerging modern worldview. The Cartesian-Newtonian clock-maker universe was being replaced by an evolutionary universe, that is, a living organism subject to the laws of growth and decay. In his

Ideen zur Philosophie der Geschichte der Menschheit (1784–91; *Outline of a Philosophy of the History of Mankind*) and *Briefe zur Beförderung der Humanität* (1793–97; *Letters for the Advancement of Humanity*), Herder affirms the plurality of human cultures and emphasizes their organic relation to their natural environment. Each nation has its own distinct character and unique quality, deposited and preserved in a people's narratives, poetry, myths, sagas, songs, and rituals. Taken together as a repository of human self-expression, aspirations, and hopes, they are a contribution in the progression toward an enlightened humanity. Whereas Herder put cultural studies on a modern footing, Immanuel Kant (1724–1804) did the same for philosophy by demolishing the centuries-old scholastic philosophy and Leibniz's (1646–1716) preestablished "best of all possible worlds"; in a second "Copernican revolution" by turning philosophical inquiry on the subject, from *what* to *how* we know, that is, on the faculties and functions of the human mind, and by formulating new answers to the basic questions What can I know? What shall I do? and What may I believe? Thus, by setting limits to human knowledge and perfectibility, the human sphere of action becomes all-important. Instead of having moral law imposed by a higher authority, the human being is empowered to find it within and to act accordingly, as formulated in the categorical imperative, "Act only on that maxim through which you can at the same time will that it should become a universal law." Schiller studied Kant so intensely that he could say, only halfjokingly, that Kant had cost him 20 years of his life: 10 to understand him and 10 to free himself of him. His philosophy is the foundation of Schiller's aesthetic writings. Although Goethe disliked abstract reasoning and preferred to derive his arguments and conclusions from sensory experience and observation, his writings echo Kant in many respects, expressing the same zeitgeist, as it were. For example, the poem *Das Göttliche* (1783; *The Divine*) also places the human being at the center of the universe and is replete with moral imperatives: "Noble be the human being, helpful, and good ... tirelessly doing what is beneficial and just, be a model [*Vorbild*] for us of those beings we divine." The human being can "discern, can choose and judge," and by doing so he can accomplish the impossible: "to give permanence to the moment." It can be said that Kant's categorical imperative becomes the basis for Goethe's theory of the symbol. The universals, such as truth, justice, God, and the good, as such unknowable, become understandable and accessible to experience through the particular act or object if done or represented in an exemplary manner. A good deed done in the fleeting moment of time will endure in its effects.

The universal imperatives are, of course, directed to all humanity. Yet the sociopolitical reality was stone-deaf, it seemed. The universal human rights of freedom, equality, and brotherhood and of life, liberty, and the pursuit of happiness, so eloquently declared in the *Rights of Man* (1789) and *The Declaration of Independence* (1776) and considered inalienable and self-evident in this post-Enlightenment period, were nowhere evident in the political reality of Europe. The French attempt to enact them failed miserably. A quote from Schiller about the French Revolution can help illustrate the glaring discrepancy between promise and reality:

> The attempt of the French people to reclaim their sacred human rights and to obtain political freedom has only brought to light their inability and unpreparedness to do so and has plunged not only that unhappy people, but a considerable part of Europe and a whole century, back into barbarism and slavery.

In general, Schiller finds in society "on the one hand, a return to the savage state; on the other, to complete lethargy: in other words, to the two extremes of human depravity, and both united in a single epoch!" Whereas in the arts human rights and aspirations are celebrated (e.g., in Schiller's *Ode to Joy* [1786] set to music by Beethoven [1770–1827] in his Ninth Symphony), the kings and the hundreds of princes, grand dukes, and dukes, each claiming a divine right, perforce deny their subjects these rights, hold them in bondage, tax them into starvation, and even sell them, as the Hessians were sold to the British to fight in colonial America. Commenting on Herder's vision of an enlightened humanity, Goethe remarks that he too believes that it will come, but not before the world has become "a big hospital" and the people each other's *Krankenwärter* (nurse). As the rulers have led their people to slaughter again and again, history is an absurd spectacle to Goethe and one to which he can respond only with sarcasm: "So that they can all kill each other, Judgment Day has been postponed." Indeed, it would be best to start all over again, as Goethe suggests in the delightful scene of *Faust II* in which Homunculus, the artificial intelligence, looks for a body, and Thales comments, "Yield to the laudable desire to begin creation anew!" The language then bursts into a paean to creation and creativity, culminating in the line, "So herrsche denn Eros, der alles begonnen!" (Let Eros prevail, who began everything!).

It is this unshakable faith in creativity and a comprehensive knowledge of the cyclical nature of natural and human evolution (i.e., the complementarity of such opposites as decay and growth, dying and becoming, and degeneration and regeneration) that made Goethe and Schiller embark on an aesthetic program of action and a series of works that showed a positive resolution of the ever-recurring struggle between barbarity and humanism and provided an alternative to the regression into barbarism. All their Sturm und Drang works had ended on a negative note: protagonists indicting and cursing a reality that denied them any meaningful activity and existence and Werther and Ferdinand and Luise in Schiller's *Kabale und Liebe* (1784; *Intrigue and Love*) committing suicide to escape from a stifling and corrupt court society dominated by a jaded aristocracy. Iphigenie, by contrast, humanizes a society by rising above political expediency and committing herself totally to the "voice of truth and humaneness." Iphigenie has been transported by Diana to be her priestess in Tauris, a culture alien to her and practicing the "law" of human sacrifice with all strangers as victims. Her brother Orestes and his friend are on a mission to steal the picture of Diana from the Taurians and bring it home to Greece. They are caught, and by law Iphigenie must sacrifice them. However, they have found an opportunity to escape, and it is at this moment that Iphigenie commits an "unheard-of deed": telling King Thoas the truth and challenging him with the words "Verdirb uns—wenn du darfst" (destroy us if your feelings as a human being let you do it). Thoas is incredulous, asking her whether she can really believe that he, "the uncivilized Scythian, the barbarian," should listen to the "voice of truth and humanity" that even the Greek Atreus did not hear. Iphigenie responds that every human being hears this voice "born anywhere under the free sky through whose bosom flows the fountainhead of life, pure and unhindered." Thoas is persuaded and blesses them when they depart. Thus, the law of human sacrifice is replaced by the law of hospitality, raising civilization a step higher in the progression of humankind. In addition, Iphigenie manages to humanize the Greek concept of inscrutable fate by replacing it with the modern concept of love when, through her sisterly love, she frees Orestes of the Eumenides that persecute him mercilessly. Not surprisingly, Schiller found the drama "astonishingly modern and ungreek." However, it does represent what the art historian Winckelmann (1717–68) had identified as the characteristics of Greek art: "a noble simplicity and tranquil grandeur." When Goethe rewrote the play during his first trip to Italy (1786–88), he read it to *St. Agatha,* a painting by Raphael, vowing that he would not let his heroine speak a word that could not also have been spoken by this saint. This is significant in two ways: for his *Kunstethos* (i.e., fusing the aesthetic with the ethical in modeling a powerfully persuasive and exemplary personality) and for his way of communicating with the objective world (be it nature or works of art), turning them into subjects, engaging them in dialogue, and giving them voice (cf. the poems "Die Metamorphose der Pflanzen" [1798; The Metamorphosis of Plants] and "Die Metamorphose der Tiere" [1820; The Metamorphosis of Animals]). In *Tasso,* Goethe communicates with the past, projecting his own situation into it, as he calls it "flesh of my flesh," and has the duke proclaim, "A barbarian is he who does not hear the voice of poetry [*Dichtung*]." The court at Ferrara has been humanized by its culture-producing activity: Petrarch, Ariosto, and all the "great names" of Italy have contributed in this cause. Yet the central question of the drama, "Wer ist denn glücklich" (Who is happy?), is answered in the negative, which is to say that no one is in a state of happiness, for happiness is in the act of *doing*. When Tasso, for example, mourns the loss of the golden age when happiness was a life of pleasure, ease, and harmony, the princess responds with a modern dialectic, namely, that "beautiful time" never was, just as it does not now exist; however, if it ever was, it certainly can come again, "only the good people will bring it back." The German for "it can come again" is "wie sie uns immer wieder werden kann," *werden* indicating that it is a process of becoming and *immer wieder* referring to the fact that in the course of a history of wars and bloodshed there have been moments of peace and harmony brought about by goodwilled people. The golden age of Greek culture was such a moment, Goethe and Schiller believed, in which in the springtime of humankind the human spirit could unfold naturally and wholly, unencumbered by any ideologies or modern fragmentation, and produce cultural objects of hitherto unimagined beauty. Once created, they stand forever as a reminder of what human creativity can achieve. Hero and poet were held in equal esteem, as they are in *Tasso*. Duke Alfons encourages and rewards both Antonio, the man of action, and Tasso, the poet, as he understands that the contributions of both are necessary for a cultured existence, which he wants to prolong as long as possible. This symbolic unity is shown when Tasso and Antonio join hands at the end of the play.

Whereas Goethe models life as it could be at a princely court, how conflicts can be resolved, and how tensions and hate can be overcome by the goodwill of well-intentioned people, in *The Maid of Orleans* Schiller models a kingship as it could be when the king fulfills his responsibility (considered as divinely ordained) of providing a "joyous existence" for the people. He does so by protecting the peace so that farmers can till their lands and townspeople can joyously go about their trades, by "leading the serfs into freedom," and by assisting the weak and punishing the evil ones. The king does not know envy: he is "a human being and an angel of mercy on this hostile earth." The throne of kings is a "refuge for the homeless," the seat of power and mercy, before which the guilty tremble and the just fear nothing. Could the "foreign king" (i.e., the English conqueror) love this country and its language, and could he be a father to its sons? Having saved France and her people from being annihilated by the British invaders, riches and fame could be Johanna's for the asking. However, when asked by the king, "How can I reward you?" she merely has two requests of the king: "Always be humane, Lord . . . do not deny justice and mercy to the least of your people." At the end she dies "heiter lächelnd" (smiling joyously) among her people. With *Tell,* Schiller moves fast-forward in the progression of humankind, not in historical but in ideal time, to the enactment of democracy. The freedom of the Swiss people and the independence of their land, which they have "created" and cultivated for over a thousand years, is on the verge of extinction because the Austrian king wants to increase his territory by annexing Switzerland. To beat the people into submission, Geßler and his henchmen inflict unspeakable atrocities on them. Because the king happens to also be the emperor, there is no authority on this earth they can appeal to. They must reach into the heavens, where the "eternal rights" are preserved "inalienable and unbreakable like the stars themselves," to reclaim and make them part of human praxis again. Because the representatives of the nobility renounce their privileges and become one with the free people, it is a "better freedom," as von Attinghausen observes, and he continues, "The old order is crumbling, the time is changing, and new life blossoms from the ruins."

Because "to provide freedom through freedom" is Schiller's definition of the aesthetic state, *Tell* can be regarded as the poetic concretization of such a state, as critics have pointed out. Beauty is similarly defined as "Freiheit in der Erscheinung" (freedom in an objective manifestation), be it in nature, art, or the individual human being. However, nature has created humans only with the capacity for choice, which can be toward either good or evil. Because the political system is still in a "barbaric" state, it is incumbent on the artist to point human progress in the "direction toward the good." As Schiller states in his *Letters on Aesthetic Education,* "Gib der Welt, auf die du wirkst, die *Richtung* zum Guten" (Give the world upon which you act the direction toward the good). Art becomes "die zweite Schöpferin" (second creator), which is to say that through art humans enter their humanity. Humans share with animals the imperative to provide for their bodily existence, but once land is cultivated to produce an abundance, humans have free time to "play": They decorate the walls of their caves, their bows and arrows, their drinking cups, and themselves, and soon this "useless" part of their existence (in a utilitarian sense) becomes "the best part of human joys" ("der beste Teil seiner Freuden"). Works of art are the depository of human joys and aspirations and, once created, are a reminder and a challenge to humans, exemplars (*Muster*) of human achievement uncorrupted by the political realities of the day.

Goethe argues in a similar way. The sociopolitical reality is a wasteland dominated by the entropic side of chaos, "decaying and dying," but there is also the creative side of chaos: the wasteland to be cultivated. "Die Zeit ist mein Besitz, mein Acker ist die Zeit" (The time allotted to me is my field to be cultivated), states Goethe in the poem "Mein Erbteil" (My Inheritance). Nature has endowed human beings with *Vernunft* (the capacity for reasoning, choosing, and making judgments); unfortunately, they use it only to be "more bestial than any beast," as Mephisto says in *Faust*. "Politicians" have done their best to prove this point. Thoas could have *not* listened to Iphigenie and continued to slaughter all "foreigners" as did Hitler, Stalin, and many other dictators in the name of whatever ideology thought up by humans. However, nature in its infinite creativity has also provided humans with the possibility of a "joyous existence," as Goethe argues in his essay *Winckelmann und sein Jahrhundert* (1805). Along the way of its evolutionary path, nature has created the "schöne Mensch," the beautiful human being, with such complex systems as the brain, the eye, and the heart that never failed to amaze Goethe. Isomorphically, human creativity also produces a beautiful product: the work of art. Whereas nature's product is momentary and perishable, the work of art endures by its form, standing before the world as an inspiration and a challenge. The words *Muster* and *Vorbild* do not point toward an unattainable goal in a utopian never-never land but literally mean to pattern and prefigure a "joyous existence" in the here and now, as part of human praxis, as part of what humans must do if they do not want to slide back into barbarity.

To counteract the bestial impulse in humans and to subvert the entrenched absolutist, hierarchical political system of their day, Goethe and Schiller take recourse to nature and art, as maintaining contact with the creative spirit manifest in both is mandatory for any regeneration and renewal of the human condition. For reorganization into a new order to occur, any complex system, such as a society, must remember and periodically confront its origins and past achievements. To overcome the fragmentation and make the human being "whole" again—in other words, for political freedom to catch up with its proclamation and prefiguration in the arts—would be a "task for more than *one* century," Schiller states in his *Letters on Aesthetic Education*. Before a "joyous existence" would be accessible to all humanity, moral improvement and the respect for human dignity would have to occur in more and more people until a critical mass is reached. From Schiller's time it took 200 years for the German people to attain political freedom in a democracy and for the former archenemies Germany, France, and England to join together in the European Union and legislate war out of existence.

RAIMUND BELGARDT

See also Johann Wolfgang von Goethe; Friedrich von Schiller; Johann Joachim Winckelmann

Further Reading

Barner, Wilfried, et al., editors, *Unser Commercium: Goethes und Schillers Literaturpolitik,* Stuttgart: Cotta, 1984

Behler, Constantin, *Nostalgic Teleology: Friedrich Schiller and the Schemata of Aesthetic Humanism,* Bern and New York: Lang, 1995

Berghahn, Klaus, *Schiller: Ansichten eines Idealisten,* Frankfurt: Athenäum, 1986

Berghahn, Klaus, editor, *Die Weimarer Klassik: Paradigma des Methodenpluralismus in der Germanistik,* Kronberg: Scriptor, 1976

Bersier, Gabrielle, "Classicism," in *A Concise History of German Literature to 1900,* edited by Kim Vivian, Columbia: Camden House, 1992

Beutin, Wolfgang, et al., *A History of German Literature,* translated by Clare Krojzl, London and New York: Routledge, 1993

Borchmeyer, Dieter, *Weimarer Klassik: Portrait einer Epoche,* Weinheim: Beltz Athenäum, 1994

Burger, Heinz Otto, editor, *Begriffsbestimmung der Klassik und des Klassischen,* Darmstadt: Wissenschaftliche Buchgesellschaft, 1971

Conrady, Karl Otto, editor, *Deutsche Literatur zur Zeit der Klassik,* Stuttgart: Reclam, 1977

Grimm, Reinhold, and Jost Hermand, editors, *Die Klassik-Legende,* Frankfurt: Athenäum, 1971

Knobloch, Hans-Jörg, and Helmut Koopmann, editors, *Schiller heute,* Tübingen: Stauffenburg, 1996

Lange, Victor, *The Classical Age of German Literature, 1740–1815,* London: Arnold, 1982

Müller-Seidel, Walter, *Die Geschichtlichkeit der deutschen Klassik,* Stuttgart: Metzler, 1983

Pickar, Gertrud Bauer, and Sabine Cramer, *The Age of Goethe Today: Critical Reexamination and Literary Reflection,* Munich: Fink, 1990

Richter, Karl, et al., *Klassik und Moderne: Die Weimarer Klassik als historisches Ereignis und Herausforderung im kulturgeschichtlichen Prozeß,* Stuttgart: Metzler, 1983

Schiller, Friedrich, *On the Aesthetic Education of Man in a Series of Letters,* edited and translated by Elizabeth Wilkinson and Leonard A. Willoughby, Oxford: Clarendon Press, and New York: Oxford University Press, 1967

Schwarzbauer, Franz, *Die Xenien: Studien zur Vorgeschichte der Weimarer Klassik,* Stuttgart: Metzler, 1993

Wende, Waltraud, *Goethe-Parodien: Zur Wirkungsgeschichte eines Klassikers,* Stuttgart: Metzler, 1995

Werner, Hans-Georg, *Literarische Strategien: Studien zur deutschen Literatur 1760 bis 1880,* Stuttgart: Metzler, 1993

Wittkowski, Wolfgang, editor, *Verlorene Klassik? Ein Symposium,* Tübingen: Niemeyer, 1986

Heinrich von Kleist 1777–1811

Throughout his short life Heinrich von Kleist was plagued by inner contradictions and external misfortunes. A Prussian aristocrat alienated from the class into which he was born, he abandoned suitable careers in the army and civil service for restless travel and the pursuit of literary projects, which failed to bring him either the fame he desired or the income he badly needed. Brilliantly gifted but neurotically maladjusted, he was torn between pedantry and passion, sensitivity and ruthlessness, and furious ambition and a paralyzing sense of inadequacy. His obsessive striving for absolute certainties was confounded by doubts. His uncompromising search for fulfillment through virtue, love, friendship, nation, nature, and art foundered on the conjunction of adverse circumstances and his own instability. Some euphoric moments apart, his dominant mood was one of despair, which led to suicide at the age of 34. It is fittingly ironic that, having been pronounced sick by Goethe and having struggled in vain for recognition in his lifetime, he has come to be considered as one of Germany's greatest writers by such major figures as Hebbel, Fontane, Kafka, and Thomas Mann.

Although he was connected to various literary circles, Kleist did not follow any particular group or direction. Fascinated by the irrational, the unconscious, and the occult and delving deep below the empirical surface of things to reveal hidden driving forces, he shared the subjectivism and spiritualism of the Romantics. Unlike the Romantics, however, he incorporated rather than glossed over the recalcitrance of objective reality in his writing, which at times brought him close to the later movement of realism. Anticipating psychoanalysis, challenging the prevailing concepts of human personality, and rejecting the philosophical, moral, and social assumptions of his time, he seems strikingly modern today. During the first half of the 20th century, critics increasingly praised his patriotism, until he became one of the figureheads of National Socialist cultural propaganda. After World War II, the critical emphasis shifted to the metaphysical and existentialist implications of his work. More recently, he has been studied from social, political, structuralist, semiotic, and narratological points of view. Despite scholars' propensity to indulge in their personal preoccupations, the multiplicity of viable interpretations bears witness to Kleist's greatness.

Kleist's central problem—documented in his correspondence and his occasional essays—was that of knowledge. At first he sought happiness through both Enlightenment rationalism and Rousseauesque sensibility, but he was shattered when some propositions of Kant—either read at firsthand or received from Fichte—seemed to confirm his suspicion, voiced in a letter to his fiancée Wilhelmine Zenge in 1801, that the intellect was "unable to decide whether what we call truth is truly the truth, or only appears so to us." He persisted in commending intuitive "feeling," most notably in three works: *Über das Marionettentheater* (1810; translated as *On a Theatre of Marionettes* and *On Puppetshows*), where he claimed that the pristine grace of an unthinking condition, which was upset by ratiocination, would be regained on a higher plane of transcendental awareness; *Über die allmähliche Verfertigung der Gedanken beim Reden* (1821; *On the Gradual Production of Thoughts Whilst Speaking*), where he asserted that ideas took shape spontaneously in the process of being articulated rather than when they were thought out in advance; and *Von der Überlegung: Eine Paradoxe* (1810: *Reflection: A Paradox*),

where he argued that action should always precede reflection. Basically, however, he believed that "feelings," being inconstant, were as unreliable as reason and that the consequent impossibility of recognizing any purpose in life made freedom an illusion and fate synonymous with chance. In addition, notwithstanding his own magnificent German style, he was troubled by the sensation that language, without which human communication was inconceivable, could only reproduce what he called in a letter to his half-sister Ulrike von Kleist in 1801 "torn fragments" and could not "paint the soul" as a whole.

Avoiding direct references to current affairs in his plays and stories, Kleist voiced his political opinions in a number of articles, chiefly in his journal *Berliner Abendblätter,* which was suppressed by the authorities soon after the start of publication. Apart from occasional bouts of nationalism nourished by his hatred of the Napoleonic occupation, he preferred republican emancipation to Prussian feudalism and absolutism. Perhaps his most unappealing piece of political agitation was the bloodthirsty anti-French diatribe *Katechismus der Deutschen* (1809; Catechism of the Germans).

Kleist's first play, *Die Familie Schroffenstein* (1803; *The Feud of the Schroffensteins*), is a Gothic melodrama with echoes of Shakespeare's *Romeo and Juliet,* in which the intuitive trust of the young lovers proves helpless against the accidents, misunderstandings, and enmities that destroy them. In this work, the very evidence of the senses is misinterpreted by both the intellect and the emotions. His next two plays mix hope with anxiety. In *Amphitryon* (1807), an adaptation of Plautus and Molière, the tragicomedy set in motion by Jupiter's impersonation of the title hero in order to seduce his wife Alkmene—paralleled by the farcical masquerade of Mercury as the servant Sosias—raises vexed questions about personal identity, the fallibility of perception, and the trustworthiness of love. The gods' abuse of the humans creates a painful sense of bewilderment in spite of some suggestions of divine favor. In *Der zerbrochne Krug* (1811; translated as *The Broken Pitcher* and *The Broken Jug*), a rural comedy with overtones of Greek and biblical myth, the truth gradually emerges as the village judge Adam convicts himself of his own advances to the virtuous Eve, but a dark background to the fun is provided through the almost fatal distrust of Eve's fiancé and the dishonesty of the supposed dispensers of justice.

Two subsequent plays, as Kleist himself noted, are complementary, with one heroine excelling in energetic activity and the other in passive submission. In *Penthesilea* (1808), a protoFreudian tragedy based on a legend from antiquity, the inefficacy of the intellect is compounded by the ambivalence of emotion as the Amazon queen, after many misunderstandings, slaughters the Greek warrior Achilles in a paroxysm of love and hate, before bringing about her own death by a sheer effort of the will. Her rebellion against an old custom forbidding Amazons to seek out their own opponents in love and war may seem to plead for individual liberty, but the lethal confusion wreaked by sadomasochistic urges predominates. In *Das Käthchen von Heilbronn* (1810; translated as *Kate of Heilbronn* and *Käthchen of Heilbronn*), a medievalizing chivalric romance, an unwavering devotion based on suprasensory promises prevails as the apparently plebeian Käthchen, who later proves to be the emperor's daughter, conquers the reluctant Count Wetter vom Strahl against all reasonable expectations, but renewed hints of sado-masochism and aristocratic despotism tarnish the celebration of intuition triumphant.

Die Hermannsschlacht (1821; Arminius's Battle)—ostensibly about the battle of the Teutoburg Forest in A.D. 9, in which the Romans were defeated for the first time on Germanic soil by the Cheruscan chieftain of the title—is little more than a tract designed to rouse Prussia and Austria against Napoléon, and it shows Kleist at his chauvinistic worst. In contrast, his vaguely historical last play, *Prinz Friedrich von Homburg* (1821; translated as *The Prince of Homburg* and *Prince Frederick of Homburg*), is generally acclaimed as his masterpiece, although it offended the Prussian nobility in its own day. Winning a battle by disobeying orders, the eponymous hero is sentenced to death for insubordination. After reaching a nadir of abject fear, he rises to welcome the prospect of atonement but is finally pardoned and rehabilitated. Thus, Kleist apparently accomplishes, in the manner of Schiller, a classical reconciliation between inclination and duty, between rebellious self-assertion and compliance with law and order. Once again, however, misconceptions abound; destiny as embodied in the all-powerful but capricious elector remains arbitrary; the glorification of the Prussian state rings hollow; and the happy ending, which fulfills the hero's initial somnambulistic mirage of love and glory, is literally called "a dream."

Among Kleist's stories, which were collected in two volumes during the last two years of his life, five are habitually regarded as outstanding. They unite extraordinary events—the traditional subject matter of the *Novelle* genre—with a wealth of accurately observed concrete facts. Their eminently dramatic qualities bears close affinities to those of the plays.

In *Das Erdbeben in Chili* (1807; The Chilean Earthquake), a young couple is lynched in a resurgence of religious bigotry that occurs after a brief idyll of pastoral peace in the open countryside following the collapse of the city. Mass hysteria, inflamed by fanatical demagogues, plays havoc with humanity, and the depravity of civilization overwhelms the purity of nature. In *Die Verlobung in St. Domingo* (1811; The Betrothal in San Domingo), set in a context of political revolution and racial strife, the hero, misinterpreting the heroine's attempt to save his life during a colonial uprising, kills her and, on learning the truth, kills himself; his story demonstrates the inability of the individual to surmount the artificial divisions between people. In *Die Marquise von O . . .* (1808; The Marquise of O—), the conundrum of the celibate but pregnant heroine is precariously resolved when she challenges the patriarchal conventions of her upper-class family in order to obtain the confession of her future husband, who raped her while she was unconscious. In *Der Zweikampf* (1811; The Duel), commonly accepted appearances prove false as the champion's belief in his lady's innocence is vindicated when he recovers from a near-fatal wound sustained in the trial by ordeal, while the villain, whose alibi rested on delusion, dies of a slight injury. In *Michael Kohlhaas* (1810), Kleist's most remarkable story, a righteous horse dealer becomes a vindictive outlaw when he is denied a fair hearing by a corrupt legal and political system that is ruled by nepotism and treachery up to the highest levels of society. With supernatural aid, Kohlhaas's grievances are redressed and his enemies are punished, but he must pay for his victory by suffering a brutal execution.

All of Kleist's plays and stories implicitly criticize contemporary social and political institutions, but the psychological, existential, and metaphysical issues that they address carry more weight. Love, trust, and intuitive confidence thrive in some cases and perish in others. In all cases, deceptive appearances, intellectual fallacies, and emotional disturbances, allied with strange coincidences and arcane interventions, proclaim the irrationality and mystery of existence.

The highly original, although not deliberately experimental, forms of Kleist's plays and stories are marked by ambiguity, irony, and paradox. His characters follow their peculiar destinies outside the realm of logic, often unaware of their own motivation. Faced with baffling situations, locked in fierce conflicts or painful isolation, and obeying impulses they can neither understand nor control, they display extreme reactions rather than normal human behavior. His superbly timed actions progress through cyclic recurrences, sudden reversals, abrupt contrasts, and complex symbolic variations on a relatively small array of puzzling themes, while his insistence on precision of detail in the midst of upheaval and confusion invests his subjective concerns with a semblance of objectivity and provides solid realistic foundations for his enigmatic visions.

His supreme achievement is his language. Flouting the rules of standard grammar, syntax, and prosody—changing the customary succession of phrases; inventing bold new metaphors; oscillating between passionate outbursts and clinical precision; blending fantasy with matter-of-factness and dryness with lyricism; alternating between luxuriant rhetoric and explosive compression; reveling in puns, quibbles, equivocations, double entendres, and relentless question-and-answer sequences; checking intricate hypotactic periods with exclamations, clarifications, and qualifications before rushing headlong to their conclusion; and, when words fail, resorting to speechless gestures, blushing, and fainting—he conveys meaning mimetically by the sound and movement of his sentences, paragraphs, and dialogues. To an unprecedented degree and rarely equaled since in German literature, he uses language not to discuss ideas in abstract conceptual terms or to supply discursive expositions, descriptions, and analyses but to re-create the very essence of experience through structure.

It is this unique command of dramatic, narrative, and linguistic devices that enables Kleist to impose an aesthetic pattern on an incomprehensible world and to turn his perplexities into magnificent art.

LADISLAUS LÖB

Biography

Born in Frankfurt, Brandenburg, 18 October 1777. Served in the Prussian army, 1792, and saw action in the siege of Mainz, 1793; promoted to second lieutenant and resigned his commission, 1799; studied law, University of Frankfurt, 1799; in Paris and Switzerland, 1800–1804; civil servant, Königsberg, 1805–6; cofounded, with Adam Müller, and edited *Phöbus*, Dresden, 1808–9; unsuccessful attempt to publish the newspaper *Germania*, Prague, 1809; edited, *Berliner Abendblätter*, 1810–11. Died (suicide) 21 November 1811.

Selected Works

Collections

Hinterlassene Schriften, edited by Ludwig Tieck, 1821
Gesammelte Schriften, edited by Ludwig Tieck, 3 vols., 1826
Werke, edited by Erich Schmidt et al., 5 vols., 1904–5
Sämtliche Werke und Briefe, edited by Helmut Sembdner, 2 vols., 1961; 5th revised edition, 1970
Selected Writings, edited and translated by David Constantine, 1997

Sämtliche Werke und Briefe in vier Bänden, edited by Ilse-Marie Barth et al., 1987–97

Plays

Die Familie Schroffenstein (produced 1804), 1803; as *The Feud of the Schroffensteins,* translated by Mary J. and Lawrence M. Price, 1916

Amphitryon (produced 1899), 1807; as *Amphitryon,* translated by Marion Sonnenfeld, 1962; translated by Charles E. Passage, in *Amphitryon: Three Plays in New Verse Translations,* 1973; translated by Martin Greenberg, in *Five Plays,* 1988

Der zerbrochne Krug (produced 1808), 1811; edited by Richard H. Samuel, 1968; as *The Broken Pitcher,* translated by Bayard Quincy Morgan, 1961; translated by Jon Swan, in *Plays,* 1982; as *The Broken Jug,* translated by Lawrence P.R. Wilson, in *Four Continental Plays,* edited by John P. Allen, 1964; translated by Roger Jones, 1977; translated by Martin Greenberg, in *Five Plays,* 1988; translated by David Constantine, in *Selected Writings,* 1997

Penthesilea (produced 1876), 1808; as *Penthesilea,* translated by Humphry Trevelyan, in *The Classic Theatre,* vol. 2, edited by Eric Bentley, 1959 (also published in *Plays,* 1982); translated by Martin Greenberg, in *Five Plays,* 1988

Das Käthchen von Heilbronn (produced 1810), 1810; as *Kate of Heilbronn,* translated by Elijah B. Impey, in *Illustrations of German Poetry,* 1841; as *Käthchen of Heilbronn; or, The Test of Fire,* translated by Frederick E. Pierce, in *Fiction and Fantasy of German Literature,* 1927

Prinz Friedrich von Homburg (produced 1821); in *Hinterlassene Schriften,* 1821; as *The Prince of Homburg,* translated by Charles E. Passage, 1956; translated by James Kirkup, in *The Classic Theatre,* vol. 2, edited by Eric Bentley, 1959; as *Prince Frederick of Homburg,* translated by Peggy Meyer Sherry, in *Plays,* 1982; translated by Martin Greenberg, in *Five Plays,* 1988

Die Hermannsschlacht (produced 1839); in *Hinterlassene Schriften,* 1821

Robert Guiscard (unfinished; produced 1901); in *Gesammelte Schriften,* 1826; as *A Fragment of the Tragedy of Robert Guiscard,* translated by Martin Greenberg, in *Five Plays,* 1988

Plays (The Broken Pitcher; Amphitryon; Penthesilea; Prince Frederick of Homburg), edited by Walter Hinderer, 1982

Five Plays (includes Amphitryon; The Broken Jug; Penthesilea; Prince Frederick of Homburg; A Fragment of the Tragedy of Robert Guiscard), translated by Martin Greenberg, 1988

Fiction

Die Marquise von O . . . , 1808; as *The Marquise of O—,* translated by Martin Greenberg, in *The Marquise of O—, and Other Stories,* 1960; translated by David Luke and Nigel Reeves, in *The Marquise of O—, and Other Stories,* 1978

Erzählungen, 2 vols., 1810–11

Michael Kohlhaas, in *Erzählungen,* 1810; translated by J. Oxenford, 1844; translated by F. Lloyd and W. Newton, 1875; translated by F.H. King, 1919; translated by James Kirkup, 1967; translated by Harry Steinhauer, in *Twelve German Novellas,* 1977; translated by David Luke and Nigel Reeves, in *The Marquise of O—, and Other Stories,* 1978; translated by David Constantine, in *Selected Writings,* 1997

Other

Briefe an seine Schwester Ulrike, edited by August Koberstein, 1860

Briefe an seine Braut, edited by Karl Biedermann et al., 1884

Über das Marionettentheater: Aufsätze und Anekdoten (published in the *Berliner Abendblätter*), 1810; edited by Helmut Sembdner, 1935; as *On a Theatre of Marionettes,* translated by G. Wilford, 1989; as *On Puppetshows,* translated by David Paisley, 1991

Geschichte meiner Seele: Das Lebenszeugnis der Briefe, edited by Helmut Sembdner, 1977

An Abyss Deep Enough: Letters of Heinrich von Kleist (includes essays), edited and translated by Philip B. Miller, 1982

Further Reading

Allan, Seán, *The Plays of Heinrich von Kleist: Ideals and Illusions,* Cambridge and New York: Cambridge University Press, 1996

Blöcker, Günter, *Heinrich von Kleist; oder, Das absolute Ich,* Berlin: Argon, 1960

Dyer, Denys, *The Stories of Kleist: A Critical Study,* London: Duckworth, and New York: Holmes and Meier, 1977

Ellis, John M., *Heinrich von Kleist: Studies in the Character and Meaning of His Writings,* Chapel Hill: University of North Carolina Press, 1979

Fricke, Gerhard, *Gefühl und Schicksal bei Heinrich von Kleist: Studien über den inneren Vorgang im Leben und Schaffen des Dichters,* Berlin: Junker und Dünnhaupt, 1929; reprint, New York: AMS Press, 1975

Gearey, John, *Heinrich von Kleist: A Study in Tragedy and Anxiety,* Philadelphia: University of Pennsylvania Press, 1968

Graham, Ilse, *Heinrich von Kleist: Word into Flesh: A Poet's Quest for the Symbol,* Berlin and New York: de Gruyter, 1977

Helbling, Robert E., *The Major Works of Heinrich von Kleist,* New York: New Directions, 1975

Hinderer, Walter, editor, *Kleists Dramen: Neue Interpretationen,* Stuttgart: Reclam, 1981

Holz, Hans Heinz, *Macht und Ohnmacht der Sprache: Untersuchungen zum Sprachverständnis und Stil Heinrich von Kleists,* Frankfurt: Athenäum, 1962

Kreutzer, Hans Joachim, *Die dichterische Entwicklung Heinrichs von Kleist,* Berlin: Schmidt, 1968

Maass, Joachim, *Kleist: Die Geschichte seines Lebens,* Bern and Munich: Scherz, 1977; as *Kleist: A Biography,* translated by Ralph Manheim, New York: Farrar, Straus, and Giroux, 1983

Mayer, Hans, *Heinrich von Kleist: Der geschichtliche Augenblick,* Pfullingen: Neske, 1962

McGlathery, James M., *Desire's Sway: The Plays and Stories of Heinrich von Kleist,* Detroit, Michigan: Wayne State University Press, 1983

Müller-Seidel, Walter, *Versehen und Erkennen: Eine Studie über Heinrich von Kleist,* Cologne: Böhlau, 1961; 3rd edition, 1971

Müller-Seidel, Walter, editor, *Heinrich von Kleist: Aufsätze und Essays,* Darmstadt: Wissenschaftliche Buchgesellschaft, 1967; 3rd edition, 1980

———, editor, *Kleists Aktualität: Neue Aufsätze und Essays, 1966–1978,* Darmstadt: Wissenschaftliche Buchgesellschaft, 1981

Sembdner, Helmut, editor, *Heinrich von Kleists Lebensspuren: Dokumente und Berichte der Zeitgenossen,* Bremen: Schünemann, 1957; 7th edition, Munich: Hanser, 1996

———, editor, *Heinrich von Kleists Nachruhm: Eine Wirkungsgeschichte in Dokumenten,* Bremen: Schünemann, 1967; 4th edition, Munich: Hanser, 1996

Stephens, Anthony R., *Heinrich von Kleist: The Dramas and Stories,* Oxford and Providence, Rhode Island: Berg, 1994

Streller, Siegfried, *Das dramatische Werk Heinrich von Kleists,* Berlin: Rütten und Loening, 1966

Wichmann, Thomas, *Heinrich von Kleist,* Stuttgart: Metzler, 1988

Michael Kohlhaas 1810
Novella by Heinrich von Kleist

The story of "one of the most upright (*rechtschaffensten*) but at the same time one of the most terrible (*entsetzlichsten*) men of his day"—a model citizen "had he not taken one virtue to excess" (*wenn er in einer Tugend nicht ausgeschweift hätte*)—runs to almost 100 immensely detailed and breathlessly action-packed pages with a seemingly endless cast of characters, making it by far the longest and most complex of Heinrich von Kleist's narratives and one of the most celebrated—and controversial—works in German literature.

It was Kleist's intention to entitle the volume of *Erzählungen* containing *Michael Kohlhaas, Das Erdbeben in Chili,* and *Die Marquise von O . . .* "moral tales." Kohlhaas the honest Brandenburg horse dealer, whose "sense of justice made him a robber and a murderer" while seeking redress—first within the law, then without—for two horses unlawfully seized and maltreated by a Saxon *Junker,* clearly embodies a moral dilemma. When this "vexatious litigant" (*unnützer Querulant*) is denied the protection of the law by nepotistic, Machiavellian, or simply corrupt tribunals, he is effectively expelled into a "state of nature" in which he must take the law into his own hands. He does so only after the most painstaking self-scrutiny—in a realistic, even conciliatory, recognition of the way of the world, that frail institution (*die gebrechliche Einrichtung der Welt,* a recurrent Kleistian motif)—but equally in the altruistic determination of "his well-bred soul" (*seine wohlerzogene Seele*) to right a wrong. His pain at witnessing the terrible state of chaos in the world (*die Welt in einer so ungeheuren Unordnung zu erblicken*) is balanced, we are told, by a sense of his own integrity (*seine Brust nunmehr in Ordnung zu sehen*); his wife's maltreatment and death after her attempted intercession on his behalf, however, ultimately tips the "goldsmith's scales" (*Goldwaage*) of his sense of justice into "the business of revenge."

This much was covered in the fragment of the story (roughly the first quarter) that Kleist published in his Dresden journal *Phöbus* in 1808. What follows is the complementary extreme to Kohlhaas's *Rechtschaffenheit,* as his feud escalates into armed rebellion (in his eyes, a "just war") against those who, however reluctantly, shield his enemy. He puts Wittenberg and Leipzig to the torch, styles himself the Archangel Michael, answerable to God alone, and issues with chiliastic fervor proclamations from "the seat of our provisional world government." According to the generally partisan narrator, however, this last act is "an hysterically twisted, pathological act" (*eine Schwärmerei krankhafter und mißgeschaffener Art*). The narrator's censoriousness here anticipates Goethe's stigmatization of the story for pursuing "a single grievance with such single-minded hypochondria" (compare Goethe's abhorrence of Penthesilea's "cannibalistic" violence). But the issue of whether we should condemn or applaud Kohlhaas, or some combination of the two, is only part of a much wider questioning of the social contract between state and individual, the relationship between what is legally and what is morally right. These arguments were familiar to Kleist from his readings of Rousseau, Garve, Kant, Gentz, Rehberg, and others, and he (anachronistically) superimposed them on the conflicting codes of Kohlhaas's own absolutist times (the *Reichlandsfrieden* of 1495 and the 1532 *Carolina* or *Strafgerichtsordnung* of Charles V, which readmitted feuding under certain conditions).

In changing the name of the historical Hans Kohlhase (of the 16th-century *Maerckische Chronic,* Kleist's source) to Michael, it is, indeed, the Archangel's role as implacable dispenser of absolute justice (whatever the price—*fiat iustitia pereat mundus*) that Kleist has arrogated to his protagonist over if not above the Christian obligation to forgive, on which both his dying wife

and—in the story's dramatic, if unhistorical, central confrontation—Martin Luther vainly insist. Luther (whose well-known letter to Hans Kohlhase of 1534 is very different from that in Kleist's version) is obliged to acknowledge that Kohlhaas has been "outlawed" (*verstoßen*) and arranges an amnesty enabling Kohlhaas to return to the social order he holds dear. But its effect is to deprive Kohlhaas once again of his autonomy, as he is implicated in a wicked henchman's violence (echoes of Schiller's *The Robbers,* and throughout of *Wallenstein* and *The Dishonoured Irreclaimable*) and enveloped in an increasingly impenetrable fog of unhappy chance and unforeseen circumstance, not least the legal paraphernalia and labyrinthine documents (we are bombarded by over 90 throughout the story) that frustrate the Kleistian ideal of direct communication—here, access to the personal source of authority. All this, combined with the scenes of surrealistic black comedy in what was understandably Kafka's *Lieblingswerk* (favorite work; Max Brod), conspires to retard a fleetingly glimpsed "happy end"—the peripeteia of the drama Kleist allegedly felt "infinitely humiliated" not to have written instead of a mere narrative.

Kohlhaas's case escalates and polarizes between separate jurisdictions. The Elector of Saxony evolves into his main antagonist, and Kohlhaas has triumphant revenge through the supernatural agency of a gypsy woman, a reincarnation of Kohlhaas's dead wife, whose mysterious prophecy of the end of the Elector's line destroys him. This intrusion of the numinous, or nemesis, as an even higher authority into a generally realistic tale was already criticized by Tieck, Kleist's first editor, as a sop to contemporary "Romantic" fashion, but it is also of a piece with the overriding "prophetic" dimension of much of Kleist's work: his vehement, if necessarily mainly covert, attacks on Napoleon, which construe the way in which the master of Europe might be overthrown by whatever means.

In the *Katechismus der Deutschen* (1809; Catechism of the Germans), "no obedience is due" to the "unpatriotic" Bonapartist King of Saxony (Friedrich August I), misled as he is—like his predecessor in *Michael Kohlhaas*—by "corrupt advisers." Kleist supported the moves of such Prussian patriots as Stein, Gneisenau, and Scharnhorst to push Friedrich Wilhelm III, King of Prussia, into a war of liberation, pending which the individual, unauthorized initiatives of Prince Louis Ferdinand and Major Ferdinand von Schill had his blessing. In *Prinz Friedrich von Homburg* (1821; *Prince Frederick of Homburg*), the Prince also "takes the law into his own hands," although he is ultimately reprieved by the wise "Great Elector" of Brandenburg. *His* predecessor in *Michael Kohlhaas* ultimately dispenses justice, although the erstwhile insurgent is executed for having violated imperial law—the highest earthly authority. But he dies—in a similarly dreamlike ending—with a clear conscience, fully reconciled, his memory vicariously honored through the ennoblement of his sons, and with the same serenity Kleist himself professed before committing suicide, shortly after the publication of *Michael Kohlhaas* and before the Prussian *Landsturmedikt* of 1813 unleashed the people against Napoleon.

FRED BRIDGHAM

Editions

First edition: in *Erzählungen,* vol. 1, Berlin: Realschulbuchhandlung, 1810

Critical edition: in *Sämtliche Werke und Briefe in vier Bänden,* vol. 3, edited by Klaus Müller-Salget, Frankfurt: Deutscher Klassiker Verlag, 1990

Translation: "Michael Kohlhaas," translated by David Constantine, in *Selected Writings*, London: Dent, 1997

Further Reading

Dyer, Denys, "*Michael Kohlhaas*," in *The Stories of Kleist: A Critical Study*, London: Duckworth, and New York: Holmes and Meier, 1977

Graham, Ilse, "*Universalium in Re: Michael Kohlhaas*," in *Heinrich von Kleist: Word into Flesh: A Poet's Quest for the Symbol*, Berlin and New York: de Gruyter, 1977

Helbling, Robert E., "The Search for Justice: *Michael Kohlhaas*," in *The Major Works of Heinrich von Kleist*, New York: New Directions, 1975

Horn, Peter, "Was geht uns eigentlich der Gerechtigkeitsbegriff in Kleists Erzählung *Michael Kohlhaas* noch an?" in *Heinrich von Kleists Erzählungen: Eine Einführung*, Königstein: Scriptor, 1978

Kittler, Wolf, "Insurrektion als staatsbürgerliche Pflicht," in *Die Geburt des Partisanen aus dem Geist der Poesie: Heinrich von Kleist und die Strategie der Befreiungskriege*, Freiburg: Rombach, 1987

Stephens, Anthony, "*Michael Kohlhaas*," in *Heinrich von Kleist: The Dramas and Stories*, Oxford and Providence, Rhode Island: Berg, 1994

Penthesilea 1808

Play by Heinrich von Kleist

Heinrich von Kleist's contemporaries greeted the publication of *Penthesilea* (1808) mostly with ridicule. They were scandalized by one of the most improbable and disturbing scenes in German literature: the Amazon queen, Penthesilea, who had entrusted Achilles with her love, feels deeply betrayed by his challenge for single combat and attacks Achilles in a fit of rage with teams of dogs and elephants, siccing a pack of dogs on him and, like a she-dog, joining them in tearing him to pieces, "blood dripping from her mouth and hands." The publisher, who had printed it sight unseen, was embarrassed and refused to market it. Goethe, to whom Kleist had sent an "Organic Fragment," declined to stage a performance, as he needed time to get acquainted with the "strange and alien regions" the play moved in. He found some parts of the tragedy "highly comical," especially the scene where Penthesilea assures Achilles that having only one breast would not diminish her love for him.

A century later, the Expressionists discovered an affinity to the "strange" world Kleist had explored. They could identify with his vision of a new human being and were captivated by the expressive power of Kleist's language: "In his own time he had to perish . . . proudly we say: we are blood of his blood, and spirit of his spirit. . . . ," "Kleist created the absolute human being—that was us! . . . the new human being was born . . . the modern human being!" (Sembdner, 1967). Kleist's "modernity" had been discovered. From rejection, ridicule, and revulsion, the pendulum of Kleist's reception had swung to extravagant praise, including "Next to Goethe's *Faust*, *Penthesilea* stands as the highest pinnacle of art"; "*Penthesilea*: a power of language, unheard of"; and ". . . the German language has never produced anything more beautiful" (Sieck). The play inspired a great number of other artists, notably Hugo Wolf, with *Penthesilea: Sym-*

phonische Dichtung; Othmar Schoeck, with *Penthesilea: Oper;* Oskar Kokoschka, with *Kleist: Penthesilea,* which consists of ten needle-etchings; and Joseph Thorak, with *Penthesilea: A Monumental Statue,* which can be seen today in Berlin-Tiergarten. Stagings of the play, however, have been rare. The original was produced for the first time on the 100th anniversary of Kleist's death on two stages in Berlin: at the Royal Theatre by Paul Lindau and at the Deutsches Theater under the directorship of Max Reinhardt. Marlene Dietrich, at age 21, played Penthesilea on this stage in a 1923 production. The 1970s and 1980s saw fewer than ten stagings, including two multimedia productions.

Penthesilea is eminently unplayable (unlike *Prinz Friedrich von Homburg* [*Prince Frederick of Homburg*] and *Der zerbrochne Krug* [*The Broken Jug*], which are frequently performed) for two reasons: the frequent use of teichoscopia and lengthy reports to convey the action, and the use of excessive imagery, similes, and extended metaphors. While the play has the most magnificent battle scenes ever created in language, they cannot be seen but must be heard by the audience. Instead of *seeing* Penthesilea and Achilles chase each other, the spectator hears images and the hyperbolic metaphors chase each other: two "stars" crashing into each other, two "bolts of lightning" shattering each other's armor. Penthesilea's horse "flies" and "devours" the road. And she dies by a metaphor ten lines long that shapes a dagger from her feelings of despair. A plethora of other images expresses the paradoxical, grotesque, bizarre, and absurd nature of life's situations—very unclassical and appealing to the modern consciousness. One of Kleist's favorite metaphors, which succinctly sums up the contradiction inherent in Penthesilea's predicament, concludes the tragedy:

> She fell because she bloomed too proud and strong!
> The dead oak withstands the storm, while the healthy one comes
> crashing down because the gale can grasp it by its crown.

Penthesilea is doomed from the beginning, not because of any character flaw (she excels in both love and war), but by the necessity of making impossible choices. Her mission as the queen of the Amazons is accomplished quickly: they have thousands of captives and are eagerly waiting for the queen to lead them home in triumph for the "sacred Rose-Festival," a time of lavish feasting and mating. But to the consternation of all, the queen now says: "Defiance and contradiction is my soul." Defiance of what? No one comprehends: the queen has gone "insane." What they do not know is that her mother had secretly divulged the name of Penthesilea's mate: "You will crown with a wreath the Pelide" (i.e., the famed Achilles, the slayer of Hector). Moreover, when she first lays eyes on him, the "God of Love" descends upon her. This is in direct contradiction to the "Law of Tanaïs," which forbids individual choice; according to this law, Mars decides, and a "Mars-Bride's" mate is whomever she captures in battle. Abiding by the "Law" and "fulfilling the last will" of her mother are both equally "sacred" to Penthesilea. Thus, having to perform two mutually exclusive duties becomes her destiny and constitutes the dramatic plot: Penthesilea must *live* and fulfill two contradictory destinies, only to be crushed in the process by the contradictions.

For a brief moment in scene 15 (the play has 24 scenes, but no acts so as not to impede its relentless action), Kleist lets the two destinies converge when Penthesilea thinks that she has conquered Achilles (her friend Prothoe had persuaded Achilles to let her think so). It is a moment of exultation: her highest and only goal in life, the summum bonum (*des Lebens höchstes Gut*) has been achieved. Thus, as she prepares for a sumptuous Rose-Festival, all the charm, grace, and tenderness of her being, "born of a nightingale," shine through and the full "radiance and splendor" of her soul unfolds. Tragically, both her state of eudaemonism and her state of despairing senseless rage are based on a false perception of reality. Achilles's challenge for single combat had been a ruse: acceding to her "whim" that she *must* conquer her beloved in combat, he had come unprepared, ready for capture and love, and not for combat. His last words— "Penthesilea! My bride! What are you doing? Is this the Rose-Festival that you promised?"—die away in the void, with no humans, no gods to hear them. This Kafkaesque scene of utter isolation epitomizes the incongruities, the glaring dissonances between the promises and the realities of life (Kafka called Kleist his "blood-brother").

Having kissed his mangled body farewell, Penthesilea joins her beloved in death, renouncing the "Law of the Amazons" and admonishing the High-Priestess: "The ashes of Queen Tanaïs—scatter them to the winds!" Thus, the text presents an indictment of a sociopolitical reality, where love is reduced to a calculable event ("yearly calculations" determine the time for the male-hunt) and where a woman has to mutilate her body and subdue her lover by the sword. The "dagger" with which Penthesilea kills herself is made from the "fires of woe and remorse" but forged also on "hope's eternal anvil" (i.e., the hope that a future generation will have laws allowing for human fulfillment). The progenitor of this generation was to be the "God of Earth," created by Penthesilea and Achilles and, thus, combining strength and beauty of soul. Prometheus would have then risen and declared to the human race: "Hier ward ein Mensch, so hab ich ihn gewollt!" (A human being is born as I had intended him/her).

Kleist had high hopes for *Penthesilea*. It was to take the place of the failed drama *Robert Guiscard*, with which he had hoped to become the foremost playwright of his nation, tearing the wreath from Goethe's brow—a situation that is mirrored in Penthesilea's relentless chase of Achilles: "the wreath of fame and glory" ever so near yet forever eluding. He said of *Penthesilea*: "My innermost being is in it . . . all the filth (*Schmutz*) as well as all the radiance and splendor (*Glanz*) of my soul." Utterly disillusioned, and also depressed by the oppressive sociopolitical conditions of his time, Kleist, too, ended his young life, departing for a "better world, where we can embrace each other with the love of angels."

RAIMUND BELGARDT

Editions

First edition: *Penthesilea: Ein Trauerspiel von Heinrich von Kleist*, Tübingen: Cotta, 1808
Critical editions: in *Sämtliche Werke und Briefe*, 3rd ed., vol. 1, edited by Helmut Sembdner, München: Carl Hanser, 1964; in *Sämtliche Werke und Briefe in vier Bänden*, vol. 2, edited by Ilse-Marie Barth and Hinrich C. Seeba, Frankfurt: Deutscher Klassiker Verlag, 1987
Translations: in *Plays*, translated by Humphry Trevelyan, New York: Continuum, 1982; in *Five Plays*, translated by Martin Greenberg, New Haven, Connecticut: Yale University Press, 1988

Further Reading
Allan, Seán, *The Plays of Heinrich von Kleist: Ideals and Illusions*, Cambridge and New York: Cambridge University Press, 1996
Angress, Ruth K., "Kleist's Nation of Amazons," in *Beyond the Eternal Feminine: Critical Essays on Women and German literature*, edited by Susan L. Cocalis and Kay Goodman, Stuttgart: Heinz, 1982
Appelt, Hedwig, and Maximilian Netz, *Heinrich von Kleist: "Penthesilea,"* Stuttgart: Reclam, 1992
Brown, Hilda, "Penthesilea: Nightingale and Amazon," *Oxford German Studies* 7 (1972)
———, *Kleist and the Tragic Ideal: A Study of "Penthesilea" and Its Relationship to Kleist's Personal and Literary Development, 1806–1808*, European University Papers: German Language and Literature, vol. 203, Bern and Las Vegas, Nevada: Lang, 1977
Chaouli, Michel, "Devouring Metaphor: Disgust and Taste in Kleist's *Penthesilea*," *German Quarterly* 69, no. 2 (1996)
Cullens, Chris, and Dorothea von Mücke, "Love in Kleist's *Penthesilea* and *Käthchen von Heilbronn*," *Deutsche Vierteljahrsschrift für Literaturwissenschaft und Geistesgeschichte* 63 (1989)
Durzak, Manfred, "Das Gesetz der Athene und das Gesetz der Tanaïs: Zur Funktion des Mythischen in Kleists *Penthesilea*," *Jahrbuch des Freien Deutschen Hochstifts* (1973)
Gallas, Helga, "Kleist's *Penthesilea* und Lacans vier Diskurse," in *Frauensprache, Frauenliteratur: Für und Wider einer Psychoanalyse literarischer Werke*, edited by Inge Stephan and Carl Pietzcker, Tübingen: Niemeyer, 1986
———, "Antikenrezeption bei Goethe und Kleist: Penthesilea—eine Anti-Iphigenie?" in *Momentum dramaticum: Festschrift für Eckehard Catholy*, edited by Linda Dietrick and David G. John, Waterloo: University of Waterloo Press, 1990
Hubbs, Valentine, "The Plus and Minus of Penthesilea and Käthchen," *Seminar* 6 (1970)
Müller-Seidel, Walter, "*Penthesilea* im Kontext der deutschen Klassik," in *Kleists Dramen: Neue Interpretationen*, edited by Walter Hinderer, Stuttgart: Reclam, 1981
Nutz, Maximilian, "Lektüre der Sinne: Kleists *Penthesilea* als Körperdrama," in *Heinrich von Kleist: Studien zu Werk und Wirkung*, edited by Dirk Grathoff and Klaus-Michael Bogdal, Opladen: Westdeutscher Verlag, 1988
Paulin, Roger, "Kleist's Metamorphoses: Some Remarks on the Use of Mythology in *Penthesilea*," *Oxford German Studies* 14 (1983)
Prandi, Julie D., "Woman Warrior as Hero: Schiller's *Jungfrau von Orleans* and Kleist's *Penthesilea*," *Monatshefte* 77 (1985)
Sembdner, Helmut, editor, *Heinrich von Kleist, "Penthesilea": Dokumente und Zeugnisse*, Frankfurt: Insel, 1967
———, editor, *Heinrich von Kleists Nachruhm: Eine Wirkungsgeschichte in Dokumenten*, Frankfurt: Insel, 1984
Sieck, Albrecht, *Kleists "Penthesilea": Versuch einer neuen Interpretation*, Bonn: Bouvier, 1976

Der zerbrochne Krug 1811

Play by Heinrich von Kleist

Der zerbrochne Krug (translated as *The Broken Pitcher* and *The Broken Jug*) was begun in Bern in 1803 and completed in Königsberg in 1806 as Kleist's entry for a competition with three other young writers: Heinrich Zschokke, Ludwig Wieland, and Heinrich Geßner. The four friends had agreed to write, respectively, a comedy, a short story, a verse satire, and a poetic idyll on the subject matter of an etching titled *Le juge ou la cruche* cassée (*The Judge or the Broken Jug*) by Jean Jacques Le Veau after a late 18th-century painting by Louis Philibert Debucourt, which in its turn was based on Jean Baptiste Creuze's acclaimed rococo painting *La cruche cassée*. Kleist won, giving the German theater one of its rare comic masterpieces.

Adapting the French model to the style of the Flemish painter David Teniers, Kleist set his play in a Dutch village in the late 17th century. The peasant woman Marthe Rull accuses Ruprecht, a young farmer engaged to her daughter Eve, of breaking the eponymous jug on a nocturnal visit to Eve's bedroom. The village judge, Adam, is obliged to investigate the case in the coincidental presence of the district judge, Walter, revealing that he himself broke the jug when, caught by Ruprecht in the act of trying to seduce Eve, he escaped through her window, losing his wig and being hit over the head in the process. Adam is sacked, and Ruprecht and Eve are united, but Marthe, with the jug still broken, is left to appeal to a higher court for any compensation.

The 13 consecutive scenes form an analytical drama of detection that rigorously observes the classical unities of time, place, and action. Kleist depicts contemporary German village life, thinly disguised by the Dutch setting, through accurately drawn rustic characters and a dialogue cast in blank verse but abounding in everyday speech rhythms, popular proverbs, colloquialisms, and dialect phrases. Parodying Sophocles' *King Oedipus* in the manner of Aristophanes, with echoes of Shakespeare's *Measure for Measure* and the Bible, he operates simultaneously at several levels of meaning. He derives broad comedy from the predicament of the corrupt judge, who, through his very evasions and subterfuges, is ironically maneuvered into convicting himself; from crude references to bodily functions and beatings; from the mock-heroic treatment of trivialities and the mock-epic breadth of detail within the tight plot; and above all from a dynamic language that, mimetically rather than discursively, turns confusion itself into art by ingenious syntactical and onomatopoeic effects, significant puns and quibbles, relentless questions and counterquestions, and extended metaphors with an independent existence of their own. However, his most serious preoccupations constantly break through the merriment.

At a social and political level, Adam's abuse of his office embodies, in grotesque distortion, Kleist's critique of the Prussian authorities while the shattered picture on the jug, which showed the Emperor Charles V handing the Netherlands over to his son Philip II, playfully suggests his distress at the disintegration of the old Holy Roman Empire and the subjugation of fragmented Germany in his own Napoleonic era. At a religious level, alluding to the myth of creation, Kleist associates Eve's purity with the innocence of Paradise and Adam's villainy with the fall of man and with the devil himself. At a philosophical level, the trial, which provides the most sustained example of Kleist's favorite device of cross-examination, dramatizes the search for knowledge that lies at the center of all his writings. Eve especially is thrown into a painful dilemma by Ruprecht's suspicions about her fidelity and Adam's threats to send Ruprecht to war if she exposes his advances. Her demand for absolute trust represents Kleist's recurrent plea for the supremacy of intuition over reason and for a belief transcending both the evidence of the senses and the conclusions of the intellect—a longing contradicted by grave doubts epitomized by his famous "Kant crisis" of 1801, when he decided that objective truth was inaccessible to

the human mind with its subjective categories of perception. The misunderstandings and errors that plague all the characters, whether by default or design, proclaim his despair over what he saw as the inability of thoughts and words to penetrate an enigmatic universe and to offer genuine communication between its baffled inhabitants. Although in this instance the truth is finally discovered, Kleist's skepticism persists as a dark background to the laughter.

The premiere at the Weimar court theater on 2 March 1808, directed by Goethe, proved a failure. Goethe himself claimed that the play, with its "otherwise witty and humorous subject matter," lacked "a swiftly executed action," whereas a local aristocrat, Henriette von Knebel, described it as "tasteless," "boring," and tainted with "moral leprosy." However, the real fault lay with Goethe, who used a more verbose discarded version of the text that he split into three acts, as well as with the actors' classically stilted technique and the audience's conventional squeamishness. The first truly successful productions were those of Friedrich Ludwig Schmidt, who also played Adam (Hamburg, 1820), and of Theodor Döring, whose acting of the part was subsequently imitated for many decades (Berlin, 1844). By the mid–19th century, Kleist's realism had come to be appreciated, and Friedrich Hebbel, for one, described the play as "one of those works against which only the audience can fail." The outstanding production in the early 20th century was Reinhard Buck's, with Emil Jannings as Adam (Berlin, 1918), later filmed by Gustav Ucicky (1937). Productions since World War II have often emphasized the existential, metaphysical, or sociopolitical aspects of the play rather than the comic. Most important, perhaps, were Hans Lietzau's (Berlin, 1980) and Dieter Dorn's (Munich, 1986) with Helmut Wildt and Rolf Boysen, respectively, as Adam; both are now available in video recordings of television performances. Although translations and adaptations exist in many languages, the difficulty of re-creating Kleist's unique style has curtailed the play's success on English-speaking stages. However, in German-speaking countries, it is unlikely to lose the exceptional position it holds in both literary history and the theatrical repertoire.

LADISLAUS LÖB

Editions

First edition: *Der zerbrochne Krug*, Berlin: Reimer, 1811
Critical edition: *Der zerbrochne Krug: Ein Lustspiel*, edited by Richard H. Samuel, London: Macmillan, 1968
Translations: *The Broken Jug*, translated by Martin Greenberg, in *Five Plays*, New Haven, Connecticut: Yale University Press, 1988; translated by David Constantine, in *Selected Writings*, London: Dent, 1997

Further Reading

Arntzen, Helmut, "Kleists *Der zerbrochne Krug*," in *Die ernste Komödie: Das deutsche Lustspiel von Lessing bis Kleist*, Munich: Nymphenburger, 1968
Delbrück, Hansgerd, *Kleists Weg zur Komödie: Untersuchungen zur Stellung des "Zerbrochnen Krugs" in einer Typologie des Lustspiels*, Tübingen: Niemeyer, 1974
Graham, Ilse, "The Broken Pitcher: Hero of Kleist's Comedy," *Modern Language Quarterly* 16 (1955)
Horn, Peter, "Das erschrockene Gelächter über die Entlarvung einer korrupten Obrigkeit: Kleists zwiespältige Komödie *Der zerbrochne Krug*," in *Heinrich von Kleist: Studien zu Werk und Wirkung*, edited

by Dirk Grathoff and Klaus-Michael Bogdal, Opladen: Westdeutscher Verlag, 1988

Michelsen, Peter, "Die Lügen Adams und Evas Fall: Heinrich von Kleists *Der zerbrochne Krug*," in *Geist und Zeichen: Festschrift für Arthur Henkel*, edited by Arthur Henkel and Herbert Anton, Heidelberg: Winter, 1977

Milfull, John, "Oedipus and Adam: Greek Tragedy and Christian Comedy in Kleist's *Der zerbrochne Krug*," *German Life and Letters* 27 (1973)

Müller, Harro, "Komödie als analytisches Drama: Kleists *Der zerbrochne Krug*," in *Dramatische Werke im Deutschunterricht*, Stuttgart: Klett, 1971; 2nd edition, 1975

Reeve, William C., *Kleist on Stage, 1804–1987*, Montreal: McGill-Queen's University Press, 1993

Rösch, Ewald, "Bett und Richterstuhl: Gattungsgeschichtliche Überlegungen zu Kleists Lustspiel *Der zerbrochne Krug*," in *Kritische Bewahrung: Beiträge zur deutschen Philologie: Festschrift für Werner Schröder zum 60. Geburtstag*, edited by Ernst-Joachim Schmidt, Berlin: Schmidt, 1974

Schneider, Karl Ludwig, "Heinrich von Kleists Lustspiel *Der zerbrochne Krug*," in *Das deutsche Lustspiel*, edited by Hans Steffen, Göttingen: Vandenhoeck und Ruprecht, 1968

Schrimpf, Hans Joachim, "Kleist: Der zerbrochne Krug," in *Das deutsche Drama vom Barock bis zur Gegenwart*, 2 vols., edited by Benno von Wiese, Düsseldorf: Bagel, 1958

Schunicht, Manfred, "Heinrich von Kleist: *Der zerbrochne Krug*," *Zeitschrift für Deutsche Philologie* 84 (1965)

Seidlin, Oskar, "What the Bell Tolls in Kleist's *Der zerbrochne Krug*," *Deutsche Vierteljahrschrift für Litteraturwissenschaft und Geistesgeschichte* 51 (1977)

Sembdner, Helmut, editor, *Heinrich von Kleist: "Der zerbrochne Krug": Erläuterungen und Dokumente*, Stuttgart: Reclam, 1973; revised edition, 1982

Voss, E. Theodor, "Kleists *Zerbrochner Krug* im Lichte alter und neuer Quellen," in *Wissen aus Erfahrungen: Werkbegriff und Interpretation heute: Festschrift für Herman Meyer zum 65. Geburtstag*, edited by Karl Robert Mandelkow et al., Tübingen: Niemeyer, 1976

Wittkowski, Wolfgang, "*Der zerbrochne Krug*: Gaukelspiel der Autorität, oder Kleists Kunst, Autoritätskritik durch Komödie zu verschleiern," *Sprachkunst* 12 (1981); as "*Der zerbrochne Krug*: Juggling of Authorities," in *Heinrich von Kleist Studies*, edited by Alexej Ugrinsky, New York: AMS Press, 1980

Zenke, Jürgen, "Kleist: *Der zerbrochne Krug*," in *Die deutsche Komödie: Vom Mittelalter bis zur Gegenwart*, edited by Walter Hinck, Düsseldorf: Bagel, 1977

Friedrich Gottlieb Klopstock 1724–1803

Friedrich Gottlieb Klopstock is a key figure in the revival of German literature in the mid–18th century. He embarked on his writing career with a mission: to raise German writing from perceived mediocrity to the heights of world literature, and to give poets a status equal to that of men of state by securing for them public recognition and financial security. While his life's work centered on the epic *Der Messias* (1748; final edition, 1799–1800; *The Messiah*), his reputation subsequently rested primarily on his odes. His cultural concerns are exemplified by *Die deutsche Gelehrtenrepublik* (1774; The German Republic of Letters), which enshrines his vision of a German cultural nation in a period of political disunity. Late in life, he was proud to be elected a citizen of the new French Republic, and he committed himself publicly to the ideals of the French Revolution.

As the culmination of his classical education at the humanist foundation *Schulpforta* (1739–45), Klopstock set out to compose a national epic, the most prestigious genre according to Renaissance tradition. *Der Messias* was designed to emulate Homer and Virgil and to take up the challenge posed by Milton's *Paradise Lost*. This took Klopstock into the heart of the literary feud between the rationalist Gottsched in Leipzig, and Bodmer and Breitinger in Zurich, who invoked the supernatural as the proper realm of poetry and advocated the imagination as the prime poetic faculty. Heralding Klopstock as the German Milton, Bodmer invited his protégé to Zurich. His support established the basis for the success of the epic, although the visit ended in acrimony owing to Klopstock's unexpectedly worldly pursuits. Financial security came from Frederick V of Denmark, who provided a modest life pension and invited Klopstock to Copenhagen, where he stayed from 1752 until 1770.

The first three cantos of *Der Messias* had been published in 1748 in the "Bremer Beiträge," an influential literary periodical edited by Klopstock's circle of friends in Leipzig, which included the brothers J.A. and J.E. Schlegel, C.F. Gellert, and the translator of Young, J.A. Ebert. Completion of the 20 cantos took until 1773, and the final version appeared only in 1799–1800. *Der Messias* can be seen as the product of gradual secularization, and it caused heated theological controversy, not least because Klopstock accorded with contemporary enlightened sensibilities by saving a repentant devil. But it was written in a spirit of faith and read primarily as a devotional work, albeit one that transcended dogmatic boundaries: even Catholic nuns were reportedly moved to tears by the Lutheran epic. There is little external action; the prime focus is on the response by angels, humans, and devils to the Passion and Resurrection. The work needs to be read intertextually, since Klopstock worked with complex levels of biblical quotation and emblematic imagery to achieve his prime aim of moving the reader—or, ideally, the listener. He rejected the alternating verse forms that had dominated German poetry since Opitz in favor of the hexameter, and he used bold inversion, expressive compounds, archaisms, and neologisms to create a varied, forceful, and emotive medium of expression with the proper classical *gravitas*.

From the 1750s, Klopstock extended his role as a religious poet to the church hymn and religious tragedy. His interest in national history culminated in a trilogy of patriotic tragedies on Arminius, who had been established by Tacitus as the "liberator" of *Germania* from Roman rule. Most influential was *Hermanns Schlacht* (1769; The Battle of Arminius), later emulated by Kleist. In the latter decades of his life, which he spent in Hamburg, Klopstock increasingly devoted himself to the cultural concerns that are at the center of *Die deutsche Gelehrtenrepublik* and to his studies of language and versification. His last major work, the fragmentary *Grammatische Gespräche* (1794; Grammatical Conversations), presents a series of lively dialogues between personified grammatical and poetic concepts that compete to establish the superiority of German over other tongues. Klopstock's prose—which includes a series of fine essays on poetics—was admired by Lessing, A.W. Schlegel, and, more recently, Arno Schmidt, who considered Klopstock to have missed his true vocation when he committed himself to a religious epic.

Throughout his career Klopstock wrote lyric poetry, mostly classical odes and elegies in which adventurous language combines with experimental form. He was the first to adapt classical meters successfully to the German language, and he emulated the Psalms in a series of elevated religious hymns (e.g., "Die Frühlingsfeier" [Spring Celebration]) that introduced free verse into German long before it became established in other European languages. His poems are both personal and public, treating friendship and love, language and poetics, cosmic visions and political events, as well as the joys of ice-skating or music. A profound sense of moral responsibility sustains his passionate odes and elegies on the French Revolution, in which he initially proclaims a new political era but then condemns Jacobin rule with a deep sense of betrayal.

Klopstock's contemporary influence was immense: at home and abroad he was celebrated as national poet, and his burial was worthy of a statesman. Lessing and Herder held him in high regard, he was a venerated mentor for Voß and the other "Göttinger Hain" poets, and his work had a powerful effect on the young Goethe and Schiller. Coleridge and Wordsworth paid him their respects in 1798, Lord Nelson and Lady Hamilton in 1800. In the 19th century, his reputation plummeted, owing to the ascendancy of Goethe as national poet and to a shift in aesthetics that sidelined the rhetorical and religious traditions from which Klopstock's work drew its strength. Selectively, however, poets have continued to take up aspects of his work: for Hölderlin, he was the supreme German poet whose odes he knew by heart; Rilke's *Duineser Elegien* (1923; *Duino Elegies*) engage with *Der Messias;* Arno Schmidt's *Gelehrtenrepublik* alludes to Klopstock's utopia; Johannes Bobrowski regarded him as his poetic master; Peter Rühmkorf discovered him as a fellow revolutionary in the years of the students' movement; and Volker Braun and Heinz Czechowski explored his work as an alternative to Socialist Realism. Critical debate is benefiting from a more historical view of the *Goethezeit* and an appreciation of the rhetorical basis of Klopstock's poetics and his cultural role in 18th-century Germany. Editorial neglect of Klopstock's works is also being remedied with the exemplary critical edition of his works and letters.

KATRIN KOHL

Biography

Born in Quedlinburg, Saxony, Germany, 2 July 1724. Theology student, University of Jena, 1745–46, and University of Leipzig, 1746–48; worked as private tutor, Langensalza, Saxony, 1748–50; traveled to Zurich at the invitation of Johann Jakob Bodmer, 1750; life pension from Frederick V of Denmark, 1751; moved to Hamburg, 1770. Married (1) Margareta (Meta) Moller, 1754 (died 1758), (2) Johanna Elisabeth von Winthem, 1791. Died in Hamburg, 14 March 1803.

Selected Works

Collections
Werke, 12 vols., 1798–1817
Sämtliche Werke, 18 vols., 1823–30
Ausgewählte Werke, edited by K.A. Schleiden, 1962
Werke und Briefe: Historisch-kritische Ausgabe, edited by Horst Gronemeyer et al., 1974–

Poetry
Der Messias, 1748; expanded editions, 1751, 1755, 1769, 1773; revised "Altona" edition, 1780; final edition, 1799–1800; translated in part as *The Messiah* by Mary Collyer and Joseph Collyer, 1763; translated by Solomon Hallings, 1810; translated by Mary Collyer and Mrs. Meeke, 1811; translated by Thomas Raffles, 1814; translated by G.H.C. Egestorff, 1821–22; translated by Catharine Head, 1826
"Auf meine Freunde," 1747; as "Wingolf," 1771
"Elegie," 1748; as "Die künftige Geliebte," 1771
"Der Zürcher-See," 1750
Ode an Gott, 1752
Geistliche Lieder, 1758–69
"Das Landleben," 1759; as "Die Frühlingsfeier," 1771
"Die frühen Gräber," 1764
"Die Sommernacht," 1766
Oden und Elegien: Vier und dreyssigmal gedrukt, 1771 [unauthorized "Darmstadt" edition]
Kleine poetische und prosaische Werke, edited by Christian Friedrich Daniel Schubart, 1771 [unauthorized edition]
Oden, 1771
"Sie, und nicht Wir: An La Rochefoucauld," 1790
"Mein Irrthum," 1793
Odes of Klopstock from 1747 to 1780, translated by William Nind, 1848
Oden, edited by F. Muncker and J. Pawel, 1889
Oden, edited by K.L. Schneider, 1966

Plays
Der Tod Adams, 1757; as *The Death of Adam*, translated by Robert Lloyd, 1763
Salomo, 1764; as *Solomon*, translated by Robert Huish, 1809
Hermanns Schlacht, 1769
David, 1772
Hermann und die Fürsten, 1784
Hermanns Tod, 1787

Other
Die deutsche Gelehrtenrepublik, 1774
Über die deutsche Rechtschreibung, 1778
Über Sprache und Dichtkunst: Fragmente, 1779–80
Grammatische Gespräche, 1794

Memoirs of Frederick and Margaret Klopstock, translated by Elizabeth Smith, 1808

Klopstock und seine Freunde: Briefwechsel der Familie Klopstock unter sich, und zwischen dieser Familie, Gleim, Schmidt, Fanny, Meta und andern Freunden, edited by Klamer Schmidt, 2 vols., 1810; as *Klopstock and His Friends: A Series of Family Letters, Written between the Years 1750 and 1803,* translated by Elizabeth Ogilvy, 1814

Klopstock, Meta, *Briefwechsel mit Klopstock, ihren Verwandten und Freunden,* edited by Hermann Tiemann, 3 vols., 1956

Briefwechsel zwischen Klopstock und den Grafen Christian und Friedrich Leopold zu Stolberg: Mit einem Anhang: Briefwechsel zwischen Klopstock und Herder, edited by Jürgen Behrens and Sabine Jodeleit, 1964

Edited Work

Meta Klopstock, *Hinterlassene Schriften,* 1759

Further Reading

Bjorklund, Beth, "Klopstock's Poetic Innovations: The Emergence of German as a Prosodic Language," *Germanic Review* 56 (1981)

Blackall, Eric A., *The Emergence of German as a Literary Language, 1700–1775,* Cambridge: Cambridge University Press, 1959; 2nd edition, Ithaca, New York: Cornell University Press, 1978

Hellmuth, Hans-Heinrich, *Metrische Erfindung und metrische Theorie bei Klopstock,* Munich: Fink, 1973

Hilliard, Kevin, *Philosophy, Letters, and the Fine Arts in Klopstock's Thought,* London: Institute of Germanic Studies, University of London, 1987

Hilliard, Kevin, and Katrin Kohl, editors, *Klopstock an der Grenze der Epochen,* Berlin and New York: de Gruyter, 1995

Kohl, Katrin, *Rhetoric, the Bible, and the Origins of Free Verse,* Berlin and New York: de Gruyter, 1990

———, *Friedrich Gottlieb Klopstock,* Stuttgart: Metzler, 2000

Kroll, Karin, "Klopstocks Bedeutung für Hölderlins Lyrik," Ph.D. diss., Universität Kiel, 1960

Lee, Meredith, *Displacing Authority: Goethe's Poetic Reception of Klopstock,* Heidelberg: Winter, 1999

Lohmeier, Dieter, *Herder und Klopstock: Herders Auseinandersetzung mit der Persönlichkeit und dem Werk Klopstocks,* Bad Homburg: Gehlen, 1968

Pape, Helmut, *Klopstock: Die "Sprache des Herzens" neu entdeckt: Die Befreiung des Lesers aus seiner emotionalen Unmündigkeit: Idee und Wirklichkeit dichterischer Existenz um 1750,* Frankfurt: Lang, 1998

Rühmkorf, Peter, "Friedrich Gottlieb Klopstock: Ein empfindsamer Revolutionär," in *Walther von der Vogelweide, Klopstock, und ich,* Reinbek bei Hamburg: Rowohlt, 1975

Schmidt, Arno, "Klopstock, oder Verkenne dich selbst!," in *Das essayistische Werk zur deutschen Literatur in 4 Bänden,* vol. 1, Zurich: Haffmans, 1988

Werner, Hans-Georg, *Friedrich Gottlieb Klopstock: Werk und Wirkung,* Berlin: Akademie, 1978

Wodtke, Friedrich Wilhelm, "Rilke und Klopstock," Ph.D. diss., Universität Kiel, 1948

Die deutsche Gelehrtenrepublik 1774
Essay by Friedrich Gottlieb Klopstock

Friedrich Gottlieb Klopstock's *Die deutsche Gelehrtenrepublik* (The German Republic of Letters) is a remarkable montage of fictional and nonfictional texts that evokes the vision of a German cultural republic through utopian historiography. The significance of the work as a whole derives as much from its cultural purpose and publication history as from its qualities as a literary text. Having built his reputation on the epic *Der Messias* (1748; final edition, 1799–1800; *The Messiah*), which was designed to establish German literature among the great literatures of the ancient and modern world, Klopstock published *Die deutsche Gelehrtenrepublik* in 1774 as a project that was intended to strengthen German cultural identity through humanist ideals. Part of this endeavor was practical: by selling the work via subscription, Klopstock experimented with a scheme designed to circumvent the publishers and booksellers, so that intellectuals might benefit fully from the proceeds of their work.

Given the political fragmentation of German-speaking territories, the project of establishing a national identity through cultural means attained considerable force in the 18th century. The lack of a cultural center was exacerbated by Frederick the Great's contempt for German language and culture—the language of the Prussian court was French, and a generous pension supported Voltaire rather than any German writer. Klopstock's utopian representation of a cultural republic in *Die deutsche Gelehrtenrepublik* was preceded by years of strategic planning to muster support for national institutions that would lay the basis for a flowering of German culture. Klopstock envisaged institutions such as a national printing works and national theater, various types of financial support for young and established scholars and writers, and a national historiography. In 1769 he published the patriotic drama *Hermanns Schlacht* (The Battle of Arminius) with a dedication to Joseph II, which was intended to galvanize the emperor into realizing these plans at the court in Vienna.

When Klopstock's scheme for national support fell on deaf ears, he turned his energies to an alternative form of self-help that would at least permit authors to retain control over their work at a time when publishers showed scant regard for matters of copyright and textual detail. Drawing on the support the "Viennese Plan" had generated among colleagues such as Lessing and the young generation of poets, he devised an ambitious subscription project, which was based on the model of Alexander Pope, who had successfully distributed his Homer translations in this way. Financially, the success of the project exceeded even Klopstock's expectations: some 3,500 subscribers committed themselves to buying the book in advance of publication; the net proceeds were around 2,000 *Reichstaler* (for comparison, the author-friendly publisher Göschen paid a generous 3,000 *Reichstaler* for Klopstock's collected works in the 1790s). But Klopstock's hopes of establishing this form of distribution foundered on its sheer complexity and, not least, on the reception of the work itself. The mixture of archaism and utopia, the unconventional form, the allusive style, and the cryptic humor rendered the work incomprehensible to the majority of recipients, and Klopstock had to abandon his plans for a second part. In a May 1774 letter to Lavater, Herder lambasted the discrepancy between the extensive preparatory publicity and the esoteric nature of the published work as "the worst farce ever performed in Germany."

Die deutsche Gelehrtenrepublik was originally conceived in the 1750s as a timeless cosmopolitan state called "Hellenopolis"; the work thus stands in the long Platonic tradition that portrays ideal republics. Klopstock drew especially on the humanist tradition of the *respublica litteraria* or *respublica eruditorum;* one prominent work in this tradition was Diego de Saavedra Fajardo's *La república literaria* (1655), which had appeared in German translations in 1748 and 1771. The allegory of learning as a state had a basis in the academies and learned societies that had been founded since the Renaissance across Europe.

The work is presented as historiography compiled by the fictional authors Salogast and Wlemar, with Klopstock figuring as the "editor." A section on the constitution and laws of the republic is followed by advice from the republic's aldermen, "Guter Rath der Aldermänner" (good advice by the aldermen), while the latter part consists of the proceedings of the most recent *Landtag* in 1772, "Geschichte des lezten Landtags." Interspersed among the proceedings are sections of epigrams, series of brief "monuments" to ancient "German" achievements, extracts from a new German grammar, treatises on a projected German dictionary and poetics, and correspondence relating to Klopstock's Vienna project. The guiding idea is the cultural competition between nations, deriving from the apologetic tradition of the Renaissance. The venerable emblematic juxtaposition of pen and sword is brought to life in the republic's use of the word as chief weapon, which culminates in a patriotic call to cultural war on the neighboring republics. While formally the work is a montage of disparate texts, it gains unity from its central concern. Strengthening German cultural identity is the prime political purpose of the fictional republic and its laws, political meetings, linguistic and literary endeavors, and historiography. It is also the prime purpose of the individual texts and the work as a whole.

Although a flop with the general public, the work inspired the young generation of poets: Goethe hailed it as "the one and only poetics of all times and peoples. The only rules that are possible!" (letter to Schönborn, 10 June 1774). That this work of cultural patriotism should have been considered a poetics indicates the powerful hold of the national idea over Klopstock's contemporaries, but it also testifies to a dissatisfaction with the normative poetics and grammars of the rationalist tradition.

Klopstock's work, a monument to the humanist tradition in 18th-century German literature, is also a pre-Romantic challenge to the regulation of the poetic spirit.

The idea of a republic of letters has been taken up in the 20th century by Hermann Hesse in *Das Glasperlenspiel* (1943; *The Glass Bead Game*), but this work draws upon the humanist tradition in general rather than Klopstock in particular. Arno Schmidt explicitly attributes his choice of title for *Die Gelehrtenrepublik* (1957; *The Egghead Republic*) to his veneration for Klopstock's work, although he draws more obviously on Jules Verne. The connection with Klopstock is one of equivalent idiosyncrasy in style and humor, but it has an opposite purpose: Schmidt's fictional author is governed by his aversion to all things German.

KATRIN KOHL

Editions
First edition: *Die deutsche Gelehrtenrepublik,* Hamburg: Bode, 1774
Critical edition: in *Werke und Briefe, historisch-kritische Ausgabe,* vol. 7/1, edited by Rose-Maria Hurlebusch, Berlin: de Gruyter, 1975

Further Reading
Hilliard, Kevin, *Philosophy, Letters, and the Fine Arts in Klopstock's Thought,* London: Institute of Germanic Studies, University of London, 1987
Hurlebusch, Rose-Maria, and Karl Ludwig Schneider, "Die Gelehrten und die Großen: Klopstocks 'Wiener Plan,'" in *Der Akademiegedanke im 17. und 18. Jahrhundert,* edited by Fritz Hartmann and Rudolf Vierhaus, Wolfenbütteler Forschungen 3, Bremen: Jacobi, 1977
Kirschstein, Max, *Klopstocks Deutsche Gelehrtenrepublik,* Berlin: de Gruyter, 1929
Pape, Helmut, "Die gesellschaftlich-wirtschaftliche Stellung Friedrich Gottlieb Klopstocks," Ph.D. diss., Universität Bonn, 1961; as "Klopstocks Autorenhonorare und Selbstverlagsgewinne," *Börsenblatt für den Deutschen Buchhandel,* Frankfurter Ausgabe 24 (1968) and 25 (1969)
Schmidt, Arno, "Klopstock, oder Verkenne dich selbst!" in *Das essayistische Werk zur deutschen Literatur in 4 Bänden,* vol. 1, Zurich: Haffmans, 1988

Alexander Kluge 1932–

During the course of his study of law at three universities in the first half of the 1950s and as an intern in the Frankfurt law practice of the politically active lawyer Helmut Becker, Alexander Kluge came into personal contact with Theodor Adorno. The popularity of the Frankfurt School, particularly at the universities in Frankfurt and Marburg, as well as the contact with Adorno helped shape Kluge's cultural criticism and his modernist aesthetics. In particular, Adorno's writings influenced his understanding of the production and reception of culture for the masses in modern capitalist society, although Kluge did not share Adorno's disdain for all forms of mass culture. On the contrary, Kluge's filmmaking and writings on film are strongly indebted to Walter Benjamin and the role Benjamin grants modern technological media in contemporary culture.

Benjamin's influence is also evident in Kluge's persistent analysis of the dis/continuities of history that had been repressed, only to resurface at crucial junctures in the life of the Federal Republic. His first literary work, *Lebensläufe* (1962; *Attendance List for a Funeral*), tells the stories of nine individuals in the Third Reich whose lives for the most part carry over into the Federal Republic. Written in part in a legal or bureaucratic dialect, these biographical sketches reveal the human side of individuals who are frustrated in their attempts to find justice in a rigid social order incapable of bridging the breach in history between the

Third Reich and the Federal Republic. The life stories of these victims put the justice system itself on trial without, however, suggesting a feasible alternative. In a similarly unsettling fashion they also reveal historical continuities that draw into question the *Stunde Null* (zero hour) notion of a clean start after 1945. Structurally, the accounts are broken both internally and among themselves into isolated fragments without transitions that bind them into a unifying whole. Alluding to his preoccupation with film at this early stage in his career, Kluge has said that the central form principle of *Attendance List for a Funeral* is actually more filmic rather than literary and that on closer inspection one can even detect the "cuts" between scenes.

The fragmentary structure of *Attendance List for a Funeral* also signifies a basic distrust of poetic fiction and its ability to convey historical reality. Kluge's short prose pieces combine quasi-historical or bureaucratic documents with fictional episodes into a docufiction format similar to that produced for the stage at the time by leading German playwrights such as Rolf Hochhuth and Peter Weiss. In his next literary work, *Schlachtbeschreibung* (1964; *The Battle*) Kluge applies the realistic method of *Lebensläufe* to a monumental event of the Nazi period, the defeat of the German Sixth Army at Stalingrad. He incorporates a broad array of private and public, personal and official, contemporary and historical texts into a loosely structured montage that illuminates the complexity of the sociohistorical network through which one must negotiate in order to understand history. These include military reports, internal messages of the Nazi leaders, sermons given by military chaplains during the battle, personal diary entries, interviews with participants, and charts showing strategic military moves. The abundance of diverse materials suggests a complex of interconnected forces and conditions that defies understanding or resistance. In this regard, the work seems to contradict Kluge's theoretical faith (see *Geschichte und Eigensinn*) that there is the potential for resistance to social forces that dominate individual human interaction.

Kluge's docufiction narratives display a tension that is central to his theory as well. His analysis (with Oskar Negt) of *Öffentlichkeit und Erfahrung* (1972; *Public Sphere and Experience*) builds on a theoretical framework derived from Jürgen Habermas but questions Habermas's reliance on rational public discourse as a sufficient agency for structuring society. Attacking what Kluge and Negt term the "kühne Fiktion" that all citizens participate in a public discourse concerned with the common good, they contend that the public sphere functions in a totalitarian manner, creating a monolithic sphere of experience that relegates all unintegrated experiences to the detached, shadowy margins of society. Thus, human experience is structured according to forms of production that exclude, suppress, or appropriate basic, but for capitalistic society, counterproductive needs of the individual—and any rational reorganization of social experience based on a critical public discourse (such as Habermas advocates) participates in this tyranny and exclusion.

Kluge's later collection of stories *Neue Geschichten* (1977; New Stories) reflect this tension between public and private modes of experience. Yet in an even more pointed fashion than in his earlier stories, they reject the traditional role of art as the preserver of authentic, individual, or subjective experience. These diverse sketches of life are set in various time periods spanning the 18th century to the present. Combining fictional documentary accounts with well-spun narratives centered around a protagonist, they point on the one hand to the unavoidable dominance of socioeconomic forces that structure life in the public sphere, while at the same time they reveal the inability of theory to encompass or explain lived experience. While Stalingrad may be seen as a (perhaps intentionally) failed attempt to illuminate history through a prism that distinguishes various categories of technical and institutional influence, *Neue Geschichten* restores the autonomy of immediate human experience. However, as Kluge slyly subverts the attempt to subjugate life to conceptual thought, he also indicates that traditional realist fiction fails in its attempt to represent autonomous subjective experience.

This theoretical objection to realist literary genres led Kluge to abandon writing in favor of film, a modern visual medium that could balance creative narrative against a technologically produced objective point of view. In the 1960s he emerged as the unofficial leader of the New German Cinema, serving as the chief spokesman for the group of young filmmakers who signed the Oberhausen Manifesto in 1962 and then spearheading the successful effort to secure funding for alternative feature films. As an adjunct professor of law, a social theorist, a critic of contemporary culture, and an author of docufiction, he was well suited to lead the push for a new mode of film production. When the breakthrough came in 1964 with the establishment of a federal fund to subsidize films by young German filmmakers, Kluge's *Abschied von gestern* (1966; *Yesterday Girl*) was one of the important debut films of the New German Cinema, having success at the box office and winning the Silver Prize at Venice in 1966.

As the early successes began to open up opportunities for Young German directors to find commercial funding, Kluge remained steadfast in his effort to develop the institutional framework for an alternative cinema. He was also able to attain substantial financing for his own film projects and became, together with Edgar Reitz, codirector of the newly constituted Ulm Institute for Film Design. He has used his position at the school to train young directors not just in the specialized skills needed for filmmaking (camera work, scriptwriting, production, directing, etc.) but also in the critical theory and modernist aesthetics that informed his own work.

What mainly distinguished Kluge from other Young German filmmakers was his faith in film as a tool for social change. During the first two decades of New German Cinema (roughly 1965–85) he expressed the optimistic conviction that film, as a medium involving collective modes of production and reception, can generate resistant forms of cultural experience. He argues that film has an advantage over reading, which takes place in isolation and thus leaves the reader more susceptible to preprogrammed needs produced by the culture industry (*Bestandsaufnahme: Utopie Film,* 1983). In his feature films Kluge develops his own style of fragmented modernist narrative that disrupts the realist illusion of conventional narrative cinema and foregrounds the constructedness of film reality. Typically these films have an alienated central protagonist, often a woman, who is adrift between social institutions that offer no anchoring or sense of direction. In *Abschied von gestern,* Anita G. is a refugee from the GDR seeking integration into West German society. The film consists of separate, often seemingly isolated incidents in her odyssey through a cold, uncaring world of monolithic rigidity and cynical disregard for fellow human beings. The episodes are only loosely connected, lacking the usual continuities of time and space or a clear unifying overriding narrative.

In his second feature film (*Die Artisten in der Zirkuskuppel: Ratlos*, 1967; *Artistes at the Top of the Big Top: Disoriented*), Kluge offers an allegorical look at the conditions for artistic production and reception in the highly charged political climate of the late 1960s. Working filmically through postulates that stem from Adorno's aesthetic theory, Kluge reflects on the dilemma of the critical artist bound by capitalistic parameters for success. Featuring an analytical approach grounded in Kluge's own theoretical writings, *Gelegenheitsarbeit einer Sklavin* (1973; *Occasional Work of a Female Slave*) examines women's emancipation in Germany as it had evolved out of and, to a large measure, in opposition to the male-dominated student movement of the 1960s. For the most part the film was poorly received by German feminists, who overlooked its theoretical framework and regarded it as a male critique of the feminist movement.

In 1975 Kluge made his one film with a more conventional narrative structure (*Der starke Ferdinand*; *Strongman Ferdinand*). Despite critical acclaim (1976 Cannes International Film Critics' Prize and Special Prize at Naples), it fared poorly at the box office, at least in part because a newspaper strike coincided with its opening, virtually eliminating essential pre-release publicity. Shortly thereafter, the volatile events of the German Autumn induced Kluge to devote his attention more fully to contemporary political issues and to reawakened questions of German history. Kluge spearheaded a speedy film project that enabled New German Cinema's leading filmmakers to respond to a nation shaken by the controversial deaths of industrialist Hans Martin Schleyer and the Baader-Meinhof terrorists in Stammheim. Premiering less than five months after the climactic events in September 1977, *Deutschland im Herbst* (1978; *Germany in Autumn*) consists of eight diverse segments stitched together skillfully by Kluge with intertitles and voiceover commentary. The film's huge box-office success spurred even greater fragmentation in Kluge's subsequent films. In *Die Patriotin* (1979; *The Patriot*) the protagonist, Gabi Teichert, a history teacher unsettled by the events of the German Autumn, goes searching for the foundations of German history. Three mini-narratives from the years 1939–45 (as well as numerous vignettes) are interspersed within the loosely constructed main narrative. His last three feature films, before he abandoned cinema for television in 1984, extend this use of multiple narratives and offer new critical perspectives on the postmodern proliferation of media images.

With the advent of private television in Germany in 1984, Kluge took up the new media in a move that, on the surface, seems to betray his ardent theoretical endorsement of film over the previous 25 years. Even as he continues to denounce television (as he had Hollywood cinema before) as cultural imperialism directed at the head of the spectator, he begins to produce television programs for the new private networks SAT 1 and RTL. First he made hour-long shows that highlighted filmmakers (*Stunde der Filmmacher*) and then shorter, more diverse "cultural windows" on high culture of all sorts: literature, film, art, theater, opera. These shorter programs are small-screen versions of his feature films—they present a montage of film citations, still photos, and Dada-like snippets of modern culture, edited into a fast-moving spectacle of images, words, music, and color.

They often imitate forms of television entertainment, inviting the viewer to see the manipulative power of television programming and its ability to stifle critical reflection. As in his filmmaking, Kluge attempts to stimulate this awareness not merely through objective distance but also by engaging the spectator's fantasy and desire. If indeed the "new media" actually produce needs and wishes in the public, then, according to one of the fundamental theoretical premises of his work, the path back to less colonized desires of the autonomous individual begins with the activation of dominant, media-induced sensibilities.

At the turn of the millennium, the jury remains out on this obstinate effort to subvert the imperialistic power of the culture industry from within, using its own most pervasive means of colonization, the pandemic medium of television.

ROGER F. COOK

See also Film and Literature

Biography
Born in Halberstadt, 2 February 1932. Studied law and history at the universities of Marburg and Frankfurt; teaches at the Institute for Film Design, Ulm, since 1962; member of the Oberhausener Group, which advocated the renewal of German cinema in light of its increasing commercialization; Kluge is known as a writer, filmmaker, critical theorist, and public intellectual; produces television programs for Germany's private stations SAT 1 and RTL, since 1985. Kleist Prize, 1985; Golden Lion Award, Venice, 1968 (for his filmic work). Currently lives in Munich.

Selected Works

Feature Films
Abschied von Gestern (*Yesterday Girl*), 1966
Die Artisten in der Zirkuskuppel: Ratlos (*Artistes at the Top of the Big Top: Disoriented*), 1967
Der große Verhau (*The Big Mess*), 1970
Gelegenheitsarbeit einer Sklavin (*Occasional Work of a Female Slave*), 1973
In Gefahr und großer Not bringt der Mittelweg den Tod (*The Middle of the Road Is a Very Dead End*), 1974
Der starke Ferdinand (*Strongman Ferdinand*), 1976
Deutschland im Herbst (*Germany in Autumn*), 1978
Die Patriotin (*The Patriot*), 1979
Der Kandidat (*The Candidate*), 1980
Die Macht der Gefühle (*The Power of Emotion*), 1983
Der Angriff der Gegenwart auf die übrige Zeit (*The Blind Director*), 1985

Docufiction
Lebensläufe: Anwesenheitsliste für eine Beerdigung, 1962; as *Attendance List for a Funeral*, translated by Leila Vennewitz, 1966
Schlachtbeschreibung: Der organisatorische Aufbau eines Unglücks, 1964; as *The Battle*, translated by Leila Vennewitz, 1967
Neue Geschichten, Hefte 1–18, 1977
Lernprozesse mit tödlichem Ausgang, 1973; as *Learning Processes with a Deadly Outcome*, translated by Christopher Pavsek, 1996

Nonfiction
Öffentlichkeit und Erfahrung: Zur Organisationsanalyse von bürgerlicher und proletarischer Öffentlichkeit (with Oskar Negt), 1972; as *Public Sphere and Experience: Toward an Analysis of the Bourgeois and Proletarian Public Sphere*, translated by Peter Labanyi et al., 1993

Filmwirtschaft in der BRD und in Europa: Götterdämmerung in Raten (with Michael Dost and Florian Hopf), 1973
Neue Geschichten, Hefte 1–18: "Unheimlichkeit der Zeit," 1977
Geschichte und Eigensinn (with Oskar Negt), 1981
Bestandaufnahme: Utopie Film (editor), 1983
Industrialisierung des Bewußtseins: Eine kritische Auseinandersetzung mit den "neuen" Medien, with Klaus von Bismarck et al., 1985
Theodor Fontane, Heinrich von Kleist und Anna Wilde: Zur Grammatik der Zeit, 1987
Massverhältnisse des Politischen: 15 Vorschläge zum Unterscheidungsvermögen (with Oskar Negt), 1992

Further Reading

Bowie, Andrew, "Individuality and Difference," *Oxford Literary Review* 7, no. 1–2 (1985)
Cook, Roger F., "Film Images and Reality: Alexander Kluge's Aesthetics of Cinema," *Colloquia Germanica* 18, no. 4 (1985)
Hansen, Miriam, "Aleander Kluge, Cinema, and the Public Sphere: The Construction Site of History," *Discourse* 6 (1983)
Hansen, Miriam, editor, *New German Critique* 49 (1990), special issue devoted to Kluge
Hummel, Christoph, editor, *Kinemathek* 63 (1983), special issue devoted to Kluge
Kaes, Anton, *From Hitler to Heimat: The Return of History as Film*, Cambridge, Massachusetts: Harvard University Press, 1989
Lewandowski, Rainer, *Alexander Kluge*, Munich: Beck, 1980
Lutze, Peter C., *Alexander Kluge: The Last Modernist*, Detroit, Michigan: Wayne State University Press, 1998
October 46 (1988) [special issue devoted to Kluge]
Pavsek, Christopher, "History and Obstinacy: Negt and Kluge's Redemption of Labor," *New German Critique* 68 (1996)
Rentschler, Eric, "Kluge, Film History, and *Eigensinn*," *New German Critique* 31 (1984)

Wolfgang Koeppen 1906–1996

Notwithstanding all the success of his postwar trilogy of novels and the high reputation that he enjoyed (and still enjoys) among critics and contemporaries in the Federal Republic, Wolfgang Koeppen remains an enigmatic figure. His literary career began in the late 1920s with the publication of short prose sketches for the communist newspaper *Die rote Fahne*. Then, between January 1931 and December 1933, he worked as a reviewer and journalist for the *Berliner Börsen-Courier*, a Jewish-run liberal newspaper. While his initial sympathies were clearly for the dispossessed and downtrodden, Koeppen's essays after Hitler's seizure of power were sympathetic to the regime and its values, although the question of whether this softening of his position was a personal accommodation or conditioned by the pressures imposed on the newspaper is still unclear.

Koeppen's first novel, *Eine unglückliche Liebe* (An Unhappy Love), appeared in 1934: it narrates a romantic relationship between Friedrich, a naïve and aimless student, and Sybille, a bohemian actress. Some critics have, perhaps generously, interpreted the setting of the novel (Switzerland) as betokening an implicit desire to escape from political pressures in Germany. Koeppen's second novel, *Die Mauer schwankt* (The Wall Sways) was published in Berlin by Bruno Cassirer, a Jewish publishing house, in 1935. It was written during Koeppen's self-imposed exile in Holland, which lasted from 1934 until 1938. The novel was reissued in 1939 by the Universitas Verlag, under the title *Die Pflicht* (Duty), after Koeppen's return from Holland. The novel has been interpreted both as a veiled attack on a nameless oppressive regime in the Balkans (and thus as an implicit critique of National Socialism) and as a vindication of order and duty (and thus as tacit support for the regime in Germany). His publishers succeeded in preventing his call up for military service, and Koeppen gained employment in the Nazi film industry during the war years. He survived the last months of the war in Feldafing on the Starnberger See. Koeppen certainly did apply to become a member of the *Reichsverband Deutscher Schriftsteller* in December 1933, and, after his return from Holland, also applied, in January 1939, to join the *Reichsschrifttumskammer*. Although his years in Holland appear to have been spent in poverty, his career in Nazi Germany was not unsuccessful. There is no evidence that Koeppen sympathized in any way with National Socialism, but, conversely, there is also little support for the theory that his life and work offer grounds to consider him an opponent of the regime. The mundane reality is that he attempted to survive as best he could. He published two stories in the *Kölnische Zeitung* in 1941, which could be interpreted as betokening a kind of "inner emigration" from political events.

Koeppen's literary reputation was shaped by the success of his trilogy of postwar novels, *Tauben im Gras* (1951; *Pigeons on the Grass*), *Das Treibhaus* (1953; The Hot House), and *Der Tod in Rom* (1954; *Death in Rome*). The first of these novels was undoubtedly a major influence on postwar literature in the new West Germany. Set in an unnamed German city, which bears a powerful resemblance to Munich, at a time which seems to be 1950, the novel recounts a day in the lives of about 30 characters, whose separate fates represent the values and attitudes of the fledgling Federal Republic. The title, a quotation from Gertrude Stein, suggests that human activity is aimless and unstructured, and certainly the disparate preoccupations of the characters imply that no meaningful pattern in their existence may be discerned. Each character, concerned with a pressing private or professional crisis, seems incapable of either resolving or communicating their problem. The background is evoked by the song "Night and Day," which echoes both the intrusion of American cultural values in Germany and the tension between African-American soldiers and a generation of Germans who were educated to believe in their cultural superiority. The climax is a speech by a visiting American intellectual, Mr. Edwin (whose theories bear a startling resemblance to T.S. Eliot's *Notes towards a Definition of Culture*), who attacks the godless values of a younger generation (Hemingway and Stein). Even as he attempts to reassert the continuity of cultural values in the Western tradition, racial violence breaks out in the streets outside.

Discontinuity and disjunction seem to prevail. Yet, paradoxically, a kind of structure is imposed by the narrative, in which disparate events are connected by the repetition of a phrase, motif, or, simply, spatial juxtaposition or simultaneity. Although cultural continuities appear to be contradicted by the chaotic events of the novel, classical and biblical allusions also abound. The novel demands a cultured readership, yet this readership is, again paradoxically, confronted with the discrepancy between the cultural archetype that they are invited to recognize and the tawdry reality of contemporary Germany. It is this ambivalence toward culture that characterizes Koeppen's own literary stance.

Das Treibhaus is sometimes read as a roman à clef about the Bonn politics of the fledgling Republic, but Koeppen is careful never to mention either the specific place or the exact time (a period nonetheless identifiable as immediately before the elections of 1953). The external events of the novel occupy the last two days of the life of the politician Keetenheuve, but the narrative is focused on the central figure's memories and reflections, which are often rendered in italics. Keetenheuve's ambivalence about his past—his opposition to Hitler drove him into exile, but also called into question his ability to speak for, and to, those Germans who had remained—is characteristic of Koeppen's own complex response to the past. Once again, the reader is confronted with a wealth of cultural allusion, but simultaneously with the failure of cultural allusion to offer a meaningful pattern with which the central character may confront contemporary society. In *Death in Rome*, Koeppen returns to the multilinear narrative of *Pigeons on the Grass*. Again, the events of two days in Rome in the present are exploited in order to explore a complex set of cultural and historical issues, which deal with the Nazi past, aesthetic modernism, sexuality, and religion, all of which are explored, somewhat implausibly, through family relationships.

Koeppen's subsequent career represents a shift away from literature toward travelogue: his three collections, *Nach Rußland und anderswohin* (1958; To Russia and Elsewhere), *Amerikafahrt* (1959; My Journey to America), and *Reisen nach Frankreich* (1961; Travels in France), chronicle the responses of a sensitive, historically and culturally informed, and unmistakably German visitor to Spain, Holland, the Soviet Union, London, Rome, the United States, and France. The pieces were commissioned by Alfred Andersch for his *Radio-Essay* program and were broadcast on the Süddeutscher Rundfunk; they were perhaps more popular even than Koeppen's novels. His skills in both confirming and undermining the expectations of German readers and listeners by offering both the stereotypical and the unexpected and by supplying both the apposite and the improbable literary association made for a highly successful recipe for a German public starved of foreign travel. Koeppen's travelogues, unlike his fiction, offered some reassuring certainties, including a sense that the new Federal Republic was part of a wider European order. At the same time, Koeppen continued to publish short stories, which were gathered in a collection entitled *Romanisches Café* (the name of a famous Berlin coffee house) in 1972. This collection effectively blurred the distinction between pieces he wrote under National Socialism and those that were the product of the postwar years: many had been published before in some guise and were simply adapted, sometimes (confusingly) under new titles. *Jugend* (Youth), an autobiographical piece, which was a minor literary success in 1976, contained some material that had appeared earlier. So did the volume of occasional essays, *Die elenden Skribenten* (1981; Wretched Scribblers), and the prose collections *Angst* (1987; Anxiety) and *Morgenrot* (1987; Dawn). All this, together with the reissuing of *Jakob Littners Aufzeichnungen aus einem Erdloch* (Jakob Littner's Notes from a Hole in the Ground) in 1992, a diary by Littner that had been ghostwritten by Koeppen in 1948, led some critics to the somewhat cynical conclusion that the relative paucity of Koeppen's literary production had forced his publishers to repackage existing material in order to keep his name in the public eye. A more charitable view was that his publishers were seeking to ensure a meager income for a writer who, despite early critical acclaim, simply did not have another major novel to offer.

Koeppen's reputation depends on his outstanding postwar novel trilogy. While the topical events that served as the trilogy's background have faded, the existential issues—power, guilt, sexuality, and death (and their wider relationship to German experience in the 20th century)—continue to fascinate readers. Koeppen's ability to conjure up a wealth of cultural allusion and his awareness that cultural allusion is mere play, that it disqualifies his characters from the business of living, both continue to make him accessible to the postmodern consciousness.

RHYS W. WILLIAMS

Biography
Born in Greifswald, 23 June 1906. Worked in a variety of poorly paid jobs in Würzburg, Berlin, and Hamburg; contributed short stories to *Die rote Fahne* and *Vorwärts* before becoming a journalist for the *Berliner Börsen-Courier*, 1931–33; emigrated to the Netherlands, 1934; returned to Germany in 1938; worked as a scriptwriter in the film industry; after 1945, worked as a freelance writer in Munich. Büchner Prize, 1962. Died in Munich, 15 March 1996.

Selected Works

Collections
Tauben im Gras/Das Treibhaus/Der Tod in Rom, 1969; as *Drei Romane*, 1972
Gesammelte Werke. 6 Bände, 1986
Eine unglückliche Liebe, 1934
Die Mauer schwankt, 1935; reissued as *Die Pflicht*, 1939
Tauben im Gras, 1951; as *Pigeons on the Grass*, translated by David Ward, 1988
Das Treibhaus, 1953
Der Tod in Rom, 1954; as *Death in Rome*, translated by Mervyn Savill, 1956; translated by Michael Hofmann, 1994
Romanisches Café, 1972
Jugend, 1976
Die elenden Skribenten, 1981
Angst, 1987
Morgenrot: Anfänge eines Romans, 1987
Es war einmal in Masuren, 1991
Jakob Littners Aufzeichnungen aus einem Erdloch, 1992

Travel Writing
Nach Rußland und anderswohin, 1958
Amerikafahrt, 1959
Reisen nach Frankreich, 1961

Further Reading
Arnold, Heinz Ludwig, editor, *Wolfgang Koeppen*, Munich: Text und Kritik, 1972
Basker, David, *Chaos, Control, and Consistency: The Narrative Vision of Wolfgang Koeppen*, Bern and New York: Lang, 1993

Burgess, Gordon, "Wolfgang Koeppen," in *The Modern German Novel*, edited by Keith Bullivant, New York: Berg, 1987

Craven, Stanley, *Wolfgang Koeppen: A Study in Modernist Alienation*, Stuttgart: Heinz, 1982

Greiner, Ulrich, editor, *Über Wolfgang Koeppen*, Frankfurt: Suhrkamp, 1976

Gunn, Richard L., *Art and Politics in Wolfgang Koeppen's Postwar Trilogy*, Bern and New York: Lang, 1983

Hanbidge, Carole, *The Transformation of Failure: A Critical Analysis of Character Presentation in the Novels of Wolfgang Koeppen*, Bern and New York: Lang, 1983

Oehlenschläger, Eckart, editor, *Wolfgang Koeppen*, Frankfurt: Suhrkamp, 1987

Treichel, Hans-Ulrich, *Fragment ohne Ende: Eine Studie über Wolfgang Koeppen*, Heidelberg: Winter, 1984

Oskar Kokoschka 1886–1980

Oskar Kokoschka's productive period as a writer was as short as his career as a painter was long. Most of his important literary works were written or published between 1907 and 1913; what appeared afterward was, with few exceptions, essayistic by-products of his art or documents of his political activism. The painter, who is often pigeonholed as a noteworthy "double talent," was in fact an important writer of considerable originality and inventiveness.

Given its innovative interplay of word and image and its secure standing as a prototype of the art of the Expressionist book, Kokoschka's very first independent publication, *Die träumenden Knaben* (1908; The Dreaming Boys), has perhaps been underrated by literary historians. This prose poem of some 250 lines, which includes two black-and-white vignettes and eight full-page color lithographs, enacts Kokoschka's transition from the *Jugendstil* of his teachers at the School of Applied Arts to his own literary and artistic proto-Expressionism. Although Kokoschka dedicated this work "to Gustav Klimt in admiration," even the illustrations feature a simplified, jaggedly drawn primitivism that belies their origins both as a tribute to the father figure of the Viennese Secession and, more mundanely, as a commission from the commercially oriented Wiener Werkstätte. The poem itself, which features a series of loosely connected dream narratives written in a rambling, but compellingly rhythmic style, represents an even more unconventional departure from established models. The insistent use of a first-person narrator coupled with unfamiliar, ethnographically inspired images creates effects that are by and large foreign to the neo-Romantic, Impressionistic verse of the time. There are, however, significant, but largely unremarked parallels with other offbeat poets. The first two stanzas of the poem—rhymed folk-song verse that contrasts sharply with the prose-poetic style of the dream visions that follow—in which the narrator describes stabbing little red fish with a knife exhibit surprising similarities to the satirical, often blackly humorous ballads of Frank Wedekind; and the evocation of emotional states through the pronounced use of color, gesture, and exotic imagery is strongly reminiscent of the poetry of Else Lasker-Schüler.

Thematically, the poem's representation of the emotional crises and sexual confusions of male puberty can be read as a counterargument to Freud's *Three Essays on the Theory of Sexuality* and to *The Interpretation of Dreams;* the poem was, in the memorable phrase of Ludwig Hevesi, "a fairy-tale book but not for the children of philistines." Neither focusing on the "physics of love," as one contemporary reviewer described *Three Essays,* nor affirming the hermeneutic in *The Interpretation of Dreams,* which reduces the chaotic imagery of dreams to rational explications, the text nonetheless engages the complexity of adolescent experience in a radically new manner. Rather than constructing a narrative that can be interpreted psychoanalytically—or analytically at all, for that matter—Kokoschka sets up a dialectic between the enigmatic simplicity of the illustrations and the explicitly exorbitant, often violent language of the text. The poem can be understood finally as the tentative exploration of a new relationship between body language and language itself, which is even expressed directly in lines such as "i . . . understood the dark words of your skin."

Such implicitly sophisticated articulations of the relationship between sexuality and textuality reveal a highly self-conscious literary artisan at work rather than the naive beginner Kokoschka later made himself out to be. In a letter written late in 1907 to his fellow art student Erwin Lang, Kokoschka reports that his "book of fairy tales" reveals a "psyche [becoming] more efficient and complex by the day." The same letter reveals that Kokoschka is already an informed reader of Karl Kraus's *Die Fackel* (*The Torch*), in which questions of sexuality and eroticism are directly linked to cultural criticism: "Fackel-Kraus has bitten the Fledermaus's lavatory attendant in the leg, because she's not wearing a dress designed by Hoffmann." This witty paraphrase of Kraus's satire on the overwrought aesthetic program of the Cabaret Fledermaus gives a strong hint of the stylistic registers of which the literarily inclined young painter was capable. Soon afterward, he would meet Adolf Loos, one of the major architects of modernism, on the occasion of the Kunstschau 1908, the signal Viennese art exhibition that enshrined Gustav Klimt as the supreme painter of the decorative style. Under Loos's influence and unstinting patronage, Kokoschka would turn away from his valuable connections with Klimt and his associates, join the circle of outsiders around Kraus, Loos, and Peter Altenberg, and eventually participate in the activities of the artists and writers brought together in Berlin by Herwarth Walden's *Der Sturm* (*The Tempest*), the first and most important Expressionist journal.

The turning point was the legendary performance of two plays, entitled at the time "Drama" and "Komödie," at the Kunstschau 1909. The first of these was *Mörder, Hoffnung der Frauen* (1910; as *Murderer the Women's Hope* and *Murderer Hope of Womenkind*), an extremely abbreviated one-act play featuring a Strindbergian "battle of the sexes." The stage directions, which include detailed descriptions of costumes and movements, are almost as extensive as the dialogue itself, and the frequent references to primary colors and light effects reflect the painter's sensibility at work. Clearly, the minimalist conception of character and the strong emphasis on costumes and sets that magnify the primal emotions conditioned the play's reception by both contemporaries and subsequent scholarship. This tendency was certainly reinforced by Kokoschka's own staging of the play in Dresden in 1917. Although scholars have tended to view *Murderer, Hope of Women* quite simply as the very "Beginning of Expressionist Drama," as one commentator put it—recently, feminist-inspired critiques have traded on what they perceive as its intentional misogynist ideology—contemporary reviews provide the impetus for a more complex response. Citing the tendency toward caricature and self-parody in Kokoschka's earliest artistic work, one critic suggested that the dramatic action, such as it was, was calculated as "ridicule of the outrageous 'Salome' mania and of overly serious, 'deep' interpretations of life." This perspective, which encourages an interpretation of the play as a corrective to those contemporary dramas that merely reproduced the fear-induced male fantasy of the castrating female, also helps explain why Kokoschka avoided using the loaded term *Weib* and chose *Frau* instead to designate his female characters. The former was associated particularly with Otto Weininger's enormously popular book *Geschlecht und Charakter* (1903; *Sex and Character*), which sets up an absolute dichotomy between male intellectuality and female sexuality that explicitly devalues the latter. Textual complexities of this kind indicate that caution is in order when positing the influence of Weininger's misogynist pseudophilosophy or even of Bachofen's notion of a progression from maternal law through sexual anarchy to patriarchy as ideological blueprints for the play's thematic concerns.

Although Kokoschka's other plays and poems of this first, crucial period are similarly concerned with sexual tension and with the clash of male and female sensibilities, his work does not succumb to rigid dichotomies. A poetic sketch published in the avant-garde journal *Der Sturm* (the original German text has the English title "The Eagle and the Girl"), which is unfortunately all but buried in the endnotes of the third volume of the collected works, pointedly contrasts the sympathetic understanding of the narrator for a little girl with the male gaze of "ten thousand glaring gentlemen." This sketch is more like Altenberg, the so-called troubadour of the female soul, than the Strindberg of *Murderer, Hope of Women,* and it suggests the necessity of reading Kokoschka's major texts more carefully and within the context of his entire, still inadequately edited oeuvre.

LEO A. LENSING

See also Der Blaue Reiter; Expressionism

Biography

Born in Pöchlarn, Austria, 1 March 1886. Moved with family to Vienna, 1887; attended elementary school and the Währinger *Staatsrealschule* in Vienna, 1892–1904; attended *Kunstgewerbeschule* (School of Applied Arts) of the Austrian Museum for Art and Industry, 1904–9; moved to Berlin and worked for *Der Sturm*, 1910; returned to Vienna and taught drawing at the alternative Schwarzwald School, 1911–12; volunteered for military service in the Austro-Hungarian Army, 1914; severely wounded in Galicia, 1915; moved to Dresden, 1917; held professorship at the Dresden Academy, 1919–23; traveled to Italy, France, Spain, and England, 1924–26; traveled to North Africa, Egypt, and the Near East; 1924–27; moved to Vienna, 1931; emigrated to Prague, 1934; fled to London, 1938; lived in London, 1939–45; served as president of the "Free German League of Culture," 1943; received British citizenship, 1947; guest lecturer in Boston, 1949; directed and taught in the "School for Seeing" at the Salzburg Summer Academy, 1952–62; moved to Villeneuve on Lake Geneva, 1953. Died in Villeneuve, Switzerland, 22 February 1980.

Selected Works

Collections
Dramen und Bilder, 1913
Vier Dramen, 1917
Schriften 1907–1955, edited by Hans M. Wingler, 1956
Das schriftliche Werk, vol. 1, *Dichtungen und Dramen*, edited by Heinz Spielmann, 1973; vol. 2, *Erzählungen*, edited by Heinz Spielmann, 1974; as *Stories from My Life*, translated by Michael Mitchell et al., 1998; vol. 3, *Aufsätze, Vorträge, Essays zur Kunst*, edited by Heinz Spielmann, 1975; vol. 4, *Politische Äußerungen*, edited by Heinz Spielmann, 1976

Plays
Mörder Hoffnung der Frauen (1909), first published in *Der Sturm*, 1910; *Hoffnung der Frauen* in *Dramen und Bilder*, 1913; as *Murderer the Women's Hope*, translated by Michael Hamburger, 1963; as *Murderer Hope of Womenkind*, translated by J.M. Ritchie, 1968
Der brennende Dornbusch, 1913; as *Schauspiel* in *Dramen und Bilder*, 1913; *Sphinx und Strohmann* (1909); as *Sphinx und Strohmann: Ein Curiosum* in *Dramen und Bilder*, 1913; as *Sphinx and Strawman, a Curiosity*, translated by Victor H. Miesel, 1970
Hiob: Ein Drama, 1917; as *Job, A Drama*, translated by Walter H. Sokel and Jacqueline Sokel, 1963
Orpheus und Eurydike, 1917; published in *Vier Dramen*, 1917

Poetry
Die träumenden Knaben, 1908

Other
Spur im Treibsand: Geschichten, 1956
Mein Leben, 1971; as *My Life*, translated by David Britt, 1974
Briefe I, 1905–1919; Briefe II, 1919–1934; Briefe III, 1934–1953; Briefe IV, 1953–1976, edited by Olda Kokoschka and Heinz Spielmann, 4 vols., 1984–88; as *Letters 1905–1976* (selections), edited by Olda Kokoschka and Alfred Marnau, translated by Mary Whittal, 1992

Further Reading

Cernuschi, Claude, "Pseudo-Science and Mythic Misogyny: Oskar Kokoschka's 'Murderer, Hope of Women'," *Art Bulletin* 81, no. 1 (March 1999)
Denkler, Horst, "Die Druckfassungen der Dramen Oskar Kokoschkas: Ein Beitrag zur philologischen Erschließung der expressionistischen Dramatik," *Deutsche Vierteljahrsschrift für Literaturwissenschaft und Geistesgeschichte* 40 (1966)
Gordon, Donald E., "Kokoschka and the Visionary Tradition," in *The Turn of the Century: German Literature and Art, 1890–1915*, edited by Gerald Chapple and Hans H. Schulte, Bonn: Bouvier, 1981
Hoffmann, Edith, *Kokoschka: Life and Work*, London: Faber, 1947
Hubert, Renee Riese, "Kokoschka, Kandinsky, and the Art of the Expressionist Book," *Forum for Modern Language Studies* 32, no. 2 (1996)

Knapp, Bettina, "Oskar Kokoschka's 'Murderer Hope of Womankind'," *Theater Journal* 35 (May 1983)

Lensing, Leo A., "Gesichter und Gesichte: Kokoschka, Kraus, und der Expressionismus," in *Oskar Kokoschka: Symposion, abgehalten von der Hochschule für Angewandte Kust in Wien vom 3. bis 7. März 1986 anlässlich des 100. Geburstages des Künstlers,* edited by Erika Patka, Salzburg: Residenz, 1986

————, "Scribblings Squids and the Giant Octopus: Oskar Kokoschka's Unpublished Portrait of Peter Altenberg," in *Turn-of-the-Century Vienna and Its Legacy: Essays in Honor of Donld G. Daviau,* edited by Jeffrey B. Berlin et al., Vienna: Edition Atelier, 1993

————, "Kokoschka lesen! Nörgelnde Anmerkungen eines Literaturhistorikers," in *Oskar Kokoschka: Aktuelle Perspektiven,* edited by Patrick Werkner, Vienna: Hochschule für angewandte Kunst Archiv und Sammlung, 1997

Rilke, Rainer Maria, *Haßzellen, stark im größten Liebeskreise—Verse für Oskar Kokoschka: Faksimile der Handschrift: Mit unveröffentlichten Briefen,* edited by Joachim W. Storck, Marbach am Neckar: Deutsche Schillergesellschaft, 1988

Schorske, Carl E., *Fin-de-siècle Vienna: Politics and Culture,* New York: Knopf, 1979

Schvey, Henry, *Oskar Kokoschka: The Painter as Playwright,* Detroit, Michigan: Wayne State University Press, 1982

Schweiger, Werner J., *Der junge Kokoschka: Leben und Werk, 1904–1914,* Vienna: Brandstätter, 1983

Shedel, James, "A Question of Identity: Kokoschka, Austria, and the Meaning of the Anschluss," in *Austrian Writers and the Anschluss: Understanding the Past—Overcoming the Past,* edited by Donald G. Daviau, Riverside, California: Ariadne Press, 1991

Timms, Edward, "Kokoschka's Pictographs: A Contextual Reading," *Word and Image* 6, no. 1 (January–March 1990)

Vergo, Peter, and Yvonne Modlin, "Murderer Hope of Women: Expressionist Drama and Myth," in *Oskar Kokoschka, 1886–1980,* London: Tate Gallery, and New York: Guggenheim Foundation, 1986

Werkner, Patrick, *Austrian Expressionism: The Formative Years,* translated by Nicholas T. Parsons, Palo Alto, California: Society for the Promotion of Science and Scholarship, 1993

Gertrud Kolmar 1894–1943

The poet, dramatist, and prose writer Gertrud Käthe Chodziesner (Gertrud Kolmar) is one of the most significant authors of the Weimar Republic. Similar to writings by Else Lasker-Schüler and Nelly Sachs, Kolmar's main topic is the problematic history and fate of German Jews. Until the venues for Jewish literature, performances, readings, and publications were closed, Kolmar played a central role in the Berlin *Kulturbund,* the Jewish cultural association. The oldest of the three children of defense attorney and German patriot Ludwig Chodziesner, whose family had come from Posnan, and his wife Elise, née Schönflies, the daughter of an established Jewish family from the Mark Brandenburg, Kolmar's family belonged to the Berlin élite. She was Walter Benjamin's favorite cousin and the sister-in-law of Hilde Benjamin, later minister of justice of the German Democratic Republic. Kolmar was a teacher for disabled children.

In the 1930s and 1940s, Kolmar experienced radical social descent, which was caused by Nazi Germany's anti-Semitic legislation. In 1938, her sister Hilde Wenzel took exile in Switzerland, but Kolmar apparently underestimated the risk of staying. Eventually, she and her father were forced to move from their suburban home into a ghetto house (*Judenhaus*), and she had to perform forced labor. In 1939, when she took steps to emigrate, she could not longer secure a visa. In 1943, a few months after her 81-year-old father's deportation to Theresienstadt, Kolmar was deported with the last Berlin Jewish workers to Auschwitz. Hilde Benjamin saved her poetry cycle *Das Wort der Stummen* (1978), and her sister Hilde Wenzel preserved the letters she had received from Kolmar and took charge of Kolmar's bequest.

Similar to other Jewish women writers of her generation, Kolmar fully embraced German language and culture but remained aware and proud of her Jewish heritage, which sustained her when she faced Nazi anti-Semitism. She dealt with Jewish concerns implicitly in the poetry cycle *Preußische Wappen* (1934; Prussian Coats of Arms) by reclaiming "German" territory from the point of view of a Jewish poet; she voiced these concerns explicitly in the novellas *Eine jüdische Mutter* (1981; *A Jewish Mother from Berlin*) and *Susanna* (1993; *Susanna*). Through her protagonists Kolmar problematizes the interaction between Jews and non-Jews in 20th-century Central Europe. She prioritizes the voices of outsiders and lets their marginalized point of view and inner struggles dominate her texts. Her subversive literary strategies and the preeminence of minority perceptions and themes within her German writings make her a major author of German-Jewish "Minor Literature," as defined by Gilles Deleuze and Félix Guattari (*Kafka: Toward a Minor Literature,* 1986).

Kolmar, a certified translator of French, English, and Russian, served as a censor of prisoners' of war correspondences in World War I. Her writing combines linguistic sensitivity with directness and clarity of style. The latter, traits of Weimar *Neue Sachlichkeit* (New Objectivity), are tempered by Kolmar's indebtedness to German classicism, Realism, and Romanticism. In her work, Kolmar's love for the Bible and Jewish mysticism, German literary discourses, personal experience, and poetic visions and inspirations also coalesce. Kolmar spent her life in Berlin, except for her studies in France, short-term assignments as a private tutor, and brief trips such as the one with Karl Josef Keller in 1934 to Hamburg and the Baltic Sea. She draws on all aspects of her experiences of spatial confinement and thwarted love and motherhood, not to mention her expertise as a teacher to articulate her engagement for the oppressed: women, Jews, the poor, the homeless, and animals. Female desire, sensuality, and the constructedness of femininity are central issues in works such as *German Sea,* a poetry cycle written under the pseudonym Helen Lodgers.

Despite the hardships that Kolmar faced in the 1930s, she was highly productive during that period. She published collections of poetry and contributed individual works to journals, magazines, and anthologies such as *Herz zum Hafen* (1933), *Die literarische Welt* (1933), *Der Weiße Rabe* (1933), and *Jüdische Lyrik der Zeit* (1938). Her two novellas, not published until after the Shoah, *Das Bildnis Robespierres* (1965), *Welten* (1947), the four-act drama *Cécile Renault,* and her extensive correspondence with her sister (1970) were produced within a decade. Kolmar's last volume of poetry, *Die Frau und die Tiere,* appeared in the fall of 1938.

Sensitive to the wider implications of the notions of "man" and "humanity," Kolmar shows that the bias against Jewish and female bodies and psyches must be linked to the Cartesian hierarchy of beings and values. She examines reality from the point of view of those who are vilified and discriminated against because of this dominant hierarchy. Her perceptions correspond in part to Benjamin's cultural criticism: both authors consider civilization the product of barbarism and reject European historiography because it reflects the victors' point of view. Thus, in *Das Bildnis Robespierre,* written between 1933 and 1934 in reaction to the Nazi takeover, Kolmar revises the official version of French revolutionary history. Emphasizing Robespierre's suffering, she portrays him as an unjustly maligned victim. More important, from an animal rights perspective, Kolmar casts humans as a species of predators.

Kolmar's assessment of the German culture to which Jews of former generations had aspired was shaped by the cataclysmic events of World War I and the rise of National Socialism. Herself a victim of middle-class morality, Kolmar, who as a young adult appears to have been coerced to undergo an abortion to accommodate her family's sense of propriety, confronts the destructive effects of secular Christian morality on women. The loss of a child and the destruction of the bond between mother and daughter are recurring themes throughout her work. Often women's issues are interconnected with Jewish concerns; *Eine jüdische Mutter* portrays an assimilated Jewish woman's loss of identity, which results from her own internalized anti-Semitism and her isolation as a woman in a patriarchal society. Alienation and disorientation are the major causes for the demise of Kolmar's women protagonists.

Kolmar's poems are mostly written from the point of view of the ones who suffer, but her narratives also explore the mind-set of the aggressors and individuals who identify with their oppressors. Such is the case with Martha Wolg (*Eine jüdische Mutter*), who mistakenly assumes that her gentile neighbors will support her in her despair over the disappearance of her daughter and that her non-Jewish lover will help her to track down the sex offender who traumatized the child. This not being the case, the distraught mother, who, out of touch with the Jewish community as well, murders her child, believing her act to be mercy killing, euthanasia. In *Susanna,* Kolmar validates a young woman's archaic, sensuous, and poetic view of the world, which is informed by Jewish themes and imagery, to illustrate that the protagonist's East European Jewish community, the setting of the novella, fails not only one of its members but also itself by conforming to secular Christian and protofascist patterns. At the eve of the Shoah, Kolmar points toward a complicity between National Socialism and the Jews who act as its facilitators by re-linquishing their traditional values and subscribe to rationalist pseudoscience and social Darwinism.

DAGMAR C.G. LORENZ

Biography

Born in Berlin, 12 October 1894. Cousin of Walter Benjamin; teacher of French and English; mail censor and translator in the prisoner-of-war camp, Döberitz, 1917–18; governess and private tutor in Ebermergen, Peine, Berlin, and Hamburg, 1919–27; language studies in Dijon, France, 1927; return to Berlin to manage her parents' household and nurse her sick mother and, after her death, her father Georg Chodziesner, 1927; attempts to emigrate to England fail, 1938; Kolmar and her father are forced to leave their residence in suburban Berlin and to move into a ghetto house; Kolmar entrusts her manuscripts to Karl Joseph Keller in Ludwigshafen, 1939; Hebrew studies, 1940; forced labor with Epeco, a company vital for the war effort, 1941; Georg Chodziesner deported to Theresienstadt, 1942. Deported to Auschwitz, where she died, 2 March 1943.

Selected Works

Poetry

Gedichte, 1917
Preußische Wappen, 1934
Die Frau und die Tiere, 1938
Welten, 1947
Das lyrische Werk, edited by Friedhelm Kemp, afterword by Hilde Wenzel, 1960
Weibliches Bildnis: Das lyrische Werk, 1960
Selected Poems of Gertrud Kolmar, translated by David Kipp, 1970
Dark Soliloquy: The Selected Poems by Gertrud Kolmar, translated by Henry A. Smith, 1975
Das Wort der Stummen, edited by Hilde Benjamin and Uwe Berger, 1978

Fiction

Eine Mutter, edited by Friedhelm Kemp, 1965
Eine jüdische Mutter, edited by Bernd Balzer, 1981; as *A Jewish Mother from Berlin,* translated by Brigitte Goldstein, 1997
Susanna, edited by Thomas Sparr, 1993; as *Susanna,* translated by Brigitte Goldstein, 1997
The Shimmering Crystal: Poems from 'Das Lyrische Werk' by Gertrud Kolmar (first bilingual edition), translated by Elizabeth Spencer, 1995

Letters

Briefe an die Schwester Hilde, edited by Johanna Zeitler, 1970
Briefe, edited by Johanna Woltmann, 1997

Further Reading

Blumenthal, Bernhardt George, *Gertrud Kolmar: Love's Service to the Earth,* Philadelphia, Pennsylvania: American Association of Teachers of German, 1969
Brandt, Marion, *Schweigen ist ein Ort der Antwort: Eine Analyse des Gedichtzyklus "Das Wort der Stummen" von Gertrud Kolmar,* Berlin: Hoffmann, 1993
Eichmann-Leutenegger, Beatrice, *Gertrud Kolmar: Leben und Werk in Texten und Bildern,* Frankfurt: Jüdischer Verlag, 1993
Erdle, Birgit R., *Antlitz, Mord, Gesetz: Figuren des Anderen bei Gertrud Kolmar und Emmanuel Lévinas,* Vienna: Passagen, 1994
Frantz, Barbara C., *Gertrud Kolmar's Prose,* New York: Lang, 1997
Hammer, Stephanie, "In the Name of the Rose: Gertrud Kolmar, Hélène Cixous, and the Poerotics of Jewish Femininity," in *Transforming the Center, Eroding the Margins: Essays on Ethnic and Cultural Boundaries in German-Speaking Countries,* edited by Dagmar C.G.

Lorenz and Renate S. Posthofen, Columbia, South Carolina: Camden House, 1998

Lorenz, Dagmar C.G., "The Unspoken Bond: Else Lasker-Schüler and Gertrud Kolmar in Their Historical and Cultural Context," *Seminar: A Journal of Germanic Studies* 4 (1993)

Lorenz-Lindemann, Karin, editor, *Widerstehen im Wort: Studien zu den Dichtungen Gertrud Kolmars*, Göttingen: Wallstein, 1996

Müller, Heidy M., *Klangkristalle rubinene Lieder: Studien zur Lyrik Gertrud Kolmars*, Bern and New York: Lang, 1996

Shafi, Monika, *Gertrud Kolmar: Eine Einführung in das Werk*, Munich: Iudicium, 1995

Smith, Henry A., editor, *Dark Soliloquy: The Selected Poems of Gertrud Kolmar*, New York: Seabury Press, 1975

Spencer, Elizabeth, editor, *The Shimmering Crystal: Poems from "Das lyrische Werk"* by Gertrud Kolmar, London: Millennium, 1995

Woltmann, Johanna, *Gertrud Kolmar: Leben und Werk*, Göttingen: Wallstein, 1995

König Rother

König Rother is a 12th-century tale of adventure, which is counted traditionally among the group of early courtly *Spielmannsepen*. The bipartite structure of the narrative, centered on the recurrent motif of bridal capture, is typical of orally transmitted epic. At the same time, contemporary political concerns transformed this popular narrative into a text that had relevance for the latter part of the 12th century. Because of the numerous Bavarian noble families named in the narrative, it is generally assumed that the audience, at least, can be located in the Upper German regions. The language of the oldest and nearly complete surviving manuscript (Heidelberg, cpg 390) shows a hybrid mix of Middle German, Bavarian, and Low Frankonian forms. Traditionally, scholars have identified the poet as a Rhine Frankonian who composed for a southern audience; more recent studies, however, have suggested that the clerical poet was of Low German descent. This combination of linguistic and geographical evidence attests further to cultural and literary exchanges that are known to have existed between the Middle German and Bavarian regions. An additional indication of oral sources may be found in similarities between the *König Rother* and the North Germanic saga tradition. Scholars have long pointed to striking motivic correspondences between *Rother* and the story of Osantrix in the 13th-century Old Norse *Thidrekssaga*. Common to both traditions are the wooing of a noble bride through messengers and the subsequent assistance of powerful giants. Several specific narrative analogues, however, restrict the parallel to the first part of *Rother*. Critical judgment has favored either a common source for both works or the incorporation of an earlier saga version of *Rother* into the story of Osantrix. Both theories presume earlier oral stages in the transmission of a popular tale of adventure. This secular background gives to *Rother* a unique position in receptive tendencies: it is one of the first narrative works preserved in German to be derived from predominantly vernacular traditions.

The young King Rother, who rules the western empire from his court in Bari, determines at the advice of his councilors to take a suitable wife. He sends emissaries to woo the daughter of Constantin, King of Constantinople. The mission ends in political disgrace when the messengers are imprisoned by the eastern ruler. In order to free his men and to complete their mission, Rother himself journeys with a small band of men (and giants) to the east. At the court of Constantin he claims to be Dietrich, who has allegedly fled because he was an enemy to Rother. In this guise Rother offers his service to Constantin and establishes his position at the eastern court. In a ruse to gain access to Constantin's daughter, Rother sends to her a silver and a golden shoe. During an ensuing private meeting, Rother betrays his identity and gains her confidence. She persuades her father to release the imprisoned messengers, who secretly recognize their lord Rother. They are entrusted fully to Rother when news is received of a military attack by Ymelot of Babylon. With Rother's strategy of surprise, the pagan forces are defeated and Ymelot is taken captive. Constantin requests that Rother deliver the welcome news to the women at court. Instead, Rother claims that Ymelot has defeated and killed Constantin and that the women should flee with him. Only after the daughter is on his ship does Rother proclaim his identity to all those remaining on shore. His ruse brings both his messengers and his bride back to Bari; during the trip Rother's bride conceives a child. At the close of the first part, political stability in the west has been restored after an upheaval during Rother's absence.

The narrative pattern of the second half mirrors the first, with an emphasis on trickery, disguise, and abduction. Upon realizing that he has been duped, Constantin agrees to a similar ruse in order to win back his daughter. A minstrel disguised as a merchant journeys to Bari and lures Rother's bride onto his ship to see its precious wares. She is then returned to Constantinople and is promised as a bride to the son of Ymelot, who has once again besieged the eastern kingdom. Rother sets out after her with a large military force, yet he enters Constantine's city in the garb of a pilgrim, accompanied by only a few others. After revealing himself to his bride, Rother surrenders and names the place where he wishes to hang. This final trick represents a confluence of past and present strategies. Rother awakens the sympathy of Count Arnolt, who was previously among his allies at Constantin's court. Rother's present troops await him at the site proposed for his hanging and respond on cue to a horn signal; they then free Rother and defeat the pagans. Constantin now regrets his treatment of Rother and prepares a ceremonial delivery of his daughter to her victorious consort. Although Constantin is spared, his political power is reduced considerably; Rother's ally Arnolt is named king of Greece. When the couple returns to Bari, the child Pippin, the father of Charlemagne, is born. A concluding segment details Pippin's elevation to knighthood and kingship in Aachen once he reaches the age of 24. At the advice of Berker von Meran, both Rother and his wife enter a cloister for their remaining days.

The contemporary political significance of *König Rother* can be related to both imperial and regional concerns. For instance, the work legitimizes the concept "empire" and its German dynasty by the resolution of tensions between western and eastern kingdoms. Rother functions as the ideal Christian emperor, whose abilities will pass on to Charlemagne and, by extension, to Barbarossa in the 12th century. The importance of regional courts and their patronage of literature in this latter period is also well supported by the text of *König Rother*. Many of the family and place names (Tengelingen, Dießen, etc.) are attested in contemporary Bavarian historical records. The figure Berker von Meran has been used to help date the work, since the noble title associated with Meran was granted only in 1152. On the basis of additional names and titles, the text of *Rother* is generally now dated within the range of 1160 to 1180. Further manuscript fragments exist from the 13th and 14th centuries. Aside from later scattered references to the protagonist's name, there is no surviving textual evidence of late medieval reworking of *König Rother*.

SALVATORE CALOMINO

See also Middle High German

Editions

First edition: *König Rother,* edited by F.H. von der Hagen, Berlin, 1808

Critical editions: *Rother,* edited by Jan de Vries, Heidelberg: Winter, 1922; *König Rother,* edited by Theodor Frings and Joachim Kuhnt, Bonn and Leipzig: Schroeder, 1922

Translations: modern German translation as *König Rother: Geschichte einer Brautwerbung aus alter Zeit,* translated by Günter Kramer, Berlin: Verlag der Nation, 1961; in English as *King Rother,* translated by Robert Lichtenstein, Chapel Hill: University of North Carolina Press, 1962

Further Reading

Bahr, Joachim, and Michael Curschmann, "Spielmannsdichtung," in *Reallexikon der deutschen Literaturgeschichte,* vol. 4, 2nd edition, Berlin: de Gruyter, 1984

Bumke, Joachim, *Mäzene im Mittelalter: Die Gönner und Auftraggeber der höfischen Literatur in Deutschland, 1150–1300,* Munich: Beck, 1979

Curschmann, Michael, *Der Münchener Oswald und die deutsche spielmännische Epik,* Munich: Beck, 1964

De Boor, Helmut, *Die deutsche Literatur von Karl dem Grossen bis zum Beginn der höfischen Dichtung: 770–1170,* Munich: Beck, 1949; 8th edition, 1971

Gellinek, Christian, *König Rother: Studie zur literarischen Deutung,* Bern: Francke, 1968

Haug, Walter, "Struktur, Gewalt, und Begierde: Zum Verhältnis von Erzählmuster und Sinnkonstitution in mündlicher und schriftlicher Überlieferung," in *Idee-Gestalt- Geschichte: Festschrift Klaus von See,* edited by Gerd Wolfgang Weber, Odense: Odense University Press, 1988

Klein, Thomas, "Zurþiðreks Saga," in *Arbeiten zur Skandinavistik,* edited by Heinrich Beck, Frankfurt: Lang, 1985

Meves, Uwe, *Studien zu König Rother, Herzog Ernst und Grauer Rock (Orendel),* Frankfurt: Lang, 1976

Ortmann, Christa, and Hedda Ragotzky, "Brautwerbungsschema, Reichsherrschaft, und staufische Politik: Zur politischen Bezeichnungsfähigkeit literarischer Strukturmuster am Beispiel des *König Rother*," *Zeitschrift für deutsche Philologie* 112 (1993)

The Saga of Thidrek of Bern, translated by Edward R. Haymes, New York: Garland, 1988

Schröder, Walter Johannes, *Spielmannsepik,* Stuttgart: Metzler, 1962; 2nd edition, 1967

———, *Spielmannsepik,* Darmstadt: Wissenschaftliche Buchgesellschaft, 1977

Stein, Peter K., "'Do newistich weiz hette getan. Ich wolde sie alle ir slagen hanc': Beobachtungen und Überlegungen zum *König Rother*," in *Festschrift für Ingo Reiffenstein zum 60. Geburtstag,* edited by Peter K. Stein, et al., Göppingen: Kümmerle, 1988

Szklenar, Hans, "König Rother," in *Die deutsche Literatur des Mittelalters: Verfasserlexikon,* 2nd edition, vol. 5, New York: de Gruyter, 1985

Urbanek, Ferdinand, *Kaiser, Grafen und Mäzene im "König Rother,"* Berlin: Schmidt, 1976

Vollmann-Profe, Gisela, *Geschichte der deutschen Literatur von den Anfängen bis zum Beginn der Neuzeit. I/2: Wiederbeginn volkssprachiger Schriftlichkeit im hohen Mittelalter (1050/60–1160/70),* 2nd edition, Tübingen: Niemeyer, 1994

Helga Königsdorf 1938–

In the epilogue to her first volume of short stories, *Meine ungehörigen Träume* (1978; My Impertinent Dreams), Helga Königsdorf acknowledges that, even as a child, she had always wanted to write. Yet in the 40 years before this public declaration, Königsdorf (also called Helga Bunke) followed a more conventional, academic path, establishing herself as a successful mathematician and becoming a professor at the Academy of Sciences in East Berlin, with responsibility for a department of probability studies and statistics. Despite her growing literary success, Königsdorf continued to work as a mathematician for many years, and much of her creative work is informed by a cross-fertilization of the scientific and the poetic.

Over the 20 years of her literary career, Königsdorf has experimented with a wide variety of narrative styles and literary forms. Two collections of short stories, *Der Lauf der Dinge* (1982; The Way Things Go) and *Lichtverhältnisse* (1988; Quality of Light), include, in the first collection, a literary reworking of Saint-Exupéry's *The Little Prince* and, in the second, a reworking of Kafka's *Metamorphosis*. *Respektloser Umgang* (1986; With a Lack of Respect) charts imaginary meetings between historical and fictional characters. *Ungelegener Befund* (1989; Inconvenient Findings) features epistolary exchanges between a lecturer and—among others—the object of his affection, a young male supervisee. In the novel *Die Entsorgung der Großmutter* (1997; Disposing of Grandmother), the grandmother of the title has more impact on those around her through her absence than ever before. Throughout, Königsdorf's narrators remain distanced from the action, dissecting, analyzing, and commenting on events and characters around them. The critical eye of the scientist is never far away, observing the incongruities and paradoxes of the societal stage on which the characters play their parts. Interwoven throughout Königsdorf's work are strong elements of irony and dark, even black, humor, as her narrators are forced to face the sham and absurdity of their situation and the fiction that they have created of their lives.

Much of Königsdorf's literary work draws on personal experience, and her work contributes greatly to the ongoing debate among writers such as Christa Wolf, Helga Schütz, and Christine Wolter on the position of women in GDR society. Königsdorf's short stories, written largely in the 1980s, are best known for the way in which they examine the role and perception of women in the personal and professional spheres of their lives, primarily through an exploration of women's relationships with male partners and colleagues. In "Bolero" (*Meine ungehörigen Träume*), perhaps Königsdorf's most famous short story, the narrator seeks in vain for the reason why, after a few months in a rather mediocre secret affair with a statistician she met at a conference, she grabs his ankles, as he leans over the balcony in her high-rise apartment, and tips him over the edge. Ten years later, in "Unterbrechung" (*Lichtverhältnisse*), Königsdorf examines the thoughts and feelings of an older mother who, going into hospital for an abortion, is faced with the news that a hysterectomy will also be performed. The objectification of the narrator by her partner, her son, and the male doctors in the hospital reveals the tension between her public family life and her private self, a theme that reappears in many of Königsdorf's novels.

A common theme, too, is the responsibility of the scientist to academic truth. A number of Königsdorf's characters face the dilemma of being rewarded for work they know is based on false premises or unsound research findings. In her first novel, *Respektloser Umgang*, with its fictitious meeting between the historical figure of Lise Meitner and a narrator who is also a scientist suffering from a debilitating disease, Königsdorf draws on her personal experience of Parkinson's Disease to broaden her discussion to questions of the academic and societal responsibility for the exploitation of scientific findings and the responsibility of the individual to stand up against oppressive and dehumanizing forces.

It is, therefore, not surprising that Helga Königsdorf should play such an important role during the events of fall 1989 in the GDR. Through her talks and political essays, she challenged the Socialist Unity Party from within to reform itself and face the challenges being posed by the GDR population. With other women writers such as Christa Wolf and Helga Schütz, she called upon the Party to acknowledge the internal difficulties the GDR was facing, and she individually apologized for the role writers had played in fabricating a public face for the system through their unwillingness to accept, even in private, that the state they supported did not uphold the socialist values in which they believed. In her continuing defense of *Menschenwürde* (human dignity) and in her demands that others should look equally critically at their own collusion, Königsdorf proved an unwelcome thorn in the side of many. She left the Party in January 1990, convinced of its inability to reform, yet was honest in her acknowledgment of the role it had played in the lives of writers such as herself: "Diese Partei ist uns Heimat gewesen . . . Die Partei war uns Vater und Mutter" (This party was our fatherland . . . The party was our father and mother). Her subsequent writings, particularly *Adieu DDR* (1990; Farewell GDR) and *Unterwegs nach Deutschland* (1995; On the Road to Germany) have, on the one hand, sought to give a voice to the experience of ordinary people in the ex-GDR in the momentous period of transition to a single German nation; on the other hand, they explore the individual's unfulfilled need to replace the familial comfort provided by the party with an alternative collective. Such collectives include a lesbian relationship in *Gleich neben Afrika* (1992; Just off Africa), the relations among tenants of a Berlin *Mietshaus* in *Im Schatten des Regenbogens* (1993; In the Shadow of the Rainbow), or a more conventional family unit in *Die Entsorgung der Großmutter*. The search for a new identity within postunification Germany that nonetheless encompasses the earlier GDR experience and the intrinsic value of maintaining one's own personal integrity are themes that Königsdorf continues to explore within both her political and literary writings.

As a writer whose creative output is firmly rooted in her own personal, professional, and political experience, Königsdorf succeeds in addressing issues that go well beyond her immediate surroundings. Even before 1990, Königsdorf's literary success was far from confined to the GDR; she enjoyed a well-established readership within the Federal Republic, and her earlier works have been translated, albeit not yet into English. This is an unfortunate oversight, for the English-speaking world has much to learn and enjoy from her keen observations on life, subtle use of irony, and unbounded dark humor.

JEAN E. CONACHER

Biography

Born in Gera, 1938. Studied physics in Jena and Berlin; completed her doctoral work in mathematics, 1963; professor at the Academy of Sciences, heading up a department of probability and statistics, 1974; writing career began in 1978 with the publication of *Meine ungehörigen Träume,* a collection of short stories; active during the *Wende* of fall 1989, publishing both literary works and political essays. Heinrich Mann Prize, GDR Academy of Arts, 1985. Currently lives in Berlin.

Selected Works

Short Stories

Meine ungehörigen Träume, 1978
Der Lauf der Dinge, 1982
Mit Klischmann im Regen, 1983
Hochzeitstag in Pizunda, 1986
Lichtverhältnisse, 1988
Die geschlossenen Türen am Abend, 1989
Ein sehr exakter Schein, 1990
Der gewöhnliche Wahnsinn, 1998

Novels
Respektloser Umgang, 1986
Ungelegener Befund, 1989
Gleich neben Afrika, 1992
Im Schatten des Regenbogens, 1993
Die Entsorgung der Großmutter, 1997

Other
1989; oder, Ein Moment Schönheit, 1990
Adieu DDR: Protokolle eines Abschieds, 1990
Aus dem Dilemma eine Chance machen, 1990
Über die unverzügliche Rettung der Welt, 1994
Unterwegs nach Deutschland: Über die Schwierigkeit, ein Volk zu sein; Protokolle eines Aufbruchs, 1995

Further Reading

Clausen, Jeanette, "Resisting Objectification," in *Studies in GDR Culture and Society 10*, edited by Margy Gerber, Lanham, Maryland: University Press of America, 1991

Conacher, Jean E, "Pressing for Change: The Case of Helga Königsdorf," in *Women and the Wende: Social Effects and Cultural Reflections of the German Unification Process*, edited by Elizabeth Boa and Janet Wharton, Amsterdam and Atlanta, Georgia: Rodopi, 1994

Gerber, Margy, "Impertinence, Productive Fear, and Hope: The Writings of Helga Königsdorf," in *Socialism and the Literary Imagination*, edited by Martin Kane, New York: Berg, 1991

Hammer, Klaus, "Mobilisierung der Humanität," *Neue Deutsche Literatur 35*, no. 8 (1987)

Kaufmann, Eva, "Haltung annehmen: Zu Helga Königsdorfs Erzählung *Respektloser Umgang*," in *DDR-Literatur '86 im Gespräch*, edited by Siegfried Rönisch, Berlin: Aufbau, 1987

Kirchner, Verena, "Helga Königsdorfs *Respektloser Umgang*," *Der Gingko-Baum 9* (1990)

Lauckner, Nancy A., "The Treatment of the Past and Future in Helga Königsdorf's *Respektloser Umgang*: 'Sich der Erinnerung weihen oder für die Zukunft antreten? Mit der Vergangenheit im Bunde'," in *Studies in GDR Culture and Society 10*, edited by Margy Gerber, Lanham, Maryland: University Press of America, 1991

Schmidt, Ricarda, "History Reflected in the Imaginary: Pre-Revolutionary Attitudes towards the Process of History in Works by Christa Wolf, Helga Königsdorf, Angela Krauss, and Irina Liebmann," in *The Individual, Identity and Innovation: Signals from Contemporary Literature and the New Germany*, edited by Arthur Williams and K. Stuart Parkes, Bern and New York: Lang, 1994

Stawström, Anneliese, "Ein bißchen Paradies: Sehr viel Hölle: Eben Leben," *Der Gingko-Baum 9* (1990)

Konkrete Dichtung *see* Concrete Poetry

Konrad von Regensburg fl. 1170

Konrad von Regensburg, known primarily as Pfaffe Konrad, names himself as the author in the epilogue to the 12th-century German *Rolandslied*: "ich haize der phaffe Chunrat." In this adaptation of the Old French *Chanson de Roland*, Konrad further praises his patrons, a certain Duke Heinrich and the "noble duchess" who helped to procure his source. Although it is generally agreed that Konrad was a lay priest, the period and location of his literary activity have caused considerable debate. The identity of Konrad has inevitably been linked to individual scholarly opinions about the real-life identity of the "Duke Heinrich" mentioned in the epilogue to the *Rolandslied*. Evidence has been presented for the sponsorship of Heinrich der Stolze, Heinrich Jasomirgott, and Heinrich der Löwe; all three were associated with Bavarian ducal houses during successive generations of the 12th century. Coincidentally, each Heinrich was married at some point to the daughter of a king, a point also highlighted in Konrad's testimonial epilogue. In recent decades critical opinion has again favored strongly the patronage of Heinrich der Löwe, who in 1168 married Matilde, the daughter of Henry II of England and Eleanor of Aquitaine. The likelihood of this Heinrich as the sponsor dates Konrad's literary activity to the period around 1170.

Although a general agreement prevails about the time of Konrad's composition, geographical associations and proof of professional status have been more elusive. Since Heinrich der Löwe was the Duke of Bavaria and Saxony, it is logical that either region could have been associated with court literature under his patronage. Most scholars have traditionally favored the location of Regensburg in Bavaria, in part because of evidence within the text of the *Rolandslied* itself. For instance, Konrad singles out Duke Naimes of Bavaria and comments on the nobleman's sword, which was allegedly forged in Regensburg. Additional place names mentioned by Konrad have been localized by some to Bavaria, but other critics have expressed skepticism. The most striking association between Konrad and Regensburg can be found in textual parallels between the *Rolandslied* and the *Kaiserchronik*, which dates from the middle of the 12th century. The latter work, a compendium of historical and legendary tales spanning the period from classical Rome up to Emperor Konrad III (1147), has been localized conclusively to Regensburg. Konrad borrows freely from and indeed cites passages from the *Kaiserchronik* in his own work. Because of this textual coincidence, earlier generations attributed authorship of the *Kaiserchronik* to Konrad. Although this thesis has been abandoned, the correspondences between the *Rolandslied* and the *Kaiserchronik* are now generally cited as evidence that connects Konrad to the literary traditions of Regensburg. A further possibility, which must for the present remain open, is that Konrad potentially contributed to a subsequent or final version of the *Kaiserchronik* (Kartschoke).

In contrast to the evidence for Regensburg, some scholars have maintained Konrad's association with Braunschweig in Saxony on political and historical grounds. As the Duke of both Bavaria and Saxony, Heinrich der Löwe's primary center of political power was his court at Braunschweig; allegedly, for political or cultural reasons, he spent far less time in Regensburg (Ashcroft). According to this line of argument, Heinrich's attempts to foster the cultural reputation of his northern territories could explain his patronage of Pfaffe Konrad's *Rolandslied* at the court in Braunschweig. In addition to supporting individual works of art such as the gospel book of Helmarshausen, Heinrich had rebuilt the Braunschweig cathedral dedicated to St. Blasius, who was also his own patron saint. Coincidentally, Pfaffe Konrad introduces the figure of St. Blasius into his adaptation of the *Rolandslied*; his reference to relics of St. Blasius has been interpreted as further proof of a northern base within Heinrich's territories. Konrad's detailed acquaintance with the Regensburg *Kaiserchronik* would then also presume a dissemination of this latter work well beyond its Bavarian origins.

Since proponents of both claims use textual references from the *Rolandslied* to support their arguments, it has been necessary to reevaluate the language or physical evidence from the surviving manuscripts. On such paleographical points, however, there has been little agreement. Nearly all documentation of the *Rolandslied* stems from the late 12th century: the Heidelberg Ms. P and Straßburg Ms. A (the latter was destroyed in 1870, although an 18th-century partial printing survives) as well as the majority of fragments attest to the popularity of the work soon after its completion. Common to all manuscripts of the *Rolandslied* is a perplexing mix of dialectal features, which has been variously interpreted. The combination of Upper and Middle German traits has been seen as evidence for the work's provenance in both Bavaria and Saxony. A compromise that continues to share some regular support is that Konrad was a Rhine Franconian working in the vicinity of Regensburg. Further paleographical evidence for a southern locale has been sought in the scribal drawings of Ms. P (and, potentially, Ms. A). The sketches can be related to stylistic features predominant in Regensburg and other southern areas. Finally, the title "Phaffe" has undergone manifold speculations. Examinations of charters at Heinrich der Löwe's courts and chancery have yielded a number of possibilities for identifying Konrad and his functions within religious, legal, or administrative circles. Although a conclusive match cannot be postulated, it is generally assumed from the religious tone of the *Rolandslied* that Konrad's theological training was predominant.

Despite Konrad's assurances that he neither expanded nor reduced his source, considerable differences exist between the *Rolandslied* and surviving versions of the *Chanson de Roland*. Nearly all commentaries on the German text emphasize the focus on crusading as a major theme, whereas the specifically national depiction of France is eliminated. In the German text, Emperor Karl or Charlemagne is depicted as the ideal Christian ruler whose religious mission has a direct association with God. In lengthy speeches and commentaries on the narrative, Konrad strengthens the religious significance of his version of the tale. Konrad's epilogue also bears the distinction of being the first German secular narrative to name its patron. Surviving manuscripts show the great popularity of Pfaffe Konrad's work until the end of the 12th century. During the following generation, Wolfram von Eschenbach drew on the *Rolandslied* for his adaptation of the chanson de geste in *Willehalm*. Pfaffe Konrad's text was supplanted in the 13th century by the *Karl* of Der Stricker; the latter reworking of the *Rolandslied* remained popular in manuscript until the 15th century. A version of Konrad's *Rolandslied* was also used as a source for the anonymous *Karlmeinet* compilation from the early 14th century.

SALVATORE CALOMINO

Biography
Names himself as Pfaffe Konrad ("phaffe Chunrat") in the epilogue to the *Rolandslied* (Heidelberg Ms. P, cpg 112), from ca. 1170. Specific biographical dates are not known, nor does evidence of other literary activity from the period survive.

Selected Works
Das Rolandslied, ca. 1170; as *Rolandslied,* edited by Carl Wesle, 1928; 3rd revised edition, edited by P. Wapnewski, 1985; as *Das Rolandslied des Pfaffen Konrad,* edited by Dieter Kartschoke, 1996

Further Reading
Ashcroft, Jeffrey, "Konrad's 'Rolandslied,' Henry the Lion, and the Northern Crusade," *Forum for Modern Language Studies* 22 (1986)

———, "Magister Conradus Presbiter: Pfaffe Konrad at the Court of Henry the Lion," in *Literary Aspects of Courtly Culture: Selected Papers from the Seventh Triennial Congress of the International Courtly Literature Society,* edited by Donald Maddox and Sara Sturm-Maddox, Woodbridge, Suffolk, and Rochester, New York: Brewer, 1994

Backes, Herbert, *Bibel und Ars praedicandi im Rolandslied des Pfaffen Konrad,* Berlin: Schmidt, 1966

Beckers, Hartmut, "'Karlmeinet'-Kompilation," in *Die deutsche Literatur des Mittelalters: Verfasserlexikon,* 2nd edition, vol. 4, New York: de Gruyter, 1983

Bertau, Karl, "Das deutsche Rolandslied und die Repräsentationskunst Heinrichs des Löwen," *Der Deutschunterricht* 20 (1968)

Bumke, Joachim, *Mäzene im Mittelalter: Die Gönner und Auftraggeber der höfischen Literatur in Deutschland, 1150–1300,* Munich: Beck, 1979

Gellinek, Christian, "The Epilogue of Konrad's 'Rolandslied': Commission and Dating," *Modern Language Notes* 83 (1968)

Kartschoke, Dieter, *Die Datierung des deutschen Rolandsliedes,* Stuttgart: Metzler, 1965

———, "Noch einmal zum 'Rolandslied,'" *Zeitschrift für deutsches Altertum* 122 (1993)

Nellmann, Eberhard, "Pfaffe Konrad," in *Die deutsche Literatur des Mittelalters: Verfasserlexikon,* 2nd edition, vol. 5, New York: de Gruyter, 1985

Ott-Meimberg, Marianne, *Kreuzzugsepos oder Staatsroman? Strukturen adeliger Heilsversicherung im deutschen "Rolandslied,"* Zurich: Artemis, 1980

——, "'Di matteria di ist scone': Der Zusammenhang von Stoffwahl, Geschichtsbild, und Wahrheitsanspruch am Beispiel des deutschen 'Rolandsliedes,'" in *Grundlagen des Verstehens mittelalterlicher Literatur: Literarische Texte und ihr historischen Erkenntniswert,* edited by Gerhard Hahn and Hedda Ragotzky, Stuttgart: Kröner, 1992

Sudermann, David P., "*Hortus Temporum:* Beginning the Middle High German 'Rolandslied,'" *Modern Philology* 92 (1995)

Vollmann-Profe, Gisela, *Geschichte der deutschen Literatur von den Anfängen bis zum Beginn der Neuzeit. I/2: Wiederbeginn volkssprachiger Schriftlichkeit im hohen Mittelalter (1050/60–1160/70),* 2nd edition, Tübingen: Niemeyer, 1994

Werner, Wilfried, *Das Rolandslied in den Bildern der Heidelberger Handschrift,* Wiesbaden: Reichert, 1977

Wesle, Carl, "Kaiserchronik und Rolandslied," *Beiträge zur Geschichte der deutschen Sprache und Literatur* (Halle) 48 (1924)

Siegfried Kracauer 1889–1966

Similar to so many of his contemporaries (Kisch, Tucholsky, Benjamin, and Bruckner), Kracauer influenced the intellectual and cultural development of the Weimar Republic as a prominent Publizist (publicist) who commented on a wide range of political, social, and cultural affairs in newspaper pieces, essays, and glosses. He qualified initially as an architect and practiced for ten years from 1911–21, but in 1920 he began contributing to the eminent liberal journal *Frankfurter Zeitung.* He rose to become editor of its feuilleton, but, as a left-wing Jew, he had to flee from Germany soon after Hitler's accession to power. Throughout the 1920s his journalistic activities kept him in close touch with the mood and feel of the times, which he sought to explain, interpret, and mediate through his writing. In common with like-minded colleagues he believed in the primacy and persuasiveness of facts, concrete information, and rational discussion, which he thought almost inevitably led to left-wing political sympathies. His strong interest in sociology—he wrote an early work entitled *Soziologie als Wissenschaft: Eine erkenntnistheoretische Untersuchung* (1922; Sociology as a Science: An Epistemological Study)—brought him into association with the famous Frankfurt Institut für Sozialforschung (Institute for Social Research), which provided much theoretical underpinning of the then fashionable Marxist analyses of German society. Despite his close collaboration and personal friendship with leading thinkers in this organization—including Theodor Adorno, Max Horkheimer, and Ernst Bloch—Kracauer disagreed with its overtly political line, preferring to maintain an independent stance of critical detachment; he was one of that class of progressive liberals described by Weber as the "floating intelligentsia." Although his intellectual development had been informed by the thought of Max Scheler and Georg Simmel—an early study of the latter remained unpublished—Kracauer's suspicion of ideological thinking that failed to be anchored in actual sociological content and reality made for an uneasy relationship between him and the Frankfurt School. When later in America a commission was obtained for Kracauer to write a study of fascist propaganda in Germany for the *Zeitschrift für Sozialforschung* (Journal of Social Research), he refused to allow the publication of his text, which had been extensively rewritten by Adorno.

The hunger for immediacy and authenticity prevalent in the Weimar Republic favored reportage and documentary, the Zeitroman (novel of actuality), and Zweck—or Gebrauchskunst (applied or useful art)—all of which were typified by the Neue Sachlichkeit (New Objectivity) movement and were congenial to Kracauer's nature and style. He recognized the significance of the social signals carried by art, and he gained a reputation for his sociologically oriented film critiques and his critical observations on other vehicles of mass entertainment. He believed that the fashion for biography in the late 1920s arose from the need to satisfy the widespread desire for authenticity. In line with the vogue for works about World War I and its aftermath, he wrote a novel himself, *Ginster* (1928; Broom), although the fact that his semiautobiographical hero stayed at home made this an ironically reverse bildungsroman.

Kracauer maintained that any particular time could be characterized more accurately by analyzing its trivial and superficial phenomena than by accepting its own verdict on itself, for he argued that the banal and insignificant unconsciously express the true reality of a period. With this conviction he looked for meaning in neglected themes and unusual social topics, seeking the dynamic of the actual in the vibrant world about him, in its hidden, unobserved, or marginalized detail. In the many apparently disparate themes that Kracauer wrote about in the 1920s, he was seeking to identify the topography of the modern (urban) consciousness, seeing the city or metropolis as a "labyrinth of fragmentary signs." The spotlight was not on high art but on the phenomena of popular mass culture, which he termed far more accurate indicators of the true temper of an epoch. The cinema and photography, revues and operetta, detective stories and biography, the street and advertisements, the circus, sport, and leisure pursuits—such heterogeneous topics attracted Kracauer's analytic gaze, for he saw his life's work as an attempt "to bring out the significance of areas whose claim to be acknowledged in their own right has not yet been recognized."

Kracauer's best-known work was also founded on this conviction. The penetrating sociological study *Die Angestellten* (1930; White Collar Workers) was first published in the *Frankfurter Zeitung* before the Wall Street crash initiated the Great Depression. It described in general terms, backed up by sometimes harrowing examples, a disturbing picture of this sector of the labor market. Kracauer explained the demoralizing effects of office rationalization on individuals who were subjected to monotonous, interchangeable work and treated as replaceable automata. He also delineated the marked hierarchical structures in business, with the consequent lack of meaningful communication vertically and distrust on all sides, which were, in turn, aggravated by the friction caused by rampant favoritism and connections; the minimally beneficial and protective roles of the arbitration courts and the ineffectual Labor Exchanges; the schemes for employee welfare, sport, and leisure whose covert aim was to polish the firm's image and strengthen staff loyalty; and the function of other establishments such as "amusement palaces," cinemas, and dance halls, which supplied the "cultural needs" of the employees. Kracauer deduced that all aspects of the relationship between a business and its staff were devised to support and confirm the "pre-established harmony" of free enterprise, and he painted a truly somber picture of the "anonymous privates of the white-collar army."

The underlying theme of the accelerating capitalist process of rationalization in the labor market, which was particularly acute in Germany in the wake of the 1924 Dawes Plan for the payment of reparations, was seen by Kracauer in human terms, with graphic descriptions of its impact on individuals. The book's sense of everyday lives in the fabric of society is more memorable than its implicit theoretical analysis; the alienation and reification of human beings is as convincingly demonstrated as it would be in a textbook. In pursuing his researches into this segment of society, Kracauer found the "exoticism of the everyday far more fantastic than any film trip to Africa," which corroborated his belief in the significance of apparently unremarkable and insubstantial aspects of the social fabric. Walter Benjamin praised the study as a "milestone on the road to politicizing the intelligentsia," and it also made a profound impact on the novelist Hans Fallada as he worked on *Kleiner Mann - was nun?* (1932; *Little Man, What Now?*). These two books defined the German Kleinbürgertum (petty bourgeoisie) in unambiguous terms on the eve of the Nazi era.

When *Die Angestellten* was consigned to the flames in 1935, along with other "subversive" literature, Kracauer had already been living in Paris for two years, where he wrote a second novel, *Georg* (1934; George), which remained unpublished until after his death, and produced his last work in German during his lifetime, *Jacques Offenbach und das Paris seiner Zeit* (1937; *Jacques Offenbach and the Paris of His Time*), which appeared simultaneously in French and English, and which examined the life of the composer as well as the social conditions of the operetta as a genre. In 1941 Kracauer sailed to New York with the help of an affidavit procured by Max Horkheimer, where he managed a bare subsistence for the next years with help from earlier émigrés and grant-giving foundations. He also found a small job in the film library of the Museum of Modern Art, where he returned to his earlier passion for the cinema. Henceforth Kracauer wrote in English. Numerous articles on varied aspects of the cinema—silent comedy, Jean Vigo, stereotypes in Hollywood, the Nazi newsreel, and the role of the spectator—added to his considerable output from the 1920s and culminated in 1947 with a major opus, *From Caligari to Hitler: A Psychological History of the German Film* (1947). This rigorously focused study presents a coherent and plausible interpretation of German films since World War I as a subconscious manifestation of the collective German psyche—the guilt, frustration, nationalism, ambition, and covert desire for authoritarianism of a nation that anticipated Hitler and that paved the way for his easy acceptance. With his conviction that the mass medium of film is a reliable seismograph of social and political forces, Kracauer contends that through an analysis of German films, "deep psychological dispositions predominant in Germany from 1918 to

1933 can be exposed—dispositions which influenced the course of events during that time and which will have to be reckoned with in the post-Hitler era." The impact of this work, controversial as it was, can be judged by the fact that the German version in 1958 was cut by half, which arouses the suspicion that it had to be made palatable for a German readership that had been intensively exposed to Nazi ideology.

A further thoughtful study of the principles and techniques of the cinematic art followed in 1960. In *Theory of Film: The Redemption of Physical Reality*, Kracauer examined coherently and expertly all the disciplines that come together in filmmaking—photography, acting, dialogue, music—as well as the role of the spectator, and the function of fact and literature, experiment and avant-garde, and adaptation. Sections of the book are constantly reprinted in volumes on film theory. During the 1950s Kracauer engaged in academic activities as research director in the Bureau of Applied Social Research at Columbia University. But after *Theory of Film* he fell silent on the genre (although he did revise the German translation of the book) and spent his remaining years engrossed in the philosophy of history. Published posthumously, *History: The Last Things before the Last* (1969), remained an uncompleted and ultimately unsuccessful attempt to bring Kracauer's disparate interests—mass culture, social analysis, and film journalism—into a coherent pattern.

ARRIGO V. SUBIOTTO

Biography

Born Frankfurt am Main, 8 February 1889. Studied architecture, philosophy, and social sciences; practiced as an architect, 1911–21, but switched to journalism; contributed essays, reviews, and glosses as a member of the staff of the *Frankfurter Zeitung*, 1920–33, where he became feuilleton editor in Frankfurt and then in charge of the cultural section in Berlin; fled to Paris, 1933, and New York, 1941; after 1937, published only in English, followed later by German translations; employed in the film section of the Museum of Modern Art during the 1940s; research director in the Bureau of Applied Social Research, Columbia University, 1952–58; to the end exile was painful for him, and assimilation difficult. Died in New York, 26 November 1966.

Selected Works

Collections
Schriften in acht Bänden, edited by Karsten Witte, 1971–76

Novel
Ginster: Von ihm selbst geschrieben, 1928

Scholarly Writing
Die Angestellten: Aus dem neuesten Deutschland, 1930
Jacques Offenbach und das Paris seiner Zeit, 1937; as *Jacques Offenbach and the Paris of His Time*, translated by Gwenda David and Erich Mosbacher, 1937
History: The Last Things before the Last, 1969; as *Geschichte - vor den letzten Dingen*, translated by Karsten Witte, 1973

Film Criticism
From Caligari to Hitler: A Psychological History of the German Film, 1947; as *Von Caligari bis Hitler: Ein Beitrag zur Geschichte des deutschen Films*, translated by Ruth Baumgarten, 1958
Theory of Film: The Redemption of Physical Reality, 1960; as *Theorie des Films: Die Errettung der äußeren Wirklichkeit*, translated by Friedrich Walter and Ruth Zellschan, 1964

Essays
Das Ornament der Masse: Essays, 1963; title essay as The Mass Ornament, translated by B. Cowell and J. Zipes, New German Critique 2, 1975

Further Reading
Arnold, Heinz Ludwig, editor, Siegfried Kracauer, Munich: Text und Kritik 68, 1980

Frisby, David, Fragments of Modernity: Theories of Modernity in the Work of Simmel, Kracauer, and Benjamin, Cambridge: Polity Press, 1985
Kessler, Michael, and Thomas Y. Levin, editors, Siegfried Kracauer: Neue Interpretationen, Tübingen: Stauffenburg, 1990
Mülder, Inka, Siegfried Kracauer, Grenzgänger zwischen Theorie und Literatur: Seine frühen Schriften (1913–1933), Stuttgart: Metzler, 1985

Karl Kraus 1874–1936

Georg Trakl and Adolf Loos called him a prophet. Thomas Mann lauded him as a master stylist. Walter Benjamin described him as a "Dämon" who had performed the "authentically Jewish salto mortale of worshipping the image of divine justice in language." Bertolt Brecht considered him to be an innovative dramatist. Franz Kafka remarked that the "truth in Kraus's writing hand" was as substantial as the one in his own. Berthold Viertel esteemed Kraus as an "Erzjude." Theodor Adorno admired his great probity and "self-immolating" spirit. Yet, at the same time, Theodor Lessing characterized Kraus as "the most radiant example of Jewish self-hatred." Anton Kuh ridiculed his elaborate dialectics and extravagant syntax. Franz Werfel figured him as a vain and shallow "Spiegelmensch." Hermann Bahr sued him for libel. Elias Canetti, a quondam disciple, ultimately decided that he was a cruel egomaniac. Arthur Schnitzler thought he was petty. Kraus was, in short and if nothing else, controversial, alternately venerated and vilified to extreme degrees.

Kraus began his artistic career as an actor. It soon became apparent that his talents in this area were limited, and he left acting after an ill-fated debut in 1893. If he couldn't be on stage, however, he would write about it. And in the early 1890s, Kraus began a spectacular, 40-year-long career in journalism by writing theater reviews for publications such as Die Gesellschaft and the Neue freie Presse. By the late 1890s, Kraus's range had become broader. He had begun writing feuilletons, a genre that he would later condemn as inherently insidious, and critical essays on a variety of cultural and political issues: Karl Lueger's political victories, the nationalist uproar over Badeni's language reforms, the demolition of the Café Griensteidl, and, most famously, Zionism. Indeed, it was with his satirical response to Zionism, Eine Krone für Zion (1898; A Crown for Zion), that Kraus attained a place of prominence in an extremely competitive journalistic milieu.

The real watershed development in Kraus's career, however, was the founding of his satirical newspaper Die Fackel, which appeared for the first time on 1 April 1899. Kraus's gesture was paradoxical. He was, in effect, rejecting Viennese journalism. Die Fackel was not the product of an editorial revolt; it was not meant to function simply as an alternative to existing newspapers. Rather, its mission was to expose the moral turpitude of the mass press. Die Fackel was a journal against journalism. And so, Kraus became one of Viennese journalism's central figures by turning away from established journalism.

Kraus's critique of the press did not simply consist of sweeping condemnations. Embedded in his satires and polemics was a sophisticated analysis that anticipated the Frankfurt School theory of the "culture industry." As noted, Kraus's animus was directed against that most prestigious and popular genre in fin de siècle Vienna's coffeehouse culture: the feuilleton. The feuilleton was deleterious, according to Kraus, because in conflating fact-based reporting and literature it attenuated both. In his infamous polemic against Heine, Heine und die Folgen (1910; Heine and the Consequences), Kraus compared the feuilleton to a venereal disease, which, carried into Germany from France by Heine, seriously jeopardized the fecundity of the German language.

According to Kraus, the inevitable concomitant of feuilletonist poetic pretensions was that reporting became unreliable and distorted by poetic whim. Indeed, Kraus saw what he perceived to be the mass press's increasing laxity with regard to checking facts as a result of the feuilletonist spirit. Forever prepared to use the threat of public humiliation as a deterrent, Kraus frequently employed hoaxes to expose editorial sloppiness. For example, in 1913, Kraus wrote to the Neue freie Presse pretending to be a seismologist who, because he happened to be underground investigating mines at the time, was able to record an otherwise undetected earthquake. The Neue freie Presse published the letter and reported the specious earthquake, furnishing Kraus with considerable grist for his satirical mill.

There is a telling subplot to this story. Kraus gave to his specious seismologist a Jewish name—Irwin Winkler. When Kraus revealed the hoax, he surmised that the seismologist's Jewish name played an important role in getting his letter published. The liberal press in general and the Neue freie Presse in particular were Jewish, according to Kraus, and gave nepotistic encouragement to their own. Kraus's readiness to integrate anti-Semitic stereotypes into his critique of the press is certainly troubling. It is also confusing, as Kraus was a fierce and enduring opponent of anti-Semitism. He converted to Catholicism in 1911, but he left the church in 1923 to protest Max Rheinhardt's involvement in the Salzburg festival. And his explicit discussion of his Jewish identity, "Er is doch e Jud" (1913; He's Still a Jew), is an exercise in paradox flaunting, a mode of cognition at which Kraus excelled and which, as Kraus well knew, many of his readers regarded as a kind of secular Talmudic practice. Here, Kraus both identifies with and distances himself from Jewish culture. He underlines his reputation as a modern-day Old Testament prophet while attacking "Jewish venality." Kraus uses most of his space in this piece, however, to debunk simplistic definitions of Jewish identity. Understandably, then, Kraus was often decried as a self-hating Jew; just as often, however, he was venerated as ur-Jewish. The question of the way in which Kraus's relation to Judaism affected his relation to language and his writing remains very much alive. In fact, for better or for worse, the majority of critical analyses of Kraus's work currently being produced in the Anglo-American world focus on his lurid, problematic Jewish identity.

To return to Kraus's analysis of the press, he claimed that mass-produced literature cannot be literature at all. Kraus may not have been a great fan of Schiller's dramas, but he certainly stands in the Schillerian tradition of aesthetic theory. For Kraus, true art, on the production as well as on the consumption end of the process, turns upon the free play of the imagination. The constraints of journalism—deadlines, fidelity to fact, and profit-mongering editors and owners—curtail free play, resulting in bad, formulaic literature. Moreover, the bad aesthetics of the feuilleton point to another level of bad ethics. Kraus argued that the feuilleton compromised the autonomy of literature. His correlative was that it dulled the poetic imagination: word choice becomes a matter of dealing with exigencies, when it should be about care and sensitivity. Within this mass market, Kraus claimed, all sense for the particularity of words is lost and, with it, all sense for particularity in general. In his essay "Die Sprache" (Language), Kraus wrote that language is the basis for all ethical activity. It is only here, in language, that we struggle to make "right decisions" without any threat of punishment. As the influential literary critic and essayist Erich Heller put it, "Kraus saw the connection between maltreated words and maltreated bodies."

If the feuilleton was bad for the feuilletonists, Kraus argued, it was even worse for the readers. Breezily impressionistic, the feuilleton subtly invaded the imagination, for by pre-packaging responses to daily events, it obviated any kind of imaginative response from the reader. As the popular imagination atrophied, it became that much more dependent on the feuilleton for imaginative responses. As the culture industry was for Horkheimer and Adorno, the feuilleton was for Kraus a perniciously self-perpetuating phenomenon. It systematically colonized the popular imagination, and, in doing so, it created mass markets for itself. Nothing could be more dangerous. Kraus believed that maintaining a humane society was a matter of maintaining the integrity of those spaces in which the imagination and basic critical faculties could grow to maturity. Accordingly, Kraus's objection to the press's invasion of the imagination found a famous complement in his attack against Sittlichkeitsgesetze, the attempts to legislate ethics, especially sexual ethics. In Sittlichkeit und Kriminalität (1908; Ethics and Criminality), he contended that Sittlichkeitsgesetze would effectively destroy Sittlichkeit or ethical life, since ethical life consisted of the process of mature deliberation that Sittlichkeitsgesetze would eliminate. Hence, Kraus's controversial defense of prostitution. If adults wished to patronize prostitutes, they should be able to do so. This decision is a personal decision—its social effects are limited—and it should therefore be made be the individual, not by the state.

Kraus also argued that legalizing prostitution would also stem the flood tide of bourgeois moral hypocrisy that he felt was particularly rampant in the liberal press. The press launched slashing invectives against prostitution and, in general, positioned itself as the custodian of good bourgeois values, even as it made large sums of money from personal ads in which men sought out women willing to be dominated in exchange for financial support. (Kraus frequently "deconstructed" such ads, laying bare not only the hypocrisy of the papers that ran them, but also the hypocrisy of the men that placed them. "Beethoven und Goethe" (1922) offers a poignant example of this process.) Indeed, according to Kraus, a press that was dependent on advertising had no business taking the moral high ground, as the judgment of such a press was severely compromised by its connection to corrupt, big-business interests. Of course, the press was itself big business, and Kraus never tired of pointing out how ruthlessly capitalistic newspaper owners influenced, and even dictated, editorial policy. Kraus's most famous (and perhaps most successful) clean-up-the-press campaign was in fact directed against Irme Békessy, a Hungarian tycoon who owned several tabloids in Vienna.

For Kraus, the corruption of the press did not stop at scandal mongering. He even claimed that the press was responsible for the great calamity of World War I. According to Kraus, the press's enervating effect on the popular imagination rendered the masses unable to imagine the horrors of modern warfare, thereby making such horrors possible. Kraus's logic on this point is straightforward. Catastrophes are major news. Newspapers profit from catastrophes. As profit-oriented institutions, large newspapers will do whatever they can to promote catastrophes. The pro-war patriotism of liberal newspapers during World War I, therefore, was a sham. It was employed to influence public opinion in favor of the war or, more precisely, it was employed so that the war would go forward, creating years of tragic, fantastically lucrative news. As Kraus portrayed them in his satires, newspaper owners were indifferent to human suffering. Hence, in his massive World War I drama Die letzten Tage der Menschheit (1919; The Last Days of Mankind), the newspaper owners and editors are painfully out of sync with the other characters. Portrayed as laughing hyenas, they dance and gloat at the end of the play, as the world is consumed by flames. Whereas everyone else is wracked by loss, grief, and gloom, they have made out well and are happy. So entrenched is their inhumanity that are able to enjoy the "destruction of the world through the black magic of newspaper ink."

The Last Days of Mankind is the best known of Kraus's dramas. He also wrote several others, including Literatur; oder, Man wird doch da sehn (1921; Literature; or, We'll Have to See), a brilliant and hilarious parody of Franz Werfel's play Der Spiegelmensch. The others are Traumstück (1923; Dream Play), Wolkenkuckkucksheim (1923; Cloud Cuckoo's Nest), Traumtheater (1924; Dream Theater), and Die Unüberwindlichen (1928; The Indomitiable Ones). In addition, Kraus published nine short volumes of poetry, all of which were entitled *Worte in Versen*. Kraus's verse is far removed from the innovative, difficult modernist poetry he admired (Kraus vigorously championed Georg Trakl and Else Lasker-Schüler). His poetry is lapidary, almost affectedly so. One is tempted to call it innocent, as its metrics are so basic and its themes so ingenuous (e.g., the death of a favorite dog). Indeed, Kraus's poems are interesting largely because they contrast so saliently with his devastatingly critical, elaborately formulated prose. Kraus was also an accomplished aphorist, who produced three volumes of aphorisms: *Sprüche und Widersprüche* (1909; Dicta and Contradictions), *Pro domo et mundo* (1912; For Home and World), and *Nachts* (1919; Nights). He was even frequently compared with Lichtenberg. Kraus was, furthermore, both a theorist of translation and a translator. When Friedrich Gundolf retranslated *Macbeth*, Kraus responded with an annihilating review, "Hexenszenen und anderes Grauen" (1926), which was rich in witticisms as well as in technical commentary. Kraus's own efforts at translating Shakespeare are, conversely, highly regarded (he translated Shakespeare's sonnets), as are his rendering of Offenbach's librettos. He put these translations or *Nachdichtungen,* as he called them, to immediate use. Of the hundreds of public readings Kraus gave, his readings of Shakespeare and Offenbach were widely considered to be the most brilliant. Public readings played a crucial role in Kraus's career. Many of his writings were first made public through public readings and published only subsequently. According to many accounts, including those of Elias Canetti and Theodor Adorno, Kraus was a fascinating lecturer whose skills as a dramatic reader may even have exceeded his accomplishments as a writer. Certainly, most of those contemporaries who were interested in Kraus viewed him as both a performer and a critic, and not simply as a critic who occasionally read from his work. Kraus's performances were set up in self-conscious opposition to the pompous settings and ornamentation of the Vienna's Burgtheater. Alone on stage, dressed in a plain black suit, with a table and a glass of water as his only props, Kraus would keep audiences riveted for hours with his intensity and virtuoso mimicry. While critics agreed that Kraus's skills as a performer were almost preternatural (for Walter Benjamin, Kraus the mimic was a kind of sublime *Unmensch*), they vigorously debated the effect of these skills. The case of Elias Canetti is instructive. Once an enthusiastic auditor, Canetti peremptorily decided that Kraus was too spellbinding on stage and that he was dangerously captivating; he then stopped attending Kraus's lectures. Even amid unanimity, Kraus managed to create controversy.

PAUL B. REITTER

See also Austria: Late Habsburg Literature in Vienna; Adolf Loos; Vienna

Biography

Born in Jicin, Bohemia, 28 April 1874. Studied law and German literature at the University of Vienna, 1892–98; contributed book and theater reviews and satirical pieces to various German and Austrian periodicals, including *Die Gesellschaft,* the *Wiener Rundschau, Die Wage,* and the *Neue freie Presse,* 1892–99; turned down an editorial position at the *Neue freie Presse* and founded *Die Fackel,* 1899, by writing every issue himself; converted to Catholicism, 1911; proposed for the Nobel Prize for literature by several professors at the Sorbonne,

Paris, 1925; published the final number of *Die Fackel,* number 922, and gave 700th public reading, 1936. Died in Vienna, 12 June 1936.

Selected Works

Collections
Werke, edited by Heinrich Fischer, 14 vols., 1952–67

Journalism
Die Fackel, 922 numbers, 1899–1936

Plays
Die letzten Tage der Menschheit, 1919; edited by Christian Wagenknecht, 1986; as *The Last Days of Mankind,* abridged and edited by Frederick Ungar, translated by Alexander Gode and Sue Ellen Wright, 1974
Literatur; oder, Man wird doch da sehn, 1921
Traumstück, 1923
Wolkenkuckkucksheim, 1923
Traumtheater, 1924
Die Unüberwindlichen, 1928

Aphorisims
Sprüche und Widersprüche, 1909
Pro domo et mundo, 1912
Nachts, 1919
Half-Truths and One-and-a-Half Truths: Selected Aphorisms, edited and translated by Harry Zohn, 1976

Other
Die demolirte Literatur, 1896
Eine Krone für Zion, 1898
Sittlichkeit und Kriminalität, 1908
Heine und die Folgen, 1910
Weltgericht, 1919
Untergang der Welt durch schwarze Magie, 1922
Literatur und Lüge, 1929
Die dritte Walpurgisnacht, 1936
In These Great Times: A Karl Kraus Reader, translated by Joseph Fabry, edited by Harry Zohn, 1976

Further Reading

Adorno, Theodor, "Sittlichkeit und Kriminalität," in *Noten zur Literatur,* Frankfurt: Suhrkamp, 1965
Benjamin, Walter, "Karl Kraus: Allmensch-Unmensch-Dämon," in *Schriften,* vol. 2, Frankfurt: Suhrkamp, 1955
Heller, Erich, "Karl Kraus: The Last Days of Mankind," in *The Disinherited Mind,* Philadelphia, Pennsylvania: Dufour and Saifer, and Cambridge: Bowes and Bowes, 1952
Iggers, Wilma Abeles, *Karl Kraus: A Viennese Critic of the Twentieth Century,* The Hague: Martinus Nijhoff, 1967
Jenaczek, Friedrich, *Zeittafeln zur Fackel,* Gräfelfing: Gans, 1965
Lensing, Leo, "'Kinodramatisch': Cinema in Karl Kraus's *Die Fackel* und *Die letzten Tage der Menschheit,*" *German Quarterly* 55, no. 4 (Fall 1982)
———, "Heine's Body, Kraus's Corpus: Sexuality and Jewish Identity in Karl Kraus's Literary Polemics against Heinrich Heine," in *The Jewish Reception of Heinrich Heine,* edited by Mark H. Gelber, Tübingen: Niemeyer, 1992
Ribeiro, António, "Karl Kraus's Modernism: A Reassessment," in *The Turn of the Century: Modernism and Modernity in Literature and the Arts,* edited by Christian Berg et al., Berlin and New York: de Gruyter, 1995
Timms, Edward, *Karl Kraus, Apocalyptic Satirist: Culture and Catastrophe in Habsburg Vienna,* New Haven, Connecticut: Yale University Press, 1986

Wagner, Nike, *Geist und Geschlecht: Karl Kraus und die Erotik der Wiener Moderne*, Frankfurt: Suhrkamp, 1982

Zohn, Harry, *Karl Kraus and the Critics*, Columbia, South Carolina: Camden House, 1997

Die Fackel 1899–1936

Satirical Journal published by Karl Kraus

Although it appeared for the first time on April Fool's Day, 1899, Karl Kraus's satirical newspaper *Die Fackel* was no joke. Vienna received *Die Fackel* with all due seriousness. According to eyewitnesses, thousands of curious literati were so transfixed by Kraus's rancorous wit and linguistic virtuousity that they stopped in the street to read the first *Fackel*. The effect was spectacular. The cover of *Die Fackel* is red, and Vienna is supposed to have turned red on the day it arrived.

Kraus soon became quite literally synonymous with *Die Fackel,* known to friends and foes alike as "der Fackelkraus." He was its sole editor from its inception until its end—or for 37 years and 922 numbers. Early contributors included Otto Stoeßl, Houston Stewart Chamberlain, and Adolf Loos. However, beginning with issue number 338 in 1911, Kraus wrote *Die Fackel* by himself.

Kraus generally published three numbers a month. Yet there were several extended cessations in its publication: once, early on, when Kraus was afflicted with nervous exhaustion, and again, only for much longer, after Hitler's ascent to power in 1933. Although the lead article in the issue that marked the resumption of publication was promisingly entitled "Warum *Die Fackel* nicht erscheint" (Why *The Torch* hasn't appeared), Kraus did little substantively to explain his initially taciturn response to Nazism.

After breaking his silence, Kraus used *Die Fackel* largely to combat Nazism, dedicating its final numbers to a capacious critique of the Nazis and fascist culture: *Die dritte Walpurgisnacht.* Kraus had made similar use of *Die Fackel* earlier. In addition, *Die Fackel* often contained Kraus's poems and aphorisms. Yet for the most part, *Die Fackel* consisted of essays and transcriptions of public lectures about Viennese culture. Kraus's topics ranged widely, encompassing everything from international relations to minute questions of syntax. Recurring themes include Viennese literature and the theater, "ethics and criminality," the legislation of ethical life, language, and, most prominently, corruption in the press.

Die Fackel was in fact founded as an anti-newspaper. Kraus began his career in the early 1890s publishing theater reviews and caustic essays on Viennese culture and politics. His *Wiener Briefe,* as such feuilletons were called, appeared in influential newspapers such as *Die Gesellschaft* and the *Neue freie Presse.* During the late 1890s Kraus developed into one of Vienna's most successful satirists. He also developed a deep-seated antipathy for the Viennese press. And so, when the *Neue freie Presse* needed to replace its satirist Daniel Spitzer, it offered the position to Kraus, who promptly declined it. Despite Kraus's precocity, the offer came as a surprise, for Kraus had been extremely critical of the paper's feuilleton editor, Theodor Herzl. The rejection was just as unexpected. The *Neue freie Presse* was Vienna's most pretigious newspaper. It was the *New York Times* of fin de siècle Vienna. Flatly declining a job at the *Neue freie Presse* was something a young journalist simply didn't do. Kraus made this unheard-of affront complete by using family money—his father was a wealthy Bohemian paper manufacturer—to start a journal that would expose and excoriate corruption in the journalism industry. That paradoxical journal-beyond-journalism was *Die Fackel*. In essay after essay, Kraus satirized the hypocrisy of the *Neue freie Presse* and, especially, that of its editor Moriz Benedikt. Kraus's critique was two-pronged. First, he objected to its fraudulent liberal moralism. For Kraus, any major newspaper that was financially dependent on advertising was bound to write in support of big business. Second, the *Neue freie Presse* was to be condemned as the arch-propagator of the feuilleton. And the feuilleton was, according to Kraus, a pernicious mixture of reporting and literature. Not only was it often factually suspect where factual accuracy should be of paramount importance, but, even worse, with its literary pretensions—its prepackaged sentiments and images—it obviated any kind of critical or imaginative response from the reader. The feuilleton therefore eroded vital critical faculties and the popular imagination. In response, Kraus established a newspaper that, beyond being explicitly critical of the mass media, would be its structural antipode: financially independent and cognitively challenging. Kraus achieved all these goals. The attacks that Kraus launched from the pages of *Die Fackel* were so annihilatingly effective that the *Neue freie Presse* found itself outmanned by a newspaper of one. Unable to exchange fire with Kraus, it attempted "to silence him to death" (*totzuschweigen*).

The influence of *Die Fackel* was both broad and profound. It was read throughout the German-speaking world—not only in major urban areas but in places such as Bukovina as well. It served as an inspirational model for Herwath Walden, whose journal *Der Sturm* was one of the most important organs of Expressionist thought, and for Ludwig von Ficker, editor of *Der Brenner.* And *Die Fackel* was an enduring source of fascination and provocation for many leading intellects: Freud, Kafka, Martin Buber, Walter Benjamin, and Arnold Schoenberg. It was the one nonacademic journal to which Gerschom Scholem subscribed in Jerusalem. So compelling was its appeal that Ludwig Wittgenstein arranged to have *Die Fackel* sent to his *Waldhütte* in Norway.

PAUL B. REITTER

Further Reading

Benjamin, Walter, "Karl Kraus: Allmensch-Unmensch-Dämon," in *Schriften*, vol. 2, Frankfurt: Suhrkamp, 1955

Bilke, Martina, *Zeitgenossen der "Fackel,"* Vienna: Löcker, 1981

Heller, Erich, "Karl Kraus: The Last Days of Mankind," in *The Disinherited Mind*, Philadelphia, Pennsylvania: Dufour and Saifer, and Cambridge: Bowes and Bowes, 1952

Iggers, Wilma Abeles, *Karl Kraus: A Viennese Critic of the Twentieth Century*, The Hague: Martinus Nijhoff, 1967

Jenaczek, Friedrich, *Zeittafeln zur Fackel*, Gräfelfing: E. Gans, 1965

Lensing, Leo, "'Kinodramatisch': Cinema in Karl Kraus's *Die Fackel* und *Die letzten Tage der Menschheit*," *German Quarterly* 55, no. 4 (Fall 1982)

———, "Heine's Body, Kraus's Corpus: Sexuality and Jewish Identity in Karl Kraus's Literary Polemics against Heinrich Heine," in *The Jewish Reception of Heinrich Heine*, edited by Mark H. Gelber, Tübingen: Niemeyer, 1992

Ribeiro, António, "Karl Kraus's Modernism: A Reassessment," in *The Turn of the Century: Modernism and Modernity in Literature and the Arts,* edited by Christian Berg et al., Berlin and New York: de Gruyter, 1995

Timms, Edward, *Karl Kraus, Apocalyptic Satirist: Culture and Catastrophe in Habsburg Vienna,* New Haven, Connecticut: Yale University Press, 1986

Wagner, Nike, *Geist und Geschlecht: Karl Kraus und die Erotik der Wiener Moderne,* Frankfurt: Suhrkamp, 1982

Zohn, Harry, *Karl Kraus and the Critics,* Columbia, South Carolina: Camden House, 1997

Die letzten Tage der Menschheit 1919

Play by Karl Kraus

Die letzten Tage der Menschheit (1919; *The Last Days of Mankind*) is widely considered to be one of the most innovative and powerful literary responses to World War I. It is also considered to be one of Karl Kraus's most important works. Yet *The Last Days of Mankind* has never been performed in its entirety. Kraus declined offers by Erwin Piscator and Max Reinhardt to put the play on stage. In 1930, Kraus himself gave public readings of the epilogue "Die letzte Nacht" (The Last Night) in Vienna and elsewhere in Austria. Heinrich Fischer and Leopold Lindtberg produced a version that ran in Vienna during the summer of 1964. To do so, they reduced the play's 200 scenes to 42.

Of course, this was Kraus's intention; in his preface to the book edition, which contains over 800 pages, Kraus wrote that the play was meant to be staged in a theater on Mars. Here on Earth, it would have to be performed over the course of ten evenings. Were it to be performed here, human audiences would not be able to bear *The Last Days of Mankind,* and not only because of its length. "For it is blood of their blood, and its contents are those unreal, unthinkable years, out of reach for the wakefulness of mind, inaccessible to any memory and preserved only in nightmares—those years when characters from an operetta played the tragedy of mankind." What follows these remarks is an extraordinarily comprehensive, formally innovative satirical representation of the war. There are no main characters (as Kraus put it, the play is "as heroless as hell"); there is no plot; and there is "no unity of space and time." The action, which consists mainly of conversations about actual events, takes place during the war years. The speakers are numerous and varied; the list of characters takes up 13 pages. They range from soldiers to Viennese maids to professors to the famous Nörgler or pessimist, whose vitriolic voice and resolute pacifism are close to, but not identical with, Kraus's own commentary on the war and antiwar stance. Accordingly, the setting moves from battlefields, to the streets of Vienna, to university seminar rooms, to military headquarters.

This colorful procession of voices or extreme polyphony has been called carnivalesque. Kraus himself described the play as "a tragic carnival." And much of the dialogue is farcical, such as the absurd sanctimonies of military leaders and the fatuous maunderings of provincial patriots. These moments contain strong resonances of Kraus's most important influences: Offenbach's operettas, Nestroy's farces, and Shakespeare's baroque comedies. *The Last Days of Mankind* is thoroughly grounded in venerable theatrical traditions.

But it is also forward-looking. First, the play expresses a particularly modern mode of despair, one that found theoretical articulation only after World War II. What Kraus satirizes is not so much the individual participants in the war as the war itself. The incongruity which his satire exposes is the disjunction between the magnitude of the catastrophe and the size of its progenitors. Its proportions are epic. They are puny. Scandal-mongering journalists are primarily responsible for the war, and so, for "the destruction of the world." In fact, the play ends with two journalists exulting over how splendidly their project has succeeded. Evil, as it turns out, is small, petty, banal. Even the grim consolation of tragedy is no longer available. The vulgar greed that caused the war is grotesque, as is its resultant senselessness. Satire, not tragedy, is the form appropriate to such a situation. Indeed, Kraus wrote in his preface that this situation is so grotesque that if it were represented faithfully it would satirize itself. It is tragic, but, tragically enough, no tragedy.

Second, the play's modernist orientation extends beyond its modern despair and its self-reflexivity, beyond its immanent hermeneutics—the explanation it contains of its own generic status. The formal construction of *The Last Days of Mankind* inspired modernist directors in the 1920s such as Piscator and Berthold Brecht, and it also anticipated the post–World War II documentary-drama. Kraus's use of blending techniques such as montage, which was to figure so prominently in Piscator's productions, secured for the play a place in the modernist canon. The sounds and images of war propaganda and sensationalist newspaper headlines swirl about, repeatedly invading elsewhere-focused ears and eyes, and thereby evoking the sensory chaos endemic to mass society, as well as the mass media's colonization of the individual imagination. Approximately half the dialogue consists of "clippings," texts quoted verbatim from various newspapers. These techniques were not only taken up by the Expressionist playwrights, but they also informed the development of the Expressionist *Großstadtroman* (big city novel). Consider, for example, Alfred Döblin's *Berlin Alexanderplatz.*

Kraus's incorporation of filmic techniques into his play does not mean he was a champion of early film. In fact, his attitude toward film was hardly enthusiastic. He sweepingly indicted the cinema as an instrument of propaganda. In scenes that are actually set in the movie houses, war footage functions as the backdrop against which discussions about how the war should be represented are played out. Kraus regarded film with skepticism, but he worked with it innovatively. Indeed, here Kraus pointed the way to the back-and-forth movement between dramatic action and projected images that was energetically employed in documentary dramas about World War II.

The Last Days of Mankind is also something of a war diary. Kraus's position shifted dramatically during the war, and the play registers these changes, resulting in a certain disjointedness of perspective. As Kraus moved toward socialism, and as his critique of the press and his pacifism became more radical, he reoriented the tenor and focus of the play accordingly. This epic antiwar jeremiad is intensely personal. It is only appropriate, then, that with the publication of *The Last Days of Mankind* Kraus erected the persona that would overshadow all his others: that of the apocalyptic satirist.

PAUL B. REITTER

Editions
First edition: *Die letzten Tage der Menschheit: Tragödie in fünf Akten mit Vorspiel und Epilog*, Vienna: Die Fackel, 1919
Critical edition: *Die letzten Tage der Menschheit*, edited by Christian Wagenknecht, Frankfurt: Suhrkamp, 1986
Translation: *The Last Days of Mankind*, abridged and edited by Frederick Ungar, translated by Alexander Gode and Sue Ellen Wright, New York: Ungar, 1974

Further Reading
Benjamin, Walter, "Karl Kraus: Allmensch-Unmensch-Dämon," in *Schriften*, vol. 2, Frankfurt: Suhrkamp, 1955
Field, Frank, *The Last Days of Mankind: Karl Kraus and His Vienna*, New York: St. Martin's Press, and London: Macmillan, 1967
Heller, Erich, "Karl Kraus: The Last Days of Mankind," in *The Disinherited Mind*, Cambridge: Bowes and Bowes, and Philadelphia, Pennsylvania: Dafour and Saifer, 1952
Iggers, Wilma Abeles, *Karl Kraus: A Viennese Critic of the Twentieth Century*, The Hague: Martinus Nijhoff, 1967
Lensing, Leo, "'Kinodramatisch': Cinema in Karl Kraus's *Die Fackel* und *Die letzten Tage der Menschheit*," *German Quarterly* 55, no. 4 (Fall 1982)
Mauthner, Franz, "Karl Kraus's *The Last Days of Mankind*," in *The Last Days of Mankind: A Tragedy in Five Acts*, by Karl Kraus, abridged and edited by Frederick Ungar, translated by Alexander Gode and Sue Ellen Wright, New York: Ungar, 1974
Ribeiro, António, "Karl Kraus's Modernism: A Reassessment," in *The Turn of the Century: Modernism and Modernity in Literature and the Arts*, edited by Christian Berg et al., Berlin and New York: de Gruyter, 1995
Snell, Mary, "Karl Kraus's *The Last Days of Mankind*," *Forum for Modern Literature* 4 (July 1968)
Timms, Edward, *Karl Kraus, Apocalyptic Satirist: Culture and Catastrophe in Habsburg Vienna*, New Haven, Connecticut: Yale University Press, 1986
Zohn, Harry, *Karl Kraus and the Critics*, Columbia, South Carolina: Camden House, 1997

Franz Xaver Kroetz 1946–

Franz Xaver Kroetz emerged on the West German theater scene in 1971 with the simultaneous premieres of his plays *Heimarbeit* (1971; *Homework*) and *Hartnäckig* (1971; Stiff-Necked). These brutal, naturalistic dramas portrayed the damaged existences of the Federal Republic's poor and underprivileged, whose inarticulateness and oppression by the crippling norms of a capitalist society led them on a course of self-destructive violence. Amid some public scandal created by the depiction of such acts as masturbation and attempted abortion directly on the stage, these plays met with general critical acclaim. Kroetz was heralded as the spokesman of the speechless, who aroused compassion for society's ignored outcasts. For the next decade, he continued to write prolifically and was one of the most-performed living playwrights in the German language.

Kroetz remained a major and influential figure in German theater throughout the 1970s and early 1980s. This was a time of radical experimentation, when a new generation of playwrights, including Peter Handke, Thomas Bernhard, Botho Strauß, and Heiner Müller, were questioning the efficacy of theater in portraying social reality and effecting social change. Drawing on the insights of critical theory, which linked the forms of social oppression to the market forces of the culture industry, this younger generation focused attention away from traditional political analysis to a close examination of the linguistic and behaviorist mechanisms at work in individuals. For many young authors, the parole of the future was formulated by Handke, who claimed that "Horvath is better than Brecht."

Ödön von Horvath's and Marieluise Fleisser's renewal and development of the *Volksstück* (folk play) in the 1920s and 1930s in particular provided the model for such authors as Martin Sperr, Rainer Werner Fassbinder, and Kroetz. In what came to be known as the "new" or "critical" *Volksstück*, these authors subverted the genre by exposing the bleak reality lurking just beneath the surface of the rural or proletarian idyll. Their plays share many elements with the plays of Handke, Strauß, Bernhard, and others—most notably the fragmentation of the individual who is manipulated by the increasingly mechanized forms of social interaction and by the near impossibility of true communication. The new *Volksstück* writers, however, attacked the often abstract and esoteric experiments of their colleagues as elitist and exclusionary and insisted on a realist program of politically engaged theater that was accessible to a wide audience.

For Kroetz, this insistence on a realist mode was not unproblematic. In fact, his best plays derive their effectiveness precisely from the tension between the "realistic" and the "abstract." His early plays are in this sense well-nigh paradigmatic. Within the extremely restricted dimensions of the domestic sphere, Kroetz "zooms in" (Mattson) with meticulous and seemingly naturalistic attention to detail on the banal lives of ordinary people. The bleak deprivation and desperation of the characters is rendered not only through explicit depictions of bodily functions and silent gestures, but also through a sparse, laconic language that does not function as a means of communication. Yet within the confines of this strictly mimetic mode, Kroetz hopes to reveal the social causes that cannot be portrayed directly on the stage. This he accomplishes through a highly analytic system of thematic motifs and linguistic devices that indirectly reveal the deforming and manipulative social structures determining the consciousness of his characters (Hoffmeister, Walther). Kroetz's dialogues—in a kind of stylized Bavarian dialect—show us the ellipses, the prefabricated phrases, and the linguistic rituals that clash sharply with the characters' communicative needs and that draw them seamlessly into such drastic acts as patricide (*Wildwechsel* [1973; Wild Game]), infanticide (*Heimarbeit* [1971; *Homework*], *Stallerhof* [1972; *Farmyard*] and *Geisterbahn* [1972; *Ghost Train*]), and reciprocal murder (*Männersache* [1971; Men's Business]).

Critics praised the "ultrarealism" (Cocalis) of these early plays, but drew attention to their inherent fatalism and to the danger that audiences might not recognize the social causes and see the catastrophic actions falsely as a result of the characters' own limitations. Even if the social critical subtexts were recognized, the extreme difference between the social "milieu" of the theatergoing public and the characters on stage might elicit little more than compassion at best or the thrill of the exotic at worst. Sensitive to these criticisms, Kroetz set out to create more average, articulate middle class characters capable of some development. In *Oberösterreich* (1974; Upper Austria), one of his most successful plays, catastrophe is avoided as a couple decides not to abort their child despite their precarious financial situation. After joining the German Communist Party in 1972, Kroetz continued to seek more positive solutions and experimented with agitprop and Brechtian techniques. These failed largely due to an all-too-narrow view of realism that put the political message directly into the mouths of the characters. With *Das Nest* (1975; *The Nest*), *Mensch Meier* (produced 1978; *Mensch Meier: A Play of Everyday Life*), and *Der stramme Max* (1979), Kroetz returned to the dramaturgy of *Oberösterreich,* further refining and developing the techniques that sought to illuminate the larger, more objective forces of social reality through the precise, mimetic portrayal of individuals in the private sphere. In these plays, the characters, brought to a state of existential crisis by such events as toxic waste dumping and the threat of unemployment, manage to avert catastrophe and find their way to a more human and humane, however precarious, existence.

Although Kroetz's characters are able to find a degree of solidarity, mutual respect, and refuge in the home and family, their fundamental socioeconomic circumstances remain unchanged. Kroetz has never been able to resolve his difficulties with the portrayal of positive solutions. Frustrated by Marxism's inability to deal with the complexity of postindustrial society and unwilling to follow the Communist program of Socialist Realism, Kroetz left the Party in 1980, occupying himself once again with questions of form. In *Nicht Fisch, nicht Fleisch* (1981; Neither Fish nor Fowl), he interwove the socioeconomic and private existential spheres as never before, but had less faith in the possibility of social change. The complex conflicts and contradictions required a highly analytical form that exploded the bounds of mimetic realism and achieved abstract, surreal dimensions. Increasingly, Kroetz's skepticism with regard to human agency manifested itself in his own existential crisis as an artist. *Furcht und Hoffnung der BRD* (1984; Fear and Hope of the FRG) is a collection of loosely connected monologues showing unemployed workers, artists, and intellectuals all caught in the same crisis of identity as they waver between despair and hope, isolation and the longing for solidarity, and impotence and the desire to act. *Bauern Sterben* (1985; Farmers Die) is a kind of negative parable laden with starkly symbolic images that thematizes the sociopolitical role of the theater as well as the catastrophic effects of technological progress and instrumental rationality on individuals (Mattson).

If Kroetz began his career with the conviction that the world is transparent and changeable, his growing skepticism brought him closer to the more self-reflective aesthetic concerns of authors such as Handke, Strauß, and Müller. Although some of his more recent work shows him in a self-absorbed struggle with artistic impotence, Kroetz's oeuvre as a whole will remain important and influential as it reflects the struggles of politically committed theater in the late 20th century.

INGEBORG WALTHER

Biography

Born in Munich, 25 February 1946. Studied acting in Munich, 1961–63, and at the Reinhardt Seminar, Vienna, 1964–66; worked as an actor in Munich, 1966–70; playwright-in-residence, Heidelberg Theater, 1972–73; worked as a laborer, truck driver, nurse, and banana cutter; cofounder of the Franz Xaver Kroetz Dramatik publishing house; actor in the television series *Kir Royal*, 1987; journalist for the Olympic Games in Seoul for *Die Welt*, 1988; Thoma Medal, 1970; Suhrkamp-Dramatiker stipendium, 1970; Fontane Prize, 1972; Critics Prize (Germany), 1973; Hanover Drama Prize, 1974; Lübke Prize, 1975; Drama Prize, Mühlheim, 1976; Grimme Prize, 1987. Currently lives in Altenmarkt.

Selected Works

Plays

Oblomov (adaptation of a novel by Ivan Goncharov) (produced 1968)
Julius Caesar (adaptation of the play by William Shakespeare) (produced 1968)
Hilfe, ich werde geheiratet (produced 1969); in *Weitere Aussichten*, 1976
Hartnäckig (produced 1971); included in *Drei Stücke*, 1971
Inklusive (radio play, 1972)
Der Mensch Adam Deigl und die Obrigkeit (from a work by Josef Martin Bauer) (television play, 1972)
Männersache (produced 1972); included in *Drei Stücke*, 1971; revised version, as *Ein Mann, ein Wörterbuch* (produced 1977); as *A Man, A Dictionary* (produced 1979); in *Farmyard, and Four Other Plays*, translated by Jack Gelber et al. 1976; as *Wer durchs Laub geht* (produced 1981); included in *Drei neue Stücke*, 1979; as *Through the Leaves* (produced 1983) translated by Roger Downey, 1983
Drei Stücke (includes *Männersache; Heimarbeit; Hartnäckig*), 1971
Wildwechsel (produced 1971), 1973
Michis Blut (produced 1971); included in *Gesammelte Stücke*, 1975; as *Michi's Blood* (produced 1975), in *Farmyard, and Four Other Plays*, translated by Jack Gelber et al., 1976
Heimarbeit (produced 1971); included in *Drei Stücke*, 1971; *Heimarbeit* translated as *Homework* (produced 1974); as *Home Work* (produced 1990), in *Gambit*, vols. 39–40, 1982
Dolomitenstadt Lienz (produced 1972), 1974
Globales Interesse (produced 1972; radio play, 1976)
Herzliche Grüße aus Grado (televised 1972; produced 1976)
Stallerhof (produced 1972); included in *Vier Stücke*, 1972; in English (produced 1974), in *Bauer, Fassbinder, Handke, Kroetz*, 1977; as *Farmyard*, in *Farmyard, and Four Other Plays*, translated by Jack Gelber et al., 1976
Oberösterreich (produced 1972; radio play, 1973; television play, 1976), 1974; as *Morecambe* (produced 1975)
Wunschkonzert (produced 1973), included in *Vier Stücke*, 1972; as *Request Concert* (as *Request Programme*, produced 1974); as *Request Concert* (produced 1981), in *Farmyard, and Four Other Plays*, translated by Jack Gelber et al., 1976
Muttertag (television play, 1975)
Geisterbahn (produced 1975); included in *Vier Stücke*, 1972; in English (produced 1975)
Lieber Fritz (produced 1975); included in *Vier Stücke*, 1972
Gute Besserung (radio play, 1972; produced 1982)
Bilanz (radio play, 1972; produced 1980)
Vier Stücke (includes *Stallerhof; Wunschkonzert; Geisterbahn; Lieber Fritz*), 1972
Münchner Kindl (produced 1973), 1974
Maria Magdalena (from the play by Friedrich Hebbel) (produced 1973), 1974
Die Wahl fürs Leben (radio play, 1973; produced 1980); included in *Weitere Aussichten*, 1976
Weitere Aussichten (televised 1974; produced 1975); included in *Weitere Aussichten*, 1976

Das Nest (produced 1975); included in *Weitere Aussichten*, 1976

Reise ins Glück (radio play, 1975; produced 1976); included in *Weitere Aussichten*, 1976

Gesammelte Stücke, 1975

Das Nest (radio and television play, 1976)

Weitere Aussichten: Ein Lesebuch, edited by Thomas Thieringer, 1976

Agnes Bernauer (from the play by Friedrich Hebbel) (produced 1977), included in *Weitere Aussichten*, 1976

Sterntäler, with Peter Zwetkoff (produced Braunschweig, 1977)

Verfassungsfeinde (televsion play, 1976; produced 1977), with *Nicht Fisch nicht Fleisch* and *Jumbo Track*, 1981

Mensch Meier (produced 1978); as *Mensch Meier: A Play of Everyday Life* (produced 1982), translated by Roger Downey, 1983

Drei neue Stücke, 1979

Der stramme Max (produced 1980); included in *Drei neue Stücke*, 1979

Nicht Fisch nicht Fleisch (produced 1981); with *Verfassungsfeinde* and *Jumbo-Track*, 1981

Stücke, 1981

Jumbo-Track, with Floh de Cologne (produced 1983); with *Nicht Fisch nicht Fleisch* and *Verfassungsfeinde*, 1981

Furcht und Hoffnung der BRD, with Alexandra Weinert-Purucker (produced 1984), 1984

Bauern Sterben: Materialien zum Stück (produced 1985), 1985

Help Wanted (produced 1985)

Stücke, 4 vols., 1989

Bauerntheater, 1991

Deal Soil (produced 1992)

Fiction

Der Mondscheinknecht, 1981

Der Mondscheinknecht: Fortsetzung, 1983

Other

Weitere Aussichten: Ein Lesebuch, edited by Thomas Thieringer, 1976; as *Ein Lesebuch: Stücke, Polemik, Gespräche, Filme, Hörspiele, Analysen*, 1982

Chiemgauer Geschichten: Bayerische Menschen erzählen, 1977

Frühe Prosa, Frühe Stücke, 1983

Nicaragua Tagebuch, 1985

Mythos und Politik: Über die magischen Gesten der Rechten, with Peter Glotz, 1985

Brasilien-Peru-Aufzeichnungen, 1991

Further Reading

Blevins, Richard W., *Franz Xaver Kroetz: The Emergence of a Political Playwright*, New York: Lang, 1983

Boa, Elizabeth, "Kroetz's *Nicht Fisch nicht Fleisch*: A Good Red Herring?" *German Life and Letters* 38 (1985)

Burger, Harald and Peter von Matt, "Dramatischer Dialog und restringiertes Sprechen: Franz Xaver Kroetz in linguistischer und literaturwissenschaftlicher Sicht," *Zeitschrift für Germanistische Linguistik* 2, no. 3 (1974)

Carl, Rolf-Peter, *Franz Xaver Kroetz*, Munich: Beck, 1978

Cocalis, Susan, "*Mitleid* and *Engagement*: Compassion and Political Commitment in the Dramatic Works of Franz Xaver Kroctz," *Colloquia Germanica* 14 (1981)

Hoffmeister, Donna L., *The Theater of Confinement: Language and Survival in the Milieu Plays of Marieluise Fleißer and Franz Xaver Kroetz*, Columbia, South Carolina: Camden House, 1983

Innes, C.D., *Modern German Drama: A Study in Form*, Cambridge and New York: Cambridge University Press, 1979

Mattson, Michelle, *Franz Xaver Kroetz: The Construction of a Political Aesthetic*, Oxford and Washington, D.C.: Berg, 1996

McGowan, Moray, "Botho Strauß and Franz Xaver Kroetz: Two Contemporary Views of the Subject," *Strathclyde Modern Language Studies* 5 (1985)

———, "'Die Stadt ist der Metzger': The Crisis of Bavarian Peasant Identity in Franz Xaver Kroetz's *Bauern Sterben*," *German Studies Review* 19, no. 1 (1996)

Panzer, Volker, "Franz Xaver Kroetz und die Kritiker," *Text und Kritik* 57 (1978)

Reinhold, Ursula, "Franz Xaver Kroetz: Dramenaufbau und Wirkungsabsicht," *Weimarer Beiträge* 22, no. 5 (1976)

Riewoldt, Otto F., editor, *Franz Xaver Kroetz*, Frankfurt: Suhrkamp, 1985

Walther, Ingeborg C., *The Theater of Franz Xaver Kroetz*, New York: Lang, 1990

Alfred Kubin 1877–1959

An associate of the Blaue Reiter (Blue Rider), Kubin was primarily a graphic artist whose essays, stories, autobiographical writings, and novel have led to his being described as a *Doppelbegabung* (dual talent). Although his graphic oeuvre, which spans some 60 years, contains many stylistic experiments, including excursions into abstraction, Kubin's distinctive style and themes were largely established by 1909.

Stylistically, the early graphic work, dating from the turn of the century, combines painstaking drawing with pale washes and incorporates a range of influences, including symbolism, the etchings of Max Klinger and Goya, and the flowing linear composition of *Jugendstil*. By 1907, however, Kubin had developed the pen-and-ink technique that he employed, with minor refinements, throughout his career. This *Psychographik* (psychographic art), as Kubin called it, is seen in his numerous book illustrations, which create intense atmospheric effects—usually of mystery or foreboding—from even commonplace objects.

Kubin's early drawings and paintings are almost obsessively concerned with a range of disturbing themes that recur, albeit in moderated form, throughout his career: sexuality (particularly sexual taboos), death, suffering, the weakness of the individual in the face of vast impersonal forces, mysticism, exoticism, and nightmarish visions. Not surprisingly, the response to Kubin's earliest work was divided: outraged critics branded his technique amateurish and his themes pathological, while admirers praised his uncompromising exploration of the subconscious. Kubin's characteristic themes can be traced to personal traumas in childhood and early manhood: the death of his mother, his early initiation into sexual play, his failure to find a socially acceptable career, his attempted suicide, his nervous breakdowns, and his strained relationship to his father. The positive responses to his early work, however, reflect that it expressed some of the more widespread anxieties and pessimism in turn-of-the-century Europe. Kubin's first exhibitions and publications also coincided with the rise of psychoanalysis and the concomitant interest in the subconscious mind.

Although he never renounced his visionary pen-and-ink technique, Kubin later developed a more accessible style of drawing, which, together with his book illustrations, brought him a larger audience during the 1920s. He illustrated many authors; the most congenial authors to his style were Edgar Allan Poe and E.T.A. Hoffmann. In late life, Kubin achieved widespread recognition and acceptance and received numerous public honors, including an honorary professorship. His tremulous lines and his use of ink blots in his last drawings, produced when he was over 80, push the "psychographic" technique to abstraction and remain an important influence on Austrian and German graphic artists.

The central themes of Kubin's early art are also to be found in his first and most important literary publication, *Die andere Seite* (1909; *The Other Side*). The events of this illustrated fantastic novel, which stands on the threshold between Decadence and Expressionism, are related by an unnamed first-person narrator, a graphic artist with marked similarities to the author. Most of the action is set in the Dream Kingdom, a secret realm somewhere in Asia that has been built by an immensely wealthy school friend of the narrator's, Claus Patera. Patera, a sworn enemy of progress, has constructed his exclusive, but run-down kingdom from old buildings that have been transported from all over Europe. Life in the twilit capital, Perle (Pearl), is initially more bizarre than disquieting, but as the novel progresses events become increasingly uncanny and horrific. Finally, the narrator, who has achieved a certain detachment by emulating a mysterious blue-eyed Asian tribe, witnesses the decline and destruction of Patera's creation. The novel culminates in orgiastic scenes of sex and violence and in a visionary conflict between the elusive (and apparently omnipresent) Patera and Herkules Bell, a U.S. millionaire who instigates a revolt to modernize and rationalize the Dream Kingdom. After the apocalyptic destruction of Perle and the death of Patera, the narrator, one of the few survivors, returns to Europe, where he spends years in asylums brooding on the tragic duality of existence. His thoughts are summed up in the novel's final sentence: "Der Demiurg ist ein Zwitter" (The demiurge is a hybrid).

Although Kubin feared that his novel would damage his established reputation, it was received enthusiastically by fellow artists such as Franz Marc and Lyonel Feininger. Later, Ernst Jünger praised the novel as an adumbration of the collapse of the old Austro-Hungarian Empire. An early psychoanalytic reading stressed the autobiographical dimension of the novel (underlined by the frontispiece, a self-portrait in the outdated costume of the Dream Kingdom) and interpreted *The Other Side* as a successful attempt to overcome psychosis artistically. Later critics focused on the philosophical and literary sources of the narrative, but given Kubin's extensive and eclectic reading, it is not surprising that no coherent system has emerged from the novel. Other readings have attempted to find models for the Dream Kingdom in visual art and sought to determine the relationship between Kubin's dual talents as an author and a graphic artist by analyzing the stylistic relationship between the text and illustrations of *The Other Side*. On the basis of similarities to Kafka's *Das Schloß* (1926; *The Castle*), it has also been suggested that Kubin's novel may have influenced the younger author, whom he met in Prague in 1911. Kubin himself, however, was dismissive

of such suggestions. More recently, the novel has been read as a recognition of the dual aspect of existence, embodied by Patera/Bell, and thus as the decisive turning point in the author's life and work, a reading that sits rather uneasily with Kubin's so-called Buddhist crisis of 1916.

Interpreting *The Other Side* is complicated by its eclectic amalgamation of images, text, philosophy (both Eastern and European), and autobiographical material. The enduring appeal of the novel for a wider audience, however, lies neither in its embodiment of a philosophy nor in its significance for Kubin's development, but rather in its grotesque mixture of comedy (often black) and horror and in its sense of intractable mystery, which is generated by its combination of realistic accuracy and indeterminacy.

Critical interest in Kubin increased during the 1960s and 1970s and has continued to the present day. Although neglected for many years, *The Other Side* is now seen as one of the most important fantastic novels in German literature. The influence of Kubin's graphic art is still evident, and exhibitions of his work continue to attract a large number of nonspecialist visitors.

STEVE RIZZA

Biography

Born in Leitmeritz, Northern Bohemia (now Litomerice, Czech Republic), 10 April 1877. Photography apprenticeship in Klagenfurt, 1892–96; attempted suicide, 1896; military service and nervous breakdown, Laibach, 1897; art studies at the private Schmidt-Reutte school and in the Gysis class of the Academy of Art, Munich, 1898–1900; first exhibition, Berlin, 1902; exhibition in Munich, 1904; move to Schloß Zwickledt near Wernstein am Inn, Upper Austria, 1906; member of the Neue Künstlervereinigung München, 1909–11; member of *Der Blaue Reiter*, 1911; regular contributor of drawings to the satirical periodical *Simplizisimus*, from 1912; first retrospective exhibition, Munich, 1921. Honorary member of the Prague Secession, 1929; member of the Prussian Academy of Arts, 1930; honorary professorship, 60th birthday exhibition, Vienna, 1937; member of the Bavarian Academy of the Fine Arts, 1949; Austrian State Prize for the Visual Arts, 1951; Republic of Austria, Grand Medal for Art and Scholarship, Vienna Secession Gustav Klimt Plaque, 1957. Died in Zwickledt, 20 August 1959.

Selected Works

Novel

Die andere Seite: Ein phantastischer Roman, 1909; as *The Other Side: A Fantastic Novel*, translated by Denver Lindley, 1967

Illustrations

Dostoyevsky, Fyodor, *Der Doppelgänger*, 1913
Hoffmann, E.T.A., *Nachtstücke*, 1913
Poe, Edgar Allan, *Das schwatzende Herz und andere Novellen*, 1909
Nerval, Gérard de, *Aurelia; oder, Der Traum und das Leben*, 1910
Poe, Edgar Allan, *Der Goldkäfer und andere Novellen*, 1910

Further Reading

Achleitner, Alois, "Kubin als Anreger Kafkas?" *Wort und Welt* 8 (1955)
Bisanz, Hans, *Alfred Kubin: Zeichner, Schriftsteller, und Philosoph*, Munich: Edition Spangenberg, 1977; Deutscher Taschenbuchverlag, 1980
Furness, Raymond S., "Cartographer of Darkness: The Nightmare World of Alfred Kubin," *Word and Image* 6, no. 1 (1990)
Hewig, Anneliese, *Phantastische Wirklichkeit: Interpretationsstudie zu Alfred Kubins Roman "Die andere Seite,"* Munich: Fink, 1967

Hoberg, Annegret, editor, *Alfred Kubin: 1877–1959* (Exhibition Catalogue), Munich: Spangenberg, 1990

Kubin, Alfred, *Aus meiner Werkstatt,* Munich: Nymphenburger Verlagshandlung, 1973

——, *Aus meinem Leben,* Munich: Edition Spangenberg, 1975

Lippuner, Heinz, *Alfred Kubins Roman "Die andere Seite,"* Bern: Franke, 1977

Rhein, Phillip H., *The Verbal and Visual Art of Alfred Kubin,* Riverside, California: Ariadne Press, 1989

Sachs, Hans, "Die andere Seite, ein phantastischer Roman mit 52 Zeichnungen von Alfred Kubin," *Imago* 1 (1912)

Schroeder, Richard Arthur, "From *Traumreich* to *Surréalité:* Surrealism and Alfred Kubin's *Die andere Seite,*" *Symposium* 30 (1976)

L

Elisabeth Langgässer 1899–1950

Best categorized as Expressionist, Elisabeth Langgässer's work as a whole is deeply influenced by the Catholic historical, theological, and literary tradition in which she was baptized. She is therefore often grouped with such writers as Gertrude von Le Fort (1876–1971), Werner Bergengruen (1892–1964), Reinhold Schneider (1903–58), and Protestant figures including Ina Seidel (1885–1974) and Jochen Klepper (1903–42), among others. As important as this religious aspect is for understanding her work, she was far from limited by it. She spoke positively of non-Christian writers and could quite energetically oppose the style of Catholic authors such as Theodor Haecker (1879–1945), for example. She was fully cognizant of the major German literary figures of her day, new directions in the novel (taken by Kafka and Joyce), and the importance of the psychoanalytic theories of Freud and Jung. She incorporated into her work themes related to the struggles of Jews in Germany and, above all, subject matter from classical myth. Jewish themes were closely personal: Her father was an "assimilated Jew" who was baptized as a Catholic prior to her birth. The father of Langgässer's first child, Cordelia, was Jewish, and as a result her daughter was declared "fully Jewish" in 1941. In spite of her adoption by Spaniards, Cordelia was deported on 10 March 1944 and transferred to Auschwitz. In 1946 Langgässer was informed of her daughter's survival and emigration to Sweden.

Using Greek and Roman sources in particular, Langgässer developed her distinctive reflections on the relationship between nature and grace, and its implications for her literary work. Thus, in her earliest poetry she linked the births of Christ and of Pan and at the end of her life the descents of Christ and Aeneas into the underworld. As her style developed, it grew more complex, and by 1947 she felt that readers required an "initiation" into her poetic corpus if they were to understand the manner in which it depicted the metamorphosis of nature (above all understood in terms of the natural world of the ancients) by her Christian vision, paralleling in part the way in which "natural" language is transformed by the artist's literary style. Daring, as she once said, to allow herself to be driven by the flow of inner images, her symbols fuse themes and patterns with a subtle irony, binding past and future, here and there, into single unified points of time and space, in an endeavor to communicate on a deeper, nonrational level. Thus, in her early novel *Proserpina* (1933), as in her later collection of short stories, *Das Labyrinth* (1949), she intertwines garden and shadow, innocence and experience, illusion and reality, peace and violence, life and death, extending the original tale of a child and a mother by and into its contemporary mythic dimensions. The history of the world as a whole is transferred into salvation history. The truth of the external is to be understood by the intuitive grasp of the internal form. As a result, critics have often pointed to the tendency in her novels for individual characters to be subsumed by general types.

Langgässer's two most significant works are her novels *Das unauslöschliche Siegel* (1946; The Indelible Seal) and *Märkische Argonautenfahrt* (1950; *The Quest*). The first is the more experimental of the two, opening and closing in the form of the drama, shifting normal plot and character development, and restructuring narrative techniques. As the title indicates, the work centers on the "indelible seal" of baptism. Seven years prior to 1914, the Jewish protagonist of the novel, Belfontaine, was baptized so as to enter a profitable marriage and was met each year on the anniversary by a blind man. When the man fails to appear, Belfontaine goes in search of him, is interned during World War I, and suffers excruciating physical, psychological, and spiritual torments. But because of the indelible character of his baptismal union with the divine, he emerges from the concentration camps of World War II as a type of the wise sage he had initially gone in search of. In *The Quest*, the search motif is framed by the life narratives and conversations of seven pilgrims en route in 1945 to a monastic house in Anastasiendorf (Resurrection-village) in the Mark of Brandenburg. Recapitulating in various ways the Argonauts' search for the Golden Fleece, as in the earlier novel, the pilgrims struggle over a complex and painful life-canvas toward the discovery of faith and certitude required in an increasingly technological and nihilistic world.

PETER C. ERB

Biography

Born in Alzey (Rhenish Hesse), 23 February 1899. Trained as a teacher and taught primary school, Darmstadt; wrote short reviews and literary pieces for local newspapers; moved to Berlin and worked with Expressionist writers associated with Martin Raske's journal *Die Kolonne;* forbidden to publish in Germany after the publication of her novel *Der Gang durch das Ried,* 1936; worked in a factory during

World War II; moved to Rheinzaubern in the Palatinate, 1948. Died in the fall of 1950.

Selected Works

Collections
Gesammelte Werke, edited by Wilhelm Hoffmann, 5 vols., 1959–64
Hörspiele, edited by Franz Pelgen, 1986

Fiction
Triptycon des Teufels, 1932
Proserpina, 1933
Der Gang durch das Ried, 1936
Rettung am Rhein; Drei Schicksalsläufe, 1939
Das unaulöschliche Siegel, 1946
Der Torso, 1947
Das Labyrinth: Fünf Erzählungen, 1949
Märkische Argonautenfahrt, 1950; as *The Quest*, translated by Jane Bannard Greene, 1951
Geist in den Sinnen behaust, 1951
Three German Stories, translated by Michael Bullock, 1984

Poetry
Der Wendekreis des Lammes: Ein Hymnus der Erlösung, 1924
Grenze: Besetztes Gebiet, Ballade eines Landes, 1932
Die Tierkreisgedichte, 1935
Gedichte, 1935
Der Laubmann an die Rose: Ein Jahreskreis, 1947
Kölnische Elegie, 1948

Letters and Essays
. . . soviel berauschende Vergänglichkeit: Briefe 1926–1950, edited by Wilhelm Hoffmann, 1954

Das Christliche der christlichen Dichtung: Vorträge und Briefe, edited by Wilhelm Hoffmann, 1961
Briefe, 1924–50, edited by Elizabeth Hoffmann, 2 vols., 1990

Further Reading

Augsberger, Eva, *Elizabeth Langgässer: Associative Reihung, Leitmotiv und Symbol in ihren Prosawerken*, Nuremberg: Carl, 1962
Dederer, Tilmann, and Karl Knapp, *Elisabeth Langgässer und Griesheim*, Griesheim: Schlapp, 1986
Edvardson, Cordelia, *Bränt barn söker sig till elden*, Stockholm: Brombergs, 1984; as *Gebranntes Kind sucht das Feuer*, translated by Anna-Liese Kornitzky, Munich: Hanser, 1986; as *Burned Child Seeks the Fire: A Memoir*, translated by Joel Agee, Boston: Beacon Press, 1997
El-Akramy, Ursula, *Wotans Rabe: Elisabeth Langgässer, ihre Tochter Cordelia und die Feuer von Auschwitz*, Frankfurt: Neue Kritik, 1997
Fliedl, Konstanze, *Zeitroman und Heilsgeschichte: Elisabeth Langgässers "Märkische Argonautenfahrt,"* Vienna: Braumüller, 1986
Johann, Ernst, et al., *Elisabeth Langgässer's Darmstädter Jahre*, Darmstadt: Liebig, 1981
Maassen, J.P.J., *Die Schrecken der Tiefe: Untersuchungen zu Elizabeth Langgässers Erzählungen*, Leiden: Universitaire Pers, 1973
Müller, Karlheinz, *Elisabeth Langgässer: Eine biographische Skizze*, Darmstadt: Gesellschaft Hessischer Literaturfreunde, 1990
Müller, Karlheinz, editor, *Vorträge: Elisabeth Langgässer Colloquium*, Darmstadt: Verlag zur Megede, 1990
Riley, Anthony William, *Elisabeth Langgässer: Bibliographie mit Nachlassbericht*, Berlin: Duncker und Humblot, 1970
Rinser, Luise, *Der Schwerpunkt*, Frankfurt: Fischer, 1960

Language *see* German Language; Middle High German; Old High German

---

Sophie von La Roche 1730–1807

Equally a representative of the Enlightenment and the movement of sensibility (Empfindsamkeit), Sophie von La Roche is arguably the most famous German woman writer of the 18th century. The publication of her successful first novel, *Geschichte des Fräuleins von Sternheim* (*The History of Lady Sophia Sternheim*) in 1771, often considered a foundational text for the female German literary tradition, established La Roche as an important and original author and marked a crucial turn in the development of gendered categories in the production and reception of modern German literature. In her subsequent writing career, which spanned three-and-a-half decades, La Roche adopted the most fashionable genres of her time, including novels, moral tales, travel literature, autobiography, and periodical literature,

to address such familiar 18th-century concerns as individual enlightenment and popular education, the primacy of friendship and the imperative of personal virtue, moral pragmatism, and the improvement of social institutions. Her work explores tensions in the changing social structures of late 18th-century Germany (and it contributed significantly to the self-definition of the emergent civil society); it did so from a perspective defined emphatically as female and through a concentration on issues of female education and personal development within socially prescribed gender roles. La Roche was instrumental in shaping a public discursive space for the female reader and writer while still emphasizing the centrality of traditional female roles in a private familial sphere.

La Roche's own biography and her literary career exemplify both the expanded possibilities of education, authorship, and public recognition for women born into privileged circumstances and the formidable constraints on women's lives in her time. The tensions La Roche experienced in her own life between her desires for education and the cultural limitations placed on female knowledge and between her roles as an author and as a woman in bourgeois and aristocratic societies, with their respective definitions of ideal femininity, are constant themes in her work. As she mediated moral philosophy, new models of subjectivity, and knowledge in many fields for her primary readers, "Germany's daughters," La Roche sought to articulate a defense of female education and a legitimation of her own authorship in order to counter social strictures against the independence and the public visibility of women. The successes La Roche had in these ventures through her fiction and through her work as an editor and publicist made possible—and delimited—a new profile for women writers and their texts.

In *Sternheim,* La Roche exploits the epistolary novel form in an innovative fashion for Germany, developing perspectivism and layers of narrative through the voices of multiple letter writers, while the letters of her sentimental heroine Sophie vouch for her "beautiful soul" and document her development. Epistolary writing continued to be a foundational conceit of La Roche's subsequent publications, and this is underscored in the titles of her works (e.g., *Rosaliens Briefe* [1779–81], *Briefe an Lina* [1785], and *Briefe über Mannheim* [1791]). By favoring letters as a formal guise for narrative, La Roche emphasized the 18th-century associations of letter writing with a style defined as feminine, natural, and authentic. By allowing for the play on the borders of autobiographical and fictional writing, this strategy was important for female authors of the time who faced censure for other forms of public expression. Epistolary fictions also underscore the significance of female friendship and dialogue. These are important themes throughout La Roche's oeuvre, which are likewise prominent features of the authorial persona she cultivates. In her novels and prose fiction, La Roche depicts middle- or upper-class female characters and their stories of subjectivity and socialization, primarily but not exclusively within the institutions of marriage and family. The psychological insight and novelty of character that La Roche's contemporaries associated with Sophie Sternheim, however, is not evident in all subsequent heroines. The author often oscillates between portraying model characters that accord with a patriarchal ideal and presenting stories of individual women that acknowledge the potential dilemmas between independent leanings and the traditional female roles of wife, mother, household manager, and regulator of domestic happiness. La Roche's fiction also encompasses excursuses and practical advice on such varied issues as agriculture and marriage (*Rosalie und Cleberg* [1791]) and reading and motherhood (*Briefe an Lina*). *See Oneida* (1798) explores with a utopian bent the possible paths to individual happiness and forms of social organization.

The Enlightenment's embrace of periodical literature as a new forum for public exchange and popular enlightenment was shared by La Roche, as editor of the journal *Pomona für Teutschlands Töchter,* which appeared monthly from 1783 to 1784. She emphasized the novelty of this periodical, which was edited by and for women, cultivated a female audience, and solicited contributions from other women, while distancing her enterprise from any potential charges of masculine learnedness. La Roche aimed to expand her readers' knowledge and to provide them with practical advice and moral guidance through fiction and poetry, letters, essays, excerpted writings of famous authors, and information about other cultures. More specifically, she focused on female cultural figures in England, Italy, and France in juxtaposition with a discussion of German issues. La Roche's knowledge of other European cultures and her interest in cultural comparison is also expressed through her extensive travel journals. In her accounts of travels to Switzerland, France, Holland, and England, La Roche offers the observations and experiences that contributed to her own education as occasions for reflection on foreign and German matters and as diversions that can both benefit and entertain her readers. She emphasizes her acquired knowledge and her perceptions of the landscapes, cultures, and social and political structures of the countries that she visits; her critical commentaries on social inequities and her judgments of institutions such as schools and factories often resemble insights later presented more politically in the writings of her granddaughter Bettina von Arnim (who lived for a time with La Roche). La Roche's desire to make known the achievements and moral merits of exemplary women was already articulated in *Sternheim,* and she pursued this goal in her fiction, travel writing, autobiographical texts, and the writings that she edited (including *Lebensbeschreibung von Friderika Baldinger* [1791]).

Scholarship on La Roche has moved from a focus on her personal life and her function as a muse for her famous male contemporaries to an interest in her work as an author in her own right. This shift was initiated largely by feminist criticism in the 1980s. Whereas most criticism has concentrated on the first novel, *Sternheim,* La Roche's entire oeuvre is now attracting scholarly interest, and recent editions of her letters and reprints of her works are making them more widely available. A recent fictional account of her life (by Renate Feyl) has also found popular resonance.

CLAIRE BALDWIN

See also Epistolary Novel

Biography

Born Marie Sophie Gutermann in Kaufbeuren, 6 December 1730. Daughter of a Protestant physician and scholar in Augsburg; influenced by and an influence on her cousin Christoph Martin Wieland; married Georg Michael Frank La Roche, 27 December 1753, the natural son of Count Stadion; served as hostess and salonnière at the court in Mainz and assisted with the count's extensive correspondence with foreign intellectuals; moved with Count Stadion to his estate, Warthausen, near Biberach, 1761; lived in the small provincial town of Bönningheim after the death of Count Stadion, 1768, where she began to work on her first novel; moved to Ehrenbreitstein, near Koblenz; her husband became chancellor of the elector of Trier, and she presided over a literary salon frequented by Wieland, the brothers Jacobi, Goethe, and Merck; moved to Speyer, 1780; traveled extensively throughout Europe, including Switzerland, 1784, France, 1785, and Holland and England, 1786; moved to Offenbach, 1786; became a full-time author after the death of her husband, supporting herself with her writing. Died in Offenbach, 18 February 1807.

Selected Works

Novels

Geschichte des Fräuleins von Sternheim. Von einer Freundin derselben aus Original-Papieren und andern zuverläßigen Quellen gezogen, edited by Christoph Martin Wieland, 1771; as *The History of Lady*

Sophia Sternheim, translated by Joseph Collyer, 1776; translated by Edward Harwood, 1776; German edition, edited by Barbara Becker-Cantarino, 1983; as *The History of Lady Sophia Sternheim*, translated by Christa Bagus Britt, 1991
Der Eigensinn der Liebe und Freundschaft, 1772
Rosaliens Biefe an ihre Freundin Marianne von St.**, 1779–81
Rosalie und Cleberg auf dem Lande, 1791
Erscheinungen am See Oneida, 1798
Fanny und Julie; oder, Die Freundinnen, 1801–2
Liebe-Hütten, 1803–4

Shorter Prose
Moralische Erzählungen im Geschmacke Marmontels, 1782–84
Briefe an Lina als Mädchen, 1785
Neuere moralische Erzählungen, 1786
Briefe an Lina als Mutter, 1795–97
Geschichte von Miß Lony und der schöne Bund, 1789

Other
Pomona für Teutschlands Töchter [periodical], 1783–84; edited by Jürgen Vorderstemann, 1987

Travel Writing
Tagebuch einer Reise durch die Schweiz, 1787
Journal einer Reise durch Frankreich, 1787
Tagebuch einer Reise durch Holland und England, 1788
Briefe über Mannheim, 1791
Erinnerungen aus meiner dritten Schweizreise, 1793

Autobiographical Writing
Schönes Bild der Resignation, 1796
Mein Schreibetisch, 1799
Herbsttage, 1805
Melusinens Sommer-Abende, 1806

Letters
Lettres de Sophie de la Roche a C.M. Wieland, edited by Victor Michel, 1938
Sophie von La Roche: Ihre Briefe an die Gräfin Elise zu Solms-Laubach 1787–1807, edited by Kurt Kampf, 1965
Wielands Briefwechsel, edited by Hans Werner Seifert et al., 7 vols., 1965–
Ich bin mehr Herz als Kopf. Sophie von La Roche. Ein Lebensbild in Briefen, edited by Michael Maurer, 1983

Edited Work
Lebensbeschreibung von Friderika Baldinger, 1791

Further Reading

Assing, Ludmilla, *Sophie von La Roche, die Freundin Wielands*, Berlin: Janke, 1859
Becker-Cantarino, Barbara, *Der lange Weg zur Mündigkeit: Frau und Literatur (1500–1800)*, Stuttgart: Metzler, 1987
———, "Freundschaftsutopie: Die Fiktionen der Sophie von La Roche," in *Untersuchungen zum Roman von Frauen um 1800*, edited by Helga Gallas and Magdalene Heuser, Tübingen: Niemeyer, 1990
———, "Sophie von La Roche (1730–1807): Kommentiertes Werkverzeichnis," *Das achtzehnte Jahrhundert* 17 (1993)
Bovenschen, Silvia, *Die imaginäre Weiblichkeit: Exemplarische Untersuchungen zu kultur-geschichtlichen und literarischen Präsentationsformen des Weiblichen*, Frankfurt: Suhrkamp, 1979
Ehrich-Haefeli, Verena, "Gestehungskosten tugendempfindsamer Freundschaft: Probleme der weiblichen Rolle im Briefwechsel Wieland—Sophie La Roche bis zum Erscheinen der *Sternheim*," in *Frauenfreundschaft, Männerfreundschaft: Literarische Diskurse im 18. Jahrhundert*, edited by Wolfram Mauser and Barbara Becker-Cantarino, Tübingen: Niemeyer, 1991
Feyl, Renate, *Die profanen Stunden des Glücks*, Cologne: Kiepenheuer und Witsch, 1996
Heidenreich, Bernd, *Sophie von La Roche, eine Werkbiographie*, Frankfurt and New York: Lang, 1986
Hohendahl, Peter-Uwe, "Empfindsamkeit und gesellschaftliches Bewußtsein: Zur Soziologie des empfindsamen Romans am Beispiel von *La Vie de Marianne, Clarissa, Fräulein von Sternheim* und *Werther*," *Jahrbuch des deutschen Schiller-Gesellschaft* 16 (1972)
Joeres, Ruth-Ellen Boettcher, "'That Girl Is an Entirely Different Character!' Yes, but Is She a Feminist? Observations on Sophie von La Roche's *Geschichte des Fräuleins von Sternheim*," in *German Women in the Eighteenth and Nineteenth Centuries: A Social and Literary History*, edited by Ruth-Ellen Boettcher Joeres and Mary Jo Maynes, Bloomington: Indiana University Press, 1986
Kastinger Riley, Helene M., *Die weibliche Muse: Sechs Essays über künstlerisch schaffende Frauen der Goethezeit*, Columbia, South Carolina: Camden House, 1986
Loster-Schneider, Gudrun, *Sophie La Roche: Paradoxien weibelichen Schreibens im 18. Jahrhundert*, Tübingen: Narr, 1995
Maurer, Michael, "Das Gute und das Schöne. Sophie von La Roche (1730–1807) wiederentdeckt?" *Euphorion* 79 (1985)
Meise, Helge, *Die Unschuld und die Schrift: Deutsche Frauenromane im 18. Jahrhundert*, Berlin: Guttandin und Hoppe, 1983
Milch, Werner, *Sophie La Roche, die Großmutter des Brentanos*, Frankfurt: Societät-Verlag, 1935
Nenon, Monika, *Autoschaft und Frauenbildung: Das Beispiel Sophie von La Roche*, Würzburg: Königshausen und Neumann, 1988
Ridderhoff, Kuno von, *Sophie von La Roche, die Schülerin Richardsons und Rousseaus*, Einbeck: Schroedter, 1895
Schieth, Lydia, *Die Entwicklung des deutschen Frauenromans im ausgehenden 18. Jahrhundert: Ein Beitrag zur Gattungsgeschichte*, Frankfurt: Lang, 1987
Touaillon, Christine, *Der deutsche Frauenroman des 18. Jahrhunderts*, Vienna: Braumüller, 1919
Wiede-Behrendt, Ingrid, *Lehrerin des Schönen, Wahren, Guten: Literatur und Frauenbildung im ausgehenden 18. Jahrhundert am Beispiel Sophie von La Roche*, Frankfurt: Lang, 1987

Else Lasker-Schüler 1869–1945

Else Lasker-Schüler is one of the major German poets of the early 20th century: her work encompasses a variety of genres and styles that range from early lyric with affinities to turn-of-the-century aesthetic movements through Expressionism to the last texts, which were written in exile during the Nazi years.

Since the appearance of her first poems in literary journals around 1900, Lasker-Schüler has been the focus of both admiration and denunciation, as well as critical debates concerning the proper classification of her oeuvre. The themes of many of her early poems, such as love and weltschmerz, together with the poems' ornamental images from nature and their still somewhat conventional verse styles, link them to *Jugendstil* (art nouveau) or to the neo-Romanticism that had begun to supplant naturalism at that time. Her first published volume, *Styx* (1902), collected texts of this type along with poems dealing with the family and biblical motifs. Her second volume, *Der siebente Tag* (1905; The Seventh Day), further develops these themes and images, but she became more creative in her verse forms, frequently employing a two- or three-line unrhymed, free-verse stanza that allowed greater play of associations. Her poem "Mein stilles Lied" ("My Quiet Song," translated in *Your Diamond Dreams Cut Open My Arteries*) begins:

Mein Herz ist eine traurige Zeit,
die tonlos tickt.

Meine Mutter hatte goldene Flügel,
Die keine Welt fanden.

(My heart is a sad time
Tonelessly ticking.

My mother had golden wings
That found no world.)

Lasker-Schüler's early poems tended to receive condemnation from conservative and patriarchal reviewers who thought her attention to the erotic was excessive, but she earned increasing admiration from artists and intellectual critics, including Peter Hille and Karl Kraus.

Although Lasker-Schüler is best known for her lyric poetry, which she continued writing until the end of her life, she also excelled in other genres, and a thorough evaluation must consider her contributions to drama, to the novel, and to graphic art, not to mention her essays and letters. *Die Nächte Tino von Bagdads* (1907; The Nights of Tino of Baghdad) combines verse and prose in an oriental fairy tale about a princess-poetess. Her personal use of the nickname Tino and the allusions in her texts to her own experience exemplify a strategy that recurs throughout her writing and caused many readers to confuse her life and art. Her often bohemian lifestyle, her theatrical readings of her works, and her own liberty with the facts of her biography also contributed to this confusion and tended to focus attention on her person as well as her texts. Lasker-Schüler's first play, *Die Wupper* (published in 1909, premiered in 1919; Dark River), received praise from knowledgeable reviewers, although critical debate has continued as to whether its naturalistic or Expressionistic currents are predominant. During the years preceding World War I, Lasker-Schüler was close to the Expressionists through her second marriage to Herwarth Walden, who produced the journal *Der Sturm* (Storm); both she and Franz Marc provided illustrations to a second oriental novel about her Joseph persona, *Der Prinz von Theben* (1914; The Prince of Thebes). Her epistolary novel of Berlin café life, *Mein Herz* (1912; My Heart), chronicles in part the breakup of her marriage to Walden and has been used to classify Lasker-Schüler as an avant-garde writer. The interaction with her artistic environment can also be seen in numerous poems and essays that she dedicated to her acquaintances: the most famous of these is the cycle of poems that resulted from her relationship with Gottfried Benn. Critics have often viewed Lasker-Schüler as an example of

Expressionism or as a precursor of that movement, but despite the presence of common elements, it would be wrong to force Lasker-Schüler's texts into any one stylistic direction or to ignore her transgressions against the limits of established categories. She drew on numerous modernist impulses, which she combined in new ways that have been both criticized as eccentric and praised as creative.

Another label frequently applied to her has been that of a Jewish poet, and, indeed, biblical and Jewish themes represent an important motif within her work. *Hebräische Balladen* (1913; *Hebrew Ballads and Other Poems*) contains her poems on Old Testament figures; in addition, the short story "Der Wunderrabbiner von Barcelona" (1921; The Miracle Rabbi of Barcelona) and the drama *Arthur Aronymus und seine Väter* (1932; Arthur Aronymus and His Fathers) deal with the relations between Christians and Jews. Lasker-Schüler's work displays a lifelong attachment to her religion and heritage: her treatments, however, are by no means orthodox, but unique artistic creations strengthened with images from a variety of sources. The Jewish elements in her work have been regarded positively by most critics, many of whom analyze the works' affinity to mysticism, but her Judaism also provoked anti-Semitic attacks. The scheduled premiere of *Arthur Aronymus* in Darmstadt in 1933 was canceled, and Lasker-Schüler herself left Germany for good in April of that year. Her travels to Palestine are the subject of *Das Hebräerland* (1937; The Land of the Hebrews); her final volume of poetry, *Mein blaues Klavier* (1943; My Blue Piano), was written during her exile in Jerusalem and contains some of her finest lyrics. The drama that she was completing at the time of her death in 1945, *IchundIch* (1970; *IandI*), was not published for 25 years because her literary executors were bewildered by its mixture of tragedy and slapstick and its cast of characters, which ranged from Faust and Hitler to the poet herself. But like most of her work, this play reveals her imaginative ability to turn unexpected combinations into challenging works of art that probe the nature of identity and its relation to external reality.

Following her death, critical reception devoted itself primarily to reviving the memory of a poet whose works had become forgotten during years of exile and war. Elements that received frequent attention were the themes of tolerance and reconciliation, which are exemplified in *Arthur Aronymus* and the dedication of *Mein blaues Klavier* to her friends in Germany. The attempt to rescue Lasker-Schüler's reputation from oblivion was intensified through generally praiseworthy responses on the occasions of anniversaries in 1965 and 1969. These critics often tended to focus on the same body of texts and to repeat views and generalizations that had become clichés, such as the dichotomies within the poet and her break with her world, along with the resulting escape into self-created inner worlds and the use of masks; her Expressionist qualities; her Jewishness; and her themes of love, play, childhood, and reconciliation. Since the 1970s, scholars and critics have turned their scrutiny to a greater number of poems as well as to the posthumous drama *IandI* and to the prose works. They have also paid closer attention to the proper relation between the poet's life and art and have become more skeptical of the generalizations that had developed. There is less willingness to accept the notion that Lasker-Schüler was divorced from the real world and social events, and approaches to the relation between her texts and reality have become more differentiated. Her late work has recently been examined in terms of exile literature, and feminist criticism has offered insightful approaches into Lasker-Schüler's concepts of identity, gender, and difference. It has found, for example, active, utopian components in her use of masks rather than mere escapism. Lasker-Schüler's work continues to provide challenges and provoke interest: recent performances, the founding of a society in her name, and the publication of both critical and popular editions indicate the enduring interest shown by scholars and the German public at large.

CALVIN N. JONES

Biography
Born in Wuppertal-Elberfeld, 11 February 1869. Moved to Berlin and abandoned her solid middle-class bourgeois background for a life of bohemianism; her poems were published in renowned journals of the literary avant-garde, such as *Fackel, Sturm, Aktion, Saturn, Neue Jugend,* and *Berliner Tageblatt;* a close friend of Gottfried Benn and the spouse (divorced) of the *Sturm* editor Herwarth Walden; eventually had to go into exile in 1937, and traveled via Switzerland to Palestine. Kleist-Prize, 1932. Died in Jerusalem, 22 January 1945.

Selected Works

Collections
Gesamtausgabe, 10 vols., 1919–20
Dichtungen und Dokumente, edited by Ernst Ginsberg, 1951
Briefe an Karl Kraus, edited by Astrid Gehlhoff-Claes, 1959
Helles Schlafen, Dunkles Wachen, selected by Friedhelm Kemp, 1962
Gesammelte Werke, 3 vols., edited by Friedhelm Kemp and Werner Kraft, 1959–62; selections from vol. 1 as *Your Diamond Dreams Cut Open My Arteries,* translated by Robert P. Newton, 1982
Werke und Briefe. Kritische Ausgabe, edited by Norbert Oellers, Heinz Rölleke, and Itta Shedletzky, 1996–

Poetry
Styx, 1902
Der siebente Tag, 1905
Meine Wunder, 1911
Hebräische Balladen, 1913; enlarged edition, 1920; as *Hebrew Ballads and Other Poems,* translated by Audri Durchslag and Jeanette Litman-Demeestère, 1980
Die gesammelten Gedichte, 1917
Theben, 1923
Mein blaues Klavier, 1943

Fiction
Das Peter Hille-Buch, 1906
Die Nächte Tino von Bagdads, 1907
Mein Herz: Ein Liebesroman mit Bildern und wirklich lebenden Menschen, 1912
Der Prinz von Theben, 1914
Der Malik, 1919
Der Wunderrabbiner von Barcelona: Erzählung, 1921
Arthur Aronymus: Die Geschichte meines Vaters, 1932
Das Hebräerland, 1937

Essays
Gesichte, 1913; enlarged as *Essays,* 1920
Ich räume auf! 1925
Konzert, 1932; as *Concert,* translated by Jean M. Snook, 1994

Plays
Die Wupper (produced 1919), 1909
Arthur Aronymus und seine Väter (produced 1936), 1932
IchundIch (produced 1979), 1970; as *I and I,* translated by Beate Hein Bennett, in *The Divided Home/Land,* edited by Sue-Ellen Case, 1992

Further Reading
Bauschinger, Sigrid, *Else Lasker-Schüler: Ihr Werk und ihre Zeit,* Heidelberg: Stiehm, 1980
Chick, Jean M., "Else Lasker-Schüler's 'Leise sagen—'," *Seminar* 24 (1988)
Cohn, Hans W., *Else Lasker-Schüler: The Broken World,* London: Cambridge University Press, 1974
Hedgepeth, Sonja M., *"Überall blicke ich nach einem heimatlichen Boden aus": Exil im Werk Else Lasker-Schülers,* New York: Lang, 1994
Hessing, Jakob, *Else Lasker-Schüler: Biographie einer deutsch-jüdischen Dichterin,* Karlsruhe: Loeper, 1985
Jones, Calvin N., *The Literary Reputation of Else Lasker-Schüler: Criticism 1901–1993,* Columbia, South Carolina: Camden House, 1994
Klüsener, Erika, *Else Lasker-Schüler in Selbstzeugnissen und Bilddokumenten,* Reinbek bei Hamburg: Rowohlt, 1980
Newton, Robert P., "Else Lasker-Schüler," in *Your Diamond Dreams Cut Open My Arteries: Poems by Else Lasker-Schüler,* translated by Robert P. Newton, Chapel Hill: University of North Carolina Press, 1982
O'Brien, Mary Elizabeth, "'Ich war verkleidet als Poet . . . ich bin Poetin!' The Masquerade of Gender in Else Lasker-Schüler's Work," *German Quarterly* 65, no. 1 (1992)
Schwertfeger, Ruth, *Else Lasker-Schüler: Inside This Deathly Solitude,* New York: Berg, 1991
Weissenberger, Klaus, *Zwischen Stein und Stern: Mystische Formgebung in der Dichtung von Else Lasker-Schüler, Nelly Sachs, und Paul Celan,* Bern and Munich: Francke, 1976

Die Wupper 1909
Play by Else Lasker-Schüler

Although best known for her poetry, Else Lasker-Schüler was also the author of three plays: *Die Wupper* (Dark River), *Arthur Aronymus und seine Väter* (1932; Arthur Aronymus and His Fathers), for which she received the Kleist prize, and the unfinished exile work *IchundIch* (*IandI*), written in the years just prior to Lasker-Schüler's death in Jerusalem in 1945. Of these three, *Die Wupper* best exemplifies its author's controversial position within German literary history, for, like Lasker-Schüler herself, the play defies categorization. Incorporating elements of naturalism, Expressionism, the fairy tale, and the *Volksstück, Die Wupper* constructs a lyrical, dreamlike world fraught with social and sexual conflicts, conflicts that take shape in and between the bourgeois and working-class spheres.

The title refers to the river that flows through the author's birthplace, Wuppertal, a city profoundly impacted by the second wave of the Industrial Revolution in the latter part of the 19th century. The broad and balanced spectrum of characters appearing in the drama reflects not only Lasker-Schüler's origins in a wealthy middle-class family but also her marginalized social status as a Jew and a woman. The action in Acts one and four is set among the working Pius and Wallbrecker families, whereas the second and fifth acts take place in the villa of the factory owners, the Sonntags. The two groups commingle during a St. Johannes

Day fair in the third act, but throughout the play, three vagrants, social and sexual outsiders (one is an exhibitionist, another a transvestite), hover at the margins, offering commentary on the play's events in an occasionally incomprehensible dialect. Given Lasker-Schüler's lifelong struggle against traditional gender categories and her own outsider status as a Jewish woman writer, it is hardly surprising that, of all of the characters in the play, she identified most strongly with one of the three vagrants, Amadeus. In her 1932 book of essays, *Konzert* (*Concert*), Lasker-Schüler wrote: "[I]f I had not unfortunately been born as Else Lasker-Schüler—in the fourth courtyard of the seventh heaven—I would be Amadeus, united with his colleagues, in the corner of the night."

Although *Die Wupper* is structured upon a clear set of social oppositions, it is sexual rather than social forces that motivate the characters, with disastrous consequences. Carl Pius seeks entrance to the world of his friend Eduard Sonntag by joining the clergy, converting to Protestantism, and attempting to marry Eduard's sister Marta. After dallying with Carl, Marta chooses a member of her own class (even though he is known to have seduced a working-class girl), leaving Carl to look for solace in alcohol. Eduard Sonntag's career plans also involve the church, but because he is dying, his dreams of a spiritual, monastic life after his conversion to Catholicism are destined to remain unfulfilled. Eduard's brother Heinrich has very different ambitions; at the fair in the third act, he attempts to escape the confines of the bourgeois world through a flirtation with working-class Lieschen Wallbrecker. Lieschen's romantic illusions are shattered when Heinrich rapes her, and Heinrich's subsequent feelings of guilt drive him to suicide.

Dagmar C.G. Lorenz has pointed to the connection between the Heinrich-Lieschen plot and Goethe's *Faust:* in both cases, a privileged man named Heinrich seduces a young girl, but "while Goethe's Gretchen is later elevated to embody the 'Eternal Feminine,' Lasker-Schüler's Lieschen remains a nobody who is sent to a reform school because her provocative sexuality is a threat to the repressive social system" (Lorenz). In *Die Wupper*, sexuality and emotion wield a power greater than that produced by wealth or status, and the former power affects members of all classes. This power is embodied in the witchlike figure of Grandmother Pius, described by one of the Sonntag's servants as "the carrousel on which all of us are riding." An actual carrousel in the third act is a place where members of both classes meet while mounted on wooden animals in incongruous pairings, such as a leopard with a lamb. Acting as fortune-teller, interpreter of dreams, and matchmaker, Grandmother Pius has the ability to cross social boundaries. By giving a voice to Grandmother Pius (along with women, children, the homeless, and the poor) and by presenting the workings of an oppressive system through their eyes, Lasker-Schüler's play offers social criticism without advocating revolution.

The lack of a clear and structured dramatic development in *Die Wupper* resulted in a generally negative reception by critics when the play was performed for the first time in 1919 in Berlin's Deutschen Theater. The five acts are not divided into scenes; moments of contact between characters are presented alongside one another in a flowing, montage-like manner, which gives the play a lyrical, dreamy quality. Unwilling to call the play a drama, critics had to search for terms with which to describe it,

such as "a series of images," "a colorful chain of folk ballads," and "a progression of lyrical scenes" (Klüsener and Pfafflin). In writing about the play in the late 1920s, however, Lasker-Schüler concurred with the critics: "[M]y *Wupper* in short cannot be called a fairy tale or a play or a drama, at most a city ballad with smoking chimneys and signals."

Another point of contention among critics concerned how best to categorize the play. Lasker-Schüler's reliance on dialect (*Wuppertaler Platt*) led most to consider it a work of naturalism. As a result, director Heinz Herald's decision to emphasize Expressionist elements in the 1919 production (aided by Ernst Simon's cubist-futurist stage sets) was considered an unfortunate mixing of stylistic elements. The second staging of *Die Wupper*, presented in 1927 in the Berlin Staatstheater, was received far more positively, primarily because director Jürgen Fehling took a realistic approach to the play, one in keeping with the spirit of Weimar's New Objectivity. The same cannot be said of the first postwar production of *Die Wupper*, in Cologne in 1958. It was marred by scandal after a Catholic newspaper, *Kirchenzeitung für das Erzbistum Köln*, called for audiences to protest against a play "as devoid of artistic content and as it is full of obscenities" (Bauschinger). Twelve years later, *Die Wupper* was chosen as the inaugural production for the new Schauspielhaus in Wuppertal, but at the last minute, after it was announced that the German president would be in attendance, administrators decided that Lessing's *Nathan der Weise* (1779; *Nathan the Wise*) would be a more acceptable choice.

The controversial reception of *Die Wupper* in the decades following World War II reflects the long and difficult reintegration of Else Lasker-Schüler, the consummate outsider, into the German literary tradition. "Every play is probably a world, an image of the author," wrote Lasker-Schüler in *Concert*. "Thus, when I regard my play from all sides, from top and bottom, I clearly recognize its similarity to me, even if my drama turned out blond and bright-eyed!"

JENNIFER REDMANN

Editions
First edition: *Die Wupper*, Berlin: Oesterheld, 1909
Critical edition: in *Gesammelte Werke*, vol. 2, edited by Friedhelm Kemp, Munich: Kösel, 1962

Further Reading
Jones, Calvin N., "Representing the People: 'Darstellung' and 'Vertretung' in Else Lasker-Schüler's Drama *Die Wupper*," *Germanic Review* 69, no. 1 (1994)
Klüsener, Erika, and Friedrich Pfafflin, editors, "Else Lasker-Schüler, 1869–1945," in *Marbacher Magazin* 71 (1995)
Krumbholz, Martin, "Hölle, Jahrmarkt, Garten Eden: Zum dramatischen Werk Else Lasker-Schülers," *Text und Kritik* 122 (1994)
Lasker-Schüler, Else, *Konzert*, Berlin: Rowohlt, 1932; as *Concert*, translated by Jean M. Snook, Lincoln and London: University of Nebraska Press, 1994
Lorenz, Dagmar C.G., *Keepers of the Motherland: German Texts by Jewish Women Writers*, Lincoln and London: University of Nebraska Press, 1997
Tyson, Peter K., "Else Lasker-Schüler's *Die Wupper*: Between Naturalism and Expressionism," *Journal of the Australasian Universities Language and Literature Association* 64 (1985)

Johann Caspar Lavater 1741–1801

Johann Caspar Lavater was one of the most singular and controversial figures on the German literary scene in the late 18th century. His life as well as his writings evince many of the emotional, irrational, antiauthoritarian, and proto-Romantic attitudes typical of the Sturm und Drang (Storm and Stress). Indeed, he persisted in such attitudes long after other writers who once embraced that movement had outgrown them. He was also a pastor, theologian, diarist, physiognomist, and Swiss patriot of tremendous celebrity, a man who corresponded with the crowned heads of Europe while also enjoying great popular acclaim. To study him, his work, and his notoriety is thus to observe a peculiar yet broad cross section of religious, intellectual, artistic, and social life at a formative stage in German cultural history.

Four episodes from Lavater's eventful life show both the force and the foibles of his character. In 1762 he exposed the corrupt and illegal practices of a well-connected official in Zurich, an act of civil courage so bold and so upsetting to local authorities that the young Lavater left Switzerland for a year. In 1769 he publicly challenged the Jewish philosopher Moses Mendelssohn to convert to Christianity unless he could refute the proof of its truth that Lavater claimed to find in the work of the scientist Charles Bonnet. Many contemporaries thought that this challenge and its aftermath showed Lavater to be tactless, indiscreet, and bigoted. In the early 1780s, moreover, he came to believe in the miracle cures supposedly effected by the quack Cagliostro, whom he repeatedly met before becoming disillusioned. His vain attempts to conceal this contact helped his enlightened opponents discredit him, as did his similar interests in exorcism and hypnotic "animal magnetism." Finally, in late 1799, after being deported and detained by Napoleonic officials, he was mortally wounded by a French soldier as he came to the aid of a compatriot in Zurich. These four episodes suggest the mix of probity, zealotry, credulity, and courage, not to mention charisma, altruism, and intuition, that manifested itself over the course of Lavater's life.

Nowhere is this odd mix more evident than in his writings. Lavater was an extremely prolific author, and his bibliography includes odes, poems, hymns, handbooks, readers, stories, verses, prayers, sermons, speeches, epics, a drama, and a cantata. The Bible was his main source for most of these works, which he addressed to children, servants, his congregation, his friends, the suffering, and the fishermen of Bremen, among others. He also published collections of all these works, edited weekly as well as monthly organs, wrote innumerable letters, and translated from the French. His most important theological text is *Aussichten in die Ewigkeit* (1768–78; Prospects of Eternity), which posits social, linguistic, metaphysical, and other attributes of life in heaven after death. His fervent Christology demonstrates his life-long search for empirical experience and immanent manifestations of transcendent religious truths. Such piety is also obvious in his *Geheimes Tagebuch von einem Beobachter seiner selbst* (1771–73; Secret Journal of a Self-Observer), a diary showing his psychological insight and self-scrutiny. Individualistic concerns likewise seem paramount in his *Physiognomische Fragmente* (1775–78; The Whole Works of Lavater on Physiognomy). Its premise that facial and other fixed physical traits are signs of morals and intellect, however, must be understood as part of

Lavater's theology: in such traits, he thought he saw proof that man is made in God's image. Anthropological and philanthropic concepts likewise inform its richly illustrated volumes, although he hardly applied them consistently or avoided dubious and less sanguine pseudoscientific implications.

Lavater's reputation and reception have both been lasting, albeit checkered. During his lifetime, reactions to him ranged from adulation to ridicule. To his supporters, he was a devout and humane visionary; to his detractors, an ignorant, self-absorbed charlatan; to others, a curious mass of contradictions. He exerted considerable influence on his contemporaries. He met almost all of the major German writers of his day, and he exchanged letters with many of the rest. He enjoyed his greatest popularity in the 1770s, although his critics included Lessing, Nicolai, Schiller, Herder, Wieland, and, above all, Lichtenberg. Goethe initially sought Lavater's friendship and collaborated on his physiognomic project but then grew increasingly irritated and distant, going so far as to avoid him in later life. The force of Lavater's personality did not lose its attraction for some of his admirers. Although his own literary texts were negligible, other authors made use of his physiognomic insights, most notably Balzac. Aphoristic collections of his homiletic and other writings were reissued throughout the 19th century and into the 20th century, and one biographer held him up as a national hero to Swiss readers in need of solace during World War II. Recent treatments of his physiognomic studies stress both their importance in art and literature, as well as the biases they betray in matters of class, gender, race, and nationality. Indirectly, those studies still inform many popular manuals on reading faces. Lavater thus seems certain to remain as fascinating and as frustrating as ever.

ELLIS SHOOKMAN

See also Zurich

Biography

Born in Zurich, Switzerland, 15 November 1741. Educated at the Collegium Carolinum, Zurich, where he studied theology, 1756–62; ordained, 1762; deacon, then pastor at the *Waisenhauskirche* (Orphanage Church) in Zurich, 1769–78, and at St. Peter's Church in Zurich, 1778–1801; married Anna Schinz, 1766, with whom he had eight children; traveled to Germany, 1774, 1782, and 1786, and to Denmark, 1793. Died 2 January 1801.

Selected Works

Collections
Sämtliche Werke, 6 vols., 1834–38
J.K. Lavaters Ausgewählte Schriften, edited by Johann Kaspar Orelli, 8 vols., 1841–44
J.K. Lavaters Ausgewählte Werke, edited by Ernst Staehlin, 4 vols., 1943
Sämtliche kleinere prosaische Schriften, 1987

Writings
Aussichten in die Ewigkeit, 1768–78
Geheimes Tagebuch von einem Beobachter seiner selbst, 1771–73; as *Secret Journal of a Self-Observer*, translated by Peter Will, 1795
Physiognomische Fragmente, 4 vols., 1775–78; as *The Whole Works of Lavater on Physiognomy*, translated from the French edition by George Grenville, 1787

Vermischte unphysiognomische Regeln, 1787; translated by Henry
   Fuseli as *Aphorisms on Man,* 1788
Ein Wort eines freyen Schweizers an die französische Nation, 1798; as
   *Remonstrance Addressed to the Executive Directory of the French
   Republic,* 1798

Further Reading

Fink, Karl Julius, "Johann Kaspar Lavater," in *German Writers from
   the Enlightenment to Sturm und Drang, 1720–1764,* Dictionary of
   Literary Biography, vol. 97, Detroit, Michigan: Gale Research, 1990
Graham, John, *Lavater's Essays on Physiognomy: A Study in the
   History of Ideas,* Bern and Las Vegas, Nevada: Lang, 1979
Jaton, Anne-Marie, *Jean Gaspard Lavater,* Lucerne: Coeckelberghs,
   1988
Lavater-Sloman, Mary, *Genie des Herzens: Die Lebensgeschichte
   Johann Caspar Lavaters,* Zurich: Mortgartenverlag, 1939
Shookman, Ellis, editor, *The Faces of Physiognomy: Interdisciplinary
   Approaches to Johann Caspar Lavater,* Columbia, South Carolina:
   Camden House, 1993
Tytler, Graeme, *Physiognomy in the European Novel: Faces and
   Fortunes,* Princeton, New Jersey: Princeton University Press, 1982
Weigelt, Horst, *Johann Kaspar Lavater: Leben, Werk, und Wirkung,*
   Göttingen: Vandenhoeck und Ruprecht, 1991

Jakob Michael Reinhold Lenz 1751–1792

Jakob Michael Reinhold Lenz holds a distinct and representative position in the German Sturm und Drang literary movement, which emerged during the second half of the 18th century and which included some of Germany's preeminent writers, including Johann Wolfgang von Goethe, Friedrich von Schiller, and Johann Gottfried Herder. Sturm und Drang writers emphasized the expression of emotion, advocated the sovereignty of the individual, and viewed nature as divinely inspired. As it is now seen, the movement complemented the Enlightenment rather than simply opposing it. Sturm und Drang poetics conceptualize the author as an *original genius,* an *alter deus,* who creates works of art according to his inspiration rather than by following the lines of normative formulae, as the reception of Aristotle's poetics in French classicist drama suggests. Lenz's groundbreaking essay *Anmerkungen übers Theater* (1774; Notes on Theater) brought forth exactly this distinction, proclaiming the supreme creative power of the artist. Prometheus was the movement's symbol and Shakespeare its model. Drama and poetry were its major domains, and Lenz is known mainly as a playwright whose tragicomic plays depict society in realistic detail and criticize its ideological foundations with great sophistication. In the historical development of German social drama, Lenz stands at the beginning of a tradition that leads—via Georg Büchner and Christian Grabbe—to Bertolt Brecht, whose 1950 adaptation of Lenz's *Hofmeister* revived scholarly and theatrical interest in the author in postwar Germany.

Lenz started his career as a playwright in the tradition of the French *comédie larmoyante* with a play entitled *Der verwundete Bräutigam* (1766; The Injured Bridegroom). Based on an actual case, the play depicts the violent conflict between a noble baron and his servant, whose attack upon his master is presented within a sociopolitical frame rather than as a purely individual misdemeanor. Lenz's unique sense for social conflicts, already noticeable here, becomes fully developed in his subsequent dramatic work. Following his arrival in Strasbourg, he wrote his best-known plays—*Der Hofmeister; oder, Die Vorteile der Privaterziehung* (1774; The Tutor), *Der neue Menoza; oder, Geschichte des cumbanischen Prinzen Tandi* (1774; translated as *The New Menoza* and *Prince Tandi of Cumba*), and *Die Soldaten* (1776; *The Soldiers*)—in short succession. All three plays are formally ambitious and excellent examples of early German tragicomedy. Signature aspects of Lenz's authorship are the frequent changes of scene, realistic and vivid prose dialogue, precision in the use of gesture, and the coupling of tragic and grotesque elements.

In *The Tutor,* Lenz thematizes the precarious existence of the bourgeois intellectual in the second half of the 18th century. Increasing in numbers, yet lacking political power, the young German intelligentsia had no defined place within traditional society, which offered them little prospect for adequate work and social promotion. The play's tutor is shown trapped between unmotivated pupils and haughty employers. Instead of defying his superiors and overcoming the confining circumstances, however, he submits to his fate, consoling himself with an illegitimate relationship with his pupil. When the affair becomes known, he flees and, upon being discovered, castrates himself, a drastic gesture that has commonly been interpreted as the ultimate expression of the "deutsche Misere" (Brecht): self-destruction in place of active resistance.

Self-doubt, self-hatred, and self-deception within a repressive social network are also central to Lenz's third major drama, *The Soldiers,* where the themes of sexuality and the military come to the fore. The plot revolves around young Marie, who is wooed and seduced by an army officer who has no interest in marrying her. Again, Lenz lays out the vast net of social conditions and circumstances that leads to Marie's seduction and downfall; the play also includes a critique of forced celibacy for members of the army. Lenz, who himself took great interest in military matters, devoted a lengthy essay, *Über die Soldatenehen* (1913; On Soldier's Marriages), to that problem; this essay is a crude but insightful and visionary work in which he makes an early case for the citizen soldier.

Between 1771 and 1776, Lenz was at his most prolific as a playwright. Despite enduring great personal hardship, he completed no less than six plays, translated five comedies by Plautus as well as two plays by Shakespeare, and concerned himself with the theoretical foundation of German drama. In his theoretical writings, Lenz historicizes the relationship between comedy and tragedy: according to Lenz, comedy precedes tragedy, because it depicts individuals as subject to external circumstances. Only after society has progressed toward more freedom, he argues, will the playwright be able to present characters who act according to their free will, which he defines as the task of tragedy.

The corpus of Lenz's work in prose is small yet of extraordinary quality. His novella *Zerbin; oder, Die neuere Philosophie* (1776; *Zerbin; or, Modern Philosophy*), for instance, which follows the demise of young Zerbin from naive idealist to ruthless cynic, is written with a dissecting coolness that is reminiscent of 20th-century short prose. Against a background of seduction and betrayal, Lenz thematizes complex moral and social questions in a lucid, poignant style that is yet to be fully appreciated. Similarly undervalued is his poetry, which attests to Lenz's pietist upbringing by often focusing on religious and moral matters. His Strasbourg poetry is distinct from Goethe's in the strong ambivalence it displays toward love and its tendency to stress loss and isolation. The conflict between Lenz's moral convictions and his sexual desire—summed up in the opening lines of "An das Herz" (1777; To the Heart), "Kleines Ding, um uns zu quälen, / Hier in diese Brust gelegt!" (Little heart, to torture us / placed into this chest.)—figures prominently in the poetry of the 1770s, and it is accompanied by moral-theological tracts that approach the issue on a theoretical level.

The reception of Lenz's work, his poetic ideas, and his life has followed two distinct paths, an artistic one and a scholarly one. The former starts with Büchner's novella *Lenz*, and the latter begins with Goethe's derogatory comments about the author in his autobiography *Dichtung und Wahrheit*. Both of these strains qualified Lenz's work by considering it primarily as a reflection of his personal life. Yet, while the literary reception, based on identification with the author, tended to view his personal struggle favorably, interpreting his mental illness as a form of refusal and as evidence of his seismographic artistic sensitivity, most literary scholarship of the 19th and early 20th century saw it as proof of his artistic inferiority, in particular in regard to Weimar classicism. With a more differentiated view of 18th-century German literature, however, Lenz's literary oeuvre has in the past decades evolved as an "alternative" to Weimar aesthetics, and he is today considered one of the foremost social critics of the period; his plays are seen as accurate depictions of contemporary society rather than mere products of an unrestrained imagination. More recently, Lenz's categorization as a realist writer has again been modified by scholarship that views the deviant, contradictory, and bizarre as constitutive elements of, rather than superfluous accessories to, his work. This has also led to increased interest in the writings of his later Russian period, which include works in all major genres as well as several translations, and to an at least partial revision of the long-held but erroneous opinion that nothing of literary significance was produced after the onset of his mental illness in the late 1770s.

MARTIN KAGEL

Biography

Born in Seßwegen, Russian Baltic Province of Livonia, 23 January 1751. Theology student, University of Königsberg, 1768–71; travel companion and tutor for two noble Latvian officers in French services, Strasbourg, 1771; associated with Goethe and the circle around J.D. Salzmann; freelance writer from 1774; cofounder, Deutsche Gesellschaft, Strasbourg, 1775; contributor to several journals, including *Der Bürgerfreund* and *Deutsches Museum*; Weimar, April to November 1776; expulsion from Weimar for unknown reasons; in southern Germany and Switzerland, 1777; signs of mental illness; stayed at J.F. Oberlin's, Waldbach, 1778; several suicide attempts; returned to Riga, 1779; St. Petersburg, 1780, and Moscow, 1781; translator, several positions as teacher and tutor, and active in the circle around Moscow freemasons I.G. Schwarz and N.I. Novikov; friendship with N.M. Karamzin, 1784–86; declining mental health through the 1780s. Died in the streets of Moscow, 23–24 May 1792.

Selected Works

Collections
Dramatischer Nachlaß, edited by Karl Weinhold, 1884
Gedichte von J.M.R. Lenz, edited by Karl Weinhold, 1891
Gesammelte Schriften, edited by Franz Blei, 5 vols., 1909–13
Briefe von und an J.M.R. Lenz, edited by Karl Freye and Wolfgang Stammler, 2 vols., 1918
Werke und Schriften, edited by Britta Titel and Hellmut Haug, 2 vols., 1966–67
Werke und Briefe, edited by Sigrid Damm, 3 vols., 1987
Werke, edited by Karen Lauer, 1992

Plays
Der Hofmeister; oder, Die Vorteile der Privaterziehung (abridged version produced 1778), 1774; edited by Michael Kohlenbach, 1986; as *The Tutor*, translated by William E. Yuill, with *The Soldiers*, 1972; translated and adapted by Pip Broughton, 1988; translated and adapted by Anthony Meech, in *Three Plays*, 1993
Lustspiele nach dem Plautus (adaptations from Plautus; includes *Das Väterchen, Die Aussteuer, Die Entführungen, Die Buhlschwester, Die Türkensklavin*), 1774
Amor vincit omnia (from Shakespeare, *Love's Labours Lost*), with *Anmerkungen übers Theater*, 1774
Der neue Menoza; oder, Geschichte des cumbanischen Prinzen Tandi, 1774; as *The New Menoza*, translated by Meredith Oakes, in *Three Plays*, 1993; as *Prince Tandi of Cumba; or, The New Menoza*, translated and edited by David Hill and Michael Butler, 1995
Die Soldaten, 1776; as *The Soldiers*, translated by William E. Yuill, with *The Tutor*, 1972; translated by Robert David MacDonald, in *Three Plays*, 1993
Die Freunde machen den Philosophen, 1776
Der Engländer, 1777
Tantalus, Dramolett 1798
Pandämonium Germanikum, edited by G.F. Dumpf, 1819
Der verwundete Bräutigam, 1766; edited by K.L. Blum, 1845
Catharina von Siena, edited by Karl Weinhold, 1884
Three Plays (includes *The Soldiers, The New Menoza, The Tutor*), 1993

Poetry
Die Landplagen, 1769
Petrarch, 1776
An den Geist, 1793
Die Liebe auf dem Lande, 1798
Eduard Allwills erstes geistliches Lied, 1828
Der verlorne Augenblick, die verlorne Seligkeit, 1828
Lied zum deutschen Tanz, 1891

Fiction
Zerbin; oder, Die neuere Philosophie, 1776
Der Landprediger, 1777
Der Waldbruder, ein Pendant zu Werthers Leiden, 1797

Other
Anmerkungen übers Theater, with *Amor vincit omnia*, 1774
Philosophische Vorlesungen für empfindsame Seelen, 1780; edited by Christoph Weiß, 1994
Versuch über das erste Principium der Moral, edited by August Stöber, 1874

Über Götz von Berlichingen, edited by Erich Schmidt, 1901

Briefe über die Moralität der Leiden des jungen Werthers, edited by L. Schmitz-Kallenberg, 1918

Über die Soldatenehen, edited by Karl Freye, 1913

Further Reading

Blunden, Allen, "J.M.R. Lenz and Leibniz: A Point of View," *Sprachkunst* 9 (1978)

Hill, David, "Stolz und Demut, Illusion und Mitleid bei Lenz," in *J.R.M.* [sic] *Lenz als Alternative,* edited by Karin A. Wurst, Cologne: Böhlau, 1992

Madland, Helga, "Gesture as Evidence of Language Scepticism in Lenz's *Der Hofmeister* and *Die Soldaten,*" *German Quarterly* 57 (1984)

Mayer, Hans, "Lenz oder die Alternative," in *J.M.R. Lenz: Werke und Schriften,* edited by Britta Titel and Hellmut Haug, Darmstadt: Wissenschaftliche Buchgesellschaft, 1966

Müller, Maria E., "Die Wunschwelt des Tantalus: Kritische Bermerkungen zu sozial-utopischen Entwürfen im Werk von J.M.R. Lenz," *Literatur für Leser* 3 (1984)

Osborne, John, *J.M.R. Lenz: The Renunciation of Heroism,* Göttingen: Vandenhoeck und Ruprecht, 1975

Rector, Martin, "Anschauendes Denken: Zur Form von Lenz' *Anmerkungen übers Theater,*" *Lenz-Jahrbuch* 1 (1991)

Scherpe, Klaus R., "Dichterische Erkenntnis und Projektemacherei: Widersprüche im Werk von J.M.R. Lenz," *Goethe-Jahrbuch* 94 (1977)

Schöne, Albrecht, "Wiederholung der exemplarischen Begebenheit: J.M.R. Lenz," in *Säkularisation als sprachbildende Kraft: Studien zur Dichtung deutscher Pfarrersöhne,* Göttingen: Vandenhoeck und Ruprecht, 1958; 2nd edition, 1968

Stephan, Inge, and Hans-Gerd Winter, *"Ein vorübergehendes Meteor"? J.M.R. Lenz und seine Rezeption in Deutschland,* Stuttgart: Metzler, 1984

Winter, Hans-Gerd, *J.M.R. Lenz,* Stuttgart: Metzler, 1987

——, "J.M.R. Lenz as Adherent and Critic of Enlightenment in *Zerbin; or Modern Philosophy* and *The Most Sentimental of All Novels,*" in *Impure Reason: Dialectic of Enlightenment in Germany,* edited by W. Daniel Wilson and Robert C. Holub, Detroit, Michigan: Wayne State University Press, 1993

Wurst, Karin A., "A Shattered Mirror: Lenz's Concept of Mimesis," in *Space to Act: The Theater of J.M.R. Lenz,* edited by Alan C. Leidner and Helga S. Madland, Columbia, South Carolina: Camden House, 1993

Siegfried Lenz 1926–

Next to Günter Grass and Martin Walser, Siegfried Lenz is the most highly acclaimed and popular living German prose writer of the older generation. Along with Grass, Walser, and Heinrich Böll, he has shaped the path of German prose since 1951. His breakthrough as a writer came in 1968 with the publication of his novel *Deutschstunde* (*The German Lesson*), a best-seller success that he was able to repeat in 1978 with his novel *Heimatmuseum* (*The Heritage*). The novels and collections of short stories Lenz has published thereafter have not been able to match these successes. His oeuvre consists mostly of novels and short stories, but it also includes dramas, radio plays, travel books, and essays.

Lenz's fictional works are written in a realistic style. He rarely experiments with form; rather, he tells a straightforward story and creates a vivid atmosphere through the use of precisely observed details. His works always carry a moral or social-critical message, make statements about the state of the world and what it should be, and confront the reader with situations that require moral decisions. In the 1950s and 1960s, Lenz's uncompromising moral standpoint manifested itself in parables of guilt and atonement; from the 1970s on, his work became less obviously didactic and more psychological in character. Following his literary theories, which he explains in his essays, he neither insults his readers nor does he force his ideas upon them; instead, he makes a pact with them and stimulates their thinking in a truly democratic manner, questioning prejudice and political dogmatism.

Lenz's short stories vary from humorous to social-critical and politically charged ones. Thus, *So zärtlich war Suleyken* (1955; So Tender Was Suleyken) is a collection of delightfully humorous stories about the idiosyncrasies and follies of the inhabitants of the imaginary village of Suleyken in Masuria, a utopian small-town society that is in stark contrast to the writer's own troubled society. Later, in the collection *Der Geist der Mirabelle: Geschichten aus Bollerup* (1975; The Spirit of the Yellow Plum: Stories from Bollerup), Lenz less successfully writes humorous tales and anecdotes about the inhabitants of an imaginary village in Denmark.

Of his dramas and radio plays, only *Zeit der Schuldlosen* (1961) is worth mentioning. It is an existentialist drama about guilt and atonement.

Some of the stories in Lenz's collection *Jäger des Spotts* (1958; Hunter of Ridicule) show the influence of Ernest Hemingway. Following Hemingway, Lenz is interested in people who fail despite great efforts but nonetheless prove themselves in the face of failure. Other stories are of a social-critical, satirical nature. Several stories in the collection *Das Feuerschiff* (1960; *The Lightship*) contain clear anti-Hemingway elements. Lenz, for example, wants to demonstrate that, in contrast to Hemingway's views, nothing ends with the end of a story, while every beginning has a story that precedes it. In the title story, Lenz condemns senseless heroism. In the social-critical stories of *Der Spielverderber* (1965; The Spoilsport), the past of the Third Reich plays the main role in influencing the present. The novella *Ein Kriegsende* (1984; An End of the War) takes up the question of conflicting duties, which links it to Lenz's earlier stories, novels, and dramas. The novella's main conflict involves assessing when a soldier must obey orders and under what conditions he has the right to disobey. The stories contained in the 1987 collection *Das serbische Mädchen* (The Serbian Girl) and in *Ludmilla* (1996) continue the social-critical thrust of his earlier stories.

Lenz's first novel, *Es waren Habichte in der Luft* (1951; Hawks Were in the Air), which depicts Finnish Karelia shortly after World War I, reflects the influence of French existentialism on German literature, as does his second novel, *Duell mit dem Schatten* (1953; Duel with the Shadow). In *Es waren Habichte in der Luft*, the Cold War, the existence of the two newly founded German states, and the flight of many Germans from East to West are present in allegorical form. *Der Mann im Strom* (1957; The Man in the River) replaces existential themes with concrete social criticism when it deals with the problems of an aging worker in a modern industrial economy. In the sports novel *Brot und Spiele* (1959; Bread and Games), Lenz criticizes the fickleness of the sports clubs, their sponsors, and the public, who all make an athlete into a hero and then drop him as soon as he no longer fulfills their wishes and dreams.

Lenz's next novels concentrate on political themes. *Stadtgespräch* (1963; The Survivor) is a novel about the question of whether a leader of the resistance against an occupying power in a Nordic country ought to give himself up in order to save 44 hostages and about the collective guilt of the townspeople. The impact of the Third Reich on the present is one of the themes of *The German Lesson*, which many critics consider Lenz's masterpiece. It is the story of the young Siggi Jepsen, the inmate of a juvenile detention center in Hamburg, whose father, a police officer in the fictional north German town of Rugbüll, had been ordered to enforce an order issued to his friend, the painter Max Nansen, not to paint any more. Whereas the policeman considers it his duty to carry out the order, the painter considers it *his* duty to continue painting. Thus, two concepts of duty that were crucial in the success of National Socialism in Germany clash with one another. Lenz's book is a "German lesson" for his readers, whom he wants to educate so that they can evaluate critically Germany's past and present. Morally correct behavior is also the theme of the novel *Das Vorbild* (1973; *An Exemplary Life*), in which Lenz demonstrates that there are no longer any universally acceptable role models for today's youth. The novel *The Heritage* traces the fate of a local history museum in Masuria from its founding through the Nazis' attempt to turn it into a German frontier museum to, after its reestablishment in Schleswig after the war, the attempt of German refugee organizations to eliminate all objects that would reveal the Polish heritage of Masuria. In stressing the right of the Poles to live in Masuria, Lenz pleads for the exercising of reason against the continuing hatred for Germany's Polish neighbors.

In *Der Verlust* (1981; The Breakdown), Lenz's hero suffers a stroke and loses his power of speech. In describing the effects of this loss on a person's ability to communicate, Lenz gives up social-critical and political themes in favor of psychology.

The theme of *Exerzierplatz* (1985; *Training Ground*) is the rebuilding of life in Germany on the basis of a military past, symbolized by an old drill ground on which the Zeller family from East Prussia has tried to build a new life after World War II. The story is paradigmatic of both the pulling together of all forces after the war to build a new society and the later quarrel between the old and the new generations in which the latter knows nothing about the hardships of the past but takes wealth and success for granted.

In his more recent novels, Lenz has returned to psychological and social critical themes without reference to the Third Reich. In *Die Klangprobe* (1990; The Sound Test), he uses a subtle love story in order to demonstrate the transitoriness of human existence, human relations, and artifacts, as exemplified by the sculptures of Hans Bode, which are crumbling as a result of air pollution. In *Die Auflehnung* (1994; The Revolt), two brothers revolt against fate: one of them is the owner of a fish farm who faces the loss of his livelihood because he is not permitted to kill the fish-eating cormorants, a protected species; the other one is a tea taster who must face the loss of his taste buds. The theme is thus the conflict of defiance and resignation, which is caused, on the one hand, by the conflict between codified law and justice and, on the other hand, by the effects of aging. In *Arnes Nachlaß* (1999; What Arne Left Behind) Lenz deals with the relationship of the individual to the group of his peers. The highly gifted young Arne Hellmann, whose father has committed suicide with the rest of his family, is marginalized by his peers. In his desperate attempts to be accepted by them, he compromises his principles by participating in a burglary and, out of shame, he commits suicide at age 15. Even in these last works, Lenz remains a moderate traditionalist who is able to tell a story and create a true-to-life atmosphere like few other contemporary writers.

HANS WAGENER

Biography

Born in Lyck, East Prussia (now Elk, Poland), 17 March 1926. Studied at the University of Hamburg, 1945–48; served in the navy during World War II; reporter, 1948–50; editor for *Die Welt*, Hamburg, 1950–51; freelance writer, 1951–; visiting lecturer, University of Houston, Texas, 1969; member, Gruppe 47; campaign speaker for the Social Democratic Party, 1965–. Schickele Prize, 1952, 1962; Lessing Prize, 1953; Hauptmann Prize, 1961; Mackensen Prize, 1962; City of Bremen Prize, 1962; State of North Rhine-Westphalia Arts Prize, 1966; Gryphius Prize, 1979; German Freemasons Prize, 1979; Thomas Mann Prize, 1984; Raabe Prize, 1987; Federal Booksellers Peace Prize, 1988; Galinsky Foundation Prize, 1989; Goethe Prize, City of Frankfurt, 1999. Honorary doctorate from the University of Hamburg, 1976; honorary doctorate from Ben Gurion University, Israel, 1993. Currently lives in Hamburg.

Selected Works

Collections
Gesammelte Erzählungen, 1970
Die Erzählungen: 1949–1984, 3 vols., 1986
The Selected Stories of Siegfried Lenz, edited and translated by Breon Mitchell, 1989
Werkausgabe in Einzelbänden, 20 vols., 1996–99
Essays, 1997

Fiction
Es waren Habichte in der Luft, 1951
Duell mit dem Schatten, 1953
So zärtlich war Suleyken, 1955
Der Mann im Strom, 1957
Dasselbe, 1957
Jäger des Spotts, 1958; as *Jäger des Spotts, und andere Erzählungen*, edited by Robert H. Spaethling, 1965
Brot und Spiele, 1959
Das Feuerschiff, 1960; as *The Lightship*, translated by Michael Bullock, 1962
Das Wunder von Striegeldorf: Geschichten, 1961
Stimmungen der See, 1962
Stadtgespräch, 1963; as *The Survivor*, translated by Michael Bullock, 1965
Der Hafen ist voller Geheimnisse: Ein Feature in Erzählungen und zwei masurische Geschichten, 1963

*Lehmanns Erzählungen; oder, So schön war mein Markt: Aus den
    Bekenntnissen eines Schwarzhändlers,* 1964
Der Spielverderber, 1965
Begegnung mit Tieren, with Hans Bender and Werner Bergengruen,
    1966
Das Wrack, and Other Stories, edited by C.A.H. Russ, 1967
Die Festung und andere Novellen, 1968
Deutschstunde, 1968; as *The German Lesson,* translated by Ernst
    Kaiser and Eithne Wilkins, 1971
Hamilkar Schass aus Suleyken, 1970
Lukas, sanftmütiger Knecht, 1970
So war es mit dem Zirkus: Fünf Geschichten aus Suleyken, 1971
Erzählungen, 1972
Meistererzählungen, 1972
Ein Haus aus lauter Liebe, 1973
Das Vorbild, 1973; as *An Exemplary Life,* translated by Douglas
    Parmée, 1976
Der Geist der Mirabelle: Geschichten aus Bollerup, 1975; as
    Geschichten ut Bollerup, translation into Low German by Reimer
    Bull, 1987
Einstein überquert die Elbe bei Hamburg, 1975
Die Kunstradfahrer und andere Geschichten, 1976
Heimatmuseum, 1978; as *The Heritage,* translated by Krishna Winston,
    1981
Der Verlust, 1981
Der Anfang von etwas, 1981
Ein Kriegsende, 1984
Exerzierplatz, 1985; as *Training Ground,* translated by Geoffrey
    Skelton, 1991
Der Verzicht, 1985
Das serbische Mädchen, 1987
Motivsuche, 1988
Die Klangprobe, 1990
Die Auflehnung, 1994
Ludmilla, 1996
Arnes Nachlaß, 1999

Plays
Das schönste Fest der Welt Haussuchung (radio plays), 1956
Zeit der Schuldlosen: Zeit der Schuldigen (radio plays), 1961; stage
    adaptation (in German), 1966
Das Gesicht: Komödie (produced 1964), 1964
Haussuchung (radio plays), 1967
Die Augenbinde; Schauspiel; Nicht alle Förster sind froh: Ein Dialog,
    1970
Drei Stücke, 1980
Zeit der Schuldlosen und andere Stücke, 1988
Schauspiele, 1996

Other
So leicht fängt man keine Katze, 1954
Der einsame Jäger, 1955
Das Kabinett der Konterbande, 1956
Flug über Land und Meer: Schleswig—Nordsee—Holstein—Ostsee,
    with Dieter Seelmann, 1967; as *Wo die Möwen schreien: Flug über
    Nordutschlands Küsten und Länder,* 1976
Leute von Hamburg: Satirische Porträts, 1968
Versäum nicht den Termin der Freude, 1970
Lotte soll nicht sterben (for children), 1970; as *Lotte macht alles mit,*
    1978
Beziehungen: Ansichten und Bekenntnisse zur Literatur, 1970
Die Herrschaftssprache der CDU, 1971

*Verlorenes Land—gewonnene Nachbarschaft: Zur Ostpolitik der
    Bundesregierung,* 1972
Der Amüsierdoktor, 1972
*Elfenbeinturm und Barrikade: Schriftsteller zwischen Literatur und
    Politik,* 1976
Die Wracks von Hamburg: Hörfunk-Features, 1978
*Himmel, Wolken, weites Land: Flug über Meer, Marsch, Geest, und
    Heide,* with Dieter Seelmann, 1979
Waldboden: Sechsunddreissig Farbstiftzeichnungen, illustrated by
    Liselotte Lenz, 1979
Gespräche mit Manès Sperber und Leszek Kolakowski, edited by Alfred
    Mensak, 1980
*Über Phantasie: Siegfried Lenz, Gespräche mit Heinrich Böll, Günter
    Grass, Walter Kempowski, Pavel Kohout,* edited by Alfred Mensak,
    1982
Fast ein Triumph: Aus einem Album, 1982
Elfenbeinturm und Barrikade: Erfahrungen am Schreibtisch, 1983
Manès Sperber, sein letztes Jahr, with Manès and Jenka Sperber, 1985
Etwas über Namen (address), 1985
Kleines Strandgut, illustrated by Liselotte Lenz, 1986
Dostojewski, der gläubige Zweifler, 1988
Am Rande des Friedens, 1989
Über das Gedächtnis, 1992
Über den Schmerz, 1998

Edited Works
Julius Stettenheim, *Wippchens charmante Scharmützel,* edited with
    Egon Schramm, 1960
Ben Witter, *Schritte und Worte,* 1990

Further Reading
Arnold, Heinz Ludwig, editor, *Siegfried Lenz,* Munich: Edition Text
    und Kritik, 1976; 2nd edition, 1982
Baßmann, Winfried, *Siegfried Lenz: Sein Werk als Beispiel für Weg und
    Standort der Literatur in der Bundesrepublik Deutschland,* Bonn:
    Bouvier, 1976; 2nd edition, 1978
Elm, Theo, *Siegfried Lenz, "Deutschstunde": Engagement und
    Realismus im Gegenwartsroman,* Munich: Fink, 1974
Murdoch, Brian, and Malcolm Read, *Siegfried Lenz,* London: Wolf,
    1978
Nordbruch, Claus, *Über die Pflicht: Eine Analyse des Werkes von
    Siegfried Lenz: Versuch über ein deutsches Phänomen,* Hildesheim
    and New York: Olms, 1996
Pätzold, Hartmut, *Theorie und Praxis moderner Schreibweisen: Am
    Beispiel von Siegfried Lenz und Helmut Heißenbüttel,* Bonn: Bouvier,
    1976
Reber, Trudis E., *Siegfried Lenz,* Köpfe des 20. Jahrhunderts, vol. 74,
    Berlin: Colloquium, 1973; 3rd edition, 1986
Russ, Collin, "Siegfried Lenz," in *Deutsche Dichter der Gegenwart: Ihr
    Leben und Werk,* edited by Benno von Wiese, Berlin: Schmidt, 1973
Russ, Colin, editor, *Der Schriftsteller Siegfried Lenz: Urteile und
    Standpunkte,* Hamburg: Hoffmann und Campe, 1973
Schwarz, Wilhelm Johannes, *Der Erzähler Siegfried Lenz,* Bern and
    Munich: Francke, 1974
Wagener, Hans, *Siegfried Lenz,* Munich: Beck, 1976; 4th edition, 1985
———, "Siegfried Lenz," in *Contemporary German Fiction Writers:
    Second Series,* Dictionary of Literary Biography, edited by Wolfgang
    Elfe and James Hardin, vol. 75, Detroit, Michigan: Gale Research,
    1988
Wolff, Rudolf, editor, *Siegfried Lenz: Werk und Wirkung,* Bonn:
    Bouvier, 1985

Gotthold Ephraim Lessing 1729-1781

In the philosophy, science, theology, and literature of the Enlightenment, man and his species—especially his capacities for inner and outward freedom, truth, knowledge, independent thought, and emotional and spiritual experience—became the object of rational inquiry. Reflecting this variety, Lessing is far more than merely the rationalist that earlier critics have seen. His early reviews show his positive response to such books that appealed not only to the mind but also to the heart, his later theological writing greater sympathy for the "feeling" than the "rational" Christian. In his early unfinished *Das Christentum der Vernunft* (first published posthumously, 1784; *The Christianity of Reason*), he articulates his belief in perfectibility, that is, in man's ability to make himself more perfect and thus ever closer to the absolute perfection that was God's alone. This idea was also central to his last completed work, *Die Erziehung des Menschengeschlechts* (1780; *The Education of the Human Race*). These notions are developed throughout his work. His dramatic and dramaturgical writing, to which they are central, effectively overcame the antagonism of the church by demonstrating the theater's potential for improving morality, taste, civilized behavior, and thinking. Lessing also used the German language to engender public discussion of issues that had hitherto been the concern of a select few.

Born a generation before Goethe and Schiller, when Latin was still widely used by scholars and theologians, French was employed by the German courts and the aristocracy, and Italian was the dominant language of plays and librettos printed in Germany, Lessing developed the expressive potential of the German language in poetry, fable, epigram, prose, drama, dramaturgy, criticism, theory, aesthetics, theology, and philosophy. A knowledge of Latin, Greek, French, English, Dutch, Italian, and Spanish, as well as extensive reading of both classical antiquity and contemporary European cultures, enriched his creative and critical writing.

Lessing's early comedies played to responsive audiences in Leipzig, Berlin, and Vienna. The prejudices of Germany society were exploited and undermined in *Der Freigeist* (1755; The Freethinker) and *Die Juden* (1754; The Jews), in which, respectively, a sincere Christian finally reveals his true faith after hiding behind a self-protective cloak of arrogant atheism, and the Christian virtues of charity and loving one's neighbor are demonstrated in a brave and well-educated traveler who later reveals that he is a Jew. *Miß Sara Sampson* (1755; *Miss Sarah Sampson*), set in a tavern on the road to Dover, was the first successful German example of the new genre of domestic tragedy. Lessing drew inspiration for this play from Seneca, English Restoration comedy, and the sentimental novels of Samuel Richardson. He acknowledged his indebtedness to Gellert, Chassiron, and Diderot for his theoretical justification of the genre in his *Theatralische Bibliothek* (1754–58; The Theater Library) and *Hamburgische Dramaturgie* (1767–68; *Hamburg Dramaturgy*). With *Emilia Galotti* (1772), which is set in Renaissance Italy, he gave an even more powerful illustration of domestic tragedy, which secured a place for the genre in the German tradition of social drama that includes writers from Goethe, Schiller, and J.M.R. Lenz to Büchner, Hebbel, and Gerhart Hauptmann. Emilia chooses death at the hand of her loving father rather than seduction by the persuasive, self-indulgent, and all-powerful monarch, Hettore Gonzaga.

Lessing's theory of tragedy was rooted in Aristotle's elaboration of the interrelated passions of pity and fear rather than in Corneille's adaptation of Aristotle into the neoclassic unities of action, time, and place. In the *Dramaturgy*, however, he refutes Aristotle's argument that characters drawn from history induce credibility. According to Lessing, it was the task of the dramatist, as Shakespeare had shown with the ghost of Hamlet's father, to make the audience believe by developing the causality of the drama's inner relationships between character and circumstance. This was the way to move the audience and to rouse the tragic passions of pity and fear. Family, domestic, and personal relations became the focus of Lessing's plays, rather than the mighty characters of history or of the grand classical manner. In these plays, he demonstrates instead how tragic circumstances could draw out the heroic potential of individuals, irrespective of social class or gender.

His most famous comedy, *Minna von Barnhelm* (1767; translated as *The Disbanded Officer, The School for Honor, Minna von Barnhelm,* and *The Way of Honour*), is set in a Berlin tavern six months after the conclusion of the Seven Years' War in 1763. It is an authentic account of war's capacity to destroy not only material circumstances but also human relations and feelings. For the same reasons for which he admired Plautus's *De captivi*, Lessing wrote this play as a light comedy with a serious message; it is playful but hard-hitting, and romantic but potentially tragic. The political setting is provided by the recent war between Prussia and Austria over Silesia, and the love intrigue is supplied by the reconciliation of a couple, a proud officer in the king of Prussia's army, Major von Tellheim, and a vivacious and emancipated Saxon lady of rank, Minna von Barnhelm, who are estranged by a war that has placed them on opposite sides.

Lessing's enduring masterpiece, the dramatic poem *Nathan der Weise* (1779; *Nathan the Wise*), opened the postwar German theater in 1945 immediately after the revelations of the horrors of the Holocaust. It is a tale in light iambic pentameter about the way in which a turbulent young Templar, born of a Muslim father and a Christian mother, is reconciled with his sister, Recha, who was adopted by Nathan the Jew soon after his wife and seven sons had been slaughtered by marauding Christian knights. The setting is Jerusalem some time between 1192 and 1193, when there was a prospect of peace between the Christian armies led by Richard I and the Mohammedan army of Salahed-Dîn. Saladin has already executed 19 Templars for breaking the truce and suddenly spares the life of the last one because of a vague facial resemblance to his deceased brother. This Templar saves Recha from the flames engulfing her house. First he believes Recha to be a Jew, Nathan's daughter. Later he is led to believe that she is a Christian. Her true origins of mixed Muslim-Christian parentage are revealed only in the final scenes to enrich the audience's understanding of the love and care with which her adoptive Jewish father has reared her. The centerpiece, the famous parable of the three rings, which is Nathan's response to Saladin's demand to learn what religion he, who is called "wise," considers to be the best, demonstrates symbolically that each of the three monotheistic religions of Judaism,

Christianity, and Islamism has the potential for establishing peaceful relations between the nations of the world.

Lessing's knowledge of the practical aspects of theater and his sensitivity to the relationship between theater, actors, and audience brought a new dimension to aesthetics. In the *Beyträge zur Geschichte und Aufnahme des Theaters* (1750; Contributions to the History and Reception of the Theater), he discusses what he considered to be Plautus's most effective comedy, *De captivi*. Pieces on sentimental comedy; English restoration comedy; Dryden's *Essay of Dramatick Poesie* (which he translated); the works of Shakespeare; the French theater of Corneille, Racine, Molière, Voltaire, Diderot, and others; the works of the ancients, including Aristotle; and translations from Greek and Latin were published in the *Theatralische Bibliothek*, the *Briefe, die neueste Litteratur betreffend* (1759–65; Letters on Recent Literature), and the *Hamburg Dramaturgy*. Early work on a manual for actors also was subsumed in this latter work. He describes the art of acting as "transitory painting," a form of moving pictures. Diderot's more static *tableaux vivants* undoubtedly influenced his thinking, but so did William Hogarth's *Analysis of Beauty* (1753) and Edmund Burke's *Inquiry into the Origins of Our Ideas on the Beautiful and the Sublime* (1757).

Lessing's correspondence, wide reading, and knowledge of Winckelmann also nourished his treatise on the sculpted Laocoön group that depicts the Greek priest's vain struggle to save his sons from the two serpents that the gods had sent to punish him for casting his spear at the wooden horse to warn the Trojans of its contents. In *Laokoon; oder, Über die Grenzen der Malerei und Poesie* (1766; translated as *Laocoön; or, The Limits of Painting and Poetry* and *Laocoön: An Essay on the Limits of Painting and Poetry*), Lessing uses his extensive knowledge of antiquity to identify the characteristically different properties of the visual and the verbal arts. According to Lessing, clouds should not be used to render something invisible on canvas, and poetry should not be content to paint pictures in words. He argues that the characteristic dimension of the visual arts is space, that of poetry time; the visual arts show events coexisting, and poetry evokes successive ones. For Lessing, the moderated cry of anguish on Laocoön's face is not the result of stoicism; it derives from the nature of Greek sculpture, which was commanded to represent beauty, not the distortion of extreme suffering. In this account, moderation stimulates the imagination more than naturalism.

A scholar, journalist, and moralist, Lessing chose controversial subjects, ran risks with the censor, fought for high standards in translation, and brought to public attention matters hitherto kept behind closed doors. He was granted permission by the son and daughter of the late Samuel Heinrich Reimarus to publish anonymously seven fragments of his work on the contradictions and improbabilities contained in the Bible. Lessing admired the work despite his disagreement with it. He added his own counterarguments to the extracts that he published under the title of *Die Fragmente eines Ungenannten* (1774–77; Fragments by an Unnamed Writer). Reimarus thought that biblical inconsistencies undermined the Christian faith. Lessing countered that it was only natural, for example, for the different accounts of the Resurrection to be contradictory since the Gospels had been written by different persons at different intervals from the event. Under attack from the Hamburg theologian Johann Melchior Goeze, Lessing replied that he published his unnamed author's

argument so that it could be refuted; he also argued that there was more to Christianity than was in the Bible and more in the Bible than had to do with Christianity. Stimulated by Lessing's series of *Anti-Goeze* (1778) and colored by personal rancor, the debate became so heated that his employer, Karl Ferdinand I, duke of Braunschweig and Lüneburg, chose to withdraw Lessing's dispensation from censorship. The printed copies of the *Fragmente* were confiscated, and henceforth Lessing had to submit his works to the censor prior to publication. The effect was minimal. He switched the theological controversy to the stage with the publication of *Nathan the Wise* and fueled controversy again when he applied the notion of perfectibility to the transmigration of souls in *The Education of the Human Race*.

Lessing's instinct was to defend those who could not defend themselves. He rehabilitated the work of a number of contemporaries and writers from the past and made public the private concerns of the Freemasons. His intention in the latter instance was to recall the essence of freemasonry and contrast it to the corruption prevailing in the Masonic lodges of the Scottish system that were presided over by his employer, Ferdinand I. With *Ernst und Falk: Gespräche für Freimaurer* (1780; translated as *Ernst and Falk* and *Lessing's Masonic Dialogues*), he played a leading part in the reform of German freemasonry while making clear his conviction that the virtues of social, religious, and racial equality, of friendship, frankness, charity, and actions for the public good were attainable by all—women as well as men, and in civil society as well as within freemasonry.

Ever since 1773, individual pieces and limited collections of Lessing's prose and dramatic writing have found skillful English translators, although there is as yet no translation of his collected works. His major plays and some of his early comedies continue to be performed at regular intervals in both German- and English-speaking theaters. Despite the immediate success of *Miss Sarah Sampson* in Germany and Austria, however, the London premiere of this play was as recent as 1990. *Laocoön* is widely read now, as it was then, by scholars and those interested in poetry, painting, sculpture, and aesthetics. His fables are occasionally taught in schools today, while his writing on theology, freemasonry, and dramatic theory continue to appeal to more specialized readers. Lessing's fundamental humanitarianism and his advocacy of searching public debate and the principles of social, racial, and religious equality ensure the continuing relevance of his work to succeeding generations.

EDWARD M. BATLEY

See also Aufklärung

Biography

Born in Kamenz, Saxony, 23 January 1729. Studied at the school of St. Afra, Meissen, 1741–46; studied theology and medicine at the University of Leipzig, 1746–48; at the University of Wittenberg, 1748, 1751–52; master of arts, University of Wittenberg, 1752; in Berlin, writer from 1748; edited, with Christlob Mylius, and contributed to *Beiträge zur Historie und Aufnahme des Theaters*, 1750; edited and contributed to *Theatralische Bibliothek*, 1754–58, and *Briefe, die neueste Literatur betreffend (Literaturbriefe)*, 1759; corresponded with Moses Mendelssohn and Friedrich Nicolai on aesthetics, 1755–56; acted as secretary to General Bogislaw von Tauentzien in Breslau, 1760–65; worked as resident drama critic to the National Theater in Hamburg, 1767–70; librarian to the Duke of Brunswick, Wolfenbüttel, 1770–81; traveled to Italy, 1775–76; member, Academy of Mannheim,

1776. Married Eva König (died 1778), 1776. Died in Brunswick, 15 February 1781.

Selected Works

Collections

Dramatic Works, edited and translated by E. Bell, 2 vols., 1878
Sämtliche Schriften, 3rd ed., edited by Karl Lachmann, revised by Franz Muncker, 23 vols., 1886–1924; reprint, 16 vols., 1979
Werke, edited by Julius Petersen and Waldemar von Olshausen, 25 vols., 1925; supplement, 5 vols., 1929–35; reprint, 1970
Werke, edited by H.G. Göpfert, et al., 8 vols., 1970–79; reprint, 1996
Werke und Briefe in zwölf Bänden, edited by Wilfried Barner et al., 1985–
Nathan the Wise, Minna von Barnhelm, and Other Plays and Writings, various translators, edited by Peter Demetz, 1991

Plays

Die junge Gelehrte (produced 1748), in *Schriften*, 1754
Die alte Jungfer, 1749
Die Juden (produced 1749), in *Schriften*, 1754
Der Freigeist (produced 1767), in *Schriften*, 1755
Miß Sara Sampson (produced 1755), in *Schriften*, 1755; edited by K. Eibl, 1971; as *Miss Sarah Sampson*, translated by David Ritterhouse, 1789; translated by E. Bell, in *World Drama*, edited by Barrett Clark, 1933
Philotas (produced 1780), 1759
Lustspiele, 2 vols., 1767
Minna von Barnhelm (produced 1767), 1767; edited by Dieter Hildebrant, 1969; as *The Disbanded Officer*, translated and adapted by James Johnstone, 1786; as *The School for Honor*, 1789; as *Minna von Barnhelm*, translated by F. Holcroft, 1805; translated by W.C. Wrankmore, 1858; translated by P. Maxwell, 1899; as *The Way of Honour*, translated by E.U. Ouless, 1929; translated by W.A. Steel, with *Laocoon* and *Nathan the Wise*, 1930; translated by E. Bell, 1933; translated by K.J. Northcott, 1972; translated by Anthony Meech, 1990
Trauerspiele, 1772
Emilia Galotti (produced 1772), in *Trauerspiele*, 1772; translated by Joseph Berrington, 1794; translated by Benjamin Thompson, 1800; translated by Edward Dvoretzky, 1962; translated by F.J. Lamport, in *Five German Tragedies*, 1969; translated by Anna Johanna Gode von Aesch, 1991
Nathan der Weise (produced 1783), 1779; edited by P. Demetz, 1966; as *Nathan the Wise*, translated by R.E. Raspe, 1781; translated by W.A. Steel, with *Laocoon* and *Minna von Barnhelm*, 1930; translated by Bayard Quincy Morgan, 1955 (also published in *Nathan the Wise, Minna von Barnhelm, and Other Plays and Writings*, edited by peter Demetz, 1991); translated by T.H. Lustig, in *Classical German Drama*, 1963; translated by Walter F.C. Ade, 1972

Other

Schriften, 6 vols., 1753–55; revised edition, 1771
Fabeln, 1759; revised edition, 1777; as *Fables*, translated by J. Richardson, 1773
Laokoon; oder, Über die Grenzen der Malerei und Poesie, 1766; as *Laocoon; or, The Limits of Poetry and Painting*, translated by W. Ross, 1836; translated by E.C. Beasley, 1853; translated by W.B. Rönnfeldt, 1895; translated by W.A. Steel, with *Nathan the Wise* and *Minna von Barnhelm*, 1930; translated by Edward Allen McCormick, 1962; as *Laocoön: An Essay on the Limits of Painting and Poetry*, translated by Edward Allen McCormick, 1984
Briefe, antiquarischen Inhalts, 2 vols., 1768
Berengarius Turonensis, 1770
Zur Geschichte und Literatur [*Wolfenbütteler Beiträge*], 3 vols., 1773–81

Anti-Goeze, 1778
Ernst und Falk: Gespräche für Freimaurer, 1780; edited by Wolfgang Kelsch, 1981; translated as *Ernst and Falk*, 1854–72; as *Lessing's Masonic Dialogues*, translated by A. Cohen, 1927; as *Ernst and Falk: Conversations for the Freemasons* (incomplete), translated by William L. Zwiebel, 1994
Die Erziehung des Menschengeschlechts, 1780; edited by Louis Ferdinand Helbig, 1980; as *The Education of the Human Race*, translated by Henry C. Robinson, 1806; translated by F.W. Robertson, 1858; translated by H. Chadwick, in *Lessing's Theological Writings*, 1956
Theologischer Nachlass, edited by K.G. Lessing, 2 vols., 1784
Theatralischer Nachlass, edited by K.G. Lessing, 2 vols., 1784–86
Literarischer Nachlass, edited by K.G. Lessing, 3 vols, 1793–95
Hamburgische Dramaturgie, 1767–68; edited by O. Mann, 1958; as *Dramatic Notes*, translated by Helen Zimmern, in *Selected Prose Works of G.E. Lessing*, edited by E. Bell, 1879; as *Hamburg Dramaturgy*, 1962
Briefwechsel über das Trauerspiel, edited by J. Schultze-Sasse, 1972
Brief aus Wolfenbüttel, edited by Günter Schulz, 1975
Meine liebste Madam: Briefwechsel, with Eva König, edited by Günter and Ursula Schulz, 1979
Gotthold Ephraim Lessing: A Selection of His Fables in English and German, translated by Lesley Macdonald and H. Weissenborn, 1979
Dialog in Briefen und andere ausgewählte Dokumente zum Leben Gotthold Ephraim Lessings mit Eva Catharina König, edited by Helmut Rudolff, 1981
Unvergängliche Prosa: die philosophischen theologischen und esoterischen Schriften (selections), edited by Konrad Dietzfelbinger, 1981
Die Ehre hat mich nie gesucht: Lessing in Berlin (selections), edited by Gerhard Wolf, 1985

Further Reading

Barner, Wilfried, *Lessing: Epoche, Werk, Wirkung*, Munich: Beck, 1975; 5th edition, 1987
Batley, Edward M., *Catalyst of Enlightenment: Gotthold Ephraim Lessing*, Bern and New York: Lang, 1990
Buchholtz, Arend, *Die Geschichte der Familie Lessing*, 2 vols., Berlin: Holten, 1909
Chadwick, Henry, editor, *Lessing's Theological Writings*, London: Adam and Charles Black, 1956
Daunicht, Richard, *Lessing im Gespräch: Berichte und Urteile von Freunden und Zeitgenossen*, Munich: Fink, 1971
Eichner, Siglinde, *Die Prosafabel Lessings in seiner Theorie und Dichtung*, Bonn: Bouvier, 1974
Garland, Henry B., *Lessing: The Founder of Modern German Literature*, Cambridge: Bowes and Bowes, 1937; 2nd edition, London: Macmillan, and New York: St. Martin's Press, 1963
Guthke, Karl Siegfried, *Gotthold Ephraim Lessing*, Stuttgart: Metzler, 1967; 3rd edition, 1979
Hoensbroech, Marion, *Die List der Kritik: Lessings kritische Schriften und Dramen*, Munich: Fink, 1976
Lamport, F.J., *Lessing and the Drama*, Oxford: Clarendon Press, and New York: Oxford University Press, 1981
Lessing, Karl Gotthelf, *G.E. Lessings Leben, nebst seinem noch übrigen litterarischen Nachlasse*, Berlin: Vossische Buchhandlung, 1793
Mauser, Wolfram, and Günter Sasse, editors, *Streitkultur: Strategien des Überzeugens im Werk Lessings*, Tübingen: Niemeyer, 1993
Metzger, Michael M., *Lessing and the Language of Comedy*, The Hague: Mouton, 1966
Rilla, Paul, *Lessing und sein Zeitalter*, Berlin: Aufbau-Verlag, 1960
Robertson, John George, *Lessing's Dramatic Theory, Being an Introduction to and Commentary on His Hamburgische Dramaturgie*, Cambridge: The University Press, and New York: Blom, 1939

Rolleston, T.W., *Life and Writings of Gotthold Ephraim Lessing*, London, 1889

Schmidt, Erich, *Lessing: Geschichte seines Lebens und seiner Schriften*, 2 vols., Berlin: Weidmann, 1884–92; 4th edition, 1923

Seeba, Hinrich C., *Die Liebe zur Sache: Öffentliches und privates Interesse in Lessings Dramen*, Tübingen: Niemeyer, 1973

Emilia Galotti 1772

Play by Gotthold Ephraim Lessing

Gotthold Ephraim Lessing's *Emilia Galotti,* his last domestic tragedy, is considered his most successful play and is one of the most discussed and disputed texts of German literature. *Emilia Galotti* was well received in Lessing's day. Christoph Martin Wieland in 1773 referred to it as "the best, original German play." Friedrich Schlegel appreciated the technical brilliance of the play and insisted that it was "a great example of dramatic algebra." Goethe incorporated the play into his famous Werther novel, but he expressed ambivalence about its rigid dramatic structure. For him, it seemed too "conceptualized" and predictable. At a time when German theater was lagging sorely behind developments in France and England, *Emilia Galotti* represented Germany's capacity to catch up to its neighbors.

As opposed to Johann Christoph Gottsched, who promoted French models of Aristotelian tragedy for German theater, Lessing introduced his German contemporaries to a new dramatic form, the domestic tragedy or bourgeois drama. George Lillo (*The London Merchant*) had already experimented with this genre in England, and Lessing had written an earlier domestic tragedy, *Miß Sara Sampson* (1755; *Miss Sara Sampson*). *Emilia Galotti* represents, however, the height of this genre in Germany and reflects theoretical discussions pertinent to the purpose and nature of the domestic tragedy outlined by Lessing himself in his *Briefwechsel* (exchange of letters) with Moses Mendelssohn and Friedrich Nicolai, his *Hamburgische Dramaturgie* (written 1767–69; *Hamburg Dramaturgy*), and his *Laokoon* (1766; *Laocoön*) essay.

Lessing referred to Emilia as a "bourgeois Virginia," which indicates his reliance for her story on Titus Livius's account of the death of Virginia in Rome in the fifth century B.C. Lessing stressed that he avoided the political implications of the Roman account and focused on the tragedy of a young girl killed by her father in order to preserve her virtue. *Emilia Galotti* shifts dramatic focus from the tensions of the high political courts and the nobility of the heroic play (external, public realms) to the middle-class, familial sphere (internal, private realms). And even in those instances where the two realms merge in ways that make such divisions murky, the overriding sentiment of the drama is "bürgerlich," that is, private, familial, and universal to all, and not bound to particular classes and ranks. The central objective of the domestic tragedy was to produce sympathy. Lessing suggested that, while not everyone could identify with the trials of a king, they could identify with the tribulations of mothers and fathers and daughters and sons. Accordingly, *Emilia Galotti* focuses on a familial crisis and, specifically, the struggle between Emilia's parents, Odoardo and Claudia, and

that between the family and the powers of the court for control over Emilia's fate.

Prominent critics such as Franz Mehring and Georg Lukács have concentrated on the juxtaposition of a bourgeois sphere in *Emilia Galotti* to an absolute monarchy. Ensuing scholarship has paid particular attention to the way that the play illustrates the virtue, morality, and goodness of the bourgeois family and contrasts it to the arbitrariness of a libertine prince. While Emilia's father is the "paragon of male virtue," who wishes to live quietly on his property outside the city and away from court, the ruling prince is willing to sign death warrants without reading them, to grant requests based solely on the supplicant's first name, and to let the Machiavellian Marinelli (the prince's confidant) guide his life, in order to seduce Emilia.

More recent scholarship has reassessed the juxtaposition of bourgeois virtue and the vices of absolutism in *Emilia Galotti*. These readings note that the prince's absolutism is balanced by his "bourgeois" embrace of the moral and familial lifestyle exhibited by Odoardo. Odoardo's bourgeois virtue, however, is weighed against the rigidity and harshness of his moral strictures, his greater interest in Appiani (Emilia's fiancé) than Emilia on their wedding day, and his cold murder of his own daughter. Indeed, the prince's rashness in the opening scenes of the play is contrasted to Odoardo's quick willingness to kill Emilia in the final moments. While earlier interpreters of *Emilia Galotti* stressed how Odoardo preserves Emilia's virtue by removing her forever from the prince's grasp, newer readings have suggested that Odoardo's action is problematic and even unconscionable, and that Lessing criticizes a bourgeois code that has become perverted and inhumane. For these readers, Emilia's death represents the bourgeois ideal of virtue driven to a point of absurdity.

Indeed, the ending of *Emilia Galotti* is one of the most-discussed problems in Lessing scholarship. The meaning of Emilia's admission to her father that she has and fears her "warm blood" has generated tremendous scholarly attention. Since Goethe's pronouncement that Emilia certainly loved the prince, the debate over whether she exhibits sentimental/sexual innocence or transgressive desire has raged on. Emilia has been considered either the completely innocent victim of the clash between bourgeois and absolute orders or the desirous, nascent lover of the prince, who is at least sentimentally complicit in his murder of Appiani.

In addition to familial and political concerns, Lessing scholarship has also concentrated on his aesthetics and, particularly, on his notions of the semiotics of visual, verbal, and dramatic signs—as outlined in the *Laocoon* essay—in order to explain the significance of the paintings of Emilia and Orsina (the prince's former mistress) in the opening scenes of the play. On one level, the discussion between the prince and the painter, Conti, invokes contemporary debates about art and drama crucial to Lessing's aesthetics and includes conversation about the nature of imitation, the representation of beauty and ugliness, the rules of visual representation, and the failure of the artist to capture the image of his imagination on the painting's surface. On another level, these paintings also function as symbols of female virtue and vice in *Emilia Galotti*. Virtue (Emilia) and vice (Orsina) are juxtaposed from the very start in their paintings. This juxtaposition, in turn, suggests the possibility of separating virtue from vice entirely. In fact, Orsina's vice is located principally in the painterly representations of her twisted, mocking mouth and Medusa eyes. Emilia, by contrast, is painted as beautiful (and innocent) beyond compare.

While some scholars have stressed that Emilia's painting represents her function in the play as an "idea of a daughter" or a "symbol of exchange" that is more important than a real-life daughter, others have focused on her development in the play from portrait to *tableau vivant* or metaphor. By the end of the play and through her death, Emilia will lose her painterly body and become another legend of a woman sacrificed by her father in order to preserve virtue. The symbolic importance of the paintings in *Emilia Galotti* suggests that they function as surfaces that project male fantasies about virtuous and transgressive women. Regardless of whether one isolates political, familial, or aesthetic concerns, the multiple and manifold interpretations of *Emilia Galotti* attest to the play's textual richness and to its status as one of Germany's finest literary productions.

SUSAN E. GUSTAFSON

See also Bourgeois Tragedy

Editions

First edition: *Emilia Galotti,* in *Trauerspiele,* Berlin: Christian Friedrich Voß, 1772

Critical editions: in *Sämtliche Werke,* 3rd ed., vol. 2, edited by Karl Lachmann, revised by Franz Muncker, Stuttgart: Göschen, 1886–1924; in *Werke und Briefe in zwölf Bänden,* vol. 7, edited by Wilfried Barner, Frankfurt: Deutscher Klassiker Verlag, 1993

Critical edition of a translation: *Emilia Galotti* in *Nathan the Wise, Minna von Barnhelm, and Other Plays and Writings,* translated by Anna Johanna Gode von Aesch, edited by Peter Demetz, New York: Continuum, 1991

Further Reading

Flax, Neil, "From Portrait to Tableau Vivant: The Pictures of Emilia Galotti," *Eighteenth Century Studies* 19, no. 1 (Fall 1985)

Graham, Ilse, "Minds without Medium: Reflections on Emilia Galotti and Werther's Leiden," *Euphorion* 56 (1962)

Gustafson, Susan E., *Absent Mothers and Orphaned Fathers: Narcissism and Abjection in Lessing's Aesthetic and Dramatic Production,* Detroit, Michigan: Wayne State University Press, 1995

Hart, Gail Kathleen, *Tragedy in Paradise: Family and Gender Politics in German Bourgeois Tragedy, 1750–1850,* Columbia, South Carolina: Camden House, 1996

Hoff, Dagmar von, *Dramen des Weiblichen: Deutsche Dramatikerinnen um 1800,* Opladen: Westdeutscher Verlag, 1989

Janz, Rolf-Peter, "'Sie ist die Schande ihres Geschlechts': Die Figur der Femme Fatale bei Lessing," *Jahrbuch der deutschen Schillergesellschaft* 23 (1979)

Kittler, Friedrich A., "'Erziehung ist Offenbarung': Zur Struktur der Familie in Lessings Dramen," *Jahrbuch der deutschen Schillergesellschaft* 21 (1977)

Lamport, F.J., *Lessing and the Drama,* Oxford: Clarendon Press, and New York: Oxford University Press, 1981

Neumann, Peter Horst, *Der Preis der Mündigkeit: Über Lessings Dramen,* Stuttgart: Klett-Cotta, 1977

Prutti, Brigitte, "Das Bild des Weiblichen und die Phantasie des Künstlers: Das Begehren des Prinzen in Lessings Emilia Galotti," *Zeitschrift für deutsche Philologie* 110, no. 4 (1991)

Rickels, Laurence A., "Deception, Exchange, and Revenge: Metaphors of Language in Emilia Galotti," *Lessing Yearbook* 16 (1984)

Schulte-Sasse, Jochen, *Literarische Struktur und historisch-sozialer Kontext: Zum Beispiel Lessings Emilia Galotti,* Paderborn: Schöningh, 1975

Seeba, Hinrich C., *Die Liebe zur Sache: Öffentliches und privates Interesse in Lessings Dramen,* Tübingen: Niemeyer, 1973

Sørensen, Bengt Algot, *Herrschaft und Zärtlichkeit: Der Patriarchalismus und das Drama im 18. Jahrhundert,* Munich: Beck, 1984

Stephan, Inge, "'So ist die Tugend ein Gespenst': Frauenbild und Tugendbegriff im bürgerlichen Trauerspiel bei Lessing und Schiller," *Lessing Yearbook* 17 (1985)

Ter-Nedden, Gisbert, *Lessings Trauerspiele: Der Ursprung des modernen Dramas aus dem Geist der Kritik,* Stuttgart: Metzler, 1986

Laokoon; oder, Über die Grenzen der Malerei und Poesie 1766
Essay by Gotthold Ephraim Lessing

Marking his debut in antiquarian research, Lessing, with his *Laocoön: An Essay on the Limits of Painting and Poetry,* soon gained a notoriety that has since remained virtually undiminished. Modern comparative analyses of the arts have confirmed the work's centrality in the debates over the meaning and validity of the Horatian dictum *ut pictura poesis* (as is painting, so is poetry). As a crystallization of many themes already current in 18th-century aesthetics, the text has also provoked extensive discussions about the nature and extent of its own originality.

An unfinished work that Lessing initially expected to complete with the publication of two additional volumes, *Laocoön* is in large part a polemic against Winckelmann. In his *Gedanken über die Nachahmung der griechischen Werke in der Malerei und Bildhauerkunst* (1755; *Reflections on the Imitation of Greek Works in Painting and Sculpture*), Winckelmann had celebrated the statue of the priest Laocoön and his sons being attacked by a pair of serpents, arguing that this work represented a Greek aesthetic ideal of "edle Einfalt und stille Größe" (noble simplicity and quiet grandeur). Whereas in Virgil's *Aeneid* Laocoön screams without restraint, observes Winckelmann, the stoic central figure in the sculpture emits only a muted sigh. Lessing responds that this contrast does not reflect the superiority of one work over the other but instead demonstrates the different generic requirements of poetry and the visual arts.

As Lessing argues, a visual representation of the priest's features contorted in pain would arouse revulsion rather than sympathy (*Mitleid*) in the beholder (Lessing went on to develop his theory of sympathy in his *Hamburgische Dramaturgie* [1767–69; *Hamburg Dramaturgy*]). Since the sculptor and painter are limited in their subject to a single moment of action, they must choose this moment so as not to overwhelm the viewer but to grant his or her imagination the greatest possible freedom ("freies Spiel"). The poet's medium, by contrast, does not impose such constraints (and may even represent ugliness to heighten its effects). The cries of Virgil's Laocoön pass within a sequence of events that cumulatively both soften the transient horror of his suffering and abundantly demonstrate the strength of his soul.

These observations lead unsystematically to the work's most concise formulation of the structural differences between writing and *Malerei,* a term that Lessing uses to embrace the plastic and pictorial arts. Lessing proposes that the "signs" employed in both painting and poetry must strive to become "natural," achieving a direct or "convenient" relation (*bequemes Verhält-nis*) to their object and thus creating the illusion of its presence. From this point, he concludes that signs juxtaposed spatially (as in the visual arts) best represent objects in space (*Körper*); signs that are arranged sequentially most effectively represent objects in time, or actions (*Handlungen*). In fact, painting may represent limited actions indirectly (*andeutungsweise*) by selecting a single moment from which the viewer can infer prior and subsequent events. Conversely, writing may describe a static object to the extent that it recasts its description as narrative. Thus, Lessing argues, Homer does not bore us by simply enumerating the details featured on Achilles's shield; rather, he gradually brings this object before our eyes by recounting the story of its creation. Despite the seeming parallelism of this scheme, however, Lessing privileges poetry because of the greater freedom that it grants the recipient's imagination.

Lessing's attempt to define the "limits" of the individual arts responds to a tradition, particularly in evidence since the Renaissance, that saw painting and poetry as two metaphors for a single activity. Opitz upheld the notion, which goes back at least to the Greek poet Simonides, of painting as "mute poetry" and poetry as a "speaking picture," and Charles Batteux stressed that the arts operated according to a single principle of imitation. Of particular concern to Lessing, however, was what he saw as a passion for enumerative description (*Schilderungssucht*) that had taken over German writing in the 18th century and which is generally associated most closely with the poetry of Brockes, Haller (Lessing famously criticizes his "Die Alpen") and Ewald von Kleist.

As critics have noted, however, neither Lessing's attempt to separate the arts nor many of his specific reasons for doing so were new. Abbé Dubos had explicitly sought to distinguish painting and poetry according to the nature of their "signs," and the Earl of Shaftesbury and Samuel Richardson had described the importance of the single "moment" as an object of visual representation. Lessing's own friend Moses Mendelssohn also published related ideas. Especially striking are similarities between *Laocoön* and Diderot's 1751 *Letter on the Deaf and Dumb,* as is the fact that Lessing postpones almost to the end of his essay acknowledging Winckelmann's *Geschichte der Kunst des Alterthums* (1764–67; *The History of Ancient Art*), in which Winckelmann draws generic distinctions that Lessing's work accuses him of having ignored.

Nonetheless, critics have consistently underscored *Laocoön*'s pivotal role in the history of aesthetics, even while considerably revising its arguments. In his *Kritische Wälder* (1769; Critical Woods) Herder chides Lessing for failing to distinguish either among the visual arts or among different genres of writing, rejects the notion that poetry should avoid the depiction of static objects, and proposes the notion of *Kraft* (force) rather than *Handlung* (action) as a key poetic principle. Dilthey, Wellek, and some Marxist critics, however, have suggested that the turn from static phenomena to the representation of action during and after the period of Sturm und Drang itself remains an enduring legacy of Lessing's aesthetics. Goethe, who in *Aus meinem Leben: Dichtung und Wahrheit* (1811–33; *The Autobiography of Goethe: Truth and Poetry*) recalls the enthusiasm with which his generation received Lessing's *Laocoön*, was inspired to write his own essay about the function of the pivotal "moment" represented by the statue. An increasing emphasis on individual expression and then naturalistic representation in the course of the 19th century discouraged efforts to distinguish sharply among different art forms; Irving Babbitt attacked this tendency in his 1910 work *The New Laokoon, an Essay on the Confusion of the Arts.* In the last decades, Lessing's essay has attracted considerable attention among critics interested in 18th-century semiotic theories. Recent work has also focused on the relation between genre and gender distinctions, as well as on representations of the human body in Lessing's text.

NICHOLAS RENNIE

See also Johann Joachim Winckelmann

Editions

First edition: *Laokoon; oder, Über die Grenzen der Malerei und Poesie,* Berlin: Christian Friedrich Voß, 1766

Critical edition: in *Werke und Briefe in zwölf Bänden,* edited by Wilfried Barner, vol. 5/2, Frankfurt: Deutscher Klassiker Verlag, 1990

Translation: *Laocoön: An Essay on the Limits of Painting and Poetry,* translated by Edward Allen McCormick, Baltimore, Maryland: Johns Hopkins University Press, 1984

Further Reading

Brodsky Lacour, Claudia, "'Is That Helen?' Contemporary Pictorialism, Lessing, and Kant," *Comparative Literature* 45, no. 3 (1993)

Gebauer, Gunter, and Tzvetan Todorov, editors, *Das Laokoon-Projekt: Pläne einer semiotischen Ästhetik,* Stuttgart: Metzler, 1984

Hamm, Heinz, "Die Argumentation des 'Laokoon' zum 'eigentlichen Gegenstand der Poesie' in ihrem wirkungsgeschichtlichen Kontext," in *Bausteine zu einer Wirkungsgeschichte: Gotthold Ephraim Lessing,* edited by Hans-Georg Werner, Berlin: Aufbau, 1984

Jacobs, Carol, "The Critical Performance of Lessing's *Laokoon,*" *Modern Language Notes* 102 (1987)

Mitchell, W.J.T., "The Politics of Genre: Space and Time in Lessing's *Laocoon,*" *Representations* 6 (1984)

Raaberg, Gwen, "*Laokoon* Considered and Reconsidered: Lessing and the Comparative Criticism of Literature and Art," in *Lessing and the Enlightenment,* edited by Alexej Ugrinsky, New York: Greenwood Press, 1986

Richter, Simon, *Laocoon's Body and the Aesthetics of Pain: Winckelmann, Lessing, Herder, Moritz, Goethe,* Detroit, Michigan: Wayne State University Press, 1992

Wellbery, David E., *Lessing's Laocoon: Semiotics and Aesthetics in the Age of Reason,* Cambridge and New York: Cambridge University Press, 1984

Nathan der Weise 1779
Play by Gotthold Ephraim Lessing

Gotthold Ephraim Lessing's *Nathan der Weise* (*Nathan the Wise*), the quintessential Enlightenment play, is his most famous drama. Indeed, as an Enlightenment defense of rationality and religious and social tolerance, it ranks in significance with Voltaire's "Traité sur la tolérance." Lessing predicted erroneously that *Nathan the Wise* would never be a very influential play and probably wouldn't be staged. He hoped rather modestly that the play would "read well" and felt that it would be successful if among a thousand readers, just one learned to doubt the evidence and universality of his own religion. By this, Lessing meant that his ideal reader would learn religious tolerance and would not continue to assume that his or her religion was exclusively true. Moreover, Lessing challenged his 18th-century German audience by introducing a positive Jewish lead character to the German stage. *Nathan the Wise* garnished very little positive critical response in Lessing's day—probably due to its controversial subject matter. Between 1933 and 1945, *Nathan the Wise* was banned in Germany because of its "pro-Jewish" and "anti-Christian" content. The emigrant Erwin Piscator produced the play for the New York Studio Theater of the New School of Social Research in 1942, and from there it went to Broadway. In Germany, directly after World War II, *Nathan the Wise* became one of the country's most popular plays.

Nathan the Wise is one of a series of works Lessing wrote in his later career that concentrated on religious issues. In fact, Lessing was embroiled in arguments about the literalness of the Bible and the nature of religion with an orthodox theologian, Johann Melchior Goeze, in the 1770s. The arguments between the two men resulted in a stream of published polemical and personal attacks. The public controversy was abruptly ended when the freedom from censorship that Lessing had as ducal librarian was withdrawn. Lessing was forbidden to engage in further printed theological debates. In response to this censorship, Lessing decided to "preach from his old pulpit, the theater" and wrote *Nathan the Wise*. As such, the play is the continuation and conclusion of Lessing's disputes with Goeze.

Nathan the Wise is set in Jerusalem during the time of the crusades and depicts cruel and vicious struggles between Christian, Jewish, and Moslem forces. The Enlightenment message of the play is that Nathan sees beyond the various and seemingly insurmountable religious divisions to the innate value of all peoples. His story illustrates how he overcomes the violence and hatred generated between the various religious camps. Indeed, Nathan raises the little Christian girl, Recha, as his own daughter, even after the Christians mercilessly slaughter his wife and seven sons. Nathan follows a code of ethics that applies equally to all peoples regardless of religious difference. He is also juxtaposed to figures such as Daja and the Patriarch who represent religious bigotry. As the philosopher Hannah Arendt has pointed out, Nathan stresses that genuine friendship transcends the artificial divisions between individuals fomented by rigid religious adherences. Essentially, the play is an optimistic tale about the triumph of humanity, friendship, and tolerance over war, prejudice, and religious fanaticism. Lessing's beliefs in the omnipotence and ultimate benevolence of God, the right and duty of everyone to exercise reason free of restriction and/or intervention by religious or secular authority, and intellectual and religious tolerance all come to the fore in *Nathan the Wise*.

Despite its overall artistic sophistication, less attention has been devoted by Lessing scholarship to the aesthetic quality of *Nathan the Wise*. The work vies with Lessing's earlier play, *Emilia Galotti* (1772), in terms of its "mathematical" fineness of dramatic structure. Its dialogic intensity is accentuated by its blank verse. Indeed, after *Nathan the Wise*, blank verse was recognized in Germany for its potential importance to the further development of drama. The play's larger dramatic structures are also unique and dramatically successful. Lessing referred to the play as a "dramatic poem." *Nathan the Wise* does not conform to a generic formula for a comedy or a tragedy but contains elements of both. In addition, the drama concerns itself with familial issues in a manner reminiscent of the bourgeois or domestic

tragedy. Lessing demonstrates here how the content of the play ought to determine its form rather than compliance to any particular generic mold.

Lessing claimed that the core of *Nathan the Wise* was the parable of the three rings, which he adapted from Bocaccio's *Decameron*. This parable, at the structural center of the play, evokes *in nuce* the major issues and concerns of *Nathan the Wise*. In an answer to Saladin's question about which religion, Christian, Jewish, or Moslem, is the most true, Nathan tells the story of a father who is supposed to pass on his ring (the true religion) to his most beloved son. Because the father loves all three of his sons equally, however, he is unable to select one over the others. He has two additional and identical rings made and on his deathbed gives each of his sons one of the rings. Nathan goes on to relate that after their father's death the sons squabble with one another over who has the true ring. Finally, they refer their argument to a judge who advises them to act as if each has the true ring. The parable underscores Nathan's message of religious tolerance. Moreover, it addresses the issue of fatherhood, which is also a central concern of the play. One might ask not only which religion is true but also who is the true father. And, in fact, throughout the play the characters discuss the status of Nathan as Recha's father. The biological father is constantly juxtaposed to the adoptive father. The family, headed by a father such as Nathan, is a utopic institution and the model of humanity. Fatherhood is also connected to many of Lessing's other critical concerns and is inextricably conjoined to issues about the truth of religion, the development of social order, rationality, and education. The parable itself represents the father's attempt to teach his sons and the rest of his family tolerance. It also has a transformative effect on Saladin, who overcomes his own intolerance and embraces Nathan as father and friend. The parable symbolizes the content of the play and demonstrates the educative function of literature. It suggests the didactic mission of *Nathan the Wise*. Under Nathan's tutelage, several characters are drawn through the course of the play from religious bigotry to familial unity and humanity. The transformations the characters experience in *Nathan the Wise* exemplify Lessing's theory of the domestic tragedy in which audience members are supposed to be transformed into better, more sympathetic subjects while viewing the play. The complex structure of education and transformation in *Nathan the Wise* has fascinated scholars from Johann Jakob Engel (1783), who referred to the play as a "pedagogical poem," to Brecht in the 1930s, who was attracted to Lessing's work as he was establishing the didactic and aesthetic underpinnings of his Epic Theater.

The structural and conceptual complexity and significance of *Nathan the Wise* ensures its place as one of Germany's greatest classics and its status as an important document of religious tolerance. At the same time, the history of its reception illustrates obscenities of censorship and intolerance that should never be forgotten.

Susan E. Gustafson

See also Moses Mendelssohn

Editions

First edition: *Nathan der Weise: Ein Dramatisches Gedicht in fünf Aufzügen,* Berlin: Christian Friedrich Voß, 1779
Critical editions: in *Sämtliche Schriften,* 3rd ed., vol. 3, edited by Karl Lachmann, revised by Franz Muncker, Stuttgart: Göschen,

1886–1924; in *Werke und Briefe in zwölf Bänden,* vol. 9, edited by Wilfried Barner, Frankfurt: Deutscher Klassiker Verlag, 1993

Translation: *Nathan the Wise,* translated by Bayard Quincy Morgan, in *Nathan the Wise, Minna von Barnhelm, and Other Plays and Writings,* edited by Peter Demetz, New York: Continuum, 1991

Further Reading

Bohnen, Klaus, "*Nathan der Weise:* Über das 'Gegenbild einer Gesellschaft' bei Lessing," *Deutsche Vierteljahrsschrift für Literaturwissenschaft und Geistesgeschichte* 3 (1979)

Bohnen, Klaus, editor, *Lessings "Nathan der Weise,"* Darmstadt: Wissenschaftliche Buchgesellschaft, 1984

Demetz, Peter, *Nathan der Weise,* Frankfurt: Ullstein, 1966

Gobel, Helmut, "'Nicht die Kinder bloß speist man mit Märchen ab': Zur Toleranzbegründung in Lessings Spätwerk," *Lessing Yearbook* 14 (1982)

Gustafson, Susan E., *Absent Mothers and Orphaned Fathers: Narcissism and Abjection in Lessing's Aesthetic and Dramatic Production,* Detroit, Michigan: Wayne State University Press, 1995

Kittler, Friedrich A., "'Erziehung ist Offenbarung': Zur Struktur der Familie in Lessings Dramen," *Jahrbuch der deutschen Schillergesellschaft* 21 (1977)

Lamport, F.J., *Lessing and the Drama,* Oxford: Clarendon Press, and New York: Oxford University Press, 1981

Leventhal, Robert S., "The Parable as Performance: Interpretation, Cultural Transmission, and Political Strategy in Lessing's *Nathan der Weise*," *German Quarterly* 61, no. 4 (1988)

Neumann, Peter Horst, *Der Preis der Mündigkeit: Über Lessings Dramen,* Stuttgart: Klett-Cotta, 1977

Piedmont, Ferdinand, "Unterdrückt und rehabilitiert: Zur Theatergeschichte von Lessing's *Nathan der Weise* von den zwanziger Jahren bis zur Gegenwart," *Lessing Yearbook* 19 (1987)

Seeba, Hinrich C., *Die Liebe zur Sache: Öffentliches und privates Interesse in Lessings Dramen,* Tübingen: Niemeyer, 1973

Sørensen, Bengt Algot, *Herrschaft und Zärtlichkeit: Der Patriachalismus und das Drama im 18. Jahrhundert,* Munich: Beck, 1984

Levin, Rahel, *see* Rahel Levin Varnhagen

Fanny Lewald 1811–1889

Fanny Lewald was one of the most respected and successful German woman authors of the mid–19th century, a period when many middle-class women took up the pen, for it was one of the few career options open to them. She published over 40 novels and short-story collections, autobiographical works, travel literature, and feminist treatises. Contemporary male critics praised Lewald for her logic and powers of reason and lauded her novels for their serious social, political, and ethical content. As naturalism sought to supplant realism in the latter part of the century, the younger generation regarded her novels as outdated, and the aesthetic criteria of the modern literary canon pushed her work further into oblivion. In the 1920s, the emancipatory tenor of Lewald's writings attracted the first wave of women scholars. Their findings were virtually obliterated during the Third Reich, when state-sanctioned scholarship afforded little sympathy for the writings of Jews and women. But Lewald's work was rediscovered in the late 1970s by a second wave of feminist scholars. Today Lewald's nonfiction, including posthumously published correspondence, has taken primacy of place, for it expands our understanding of 19th-century European political and social issues. Most recently, however, scholarly attention has focused on the structure and diction of Lewald's later fiction to establish whether it belongs to the Biedermeier/*Vormärz* period (the period preceding the revolutions of 1848) or to realism, which came into its own in Germany in the second half of the 19th century. This line of inquiry should demonstrate Lewald's desire to be understood as an author of realism who was fully engaged in the contemporary debates and experimentation about how mimesis was best to be achieved.

Fanny Lewald's early writing career places her among the authors of the *Vormärz,* a period when liberals and democrats sought constitutionally to unify the disparate German states in order to combat political oppression and to relieve the increasing impoverishment of the lower classes. As a woman and a Jew, doubly an outsider, Lewald sympathized with the marginalized. Her early fiction, published anonymously at her father's request so as not to discredit the family, treats issues affecting women and Jews. *Clementine* (1842) reveals the stultifying effects of arranged marriages; *Jenny* (1843) demonstrates the oppression of the Jews in Germany; *Eine Lebensfrage: Roman* (1845; A Vital Issue: A Novel) defends the right to divorce; and *Diogena: Roman von Iduna Gräfin H . . . H . . .* (1847; Diogena: A Novel by Iduna Countess H . . . H . . .) satirizes the overblown expectation, encouraged in Lewald's view by frivolous women's novels, that the "right man" is the sole source of fulfillment in a woman's life. The first novel she published under her name, *Prinz Louis Ferdinand: Roman* (1849; *Prinz Louis Ferdinand: A Novel*), a re-creation of Berlin salon life in the Romantic period, is also her only novel in which historical figures are the main protagonists. A scathing indictment of the Prussian King Frederick Wilhelm III's political impotence during the early period of the Napoleonic invasions, the novel indirectly criticizes the contemporary king's (Frederick Wilhelm IV) political and social inaction. It unleashed a storm of controversy among both liberals and conservatives, for in it the Jewish *salonière* Rahel Levin is in love with the profligate, if heroic, Prince Louis Ferdinand. Lewald thus alienated members of the Rahel cult, including her surviving husband, Varnhagen von Ense, and devotees of the Hohenzollern court, who were indignant at the portrayal of friendship between a Jewish woman and the prince, although the two had, indeed, been friends, but not romantically attached. Lewald vowed never again to write a historical novel. Ironically, this was the first of her works to be republished in 1859—with a new subtitle, "ein Zeitbild" (A Depiction of the Times).

After treating the death throes of the revolution—the 1849 uprising in Baden—in *Auf rother Erde* (1850; On Red Soil) and publishing a series of short novels set in the period of the French Revolution, including *Der Seehof* (1859; *Lake House*), Lewald embarked on longer novels for which many decisive moments in European history—the French Revolutions of 1789 and 1830, the period of Napoleonic occupation and the Wars of Liberation, and the Revolutions of 1848—serve as the framework. The novels *Wandlungen* (1853; Transformations), *Von Geschlecht zu Geschlecht* (1864–66; From Generation to Generation), and *Die Familie Darner* (1887; The Darner Family) also treat one of the central themes of German Realism: the decline of the aristocracy and the rise of the middle classes. In *Wandlungen,* moreover, three woman break the barriers of class and gender to achieve financial and artistic autonomy. *Die Familie Darner,* in which characters examine and rectify their prejudices, can be considered a radically altered companion piece to *Prinz Louis Ferdinand,* for both novels are set in roughly the same time period. Whereas the latter emphasizes the societal alienation and disharmony in Prussia when it reached its nadir in 1806, the treatment of the 1813 Prussian victory over Napoléon's army in *Familie Darner* may be viewed as a veiled celebration of German unification under Bismarck in 1871. Because Lewald was solely dependent on her writings for subsistence, she was not above producing popular entertainments or reprising often touched-upon themes, even though she prided herself that her subject matter was never frivolous.

Lewald's perceptiveness and descriptive powers manifest more frequently and efficaciously in her nonfiction than in her fiction, where character development is sometimes sacrificed to polemics. She correctly claimed that her post-1848 novels were less tendentious than her early works, and, indeed, her diction was more muted; from a sociohistorical perspective, however, her major works never eschewed the middle-class individualist ideology that argued that society and the political system must be structured so as to allow each person to develop to his or her fullest capacity.

Her travel writings were an immediate success. Critics considered *Italienisches Bilderbuch* (1847; *The Italians at Home*) to be better than Charles Dickens's account of his travels in Italy, which were published in the same year. In her book, Lewald displays a lively interest in the Italian people and an open-minded appreciation of the differences between the German and the Italian cultures. *Erinnerungen aus dem Jahre 1848* (1850; *A Year of Revolutions: Fanny Lewald's "Recollections of 1848"*) is an informative and moving account of the French and German people's aspirations to liberty and opportunity. This memoir and Lewald's autobiography, *Meine Lebensgeschichte* (1861–62; *The Education of Fanny Lewald*), were the first of her works to be republished recently in Germany, albeit in abridged form. The autobiography has been of particular interest to feminist scholars because, while tracing Lewald's development up to her emerging success as an author, it reveals how she was stunted by patriarchy and long deprived of meaningful work. That the Markuses were Jews and the family's economic stability was at times challenged compounded Lewald's difficulties, but she perceived strictures of gender to be harsher than those of ethnicity. The autobiography also contains illuminating descriptions of household management, education, and religious practices of the period, as well as vignettes of women authors in Berlin literary

circles. Throughout, the reader grows to understand the impact of historical events on the lives of ordinary citizens.

When Lewald became increasingly impatient with Prussian politics in the 1860s, she redirected her energies to the women's movement that was then gaining momentum. She never was actively engaged in any organizations or in public speaking, but *Osterbriefe für die Frauen* (1863; Easter Letters on Behalf of Women) recommends measures to improve the lot of domestic workers, many of whom had come to the burgeoning city from the provinces and lived and worked in deplorable conditions. *Für und wider die Frauen* (1870; On Behalf of and against Women), concerned primarily with middle-class women, advocates education and the right to meaningful work. While Lewald does not drastically exceed the bounds of bourgeois ideology and while the ideas of these treatises are not entirely original, both John Stuart Mill and Gertrud Bäumer, a turn-of-the-century feminist leader, considered them the best documents of the first feminist movement.

The gradual reissuing in German of Lewald's key works should make her writings more easily accessible to German studies scholars, although many of the post-1848 novels are too lengthy and unwieldy for commercial republication. Recent translations of Lewald's autobiography and her observations on the 1848 revolutions will gain for Lewald nonspecialist readers who are interested in social and political history.

IRENE STOCKSIEKER DI MAIO

Biography

Born in Königsberg, Prussia (now Kaliningrad, Russia), 24 March 1811. Reached the highest grade in the Ulrich School, a private coeducational institution, at the age of 11, but unable to pursue further education because of her sex; baptized and confirmed a Lutheran, 24 February 1830, an act she regretted; family name changed from Markus to Lewald, 1831; moved to Berlin in 1845, permanent residence there in the early 1850s; married the publicist Adolph Stahr, 1855; travel to Italy, England, Scotland, France, and Switzerland; freelance author throughout her life. Died 5 August 1889.

Selected Works

Novels

Jenny, 1843
Prinz Louis Ferdinand: Roman, 1849; as *Prinz Louis Ferdinand,* translated by Linda Rogels-Siegel, 1988
Der Seehof, 1859; as *Lake House,* translated by Nathaniel Greene, 1861
Das Mädchen von Hela: Ein Roman, 1860; as *The Mask of Beauty: A Novel,* translated by Mary M. Pleasants, 1894
Von Geschlecht zu Geschlecht (*Der Freiherr* and *Der Emporkömmling*), 1864, 1866
Die Erlöserin: Roman, 1873; as *Hulda; or, The Deliverer: A Romance,* translated by Mrs. A.L. Wister, 1874
Die Familie Darner: Roman, 1887

Other

Italienisches Bilderbuch, 1847; as *The Italians at Home,* translated by Rachel, Countess d'Avigdor, 1848
Erinnerungen aus dem Jahre 1848, 1850; as *A Year of Revolutions: Fanny Lewald's "Recollections of 1848,"* translated by Hanna Ballin Lewis, 1997
England und Schottland: Reisetagebuch, 1851–52
Wandlungen, 1853

Meine Lebensgeschichte, 1861–62; as *The Education of Fanny Lewald*, translated by Hanna Ballin Lewis, 1992

Osterbriefe für die Frauen, 1863

Für und wider die Frauen: Vierzehn Briefe, 1870

Gefühltes und Gedachtes (1838–1888), edited by Ludwig Geiger, 1900

Römisches Tagebuch 1845–46, edited by Heinrich Spiero, 1927

Further Reading

Di Maio, Irene Stocksieker, "Reclamation of the French Revolution: Fanny Lewald's Literary Response to the *Nachmärz* in *Der Seehof*," in *Geist und Gesellschaft: Zur deutschen Rezeption der Französischen Revolution*, edited by Eitel Timm, Munich: Fink, 1990

———, "Jewish Emancipation and Integration: Fanny Lewald's Narrative Strategies," in *Autoren damals und heute: Literaturgeschichtliche Beispiele veränderter Wirkungshorizonte*, edited by Gerhard Peter Knapp, Amsterdam and Atlanta, Georgia: Rodopi, 1991

Gudrun, Marci-Boehncke, *Fanny Lewald: Jüdin, Preussin, Schriftstellerin: Studien zu autobiographischem Werk und Kontext*, Stuttgart: Heinz, 1998

Lewis, Hanna Ballin, "Fanny Lewald and the Revolutions of 1848," in *Horizonte: Festschrift für Herbert Lehnert zum 65. Geburtstag*, edited by Hannelore Mundt et al., Tübingen: Niemeyer, 1990

———, "The Misfits: Jews, Women, Soldiers, and Princes in Fanny Lewald's *Prinz Louis Ferdinand*," in *Crossings/Kreuzungen: A Festschrift for Helmut Kreuzer*, edited by Edward Haymes, Columbia, South Carolina: Camden House, 1990

Schneider, Gabriele, *Vom Zeitroman zum "stylisierten" Roman: Die Erzählerin Fanny Lewald*, Frankfurt: Lang, 1993

van Rheinberg, Brigitta, *Fanny Lewald: Geschichte einer Emanzipation*, Frankfurt and New York: Campus, 1990

Ward, Margaret E., "*Ehe* and *Entsagung*: Fanny Lewald's Early Novels and Goethe's Literary Paternity," *Women in German Yearbook* 2 (1986)

Watt, Helga Schutte, "Fanny Lewald und die deutsche Misere Nach 1848 im Hinblick auf England," *German Life and Letters* 46, no. 3 (1993)

Georg Christoph Lichtenberg 1742–1799

Georg Christoph Lichtenberg has emerged as one of the most important writers of the German Enlightenment, although not for the reasons for which he was famous in his lifetime. Rarely in literature has the posthumous evaluation of an author depended so much on something about which his contemporaries knew so little. To students and colleagues at the University of Göttingen, he was a highly regarded and frequently entertaining teacher with a strong experimental bent, the editor of a widely read handbook on the natural sciences, and a respected authority on scientific issues and debates; to the public at large, he was the editor of a popular almanac, a congenial commentator on William Hogarth's engravings, and a witty satirist. At the time of his death, Lichtenberg would have been the first to admit that, if judged by the conventional notions of artistic and scientific achievement of his day, he did not live up to the arsenal of wit and talent that he had at his disposal. His early scientific claim to fame, the serendipitous discovery of the so-called Lichtenberg Figures, remained a curiosity without any practical consequences; some of the disciplines that he had ably popularized and commented upon were slowly leaving him behind; his celebrated forays into the public as a satirical debunker of Johann Caspar Lavater's physiognomy, Johann Heinrich Voß's awkward spelling reforms, and other fashions and crazes that swept through Germany were a thing of the past; and none of his numerous literary daydreams had amounted to anything.

What assured his reputation was the posthumous publication, in increasingly detailed and meticulous editions, of his *Sudelbücher* (Waste Books). Begun in 1764, they comprise a set of notebooks into which "I write everything the way I see it or as my thinking tells me to." Never intended for publication, they served as a paper dragnet in which Lichtenberg recorded ideas, notes, quotes, jokes, puns, idioms, trivia, confessions, and observations, many of which subsequently secured his position as the foremost German writer of aphorisms. Pronounced by Nietzsche to be one of the few German books worth reading, the disjointed, fragmentary, and, as it were, undigested writings in the *Sudelbücher* seem more in tune with present times, which has led some critics to depict Lichtenberg as a precursor of a modern, even poststructuralist poetics.

What emerges from the *Sudelbücher*—as well as from Lichtenberg's lively and informative letters—is a perspicacious, frequently whimsical observer whose world, after two invigorating trips to England, was restricted to "a girl, 150 books, a few friends, and a view about four miles in diameter." This did not prevent him from becoming an engaged critic who embodied the most advanced features of the German Enlightenment. He ridiculed the backwardness of the German principalities, the continuing reign of prejudice and superstition in an age of reason, and the cult of sentimentality (*Empfindsamkeit*) propagated by younger authors (including the young Goethe). His own literary tastes went more toward Shakespeare and Laurence Sterne, whose novels came closest to his own aborted projects. His pronounced Anglophilia, most noticeable in his detailed commentaries on Hogarth, was also evident in his many reflections on the operations of the human mind, in which he showed himself to be a disciple of the early psychological tradition of John Locke and David Hartley. His criticisms of Lavater's physiognomy, Voß's orthography, and Lavoisier's chemical terminology had their roots in his experimental and, as it were, subjunctive way of thinking. For Lichtenberg, it was less a matter of falsifying claims than of altering them by incessantly asking whether the objects under investigation could not be seen in a different way. Hence, it was imperative never to postulate a fixed, immutable connection between sign and meaning—such as Lavater's physiognomy had done between facial features and moral character—and never to abrogate discussions by imposing signs that act as exclusionary definitions—as Lavoisier's new chemical terminology appeared to be doing. Rather, according to

Lichtenberg, words should be experimented on so as to reveal their signifying potential and, thus, to achieve "new glimpses through old holes."

By focusing on the central importance of language, Lichtenberg at times anticipated modern language philosophy. If, as stated in one of the most famous entries, "our false philosophy is embodied in the language of the whole," then "we cannot reason without reasoning incorrectly." Subsequently, he states that philosophy must withdraw from the high realm of concepts and ideas and restrict itself to "an improving of linguistic usage." A cloud of Enlightenment philosophy is distilled to a few drops of linguistic criticism; this linguistic turn helps explain why Lichtenberg was so important to Wittgenstein and the Vienna Circle. Likewise, suggestions to rephrase "I think" as "it thinks"—analogous to "it thunders"—point ahead to the 20th-century inversion of the relationship between language and subject in which subjects no longer speak but are spoken by language. Finally, his remarks on the "paradigms" of science have been said to anticipate Thomas Kuhn's theory of scientific revolutions.

It remains a matter of debate as to what extent the singular character of his work was influenced by his physical condition. Evidence suggests that Lichtenberg suffered from kyphoscoliosis, a deformation of the breastbone that resulted in stunted growth, a hunchback-shaped deformation of the rib cage, and ongoing health troubles that worsened in 1789 and plagued him for the last ten years of his life. The deterioration of his health was accompanied by a change of mood, which is reflected in his private writings. Lichtenberg had married his housekeeper, Charlotte Kellner, and was beset by financial worries about his growing family. As a staunch loyalist to George III, he opposed the French Revolution, espoused a growing conservatism, and at times exhibited—a characteristic critics have not yet adequately dealt with—an anti-Semitic streak. While he did not lose any of his esprit or literary talent, he experienced growing doubts about whether his fellow humans were really capable of the great Enlightenment project of learning to think for themselves. Human nature seemed too prevalent and too much in need of gentle but firm instruction. "Therefore," he wrote in his last letter to his brother, "all that the really wise men can do is to guide everything towards a good goal, and yet to take men as they are."

GEOFFREY WINTHROP-YOUNG

Biography

Born in Oberramstadt, near Darmstadt, 1 July 1742. Studied mathematics, astronomy, and natural sciences, University of Göttingen, 1763–70; appointed Extraordinary Professor at Göttingen, 1770; traveled to England in the spring of 1770 and then again for an extended visit from August 1774 to December 1775, during which time he was in personal contact with the royal family and the actor David Garrick, among others; appointed professor in Göttingen, 1775; discovered the Lichtenberg figures, 1777, and erected Germany's first lightning conductor, 1780; edited four extensively revised editions of Johann Polycarp Erxleben's *Anfangsgründe der Naturlehre*, one of the most widely used science handbooks of its day; edited the *Göttinger Taschen Calendar*, 1777–99, and co-editor, with Georg Forster, of the *Göttingische Magazin der Wissenschaften und Litteratur*, 1780–85. Died in Göttingen, 24 February 1799.

Selected Works

Lichtenberg's Visits to England, As Described in His Letters and Diaries, edited by Margaret Laura Mare, translated by W.H. Quarrell, 1938

The Lichtenberg Reader: Selected Writings of Georg Christoph Lichtenberg, edited, translated, and introduced by Franz H. Mautner and Henry Hatfield, 1959

Lichtenberg's Commentaries on Hogarth's Engravings, translated with an introduction by Innes and Gustav Herdan, 1966

Schriften und Briefe, 4 vols., edited by Wolfgang Promies, 1967–92

Briefwechsel, 4 vols., edited by Albrecht Schöne and Ulrich Joost, 1983–92

Aphorisms, translated by R.J. Hollingdale, 1990

Further Reading

Baasner, Rainer, *Georg Christoph Lichtenberg*, Darmstadt: Wissenschaftliche Buchgesellschaft, 1992

Brinitzer, Carl, *G.C. Lichtenberg: Die Geschichte eines gescheiten Mannes*, Tübingen: Wunderlich, 1956; translated as *A Reasonable Rebel: Georg Christoph Lichtenberg*, London: George Allen and Unwin, and New York: Macmillan, 1960

Buechler, Ralph W., *Science, Satire, and Wit: The Essays of Georg Christoph Lichtenberg*, New York: Lang, 1990

Craig, Charlotte M., editor, *Lichtenberg: Essays Commemorating the 250th Anniversary of His Birth*, New York: Lang, 1992

Gravenkamp, Horst, *Geschichte eines elenden Körpers: Lichtenberg als Patient*, Göttingen: Wallstein, 1989; 2nd edition, 1992

Heißenbüttel, Helmut, "Georg Christoph Lichtenberg—der erste Autor des 20. Jahrhunderts," in *Aufklärung über Lichtenberg*, edited by Helmut Heißenbüttel, Göttingen: Vandenhoek und Ruprecht, 1974

Joost, Ulrich, *Lichtenberg der Briefschreiber*, Göttingen: Wallstein, 1990

Lorenz, Dagmar C.G., "Lichtenberg—das Maß aller seiner Dinge: Der politische und soziale Aspekt in einem egozentrischen Weltbild," *Lessing Yearbook* 10 (1978)

McCarthy, John, "Lichtenberg as Post-Structuralist," *Studies on Voltaire and the Eighteenth Century*, no. 305 (1992)

Schöne, Albrecht, *Aufklärung aus dem Geist der Experimentalphysik: Lichtenbergsche Konjunktive*, Munich: Beck, 1982; 3rd edition, 1993

Stern, J.P., *Lichtenberg: A Doctrine of Scattered Occasions*, Bloomington: Indiana University Press, 1959; London: Thames and Hudson, 1963

Liedermacher

Wolf Biermann allegedly coined the term *Liedermacher* in 1961, a reference to Bertolt Brecht's description of his own trade as a *Stückeschreiber* (writer of theater pieces). The term was intended to reflect the *Gebrauchswert*, or the practical value of the product—the song with its potential for direct communication to large audiences could be used as a tool of political enlightenment. The term also has handicraft associations, which reflect its origins in the street ballad, the *Bänkelsang* or *Moritat* of the medieval marketplace. Since the early 20th century, however, it has also enjoyed the status of a literary genre—not least due to the satirical ballads of Frank Wedekind, Bertolt Brecht, and the 1920s cabaret songs of Kurt Tucholsky and Walter Mehring. In these examples, a satirical "view from below" is presented via literary devices and poetic images. In this respect, the term *Liedermacher* encapsulates the clash between high and low cultural values, the poetic and the profane. This clash enables the traditional ironical perspective that has constituted the driving force of the genre, as exemplified by Brecht's *Legende des toten Soldaten* (1918; *Ballad of the Dead Soldier*).

The literary upgrading of the German street ballad differentiates it from its British or U.S. counterparts, neither of which have been viewed as separate from traditional folk music. The German variant has also frequently looked to France for inspiration. The 15th-century vagabond bard François Villon is a father figure of modern *Liedermacher*, the chansons of Pierre Jean de Béranger had a strong influence on German *Spottdichter* (Poets of Scorn) of the 1848 revolution, the Montmartre cabarets of the late 19th century formed the model for the German literary cabarets of the early 20th century, and chansonnier George Brassens gave a major stimulus to the singer-songwriters that gathered at the Burg-Waldeck festivals from 1964 to 1968.

This recent development in German *Liedermacher* was initially inspired by a further foreign influence: the folk and protest song revival of the United States and Great Britain. Singers such as Hein and Oss Kröyer and Peter Rohland responded by reviving democratic traditions in German folk song, performing alongside proponents of the political chanson variety, which included Franz-Josef Degenhardt, Walter Moßmann, and Dieter Süverkrüp. Degenhardt in particular achieved widespread popularity with songs such as *Spiel nicht mit den Schmuddelkindern* (1965; Don't Play with the Scruffy Kids), which undermined the new image of idyllic social harmony in the Federal Republic. In 1972, he reached number one in the charts with *Befragung eines Kriegsdienstverweigerers* (Interrogation of a Conscientious Objector). By this time, his songs had become overtly political, as he campaigned for a People's Front between the Social Democratic Party (SPD) and the Communist Party (DKP). With the floundering of the protest movement, a trend toward the more subjective set in among *Liedermacher* from the mid 1970s. A prominent example is Konstantin Wecker. While some of his songs celebrate a lifestyle of anarchic hedonism, others, including *Willy* (1977), deal with themes such as resurgent neo-Nazism. Wecker's work embodies the aforementioned conflict between the high and the low; his classically trained voice and operatic Orff-inspired arrangements clash with the rough-hewn Tucholsky-influenced lyrics, often sung in Bavarian dialect.

In the GDR, the genre developed along different lines. In the early 1960s, the revolutionary song of Brecht and Hanns Eisler was already a nurtured tradition. This was soon to accommodate the Western folk wave that arrived in East Berlin via radio and guests such as Pete Seeger. Meanwhile, a more eclectic jazz and "Lied" scene had emerged around figures such as Wolf Biermann and Eva-Maria Hagen. Recognizing the communicative power of the song, the SED took two extreme measures: the prohibition of Biermann's songs and the hijacking of the popular *Hootenanny-Klub-Berlin*. Biermann, demonstrating influences from Villon and Heinrich Heine through to Brecht/Eisler and Brassens, nonetheless recorded a string of classic LPs during his 11-year ban. In 1976, he was stripped of his GDR citizenship and refused reentry after being allowed out for a performance in Cologne. In 1967, the *Hootenany-Klub*'s name was forcibly changed to the *Oktoberklub*, which prompted the departure of Bettina Wegner. The group was henceforth misused alongside other *Singegruppen* as an instrument of mass propaganda. From 1970 to 1990, East Berlin was host to the annual International Festival of the Political Song, a socialist showcase event that simultaneously permitted a forum for considerable artistic interchange.

Their importance waning in West Germany by the 1980s, *Liedermacher* concerts in the GDR helped substitute for the lack of open debate right up until 1989. By the late 1970s, the collective agitative approach had been replaced by a more subjective, critical style as the *Oktoberklub* generation (including Barbara Thalheim) grew disillusioned and new singers emerged. In the aftermath of Biermann, the practice of codifying messages in poetic metaphors as a means of evading censorship had become widespread. This strategy mirrored literary trends and was particularly apparent in the songs of Hans-Eckardt Wenzel and Steffen Mensching. In the GDR's latter years, the strained political climate was reflected in the expulsion of singer Stephan Krawczyk to the West in 1988. Due to the popularity of the genre, however, the state label Amiga relented and released acclaimed records by Wenzel, Thalheim, and Gerhard Gundermann. During the *Wende* of 1989–90, concerts such as Wenzel and Mensching's *Letztes aus der Da Da eR* (a play on the words "Dada" and "DDR") functioned as a satirical comment on the fast-changing events.

Since German unification, interest in *Liedermacher* has been low. The genre thrived on the ideological conflict of the Cold War and on the belief that socialism was reformable. Many singers, bereft of an ideal or a tangible common oppressor, have fallen silent. Others, playing to a limited commercial market, deal with themes such as recurring German nationalism, the environment, or, in the East, the turmoil of cultural uprooting since absorption into the Federal Republic. Those performing in the wider rock market, including Udo Lindenberg, Herbert Grönemeyer, Wecker, and Gundermann (up until his premature death in 1998), continue to play to larger audiences. The latter's popularity was based on his vivid depiction of everyday life from the perspective of the unemployed ex-GDR worker.

DAVID ROBB

See also Wolf Biermann

Further Reading

Bullivant, Keith, "The 'German Question' in German Letters II: 'Liedermacher,'" in *The Future of German Literature*, Oxford and Providence, Rhode Island: Berg, 1994

"Deutsche Liedermacher 1970–1996," *Literatur für Leser* 3 (1996) (with contributions from Reinhold Grimm, Caroline Molina y Vedia, David Robb, Jay J. Rossellini, and Richard Rundell)

Henke, Matthias, *Die großen Chansonniers und Liedermacher: Wichtige Interpreten, bedeutende Dichtersänger,* Düsseldorf: Econ Taschenbuch, 1987

Kirchenwitz, Lutz, *Folk, Chanson, und Liedermacher in der DDR: Chronisten, Kritiker, Kaisersgeburtstagssänger,* Berlin: Dietz, 1993

Riha, Karl, *Morität, Bänkelsong, Protestballade: Zur Geschichte des engagierten Liedes in Deutschland,* Frankfurt: Fischer, 1975

Robb, David, *Zwei Clowns im Lande des verlorenen Lachens: Das Liedertheater Wenzel und Mensching,* Berlin: Links Verlag, 1998

Rothschild, Thomas, *Liedermacher 23 Porträts,* Frankfurt: Fischer, 1980

Schwarz, Petra, and Wilfried Bergholz, *Liederleute: 28 Porträts,* Berlin: Lied der Zeit, 1989

Liselotte von der Pfalz (Elisabeth Charlotte d'Orléans) 1652–1722

During the 17th century, German women's literature was still mostly limited to religious topics dealt with by members of the aristocracy and upper bourgeoisie. Only a few women such as Maria Cunitz (1610–64) and Maria Sibylla Merian (1647–1717) had access to an academic education through home schooling at the hands of their fathers, husbands, or brothers and found enough societal freedom to write about their scholarly investigations. Anna Maria of Schurmann (1607–78) acquired an impressive body of knowledge along with her brothers, and she even attended the University of Utrecht and later became a European celebrity. But at the age of 62, to the shock and disbelief of most intellectuals, she turned away from her worldly life and joined an itinerant Pietist group. Further, a few duchesses such as Sophie Elisabeth (1613–76) and Sibylle Ursula (1629–71) of Brunswick-Lüneburg were dedicated religious poets, dramatists, and novelists, but most other Baroque women were excluded from public literary circles. Instead, they composed their texts only for private reading groups at the courts and in the cities and had almost no chance of publishing any of their texts. The outstanding lyric poetry by Catharina Regina von Greiffenberg (1633–94), almost exclusively religious in nature, appealed to a Protestant audience but did not represent a breakthrough for early-modern German women writers. Even though the world of the absolutist courts in 17th-century Europe established a cultural platform for all its members to participate, the overpowering male dominance was not shaken at all. Women continued to be relegated to their private spheres and had to make do with the limited resources available to them. Three French women writers, Marie de Sévigné (1626–96), the so-called Babet (1638–1701), and Ninon de Lenclos (1620–1705), however, emerged as leading epistolary authors of their times, and they were highly regarded for their witticism, literary qualities, and ethical standards. The only comparable figure in German literature proves to be Liselotte von der Pfalz (Elisabeth Charlotte d'Orléans), later the wife of the French dauphin. She was remarkable not only for the incredible output of letters, but also for her decision to resort to her native German during a time when most correspondence and public discourse was carried out in French.

Elisabeth was born in Heidelberg on 27 May 1652, as the daughter of the Elector of the Palatinate, Karl Ludwig, and his wife Charlotte, Countess of Hesse-Kassel. Her parents divorced a few years later, and her father remarried the noble chambermaid Luise of Degenfeld on 6 January 1658. In the same year Elisabeth went to live with her aunt, Sophie, Duchess of Brunswick-Lüneburg, with whom she spent four happy years. In 1671, she was wedded, against her will, after having rejected several marriage proposals, to Philip of Orléans, brother of the French king Louis XIV, in Châlon, and she was forced to convert to Catholicism. Although Elisabeth strongly disliked her husband, the couple had three children: Alexandre Louis d'Orléans, Duke of Valois, Philip, Duke of Orléans, and Elisabeth Charlotte. In her letters she bitterly complained about her husband, who turned out to be homosexual and exclusively interested in jewels, parties, and court intrigue. By contrast, Elisabeth enjoyed the outdoors and despised the artificial attention to the external appearance that was so important at the court. Remarkable for her time, but not surprising considering the cultural clash between Elisabeth and the French world, she rejected the aristocratic lifestyle at the royal court of Versailles and mostly withdrew to her private chambers. Nevertheless, she later became famous for her extensive correspondence with friends and relatives to whom she wrote approximately 40,000 to 50,000 letters, mostly in German. This choice was contrary to the fashion of her time, which favored French in oral and written communication. In this decision she became a forerunner of enlightened 18th-century German writers such as Louise Gottsched, née Kulmus (1713–62), her husband Johann Christoph Gottsched (1700–1766), Christiane Mariane von Ziegler née Romanus (1695–1760), and Christoph Martin Wieland (1733–1813). Only about 20 percent of her correspondence has so far been published, but the extant letters prove her literary abilities, her critical perception of Baroque culture, and her radical rejection of the pompousness of the French aristocracy. Elisabeth's style was refreshingly direct, open-minded, at times crude and unpolished, but also highly vivacious, humorous, and realistic. Women's freedom to utilize epistolary form for their literary interests, however, ended in Germany when C.F. Gellert published his learned treatise on the proper form of letter writing according to scholarly traditions in 1742.

Elisabeth severely suffered from homesickness throughout her life in Versailles, but she could never return to the Palatinate. She bitterly complained about the War of the Grand Alliance (1688–97), in which her home country was burned and destroyed by her brother-in-law, King Louis XIV, who had claimed that territory for France as his sister-in-law's rightful inheritance after her brother, the Elector Karl, had died, leaving no other male successor to the throne. When Louis's armies could not hold on to the Palatinate, they withdrew to France leaving behind a charred country. Elisabeth had no other recourse to protest against Louis's military policy except for her letters. Elisabeth's husband died in 1701, and she passed away in Versailles on 8 December 1722.

In this extensive correspondence, carried out throughout her whole life, Elisabeth provides an insightful portrait of French courtly life and critically analyzes French and German politics from a woman's perspective. Many of her letters contain simple tidbits of political intrigues, love affairs, and scandals and extensive information about aristocratic entertainment and, particularly, her personal experiences as a high-ranking member of the French-German nobility at the time of absolutism and Baroque. Moreover, Elisabeth's correspondence contains important statements about European politics, rulers, ministers, and other aspects of the royal courts, including the Vatican. Consequently, many 18th- and 19th-century historians and literary scholars translated and edited her letters and treated them as significant cultural-historical documents.

ALBRECHT CLASSEN

Biography
Born in Heidelberg, 27 May 1652. Lived with her aunt, Sophie, Duchess of Brunswick-Lüneberg, 1658–62; wedded against her will to Philip of Orléans, brother of Louis XIV, in Châlon, and forced to convert to Catholicism, 1671; rejected the aristocratic lifestyle at Versailles and withdrew to her private chambers; became famous for her extensive correspondence with her friends and relatives, to whom she wrote approximately 40,000–50,000 letters (only about 20 percent of which have been published), mostly in German (contrary to the fashion of her time, which favored French); bitterly complained about the War of the Grand Alliance, 1688–97, in which her home country was burned and destroyed by her brother-in-law, Louis XIV, who claimed that territory for France as his sister-in-law's rightful inheritance after her brother, Elector Karl, died and left no male successor to the throne. Died in Versailles, France, 8 December 1722.

Selected Works

Letters
Briefe aus den Jahren 1676–1722, edited by Wilhelm Ludwig Holland, 1867–81

Letters from Liselotte, Elisabeth Charlotte, Princess Palatine and Duchess of Orléans, "Madame," 1652–1722, translated and edited by Margaret Kroll, 1970

A Woman's Life in the Court of the Sun King: Letters of Liselotte von der Pfalz, Elisabeth Charlotte, Duchesse d'Orléans, translated by Elborg Forster, 1984

Further Reading
Blackwell, Jeannine, and Susanne Zantop, editors, *Bitter Healing: German Women Writers from 1700 to 1830: An Anthology,* Lincoln: University of Nebraska Press, 1990
Classen, Albrecht, "Female Epistolary Literature from Antiquity to the Present: An Introduction," *Studia Neophilologica* 60 (1988)
———, "Elisabeth Charlotte von der Pfalz, Herzogin von Orléans: Epistolare Selbstbekenntnisse und literarisches Riesenunternehmen," *Archiv für Kulturgeschichte* 77, no. 1 (1995)
Eberlein, Harold Donaldson, *The Rabelaisian Princess: Madame Royale of France,* New York: Brentano's, 1931
Forster, Elborg, editor and translator, *A Woman's Life in the Court of the Sun King: Letters of Liselotte von der Pfalz, 1652–1722,* Baltimore, Maryland: Johns Hopkins University Press, 1984
Kiesel, Helmuth, "Herzogin Elisabeth Charlotte von Orleans, gen. Liselotte von der Pfalz," in *Deutsche Dichter des 17. Jahrhunderts: Ihr Leben und Werk,* edited by Harald Steinhagen and Benno von Wiese, Berlin: Schmidt, 1984
Kroll, Maria, editor and translator, *Letters from Liselotte: Elisabeth Charlotte, Princess Palatine and Duchess of Orléans, "Madame" 1652–1722,* London: Gollancz, 1970
Liselotte von der Pfalz: Madame am Hofe des Sonnenkönigs, Catalogue for the Exhibition in Heidelberg on the occasion of the 800th Anniversary, September 21, 1996 to January 26, 1997, Heidelberg: HVA, 1996
Mattheier, Klaus J., et al., editors, *Pathos, Klatsch, und Ehrlichkeit: Liselotte von der Pfalz am Hof des Sonnenkönigs,* Tübingen: Stauffenburg, 1990
Nickisch, Reinhard M.G., "Briefkultur: Entwicklung und sozialgeschichtliche Bedeutung des Frauenbriefs im 18. Jahrhundert," in *Vom Mittelalter bis zum Ende des 18. Jahrhunderts,* Deutsche Literatur von Frauen, edited by Gisela Brinker-Gabler, vol. 1, Munich: Beck, 1988
Woods, Jean M., and Maria Fürstenwald, *Schriftstellerinnen, Künstlerinnen, und gelehrte Frauen des deutschen Barock: Ein Lexikon,* Stuttgart: Metzler, 1984

Oskar Loerke 1884–1941

In his day, Oskar Loerke was one of the most active and influential of all writers at work in Germany. As a publisher's reader, trade representative, and reviewer; as the author of two novels, together with numerous short stories, essays, and works on music; and as the editor of an astonishing variety of different texts, his presence on the literary scene was ubiquitous and his importance is hard to overestimate. And yet, in his diaries, Loerke is constantly complaining of neglect because what he really wanted all his life was proper, public recognition of what posterity has, indeed, come to regard as his most important achievement: the poems that he collected into a carefully crafted heptameron and a few supernumerary sequences.

As a poet, Loerke is often regarded as an early and outstanding practitioner of *naturmagische Lyrik* (magic realist nature poetry), whose influence on Wilhelm Lehmann, Günter Eich, Karl Krolow, and others is acknowledged to be profound. Similar to their works, his poems are concerned above all with that art of condensation and extrapolation in which the reality of things is held fast through the invocation of their metaphysical implications. They are almost always written in strict forms, because for him the accident of rhyme bespeaks metaphysical connectedness. But within these, Loerke is able to achieve extreme precision of imagery and cadence, often at the expense of superficial musicality. As a result, there is something of a Neue Sachlichkeit or New

Objectivity about them. And unlike the ecstatic outpourings of certain other Expressionists, they demand to be reread.

Loerke, born in 1884, was of the Expressionist generation, and it was on the back of Expressionism that he achieved his greatest success, when, after his journeyman overture *Wanderschaft* of 1911, his second collection, originally published in 1916 as *Gedichte* (Poems), was reprinted in 1929 under the title *Pansmusik*. The whole book is indelibly influenced by the trip that the Kleist Prize made possible. Indeed, it is structured as a journey to the East, encompassing the city and the country, the sea and its islands, and subsuming them all to the synesthetic pantheism of the title poem.

Pansmusik weaves the song of the goat-footed god out of a combination of sky, light, and the river on whose banks he had grown up. The "heimliche Stadt" that furnishes the title of the next collection harbors an ambiguity famously explored by Freud. By the time the book appeared in 1921, Loerke had definitely made Berlin his home. After all, he had been working as publisher's reader for Samuel Fisher for four years. But beyond and behind this familiar city, Loerke was concerned to conjure another city that is unfamiliar and almost uncanny, a "secret city" that is largely but not exclusively a city of night and winter and that mysteriously corresponds to the mausoleum city that is Pompeii.

The fourth collection of the seven is the pivotal one, and its title, *Der längste Tag* (1926; The Longest Day), strongly underlines this feeling, as does the final poem "Sonnwendabend," which has a solstice in its title. The book is full of more-or-less magical, more-or-less circular journeys that bring the lyric subject back to himself. There is bitterness, doubt, and questioning in it. But there is also a sense of purpose and structure, almost of fate, almost of resignation in the collection.

After the longest day, all that remains is a descent into darkness. To show that things are not as simple as that, however, Loerke's next collection, *Atem der Erde* (1930; Breath of Earth), begins with childhood and a poem that insists that the symbolic solstice is infinitely deferrable. What follows is a mirror image of the progress of *Pansmusik*: a journey back from the Atlas mountains and far distances to the city, the dreaming self, and the Other. And here, questions of circularity or finality, of fellowship and the permanence of art, are asked with an existential urgency, which, however, is always seen as arising from the various landscapes, trees, and cultural artifacts described.

The last two books of the heptameron, *Silberdistelwald* (1934; Silver Thistle Wood) and *Wald der Welt* (1936; Forest of the World), were pressed together by the threat of Nazism. Now nature has become a "Gericht," a place of judgment; the question of transience is fraught with a new moral urgency; and the garden, which Loerke had acquired in 1930, figures as the locus classicus of inner emigration. The "Tafelrunde" or round table is dangerously close to the "Verstoßenen," or outcasts, who in turn have much in common with the poets of the Thirty Years' War. The world in which they live has become an underworld, an Atlantis, a city of night. But the painted vases that outlive the submerged city give notice of the ethical and political durability of art. And that is why they are surrounded, in the positive half of the diptych, by "Tröstungen," consolations, and "das alte Dasein," the old existence.

This old existence, in which spiritual communion is possible across distances of time and space, and in which the contingencies of life can be subsumed into the transcendent reality of a work of art, is the heart of Loerke's entire oeuvre and the essence of his magic. And his struggle to keep faith with it in his last works painfully epitomizes the paradoxes of inner emigration, as when an anthology celebrating the spiritual and intellectual achievements of German culture ("Deutscher Geist," 1940) became misreadable as a celebration of the spirit of Germanness. Loerke himself was in no doubt that these paradoxes materially helped to bring about his death in 1941. As with the other images and impulses of his artistic life, however, the exactitude with which he catalogued them and the truth he was able to achieve despite external constraints have helped to ensure for him a permanent place in German literature.

ROBERT GILLETT

Biography

Born in Jungen an der Weichsel, 13 March 1884. Studied German literature, philosophy, history, and music in Berlin; discontinued his studies after first literary publications; in the Sahara and Italy on a travel grant; became a reader for the Fischer Verlag, 1917; in 1927 he became a secretary of the poetry section in the Prussian Academy of the Arts, an appointment he lost in 1933. Kleist-Prize, 1913. Died in Berlin-Frohnau, 24 February 1941.

Selected Works

Collections

Die Abschiedshand: Letzte Gedichte, edited by Hermann Kasack, 1949
Reden und kleinere Aufsätze, edited by Hermann Kasack, 1957
Gedichte und Prosa, edited by Peter Suhrkamp, 2 vols., 1958
Reisetagebücher, edited by Heinrich Ringleb, 1960
Der Bücherkarren: Besprechungen im Berliner Börsen-Courier 1920–1928, edited by Hermann Kasack, 1965
Literarische Aufsätze aus der "Neuen Rundschau" 1909–1941, edited by Reinhard Tgahrt, 1967
Die Gedichte, edited by Peter Suhrkamp, revised by Reinhard Tgahrt, 1984
Tagebücher 1903–1939, edited by Hermann Kasack, 1986
Was sich nicht ändert: Gedanken und Bemerkungen zu Literatur und Leben, edited by Reinhard Tgahrt, 1996

Fiction

Vineta, 1907
Franz Pfinz, 1909
Der Turmbau, 1910
Chimärenreiter, 1919
Das Goldbergwerk, 1919
Der Prinz und der Tiger, 1920
Der Oger, 1921

Poetry

Wanderschaft, 1911
Gedichte, 1916; as *Pansmusik*, 1929
Die heimliche Stadt, 1921
Der längste Tag, 1926
Atem der Erde, 1930
Der Silberdistelwald, 1934
Der Wald der Welt, 1936
Der Steinpfad, 1938
Kärntner Sommer, 1939

Essays

Zeitgenossen aus vielen Zeiten, 1925
Das alte Wagnis des Gedichts, 1935

Das unsichtbare Reich: Johann Sebastian Bach, 1935
Anton Bruckner: Ein Charakterbild, 1938
Hausfreunde, 1939

Further Reading

Gebhard, Walter, *Oskar Loerkes Poetologie*, Munich: W. Fink, 1968
Tgahrt, Reinhard, editor, *Oskar Loerke: Marbacher Kolloquium, 1984*, Mainz: Hase und Köhler, 1986
————, editor, *Zeitgenosse vieler Zeiten: Zweites Marbacher Loerke-Kolloquium 1987*, Mainz: Hase und Köhler, 1989
————, editor, *Drittes Marbacher Loerke-Kolloquium 1997*, Mainz: Hase und Köhler, 1999
Tgahrt, Reinhard, and Tilman Kröner, editors, *Oskar Loerke 1884–1964: Eine Gedächtnisausstellung zum 80. Geburtstag des Dichters*, Stuttgart: Turmhaus-Druckerei, 1964

Daniel Casper von Lohenstein 1635–1683

The works of Daniel Casper von Lohenstein mark an extreme development in the style and content of German Baroque literature. Writing in the latter half of the 17th century, Lohenstein combined his vast legal and historical knowledge with a radically complicated literary style to produce some of the most highly praised and, subsequently, unanimously condemned works of the era. His dramas, for which he is best known, feature a style characterized by extravagant metaphorical constructs. Compressed and often abstruse emblematic images fill the dialogue of these plays. No conceit is too rare nor any syntax too complex when his characters surge into the full rhetorical mode that characterizes these works. Extensive footnotes, often longer than the plays themselves, document the historical and scholarly sources Lohenstein felt necessary for an appropriate understanding of his efforts. Similarly, his massive novel *Großmüthiger Feldherr Arminius* (1689–90) features encyclopedic learning couched in a prose style fully as florid as that of the dramas. In both instances, and in his poetry as well, Lohenstein showed a predilection for extreme subject matters, including a remarkable concentration on the themes of sex and violence. This last subject focus has been at least partially responsible for the renewed interest in his works during the latter half of the 20th century.

At the age of 15, Lohenstein composed his earliest drama, *Ibrahim Bassa* (1650). This play, along with his final effort, *Ibrahim Sultan* (1673), reflects something of the anti-Turkish sentiment that filled an age when the Turks were an active threat to Central Europe. After all, the Turks would stand before the walls of Vienna only a few years after Lohenstein's death. This first production, however, is relatively restrained in its depiction of the Turkish sultan's desire for Ibrahim's wife, and only through the machinations of his evil courtiers does the sultan arrive at a device to eliminate her husband. The same cannot be said for *Ibrahim Sultan*. Here Lohenstein pillories the decadent Turkish court headed by the historically based Sultan Ibrahim. This reprehensible monarch embodies the stereotypical vices of the "lustful Turk." Along with other crimes, he assaults his sister-in-law and rapes a young girl before he is finally deposed and assassinated. The only ray of hope comes from the indication in the choruses that the Holy Roman Empire is destined to subjugate this barbaric Turkish state.

Lohenstein's homage to the Austrian Habsburgs and their empire appears repeatedly in his plays. In his two dramas *Cleopatra* (1661) and *Sophonisbe* (1680), he shows how the devious sensuality of these southern Mediterranean queens proves overwhelming for weaker male figures of Antonius and Masinissa. But their seductive wiles are no match for the coldly rational self-control of Rome's representatives, Augustus and Syphax, the putative forebears of the Holy Roman Empire. Both male figures embody the role of historical fate that Lohenstein saw as implicit in the transition of world power from Egypt and Carthage to Imperial Rome and the Habsburg-controlled German Empire of Lohenstein's day.

As in the previous two plays, the eponymous heroines of the remaining dramas, *Agrippina* (1665) and *Epicharis* (1665), are dominant female characters. Lohenstein's female protagonists have little in common with the saintly and long-suffering women of such contemporary martyr dramas as Gryphius's *Catharina von Georgien*. Two factors are at work here. The first is that Lohenstein's women are made of sterner stuff; they actively work at controlling their own destiny rather than passively suffering the whims of a male tyrant. Second, a drive to power dominates their actions. No female restraints apply as they repeatedly employ whatever force or trickery is necessary in order to preserve or extend their influence.

Agrippina, the drama of Nero's mother, epitomizes the sexual extremes associated with Lohenstein's work that caused 19th-century critics such dismay. Fearful that Nero's new mistress will cause her to lose control over the emperor, Agrippina sets out to restore her domination by seducing her own son. When her staged attempt fails at the last moment—due only to an unanticipated interruption—Nero recognizes his danger and arranges to have her killed. This in turn leads to a concluding chorus in which the Furies torture Nero with visions of ultimate retribution. In *Epicharis*, Lohenstein provides an unremittingly bloody spectacle. Leader of a conspiracy to overthrow the tyrant Nero, Epicharis lies, deceives, and finally commits suicide in defense of her cause. The main theatrical impact comes, however, from the almost countless forms of torture and execution that are performed on the open stage in full view of the public.

At the time of his death, Lohenstein's sole novel, *Arminius*, remained a fragment even though the published edition ran to over 3,000 pages of double-column print. Written in the conventions of historical courtly fiction, *Arminius* conforms only loosely to the history of the Germanic chieftain who handed the Romans their first serious defeat in the north. The larger purpose, however, is a glorification of the Germanic tradition as opposed to the Roman past and the French present. In this roman à clef, contemporary readers easily recognized the Austrian Emperor

Leopold behind the Germanic hero. On the stylistic level, lavishly portrayed exotic settings and customs fill the novel while language luxuriates in its own powers in what some critics have called the apex of Baroque ornateness.

Raised to the heights by his contemporaries, Lohenstein's critical standing plummeted in the Enlightenment and has risen again only in the last half century. The rational thinkers of the 18th century found little joy in his difficult verse and obscure imagery. They saw in him the worst sort of Baroque bombast. The 19th century, while more open to his linguistic adventures, had little patience with his subject matter. More recent evaluations of his accomplishments have been twofold. First, there has been a greater recognition of the rhetorical and emblematic assumptions underlying his work and, by extension, a greater understanding of both what he was attempting and what he achieved. Second, critics have become more interested in the role of the imminent in his works. His protagonists struggle and die in their own world. There is no second chance or reward in the afterlife. The theme of the accumulation and retention of power in this world caught and clearly held the attention of this skillful lawyer, occasional diplomat, dramatist, novelist, and universally knowledgeable scholar.

BARTON W. BROWNING

Biography
Born in Nimptsch, near Breslau, 25 January 1635. Began studying law at the University of Leipzig at the age of 16, and completed his studies in 1655; grand tour of central Europe; appointment as legal council to the city of Breslau, 1669; diplomatic missions at the Imperial Court leading to appointment as senior legal council of Breslau and imperial counselor, 1675. Died 28 April 1683.

Selected Works

Collections
Türkische Trauerspiele, edited by Klaus Günther Just, 1953
Römische Trauerspiele, edited by Klaus Günther Just, 1955
Afrikanische Trauerspiele, edited by Klaus Günther Just, 1957

Dramas
Ibrahim Bassa, 1650
Cleopatra, 1661
Agrippina, 1665
Epicharis, 1665
Ibrahim Sultan, 1673
Sophonisbe, 1680; translated by M. John Hanack, 1992

Novel
Großmüthiger Feldherr Arminius, 1689–90

Poetry
Lyrica, die Sammlung "Blumen" (1680) und "Erleuchteter Hoffmann" (1685): Nebst einem Anhang. Gelegenheitsgedichte in separater Überlieferung, edited by Gerhard Spellerberg, 1992

Further Reading
Aikin, Judith Popovich, *The Mission of Rome in the Dramas of Daniel Casper von Lohenstein: Historical Tragedy as Prophecy and Polemic,* Stuttgart: Heinz, 1976
Asmuth, Bernhard, *Daniel Casper von Lohenstein,* Stuttgart: Metzler, 1971
Best, Thomas W., "On Lohenstein's Concept of Tragedy," *Euphorion* 80 (1986)
Gillespie, Gerald Ernest Paul, *Daniel Casper von Lohenstein's Historical Tragedies,* Columbus: Ohio State University Press, 1965
Just, Klaus Günther, *Die Trauerspiele Lohensteins: Versuch einer Interpretation,* Berlin: Schmidt, 1961
Kayser, Wolfgang, "Lohensteins 'Sophonisbe' als geschichtliche Tragödie," *Germanisch-romanische Monatschrift* 29 (1941)
Martino, Alberto, *Daniel Casper von Lohenstein: Geschichte seiner Rezeption,* Tübingen: Niemeyer, 1978
Plume, Cornelia, *Heroinen in der Geschlechterordnung: Weiblichkeitsprojektionen bei Daniel Casper von Lohenstein und die "Querelle des femmes,"* Stuttgart: Metzler, 1996
Spellerberg, Gerhard, *Verhängnis und Geschichte: Untersuchungen zu den Trauerspielen und dem "Arminius"-Roman Daniel Caspers von Lohenstein,* Bad Homburg: Gehlen, 1970
Wichert, Adalbert, *Literatur, Rhetorik, und Jurisprudenz im 17. Jahrhundert: Daniel Casper von Lohenstein und sein Werk: Eine exemplarische Studie,* Tübingen: Niemeyer, 1991

Adolf Loos 1870–1933

The architect, theorist, and writer Adolf Loos is considered a most important proponent for, and practitioner of, the modern style in architecture in Europe at the beginning of the 20th century. Walter Gropius, the founder of the Bauhaus, considered Loos one of the few architects who, in 1900, had already formulated the directives that later shaped the modern, functionalist building style. The financially hazardous visit to the United States that the 23-year-old student from Dresden Technical University embarked upon in 1893 has to be regarded as a catalytic event in this process. During his three-year stay, Loos familiarized himself with the architecture of the Chicago School, the high-rise projects of Louis Sullivan in Chicago and St. Louis, and the early New York skyscrapers. Sullivan's essay "Ornament in

Architecture" (1892), which argued for a critical attitude toward ornament in the context of the emerging building style, is assumed to have influenced the young Austrian architect.

In 1896, Loos returned to Vienna, where the Secession movement was taking shape to become official in 1897. The U.S. experience had sensitized Loos in two directions simultaneously. He began critiquing the eclectic historicism of the Ringstraße architecture while at the same time ridiculing the innovative attempt of the Secessionists Joseph Maria Olbrich and Josef Hoffmann at a modern alternative to the historicist tradition by means of their art nouveau and proto-art deco styles. Loos began publishing his polemical statements against the decorative approach to design in *Die Zeit* and *Die Neue Freie Presse,* as well as in his own short-lived journal *Das Andere* (two issues in 1903). He also attacked the decorative movement at a different front, namely, in the interiors that he executed at the time. The Café Museum (1899, partly destroyed), which was located in the proximity of Olbrich's Secession building, was one such statement. Loos was in no way displeased that his design of radical simplicity, without ornaments and with (then) ordinary Thonet chairs, was nicknamed "Café Nihilismus." In 1898, the article "Die Potemkin'sche Stadt" (Potemkin—or Fake—City) appeared in the journal of the Secession, *Ver Sacrum*. In this article, Loos turned against the "hypocrisy" of the false Renaissance and neo-Baroque facades of the palatial Ringstraße buildings; they appeared to him, with their plaster of Paris imitations, as pompous simulacra of authentic Viennese Baroque ornamentation.

Loos's writing and designing activities after 1898 converged most intensively around 1910, when he gave a talk with the title "Ornament und Verbrechen" (Ornament and Crime) at the Akademischer Verband für Literatur und Musik in Vienna and completed the building for the clothier Goldman und Salatsch at the Michaelerplatz, now called the "Loos-Haus" (restored). The essay, which is frequently cited and alluded to in German-language cultural discourse, is usually dated in posthumous editions as having appeared in 1908. New research (Rukschio) claims that "Ornament und Verbrechen" was given in 1910, repeated in 1913 when it was first published in French, and eventually published in German on 24 October 1929, in *Frankfurter Zeitung*. The essay begins with an embrace of a primitivist aesthetic in the framework of an emphatic, untheorized anthropology of art: "The first ornament was the cross and was of erotic origin: a horizontal line—woman. A vertical line: man penetrating." Throughout the text Expressionist fervor and deliberate crudeness create involuntary comic effects: "Modern man who tatoos himself is a criminal or a degenerate." He also states: "He who goes to listen to the ninth symphony and then sits down to draw a wallpaper pattern, is either a crook or a degenerate." Portraits of Adolf Loos in architectural histories generally omit a discussion of the essay. The piece does, however, contain the reflections—then unprecedented—that influenced architectural modernism and the 20th-century aesthetic sensibility in general: "Evolution of culture is identical to removing the ornament from the ordinary object of use." Reading this statement today, we associate it with the evolution of the Bauhaus design aesthetic. Other important observations are: "Since the ornament is no longer organically linked with our culture, it is no longer an expression of our culture" and "Lack of ornament is a sign of spiritual power. Modern man uses the ornaments of earlier and foreign cultures at will. His own invention is focused on other things."

For Loos, these "things" were first and foremost the attempt of the modern architect to use the very properties of a material as an expressive form. Loos demonstrated this most convincingly in the facade of the Loos-Haus (which also shows the architect's admiration for classicists such as Palladio and Schinkel). The green marble that is arranged in a functionalist manner is decorative only because of its nature as a richly textured, traditional stone; for Loos, this represents the true ornament of nature, because it is not made with human hands. Mies van der Rohe's Barcelona Pavilion of 1929 develops Loos's treatment of marble further; sharing Loos's condemnation of imitating one

material with another, the Bauhaus also emancipated many ordinary building materials, even concrete, to an aesthetic status.

In 1910, Loos also completed Haus Steiner. The early historian of architectural modernism, Nikolaus Pevsner, said that any uninitiated observer would date this house in the years 1924 to 1930 or even later. The Steiner House is a key monument of the modern movement in architecture and anticipated the cubic forms of the International style; it was the first time concrete was used in the construction of a private house. The broad influence that Loos's Viennese houses and Haus Müller in Prague (1928–30) exerted on the development of modernist building styles can only be noted in passing. Loos's influence is also felt in the house that Ludwig Wittgenstein designed for his sister in Vienna, now an embassy.

Not enthusiastic about the reception of his work in Vienna, Loos left for Paris in 1922, where his collection of early essays had been well received (published in German as *Ins Leere gesprochen* in 1921 [*Spoken into the Void*]). Apart from numerous unexecuted designs during that time, his house for the Dadaist Tristan Tzara was completed. Among the planned work was the entry for the *Chicago Tribune* Tower competition (1922), which proposed a skyscraper with 22 floors in the shape of a Doric column. The "bewohnte Säule" (inhabited column), one the most reproduced architectural designs, gained particular respect with postmodern architects in the 1980s. Robert Stern recreated a pastiche of Loos's design as a work of graphic art, and Ricareo Bofill built apartment houses in Paris using the inhabited column idea. Inspired by postmodernist quotation practices, the Belgian architect Bob van Reeth executed a flamboyant project first imagined by Loos: "Ein Haus für Josephine Baker." What had to remain a design in 1920s Paris was built in 1985 in Antwerp, and it now tells a lively story of intertextuality in architecture.

The purist and iconoclast Adolf Loos remained controversial until his death in 1933. While his fame as architectural pioneer is secured, that of the writer Loos is considered modest. It should be remembered that he came from an exclusively technical background and had little formal schooling in the humanities. It is therefore not surprising that his journalistic writings do not match the polished verbal wit of his ally Karl Kraus and others of the Viennese feuilleton; nor does his polemical playlet *Das Scala-Theater in Wien* (collected in *Spoken into the Void*) impress us today. He nevertheless had the respect of intellectuals such as Hermann Broch, who was clearly affected by Loos's decisive modernist stand. The Viennese novelist was one of the first to write on Loos, and in the 1920s he styled the interior of his Teesdorf home after Loos.

INGEBORG HOESTEREY

See also Karl Kraus

Biography

Born in Brno, Moravia, 10 December 1870. Trained as a bricklayer, 1887; studied building engineering at various trade schools and enrolled in the Technische Hochschule, Dresden, 1889; served in the army; applied to the Academy of Art, Vienna; completed his courses in Dresden, 1892–93; three-year visit to the United States, beginning 1893; worked as a journalist for the *Neue Freie Presse*, 1897–1900; private architectural practice, Vienna, 1897–1922; appointed chief architect, municipal housing department, Vienna, 1920; lived and worked in Paris, 1922–27; returned to Vienna to practice architecture,

1927–33; founder of the Free School of Architecture. Died in Kalksburg, Austria, 23 August 1933.

Selected Works

Writings

Ins Leere gesprochen, 1921; as *Spoken into the Void: Collected Essays, 1897–1900*, translated by Jane O. Newman and John H. Smith, 1982

Trotzdem, 1900–1930, 1931

Die Potemkin'sche Stadt: Verschollene Schriften, 1897–1933, edited by Adolf Opel, 1983

Further Reading

Adolf Loos, zum 60. Geburtstag am 10. Dezember 1930: Festschrift, Vienna: Lanyi, 1930

Lustenberger, Kurt, *Adolf Loos*, Zurich: Artemis, 1994

Münz, Ludwig, and Gustav Künstler, *Der Architekt Adolf Loos*, Vienna: Schroll, 1964; as *Adolf Loos: Pioneer of Modern Architecture*, translated by Harold Meek, London: Thames and Hudson, and New York: Praeger, 1966

Rukschcio, Burkhardt, and Roland L. Schachel, *Adolf Loos: Leben und Werk*, Vienna: Residenz, 1982

Ludwigslied 881–882

Epic Poem

The Old High German *Ludwigslied* is a ninth-century poem in 59 long-lines, rhymed at the caesura and grouped together as 22 strophes of two or three lines. It is preserved in a monastery in what is now France, in a manuscript that contains primarily Latin and Old French material. Moreover, the *Ludwigslied* is a poem praising and celebrating a victory by a West Frankish—we might now say French—king.

The hero of the poem is Louis III, great-grandson of Charlemagne, who succeeded his father as king of the West Franks, of the French part of Charlemagne's empire in 879, while still a teenager. He ruled together with his even-younger brother Carloman. His age made him vulnerable, but in spite of opposition he maintained his throne, and in 881, he assisted his brother in repelling the attacks of a pretender to the throne, Boso, duke of Provence, on Carloman's southern part of the West Frankish kingdom.

In July 881, Louis rode northward again to face another threat, this time from the Vikings, who had been making frequent attacks on the coast of Northern France and the Low Countries. Louis met them at Saucourt in Picardy on 3 August 881 and defeated them. This was a matter of considerable importance, as the Vikings were a powerful force, and the king himself was praised particularly in contemporary chronicles. In fact, the triumph was short-lived. Although Louis was planning to consolidate his victory, he died almost exactly a year later, on 5 August 882, and Carloman died soon after.

The *Ludwigslied* was probably composed at the monastery of St. Amand in Picardy, which had an international reputation for scholarship and which attracted aristocratic members, including, presumably, the Rhinelander who composed the poem while the king was still alive. God is asked in the poem itself to grant him long life. By the time the version we have was written down, however, Louis was dead and a heading had to be added dedicating the work to his memory. The manuscript was first identified in the 17th century, lost for nearly 200 years, and rediscovered in Valenciennes by Heinrich Hoffmann von Fallersleben in 1839.

The poem presents a series of events, and when it was written, it would have provided valuable support for the young king's cause. As a piece of historical writing it is theocentric. God is in control of all human events, but the characters involved are not given special knowledge of how events will turn out. Although the work centers on the Viking battle, the poet is more concerned to present a reason for the Viking attacks, and he sees this in God's desire first to test the young king and second to punish the sinfulness of the Frankish people. The king is presented as having lost his father when young—as indeed he did—and as having been protected by God (a good propaganda point), who provided him with loyal supporters. At this point, and while Louis is away (we are not told in the poem where or why), the Vikings come with their double purpose. Although chronicles sometimes present them as monsters and at least as anti-Christian, here they are just referred to as "Norsemen" or "heathens." Since they are instruments used by God, they have no real identity. The Franks are punished for their sins (this interpretation of events was common in the period), and eventually God recalls Louis to help. Louis agrees to fight as best he can—he is given no special promise of victory—raises his war banner, and leads his men into battle singing the *Kyrie eleison* (Lord have mercy). The final lines of the poem place historically verifiable statements ("Louis was victorious") against theocentric interpretations ("God gave him the victory"). The concluding lines ask that God preserve the king, but this did not happen.

That the poem is rhymed places it in the tradition of Latin-influenced religious writings in which the form was developed in German, and the poem, propaganda when composed and a memorial piece when committed to manuscript, echoes Latin theological and historical poems. It records events and details that can be confirmed from other sources: that Louis was young when he became king and that he defeated the Vikings. Other elements are potentially factual, such as his address to his troops, or the singing of the *Kyrie*. But it is also a work of literature, selecting events and interpreting them first in a manner favorable to the king and second in a theological manner, asking why the Vikings were sent. This approach does not constitute what has been called a *Drahtpuppengesinnung* (puppet mentality). God may be in control of history, but He is outside time; the participants within the events have to act as best they can, and Louis says as much to his soldiers before the battle. As a panegyric and as propaganda, the work is straightforward, presenting Louis as having God on his side. In its ultimate form as a memorial poem, it has an exemplary function in demonstrating how a Christian king ought to behave.

The poem omits dates and places, presumably because the victory was so famous (certainly immediately afterward), and this has led to attempts to see the poem as being about the East Frank (German) King Ludwig III; however, he never enjoyed such a clear victory over the Vikings, and other facts given in the *Ludwigslied* do not match his career. Nevertheless, there is a historian's attempt to explain why things happen; we might nowadays come to different conclusions, but the poet's theocentric view was valid for the time and indeed for many centuries thereafter.

The manuscript text is inscribed to the blessed memory of King Louis, son of Louis, who was also a king. Any question of disputed kingship is ruled out in this heading even after his death, but whatever the political intent of the poem when it was composed, the Church has placed the events described and the battle into a much more consistent context and has assimilated the hero. Arguments in criticism about whether the work is Germanic-heroic or Latin-Christian are less than relevant, since the work is both. Louis behaves like an idealized Frankish warrior king, but he does this in a Christian framework, defending his own people, who are also God's people—God tells him this.

The Old High German *Ludwigslied,* concerned with a contemporary event, is comparable not only to Latin panegyrics but also to later battle poems, such as the Anglo-Saxon *Battle of Maldon,* or the French *Chanson de Roland* (*Song of Roland*) in its Christianization. It may have been intended as propaganda, but it uses historical analysis in describing and also explaining given events. It has survived as a memorial to a victorious Christian warrior hero.

BRIAN MURDOCH

See also Old High German

Further Reading

Bostock, John Knight, *A Handbook on Old High German Literature,* Oxford: Clarendon Press, 1955; 2nd edition revised by K.C. King and D.R. McLintock, 1976 (with translation of the poem)

Braune, Wilhelm, editor, *Althochdeutsches Lesebuch,* Tübingen: Niemeyer, 16th edition revised by Ernst Ebbinghaus, 1979 (includes the poem)

Combridge, Rosemary N., et. al., editors, *"Mit regulu bithuungan": Neue Arbeiten zur althochdeutschen Poesie und Sprache,* Göppingen: Kümmerle, 1989

Groseclose, J. Sidney, and Murdoch, Brian O., *Die althochdeutschen poetischen Denkmäler,* Stuttgart: Metzler, 1976

Harvey, Ruth, "The Provenance of the Old High German Ludwigslied," *Medium Aevum* 14 (1945)

Murdoch, Brian, "Saucourt and the Ludwigslied," *Revue belge de philologie et d'histoire* 55 (1977)

———, *The Germanic Hero,* London and Rio Grande, Ohio: Hambledon, 1996

Schlosser, Horst Dieter, editor, *Althochdeutsche Literatur,* Frankfurt: Fischer, 1970; revised edition, 1989 (includes poem)

Schwarz, Werner, "The *Ludwigslied*: A Ninth-Century Poem," *Modern Language Review* 42 (1947)

Steinmeyer, Elias von, editor, *Die kleineren althochdeutschen Sprachdenkmäler,* 1916; reprinted as 2nd edition, Berlin: Weidmann, 1963 (includes poem)

Georg Lukács 1885–1971

Born into a prominent Hungarian-Jewish banking family, Georg (György) Lukács became one of the 20th century's foremost Marxist theorists and is considered a principal influence in the development of socialist realism. His voluminous publications address literary studies, literary theory, philosophy, political theory, and economics. Spanning nearly 70 years, his career is commonly divided into three periods: 1902–18, 1919–56, and 1957–71. The two junctures were created by his decision to join the Communist Party (December 1918) and his half-year imprisonment (1956–57) and ten-year suspension of party membership following the failed Hungarian uprising of 1956. Each of these breaks in his career was accompanied by a new direction, or new focus, in his writings, but in spite of historical vicissitudes and their impact on Lukács's life, the thematic content of his works, along with his literary taste, remained remarkably consistent.

Already a public figure in his late teens, Lukács's career began in 1902 with reviews of contemporary dramas written for prestigious Hungarian literary journals, such as *Magyar Szalon.* His first "serious" work, an essay on Novalis published in 1907 by *Nyugat* (West), was subsequently combined with nine other essays and appeared as a book both in Hungarian and in German. This first book, *Die Seele und die Formen: Essays* (1911; *Soul and Form*), also marked the beginning of Lukács's turn to German, which he subsequently used almost exclusively for works with international relevance and scope.

Soul and Form, often interpreted as a collection of unconnected essays reflecting Lukács's "romantic anti-capitalist" phase (Löwy), postulates the freedom of the "essay" as a form and uses this freedom both to evoke the mood of (neo)Romanticism and to pay homage to its luminaries (e.g., Laurence Sterne, Novalis, Kierkegaard, and Stefan George). But the lyrical tone masks Lukács's self-reflexive skepticism: despite his attraction to the spirit of Romanticism, Lukács distances himself by stressing the aesthetic and hence ethical danger implicit in the movement's increasingly radical abandonment of form. These seminal essays thereby set up the paradox evident in most of Lukács's subsequent writings, a paradox that has complicated the task of his interpreters. Although he criticized the socially alienating effect of modernity and advocated cultural renewal and even political revolution, Lukács remained aesthetically conservative, rejecting not only Romanticism (and its descendants) but ironically even those movements such as Expressionism, whose aesthetic programs embodied the very revolution he sought. Instead, Lukács increasingly advocated the literary products of the "great" 19th-century European "realists," especially Balzac and Tolstoy, chronologically flanked by Goethe and Thomas Mann.

While Lukács's literary canon became entrenched only after his conversion to Marxism, his revolutionary antibourgeois stance is already evident in *Esztétikai kultúra* (1913; *Aesthetic Culture*), his last major work in Hungarian. Originally an essay from 1910, it attacks bourgeois decadence and calls for the destruction of Western culture at the hands of the proletariat. This "anticapitalist," although hardly "romantic" (in the conventional sense) rhetoric sets up Lukács's later acceptance of the Russian Revolution and even Lenin's Bolshevism.

The years surrounding the outbreak of World War I were dominated by the planned book on Dostoevskii, which would also reflect Lukács's fascination with Russia. While in Heidelberg, shortly before the outbreak of the war, Lukács's membership in Max Weber's circle augmented his interest in sociological processes, such as those suggested by Ferdinand Tönnies, who argued that original human organization had been *communal,* replaced in the modern West by *society.* For Lukács, preindustrial Russia was still a *community* and could function as a beacon to the West because it had not yet become "corrupted." This essential quality of hope was most clearly evident in Dostoevskii's novels.

Lukács never completed his book on Dostoevskii, although extensive notes (*Dostojewski Notizen,* 1985) were found in a bank vault and published posthumously. Instead, he wrote the extended essay *Die Theorie des Romans* (1920; *The Theory of the Novel*), which continues to be an original and relevant examination of the novel, viewed from a historical and sociological perspective. Although it ends with an invocation to Dostoevskii, *Theory of the Novel*'s main task is to expand on Hegel's thesis that the novel is modernity's variant of the ancient epic. While the epic was first sung, then written, in verse and reflected the "totality" of an age during which the individual was "at one" with the cosmos, the novel—written in prose—reflects prosaic modernity in which God is dead and mankind, cast adrift, suffers from "transcendental homelessness." While the novel—like its ancestor the epic—attempts to portray "totality," the reality of modernity undermines the possibility that this portrayal can be successfully achieved. Novels therefore focus either on the introspective self-absorbed individual or on episodic adventure. The only novel that Lukács considered at least a partial reintegration of this interior/exterior split is Goethe's *Wilhelm Meisters Lehrjahre* (1795; *Wilhelm Meister's Apprenticeship*).

The outbreak of the Russian Revolution was initially welcomed by Lukács's intellectual circle (the "Sunday Circle"), although Lukács subsequently wrote against the radical ethic of Bolshevism ("Bolshevism as a Moral Problem," 1918). But by the time this attack was published, Lukács had nevertheless joined the Communist Party, surprising his colleagues with his sudden change of mood and causing one to remark "Saul became Paul." Lukács scholarship ever since has tended to accept his decision as a "leap of faith," constituting a "radical break" with the past, thereby disregarding clear indications in his pre-1918 publications of an explicit "road to Marx."

Several essays followed during early 1919 that deal with tactical issues concerning the practical implementation of Marxism. These accompanied Lukács's political activities as a commissar during the short-lived Hungarian Soviet of 1919. Lukács used his position to confiscate private art collections and to order the court-martial and public execution of eight soldiers who had reportedly deserted their posts. After the Béla Kun government collapsed, Lukács was forced to flee Hungary and seek asylum in Vienna, where he was arrested for a short period.

The 1920s were highlighted by *Geschichte und Klassenbewußtsein* (1923; *History and Class Consciousness*), considered by many to be the most significant work of theoretical Marxism since *Das Kapital.* The work was not well received in Moscow at the Fifth Comintern Congress, where Lukács was accused of straying from orthodoxy, because he showed Hegel—especially the dialectical method—to be an important precursor of Marxism, even though Marx had declared Hegel a "dead dog."

During the 1930s, after a brief stay in Berlin (1931–33), Lukács took up residence in the Soviet Union, where he would stay until the occupation of Budapest by the Red Army in 1945. Following the politically damaging publication of his *Blum-Theses* (1928), which theorizes "democratic dictatorship," Lukács returned to literary studies. This same period (1933–45) also poses ongoing problems for Lukács's scholarship because of essentially unresolvable questions concerning his acceptance of and complicity in Stalin's regime. By his own subsequent admission, Lukács was the only Hungarian intellectual residing in the Soviet Union who did not fall victim to the purges and who returned alive to Hungary after the war. Much of his literary analysis is "tainted" with gratuitous comments echoing Stalinist rhetoric. Lukács insisted that he was obliged to insert "crude Stalinisms" to ensure publication. Nevertheless, in the 1968 interview that formed the basis of his (auto)biography *Gelebtes Denken* (1981; *Record of a Life*), he admitted that he still agreed with Stalin on many issues, including his opposition to Trotsky, the policy of "socialism in one country," and the purges against Bukharin and others.

Lukács's defenders argue that his preoccupation with literature—especially Goethe of the Weimar period—was simultaneously a retreat from political activity and a gesture advocating the humanistic and cosmopolitan ideals of Germany's most "European" author (Fehér). During these Moscow years, Lukács wrote the essay collection *Goethe und seine Zeit* (1947; *Goethe and His Age*), the *Faust-Studien* (1940; as "Faust Studies," in *Goethe and His Age*), the influential *Der historische Roman* (1955; *The Historical Novel*), and *Der junge Hegel* (1948; *The Young Hegel*). His central preoccupation was the study of "realism" and defense of the 19th-century bourgeois-realistic tradition, which was under attack from the newly emerging socialist-realist school. Lukács based his defense of "bourgeois" literature on the newly discovered "*Realism*"-letter written in 1888 from Friedrich Engels to Margaret Harkness, wherein Engels describes the "triumph of realism" in works by authors such as Balzac who, despite their own class background and political leanings, nevertheless portrayed the social realities of a decaying society and its ills. The "great" realists, Lukács similarly argued, shared this ability to portray society commensurate with and reflective of the Marxian critique and in harmony with a Marxist teleological historiography. Such validations of Marxist theory came from non-Marxist or even pre-Marxist authors such as Goethe, Walter Scott, Balzac, Tolstoy, Keller, Storm, Fontane, and Thomas Mann—"great realists" who were like the "great elephants living in the plains," as compared with the rabbits (socialist realists) on the mountain peak. Just because they are at a higher elevation (level of consciousness), Lukács explained, the rabbits should not think themselves greater than the elephants. This comparison, consistent with Lukács's literary taste, underscores the aesthetic conservatism he preached.

During the Moscow years, Lukács also began to recharacterize Sturm und Drang (Storm and Stress), the literary period commonly perceived as a pre-Romantic revolt against the strictures of Enlightenment rationalism. However, Lukács wanted to argue that, even as a young "Stürmer und Dränger," Goethe had consistently supported the basic populist, antiabsolutist ideals expressed subsequently by the French Revolution. This necessitated a redefinition of Sturm und Drang as being a phase—albeit extreme—within the Enlightenment and faithful to its fundamental goal, which stressed the development of the individual (*Skizze einer Geschichte der neueren deutschen Literatur*, 1953). Lukács's reading, also informed by the ongoing political-intellectual struggle between communism and fascism, polarized Western thought into two camps. On the one side was Enlightenment rationalism (including Sturm und Drang), which culminated with Marx, Lenin, and Stalin (whom Lukács considered to be "hyper-rational"), while on the other side ran a reactionary countercurrent of irrationalism, specifically in German thought, stretching from Romanticism to fascism, evident in Novalis, Schopenhauer, Wagner, Nietzsche, Spengler, and culminating in Hitler. This strand of thought was responsible for the "destruction of reason" evident in 20th-century German politics and art, a thesis Lukács presented in a much-criticized book *Die Zerstörung der Vernunft* (1954; *The Destruction of Reason*).

While the ideological stamp of Lukács's post-1918 writings is evident, it is interesting that they delineate the same aesthetic already formulated in the 1907 "Novalis" essay, the same position he advocated in the famous "Expressionism-debate" between Brecht and Lukács, conducted in the literary journal *Das Wort* during 1937–38 and continued in his published correspondence with socialist author Anna Seghers in 1938–39. While Brecht argued that Joyce, Döblin, and Kafka were worthy models for socialist realist writers, Lukács dismissed their works as distortions of reality and Expressionism itself as empty formalism. Lukács later praised Brecht at his death in 1956, and while imprisoned in a Romanian castle (1956–57), Lukács supposedly remarked that "Kafka was a realist" after all.

The years from 1957 until his death of cancer in 1971 were devoted to multivolume works on aesthetics, ethics, and ontology, in order to complete the comprehensive foundation of theoretical Marxism as a total system. Lukács also witnessed the major revival of interest in *History and Class Consciousness*, reprinted in 1968 in volume two of Luchterhand's planned edition of his complete works (*Werke*) and used as a handbook of sorts by the student movements, especially by neo-Marxists such as Herbert Marcuse. Lukács had already influenced the founding members of the Frankfurt School—Theodor Adorno and Max Horkheimer—who were especially indebted to Lukács's earlier writings, to his conception of reification, and to his ideological linkage between capitalism and fascism, even if they were aesthetically less conservative and philosophically more willing to see tensions within the Enlightenment itself.

While Lukács's perceived relevance has fluctuated with the political fortunes of Marxism, his publications on the novel and on certain authors remain exemplary analyses using a Marxist methodology. As one of the 20th century's most notable intellectuals, Lukács's writings eloquently mirror 70 years of cultural history, from fin de siècle ennui to the politically polarized world of the Cold War. No history of German literature or its reception during the 20th century can be complete without reference to his work.

NICHOLAS VAZSONYI

See also Marx and Marxism

Biography

Born in Budapest, 13 April 1885. Ph.D. at the University of Budapest, 1906; studied privately with Heinrich Rickert in Heidelberg, 1912–15; commissar for public education under Béla Kun, 1919; with the Marx-Engels-Lenin Institute, Moscow, 1929–30; researcher with the Institute of Philosophy, Soviet Academy of Sciences, Moscow, 1933–44; professor of aesthetics and cultural philosophy, University of Budapest, 1945–56; Minister of Culture under Imre Nagy, 1956. Goethe Prize, 1970. Died in Budapest, 4 June 1971.

Selected Works

Collections
Werke, 1962–

Nonfiction
Die Seele und die Formen: Essays, 1911; as *Soul and Form*, 1974
Entwicklungsgeschichte des modernen Dramas, 2 vols., 1912; abridged version as *The Sociology of Modern Drama*, 1965
Esztétikai kultúra, 1913; translated as *Aesthetic Culture* in *The Lukács Reader*, edited by Arpad Kadarkay, 1995
Taktik und Ethik, 1919; selections as *The Question of Parliamentarianism and Other Essays*, 1972; as *Tactics and Ethics: Political Essays, 1919–1929*, 1975
Die Theorie des Romans: Ein geschichtsphilosophischer Versuch über die Formen der großen Epik, 1920; as *The Theory of the Novel: A Historico-Philosophical Essay on the Forms of Great Epic Literature*, 1971
Geschichte und Klassenbewußtsein: Studien über marxistische Dialektik, 1923; as *History and Class Consciousness: Studies in Marxist Dialectics*, 1971
Gottfried Keller, 1940
Faust-Studien, 1940; as "Faust Studies," in *Goethe and His Age*, 1978
Balzac, Stendhal, Zola, 1945
Goethe und seine Zeit, 1947; as *Goethe and His Age*, 1965
Der historische Roman, 1955; as *The Historical Novel*, 1962
Der junge Hegel: Über die Beziehungen von Dialektik und Ökonomie, 1948; as *The Young Hegel: Studies in the Relations between Dialectics and Economics*, 1975
Essays über Realismus, 1948; as *Studies in European Realism: A Sociological Survey of the Writings of Balzac, Stendhal, Zola, Tolstoy, Gorki, and Others*, 1950
Karl Marx und Friedrich Engels als Literaturhistoriker, 1948
Skizze einer Geschichte der neueren deutschen Literatur, 1953
Thomas Mann, 1949; as *Essays on Thomas Mann*, 1965
Existentialismus oder Marxismus? 1951
Deutsche Realisten des 19. Jahrhunderts, 1951
Balzac und der französische Realismus, 1952

Der russische Realismus in der Weltliteratur, 1952
Die Zerstörung der Vernunft, 1954; as *The Destruction of Reason,* 1980
Beiträge zur Geschichte der Ästhetik, 1954
Wider den missverstandenen Realismus, 1958; as *The Meaning of Contemporary Realism,* 1963; as *Realism in Our Time: Literature and the Class Struggle,* 1964
Schriften zur Literatursoziologie, edited by Peter Ludz, 1961
Die Eigenart des Ästhetischen, 2 vols., 1963
Deutsche Literatur in zwei Jahrhunderten, 1964
Der junge Marx: Seine philosophische Entwicklung von 1840 bis 1844, 1965
Schriften zur Ideologie und Politik, 1967
Die Grablegung des alten Deutschland: Essays zur deutschen Literatur des 19. Jahrhunderts, 1967
Frühschriften, 1967
Probleme des Realismus, 3 vols., 1967–71
Probleme der Ästhetik, 1969
Writer and Critic and Other Essays, 1971
Ästhetik, 4 vols., 1972
Marxism and Human Liberation: Essays on History, Culture, and Revolution, 1973
Frühe Schriften zur Ästhetik, 2 vols., 1974, 1975
Politische Aufsätze, 1975
Kurze Skizze einer Geschichte der neuen deutschen Literatur, edited by Frank Benseler, 1975
Kunst und objektive Wahrheit: Essays zur Literaturtheorie und Geschichte, 1977

Other

Levelézése [selected correspondence], 1981
Record of a Life: An Autobiographical Sketch, edited by István Eörsi, 1983

Georg Lukács: Selected Correspondence, 1902–1920, edited and translated by Judith Marcus and Zoltán Tar, 1986

Further Reading

Bernstein, J.M., *The Philosophy of the Novel: Lukács, Marxism, and the Dialectics of Form,* Brighton: Harvester, and Minneapolis: University of Minnesota Press, 1984

Fehér, Ferenc, "Lukács in Weimar," in *Lukács Reappraised,* edited by Agnes Heller, New York: Columbia University Press, 1983; as *Lukács Revisited,* Oxford: Blackwell, 1983

Gallée, Caroline, *Georg Lukács: Seine Stellung und Bedeutung im literarischen Leben des SBZ/DDR 1945–1985,* Tübingen: Stauffenberg, 1996

Gluck, Mary, *Georg Lukács and His Generation, 1900–1918,* Cambridge, Massachusetts: Harvard University Press, 1985

Kadarkay, Arpad, *Georg Lukács: Life, Thought, and Politics,* Oxford and Cambridge, Massachusetts: Basil Blackwell, 1991

Lapointe, François, *Georg Lukács and His Critics: An International Bibliography with Annotations (1910–1982),* Westport, Connecticut: Greenwood Press, 1983

Löwy, Michael, "Naphta or Settembrini? Lukács and Romantic Anticapitalism," *New German Critique* 42 (1987)

Marcus, Judith, "Georg Lukács and Thomas Mann: Reflections on a Relationship," in *Georg Lukács: Theory, Culture, and Politics,* edited by Judith Marcus and Zoltán Tarr, New Brunswick, New Jersey: Transaction Publishers, 1989

Pike, David, *Lukács and Brecht,* Chapel Hill: University of North Carolina Press, 1985

Sim, Stuart, *Georg Lukács,* New York: Harvester Wheatsheaf, 1994

Vazsonyi, Nicholas, *Lukács Reads Goethe: From Aestheticism to Stalinism,* Columbia, South Carolina: Camden House, 1997

Martin Luther 1483–1546

Not unlike the Italian Renaissance, the Reformation in Germany is one of those momentous events that profoundly changed the history of the Western world. It divided the Christian Church and put an end to the absolute authority that Roman Catholicism had exercised not only in religious matters but in all areas of human endeavor throughout the Middle Ages. It deeply affected European politics for the ensuing centuries, and it changed social and economic conditions in territories and states that adopted the new faith, but also in areas that remained loyal to Rome.

Luther's reforms were based on biblical exegesis: according to Luther, neither the writings of the Church fathers, nor the proclamations of Church Councils, nor the encyclicals of the Pope, but Scripture and Scripture alone contains evangelical truth. This premise also beckoned the common man to become a reader. The image of a Christian reader in search of a divine revelation embedded in a text foreshadows another image: that of a critical reader and a secular text. Since the truth to be found in Scripture must be discovered individually, the stage is set for the analogous scene: the individual, independent of all traditional authority, in search of a secular truth. To attribute to Protestantism a seminal role in the rise of the autonomous individual might be an overstatement, but it would be difficult to deny it a contributing function.

It is ironic that almost none of these effects of the Reformation were intended by its instigator. When Martin Luther, a monk and a professor of Bible at the University of Wittenberg, published his famous *Ninety-Five Theses* in 1517, he was extending an invitation to his learned colleagues to discuss his views on the sale of indulgences, the nature of penance, and divine grace. Like many others before him, he intended to reform the Church, not to break it apart. Luther presented his theses in a rather modest fashion. He did not question the authority of the Church to sell indulgences or the dogma upon which it was based. But he argued on biblical evidence that they could only relieve the sinner of those punishments imposed by the Church, and he condemned the practice of offering forgiveness for all conceivable sins, even those not yet committed, to anyone ready to pay for it.

Luther was certainly not the first to recognize the need for reforms. What distinguished him from his predecessors was that he was both an astute theologian and an effective popular publicist. Even that would not have spared him the fate of a Johan

Hus if it were not for the geopolitical circumstances in which he found himself and the widely held conviction that the millennium was near. The publication of the *Ninety-five Theses*, addressed to Albrecht von Mainz, probably displayed in Wittenberg, and sent to potential discussants, is generally regarded as the beginning of the Reformation. A German version, freed of the work's lengthy biblical justifications, stresses what has become the core of Lutheranism: the notion that human salvation is a gift from God and is freely given to the faithful. According to this view, man can prepare himself to become the vessel of faith, but the divine gift of faith is reserved for those whom the Holy Spirit chooses.

The theological and social implications of Luther's *sola fide* (by faith alone) are enormous. To realize that salvation is not the reward for a good and pious life but a result of the gift of faith is to feel free—freed from the canon of laws of the Old Testament and relieved of the "meritorious" if burdensome "good deeds" that had in various degrees become an integral part of every Christian's life from childhood to old age. Luther's interpretation of Paul (Romans 1:17 and 3:28), however, not only deprives the individual of the possibility to contribute toward his own salvation but also leaves the burning question of his ultimate fate unanswered. Although foreknown by God, the reason for human salvation or eternal damnation lies beyond human comprehension. The problem, whether human deeds have merit before God, involved Luther in an extended controversy with Erasmus; the question of man's ultimate fate—can he in his earthly existence be certain of salvation?—found an answer of sorts in the theologies of Müntzer and Calvin.

Intimately linked to the concept of salvation through faith alone is Luther's doctrine of a common priesthood of all believers. If the gift of faith lies beyond human comprehension, then saints, priests, or the Church itself cannot assume a mediatory role. Luther makes this point most forcefully in *An den christlichen Adel deutscher Nation* (1520; To the Christian Nobility of the German Nation). Through baptism, he argues, all Christians have become priests, and as such, their understanding of the evangelical message is as valid (or as false) as that of any other Christian. The ultimate authority in these exegetical matters thus rests not with the Pope, who claimed it, but in the Bible itself. And Luther does not fail to point out that this example of papal privilege has no scriptural basis, but is of human origin. It was, in fact, decreed in 1145 (*Decretum Gratiani*).

In 1520, Luther published three important papers: the programmatic *Address to the Christian Nobility*, the *De captivitate ecclesiae babylonica* (On the Babylonian Captivity of the Church), in which he espouses his views on the sacraments—instead of the traditional seven he posits in essence only one, Christ—and, in Latin and German, his *Von der Freyheyt egniss Christen menschen* (On the Freedom of a Christian). The latter work, conceived to placate Pope Leo X and dedicated to him, emphasizes the freedom of the elect, a freedom that can with equal justification be called the elect's bondage. But Pope and Curia were not placated. Their attempts to extradite the German heretic to stand trial in Rome, however, were thwarted by Elector Prince Frederick the Wise of Saxony, Luther's employer and sovereign. At his insistence, the disputations with the emissaries of the Curia took place on German soil. Even after the bull *Exsurge Domine* (i.e., the papal ban) had arrived in Wittenberg, the elector refused to abandon his protégé. He managed to obtain

free conduct for Luther so that he could defend himself at the Diet of Worms in 1521. Standing before the assembled dignitaries of the empire, Luther again refused to recant and repeated that he would accept no authority other than the Bible itself. In the Edict of Worms, the emperor's ban was added to the condemnation by the Church. Not only was Luther declared an outlaw, his writings were banished, and action was threatened against his supporters.

At this point, the undaunted Luther had become a popular hero in Germany. That a German monk had defied Rome and had firmly defended his convictions at Worms stirred popular sentiment. There is also a noticeable undercurrent in some of Luther's writings that seems aimed at creating feelings of national pride. His anti-Roman stance accounts for some of this; the message to his "dear Germans" that they were burdened with unjust financial obligations by a greedy and corrupt Roman clergy was eagerly received. It is also conceivable that the public forum afforded him by the Leipzig debate (with Eck), the confrontation with Cajetan in Augsburg, and the much publicized refusal to recant at the Diet of Worms all enhanced rather than diminished the cause of the new doctrine despite the condemnations that followed. It is not entirely clear if the protective measures of Frederick the Wise were necessary when he spirited the returning Luther to his castle in Thuringia. But it afforded the embattled Reformer some respite. Protected behind the walls of the Wartburg, he translated the New Testament from the original Greek into German.

Although the Edict of Worms threatened the existence of Lutheranism in its infancy, it failed to stop the spread of the Reformation. In 1524, Philipp of Hesse joined the Lutheran side. "Evangelical" reforms were introduced in northern and northeastern territories of the empire and in many imperial cities. This was accompanied by a considerable amount of social upheaval: church lands and monasteries were expropriated, and sacred images and statues were destroyed. There was a very real danger that the work of the reformers would be associated with mob rule. It is conceivable that Luther's repeated insistence on total obedience to all civil authority and, furthermore, his incredibly harsh condemnation of the very reasonable demands of the insurgent peasants in 1525 have their roots here. But true to his *sola scriptura* (through Scripture alone), he justifies his views with biblical quotations in both cases.

A second problem, one that plagues Protestantism to this day, has a doctrinal basis. To abolish the regulatory role of popes, church councils, and the priesthood in all doctrinal matters and to encourage every believer to discover on his own how God reveals Himself to him both render futile any attempt to establish a unified church. Sectarianism is the obvious consequence. This is one of the problems that occupied Luther until his death in 1546. Yet another, even more urgent matter was to gain legitimacy for his movement.

At the first Diet at Speyer (1526), Luther's supporters had negotiated a temporary standoff: until a final solution was found at a Council or National Assembly, individual princes were permitted to follow their own conscience in dealing with the Reformation. But the negotiated truce came to an end at the second meeting of the Diet in Speyer in 1529. An unexpectedly harsh and uncompromising proclamation by the absent Emperor was presented by his brother, Ferdinand II, with the result that the Catholic majority voted to repeal the decision of the previous

Diet. (It was discovered only in this century that Charles' Proclamation had never reached Speyer and that the document presented had been a forgery.) The objections of those members who had already introduced Lutheran reforms in their regions earned them the name "Protestants." Alliances of Protestant and of Catholic princes followed, and the ensuing War of Schmalkalden (1546) ended with a victory of the imperial Catholic armies.

The document that defined the new creed at the 1530 Diet of Augsburg, the *Confessio Augustana*, legitimized Lutherans but excluded Calvinists. It was authored primarily by Luther's close friend and ally, the humanist Melanchthon, while Luther followed the proceedings from the nearby fortress at Coburg. The formula that established a limited and very tenuous religious tolerance (at the 1555 Diet of Augsburg, after Luther's death), *cuius regio eius religio* (liberally translated: you must adopt the religion of your reigning prince), left the decision whether a territory was to join the Reformation to its ruling prince. Dissenters were to be allowed to leave the region.

At the end of his life, Luther could look back on some incredible achievements. By leaving monastic life and marrying Katharina von Bora, a former nun, he had relegated to history the valorization of a form of life that had existed for a millennium. He had completed (in 1534) and repeatedly revised his translation of the Bible. He had instituted a new church, and he had lived to see his followers gain legal acceptance from a reluctant emperor. But his record is not without blemish: as a polemicist, he seemed determined to outdo the worst offenders among his contemporaries in crudeness and vulgarity. And while he talks throughout most of his life in similar terms about the Pope, Catholics, Anabaptists, Turks, Jews, and other "heretics" and "heathens," there is a dramatic change in his attitude toward Jews in 1543. In this year, possibly because his hopes for mass conversions of Jews had not been realized, he published some of the worst anti-Semitic propaganda of his age, in which he suggested that synagogues be burned, Hebrew books be destroyed, and—if that did not yield results—Jews be driven out of the country "like mad dogs."

The religious peace concluded at the 1555 Diet of Augsburg (after Luther's death), with its acceptance of two denominations, was a far cry from postulates of religious tolerance of the European Enlightenment (e.g., Locke, Voltaire, and Lessing). The choice, afforded not to the individual but to the individual prince, did not forestall efforts to gain or regain new or old claims, but it strengthened an already existing process: a vitalization of regional, monarchical government at the expense of a centralized, imperial administration. It also ended the unity of church and state, which had been preserved throughout the Middle Ages and was later revived as a dream by Romantic thinkers in the 19th century.

GERD HILLEN

See also German Language; Religion and Literature

Biography

Born in Eisleben, Thuringia, 1483. Educated at Mansfeld, Magdeburg, and Eisenach; at the University of Erfurt, 1501–5; entered an Augustinian monastery in 1505; ordained in 1507; doctor of theology, University of Wittenberg, 1512; professor of philosophy at the University of Wittenberg, 1508; lectured at Erfurt, 1509–10; returned to teach at University of Wittenberg, 1512-18; published his 95 theses, 31 October 1517; publically burned a papal bull demanding retraction of his writings and lectures, 1520; excommunicated, 1520; appeared before the Imperial Diet at Worms, April 1521, where he was outlawed; translated the New Testament, 1522; married Katharina von Bora, 1525; active in the reorganization of the church of Saxony, 1526–29. Died 18 February 1546.

Selected Works

Collections
Werke [Weimar edition], edited by J.C.F. Knaake et al., 110 vols., 1883–
Works [American edition], edited by Jaroslav Pelikan and Helmut T. Lehmann, 55 vols., 1955–
Selections, edited by J. Dillenberger, 1961
Selected Political Writings, edited by J.M. Porter, 1974

Theological Writings
An den christlichen Adel deutscher Nation, 1520
De captivitate ecclesiae Babylonica (Von der babylonischen Gefangenschaft der Kirche), 1520
Von der Freyheyt eyniss Christen menschen, 1520
Ein Sendbrief von Dolmetschen, 1530
Tischreden, 1566

Poetry
Geystliche gesangk-Buchleyn, 1524 (hymns)
Enchiridion geystlicher geseng, 1524 (hymns); expanded edition, 1545

Translations
Bible (New Testament), 1522
Etliche Fabeln aus Esopo, 1530
Bible (Old Testament), 1534

Further Reading

Bainton, Roland Herbert, *Here I Stand: A Life of Martin Luther*, New York: Mentor, 1950; London: Hodder and Stoughton, 1951
Becker, Reinhard P., *German Humanism and Reformation*, New York: Continuum, 1982
Blickle, Peter, *Die Reformation im Reich*, Stuttgart: Ulmer, 1982; 2nd edition, 1992
Bornkamm, Heinrich, *Das Jahrhundert der Reformation: Gestalten und Kräfte*, Göttingen: Vandenhoeck und Ruprecht, 1961; 2nd edition, 1966
Brecht, Martin, *Martin Luther*, 2 vols., translated by James Schaff, Philadelphia, Pennsylvania: Fortress Press, 1985–93
Buck, August, editor, *Renaissance, Reformation: Gegensätze und Gemeinsamkeiten*, Wiesbaden: Harrassowitz, 1984
Buck, Lawrence P., and Jonathan W. Zophy, editors, *The Social History of the Reformation*, Columbus: Ohio State University Press, 1972
Edwards, Mark U., *Luther's Last Battles: Politics and Polemics, 1531–46*, Ithaca, New York, and London: Cornell University Press, 1983
Hoffmeister, Gerhart, editor, *The Renaissance and Reformation in Germany*, New York: Ungar, 1977
Hubatsch, Walther, editor, *Wirkungen der deutschen Reformation bis 1555*, Darmstadt: Wissenschaftliche Buchgesellschaft, 1967
Junghans, Helmar, *Martin Luther in Two Centuries: The Sixteeenth and the Twentieth*, translated by Katharina Gustavs and Gerald S. Krispin, St. Paul, Minnesota: Lutheran Brotherhood Foundation, 1992
Nipperdey, Thomas, *Reformation, Revolution, Utopie: Studien zum 16. Jahrhundert*, Göttingen: Vandenhoeck und Ruprecht, 1975
Todd, John Murray, *Luther: A Life*, London: Hamilton, and New York: Crossroads, 1982

M

Magdeburg, Mechthild von, *see* Mechthild von Magdeburg

Heinrich Mann 1871–1950

Although long overshadowed in critical esteem by his younger brother Thomas, Heinrich Mann was an independent, innovative writer with two major strengths: he wrote works of critical realism that attempted to re-create the essence of a whole society and satire that leaned toward the grotesque. He is thus closer to the French novel than to the German mainstream, which explains both critics' aloofness (although even Gottfried Benn praised his technique) and his slow assimilation into the German literary canon. His artistic pedigree contains the names of Flaubert (for the concept of the outsider-artist), Balzac and Zola (for the combination of social realism with monomaniacal grotesque), and Rousseau (for the spirit of 1789 and republican democracy) rather than any German ancestors. By gradual shifts of attitude, he went from being the eldest son of a respected senator of a Hanseatic city to becoming an honored cultural figure of a communist state. Always his own man, he rarely followed a literary fashion, whereas in social satire, activist essay writing, and the historical novel, he was an innovator at different periods. He saw writing as an ethical business, a project that involved improving the world. Two of his novels are famous—*Der Untertan* (1918; translated as *The Patrioteer, Little Superman, Man of Straw,* and *The Loyal Subject*), for its panorama of the Wilhelminian middle class, and *Professor Unrat* (1905; also published as *Der blaue Engel;* translated as *The Blue Angel*), which was the basis of the film *The Blue Angel.*

At 20, fashionably apolitical, he embraced decadent style, writing about interestingly pale fin de siècle ladies. A little later he penned cultural-political essays on the spiritualization of life through art in conservative periodicals; he even edited a reactionary magazine. With *Im Schlaraffenland* (1900; translated as *In the Land of Cockaigne* and *Berlin: The Land of Cockaigne*), he brought conservative attitudes to bear on modern society and discovered his satirical bent, attacking the selfish modern liberal capitalist. His awareness of how his admired France differed from Wilhelminian Germany then made him see the aim of ennobling society differently; at this time, his satire grew more full-blooded, and he concentrated henceforth on the use and misuse of power. *The Blue Angel,* his main early social-realist novel, develops his dialectic of the Second Reich: tyrant and subject. The small-town schoolmaster is a tyrannical accredited authority; but he is also a subject, a civil servant. When infatuation throws him out of his routine, he shows the repressed anarchist and looses a wave of hysteria and crime. In this work, Mann combines exact descriptions of a petty-minded society with zestful quirkiness. The next major project, spanning two decades, was the trilogy of the Wilhelminian mentality (*The Loyal Subject* on the middle class, *Die Armen* [1917; The Poor] on the workers, and *Der Kopf* [1925; The Head] on the makers and would-be makers of policy).

From about 1910, he wrote many essays to build an informed, progressive readership, believing that the creative writer has a public responsibility to preach reason and ethics. The programmatic *Geist und Tat* (Intellect and Deed), years ahead of its time, inaugurated activism, encouraging younger committed writers who, around 1919, seemed his protégés. His political stance at this time was that of an old-fashioned liberal, which made him seem dangerously radical to the authorities. From 1914 on, pacifist and antinationalist, he defiantly wrote essays on French topics, with scarcely veiled criticisms of contemporary Germany. *Die Armen* propounds an alliance of the liberal and the socialist.

In the chaos of 1918–19, Mann engaged in politics: at that time, he hoped that the working class would defend morality and democracy better than his own class. But he never wanted revolution; rather, he advocated honesty, reconciliation, social justice, and left-liberal leadership. A series of essays in 1923 bid for direct political influence. Mann satirized the powerful infla-tion speculator Hugo Stinnes in his small masterpiece *Kobes* (1925; Kobes), analyzing capitalist ideology in surrealist, expres-sive style. Hitler swept away all that Mann tried to do in the 1920s—supporting Franco-German reconciliation and a United States of Europe, producing political and cultural essays, presid-ing over the Sektion für Dichtkunst (Literature Section) of the Prussian Academy, campaigning against censorship and class justice, and fostering theater as an educational organ and film as an art for the masses. The varied, experimental 1920s novels largely failed to convince critics or the public; except for *Der Kopf*, the subject of some recent studies, they are still largely ne-glected. *Der Kopf* has been criticized for its rambling plot, ab-stractness, and confusing use of caricature and pastiche; Mann was convinced, however, that he had found a way to propagate morality in public life through literature.

When Hitler became *Reichskanzler*, Mann fled to France; his works were burned by the Nazis. Moving leftward again, he es-poused an almost communistic theory of fascism as the continua-tion of capitalist pseudodemocracy; as the Soviet Union seemed the only power willing to oppose Hitler, Mann set aside his suspi-cions and hailed it as successor to the spirit of the French Revolu-tion. Active in the Popular Front and integrated into the French critical intelligentsia, he wrote political articles and his great con-tribution to the historical novel, *König Henri IV* (*Die Jugend des Königs Henri Quatre* [1935; translated as *Young Henry of Navarre*, *The Youth of Henri IV*, and *King Wren: The Youth of Henri IV*]; *Die Vollendung des Königs Henri Quatre* [1938; translated as *Henri Quatre, King of France*, and *Henry, King of France*]). The 16th-century ruler appears as a revolutionary from above and model humanitarian ruler who harnesses the people's goodness and the advice of thinkers: Henri is a utopian, humane contrast to the cult of Hitler. Mann's theory of world improve-ment appears here in a rather pessimistic form: the common peo-ple need to be raised to the level of intellect before they can exercise power responsibly. The novel was praised by Georg Lukács as progressive and compatible with socialist realism.

Forced to flee Europe, yet unable to reach the American public with his subsequent works, Mann had no use for the United States. He completed the complex, unusually structured mem-oirs *Ein Zeitalter wird besichtigt* (1945; An Age Is Inspected), again demanding revolution from above—with Henri and Lenin as models. After the war, the award of the East German *Nationalpreis*, with the offer of the presidency of the revived Prussian Academy, touched him. Despite doubts, he would have gone to East Germany—if it had not been for his death—pre-sumably to resume, to the discomfort of the government, his role as the conscience of the society.

Seen as too political, Mann was long disregarded in West Ger-many. Only the leftward movement of the 1960s and the cente-nary of his birth in 1971 brought about wider interest, some television adaptations, and research activity. Gradually, his avant-garde works were studied alongside the more accessible ones.

ALFRED D. WHITE

Biography

Born in Lübeck, 27 March 1871. Brother of the writer Thomas Mann. Apprentice in the Dresden firm of Zahn and Jaensch, booksellers, 1889–91; worked for S. Fischer, publisher, in Berlin, 1891; in a sanatorium for tuberculosis, Germany and Switzerland, 1891–93; in France, Italy, and Munich, 1893–94; in Rome and Palestrina with Thomas Mann, 1895–96; in Rome, 1896–98; in Northern Italy, Tyrol, and Munich, 1898–1910; in southern France, northern Italy, and Munich, 1910–14; editor of *Das zwanzigste Jahrhundert*, 1895–96; alienated from brother Thomas Mann, 1914–22; in Munich, 1914–25; in Munich and Berlin, 1925–28; in Berlin, 1928–33; during 1920s, journalistic and lecturing work; chairman of the *Volksverband für Filmkunst*, Berlin, 1928; president of the literary section of the Prussian Academy, 1931 (dismissed 1933); German citizenship revoked, 1933; Czech citizen, 1935; in exile in Nice, 1933–40; leader of and writer for *Dépêche de Toulouse*; president of the *Bund freiheitlicher Sozialisten*, 1937; flees via Spain to the United States, 1940; in Los Angeles, California, 1940–50; writer for Warner Brothers Film Studios, Hollywood, California, 1940–41. Honorary doctorate from Humboldt University, Berlin, 1947; German National Prize, first class, GDR, 1949; president of Academy of Arts, GDR, 1950. Died in Santa Monica, California, 12 March 1950.

Selected Works

Collections

Gesammelte Werke, 4 vols., 1909
Gesammelte Romane und Novellen, edited by Kurt Wolff, 10 vols., 1917
Drie Akte: Der Tyrann; Die Unschuldige; Varieté, 1918
Gasammelte Werke, edited by Paul Zsolnay, 13 vols., 1925–32
Ausgewählte Werke in Einzelausgaben, edited by Alfred Kantorowicz and Heinz Kamnitzer, 13 vols., 3 supplements, 1951–62
Gesammelte Werke in Einzelausgaben, 18 vols., 1 supplement, 1958–88
Gesammelte Werke, edited by Sigrid Anger, 1965–
Werkauswahl, 10 vols., 1976
Studienausgabe in Einzelbänden, 1986–
Gesammelte Werke in Einzelbänden, 1994–

Fiction

In einer Familie, 1894; revised edition, 1924
Das Wunderbare und andere Novellen (stories), 1897
Ein Verbrechen und andere Geschichten (stories), 1898
Im Schlaraffenland, 1900; as *In the Land of Cockaigne*, translated by Axton D.B. Clark, 1929; as *Berlin: The Land of Cockaigne*, translated by Clark, 1929
Die Göttinnen; oder, Die drei Romane der Herzogin von Assy, 1903; Part I only as *Diana*, translated by E. Posselt and E. Glore, 1929
Die Jagd nach Liebe, 1903
Professor Unrat; oder, Das Ende eines Tyrannen, 1905; as *Der blaue Engel*, 1947; as *The Blue Angel*, translated anonymously, 1931; translated by Wirt Williams, 1959; as *Small Town Tyrant*, translated by Wirt Williams, 1944
Flöten und Dolche (stories), 1905
Mnais und Ginevra (stories), 1906
Schauspielerin (stories), 1906
Stürmische Morgen (stories), 1906
Zwischen den Rassen, 1907
Die Bösen (stories), 1908
Die kleine Stadt, 1909; as *The Little Town*, translated by Winifred Ray, 1930
Das Herz (stories), 1910
Die Rückkehr vom Hades (stories), 1911
Auferstehung, 1913
Novellen, 2 vols., 1917
Die Armen, 1917
Bunte Gesellschaft (stories), 1917
Der Untertan, 1918; edited by Peter-Paul Schneider, 1993; as *The Patrioteer*, translated by Ernest Boyd, 1921; as *Little Superman*,

translated by Boyd, 1945; as *Man of Straw,* translated by Boyd, 1947; as *The Loyal Subject,* translated by Boyd, adapted, with new portions translated by Daniel Theisen, edited by Helmut Peitsch, 1998

Der Sohn, 1919

Die Ehrgeizige (stories), 1920

Die Tote und andere Novellen (stories), 1921

Abrechnungen (stories), 1924

Der Jüngling (stories), 1924

Der Kopf, 1925

Kobes, 1925

Liliane und Paul, 1926

Mutter Marie, 1927; as *Mother Mary,* translated by Whittaker Chambers, 1928

Eugénie; oder, die Bügerzeit, 1928; as *The Royal Woman,* translated by Arthur J. Ashton, 1930

Sie sind jung (stories), 1929

Die große Sache, 1930

Ein ernstes Leben, 1932; as *The Hill of Lies,* translated by Edwin and Willa Muir, 1934

Die Welt der Herzen (stories), 1932

Die Jugend des Königs Henri Quatre, 1935; as *Young Henry of Navarre,* translated by Eric Sutton, 1937; as *The Youth of Henri IV,* 1937; as *King Wren: The Youth of Henri IV,* translated by Eric Sutton, 1937

Die Vollendung des Königs Henri Quatre, 1938; as *Henri Quatre, King of France,* translated by Eric Sutton, 1938–39; as *Henry, King of France,* translated by Sutton, 1939

Lidice, 1943

Der Atem, 1949

Empfang bei der Welt, 1956

Die traurige Geschichte von Friedrich dem Großen: Fragment, 1960

Plays

Die Unschuldige, in *Das Herz,* 1910

Der Tyrann (produced 1910), in *Die Bösen,* 1918

Schauspielerin, 1911

Die große Liebe, 1912

Madame Legros (produced 1917), 1913

Brabach (produced 1919), 1917

Varieté, in *Drei Akte,* 1918

Der Weg zur Macht (produced 1920), 1919

Das gastliche Haus (produced 1927), 1924

Bibi (produced 1928), in *Sie sind jung,* 1929

Szenen aus dem Nazileben, in *Der Haß,* 1933

Die Rede, in *Es kommt der Tag,* 1936

Das Strumpfband, 1965

Other

Eine Freundschaft: Gustave Flaubert und George Sand (essays), 1905

Macht und Mensch (essays), 1919

Diktatur der Vernunft: Reden und Aufsätze (essays), 1923

Sieben Jahre: Chronik der Gedanken und Vorgänge (essays), 1929

Geist und Tat: Franzosen 1780–1930 (essays), 1931

Fünf Reden und eine Entgegnung zum sechzigsten Geburtstag, 1931

Das öffentliche Leben (essays), 1932

Der Haß: Deutsche Zeitgeschichte (essays), 1933

Der Sinn dieser Emigration, 1934

Es kommt der Tag: Deutsches Lesebuch, 1936

Hilfe für die Opfer des Faschismus: Rede 1937, 1937

Was will die deutsche Volksfront? 1937

Mut (essays), 1939

Ein Zeitalter wird besichtigt (autobiography), 1945

Briefe an Karl Lemke 1917 bis 1949, 1963

Briefe an Karl Lemke und Klaus Pinkus, 1963

Briefwechsel 1900–1949, with Thomas Mann, edited by Ulrich Dietzel, 1969; also edited by Hans Wysling, 1968; extended edition, 1984; 3rd extended edition, 1995

Verteidigung der Kultur: Antifaschistische Streitschriften und Essays, 1971

Briefe an Ludwig Ewers 1889–1913, edited by Ulrich Dietzel and Rosmarie Eggert, 1980

Briefwechsel, with Barthold Fles, edited by Madeleine Rietra, 1993

Translations

Alfred Capus, *Wer zuletzt lacht,* 1901

Anatole France, *Komödiantengeschichte,* 1904

Choderlos de Laclos, *Gefährliche Freundschaften,* 1905; as *Schlimme Liebschaften,* 1920; as *Gefährliche Liebschaften,* 1926

Edited Work

The Living Thoughts of Nietzsche, 1939

Further Reading

Allison, J.E., "An Analysis of the Nietzschean Wille zur Macht, as portrayed in Heinrich Mann's *Professor Unrat,*" *New German Studies* 7, no. 3 (1979)

Gross, David, *The Writer and Society: Heinrich Mann and Literary Politics in Germany 1890–1940,* Atlantic Highlands, New Jersey: Humanities Press, 1980

Haupt, Jürgen, *Heinrich Mann,* Stuttgart: Metzler, 1980

Jasper, Willi, *Der Bruder: Heinrich Mann—eine Biographie,* Munich: Hanser, 1992

Metzger, Michael M., "Heinrich Mann," in *German Fiction Writers 1885–1913,* edited by James N. Hardin, Detroit, Michigan: Gale Research, 1988

Sommer, Fred, "Nostalgia, Francophilia, and the Agony of Hitlerism: The Autobiographies of Heinrich Mann and Stefan Zweig," *New German Studies* 16, no. 2 (1990–91)

Der Untertan 1918

Novel by Heinrich Mann

Der Untertan (translated as *The Patrioteer, Little Superman, Man of Straw,* and *The Loyal Subject*), Heinrich Mann's devastating satire of the German bourgeois, the obsequious but opportunistic loyal subject of Kaiser Wilhelm II in the 1890s, had appeared in serialization from January to August 1914, when at the outbreak of World War I, editor and author, anticipating censorship, agreed to abruptly terminate publication without any explanation to the readers. Shortly after the defeat of Germany in November 1918, *The Loyal Subject* was published in a first edition of 100,000 copies, which were sold in only a few weeks; in the numerous reviews that appeared throughout central Europe, Mann's controversial novel was either praised as a brilliant satire and prophetic work (prophesying the German chauvinism that culminated in the war) or criticized as literary pamphleteering that had been inspired by the author's alleged hatred of Germany. Mann himself received not only open letters of condemnation but also death threats from reactionary circles.

Mann develops his main character, Diederich Heßling, whose name suggests a hateful (*Haß*) and repulsive (*häßlich*) person, through childhood (with an authoritarian father, whom he fears, but admires, and a doting, sentimental mother, whom he scorns), school (fearing his teacher, but bullying a Jewish classmate), and university (drinking with his neo-Teuton fraternity brothers and learning to shout praises of the kaiser and to quote his denunciations of such "subversive enemies" as socialists, liberals, and Jews). When Heßling returns home to Netzig (the related word "Netz" has the figurative meaning of "hick-town") to take over his deceased father's paper factory, he proceeds to conquer (*erobern*) the community for the kaiser by ruining leaders of the liberal establishment in court cases involving lèse-majesté and libel over a fraudulent land deal and by conspiring with the (equally unscrupulous) Social Democratic foreman in his factory to defeat the liberals in the local elections.

In his rise to local power, Heßling is satirically portrayed as a mini-kaiser, with the same threatening mustache turned up at right angles, the same eyes flashing with catlike ferocity, and, above all, the same pontifical manner of speaking. Whether admonishing his factory workers, testifying in court cases against liberal defendants, accepting admission to the Veterans' Association (even though he never served in the military), or exhorting the "good," "loyal" citizens of the Kaiser's Party against the "unpatriotic elements" of the People's Party, Heßling quotes incessantly from the kaiser's own public pronouncements, and this relentless satire culminates in Heßling's oration at the end of the novel when he dedicates a monument to the centenary of the kaiser's grandfather, Wilhelm I (1797–1888). Ironically, however, his speech is drowned out by a torrential rain, which forces Heßling and his audience to disperse. On the way home, Heßling checks the house he has rented to Herr Buck, the veteran of the failed 1848 Revolution and grand old man of Netzig, whom he has ruined politically and financially. Old Buck, who is on his deathbed, expires at the sight of Heßling appearing in the doorway, and one of those in attendance cries out: "He has seen something! He has seen the Devil!" With Old Buck, liberalism dies in Netzig, just as its last chance in the Kaiserreich had been lost with the premature death of the liberal Kaiser Friedrich III and the accession of his son, Wilhelm II, to the throne in 1888.

Perhaps only Mann's earlier novel *Professor Unrat* (1905; translated as *The Blue Angel* and *Small Town Tyrant*), a bitter satire of the pedantic and tyrannical schoolmaster of the day, is better known today than *The Loyal Subject*, but the former's reputation is based more on the later film version (1930) under the title *Der blaue Engel* (shot simultaneously in English as *The Blue Angel*), with Emil Jannings and Marlene Dietrich in the principal roles. The East German film version (by Wolfgang Staudte, 1951) of *Der Untertan*, however, is but another document in the controversial reception of this novel to the present day.

Late in life, Mann noted, with both irony and annoyance, that the Germans published and reprinted his novel whenever they lost a war. Indeed, *Der Untertan* was a best-seller again after World War II. At first, however, it only achieved this popularity in East Germany, where it was celebrated as the original antifascist novel, while in West Germany, and now in reunited Germany, the novel has remained subject to a fierce debate over its historical accuracy, prophetic vision, and literary quality. Diederich Heßling is considered to be either "the quintessential Wilhelminian German" or too "bad" to be "true"; *The Loyal Subject* is ranked by some among the great works of world literature but dismissed by others who claim that satire is by definition an inferior form of art.

The Loyal Subject was the first of Mann's novels to be translated into English; the different English titles reflect the changing reception of the original. Published in 1921, *The Patrioteer* (a recently coined word, analogous to "profiteer") accentuated the German chauvinism that led to World War I. When it was reissued in 1945, the novel was again interpreted as a prophetic work, this time anticipating Nazism. The new title, *Little Superman,* a translation of Nietzsche's "Übermensch," which, unfortunately, may have reminded American readers more of the comic-strip hero created in the 1930s, ironically characterized the "little" or "typical" German who enthusiastically supported Hitler. *Man of Straw* (1947) identifies the representative main character as a straw image of the kaiser, thus returning the novel to its historical focus; similar to the first two titles, however, it is not as accurate a translation as *The Loyal Subject* (1998), which exposes the inherent incompatibility of the subject-ruler relationship with a democratic society. It is the critical treatment of this conflict between authority and democratic principles that makes *The Loyal Subject* one of the great political novels of the 20th century.

FREDERICK BETZ

Editions

First edition: *Der Untertan,* Leipzig: Wolff, 1918

Critical editions: in *Gesammelte Werke,* edited by Sigrid Anger, vol. 7, Berlin: Aufbau, 1965; edited by Peter-Paul Schneider, Frankfurt: Fischer Taschenbuch, 1991; Munich: Deutscher Taschenbuch, 35th printing, 1993, with companion volume of *Erläuterungen und Dokumente,* by Frederick Betz, Stuttgart: Reclam, 1993

Translations: *The Patrioteer,* translated by Ernest Boyd, New York: Harcourt Brace, 1921. Boyd's translation was later reissued under two different titles: *Little Superman,* New York: Creative Age Press, 1945, and *Man of Straw,* London and New York: Hutchinson International Authors, 1947; *Man of Straw,* Harmondsworth and New York: Penguin, 1984; *Man of Straw,* London, New York: Penguin Books, 1992. In the 1947, 1984, and 1992 editions, Boyd, who died in 1946, is no longer identified as the translator. Boyd's outdated, inadequate, and incomplete translation has now been adapted, with new portions translated by Daniel Theisen, and edited by Helmut Peitsch, under the title *The Loyal Subject,* New York: Continuum, 1998

Further Reading

Emmerich, Wolfgang, *Heinrich Mann: "Der Untertan,"* Munich: Fink, 1980

Hardaway, R. Travis, "Heinrich Mann's 'Kaiserreich'-Trilogy and His Democratic Spirit," *Journal of English and Germanic Philology* 53 (1954)

Kowal, Michael, "Heinrich Mann and *Der Untertan,*" *Nation* 225 (8 October 1977)

Scheuer, Helmut, "Heinrich Mann: *Der Untertan,*" in *Romane des 20. Jahrhunderts,* 2 vols., Stuttgart: Reclam, 1993

Siefken, Hinrich, "Emperor William II and His Loyal Subject: Montage and Historical Allusions in Heinrich Mann's Satirical Novel *Der Untertan,*" *Trivium* 8 (1973)

Thomas, Lionel, *Heinrich Mann's "Kaiserreich" Trilogy with Special Reference to Der Untertan,* Leeds: Leeds Philosophical and Literary Society, 1977

Klaus Mann 1906–1949

Klaus Heinrich Thomas Mann's middle names place him within a literary-familial constellation that both spurred and frustrated his literary aspirations. Both his father, Thomas Mann, and his uncle, Heinrich Mann, had a profound impact on Mann's literary works. With his father he shared a passion for Romantic irrationalism and doomed eroticism that culminated in death; with his uncle he shared a love of French cosmopolitanism and progressive politics. Mann's prolific body of writing included novels, plays, cabaret texts, journalism, essays, literary and political criticism, travel literature, biographies, and, despite the relatively brief duration of his life, three autobiographies. Most of his works were marked by controversy—several by scandal.

Mann's works may be divided into three groups. The first comprises his writings prior to 1932, which were a paean to youth, and which borrowed from Wedekind, Gide, Cocteau, and others whose works challenged established mores. His second and most productive period, during the years of the Third Reich, featured fictional and nonfictional antifascist writings that contained increasingly urgent calls for political engagement. Here, Mann moved from an aesthete to a moralist. The final phase of his writing was marked by deracination and despair; it consisted of diffuse literary fragments and translations of his earlier English-language works into German.

Klaus Mann's first novel, *Der fromme Tanz* (1925; *The Pious Dance*), was intended, as Mann wrote in the book's foreword, "to be nothing more than an interpretation, expression, description, and confession of [the] younger generation, its urgency, its perplexity—and perhaps its high hopes." This statement summarizes Mann's central concerns throughout the 1920s. His dramas of that period (*Anja und Esther* [1925; Anja and Esther], *Revue zu Vieren* [1926; Four in Revue], and *Geschwister* [1930; Siblings]) are of negligible literary merit, but all enjoyed their own succès de scandale throughout Germany owing to their themes of adolescent longing, egotistic self-indulgence, and rebellion against sexual norms.

With the publication of his earliest writings, which also included a prose collection, *Vor dem Leben* (1925; Before Life), Mann was lambasted in the press for unabashedly exploiting his family connections. Following up on the notoriety attached to Klaus Mann's budding popularity, Bertolt Brecht jested in an essay, "The whole world knows Klaus Mann, the son of Thomas Mann. By the way, who is Thomas Mann?"

Recasting themselves as the "literary Mann twins," Mann and his sister Erika Mann, who were one year apart in age, traveled around the world. They financed their stays with two book-length travel accounts, *Rundherum* (1929; Roundabout) and *Das Buch von der Riviera* (1931; The Riviera Book). Mann's self-indulgent attitude found full expression in these works.

Mann's novels and biographies contain an unusually high degree of self-portraiture. His novelistic biographies of Alexander the Great (*Alexander: Roman der Utopie* [1929; *Alexander: A Novel of Utopia*]) and Tchaikovsky (*Symphonie pathétique: Ein Tschaikowsky-Roman* [1935; *Pathetic Symphony: A Novel about Tchaikovsky*]), and his books on King Ludwig of Bavaria (*Vergittertes Fenster* [1937; Barred Window]), and Gide (*André Gide and the Crisis of Modern Thought* [1943]) reveal nearly as

much about their author as their ostensible subjects. Mann's other novels are similarly self-revelatory; in *Treffpunkt im Unendlichen* (1932; Meeting Point in Infinity) alone, Mann creates three fictional counterparts for himself, including Richard, whose suicide in France prefigures Klaus Mann's own suicide 17 years later under eerily similar circumstances.

Klaus Mann had a penchant for committing even the minutest details of his life to paper, completing no fewer than three book-length autobiographies. The first of these, *Kind dieser Zeit* (1932; Child of the Times), was published when he was only 26. Although it is in part an unblushing celebration of himself, *Kind dieser Zeit* also contains insightful discussions devoted to issues of social and political significance. The second, *The Turning Point* (1942), which he wrote in English, was perhaps his finest work; the *Herald Tribune* compared its style and language to Proust and Virginia Woolf. As its subtitle suggests ("Thirty-five Years in This Century"), the book chronicles the turbulent era of which Mann was a part. The third, *Der Wendepunkt* (1952; The Turning Point), is Mann's own German translation of *The Turning Point*, which updated and revised the earlier work for a German readership. Moreover, Mann was a devoted diarist; his diaries have been published in six volumes (*Tagebücher*, 1989–91).

Although Mann continued to write novels in exile, including *Flucht in den Norden* (1934; *Journey into Freedom*) and *Der Vulkan* (1939; The Volcano), both of which depict the quandaries facing emigrants who grapple with life abroad and reflect on the political situation at home, he turned increasingly to journalism and lecturing to register his opposition to fascism directly.

After leaving Germany on 13 March 1933 (he appeared on the Third Reich's first blacklist [issued 23 April 1933] of banned authors, and he was officially expatriated on 1 November 1934), Mann spent his initial period abroad hovering near the German border. While in Amsterdam, he launched a journal in September 1933: *Die Sammlung* (The Collection). This journal became a leading voice of early German exile, and it is considered to be the finest cultural journal in German of its time. *Die Sammlung*'s original patrons were Aldous Huxley, André Gide, and Heinrich Mann. Conspicuous by his absence was Thomas Mann, who at that time feared formal affiliation with the exile community. After the journal folded in August 1935, Mann collaborated with his sister Erika Mann on her literary cabaret *Die Pfeffermühle* (The Peppermill), for which he composed songs and sketches. Mann emigrated to the United States in 1938.

Unlike many fellow émigrés, Mann acquired complete fluency in English soon after his arrival in the United States and became a well-regarded lecturer and journalist. He was also the co-author, with his sister Erika, of *Escape to Life* (1939) and *The Other Germany* (1940). Both works attempt to clarify the situation of German exiles. Mann lectured widely on political themes, reported from the front lines in Spain in 1938, served in the U.S. Army, and, in 1941, founded the English-language journal *Decision*, whose fusion of literary and political pieces took up the goals of *Die Sammlung*. Its illustrious contributors included W.H. Auden, Sherwood Anderson, Somerset Maugham,

Stephen Spender, and Jean-Paul Sartre. The journal succumbed to financial difficulties barely one year after its promising debut.

The novel that assured Mann's place in literary history was *Mephisto* (1936; *Mephisto*), a scathing satire about Germany under Hitler. This novel later entered the international limelight with an Academy Award-winning cinematic rendition by the Hungarian director István Szábo (1981). Subtitled "Novel of a Career," the book tells of an opportunistic actor who abandons moral and political scruples to rise to the top of the theater world. The main character, Hendrik Höfgen, unmistakably resembles Gustaf Gründgens, whose most famous stage role was Mephistopheles in Goethe's *Faust*. Critics contended that the book was a defamatory roman à clef, although Mann insisted that the characters were general *types* rather than specific *portraits*. After a series of libel suits in the 1960s and 1970s, *Mephisto* became the only book to be prohibited from publication in the Federal Republic of Germany. The publisher Rowohlt defied this prohibition by printing the novel in 1981, but this action met with no legal incident, and the work became a runaway best-seller and received acclaim from foreign editions in over 20 languages.

Mann's last known project, tellingly titled *The Last Day,* was planned as a novelistic dissection of Cold War tensions that drive Julian, the central character, to suicide. This project and other planned publications remained fragments when Mann, similar to several of his fictional counterparts, brought his own life to an end.

Beginning with the 1981 edition of *Mephisto* and extending throughout the 1990s, a Klaus Mann renaissance on both sides of the Atlantic has seen a spate of translations and reissues of the author's works, as well as critical essays and monographs.

SHELLEY FRISCH

Biography
Born in Munich, 1906. Son of the writer Thomas Mann. Worked as dramatist, novelist, essayist, theater critic, journalist, biographer, lecturer, and cabarettist; founded two journals, *Die Sammlung* and *Decision;* emigrated to the United States, 1938; mobilized the exile community in the fight against fascism. Died (suicide) in Cannes, 1949.

Selected Works

Novels
Der fromme Tanz, 1925; as *The Pious Dance,* translated by Laurence Senelick, 1987

Alexander: Roman der Utopie, 1929; as Alexander: A Novel of Utopia, translated by Marion Saunders, 1930
Treffpunkt im Unendlichen, 1932
Flucht in den Norden, 1934; as *Journey into Freedom,* translated by Rita Reil, 1936
Symphonie pathétique: Ein Tschaikowsky-Roman, 1935; as Pathetic Symphony: A Novel about Tchaikovsky, translated by Hermon Ould, 1938
Mephisto: Roman einer Karriere, 1936; as Mephisto, translated by Robin Smyth, 1977
Der Vulkan: Roman unter Emigranten, 1939

Dramatic Works
Anja und Esther, 1925
Revue zu Vieren, 1926
Geschwister, 1930; as *Siblings,* translated by Tania Alexander and Peter Eyre, 1992

Other
Rundherum, with Erika Mann, 1929
Das Buch von der Riviera, with Erika Mann, 1931
Kind dieser Zeit, 1932
Vergittertes Fenster, 1937
Escape to Life, with Erika Mann, 1939
The Other Germany, with Erika Mann, 1940
The Turning Point, 1942
André Gide and the Crisis of Modern Thought, 1943
Der Wendepunkt, 1952
Briefe und Antworten, edited by Martin Gregor-Dellin, 1968–69
Tagebücher, edited by Joachim Heimannsberg et al., 6 vols., 1989–91

Further Reading

Arnold, Heinz Ludwig, editor, "Klaus Mann," *Text und Kritik* 93–94 (January 1987)
Frisch, Shelley, "The Americanization of Klaus Mann," in *Kulturelle Wechselbeziehungen im Exil—Exile across Cultures,* edited by Helmut Pfanner, Bonn: Bouvier, 1986
———, "The Turning Down of *The Turning Point:* The Politics of Non-Reception in the Adenauer Era," in *Die Resonanz des Exils,* edited by Dieter Sevin, Amsterdam and Atlanta, Georgia: Rodopi, 1992
Kroll, Fredric, et al., editors, *Klaus-Mann-Schriftenreihe,* 6 vols., Wiesbaden: Blahak, 1976–
Naumann, Uwe, "Mit den Waffen des Geistes: Klaus Mann im Zweiten Weltkrieg," in *Der Zweite Weltkrieg und die Exilanten: Eine literarische Antwort,* edited by Helmut Pfanner, Bonn: Bouvier, 1991
Spangenberg, Eberhard, *Karriere eines Romans: "Mephisto," Klaus Mann, und Gustaf Gründgens,* Munich: Ellermann, 1982
Wolff, Rudolf, editor, *Klaus Mann: Werk und Wirkung,* Bonn: Bouvier, 1984

Thomas Mann 1875–1955

Thomas Mann and Bertolt Brecht, the conservative bourgeois novelist and the communist bohemian playwright, were long considered the most representative authors of modern Germany. In very different ways, they were both deeply affected by its dramatically changing culture and society, which Mann, the late Romantic, strove to preserve, and which Brecht, the young rebel, struggled to change. With the growing distance to these contested times, Mann's life and work emerges more and more as a *grand récit,* which arguably renders the complexities and contradictions of Germany in the first half of the 20th century most comprehensively.

At the young age of 25, Mann published *Buddenbrooks: Verfall einer Familie* (1901; *Buddenbrooks: The Decline of a Family),* his first novel, which soon established him as the principal

German expositor of Europe's cultural epoch of decadence, which took place around the turn of the century. The novel chronicles the rise and fall of several generations of a merchant dynasty in northern Germany whose final economic decline is associated with an unfolding aesthetic sensibility. The author had modeled plot and personalities of his novel partially after members of his own family. Mann's early novellas, notably *Der kleine Herr Friedemann* (*Little Herr Friedemann*), *Tristan,* and *Tonio Kröger,* which all appeared in 1903, are colorful variations of the theme of decadence. They increasingly instrumentalize the Wagnerian technique of the leitmotiv, thereby orchestrating a variety of decadent themes such as the concept of *l'art pour l'art,* the figure of the dilettante, and the cultural complex of decay and regeneration. Together, these tropes create an ambivalent reality, vascillating between art and life, that is both doomed to fail and determined to thrive. Its decadent gloom and glory are, above all, inspired by Schopenhauer, Wagner, and Nietzsche, the intellectual godfathers of the young author's unfolding literary universe. Of his early works, *Tonio Kröger* was to become not only Mann's own favorite novella in later years, its youthful hero also grew into an icon of adolescence; his search for an authentic self and struggle for self-expression in art has fascinated generations of readers and writers from T.S. Eliot and Kafka to Czeslaw Milosz.

In 1905, Mann matched his growing literary reputation by marrying into a well-established German Jewish family in Munich; he soon presided over an ever-expanding household, which included six children, maids, and a chauffeur. In 1912, Mann's most famous novella, *Der Tod in Venedig* (*Death in Venice*), appeared. It is the portrait of an aging German author, a model of his class and master of its culture, who embarks on a journey to Venice, where he falls passionately in love with a beautiful young boy. A lifetime of dedication to the laws of logos, a lifetime of reason, sensibility, and literary production, falls prey to the lures of eros, passion, sensuality, and self-abandon. More than in any other of Mann's novellas, the protagonist's fantasies crystallize with sparkling eloquence into mythopoetic epiphanies, which in turn represent and reflect Nietzsche's most influential mythic model, the perennial agon between Apollo and Dionysus.

The outbreak of World War I also launched Mann's long-lasting career as a political writer. His essay "Gedanken im Kriege" (1914; "Thoughts in the War") is a highly belligerent diatribe against France, which doubles as a showcase and showdown of German *Kultur* versus French Civilization. With its sweeping polemics, it is emblematic of the best and the worst of Mann's powers of persuasion. As he whipped Wilhelmine warriors into a crusade for German greatness, he was also decades later capable of stirring the political passions of his audience against the surging forces of fascism.

Mann's voluminous *Betrachtungen eines Unpolitischen* (1918; *Reflections of a Nonpolitical Man*) appeared at the end of World War I. They represent a last ditch effort to define and defend his cultural heritage and identity, which was so deeply grounded in the political traditions of the Wilhelmine monarchy. It was a reactionary revolt for a thoroughly lost cause. In the following years, he transformed himself systematically into a politically as well as culturally progressive representative of Weimar Germany. In 1924, his epic and encyclopedic bildungsroman, *Der Zauberberg* (*The Magic Mountain*), was published. Originally

conceived as a satirical counterpiece to *Death in Venice,* it grew into a multifaceted monument, reflecting and refracting contemporary civilization and its many discontents. High up in a sanitarium of the Swiss Alps, Europe's moribund social and intellectual elite engages in a variety of erotic and intellectual adventures and experiments, exploring and expanding the limits of the human condition. Their humanist areas of inquiries range from the ancient Eleusinian mysteries to contemporary psychoanalytical theories; their ideologies link the Catholic utopia of the Jesuit Counter Reformation with the communist agenda of world revolution. Naphta and Settembrini, the most prominent patients-cum-philosophers of *The Magic Mountain,* are the exemplary proponents of increasingly antagonistic weltanschauungen, which were soon to split Europe into two politically opposite camps. Hans Castorp, the novel's central protagonist, is caught in the middle of his mentors' Manichean mind games and captivated by their dialectical erudition and cultural sophistication. In his state of constant confusion and fascination and in his struggle for mediation and clarification, Castorp personifies his contemporary Germany in search for its modern identity.

As a whole, *The Magic Mountain* stands as a veritable summit and summa of Europe's culture on the eve of World War I. Privately, this novel earned its author the affectionate accolade "The Magician"; publicly, it won him critical acclaim as one of Germany's and Europe's most complex authors. The final years of the Weimar Republic not only saw him crowned with the Nobel Prize for literature but also engaged as an increasingly outspoken critic of the growing movement of National Socialism. In public appearances ranging from Vienna to Berlin, he warned his countrymen not to regress into the murky realms of a "blood and soil" ideology, whose corrupted mother-myth promised Germany, exhausted by economic troubles and political strive, a mystical rebirth as a Nietzschean nation of strong "blond beasts." Abroad on a European tour lecturing on Richard Wagner when Hitler came to power, Mann decided not to return to his native land.

Having been passionately and finally painfully German, the exiled Mann changed his citizenship twice, first becoming a citizen of Czechoslovakia, then of the United States. During his early years of exile in France, Switzerland, and the United States, he sustained himself mentally as well as financially through the elaborate production of his most voluminous work, *Joseph und seine Brüder* (1933–43; *Joseph and His Brothers*), a tetralogy comprising some 2,500 pages. A revisiting and a revisioning on a Homeric scale of the Old Testament story of Joseph's exile in Egypt, the work is grounded in the then latest theories of biblical mythography and cultural anthropology and teems with personal and political allusions to Mann's own life and times. For example, the economic plans and policies of Joseph, the Provider, in Egypt are fashioned after Franklin Roosevelt's New Deal. The American president was to return the favor by recommending the expatriot novelist for the office of president of a future, postfascist Germany. In the wake of his 16-year-long research and recreation of the Joseph story, Mann wrote two additional novellas that have the mythic world of the Middle and Far East as their backdrop: *Die vertauschten Köpfe: Eine indische Legende* (1940; *The Transposed Heads*) and *Das Gesetz* (1944; *The Tables of the Law*). In the first novella, the author reimagined the contradictions of art and life, the central conundrum of his earlier work, through the oriental myth and make-believe of the

Great Maya, whose matriarchal mystique was the original source of inspiration for Schopenhauer's magnum opus *The World as Will and Representation.* The latter novella revises the Moses myth through a Freudian focus, portraying the great lawgiver and founding father of a chosen people as a man of intense sexual and spiritual yearnings. In addition, the legend and legacy of the Mount Sinai story serves as a multiply inscribed pre-text, whose cryptic references correspond—across the millennia—to Moses' ultimate antagonist, Adolf Hitler. Mann's subsequent *Lotte in Weimar* (1939; translated as *Lotte in Weimar* and *The Beloved Returns*) represents his first major fictional preoccupation and the beginning of his identification with Goethe, the incarnation of the other classical Weimar and the archrepresentative of German culture at its best. In his later life, Mann would increasingly indulge himself in such an ironic *imitatio Goethe,* thereby pursuing and practicing his own theory that a "great man" will invariably follow in the footsteps of a former "great man" of culture and history.

During his years in the United States, Mann became not only the most prominent deputy of German culture but also the most vocal adversary of the Third Reich. In numerous lecture tours crisscrossing the North American continent, the self-proclaimed "itinerant preacher of democracy" promised its coming victory while at the same time warning of the growing menace of Nazi Germany. Beyond his American audience, he also attempted to reach his compatriots across the Atlantic through frequent broadcasts on the BBC called "Deutsche Hörer" ("Listen, Germany"), endeavoring to open German eyes to the true nature of fascism.

In contrast to his unequivocal denunciation of Hitler in his British broadcast messages, Mann pursued quite a different path in an essay of 1939. In this essay, he delineates several biographical and psychological similarities between himself, the young decadent *littérateur* turned Nobel laureate, and the ex-Austrian *peintre maudit,* now the most powerful politician and mass-media magician of Germany. Through these uncanny elective affinities, Mann explored and exorcised some of his own youthful national-chauvinistic tendencies. The Nietzschean "Will to Power" associated with both figures made them perfect parodic antipodes in a doomed world of culture and politics. Mann called his essayistic fantasy of this satirical sibling rivalry "Ein Bruder" ("A Brother").

With his magisterial novel *Doktor Faustus: Das Leben des deutschen Tonsetzers Adrian Leverkühn, erzählt von einem Freunde* (1947; *Doctor Faustus: The Life of the German Composer, Adrian Leverkühn, as Told by a Friend*), Mann wrote the ponderous and, some critics argue, even more problematic counterpart to his frivolous fraternizing with the führer. Leverkühn's life and work are a provocatively speculative allegory on Germany's creative and destructive genius as it unfolds throughout the centuries; the work culminates in the disastrous and, if read in light of the Faust fable, demonic events of Nazi Germany. Splitting his emotional loyalties between the protagonist and the narrator of the novel, Mann invents and invests himself twice—and larger than life—in the cultural triumphs and historical traumas of his increasingly schizoid nation. He took his literary labor of love and mourning very personally. "Where I am, there is Germany" became one of his most quoted, applauded, and derided statements during these years in exile. In retrospect, he could not have been more correct. No other

German author such as Mann had experienced and fictionalized the aesthetic and political developments of his country and had identified with the most (in)famous men of his great culture and its even greater catastrophe.

The year 1945 brought the end of Word War II but not the end of Mann's involvement in national and international politics. Through numerous committees and public lectures, he attempted to moderate and mediate the growing differences between the Soviet Union and the United States (echoes of Castorp, caught between Naphta and Settembrini). During the following years, however, Mann appeared more and more like a crier in the wilderness, his messages drowned out by the rising clamor of the Cold War. Soon, the once idolized "itinerant preacher of democracy" found himself, together with other members of his family, suspected of being a fellow traveler of an international communist conspiracy. In 1952, the Mann family pulled up stakes one more time and moved back to the Old World, settling in Zurich, neutral Switzerland. The author's last official visit to Germany resonates with the tragic irony of its cultural history. To avoid provoking either part of his divided country, he gave his anniversary speech on Goethe, his beloved alter ego, in both Frankfurt and Weimar. It was a gesture of highly symbolic significance. By now, Goethe's *Faust,* his ominous pact and his proverbial "two souls," had, indeed, become a self-fulfilling prophecy for modern, divided Germany. By honoring Goethe on both sides of the political divide, Mann paid his last tribute to the pathetic fallacy of Faustus/Germany.

While researching and writing *Doctor Faustus,* Mann also drew on the medieval legends of the *Gesta Romanorum,* which in turn became the source of inspiration for his penultimate novel, *Der Erwählte* (1951; *The Holy Sinner*). It is an imaginative revisiting of the medieval vita of Pope Gregory the Great, a dazzling period piece of courtly love, replete with monstrous sexual aberrations and miraculous spiritual redemption. The novel also exemplifies Mann's most advanced stylistic and linguistic experimentation with hybridized forms of French, English, and Lutheran German. It is no coincidence that this exemplary (im)morality play about a great sinner and saint deploys and displays Mann's most purple prose. In its linguistic brio and stylistic brilliance, the novel is Mann's poetic paean to a "sacred" world—in the most original sense of the word as both "holy" and "horrible"—as such, the work's worldview reflects the history of mankind as primarily determined by the extraordinary (mis)deeds of its "great men."

In Mann's last novel, *Bekenntnisse des Hochstaplers Felix Krull: Der Memoiren erster Teil* (1954; *Confessions of Felix Krull, Confidence Man: The Early Years*), the many contradictions of art and life, the lasting leitmotif of Mann's career, find their final reconciliation of sorts in a synthesis of sublime sentimentality. Felix Krull, the charming impostor, is Mann's *Lebenskünstler* par excellence, an artist of life and—for that matter—love, whose beguiling beauty and iridescent identity make him the object of desire of women and men alike. In embarking on his Iberian itinerary, pursuing happiness and courting disaster, Felix Krull is following the path of the picaro, the most prominent protagonist figure in Spanish literature; this strategy turns the Faustian quest for knowledge into an erotic adventure—an *éducation sentimentale* of body and mind. As such, Felix Krull embodies and enacts Mann's own lifelong dreams and desires, as well as the vagaries and vicissitudes of his artistic biography. Similar to a baroque picaro in bourgeois disguise, the author, too, had experienced the world as a Wheel of Fortune that had extolled and exiled, honored and humiliated him time and time again. In his art, Mann re-created his life and times more and more as a literary *teatrum mundi,* a colorful spectacle of human masks and of humanity's timeless myths.

Thomas Mann's reception after World War II was as variegated as his literary production. Soon canonized in East Germany as a progressive precursor of socialist realism, he was repeatedly calumniated by conservatives in West Germany, primarily for having critically distanced if not disassociated himself from his country. In the Anglo-American world, the "Stature of Thomas Mann" (Neider) continued to loom large as modern Germany's most profound if not dauntingly difficult author and most outspoken advocate of freedom and democracy. The many official activities associated with Mann's 100th anniversary in 1975 in Germany, however, stood in stark contrast to his reserved reception by a younger generation of German readers and writers. In a decade of antiestablishment sentiments and countercultural iconoclasm, Mann was perceived as a bourgeois *embarras de richesse,* overbearing in his accomplishments and outmoded in his concept of culture. The politics and aesthetics of the expatriot author, his increasingly liberal leanings and socialist sympathies, as well as his *Greisen-Avantgardismus* (Schröter), that is, the experimental, even campy conceptualizations of his late works, were hardly known.

The beginning of the publication of his diaries in the early 1980s, however, marked a renewed interest in Thomas Mann. With the last of the ten volumes published in 1995, this posthumous oeuvre comes close to matching the 13 volumes of the standard German edition of his work proper. These diaries have yielded a plethora of uncensored personal and political, literary, and historical observations, which add up to a elaborate running commentary on the most turbulent decades in German history. The first of his published diaries, for example, covers the years 1918 to 1921, when Mann witnessed the labor pains of his country's nascent democracy firsthand in its most violent form, that is, in Munich's short-lived Soviet Republic of 1919. During this period of political turmoil, rampant with street fights and culminating in the vicious assassination of some of its political leaders, Mann, too, repeatedly feared for his own life. In addition to the many close-ups of political and historical events, the diaries reveal behind the well-composed public persona a highly complicated and vulnerable personality—a vita as wound. At its core lies the author's lifelong agony with his persistently suppressed and sublimated homosexuality. It constitutes the true psychological subtext for Mann's literary antagonism between art and life; its subcutaneous conflicts characterize and challenge almost all of his literary protagonists. Mann's diaries contain countless erotic reveries and sexual references, ranging from his enraptured glimpses of handsome young men in various stages of dress—including his own adolescent son—to the melancholy memories of his largely unrequited romances. In their elegiac musings, these entries belong to the most moving passages in the work of this last and most eloquent epigone of the romantic *Liebestod,* whose enigma of erotic excess so haunted Germany's late 19th-century culture. In this context, Mann's novella *Death in Venice* not only stands as a master narrative of literary modernity but also emerges as "a revolutionary breakthrough in the expression of gay desire" (Heilbut). Luchino Visconti's filmic version of *Death in Venice* (1970) and Benjamin Britten's musical rendition (1973) have long been classics of gay cinema and opera.

The years 1995 and 1996 saw the publication of no less than four voluminous biographies of Thomas Mann by German, British, and American authors. All these works, although of various quality, paint a multifaceted picture of Mann, whose life and work serve to reflect modern Germany's complicated culture and history. Unique among his contemporaries, Mann's oeuvre evolved and expanded from an exclusively national perspective into a truly international worldview. Its widening horizons also encompass a progression from the preoccupation with individual psychology to the exploration of universal mythologies. This development engages a wide variety of cultural movements and critical models, ranging from German Classicism and Romanticism to Marxist theory, matriarchal mythography, Freudian psychoanalysis, and the musicology of the Frankfurt School. Seen together, they constitute a veritable metanarrative of German and Judeo-Christian traditions. By all accounts, the work of this last *poeta doctus* stands as a formidable bulwark of *Bildung,* representing the quintessence of Germany's modern intellectual history—as if to shore it up one more time against its imminent political collapse. In this endeavor, Mann emerges as a central contributor to that Western project that Adorno and Horkheimer defined and delineated as the *Dialectic of Enlightenment.* The frequent illumination of both sides of an issue and the negotiations of its various contradictions and underlying similarities became Mann's characteristic trademarks, establishing him as modern Germany's foremost master of ambivalences and ironies.

By the same token, Mann was not only an accomplished architect of serious thoughts and complex stories but also their most skillful and playful underminer. In almost all of his epic works, he probed deeper layers of literary traditions and dismantled their cultural conventions, turning them with care and cunning into complex parodies. For it was Mann's humanist credo that these parodic parings would reveal the "unity of the human spirit" at the heart of all culture ("Die Einheit des Menschengeistes," 1932).

New Historicism and the theories of postmodernism, the most influential academic discourse formations of the 1980s and the 1990s, find in Mann's voluminous work an ideal quarry for their epistemological inquiries. New Historicism's privileged paradigm of "thick description" (Clifford Geertz) and "cross-cultural montage" (Dominick LaCapra) are congenial concepts for explicating Mann's metanarratives and their multiple encodings. Likewise, New Historicism's principal tenets of exchange, circulation, and renegotiation, which draw upon the central modi operandi of the mercantile world, meet in Mann, the prodigal son of a merchant dynasty, a skilled economist, savvy in the art of recycling knowledge and producing cultural surplus value.

Closely related to the tenets of New Historicism are the theories of postmodernism, which can also shed new light on Mann's literary and cultural archeology. His parodic deconstruction of traditions and their experimental montage are characteristic features of the postmodern imagination. In addition, his strategies of merging mythic and modern times and paradigms anticipate postmodernism's most popular trajectory—"back to the future." They interface both with the religious syncretism of New Age spirituality and—*mutatis mutandis*—with the sexual revolution of the 20th century. Mann's lifelong struggle with gender identity is part of this revolution to liberate and celebrate (wo)man's original polymorphous sexuality. Last but not least, Mann's systematic refocusing of Western civilization through the kaleidoscope of a multicultural consciousness represents a central aspect of the unfinished project of postmodernity.

FREDERICK A. LUBICH

Biography

Born in Lübeck, North Germany, 6 June 1875. Brother of the author Heinrich Mann; father of the authors Erika and Klaus Mann. Left Lübeck Gymnasium without Abitur, 1894; joined his mother in Munich, where he started working for an insurance company; in Rome with his brother Heinrich, 1896–98, where he began work on *Buddenbrooks;* worked as writer and editor for the satirical journal *Simplicissimus,* 1898–1900; lecture tours throughout Germany and Switzerland, with intermittent travel to Italy; public declaration of conversion to democracy in Berlin lecture "Von deutscher Republik" ("On the German Republic"), 1922; traveled in Egypt and Palestine, 1930; emigrated to Sanary-sur-Mer, France, then Küsnacht, near Zurich; visit to the United States, 1934; lost German citizenship, 1936; citizen of Czechoslovakia, 1936; moved to the United States, 1938; lecturer in the Humanities at Princeton University, 1938; moved to California, 1940; United States citizenship, 1944; returned to Europe and settled in Zurich, 1952; annual visits to Germany. Nobel Prize in literature, 1929. Died 12 August 1955.

Selected Works

Collections

Gesammelte Werke in dreizehn Bänden, edited by Hans Bürgin and Peter de Mendelssohn, 1990

Fiction

Buddenbrooks: Verfall einer Familie, 1901; as *Buddenbrooks: The Decline of a Family,* translated by H.T. Lowe-Porter, 1924; translated by John E. Woods, 1993
Tristan: Sechs Novellen (including *Tonio Kröger*), 1903; three novellas translated by H.T. Lowe-Porter, in *Death in Venice, Tristan, and Tonio Kröger,* 1929
Königliche Hoheit, 1909; as *Royal Highness: A Novel of German Court-Life,* translated by Cecil Curtiss, 1916; translated by H.T. Lowe-Porter, 1939
Der Tod in Venedig, 1912; edited by T.J. Reed, 1983; as *Death in Venice,* translated by Kenneth Burke, 1925; revised edition, 1970; translated by H.T. Lowe-Porter, 1928 (also published in *Stories of Three Decades,* 1936, and in *Death in Venice: And Seven Other Stories,* 1936); translated by David Luke, in *Death in Venice and Other Stories,* 1988 (also published in *Death in Venice* [critical edition], edited by Naomi Ritter, 1998); translated by Clayton Koelb, 1994; translated by Stanley Applebaum, 1995; translated by Joachim Neugroschel, in *Death in Venice and Other Tales,* 1998
Betrachtungen eines Unpolitischen, 1918; as *Reflections of a Nonpolitical Man,* translated by Walter D. Morris, 1983
Der Zauberberg, 1924; as *The Magic Mountain,* translated by H.T. Lowe-Porter, 1927; translated by John E. Woods, 1995
Mario und der Zauberer, 1930; as *Mario and the Magician,* translated by H.T. Lowe-Porter, 1931
Joseph und seine Brüder, 4 vols., 1933–43; as *Joseph and His Brothers,* 1934–44
　Die Geschichten Jaakobs, 1933; as *The Tales of Jacob,* translated by H.T. Lowe-Porter, 1934
　Der junge Joseph, 1934; as *Young Joseph,* translated by H.T. Lowe-Porter, 1935

Joseph in Ägypten, 1936; as *Joseph in Egypt,* translated by H.T. Lowe-Porter, 1938
Joseph, der Ernährer, 1943; as *Joseph the Provider,* translated by H.T. Lowe-Porter, 1944
Lotte in Weimar, 1939; as *Lotte in Weimar,* translated by H.T. Lowe-Porter, 1949; as *The Beloved Returns,* translated by Lowe-Porter, 1940
Die vertauschten Köpfe: Eine indische Legende, 1940; as *The Transposed Heads,* translated by H.T. Lowe-Porter. 1941
Das Gesetz, 1944; as *The Tables of the Law,* translated by H.T. Lowe-Porter, 1945
Doktor Faustus: Das Leben des deutschen Tonsetzers Adrian Leverkühn, erzählt von einem Freunde, 1947; as *Doctor Faustus: The Life of the German Composer, Adrian Leverkühn, as Told by a Friend,* translated by H.T. Lowe-Porter, 1948; as *Doctor Faustus,* translated by John E. Woods, 1997
Der Erwählte, 1951; as *The Holy Sinner,* translated by H.T. Lowe-Porter, 1951
Bekenntnisse des Hochstaplers Felix Krull: Der Memoiren erster Teil, 1954; as *Confessions of Felix Krull, Confidence Man: The Early Years,* translated by Denver Lindley, 1955

Other

Vom zuküftigen Sieg der Demokratie, 1938; as *The Coming Victory of Democracy,* translated by Agnes E. Meyer, 1938
Tagebücher, 1918–21, 1933–34, 1935–36, 1937–39, 1940–43, edited by Peter de Mendelssohn, 1979–82; *Tagebücher, 1944–46, 1946–48, 1949–50, 1951–52, 1953–55,* edited by Inge Jens, 1986–95; selections as *Diaries 1918–39,* translated by Richard and Clara Winston, 1982

Further Reading

Hamilton, Nigel, *The Brothers Mann: The Lives of Heinrich and Thomas Mann, 1871–1950 and 1875–1955,* New Haven, Connecticut: Yale University Press, 1979
Hayman, Ronald, *Thomas Mann: A Biography,* New York: Scribner, 1995; London: Bloomsbury, 1996
Heilbut, Anthony, *Exiled in Paradise: German Refugee Artists and Intellectuals in America, from the 1930s to the Present,* New York: Viking Press, 1983
———, *Thomas Mann: Eros and Literature,* London: Macmillan, 1995; New York: Knopf, 1996
Koopmann, Helmut, editor, *Thomas-Mann-Handbuch,* Stuttgart: Kröner, 1990; 2nd edition, 1995
Lubich, Frederick A., "'Fascinating Fascism': Thomas Manns 'Das Gesetz' und seine Selbst-de-Montage als Moses-Hitler," *German Studies Review* 14, no. 3 (1991)
———, "Horrible Humanist—Hippest Humanist: Recent Thomas Mann Biographies," *German Studies Review* 21, no. 1 (1998)
Martin, Robert K., "Walt Whitman and Thomas Mann," *Walt Whitman Quarterly Review* 4 (1987)
Neider, Charles, editor, *The Stature of Thomas Mann,* New York: New Directions, 1947; London: Owen, 1951
Reed, T.J., *Thomas Mann: The Uses of Tradition,* Oxford: Clarendon Press, 1974; 2nd edition, Oxford: Clarendon Press, and New York: Oxford University Press, 1996
Reich-Ranicki, Marcel, *Thomas Mann and His Family,* translated by Ralph Manheim, London: Collins, 1989
Schröter, Klaus, *Thomas Mann in Selbstzeugnissen und Bilddokumenten,* Reinbek bei Hamburg: Rowohlt, 1964
Vaget, Hans Rudolf, *Thomas Mann-Kommentar zu sämtlichen Erzählungen,* Munich: Winkler, 1984
Winston, Richard, *Thomas Mann: The Making of an Artist, 1875–1911,* New York: Knopf, 1979; London: Constable, 1982
Wysling, Hans, and Yvonne Schmidlin, editors, *Thomas Mann: Ein Leben in Bildern,* Zurich: Artemis, 1994

Yourcenar, Marguerite, "The Humanism of Thomas Mann," *Partisan Review* (Spring 1956)

Doktor Faustus 1947

Novel by Thomas Mann

Thomas Mann's "most direct, most personal, and most passionate novel" (as he described in a letter of 3 December 1949 to Agnes Meyer), his adaptation of the medieval German myth of Faust, best known in Goethe's dramatic adaptation, was written in German between 1943 and 1947 during his exile in the United States. (In 1949, Mann published his own account of the writing of the novel, *Die Entstehung des Doktor Faustus: Roman eines Romans* [*The Genesis of a Novel*]; recent research has given a much more comprehensive picture.) In *Doktor Faustus* (*Doctor Faustus*), Mann took up one of his earliest ideas, first sketched in 1901, and made use of much material from early notebooks, as he turned his back on the Goethean version and returned to the medieval chapbook tradition.

The novel is, as its subtitle indicates, a recasting of the myth of the medieval German necromancer and magician who sells his soul to the devil in order to gain 24 years of superhuman ability before the devil claims his part of the bargain. For Mann, the paradigmatic representative of modern cultural history had to be a composer, a custodian of the "machtgeschützte Innerlichkeit" (interiority protected by power). Leverkühn, his Faustus, a genius who wittingly contracts syphilis, achieves his Promethean task in the following 24 years. He defines this task as the breakthrough from the staleness of tradition, which he believes is turning into a parody of itself, to a new mode of musical expression (in itself an adaptation of Arnold Schoenberg's 12-tone technique). The young Leverkühn also recognizes in Beethoven's music the abstract Promethean, and thus Faustian, nature of music itself: "the highest energy . . . but without an object." As "energy . . . in its actuality," it has a quality that appears to him as almost equivalent to "a definition of God. *Imitatio Dei*—I am surprised it is not forbidden."

The tale of this life spans the years 1885 to 1940 (by 1930, Leverkühn is reduced by a paralytic shock to madness, reverting to the state of "the most docile of children"). Its cultural and historical context is given in detail for three significant periods of his life: his student years in Halle (1904–5), his time near Munich in 1913–14, and the early years of the Weimar Republic in Munich at about 1920. The novel is presented in the form of a biography, written after Leverkühn's death by Serenus Zeitblom, a dissident teacher of classical studies who is dismissed from his post by the Nazis for his humanist convictions. It adopts the tone of personal witness by a childhood friend who insists that his first-person account is not a novel and that he is not a storyteller. We become involved in his attempt to achieve the impossible by writing, between 23 May 1943 and the looming end of the war in 1945, and without any hope of publication, an imperfect and "assuredly very premature" version of the life of a "musician of genius."

The narrative stance colors the dark tale with personal affection, foreboding, and the irony caused by Zeitblom's long-winded, pedantic humanist perorations. It also gives Mann's complex novel characteristics of the *Zeitroman* (tracing key developments in German cultural history to 1945), the *Entwicklungsroman,* and the *Künstlerroman* (tracing the development and education of an artist obsessed with perfecting his art while increasingly withdrawing from society). It is rich in cultural and linguistic resonances and allusions, and in uncanny montage of direct and indirect references, both to the medieval world of Luther and Dürer and to the more contemporary world of the life and work of Nietzsche, Schoenberg, and Adorno. The many very personal allusions to Mann's own life and family add further complexity to the text. The novel also makes heavy demands on the reader through its skillful use of varied linguistic registers, from the archaic German of Leverkühn's letters to the endless elasticity of Zeitblom's writing, from the parody of German students' intellectual pretentiousness to the mock-medieval simplicity of the elflike child Echo, who dies brutally from meningitis.

Mann's complex critique of Germany's cultural heritage plays on the reader's ability to respond to the many conflicting signals embedded in the text and on the reader's willingness to suspend premature judgment and disbelief in favor of focusing upon its engaging game with tradition, real and fictional. Whatever the thousands of critical studies have suggested over the last 50 years, the novel will immediately engross the sophisticated reader. Part of the reader's fascination is the interaction between the different time levels in the novel. The attempted biography, which leads to personal catastrophe, is written against the historical background of the impending German catastrophe of 1945, and these stories are overshadowed by the narrator's apprehension about both catastrophes. He knows that his tale must lead to the collapse of Leverkühn, which is the terrible price the character pays for the artistic achievement he owes to his Satanic syphilitic infection. The reader knows how the war will end.

The marked contrast in attitude and language between the well-meaning and pedantic humanist biographer Zeitblom, whose own life is closely entertwined with that of his inspired, demonic friend, and the world and language of the latter, whose links with a medieval and Lutheran past are forever present, is captivating. The rich and unconventional musical education of Leverkühn, temporarily interrupted by the study of theology at Halle/Wittenberg, leads after experiments with various forms, which he quickly masters to the point of parody, to the discovery of his own form of composition. Music is Leverkühn's Faustian temptation, and the temptation that it offers stems from its pseudo-theological base: it is a "magic marriage between theology and the so diverting mathematics."

As a young composer, Leverkühn first senses in the "brevity and condensation" of his experimental *Brentano Songs* the constructivist potential, but also the severe limitations, of composing in a style so strict that a whole lied results from the five tones h, e, a, e, and es. In these notes are magically encoded the mythical name of the prostitute, Hetaera Esmeralda, to whom, despite her warning, he owes his infection. (The notes h and es become b and e-flat in English terminology, which suggests some the insuperable difficulties of playing Mann's allusive games in translation.) After composing these songs, Leverkühn dreams of a composition based on the use of "the twelve letters of the tempered semitone alphabet." In it there would not be a free note, since all must demonstrate their relation to a fixed fundamental series, a strict and all-encompassing order similar to the magic square of numbers in his study. He finally achieves that ambition when he turns the mythical pattern of his own case into a work of art. His symphonic cantata *Lamentations of Dr. Faustus,* based on the 12 syllables of the last words of the dying Faustus to his assembled students ("For I die as a good and as a bad Christian"), is a mammoth variation piece of lamentation, lasting an hour and a quarter. It is his discovery of 12-tone music that provides the hoped-for breakthrough to perfect order that has no room for subjective emotion. It also marks the end of his striving.

The inevitability of Leverkühn's progress to his own catastrophe, which so strongly marks Mann's treatment of the myth, is predicted by the satanic figure whom Leverkühn sees at Palestrina in Italy, five years after his infection. This figure restates Mann's old conviction: "The artist is the brother of the criminal and the madman." The condition that controls the deal is the emotional deprivation from love. The icy detachment, the "Kälte" surrounding the genius, parasitic on those closest to him, is an issue that originated from Mann's own artistic career. He had also treated it in *Lotte in Weimar* (1939; translated as *Lotte in Weimar* and *The Beloved Returns*) to quite different effect, emphasizing in Goethe's case that, by personal sacrifice and through the metamorphosis of human experience into the lovely perfection of art, the artist gives joy to many. In Leverkühn's case, the climax of his achievement is very different, a reversal of Beethoven's Ninth Symphony; its "Ode to Joy" becomes an "Ode to Sorrow." It leaves the demonic Faustus lost in hopelessness and holding on to the disillusionment of his despair, except that his work's last dying note, the high *g* of a cello, might be a symbol of hope beyond hopelessness, a light in the night.

Introducing this piece to his friends in a long address in archaic medieval language, full of references to the Faustus tradition, Leverkühn collapses in a paralytic stroke, the "burnt-out husk of his own personality." To their total disbelief, he had just confessed that for 24 years he had, through Hetaera Esmeralda, been wedded to Satan. Strangely, in his suffering he has acquired, as Zeitblom notices, some Christlike figures.

As a young author, Mann had attached the Ibsen motto "to write is to sit in judgment on oneself" to his first collection of *Novellen;* in *Doctor Faustus* he does just that, with a passion and a relentless insistence that are hard to fathom unless we realize the extent to which this musical German magician is another Thomas Mann, a "Zauberer" (Mann's nickname at home) who thought of his artistic fictional writing as "musizieren," while characterizing the essays and speeches that expressed his opinions as mere hackwork.

HINRICH SIEFKEN

Editions

First edition: *Doktor Faustus: Das Leben des deutschen Tonsetzers Adrian Leverkühn, erzählt von einem Freunde,* Stockholm: Bermann-Fischer, 1947

Translations: *Doctor Faustus: The Life of the German Composer, Adrian Leverkühn, as Told by a Friend,* translated by H.T. Lowe-Porter, London: Secker and Warburg, 1948; as *Doctor Faustus,* translated by John E. Woods, 1997

Further Reading

Fetzer, John Francis, *Music, Love, Death, and Mann's Doctor Faustus,* Columbia, South Carolina: Camden House, 1990

——, *Changing Perceptions of Thomas Mann's Doctor Faustus: Criticism 1947–1992,* Columbia, South Carolina: Camden House, 1996

Heftrich, Eckhard, *Vom Verfall zur Apokalypse,* Frankfurt: Klostermann, 1982

Kaufmann, Fritz, *Thomas Mann: The World as Will and Representation,* Boston: Beacon Press, 1957

Koopmann, Helmut, *Der schwierige Deutsche: Studien zum Werk Thomas Manns,* Tübingen: Niemeyer, 1988

Lehnert, Herbert, and Peter C. Pfeiffer, editors, *Thomas Mann's Doctor Faustus: A Novel at the Margin of Modernism,* Columbia, South Carolina: Camden House, 1991

Reed, T.J., *Thomas Mann: The Uses of Tradition,* Oxford: Clarendon Press, 1974; 2nd edition, Oxford: Clarendon Press, and New York: Oxford University Press, 1996

Thomas Mann Jahrbuch, vol. 7 (1994) (papers from the Lübeck Kolloquium, 1993, "Thomas Mann und die Musik")

Wolff, Rudolf, editor, *Thomas Manns Dr. Faustus und die Wirkung,* 2 vols., Bonn: Bouvier, 1983

Wysling, Hans, and Yvonne Schmidlin, editors, *Bild und Text bei Thomas Mann: Eine Dokumentation,* Bern and Munich: Francke, 1975; 2nd edition, 1989

——, editors, *Notizbücher: Edition in zwei Bänden,* Frankfurt: S. Fischer, 1991–92

Der Tod in Venedig 1912

Novella by Thomas Mann

The novella *Der Tod in Venedig* (*Death in Venice*) is among the most important texts of one of the foremost authors of the 20th century. Thomas Mann wrote it after vacationing in Venice in 1911, and it has since enjoyed perennial popularity and high critical acclaim throughout the world. Its story of the respected but burnt-out Gustav von Aschenbach, an aging writer who ogles a Polish boy on the Lido and who is haunted by Dionysian dreams and misled by Platonic concepts of beauty, raises general issues of moral dissolution, cultural decadence, sexual preference, and literary aesthetics. It treats such issues in ways closely tied to Mann's career, as well as to the course of German history, and it has inspired not only several hundred scholarly studies but also creative efforts in film, music, fiction, ballet, and the visual arts. Its status as a classic thus seems assured.

The novella itself, however, casts doubt on the concept of the literary "classic." Aschenbach's own work has achieved this distinction, but his professional success has come at a terrible psychic cost. He has been ennobled for writing prose so polished that it is emulated in schools, but he has neglected his personal life and repressed his sensual needs so severely that they return to plague him far more than the cholera in Venice. He has also achieved moral resolve only by renouncing his skeptical insight into the abyss of the human condition. That he comes from a long line of German civil servants and that his moral model is Frederick the Great lend the resulting aesthetic simplification national and historical import. When smitten with the beauty embodied by young Tadzio, he evinces a fascination with death that recalls German Romanticism and demonstrates Mann's indebtedness to Platen, Schopenhauer, Nietzsche, and Wagner (Wagner actually had died in Venice). That art can reveal its truths only through our senses, however, as Aschenbach comes to realize, is an aesthetic conundrum as old as Plato, whose *Phaedrus* Aschenbach dimly recalls in the last throes of his fatal passion. His death thus ends a writer's life and a life's work that had become morally dubious. Mann thereby conveys a cultural malaise besetting much of Europe before World War I.

Mann often posited tension, including the kind that kills Aschenbach, between the life of the mind and life itself. He had seemed to ease such tension in *Tonio Kröger* (1903), for example, but it recurs even more acutely in *Doktor Faustus* (1947; *Doctor Faustus*). *Death in Venice* treats this issue at a low point in Mann's career. Like Aschenbach, Mann had then gained literary fame but found finishing new works increasingly difficult. By attributing his own incomplete texts to Aschenbach, however, he exorcised a problematic part of himself, a strategy that helped him avoid his protagonist's tragic fate. His plot is seamlessly woven, held together by other enigmatic characters, and the events that he relates seem to occur on a mundane as well as an abstract, allegorical level. He adapts several passages from Plato, Xenophon, and more modern sources, practicing the technique of "montage" used in his other texts as well. Ironically, the most outstanding feature of *Death in Venice* may well be its prose style, which is so highly refined and suited to its subject as to seem at odds with the novel's apparent message. Aschenbach, his author, and the narrator that stands between them, not to mention many other characters and episodes, often intersect amid such artful ambivalence.

The critical and scholarly reception of the novella has confirmed its strong popular impact. Initial reactions to it were by and large favorable. Mann's brother Heinrich noted its implicit critique of Wilhelminian society, while Hermann Broch read it as a commentary on realism and idealism; D.H. Lawrence cited its sinister symbols and tired unwholesomeness. For the rest of Mann's life, it was interpreted in similarly diverse ways. Georg Lukács liked its exposé of Prussian composure, while Oskar Seidlin admired its stylistic finesse. In the 20 years following Mann's death in 1955, studies showed, among other things, how *Death in Venice* combines psychology and myth, Goethe and the ancient Greeks, and its author's famous irony. Thanks to archival research and the editorial work of scholars such as Herbert Lehnert, Hans Wysling, Manfred Dierks, T.J. Reed, and Hans Vaget, the centennial of Mann's birth was celebrated in 1975 with numerous books and articles about the novella, studies that spanned the entire range of academic fashions and intellectual trends. Since then, the publication of Mann's diaries has revealed in detail his lifelong homosexual leanings, which has tempted some critics to reduce the novella to an autobiographical "coming out." Other approaches to it have located it in the history of the novella as a literary genre, compared it to texts such as Gide's *Immoraliste* and Conrad's *Heart of Darkness*, linked it to other stories set in Venice, and subjected it to repeated psychoanalytic treatments. It thus seems to offer something for almost every conceivable scholarly taste.

Death in Venice also owes some of its appeal to its many adaptations in other media. It has been published in several handsomely illustrated editions, and its scenes have often provided subjects for other drawings and paintings as well. Its two most prominent adaptations, however, both date from the early 1970s. Luchino Visconti's film *Morte a Venezia* (1970) transforms Aschenbach into a composer resembling Gustav Mahler, whose death in 1911 had moved Mann to ascribe to his protagonist the famous composer's facial features. Visconti's soundtrack, consisting largely of excerpts from Mahler's symphonies, is no substitute for Mann's indirect discourse, however, and Aschenbach accordingly appears to be little more than an overwrought pederast. Visconti's use of flashbacks, some alluding to Mann's *Doctor Faustus* as a further means of explaining Aschenbach's art and psychology, has likewise struck many critics as mistaken. Its defenders and detractors alike, however, praise the film for conveying the atmosphere and the attitude of a long-gone *haute bourgeoisie*. In any case, sales of Mann's novella tripled soon after the film was released. Benjamin Britten's opera *Death in Venice* (1973) has been less controversial. Thanks in part to Myfanwy Piper's libretto, its Aschenbach clearly expresses his larger thoughts aloud, while its Tadzio remains silent, as does Mann's, dancing his role instead. While dance figures prominently in Britten's staging, Mann's story has also occasioned at least one full-fledged ballet.

The most telling sign of the work's influence, however, may be its presence in books by other authors. Wolfgang Koeppen's *Der Tod in Rom* (1954; *Death in Rome*), for example, is a novel that takes Mann's final lines about the world's being respectfully shocked by the news of Aschenbach's death and then turns them into a postwar reflection on the evil legacy of the Holocaust. By contrast, Anthony Appiah's *Another Death in Venice* (1995) is a mystery novel that merges the names of Aschenbach and the American art collector Peggy Guggenheim in the character "Peggy Aschenheim." Indeed, the expression "Death in Venice" can be found in the titles of books and articles having nothing to do with Mann, both in academic analyses of other writers and in British and American magazines that report on events as diverse as film festivals and art exhibits in Italy, on villas and gardens in Florida, and on crime, cocaine, and diseased ducks in Venice, California. Aschenbach's story thus seems to have become proverbial, a fact that indirectly confirms its serious, lasting import.

ELLIS SHOOKMAN

Editions

First editions: *Der Tod in Venedig*, in *Neue Rundschau* 23, nos. 10 and 11 (October and November 1912); *Der Tod in Venedig*, Munich: Hyperion, 1912

Critical edition: *Der Tod in Venedig: Texte, Materialien, Kommentar; mit den bisher unveröffentlichten Arbeitsnotizen Thomas Manns*, edited by T.J. Reed, Munich: Hanser, 1983

Translations: *Death in Venice*, translated by Kenneth Burke, New York: Knopf, 1925, revised edition, New York: Modern Library, 1970; translated by H.T. Lowe-Porter, London: Secker, 1928; New York: Knopf, 1930 (also published in *Stories of Three Decades*, London: Secker, and New York: Knopf, 1936, and in *Death in Venice: And Seven Other Stories*, New York: Vintage, 1936); translated by David Luke, in *Death in Venice and Other Stories*, New York: Bantam, 1988; translated by Stanley Applebaum, New York: Dover, 1995; translated by Joachim Neugroschel, in *Death in Venice and Other Tales*, New York: Viking, 1998

Critical editions of translations: *Death in Venice: A New Translation, Backgrounds and Contexts, Criticism*, translated and edited by Clayton Koelb, New York and London: Norton, 1994; and see Ritter, below

Further Reading

Bahr, Ehrhard, *Thomas Mann: Der Tod in Venedig*, Stuttgart: Reclam, 1991

Berlin, Jeffrey B., and Richard H. Lawson, *Approaches to Teaching Mann's Death in Venice and Other Short Fiction*, New York: Modern Language Association of America, 1992

Bloom, Harold, editor, *Thomas Mann*, New York: Chelsea House, 1986

Koopmann, Helmut, editor, *Thomas-Mann-Handbuch*, Stuttgart: Kröner, 1990; 2nd edition, 1995

Kurzke, Hermann, *Thomas Mann: Epoche, Werk, Wirkung*, Munich: Beck, 1985

Mitchell, Donald, editor, *Benjamin Britten: Death in Venice*, Cambridge and New York: Cambridge University Press, 1987

Nicklas, Hans W., *Thomas Manns Novelle Der Tod in Venedig: Analyse des Motivzusammenhangs und der Erzählstruktur*, Marburg: Elwert, 1968

Reed, T.J., *Death in Venice: Making and Unmaking a Master*, New York: Twayne, 1994

Renner, Rolf Günter, *Das Ich als ästhetische Konstruktion: "Der Tod in Venedig" und seine Beziehung zum Gesamtwerk Thomas Manns*, Freiburg: Rombach, 1987

Ritter, Naomi, editor, *Death in Venice: Complete, Authoritative Text with Biographical Contexts, Critical History, and Essays from Five Contemporary Critical Perspectives*, Boston: Bedford, 1998 [includes David Luke's translation of the text]

Vaget, Hans Rudolf, *Thomas Mann—Kommentar zu sämtlichen Erzählungen*, Munich: Winkler, 1984

Tonio Kröger 1903

Novella by Thomas Mann

A collection of six novellas entitled *Tristan* was published in 1903, but the story that Thomas Mann selected as the title for the whole collection turned out not to be its most famous piece. Instead, it was the story called *Tonio Kröger*, which became one of Mann's best-loved works, not least because it is considerably shorter and more accessible than his full-length novels, and yet it encapsulates one of Mann's lifelong preoccupations: the dilemma of the artist who is torn between conflicting parts of his nature.

In formal terms, the story of Tonio is beautifully simple: a symmetrical narrative structure with nine sections. The first four are a series of stylized reminiscences on the artist's childhood, depicting in evocative terms a lonely young boy who desperately longs to belong to the blond-haired, blue-eyed society of the merchant class yet finds that his dark looks and his passion for poetry exclude him from that uncomplicated existence. The young Tonio envies the likes of his school friend Hans or the beautiful Ingeborg, hoping to be granted a small place in their circle of friends, though all the while he knows that they can never understand or truly accept him. He both admires and despises their lifestyle and cannot find a way to integrate himself: his clumsy attempts at joining their dance arouse mockery or, at most, pity, and his attempts to introduce Hans to the delights of literature meet with blank incomprehension. Evidently, this tension has not been resolved by his decision as a young man to move to a more relaxed, artistic location in the south, and so, in the pivotal fifth section, he decides to make a trip back to the northern German town of his birth. The last four sections are a revisiting of each of the four memories in reverse order, as if he is retracing the key phases in his own personal development. He finds people, images, and events that cause him to relive the paradoxes of his childhood, but this time with all the analytical powers of an adult and all the painful awareness of a creative artist. The story ends with a reassertion of Tonio's dilemma: a man who feels caught in the space between two worlds.

The dual forces in the story operate on many levels, and this is one of the most enduring qualities of the work. From the title page onward is paradox and contrast: the main character's name symbolizes both the strictly moral, patrician code of the north (Kröger) and the more exotic, bohemian lifestyle of the south (Tonio). The world of his father is materialistic, controlled, and predictable. The healthy, blond children of the north adore active, concrete pursuits and excel at sports and dancing. Tonio, however, has inherited from his mother a love of music and the arts and a tendency to be drawn into the excesses of emotion, whether these be literary or, later as a young adult, moral. In fact, Tonio is not completely happy in either of these two worlds. The stiff Protestant lifestyle, symbolized by the formal clothing and the steely gray cityscape, stifles him. However, the image of gypsies in a green wagon is used to indicate his fear of the opposite—of formlessness, aimlessness, and chaos. Tonio's father, the archetypal patriarch, wears one solitary wildflower on his lapel as a tiny sign of something outside the confines of his narrow world. In a kind of reversal of this, Tonio lives the life of an artist but wears the formal suit of the bourgeoisie, as if to give himself a hold on the world of order and control. As a result, Tonio finds himself on the edge of both worlds, caught between north and south, father and mother, life and art, innocence and experience, and control and disintegration.

The story can be read as a semiautobiographical account of Mann's early life, and this was Mann's favorite of all his stories. In many ways, it was prophetic because Mann's later works return again and again to this unresolved personal tension. Many of Mann's fictional characters rework the dilemma of Tonio: the early character Hanno Buddenbrook (*Buddenbrooks* [1901]) had started off the theme as the gifted but sickly son and last heir of a patrician family. Knowing that his musical genius is of no use in the world he is to live in, he draws a line under his name in the family tree and dies soon after. In *Tonio Kröger*, the final paragraph hints that there might be some kind of future for the tortured artist: He will live on the edge of two worlds, uncomfortable though this position is, and he will use this distancing effect to fashion great art. This idea was no doubt partly influenced by the work of Schopenhauer, the melancholy philosopher similarly torn between the demands of real life and the attractions of pure reflection. Later reincarnations of Tonio explore different endings. Gustav Aschenbach, in *Der Tod in Venedig* (1912; *Death in Venice*), is a washed-up, seedy figure who illustrates incidentally another ambivalence that is present in the figure of Tonio, namely, a love for physical beauty in both male and female form. Adrian Leverkühn, in *Doktor Faustus* (1947; *Doctor Faustus*), is a musician who, in the tradition of Faust stories, makes a pact with the devil, showing again the power of art as both a creative and a destructive force.

Tonio Kröger manages to convey many of the pressing cultural tensions of its day, including the fin de siècle decadence and the sinister influence of Nietzsche's will to power, Wagnerian excesses, and the tortured alienation of early nihilists and existentialists. Political ideas are less important to Mann's writings at this stage, and yet there is a sense in which Tonio's personal struggle embodies the complicated society that eventually was to give birth to National Socialism. The story depicts a striving for order (and yet a longing for absolutes), for greatness, and for freedom from the daily constraints and humiliations of bourgeois life. In the end, some kind of resolution is found, perhaps not in the person of Tonio, who fails to convince himself or his reader that he is truly an artist or a pillar of bourgeois society, but in the work itself: a well-crafted, deeply moving story in which perfection of form holds together some of the early 20th century's most conflicting and disturbing ideas.

LINDA ARCHIBALD

Editions

First edition: in *Tristan: Sechs Novellen*, Berlin: Fischer, 1903
Critical edition: in *Gesammelte Werke in dreizehn Bänden*, edited by Hans Bürgin and Peter de Mendelssohn, Frankfurt: Fischer Taschenbuch Verlag, 1990
Translation: in *Death in Venice, Tristan, and Tonio Kröger*, translated by H.T. Lowe-Porter, New York: Knopf, 1929

Further Reading

Bennet, Benjamin, "Structure, Parody, and Myth in *Tonio Kröger*," in *Thomas Mann*, edited by Harold Bloom, New York: Chelsea House, 1986
Böhm, Karl Werner, *Zwischen Selbstzucht und Verlangen: Thomas Mann und das Stigma Homosexualität: Untersuchungen zu Frühwerk und Jugend*, Würzburg: Königshausen und Neumann, 1991
Heller, Erich, *Thomas Mann: The Ironic German*, London: Secker and Warburg, 1958; reprint, Cambridge: Cambridge University Press, 1981
Hinton, Thomas, R., *Thomas Mann: The Mediation of Art*, Oxford: Clarendon Press, 1956
Hirschbach, Frank Donald, *The Arrow and the Lyre: A Study of the Role of Love in the Works of Thomas Mann*, The Hague: Nijhoff, 1955
Wilkinson, E.M., "*Tonio Kröger*: An Interpretation," in *Thomas Mann: A Collection of Critical Essays*, edited by Henry Caraway Hatfield, Englewood Cliffs, New Jersey: Prentice Hall, 1964

Der Zauberberg 1924

Novel by Thomas Mann

Originally designed as a satirical counterpiece to *Der Tod in Venedig* (1912; *Death in Venice*), Thomas Mann's *Der Zauberberg* (1924; *The Magic Mountain*) grew in the 12 years of its creation into a multilayered bildungsroman, an exemplary novel of a protagonist's personal development and cultural education. It represents and reflects, arguably like no other literary work of its time, the zeitgeist of this exceptionally momentous period in German history, which was marked by the dramatic decline of the Wilhelmine Empire, World War I, and the creation of the Weimar Republic.

Hans Castorp, the novel's main protagonist, is a young engineer from Hamburg who embarks on a three-week visit to his cousin Joachim Ziemßen in the elegant Berghof sanitarium in Davos high up in the Swiss Alps. He soon succumbs completely to its contagious climate of disease and decadence. The famous resort turns out to be a frivolous refuge for Europe's haute bour-

geoisie and its world-weary aristocracy, who cultivate if not simulate in this rarefied atmosphere a variety of fashionable maladies. For example, the fits and foibles of hysteria, the fin de siècle's most privileged pathology, enjoys an immense popularity among the Berghof's latter-day Victorians, whose moribund desire for life and love is always overshadowed by the omnipresence of death. Very much intrigued by their daily fears and follies, the highly impressionable Castorp soon becomes deeply involved in a variety of adventures of the heart as well as experiments of the mind, indulging in obsessions and preoccupations that extend his original three-week visit to a full seven years.

In a continuous state of feverish excitability, Castorp falls in love, overtly with Madame Chauchat, the reigning femme fatale of the *Magic Mountain*, and covertly with his cousin, a Prussian paragon of military masculinity. In this erotic double bind and bondage to two seemingly forbidden and forbidding objects of desire, Castorp embarks on high-spirited flights of fancy, which frequently oscillate between pathos and pastiche, often merging the downright silly and comic with the most cosmic and sublime. The first part of the novel climaxes in a mock-heroic staging of the Walpurgis Night, the concluding scene of Goethe's *Faust*, part one, which metamorphoses into a cross-dressing carnival, abundantly laced with classical allusions and strongly underpinned by an impassioned quest for carnal knowledge. In a final charade, Castorp gushingly celebrates Chauchat's feminine mystique through Walt Whitman's homoerotic hymn to the male body beautiful, veiling his coming-out—*avant la lettre*—in an impeccable French translation. Castorp's linguistic labor of love is not lost on his object of adoration.

Analogous to the second part of Goethe's *Faust*, the second part of Mann's *Magic Mountain* raises the protagonist's errant erotic drives and human strivings more and more onto humanist and even metaphysical planes. Naphta and Settembrini, Castorp's intellectual mentors and philosophical sparring partners through major segments of the narrative, become mouthpieces for increasingly regressive and progressive political agendas and social utopias, respectively. Their endless debates and discussions amount to veritable "operationes spirituales" (chapter 6), which systematically transcend and interface the humanist disciplines of literature, history, philosophy, politics, and religious study. To varying degrees, they both envision a redemptive history that promises to emancipate mankind from all forms of repression and oppression—be they sexual, social, or spiritual. Such utopian projects toward global revolution and redemption were grounded in contemporary antagonistic models of Germanic *Kultur* versus Roman civilization, Eastern absolutism versus Western liberalism, polarizations that—as the 20th century has shown—were to cause civilizational breaks and catastrophes unprecedented in human history.

The most telling manifestation of Naphta's and Settembrini's many utopian ambitions and contradictions is Mynheer Peeperkorn. An extremely charismatic personality, Peeperkorn playfully impersonates the mythic prototypes of Dionysus and Christ, of sensual martyr and spiritual messiah, thereby enthralling his captive audience into a mesmerized, self-abandoned entourage. With his drunken orgies and delirious oratories, spectacles both powerful and pathetic, he emerges as a pathbreaking avatar of the modern *Massenführer*, the coming political mystagogues and masterminds of Western fascism and Eastern communism.

True to his dialectical principles of contrasting if not collapsing opposites, Mann continuously alternates and interlaces narrative modes and philosophical models: logos and eros, sensuality and spirituality, and progressive enlightenment and regressive mysticism—these are the primary dynamics and dichotomies of the novel. Their common denominator is the archetypal contradiction between culture and nature. Accordingly, the novel's numerous chapters, full of animated and agonizing exchanges between humans and ideas, are systematically contrasted with chapters that reflect nature's supreme serenity, whether in turmoil or tranquillity.

Nature's equivocal powers unfold most dramatically in the central chapter, entitled "Snow." Attracted by the magnificence of the mountains, which are then deeply covered in snow, Castorp ventures one day higher and higher into the wintry wilderness, only to be finally overwhelmed by a blizzard. In its chaos, he experiences the ultimate wonder and terror of nature, envisions death and rebirth through the elemental might of Mother Nature in a kaleidoscope of mythopoetic epiphanies. This pivotal chapter is complemented by the chapter "Fullness of Harmony" toward the end of the novel. As in the magical world of snow and its whirling storm, Castorp becomes more and more immersed in an all-enveloping universe of sound in which the elemental forces of nature are replaced by culture's most abstract form of expression. By playing his gramophone, the enraptured protagonist experiences—again and again—life, love, and death melodramatically through the great masterworks of his most cherished composers.

Underlying the narrative of *The Magic Mountain* is a contemporary (un)consciousness, whose source and essence has been increasingly extrapolated by critics as unadulterated Freudian psychology. Originally very resistant to the nascent movement of analytical theory, the author of *The Magic Mountain* soon graduated from mocking to mimicking its tenets and, ultimately, to modeling them into the very fabric of the novel. Psychological behavior patterns such as resistance, projection, and sublimation, as well as the theories of symbolic dreams and sexual drives, permeate virtually all human agendas and arenas of the novel. Its psychoanalytical thrust culminates in the chapter "Highly Questionable," which explores the occult phenomena of parapsychology, that borderline world where absolute truth and treachery inextricably merge.

Castorp's extensive and diverse explorations of the mysteries of life and death come to an abrupt end with the outbreak of World War I. Full of patriotic passions and chiliastic visions, he storms and stumbles through the battlefields and finally disappears—and with him the last true representative of the German bildungsroman. Goethe's novel *Wilhelm Meister* initiated this tradition; Mann's *Magic Mountain* represents the closure and culmination of its aesthetic reception. The German *Bildungsbürgertum*, a social elite, characterized by culture and property (*Bildung und Besitz*), had derived its ethos and identity to a large degree through Goethe's literary models and their classical humanist idealism. From its very inception during the time of the French Revolution, however, the German bourgeoisie had to compensate for their political impotence through their cultural prowess. With Castorp's descent onto the battlefields of France, this sense of a sublime if not superior German cultural identity collapsed unsalvageably. The bloody birth of the Weimar Republic out of the agony of World War I brought forth a new kind of cultural prototype: the socially critical citizen and politically engaged author. Thomas Mann, too, would soon practice and perfect that role—especially as an expatriot in the United States in his formidable crusade against his greatest antagonist, Adolf Hitler, the ultimate corrupter of humanist ideals and utopian visions.

Upon publication, *The Magic Mountain* soon established itself as a literary landmark, as an eloquent and erudite monument to Western civilization, its many cultural achievements, and—vice versa—its political and psychological discontents. On a par with such masterworks of European modernism as James Joyce's *Ulysses* and Marcel Proust's *A la recherche du temps perdue*, Mann's multifaceted novel had the additional edge of a European *Zeitroman*, of being able to offer a complex contemporary panorama of old-world cultural traditions that were in a politically dramatic transformation. In the early 1940s, even Hollywood became interested in turning Mann's *Magic Mountain* into a major movie picture, and Greta Garbo and Montgomery Clift were considered for the leading roles. It never happened.

In recent decades, the novel inspired a plethora of scholarly interpretations. Following Mann's own assessment of his novel as a "swan song" of a doomed world order (*Einführung*), its epochal story was interpreted as an "epic of diseases" (Weigand, 1986), and the adventures of its protagonist were illuminated through the medieval model of the knightly quester and his search for the Holy Grail (*Einführung*). More recent interpretations have anchored the novel's narrative in Homer's *Odyssey* and Virgil's *Aeneid* (Frizen) and adumbrated its hero's many extravagant excursions as a "Descent into Hades" (Wysling). This symbolic territory was analyzed, in turn, as the Faustian "Realm of the Mothers," whose archetypal womb and tomb topography figures as the mythic matrix of all matriarchal utopias (Lubich). Conversely, the most recent interpretation of *The Magic Mountain* highlights its epistemological labyrinth as a postmodern hypertext and declares Castorp, the searcher for universal knowledge, as literally "made for the Internet" (Heilbut). In the early 1980s, Hans Geißendörfer's filmic rendition with an international cast brought Mann's *Magic Mountain* to a wider audience. As ambitious as this film project was, it only proved that the medium of cinematography cannot do justice to the multiple significations of Mann's "most complex creation" (Reed).

FREDERICK A. LUBICH

See also Bildungsroman

Editions

First edition: *Der Zauberberg*, Berlin: S. Fischer, 1924
Translations: *The Magic Mountain*, translated by H.T. Lowe-Porter, New York: Knopf, and London: M. Secker, 1927; also translated by John E. Woods, New York: Knopf, 1995

Further Reading

Abbott, Scott, H., "'Der Zauberberg' and the German Romantic Novel," *Germanic Review* 55, no. 4 (1980)
Bloom, Harold, editor, *Thomas Mann's The Magic Mountain*, New Haven, Connecticut: Chelsea House, 1986
Frizen, Werner, "Zeitenwende: Über theopolitische Grundmotive in Thomas Manns 'Zauberberg,'" in *Internationales Thomas-Mann-*

Kolloquium 1986 in Lübeck, edited by Cornelia Bernini et al., Thomas-Mann-Studien, vol. 7, Bern: Francke, 1987

Heftrich, Eckhard, *Zauberbergmusik: Über Thomas Mann,* Frankfurt: Klostermann, 1975

Heilbut, Anthony, *Thomas Mann: Eros and Literature,* London: Macmillan, 1995; New York: Knopf, 1996

Koopmann, Helmut, editor, *Thomas-Mann-Handbuch,* Stuttgart: Kröner, 1990; 2nd edition, 1995

Lubich, Frederick A., "Thomas Manns *Der Zauberberg:* Spukschloß der Magna Mater oder Die Männerdämmerung des Abendlandes," *Deutsche Vierteljahrsschrift für Literaturwissenschaft und Geistesgeschichte* 67, no. 4 (1993)

Mann, Thomas, "Einführung in den 'Zauberberg': Für Studenten der Universität Princeton" (1939), in *Gesammelte Werke in dreizehn Bänden,* vol. 11, Frankfurt: Fischer, 1990

Passage, Charles, E., "Hans Castorp's Musical Incantations," *Germanic Review* 28 (1963)

Reed, T.J., *Thomas Mann: The Uses of Tradition,* Oxford: Clarendon Press, 1974; 2nd edition, Oxford: Clarendon Press, and New York: Oxford University Press, 1996

Sauereßig, Heinz, editor, *Besichtigung des Zauberbergs,* Biberach an der Riss: Wege und Gestalten, 1974

Weigand, Hermann J., *Thomas Mann's Novel, Der Zauberberg,* New York and London: Appleton-Century, 1933; reprinted as *The Magic Mountain: A Study of Thomas Mann's Novel, Der Zauberberg,* Chapel Hill: University of North Carolina Press, 1965

——, "Disease," in *Thomas Mann's The Magic Mountain,* edited by Harold Bloom, New Haven, Connecticut: Chelsea House, 1986

Wysling, Hans, "Der Zauberberg," in *Thomas-Mann-Handbuch,* edited by Helmut Koopmann, Stuttgart: Kröner, 1990

Manuscripts (Medieval)

All items written by hand (*Handschriften*) can be included in the category of manuscripts, but it is most common to restrict the term to books, as opposed to letters, deeds, and other documents of relatively short length (diplomatics). The history of the handwritten book is closely tied to the development of materials and formats found to be more suitable to contemporary needs than those previously available; thus, the use of parchment versus papyrus and the codex or book form versus the roll are what most distinguished a manuscript during the medieval period, although these others continued to find some applications. The transmission of texts from late antiquity to the Middle Ages took place in a relatively few locales in Germany—those with strong ties to the political and ecclesiastical centers at the fault line between the late Roman Empire and Germania magna such as Köln, Mainz, Trier, and Augsburg. Only those Germanic tribes that had been in close contact with the Latin world could boast of an early manuscript culture, and only the Goths, with Bishop Wulfila's Bible translation, would produce a Germanic text that was still transmitted after the fall of the Roman Empire at the end of the fifth century. The Latin tradition was to survive in relatively obscure outposts among monastic communities involved in missionary work among the Anglo-Saxons, in Ireland, and in Verona and Tours.

Manuscripts produced in Germany before the Carolingian revival were also connected to centers of monastic missions, most notably Weissenburg, Echternach, Weltenburg, Reichenau, and St. Gall. These were strongly influenced by the Anglo-Irish tradition, both in terms of scripts and illumination. The first golden age of manuscript production in the German-speaking empire was introduced by the Carolingian dynasty, most notably by Charlemagne (768–814) himself. Aside from his interest in the German language, Charlemagne recognized the value of manuscripts as representational objects not only for ecclesiastical organization and standardization but also as symbols of the court's power. Charlemagne's court school was instrumental in developing a standard script (Carolingian minuscule) and critical redactions of biblical and classical literature. Over 7,000 manuscripts and fragments from the eighth and ninth centuries have survived. These manuscripts were distributed and copied in the monastic centers of the empire, thus creating a cross-regional standard for both texts and artistic styles. This standard, in conjunction with the Benedictine movement, gave rise to a manuscript culture that soon saw itself able to produce works in the vernacular—at first, glosses of Latin and snippets of heroic poetry, but then the great metrical gospel harmony of Otfrid von Weissenburg around 870. The manuscripts made of this work include corrections in Otfrid's own hand as well as exemplars produced as gifts to friends and dignitaries. Nevertheless, it was Latin that remained the language of almost all manuscripts, and scribes were relatively fluent in at least written Latin throughout the Middle Ages.

Manuscript production itself was an extremely costly and time-consuming process. The skins necessary for the parchment often numbered in the hundreds, even for a single book, and this alone represented an enormous cost in terms of livestock. The process to prepare and treat the skins in order to present a suitable writing surface was arduous and required considerable resources in terms of time and manpower. The actual handwriting was, of course, the main step in production, and for this it was necessary to have trained scribes and an organized scriptorium and library that could provide the texts to be reproduced and the training necessary to copy them accurately and legibly. Finally, the various sections, or quires, of parchment had to be gathered together and bound so as to form a cohesive whole that would withstand frequent use over many years. The total investment in a manuscript, even one lacking ornamentation or artwork, represented the work of dozens of laborers, scribes, and artisans over a period of perhaps a year or more. When costly materials such as gold leaf or silver ink were used, or elaborate works of art found expression on parchment, the manuscript became priceless; when such a manuscript was associated with a holy figure such as St. Boniface, it became a relic. These manuscripts were valued as objects of great beauty and also continued to serve both the church and the secular leadership as representations of power and wealth.

Renewed interest in literary achievement was demonstrated by the Hohenstaufen dynasty, and the works of great German poets such as Wolfram von Eschenbach, Hartman von Aue, and Gottfried von Straßburg encouraged the increased production of manuscripts when the demand for written, as opposed to oral, testimony to these works was made by the nobility. These efforts were to become more rationalized and consolidated with the advent of the first German universities, which were founded in the middle of the 14th century. It became characteristic of these institutions of learning that the students provided their own copies of texts, and so manuscripts and their production became an active means to pass on and spread secular as well as theological knowledge. University lectures often consisted of masters reading and commenting on texts, which were then copied verbatim by the attending students. The increased demand for books among the laity also gave rise to an increased market for professional copyists. As the pretension to literacy and education took on greater meaning among the upper classes, the growth of cities and a wealthy merchant class created a new market for books and booksellers. With the introduction of paper and its indigenous production in Germany beginning around 1390, the basic material for manuscripts became affordable enough for a kind of mass production. The step to printing reduced the other main cost factor in book production, that is, the time it took to copy a manuscript by hand. Manuscripts continued to be produced after the advent of printing around 1450, but their numbers became insignificant by the 16th century when compared to the over 20,000 surviving manuscripts written in Germany in the 15th century alone. Although many early prints were still colored by hand, the printed book represented a technological advance that forever relegated manuscript production to an anachronistic pastime.

WILLIAM WHOBREY

Further Reading

Avrin, Leila, *Scribes, Script, and Books: The Book Arts from Antiquity to the Renaissance,* Chicago: American Library Association, 1991

Banks, Doris, *Medieval Manuscript Bookmaking: A Bibliographic Guide,* Metuchen, New Jersey: Scarecrow Press, 1989

Bischoff, Bernhard, *Latin Palaeography: Antiquity and the Middle Ages,* Cambridge: Cambridge University Press, 1990; originally as *Paläographie des römischen Altertums und des abendländischen Mittelalters,* Berlin: Schmidt, 1979

Brownrigg, Linda, editor, *Making the Medieval Book: Techniques of Production,* Los Altos Hills, California: Anderson-Lovelace, 1995

Diringer, David, *The Hand-Produced Book,* New York and London: Hutchinson, 1953

Ganz, Peter F., editor, *The Role of the Book in Medieval Culture,* Turnhout: Brepols, 1986

Harmon, James A., *Codicology of the Court School of Charlemagne: Gospel Book Production, Illumination, and Emphasized Script,* Frankfurt and New York: Lang, 1984

Levarie, Norma, *The Art and History of Books,* New York: Heineman, 1968; New Castle, Delaware: Oak Knoll Press, 1994

Maniaci, Marilena, and Paola Munafò, editors, *Ancient and Medieval Book Materials and Techniques,* 2 vols., Vatican City: Biblioteca Apostolica Vaticana, 1993

McKitterick, Rosamond, *The Carolingians and the Written Word,* Cambridge and New York: Cambridge University Press, 1989

Putnam, George, *Books and Their Makers during the Middle Ages, 476–1600,* 2 vols., New York: Hillary House, 1962

Rück, Peter, and Martin Boghardt, editors, *Rationalisierung der Buchherstellung im Mittelalter und in der frühen Neuzeit,* Marburg: Institut für Historische Hilfswissenschaften, 1994

Wattenbach, Wilhelm, *Das Schriftwesen im Mittelalter,* Leipzig: Hirzel, 1871; reprint, Graz: Akademische Druck- und Verlagsanstalt, 1958

Marx and Marxism

Karl Marx (1818–83), along with his great friend and collaborator Friedrich Engels (1820–95), claimed to have made the theory of communism truly scientific and revolutionary. Their lifelong mission was to develop the insights of their materialist outlook on history and to apply them to the task of establishing a classless society. Marx's own writings range from rigorous economic analyses and historiography to political pamphlets, journalism, and a bulk of personal correspondence that exhibits his international socialism; all express a call to working men of all countries to unite against capitalism. As a propagandist Marx is unsurpassed. In the *Manifest der Kommunistischen Partei* (1848; *Communist Manifesto*), his attempt to explain the nature of capitalism and to predict its downfall was a potent combination of scientific analysis and prophecy that inspired generations of workers in the industrialized countries of Europe and the United States. Marxism's most spectacular successes, however, were in revolutionary Russia, China, and Cuba, where it became the ideology that united the workers and peasants.

Marx took inspiration from his great predecessor Hegel (1770–1831), who had proposed that history is a record of the struggles of Spirit (or God) toward its full realization as absolute self-knowledge. To Hegel, the material world, human institutions, the state of the arts and sciences at a given time, and even human nature itself are all manifestations of the progress of Spirit toward perfection. Spirit's principle of self-change is the *dialectic,* the working out in conflict of its inner contradictions. Spirit's change and development, driven by the dialectical struggle of its opposite tendencies, is never a smooth procession of change. It is change in which periods of slow development may culminate in a sudden leap forward, sometimes out of what look to be the most unpromising and repressive of circumstances. The Enlightenment, for example, took shape against a background of religious fanaticism and persecution. Hegel was himself one of the great spokesmen of a romanticism that celebrated Spirit on a much grander scale than hitherto, when its own nature appears to it as potentially unbounded.

This account of historical change, with its romantic intimations, greatly appealed to Marx. But he was not impressed by the notion of Spirit as the bearer of historical progress. Initially, in his humanist phase, he replaced Spirit by man and made human fulfillment in communism the true end of history. Later, in the interests of his materialism proper, he said Hegel's system had to be "stood on its head." It was not, for Marx, the contradictions within Spirit's being that pushed history forward but the contradictions within the material production of the life of human beings. It is to this "mode of production" to which we must look to explain the behavior of human beings, their conflicts, their thoughts and ideas, and their political, artistic, and scientific achievements. According to Marx, understanding the material basis of human life and society in all its complexity, including its exploitative mechanisms, was the first step to human freedom.

The beginnings of Marxism can be discerned in the *Economic and Philosophic Manuscripts of 1844,* a collection of writings most notable for a vigorous humanism in which Marx sees human beings to be alienated by capitalism from the processes and products of their own labor, their own distinctive species powers, and their fellow human beings. Labor, man's unique capacity to act upon nature, is lauded by Marx as Promethean. Unlike with other animals, nature is not present immediately or adequately to man, who is a being with a potential to appreciate the world as the creation of his species powers. In capitalism, however, the products of his labor come to stand in an alien and dominating otherness to him. Just as in religion, when human beings subject themselves to a being who is really the alien presentation of their own nature, in capitalism they submit to the alien power of the commodity. The more they create material riches, the more they plunge themselves into poverty and cut themselves off from the potential of their many-sided nature. The solution to this predicament is communism, a system in which "the wealth of human need takes the place of the wealth and poverty of political economy." Communism sees "the complete restoration of man to himself as a social, i.e. human being, a restoration which has become conscious and which takes place within the entire wealth of previous periods of development." In the *1844 Manuscripts,* Marx looks to communism to make the dream of the many-sided human being come true. Human advancement, which "takes place within the entire wealth of previous periods of development," eventually ends in the society that produces man "in all the richness of his being, the rich man who is profoundly and abundantly endowed with all the senses."

Marx's early writings outline an active materialism that takes issue with earlier materialists, including his contemporary Ludwig Feuerbach (1804–72), whom he claimed failed to see that the empirical, sensuous world of man is not eternally given but is the outcome of human labor power. According to Marx, they fatally underestimate man's capacity for practical action, and this criticism underlies his famous aphorism in the "Theses on Feuerbach": "Hitherto philosophers have interpreted the world. The point is to change it." Thereafter, Marx undertook an ever more rigorous analysis of political economy in a series of works from

Die heilige Familie (1845; *The Holy Family*) to *Grundrisse der Kritik der politischen Ökonomie* (1857–58; *The Grundrisse*), the *Zur Kritik der politischen Ökonomie* (1859; *A Contribution to the Critique of Political Economy*), and the three volumes of *Das Kapital* (1867; *Capital*). *Die deutsche Ideologie* (1846; *The German Ideology*) is a philosophical polemic against Feuerbach and other radical descendants of Hegel such as Max Stirner (1806–56) and Bruno Bauer (1809–82). To the philosophical idealism of these "ideologists," Marx counterposes his materialist standpoint, abandoning in the process his own "erstwhile philosophical consciousness." Whereas his opponents believed that the false ideas and imaginings that beset and divide human beings originate in the mind and can thus be corrected by philosophy, Marx held that ideological divisions, whether political, moral, or religious, could be traced back to their material relations within production. For Marx, it was not consciousness that determined social life. It was the other way around. Only a revolution in the material organization of life could free human beings, not a revolution in thought alone. Throughout *The German Ideology,* Marx consistently argues for the empirical status of his approach to history, stating that, "when reality is depicted, philosophy as an independent branch of knowledge loses its medium of existence."

The *Communist Manifesto*'s proclamation that "the history of all hitherto existing society is the history of class struggles" follows from Marx's assumption that, only when the determining role of the forces of production and their social relations (the economic mode of production) is acknowledged, does history become intelligible; only then, in turn, can fundamental questions be asked about history. Applying this method, it will be found that history is no mere chronicle, but that there is a necessity within the unfolding of events. Rapid advances in a society's forces of production produce inevitable tensions within its overall structure. In a revolutionary epoch, these tensions lead to the forcible overthrow of the hitherto dominant class. According to Marx, this happened in the revolutionary struggles in Europe of 1789–1848, when the foundations of industrial society were being laid. Of the contending classes in this period, the bourgeoisie was mainly victorious, defeating feudal and landed interests. To Marx, however, its success would prove short-lived once the masses became conscious of the exploitative nature of capitalism and broke their links with the liberal parties.

The *Communist Manifesto* is a peculiar combination of scientific analysis and apocalyptic prophecy. In this work, Marx welcomes capitalism as the progressive outcome of previous economic conditions and class struggles, but only as a staging post on the path to communism. To the proletariat Marx assigns the epic role of securing the communist future. Communists themselves, who are the most "advanced and resolute section of the working class parties of every country," are to play a leading role in this process. Marx demarcates the communist position from a range of other socialist positions, variously called utopian socialism, petty bourgeois socialism, conservative or bourgeois socialism, and German or "true" socialism. He is particularly hard on the last group, attacking its philosophical sentimentalism and adding that in Germany "it spread like an epidemic." The *Communist Manifesto* also makes his position on political violence clear. The ends of communism can be attained only by "the forcible overthrow of all existing social conditions." Marx's skill as a propagandist in the *Communist*

Manifesto is highlighted by a flair for aphorisms such as "the ruling ideas of each age have ever been the ideas of its ruling class," "the executive of the modern state is but a committee for organizing the affairs of the ruling class," and "in place of the old bourgeois society . . . we shall have an association where the free development of each is the condition for the free development of all." It concludes with the buoyant sentiment that "the proletarians have nothing to lose but their chains."

Marx's scientific inquiries culminated in *Das Kapital,* which attempted to reveal both the objective nature of the exploitative relations between capitalist and worker and the way in which capitalism necessarily subordinates labor to capital. According to Marx, the worker's labor power is a commodity that the capitalist buys along with other commodities such as equipment and raw materials. But the commodity of human labor power, unlike other commodities, is a source of what Marx calls "surplus value." Human labor power, working through machinery and raw materials, adds value to the eventual products of this labor. But the worker does not receive the full value of his contribution to the labor process, in the form of wages. If he did, there would be no profit for the capitalist. The extraction of surplus value—profit—from the worker's activity is thus exploitative, and this Marx takes himself to have empirically demonstrated. The worker is forced to sell his labor power at a price that effectively swindles him out of its real value. The capitalist is then able to accumulate surplus value and reinvest it in the pursuit of yet more surplus value. The logic of this system for Marx was that society would inevitably split into two hostile camps, with the increasingly impoverished mass of workers on one side and the capitalists on the other.

Somewhat unexpectedly, and to Marx's delight, his theories became popular in Russia, where capitalism was largely undeveloped. Of the leading Bolsheviks, Lenin (1870–1922) made the most significant theoretical additions to Marxism; these contributions were so significant that the term *Marxist Leninism* became common currency in Marxist circles. Lenin emphasized the role of a vanguard revolutionary party and a dictatorship of the proletariat in establishing socialism; these were notions to which Marx had gestured in his earlier work. It is often acknowledged that the ideals of the October Revolution were corrupted during and after the power struggles in the Soviet Union after Lenin's death. These culminated in the period of the Stalin personality cult and terror, when many of the October Bolsheviks such as Kamenev, Zinoviev, and Bukharin were executed. Stalin's main protagonist, Leon Trotsky, was murdered in Mexico City in 1940. The Soviet state remained an instrument of terror until Stalin's death in 1953 and the subsequent execution of Beria, the head of the KGB. The Chinese revolution led by Mao in 1936 similarly collapsed into personality cults and power struggles within the elite; these collapses eventually led to the fiasco of the cultural revolution in the 1960s, which, among other things, attacked intellectual life and campaigned against all things Western, even the music of Beethoven.

In the West, where the nearest thing to a revolution was the brutally suppressed Spartacus uprising in Germany (1919) led by Rosa Luxemburg and Karl Leibnecht, perhaps the most common feature of the deliberations of Marxist thinkers has been their attention to the *interaction* of economic base and its ideological superstructure, which has been said to have been neglected by Marxists of the second international such as Kautsky

and even by Marx himself. A crude form of economic determinism certainly became the official creed in the Soviet Union. By contrast, thinkers such as George Lukács (1885–1970), Antonio Gramsci (1891–1937), Louis Althusser (1918–90); members of the Frankfurt School in prewar Germany such as Herbert Marcuse (1898–1979), Erich Fromm (1900–1980), Walter Benjamin (1892–1940), Theodor Adorno (1903–70), and Max Horkheimer (1895–1970); and heirs of the Frankfurt School such as Jurgen Habermas (1929–) have emphasized the ideological resources of capitalism in sustaining and reproducing itself. This body of work was undertaken partly to explain how, contrary to Marx's expectations, capitalism had managed to remain dynamic and even to improve general living standards. In their various ways, these thinkers stressed the notion of dialectical interaction between economic base and superstructure, rejecting the notion of ideology as a mere reflection of material processes (a view arguably present in *The German Ideology*). Gramsci's notion of hegemony and Althusser's notion of the "ideological state apparatuses," for example, both indicate that manufacturing ideology through institutions such as religious organizations, schools, and the mass media is more vital to maintaining ruling class power than the use of force. Ideological hegemony was Gramsci's answer to the puzzle of how capitalism had been able to survive in the bourgeois democracies of the West. Given the cultural hegemony of the bourgeoisie, a proletarian revolution was impossible. To succeed, the workers would have to establish such cultural hegemony themselves.

The Frankfurt School, notably Adorno and Marcuse, analyzed the notion of the "culture industry," pointing to the mass production of cultural opiates, including popular music, films, journalism, and television, to keep the masses in a state of servile contentment. The culture industry, in turn, was partly the outcome of the reactionary use of science and technology, which founded the appearance of human well-being upon the abuse of nature and the subjection of human beings to the scientific values of measurement, predictability, and control. To them, the great mission of the Enlightenment, of which traditional Marxism was an extension, had miscarried. Instead of being liberated by scientific reason, men were increasingly enslaved by it. Technology was itself a form of ideology. According to Marcuse, people began to find their souls in their automobiles, kitchen equipment, and hi-fi systems. Through its sheer productivity, capitalism thus established control over the workers by promoting "one-dimensional" thinking, which was unable to conceptualize any radical alternatives to the system.

There have been arguments within the Marxist tradition on the issue of the theoretical continuity between Marx's early humanist writings and his so-called mature works. Some members of the Frankfurt School, notably Marcuse and Fromm, found inspiration more in the young, humanist Marx than in the later Marx. Althusser, however, took the opposite approach. He judged Marx's great achievement as the discovery of a "problematic" based upon an entirely new object: *the mode of production.* A problematic is the form in which problems must be posed in order to produce knowledge. For Althusser, it was the concepts of economic base and social, legal, and ideological superstructure that enabled Marx to pose questions about social formations in a form that allowed for genuinely scientific insight. For this reason, Althusser rejects the idea that Marx continued to work in the problematics of humanism, Hegel, or earlier political economists. Indeed, it was necessary for Marx to break free from those problematics. Working within them, he would have been restricted to their conceptual appraisal of the world. There was thus an "epistemological break" between the problematic of Marx's early humanism and that of *Capital*, Marx's truly scientific achievement.

Marxism still survives as an academic discipline in the arts, social sciences, and cultural studies, but it seems to have lost touch with everyday life. The collapse of the Soviet Union, the power of the culture industry, the triumphant progress of science and technology, cultural pluralism, and the current lack of taste for grand theories all count against its popular appeal. The notion of an industrial working class, in the sense of one that has "nothing to lose but its chains," is no longer real. As a consequence, at the start of a new millennium the socialist millenium seems as far away as ever.

ALASTAIR MCLEISH

See also Frankfurt School; Georg Lukács

Selected English-Language Editions of Marx's Works

Marx, Karl, *Early Writings of Karl Marx,* translated by Rodney Livingstone and Gregor Benton, with an introduction by Lucio Colletti, Harmondsworth: Penguin, 1975

Marx, Karl, and Friedrich Engels, *The German Ideology, Part 1: With Selections from Parts 2 and 3, together with Marx's "Introduction to a Critique of Political Economy,"* edited and with an introduction by C.J. Arthur, New York: International, 1970

——, *The Holy Family,* in *Karl Marx, Frederick Engels: Collected Works,* vol. 4, translated by Richard Dixon et al., London: Lawrence and Wishart, and New York: International, 1975–

Marx, Karl, *The Poverty of Philosophy,* with an introduction by Friedrich Engels, in *Karl Marx, Frederick Engels: Collected Works,* vol. 6, translated by Richard Dixon et al., London: Lawrence and Wishart, and New York: International, 1975–

Marx, Karl, and Friedrich Engels, *The Communist Manifesto: A Modern Edition,* with an introduction by Eric Hobsbawm, London and New York: Verso, 1998

——, *Capital,* in *Karl Marx, Frederick Engels: Collected Works,* vols. 35–37, translated by Richard Dixon et al., London: Lawrence and Wishart, and New York: International, 1975–

Marx, Karl, *Grundrisse: Foundations of the Critique of Political Economy,* translated by Martin Nicolaus, London: New Left Review, and New York: Random House, 1973

Marx, Karl, and Friedrich Engels, *Collected Works,* translated by Richard Dixon et al., London: Lawrence and Wishart, and New York: International, 1975–

Further Reading

Adorno, Theodor W., and Max Horkheimer, *Dialektik der Aufklärung,* Amsterdam: Querido, 1947; as *The Dialectic of Enlightenment,* New York: Continuum, 1972

Althusser, Louis, *Pour Marx,* Paris: Maspero, 1965; as *For Marx,* London: Lane, and New York: Pantheon, 1969

——, *Lénine et la philosophie,* Paris: Maspero, 1969; as *Lenin and Philosophy and Other Essays,* translated by Ben Brewster, London: New Left Books, 1971

Althusser, Louis, and L. Balibar, *Lire le Capital,* Paris: Maspero, 2 vols., 1965; as *Reading Capital,* translated by Ben Brewster, London and New York: Verso, 1979

Bloch, Ernst, *Das Prinzip Hoffnung,* Berlin: Aufbau, 3 vols., 1954–59; as *The Principle of Hope,* Cambridge, Massachusetts: MIT Press, 3 vols., 1986

——, *Geist der Utopie,* Munich: Duncker und Humblot, 1918

Gramsci, Antonio, *Selections from the Prison Notebooks,* edited by Quintin Hoare and Geoffrey Nowell-Smith, London: Lawrence and Wishart, 1971; New York: International, 1972

Hook, Sidney, *From Hegel to Marx: Studies in the Intellectual Development of Karl Marx,* New York: Reynal and Hitchcock, and London: Gollancz, 1936

Lenin, Vladimir Ilich, *Essential Works of Lenin,* edited by Henry M. Christman, New York: Bantam Books, 1966

Lukács, Georg, *Geschichte und Klassenbewusstsein: Studien über marxistische Dialektik,* Berlin: Malik, 1923; as *History and Class Consciousness: Studies in Marxist Dialectics,* Cambridge, Massachusetts: MIT Press, 1971

——, *Der junge Hegel: Über die Beziehung von Dialektik und Ökonomie,* Zurich: Europa, 1948; as *The Young Hegel: Studies in the Relations between Dialectics and Economics,* London: Merlin Press, 1975; Cambridge, Massachusetts: MIT Press, 1976

Marcuse, Herbert, *Reason and Revolution,* London and New York: Oxford University Press, 1941

——, *One Dimensional Man,* London: Routledge and Kegan Paul, and Boston: Beacon Press, 1964

McLellan, David, *Karl Marx: His Life and Thought,* London: Macmillan, 1973; New York: Harper and Row, 1974

Ollman, Bertell, *Alienation: Marx's Conception of Man in Capitalist Society,* Cambridge: Cambridge University Press, 1971

Mastersingers

The mastersingers are most familiar today through Richard Wagner's opera *Die Meistersinger von Nürnberg* (*The Mastersingers of Nuremberg*), completed in 1867 and first performed in Munich in 1868. Based on the composer's reading of Jacob Grimm's *Über den altdeutschen Meistergesang* (1811; On the Old German Art of Mastersong) and Johann Christoph Wagenseil's *Von der Meistersinger holdseliger Kunst* (1697; On the Sweet Art of the Mastersingers), the opera presents a romantic-poetic picture of the world of the 16th-century mastersingers.

Though the art of the mastersingers has its roots in the work of medieval professional itinerant poets who were dependent on aristocratic patrons, its most remarkable phase is the institutionalized form it attained in the early-modern period when amateur singers, largely (but not exclusively) craftsmen and artisans of the middle and lower classes, organized themselves into *Singschulen* (singing schools). These fraternities, whose activities were influenced by the late-medieval guild system, flourished especially in the 15th and 16th centuries not only in Nuremberg but also in about 25 other towns, mostly imperial cities in southern Germany, as well as in Austria (Schwaz, Steyr, Wels) and elsewhere (such as Breslau in Silesia and Iglau in Moravia). Several of these *Singschulen* endured for as long as 300 years or more, such as in Mainz (allegedly founded by Frauenlob ca. 1310 and existing until 1600), Augsburg (1449–1772), Nuremberg (1450–1774), Strasbourg (1492–1780), Ulm (1517–1839), and Memmingen (1600–1875). The last Memmingen mastersinger died as recently as 1922.

Just as the medieval craft guilds jealously watched over their traditions and privileges, so too the 15th- and 16th-century *Singschulen* promoted their art through enforcement of a strict code of practice. The mastersingers viewed their activities as an extension of the song contests of the Middle Ages (of the kind depicted in Wagner's *Tannhäuser*), and accordingly, a competitive spirit was of the essence. Members progressed from grade to grade through public demonstration of their abilities. The absolute novice was termed a *Schüler* (pupil), while one who had learned the basic rules was a *Schulfreund* (schoolfriend); a member able to sing five or six songs faultlessly was a *Singer* (singer), while one who could compose new words to be set to existing tunes was a *Dichter* (poet). The highest title, *Meister* (master), was reserved for those who composed not only original words but also an original tune.

The focus of activity of the *Singschule* was the regular public concert, usually held monthly in a church, at which only religious songs were sung; this was followed by the private *Zechsingen* (concert held in a room in an inn), at which secular songs would be sung but where it was still a requirement for the content of the songs to reflect Christian morality. The performers, singing solo and unaccompanied, competed for prizes that initially took the form of a crown, wreath, or chaplet of flowers, or an image of King David, the psalmist, but later, even cash rewards were offered. Songs were composed and sung according to the strict rules of the *Tabulatur*, the earliest surviving example of which, from Nuremberg, dates from 1540. Though details might differ slightly from place to place, the Nuremberg model was generally influential, not least through being disseminated through Adam Puschman's *Gründlicher Bericht des deutschen Meistergesanges* (1571). Observance of the rules was monitored by up to four *Merker* (judges) hidden from view behind a curtain, each of whom would be assigned a specific set of tasks, whether assessing the linguistic quality, checking the stanzaic form (the number of lines, the correct number of syllables per line, and the rhyme scheme against a written skeleton plan—a difficult task given the complexity of some stanzas, e.g., Hans Folz's *Freier Ton* with its 28 lines and 11 rhymes, while some later examples had more than 100 lines!), the melody, or the content of the song (especially, after the Reformation, checking it against Luther's Bible for inaccuracies of doctrine or detail). Hans Sachs (1494–1576), the most famous of the Nuremberg mastersingers, who penned an astonishing 4,285 mastersongs (of which slightly more than half were on secular subjects, reflecting his voracious reading) employing more than 300 different strophic forms, himself served as *Merker* from 1555 to 1561.

The mastersingers saw themselves as the heirs to the poetic tradition of the Middle Ages. They subscribed to the (chronologically impossible) myth that in the year 962 "12 old masters" had been inspired by God to practice the art of poetry in German. Foremost among these were "the four crowned masters"

(allegedly crowned by Emperor Otto the Great): Heinrich von Mügeln (d. after 1371), Frauenlob (d. 1318), Marner (ca. 1230–70), and Regenbogen (d. after 1318), whose *lange Töne* (long stanzas) each aspirant was required to master. Regarding their art as a craft whose skills could be learned, the mastersingers tended to emphasize mastery of form (as a reflection of the Divine Order) rather than poetic inventiveness or literary quality, which explains why little of lasting merit was produced.

The songs of the mastersingers invariably comprised an odd number of stanzas. As in many songs of their medieval predecessors, the stanzaic form was tripartite, the first two sections being metrically and musically identical, while the final section differed both in meter and melody. But while they inherited this form from the minnesingers, the poets of courtly love, their songs dealt mostly with religious topics (such as the Creation, the Trinity, the Virgin Mary, or the Nativity, Passion, and Resurrection of Christ) or didactic subjects (the seven liberal arts, for example). Through their songs the mastersingers, whose very designation, although deriving immediately from the practices of the craft guilds, ultimately embodied the notion of the learned poet, the *poeta doctus*, contributed to the general education of their contemporaries.

Since *Meistersang* was a form of institutionalized art, constrained by a canon of rules into uniformity, the characteristic voice of an individual poet is difficult to discern. The songs were regarded as the property of the group, and individuals were generally not permitted to publish their own songs (some 16,000 songs survive in about 120 manuscripts from the 15th to 18th centuries). But while the majority of the mastersingers were undistinguished and indistinguishable, one or two have left a mark as individuals. Hans Sachs has already been mentioned, but another important figure is Hans Folz (ca. 1435–1513), who seems to some extent to have questioned the value of trying to emulate the "12 old masters" of whom his contemporaries had but the haziest of notions. It became a requirement in Nuremberg (and subsequently elsewhere) that, in order to qualify for the title of master, an aspirant must compose a new melody to words of his own invention. Hans Sachs himself composed 13 original melodies, one of which, his *Silberweise* (ca. 1513; Silver Air), appears to have been the model for the tune of Luther's famous hymn *Ein feste Burg ist unser Gott* (A Safe Stronghold). In one virtuoso piece, *Die 13 verwandelten Frawen* (The 13 Metamorphosed Ladies), Sachs uses each of his 13 original melodies in turn. Hans Sachs himself praised 12 modern masters as the pride of the Nuremberg *Singschule*: Kunrad Nahtigall, Fritz Zorn, Vogelsang, Herman Oertel, Fritz Ketner, Merten Grim, Sixt Beckmesser, Gostenhof, Hans Schwarz, Ulrich Eislinger, Hans Folz, and his own teacher, Lienhart Nunnenbeck, names many of which we recognize from Wagner's *Die Meistersinger von Nürnberg*.

JOHN L. FLOOD

See also Hans Sachs

Further Reading

Bell, Clair Hayden, *The Meistersingerschule at Memmingen and Its "Kurtze Entwerffung,"* Berkeley: University of California Press, 1952
——, "A Glance into the Workshop of Meistergesang," *PMLA* 68 (1953)

Brunner, Horst, *Die alten Meister: Studien zu Überlieferung und Rezeption der mittelhochdeutschen Sangspruchdichter im Spätmittelalter und in der frühen Neuzeit*, Munich: Beck, 1975

———, "Meistergesang," in *Literatur Lexikon*, edited by Walther Killy, Gütersloh: Bertelsmann, 1993

———, "Meistergesang," in *The New Grove Dictionary of Music and Musicians*, edited by Stanley Sadie, London: Macmillan, 1980

———, editor, *J. Chr. Wagenseil, "Buch von der Meister-Singer holdseligen Kunst" (Altdorf 1697)*, Göppingen: Kümmerle, 1975

Brunner, Horst, and Burghart Wachinger, editors, *Repertorium der Sangsprüche und Meisterlieder des 12. bis 18. Jahrhunderts*, 16 vols., Tübingen: Niemeyer, 1986–97

Drescher, Karl, editor, *Nürnberger Meistersinger-Protokolle von 1575–1689*, 2 vols., Stuttgart and Tübingen: Litterarischer Verein, 1897; reprint in 1 vol., Hildesheim: Olms, 1963

Klesatschke, Eva, "Meistergesang," in *Deutsche Literatur: Eine Sozialgeschichte*, edited by Horst Albert Glaser, Reinbek bei Hamburg: Rowohlt, 1980

Klesatschke, Eva, and Horst Brunner, editors, *Meisterlieder des 16. bis 18. Jahrhunderts*, Tübingen: Niemeyer, 1993

Könneker, Barbara, *Hans Sachs*, Stuttgart: Metzler, 1971

Nagel, Bert, *Meistersang*, Stuttgart: Metzler, 1962

Nagel, Bert, editor, *Meistersang: Meisterlieder und Singschulzeugnisse*, Stuttgart: Reclam, 1965

———, editor, *Der deutsche Meistersang*, Darmstadt: Wissenschaftliche Buchgesellschaft, 1967

Petzsch, Christoph, "Zur sogenannten, Hanz Folz zugeschriebenen Meistergesangreform," *Beiträge zur Geschichte der deutschen Sprache und Literatur* 88 (Tübingen, 1966)

Rettelbach, Johannes, *Variation, Derivation, Imitation: Untersuchungen zu den Tönen der Sangspruchdichter und Meistersinger*, Tübingen: Niemeyer, 1993

Schanze, Frieder, *Meisterliche Liedkunst zwischen Heinrich von Mügeln und Hans Sachs*, 2 vols., Munich and Zurich: Artemis, 1983–84

Taylor, Archer, *The Literary History of Meistergesang*, London: Oxford University Press, and New York: Modern Language Association of America, 1936

Taylor, Brian, "The Historical Mastersingers: What Were They Really Like?" *Wagner in Australia* 1 (1988)

Taylor, Brian, editor, *Adam Puschman, "Gründlicher Bericht des deutschen Meistergesangs" (Die drei Fassungen von 1571, 1584, 1596)*, 2 vols, Göppingen: Kümmerle, 1984

Karl May 1842–1912

Karl May was and remains the best-selling fiction writer in the German language. No one knows how many volumes of his works have been sold, especially after his copyright fell into the public domain in 1962; estimates begin at 100 million. He has become the most universally shared reading experience of German boys and girls, and it is possible that his works have displaced even the Bible. While the popularity of his works has been declining, sales continue to hover around a quarter of a million volumes a year. Although perhaps best understood as a writer for young readers, May remains a presence in the cultural memory of many adults, and a large philological and scholarly corpus has grown up around him.

May was born into a community of weavers that had become desperately impoverished owing to technological obsolescence. He became blind shortly after birth, a circumstance to which he ascribed his predilection for fantasy, and his sight was not restored until he was five years old. His family struggled to give him an education, sending him eventually to a teachers' school. There began a curious series of delinquencies, thefts, and swindles with false identities that resulted in his expulsion from school and arrest, and prison terms totaling eight years. In prison he began to think that writing might be a more practical use of his imagination than crime, and he began a career of writing magazine stories and subliterary serial novels. His breakthrough to fame, however, came in the 1880s and 1890s with a series of stories and novels set in two exotic settings: the American West and the Near East.

May's works had a very complicated publication history, but in the form in which they came to be widely read they are known as *Winnetou* in four volumes (1893–1910), *Durchs wilde Kur-distan* and *Durch die Wüste* (1892, 1896; *In the Desert*), *Von Bagdad nach Stambul* (1892; *The Caravan of Death*), *In den Schluchten des Balkan* (1892: *The Secret Brotherhood*), *Durch das Land der Skipetaren* (1892; *The Evil Saint*), and *Der Schut* (1892; *The Black Persian*). In general these works belong to a mode of exotic adventure writing drawn, especially in May's case, from fiction, travel books, and anthropological and linguistic studies of the past in which he was especially well read and from which he drew in an elaborate system of plagiaristic synthesis. Among his sources were James Fenimore Cooper and such German-language writers as Charles Sealsfield and Friedrich Gerstäcker.

The pecularity of these lively and unremittingly suspenseful narrations came to be their progressive erasure of the boundary between fiction and lying. The reader is encouraged to identify the protagonist with the author himself. In the stories of the American West, he is the universally competent Old Shatterhand, a German "greenhorn" who has acquired skills surpassing those of all frontiersmen and even the Indians by reading books in his homeland (presumably May's) and who forms a partnership with the ideal Indian, Winnetou. In the Near Eastern tales, he is Kara ben Nemsi ("Karl the German"), equipped with similar superhuman skills. In time May claimed to know hundreds of Indian dialects and North African languages and displayed exotic weapons and hairs from Winnetou's head. In fact, he visited North Africa for the first time in 1899–1900 and the United States in 1908, long after his public persona had been established. Inevitably, his imposture became obvious, leading to a campaign of exposure that embittered the last years of his life and caused him to reflect on his psychological disposition, which he came to self-diagnose as a form of schizophrenia. In the long run, however, the unmasking of his fraudulence in no way inhibited the conquest of the reading public.

May's fiction has two main aspects. One is the sheer entertainment of suspense and adventure, the endless story of danger encountered and escaped, crime and punishment, stalking and ambush, mystery and solution, a template for generations of children's games, wherever there might be a field, a hill, or a ravine. But the other is a conservative moralism, muscularly Christian and monarchist, antidemocratic, antisocialist, and antifeminist. Above all, the implications are intensely nationalistic. All the good white men in the American West, starting with Old Shatterhand, are Germans; they are allied with the noble Indians against the avaricious Yankees and their degenerate Indian allies. Thus, May created in German culture not only an enduring fascination with Indians and their culture but also a curious notion of a German-Indian affinity, two peoples oppressed by the crass and the unspiritual but destined to triumph. To this day Germans celebrate this affinity in museums, Indian encampments, festival reenactments of May's tales, and a series of popular films.

One can, to be sure, overestimate May's ideological influence on the German people. Since everyone read him, from Adolf Hitler to Albert Schweitzer, he cannot be held responsible for every reader's behavior. Furthermore, in the course of time, he became notably pacifist and, in his late, so-called mystical works, *Ardistan und Dschinnistan* (1909: *Ardistan and Djinnistan*) and the fourth volume of *Winnetou* (1910), he propagated a utopian vision of reconciliation among warring peoples. If he had not died in 1912, but had lived another two or three years, it is not impossible that he would have become an opponent of World War I, with consequences that are fascinating to contemplate. But it is perhaps significant that the most spectacularly successful German writer about the United States, although he had some international success, never found an American readership; an ambitious effort in 1977 to propagate him in English translation failed completely. A systematic American perspective on the phenomenon remains to be achieved.

JEFFREY L. SAMMONS

See also Popular Literature

Biography

Born in Ernstthal, 25 February 1842. Sentences served in jail, workhouse, and prison, 1862, 1865–74; editor in the publishing house of Münchmeyer, Dresden, 1875–77; freelance writer from 1877. Died in Radebeul, 30 March 1912.

Selected Works

Collections

Gesammelte Werke, edited by E.A. Schmid et al., 65 vols., 1913–39
Gesammelte Werke, edited by E.A. Schmid, 74 vols., 1949–65
Karl Mays Werke: Historische-kritische Ausgabe, edited by Hermann Wiedenroth and Hans Wollschläger, 99 vols., 1987–

Fiction

Auf hoher See gefangen, 1879
Das Waldröschen oder Die Verfolgung rund um die Erde, 1882–84
Die Liebe des Ulanen, 1883–85; expanded editions, 1905–6
Deutsche Herzen—Deutsche Helden, 1885–87
Der vorlorene Sohn oder der Fürst des Elends, 1885–87
Der Weg zum Glück, 1886–87
Durch das Land der Skipetaren, 1892; as *The Evil Saint*, translated by Michael Shaw, 1979
Durch Wüste und Harem, 1892; republished as *Durch die Wüste*, 1896; as *In the Desert*, translated by F. Billerbeck-Gentz, 1955
Durchs wilde Kurdistan, 1892; as *In the Desert*, translated by Michael Shaw, 1977
In den Schluchten des Balkan, 1892; as *The Secret Brotherhood*, translated by Michael Shaw, 1979
Der Schut, 1892; as *The Black Persian*, translated by Michael Shaw, 1979
Von Bagdad nach Stambul, 1892; as *The Caravan of Death*, translated by Michael Shaw, 1979
Die Sklavenkarawane, 1893
Winnetou, der rote Gentleman [Parts I–III], 1893; abridged as *Winnetou, the Apache Knight* and as *The Treasures of Nugget Mountain*, translated by Marion Ames Taggart, 1898; Parts I and III as *Winnetou*, translated by Michael Shaw, 1977
Am Rio de la Plata, 1894
Am stillen Ocean, 1894
Orangen und Datteln: Reisefrüchte aus dem Oriente, 1894
Der Schatz im Silbersee, 1894
In den Cordilleren, 1894–95
Old Surehand [Parts I and II], 1894–95; abridged as *Captain Cayman*, translated by Fred Gardner, 1971
Im Lande des Mahdi, 1896
Old Surehand [Part III], 1896
Satan und Ischariot, 1896–97
Der Oelprinz, 1897
Im Reiche des silbernen Löwen, 1898–1903
Ardistan und Dschinnistan, 1909; as *Ardistan and Djinnistan*, translated by Michael Shaw, 1977
Winnetou [Part IV], 1910

Essays

Und Frieden auf Erden, 1904
Mein Leben und Streben: Selbstbiographie, 1910

Further Reading

Berman, Nina Auguste, *Orientalismus, Kolonialismus und Moderne: Zum Bild des Orients in der deutschsprachigen Kultur um 1900*, Stuttgart: M und P, 1997
Cook, Colleen, "Germany's Wild West Author: A Researcher's Guide to Karl May," *German Studies Review* 5 (1982)
Doerry, Karl W., "Karl May," in *Nineteenth-Century German Writers*, Dictionary of Literary Biography, vol. 129, edited by James Hardin and Siegfried Mews, Detroit, Michigan, and London: Gale Research, 1993
Hohendahl, Peter Uwe, "Von der Rothaut zum Edelmenschen: Karl Mays Amerikaromane," in *Amerika in der deutschen Literatur: Neue Welt, Nordamerika, USA*, edited by Sigrid Bauschinger, Horst Denkler, and Wilfried Malsch, Stuttgart: Reclam, 1975
Lowsky, Martin, *Karl May*, Stuttgart: Metzler, 1987
Sammons, Jeffrey L., *Ideology, Mimesis, Fantasy: Charles Sealsfield, Friedrich Gerstäcker, Karl May, and Other German Novelists of America*, Chapel Hill: University of North Carolina Press, 1998
Schmiedt, Helmut, *Karl May: Studien zu Leben, Werk und Wirkung eines Erfolgschriftstellers*, Königstein: Hain, 1979
Ueding, Gert, and Reinhard Tschapke, editors, *Karl-May-Handbuch*, Stuttgart: Kröner, 1987
Wohlgschaft, Hermann, *Große Karl May Biographie: Leben und Werk*, Paderborn: Igel, 1994
Wollschläger, Hans, *Karl May in Selbstzeugnissen und Bilddokumenten*, Reinbek bei Hamburg: Rowohlt, 1965

Mechthild von Magdeburg ca. 1207–ca. 1282

Within the *Frauenmystik* (female mysticism) of the 12th to the 14th centuries, Germany's Mechthild von Magdeburg's sole book, *Das fließende Licht der Gottheit* (*The Flowing Light of the Godhead*), written between ca. 1250 and ca. 1282, is regarded as a singular and strikingly lyrical expression of affective mysticism. Mechthild's Low German text has not survived; her writings reach the modern reader through the filter of a mid-14th-century translation of it into the Alemannic dialect of High German by Heinrich von Nördlingen.

The 267 individual passages of *The Flowing Light of the Godhead* are divided into seven books. Some of these passages comprise a few lines, others extend to pages; some are linked thematically with what precedes and follows, but the majority of them stand as independent units. As an integral literary work, *The Flowing Light of the Godhead* eludes categorization in terms of genre, containing as it does visions, revelations, auditions, dialogues, prayers, hymns, letters, allegories, parables, and narratives. As the narrator, Mechthild casts herself in the role of visionary, lover, prophet, teacher, critic, counselor, and mediator. She is boldly eclectic in her use of stylistic devices to convey her experiences, thoughts, and feelings and employs lyrical, epic, dramatic, and didactic elements. The sense of structural fluidity in *The Flowing Light of the Godhead* is enhanced by a prose that transmutes easily into verse through the use of colon rhyme, that is, the linking of phrases by assonance. The unity and coherence of *The Flowing Light of the Godhead* reside in the persona of the author and her spiritual biography. Of fundamental importance in Mechthild's writings is the love shared by God and his creation mankind, and this she expresses most powerfully and memorably in her descriptions of the encounters between the loving soul and her bridegroom Christ.

Although modern scholars may struggle to categorize *The Flowing Light of the Godhead* as a literary work and to identify cohesive structural patterns in that work, Mechthild herself quite clearly had a sense of the unity of her writings, referring to them programmatically as a "book." For Mechthild, the individual passages were all manifestations of the inspiration she received from God. Indeed, God is presented as the "author" of her work and Mechthild herself as but the instrument. Feminist interpretations of medieval women's mystical writing in the last two decades have thrown into sharp relief how women who were increasingly denied clerical authority could claim authority through direct communion with God. Throughout *The Flowing Light of the Godhead*, Mechthild expresses her sense of her unworthiness, inadequacy, and vulnerability to criticism, projecting an image of herself as a simple, untutored woman. God's reassurance that it is her very lack of education that makes her a worthy recipient for his favor (e.g., in books II and IV), however, places Mechthild beyond criticism by invoking the tradition of *docta ignorantia* and *sancta simplicitas*. Although Mechthild's writings explicitly reinforce the authority of the Church and the clergy, she nonetheless feels empowered by God to attack the priesthood for its spiritual shortcomings (e.g., in book VI).

Mechthild appears to have been born into a wealthy family, possibly a noble one, and to have received an education befitting her social status. She informs her reader that she can read and write, although she claims to be unversed in Latin. It is evident from her writings that Mechthild was well acquainted with the Bible (in particular the Song of Songs, the Psalms, the Gospels, and Revelation), methods of biblical exegesis, and the liturgy. Beyond that, she freely employs images from the Neoplatonic tradition and the courtly love lyric. Although Mechthild did not benefit from the Latin-based theological education of the convent, there is nonetheless evidence of the influence of the following in her writings: Augustine, Bernard of Clairvaux, Hugh and Richard of St. Victor, Pseudo-Dionysius, and Joachim of Fiore. It is generally assumed that these influences were mediated to her through sermons and instruction by the Dominicans.

The first evidence of the reception of Mechthild's work is to be found in the Latin translation, completed by the end of the 13th century, of the first six of her seven books by Dominicans from Halle. The *Lux divinitatis fluens in corda veritatis* (The Light of the Divinity Flowing into the Hearts of Truth) is not an entirely faithful translation, for some of Mechthild's more erotic imagery, her fierce attacks on contemporaries, and passages of questionable theology are tempered. Furthermore, the material has been radically reordered. Whereas in *The Flowing Light of the Godhead* it would seem that passages appear in chronological order, they are grouped according to theme in the *Lux divinitatis*.

It would seem that Mechthild spent the greater part of her adult life as a Beguine, that is, as a member of a community of women who chose to lead a life of voluntary poverty, chastity, and religious devotion in the secular world. The unregulated lives of the Beguines became a cause for suspicion and concern in clerical circles in the 13th century, and it could be that this suspicion fueled Mechthild's sense of vulnerability. It is nonetheless evident from the prefaces to *The Flowing Light of the Godhead* and the prologue to the *Lux divinitatis* that the Dominicans were supportive of Mechthild and promoted her writings. Mechthild reciprocated in her fulsome praise of their order and its founding father, and she supported them in their conflict with the secular clergy over matters of pastoral care.

Mechthild spent the last years of her life in the convent of St. Mary at Helfta. By the end of the 13th century, the books recording the revelations and visions accorded to Mechthild's younger contemporaries and kindred spirits, Mechthild von Hackeborn and Gertrude the Great, the *Liber specialis gratiae* (*The Book of Special Grace*) and the *Legatus divinae pietatis* (*The Herald of Divine Love*), together with Mechthild's own writings, established Helfta as a center for women's visionary mysticism. Mechthild von Hackeborn's and Gertrude's books were, however, to enjoy a greater circulation than Mechthild von Magdeburg's more idiosyncratic work. The integrity of *The Flowing Light of the Godhead* was not respected after the mid–14th century, and it survived thereafter only into the beginning of the 16th century in selected anonymous passages in manuals of piety.

ELIZABETH A. ANDERSEN

Biography

Born near Magdeburg, ca. 1207. Became a Beguine, ca. 1230/35; entered Benedictine convent as Cistercian nun at Helfta, near Eisleben, ca. 1270. Died in Helfta, ca. 1282.

Selected Works

Writings

Das fließende Licht der Gottheit, translated [from Low German to High German] by Heinrich von Nördlingen, ca. 1344; translated into modern German by Margot Schmidt, 1995; as *The Flowing Light of the Godhead,* translated by Frank Tobin, 1998

Further Reading

Bynum, Caroline Walker, "Women Mystics in the Thirteenth Century: The Case of the Nuns of Helfta," in *Jesus as Mother: Studies in the Spirituality of the High Middle Ages,* Berkeley: University of California Press, 1982

Hollywood, Amy, *The Soul as Virgin Wife: Mechthild of Magdeburg, Marguerite Porete, and Meister Eckhart,* Notre Dame, Indiana: University of Notre Dame Press, 1995

Mohr, Wolfgang, "Darbietungsformen der Mystik bei Mechthild von Magdeburg," in *Märchen, Mythos, Dichtung: Festschrift zum 90. Geburtstag Friedrich von der Leyens,* edited by Hugo Kuhn and Kurt Schier, Munich: Beck, 1963

Neumann, Hans, "Beiträge zur Textgeschichte des 'Fließenden Lichts der Gottheit' und zur Lebensgeschichte Mechthilds von Magdeburg," in *Altdeutsche und altniederländische Mystik,* edited by Kurt Ruh, Darmstadt: Wissenschaftliche Buchgesellschaft, 1964

Ruh, Kurt, "Mechthild von Magdeburg," in *Frauenmystik und Franziskanische Mystik der Frühzeit,* Geschichte der abendländischen Mystik, vol. 2, Munich: Beck, 1993

Tobin, Frank J., *Mechthild von Magdeburg: A Medieval Mystic in Modern Eyes,* Columbia, South Carolina: Camden House, 1995

Wiethaus, Ulrike, *Ecstatic Transformation: Transpersonal Psychology in the Work of Mechthild von Magdeburg,* Syracuse, New York: Syracuse University Press, 1996

Medieval Manuscripts *see* Manuscripts (Medieval)

Meister Eckhart ca. 1260–1328

Meister Eckhart is, alongside Mechthild von Magdeburg, the key figure of mysticism in late-medieval Germany. This mysticism arose in the context of the turn to more individualized forms of spirituality that developed in the trade centers of Europe (Lombardy, northeastern France, Flanders, and the Rhineland) from the 12th century onward. By actively cultivating the individual's inner life and sense of responsibility, late-medieval German mysticism prefigured aspects of modern forms of subjectivity. Meister Eckhart's particular contribution to this mysticism is the place that his texts give to rational self-analysis in the process of spiritual development without losing contact with the longing for God that Eckhart shared with the spiritually inclined nuns and beguines who to a great extent comprised his congregation. Eckhart's sermons represent a radical reformulation of apostolic ideals by a thinker who was close to the women to whom he preached and who enjoyed an incomparable grounding in the academic philosophy of the period.

Texts by Eckhart survive in both Latin and Middle High German. The Latin texts are primarily academic in nature and include scholarly disputations such as the *Quaestiones Parisienses* (1302–3; *Parisian Questions*), biblical commentaries (Genesis, Exodus, Ecclesiastes, and John's Gospel), sermons, and the prologue to an *Opus Tripartitum* (1302–3 or 1311–13; Tripartite

Work) that Eckhart conceived along the lines of Thomas Aquinas's *Summa theologica* at the time of one of his own appointments in Paris. The German works are primarily pastoral and include sermons (115 have so far been accepted as authentic) and treatises: *Die rede der underscheidunge* (1294–98; *Talks of Instruction*); the *Liber "benedictus"* (1314–23; "Blessed" Book), which contains both "Daz buoch der goetlîchen troestunge" (Book of Divine Consolation) and the sermon "Von dem edeln menschen" (On the Noble Man); and, finally, "Von abgescheidenheit" (Of Detachment), a text whose authenticity is still in doubt. While it was at one time thought that the sermons were passed down on the basis of notes taken by the friars and nuns who listened to Eckhart preach, it is now believed that the texts are no less authoritative than those of the Latin or German treatises, which are known to stem from Eckhart's hand. The sermons were also edited or approved by Eckhart before they were issued in written form.

Eckhart's writings can be divided up in various ways. The earliest German texts—*Die rede der underscheidunge,* which Eckhart addressed to novices while he was prior of the Dominican friary in Erfurt—can be separated from later German works, which more obviously show the signs of Eckhart's academic training. The sermons gathered in the manuscript known as the

Paradisus anime intelligentis (sermons 7, 9, 20B, 32, 33, 37, 38, 43, 56, 57, 60, 70, 72, 80, 82, 84, and 85 [in both *Die deutschen und lateinischen Werke* and *Werke,* edited by Largier]) are thought to belong to the period immediately after Eckhart's first Parisian appointment and show traces of the debates between Dominicans and Franciscans as to whether intellect or the will was the faculty of knowledge of God. Other sermons (sermons 1, 10–15, 18, 19, 22, 25, 26, 35, 37, 49, 51, 59, and 79) appear to stem from Eckhart's final years in Cologne, and there has been speculation that the sermon on the text "Blessed are the poor in spirit" (sermon 52) might even date from the period after inquisitorial proceedings had been initiated against Eckhart. The pastoral German texts can be separated from the academic Latin works, while these in their turn can be divided up into different periods, with the *Quaestiones Parisienses* reflecting Eckhart's encounter with Franciscan theology at the Sorbonne. With their stress on the intellectuality of God, by contrast, the incomplete *Opus Tripartitum* and the commentary on St. John reflect a conceptual shift away from the *Quaestiones Parisienses* to a position closer to that of Eckhart's pre-Parisian texts, which emphasize God's being.

Eckhart's own texts do not strictly observe these divisions. For instance, Eckhart does not consistently privilege intellect over will or love in the sermons collected in *Paradisus anime intelligentis* (e.g., sermon 60). Nor does he consistently move away from the Parisian emphasis on intellectuality to a later interest in God's being, but he can at any moment defend a position beyond both terms (e.g., sermons 2 and 7). Such nonobservation seems to be a part of Eckhart's method. He did not attempt to elaborate a system (even the *Opus Tripartitum,* had it been completed, would not have offered an exhaustive account of Eckhart's position, but would merely have clarified those issues on which he thought he had something new to say, [see Largier, editor, *Werke,* vol. 2, p. 462]). His interventions in both the sermons and the treatises were instead strategic, engaging with concepts in order to push beyond them. In this respect it is more useful to view Eckhart's texts as part of a single project that responds differently to different situations, rather than to impose on them a strict periodization.

Eckhart's project can be summed up with a sentence from the *Die rede der underscheidunge:* "Nim dîn selbes war, und swâ dû dich vindest, dâ lâz dich; daz ist daz aller beste" (Examine yourself and wherever you find yourself, take leave of yourself—that is the best thing of all). The self that Eckhart is encouraging his listeners to abandon is not an abstract entity. Rather, Eckhart focuses on the accumulated habits and assumptions by which individuals impose structure and security on their life. In the case of Eckhart's monastic audience of the early 14th century, this meant the self-castigating regimen to which devout nuns and friars subjected themselves (including fasting, vigils, sleeping on boards, and self-laceration) in the hope of guaranteeing their salvation, or of forcefully generating a form of mystical rapture. Eckhart encourages his audience to forego such false security. There is no single, guaranteed path to God. Rather, Eckhart suggests in *Die rede der underscheidunge* that each individual must find his or her own way—giving up one or two words they particularly cling to, rather than renouncing speech altogether.

Eckhart engages with the behavior and ascetic routines of his audience, but he also addresses the assumptions behind this behavior, criticizing the quasi-economic attitude that assumes its good works will be adequately rewarded (sermon 1). Similar to other representatives of the apostolic life, Eckhart criticizes the calculating assumptions of a nascent economic rationality. He equally calls into question other conceptual assumptions, bidding his audience to take leave of the categories of time, space, number, and, indeed, God, since individuals only need a concept of God to the degree that they are separated from divinity (sermon 52).

The union with God in which this process of self-overcoming culminates is frequently described by Eckhart using two groups of metaphors, those associated with Christ's incarnation, and others associated with the idea of a spark (*vünkelîn*) or ground of the soul. Christ's incarnation is not treated as a historical event. Rather, God is said to give birth to his son continuously in a process that occurs in the souls of individuals who have sufficiently rid themselves of psychological rigidity, and to which these souls themselves can actively contribute (sermon 2). The metaphors associated with the spark of the soul similarly express the potential proximity between God and man. Indeed, in some texts, Eckhart even goes so far as to put this attribute of the soul on the same level as God, calling it "ungeschaffen und ungeschepfelich" (uncreated and uncreatable, sermon 13), not a product of God, but a part of him. In general, however, the terms themselves are less important than the dynamic that they express. Eckhart does not develop a systematic terminology. One of his clearest expressions of the idea of the spark of the soul (sermon 2) is achieved precisely by abandoning the metaphor of the spark to replace it with another—the "castle" or *bürgelîn,* a place so pure that to enter it God himself must change, giving up his division into Father, Son, and Holy Spirit to become absolute simplicity. Eckhart wanted his listeners to relinquish all forms of rigid behavior, and his sermons themselves frequently enact this process of self-transcendence, setting up a proposition only to push triumphantly beyond it with the frequently recurring refrain: "but I say more." Eckhart's flights of rhetorical daring are engineered to reinforce at a formal level the process of "durchbrechen" (breaking through, sermons 29 and 52), of casting aside habits and concepts that his treatises and sermons address in their content.

This dynamic helps clarify three aspects of Eckhart's doctrine: its relation to scholastic philosophy, its relation to the women's spirituality of the period, and its eventual condemnation for heresy. Eckhart's texts are steeped in the philosophical tradition in which he had been educated—St. Augustine, Albert the Great, and Thomas Aquinas. Where he takes up particular themes or appropriates arguments from existing authorities (such as his use of the concept of analogy to describe man's participation in the divine attribute of justice in "Daz buoch der goetlîchen troestunge" [The Book of Divine Consolation]), however, his purpose is never purely intellectual. Eckhart argues with the tools developed by philosophers ("rationes naturales philosophorum"), but only because they further his spiritual project. Reason is, for him, an emancipatory force, but not an end in itself. Unlike nominalist contemporaries such as William of Ockham, Eckhart does not separate out logical argument from revelation but uses argument in the service of spiritual development.

This leads to the question of Eckhart's relation to the women to whom he preached. A number of critics (Langer, Schweitzer) argue that Eckhart takes up the irrational, and potentially hereti-cal spirituality prevalent in the nunneries of the era and rational-izes it, breaking its attachment to particular somatic states. This argument rightly stresses the degree to which Eckhart's thought develops in dialogue with women's spirituality, but it obscures Eckhart's motivation for criticizing it. The nuns enjoyed only a rudimentary education and so had not been able to develop the analytic powers attainable by a friar such as Eckhart. As a con-sequence, their horizons were limited much more by the cycle of the Church calendar and by the symbols of official iconography (Christ's wounds, Christ appearing in the oblate, etc.). Eckhart encouraged them to break ties with the routine of litany and symbols and, indeed, to give up their attachment to the particu-lar states of ecstasy (sermon 86). In so doing, Eckhart was not so much questioning the "irrational" longing of the nuns as fur-thering it with the analytic tools at his disposal.

Eckhart's openness to the nuns' longing also led to the con-demnation of his teaching as heretical. Some critics (Trusen, Davies) play down the conflict between Eckhart and the Church; other critics (Suárez-Nani, Lerner) have found both theological and historical evidence to support the view that the ecclesiastical authorities had substantial reasons for proscribing his teaching. Eckhart did not believe himself to be a heretic and publicly re-nounced any errors he may unwittingly have propagated. At the same time, his texts constantly undermined the rigid conceptual framework by which the Church sought to regulate religious longing, for even though Eckhart respected hierarchy and dogma, he would never privilege either notion over the needs of genuine spiritual development.

Many thinkers live on through a process of misappropriation and unacknowledged influence. In the case of Eckhart, this ten-dency has been exacerbated by his condemnation and the frag-menting effect this had on the transmission of his texts. After the condemnation, his followers in Cologne continued to copy and issue his writings, but they focused on the Latin works, avoiding the more problematic formulations of the German sermons and effectively sanitizing the teaching even as they preserved it. Simi-larly, when Heinrich Seuse (1295/97–1366) defended Eckhart in his *Das Büchli der Warheit* (1327–29; *Book of Truth*), he did so at the cost of changing Eckhart's priorities and allowing the ob-servation of a doctrinal framework to take precedence over the project of spiritual self-development. Eckhart's German texts survived in scattered groups: some were gathered into general collections of sermons such as the *Paradisus anime intelligentis* that was collated in the mid–14th century, and others were transmitted anonymously or under other people's names. When the sermons of Johannes Tauler (ca. 1300–1361, alongside Seuse the most important follower of Eckhart) were printed in 1521–22, the book included an appendix of sermons actually by Eckhart. It was in this misattributed form that Eckhart's ideas could influence Reformation debates.

Such misattribution makes it difficult to trace Eckhart's influ-ence between the 16th and the 18th centuries. His ideas were first consciously reappropriated in the first half of the 19th cen-tury (by Hegel, Franz von Baader, and Karl Rosenkranz). Musil drew on Eckhartian themes in his work (*Der Mann ohne Eigen-schaften* [1930–42; *The Man without Qualities*]), as did Carl Jung, Martin Heidegger (redeploying the mystical term *Gelassenheit* or "detachment"), Ernst Bloch, Erich Fromm (*To Have or to Be*, 1976), Ingeborg Bachmann ("Das dreißigste Jahr," [1961; The Thirtieth Year]), and Paul Celan. Most recently, parallels have been seen between Eckhart's project and that of deconstruction, particularly the work of Jacques Derrida.

BEN MORGAN

Biography

Born in Tambach, south of Gotha, ca. 1260. Entered the Dominican order; studied at the Dominican *Studium generale* in Cologne, probably under Albert the Great, and in Paris; Reader of the Sentences, Paris, 1293–94; prior of Dominican convent, Erfurt, 1294–98, and vicar of Thuringia, 1294–1302; appointment to the Dominican chair in theology, University of Paris, 1302–3; provincial of Dominican province of Saxony, 1303–11; given additional responsibilities as vicar general of Bohemia, 1307; second appointment to the Dominican chair, University of Paris, 1311–13; sent to Strasbourg as vicar of the master general with special responsibility for discipline in women's communities, 1314–1323; moved to Cologne, probably as master at the Dominican *Studium generale,* 1323; inquisitorial proceedings initiated against him by Henry of Virneburg, Archbishop of Cologne, 1326; made public declaration of orthodoxy in the Dominican church in Cologne, 13 February 1327; inquisitorial proceedings transferred to Avignon, 1327–1328; papal bull *In agro dominico* published after Eckhart's death by John XXII condemning 28 propositions, 27 March 1329; Dominican order initiates investigation that acquits Eckhart of charges of heresy, 1980. Circumstances of death unknown; probably died in Avignon, 1328.

Selected Works

Collections

Deutsche Mystiker des vierzehnten Jahrhunderts, vol. 2, *Meister Eckhart,* edited by Franz Pfeiffer, 1857
Meister Eckhart und seine Jünger: Ungedruckte Texte zur Geschichte der deutschen Mystik, edited by Franz Jostes, 1895
Paradisus anime intelligentis (Paradis der fornunftigen sele), edited by Philipp Strauch, 1919
Die deutschen und lateinischen Werke, edited by the Auftrag der Deutschen Forschungsgemeinschaft, 10 vols., 1936–
Master Eckhart: Parisian Questions and Prologues, translated by A. Maurer, 1974
Sermons and Treatises, translated and edited by M.O'C. Walshe, 3 vols., 1979–85
Meister Eckhart: The Essential Sermons, Commentaries, Treatises, and Defense, translated and edited by Edmund Colledge and Bernard McGinn, 1981
Meister Eckhart: Teacher and Preacher, edited by Bernard McGinn, translated by Frank Tobin and Elvira Bogstadt, 1986
Werke, edited by Niklaus Largier, 2 vols., 1993
Selected Writings, translated and edited by Oliver Davies, 1994

Trial Documents

Daniels, P. Augustin, "Eine lateinische Rechtfertigungsschrift des Meister Eckhart," *Beiträge zur Geschichte der Philosophie des Mittelalters* 23, no. 5 (1923)
Laurent, M.-H., "Autour du procès de Maître Eckhart: Les documents des archives vaticanes," *Divus Thomas,* 3rd series, 13 (1936)
Pelster, Franz, "Ein Gutachten aus dem Eckehart-Prozeß in Avignon," *Beiträge zur Geschichte der Philosophie des Mittelalters,* supplementary vol. 3, no. 2 (1935)
Gabriel Théry, "Édition critique des pièces relatives au procès d'Eckhart contenues dans le manuscrit 33b de la bibliothèque de Soest," *Archives d'histoire doctrinale et littéraire du moyen âge* 1 (1926/27)

Further Reading

Cormeau, Christoph, editor, "Mystik," *Zeitschrift für deutsche Philologie* 113 (1994)

Davies, Oliver, *Meister Eckhart: Mystical Theologian*, London: SPCK, 1991

Derrida, Jacques, "Comment ne pas parler: Dénégations," in *Psyché: Inventions de l'autre*, Paris: Galilee, 1987

Grundmann, Herbert, *Religious Movements in the Middle Ages: The Historical Links between Heresy, the Mendicant Orders, and the Women's Religious Movement in the Twelfth and Thirteenth Century, with the Historical Foundations of German Mysticism*, translated by Steven Rowan, Notre Dame, Indiana: University of Notre Dame Press, 1995

Hollywood, Amy, *The Soul as Virgin Wife: Mechthild of Magdeburg, Marguerite Porete, and Meister Eckhart*, Notre Dame, Indiana: University of Notre Dame Press, 1995

Langer, Otto, *Mystische Erfahrung und spirituelle Theologie: Zu Meister Eckharts Auseinandersetzung mit der Frauenfrömmigkeit seiner Zeit*, Munich: Artemis, 1987

Largier, Niklaus, "Perspektiven der Forschung, 1980–1993," *Zeitschrift für deutsche Philologie* 114, no. 1 (1995)

Lerner, Robert E., "New Evidence for the Condemnation of Meister Eckhart," *Speculum* 72, no. 2 (1997)

McGinn, Bernard, "Eckhart's Condemnation Reconsidered," *Thomist* 44 (1980)

Ruh, Kurt, *Meister Eckhart: Theologe, Prediger, Mystiker*, Munich: Beck, 1985; 2nd edition, 1989

——, "Meister Eckhart," in *Die Mystik des deutschen Predigerordens und ihre Grundlegung durch die Hochscholastik*, Geschichte der abendländischen Mystik, vol. 3, Munich: Beck, 1996

Schweitzer, Franz-Josef, *Der Freiheitsbegriff der deutschen Mystik: Seine Beziehung zur Ketzerei der "Brüder und Schwestern vom Freien Geist," Mit besonderer Rücksicht auf den pseudoeckartischen Traktat "Schwester Katrei" (Edition)*, Frankfurt: Lang, 1981

Steer, Georg, and Loris Sturlese, editors, *Lectura Eckhardi: Predigten Meister Eckharts von Fachgelehrten gelesen und gedeutet*, Stuttgart: Kohlhammer, 1998

Suárez-Nani, Tiziana, "Philosophie- und theologiehistorische Interpretationen der in der Bulle von Avignon zensurierten Sätze," in *Eckardus Theutonicus, homo doctus et sanctus: Nachweise und Berichte zum Prozeß gegen Meister Eckhart*, edited by Heinrich Stirnimann et al., Freiburg: Universitätsverlag, 1992

Tobin, Frank, *Meister Eckhart: Thought and Language*, Philadelphia: University of Pennsylvania Press, 1986

Trusen, Winfried, *Der Prozeß gegen Meister Eckhart: Vorgeschichte, Verlauf, und Folgen*, Paderborn: Schöningh, 1988

Meistersinger *see* Mastersingers

Moses Mendelssohn 1729–1786

Moses Mendelssohn is widely regarded as the first protagonist of a German-Jewish culture, after more than 1,000 years in which Jews had lived in Germany but were forced to keep to themselves. After centuries of persecution and ignorance of Jewish culture, religion, and ways of life, the young poet Gotthold Ephraim Lessing wrote a play entitled *Die Juden* (1754; The Jews), which challenged anti-Jewish prejudices. A new era seemed to have begun, of which Mendelssohn, his lifelong friends Lessing, and the publisher Friedrich Nicolai are held to be the flagships—Mendelssohn by virtue of his contribution to German philosophy and literary criticism and by his guiding of fellow Jews to emancipation and participation in German culture. Nonetheless, Mendelssohn always remained deeply rooted in Judaism. His later life was almost entirely devoted to attempts to reform German Judaism during a period of instability and inner crisis.

Mendelssohn was born in 1729, in Dessau, as the son of a Tora scribe. His native tongue was Yiddish, and he received a traditional Jewish education mainly based on the study of the Holy Scriptures and the Hebrew language. At the age of 14, Mendelssohn followed his teacher David Fränkel to Berlin. After years of poverty that did permanent damage to his health, Mendelssohn became a tutor to the sons of a Jewish silk merchant. His spare time was devoted to the study of German, modern and classical languages, philosophy, literature, and sciences. By the time he met Lessing in 1754, Mendelssohn already personified both the Jewish scholar and the modern intellectual. Lessing encouraged him to write and publish in German. In 1763 Mendelssohn won first prize in a competition at the Prussian Academy of Science for his paper "Abhandlung über die Evidenz in metaphysischen Wissenschaften" (Treatise concerning Evidence in the Metaphysical Sciences). In 1755 he published

"Briefe über die Empfindungen" (Letters about Sensory Experience), a contribution to the theory of aesthetics. He wrote literary reviews in Nicolai's periodicals *Bibliothek der schönen Wissenschaften und der freien Künste* and *Briefe die neueste Literatur betreffend*, which made him part of the cultural avantgarde: in French-dominated Prussia it was still considered "antiestablishment" to read and write German literature. At the same time he tried to establish a Hebrew periodical (*Kohelet Musar*) and published a commentary in Hebrew on the logic of Maimonides.

In 1762 Mendelssohn married Fromet Guggenheim. Only then was he granted a residence permit by the king, although it applied neither to his wife nor to the six children who were to be born to them in the following years. Emancipation was still decades away, and Prussian Jews lived in uncertainty. Mendelssohn became a clerk and later a partner in Isaak Bernhard's silk business, something that enabled him to make a living. Until his death in 1786 he was able to devote only his spare time to his philosophical and literary work.

In 1767 Mendelssohn published *Phädon; oder, Über die Unsterblichkeit der Seele* (Phaedon; or, The Immortality of the Soul) one of his major works on the philosophy of religion, in which he tries to harmonize enlightened rationalism with fundamental religious issues such as the immortal soul. The book became what we would call in modern terms a best-seller, and this made Mendelssohn famous throughout Europe. Radical enlightened thinking had begun to question the established religions, which led to a growing feeling of uncertainty. Mendelssohn's book seemed to offer a remedy. For progressive Christian theologians it became a matter of principle to convince the author of *Phaedon* of the supremacy of Christianity. An open attempt to do so was made in 1769 by the Swiss clergyman Johann Kaspar Lavater. He dedicated his translation of a modern Calvinist apology of Christianity to Mendelssohn and asked him to draw the obvious conclusion. Mendelssohn felt trapped. The precarious situation of the Jews did not allow a discussion of this fundamental issue, but Lavater forced him to make a public statement. In 1770 *Schreiben an den Herrn Diaconus Lavater zu Zürich* (Letter to Mr. Lavater of Zurich) was published, which avoided an answer to Lavater's question and instead explained why Mendelssohn could not join a dispute on the supremacy of any religion. The public debate continued even after Lavater apologized. The affair left Mendelssohn shattered in his former conviction that modern society would accept Jews for their merits, despite their religion. After a long period of illness and depression he managed a spiritual recovery and continued with his work, although with a different focus.

Mendelssohn dedicated the last ten years of his life to the improvement of the social and civic status and to the education of Jews in Germany. In several cases he used his connections to help Jewish communities threatened by oppressive legislation. He also wrote an explanation of the Jewish laws of matrimony and composed a Jewish oath to the Prussian authorities. He initiated the famous essay "Über die bürgerliche Verbesserung der Juden" (On the Social Advancement of the Jews) by Christian Wilhelm von Dohm. In an attempt to modernize Jewish culture in Germany, Mendelssohn translated the Pentateuch into German. Written in Hebrew characters and with a commentary in Hebrew (1780–83), it targeted a Jewish audience. Translations of the books of Psalms and Song of Songs followed in 1783 and 1788 (posthumously), respectively. He also wrote an introduction to a new edition and translation of Manasse Ben Israel's *Vindiciae Judaeorum*, originally published in Amsterdam in 1656. Here, for the first time, Mendelssohn turned the status of Jews into the main topic, criticizing both Christian society and Jewish orthodoxy for what had become of the Jews. Continuing this theme, Mendelssohn's book *Jerusalem*, published in 1783, deals with the question of religion and the state and presents a vision of a tolerant society.

Mendelssohn died on 4 January 1786 in Berlin. He remained active during his last years: in 1784, *Die Sache Gottes* (The Case of God) was published. In *Morgenstunden* (Morninghours), published in 1785 and originally intended for the instruction of his eldest son, Mendelssohn returned to the religious-philosophical topics outlined in *Phaedon*. His last months were darkened by a controversy over the late Lessing's attitude to Spinoza, which led to his last work, *An die Freunde Lessings* (1786; To Lessing's Friends).

While taking the manuscript to the printer, he caught a cold from which he died shortly afterwards, mourned by Jews and non-Jews alike.

GERTRUD REERSHEMIUS

See also Aufklärung

Biography

Born in Dessau, 26 September 1729. Self-study of languages, philosophy, and literature; Talmud study at Bet Hamidrash in Dessau, from 1735; lived in Berlin, studying Talmud with David Fränkel, from 1743; worked in Berlin, copying Hebrew texts; became tutor in house of Isaak Bernhard, 1750; Greek lessons with Friedrich Nicolai, 1757; became bookkeeper for silk manufacturing firm of Bernhard, 1754; led firm from 1761; friendship with Lessing, from 1753, with Nicolai, from 1754, and with Abbt, from 1761; received protected status as Jew through intervention of Marquis d'Argens; active as literary critic for *Bibliothek der schönen Wissenschaften und der freyen Künste, Briefe die Neueste Literatur betreffend*, and *Allgemeine deutsche Bibliothek*, from 1757. First prize in essay competition of Berliner Akademie, 1763; became member of Berliner Akademie, 1771. Died in Berlin, 4 January 1786.

Selected Works

Collections

Gesammelte Schriften, edited by G.B. Mendelssohn, 7 vols., 1843–45; reprint, 1972–76

Gesammelte Schriften: Jubiläumsausgabe, edited by I. Elbogen et al., 20 vols., 1929–38; reprint, 1971

Moses Mendelssohn: Selections from His Writings, edited and translated by Eva Jospe, 1975

Essays

Philosophische Gespräche, 1755

Über die Empfindungen, 1755

Abhandlung über die Evidenz in den metaphysischen Wissenschaften, 1764

Phädon; oder, Über die Unsterblichkeit der Seele, 1767; as *Phaedon; or, The Death of Socrates*, 1789

Anmerkungen zu Abbts freundschaftlicher Correspondenz, 1782

Jerusalem; oder, Über religiöse Macht und Judentum, 1783; as *Jerusalem: A Treatise on Ecclesiastical Authority and Judaism*, translated by M. Samuels, 1838

Über die Frage: was heißt aufklären? 1784

Morgenstunden; oder, Vorlesungen über das Daseyn Gottes, 1785
An die Freunde Lessings, edited by J.J. Engel, 1786

Further Reading

Altmann, Alexander, *Moses Mendelssohn: A Biographical Study,* London: Routledge, and Philadelphia, Pennsylvania: Jewish Publication Society of America, 1973

Knobloch, Heinz, *Herr Moses in Berlin: Auf den Spuren eines Menschenfreundes,* Berlin: Der Morgen, 1979

Sorkin, David, *Moses Mendelssohn and the Religious Enlightenment,* London: Halban, 1996

Srowig, Regina, *Religion und Aufklärung bei Moses Mendelssohn,* Marburg: Tectum, 1996

Sophie Mereau 1770–1806

Sophie Mereau, as she is usually known, belongs to a generation set on the borderline between the Enlightenment and classicism of the later 18th century and the first generation of the German Romantics, most of whom were born a few years later. Thus, her works exhibit some of the characteristic themes and styles of the 18th century but also incorporate Romantic sensibilities and desires.

She came to write at a time when educated women, despite the prejudices of the age, were beginning to make their mark on the literary scene in the German-speaking countries. During her life, and until quite recently, she shared the fate of many female writers in being characterized as only on the margin of contemporary literary activity and primarily in connection with male writers in their orbit—in her case, with one of the major names of the Romantic period, Clemens Brentano, whom she eventually married. The impressive range of her achievements, however, encompasses translations from many European languages, a journal for women, short stories, drama, lyric poetry, and work in the new genre of the 18th century, the novel, in which many women were already beginning to express themselves. She was one of the earliest female professional writers in Germany who attempted to make a living by the pen.

Much of her earlier poetry, including an enthusiastic 1790 ode on the French Revolution, was first published in journals such as Schiller's *Thalia* and *Die Horen*. Shorter items such as the two poems entitled "Frühling" (Spring) present the poet as a child of mother nature. The sense of the free development of human potential, one of her favorite themes, comes through in a poem like "Gebet" (Prayer). The realization of erotic love is evident throughout her work, notably in the somewhat longer poem "Schwärmerey der Liebe" (Reverie of Love), where the life-enhancing effect of love and a sense of the unity of lovers, even after death, make an impressive finale. The harmony of nature can, however, be perverted, as in a well-known poem "An einen Baum am Spalier" (To a Tree on a Trellis), where the artificiality of attaching a tree to a wall, and not allowing it free growth, suggests an obvious human analogy.

Also impressive is the sustained quality of Mereau's longer poems. "Schwarzburg" celebrates an idyllic spot in the Schwarza valley where she lived for a while; the free development of the individual in nature rises to a transcendental experience as she and an imagined ideal lover ascend to the summit of the hill. "Der Garten zu Wörlitz" (The Garden at Wörlitz) contrasts the artificial formal garden with the energy of the untrammeled forces of nature. Later, Mereau composed an ambitious longer poem "Serafine," set partly in Spain but mainly in India, about a beautiful angelic woman who comes down to earth, eventually dying and being reunited with the forces of cosmic harmony. Almost all of these poems were gathered together in the collections *Gedichte* (1800–1802; Poems) and *Der Sophie Mereau Gedichte* (1805; The Poems of Sophie Mereau).

Journals produced by women for female consumers were already a feature of the age, and in 1800–1802, Mereau brought out two volumes of her own journal, *Kalathiskos,* the name of which means a little basket of useful things for women. There are contributions from her older sister Henriette and some items by Clemens Brentano, but she herself produced the majority of the writings. They include translations from various languages, including her new translation of Montesquieu's *Lettres Persanes,* poems and stories, and an extensive essay on Ninon de Lenclos, a French freethinker of the previous century. Although the initiative was carried out at least partly for financial reasons, it also gave her an opportunity to show something of the range of her interests.

Mereau's novels, similar to many novels written by women from the later 18th century onward, contain a strong autobiographical element and reflect her difficult marriages and personal relationships, as well as her desire for freedom and personal fulfillment, especially in the erotic sphere. *Das Blüthenalter der Empfindung* (1794; The Blossom-Age of Sentiment) is a short novel with a complex plot and a male hero; it was produced anonymously, although the fact that the author is female is revealed in the foreword. Set in Italy, France, and the Swiss Alps, it charts the quest for a love that will be free from the constraints of society, especially the constraints experienced by women, often through marriage or family pressures. The tone is occasionally radical, especially on the question of the rights of women. Society is presented as the enemy to the individual's desire for fulfillment, and there is a certain logic, therefore, to the sudden introduction at the end of the lovers' decision to emigrate to the United States, the New World where the old social order may no longer hold sway. Her extended epistolary novel, *Amanda und Eduard* (1803; Amanda and Eduard), has a complex narrative that is set in Italy and explores the enlivening effect of erotic love on the personality of the individual. The liberating moments in a natural setting are again particularly striking. Parallels have been found between this text and her love letters to a student, Johann Heinrich Kipp. There are many references to the literature of the age, especially the works of Goethe and Schiller, and some signs of her contact with the Romantic movement are suggested by the lyrical interludes in the second part. The more radical questioning of the earlier novel is largely absent here and the attitude toward marriage less negative. Again, the three positive forces are freedom, nature, and love, and the cosmic harmony of the two lovers survives even the death of Amanda at the end of the novel.

There is a consistency of theme in Mereau's work that comes to the fore in most of her productions, and we can sense in her works the energy of an intelligent woman writing at a crucial and transitional phase of German literature and culture.

ANTHONY J. HARPER

Biography

Born Sophie Friederike Schubart in Altenburg, 28 March 1770. Educated by private tutors; first poetry written, 1790; death of father Gotthelf, 1791; married Professor Friedrich Ernst Karl Mereau; moved to Jena, 1793; birth of son Gustav, 1794; daughter Hulda, 1797; affair with student Johann Heinrich Kipp, 1794–95; publications in Schiller's journals, from 1796; first meeting with Clemens Brentano, 1798; death of Gustav; separated from husband; moved to Camberg, 1800; divorced; moved to Weimar, 1801; married Brentano; moved to Marburg, 1803; birth and death of son Achim Ariel; moved to Heidelberg, 1804; birth and death of daughter Joachime, 1805. Died in childbirth in Heidelberg, 31 October 1806.

Selected Works

Collections
Liebe und allenthalben Liebe: Werke und autobiographische Schriften, 3 vols., edited by Katharina von Hammerstein, 1997

Writings
Das Blüthenalter der Empfindung, 1794; reprint, edited by Herman Moens, 1982
Gedichte, 2 vols., 1800–1802
Kalathiskos, 2 vols., 1801–2; edited by Peter Schmidt, 1968
Amanda und Eduard, 2 vols., 1803; edited by Bettina Bremer and Angelika Schneider, 1993
Der Sophie Mereau Gedichte, 1805
Bunte Reihen Kleiner Schriften, 1806

Further Reading

Brandes, Ute, "Escape to America: Social Reality and Utopian Schemes in German Women's Novels around 1800," in *In the Shadow of Olympus: German Women Writers around 1800*, edited by Katherine Goodman and Edith Josephine Waldstein, Albany: State University of New York Press, 1992

Bremer, Bettina, "Sophie Mereau: Eine exemplarische Chronik des Umgangs mit Autorinnen des 18. Jahrhunderts," *Athenäum* 5 (1995)

Bürger, Christa, "'Die mittlere Sphäre,' Sophie Mereau: Schriftstellerin im klassischen Weimar," in *Deutsche Literatur von Frauen*, edited by Gabriele Brinker-Gabler, Munich: Beck, 1988

———, *Leben Schreiben: Die Klassik, die Romantik, und der Ort von Frauen*, Stuttgart: Metzler, 1990

Fleischmann, Uta, *Zwischen Aufbruch und Anpassung: Untersuchungen zu Werk und Leben der Sophie Mereau*, Frankfurt and New York: Lang, 1989

Gersdorff, Dagmar von, *Dich zu lieben kann ich nicht verlernen: Das Leben der Sophie Mereau*, Frankfurt: Insel, 1984

Goozé, Marjanne E., "Sophie Mereau," in *An Encyclopaedia of Continental Women Writers*, edited by Katharina M. Wilson, vol. 2, New York and London: Garland, 1991

Hammerstein, Katharina von, *Sophie Mereau-Brentano: Freiheit, Liebe, Weiblichkeit: Trikolore sozialer und individueller Selbstbestimmung um 1800*, Heidelberg: Winter, 1994

Kastinger Riley, Helene M., *Die weibliche Muse: Sechs Essays über künstlerisch schaffende Frauen der Goethezeit*, Columbia, South Carolina: Camden House, 1986

Schwarz, Gisela, *Literarisches Leben und Sozialstrukturen um 1800: Zur Situation von Schriftstellerinnen am Beispiel von Sophie Brentano-Mereau geb. Schubart*, Frankfurt and New York: Lang, 1991

Vansant, Jacqueline, with Walter Arndt, "Sophie Mereau," in *Bitter Healing: German Women Writers from 1700 to 1830, an Anthology*, edited by Jeannine Blackwell and Susanna Zantop, Lincoln and London: University of Nebraska Press, 1990

Merseburger Zaubersprüche

The small pieces in Old High German usually known as the *Merseburger Zaubersprüche* (Merseburg Charms) consist of two passages in a central German dialect that are written out continuously but in fact are in alliterative verse, written in the tenth century on a blank page in a manuscript that contains liturgical material in Latin and a fragment of a prayer in German. The first of these works, which consists of four long-lines, seems to describe how Valkyries released some prisoners, and then it adds the command: "escape from the bonds." The second piece, separated from the first by a sign that might mean "another," tells first how Phol (who is unknown and has been identified variously; for example, as Apollo or as St. Paul) and Woden were riding in a forest when Woden's horse sprained a foot. A number of goddesses (there are either four separate or two double names; there are no capital letters in the original to help us determine this) try to cure it, but then Woden himself cures the sprain. The last part of the piece, which is poetically forceful, commands that bone be joined to bone, blood to blood, and limb to limb. The German material is then followed on the manuscript page by a prayer in Latin prose asking for God's help for an individual (whose name can be added). This prayer is integral to the whole and presumably made the earlier material acceptable to the church.

The first Old High German piece is often interpreted as being magic for the release of prisoners and the second as a magic spell to cure a horse. Both of these interpretations are questionable, and the concept of the magic charm as such is a difficult one in the Christian Middle Ages. Possibly these fragments of Old High German verse do preserve some elements of pre-Christian magic spells, and certainly they refer to pagan gods and magic figures. However, they were written down by a monk into a theological manuscript, and the Latin prayer attached to them is part of their function. They are clearly designed to have a curative effect: both refer to things that have happened, and both command a cure, although the Latin prayer attached makes it into a request rather than a demand.

Although the Merseburg pieces are unusual in referring to pagan figures, they have to be viewed beside the other Old High German charms, of which there are several. Typically, a charm will describe a situation (usually involving Christian figures—there is a charm similar to the second Merseburg piece in which Christ works the charm) and then call for a cure, but it will also prescribe, for example, three Our Fathers or three Amens. The pagan elements, even when they are still visible (and usually they are not, beyond the fact of the use of magic as such), are counterbalanced by the Christian prayer that asks that God's will be done or requests (in the word "amen") that God should "let it be."

The Old High German charms are primarily for transient traumatic situations—that is, for medical conditions that are not long lasting, such as sprains, cramps, nosebleeds, and other problems that would pass of their own accord relatively quickly. There are in addition charms against epilepsy (containing a possible reference to another pre-Christian Germanic god, Thor), but the epileptic fit, however alarming, is also something that does not last. Pronouncing the words of a charm, and perhaps more important, also saying a familiar prayer several times, would at least calm the patient in any case and therefore would have a positive therapeutic effect.

The charms as we have them in Old High German fall between what we might think of as medicine proper (that is, the use of selected ingredients to effect a cure) and the general prayer, although since all those that survive in German are Christianized, they are far closer to the latter. Indeed, they have a strong structural similarity to the prayers of request known as collects, and in early German we do find prayers asking that specific potential problems may be averted. The Old High German charms, and especially the Merseburg pieces, seem to apply to situations that have happened (i.e., they are not prophylactic), but they call at the most for actions and words rather than ingredients. In the Middle Ages they are found both in liturgical contexts (as here) and also in medical ones, and medical writings will sometimes combine actual pharmacy with charms; we may remember, too, that medical recipes themselves are sometimes found together with cookery recipes. This state of affairs is matched in many other languages in the Middle Ages, and indeed in earlier and later civilizations. There are charms not unlike some of the early German ones in ancient Indian writings, and a charm very much like the second Merseburg piece was collected from oral sources in Scotland in the 19th century.

Since all the other surviving Old High German charms are for (usually) identifiable problems that were at least potentially curable, and since prisoners manifestly do not escape by magic, it is likely that the first is a charm for temporary paralysis or cramp from which the "prisoner" had to be freed. The second situation refers to a horse, but the charm might apply to any sprain, and the prayer refers to people. Some Old High German charms are aimed at animals, particularly horses, but the majority have to do with human conditions. Whatever the original use may have been of the clearly pagan parts of the Merseburg pieces, they are now Christianized poems that command a cure but then express the hope that God will permit it. The names of the pagan gods in the charm are unclear, but it is doubtful whether they would even have been acknowledged much more than we might the names of Woden and Thor in the names of the days of the week: they are likely to have become simply abracadabra words.

BRIAN MURDOCH

Further Reading

Bostock, J. Knight, *A Handbook on Old High German Literature,* Oxford: Clarendon Press, 1955; 2nd edition revised by K.C. King and D.R. McLintock, 1976

Braune, Wilhelm, editor, *Althochdeutsches Lesebuch,* Tübingen: Niemeyer, 16th edition revised by Ernst Ebbinghaus, 1979 (includes edition of the text)

Eis, Gerhard, *Altdeutsche Zaubersprüche,* Berlin: de Gruyter, 1964

Groseclose, J. Sidney, and Brian Murdoch, *Die althochdeutschen poetischen Denkmäler,* Stuttgart: Metzler, 1976

Geier, Manfred, "Die magische Kraft der Poesie," *Deutsche Vierteljahresschrift* 56 (1982)

Ködderitzsch, Rolf, "Der 2. Merseburger Spruch und seine Parallele," *Zeitschrift für celtische Philologie* 33 (1974)

Murdoch, Brian, "But Did They Work? Interpreting the Old High German Merseburg Charms in their Medieval Context," *Neuphilologische Mitteilungen* 89 (1988)

Murdoch, Brian, "Drohtin, uuerthe so! Zur Funktionsweise der althochdeutschen Zaubersprüche," *Literaturwissenschaftliches Jahrbuch der Görres-Gesellschaft* 32 (1991)

Schlosser, Horst Dieter, editor, *Althochdeutsche Literatur,* Frankfurt and Hamburg: Fischer, 1970; revised edition, 1989 (with texts and modern German translations)

Steinmeyer, Elias von, editor, *Die kleineren althochdeutschen Sprachdenkmäler,* 1916; reprinted as 2nd edition, Berlin: Weidmann, 1963 (includes text)

Conrad Ferdinand Meyer 1825–1898

Conrad Ferdinand Meyer's road to literary success was slow and arduous. Given the early loss of a father he adored, his deeply troubled relations with his mother, and his own neurasthenic disposition, it took him decades to establish some self-confidence, to distance himself from Romanticism, and to find not only his own subject matter but also his own voice. Meyer was in his mid-40s when the publication of *Huttens letzte Tage* (1871; Hutten's Last Days)—a verse epic about the final days of the valiant 16th-century humanist and his fight for a strong, unified Germany—established his literary reputation. For the next 20 years, until his breakdown in 1891, Meyer wrote widely acclaimed historical novellas, ballads in the manner of Schiller, and a collection of poems that made him the most prominent poet of the period. His emergence on the literary scene coincided with Bismarck's triumph—Germany's long-awaited unification and the founding of the Second Empire—events that Meyer followed with admiration, not to say envy, from his peaceful home on Lake Zurich. Whereas Gottfried Keller became the enthusiastic spokesman of Swiss democracy on the move, Meyer took many of his cues from Imperial Germany, most important its historicist approach to the past and its cult of great political personalities. A patrician by origin and inclination, Meyer—similar to Jacob Burckhardt, whose seminal study of Italian Renaissance culture had a profound impact on his writings—considered democracy a gateway to mediocrity. Judging from a comment he made to his publisher, however, this bias was also the result of deep-seated personal anxieties: "The mediocre saddens me because it finds within myself a kindred material—therefore, I am seeking the great with such yearning."

Meyer's narratives remain interesting to today's reader because what might at first appear as an uncritical auctorial fascination with ruthless politics and violence is in fact undermined by complex, frequently self-referential narrative strategies, as well as by profound psychological insights into the minds of his tragically conflicted heroes and their relationship to conscience and power in times of political change and upheaval. Such heroes include Thomas Becket, the chancellor of Henry II and archbishop of Canterbury in *Der Heilige* (1880; translated as *The Chancellor's Secret* and *The Saint*); Fernando Pescara, the Habsburg condottiere in 16th-century Italy in *Die Versuchung des Pascara* (1887; translated as *The Tempting of Pescara* and *Pescara's Temptation*); and Jürg Jenatsch, the Grison freedom fighter during the Thirty Years' War in *Jürg Jenatsch* (1876). Influenced by Friedrich Theodor Vischer's *Kritische Gänge* (1844; Critical Errands), with its strong endorsement of realism, Meyer was committed to present his subject matter, which he drew from various historical sources—from Ferdinand Gregorovious and Burckhardt, mostly—as objectively as possible. He achieved this objectivity both through highly stylized language that stays clear of regionalisms and sociolects and through a number of narrative techniques such as the assembly of a wide array of subjective, frequently contradictory perspectives, which, in their totality, approximate objective truth. He also used the construction of intricate frames to distance and modify characters and events of the central story in works such as *The Saint* and *Die Hochzeit des Mönchs* (1884; translated as *The Monk's Wedding, The Monk's Marriage,* and *The Marriage of the Monk*). Because of these characteristics, Meyer's novellas are generally considered representative examples of German bourgeois realism despite the fact that they but rarely touch on middle-class life. Tellingly, his foray into the representation of the middle class, *Der Schuß von der Kanzel* (1878; *The Shot from the Pulpit*), is a humorous boy-gets-girl story.

Although Meyer occasionally referred to his poems as "my little things," critics have agreed about their great artistry. In his ballads, Meyer typically focuses on the psychological responses of a central character caught up in a highly dramatic situation, often at a historically portentous moment. Most famous among them and excelling by its craftsmanship is *Die Füße im Feuer* (*The Feet in the Fire*). His lyrical poems in the collection *Gedichte* (1882; Poems), as well as a handful of poems that he wrote after 1882, reveal their affinity with French symbolism and anticipate 20th-century developments of the genre. In *Zwei Segel* (*Two Sails*), both a love poem and a *Dinggedicht* (poem focused on a single object), the image of two sails in motion symbolizes love: concentrating on a single motif and avoiding directly expressed emotion, Meyer conveys intense feelings with nonconfessional strategies. Some of the best Meyer scholarship has been devoted to the close analysis of successive versions of an individual poem, charting the evolution from its tentative beginnings to the final text, as in the case of *Der römische Brunnen* (*The Roman Fountain*). Such studies have revealed Meyer's unfailing commitment to concise poetic expression and lucidity of style.

Meyer reached mostly conservative readers of the educated middle and upper classes (*Bildungsbürgertum*), especially during the last decades of the 19th century, which were marked by major intellectual and social changes, and then again during the Weimar Republic, when political uncertainties became a threat to many. His aristocratic tenor, his honed language, and his rootedness in history, tradition, and culture secured him a public that distanced itself from authors who challenged the status quo and sought nonconventional modes of literary expression. In the 1950s and 1960s, critical studies tended to focus on biographical questions, Meyer's narrative techniques, or close readings of his poetry. Although his works are widely available and continue to appear on school and university reading lists, critical interest in Meyer has been on a steady decline since the late 1960s. Nowadays, professional publications about Meyer and his works are few and far between.

Othmar Schoeck and Arnold Schoenberg are among the composers who used Meyer poems as lieder texts. Two screen versions by the internationally acclaimed director Daniel Schmid—*Violanta* (1977; the adaptation of *Die Richterin* [1885; *The Judge*]) and *Jenatsch* (1987; a thriller loosely based on *Jürg Jenatsch*)—have not been successful in bringing Meyer back to the attention of a broader public.

TAMARA S. EVANS

Biography

Born in Zurich, Switzerland, 11 October 1825. Attended the University of Zurich, 1844–45; years of social isolation; suffered a mental breakdown, 1852; several months at Préfargier, a clinic near Neuchâtel; private study of art, literature, and history in Paris and Munich, 1857,

Rome, Florence, and Siena, 1858, Lausanne, 1860–61, and Verona and Venice, 1871–72; from 1877 on in Kilchberg; acquainted with Gottfried Keller, Julius Rodenberg, Paul Heyse, and Louise von François; confinement in Königsfelden, 1892–93. Honorary doctorate from the University of Zurich, 1880; Bavarian Order of Maximilian, 1888. Died 28 November 1898.

Selected Works

Collections

Sämtliche Werke, edited by Hans Zeller and Alfred Zäch, 15 vols., 1958–96

Werke, edited by Heinz Schöffler, 2 vols., 1967

Werke, edited by Gerhard Stenzel, 2 vols., 1968

Werke, edited by Helmut Brandt, 2 vols., 1970

The Complete Narrative Prose of Conrad Ferdinand Meyer, translated by George F. Folkers, David B. Dickens, and Marion W. Sonnenfeld, 2 vols., 1976

Gesammelte Werke, edited by Wolfgang Ignée, 5 vols., 1985

Poetry

Huttens letzte Tage, 1871

Gedichte, 1882

Fiction

Das Amulett, 1873; as *The Amulet,* translated by George F. Folkers, in *The Complete Narrative Prose,* 1976

Jenatsch, 1876; as *Jürg Jenatsch,* translated by David B. Dickens, in *The Complete Narrative Prose,* 1976

Der Schuß von der Kanzel, 1878; as *The Shot from the Pulpit,* translated by George F. Folkers, in *The Complete Narrative Prose,* 1976

Der Heilige, 1880; as *The Chancellor's Secret,* translated by Mary J. Taber, 1887; as *The Saint,* translated by Edward Franklin Hauch, 1930; also translated by George F. Folkers, in *The Complete Narrative Prose,* 1976; W.F. Twaddell, 1977

Plautus im Nonnenkloster, 1882; as *Plautus in the Convent,* translated by William Guild Howard, with *The Monk's Marriage,* 1965; also translated by Marion W. Sonnenfeld, in *The Complete Narrative Prose,* 1976

Gustav Adolfs Page, 1882; as *Gustav Adolf's Page,* translated by David B. Dickens, in *The Complete Narrative Prose,* 1976

Das Leiden eines Knaben, 1883; as *The Tribulations of a Boy,* translated by E.M. Huggard, 1949; as *The Sufferings of a Boy,* translated by Harry Steinhauer, 1969; as *A Boy Suffers,* translated by David B. Dickens, in *The Complete Narrative Prose,* 1976

Die Hochzeit des Mönchs, 1884; as *The Monk's Wedding,* translated by S.H. Adams, 1887; as *The Monk's Marriage,* translated by William Guild Howard, with *Plautus in the Convent,* 1965; as *The Marriage of the Monk,* translated by Marion W. Sonnenfeld, in *The Complete Narrative Prose,* 1976

Die Richterin, 1885; as *The Judge,* translated by Marion W. Sonnenfeld, in *The Complete Narrative Prose,* 1976

Die Versuchung des Pescara, 1887; as *The Tempting of Pescara,* translated by Clara Bell, 1890; as *Pescara's Temptation,* translated by George F. Folkers, in *The Complete Narrative Prose,* 1976

Angela Borgia, 1891; as *Angela Borgia,* translated by Marion W. Sonnenfeld, in *The Complete Narrative Prose,* 1976

Other

Louise von François und Conrad Ferdinand Meyer: Ein Briefwechsel, edited by Anton Bettelheim, 1905; revised edition, 1920

Briefwechsel zwischen Conrad Ferdinand Meyer und Gottfried Keller, 1908

Briefe Conrad Ferdinand Meyers nebst seinen Rezensionen und Aufsätzen, edited by Adolf Frey, 2 vols., 1908

Conrad Ferdinand Meyer und Julius Rodenberg: Ein Briefwechsel, edited by August Langmesser, 1918

Briefe von Conrad Ferdinand Meyer, Betsy Meyer, und J. Hardmeyer-Jenny, edited by Otto Schulthess, 1927

Johanna Spyri—Conrad Ferdinand Meyer: Briefwechsel 1877–1897, edited by Hans and Rosemarie Zeller, 1977

Translation

Augustin Thierry, *Erzählungen aus den merowingischen Zeiten mit einleitenden Betrachtungen über die Geschichte Frankreichs,* 1855

Further Reading

Baumgarten, Franz Ferdinand, *Das Werk Conrad Ferdinand Meyers: Renaissance-Empfinden und Stilkunst,* Munich: Beck, 1917

Brunet, Georges, *C.F. Meyer et la nouvelle,* Paris: Didier, 1967

Burkhard, Marianne, *Conrad Ferdinand Meyer,* Boston: Twayne, 1978

Gerlach, U. Henry, *Conrad Ferdinand Meyer Bibliographie,* Tübingen: Niemeyer, 1994

Henel, Heinrich, *The Poetry of Conrad Ferdinand Meyer,* Madison: University of Wisconsin Press, 1954

Hohenstein, Lily, *Conrad Ferdinand Meyer,* Bonn: Athenäum, 1957

Isaak, Gudrun, *Der Fall C.F. Meyer: Außerliterarische Faktoren bei der Rezeption und Bewertung eines Autors,* Frankfurt, Bern, and Cirencester: Lang, 1980

Jackson, David, *Conrad Ferdinand Meyer in Selbstzeugnissen und Bilddokumenten,* Reinbek bei Hamburg: Rowohlt, 1975

Jesiorkowksi, Klaus, "Die Kunst der Perspektive: Zur Epik Conrad Ferdinand Meyers," *Germanisch-romanische Monatsschrift* 17 (1967)

Kittler, Friedrich A., *Der Traum und die Rede: Eine Analyse der Kommunikationssituation Conrad Ferdinand Meyers,* Bern: Francke, 1977

Laumont, Christof, *Jeder Gedanke als sichtbare Gestalt: Formen und Funktionen der Allegorie in der Erzähldichtung Conrad Ferdinand Meyers,* Göttingen: Wallstein, 1997

Mullen, Inga E., *German Realism in the United States: The American Reception of Meyer, Storm, Raabe, Keller, and Fontane,* New York and Bern: Lang, 1988

Schmid, Karl, "Conrad Ferdinand Meyer und die Grösse," in *Unbehagen im Kleinstaat,* Zurich: Artemis, 1963

Staiger, Emil, "Das Spätboot: Zu Conrad Ferdinand Meyers Lyrik," in *Die Kunst der Interpretation,* Zurich: Atlantis, 1955

Wiesmann, Louis, *Conrad Ferdinand Meyer: Der Dichter des Todes und der Maske,* Bern: Francke, 1958

Die Hochzeit des Mönchs 1884
Novel by Conrad Ferdinand Meyer

Of the 11 novellas Conrad Ferdinand Meyer wrote in the 1870s and 1880s, *Die Hochzeit des Mönchs* (*The Marriage of the Monk*) is probably his most famous, and it is generally considered among the most significant examples of historical realism. Nowadays, however, its reputation rests less on the theme of the defrocked monk, as provocative as this may have been to readers in the era of the *Kulturkampf,* and more on the form, a very intricate frame story referred to by Meyer himself as a "non plus ultra" and, indeed, not repeated in his subsequent work.

The work's complicated structure did not diminish the general readership's appreciation of its high drama, which it presented in the historicist mode of the day. Despite the initial misgivings of Hermann Haessel, Meyer's publisher, *The Marriage of the Monk* went into its ninth edition in 1892. It was translated into English as early as 1887, and an illustrated translation into Italian followed that same year. Critics whose opinion Meyer respected (among them Paul Heyse, Louise von François, Julius Rodenberg, and Otto Brahm), however, had mixed reactions to the formal aspects of the work. To some, the novella was too mannered; to others, the frame structure, reproducing the act of narration, seemed "enigmatic." In a letter to Heyse, Meyer justified his choice of such a complicated structure as "instinctive," as a device "to soften the harshness of the main story and to keep the subject matter at a safe distance" from himself. While the main story of *The Marriage of the Monk* combines the theme of the defrocked monk (a motif occurring elsewhere in his works) with a tale from Machiavelli's *Istorie fiorentine* (1532; *Florentine History*) about a violent feud that erupts between several families when a young man breaks his engagement after having fallen in love with another woman, some of Meyer's very private ordeals are also imprinted in the text, including the reclusive years of his youth and the precarious position in which he found himself when the relationship between his wife and his much-beloved sister Betsy began to deteriorate. As early as 1898, Sigmund Freud, an admirer of the novella, pointed out that the monk "is a 'frater,' a brother." It is not surprising that for these reasons alone the distancing device of the frame was, as Meyer put it, "altogether necessary."

The frame story is set in early-14th-century Verona. Dante Alighieri, in exile at the court of Cangrande, joins a group of courtiers telling stories about "sudden career changes" and himself eventually contributes a story that he develops from a tombstone inscription. In this story, Astorre, a monk in 13th-century Padova and the only surviving male descendant of his family, is tricked by his dying father to break his vows so that he can be betrothed to Diana, the bride of his deceased brother. Having left monastic discipline behind, Astorre loses all self-control and secretly marries Antiope, whose sweetness and vulnerability have unleashed his passion. At the close of Dante's narrative, on the occasion of the frenzied, carnivalesque wedding celebrations, Diana murders Antiope, and Astorre kills Diana's steadfast brother Germano and wounds himself mortally when running into Germano's drawn sword.

Psychoanalytic approaches to the novella focus on Astorre's ascetic life, which has not helped him control his instincts but instead has given both his libido and his psyche a sadistic direction (Jackson); alternatively, a Lacanian reading has been suggested by Downing. The question of Astorre's guilt has been a frequent focus in Meyer criticism. According to some, he is guilty either of betraying his monastic vows (von Wiese), of breaking his engagement to Diana (W.D. Williams), or of having disturbed the moral order of the world (Martini). Others have shifted the blame away from the protagonist and have held society's questionable principles of action responsible for the tragedy (Shaw).

If the novella does not provide an easy answer to the question of guilt, it is because Meyer shies away from unequivocal definitions of what constitutes guilt and innocence (see the many ambiguities permeating his other works, including *The Saint, A Boy Suffers,* and *Pescara's Temptation*). Instead, Meyer impresses upon his readers the difficulty of judging events and characters both in the frame story and the main story. Dante's first-person narrator (Christof Laumont is the most recent critic to distinguish the position of the internal narrator from Dante's position) expresses uncertainty on several occasions, and Dante himself, despite his narratorial control, makes mistakes, allows personal resentments to shape his tale, admits to changing his convictions according to context, and adjusts the represented reality in his story to the expectations of his audience. Dante's full understanding of the events he narrates is limited even further by the spirit of the times he lives in: according to Meyer, he "represents the Middle Ages pure and simple."

Borrowing the names, features, and chief motivations of his listeners to develop the main characters of his tale, Meyer's Dante creates multiple mirroring effects. The frame figures, who feel personally involved and take sides with their counterparts in the embedded story, provide ruptures in perspective by breaking in repeatedly to ask questions, to disagree with some of Dante's authorial decisions, or to point out inconsistencies in his narrative. With its symmetrical constellations, its doublings and double entendres, the novella is predominantly structured by the principle of duality; desires and identities are transferred from the frame to the embedded story and vice versa.

It has been pointed out (Downing, Laumont) that Dante's gesture of holding a pen and crossing out a particular comment stands metonymically for the poetological purpose of the frame construction: Dante's storytelling is an allegory of writing. Both Dante's listeners and Meyer's readers are to understand that stories are subject to conditions of narration and principles of invention. More than any other novella by Meyer, *The Marriage of the Monk* is a transitional work; it combines thematic and stylistic elements of 19th-century historical realism with narrative strategies that reveal the illusionism of that very tradition and thus anticipate 20th-century developments in fiction.

TAMARA S. EVANS

Editions

First edition: *Die Hochzeit des Mönchs*, Leipzig: Haessel, 1884
Critical edition: in *Sämtliche Werke*, edited by Hans Zeller and Alfred Zäch, vol. 12, Bern: Benteli, 1961
Translation: *The Marriage of the Monk*, translated by Marion W. Sonnenfeld, in *The Complete Narrative Prose of Conrad Ferdinand Meyer*, vol. 2, Lewisburg, Pennsylvania: Bucknell University Press, 1976

Further Reading

Downing, Eric, "Double Exposures: Repetition and Realism in Meyer's *Die Hochzeit des Mönchs*," *Deutsche Vierteljahrsschrift* 68 (1994)
Evans, Tamara, "Die Ironisierung des Erzählens: *Die Hochzeit des Mönchs*," in *Formen der Ironie in Conrad Ferdinand Meyers Novellen*, Bern and Munich: Francke, 1980
Feise, Ernst, "*Die Hochzeit des Mönchs* von Conrad Ferdinand Meyer: Eine Formanalyse," in *Xenion: Themes, Forms and Ideas in German Literature*, Baltimore, Maryland: Johns Hopkins University Press, 1950 [Originally in *Monatshefte* 30 (1938)]
Jackson, David A., "Dante the Dupe in C.F. Meyer's *Die Hochzeit des Mönchs*," *German Life and Letters* 25 (1971–72)
Jacobson, Manfred R., "The Two Faces of Dante: Fate and the Artist in C.F. Meyer's *Die Hochzeit des Mönchs*," *Trivium* 16 (1981)
Laumont, Christof, *Jeder Gedanke als sichtbare Gestalt: Formen und Funktionen der Allegorie in den Erzähldichtung Conrad Ferdinand Meyers*, Göttingen: Wallstein, 1997
Martini, Fritz, *Deutsche Literatur im bürgerlichen Realismus*, Stuttgart: Metzler, 1964

Nehring, Wolfgang, "The Representation of Reality in the Narrative Prose of Conrad Ferdinand Meyer: As Seen in *Die Hochzeit des Mönchs*," *Pacific Coast Philology* 16, no. 2 (1981)

Plater, Edward M.V., "The Figure of Dante in *Die Hochzeit des Mönchs*," *Modern Language Notes* 90 (1975)

Reinhardt, George W., "Two Romance Word Plays in C.F. Meyer's *Novellen*," *Germanic Review* 46 (1971)

Shaw, Michael, "C.F. Meyer's Resolute Heroes: A Study of Beckett, Astorre and Pescara," *Deutsche Vierteljahrsschrift* 40 (1966)

Stauffacher, Werner, "Erzählen des Erzählens: Zu C.F. Meyers *Hochzeit des Mönchs*," American Association of Teachers of German, *Proceedings of the 42nd Annual Meeting, Bonn, Germany, June 27–July 2, 1974*, edited by Reinhold Grimm, Philadelphia, Pennsylvania: AATG, 1975

Wiese, Benno von, "Conrad Ferdinand Meyer: *Die Hochzeit des Mönchs*," in *Die deutsche Novelle von Goethe bis Kafka*, edited by Benno von Wiese, Düsseldorf: Bagel, 1957

Gustav Meyrink 1868–1932

Gustav Meyrink is still generally known as the author of *Der Golem* (1915; *The Golem*), which reflects the continuing popularity of his best-known work. German academic critics, by contrast, long consigned his work to the category of *Trivialliteratur* (popular fiction); the first edition of the Frenzels's *Daten deutscher Dichtung* (1953), for example, does not list one work by Meyrink.

The increased importance given to the literature of the occult and the fantastic over the last three decades has led to something of a critical reevaluation of Meyrink (see Cersowsky and Geißler). Instead of being cited as a minor body of work on the periphery of the Kafka constellation, he is now often treated in his own right as one of the key representatives of "magic Prague" (Ripellino).

Meyrink is sometimes claimed as an Expressionist. Although both he and the Expressionists rejected the materialism of bourgeois society, and although there is a clear parallel between the brooding atmosphere of *The Golem* and Expressionist films, there is no stylistic similarity between Meyrink's novels and stories and literary Expressionism, and his exploration of the occult is very different from their rather abstract spirituality.

Outside academic circles, there have always have been readers for whom Meyrink's novels are not literature, whether "trivial" or not, but prophetic texts embodying esoteric wisdom. In this, they are following Meyrink's own description (written in the 1920s) of his works as having "more or less nothing to do" with literature; instead, he claims that what he writes is "'magic'—suggestion—and therefore not bound by the recipes and rules of 'artistic structure'." This is the obverse of the view held by many literary critics (both contemporary with Meyrink and more recent)—that, after *The Golem*, Meyrink's novels increasingly became mere packaging for his esoteric teachings.

Meyrink began his literary career as a writer of short stories. He eventually wrote about 60 short stories, over two-thirds of which first appeared in the satirical magazine *Simplicissimus*, most between 1901 and 1908. These stories contain many disparate elements—fantasy, horror, humor, satire, the supernatural, occult, macabre, grotesque—and often skip from one element to another in confusing fashion. Their main thrust, however, is satirical, and they quickly made Meyrink a popular name with the younger generation of writers and artists. He attacked the philistine complacency of the bourgeoisie that buttressed the authority of the state. His sharpest satire was reserved for that most sacred of sacred cows in Imperial Germany, the army, and he lampooned the mindless incompetence of the military in stories such as *Schöpsoglobin* (1906; *Wetherglobin*). During World War I, he was attacked in articles by nationalist critics and by nationalist hooligans, who threw stones at his windows.

The grotesque and the occult are the two elements that dominate Meyrink's first novel, *The Golem*. The work does not recount the Jewish legend of the golem and Rabbi Loew but uses the eponymous figure symbolically, as a mysterious presence embodying the spirit of the old Jewish quarter and representing something of the past life of the hero, Athanasius Pernath.

The Golem took a long time to write, and there are several reports of Meyrink needing help to restrict and order the large number of episodes and figures. In its final form it is still rather loosely structured, and this contributes to the effectiveness of the novel. It helps build up the nightmarish atmosphere, which is a great part of the novel's popular appeal. The disjointed narration also reflects the situation of the hero, whose loss of memory has led to a loss of identity. Finally, the loose structure adds to the sense of a universe that is not accessible to rational explanation; this structure thus underpins both the novel's esoteric message and its literary power.

Meyrink's next novel, *Das grüne Gesicht* (1916; *The Green Face*), reads rather like an attempt to repeat the success of *The Golem*, with Amsterdam replacing Prague as the work's background. It contains some effective writing, including the descriptions of Amsterdam and the cataclysm in which the novel culminates, but its effectiveness as literature is diminished by the way the occult scenes tend to degenerate into preaching.

Walpurgisnacht (1917; *Walpurgisnacht*) is something of a return to the earlier Meyrink of the satirical stories, especially in its grotesque portrayal of the fossilized aristocratic and bureaucratic German society that has shut itself away in the Hradschin high above Prague. The clash of imperial order with the fanatical revolutionary nationalists, with which the novel ends, takes on apocalyptic proportions that suggest the end of the world rather than the clash of two political ideologies.

The occult—both as theme and imagery—in *The Golem* is based largely on the Cabala and the tarot, while yoga exercises provide the spiritual teaching in *The Green Face*. Meyrink's fourth novel, *Der weiße Dominikaner* (1921; *The White Dominican*), has been called his "Tao book." The path of the Tao, which the hero follows, is one of the reasons for the book's lack of action, and this, together with the sentimental characterization of some characters, makes it the book that is likely to be of least interest to the general reader among Meyrink's novels; a French critic (Heym), however, has also called it "the most profound of Meyrink's novels, and also the most authentic."

There is doubt as to whether *Der Engel vom westlichen Fenster* (1927; *The Angel of the West Window*), based on the life of the Elizabethan magus John Dee, is by Meyrink at all. An old friend of Meyrink's, F.A. Schmid-Noerr, claimed that he wrote the novel but that they agreed to publish it under Meyrink's—more famous—name and to share the advance. This novel certainly differs from Meyrink's other novels in many ways: the historical setting; the style, especially the passages of pastiche old German; the hothouse eroticism; and the lack of the spiritual didacticism, which was particularly strong in *The White Dominican*. The latter point probably works to the book's advantage as literature. It means that the occult background, which here focuses on alchemy, is integrated into the work's overall aesthetic structure. This integration produces a richly textured novel, which can stand as a summation of Meyrink's preoccupation with the occult.

It is as one of the main representatives of the early 20th-century search for spiritual renewal through occult and esoteric teachings that Meyrink will be remembered, as well as for his satires on Imperial Germany in his early stories.

MICHAEL MITCHELL

See also Prague

Biography

Born in Vienna, 19 January 1868. Educated in Munich, 1874–80, Hamburg, 1881–83, and Prague, 1883–89; founded a bank in Prague; went bankrupt, 1902; in Vienna, 1904; edited *Der liebe Augustin;* moved to Munich, 1907; eventually settled in Starnberg, 1911; translated the novels of Dickens and wrote comedies with Roda Roda, 1909–14; rejected offer of membership of Varnbüler family, 1919; edited a series of occult and esoteric books, 1919–25. Died in Starnberg, 4 December 1932.

Selected Works

Collections
Gesammelte Werke, 6 vols., 1917

Fiction
Des deutschen Spießers Wunderhorn, 1913; many of the stories included in *The Opal (and Other Stories)*, translated by Maurice Raraty, 1994
Der Golem, 1915; as *The Golem*, translated by Mike Mitchell, 1995
Fledermäuse, 1916
Das grüne Gesicht, 1916; as *The Green Face*, translated by Mike Mitchell, 1992
Walpurgisnacht, 1917; as *Walpurgisnacht*, translated by Mike Mitchell, 1993
Der weiße Dominikaner, 1921; as *The White Dominican*, translated by Mike Mitchell, 1994
Der Engel vom westlichen Fenster, 1927; as *The Angel of the West Window*, translated by Mike Mitchell, 1991
Das Haus zur letzten Latern: Nachgelassenes und Verstreutes, edited by E. Frank, 1973

Further Reading

Cersowsky, Peter, *Phantastische Literatur im ersten Viertel des 20. Jahrhunderts*, Munich: Fink, 1983; 2nd edition, 1989
Geißler, Rolf, "Zur Lesart des magischen Prag (Perutz, Meyrink, Kafka)," *Literatur für Leser* (1989)
Goldsmith, Arnold L., "Gustav Meyrink and the Psychological Gothic," in *The Golem Remembered, 1909–1980: Variations of a Jewish Legend*, Detroit, Michigan: Wayne State University Press, 1981
Heym, Gérard, "Le Dominicain blanc," in *Gustav Meyrink*, edited by Yvonne Caroutch, Paris: Edition de l'Herne, 1976
Mitchell, Michael, "Gustav Meyrink," in *Major Figures of Austrian Literature: The Interwar Years 1918–1938*, edited by Donald G. Daviau, Riverside, California: Ariadne Press, 1995
Qasim, Mohammad, *Gustav Meyrink: Eine monographische Untersuchung*, Stuttgart: Heinz, 1981
Ripellino, Angelo Maria, *Praga Magica*, Turin: Einaudi, 1973; as *Magic Prague*, Berkeley: University of California Press, 1973; London: Macmillan, 1994
Smit, Frans, *Gustav Meyrink: Auf der Suche nach dem Übersinnlichen*, Munich: Langen Müller, 1988

Middle High German

It is most common to define Middle High German (MHG) and its literature linguistically and chronologically—to set it apart from what came before and after, namely, Old High and Early New High German—thus placing it in its phonetic and orthographic development roughly between the years 1000 and 1400.

In geographic terms, MHG is distinct from various forms of Low German spoken in northern Germany, but in its written form it developed into a kind of standard, supraregional medieval language. Middle High German served to establish German as a literary language in its own right, alongside Latin and in competition with French as the language of courtly literature. Throughout the 11th century and the first half of the 12th century, the literature remained that of the church. It was not until the middle of the 12th century that a new type of profane entertainment literature arose, and MHG was to become the means to represent the new ideals of chivalry and service. This literature must be closely linked to the rise of the Hohenstaufen dynasty; its competition with other courts, notably that of Henry the Lion; and its expansionist, even universal ambitions.

An early representative of this new literature was Lamprecht's *Alexanderlied* (ca. 1150), an epic tale set in the ancient world with Alexander the Great as its hero. The narration introduced French literary tastes and a notably profane hero as models for the future. Konrad's *Rolandslied* (ca. 1170) also updated an earlier hero, this time Charlemagne, in its use of a French original. The crusading theme further increased the relevance of such works for a contemporary audience, who were mostly members of the noble classes and fighting elite. This elite soon produced a number of highly talented and learned poets from its own ranks, and these poets expressed themselves in a number of different genres and poetic forms. The list of poets ranges from the emperor Henry VI to court ministers and crusaders such as Friedrich von Hausen. The concerns voiced were no longer strictly those of the clergy, but included themes of love, warfare, and rule. The expression of love and the knight's service of the lady became a favorite form of lyrical and musical performance. The *Minnesang*, or love lyric, was written and performed at court by wandering singers, themselves knights and nobles, and was likely influenced by similar movements in Provence, Moorish Spain, and the Levant. These songs were a highly stylized and idealized form of poetry that had little grounding in reality. Women were politically virtually powerless, yet in song they were given a dominant voice by male poets and commanded men as their servants. The service of women embodied the virtues of sacrifice and fortitude, and the men fantasized themselves in dangerous situations always one step ahead of the woman's husband. Early representatives from the southern German area include Der Kürenberger, Dietmar von Eist, and Albrecht von Johannsdorf.

The search for love and social recognition was also carried over to another verse form, the heroic epic. The same poets who wrote about love also debated the ethical dilemmas of conflict and leadership. In such works as Wolfram von Eschenbach's *Parzival* (ca. 1210), Hartmann von Aue's *Erec* (ca. 1185) and *Iwein* (ca. 1200), and Ulrich von Zatikhoven's *Lanzelet* (ca. 1195), the legends of Arthur and his knights served as models for proper or improper behavior; the situations depicted tested the knight's courage as well as his manners. These loose translations and expansions of the French works of Chrétien de Troyes were thoroughly original in their approach to verse and themes. Ancient matter was used to the same purpose, be it Germanic, as in the anonymous *Nibelungenlied* (ca. 1200) or *Kudrun* (ca. 1230), or classical, as in Heinrich von Veldecke's *Eneid* (ca. 1180) or Herbort von Fritzlar's *Lied von Troja* (ca. 1190). The heroic tradition was subsequently subsumed by the search for examples of masculine and feminine virtue. The warrior elite saw its own questions reflected in the struggles of knights against fantastic monsters and evil men. Gottfried von Straßburg's *Tristan und Isolt* (ca. 1210) continued this pattern, but raised disturbing questions about the role of love and adultery in an ordered society. Monastic and mystic traditions of isolation and exile also made the answers to such questions more complex. The influence of the church in this debate remained strong, as evidenced by the important role of the religious orders fighting in Palestine. This more realistic perspective found itself the subject of numerous crusader poems as well as Wolfram's epic *Willehalm* (ca. 1215). Religious debates and the continued popularity of saintly heroes led to MHG works such as Hartmann von Aue's *Gregorius* (1187–89). Based on the Oedipus myth, this work raises questions of sin and redemption outside the traditional courtly scenario.

Already by the first decade of the 13th century, a trend toward parody marked an internal conflict between the poets and their treatment of themes. Walther von der Vogelweide distanced himself from his teacher Reinmar der Alte and began to write politically and socially critical songs as well as to develop a view of a kind of *minne* that strives for the happiness of both partners. Neidhart von Reuental took this movement to an extreme by situating lovers in the lower classes while often viewing love through the eyes of mothers and daughters. With Walther's death around 1230, the death of Emperor Frederick II in 1250, and the subsequent demise of the Hohenstaufens, the classical period of MHG literature came to an end. What followed was certainly of literary merit, but the age lacked an abundance of talented poets and a sense of cohesiveness. The prolific Konrad von Würzburg and others continued to present entertaining tales to courtly audiences, but their works already glance back to the greats as authorities. The rise of the cities and their merchant classes, the preaching monastic orders, and the loss of the crusader states created a new sense of direction for medieval societies. The search for answers moved away from the courts to mystics and moralists, while by the 15th century entertainment was provided by the *Meistersinger*, who looked back on the golden age of MHG literature for inspiration.

WILLIAM WHOBREY

See also German Language; Old High German

Further Reading

de Boor, Helmut, *Die höfische Literatur: Vorbereitung, Blüte, Ausklang, 1170–1250*, Munich: Beck, 1953; 11th edition, 1991

Bumke, Joachim, *Höfische Kultur: Literatur und Gesellschaft im hohen Mittelalter*, Munich: Deutscher Taschenbuchverlag, 1986; as *Courtly Culture: Literature and Society in the High Middle Ages*, translated by Thomas Dunlap, Berkeley: University of California Press, 1991

——, *Geschichte der deutschen Literatur im hohen Mittelalter*, Munich: Deutscher Taschenbuchverlag, 1989

Ehrismann, Gustav, *Geschichte der deutschen Literatur bis zum Ausgang des Mittelalters*, 4 vols., Munich: Beck, 1918–1935

Ehrismann, Otfrid, *Ehre und Mut, Aventiure und Minne: Höfische Wortgeschichten aus dem Mittelalter*, Munich: Beck, 1995

Gibbs, Marion E., *Medieval German Literature: A Companion*, New York: Garland, 1997

Hardin, James, and Will Hasty, editors, *German Writers and Works of the High Middle Ages: 1170–1280*, Dictionary of Literary Biography, vol. 138, Detroit, Michigan: Gale Research, 1994

Nagel, Bert, *Staufische Klassik: Deutsche Dichtung um 1200*, Heidelberg: Stiehm, 1977

Schweikle, Günther, *Minnesang in neuer Sicht*, Stuttgart: Metzler, 1994

Stammler, Wolfgang, editor, *Die deutsche Literatur des Mittelalters: Verfasserlexikon*, Berlin: de Gruyter, 5 vols., 1933–1955; 2nd edition, 1977–

Minnesang

The term *Minnesang* (Middle High German [MHG]; *minne* "love" + *sanc* "song") designates the German variant of the secular love lyric that was performed at the courts of the nobility all over Western Europe in the Middle Ages. Love in this lyric is typically conceptualized as a form of feudal service rendered by the subservient male lover to his lady; the song is characteristically a first-person monologue uttered by this lover, who woos the lady, petitions her, praises her beauty and her noble virtues, and articulates his frustration and suffering but also his persistence when his service invariably goes unrewarded. This paradigm of "courtly love"—the MHG term is *hôhe minne* (high love)—predominates in Minnesang, although it is by no means the only one; the surviving corpus of lyrics contains a variety of paradigms, speaking roles, discourse forms, and perspectives. Alongside songs of courtly love there are lyrics celebrating reciprocal love; female as well as male personae (although there were no women minnesingers); and dialogue songs and "objective genres" containing third-person narrative, including dawn songs and pastourelles.

The social locus of Minnesang was the court; a central task of interpretation is therefore to elucidate what function and meaning the lyric had for its courtly audience and its performers (who were often, but not exclusively, noblemen themselves). There is very little historical documentation of performance, with the consequence that interpretations and explanations are hypothetical and often controversial. The central points at issue in modern scholarship are whether Minnesang was a ritual that had the primary function of expressing and fostering the self-image of a social elite or was an autonomous art form that was cultivated and valued for aesthetic reasons, whether Minnesang articulated and addressed real experiences and emotions or was fictive, whether the songs' verbal content and themes are to be interpreted as being literally about love or as codes for other, nonerotic, concerns (for example, a desire for recognition and preferment at court). Most likely, the function and the meaning of the lyric varied according to context and time, making it likely that no single theory will account for all of Minnesang throughout its long history.

The earliest attested Minnesang dates from ca. 1150–ca. 1180; this "Danubian" lyric (so called because of its geographical provenance) is distinctive because it does not follow the courtly love paradigm and because a high proportion of the (typically monostrophic) songs are given to female lyric personae. These *Frauenstrophen* (women's strophes) do not articulate authentic feminine experiences but represent male preconceptions about femininity. The Danubian lyric appears to be an indigenous tradition; it was eclipsed in the period ca. 1170–ca. 1190, as German courts became increasingly influenced by the more advanced literary culture of France. Poets such as Heinrich von Veldeke (active ca. 1165–85), Friedrich von Hausen (ca. 1170–90), and Rudolf von Fenis (ca. 1180–90) imitated the content (courtly love paradigm) of troubadour and trouvère lyrics, and also their characteristic form (polystrophic canzone: a song consisting of stanzas with tripartite musical and metrical structure). This style, which henceforth became the norm in Minnesang, was developed along independent lines by the lyric poets of the *Blütezeit* (period of florescence) of medieval German literature: Hartmann von Aue (ca. 1180–1200), Albrecht von Jo-

hansdorf (ca. 1180–1210), Reinmar (ca. 1190–1210), Heinrich von Morungen (ca. 1190–1220), Walther von der Vogelweide (ca. 1198–1227), Wolfram von Eschenbach (ca. 1200–1220), and Neidhart von Reuental (ca. 1210–40). In this period Minnesang attained a high level of self-conscious artistry; its salient features were the virtuoso handling of received models and the innovation of new ones; the deployment of humor, irony, and parody; and the fashioning by individual poets of a distinctive authorial personality. The remainder of the 13th century witnessed the continuing trend toward making Minnesang an artifact; the three leading trends were classicism, mannerism, and parody. There were poets who imitated the by then revered *Blütezeit* "classics"; a notable example is Ulrich von Liechtenstein, who embedded his songs in a fictive autobiography, the *Frauendienst* (1255; Service of Ladies). Mannerism manifested itself in the *geblümter Stil* (florid style) associated with Burkhart von Hohenfels (ca. 1210/1230) and in the formal virtuosity of Gottfried von Neifen (ca. 1235/1255); parody is the hallmark of Neidhart's imitators, of whom Steinmar (ca. 1295) is one of the most original. The 14th century is the period of the waning of Minnesang as a living form of courtly culture. In response to economic crisis, the plague, and religious schism, court literature turned to didactic modes and genres that provided the troubled aristocracy with ideological reassurance; Minnesang was not well adapted for this role. The love lyrics that were produced in the 14th and early 15th centuries is often highly personalized; it was also a vehicle for displaying mastery of the genre's thematic, formal, and rhetorical repertoire. Important figures from this period are the Monk of Salzburg (ca. 1350–75), Eberhard von Cersne (ca. 1400), Hugo von Montfort (d. 1423), and Oswald von Wolkenstein (d. 1445).

One development around the turn of the 14th century is of momentous significance for Minnesang: the compilation of lyric texts in large-scale manuscript collections. Some manuscripts were collections of lyrics by several poets (the most impressive example is the large Heidelberg manuscript, probably produced in Zurich in the early 14th century; it contains around 6,000 strophes by 140 poets). Others are author-based (the Berlin Neidhart manuscript from the late 13th century); in a few cases, authors such as Hugo von Montfort and Oswald von Wolkenstein appear to have commissioned manuscripts themselves. The production of these manuscripts is important in two ways. First, it marks the transition of Minnesang from performance art to written text: very few manuscripts include music. Second, the manuscripts are the principal source of our knowledge of Minnesang today. At the same time, they condition our knowledge in crucial respects. The manuscript compilers wrote down what was available to them and what they considered worth preserving; our picture of Minnesang is therefore refracted through their habits of compilation and their tastes. Perhaps more seriously, the preservation of the lyrics largely as words without music severely impedes our appreciation of Minnesang as *song*. We can, however, recover something of the performance reality from the manuscript evidence. Where the same text is preserved in more than one manuscript, there are often differences in the wording and in the sequence and the number of strophes. These variants, which traditional textual philology dismissed as scribal "errors," are currently considered as legitimate alternative versions; their analysis affords us at least some insight into how lyrics could mutate with each new performance.

MARK CHINCA

See also Sangspruchdichtung

Further Reading
Bergner, Heinz, editor, *Lyrik des Mittelalters: Probleme und Interpretationen*, 2 vols., Stuttgart: Reclam, 1983
Dronke, Peter, *The Medieval Lyric*, London: Hutchinson, 1968; 3rd edition, Woodbridge and Rochester, New York: Brewer, 1996
Edwards, Cyril, et al., editors, *Lied im deutschen Mittelalter: Überlieferung, Typen, Gebrauch*, Tübingen: Niemeyer, 1996
Fromm, Hans, editor, *Der deutsche Minnesang: Aufsätze zu seiner Erforschung*, 2 vols., Darmstadt: Wissenschaftliche Buchgesellschaft, 1961; 6th edition, 1985
Holznagel, Franz-Josef, *Wege in die Schriftlichkeit: Untersuchungen und Materialien zur Überlieferung der mittelhochdeutschen Lyrik*, Tübingen and Basel: Francke, 1995
Kasten, Ingrid, *Frauendienst bei Trobadors und Minnesängern im 12. Jahrhundert: Zur Entwicklung und Adaption eines literarischen Konzepts*, Heidelberg: Winter, 1986
Kuhn, Hugo, *Minnesangs Wende*, Tübingen: Niemeyer, 1952; 2nd edition, 1967
Räkel, Hans-Herbert, *Der deutsche Minnesang: Eine Einführung mit Texten und Materialien*, Munich: Beck, 1986
Ranawake, Silvia, *Höfische Strophenkunst: Vergleichende Untersuchungen zur Formentypologie von Minnesang und Trouvèrelied an der Wende zum Spätmittelalter*, Munich: Beck, 1976
Sayce, Olive, *The Medieval German Lyric, 1150–1300: The Development of Its Themes and Forms in Their European Context*, Oxford: Clarendon, and New York: Oxford University Press, 1982
Schilling, Michael, and Peter Strohschneider, editors, *Wechselspiele: Kommunikationsformen und Gattungsinterferenzen mittelhochdeutscher Lyrik*, Heidelberg: Winter, 1996
Schweikle, Günther, *Minnesang*, Stuttgart: Metzler, 1989
Tervooren, Helmut, editor, *Gedichte und Interpretationen: Mittelalter*, Stuttgart: Reclam, 1993

Minority Literature

The term *minority literature* can be seen specifically as an attempt to recognize the existence and writings of ethnic and other minorities. It is a term that is deeply contested by those writers who see themselves as marginalized by such a categorization.

Unlike other literary movements that allow themselves to be located and understood within the German cultural system, "minority literatures" have participated mostly as absence. A homogeneous perception of what is German has precluded any investigation of texts written by migrants to Germany as a vital component of German literature. Nevertheless, this literature has been making its presence increasingly felt since the late 1980s, and a special issue on minorities in German culture was published by the journal *New German Critique* in 1989. To quote one of the contributors to this issue, "Why are certain representations, that is, linguistic, social, and political perceptions of the other's reality, validated by the dominant culture, while others are discredited?"

In talking about minority literatures, we need to differentiate between two groups. One of them pertains to the *Gastarbeiter* (guest workers) who signed contracts with the government of the Federal Republic of Germany to help rebuild a war-torn Germany in the aftermath of World War II. Some of these workers began writing in German or having their works translated into German. The term *guest worker* was used as a linguistic leverage against foreigners, for it stressed their guest, that is, transitory status in Germany and also their position as workers who were subject to the will of their employer. Quite different is the other group whose voice has been making itself heard since the mid-1980s and who call themselves Afro-Germans.

Writings by guest workers were initially published under the rubric of "exotic" writings. It would seem that underlying this willingness to publish such writings was a hope that minority literatures would not endure long enough to warrant inclusion in the German literary canon. Hence, German readers of these texts brought a good deal of sympathy to them. Such writing seemed to appease their bad conscience about the miserable living conditions that the workers had to endure. It is ironic that readers' expectations of portraits of unmitigated woe in these writings resulted not only in framing the writers in even more stereotypical forms but also led the readers to dismiss such literature very quickly as interesting but dispensable. In other words, the writers were rewarded only for writing in graphic and sentimental detail the anguish that they endured in Germany. What neither the German government nor the readers had foreseen was that many workers stayed on in Germany long after the late 1940s.

Attempts to find more sensitive terms for minority literatures resulted in the title *Eine nicht nur deutsche Literatur* (A Not Merely German Literature), coined at the 1985 Bad Homburg conference on German literature by nonnative writers. *Minority literature* gained recognition through two anthologies in the early 1980s, as well as through special issues of cultural and academic journals (*Kürbiskern* [1979; Pumpkin Seed], *Zeitschrift für Kulturaustausch* [1985; Journal for Cultural Exchange]). Franco Biondi, Rafik Schami, Jusuf Naoum, and Suleman Taufiq, editors of the series *Südwind Gastarbeiterdeutsch* (Southwind Guest Worker German), first used the term *Literatur der Betroffenheit* (literature of consternation) in *Zu Hause in der Fremde* (1984; At Home Abroad) and attempted to employ their texts to foster political unity and solidarity among workers. In 1980, they created a multinational association for literature and the arts (Polynationaler Literatur- und Kunstverein [Polynational Literary and Cultural Organization], or Polikunst) for foreign authors and artists. In 1987, the Poli-Kunstverein was dissolved and the name *Südwind Gastarbeiterdeutsch* was changed to *Südwind Literatur*--indicating a shift from political to more literary concerns. Although these writers claimed that cultural resistance was still their agenda, it was not apparent in their publications.

The accent seemed to be more on social integration, as in the case of Yüksel Pazarkaya, whose writings represented a position of cultural exchange that was less adversarial.

Irmgard Ackermann and Harald Weinrich of the Foreign Language Institute in Munich took the initiative of fostering writings by non-Germans and published three volumes containing award-winning articles: *Als Fremder in Deutschland* (1982; As a Stranger in Germany); *In zwei Sprachen leben* (1983; Living in Two Languages); and *Türken deutscher Sprache* (1984; German-Speaking Turks). This visibility has, however, been a mixed blessing, because it still contains these writers in a special province devoted to the "other." It is very similar to the kind of tokenism by which texts are allotted a place in the archive of "Third World Literature," thereby mystifying and trivializing them.

Although *Ausländerinnenliteratur* (literature by foreign women) is in all the above anthologies, the writings of these and other women have earned recognition only in the last two decades. The first women guest workers who came to the Federal Republic had no educational background within their culture. They either accompanied their husbands or fathers or came alone with the intention of supporting their families, who either followed them or remained at home. These women's life experiences became a reality for the general reading public when in 1978, a German woman, Marianne Herzog, edited and revised an audiotape about a Yugoslavian woman Vera Kamenko, who was jailed for having beaten and killed her son. The Turkish writer Saliha Scheinhardt used a similar approach (*Frauen, die sterben, ohne daß sie gelebt hätten* [1983; Women Who Die without Having Lived] and *Drei Zypressen* [1983; Three Cypresses]) in documenting the miserable lives of these women. Although such writings were thought provoking and sought insights into the situation of Turkish girls and women, the women were portrayed as being so regularly and incessantly victimized by Turkish men that it served to increase prejudice rather than to reduce it. Some texts tried to make Germans realize that these women's lives were unfulfilled, but this style of writing again evoked old stereotypes about the "poor but happy" people from the south. There were also several volumes of case studies on women of different nationalities (for example, Hanne Straube and Karin König, editors, *Zuhause bin ich "die aus Deutschland": Ausländerinnen erzählen* [1982; At Home I Am "The One from Germany": Foreign Women Narrate]).

One example of a more differentiated way of describing experiences is Alev Tekinay's text in *Eine Fremde wie ich* (Hülya Özkan and Andrea Wörle, editors, 1985), where she warns against the danger of assimilation and simultaneously stresses the impossibility of going back. Melek Baklan discusses the difficulties in leaving a traditional family situation in Turkey that has become oppressive and in nonetheless viewing that family as a lost support system when one is on one's own in Germany (see Luisa Costa-Hölzl and Eleni Torossi, editors, *Freihändig auf dem Tandem* [No Hands on the Tandem], Kiel: Neuer Malik Verlag, 1985). The Portuguese Luisa Hölzl discusses issues of different moral standards with which foreign women are confronted (*Als Fremder in Deutschland* [1982; As a Foreigner in Germany]). All these writers have in common their criticism of German society, especially the prejudices rampant in all public places and institutions. Solutions are not offered; neither are they possible.

The second and third generation of German texts by women of different colors and ethnicities are characterized by different senses of self-esteem, although there still seems to be no other alternative to conformity (see works by Zehra Çirak, Yasmin Erönü, Hülya S. Özkan, and Alev Tekinay). But their texts are invaluable in their diversity and the manner in which they problematize simplistic notions of "we" and "they." Issues such as xenophobia, integration, and problems of identity formation are crucial for these writers.

In 1994, the yearly *Bericht der Beauftragten der Bundesregierung für die Belange der Ausländer über die Lage der Ausländer in der Bundesrepublik Deutschland* (Report by the Delegates of the Federal Government on the Concerns of Foreigners about the Situation of Foreigners in the Federal Republic of Germany) published statistics about minorities updated only to 1991. Conspicuously missing from this list were Afro-Germans and Southeast Asians. Of the 100,000 people of color in Germany, about 30,000 are estimated to be Afro-Germans. Other estimates put their number between 50,000 to 100,000. In other words, no census category is available to identify the increasing number of Germans of color. The assumption that being German means "white," moreover, makes Afro-Germans veritably invisible. Their fight for survival has been documented only recently by May Ayim and Dagmar Schultz in their path-breaking work *Farbe bekennen: Afro-deutsche Frauen auf den Spuren ihrer Geschichte* (1992; Afro-German Women in Search of Their History). *Afreta* and *afro look*, journals written and edited by Afro-Germans, cannot be found on the shelves of bookstores in Germany. The concept "Afro-German," however, has forced a reevaluation of the otherwise unquestioningly accepted national category "German" and the equally unproblematized racist category "black." A second volume entitled *Entfernte Verbindungen* (1993; Remote Connections), also published by the Orlanda Frauenverlag (Orlanda Publishing House for Women) and edited by Ika Hügel, Chris Lange, May Ayim, Ilona Bubeck, Gülsen Aktas, and Dagmar Schultz, is deeply concerned with the increasing racism, anti-Semitism, and class oppression in Germany. The contributors to this volume are not restricted to Afro-Germans but come from many ethnic backgrounds.

A similar destiny of absence and invisibility envelops Asian writers living and writing in Germany. Born in India in 1969, Anant Kumar began his studies of German literature and linguistics at the University of Kassel in 1991 and is now completing his master's degree with a thesis on Alfred Döblin's *Manas*. Since 1992, several of his texts have been published in literary journals in Germany. *Fremde Frau—Fremder Mann* is his first poetry collection. It was nominated in 1997 for the V.O. Stomps Prize, which is awarded every two years by the city of Mainz for literary work published by small presses. He does not allow his poetry to be consumed as part of the exotic scene. There is an urgency in it that forces the reader/listener to rethink what it means to write in a particular language. Kumar has made a conscious decision by choosing German as his language. He sees himself primarily as a writer and recognizes his Asian identity as one component of the plurality of identities that he harbors within himself. In his poem "Sprache und Kultur" (1998; Language and Culture) he says: "Literatur ist Literatur! / Literatur kennt keine Grenzen!" (literature is literature! / literature knows no boundaries!). This is a sentiment widely echoed by the younger generation of "minority" writers. The Turkish writer Zehra Çirak makes a similar appeal to the reader in her poem "Kulturidentität" (1986; Cultural Identity). She asks: "Ist das etwas, womit ich mich wieder- / erkenne, oder ist das etwas womit andere / mich einordnen können?" (Is that something in which I recognize myself, / or is it something with which / others can classify me?). This is a resistance to *Verschubladisierung*, a word that has been coined by Çirak to denote the tendency on the part of the German reader to categorize and stereotype: the word *Schublade* means a (desk) drawer; hence, *Verschubladisierung* literally means the attempt to pigeonhole.

Interestingly, Germany is not the only country where a monolithic white Germanness is being challenged. In 1995–96 a workshop took place in Austria, and writers from different ethnic backgrounds participated with texts and discussions. The organizers of this workshop published the participants' contributions in an anthology entitled *JEDER IST anderswo EIN FREMDER* (EVERYONE IS somewhere A FOREIGNER). The wide spectrum of writing encompasses problems similar to those articulated in Germany. Some names associated with "minority" writing in Austria are Senol Akkilic, Reza Ashrafi, Milo Dor, Mario Horvath, Obrad Jovanovic, and Mario Ruthofer.

Since the unification of Germany, the rhetoric of "We Germans" has become more insidious—since it does not reflect upon the category "we" and its consequences. Minorities have become an incessant target for violence because they signify an element that can potentially disrupt and destabilize the search for a "German" identity. Such disruption, however, needs to be seen as a powerful force in continually revitalizing German writing.

KAMAKSHI P. MURTI

See also May Ayim

Further Reading
Ackermann, Irmgard, and Harald Weinrich, editors, *Eine nicht nur deutsche Literatur: Zur Standortbestimmung der "Ausländerliteratur,"* Munich: Piper, 1986

Bade, Klaus J., editor, *Deutsche im Ausland—Fremde in Deutschland: Migration in Geschichte und Gegenwart*, Munich: Beck, 1992
Boehncke, Heiner, and Harald Wittich, editors, *Buntesdeutschland: Ansichten zu einer multikulturellen Gesellschaft*, Reinbek bei Hamburg: Rowohlt Taschenbuch, 1991
Castles, Stephen, et al., *Here for Good: Western Europe's New Ethnic Minorities*, London: Pluto Press, 1984
Dönhoff, Marion, *Weil das Land sich ändern muß: Ein Manifest*, Reinbek bei Hamburg: Rowohlt, 1992
Hourani, Albert Habib, *Islam in European Thought*, Cambridge and New York: Cambridge University Press, 1991
Internationaler Germanisten-Kongreß, *Begegnung mit dem Fremden: Grenzen, Traditionen, Vergleiche: Akten des I. Internationalen Germanisten-Kongresses, Tokio, 1990*, Munich: Iudicium, 1991
JanMohamed, Abdul R., and David Lloyd, editors, *The Nature and Context of Minority Discourse*, New York: Telos Press, 1987; Oxford and New York: Oxford University Press, 1990
Martin, Peter, *Schwarze Teufel, edle Mohren: Afrikaner im Bewußtsein und Geschichte der Deutschen*, Hamburg: Junius, 1993
Pazarkaya, Yüksel, *Rosen im Frost: Einblicke in die türkische Kultur*, Zurich: Unionsverlag, 1982
Schmalz-Jacobsen, Cornelia, and Georg Hansen, *Ethnische Minderheiten in der Bundesrepublik Deutschland: Ein Lexikon*, Munich: Beck, 1995
Special Issue on Minority Literature, *New German Critique* 46 (1989)
Stienen, Inga, *Leben zwischen zwei Welten: Türkische Frauen in Deutschland*, Weinheim: Quadriga, 1994
Teraoka, Arlene Akiko, "Turks as Subjects: The Ethnographic Novels of Paul Geiersbach," in *Culture/Contexture: Essays in Anthropology and Literary Studies*, edited by E. Valentine Daniel and Jeffrey M. Peck, Berkeley: University of California Press, 1996
Wägenbaur, Thomas, "Kulturelle Identität oder Hybridität? Aysel Özakins *Die blaue Maske* und das Projekt interkultureller Dynamim," *LiLi* 97 (1995)
Wierlacher, Alois, et al., editors, *Hermeneutik der Fremde*, Munich: Iudicium, 1990
Wierlacher, Alois, editor, *Das Fremde und das Eigene: Prolegomena zu einer interkulturellen Germanistik*, Munich: Iudicium, 1985
———, editor, *Perspektiven und Verfahren interkultureller Germanistik: Akten des I. Kongresses der Gesellschaft für Interkulturelle Germanistik*, Munich: Iudicium, 1987

Die Moderne

There are various ways of seeing what has been called the modern movement, modernity, modernism, or *Die Moderne*. The first perspective is close to avant-garde, implying that each wave of conscious innovation since about 1885, up to or even including postmodern trends, has been a fresh modernism. Premodern works either fail to respond to modern conditions, or they do so only with conventional aesthetics and conventional psychology. But works that consciously and innovatively react, positively or negatively, to changes—social and mental—since the Industrial Revolution can be claimed for modernism. In these works, the worldviews that had so far sufficed, with their divine world order (or, at least, comprehensible meaning of things), their cultivation of individual identity as a progressive ideal, and their Aristotelian or Platonic aesthetics, become highly suspect. Moral stances dissolve into appreciations of dilemmas. Belief in timeless entities such as nation and heredity yields to skepticism about all groupings that restrict freedom. Facts are revealed as a construct of memory and convention. Narrative is suspect, identity is dubious, and time is questioned. Sexual and gender roles are deconstructed. Obscurity is embraced: clarity would mean oversimplification. Seeing modernism in this way thus leads to the listing of diverse characteristics (including shock, discontinuity, crisis, nonrepresentationalism, mannerism, plight, alienation, fragmentation, objectifying the subjective, chaos, creation and destruction, and synchronicity) without finding a single criterion of definition.

The second perspective on modernism comes from the narrow, anglophone definition of modernism, which is exemplified in works by Joyce, Lawrence, Gertrude Stein, and Virginia Woolf; the search for continental European equivalents have often found apparent success in identifying Thomas Mann's ironic deconstruction of narrative and Kafka's shifting realities as modernist. But there is much more German modernism in this sense, even if one only considers narrative literature. For instance, Hofmannsthal and Schnitzler engaged in depth psychology. Rilke (*Aufzeichnungen des Malte Laurids Brigge* [1910; *The Notebook of Malte Laurids Brigge*]), Carl Einstein (*Bebuquin*, 1912), Musil (*Der Mann ohne Eigenschaften* [1930–43; *The Man without Qualities*]), Hans Henny Jahnn (*Perrudja*, 1929), and Frisch (*Mein Name sei Gantenbein* [1964; *A Wilderness of Mirrors*]) all undermine the role of reality and substitute a shifting potentiality. Broch turns his novel (*Die Schlafwandler* [1952; *The Sleepwalkers*]) into a set of parallel plots and excursuses—and so on.

A third perspective sees modernism as an experience of a crisis in culture across Europe between about 1885 and 1918, which comprehends an onset of doubt in the ability of discursive language to represent or logically articulate the world as causally coherent. There is no real pattern of responses to this, but reactions can be roughly grouped in the following categories: conservative, seeking to reaffirm the power of language to grasp realities and to distill metaphysical significance from them (Rilke's poetry); revisionist, wishing to bring in some fresh value to language or to make words usable in some new way and thus hoping to rescue the wholeness of expressible meaning (Stramm's poetry); and radical, abandoning the nexus of signifier and signified altogether (Ball's poetry). These groupings cut across conventional literary movements.

The architectural critic defines modernism roughly as the replacement of beautiful form by effective function. The shape of modernist drama, similarly, depends on what the playwright thinks vital rather than a convention of a plot fitting into five acts. In such models, the writer responds to life in the industrial era by projecting a form that itself expresses these conditions—carrying subjectivity further and further, or inventing new forms to express social involvement. Thus, literature itself can be seen as functional, playing a part in the propagation of human freedom, whether by the exploration of individual eccentricities, the satirical exposure of society's wrongs, or the employment of utopian attitudes. As a consequence, formal innovation can serve functional purposes. For instance, complex techniques reflect the mazelike structure of modern mentality. Further, the division of genres is subverted by the introduction of autobiographical, autothematic, and invented elements together. For this perspective on modernism, the modern world is humankind's plaything. The modernists celebrate the achievements of this play—the city and the machine; or they repeat playing at or producing, alternately, pleasing forms, teasing allusions, appeals to the subconscious, montages, and collages, all of which experimentally cut the bonds of logic. The appearance of naturalness, hitherto important, is abandoned: modernism is proud to be seen to be art.

Die Moderne, a feminine noun, is the German-speaking world's particular contribution to the vocabulary of modernism. Coined in 1886, it first referred to Berlin naturalism but was reinvented in 1890 to denote the first attempts to move beyond naturalism. By 1891, *Die Moderne* in this sense was established, and a short-lived eponymous periodical appeared, but the word still occurred to denote naturalism, and already a writer could state that any attempt to define it would be contrary to its inmost being! From this promising start, *Die Moderne* has often been perceived as an epoch (embracing a number of movements in the narrower sense) in literature and other arts in German-speaking countries between about 1885 and 1914, from naturalism to early Expressionism, always future-directed, generally stressing the inevitability of and need for progress. Although many critics refer to the wider, longer-lasting, international modern movements sketched above as *Die Moderne,* the narrower definition will be adopted here.

Die Moderne sought above all to revalue identity. The grand narratives of the 19th century influenced it in various ways: Darwin and Spencer for a nonreligious view of man and society, Freud for a new interpretation of the mind, and Nietzsche for the problematization of language as a key criterion of modernity. Modern life and sensibility demanded new modes of expression. Belief in progress justified jettisoning all old precedents and authorities, in philosophy or in literature, in concurrence with Nietzsche's revaluation of all values. *Die Moderne* consisted of young movements (nobody over 40 played a leading active role), centered on particular places (notably Berlin, Vienna, and Munich), giving themselves programmatic names such as *Jung Wien* (Young Vienna) or *die Jüngstdeutschen* (The Latest Germans), which referred back to "das junge Deutschland."

The first movement of *Die Moderne* was naturalism. Literary form was loosened, and writers came to grips with the fact that industrial and urbanized society had already altered human psychology. An aesthetics to match modern science, naturalism propounded modern ethics and the social question. In Berlin, naturalism remained the dominant literary tendency from about 1885 to 1900. Munich naturalism had a shorter life, and it has worn less well. Vienna naturalism was even less obvious: the pioneering periodical *Moderne Dichtung* set out in 1890 with a naturalist manifesto and invited Ibsen to a banquet in 1891, before becoming the *Moderne Rundschau* and printing Schnitzler and Hofmannsthal.

Viennese writers reacted quickly against naturalism—Bahr's influential essay *Die Überwindung des Naturalismus* (1891; The Conquest of Naturalism) is indicative—taking up subjective, psychologically analytic modes. Even in its first issue, *Moderne Dichtung* published Bahr's confused yet seminal essay *Die Moderne,* which introduces the notes of nervous Romanticism and decadence characteristic of Viennese *Moderne.* In this essay, the situation of the age in general and literature in particular is seen as a dying, from which only a savior, perhaps a Nietzschean superman, can rescue it. Similar to the naturalists, Bahr apostrophizes truth as the means to this salvation—but he means a subjective truth, a matter of the psyche, experienced by each individual through sensibility. According to Bahr, the objectively new will be recognized only when it appears in the soul of the new man. After Bahr, literature was seen as psychological exploration.

Bahr's mission to oppose a specifically Austrian voice, idealist and open to other literatures, to the threatening cultural hegemony of Berlin (which in turn reflected the increasing political predominance of the German Empire) and its materialist naturalism took shape when he recognized in Hofmannsthal, still a schoolboy, the creative genius who could realize his aims—and who intuitively grasped them. Thus began *Die Moderne*'s most characteristic movement, known by the largely coterminous designations neo-Romanticism (idealism, taking up the insights of Romanticism), decadence, Impressionism (conversion of sense impressions into thought by way of feeling), symbolism (metaphorical expression, externalizing the internal), and fin de siècle (topicality, looking to the next century). Lyric poetry and poetic drama were the fortes of symbolism, and by his late poetry, Rilke eventually overtook the reputations of George and Hofmannsthal.

Three different directions of German literature may be mentioned as starting under the auspices of *Die Moderne*. First, a Viennese psychological school was pioneered by Schnitzler and Hofmannsthal. A line goes from them to Broch, Doderer, and Canetti. Second, there were conservative literary tendencies, particularly Heimatliteratur, working consciously against the background of the modern world and trying to influence the future by reversion toward the past, individualism, and the rural—away from the mass and the urban. Theories of Blut und Boden, heredity and the soil, although programmatically disregarding industrial society and the crises of the age, were an offshoot of naturalism. Third, there was the fantastic experimental style of poetry founded by Arno Holz, which can be followed through Paul Scheerbart, Schwitters, and Hans Arp to the Wiener Gruppe.

Die Moderne was not tied to one political line, and most of its members would have defended the primacy of the aesthetic over the topical, or form over content; but it generally saw its strivings for progress, freedom, and youth as more liberal or socialist than conservative. Progressive ideas, including women's emancipation, free love, careers for women, theater reform, republicanism, and the abolition of censorship, characterize *Die Moderne*. Kaiser Wilhelm II himself attacked the libertarian ideology of *Jugendstil*. Munich *Moderne*, under the clerical Bavarian censorship, led the fight for freedom; Wedekind had a running battle with the censors.

Institutionally, *Moderne* as urban culture centered around cafés. The Griensteidl in Vienna and the Café des Westens in Berlin shared the nickname Café Größenwahn (*folie de grandeur*). For weight of talent, the Griensteidl wins: Bahr, Schnitzler, Hofmannsthal, Beer-Hofmann, Kraus, and Altenberg met there, as did socialist politicians and publicists. In *cafés, littérateurs,* actors and other theatrical people, artists of all kinds, critics, and politicians discussed the latest developments and read the daily and weekly press. Literary cabarets, notably the Elf Scharfrichter (11 Executioners) in Munich, easily arose from café backgrounds. Loose associations for the propagation of modernity in verse, theater, or art were also founded there: Munich had the Nebenregierung (Spare Government), a group of young satirically minded authors, artists, musicians, and actors associated with the Dichtelei café. Plans for periodicals were discussed, and careers were furthered.

Some institutions of *Die Moderne* were concentrated in one place. Thus, Berlin had the leading publisher for modernist literature (Samuel Fischer) and the largest and most varied theater scene. As a consequence, it attracted cultural leaders: Max Reinhardt, of Austrian origin, Munich-influenced, went there to found his cabaret stage Schall und Rauch (Sound and Fury) and, eventually, his Deutsches Theater (German Theater). Ernst von Wolzogen found the right atmosphere for his musical cabaret, or Überbrettl, the springboard for Berlin's early Expressionist cabarets.

Munich modernism, less unitary than that of Berlin or Vienna, espoused a range of advanced ideas—*George-Kreis* aristocratism, the woolly mysticism of the *Kosmiker* (cosmics) around Ludwig Derleth, and Erich Mühsam's anarchism. Munich also attracted young writers. Rilke came to cultivate influential contacts. Thomas Mann explored the outsiders and the oddball intellectuals of the Munich avant-garde. Heinrich Mann visited regularly, developing as a social novelist between the naturalist and psychological schools. Wedekind explored drama to unmask the individual personality in an age of repression and hypocrisy. Munich also became the center of periodical publishing. Albert Langen moved there from Leipzig to found his satirical magazine *Simplicissimus* in a congenial environment. This and another Munich periodical, *Jugend* (Youth), made *Die Moderne* accessible to progressive elements of the *Bürgertum* (middle classes). They united literary and visual innovation and gave work to young authors and artists. In *Simplicissimus*, Wedekind's disrespectful verses, Ludwig Thoma's satires, and Thomas Theodor Heine's cartoons complemented each other. With *Jugend* and *Die Insel* (The Island), Munich became the center of book art and the decorative periodical.

Die Moderne existed in other arts and studies, too. In Berlin, Vienna, and Munich, young painters formed a *Secession* in defiance of the established academies; Max Liebermann, Lovis Corinth, Gustav Klimt, Wassily Kandinsky, and Oskar Kokoschka are inseparable from *Die Moderne*. Gerhart Hauptmann's *Die Weber* (1892; *The Weavers*) was the literary inspiration for Käthe Kollwitz's graphic cycle *Weberaufstand*, which brought her into conflict with the kaiser. In architecture, department stores and industrial buildings in Berlin (Messel, Behrens) were prominent; galleries and mansions in Vienna (Olbrich, Loos) were also well known. In Vienna and Munich, there was much stress on applied art and crafts. Most closely linked with *Die Moderne* was *Jugendstil*, the art of floral decoration and sinuous line, which was found in Viennese art, decorative arts in Munich (the name comes from an association with *Jugend*'s graphic artwork), and the verse of Otto Julius Bierbaum, poet of the dance. Viennese music, with Mahler and Schoenberg, rounds out the picture.

Philosophy, psychology, social studies, and even aspects of science and economics participated in *Die Moderne*, especially in Vienna, where Freud and Weininger worked, and where Ernst Mach, the proponent of an antimetaphysical philosophy of science, discussed literature and psychology with Bahr. Mach's theory of the interplay of outer reality and inner receptivity reduces the role of the unique individual; Musil's man without qualities originated within this conceptual environment.

Expressionism began in the second generation of *Die Moderne*, from about 1908 (Georg Heym). Starting as the culmination of *Die Moderne*, the most personal avatar of the negative response to modernity—with egocentric, hymnic, distressed lyrics, and apocalyptic visions—goes on to tormented dramas and a strain of activism propagating idealist world visions amid the breakdown occasioned by the experience of World War I; this closeness to current affairs was alien to *Die Moderne* and marked its end. Dada, subverting all existing concepts of language, art, and society, still had elements of *Die Moderne*, but they were radicalized beyond recognition. Techniques (montage) and attitudes (closeness to communism, reception of Marx) almost unknown to *Die Moderne* emerged. Today's critical tendency is to see later Expressionism and Dada as a second, radical wave of modernism. Then came the behaviorism of *Neue Sachlichkeit,* the first specifically 20th-century theory that challenged the ideologies of *Die Moderne.*

The politicization of literature after 1914 does not always favor modernism in the wider sense (socialist realism depends on premodern attitudes), let alone *Die Moderne.* Existentialism and its literary scions tended to revive it: Sartre offered perhaps the last grand narrative, and highly abstract treatments of basic human problems were possible. Relevance beyond the individual subjectivity, however, was not claimed; World War II, the Shoah, and nuclear warfare made ideas of general progress hard to sustain; and political commitment became obligatory. The vogue of existentialism in West Germany after 1945 connected with the so-called *klassische Moderne,* a mixture of elements from such writers as Eliot, Valéry, and Joyce, with techniques that had been in disfavor under Hitler. Hermetic poetry came into vogue; Thomas Mann remarked that only novels that don't look like novels could be taken seriously.

ALFRED D. WHITE

See also Avant-Garde; Der Blaue Reiter; Dadaism

Further Reading

Huyssen, Andreas, and David Bathrick, editors, *Modernity and the Text: Revisions of German Modernism,* New York: Columbia University Press, 1989

Petersen, Jürgen H., *Der deutsche Roman der Moderne: Grundlegung, Typologie, Entwicklung,* Stuttgart: Metzler, 1991

Schmitz, Walter, editor, *Die Münchner Moderne: Die literarische Szene in der "Kunststadt" um die Jahrhundertwende,* Stuttgart: Reclam, 1990

Schutte, Jürgen, and Peter Sprengel, editors, *Die Berliner Moderne, 1885–1914,* Stuttgart: Reclam, 1987

Sheppard, Richard, "Modernism, Language, and Experimental Poetry: On Leaping over Bannisters and Learning How to Fly," *Modern Language Review* 92, no.1 (1997)

Wunberg, Gotthart, and Johannes J. Braakenburg, editors, *Die Wiener Moderne: Literatur, Kunst, und Musik zwischen 1890 und 1910,* Stuttgart: Reclam, 1981

Libuše Moníková 1945–1998

Libuše Moníková extends the tradition of Prague German literature and, more specifically, carries the legacy of Franz Kafka into the second half of the 20th century. Drawing inspiration also from the works of Arno Schmidt, Jorge Borges, James Joyce, and Thomas Pynchon, her writing exhibits the narrative techniques and stylistic features of postmodern literature such as pastiche, intertextuality across many disciplines, and metafiction. Her central themes include various forms of discrimination, issues of power and domination in political as well as personal contexts, and the representation of history. Moníková wrote in German, a language foreign to her, and she addressed a German and Western audience unfamiliar with her place of origin, Czechoslovakia. Her exile and the troubled history of her native country were the original motivation for her writing, but she situated her narratives all over Europe and beyond. Following her motto taken from Arno Schmidt, "Wer nicht liest, kennt die Welt nicht" (Whoever does not read, does not know the world), she constructed her fictional universe by incorporating detailed facts, ideas, anecdotes, and terminology from countless fields of human knowledge into her prose. This is especially true of her large third novel, *Die Fassade* (1987; *The Façade*), which won the prestigious Döblin Prize and established Moníková as a major literary voice in late 20th-century Germany.

Because of the themes of her first two novels, Moníková was initially read primarily in feminist circles. The use of the backdrop of European history in her third and subsequent novels and in many of her essays led to a wide readership in European countries. Her foreign origin has led to the categorization of her work as *AusländerInnenliteratur, MigrantInnenliteratur, Minderheit-*

enliteratur, or, most recently, *multikulturelle Literatur* (literature by foreigners, migrant literature, minority literature, multicultural literature). Moníková, however, vehemently objected to being classified in any of these categories. She called herself a Czech citizen, but a German writer—since she only ever wrote literature in German. Recent debates about her work have addressed issues of gender, national belonging, and the rewriting of history.

In her first novel, *Eine Schädigung* (1981; An Injury), Moníková uses the woman's point of view to describe the physical and emotional lacerations incurred by a gendered form of violence. The central character, Jana, is raped by a police officer in the deserted Prague government district but manages to kill him with his club and dispose of his body. The novel focuses on her slow recovery. But the personal account of postrape trauma only thinly veils the political subtext: *Eine Schädigung* is dedicated to Jan Palach, the Prague student who immolated himself to protest the 1968 Soviet occupation of Czechoslovakia. Moníková's novel is thus also an allegorical representation of the rape of her home country by a colonial oppressor.

Her second novel, *Pavane für eine verstorbene Infantin* (1983; Pavane for a Deceased Princess), again focuses on issues of power, this time in quotidian incidents of oppression, exclusion, and marginalization. Francine, the main figure, faces these issues as a female in predominantly male academia, as a foreign national, and as the survivor of her sister's cruel power games in childhood. She counteracts her various displacements by physically acting out the imposed restrictions: even though she can walk she starts using a wheelchair. It provides her with a place of power, turns into a fetish of projected dependencies, and is then destroyed in effigy. In this way, Francine can then walk away from her displacements and come into her own.

Moníková forged new territory with her third and most prominent novel, *The Façade*. Its characters are four male artists, engaged in the Sisyphean task of restoring the facade of a famous Bohemian Renaissance castle and bounced from one adventure to the next on an eventful journey east into the depths of the Soviet Union. In true postmodernist fashion, the author rewrites the genre of the picaresque novel, with its slapstick humor and biting political satire, while incorporating colorful as well as intellectual digressions into fields such as geology, anthropology, and entomology, and spiking her text with innumerable literary, cultural, and historical allusions and quotations. The castle facade, whose serial images can be read as an allegory of history and of the fragmented national biography, functions as a visual representation of the narrative composition of the novel. The focus on the *process* of image restoration lays bare the narrative framing of history and makes the novel an allegory of historiography. The inserted drama concerning 19th-century Czech National Revival as well as the constant undermining of Cold War communist ideology further contribute to the novel's function as a dissident counterproduction to the official representations of East Central European history.

In *Treibeis* (1992; Drift Ice), history remains on center stage, as Prantl, a middle-aged schoolteacher living in Greenland, meets another Czech exile, Karla, a young stunt woman in the film industry. In their lovers' discourse they try to recreate their lost homeland only to find that their images do not correspond. Prantl's World War II memories of being a resistance parachutist seem disconnected with Karla's experience of exile after the 1968 Soviet occupation. Neither individual nor collective memory seems to provide them with a sense of national identity. Instead, personal as well as political histories appear as a series of displacements, simulations, and border crossings between fiction and reality.

Moníková's last completed novel, *Verklärte Nacht* (1996; Transfigured Night), uses themes, motifs, and a narrative style reminiscent of her first two novels and extends the project of writing a Czech national biography up to the present time. The end of the state of Czechoslovakia in 1993 is projected onto the life and body of the protagonist, Leonora, an internationally renowned dancer and choreographer visiting her native Prague. Leonora's search for her country is a desperate effort against "collective forgetting" in the face of Westernization after the Velvet Revolution and—as in 1938, through Hitler, and again in 1968, through the Soviet invasion—yet another annihilation of the nation with which she identifies. The novel becomes a dance of death and requiem as well as a near-death experience in which Leonora hallucinates embodiments of three mythical-historical female figures, each one of them immortal in her own way. Her passage through death and eventual love for a German with roots in the *Sudentenland* moves the narrative from a solo to a pas de deux with a role reversal in the dance of love—love for each other, for Prague and Bohemia, for the Czechs and the Slovaks, and for Germany and Europe.

In addition to her five novels, Moníková published a collection of short plays, *Unter Menschenfressern: Ein dramatisches Menü in vier Gängen* (1990; Among Cannibals: A Dramatic Meal with Four Courses), and two essay collections, *Schloß, Aleph, Wunschtorte* (1990; Castle, Aleph, Dream Cake) and *Prager Fenster* (1994; Prague Windows). Using the form of pastiche for the dramas, the author cannibalizes historical accounts (of Mozart's funeral) and literary texts (Nestroy, Shakespeare, and Arno Schmidt) for the pleasure derived from skillful play with intertextuality. The work of some literary precursors is also at the center of the essays in her first collection, in which Moníková analyzes totalitarian power structures in the works of Kafka and Wedekind, and linguistic categorizations and myth in the works of Borges. In her second essay collection, she focuses on recent European political developments up to the Velvet Revolution and its aftermath, while tracing their roots in the turning points of Czechoslovakia's national biography.

The writing of Libuše Moníková contributes a new perspective to contemporary German literature both in terms of its wide-ranging topics and its sophisticated narrative techniques. The combination of the author's keen eye for social and political injustice, her love of detailed factual knowledge, and the rich of her cultural allusions makes her texts distinctive in European postmodern literature.

HELGA G. BRAUNBECK

Biography

Born in Prague, Czechoslovakia (now the Czech Republic), 30 August 1945; Studied English and German literature at Charles University, Prague, 1963–68; doctoral degree with a dissertation on the comparison of Shakespeare's and Brecht's *Coriolanus*, 1970; lecturer in language and literature, Charles University, and in factories in Prague, 1968–71; moved to West Germany, 1971; worked as a lecturer in German, comparative literature, and women's literature at the universities of Kassel and Bremen; teacher in Bremen, 1978–81; freelance writer living in Berlin and Prague, 1981–98; held the post of Stadtschreiberin in Mainz, 1994. Ehrengabe des Kulturkreises des Bundesverbands der Deutschen Industrie (BDI), 1984; Döblin Prize, 1987; Kafka Prize (Austria), 1989; Chamisso Prize, 1991; Berlin Literature Prize, combined with Johannes Bobrowski Medal, 1992; International Literature Prize Vilenica (Slowenia), 1993; Literature Prize of ZDF (second public television channel) combined with the Literature Prize of the city of Mainz, 1994; Roswitha von Gandersheim Medal, 1995; Bundesverdienstkreuz am Bande, for literary achievement and achievements in German-Czech relations, 1996; Arno Schmidt stipend, 1997; Thomas Masaryk Medal (Czech Republic), 1997; various memberships in scholarly societies. Died in Berlin, 12 January 1998.

Selected Works

Fiction
Eine Schädigung, 1981
Pavane für eine verstorbene Infantin, 1983
Die Fassade, 1987; as *The Façade*, translated by John E. Woods, 1991
Treibeis, 1992
Verklärte Nacht, 1996
Excerpt from the novel fragment "Jakub Brandl," *Akzente* 6 (1997)

Essays
Schloß, Aleph, Wunschtorte, 1990
Prager Fenster, 1994

Play
Unter Menschenfressern: Ein dramatisches Menü in vier Gängen, 1990

Television Film
Wer nicht liest, kennt die Welt nicht—Grönland Tagebuch (produced 13 December 1994)

Further Reading

Braunbeck, Helga, "The Body of the Nation: The Texts of Libuše Moníková," *Monatshefte* 89, no. 4 (1997)

Braunbeck, Helga, and Libuše Moníková, "Gespräche mit Libuše Moníková," *Monatshefte* 89, no. 4 (1997)

Cramer, Sybille, et al., "Libuše Moníková im Gespräch mit Sibylle Cramer, Jürg Laederach, und Hajo Steinert," *Sprache im technischen Zeitalter* 119 (September 1991)

Engler, Jürgen, "Gespräch mit Libuše Moníková: 'Wer nicht liest, kennt die Welt nicht'," *neue deutsche literatur* 45, no. 515 (1997)

Haines, Brigid, "'New Places from Which to Write Histories of Peoples': Power and the Personal in the Novels of Libuše Moníková," *German Life and Letters* 49, no. 4 (1996)

Jankowsky, Karen Hermine, "Remembering Eastern Europe: Libuše Moníková," in *Women in German Yearbook 12*, edited by Sara Friedrichsmeyer and Patricia Herminghouse, Lincoln and London: University of Nebraska Press, 1996

———, "Between 'Inner Bohemia' and 'Outer Siberia': Libuše Moníková Destabilizes Notions of Nation and Gender," in *Other Germanies: Questioning Identity in Women's Literature and Art*, edited by Karen Hermine Jankowsky and Carla Love, Albany: State University of New York Press, 1997

Krumme, Lothar, "Ausschluß aus den Zirkeln: Über die ersten beiden Prosatexte von Libuše Moníková," in *Bausteine zu einer Poetik der Moderne: Festschrift für Walter Höllerer*, edited by Norbert Miller et al., Munich: Hanser, 1987

Kublitz-Kramer, Maria, "'Was man nicht erfliegen kann, muß man erhinken': Auf den 'Straßen des weiblichen Begehrens': Libuše Moníkovás Erzählung *Pavane für eine verstorbene Infantin*," in *Textdifferenzen und Engagement: Feminismus, Ideologiekritik, Poststrukturalismus*, edited by Cornelia Weiss and Maria Kublitz-Kramer, Pfaffenweiler: Centaurus, 1993

Modzelewski, Jozef A., "Libuše's Success and Francine's Bitterness: Libuše Moníková and Her Protagonist in *Pavane für eine verstorbene Infantin*," in *The Germanic Mosaic: Cultural and Linguistic Diversity in Society*, edited by Carol Blackshire-Belay, Westport, Connecticut and London: Greenwood Press, 1994

Trumpener, Katie, "Is Female to Nation as Nature is to Culture? Božena Němcová, Libuše Moníková, and the Female Folkloric," in *Other Germanies: Questioning Identity in Women's Literature and Art*, edited by Karen Hermine Jankowsky and Carla Love, Albany: State University of New York Press, 1997

Vedder, Ulrike, "Libuše Moníková," in *Kritisches Lexikon zur deutschsprachigen Gegenwartsliteratur*, no. 51, Munich: Edition Text und Kritik, 1982

———, "Mit schiefem Mund auch 'Heimat': Heimat und Nation in Libuše Moníkovás Texten," *Monatshefte* 89, no. 4 (1997)

Christian Morgenstern 1871–1914

Christian Morgenstern is the greatest comic poet in German, the only one worthy of comparison to Lewis Carroll. His four volumes of brilliant and bizarre lyric fantasies—*Galgenlieder* (1905; translated as *The Gallows Songs* and *Songs from the Gallows*), *Palmström* (1910), *Palma Kunkel* (posthumous, 1916), and *Der Gingganz* (posthumous, 1919), later published collectively as *Alle Galgenlieder* (1932)—are for many speakers of German the funniest and most exhilarating documents in the language. Morgenstern himself considered these works to be something of a sideline. He wrote an equal quantity of religious-philosophical verse, as well as aphorisms and essays, but few readers in recent years have valued this material as highly as he did, in spite of its obvious sincerity (a long struggle with debilitating tuberculosis underlay the poetic images of impending death). Morgenstern the religious thinker—borrowing themes from Dostoevsky, Nietzsche, various strains of Christianity, and (after 1909) the anthroposophy of Rudolf Steiner—cultivated a distinctive mode of verse meditation that has plausibly been discussed in connection with Rilke. He did not, however, develop an equally striking *poetics,* as Rilke certainly did. Morgenstern's serious verse is always technically competent, often elegant; but his indispensable contribution to German literature is in the realm of the comic imagination.

The writing of "gallows songs" began in Berlin around 1895 as an exercise in black humor among youthful friends. Later the vaudeville of Ernst von Wolzogen became the natural (or supernatural) home of Morgenstern's moonsheep, hangman's daughter, midnight mouse, and assorted other grotesqueries. But it

soon became obvious that more was at stake here than bravado and high jinks. The alienated perspective from gallows hill made it possible for the young poet to venture a wide variety of linguistic and metaphysical sallies. He exploited ambiguities that native speakers of a language have usually trained themselves not to notice (*elf* means "eleven" but—capitalized—also "elf"); reversals that would never occur to the pragmatic citizen (if you wear a *Weste* over your paunch, why not an *Oste* over your back?); and dead metaphors just waiting for sundown so that they can return as vampires (the word for "bootjack," *Stiefelknecht*, means literally "boot servant"—it's *so* hard for a boot to get good domestic help these days). He also played with extended idioms (who washes your dirty towel when you "throw in the towel"?—or, as they say in German, you "throw your shotgun into the wheat field" [Morgenstern, by the way, is the undisputed master of confusing multiple parentheses]); anthropomorphisms (what would it be like to be a funnel?); reifications (how much for a dozen doughnut holes?—no, not the pieces of dough that have been removed, but the holes themselves; Morgenstern plays the same game with a picket fence); graphic representations (German script makes *Nilpferd* [hippopotamus] look very much like *Stilpferd* [style horse]); crazy inventions (the lamp that instantaneously turns broad daylight into pitch blackness is the grandfather of Woody Allen's machine for deboning fish [or, alternatively, reinserting the bones into a fish]); and imaginary beings.

English versions of the *Galgenlieder* illustrate the fact that like all ostentatiously "untranslatable" poets, Morgenstern actually "translates" relatively well into other languages. The reason is clear: when the original poem is freely inventive, the imitator has license to invent in the same spirit. (There exist at least three good German translations of the "Jabberwocky," but none of the far simpler "The Owl and the Pussycat.") Thus, paradoxically, the Anglophone reader can enjoy multiple approaches to this most German of German poets in brilliant versions by Max Knight (especially), as well as Walter Arndt, David Slavitt, and others. (One problem: the parodies of German bureaucratic language are never quite as chilling in English.) It may be mentioned that Morgenstern himself was an important translator—of Ibsen and Hamsun.

In the context of early 20th-century philosophy, Morgenstern's fantasy creations can be understood as a reaction to materialism and to various strains of skeptical nominalism in the work of Hugo von Hofmannsthal, Fritz Mauthner (an explicit target of satire at the end of *Alle Galgenlieder*), Karl Kraus, Ludwig Wittgenstein, and others. If the philosophers saw their task as the demystifying of philosophical problems through the systematic elimination of linguistic phantoms (purely verbal entities), Morgenstern found spiritual value in the poetic cultivation of precisely those phantoms. In fact, a whole gallery of brave and delicate monsters (such as the celebrated "Werwolf") could be conjured up by the poet from mere contingencies of phonology, morphology, syntax, onomastics, and idiomatics. Just as the music synthesizer produces sounds that no musician has ever coaxed out of a conventional instrument, so Morgenstern produced a galaxy of hitherto unimaginable alternative worlds by directly twiddling the knobs and dials of the German language. In this project the comedian and the philosopher met.

H. STERN

Biography

Born in Munich, 6 May 1871. Studied political economy in Breslau; diagnosed with tuberculosis, 1893; broke off studies and recuperated in Switzerland; studied art history and archaeology in Berlin, 1894 (did not complete degree); worked at *Tägliche Rundschau* and *Freie Bühne*, from 1894; wrote feuilletons for *Kunstwart;* translated Strindberg, Ibsen, Björnstjerne Björnsons, from 1897; worked as journalist in Italy, 1902; worked as reader for theatrical publisher Felix Bloch Erben and for Verlag Cassirer in Berlin, 1903; published poetry with Cassirer, from 1905. Died in Merano, Italy, 31 March 1914.

Selected Works

Collections
Alle Galgenlieder, 1932
Gesammelte Werke in einem Band, edited by Margareta Morgenstern, 1965
Kindergedichte, 1965
Sämtliche Dichtungen, edited by Heinrich O. Proskauer, 17 vols. and index vol., 1971–80
Jubiläumsausgabe, edited by Clemens Heselhaus, 4 vols., 1979

Poetry
In Phanta's Schloß: Ein Cyklus humoristisch-phantastischer Dichtungen, 1895
Auf vielen Wegen, 1897
Ich und die Welt, 1898
Ein Sommer, 1900
Und aber ründet sich ein Kranz, 1902
Melancholie, 1906
Einkehr, 1910
Ich und Du, 1911
Wir fanden einen Pfad, 1914

Nonsense Verse
Galgenlieder, 1905; contained in *Alle Galgenlieder*, 1932; as *The Gallows Songs*, translated by Max Knight, 1963; as *Songs from the Gallows*, translated by Walter Arndt, 1993
Palmström, 1910; contained in *Alle Galgenlieder*, 1932
Palma Kunkel, 1916; contained in *Alle Galgenlieder*, 1932
Der Gingganz, edited by Margareta Morgenstern, 1919; contained in *Alle Galgenlieder*, 1932
Die Schallmühle, edited by Margareta Morgenstern, 1928

Parody
Horatius travestitus: Ein Studentenscherz, 1897

Letters
Ein Leben in Briefen, edited by Margareta Morgenstern, 1952
Alles um des Menschen Willen: Gesammelte Briefe, 1962

Aphorisms
Stufen: Eine Entwicklung in Aphorismen und Tagebuch-Notizen, edited by Margareta Morgenstern, 1918

Further Reading
Hofacker, Erich P., *Christian Morgenstern*, Boston: Twayne, 1978
Janik, Allan, and Stephen Toulmin, *Wittgenstein's Vienna*, New York: Simon and Schuster, 1973

Irmtraud Morgner 1933–1990

Irmtraud Morgner established herself as a writer during the 1960 and belongs to the second generation of women writers in the German Democratic Republic (GDR), alongside authors such as Christa Wolf, Helga Königsdorf, and Maxi Wander. They followed in the footsteps of a first generation of GDR women writers whose key figure was Anna Seghers and preceded a third generation, represented by authors such as Kerstin Hense and Gabriele Kachold. Similar to many other authors of her time, Morgner believed that, despite all critical reservations regarding the GDR, her writing would make a contribution toward socialism, which was regarded as defective, yet still seemed an alternative to capitalism for which it was worth fighting. In this respect she is a typical representative of GDR literature, but her creation of new narrative structures, unusual montage techniques, extensive use of the doppelgänger motif as well as science-fiction topoi in her works, and unconventional approach to the literary heritage all make her quite an exceptional case in GDR literature.

She is regarded as one of the GDR's best storytellers and, since the publication of *Leben und Abenteuer der Trobadora Beatriz nach Zeugnissen ihrer Spielfrau Laura* (1974; The Life and Adventures of Beatrice the Troubadour), the most outspoken feminist author of her generation. She had a seminal influence on the Germanist debates about a female aesthetic during the 1970s by exploring themes such as the relationship between the sexes, the supernatural, eroticism in everyday life, and alternative modes of creativity.

During the 1970s, along with authors such as Christa Wolf, Morgner rediscovered Romantic writers such as E.T.A. Hoffmann, Hölderlin, and Jean Paul as a source of inspiration, and subsequently, Romantic themes and modes of writing fed quite significantly into the development of her own brand of feminist fantasy.

Since then, her literary works have become associated with innovative montage techniques, subtle humor, and the extensive use of elements of fantasy. Knowing that these did not seem to fit into the narrow conceptual framework of socialist realism, she argued the case for fantasy, claiming it to be a legitimate means of articulating constructive social criticism. Indeed, Morgner's defense of fantasy as a realistic mode of representation must be seen as a response to the prescriptive concepts associated with socialist realism. Having succeeded in arguing the case, she gained official acceptance into the realist canon of the GDR, a prerequisite for getting her works published. Morgner's emancipation from the narrow restrictions of socialist realism (and more specifically, the brand of socialist realism defined in the first Bitterfeld conference) was not easily achieved; this struggle, however, ultimately led to a mode of writing that gained her international reputation, especially among feminist writers and theorists.

In her first publications, *Das Signal steht auf Fahrt* (1959; Green Light) and *Ein Haus am Rande der Stadt* (1962; A House in the Suburbs), she adheres to the political and cultural demands formulated in April 1959 in Bitterfeld to an extent that is representative but almost embarrassing. In both cases, the content (the metamorphosis of a petit bourgeois into a socialist worker) and mode of narration (adhering to the doctrine of socialist realism) serve to use literary means for political ends. Both works received much praise from official institutions. Morgner, however, later distanced herself from her early writings.

With regard to content, Morgner's story *Notturno* (1964; Nocturne) is still committed to the principles of socialist realism, although in its form it hints at some of the main aspects of her later writings: it veers toward Romanticism and fantasy, away from an omniscient style of narration. In all prose works that follow, we can see the further development and deepening of these features. This development and the uncompromising and fearless exploration of themes relating to female emancipation that gained ever more importance in her writing drew the attention of literary critics in both East and West Germany to her works.

The quest for women's emancipation in terms of sexual liberation and self-determination is the dominant theme in all her later works, particularly *Leben und Abenteuer der Trobadora Beatriz nach Zeugnissen ihrer Spielfrau Laura* and *Amanda* (1983). The latter was originally planned as the first two parts of a trilogy, which remained unfinished.

The female protagonists in these works are all strangely decentered, off-balance, and split personalities in need of complementation and in search of a "better half"—a double in the truly Romantic tradition. They live out a dilemma: in order to cope with everyday life, they have to accept limitations that often result in damage to their true selves, but in order to fulfill their true ambitions and potential, they need their other half. In their desire and struggle to become whole again, they go through supernatural experiences that challenge reality and traditional assumptions about reality as such. It is socialist reality in particular that seems constantly to oppose the search for joie de vivre (not unlike the Freudian pleasure principle) as presented and pursued by Morgner's women. In Morgner's feminist critique of the prevailing myths of patriarchal history, she questions humanist categories of self and (wo)man's ability to change, exposing the underlying links between patriarchal systems and so-called humanist values and attitudes. This clearly relates not only to the reality surrounding the author and her literary figures but also to the officially prescribed doctrine of socialist realism that stabilized the East German patriarchal system and its practices; in this system, there was no space for Morgner's emancipated women, their demands, and their way of life.

It is therefore not surprising that Morgner's work was subject to severe censorship that tried to fit her into the narrow corset of socialist realism. Her novel *Rumba auf einen Herbst* (1965, published posthumously in 1992; Rumba in Autumn) did not get permission for publication, and numerous passages had to be rewritten and changed. Yet despite all the necessary compromises the author had to accept, she did not allow herself either to be iconized or to become part of the conformist literary establishment of the GDR. On the contrary, she rose to the challenge and developed her own unmistakable style, which is possibly best described by the term *fantastical realism*.

ASTRID HERHOFFER

Biography

Born in Chemnitz/Karl-Marx-Stadt, 22 August 1933. Studied German literature at the University of Leipzig, 1952–56; worked as editorial assistant for *Neue Deutsche Literatur,* a journal published by the GDR Writers' Association; freelance writer since 1958. Died in East Berlin, 7 May 1990.

Selected Works

Das Signal steht auf Fahrt, 1959
Ein Haus am Rande der Stadt: Roman, 1962
Notturno: Erzählung, 1964
Hochzeit in Konstantinopel, 1968
Gauklerlegende: Eine Spielfraungeschichte, 1970
Die wundersamen Reisen des Gustav Weltfahrers: Lügenhafter Roman mit Kommentaren, 1972
Leben und Abenteuer der Trobadora Beatriz nach Zeugnissen ihrer Spielfrau Laura: Roman in dreizehn Büchern und sieben Intermezzos, 1974
Geschlechtertausch: Drei Geschichten über die Umwandlung der Verhältnisse, by Sarah Kirsch, Irmtraud Morgner, Christa Wolf, 1980
Amanda: Ein Hexenroman, 1983
Der Schöne und das Tier: Eine Liebesgeschichte, 1988
Rumba auf einen Herbst: Roman, 1992
Das heroische Testament: Roman in Fragmenten, edited by Rudolf Bussman, Luchterhand: Frankfurt, 1998

Further Reading

Gerhardt, Marlis, editor, *Irmtraud Morgner: Texte, Daten, Bilder,* Darmstadt: Luchterhand, 1990

Hanel, Stephanie, *Literarischer Widerstand zwischen Phantastischem und Alltäglichem,* Pfaffenweiler: Centaurus, 1995

Lewis, Alison, *Subverting Patriarchy: Feminism and Fantasy in the Works of Irmtraud Morgner,* Oxford and Washington, D.C.: Berg, 1995

Scherer, Gabriela, *Zwischen "Bitterfeld" und "Orplid": Zum literarischen Werk Irmtraud Morgners,* Bern and New York: Lang, 1992

Wolf, Christa, "Der Mensch ist in zwei Formen ausgebildet: Zum Tode von Irmtraud Morgner," *Die Zeit,* 11 May 1990

Eduard Mörike 1804–1875

Eduard Mörike is considered a premier poet of the 19th century. His early writings have much in common with the Romantics who preceded him, particularly an emphasis on nature poetry and an interest in dreams, fantasy, and fairy tales. More important, however, was the influence of Goethe, whose model determined the entire trajectory of Mörike's artistic development. Often called Goethe's "spiritual son," Mörike is considered the inheritor of a Goethean lyricism that echoes in the imagery and rhythms of his poems. While his early poetry registers both melancholic moods and moments of ecstatic bliss in diverse lyrical forms, his mature poems avoid subjective excesses and assume the limiting and self-protective structures of a Goethean neoclassicism. Despite the recurring scholarly discussions of his epigonal status, Mörike continues to be cited as one of the most innovative poets of the 19th century. Pointing to his mastery of forms and his insistence on beauty as an absolute value, scholars have portrayed him as a precursor of *l'art pour l'art* aestheticism. His so-called *Dinggedichte* (thing poems), while appropriating Greek and Goethean models, also anticipate Rainer Maria Rilke's iconic symbolist poetry. The brooding aspect of his poetry has been isolated to create the image of an "existential" poet exposed to the forces of being by the post-Romantic loss of metaphysical beliefs. Another common image of Mörike is that of a provincial poet; he is often linked to the Biedermeier attitude, which involves an apolitical acceptance of authority, a contentment within limitations, and a nostalgia for a simpler, more idyllic age. Because much of his writing lacks explicit political content, critics have cast Mörike as a "pure" lyrical poet whose poetry is in service only to the play of language as it forms the human psyche. Despite his recognized status in the German canon, however, Mörike has never enjoyed wide popularity, which is attributable to the parochial nature of his interests and to his hermetic artistic posture. Mörike also remains largely unknown in the English-speaking world, where his finely nuanced poetry, firmly fixed in its German idiom and historical context, resists adequate translation. Outside Germany, his poetry is known almost exclusively as the texts of classical lieder by Robert Schumann and Hugo Wolf.

Between 1827 and 1832, Mörike wrote some of his best and most-anthologized poetry, much of it nature poetry, including "Septembermorgen" (September Morning) and "Um Mitternacht" (At Midnight), both written in 1827, as well as "Im Frühling" (In Spring) and "Mein Fluß" (My River), both written in 1828. In these early poems, a monological lyric voice emerges that seeks to merge with its external surroundings. Such appeals to nature, however, typically only confirm the primacy and isolation of the self. The exemplary poem "Besuch in Urach" (1827; Visit in Urach) narrates the poet's return to the idyllic site of his preparatory schooling. Caught in regressions to the past, the lyric I seeks a heightened sense of identity and self-understanding through an intensified experience of the present, only to realize that all experience is mediated by *Erinnerung* (subjective memory). "Besuch in Urach" conveys the frustration of Mörike's desire for an *unio mystica* with a nature that remains "orphaned," unable to rise out of its own enigma. Critics have seen "Besuch in Urach" as a turning point in the history of poetry because it challenges Goethe's imperative that poetry must be *Erlebnislyrik,* that it must avoid the dangers of subjective reminiscence and articulate the immediate experience of present reality. Blocked from the self-completion that Goethe's view of nature promised, the writing subject in Mörike's poems must render and unify its subjectivity apart from the external world. Prefiguring the modern artist's descent into interiority, Mörike's natural imagery becomes increasingly opaque and aestheticized, or, as James Rolleston remarks (in Adams, 1990), Mörike's perceptions of natural phenomena are converted immediately into cultural events. The diminishment of artistic authenticity created by his belated historical position may account for the emotional ambiguity expressed in poems such as "Im Frühling," where inner feelings saturate external phenomena that serve as metaphors for the poet's moods:

> I think of this, I think of that,
> I long for something, yet do not know really what:
> Half is desire, half is lament;
> My heart, tell me,
> What memories are you weaving
> In the twilight of golden green branches?
> —Old unnamable days!

This melancholic mixture of pleasure and pain occurs with increasing frequency and refinement in Mörike's works as he, more than any poet of his age, invents a somatic poetry to record the impulses of the body and their relation to individual identity.

In 1830, Mörike wrote a series of love sonnets inspired by his fiancée, Luise Rau. Commemorating more than just the ill-fated affair with Rau, these poems mark a shift in Mörike's technique: rather than releasing pent-up youthful emotion in the expressive style of the young Goethe or the Romantics, Mörike employs the strict and regular sonnet form to conserve and purify feelings, thereby containing and idealizing human subjectivity. This formal move also exhibits Mörike's increasing attempts to turn his art to therapeutic uses. From his earliest years, Mörike had experienced a pattern of psychosomatic illness, and throughout his life he would suffer from ailments of nonspecific origin, which he attributed to his psychic fragility. Recognizing the necessity of preserving psychic balance, he began seeking emotional refuge in a more meditative approach to his art, which is depicted in the sonnet "Zu viel" (Too Much), where the poet speaks of a soothing descent into the "Abgrund der Betrachtung" (abyss of contemplation).

Following the model of the Goethean bildungsroman, Mörike interpolated the 1830 sonnet cycle and many other early poems into his only novel, *Maler Nolten* (1832; The Painter Nolten). While on one level, *Maler Nolten* is a *Künstlerroman* (artist's novel) and thus a vehicle for Mörike's aesthetic views, the problems of the artist are intertwined with and to an extent overshadowed by the psychological problems of its characters, whose emotional entanglements and their fateful consequences are the novel's central concern. Theobald Nolten, a sensitive, introverted artist whose style is a blend of the classical and the Romantic, reflects the author's struggle with Romantic influences and his Goethe-like efforts to master them. Nolten's tragic flaw resides in the narcissistic delusion that art will enable him to transcend the inevitable pain and conflict of human existence. The painter's inclination to withdraw into a hermetic realm of art mirrors Mörike's desire to escape the threatening emotional excesses of interpersonal relationships. Remarkable for its many anticipations of modern psychoanalysis, *Maler Nolten* has nevertheless been criticized for its technical deficiencies and for a derivative prose style indebted to Goethe's *Wilhelm Meisters Lehrjahre* (1795–96; *Wilhelm Meister's Apprenticeship*). At the same time, S.S. Prawer argues that *Maler Nolten* is an "anti-Meister," a revisionary response to *Wilhelm Meister's Apprenticeship* that rejects the ordered Enlightenment society that produced Goethe's hero.

Writings of the later 1830s move away from the angst-ridden atmosphere of *Maler Nolten,* as Mörike struggles to cope with his psychosomatic ailments. Following the bourgeois trend of the Biedermeier period, Mörike restricts his "unhealthy" literary pursuits, turning to the classical tradition and to less-refined folk poetry in order to develop an aesthetic "diet" that he hopes will provide greater psychic stability. In these years, Mörike devoted himself to translations of Greek pastoral poetry, published in 1840 as *Classische Blumenlese* (Classical Anthology), as well as to writing neoclassical poems that commemorate quotidian objects and events. In 1837 and 1838, he produced many of his best folk ballads, as well as the long poems "Märchen vom sichern Mann" (Tale of the Trusty Man) and "Wald-Idylle" (Forest Idyll), both of which assimilate earthy Swabian humor and elements of Greek and Germanic mythology into classical verse forms. Also important during this period are several short prose works, especially the tale entitled "Der Schatz" (1839; The Treasure), a *Kunstmärchen* (literary fairy tale) distinguished by its sophisticated prose style and its narrative composition, which, like that of *Maler Nolten,* is complex and experimental.

More than any other work, "Der alte Turmhahn" (The Old Weathercock), begun in 1840 and finished over a decade later, has contributed to the perception of Mörike as a happy-go-lucky Biedermeier parson. A lengthy poem written in doggerel laced with Swabian dialect, "Der alte Turmhahn" seems autobiographical, but it is better understood as a self-conscious idealization of the country parson's contemplative existence. Conventionally read as

a portrayal of the cozy domestic life Mörike is supposed to have led, the poem was written during a period of physical and financial adversity starkly contrasting the idyllic setting and tone of the poem. The 1840s also yielded Mörike's finest neoclassical poems, most notably "Die schöne Buche" (1842; The Beautiful Beech Tree), an excellent example of the concretely imagistic tendency of his mature lyric poems. Written in carefully measured distichs, the poem captures and contains the sublime melancholy of the poet by re-creating the artlike symmetry of a well-formed tree. Although standing in a classical *locus amoenus,* the tree is surrounded by a "daemonic solitude" that evokes in the lyric I a sense of the distance created by the autonomy of the natural object, which in turn intensifies the poet's isolation and self-containment. This poem may be read as a realization of Walter Benjamin's belief that meaningful transactions between the melancholic and the world take place through things rather than people; that the melancholic projects his heavy temperament outward onto massive objects capable of absorbing Saturnine passions. Considered by Heinrich Henel to be a "Kopernikanische Drehung" (Copernican revolution) in the German lyric tradition, this poem and others like it came to be called *Dinggedichte,* whose form and implied aesthetic ethos are elaborated in subsequent poems by Conrad Ferdinand Meyer and Rilke.

In 1846, Mörike wrote the celebrated poem "Auf eine Lampe" (On a Lamp), considered to be the apotheosis of his *Dinggedichte.* An apostrophe to a forgotten artifact, "Auf eine Lampe" evokes a Biedermeier nostalgia for a bygone era of finer sensibility. The lamp's porcelain body, graced with ivy, displays images of classical antiquity. As a poem that tries to transform verbal art into an aesthetic object with sensuous presence, "Auf eine Lampe" has often been compared to John Keats' iconic poem "Ode on a Grecian Urn" (1820). Although its imagery and classical trimeters appropriate antique traditions, it is a protomodernist poem that moves beyond classical-Romantic conventions toward a symbolist aesthetic, voiced in the poem's final line: "Was aber schön ist, selig scheint es in ihm selbst" (What is beautiful, however, appears [or shines] blessed in itself). In the early 1950s, "Auf eine Lampe" became the focus of a now-famous critical dialogue between the philosopher Martin Heidegger and the preeminent Swiss Germanist Emil Staiger. Their debate concerned the interpretation of the word *scheint*—Staiger arguing that it must mean "appears," Heidegger advancing an Hegelian argument for understanding *scheint* as "shines." While they agreed that the poem is essentially elegiac—the lamp is a neglected relic (as Mörike in his own time was overlooked)—they disagreed about the source of its melancholy mood. Staiger attributed it to Mörike's belated arrival on the literary scene, thus promoting the image of Mörike as epigone; Heidegger maintained that the "shining" of the lamp is informed by the Hegelian thesis that beauty determines itself as the sensory manifestation of the idea.

While it may be argued that, in the 1840s, with such poems as "Die schöne Buche" and "Auf eine Lampe," Mörike reached the threshold of his potential as lyric poet, after which his creative productivity waned, his talent for prose seems to have flourished in the 1850s. In 1852, he wrote "Das Stuttgarter Hutzelmännlein" (The Stuttgart Goblin), a folktale so authentic sounding that his friends accused him of cribbing from existing legends. Although he did raid the storehouse of German folktales for his materials, Mörike's singular blend of fantasy and realism remains a unique achievement in German literature. The realistic novella *Mozart auf der Reise nach Prag* (1856; *Mozart's Journey to Prague*) is Mörike's best-known prose work. Although less directly autobiographical than *Maler Nolten*, *Mozart's Journey to Prague* is Mörike's mature attempt at literary self-portraiture and self-analysis. Set in 1787, the year Wolfgang Amadeus Mozart traveled to Prague to conduct the first performance of his opera *Don Giovanni*, the novella offers a detailed and historically accurate picture of a fictional day in the life of the composer. Mörike had a lifelong fascination for Mozart, probably due to a perceived affinity in their mode of creativity, which emerges as a central theme in the novella. In a key scene, Mozart plucks an orange from the garden of an aristocrat, the sight of which evokes a childhood memory, which in turn triggers the spontaneous formulation of a musical theme needed to complete the opera *Don Giovanni*. Mozart's creative reverie, with its implied link to unconscious processes, corresponds with Mörike's mode of *Erinnerung*—creativity as an imaginative re-creation of the past, inspired by encounters with concrete objects. When, in the story, Mozart performs the inspired finale of *Don Giovanni*, it is described as "eine gemalte Symphonie" (a painted symphony), a metaphor that also characterizes the synesthetic reconciliation of image and sound in Mörike's protosymbolist poetry. The story ends on an ominous note with the poem "Denk es, o Seele!" (Ponder it, O Soul!), which foreshadows both Mozart's premature death and Mörike's growing dread of his own mortality.

Some critics read *Mozart's Journey to Prague* as the death knell for Mörike's creativity. The Mozart novella itself, despite its identification with the free-flowing creative productivity of the genial composer, took Mörike some eight years to complete. In his final years, apart from minor literary projects such as *Anakreon und die sogenannten anakreontischen Lieder* (1864; Anacreon and the So-Called Anacreontic Songs)—a modest revision of preexisting translations—Mörike produced only a handful of published poems. Several of these, however, rank with his best. In the iconic mode of "Auf eine Lampe," the neoclassical cycle "Bilder aus Bebenhausen" (1863; Pictures from Bebenhausen) is a symbolic attempt to preserve the aestheticized object (here a Cistercian monastery) in historical memory by documenting it as a cultural artifact. "Erinna an Sappho" (1863; Erinna to Sappho) is a meditation on death, often cited for its protomodernist blending of formal elements.

JEFFREY ADAMS

Biography

Born in Ludwigsburg, 8 September 1804. Curate in Möhringen, 1827, Plattenhardt, 1829, and Owen and Ochsenwang, 1832; vicar, Cleversulzbach, 1834; worked as a journalist; pensioned in 1843; lived in Schwäbisch-Hall and in Bad Mergentheim, 1844–75. Died 4 June 1875.

Selected Works

Collections

Werke, edited by Harry Maync, 1909; revised, 1914
Werke und Briefe, edited by Herbert Göpfert, 1954
Sämtliche Werke, edited by Gerhart Baumann, 3 vols., 1954–59
Werke und Briefe. Historisch-kritische Ausgabe, edited by Hans-Henrik Krummacher, Herbert Meyer, and Berhnard Zeller, 15 vols., 1968–86
The Complete Poems, 1969

Poetry

Gedichte, 1838; revised editions 1848, 1856, 1867
Poems, translated by Norah K. Cruickshank and Gilbert E. Cunningham, 1959

Fiction

Maler Nolten, 1832
Iris: Eine Sammlung erzählender und dramatischer Dichtungen, 1839
Idylle vom Bodensee, 1846
Das Stuttgarter Hutzelmännlein (stories), 1853
Mozart auf der Reise nach Prag, 1856; as *Mozart's Journey from Vienna to Prague*, translated by Florence Leonard, 1897; as *Mozart on the Way to Prague*, translated by Walter and Catherine Alison Philips, 1934; as *Mozart's Journey to Prague*, translated by Leopold von Loewenstein-Wertheim, 1957
Die Historie von der schönen Lau, 1873

Other

Mörike-Storm Briefwechsel, 1919
Gedichte und Briefe an Seine Braut Margarete V. Speeth, edited by Marie Bauer, 1906
Eines Dichters Liebe: Eduard Mörike's Brautbriefe, edited by Walther Eggert Winbegg, 1911
Eduard Mörike: Briefe, edited by Friedrich Seebass, 1939
Briefe, edited by Gerhart Baumann, 1960
Briefe an seine Braut Luise Rau, edited by Friedhelm Kemp, 1965

Translations

Classische Blumenlese, 1840
Theokritos, Bion und Moschos, 1855
Anakreon, 1864

Further Reading

Adams, Jeffrey, "The Scene of Instruction: Mörike's Reception of Goethe in *Besuch in Urach*," *Deutsche Vierteljahrsschrift* 3 (1988)
Adams, Jeffrey, editor, *Mörike's Muses: Critical Essays on Eduard Mörike*, Columbia, South Carolina: Camden House, 1990
Bennett, Benjamin, "The Politics of the Mörike-Debate and Its Object," *Germanic Review* 68, no. 2 (1993)
Doerksen, Victor G., editor, *Eduard Mörike*, Darmstadt: Wissenschaftliche Buchgesellschaft, 1975
Fliegner, Susanne, *Der Dichter und die Dilettanten: Eduard Mörikes Lyrik und die bürgerliche Geselligkeitskultur des 19. Jahrhunderts*, Stuttgart: Metzler, 1991
Henel, Heinrich, "Erlebnisdichtung und Symbolismus," in *Zur Lyrik-Diskussion*, edited by Reinhold Grimm, Darmstadt: Wissenschaftliche Buchgesellschaft, 1974
Holthusen, Hans-Egon, *Eduard Mörike in Selbstzeugnissen und Bilddokumenten*, Reinbek bei Hamburg: Rowohlt, 1971
Prawer, S.S., "Mignon's Revenge: A Study of *Maler Nolten*," *Publications of the English Goethe Society* 25 (1956)
Sammons, Jeffrey L., "Fate and Psychology: Another Look at *Maler Nolten*," in *Lebendige Form: Festschrift für Heinrich E.K. Henel, Interpretationen zur deutschen Literatur*, edited by Jeffrey L. Sammons and Ernst Schürer, Munich: Fink, 1970
Slessarev, Helga, *Eduard Mörike*, New York: Twayne, 1970
Staiger, Emil, Martin Heidegger, and Leo Spitzer, "A 1951 Dialogue on Interpretation," translated by Berel Lang and Christine Ebel, *Publications of the Modern Language Association* 105 (May 1990)
Stern, J.P., "Eduard Mörike: Recollection and Inwardness," in *Idylls and Realities*, New York: Ungar, and London: Methuen, 1971
von Heydebrand, Renate, *Eduard Mörikes Gedichtwerk*, Stuttgart: Metzler, 1972
von Wiese, Benno, *Eduard Mörike*, Tübingen: Wunderlich, 1950

Karl Philipp Moritz 1756–1793

The bicentenary in 1993 of Karl Philipp Moritz's death has led to a resurgence of interest in this author of the late Enlightenment, who had been largely neglected for much of the 20th century. Moritz's interests were varied and his output diverse, yet he is indisputably known for just one work: his autobiographical novel *Anton Reiser* (1785–90; *Anton Reiser*). This is particularly true in the English-speaking world, for it is upon this work that translators have concentrated, especially in recent years. We derive much of our knowledge of the author's early life from *Anton Reiser*: it conveys his personal struggle with the harsh circumstances of an unhappy childhood in a pietistic household, his apprenticeship at a hatmaker's in Brunswick, and his craving for an education and a niche in life. While the novel is of value as a social record of the times, the focus of interest is unquestionably the protagonist. In its reflective appraisal of the central character's development and the forces that shaped his life, the novel dissects the past of an author who is interested in psychological investigation, places himself at a distance from what he has undergone, and objectively analyzes his own case. Reiser's sense of inferiority and his insecurity are intensified by a traumatic series of dashed hopes, lack of progress, and social exclusion. At best, his existence is mundane and monotonous, a condition that he detests and from which he attempts to escape, at first by immersing himself in literature (feeling particular affinity with Goethe's *Werther* in his suffering) and, later, in the theater, where he strives to be accepted into a company of actors, thus entering a world of illusion. The errors and delusions of the fantasy-driven, Romantic search for a new and more fulfilling existence are sharply exposed by the coolly rational narrator's irony.

The two *Andreas Hartknopf* novels (1786 and 1790), written at the same time as *Anton Reiser,* also present a wanderer in the figure of a blacksmith who becomes a journeyman and, eventually, a pastor with a pedagogical bent. These novels are satirical in mode and cast in the form of a parable about a man who, in his attempt to help his fellow beings, is exposed to benevolent and hostile forces and, finally, martyrdom. Among Masonic influences and symbols, numerous allusions to the New Testament point to a parodic analogy between this man and Christ. Moritz's last novel, *Die neue Cecilia* (The New Cecilia), an epistolary work in the wake of *Werther,* although with several correspondents, remained a fragment and was only published posthumously in 1794. Very different in style and subject matter from his previous narratives, it relates a tragic love relationship between a bourgeois girl and a relative of the pope in a more structured manner than its somewhat shapeless predecessors, which are mainly held together by images and motifs. *Die neue Cecilia* combines the weight given to the aesthetic in its discussions of art with strikingly visual scenes, as it paints the views of Rome, the city that Moritz had come to know so well.

Blunt; oder, der Gast (1781; Blunt; or, the Guest), Moritz's only—and not very accomplished—drama, displays fatalistic and tragic elements in the forces that drive a father, unaware of the identity of his guest, to murder for financial gain a man who is in fact his long-departed son. The most singular feature of this derivative drama is its existence in two versions, which end on startlingly different notes: unrelieved tragedy, or, alternatively, the happiness of reconciliation.

In 1786, Moritz gave up his post at the Gymnasium zum Grauen Kloster in Berlin to go to Italy, where he met and formed a close friendship with Goethe. His journeys to Italy and a decade earlier to England gave rise to travelogues in the form of short essayistic portraits, ostensibly written as letters, dealing with a series of topics and impressions. In part, they are the record of a journey: in England, one such journey took him, mostly by foot, from London to the caves of the Peak District of Derbyshire. The engaging account (more personal than his observations on Italian culture) that emerged from his stay was translated into English soon after its publication and also spawned contemporary imitations in Germany; it combines informative presentations on the customs, democratic traditions, and cultural life of the capital city with a more individual section on the author's experiences of walking through the English countryside. Moritz is successful in capturing the visual wonders of the natural surroundings, noting social attitudes, and conveying the less admirable social indices betrayed by his reception at the inns en route.

While not a leader in any theoretical field, Moritz engaged in a range of contemporary issues. *Versuch einer deutschen Prosodie* (1786; Attempt at a German Prosody) takes up the metrical problem, much debated at the time, of accommodating the stress patterns of German verse within the quantities of classical meters; this was an essay that Goethe declared was highly influential upon the way in which he recast *Iphigenie auf Tauris* from prose into iambic verse. Within this work, Moritz also set out his theory of poetry, arguing that a poem does not progress in a linear manner, but in patterns of rhythm and sound. *Über die bildende Nachahmung des Schönen* (1788; On the Creative Imitation of the Beautiful) contributes to the discussion of imitation in 18th-century aesthetics; Moritz here sees the work of the creative artist as "im Kleinen ein Abdruck des höchsten Schönen im großen Ganzen der Natur" and draws distinctions between the concepts of *das Schöne* (the beautiful), *das Gute* (the good), *das Edle* (the noble), and *das Nützliche* (the useful). *Götterlehre oder mythologische Dichtungen der Alten* (1791; Mythological Tales of the Ancients) stresses the power of the imagination and treats mythological stories as the products of its language and creativity. Further indications of the breadth of Moritz's interests include his studies of language, lectures on style, a handbook on the art of writing letters, and his editorship of and contributions to the ten volumes of *Magazin zur Erfahrungsseelenkunde* (1783–93; Journal of Empirical Psychology), a periodical dealing with psychological investigation, with an emphasis in its early years on factual data and clinical cases.

I.A. WHITE

Biography

Born in Hameln, 15 September 1756. Studied theology, University of Erfurt, 1776–77, and University of Wittenberg, 1777–78; master's degree from Wittenberg, 1779; teacher, Konrector (assistant headmaster), and professor at schools in Berlin, 1778–86; editor of *Magazin zur Erfahrungsseelenkunde,* 1783–93, and of the *Berliner privilegierte Zeitung* (*Vossische Zeitung*), 1784–85; journey to Italy (1786–88); appointed professor of the theory of the fine arts at the Königlich Preußische Akademie der mechanischen Wissenschaften und der freyen Künste zu Berlin, 1789. Died in Berlin, 26 June 1793.

Selected Works

Collections
Werke, edited by Horst Günther, 3 vols., 1981
Schriften, edited by Petra and Uwe Nettelbeck, 30 vols., 1986–

Fiction
Anton Reiser: Ein psychologischer Roman, 1785–90; as *Anton Reiser:
  A Psychological Novel*, translated by P.E. Matheson, 1926; translated
  by John R. Russell, 1996; translated by Ritchie Robertson, 1997
Andreas Hartknopf: Eine Allegorie, 1786
Andreas Hartknopfs Predigerjahre, 1790
Die neue Cecilia, 1794

Play
Blunt; oder, der Gast, 1781

Nonfiction
Reisen eines Deutschen in England im Jahr 1782, 1783; as *Travels,
  Chiefly on Foot, through Several Parts of England*, translated
  anonymously, 1795; as *Journeys of a German in England: A Walking
  Tour of England in 1782*, translated by Reginald Nettel, 1965
Versuch einer deutschen Prosodie, 1786
Über die bildende Nachahmung des Schönen, 1788
Götterlehre oder mythologische Dichtungen der Alten, 1791
Reisen eines Deutschen in Italien in den Jahren 1786 bis 1788,
  1792–93

Further Reading
Boulby, Mark, *Karl Philipp Moritz: At the Fringe of Genius*, Toronto
  and Buffalo, New York: University of Toronto Press, 1979
Buhofer, Annelies Häcki, editor, *Karl Philipp Moritz:
  Literaturwissenschaftliche, linguistische und psychologische
  Lektüren*, Tübingen: Francke, 1994
Fontius, Martin, and Anneliese Klingenberg, editors, *Karl Philipp
  Moritz und das 18. Jahrhundert: Bestandaufnahmen, Korrekturen,
  Neuansätze*, Tübingen: Niemeyer, 1995
Karl Philipp Moritz, Text und Kritik 118/119 (1993)
Müller, Lothar, *Die kranke Seele und das Licht der Erkenntnis: Karl
  Philipp Moritz' "Anton Reiser,"* Frankfurt: Athenäum, 1987
———, "Karl Philipp Moritz: Anton Reiser," in *Romane des 17. und
  18. Jahrhunderts, Interpretationen*, Stuttgart: Reclam, 1996
Vosskamp, Wilhelm, "Poetik der Beobachtung: Karl Philipp Moritz'
  Anton Reiser zwischen Autobiographie und Bildungsroman," *Études
  Germaniques* 51 (1996)
White, I.A., "'Die zu oft wiederholte Lektüre des Werthers': Responses
  to Sentimentality in K.P. Moritz's *Anton Reiser*," *Lessing Yearbook*
  26 (1994)

Heiner Müller 1929–1995

Heiner Müller is the most important playwright to emerge out of
the German Democratic Republic (GDR). In communist East
Germany, his work was for decades subjected to the vagaries of
state-directed cultural policy. In the West, in the wake of the political failures of 1968, he offered an alternative to the socially
critical drama of liberal moralists such as Max Frisch, Friedrich
Dürrenmatt, and Rolf Hochhuth, and to the openly didactic theater of left-wing authors such as Peter Weiss, Heinar Kipphardt,
and Franz-Xaver Kroetz. The inheritor of Brecht's mantle as political dramatist, Müller became the most hotly debated, and the
most performed, dramatist writing in German.

Müller's art is characterized by a constant search for new dramatic forms and by a gradual broadening of thematic concerns:
the initial focus on communism in East Germany gives way to an
interest in German history and the legacy of National Socialism;
the examination of the contradictions of the Soviet Revolution
turns into a critical assessment of the communist utopia; the investigation of European history yields a pessimistic analysis of
modern civilization. The individual, in Müller's increasingly
complex and dense scenarios, becomes the force field in which
conflicting historic and political forces intersect. Especially with
his later collages of provocative, often violent, dramatic images,
Müller became a major participant in international debates on
modern subjectivity, the limits of instrumental reason, postmodernity, global politics, imperialism, national identity, and
gender issues.

Müller's early plays are usually referred to as "Produktions-
stücke," dramas that deal with the difficulties of building a communist society. *Der Lohndrücker* (1958; The Rate Buster;
translated as *The Scab*), written with his wife, Inge, examines the
problems besetting the new social order by employing the motif
of a circular furnace that needs to be repaired without halting
production. The play aims at a critique of the GDR from a non-
conformist Marxist perspective. Like some of his later works,
notably *Die Korrektur* (1959; The Correction), *Die Umsiedlerin;
oder, Das Leben auf dem Lande* (1975; The Resettled Woman;
or, Life in the Country), and *Der Bau* (1974; Construction), it
was banned from public performance. Yet at the same time,
Müller also received major literary awards, highlighting the ambivalences of communist cultural policies.

Faced with harassment and censorship, Müller turned to
adaptations of ancient myths, addressing pertinent political
questions in a more abstract guise. Verse plays such as *Herakles
5* (1966; Heracles 5), *Philoktet* (1966; Philoctetes), and *Der Horatier* (1975; The Horatian) can be read as parables of ruthless
realpolitik, in which the abuse of power destroys the individual.
Mauser (1976; Mauser), an effort to revitalise the *Lehrstück* tradition of didactic drama in direct response to Brecht's *Die Mass-*

nahme (1931; *The Measures Taken*), is set in the Russian Revolution and examines the paradox of political violence that turns against the very people it ostensibly aims to liberate.

Three plays from the 1970s shift the focus to German history, employing a collage of "synthetic fragments": disparate episodes loosely linked by a common theme. In provocative tableaus ranging from the reign of Frederick the Great to the 1953 workers' uprising in East Berlin, *Germania Tod in Berlin* (1977; *Germania Death in Berlin*), *Die Schlacht* (1975; translated as *The Slaughter* and *The Battle*), and *Leben Gundlings Friedrich von Preußen Lessings Schlaf Traum Schrei* (1977; *Gundling's Life Frederick of Prussia Lessing's Sleep Dream Scream*) challenge official GDR historiography. The plays question the foundational myth (ironically evoked here as "immaculate conception") of the GDR as an antifascist alternative to a West Germany tainted by National Socialism and suggest disturbing continuities between Prussian authoritarianism and the GDR variant of Stalinism. Müller returns to these concerns and to similar dramatic techniques in his two final major plays. *Wolokolamsker Chaussee* (1988; translated as *Volokolamsk Highway* and *The Road of Tanks*) addresses the petrification of the communist ideal into a soulless bureaucracy; *Germania 3: Gespenster am toten Mann* (1995; Germania 3 Ghosts on the Dead Man) places the failure of the GDR against the backdrop of the catastrophes of Stalinism and German fascism.

Beginning with *Die Hamletmaschine* (1977; *Hamletmachine*), Müller widens the focus to investigate the foundations of European civilization itself. Using Shakespeare's wavering intellectual as a prism, Müller adopts a monologic mode of writing that offers a bleak assessment of human agency in a world of universal destruction. *Der Auftrag* (1981; translated as *The Mission* and *The Task*) features more traditional dramatic elements, such as dialogue, plot, and sharply defined characters. In a remarkable effort to contemplate questions of political agency from a non-European perspective, the play explores the failure to export the French Revolution to Jamaica. Müller's tightly structured exploration of gender politics and instrumental reason, *Quartett* (1981; *Quartet*), based on Laclos's 18th-century novel *Les Liaisons dangereuses* (*Dangerous Liaisons*), presents two antagonists who exchange roles in a dazzlingly complex battle for power. *Verkommenes Ufer Medeamaterial Landschaft mit Argonauten* (1983; translated as *Despoiled Shore Medeamaterial Landscape with Argonauts* and *Waterfront Wasteland Medea Material Landscape with Argonauts*) addresses similar issues, once again drawing upon Greek mythology. Set in a post-apocalyptic no-man's-land, three overlapping monologues (to be performed simultaneously) present Medea's murder of her children as a logical consequence of colonial and gender oppression.

Most of Müller's plays could not be performed in the GDR until the liberalization of the 1980s. Müller did not share the hope of many GDR citizens that the system could be reformed from within. For years, he had occupied a special position, enjoying considerable privileges, notably the ability to travel and to publish in the West. He had achieved international recognition, receiving virtually every major literary award in East as well as West Germany. After the unification of Germany of 1990, Müller turned to the more intimate form of poetry, a move not surprising if one remembers that his monologic theater texts and the performances of prose pieces such as *Bildbeschreibung* (1984; translated as *Explosion of a Memory/Description of a Picture* and *Explosion of a Memory*) and verse poems such as *Mommsens Block* (1993) render genre distinctions largely obsolete. In innumerable interviews, talk show appearances, and essays, Müller railed against the ostensible triumph of capitalism, insisting that the East German experience, despite its failure, should not be overlooked. Never afraid of controversy, and skillfully exploiting his celebrity status in the media, Müller rejected what he viewed as the commodification of culture in a market economy. In his work as director he incessantly reworked (some would say, recycled) his texts and those of other authors, notably Brecht, turning the theater into a public space in which historical memory is kept alive. It is perhaps this insistence on the vital function of theater as a means of societal self-reflection that will remain Müller's most important legacy.

CHRISTIAN ROGOWSKI

Biography
Born in Eppendorf, 9 January 1929. Worked in a library, as office clerk, and then as a journalist and freelance writer; editor of *Junge Kunst;* on the staff of Maxim-Gorki-Theater, 1958–59, the Berliner Ensemble, 1970–76 and 1992–95, the Berlin Volksbühne, 1976–88, Deutsches Theater 1988–91. Heinrich Mann Prize, 1959; Erich Weinert Medal, 1964; BZ Critics Prize, 1970, 1976; Lessing Prize, 1975; Büchner Prize, 1985; GDR National Prize, 1986; European Theater Award, 1994. Died in Berlin, 30 December 1995.

Selected Works

Collections
Werke, edited by Frank Hörnigk, 1998–

Plays
Zehn Tage, die die Welt erschütterten (after John Reed's *Ten Days That Shook the World*) (produced 1957), with Hagen Müller-Stahl, in *Junge Kunst,* 1957
Der Lohndrücker (produced 1958), with Inge Müller, 1958; in *Geschichten aus der Produktion I,* 1974; as *The Scab,* translated by Carl Weber, in *The Battle: Plays, Prose, Poems,* 1989
Klettwitzer Bericht (produced 1958), with Inge Müller, in *Junge Kunst,* 1958
Die Korrektur (produced 1958), with Inge Müller, 1959; in *Geschichten aus der Produktion I,* 1974; as *The Correction,* translated by Carl Weber, in *Hamletmachine and Other Texts for the Stage,* 1984
Herakles 5 (produced 1974), with *Philoktet,* 1966; as *Heracles 5,* translated by Carl Weber, in *The Battle: Plays, Prose, Poems,* 1989
Philoket (produced 1968), with *Herakles 5,* 1966; as *Philoctetes* (produced 1986), translated by Oscar Mandel and Maria Kelsen Feder, in *Philoctetes and the Fall of Troy,* 1981
Ödipus Tyrann (after Sophocles and Friedrich Hölderlin) (produced 1967), 1969; in *Mauser* (collection), 1978
Prometheus (after Aeschylus) (produced 1969), in *Geschichten aus der Produktion 2,* 1974
Zement (from a novel by Fyodor Gladkov) (produced 1973), in *Geschicten aus der Produktion 2,* 1974; as *Cement* (produced 1981), translated by Helen Fehervary et al., 1979
Traktor (produced 1975), in *Geschichten aus der Produktion 2,* 1974; as *Tractor,* translated by Carl Weber, in *The Battle: Plays, Prose, Poems,* 1989
Der Bau (based on Erik Neutsch's novel, *Der Spur der Steine*) (produced 1980), in *Geschichten aus der Produktion 1,* 1974
Geschichten aus der Produktion 1 and 2, 2 vols., 1974
Drachenoper (libretto to the opera *Lanzelot,* by Paul Dessau) (produced 1969), with Ginka Tscholakowa, in *Theater-Arbeit,* 1975

Horizonte (from a work by Gerhart Winterlich) (produced 1969), in
   Theater-Arbeit, 1975
Weiberkomödie (from a radio play by Inge Müller) (produced 1970), in
   Theater-Arbeit, 1975
Die Umsiedlerin; oder, Das Leben auf dem Lande (produced 1961),
   1975; revised version as *Die Baueren* (produced 1975), in *Stücke*,
   1975
Macbeth (from the play by William Shakespeare) (produced 1972), in
   Stücke, 1975
Der Horatier (produced 1973), in *Stücke*, 1975; as *The Horatian*,
   translated by Helen Fehervary and Marc Silberman, in *Minnesota
   Review* NS 6, 1976; translated by Carl Weber, in *The Battle: Plays,
   Prose, Poems*, 1989
Die Shlacht (produced 1975), in *Die Umsiedlerin; oder, Das Leben auf
   dem Lande*, 1975; with *Traktor* and *Leben Gundlings Friedrich von
   Preussen Lessings Schlaf Traum Schrei*, 1977; as *The Slaughter:
   Scenes from Germany*, translated by Marc Silberman et al., in
   Theater (Yale) 17, no. 2, 1986; as *The Battle*, translated by Carl
   Weber, in *The Battle: Plays, Prose, Poems*, 1989; as *Slaughter*,
   translated by Marc von Henning, in *Theatremachine*, 1995
Theater-Arbeit, 1975
Stücke, 1975
Mauser (from the novel *And Quiet Flows the Don*, by Sholokhov)
   (produced in English, 1975; in German, 1980), in *Alternative* 11,
   1976; in *Mauser* (collection), 1978; translated by Helen Fehervary
   and Marc Silberman, in *New German Critique* 8, 1976; translated by
   Carl Weber, in *The Battle: Plays, Prose, Poems*, 1989
Leben Gundlings Friedrich von Preussen Lessings Schlaf Traum Schrei
   (produced 1979), with *Die Schlacht* and *Traktor*, 1977; in *Herzstück*,
   1983; as *Gundling's Life Frederick of Prussia Lessing's Sleep Dream
   Scream*, translated by Carl Weber, in *Hamletmachine and Other
   Texts for the Stage*, 1984
Germania Tod in Berlin (produced 1978), 1977; as *Germania Death in
   Berlin*, translated by Carl Weber, in *Explosion of a Memory:
   Writings*, 1989
Die Hamletmaschine (produced 1979), in *Theater heute* 12, 1977; in
   Mauser (collection), 1978; as *Hamletmachine* (produced 1984),
   translated by Carl Weber, in *Hamletmachine and Other Texts for the
   Stage*, 1984; as *The Hamletmachine*, translated by Marc von
   Henning, in *Theatremachine*, 1995
Fatzer (after Bertolt Brecht) (produced 1978)
Mauser (collection), 1978
Der Auftrag (produced 1980), with *Der Bau* and *Herakles 5*, 1981; as
   The Mission; or, Memory of a Revolution (produced 1982), in
   Gambit 39–40, 1982; as *The Task* (produced 1989), translated by
   Carl Weber, in *Hamletmachine and Other Texts for the Stage*, 1984;
   as *The Mission*, translated by Marc von Henning, in *Theatremachine*,
   1995
Quartett (from the novel *Les Liaisons dangereuses*, by Choderlos de
   Laclos) (produced 1982), 1981; in *Herzstück*, 1983; as *Quartet*
   (produced 1983), translated by Karin Gartzker and Geoffrey Davis,
   in *GDR Monitor*, 1983; translated by Carl Weber, in *Hamletmachine
   and Other Texts for the Stage*, 1984; translated by Marc von
   Henning, in *Theatremachine*, 1995
Verkommenes Ufer Medeamaterial Landschaft mit Argonauten
   (produced 1983), in *Herzstück*, 1983; as *Despoiled Shore
   Medeamaterial Landscape with Argonauts*, translated by Carl Weber,
   in *Hamletmachine and Other Texts for the Stage*, 1984; as *Medea
   Plays: Medea Game and Waterfront Wasteland* (produced 1990); as
   Waterfront Wasteland Medea Material Landscape with Argonauts,
   translated by Marc von Henning, in *Theatremachine*, 1995
Wladimir Majakowski: Tragödie (produced 1983)
Herzstück (produced 1981), 1983; as *Heartpiece*, translated by Carl
   Weber, in *Hamletmachine and Other Texts for the Stage*, 1984; as
   Heartplay, translated by Marc von Henning, in *Theatremachine*,
   1995

Bildbeschreibung (produced 1985), 1984; as *Explosion of a
   Memory/Description of a Picture*, in *Explosion of a Memory:
   Writings*, translated by Carl Weber, 1989; as *Explosion of a Memory*,
   translated by Marc von Henning, in *Theatremachine*, 1995
Hamletmachine and Other Texts for the Stage, translated by Carl
   Weber, 1984
Wie es euch gefällt (from the play *As You Like It*, by William
   Shakespeare) (produced 1968), in *Shakespeare Factory 1*, 1985
Shakespeare Factory 1, 1985
The CIVIL warS: a tree is best measured when it is down ("Cologne
   section," produced 1984), with Robert Wilson, 1985
Quai West (from a work by Bernard-Marie-Koltès) (produced 1986)
Prologue to *Alcestis* (produced 1986)
Wolokolamsker Chausee (produced 1988), with *Die Schlacht*, 1988; as
   Volokolamsk Highway, translated by Carl Weber, in *Explosion of a
   Memory: Writings*, 1989; as *The Road of Tanks*, translated by Marc
   von Henning, in *Theatremachine*, 1995
Revolutionsstücke, edited by Uwe Wittstock, 1988
Anatomie Titus Fall of Rome (produced 1985), in *Shakespeare Factory
   2*, 1989
Hamlet (from the play by William Shakespeare) (produced 1977), with
   Matthias Langhoff, in *Shakespeare Factory 2*, 1989
Shakespeare Factory 2, 1989
Der Arzt wider Willen (from a work by Molière) (produced 1970), with
   Benno Besson, in *Kopien 1*, 1989
Die Möwe (from a work by Anton Chekhov) (produced 1972), with
   Ginka Tscholakowa, in *Kopien 2*, 1989
Stücke: Text über Deutschland (1957–1979), edited by Frank Hörnigk,
   1989
Kopien 1 and 2, 2 vols., 1989
Herakles 13, 1991; as *Heracles 13*, translated by Marc von Henning, in
   Theatremachine, 1995
Mommsens Block, 1993; as *Mommsen's Block* (produced 1994),
   translated and edited by Carl Weber, in *DramaContemporary:
   Germany*, 1996
Germania 3: Gespenster am toten Mann, 1995

Other
Rotwelsch, 1982
"Ich bin ein Neger": Diskussion mit Heiner Müller, with Eva-Maria
   Viebeg, 1986
Gesammelte Irrtümer: Interviews und Gespräche, 1986
Explosion of a Memory: Writings (includes plays), edited and translated
   by Carl Weber, 1989
Erich Fried—Heiner Müller, ein Gespräch, 1989
The Battle: Plays, Prose, Poems, edited and translated by Carl Weber,
   1989
Gesammelte Irrtümer 2: Interviews und Gespräche, 1990
Heiner Müller "zur Lage der Nation" (interview), with Frank M.
   Raddatz, 1990
Ein Gespenst verläßt Europa, photographs by Sibylle Bergemann, 1990
Germania (interviews and texts), translated by Bernard and Caroline
   Schutze, edited by Sylvère Lothringer, 1990
Jenseits der Nation (interview), with Frank M. Raddatz, 1991
Gedichte, 1992
Krieg ohne Schlacht, 1992; expanded edition, 1994
Ich hab zur Nacht gegessen mit Gespenstern, 1993
Gesammelte Irrtümer 3: Texte und Gespräche, 1994
Ich schulde der Welt einen Toten: Gespräche, 1995
Theatremachine, translated and edited by Marc von Henning, 1995
Ich bin ein Landvermesser: Gespräche, neue Folge, 1996

Further Reading

Arnold, Heinz-Ludwig, editor, *Heiner Müller*, Munich: Text und Kritik,
   1982; 2nd edition, 1997

Fischer, Gerhard, editor, *Heiner Müller: Contexts and History,* Tübingen: Stauffenburg, 1995

Herzinger, Richard, *Masken der Lebensrevolution: Vitalistische Zivilisations- und Humanismuskritik in Texten Heiner Müllers,* Munich: Fink, 1992

Hörnigk, Frank, editor, *Heiner Müller Material: Texte und Kommentare,* Göttingen: Steidl, 1989

Kalb, Jonathan, *The Theater of Heiner Müller,* Cambridge and New York: Cambridge University Press, 1998

Raddatz, Frank-Michael, *Dämonen unterm roten Stern: Zu Geschichtsphilosophie und Ästhetik Heiner Müllers,* Stuttgart: Metzler, 1991

Scheid, Judith R., editor, *Zum Drama in der DDR: Heiner Müller und Peter Hacks,* Stuttgart: Klett, 1981

Schivelbusch, Wolfgang, *Sozialistisches Drama nach Brecht: Drei Modelle: Peter Hacks, Heiner Müller, Hartmut Lange,* Neuwied: Luchterhand, 1974

Schmid, Ingo, and Florian Vaßen, *Bibliographie Heiner Müllers,* Bielefeld: Aisthesis, 1993

Schulz, Genia, *Heiner Müller,* Stuttgart: Metzler, 1980

Silbermann, Marc, *Heiner Müller,* Amsterdam: Rodopi, 1980

Teraoka, Arlene, *The Silence of Entropy or Universal Discourse: The Postmodern Poetics of Heiner Müller,* Frankfurt and New York: Lang, 1985

Tschapke, Reinhard, *Heiner Müller,* Berlin: Morgenbuch, 1996

Wieghaus, Georg, *Heiner Müller,* Munich: Beck, 1981

Germania Tod in Berlin 1977

Play by Heiner Müller

Germania Tod in Berlin (*Germania Death in Berlin*) is Heiner Müller's most comprehensive historical play. It was begun in 1956, completed during Erich Honecker's political thaw in 1971, published in 1977, and first performed, but only in West Germany, in 1978. It is a montage of 13 scenes in which episodes set in the German Democratic Republic (GDR) between 1949 and 1953 alternate with episodes from early Germanic, Prussian, and German history. Müller deploys a Baroque mixture of styles from one scene to the next—laconic realism, cartoon comedy, circus clowns, even an extended quotation from Tacitus—to demonstrate the historical factors that shaped the German mentality, and in its turn, GDR socialism.

"Street 1," the brief first scene, is a powerful annotation of Spartakus Week, the abortive revolution in 1919, and shows starving children manipulated by outsize bourgeois figures. In "Street 2" a jubilant loudspeaker proclaims the founding of the GDR in 1949 to an unenthusiastic passing crowd. In "Brandenburg Concerto 1" two clowns deconstruct the myth of Frederick the Great as the enlightened ruler of responsible citizens and unmask him as a callous commander of willing cannon fodder. In "Brandenburg Concerto 2" a hero of labor chokes on caviar at his award ceremony but brushes aside advances from the ghost of Frederick. The worker is emancipated, but the party bosses adopt the trappings of a ruling class. "Homage to Stalin 1" follows a moment of cannibalism at Stalingrad with a grotesque scene of masturbation and self-destruction among the Nibelungs, the Germanic heroes whom Wagner romanticized in *The Ring*. Germanic myth is made to provide the founding image of German militarism and self-destructive fanaticism.

"Homage to Stalin 2" is a bar scene. It is 1953. Stalin has just died, and the bawdy drinkers raise subversive voices.

These episodes are self-contained and constructed to make historical points. There is no plot, but the GDR scenes provide the spine of the action, beginning with the founding of the East German Communist state and ending with the Berlin rising of 14 June 1953. This revolt of the Berlin workers against the "workers' and peasants' state," long a taboo subject in the GDR, lies at the heart of Müller's project, in which the only recurring figures are Young Bricklayer, Whore 1, and Hilse. The bricklayer naively falls for Whore 1 in the second scene and courts her again in the sixth, to general amusement. By the last scene he knows her trade but sticks to her nonetheless. What would you do, he asks the old Communist Hilse, if the party you had slaved and suffered for turned out to have prostituted itself? His problems with his girl and his Party are analogous. This dilemma is also Müller's, as he demonstrates in *Die Hamletmaschine* (1977; *Hamletmachine*), where he imagines himself on both sides in the 1956 Budapest rising, split between the Party (as a committed Communist) and the insurgents (as a utopian socialist). *Germania* is a coded critique of real socialism in the GDR, which had prostituted itself to Stalinism.

Scene 7, "The Holy Family," is a grotesque parody of the Nativity, in which Hitler fathers the Federal Republic on a female Goebbels in the form of a *Contergan-Wolf* (thalidomide wolf) in sheep's clothing. Germania acts as midwife and the gift-bearing Magi are the United States, France, and Britain. For Georg Hensel in the *Frankfurter Allgemeine Zeitung*, this was shrill GDR propaganda; for Müller it was over-the-top satire on that same propaganda. Hilse (the name comes from the docile proletarian in Gerhart Hauptmann's *Die Weber* [1892; *The Weavers*]) appears as the Old Man who welcomes the new GDR in scene 2 and as the loyal Communist in scene 6. In scene 8, "The Workers' Monument," he refuses to join the 1953 Berlin rising and is stoned by skinheads. The Activist in scene 4 also has his head bandaged, signs that active conformity is not popular. Life in the GDR is seen from the point of view of the workers for whom the state exists, but whose support it has failed to win. They are a motley band—an ex-Nazi general, a demoted GDR minister, a fat bricklayer, a one-time Communist who noticed that the leaders never risked their necks—but strikers all, united in their resistance to more work for the same money. In the final deathbed scene, "Death in Berlin," the Young Bricklayer feeds Whore 1 (whom Hilse mistakes for Rosa Luxemburg) the words that sustain the dying man's delusion that the red flag will one day fly over Rhine and Ruhr in a Germany united under Communism, an ending that both exposes and sympathizes with the veteran Communist's delusion.

"Brothers 1" is a confrontation from Tacitus's Annals from A.D. 16 of two brothers, one in Roman imperial service, the other leading his native tribe. In "Brothers 2" two brothers are in prison—one an ex-Communist who has been tortured into becoming a storm trooper, the other a Communist who has deviated from the Party line—both would-be servants of Moscow who have come unstuck. As the Russian tanks roll in to quell the 1953 rising, the other prisoners kill the Communist. In this scenario there are no positive roles. The storm trooper has been tortured by his enemies, then ostracized by his friends; the Communist has been victimized by the Party yet sides with the Russian tanks rather than with his fellow German protestors.

Scene 11, "Nightplay," might be read as stage directions for a mime but is more plausible as a monologue. A dummy plastered with posters trips over a threshold, pulls off his offending limbs, is blinded, and finally develops a mouth to scream. Is the dummy the ruling Socialist Unity Party, or the people of the GDR, stumbling into a new world, mutilating itself with purges, blinding itself with censorship, finally perhaps acquiring a voice? History is an apocalyptic vision in which imperial wars merge into one long historical catastrophe, and Napoléon and Caesar rub shoulders with the Nibelungs and Stalin. The play is bleak and violent, yet observed with a sardonic wit that bespeaks a wish that things might be otherwise. This is remote from the clear-cut issues of Brecht's plays. Müller seems to suggest that 1953 was the GDR's last chance, and it missed it.

HUGH RORRISON

Editions

First edition: *Germania Tod in Berlin,* Berlin: Rotbuch-Verlag, 1977
Translation: *Germania Death in Berlin,* translated by Carl Weber, in *Explosion of a Memory: Writings,* New York: PAJ Publications, 1989

Further Reading

Eke, Norbert Otto, *Heiner Müller: Apokalypse und Utopie,* Paderborn: Schöningh, 1989
Emmerich, Wolfgang, "Der Alp der Geschichte," in *Deutsche Misere einst und jetzt: Die deutsche Misere als Thema der Gegenwartsliteratur/Das Preussensyndrom in der Literatur der DDR,* edited by Paul Gerhard Klussmann and Heinrich Mohr, Bonn: Bouvier, 1982
Hermand, Jost, "Fridericus Rex," in *Dramatik der DDR,* edited by Ulrich Profitlich, Frankfurt: Suhrkamp, 1987
Kalb, Jonathan, *The Theater of Heiner Müller,* Cambridge and New York: Cambridge University Press, 1998
Klein, Christian, *Heiner Müller; ou, L'idiot de la république,* Bern: Lang, 1992
Klussmann, Paul Gerhard, "Heiner Müllers *Germania Tod in Berlin,*" in *Geschichte als Schauspiel,* edited by Walter Hinck, Frankfurt: Suhrkamp, 1981
———, "Deutschland-Denkmal: Umgestürzt. Zu Heiner Müllers *Germania Tod in Berlin,*" in *Deutsche Misere einst und jetzt: Die deutsche Misere als Thema der Gegenwartsliteratur/Das Preussensyndrom in der Literatur der DDR,* edited by Paul Gerhard Klussmann and Heinrich Mohr, Bonn: Bouvier, 1982
Rischbieter, Henning, "Nur heilloser Schrecken, *Germania Tod in Berlin,* und den Münicher Kammerspielen," *Theater Heute* 6 (1978)
Schulz, Genia, *Heiner Müller,* Stuttgart: Metzler, 1980
Wieghaus, Georg, *Zwischen Auftrag und Verrat: Werk und Ästhetik Heiner Müllers,* Frankfurt: Lang, 1984

Die Hamletmaschine 1977

Play by Heiner Müller

Die Hamletmaschine (*Hamletmachine*), written in 1977, represents a radical break with the various modes of drama to which Heiner Müller's writing is indebted, including Brecht's epic theater, highly stylized reworkings of ancient myths, Artaud's theater of cruelty, and the fragmentary dramaturgy of Georg Büchner. Müller's self-professed "obsession" with the Hamlet story led him first to undertake a translation and adaptation of Shakespeare's five-hour play. From this endeavor emerged what he calls a "shrunken head" version, a dense nine-page collage that distills certain key historical and political aspects of the Hamlet story and that pushes the limits of what can be performed on stage (the first attempt at producing the play, in Cologne, was in fact abandoned; see Girshausen, 1978).

Müller dispenses with most elements that traditionally characterize drama, such as discernible characters, a clearly defined temporal and spatial setting, the unfolding of a dramatic conflict, and plot development. It is largely left open to the director to decide which lines are to be spoken by which actors; only occasionally are lines clearly assigned to a specific personage. We are confronted with a kind of associative prose poem, a blueprint for a performance event set in an abstract postapocalyptic world of "the ruins of Europe." Any attempt to explicate Müller's multilayered piece—including this one—necessarily privileges certain aspects over others, which runs the risk of misrepresenting a work that, in many ways, renders a unified reading impossible.

Hamletmachine is divided into five sections (echoing the five acts of Shakespeare's original). Sections 1 and 4 appear to represent reflections associated with a male speaking subject whose words evoke aspects of Hamlet's predicament, centering on his inability to act. Sections 2 and 5 focus on a female subject, with Ophelia becoming an emblem of women's oppression. Only in section 3, which bears the musical title "Scherzo," do we find a reduced semblance of dialogue, when the Hamlet subject and the Ophelia subject meet. Interestingly enough, their interaction involves an effort on the part of the male subject to exchange subject positions: by "becoming" a woman, Hamlet tries to eschew the political responsibility placed upon him. The motifs of social role-playing, theatrical play-acting, and political action are here intricately and inextricably intertwined; an examination of gender issues is combined with an extended self-reflection of the problematic status of drama and a profound exploration of the problem of political agency.

In his treatment of the Hamlet story, Müller differs from his predecessors, among them Goethe, the German Romantics, Chekhov, Joyce, and Alfred Döblin, by giving equal attention to the predicament of the female subject, Ophelia. Through a multitude of literary and historical allusions, Müller encourages the reader/viewer to reflect on the historical, personal, and political issues raised by the Hamlet/Ophelia story. The stage instructions evoke powerful dramatic images that are difficult, if not impossible, to render in an actual performance: Ophelia, for instance, is supposed to appear with a clock in place of her heart, an image that later is transformed into a "madonna with breast cancer," which in turn suggests the general status of women as victims rather than as agents of history. The complex network of verbal allusions and the profusion of surreal, often puzzling, dramatic images lend the text a centrifugal energy that dissolves standard notions of history on the most abstract level. At the same time, Müller offers here his most personal reflection about his own status as an East German intellectual caught between two power blocs during the Cold War, culminating in the dramatic gesture of having a photograph of the author torn to pieces on stage.

In particular, Müller's scenario addresses the great (botched) utopian transformations of European history such as the Bolshevik Revolution of 1917, the Hungarian Uprising of 1956, and the Prague Spring of 1968. Hamlet can be read as the left-wing intellectual who is interested in political change, but hampered in his initiative by the ghost of the "father"—the specter of Stalinism. Section four, "Pest in Buda/Battle for Greenland," features an extended soliloquy describing a coming uprising, which, in retrospect, appears oddly prophetic of the demise of communism in the late 1980s. Müller himself exploited this historical irony by inserting *Hamletmachine* into his own production of Shakespeare's *Hamlet* at the Deutsches Theater, Berlin (March 1990), rehearsals for which ran parallel to the momentous events of the fall of 1989.

Müller is clearly indebted to Walter Benjamin's notion of European history as perennial catastrophe. His Hamlet voices ennui, an unwillingness to enter the chain of political violence. All the same, Müller's Hamlet ends up climbing into his dead father's armor and taking an ax to smash open the heads of three former harbingers of political hope—Marx, Lenin, and Mao—who appear here in feminized guise as three nude women. Hamlet, paradoxically, both joins and destroys the order of the founding fathers of communism. By way of contrast, Ophelia appears to discover a politically "progressive" voice. Yet, in the text's bizarre final image, her call to violent rebellion is drowned out as she, seated underwater in a wheelchair, is wrapped in gauze by two men in white smocks until nothing remains on stage but her motionless embalmed cocoon. Armor versus cocoon: men turn to mindless violence, while women are rendered silent. Müller presents European history as a "Hamlet machine," an apparatus that produces "Hamlets," male subjects incapable of fruitful political action, and "Ophelias," female subjects whose very attempts to escape and challenge the structures of oppression lead to madness and self-destruction.

As a daring dramatic experiment, *Hamletmachine* provides a unique, yet extraordinarily fruitful challenge to critics and to the theater alike. The piece has in fact been produced frequently, and with considerable success, sometimes by directors such as Robert Wilson (1986) who deliberately ignore the stage instructions and invent their own dramatic imagery to go with Müller's text. It has also provided the basis for an opera by Wolfgang

Rihm (Nationaltheater Mannheim, 1987). Müller himself participated in a radio production of the piece with music by avant-garde pop band Einstürzende Neubauten (Rundfunk der DDR, Berlin, 1990).

CHRISTIAN ROGOWSKI

Editions
First edition: *Die Hamletmaschine*, in *Theater heute* 12 (1977); also in *Mauser*, Berlin: Rotbuch, 1978
Translations: *Hamletmachine*, translated and edited by Carl Weber, in *Hamletmachine and Other Texts for the Stage*, New York: PAJ, 1984; *The Hamletmachine*, translated and edited by Marc von Henning, in *Theatremachine*, London: Faber, 1995

Further Reading
Eke, Norbert Otto, "'Ein inkommensurables Produkt, geschrieben zur Selbstverständigung': *Die Hamletmaschine*," in *Heiner Müller: Apokalypse und Utopie*, Paderborn: Schöningh, 1989
Girshausen, Theo, editor, *Die Hamletmaschine: Heiner Müllers Endspiel*, Cologne: Prometh, 1978
Guntermann, Georg, "Heiner Müller: *Die Hamletmaschine*: Das Drama der Geschichte als Kunst-Stück," in *Deutsche Gegenwartsdramatik*, 2 vols., edited by Lothar Pikulik et al., Göttingen: Vandenhoeck und Ruprecht, 1987
Petersohn, Roland, "Die *Hamlet*-Variationen: Die zerstörte Obession: Von Shakespeares *Hamlet* zu Müllers *Die Hamletmaschine*," in *Heiner Müllers Shakespeare-Rezeption: Texte und Kontexte*, Frankfurt and New York: Lang, 1993
Raddatz, Frank-Michael, "*Die Hamletmaschine*: Geschichte und Subjektivität," in *Dämonen unterm roten Stern: Zu Geschichtsphilosophie und Ästhetik Heiner Müllers*, Stuttgart: Metzler, 1991
Scheer, Edward, "'Under the Sun of Torture': A New Aesthetic of Cruelty: Artaud, Wilson and Müller," in *Heiner Müller: Contexts and History*, edited by Gerhard Fischer, Tübingen: Stauffenburg, 1995
Schulz, Genia, "*Die Hamletmaschine*," in *Heiner Müller*, Stuttgart: Metzler, 1980
Teraoka, Arlene Akiko, "The Entropy of Bourgeois Drama: *Die Hamletmaschine* (1977)," in *The Silence of Entropy or Universal Discourse: The Postmodernist Poetics of Heiner Müller*, New York: Lang, 1985

Herta Müller 1953–

Herta Müller is one of the most remarkable and original voices in contemporary German-language literature. Her 1984 debut in the Federal Republic of Germany with the publication of *Niederungen* (*Nadirs*) put her on the literary map: the book was reviewed widely and enthusiastically, and the author was hailed as a "discovery."

A descendant of Swabians who had settled in Romania in the 18th century, Müller grew up in a German enclave in the Banat region of Romania, and her first texts were published in German in Bucharest. She began writing from a position as a triple outsider: as a member of a linguistic minority in Romania, as a dissident against Ceauşescu's political dictatorship in Romania, and as an author in opposition to the traditions, values, and folk-

loristic literature cherished by the Romanian-German community. In addition, she was writing as a woman about—and against—a strongly patriarchal community.

Her writing is preceded by—and often associated with—the work of writers such as Rolf Bossert, Gerhardt Csejka, Gerhard Ortinan, William Totok, Richard Wagner, and Ernest Wichner, who in 1972 formed the so-called Aktionsgruppe Banat (Banat Action Group). Their experimental texts broke with the standards of traditional Romanian-German literature, taking advantage of a temporary atmosphere during the early 1970s of support for linguistic and cultural minority communities and for aesthetic innovation and experimentation in general. Müller subsequently formed close friendships (she was married to

Richard Wagner) with members of the group, which was suppressed in 1975.

Müller's Banat-Swabian background is reflected and thematized extensively in *Nadirs*. The title story (which runs to 77 pages), told from the point of view of a child, portrays life in the rural German Banat as an anti-idyll marked by stagnation, claustrophobia, and decay. The village community is governed by intolerance and a stifling insistence on conformity, family life is devoid of warmth or tenderness, relationships and behavior are marked by barely suppressed aggressions and violence, and fascist tendencies go hand in hand with a nostalgia for the Germany of National Socialism (a number of the men—among them Müller's father—had been members of the SS).

Herta Müller's literary uncovering of the darker side of the German traditions and virtues upon which the Banat-Swabians prided themselves stirred up the community. When the *Neue Banater Zeitung* published her grotesquely comical short text "Das schwäbische Bad" (The Swabian Bath) in 1981 (later included in *Nadirs*), readers for the most part were outraged and branded the author a "Nestbeschmutzer" (someone who soils her own nest). Both detractors and defenders read Müller's texts as pure autobiographical truth, a tendency that continued to some degree in early Müller criticism.

Müller's texts to date can be roughly divided into three groups: fictional texts written in Romania, those written after she emigrated to Germany, and a body of nonfiction, including poetological texts. The texts written before she emigrated, including *Niederungen*, *Der Mensch ist ein großer Fasan auf der Welt* (1986; *The Passport*), and *Barfüßiger Februar* (1987; February on Bare Feet) (the latter collection makes available a number of texts previously published in Romania as *Drückender Tango* [Oppressive Tango]), draw primarily on Müller's experiences in the Banat community. *The Passport* focuses on the miller Windisch's attempt to attain passports and emigrate to Germany with his family, presenting a village community marked by resentment, corruption, and exploitation, including exchanges of political for sexual favors, which are carried out at the expense of women. All three collections offer prose sketches with little or no plot, and Müller's language in these early texts on occasion has a distinct Expressionist flavor.

Müller's first text after she left Romania presents a strongly autobiographical account of emigration to Germany. The protagonist of *Reisende auf einem Bein* (1989; *Traveling on One Leg*), Irene, views West German life and culture through the eyes of an outsider—someone at home neither in the country and society she has left nor the one she has now joined.

Müller's later fictional texts (written after the collapse of the Ceauşescu regime in Romania) revisit the experience of living in Romania once again, this time providing much more explicit accounts of life under Ceauşescu: its mechanisms of repression, surveillance, and intimidation; the way in which these mechanisms undermined and destroyed relationships; and the numbness, fear, and suspicion that pervaded everyday life. With stronger plot lines, *Der Fuchs war damals schon der Jäger* (1992; The Fox Was the Hunter Even Back Then) and *Herztier* (1994; *The Land of Green Plums*), as well as Müller's most recent novel, *Heut wär ich mir lieber nicht begegnet* (1997; Today I Would Have Preferred Not to Encounter Myself), detail how their respective protagonists' lives are affected and disrupted by the living conditions associated with a dictatorship. *The Land of Green Plums* follows the fate of a female narrator and three male friends who are modeled on members of the Aktionsgruppe Banat and intersperses their stories with flashbacks to the narrator's childhood, in which she remembers the mechanisms of repression and intimidation at work previously; these strategies help us realize that the localized, provincial realm and the social landscape of a totalitarian regime dovetail neatly, with surveillance and merciless control at work in both.

Finally, Müller has published a number of poetological and nonfictional texts. In particular, the five lectures on poetics that form the body of *Der Teufel sitzt im Spiegel: Wie Wahrnehmung sich erfindet* (1991; The Devil Sits in the Mirror: How Perception Invents Itself) offer detailed insights into Müller's craft and her background. In a category of its own is a set of collages, *Der Wächter nimmt seinen Kamm* (1993; The Guard Takes His Comb), verbal-visual texts that take up the central issues of Müller's work in more oblique and playful ways.

Müller herself has frequently objected to a reading of her texts as autobiographical; she emphasizes instead what she calls the "autofictional," the combination of memory, perception, and invention that marks her work, as well as the extent of linguistic and narrative stylization involved in her work (she cites Peter Handke and Thomas Bernhard as early influences). In Müller's texts, realistic and often graphic perceptions are highly mediated, rendered in a language that draws attention to itself and defamiliarizes its objects. Her technique is characterized in particular by the following strategies: (1) A scalpel-like gaze that focuses on details and seems virtually to dissect that upon which it is trained; (2) highly creative and unorthodox imagery that conveys perceptual intensity, employs original metaphors, occasionally transgresses the rules of orthodox language use, and frequently borrows from the poetic richness of the Romanian language; (3) insistently simple paratactical sentence construction, reductive and repetitive phrases, and the absence of explicit connections between statements and observations; (4) a graphic emphasis on disturbing and repulsive elements—in her texts, slime, filth, sweat and other body secretions, rot, and unpleasant odors all figure prominently. Death is a pervasive motif—as a conspicuous element of village life, as a consequence of totalitarian oppression in Romania, and in connection with the fascist heritage of the Banat Germans.

Müller's texts challenge readers through their combination of obliqueness and drastic expression. They present a fragmented, dissociated world without overt cohesion and with only isolated and precarious moments of contentment—a social realm whose protagonists appear numb and anxious, paralyzed by forces beyond their control, and unable to shape their own lives. Her vivid and detailed depiction of life under oppression is rendered in striking images and a style that places her in the tradition of modern nonrealist literature.

Sabine Gross

Biography

Born in Nitzkydorf, in the Banat region of Romania, 17 August 1953. Studied German and Romanian literature in Timişoara and worked as a translator, 1976–79, and Geman Teacher, 1979–83; after an uncensored version of *Niederungen* was published in Germany in 1984, she was denied permission to either work or publish in Romania and devoted herself exclusively to writing; emigration application granted and moved to the Federal Republic of Germany, 1987. Ricarda Huch Prize, Darmstadt, 1987; Marieluise Fleißer Prize, Ingolstadt, 1989; Kleist Prize, 1994; IMPAC Dublin Literary Award, 1998; member of the

German Academy for Language and Literature, 1995. Currently lives in Berlin.

Selected Works

Fiction

Niederungen, 1984; as *Nadirs*, translated by Sieglinde Lug, 1999
Drückender Tango, 1984
Der Mensch ist ein großer Fasan auf der Welt, 1986; as *The Passport*, translated by Martin Chalmers, 1989
Barfüßiger Februar, 1987
Reisende auf einem Bein, 1989; as *Traveling on One Leg*, translated by Valentina Glajar and André Lefevere, 1998
Der Teufel sitzt im Spiegel: Wie Wahrnehmung sich erfindet, 1991
Der Fuchs war damals schon der Jäger, 1992
Eine warme Kartoffel ist ein warmes Bett, 1992
Der Wächter nimmt seinen Kamm, 1993
Herztier, 1994; as *The Land of Green Plums*, translated by Michael Hofmann, 1996
Heute wär ich mir lieber nicht begegnet, 1997

Other

Hunger und Seide, 1995
In der Falle (lectures on poetics), 1996

Further Reading

Bauer, Karin, "Tabus der Wahrnehmung: Reflexion und Geschichte in Herta Müllers Prosa," *German Studies Review* 14, no. 2 (1996)
Eke, Norbert Otto, editor, *Die erfundene Wahrnehmung: Annäherung an Herta Müller*, Paderborn: Igel, 1991
Haupt-Cucuiu, Herta, *Eine Poesie der Sinne: Herta Müllers "Diskurs des Alleinseins" und seine Wurzeln*, Paderborn: Igel, 1996
Köhnen, Ralph, editor, *Der Druck der Erfahrung treibt die Sprache in die Dichtung: Bildlichkeit in Texten Herta Müllers*, Frankfurt and New York: Lang, 1997
Krauss, Hannes, "Fremde Blicke: Zur Prosa von Herta Müller und Richard Wagner," in *Neue Generation, Neues Erzählen: Deutsche Prosa-Literatur der achtziger Jahre*, edited by Walter Delabar et al., Opladen: Westdeutscher Verlag, 1993
Monatshefte 89, no. 4 (1997) Special Issue: *Libuše Moníková / Herta Müller: Sprache, Ort, Heimat*, edited by Sabine Gross
Ottmers, Clemens, "Schreiben und Leben: Herta Müller, *Der Teufel sitzt im Spiegel: Wie Wahrnehmung sich erfindet*," in *Poetik der Autoren: Beiträge zur deutschsprachigen Gegenwartsliteratur*, edited by Paul Michael Lützeler, Frankfurt: Fischer, 1994
Zierden, Josef, "Herta Müller," in *Kritisches Lexikon zur deutschsprachigen Gegenwartsliteratur*, Munich: Edition Text und Kritik, 1995

Munich

Munich (population 1.2 million) is the capital of Bavaria and Germany's third largest city. Just over half the population is Roman Catholic; one-fifth is Protestant. Noted for its theaters, opera, museums, art galleries, and four leading orchestras, present-day Munich is the product of an 800-year history of attracting leading cultural innovators.

The city has its origins in an act of economic aggression, when in 1158 the Guelph Henry the Lion destroyed a bridge over the Isar at Oberföhring owned by the bishop of Freising and built a new one at the site where monks from Tegernsee monastery had settled (*zu den Munichen* [at the place of the monks]). The lucrative salt-trade route was thereby diverted to Munich, which yielded valuable income from tolls. The Wittelsbachs became dukes of Bavaria when Henry fell out of favor and Emperor Frederick Barbarossa made Otto I ruler of Bavaria. In 1255, the Wittelsbach duke, Ludwig II, took up residence in Munich, making it his capital. Under Ludwig IV, Munich became the cultural capital of the Holy Roman Empire in 1328.

With the accession of Albrecht V to Electoral Duke, the tradition of patronage of the arts by Wittelsbach rulers began in earnest. Albrecht summoned the Jesuits to Munich, who opened their Gymnasium in 1559. The expulsion from Munich of Protestant literary figures such as historian Johann Turmair (Aventinus) and Martin Balticus indicated a loss of intellectuals that was only slowly compensated for by the newly arrived Jesuit order. Albrecht's lasting contribution to the cultural life of the city was his purchase of the libraries of J.A. Widmanstetter

(1558), Jakob Fugger (1571), and Hartmann Schedel (1571), which became the core of the court library and, later, the Bavarian State Library. Further, with the art collection in the Münzhof and the Antiquarium, this Wittelsbach ruler founded the first German museums.

As a center of the Counter Reformation, Munich experienced a surge of cultural activity during the 17th and 18th centuries. Under Maximilian I, the city ranked behind only Augsburg and Prague as a center for the arts in Europe. An admirer of Dürer, Maximilian acquired *The Four Apostles*, which can still be seen in the Alte Pinakothek. Contributors to Munich's literary culture at this time included Aegidius Albertinus, a Dutchman, who furthered the literary use of Bavarian German in his almost 50 books. Through his translation of Mateo Alemán's *Guzmán de Alfarache* (1599; *Der Landstörzer Gusman von Alfarache* [The Vagabond Gusman of Alfarache]), Albertinus advanced the genre of the picaresque novel in German literature before Grimmelshausen. Jakob Biedermann arrived in Munich in 1606, where, three years later, the boys of the Jesuitengymnasium performed his *Cenodoxus*, the most prominent example of the prodigious tradition of Latin Jesuit dramas, which extended unbroken from 1560 to 1773.

The progress of the Enlightenment was slow in Munich. Nonetheless, Eusebius Amort, Agnellus Kandler, and Gelasius Hieber attempted in 1719 to found an academy comparable to the Akademie der Wissenschaften in Berlin (founded in 1700). They were unsuccessful with their academy, but in 1722 they launched the literary and scholarly journal *Parnassus Boicus,* which, before its demise in 1740, programmatically advanced the use of German as a language of science and culture. In 1759, the Bavarian Academy of Sciences was finally founded. One of its members, the multifaceted Lorenz Westenrieder, became the foremost representative of the belated Enlightenment in Munich. His considerable literary output included the most important 18th-century Bavarian novel, *Leben des guten Jünglings Engelhof* (1781; Life of the Good Youth Engelhof).

After Napoléon had made Bavaria a kingdom on 1 January 1806, King Maximilian I Josef, with his factotum minister Maximilian, count of Montgelas, determined the political shape of Bavaria as the first German constitutional monarchy (1818). They also shaped the physical appearance of its capital with the creation of the Max-Vorstadt and expansion to the north and west. In the early 19th century, rapid secularization in Bavaria brought valuable libraries, manuscripts, and religious art and artifacts into royal (later state) collections in the city and decimated centuries-old centers of teaching and learning in the Bavarian provinces. The university, founded in Ingolstadt in 1472 and moved to Landshut in 1802, was finally transferred to Munich in 1825; as today's Ludwig-Maximilians-Universität, it is the second-largest in Germany, with 63,000 students.

Already as crown prince, Ludwig I developed plans for monumental buildings in classical style, inspired by visits to Rome and Greece. With master builders Leo von Klenze and Friedrich von Gärtner, he executed the Königsplatz (with the Glyptothek, Antikensammlung, and Propyläen evoking ancient Greek models), the Odeonsplatz (with the Feldherrnhalle derived from the Loggia dei Lanzi in Florence), the Alte and Neue Pinakothek, the Ludwigstrasse (inspired by Rome's Via del Corso, with the Siegestor [in Roman style], the Ludwigskirche, the State Library, and the University), and the expansion of the Residenz.

The Munich of Maximilian I and Ludwig I was home to important writers of German Romanticism, among them the Görres circle and F.W.J. Schelling. Ludwig's favorable disposition toward German nationalism; his romantic espousal of antiquity, the Middle Ages, and Catholicism; and his lax enforcement of the Karlsbad Decrees (1819) made Munich an attractive place for anti-Restoration minds after the Congress of Vienna. Heinrich Heine sought employment at the university during his stay (1827–28), Friedrich Hebbel was a student in the city from 1836 to 1839, and Clemens Brentano was a Munich resident between 1833 and 1842 and wrote *Gockel, Hinkel, und Gackeleja* (1838; *Gockel and Scratchfoot*) there. In Gottfried Keller's work, his experiences in Munich (1840) provide the basis for significant parts of *Der grüne Heinrich* (1853–55; *Green Henry*).

Under Maximilan II, literature assumed a more prominent place in Wittelsbach cultural policy. The well-established tradition of inviting outsiders to Munich to enrich the cultural mix was continued in the summoning of *Nordlichter* (Northern Lights), who included men of medicine and science as well as literary luminaries. To the displeasure of local writers and artists, northerners Friedrich Bodenstedt, Emanuel Geibel, Paul Heyse (Nobel Prize in literature in 1910), Adolf Friedrich von Schack, and others were granted the favor of the court. These literary figures, under Heyse's direction, formed the Münchner Dichterkreis in 1857. This group, also known as the Krokodil, survived until 1883 and adhered to the classical formal strictures propounded by Geibel. Among the poets who represented popular

taste in Bavarian idiom during this era were Franz von Kobell and Karl Stieler—with their images of rural life, rustic characters, and customs—and Franz von Pocci, who advanced the cause of children's literature and serial publications.

Where Maximilian's energies were directed toward establishing Munich's position as the intellectual center of a modern Bavarian state and toward the physical progress of the city, his successor, Ludwig II, preferred to indulge his architectural fantasies in the Bavarian landscape. Apart from his sponsorship of Richard Wagner, Ludwig II's personal impact on the cultural life of the city was inconsiderable. Wagner lived in Munich from 1864 to 1865 and premiered *Tristan und Isolde* (1865), *Die Meistersinger von Nürnberg* (1868), *Das Rheingold* (1869), and *Die Walküre* (1870) in the city.

At the close of Ludwig II's reign, the kingdom's coffers were empty, and thus financial support for the arts was no longer possible. And yet the lively artist community in Munich and Schwabing at the turn of the century prompted Thomas Mann's formulation in *Gladius Dei* (1902), "München leuchtete" (Munich was shining). In the Prinzregentenzeit (1886–1912), the literary culture of the rapidly growing city (population 500,000 in 1900) emancipated itself from royal patronage and flourished as a broad, middle-class institution excelling in popular entertainment, satirical and bohemian diversion, and high art of the most elitist stripe.

Frank Wedekind came to live in Munich in 1889 and wrote his "children's tragedy," *Frühlings Erwachen* (Spring Awakening), in 1891. Mixing sexuality and youthful insecurity with the grotesque, Wedekind scandalized the bourgeois theater and propelled German drama into modernism. Wedekind's role as a writer and performer in Munich's Elf Scharfrichter (Eleven Executioners) cabaret (1901–3) and as a contributor to the satirical weekly *Simplicissimus* (1896–1944, 1954–67) put him in the middle of the city's energetic literary activity and in jail (for insulting the kaiser). The cabaret, *Simplicissimus,* and *Jugend* (1896–1940, from which *Jugendstil* [Art Nouveau] derived its name) were central to Munich's modernist movement and—with the painters of *Der Blaue Reiter* (The Blue Rider)—placed the city with Berlin and Vienna at the forefront of avant-garde culture in Europe.

Elitists Stefan George and Rainer Maria Rilke worked repeatedly in Munich at the turn of the century but never sought each other out. The poetry of George and Rilke holds an unchallenged place in the canon of German literature as does that of other Munich residents of this era: Erich Mühsam, Ricarda Huch, Gustav Meyrink, Otto Julius Bierbaum, and Heinrich and Thomas Mann (Nobel Prize in Literature in 1929). Thomas Mann lived in the city from 1893 until his exile in 1934, and it remained a formative element of his work.

A resurgent Bavarian literature centered in Munich asserted itself at the turn of the century, beginning with Josef Ruederer's *Die Fahnenweihe* (1895; The Consecration of the Flag) and Ludwig Thoma's rural tales from Dachau, *Agricola* (1897). This wave brought the alpine novels of Thoma's close friend Ludwig Ganghofer, the narratives of the tormented Lena Christ, the humorous tales of Eduard Stemplinger, and Georg Queri's songs, literary sketches, and collections of folk material. Of these writers, Thoma found the widest audience outside Bavaria.

Critical voices became ever harder to find in the Munich of the 1920s. In song and on the small stage, Karl Valentin, whose films, sketches, and songs with Liesl Karlstadt assaulted the relationship between language and reality, developed into an uncomfortable figure for the authorities in the Third Reich. Valentin spanned literary genres and epochs; Bertolt Brecht drew on Valentin's aesthetics in developing the theory of Epic Theater and *Verfremdungseffekt* (Alienation Effect). Valentin (*Familiensorgen* [1943; Family Problems]) also anticipated Beckett's theater of the absurd. Thoma's heir as storyteller of the Bavarian condition was Oskar Maria Graf, especially in his *Das bayerische Dekameron* (1928; Bavarian Decameron). Graf remained true to his socialist convictions (he had supported the 1917 Bavarian revolution of Kurt Eisner, Gustav Landauer, and Erich Mühsam) and considered it a personal insult when Hitler's incendiaries did not burn his work in 1933. Lion Feuchtwanger valued Graf's coarse directness above Thoma's lighter touch. Feuchtwanger, born in Munich and a resident (with interruptions) until 1925, renounced an academic career to produce such historical novels as *Jud Süß* (1925; *Jew Süß*), *Die hässliche Herzogin Margarete Maultasch* (1923; *The Ugly Duchess: An Historical Romance*), and *Erfolg* (1930; *Success*), which traces the rise of National Socialism.

Munich was an important breeding ground for National Socialism in the 1920s; the first meetings of the NSDAP (National Socialists) and the Hitler-Putsch (1923) took place there. Later designated "Hauptstadt der Bewegung" (Capital of the Movement, 1935–45) by Adolf Hitler, Munich attracted authors sympathetic to the movement: Edwin Erich Dwinger, Josef Ponten, Hanns Johst, Paul Alverdes, Will Vesper, and Erwin Guido Kolbenheyer.

Inescapably identified with the Munich Agreement (1938) between Hitler, Chamberlain, Deladier, and Mussolini, the Bavarian capital is linked with some of the darkest moments of prewar and wartime history. In 1937, Munich was the site of the *Entartete Kunst* (Depraved Art) exhibition, which vilified modern painting and sculpture; in 1939, an attempt on Hitler's life in the Bürgerbräu-Keller failed; in 1943, the protests of Hans and Sophie Scholl and the White Rose resistance movement ended with the execution of its members.

During the decades of the Cold War and the division of Berlin, Munich acquired the popular appellation "the secret capital of Germany." These 40 years saw the city reach a population of 1 million (1957), surpass other Bavarian cities (Nuremberg, Augsburg, Schweinfurt, and Würzburg) as a center of industry (1964), host the Olympic Games (1972), and become the second publishing city in the world after New York (in 1982, over 300 Munich publishers produced approximately 10,000 new titles).

In the 1960s and 1970s, a contemporary variant of the traditional *Volksstück* emerged, which critiqued social complacency and repression in Bavaria during the economic miracle and the ensuing years. Picking up where Marieluise Fleißer had left off, Martin Sperr in *Jagdszenen aus Niederbayern* (1966; Unting Scenes from Lower Bavaria) and Rainer Werner Fassbinder in *Katzelmacher* (1968) laid the groundwork on which Franz Xaver Kroetz continued to build during the 1970s. Kroetz's *Heimarbeit, Hartnäckig,* and *Michis Blut* (1971; Homework, Stubborn, and *Michi's Blood*), *Globales Interesse* (1972; Global Interest), *Münchner Kindl* (1973; Munich Child), and *Das Nest* (1975; The Nest) all premiered in Munich. The use of Bavarian-colored language was shared by these authors and the poets of the Friedl Brehm Verlag (Feldafing), who moved dialect poetry

out of the domain of *Heimatlyrik* and into the literary avant-garde. Among the Munich writers in Brehm's group were Josef Wittmann, Benno Höllteufel (Carl Ludwig Reichert and Michael Fruth), and Bernhard Setzwein. Brehm's journal *Schmankerl* (1969–86) frequently engaged in critical exchange with the dialect poets of the Munich *Turmschreiber* (Tower Writers) group, whose most prolific members, Helmut Zöpfl, Franz Ringseis, Herbert Schneider, and Leopold Kammerer, tended to adhere to established formal and thematic traditions.

Two of the most conspicuously successful German novelists of the 1970s and 1980s were residents of Munich. Michael Ende's children's tales about Jim Knopf placed him in the forefront of that genre, while his fantastic-realist novels, *Momo* (1973) and *Die unendliche Geschichte* (1979; The Never-Ending Story), acquired cult status among the ecologically sensitive, antiestablishment Green movement. Patrick Süskind's stage success with *Der Kontrabass* (1981; The Double-Bass) was followed in 1985 by his genre-bending, postmodern novel of murder and aroma, *Das Parfum* (Perfume), which dominated the best-seller lists of *Der Spiegel* and the *New York Times* for extended stretches.

Munich awards three literary prizes annually, one prize that alternates between literary and journalistic recipients, two prizes for cabaret or small-stage performance, and four prizes that support film. The Bavarian Academy of Sciences in Munich sponsors the Bayerisches Wörterbuch project (founded 1911), which began publishing its dictionary in 1995. The Ludwig-Maximilians-Universität established its Institut für Bayerische Literaturgeschichte in 1985. This institute produces a quarterly journal, *Literatur in Bayern* (1985–), which is charged with documenting, critically engaging, and supporting the literary life of Bavaria. The Munich Literaturhaus was opened in 1997.

CHRISTOPHER J. WICKHAM

Further Reading

Biller, Josef H., and Hans-Peter Rasp, *München: Kunst und Kulturlexikon: Stadtführer und Handbuch,* Munich: Süddeutscher Verlag, 1972, 4th edition, Munich: Südwest, 1997

Bosl, Karl, editor, *Bosls Bayerische Biographie: 8000 Persönlichkeiten aus 15 Jahrhunderten,* Regensburg: Pustet, 1983

Dünninger, Eberhard, and Dorothee Kiesselbach, editors, *Bayerische Literaturgeschichte: In ausgewählten Beispielen,* 2 vols., Munich: Süddeutscher Verlag, 1965–1967

Hubensteiner, Benno, *Bayerische Geschichte: Staat und Volk, Kunst und Kultur,* Munich: Süddeutscher Verlag, 1977

Jelavich, Peter, *Munich and Theatrical Modernism: Politics, Playwriting, and Performance, 1890–1914,* Cambridge, Massachusetts: Harvard University Press, 1985

Nöhbauer, Hans F., *Kleine bairische Literaturgeschichte,* Munich: Süddeutscher Verlag, 1984

Reiser, Rudolf, *Glanzlichter bayerischer Geschichte: Aus Naturwissenschaft, Technik, Kultur, und Kunst,* Munich: Ehrenwirth, 1988

———, *Zwei Jahrtausende Bayern in Stichworten: Daten, Namen, Fakten,* Munich: Ehrenwirth, 1988

Sackett, R.E., *Popular Entertainment, Class, and Politics in Munich 1900–1923,* Cambridge, Massachusetts: Harvard University Press, 1982

Wadleigh, Henry Rawle, *Munich: History, Monuments, and Art,* London: Unwin, and New York: Stokes, 1910

Weber, Albrecht, editor, *Handbuch der Literatur in Bayern: Vom Frühmittelalter bis zur Gegenwart,* Regensburg: Pustet, 1987

Zehetner, Ludwig, *Das bairische Dialektbuch,* Munich: Beck, 1985

Robert Musil 1880–1942

Among the authors who made substantial contributions to our image of modernism, Robert Musil has for many years remained in the shadow of others such as Joyce, Proust, Kafka, and Thomas Mann. Changing views of the modern period, including theories of postmodernism, have led to an increasing recognition of his importance. His work has been interpreted as being located on the threshold between modernism and the postmodern. In particular, his huge and unfinished novel, *Der Mann ohne Eigenschaften* (1930–43; *The Man without Qualities*), has been read as a major tribute to the literary and philosophical shaping of the century. Musil himself once said that his motivation for writing was to contribute to the intellectual mastering/overcoming (*Bewältigung*) of his time. He had studied civil engineering and philosophy and was well-informed about research in physics and experimental psychology, but he was also one of the very few authors of fiction in this century who made original contributions to theoretical knowledge. His oeuvre, in a more fundamental way than that of other writers, crosses the line between literature and philosophical discourse, which from early Romanticism on had become permeable, and which from the end of the 19th century was blurred. Musil was not only a *poeta doctus,* a writer well aware of philosophical and scientific theory, but his prose is symptomatic of the modern fusion of philosophical thought and literary imagination.

In a self-conscious fashion, Musil's work is European, using, without a trace of nostalgia, the Austro-Hungarian Empire (for the "k.k." of the double monarchy, he invented the term *Kakanien*) as a model for the combination of diversity and homogeneity that has become characteristic of Western and Central European cultures from the Enlightenment forward. The geographical and mental centers of his life were Vienna and Berlin, where he spent most of his life, with a few short excursions to Italy and Paris. Shortly after Hitler came to power in 1933, he left Berlin and returned to Vienna. In 1938, after the annexation of Austria, he left for Switzerland and died under miserable circumstances in Geneva in 1942. Musil led an uneventful life in seclusion, entirely devoted to writing. In terms of the banalities and repetitiveness of modern life, his life was symptomatic of modern reality. The exception was World War I. Similar to most other authors of his generation, he shared the enthusiasm for the outbreak of the war, and he later wrote about these weeks as a time that made an end of the monotony and fragmentation of life. This celebrated union and reconciliation was experienced as a collective ecstasy, which made a life that had lost meaning meaningful again, and it joined together a society that had been demolished into disjointed fragments. The experience of August 1914 (*Augusterlebnis*) was interpreted as a breakthrough of displaced desires. For Musil, as for many others, disillusionment with the realities of the war came quickly. However, Musil turned the memory of August 1914 into a model for an individual and collective experience that had the power to achieve the longed-for unity and cohesion that had been lost in the modern world. His title *Vereinigungen* (1911; *Unions*) preceded the war, but its basic aim of a confluence of divergent interests into a unified life of a shared reality was confirmed by the experience of August 1914 and remained a dominant strand in Musil's writing. It was carried over into his great novel, where

it is one of its organizing principles and the focal point for the Ulrich-Agathe relationship.

In contrast to this ideal, Musil was an outsider in both his life and literary career. He joined no literary group or school; even at the time when he was increasingly recognized as a serious and innovative author during the 1920s, he remained at the margin of social and literary life. He consistently subordinated his life to writing. On several occasions he turned down job offers that would have secured his financial situation. As a result, he was subjected to a life of great insecurity and financial hardship, which ended in extreme poverty. Given his military and technological background and interests, it is surprising that Musil should have turned to literature. Only a few literary authors can be said to have had a noticeable influence on him (among them Paul Valéry, Dostoyevsky, Maurice Maeterlinck, and Hugo von Hofmannsthal). He held most of the literature of his time in low esteem and was particularly scornful of literature that provided an easy emotional identification and a pseudo-profoundness ("Tiefsinn"). More important for the creation of his intellectual cosmos were philosophers, scientists, and anthropologists, among them Nietzsche, Husserl, Ernst Mach, Emerson, and Ludwig Klages. His ideal was an attitude toward life and literature that combined philosophical reflection with the impartial perspective of a scientifically trained observer. In an early diary entry he speaks of a "monsieur le vivisecteur" who perceives the world through the glass of a windowpane or a thick layer of ice. From early on, however, Musil juxtaposes this perspective with an equally significant position, based not upon observation but upon introspection and ecstatic practices. Giving access to an invisible world, ecstasy, imagination, and mystical experiences are not constructed as opposites to the reality of the sciences, but as its complement. For Törleß, the hero of his early novel *Die Verwirrungen des Zöglings Törleß* (1906; *Young Törless*), the square root of minus one and mathematical questions of number theory (imaginary numbers) turn into existential problems about defining the limits of existence. This polarity of the world and the self provided Musil with a basic framework for the construction of the literary world in his two novels, short prose texts, essays, and dramas. Indicative of this basic concern are *Young Törless,* his collection of stories *Unions,* and his essays, which were devoted to contemporary issues in the wake of World War I and to problems of aesthetics and ethics.

Young Törless is an example of his preoccupation with questions of the constitution of reality. The narration follows literary conventions. It is set in a military academy for cadets, which is isolated in a remote location at the margin of the Austrian Empire. These external conditions enable the narration to focus on a microspace made up of dorms, classrooms, a courtyard, and a secret "red chamber," with rare excursions into the immediate environment of a village, where a café and a prostitute are the major objects of attention. The story fuses problems of puberty and interpersonal relations, including sadistic and masochistic excesses, and questions of cognition and the perception of reality. The plot is straightforward. A small sum of money is missing, and when one of the cadets discovers who has stolen it, the culprit is made the object of inquisitory nightly sessions in the red chamber, including torture and dilettantic experiments with hypnosis. Two boys of the group of four and the victim are linked together by their sadistic and complementary masochistic drives, while Törleß, the main character, does not actively participate in the physical torture. He remains in the role of a distanced observer who nonetheless inflicts the gravest psychological pain on the victim. In the end, these secret sessions are discovered, and after being examined by the teachers, Törleß is dismissed from school. His mother comes to take him back home. This is not one of the novels about education or generational conflict, which were popular around the turn of the century. Rather, the constellation of characters in combination with the psychological disturbances resulting from puberty and the artificial, remote environment provide the narrator with the opportunity of exploring philosophical and psychological questions, thereby exposing the two opposite currents running through Musil's writing: a scientific, naturalistic one and a speculative, transcendental one.

His works have been read as reflections of his biography. While it is not difficult to trace models for many events and figures in his novels and stories to his life, his concept of the literary is hostile to a biographical reading of literature. His texts never attempt realistic representations of nonliterary reality. Indeed, beginning with his first literary texts, Musil struggled with the problem as to what constitutes reality. His novel *Young Törless* is an early example of his main concern with a reality that extends into the imaginary, and with the instability ("das Unfeste") at the core of a seemingly solid reality. The present, he once remarked, is but a hypothesis that has not yet been superseded by coming events. His philosophical and literary positions were informed by his knowledge of experimental psychology and post-Newtonian theoretical physics. His life and literary pursuits were invested in a continuous process of reflection on the basic question as to the constitution of reality, the subject, and their possible forms of correlation. He created the intellectual framework for this lifelong pursuit during his years in Berlin where, until 1910, he studied philosophy, completed his doctoral thesis on Ernst Mach, and immersed himself in the philosophical and psychological (*Gestaltpsychologie*) debates of the period. During these years, he also conceived many ideas for the literary projects that were to form the center of his productivity; some were never pursued in detail, while others, including the first plans of *The Man without Qualities,* turned into lifelong preoccupations. After agonizing over them for two years, he also completed his first experimental prose texts, "Die Vollendung der Liebe" and "Die Versuchung der stillen Veronika," which appeared in 1911 under the title *Vereinigungen* ("Unions: The Perfecting of a Love" and "The Temptation of Quiet Veronica" are translated in *Tonka and Other Stories,* 1965). They can be seen as a prelude to and early example of his experimental approach to narration, which, in later years, was concerned with the nonobservable, but broke away from the conventional psychological model of depicting the invisible world of the soul. They met with a cool public response and rejection by many critics.

During these years, he also designed his drama *Die Schwärmer,* published after the war (1921; *The Enthusiasts*), which made an attempt to translate into gestures and theatrical images the irreconcilable clash between the "structure of reality" and the life of the soul. This remained the central problem of Musil's literary characters and was pushed to the limits by the brother-sister relationship in the novel. This was also the time at which Musil developed his lasting fascination with potentiality. The given and present reality, he reasoned, was only one of many possibilities that had materialized. He saw no logic in this development, and he thought that reality, rather than being the inevitable consequence of the past, had to be seen as dependent on chance and the contingencies of incidental constellations. Ulrich, the protagonist of *The Man without Qualities,* reasons as a schoolboy that while creating the world, God thought he might as well do it differently. And later Ulrich argues that if there is a sense for the real, there must also be a sense for the potential. This strong sense of the counterfactual is at the center of Musil's literary imagination, and he developed a writing technique that, by merging philosophical reflection, psychological studies, and literary metaphor, created a considerable freedom from the restrictions of genre and conventional literary language. He used the term *essayism* for this attempt at developing an appropriate literary language for dissolving the given object into the flux of changing perspectives and capturing the anti-Hegelian spirit of potentiality. In terms of plot and constellations for action, it was the expedition into the unknown rather than planned projects, departure rather than arrival, new beginnings rather than results, and openness rather than security that corresponded to his view of fleeting reality.

In the wake of the war, Musil developed his theory of "Gestaltlosigkeit," which emphasized that plasticity was the anthropological condition of humankind. The unprecedented cruel behavior of civilized men during the war had demonstrated, he argued, that no definitive definition of man was possible. Rather than trying to define the ideal man, it had to be acknowledged that the gestalt of human beings varied in infinite mutations according to the varying conditions of life. Ulrich's characterization as a man without qualities, which could as well be translated as an absence of properties or of distinguishing attributes, is a reflection of this anthropological relativism in relation to the definition of the human ideal.

Musil is best known as the author of *The Man without Qualities,* a novel with an insignificant plot. It uses and at the same time subverts traditional forms of narration. The novel's protagonist, Ulrich, takes a one-year "leave from his life." During that time he is exposed to a wide range of social actions and private situations that create opportunities to explore the conditions of constructing reality and biography. The intricate net of actions can be reduced to three interrelated cycles. The first revolves around the satirical "parallel action," a major political project that aims at counterbalancing the envisaged celebration of the German kaiser's 30th year of reign by the Austrian emperor's celebration of his 70th inauguration in 1918, the year that, in real history, saw the collapse of both empires. The second deals with Ulrich and Agathe, who are twins but have not seen each other since early childhood. At the occasion of their father's death, they meet and begin an intensive relationship—Musil was uncertain as to whether it would lead them to incest. The third explores the tempestuous adventures of Clarisse, a character in the orbit of Nietzsche's philosophy of situations of extremity who lives at the verge of madness. All lines, Musil unequivocally stated at several occasions, lead into the war. It is difficult to determine, however, what he meant by the term *war,* and, given his *essayistic* manner of writing, he himself might not have known.

While this is one of the longest novels of the century, which kept Musil occupied from the time he conceived it prior to World War I up until his last day, there are nonetheless good reasons to read Musil as a master of the small form. His entire oeuvre, including the long novel, are refractions of the world in the mode of minimalism. Not only are his short texts, some as short as Kafka's parables, among the best he has written, but he was skillful in disintegrating narrative techniques of the grand genre, the novel, into loosely connected small fragments. In the absence of continuity and logical progression, he perceived life as dispersed into inconsistent facets. It was no longer possible for literature to approach life by simply narrating a story, for everything substantial in reality had lost its narratability (life had become "unerzählerisch"). Life no longer followed a thread but was spread on an infinitely entangled plane ("sich in einer unendlich verwobenen Fläche ausbreitet"). The ever-changing structure of his unfinished huge project, which he called a *novel,* and which transformed his own life into an increasingly painful operation of literary production, provided nothing but an open-ended framework for preventing these facets from falling into incoherence, unintelligibility, and mere subjective arbitrariness.

Musil perhaps draws upon his own experiences in presenting his alter ego, Ulrich, as trained in the sciences and thinking highly of the ideal of scientific precision. At the same time, Ulrich also follows Musil himself in not being satisfied with the answers to the important questions of life that scientific inquiry is capable of giving. Questions of real significance for life will never be answered by knowledge based on empirical research. The examples of Moosbrugger, the killer of a prostitute, or the impetuous Clarisse demonstrate that an attempt to reconstruct life in terms of rational discourse is in vain. In Musil's view, it is not possible to find a rational justification for a specific form of life. Ultimately, action in Musil's novel, and this includes the actions of the rational Ulrich, is without recourse to reason and rational justification. It was already Törleß's discovery that the rational is grounded in the nonrational. He was disturbed by his discovery that finite beings are capable of thinking the infinite. This discovery, later shared by Ulrich, does not lead to religious faith or to the return of metaphysics but to developing an attitude complementing that of the scientist, which could be called transcendental speculation. Musil was not content with the position of epistemological and ethical indeterminacy nor with clinging to systemic definitions at a time when the sciences themselves had begun eroding the very basis of this Newtonian concept of reality. He believed that no careful balancing act was possible in the way Kant had balanced abstract categories with the world of the senses. An irreconcilable rift needed to be acknowledged, he argued, as a precondition of coming to terms with the modern condition. *The Man without Qualities* can be read as a literary experiment investigating the implications of this erosion for the concrete acts of constructing life and developing reasons for the very *thing* of living by exploring other forms of life.

Musil's work addresses the ever looming threat of incoherence and madness, and it is itself an example of modern literature verging on the threshold of losing its grip on reality and slipping into the nonsensible. For Musil (and many of his contemporary authors) this dubious condition of the modern self in the world is ambivalent—threatening and, at the same time, an object of desire. The experiences of sense slipping away and the intelligibility of reality fading are, in Musil's view, borderline experiences that define human existence in a fundamental way. From his first novel *Young Törless* until the last chapter of his unfinished novel, Musil fantasized about the possibility of leaving one's own mind behind and slipping into a state of other-mindedness. He was infatuated with European and Asian mysticism as well as anthropological accounts of trance and magical practices (Lévy-Bruhl), and he excerpted material from Klages's *Vom kosmogonischen Eros* (Of Cosmogenic Eros). For such experiences of the transcendent, Musil invented the name "der andere Zustand" and reflected on it as a subjective as well as a shared experience (between Ulrich and Agathe). The openness of the "novel" provided him with the literary means for exposing these questions and developing strategies for exploring them in depth.

The much-misunderstood name "der andere Zustand" is Musil's attempt to explore the consequences of radical epistemological and ethical relativism. If the structure of the world is determined by the mind and the process of perception, the question arises as to what the world looks like in another mind. The world is *our* world and differs from that of other times and cultures because *our* mind is structured in a specific way. Our world, then, represents one possibility among other, equally possible worlds. This is young Ulrich's idea, minus God as the creator. But what would this other world be like? If we were other-minded, what kind of world would we live in? Is it at all possible to envision a world that is not ours, such as the world of a shaman? Musil's project was concerned with exploring the potential of literature for imagining such a counterfactual, alternative world. The "andere Zustand" has been interpreted as his modern version of utopia. However, there is a fundamental difference between utopia as an imagined world based on our own experiences and extending into our own hopes and a world constructed by a different mind. Musil's imagined figures are hovering at the verge of complete incoherence and madness in order to explore what it might be like to be other-minded and live in a world that fundamentally differs from *our* world. The mere severing of ties to our world does not in itself lead to the experience of another world but just to the absence of the familiar order. This is the experience of Moosbrugger and Clarisse, whose world is slipping into inconsistency and incoherence. The "andere Zustand," however, is Musil's attempt to do away with both the centered self and a responding and coherent space and to create images that are capable of explaining what it means to be out of one's own world. This is why accounts of mystic experiences fascinated him: they seemed to offer a language capable of describing what it is like to replace *our* self and *our* world with a different self and its different world. It is literature, and not philosophy or psychology, that, in Musil's view, is fit to provide the means for investigating this state of other-mindedness.

In an attempt to overcome the modern divide and to introduce the scientific ideal of precision into matters of life, Ulrich suggests the creation of a world secretariat for precision and soul ("Erdensekretariat der Genauigkeit und Seele") and adds that all other tasks have become obsolete and immaterial. Despite its satirical wording, this suggestion is meant deadly earnest. Many people, Musil wrote, perish through their attempt at leading a life. He was convinced that the literary imagination was well equipped for responding to the question that was first asked by Socrates: How shall we live? And he set out to reshape the novel to make it fit for responding to this question that had not lost its relevance but had been radically transformed under the conditions of modernity when the sciences had finally replaced metaphysics.

BERND HÜPPAUF

Biography

Born in Klagenfurt, Austria, 6 November 1880. Engineering student at Technische Hochschule, Brno, 1898–1901; philosophy student, University of Berlin, 1903–5, Ph.D., 1908; served in the military, 1901–2; served in the Austrian army, 1914–16; hospitalized, 1916; editor of army newspaper, 1916–17; worked as an instructor for civil engineering at the Technical University of Stuttgart, 1902–3; in Berlin, 1903–11; archivist in Vienna, 1911–13; editor of *Die Neue Rundschau*, Berlin, 1914; worked in the press section of the office of foreign affairs, Vienna, 1919–20; consultant to the defense ministry, 1920–22; freelance writer in Vienna, then moved to Berlin, 1931–33, Vienna, 1933–38, and Switzerland, 1938–42. Bronze cross for military service; Kleist Prize, 1923; City of Vienna Prize, 1924. Died 15 April 1942.

Selected Works

Collections

Gesammelte Werke in Einzelausgaben, edited by Adolf Frisé, 3 vols., 1952–57; revised edition, 2 vols., 1978
Gesammelte Werke in neun Bänden, edited by Adolf Frisé, 1978

Fiction

Die Verwirrungen des Zöglings Törless, 1906; as *Young Törless*, translated by Eithne Wilkins and Ernst Kaiser, 1955
Vereinigungen (includes the stories "Die Vollendung der Liebe" and "Die Versuchung der stillen Veronika"), 1911; as "Unions: The Perfecting of a Love" and "The Temptation of Quiet Veronica," in *Tonka and Other Stories*, translated by Eithne Wilkins and Ernst Kaiser, 1965
Drei Frauen (includes the stories "Grigia," "Die Portugiesin," and "Tonka"), 1924; in *Five Women*, translated by Eithne Wilkins and Ernst Kaiser, 1965; as *Tonka and Other Stories* (includes translation of *Vereinigungen*), 1965
Der Mann ohne Eigenschaften, completed by Martha Musil, 3 vols., 1930–43; edited by Adolf Frisé, 1952; revised edition, 1965; as *The Man without Qualities*, translated by Eithne Wilkins and Ernst Kaiser, 3 vols., 1953–60; translated by Sophie Wilkins and Burton Pike, 2 vols., 1995
Tonka and Other Stories (includes the stories in *Vereinigungen* and *Drei Frauen*), translated by Eithne Wilkins and Ernst Kaiser, 1965

Plays

Die Schwärmer, 1921; as *The Enthusiasts*, translated by Andrea Simon, 1982
Vinzenz und die Freundin bedeutender Männer, 1923

Other

Beitrag zur Beurteilung der Lehren Machs, 1908; as *Mach's Theories*, translated by Kevin Mulligan, 1982
Das hilflose Europa, 1922
Nachlass zu Lebzeiten, 1936; as *Posthumous Papers of a Living Author*, translated by Peter Wortsman, 1987
Theater: Kritisches und Theoretisches, edited by Marie-Louise Roth, 1965
Der Deutsche Mensch als Symptom, edited by Karl Corino and Elisabeth Albertsen, 1967
Briefe nach Prag, edited by Barbara Köpplova and Kurt Krolop, 1971
Tagebücher, edited by Adolf Frisé, 2 vols., 1976; as *Diaries 1899–1941*, translated by Philip Payne, 1998

Texte aus dem Nachlass, 1980
Briefe 1901–1942, edited by Adolf Frisé, 2 vols., 1981
Selected Writings, edited by Burton Pike, 1986
Precision and Soul: Essays and Addresses, edited and translated by Burton Pike and David S. Luft, 1990

Further Reading

Arnold, Heinz Ludwig, editor, *Robert Musil*, Text und Kritik, vol. 21/22, Munich: Edition Text und Kritik, 1983
Arntzen, Helmut, *Musil-Kommentar*, 2 vols., Munich: Winkler, 1980–82
Berghahn, Wilfried, *Robert Musil in Selbstzeugnissen und Bilddokumenten*, Reinbek bei Hamburg: Rowohlt, 1963
Corino, Karl, *Robert Musil: Leben und Werk in Bildern und Texten*, Reinbek bei Hamburg: Rowohlt, 1988
Dinklage, Karl, editor, *Robert Musil: Leben, Werk, Wirkung*, Reinbek bei Hamburg: Rowohlt, 1960
Hickman, Hannah, *Robert Musil and the Culture of Vienna*, London: Croom Helm, 1984
Luft, David S., *Robert Musil and the Crisis of European Culture, 1889–1942*, Berkeley: University of California Press, 1980
O'Connor, Kathleen, *Robert Musil and the Tradition of the German Novelle*, Riverside, California: Ariadne Press, 1992
Peters, Frederick, *Robert Musil: Master of the Hovering Life*, New York: Columbia University Press, 1978
Rogowski, Christian, *Implied Dramaturgy: Robert Musil and the Crisis of Modern Drama*, Riverside, California: Ariadne Press, 1993

Der Mann ohne Eigenschaften 1930–1943
Novel by Robert Musil

Written between 1924 and 1942, Robert Musil's *Der Mann ohne Eigenschaften* (1930–43; *The Man without Qualities*) is one of the monuments of 20th-century literature. Its impact has been enormous but, similar to the impact of Proust's *À la recherche du temps perdu* (1913–27; *In Search of Lost Time*), diffuse. Neither of these great novels lends itself to imitation but rather to experience, study, and thought. The greatest impact of *The Man without Qualities* is to be found in its effect on individual readers. Musil's novel has kept its modernity: its central concern, how we are to reconstruct appropriate moral values in a world transformed by science and the disappearance of the values of an earlier time, is as urgent today as it was when Musil was writing.

Musil was trained as a scientist, and science had, by the beginning of the 20th century, lost its metaphysics, basing itself instead on probability and functional relativity rather than on absolute first principles. The transient, symbolic, and tentative nature of thought in nonscientific fields came to be true of science as well. There was a new opportunity, after the 19th century's rationalistic positivism, to reconcile humanistic and scientific endeavor, and Musil, as a trained psychologist, mathematician, and engineer, widely read in philosophy, was well situated to try to bring about this reconciliation.

Musil's goal was to reconcile the irrational with the rational, to unite precision with soul, and to reach out toward new basic moral principles that could govern peoples' actions in a world that had done away with fixed principles. In *The Man without Qualities* this problem devolves on the central character, Ulrich, a mathematician by profession, with the independent narrator looking over his shoulder.

Musil's fiction was experimental from the beginning, but in *The Man without Qualities* his "thought-experiment" is on a far larger scale than in anything else he wrote. Thematically related to his first novel, *Die Verwirrungen des Zöglings Törless* (1906; *Young Törless*), his short stories, and his two plays, *The Man without Qualities* vastly expands his canvas. Rejecting the concept of narrative order in this novel, he chose instead to base his narrative on the tangled web of ideas and feelings as characters perceive or experience them at given moments in given situations. Musil's central technique of "essayism," in which scenes of this kind are interspersed with interwoven authorial commentary, bridges the solipsistic lives of his characters and makes them representative of Western culture in crisis. The concept of linear chronological time fades into a shadowy background, becoming an ironic setting for its foreground. (*The Man without Qualities* opens in August 1913; unfinished and unfinishable, however, it never reaches August 1914.) The characters are caught in human predicaments that reflect those of an entire culture, and they head unawares toward destruction.

Ulrich is taking a year off to decide how to take life seriously. He is a financially independent and marvelously gifted man with every talent, none of which he is able to use in the service of the hollow social, political, and cultural reality of the last years of the old Austrian Empire, which the novel calls "Kakania." Ulrich's situation is one of social paralysis and furious intellection. His highest, almost mystical belief is in possibility, an offshoot, of course, of probability theory: anything that happens is only one of a number of random possible things that might have happened in its place, and of no greater potential value than any of the possibilities that did not make it as far as reality. The conglomerate nature of the Austrian Empire, containing as it did many clashing minority languages and cultures clamoring for recognition and separation—possibilities struggling mightily to become actualities—gave Musil a perfect paradigm in the real world for an old order of thought that needed to be superseded by new values.

Since accident or contingency rather than necessity rules possibility, almost any scene in the novel could be expanded in any direction at will, or other scenes inserted. And since the scenes are situated in the momentary envelopes of the characters' thoughts and feelings, eschatology, the sense of an ending toward which the whole is driving, disappears except as a remote, ironic undertone. The posthumous material, a great mass of early and late drafts that is now partially available in translation, contains the most varied ideas for the novel, as well as many alternative versions of scenes that found their way into the novel as we now have it; there are, however, no indications of what final form Musil would have given it. Critics have been arguing for years about what Musil's final intentions might have been, but this will always remain a matter for conjecture.

The portions of *The Man without Qualities* published in Musil's lifetime, in 1930 and 1932–33, were critically acclaimed. Elias Canetti, Ingeborg Bachmann, and Thomas Mann are among many who have paid tribute to Musil's epic novel. Today it is frequently ranked with Proust's *In Search of Lost Time* and Joyce's *Ulysses* as one of the three greatest modern novels.

BURTON PIKE

Editions

First edition: *Der Mann ohne Eigenschaften*, vols. 1–2, Berlin: Rowohlt, 1930–33; vol. 3, completed by Martha Musil, Lausanne: Impremerie centrale, 1943

Authoritative edition: in *Gesammelte Werke in neun Bänden*, vols. 1–5, edited by Adolf Frisé, Reinbek: Rowohlt, 1978

Translations: *The Man without Qualities*, translated by Eithne Wilkins and Ernst Kaiser, 3 vols., London: Secker and Warburg, and New York: Coward-McCann, 1953–60; this translation is based on the edition of Musil's *Gesammelte Werke in Einzelausgaben* of the 1950s. The authoritative translation is *The Man without Qualities*, translated by Sophie Wilkins and Burton Pike, 2 vols., New York: Knopf, 1995; this translation is based on the authoritative 1978 edition of Musil's *Gesammelte Werke in neun Bänden*, edited by Adolf Frisé, and it contains much material not in the translation from the 1950s.

Further Reading

Dahan-Gaida, Laurence, *Musil: Savoir et fiction*, Saint-Denis: Presses Universitaires de Vincennes, 1994

Heydebrand, Renate von, *Die Reflexionen Ulrichs in Robert Musils Roman "Der Mann ohne Eigenschaften,"* Münster: Aschendorff, 1966

Honold, Alexander, *Die Stadt und der Krieg: Raum- und Zeitkonstruktion in Robert Musils Roman "Der Mann ohne Eigenschaften,"* Munich: Fink, 1995

Janik, Allan, and Stephen Edelston Toulmin, *Wittgenstein's Vienna*, New York: Simon and Schuster, and London: Weidenfeld and Nicolson, 1973

Luft, David S., *Robert Musil and the Crisis of European Culture, 1880–1942*, Berkeley: University of California Press, 1980

Payne, Philip, *Robert Musil's "The Man without Qualities": A Critical Study*, Cambridge: Cambridge University Press, 1988

Roth, Marie-Louise, *Robert Musil: Ethik und Ästhetik*, Munich: List, 1972

Schöne, Albrecht, "Zum Gebrauch des Konjunktivs bei Robert Music," *Euphorion* 55 (1965)

Die Verwirrungen des Zöglings Törleß
1906
Novel by Robert Musil

Robert Musil's first novel, *Die Verwirrungen des Zöglings Törleß* (*Young Törless*), marked a new departure in German prose. It employs a scientific precision of observation and language to analyze the bewildering psychology of a developing adolescent. It has been called a forerunner of Expressionism, but two of its characters, Beineberg and Reiting, prefigure the mentality of Nazism. It was also made into an excellent movie by Volker Schlöndorff in 1966 (*Young Törless*).

This novel is a study of the coalescing of Törleß's personality as the result of his experiences in a military boarding school, when he is away from his parents for the first time. It explores the inadequacy of language to represent the complexity of feelings and perceptions associated with the process of a person's development, and it experiments with using metaphor to convey the subtle interaction of perceptions, feelings, and ideas that occur during that psychological process.

The school that is the novel's setting educates upper-class Austrians to be the future leaders of the Austrian Empire. It is an education whose values are totally at variance with—and dangerously oblivious to—the turbulent and in part malevolent emotions and attitudes of the pupils. These emotions and attitudes threaten in many ways to undermine the school's outmoded, idealistic notion of *Bildung* (education) as a system of fundamental order in a fundamentally ordered world. The threat to order by Beineberg's and Reiting's appeal to individual and mass hysteria makes this novel an uncomfortable (and, of course, unwitting) precursor of the rise of fascism, and thus makes it still relevant in today's world. *Young Törless* is not a political novel, but it presents a clearly implied picture of the old Austrian Empire as a nation out of the modern mainstream. This empire was a far-flung pluralistic conglomeration, multiethnic and multilingual, with a weak sense of nation; Musil was to memorialize it as Kakanien in *Der Mann ohne Eigenschaften* (1930–43; *The Man Without Qualities*).

Musil's central concern in this novel, which marks it as one of the first major experiments in literary modernism, is its paradoxical attitude toward language. Language reduces the complex tangle of rational and irrational processes that together make up human thinking to a single strand, which, in turn, falsifies them. In this novel, Musil wants to develop a language that will be adequate to rendering the thinking process in all its complexity, that will fuse the rational and irrational elements of experience. As a consequence, Musil's language is on the one hand, extremely analytical—the narrator is a detached, observing adult, a kind of hovering scientist who dissects Törleß' reactions—and, on the other hand, extremely metaphorical. A rich swarm of metaphors aims to recreate with precision in the reader the irrational emotions that the boy Törleß experiences in various confrontations. Musil was a trained mathematician and psychologist, and one of the most important aspects of this novel is the striking and confident way in which it brings science into the realm of aesthetic belles lettres.

Musil was not interested in reclaiming traditional moral values; as a scientist he reports and analyzes. Musil was aiming to create a new *kind* of aesthetics. Since *Young Törless* was well received when it was published and quickly recognized as a pathbreaking achievement, it represents a major contribution to the development of literary modernism.

Musil had a strong interest in the irrational and its connection to the rational world. The unconscious and the irrational did not interest him as such; he was intrigued by them only when they emerge at the boundary at which they become conscious and a determining factor in a person's behavior. (Musil's psychological training was as a behaviorist; he had little patience with psycho-analysis.) The central vision of the irrational in the novel occurs when Törleß, lying on his back, looks up at the sky and is suddenly struck by what the mathematical concept of infinity must *mean*. His shock of recognition and his inability to integrate the concept of infinity with his reaction to it can only be expressed in a series of metaphors. The same is true as he tries to integrate the concept of irrational numbers into the ordered scheme of things, or when he tries to put into words his powerful sexual feelings. When at the novel's end he tries to explain the complexity of his feelings to the school's board of inquiry in their rational language, they don't understand what he's talking about.

The characters in this novel are credible, complex, and three-dimensional in a way that was to elude Kafka and the young Thomas Mann. This stage in Törleß's life presents vividly an adolescent in whom character, attitudes, and experience are gradually coalescing into the later, fixed personality of the adult—an adult who in later life, as projected by the narrator, will not be particularly ideal or sympathetic. The other characters in the novel, even the minor ones, are presented dispassionately as living in their own solipsistic worlds.

Musil's invention of a new literary technique and his ability to handle its complexities so brilliantly marked the arrival of a major literary talent and one of the first achievements of modernism. The influential critic Alfred Kerr greeted the novel in a glowing review when it was published.

BURTON PIKE

Editions

First edition: *Die Verwirrungen des Zöglings Törless*, Vienna: Wiener Verlag, 1906
Translation: *Young Törless*, translated by Eithne Wilkins and Ernst Kaiser, New York: Pantheon, and London: Secker and Warburg, 1955

Further Reading

Brosthaus, Heribert, *Der Entwicklungsroman einer Idee*, Würzburg: Gugel, 1969
Corngold, Stanley, "Patterns of Justification in *Young Torless*," in *Neverending Stories: Toward a Critical Narratology*, edited by Ann Clark Fehn et al., Princeton, New Jersey: Princeton University Press, 1992
Kontje, Todd, "Organized Violence/Violating Order: Robert Musil's *Die Verwirrungen des Zöglings Törleß*," *Seminar* 24, no. 3 (1988)
Stern, J.P., "History in Robert Musil's *Törleß*," in *Teaching the Text*, edited by Susanne Kappeler and Norman Bryson, London and Boston: Routledge, 1983
Varsava, Jerry A., "Törless at the Limits of Language: A Revised Reading," *Seminar* 20, no. 3 (1984)

Mystery Plays

The term *mystery play* derives from the medieval French word *mystère*, which denotes any serious play, not necessarily one on a religious subject. (Despite the medieval English usage, it has nothing to do with trade guilds.) Today, the word denotes any medieval religious play; the corresponding German *Mysterienspiele*, however, is rarely used, since scholars prefer to emphasize the differences between liturgical and nonliturgical plays and between Easter plays, Passion plays, and Corpus Christi plays.

German scholars use the term *Osterfeiern*, Easter Offices, to characterize the oldest liturgical dramas from the German-speaking area, which were sung in Latin by clergy and choir members wearing vestments as part of the divine service, notably on Easter Day. They are a European phenomenon, but the great majority of the extant texts come from the area of the old German Empire (*Reich*).

The surviving texts suggest that nonliturgical religious plays begin to be written in German from about 1250, although just how and why the transition to writing in German comes about is unclear. The great majority of plays continue to emphasize the importance of Easter. Passion plays (*Passionsspiele*), dealing with the events culminating in Christ's crucifixion and resurrection, seem to be a spontaneous new development deriving from the spirituality of that age, which concentrated on the figure of the suffering Christ. Some plays limit themselves to the few days preceding Holy Week, others include scenes from Christ's earlier ministry, and others include Old Testament scenes considered to have prefigurative significance. Texts such as the Lucerne Passion play, make clear that they aim to teach about Christianity along with praising God and honoring their city. Easter plays (*Osterspiele*) begin with Easter morning. The greatest difficulty in interpretation is presented by manuscripts such as the *Innsbrucker Osterspiel* (1391; Innsbruck Easter Play). The work's stage directions suggest that a section of text was sung in Latin followed by spoken German that was a close or free rendering of the sung Latin text. Usually the Latin is not given in full but is restricted to an incipit, one line or a single word.

Several towns developed a tradition of regular performances of a Passion play involving the whole community. Unlike the liturgical plays, these works were performed outdoors, usually on the principal square of the town, on which stands ("bleachers") for spectators and other major structures were erected at municipal expense. The best documented of these series were the performances in Lucerne between 1453 and 1616, by which time other kinds of drama were well established. The tradition persisted in Lucerne, which was the only German-speaking Swiss canton to remain Catholic after the Reformation. Although the Reformation made good use of theater and dramatizations of biblical material, Protestants were generally hostile to the portrayal on stage of Christ's suffering. The Lucerne manuscripts and other material concerning the organization of the performance—including the famous stage plans for the two days of the 1583 performance—have survived thanks to the deliberate effort of Renward Cysat, the town clerk and, in effect, the roving ambassador of the city state of Lucerne. (Cysat was also the director [*Regent*] of three performances; his death in 1614 caused the postponement of the final performance.)

Citizens vied with one another to have a part in these productions; they had to provide their own costumes and small properties and to pay on a sliding scale for the text of their parts. All the actors entered in a procession at the start of the 12-hour performance and sat in stalls around the acting area except when involved in a scene. With this simultaneous staging (*Simultanbühne*), it was possible to have one scene with dialogue and another mimed scene going on simultaneously.

Tyrol, straddling the Austrian-Italian border, is another area from which a group of texts survive, again due to the efforts of one man, Vigil Raber, a professional painter, who was involved in the organization of several performances in Bozen (now known officially by its Italian name Bolzano) and Sterzing (now Vipiteno) between 1510 and his death in 1552.

Corpus Christi processions became commonplace after the introduction of this feast in 1264, but in the German-speaking area, only a few plays resulted. Surviving material from Freiburg im Breisgau shows the procession evolving into a processional play. We also have extant a small number of plays on separate episodes from the Easter season—the Last Supper, the Deposition of Christ's body from the Cross, his appearance to two disciples on the way to Emmaus (known by the Latin name, *Peregrinus* [Pilgrim]), and related material such as the life of Mary Magdalene, the Ascension, and the Assumption of Mary.

The German-speaking area has far fewer saints' plays than France and also relatively few plays concerned with the Christmas season. Short plays dramatizing Old Testament episodes are rare but include from Tyrol a David and Goliath play. We know the names of directors of performances, such as Cysat and Raber, but the plays are almost always anonymously authored; in some cases, clergy approval of the theological correctness of texts had to be obtained before performances were authorized.

Our picture of how widespread dramatic performances were in the medieval period has been changed radically in recent decades, notably by the appearance of Bernd Neumann's *Geistliches Schauspiel*. As he makes clear, however, the picture is still far from complete; many more archives remain to be checked thoroughly, especially in the area of the former German Democratic Republic. For the moment, we have the impression of certain areas or centers being especially prolific, such as Hessen around Frankfurt am Main, from where records of performances of various kinds of plays survive. In the longer term, this impression may prove illusory, and the final picture may be more even.

JOHN E. TAILBY

Further Reading

Bergmann, Rolf, *Katalog der deutschsprachigen geistlichen Spiele und Marienklagen des Mittelalters,* Munich: Beck, 1986

Brett-Evans, David, *Von Hrotsvit bis Folz und Gengenbach: Eine Geschichte des mittelalterlichen deutschen Dramas,* 2 vols., Berlin: Schmidt, 1975

Evans, Marshall Blakemore, *The Passion Play of Lucerne,* New York: Modern Language Association of America, and Oxford: Oxford University Press, 1943

Linke, Hansjürgen, "Germany and German-speaking Central Europe," in *The Theatre of Medieval Europe*, edited by Eckehard Simon, Cambridge and New York: Cambridge University Press, 1991

Meredith, Peter, and John E. Tailby, editors, *The Staging of Religious Drama in Europe in the Later Middle Ages: Texts and Documents in English Translation*, Kalamazoo: Western Michigan University Press, 1983

Muir, Lynette R., *The Biblical Drama of Medieval Europe*, Cambridge and New York: Cambridge University Press, 1995

Neumann, Bernd, *Geistliches Schauspiel im Zeugnis der Zeit: Zur Aufführung mittelalterlicher religiöser Dramen im deutschen Sprachgebiet*, 2 vols., Munich: Artemis, 1987

Schottman, Brigitta, editor and translator, *Das Redentiner Osterspiel*, Stuttgart: Reclam, 1975

Touber, Anthonius H., *Das Donaueschinger Passionsspiel*, Stuttgart: Reclam, 1985

Young, Karl, *The Drama of the Medieval Church*, 2 vols., Oxford: Clarendon Press, 1933

Mysticism

Although mysticism as a religious, spiritual, and literary movement reached its highest development in 13th- and 14th-century Europe, almost all world religions at all times of human history report mystical phenomena and visions experienced by religious men and women. Even though today these phenomena are less reported and generally regarded as obscure and sometimes even as a sign of mental illness, mysticism as a paranormal phenomenon has also occurred in the 20th century in both the Eastern and the Western world, and it is still often considered as a stage of divine illumination. Philosophers such as Martin Buber (1878–1965) and writers such as Robert Musil (1880–1942) have demonstrated that mysticism has a vitality and profound meaning for their work.

Mysticism (Greek "myo," to close, or to keep silent) basically means the experience of visions and revelations of divine matters. The mystic perceives images of the Godhead or saints, and in this vision a discussion often follows that implies concrete messages for the seer. The mystical experience is mostly preceded by intensive fasting and praying, deprivation of sleep, and other forms of deliberate asceticism, all of which lead to a kind of rapture, which in turn could involve a spiritual revelation. Modern visionaries often seek to gain access to these out-of-the-world experiences by means of drugs, whereas medieval mystics relied on natural resources and theological practices to prepare themselves for the spiritual epiphany. Other situations such as deep sleep or unconsciousness, the heavy loss of blood, or hunger could also trigger mystic experiences. True mysticism is a religious phenomenon that claims that a divine force enters the mystic's mind and communicates with him or her, creating a type of ecstasy.

The earliest medieval mystical visions were reported by male clerics such as Bishop Gregory of Tours, in his *Historia Francorum* (583), and Pope Gregory the Great, in his *Dialogi de vitis patrum Italicorum* (594). Some of the revelations took the mystics on fantastic visionary journeys through the universe, hell, purgatory, and heaven and put them in direct contact with the Godhead. Such was purportedly the case for the Holstein farmer Gottschalk, who after his return or recovery provided an extensive account of his divine experiences to two priests in 1190.

Irrespective of how we would view the religious experience of any of the mystics throughout the centuries, most of them felt a strong urge to discuss their visions in amazingly expressive images and in highly eloquent fashions. Medieval Europe witnessed, at least since the sixth century and certainly until as late as the 15th century, an enormous outburst of mystical literature, which scholarship has only recently begun to appreciate as highly valuable poetic, historical, and religious documents. To name but a few, the 11th-century Hugo of Flavigny composed his *Chronicon*, and his contemporary Petrus Damiani wrote his *De variis miraculis narratio*; Elisabeth von Schönau (ca. 1129–64) and Hildegard von Bingen (1098–1179) produced outstanding literary accounts of their revelations in the 12th century; and the 13th-century Dutch beguine Hadewijch and the North German nuns Mechthild von Magdeburg (ca. 1208–82/97), Gertrud the Great (1265–1301/2), and Mechthild von Hackeborn (1241/42–99) dictated their breathtaking and aesthetically powerful visions to their confessors and scribes. During the 14th century, the Swedish mystic Birgitta of Sweden, the French mystic Marguerite Porete, and the Italian mystic St. Catherine of Siena wrote extensively about their revelations; at the turn of that century, the English mystic Margery Kempe produced a highly curious autobiographical account of her mysticism. In the 15th century, the German mystic Magdalena Beutler of Freiburg and the Dutch mystic Mary of Nijmeghen copied down their own spiritual visions. The 14th century also witnessed the emergence of a number of so-called *Sister Books*, collections of texts written by female authors in South German and Swiss Dominican convents.

Mysticism proved to be an essential vehicle for many medieval women to explore the world of literacy because they claimed that a divine voice encouraged them to put down their revelations in writing. Although no medieval German woman writer is known to have been involved in secular literature, in the world of religious experiences they quickly proved to be superb writers and narrators who dramatically succeeded in expressing their visions in strong and meaningful literary terms and images. Hildegard von Bingen wrote in Latin about her startling revelations in various books. More typical of medieval women's level of education, Mechthild von Magdeburg and the many South German Dominican nuns such as Elsbeth Stagel did not know Latin and resorted to the vernacular, and so they nonetheless contributed in their own way to medieval German literature. Surprisingly, as we can tell from the use of similar genres and poetic images, these mystical accounts reflect a deep familiarity with courtly literature. The mystics relied heavily on courtly models in order to come to terms with the ineffable and to provide concrete expressions for their visions. Consequently, many of the mystical accounts contain shockingly erotic passages in which the visionaries report their intimate union with the Godhead, the so-called *unio mystica*.

As mysticism was always a form of highly private, intimate experience, the written accounts often transformed into intensively autobiographical confessions that involved dialogues between the soul and the Godhead. Mechthild von Magdeburg also carefully outlined the way in which she was charged with writing down her vision and indicated that a full understanding of her work would be possible only after nine readings of her text. Many times the female mystics resorted to nuptial images, since they perceived themselves as God's brides. Their supposed intensive experiences as God's mother and nurse also played a significant role in their mysticism and writing, perhaps in imitation of the Virgin Mary and her suckling of the Christ child. Moreover, the mystics quite commonly reported having been witnesses of Christ's crucifixion and then having experienced a form of stigmatization on their own bodies.

German women's mysticism in the 12th and 13th centuries was influenced both by older traditions established by Hildegard von Bingen and Elisabeth von Schönau and by male mysticism that had been developed in earlier centuries and had been closely linked with early forms of scholasticism. The founder of the Cistercian order, Bernhard of Clairvaux (1090–1153), who corresponded with Hildegard von Bingen and admired her for her visionary power, became one of the most significant sources for German female mysticism because of his interpretation of the Song of Songs. In particular, the Franciscan David von Augsburg (ca. 1200–1272), the Dominican Meister Eckhart (1260–1328), and his disciples Johannes Tauler (ca. 1300–1361) and Heinrich Seuse (ca. 1295–1366) dominated late-medieval mysticism. Both they and their female contemporaries were responsible for far-reaching innovations in the German language, because they had to struggle to express all their visions and experiences in appropriate terms that often were not yet available. Many abstract nouns still in use today, with endings such as "-ung(e)," "-heit," "-keit," and "-nis," and many adjective terms to express the ineffable, including "unbegrîfelîch," "unsprechlîch," and "unsehelîch," came into use only because the mystics and scholastics coined them in order to describe their revelations to their readers.

Another outstanding feature of the mystics' language was the use of paradox, oxymorons, and imagery from hymns. In particular, the reflections of the Song of Songs in the Old Testament can be traced within many mystical discourses. One of the most impressive contributions of German mysticism to language and literature was the development of highly expressive imagery for metaphysical experiences that refute any rational explanation but invite emotional-religious admiration and imitation.

Medieval mysticism continued its influence far into the modern age, and traces of mysticism can be seen in the work of such personalities as Martin Luther (1483–1546), Jakob Böhme (1575–1624), Angelus Silesius (1624–77), and Catharina Regina von Greiffenberg (1633–94). Mystical experiences have also been claimed for Hugo von Hofmannsthal's "Chandos-Brief" (1902; Lord Chandos Letter), Rainer Maria Rilke's *Stunden-Buch* (1905; Book of Hours), Alfred Döblin's *November* (1939–50), Hermann Broch's *Tod des Vergil* (1945; Death of Virgil), and Peter Handke's "Die Wiederholung" (1986; The Repetition).

ALBRECHT CLASSEN

See also Jakob Böhme; Hildegard von Bingen

Further Reading

Bynum, Caroline Walker, *Jesus as Mother: Studies in the Spirituality of the High Middle Ages*, Berkeley: University of California Press, 1982
Clark, Anne L., *Elisabeth of Schönau: A Twelfth-Century Visionary*, Philadelphia: University of Pennsylvania Press, 1992
Classen, Albrecht, "Flowing Light of the Godhead: Binary Oppositions of Self and God in Mechthild von Magdeburg," *Studies in Spirituality* 7 (1997)
Dinzelbacher, Peter, *Mittelalterliche Frauenmystik*, Paderborn: Schöningh, 1993
Dinzelbacher, Peter, editor, *Wörterbuch der Mystik*, Stuttgart: Kröner, 1989
Foley-Beining, Kathleen, *The Body and Eucharistic Devotion in Catharina Regina von Gireffenberg's "Meditations,"* Columbia, South Carolina: Camden House, 1997
Hernández, Julio A., *Studien zum religiös-ethischen Wortschatz der deutschen Mystik*, Berlin: Schmidt, 1984
Lewis, Gertrud Jaron, *Bibliographie zur deutschen Frauenmystik des Mittelalters*, Berlin: Schmidt, 1989
———, *By Women, for Women, about Women: The Sister-Books of Fourteenth-Century Germany*, Toronto: Pontifical Institute of Mediaeval Studies, 1996
McGinn, Bernard, editor, *Meister Eckhart and the Beguine Mystics: Hadewijch of Brabant, Mechthild of Magdeburg, and Marguerite Porete*, New York: Continuum, 1994
Petroff, Elizabeth, editor, *Medieval Women's Visionary Literature*, New York and Oxford: Oxford University Press, 1986
Ruh, Kurt, *Geschichte der abendländischen Mystik*, 3 vols., Munich: Beck, 1990–96
Szarmach, Paul E., editor, *An Introduction to the Medieval Mystics of Europe: Fourteen Original Essays*, Albany: State University of New York Press, 1984
Tobin, Frank, *Mechthild von Magdeburg: A Medieval Mystic in Modern Eyes*, Columbia, South Carolina: Camden House, 1995
Wagner-Egelhaaf, Martina, *Mystik der Moderne: Die visionäre Ästhetik der deutschen Literatur im 20. Jahrhundert*, Stuttgart: Metzler, 1989

Mythology

Derived from the ancient Greek word for speech and fable, mythology, in its original meaning, comprises a society's traditional narratives of the actions of its gods and heroes, the creation and end of civilizations or the world, and any other existentially significant circumstances or changes. As such, mythologies and their constitutive elements, myths, function as a collective cognitive means of making sense of the world and its conditions by attaching value. In later usage, the term has also come to denote any theoretical or artistic treatment of myths. In European culture, ancient Greek mythology has remained the first point of reference; in Greek culture, one also finds the contrasting distinction between *mythos,* the image of a concept, and *logos,* its conceptual abstraction, which has defined the treatment of myth, the mythic, and mythology ever since. While mythic conceptualizing operates through images and narratives to make understandable the abstract and the spiritual—that which is beyond the grasp of empirical experience—the *logos* operates with abstract concepts that are arrived at through reflective analysis. Evidently, the mythic approach to the world and existence is based on a knowledge derived from believed facts, whereas the analytical one is based on knowledge derived from critical investigation.

It is generally accepted that the mythic type of mental activity and resulting worldview preceded the logos-based view in human intellectual history, a premise that has formed the basis for a lengthy discussion regarding the merits and utility of myth: do myths contain (their own) immutable truths or are they merely unreasonable superstitions and fanciful lies made up by either ignorant or scheming early thinkers, which can be brushed aside by the penetrating and illuminating power of analytical reason and discourse? As soon as analytical abstraction occurs, the latter view gains ground, as it did once Greek philosophy had established schools of abstract thought. (In these opposed evaluations originates the twofold meaning of *myth,* as something without factual basis or as something pervasive and powerful.) Throughout the premedieval and medieval periods, Christian dogma remained hostile toward ancient or local mythology due to the fact that they were pagan (and rival systems of existential meaning), but Christianity itself was eventually identified as a mythological system in the course of the modern period, in keeping with the assertion of abstract analysis from the Renaissance onward. From the Renaissance, which brought ancient mythology back into the view of thinkers and artists, to the Enlightenment, myths, if they were not considered barbarous superstitions, tended to be interpreted as allegories—something that *chooses* to express an abstract concept through a decorative image, which in turn requires (analytical) decoding.

Prepared by the late Enlightenment, the understanding of myth underwent a radical and lasting change during the Romantic movement, which had a significant bearing on the development of Romantic theories of art and teleologies of history. In a world whose religious and spiritual foundations had been irreparably shaken by the relentlessly dissolving operations of rationalist analysis, the substantiating and synthesizing pictorial power of the mythic image or narrative was reevaluated as revelatory, as an insoluble last entity of meaning. Its all-inclusive, timeless completeness came to be seen as the only way fit to make sense of the proliferating empirical or theoretical data of rationalist analysis. Thus, myth became significant (again) in its own right rather than as allegorical decoration. The Romantic discovery of an individual's or society's need for myth, which, in its precise naming of the needed entity as "myth," was particular to German Romanticism, and which constituted one of its defining features, is generally referred to as the formulation of Neue Mythologie (New Mythology). The groundwork was laid by C.G. Heyne, whose Enlightened inquiry into ancient mythology in the third quarter of the 18th century identified mythic expression as the inevitable prerationalist mode of conceptualizing, which grew out of and served the limited intellectual conditions of primitive humanity.

Soon this new concept of early human conceptualizing was, by Heyne's pupil J.G. Eichhorn, applied to the Bible, establishing, for example, the Old Testament as ancient Hebrew mythology. Also investigating "early literature," J.G. Herder stressed the poetic quality of these ancient sacred texts, or myths. The equation of sacred text with myth and poetry facilitated the (Romantic) conclusion that all genuine poetry had mythic potential, which, notwithstanding the antiquity of the mythic method, had a significant role to play in modern thought. Regarding literature, the notion of the need for mythology is prevalent in many theoretical texts of the *Frühromantik* (Early German Romanticism); this notion is, perhaps, most clearly formulated in Friedrich Schlegel's *Gespräch über die Poesie* (1800; *Dialogue on Poetry*), especially its "Rede über die Mythologie" ("Speech on Mythology"). A new mythology was required for the creation of genuine poetry, as it provided poetry's intellectual and artistic framework, making possible literature's functioning as a source of existential meaning analogous to that of original mythology. Romantic literary theory defined literature as capable of assuming the function of a mythic and, hence, revelatory sacred text and characterized art in general as capable of fulfilling the functions of religion. While the perpetually and bottomlessly fragmenting effect of critical analysis—which caused the crisis of reason that came to a head at the close of the Enlightenment as a consequence of the political and intellectual earthquakes associated with the French Revolution—had led the Romantic thinkers back to an "old" mode of conceptualizing, and while, amid the discussions of Greek myth and the new reception of oriental mythology, keen attempts were being made to unearth a northern mythology based on Germanic and Celtic myth, which could compare with its classical counterpart, the recourse to an old model was not to entail a retarding regress to a superseded intellectual condition. It was clear to the Romantic theoreticians that a new mythology would have to incorporate the intellectual development humanity had achieved: it was to go beyond pure reason and rationalism, not to deny or annul it. Friedrich Schlegel suggested in his "Rede über die Mythologie" that the New Mythology should "auf dem ganz entgegengesetzten Wege . . . uns kommen [sic], wie die alte ehemalige" (come to us on the path entirely opposite to the old one) and that it "muß . . . aus der tiefsten Tiefe des Geistes herausgebildet werden; es muß das künstlichste aller Kunstwerke sein, denn es soll alle andern umfassen" (must be created out of the deepest depth of the mind; it must be the most artful of all artworks, for it is to encompass all others). As such, it could unite within itself all achievements of the human mind and would amount to a consummate expression.

The idea of myth being the beginning as well as the end of all human intellectual endeavors, albeit in distinct manifestations, also informed the notions of history within German Idealism. The teleological panoramas of intellectual world history as conceived by F.W.J. Schelling in his *System des Tranzendentalen Idealismus* (1800; *System of Transcendental Idealism*) and by J.G. Fichte in his *Grundzüge des gegenwärtigen Zeitalters* (1803–4; *Characteristics of the Present Age*) assume an original state, in which the intellect is at rest but fully unconscious in its submergence in nature, and which they linked to original myth. With the first stirrings of intellectual activity, this state of equilibrial rest is broken, and history begins as the human being embarks on its conquest of knowledge by analytical means. Once this is complete, at some future point in time, a second mythic state is reached, in which the intellect is again at rest but is now in a fully conscious self-reflexive state.

As in literary theory, the Romantic mythic denotes consummate completeness and potential or fulfilled knowledge. It shares with the original mythologies the trust in the ultimate insoluble truth of the mythic image. Such dispensing of truth and meaning was becoming most desirable in a century whose intellectual and political changes were underpinned by dramatic economic change: by mid-century, the Industrial Revolution had spread into most European countries and fundamentally transformed the lives of many within one or two generations. The Romantic notions of mythically sustained art, history, and life have had a pervasive influence on the intellectual and artistic landscapes of the 19th and 20th centuries. They found one of their most enduring artistic realizations in Richard Wagner's monumental music dramas. In the border area between intellectual history and politics, relying on the collective and legitimizing nature of mythmaking, these influences activated the intense 19th-century interest in national myths, which were considered to carry the essence of a nation and to point to its origin as well as to its destiny, thus contributing to national legitimization. In Germany, attention focused on the Nibelungen material in this respect.

In the course of the 19th century, myth and mythologies attracted considerable scientific attention in the fields of comparative mythology, linguistics, ethnology, anthropology, folklore studies, and, toward the end of the century, perhaps most crucially in the work of Sigmund Freud and the budding science of psychology. Freud's discovery and scientific investigation of the different layers of human consciousness through psychoanalysis led to the acknowledgment of an unconscious framework of coherent subconscious relations whose inherent logic is inaccessible to the conscious rationality of the individual as those relations precede (or interfere with) the development of independent individual rationality. Freud's findings laid the basis for the recognition of nonrationalist and unconscious motives for human behavior and modes of understanding. Seeing striking correlations between the stages (and failures) of psychological development and the events and circumstances depicted in ancient mythology, Freud used the old names for his discoveries. The most famous of these correlations is the Oedipus complex, named after the legendary Greek king. Freud's pupil Carl Gustav Jung extended the theory of the close relation between the workings of the human unconscious and mythic conceptualizing by dividing the unconscious into a personal and a collective unconscious. According to Jung, the latter is constructed around collective mythical archetypes that owe their existence to universal human experiences inscribed in the unconscious by race memory, directing human behavior and conceptualizing from the most unconscious levels of the mind. Thus, analytical science found the products of the first mental and intellectual activities still active within the human mental makeup. Myth and mythology have remained important categories in the 20th century for the investigation of mental processes in psychology, linguistics, and cultural studies; 20th-century philosophy, too, took up the discussion of myth as a basis for a valid epistemology.

In the 1920s, the neo-Kantian philosopher Ernst Cassirer, characterizing the human being as a "symbolic animal," presented the mythic mode as the earliest of the symbolic frameworks through which the world is apprehended conceptually (the theoretical-analytical was the last). Cassirer equated all frameworks regarding their effectiveness, thus putting a historical perspective on Kant's idea of the universal nature of the constitution of knowledge. All discussions of myth and mythology focus in one way or other on the relation between *mythos* and *logos,* the image and its deconstruction. Hans Blumenberg suggested in 1979 that the two entities should not be seen as chronologically successive but that the logical faculty of the intellect was already at work when *mythos* was being created; thus, *mythos* and *logos,* although distinct in appearance, form an intellectual unit, as both represent intellectual attempts at generating meaning. Once myth has been created, the *logos* will proceed to work on it, which will inevitably lead to the abstraction of the concrete image. The idea of an underlying unity between the mythic and the analytic mode of conception was further elaborated by Kurt Hübner, who showed that myth and science are based on identical structures and that investigative science, too, rests on "final facts," which are taken as insoluble, but which are in the final analysis assumptions, acts of faith.

The crisis of reason, which initiated the modern interest in myth at the end of the 18th century, appears to remain unsolved, with reason recognized as a function rather than a self-sufficient content, while the last "Urgrund," the eternally insoluble, remains to be found only by setting rather than deducing it. *Mythos* and *logos,* although based on the same structures and attempting to answer to the same human need, remain distinct modes of intellectual activity. Myth, with its advantage of setting meaning by simply showing rather than proving it, has been recognized as the necessary starting point for the formation of any worldview. Since the call for the New Mythology, myth has, exonerated from the irrational, become instated as a prerational or even pararationalist mode of conceptualizing.

MAIKE OERGEL

Further Reading

Barthes, Roland, *Mythologies,* Paris: Seuil, 1957; as *Mythologies, Selected and Translated by Annette Lavers,* London: Cape, 1972, reprinted: London: Vintage, 1993

Blumenberg, Hans, *Arbeit am Mythos,* Frankfurt: Suhrkamp, 1979

Bohrer, Karl Heinz, editor, *Mythos und Moderne: Begriff und Bild einer Rekonstruktion,* Frankfurt: Suhrkamp, 1983

Cassirer, Ernst, *Philosophie der symbolischen Formen,* 3 vols., Berlin: Cassirer, 1923–29; as *The Philosophy of Symbolic Forms,* New Haven, Connecticut: Yale University Press, 1953–57

——, *Sprache und Mythos,* Leipzig: Teubner, 1925; as *Language and Myth,* New York: Harper, 1946

Eichhorn, Johann Gottfried, *Urgeschichte,* edited by Johann Philip Gabler, 3 vols., Altdorf and Nuremberg: Monath und Kussler, 1790–93

Eliade, Mircea, *Cosmos and History: The Myth of the Eternal Return,* New York: Harper, 1959

Falck, Colin, *Myth, Truth, and Literature: Towards a True Postmodernism,* Cambridge and New York: Cambridge University Press, 1991; 2nd edition, 1994

Feldman, Burton, and Robert D. Richardson, *The Rise of Modern Mythology, 1680–1860,* Bloomington and London: Indiana University Press, 1972

Fichte, Johann Gottlieb, "Grundzüge des gegenwärtigen Zeitalters," in *Fichtes Werke,* edited by Immanuel Hermann Fichte, 8 vols., Berlin: Veit, 1845–46, reprinted Berlin: de Gruyter, 1971, vol. 7; as *Characteristics of the Present Age, Fichte's Popular Works,* 2 vols., vol. 2, London: Chapman, 1849

Frank, Manfred, *Der kommende Gott,* Vorlesungen über die Neue Mythologie, vol. 1, Frankfurt: Suhrkamp, 1982

——, *Gott im Exil,* Vorlesungen über die Neue Mythologie, vol. 2, Frankfurt: Suhrkamp, 1988

Freud, Sigmund, *Totem und Tabu,* Leipzig: Heller, 1913; as *Totem and Taboo: Some Points of Agreement between the Mental Lives of Savages and Neurotics,* London: Routledge, 1960

Hübner, Kurt, *Die Wahrheit des Mythos,* Munich: Beck, 1985

Jung, Carl Gustav, *Von den Wurzeln des Bewußtseins,* Zurich: Rascher, 1954; as *The Archetypes and the Collective Unconscious,* 2nd edition, London: Routledge and Kegan Paul, 1968; reprinted, 1990

Oergel, Maike, *The Return of King Arthur and the Nibelungen: National Myth in 19th-century German and English Literature,* Berlin and New York: de Gruyter, 1998

Schelling, Friedrich Wilhelm Josef, *Philosophie der Kunst,* in *Schellings Werke,* edited by Manfred Schröter, vol. 3, 13 vols., Munich: Beck, 1927–59; reprinted, 1962–66

——, *Philosophie der Mythologie,* in *Schellings Werke,* edited by Manfred Schröter, vol. 5, 13 vols., Munich: Beck, 1927–59; reprinted, 1962–66

——, *System des Transzendentalen Idealismus,* in *Schellings Werke,* edited by Manfred Schröter, vol. 2, 13 vols., Munich: Beck, 1927–59; reprinted, 1962–66; as *The System of Transcendental Idealism (1800),* Charlottesville: University Press of Virginia, 1978

Schlegel, Friedrich, *Gespräch über die Poesie,* in *Kritische Friedrich Schlegel-Ausgabe,* edited by Ernst Behler, vol. 2, Munich: Schöningh, 1958–87; as *Dialogue on Poetry and Literary Aphorisms,* University Park and London: Pennsylvania State University Press, 1968

Shaffer, Elinor, *"Kubla Khan" and the Fall of Jerusalem: The Mythological School in Biblical Criticism and Secular Literature,* Cambridge and New York: Cambridge University Press, 1975

Vickery, John, editor, *Myth and Literature: Contemporary Theory and Practice,* Lincoln: University of Nebraska Press, 1966

N

Sten Nadolny 1942–

With the publication of his second novel in 1983, *Die Entdeck-ung der Langsamkeit* (*The Discovery of Slowness*), Sten Nadolny has recently become one of a number of contemporary German novelists to enjoy both popular and critical success in Germany and abroad. Despite the commercial success of that novel and his 1994 novel *Ein Gott der Frechheit* (1994; *A God of Impertinence*), however, critics and scholars have only more recently begun to devote much study to his novels and literary technique; this neglect, perhaps, is due in part to his relatively small literary output.

Nadolny began his literary career as an occasional essayist and short-story writer. Having studied history, he worked as a history teacher before embarking on a career as a novelist. As a result, his novels are characterized by the extensive research and attention to detail that one would expect from a historian turned novelist. While such an approach has at times invited stylistic criticism, his dedication to and belief in literary narrative, out-lined quite succinctly in a series of lectures on poetics he gave at the University of Munich in 1990, *Das Erzählen und die guten Absichten* (Storytelling and Good Intentions), has imbued his novels not only with interesting protagonists but also with en-gaging story lines.

In his poetics lectures, Nadolny follows the recent tradition of discussing the process of literary creativity more than his own conception of literary poetics. As the title indicates, the notion of storytelling (*Erzählen*) is central to all of his works, and he de-fines literary storytelling as the construction of an ordered series of those details at hand. Thus, he sees his task as a writer as con-structing a meaningful order from the observations collected around him. In this way, Nadolny presents himself as a social commentator and critic, a role that becomes evident in his nov-els—texts that are both observations on and critiques of contem-porary society.

Nadolny's debut novel, *Netzkarte* (1981), is schematically typical of his other novels. The story follows the exploits of its protagonist, Ole Reuter, a traveler who purchases an unlimited train ticket and begins traveling somewhat aimlessly around Germany. The episodic nature of the novel allows for both the exploration of Reuter's own search for understanding as well as his critique of the world around him. Nadolny expands on this same technique in his next novel, *The Discovery of Slowness*, a fictionalized account of the life of the real-life sailor and explorer John Franklin. As the title suggests, the novel explores the merits of slowness as a counterpoint to an increasingly rapid and tech-nological society. The result of such developments has led, Nadolny argues, to the isolation of the individual or, at least, those less acclimated to society. As such, the novel is as much a plea for individuality as it is a plea for respect for the individual, two themes explored in greater detail in his next novel.

Nadolny's third novel, *Selim; oder, die Gabe der Rede* (1990; *Selim; or, the Gift of Speech*), has enjoyed perhaps the greatest degree of critical attention and has also been the focus of a de-bate in American German studies concerning minority represen-tation in German literature and culture studies. In an essay on the origins and inspiration for the novel ("'Wir' und 'Die'— Erzählen über Fremde" ["'Us and Them': Stories about Strangers"]), Nadolny recounts that the impetus for the book was his desire to write a novel as a means of helping him under-stand a Turkish friend as well as Germany as a multicultural so-ciety. The novel begins as a third-person narrative with the German protagonist, Alexander, a former soldier who befriends a Turkish immigrant worker, Selim, in the 1960s. Throughout the course of the novel, Nadolny presents not only the develop-ment of their friendship but a portrait of Germany's recent multicultural history. In the last third of the novel, the narrative perspective switches to the first person, and it then becomes clear that Alexander is writing his own story. In this way, Nadolny problematizes not only the process of writing as a means of cre-ating identity (a process that he outlines theoretically in his poet-ics lectures) but also the importance of speech and storytelling, skills that the Western Alexander admires in the Turkish Selim, for whom they are one and the same.

In his essay on the novel, Nadolny admits that his intention was to write a colonial novel that takes place within the borders of Germany. Consequently, critics have seized upon this point to analyze Nadolny's methodological and ideological stance, raising concerns about his portrayal of the "Other" as embodied in his representation of Turkish-Germans as well as his references to Turkish and German history. While critics are divided as to the degree to which his characterizations are stereotypical and West-ernized, the novel remains one of the first serious attempts by a German writer to deal with minority representation in literature.

For his 1994 novel *The God of Impertinence*, Nadolny chose to intermingle the contemporary and the antique worlds to write a humorous novel, which is again thematically reminiscent of his previous works. Hermes, the god of insolence, chaos, and turmoil, is freed into a modern world in which the other gods of antiquity are no longer present. Similar to Ole Reuter and John Franklin before him, Hermes is a traveler who journeys through the modern world in the tradition of the *Schelm* or picaro, discovering and commenting on society and its foibles. Later, it falls upon him to save the world from destruction, and it is his task to convince the powers that be that the world is, indeed, worth saving. In this regard, Nadolny returns to familiar territory by exploring the dichotomies of modern society: order versus chaos, technological advances versus tradition, and conservatism versus freedom and flexibility. As a result of the novel's humor and playfulness, it became a best-seller in Germany, but it also met with mixed reviews from critics. While some found the novel entertaining, many criticized Nadolny's idealism and didacticism. Not surprisingly, the novel enjoyed a greater degree of critical success in the United States, where light, entertaining novels are often better received.

Among the recent works of contemporary German writers, Nadolny's novels have enjoyed both critical and commercial success. As a result of his ability to combine well-written narratives with complex social and literary themes, he is often cited, along with Uwe Timm, Patrick Süskind, and Christoph Ransmayr, as a novelist who has been able to overcome the so-called crisis of narration of the 1960s and 1970s.

DAVID N. COURY

Biography

Born near Berlin, 1942. Son of the writers Isabellan and Burkhard Nadolny. Brought up in Bavaria; Ph.D. in history, Freie Universität, Berlin; history teacher and production manager in the film industry. Ingeborg Bachmann Prize (for *Die Entdeckung der Lansamkeit; The Discovery of Slowness*); Hans Fallada Prize, 1985; Premio Vallombrosa, 1986. Currently lives in Berlin and Munich.

Selected Works

Netzkarte, 1981

Die Entdeckung der Langsamkeit, 1983; as *The Discovery of Slowness,* translated by Ralph Freedman, 1987

Selim; oder, die Gabe der Rede, 1990

Das Erzählen und die guten Absichten (Münchner Poetik-Vorlesungen), 1990

Ein Gott der Frechheit, 1994; as *The God of Impertinence,* translated by Breon Mitchell, 1997

Further Reading

Adelson, Leslie, "Opposing Oppositions: Turkish-German Questions in Contemporary German Studies," *German Studies Review* 17, no. 2 (1994)

Bunzel, Wolfgang, editor, *Sten Nadolny,* Eggingen: Isele, 1996

Magris, Claudio, "Verteidigung der Gegenwart: Sten Nadolnys *Die Entdeckung der Langsamkeit,*" *German Quarterly* 63, no. 3–4 (1990)

Wittstock, Uwe, "Das souveräne Erzählen und die Hühnerknochen," in *Leselust: Wie unterhaltsam ist die neue deutsche Literatur?* Munich: Luchterhand, 1995

Napoleonic Era

The name and fame of Napoléon spread throughout Europe with considerable speed, beginning in 1793 when he helped to drive the British from Toulon. Soon thereafter he conducted the military campaigns in Northern Italy, driving out the Austrians; he then embarked on the invasion of Egypt, which ended with the destruction of the French fleet in the Battle of the Nile by the British under Admiral Nelson on 1 August 1798. But it is only with the coup d'état of Brumaire 18 (9 November 1799) and his assumption of the role of First Consul (of three) that the Napoleonic era began in earnest.

From the German perspective one can distinguish three periods. The first was from 1799 to 1806, the time of the ascendance of Napoléon, which culminated in his crowning himself Holy Roman Emperor. The second period included the French occupation of German-speaking lands and a bewildering array of alliances for and against Napoléon, mainly from 1806 until 1812 (to be sure, French troops had already crossed the Rhine in 1792, shortly after the artillery duel known as the "cannonade of Valmy," which Goethe witnessed, and which caused the Prussian armies to retreat). The third period started with the Russian campaign of 1812 and the battle of Leipzig, both defeats for Napoléon, continued with the Wars of Liberation, and ended with the final defeat at Waterloo on 18 June 1815.

It is important to note that the alliances German nobles formed with or against Napoléon led to utterly kaleidoscopic wars. German-speaking soldiers wearing different uniforms confronted each other, as Ludwig Tieck portrayed in his 1830 story *Zauberschloss,* where father and son encounter each other as combatants. In the battle of Jena in 1806, for example, 177,376 French soldiers fought side by side with 31,187 German-speaking soldiers from the lands now subsumed under the "Confederation of the Rhine," and approximately 200,000 German-speaking troops were part of the Grande Armée that was decimated by the Russian winter of 1812.

The presence in Germany of French troops, diplomats, and nobility from the early 1790s until 1815 was pervasive, shaped the sense of cultural identity of the German-speaking lands, and contributed to the desperation felt and articulated by many who had initially pinned their hopes on the ideals of the French Revolution but who were soon disillusioned by the reality of yet another military conquest. Reaction ranged from unwavering support by those who gained long-overdue enfranchisement, including the Jewish Germans in the Rhineland (such as Heine), to skepticism and hatred. Napoléon can be found on a scale of values with Christ at one end and Satan or at least Attila the Hun on the other.

In German-speaking lands, the initial reaction to Napoléon in the role of Consul was generally positive. Roman republican virtues seemed to be incarnate, and the pervasive hope for constitutions or at least constitutional monarchies was alive among progressive forces in the German lands. But as Napoléon assumed more and more aristocratic trappings, entwining himself by marriage and other means within the monarchies of Europe, disillusionment grew rapidly. Beethoven's grand gesture, erasing the dedication "Napoleon" from the title page of his third symphony in 1804, remains the most visible signpost pointing to the realization that the republican masks merely disguised the face of yet another French conqueror with Cesarean ambitions.

Even in the midst of French occupation, however, many found ways to accommodate themselves. Jacob Grimm became a librarian in Kassel for the private library of Napoléon's brother Jerôme, and Goethe was impressed by the very fact that the emperor deigned to meet with him in Erfurt (in 1808); Hegel, who put the finishing touches on his *Die Phänomenologie des Geistes* (1808; *Phenomenology of Spirit*) on the eve of the battle of Jena, swooned over what he saw as a *Weltgeist* represented by Napoléon. Many, of course, begrudgingly acknowledged the utility of having fewer princelings and working toward the reduction of the bewildering particularism that ruled the German day. In fact, the *Code Napoléon* did bring a measure of civil order into innumerable conflicting bureaucracies and genuine progress for disenfranchised.

The reaction of German writers to Napoléon varied from the enthusiastically pro-Napoléon anecdote of Johann Peter Hebel, *Kaiser Napoleon und die Obstfrau in Brienne* (Emperor Napoléon and the Fruit Vendor of Brienne, published in *Rheinischer Hausfreund*) to Zacharias Werner's historical drama *Attila König der Hunnen* (Attila, King of the Huns), both of which were published in 1808. Very vocal in the anti-Napoléon camp was Heinrich von Kleist, who in his drama *Die Herrmannsschlacht* (1808–9; Arminius's Battle) tried to exhort his countrymen to rise up against Napoléon as the Germanic chieftain did against Roman occupation in A.D. 9. Not all critical voices were as unmistakable as Kleist's. Achim von Arnim in his novel *Die Kronenwächter* (1810; The Crown Guardians) smuggled another Attila tale into his text, and of course Napoléon is the Hun.

Without necessarily mentioning Napoléon or specific battles, war looms in the background of many important works. In Goethe's *Wahlverwandschaften* (1809; *Elective Affinities*), the major is currently not engaged in warfare, but when Eduard is at his wits' end, war is there as a conveniently risky and manly occupation. In Brentano's *Die Geschichte vom braven Kasperl und dem schönen Annerl* (1817; *The Story of the Honest Caspar and Fair Annie*), tragedy takes its course because of Kasperl's exaggerated sense of (military) honor. Heine's famous poem "Die Grenadiere" (1819), by contrast, is a sentimental paean on Napoléon from the point of view of soldiers whom he so valiantly abandoned in Russia. In Heine's *Ideen: Das Buch Le Grand* (1826; Ideas: The Book Le Grand), Napoléon is celebrated as a progressive force, and his visit to Heine's hometown,

Düsseldorf, is recalled with enthusiasm. Equally enthusiastic is the portrayal of Napoléon in Wilhelm Hauff's story *Das Bild des Kaisers* (1828; The Portrait of the Emperor).

The figure of Napoléon continued to loom in German literature long after his death. Christian Dietrich Grabbe's *Napoleon; oder, Die Hundert Tage* (1831; Napoléon; or, The One Hundred Days), written between 1829 and 1831, is one of the earliest, serious, and grandiose attempts to represent the Napoleonic era on the stage. A complete performance, incidentally, was not given until 1895.

Specific representations of Napoléon in literary works, however, are less important than what the figure of Napoléon represents in the broader context of the history of Europe. Franz Schnabel, the great historian of the 19th century, saw Napoléon's conquests and reorganization of Europe as an effort similar to the Roman conquests. They usually required standardization of weights and measures, laws, and governments, and they promoted urban design as geometrical as possible. The price of the integration and unification was the eradication of whatever was local, traditional, nonconforming, inconvenient, particular, or crooked. Napoléon represented once again quintessentially urbane, Cesarean values that necessitated the suppression or at least the subordination of the individual. Napoléon was thus a leading figure in one of the acts of the European drama of the tug-of-war between the particular and the uniform.

MICHAEL BACHEM

See also Restoration

Further Reading

Addington, Larry H., *The Patterns of War since the Eighteenth Century,* Bloomington: Indiana University Press, 1994

Amoretti, G.V., "Napoleone e Goethe," *Dialoghi: Rivista Bimestrale di Letteratura, Arti, Scienze* 18 (1970)

Ancelet-Hustache, Jeanne, "Napoleon jugé par les écrivains allemands de son temps," *Europe: Revue Litteraire Mensuelle* 480–81 (1969)

Brose, Eric Dorn, *German History, 1789–1871: From the Holy Roman Empire to the Bismarckian Reich*, Providence, Rhode Island: Berghahn Books, 1997

Esdaile, Charles, "Popular Resistance in Napoleonic Europe," *History Today* 48 (1998) Hermand, Jost, "Napoleon oder Don Quichote: Zur Kontroverse über den Kometen," *Hesperus: Blätter der Jean Paul Gesellschaft* 30 (1967)

Lützeler, Paul Michael, "The Image of Napoleon in European Romanticism," in *European Romanticism: Literary Cross-Currents, Modes, and Models,* edited by Gerhart Hoffmeister, Detroit, Michigan: Wayne State University Press, 1990

Thompson, Martyn P., "Ideas of Europe during the French Revolution and Napoleonic Wars," *Journal of the History of Ideas* 55 (1994)

Trapp, Frithjof, "Napoleon redivivus: Zu Walter Hasenclevers *Abenteuer in sieben Bildern*, Napoleon greift ein," *German Life and Letters* 43–45 (1992)

Ziolkowski, Theodore, "Napoleon's Impact on Germany: A Rapid Survey," *Yale French Studies* 26 (1960/61)

Nationalism and Nationhood

The concept of the German nation in itself and in its relation to language and literature has long been problematic. Discussions of German nationhood since 1945 (and indeed before), overshadowed by the development of nationalism in its most virulent racist form during the Third Reich, have tended to ignore a wider context.

On the one hand, non-German minorities have lived in the German-speaking lands throughout most of their history. They include Sorbs (Wends), Jews, Huguenots, Salzburg Protestants, Polish migrant workers toward the end of the 19th-century, and *Fremdarbeiter* from developing countries after World War II. On the other hand, German minorities have for centuries lived outside Germany, Austria, and Switzerland in places such as Denmark, Poland, Czechoslovakia, the South Tyrol, the Baltic region, Russia, Transylvania, the Americas, and the overseas colonies established during the later years of the Second Reich. It is one of the ironies of history that more people with German as their first language now live within the borders of Germany, Austria, and Switzerland than at any time since the Middle Ages.

Except during the Third Reich, a united Germany has had a federal structure, and regional differences have been as important for literature as for politics. Some major writers, as well as a host of minor ones, have been closely associated with particular regions, provinces, or political constructs that have enjoyed a degree of autonomy. One thinks of the links between Kleist, Alexis, and Fontane and Prussia, of others with Scandinavia, Alsace, the Baltic lands, Bukovina, and Transylvania. While the list of writers forced by political circumstances to emigrate is long, many also left their homeland voluntarily, drawn to a more stimulating cultural ambience, in Italy especially, or to more exotic locations.

Central to the relation between German-speaking writers and the nation has been the discrepancy between political and cultural nationhood. While Walther von der Vogelweide's "Preislied" of 1203, with its definition of national characteristics within named geographical boundaries, is singular in its time, a sense of what came to be defined as the *Kulturnation* was fostered at least as early as the beginning of the 16th century, when some humanists threw in their lot with the Reformation. Consequently, the transition to the Renaissance was complicated by the need to draw away from the religious tutelage of Rome and establish a degree of cultural independence. The translation of the Bible by Martin Luther brought a measure of linguistic unity, but in attacking the papacy for spiritual, not political, reasons, and in supporting the existing political structure, he discouraged any trend toward German unity and was therefore not the nationalist he appeared to be to the 19th century.

In the 17th century, poets lamented the condition of a nation devastated by war, yet the foreign intervention prompted by the religious divisions within Germany produced no xenophobic reaction. A process of cultural identity formation was continued by the *Sprachgesellschaften* and by linguists such as Schottel, then in the 18th century by efforts to counter French cultural supremacy, especially in the theater, by setting up alternative models (Shakespeare, Ossian, folk songs, and the Gothic style, which was assumed for a time to be quintessentially German). There was a national dimension to the reaction of the middle class, with its value system grounded in pietism and then promoted by the popularization of the Enlightenment in the moral weeklies and the novel, to the artificiality of court manners and art forms (e.g., opera) that were imported from France and Italy. During the Seven Years' War, the literary support for the cause of Friedrich II of Prussia had protonationalist overtones. With Herder, cultural identity, essentially popular and locally defined, neither exclusive to Germany (or a privileged group of nations) nor identified with an existing state, remained in harmony with Enlightenment universalism. Patriotism as a cultural phenomenon was seen as invigorating society but not as the instrument of state power. Schiller, in the unpublished fragment "Deutsche Größe," rejoiced in the separation of culture and politics yet implicitly rejected thereby a form of state with which the middle class was out of sympathy.

The French Revolution, therefore, presented an alternative that the advocates of the *Kulturnation* could not ignore. Their attitude changed from enthusiastic support to outright rejection of a political system maintained by violence, however democratic it claimed to be. They took their stand on a cosmopolitan cultural ideal until the military consequences of the Napoleonic system became intolerable and divided them. The extent of popular support for the nationalism that inspired the War of Liberation of 1813–15 remains a matter of debate; there can be no doubt, however, that it was promoted by writers (Fichte, Arndt, Jahn, Körner, and Schenkendorf) and that it had long-term effects. Although a popular force that was initially regarded with suspicion by the restored monarchical system, it underwent a metamorphosis in which its democratic potential was stifled. Its association with Romanticism (Arnim and Brentano in *Des Knaben Wunderhorn,* Jakob Grimm in *Deutsche Mythologie*) and historicism produced an amalgam present in a number of foundation myths: the defeat of the Romans by Arminius/Hermann in A.D. 9, the medieval epic the *Nibelungenlied,* the legend of the Emperor Friedrich Barbarossa's confinement within the Kyffhäuser mountain, and the allegorical figure of Germania. Literary treatments of these myths, occasionally the work of major writers (Kleist, Hebbel), were not always composed to foster popular nationalism, but they were inevitably associated with the monuments that were erected as testimonies to national feeling at this time. With the unification of Germany under Prussian hegemony, nationalism became firmly anchored to the monarchical system, which had previously either rejected it or viewed it in purely cultural terms. There were those who criticized this development (Heine, Herwegh, Grillparzer, and Nietzsche), but their voices were drowned by others, including Geibel and Freytag.

In the 20th century, nationalism, as expressed in the *Heimatkunst* movement and then in the propagandist literature during and after World War I, whether it took crude (Lissauer, Löns) or elitist (Thomas Mann, *Betrachtungen eines Unpolitischen;* George, *Das neue Reich*) forms, ceased to imply support for the Wilhelminian establishment; at the same time, it became increasingly exclusive (anti-Semitic) and expansive. The tragedy of the Weimar Republic lay in a polarization of politics that prevented the left (Heinrich Mann, Tucholsky) from offering a resentful majority a national vision compatible with reconciliation and capable of competing with the revanchism of the right. On the level of cultural debate, nationalism was given an irrational dimension (Wilhelm Schäfer, *Dreizehn Bücher der deutschen Seele*) that left it wide open to corruption and appropriation by the *völkisch* movements eventually absorbed into National Socialism. Writers forced into exile during the Third Reich, while rightly convinced that they represented "das bessere Deutschland," were divided between those (mainly Marxists, e.g., Brecht, Becher) who saw socioeconomic factors as paramount in the drift to Nazism and any future reconstitution of Germany, and those (e.g., Thomas Mann, *Deutschland und die Deutschen*) who looked for deeper roots in the historical development of national character.

Postwar writers were inevitably caught up in the ideological debates created by the East-West division and came to occupy a middle position, which is evident in the revival of the *Kulturnation* idea by Günter Grass. Formulated long before the *Wende* (turn) of 1989–90, this idea has since grounded Grass's criticism of the haste and insensitivity that he maintains has been demonstrated by the West during and after the unification process. His view has been supported by writers from the former GDR (Stefan Heym, Heiner Müller, and Christa Wolf), challenged by Martin Walser and Dieter Wellershoff, and set in a wider context in the very different contributions of Wolf Biermann, Hans Magnus Enzensberger, and Botho Strauß. At the same time, Austrian (Gerhard Roth, Turrini, Scharang, and Menasse) and Swiss (Frisch, Bichsel, Marti, and Muschg) writers have been anxious to ensure that their much smaller countries, in which foundation myths (associated with the Habsburg dynasty and Wilhelm Tell) have been equally strong, do not adopt an inward-looking posture in reaction to immigration, pressures from more powerful neighbors, and globalization.

MALCOLM HUMBLE

See also Johann Gottlieb Fichte

Further Reading

Bade, Klaus J., editor, *Deutsche im Ausland: Fremde in Deutschland, Migration in Geschichte und Gegenwart,* Munich: Beck, 1992

Borst, Arno, "Barbarossas Erwachen: Zur Geschichte der deutschen Identität," in *Identität*, edited by Odo Marquard and Karlheinz Stierle, Munich: Fink, 1979

Craig, Gordon A., *Die Politik der Unpolitischen: Deutsche Schriftsteller und die Macht, 1770 bis 1871,* Munich: Beck, 1993; as *The Politics of the Unpolitical: German Writers and the Problem of Power,* Oxford and New York: Oxford University Press, 1995

Gössmann, Wilhelm, "Deutsche Nationalität und Freiheit: Die Rezeption der Arminius-Gestalt in der Literatur von Tacitus bis Heine," *Heine Jahrbuch* 16 (1977)

Gössmann, Wilhelm, and Klaus-Hinrich Roth, editors, *Poetisierung—Politisierung: Deutschlandbilder in der Literatur bis 1848,* Paderborn: Schöningh 1994

Hermand, Jost, "Braut, Mutter oder Hure? Heiner Müllers Germania und ihre Vorgeschichte," in *Sieben Arten an Deutschland zu leiden,* Königstein: Athenäum, 1979

Hinderer, Walter, editor, *Geschichte der politischen Lyrik in Deutschland,* Stuttgart: Reclam, 1978

Keller, Ernst, *Nationalismus und Literatur: Langemarck, Weimar, Stalingrad,* Bern and Munich: Francke, 1970

Langguth, Gerd, editor, *Autor, Macht, Staat: Literatur und Politik in Deutschland, Ein notwendiger Dialog,* Düsseldorf: Droste, 1994

Magris, Claudio, *Der Habsburgische Mythos in der österreichischen Literatur,* Salzburg: Müller, 1966

Mayer-Iswandy, Claudia, *Zwischen Traum und Trauma: Die Nation,* Tübingen: Stauffenburg, 1994

Scheuer, Helmut, "Die Dichter und ihre Nation: Ein historischer Abriß," *Deutschunterricht* 42, no. 4 (1990)

Scheuer, Helmut, editor, *Dichter und ihre Nation,* Frankfurt: Suhrkamp, 1993

Wiegels, Rainer and Winfried Woesler, editors, *Arminius und die Varusschlacht: Geschichte, Mythos, Literatur,* Paderborn: Schöningh, 1995

Wiese, Benno von, and Rudolf Henß, editors, *Nationalismus in Germanistik und Dichtung: Dokumentation des Germanistentages in München vom 17. - 22. Oktober 1966,* Berlin: Schmidt, 1967

Wülfing, Wulf, et al., *Historische Mythologie der Deutschen, 1798–1918,* Munich: Fink, 1991

National Socialism

Once in power after January 1933, the Nazis made their intentions regarding literature very clear. On 10 May 1933, students and young Nazis entered libraries, took books by Jewish, Marxist, and other writers felt to be out of sympathy with the new regime, and burned them publicly outside universities. In Berlin, Goebbels made an aggressive speech. Almost immediately, an exodus of writers began, and in a short time over 2,000 writers had left the country. One of the Nazi key words was "Gleichschaltung," an electrical term meaning switching over to the same current. In reality it meant the complete subjection of all activities, including literary, to the National Socialist ideology. For example, the literary section of the Akademie der Künste was "gleichgeschaltet," that is, brought into line. Heinrich Mann, Thomas Mann, Alfred Döblin, and many other established figures were forced to resign and were replaced by writers such as Hans Grimm, Erwin Guido Kolbenheyer, and the rabid anti-Semite Will Vesper. Another favorite word of the Nazis was "Weltanschauung" (world view). Hitler was convinced that the Nazi revolution would not be successful until his world view was accepted by all Germans. Central to this world view was the racial doctrine of Aryan superiority and Jewish inferiority. Jews would have no further part to play in German life or culture.

The Burning of the Books was a symbolic act that indicated the destruction of Weimar culture. This was followed by the banning of books through the publication of official blacklists. Other lists followed and indicated officially approved books. Often attributed to Goebbels or Goering is the saying: "every time I hear the word culture, I reach for my revolver." In fact, these words come from the play *Schlageter* (1933) by Hanns Johst, a former Expressionist, who dedicated this play to Adolf Hitler. Out of context, the saying is misleading, because it suggests that the Nazis despised culture. In fact, they took it very seriously, so much so that they endeavored to organize every aspect of it for their purposes. To bring about the desired "Gleichschaltung" and the propagation of the desired world view, a "Reichskulturkammer" (RKK) was set up by Goebbels. This RKK removed culture from the regional control that it had enjoyed and centralized that control. The Reich Cultural Chamber had seven separate departments, which covered all aspects of culture. The literary chamber was called the "Reichsschrifttumskammer" (RSK). All writers had to register with it. Only Germans could be members; all Jews were excluded. In addition to the RKK and the RSK, there was also the "Reichsstelle zur Förderung des deutschen Schrifttums." This Reich Center for the Advancement of German Writing was in direct competition with Goebbels's Propaganda Ministry and the RSK. The foundations of this organization went back to the "Kampfbund für deutsche Kultur" (Fighting Union for German Culture), which was founded in 1929 by Alfred Rosenberg, the author of *Mythos des zwanzigsten Jahrhunderts* (1930; *Myth of the Twentieth Century*) and the chief ideologue of the Nazi Party. In addition to the Rosenberg and the Goebbels organizations, the "Parteiamtliche Prüfungskommission" (PPK) also came into being. This Party Supervisory Commission, under the direction of Reichsleiter Philipp Bouhler, had the task of checking all publications for deviations from the party's ideology. Literature in the Reich was thereby subject to control by a three-fold bureaucracy. But in addition to control, there was also encouragement. The Nazis took literature seriously. For those prepared to work with them, there were Writers Days, Book Weeks, and countless prizes and conferences. Despite the negative impression made by the exodus of so many literary stars from the Weimar Republic, a semblance of literary culture was preserved.

Some Nazi literature has a certain notoriety to this day. Nazi lyric poetry was generally disastrous, but the words and music of the Horst Wessel Song of the Nazi "martyr" still evoke ominous images of glamorous uniforms and marching men. The urban setting of the film *Hitlerjunge Quex* (1932; *Quex of the Hitler Youth*), based on the novel by Alois Schenzinger, conjures up realistic images of street-fighting between communists and Nazis; this work was far removed from the boring blood and soil novels of healthy German peasants preferred by the Nazi ideology. Yet despite the fact that the massive Nazi bureaucracy apparently controlled all aspects of culture, some breathing space was allowed. Open resistance to the regime was out of the question, but not everything non-conformist was banned. Many writers from the despised Weimar Republic had decided against emigration, and Reinhold Schneider, Werner Bergengruen, and Ernst Wiechert were among those who discovered that forms of "Inner emigration" were possible, although the slightest deviation could result in transportation to a concentration camp, as in the case of Wiechert. While the Nazis banned all progressive, avantgarde, or socialist literature and while absolutely no kind of resistance utterance was permitted, they actively encouraged traditional forms, an aspect which the Nazi sympathizer and prizewinner Josef Weinheber exploited in his classical poetry. But the glorification of the fighting soldier was what the Nazis really preferred; hence, Ernst Jünger, although no Nazi, saw his World War I works made available in large numbers, and even his *Auf den Marmorklippen* (1939; *On the Marble Cliffs*) was sent to front-line soldiers—although it was an ambivalent tale about a dangerous dictator.

Ernst Jünger was a survivor who has continued to fascinate modern readers. It is, however, to another body of writers that attention has turned more recently. Jünger was by no means the only non-Nazi to enjoy favorable publishing conditions throughout the Nazi period. Writers who come into this category are: Wolfgang Koeppen, Felix Hartlaub, Karl Krolow, Johannes Bobrowski, Peter Huchel, and Günther Eich, some of whom were to become leading figures in East and West Germany after the war. Despite government controls and strict censorship, the period between 1933 and 1945 cannot be reduced to literature produced strictly along party lines.

J.M. RITCHIE

See also Fascism and Literature

Further Reading

Denkler, Horst, and Karl Prümm, editors, *Die deutsche Literatur im Dritten Reich: Themen, Traditionen, Wirkungen*, Stuttgart: Reclam, 1976

Gilman, Sander L., editor, *NS-Literaturtheorie: Eine Dokumentation*, Frankfurt: Athenäum, 1971

Hartung, Günter, *Literatur und Ästhetik des deutschen Faschismus*, Berlin: Akademie, 1983

Ketelsen, Uwe-Karsten, *Völkisch-nationale und nationalsozialistische Literatur in Deutschland, 1890–1945*, Stuttgart: Metzler, 1976

———, *Literatur und Drittes Reich*, Schernfeld: SH-Verlag, 1992; 2nd edition, 1994

Loewy, Ernst, and Hans-Jochen Gamm, editors, *Literatur unterm Hakenkreuz: Das dritte Reich und seine Dichtung*, Frankfurt: Europäische Verlagsanstalt, 1966; 3rd edition, 1977

Ritchie, J.M., *German Literature under National Socialism*, London: Croom Helm, and Totowa, New Jersey: Barnes and Noble, 1983

Schäfer, Hans Dieter, *Das gespaltene Bewußtsein: Über deutsche Kultur und Lebenswirklichkeit, 1933–1945*, Munich: Hanser, 1981; 3rd edition, 1983

Schonauer, Franz, *Deutsche Literatur im Dritten Reich: Versuch einer Darstellung in polemisch-didaktischer Absicht*, Freiburg: Walter, 1961

Thunecke, Jörg, editor, *Leid der Worte: Panorama des literarischen Nationalsozialismus*, Bonn: Bouvier, 1987

Vondung, Klaus, *Völkisch-nationale und nationalsozialistische Literaturtheorie*, Munich: List, 1973

Wulf, Josef, editor, *Literatur und Dichtung im Dritten Reich: Eine Dokumentation*, Gütersloh: Mohn, 1963

Naturalism

German Naturalism, a term applied, mainly in retrospect, to the period from approximately 1882 to 1892, designates an amorphous movement of youthful literary revolutionaries who were intent upon replacing what they considered a superannuated, calcified idealism with a modern, hard-edged realism. Following a trend begun earlier, particularly in France and Scandinavia, they aspired to a literature that would reflect contemporary social, scientific, and philosophical thought. Within a brief period, Germany had experienced rapid advances in natural science and sociology, a new antimetaphysical outlook based on the theories of Charles Darwin, the positivism of Auguste Comte and Hippolyte Taine, the atheistic materialism of Ludwig Feuerbach, and the socialism of Marx and Engels. As one representative of the movement later recalled, a distinctive feature of the time was a confidence in science to solve all human problems and free mankind from the atavisms of superstition and religion.

Unfortunately, such optimism contrasted sharply with contemporary conditions. The unification of Germany after its victory over France in 1871 and its ascendancy under Bismarck to the rank of a world power were both accompanied by virulent nationalism. The rise of labor-saving technology during the industrial revolution widened the gap between an oppressed proletariat and a complacent bourgeoisie The sudden shift from agrarian, handicraft employment to factory production also strained the economic system, and the rapid growth of cities (Berlin in particular) concentrated the misery of the disenfranchised. Finding an appropriate literary form for expressing such conditions required trial and error, but it was eventually accomplished by an intensification of earlier foreign and domestic trends. The process took place in several phases, is documented in contemporary periodicals, and is mainly identified with the cities of Munich and Berlin.

Because of what was considered the sorry state of literature in Germany—one dominated by mediocre French imports and popular epigones such as Emanuel Geibel and Paul Heyse—much of early naturalist criticism was combative in tone. Among the earliest initiators of a reaction against the status quo were the brothers Heinrich and Julius Hart. In their magazine *Kritische Waffengänge* (1882–84; Critical Passages at Arms), they pilloried the literary establishment while expressing hope for the future. Anticipating an impending "great literary epoch," their program still stressed a proper balance between realism and idealism, and between cosmopolitanism and a "healthy" nationalism. With a bias for lyric poetry, they showed little interest in the social criticism so typical of later naturalists.

The same can hardly be said of *Die Gesellschaft* (Society). This Munich periodical, founded in 1885 and edited by Michael Georg Conrad, favored prose, emphasized social problems and, through a diverse cadre of contributors, blindly attacked both living and dead authors. Although the initial attacks were aimed primarily at contemporaries, zeal for the destruction of the old, ostensibly in preparation for the new, soon ran riot until even Goethe and Schiller were subjected to the vilest vituperation, while members of Conrad's inner circle such as the self-proclaimed literary messiah Carl Bleibtreu (whose book *Die Revolution der Literatur* [1886; The Revolution of Literature] became a pacemaker for destructive criticism) were wildly lauded. While praising truth, modernity, and nationalism, Conrad stressed the latter. In terms chillingly familiar to the 20th century, he located the "secret" of art in Blut und Boden (blood and soil) and allowed contributors freely to indulge their anti-Semitism. On a positive note, Conrad was largely responsible for introducing a new image of Emile Zola to Germany. Previously denounced as a cynical pornographer, Conrad saw him as a courageous loner who dared to expose the evils of society and shared Zola's view that literature should become more scientific.

By 1886, with the founding of the Berlin literary society Durch (Through), the more significant discussions of naturalism had shifted to that city and are best illustrated by analyzing the work of two society members: Wilhelm Bölsche and Arno Holz. Bölsche's book *Die naturwissenschaftlichen Grundlagen der Poesie* (1887; The Natural Science Foundations of Literature) exemplifies the movement's new sobriety. Deploring unprincipled attacks on the German literary tradition and urging an intensified cross-fertilization of science and literature, he hoped to exploit the advances of the former to benefit the latter, while stripping such concepts as the freedom of the will of their metaphysical overtones. Holz, the best-known German Naturalist theoretician, carried the idea of a scientifically oriented literature to near absurdity. His *Die Kunst: Ihr Wesen und ihre Gesetze* (1891; Art: Its Essence and Its Laws) is an attempt to reduce literature to a manufactured product. Starting from Zola's equation "art = nature-x," in which x represents the "temperament" of the artist, Holz, who rejected the concept of artistic genius, strove to eliminate the x completely in favor of a totally objective depiction of reality. Although later admitting the futility of this ambition, Holz's language experiments in the novella *Papa Hamlet* (1889) and the drama *Familie Selicke* (1890; The Selicke Family), both written in collaboration with Johannes Schlaf, produced a new, hyperrealistic language that was capable of expressing the psychological nuances of fictional characters.

With the 1889 founding of the Verein Freie Bühne (Free Stage Society) and the 1890 periodical *Freie Bühne für modernes Leben* (Free Stage for Modern Life) in Berlin, the movement entered its most productive phase, and Otto Brahm, who served as both the theater director of the stage society and the editor of the periodical, must be credited with guiding the movement to its most significant accomplishments. With his preference for the dramatist Henrik Ibsen over the novelist Zola, and with his vigorous promotion of the naturalistic dramas of Gerhart Hauptmann, Brahm retreated from the movement's extreme forms to a more humanistically oriented literature. Never a "consequent" naturalist in the Holz vein, he saw the movement as part of an evolving continuum and, while not averse to social criticism, emphasized artistry over content. Seen in retrospect and from an international perspective, the movement produced only one author of lasting significance: Gerhart Hauptmann—and even he resisted the naturalist label that was applied to his works. Nevertheless, naturalism is usually regarded as the beginning phase of modern German literature. With its intensification of the realistic tendencies within earlier literary movements such as Storm and Stress and Young Germany (not to mention in certain authors such as Georg Büchner), and its innovations in language and subject matter (e.g., social problems), naturalism's impact on such 20th-century authors as Thomas Mann and Bertolt Brecht is indisputable.

WARREN R. MAURER

See also Bismarck Era; Gerhart Hauptmann

Further Reading

Hoefert, Sigrid, *Das Drama des Naturalismus,* Stuttgart: Metzler, 1968; 2nd edition, 1973

Marshall, Alan, *The German Naturalists and Gerhart Hauptmann: Reception and Influence,* Frankfurt: Lang, 1982

Maurer, Warren R., *The Naturalist Image of German Literature: A Study of the German Naturalists' Appraisal of Their Literary Heritage,* Munich: Fink, 1972

——, "Gerhart Hauptman in the United States," in *The Fortunes of German Writers in America: Studies in Literary Reception,* edited by

Wolfgang Elfe et al., Columbia: University of South Carolina Press, 1992

——, *Understanding Gerhart Hauptmann,* Columbia: University of Southern Carolina Press, 1992

Mews, Siegfried, "Naturalism," in *A Concise History of German Literature to 1900,* edited by Kim Vivian, Columbia: Camden House, 1992

Möbius, Hanno, *Der Naturalismus: Epochendarstellung und Werkanalyse,* Heidelberg: Quelle und Meyer, 1982

Osborne, John, *The Naturalist Drama in Germany,* Manchester: Manchester University Press, and Totowa, New Jersey: Rowman and Littlefield, 1971

Pascal, Roy, *From Naturalism to Expressionism: German Literature and Society, 1880–1918,* London: Weidenfeld and Nicholson, and New York: Basic Books, 1973

Schutte, Jürgen, *Lyrik des deutschen Naturalismus (1885–1893),* Stuttgart: Metzler, 1976

Nazi Party *see* National Socialism

Neidhart (von Reuental) ca. 1180/90–ca. 1240

The poet Neidhart competes with Walther von der Vogelweide as the most popular vernacular lyricist of the German Middle Ages. He is, at first glance, certainly the most prolific: approximately 1,500 stanzas (around 150 songs) survive under his name in 25 manuscripts (13th–15th centuries) and three imprints (16th century). By contrast, we only have some 490 extant stanzas for Walther. The bulk of these Neidhart texts, however, have come down to us outside the customary channels for Minnesang, the courtly love poetry of medieval Germany. Most are found in 15th-century sources, some 200 years younger than the author and more than 100 years younger than the standard Minnesang manuscripts of the late 13th and early 14th centuries. Moreover, by 1400, Neidhart had become a figure of legend, appearing as the quintessential *Bauernfeind* (enemy of peasants) in epics (Heinrich Wittenwiler's *Ring*), fabliaux (especially the chapbook *Neidhart Fuchs*), and carnival plays (so-called *Neidhartspiele*). Generations of scholars have since taken pains to separate the "real" Neidhart from Pseudo-Neidhart impostors—the assumed authors of the songs of late transmission—as well as from the Neidhart of folklore. For a late medieval audience, however, there was only one Neidhart, and more recent scholarship, represented above all by Günther Schweikle, has argued that the division of Neidhart's songs into categories of *echt* (authentic) and *unecht* (inauthentic) is itself a pseudodivision. Whatever the case, no other medieval author so well exemplifies the mutability of early (originally oral) texts, the thin line between fact and fiction, and the resulting conundrums of literary scholarship.

The debate begins with the author's name: "Neidhart" or "Neidhart von Reuental." In early Minnesang manuscripts, as well as in narrative works such as Wolfram von Eschenbach's *Willehalm* or Wernher der Gartenaere's *Helmbrecht,* he appears simply as *(Her) Nîthart* ([Sir] Neidhart). The singer in Neidhart's songs, however, often associates himself with a certain Riuwental (Reuental). Other figures similarly refer to a "knight of Riuwental," and two late sources identify the author as "Her Nithard van dem Ruwental" or "Heer Nytert van Ruwendael." Early scholars suspected that the "knight of Riuwental" must be the author himself, but this theory has increasingly found its detractors. Despite candidates such as Rewental near Freising and Reintal by Landshut, no one has conclusively identified a 13th-century village or parish by the name of Riuwental. More important, Neidhart's songs consistently play upon Riuwental's metaphorical overtones as "Reuen-Tal," or "Vale of Sorrows," making it nearly impossible to ascertain whether Riuwental is an actual place or merely a poetic construct. Current research now takes a conservative approach, preferring simply "Neidhart" over "Neidhart von Reuental."

Further biographical details, garnered from Neidhart's songs, are equally vague and are reliable only if the Riuwental persona is autobiographic. One event alone seems relatively certain: ca. 1230, the author moved from Bavaria to Medelicke (likely present-day Mödling), where he entered the service of Friedrich II of Austria. Neidhart subsequently apostrophized his patron in several stanzas, but he made no mention of Friedrich's death in 1246, suggesting that the author had passed away by this date. Other circumstances of Neidhart's life—knighthood, a wife and children, and participation in a crusade—are likely but remain speculative.

Happily, the songs themselves amply reward all efforts to become better acquainted with their author. Neidhart's oeuvre is *Dörperpoesie*, drawing its vibrancy from the ironic transposition of courtly ideals to the village, home of the *dörper* (boor). Unlike the Neidhart of legend, the author is not necessarily ill-disposed to peasants. Rather, the *dörper* symbolizes all that is uncourtly. This allows on the one hand for a frank treatment of "uncivilized" topics such as the open expression of sexual desire, especially as compared to the ritualized abnegation found in courtly love (*hohe Minne*). On the other hand, the frequently unsuccessful attempts by the singer, who adheres to courtly norms such as *êre* (honor), *zuht* (propriety), and *mâze* (moderation), to partake in the gaiety of the loutish *dörper* points to the limits of courtly values and, conversely, to the need to adhere to such values if they are to survive. Set against this backdrop, Neidhart, similar to Walther and other contemporary authors, ultimately sounds a lament on the failure of courtly culture to reconcile secular and religious ideals: "bî der werlde niemen lebet sünden vrî: ja ist ez sô ie lenger sô ie boeser in der kristenheit" (no one in this world lives without sin: indeed, as time goes on, things grow worse in all Christendom).

Formally, Neidhart's songs fall into two main categories, *Sommerlieder* (summer songs) and *Winterlieder* (winter songs). Both take their name from the imagery of the *Natureingang* (nature introduction), which can range from a few lines to four full stanzas and which expresses the singer's joy or sorrow according to the season. The snow and barren trees of the *Winterlieder* customarily introduce monologic laments that deal with unhappy courtships and the singer's village rivals. They are composed in the tripartite *Stollenstrophe* typical for most Minnesang: two metrically identical *Stollen* of 2 to 6 lines of varying length, together forming the *Aufgesang*, are followed by the metrically independent *Abgesang* of 2 to 13 lines, which completes the stanza; up to 14 stanzas can comprise one song. Subcategories of the *Winterlied* genre are the so-called *Werltsüeze* songs (laments on "Dame World") or the *Frîderun* songs (in which Neidhart laments the plunder of Frîderun's mirror by the peasant Engelmâr, symbolic for the loss of joy). Further, certain stanza types appear mainly in the winter songs: *Trutzstrophen* (counterstanzas, in which fictitious opponents of Neidhart speak), *Bittstrophen* (petitionary stanzas, in which the author requests favors, including a house, from Friedrich of Austria), and *Bilanzstrophen* (accounting stanzas, in which Neidhart takes stock of his poetic production). Conversely, images of flowers and green meadows open the dialogic *Sommerlieder*, in which either a mother and daughter or two playmates (*Gespielinnen*) discuss the younger women's (but at times the mother's) wish to dance and their desire for the knight of Riuwental. Strophic form also distinguishes the *Sommerlieder*: here, Neidhart employs the *Reienstrophe*, 4 to 17 line stanzas based predominantly on couplets of varying length. Its name stems from the *Rei(g)en*, a dance in which participants moved in a circle. The *Winterlieder* are dance songs as well, and melodies

a total of 55 songs survive, an astonishing amount considering that only some 50 (reconstructed) melodies survive for all other Minnesingers.

Currently, Ulrich Müller, Ingrid Bennewitz-Behr, and Franz Viktor Spechtler have undertaken a new edition of Neidhart's songs (without "pseudo" divisions). The project has already produced an analysis of the Riedegg manuscript, the oldest Neidhart source and the basis for the early editions of Moriz Haupt (1858) and Edmund Wießner (1923), and a transcription of the Ried manuscript of the 15th century, the largest collection of Neidhart songs (1,098 stanzas). The edition's inclusion of late sources such as the Ried manuscript, containing hitherto "inauthentic" *Schwanklieder* (versified fabliaux) significant for the development of the Neidhart legend, will undoubtedly contribute to further debate upon one of the most fascinating figures of the German Middle Ages.

GLENN EHRSTINE

Biography
Born ca. 1180/90, likely in Bavaria. First songs ca. 1210/20. Participated in crusade, either 1217–21, 1228–29, or both. Moved from Bavaria to Mödling by Vienna, ca. 1230, subsequently in the service of Friedrich II of Austria. Possibly married with children. Died ca. 1240.

Selected Works

Writings
Neidhart von Reuental, edited by Moriz Haupt, 1858; reprinted in *Neidharts Lieder*, edited by Ulrich Müller, et al., 1986
Die Lieder Neidharts, edited by Edmund Wießner and Paul Sappler, 4th edition, 1984
The Songs of Neidhart von Reuental, edited by A.T. Hatto and R.J. Taylor, 1958
Materialien zur Neidhart-Überlieferung, edited by Dietriche Boueke, 1967
Neidhartspiele, edited by John Margetts, 1982

Further Reading
Bennewitz-Behr, Ingrid, *Original und Rezeption: Funktions- und überlieferungsgeschichtliche Studien zur Neidhart-Sammlung R*, Göppingen: Kümmerle, 1987
Bennewitz-Behr, Ingrid, and Ulrich Müller, "Grundsätzliches zur Überlieferung, Interpretation, und Edition von Neidhart-Liedern: Beobachtungen, Überlegungen, und Fragen, exemplifiziert an Neidharts Lied von der *Werltsüeze*," *Zeitschrift für deutsche Philologie* 104, no. 1 (1985)
Beyschlag, Siegfried, "Neidhart und Neidhartianer," in *Die deutsche Literatur des Mittelalters: Verfasserlexikon*, edited by Kurt Ruh, et al., vol. 6, Berlin and New York: de Gruyter, 1977
Birkhan, Helmut, editor, *Neidhart von Reuental: Aspekte einer Neubewertung*, Vienna: Braumüller, 1983
Brunner, Horst, editor, *Neidhart*, Darmstadt: Wissenschaftliche Buchgesellschaft, 1986
Gaier, Ulrich, *Satire: Studien zu Neidhart, Wittenwiler, Brant, und zur satirischen Schreibart*, Tübingen: Niemeyer, 1967
Goheen, Jutta, *Mittelalterliche Liebeslyrik von Neidhart von Reuental bis zu Oswald von Wolkenstein: Eine Stilkritik*, Berlin: Schmidt, 1984
Jackson, William E., "Neidhart von Reuental," in *German Writers and Works of the High Middle Ages: 1170–1280*, Dicitonary of Literary Biography, vol. 138, edited by James Hardin and Will Hasty, Detroit, Michigan: Gale Research, 1994
Müller, Ulrich, "Mündlichkeit und Schriftlichkeit: Probleme der

Neidhartüberlieferung," in *Textkonstitution bei mündlicher und bei schriftlicher Überlieferung,* edited by Martin Stern, Tübingen: Niemeyer, 1991

Schweikle, Günther, *Neidhart,* Stuttgart: Metzler, 1990

Simon, Eckehard, *Neidhart von Reuental: Geschichte der Forschung*

und Bibliographie, Cambridge, Massachusetts: Harvard University Press, 1968

———, *Neidhart von Reuental,* Boston: Twayne, 1975

Wießner, Edmund, *Kommentar zu Neidharts Liedern,* Leipzig: Hirzel, 1954

Johann Nepomuk Nestroy 1801–1862

Johann Nestroy is now commonly acknowledged as one of the foremost writers of satiric comedy in the German language, but for the greater part of the almost 140 years since his death, his work was neglected as a purely local affair, lacking literary or intellectual weight. His work was also sentimentalized or politicized as folk art and even denounced as the voice of the gutter. For many decades his *Lokalpossen* (farces of local life) were considered inseparable from the unique stage personality of their author, and only a select few were regularly performed, even after collected editions became available. In addition, appreciation was impeded, both in the theater and academia, by dogmatic conceptions of comedy as a dramatic genre and by an unwillingness to recognize the literary legitimacy of satiric aggression as opposed to the reconciling, transfiguring spirit of poetic *Humor.* A balanced judgment has had to break down such barriers and take account of the very breadth of Nestroy's achievement and the range of perspectives from which his plays must be approached. The statistics alone bear witness to a life lived obsessively within and for the stage, both as a performer and writer. His long and prolific career spanned more than 40 years, producing over 80 plays in a variety of forms of popular comedy, with an acting repertoire of 880 roles in grand opera, parody, farce, vaudeville, social drama, and operetta. On one level, Nestroy is the successor to a long tradition of actor-playwrights, and his comedy is the culmination of a popular theater that stretches back to the court and Jesuit drama of the Baroque era via the crude peasant *Hanswurst* farce of the early 18th century and the institutionalizing of a more didactic local comedy during the 1780s, many of the conventions and stock themes of which became the material of Nestroy's parody. But his work belongs equally to the international theater industry of his own time. The essence of Nestroy's originality lies in what has been called "creative adaptation" (Yates): almost all his work has now been traced to contemporary sources—tales, novels, and, above all, stage works—and it amounts to an ongoing process of commercial and cultural cross-fertilization, often across frontiers and languages. On another level, these comedies give voice to an entire era in Viennese, German, and European society, not just in their thematic wealth, which reflects the evolving social and political experiences of four decades, but also in their contribution to a literary-dramatic critique of that society's language. In the *Sprachspiel* (play with language) that characterizes his work, Nestroy offers a satiric commentary, comparable with that of Grabbe, Büchner, and Heine, on the communicative norm of metaphorical speech that passes from the Romantics and Jean Paul, who framed it as a language of poetic freedom, to Görres,

Börne, and the writers of *Jungdeutschland,* and from there, through the models of journalism and trivial literature, to the general 19th-century rhetoric of subjectivist and idealist pathos.

Amid the complexity of Nestroy's relationship with his time, three aspects have figured most prominently in the heritage of his work in the 19th and, especially, in the 20th centuries. In the first place, as a theater that grows out of, and interacts with, a local tradition and a specific public, these *Lokalpossen* have been cited as a model for a new and critical *Volksstück* (folk drama). From Anzensgruber to Horváth, Bauer, and Turrini, later writers have seen in Nestroy the outstanding example of a theater for and about the people, which combines popular entertainment with fundamental questions of communal values and identities. At the same time, with Horváth, but then again with the experimentalists of the 1960s, above all the earlier work of Peter Handke, it is Nestroy's language consciousness that has made him a writer of our time, one for whom words can never be reduced to a mere medium of social discourse but become their own reality—explored, rehearsed, and enacted in the expression of meaning. Finally, the modernity of Nestroy's work has been evident in the revaluation of comedy, satire and parody in general, and above all with the propagation of forms of "open" theater, where the fiction of the stage becomes the instrument of an anti-illusionist interplay between dramatist, actors, and public. Since the 1920s, the fusion achieved in Nestroy between polemical intention, rational analysis, and aesthetic structures—verbal wit, song, dance, and gesture—can be seen to anticipate Brechtian alienation techniques and goes far beyond the traditional comic complicity of stage and audience in farce in its activation of audience response.

It was Karl Kraus, in his celebrated essay on the 50th anniversary of Nestroy's death, *Nestroy und die Nachwelt* (1912; *Nestroy and Posterity*), who first saw in Nestroy a creator of satiric comedy of a European rank. Far from being harmless fun, these *Lokalpossen,* Kraus argued, were "dynamite wrapped in cotton-wool," driven by a satiric spirit through which, for the first time in German literature, "language itself reflected on the things it expressed." In this view, wordplay becomes not just the comic form of this satire but its true subject. In Nestroy's earlier work, this sensitivity toward words and what they may conceal and reveal builds on the relatively naive wordplay and situation comedy of his predecessors in the Viennese popular theater. Soon, however, elements of comically inappropriate speech are integrated into a comprehensive *Sprachspiel,* where the wordplay is no longer just accidental and occasional but gives the entire dramatic fiction a parodic quality. Here, literary-theatrical pathos, the juxtaposing of registers, reactivated cliché, idiom, and proverb, chains of metaphor, allegorical abstraction, mock-quotation, pseudoscientific jargon, effects of alliteration, assonance, repetition, and a wealth of forms of ambiguity are seen to be the constituents of a rhetoric of quotation, mobilized by a society of role players. While the protagonists may remain ignorant of the ambivalence of their speech, their rhetoric betrays the rise of a problematic individualism, in which the apparent certainties of social discourse are deployed with an assertiveness that signals the end of the old Viennese order. Throughout his work, it is the comic ambiguity of Nestroy's dialogue that offers the hope of satiric negation and release, of winning from language a new self- and social consciousness.

When in 1831 Nestroy returned to Vienna to join Karl Carl's ensemble at the Theater an der Wien, he had already made his name as a performer of the grotesque parody that was to demolish the now empty shell of traditional Viennese popular comedy. The old magic and allegorical elements of that comedy had survived into the early 19th century, most notably in the portrayal of the dual reality of human and spirit worlds, where the higher *Zauberwelt* (magic world) still exercised a certain corrective force in the *Besserungsstück,* the comedies about misfits and miscreants who are restored to the proper path. Steadily, however, in the never-ending flow of entertainment pieces by J.A. Gleich, Adolf Bäuerle, and Karl Meisl, the representation of order and authority exhausts itself in sterile reproduction: the conventions are observed, but the interest is maintained only through gentle travesty and parody. Despite accusations leveled against him during and after his lifetime, Nestroy did not destroy the old stage, nor did he undermine Ferdinand Raimund's attempt to renew it: in the face of social and cultural change, it had already run its full course. Nestroy's parody of the language of the magic play shows the emptiness and absurdity of the pretense to moral norms where these are already reduced to fictions of self-assertion. When, in *Der konfuse Zauberer* (produced 1832; The Confused Magician) and other early *Zauberspiele,* the spirits can only quote the stock phrases of their allegorical selves, the action grinds to a halt in senseless automatism. At the same time, in adaptations of the *Besserungsstück* such as *Die Verbannung aus dem Zauberreich* (produced 1828; The Banishment from the Magic Realm) and Nestroy's greatest career success, *Der böse Geist Lumpazivagabundus* (produced 1833; The Evil Spirit Lumpazivagabundus), the challenge to social order is drastic and uncompromising. Where the barely redeemed good-for-nothing Longinus and the completely irredeemable Knieriem, the connoisseur of destructive comets and prophet of drunken despair, each insist on their right to their disreputable identities, the ironic facade of final harmony is refuted.

Nestroy's *Zauberspiele* can be seen as comedies of comic, and sometimes bitter, disillusion in which the traditional genre serves merely as the occasion for the subversive creativity of parody. Likewise, his adaptation of his sources throughout his career can be described as following the same quasi-parodic pattern: the comic localizing, and often trivializing, of the original theme and language to a Viennese idiom, and the exploiting of the ambiguities of a dialogue of *Sprachspiel* to reveal dimensions of motivation, characterization, and situation comedy generally lacking in the original. The process of *Verwienerung* (localization into the Viennese milieu) in Nestroy's drama is never aimed at merely naturalistic dialect effects: it is, as Kraus said, not a crutch but an artistic means and an integral part of this comedy of language.

To what extent the ambiguities function as explicit parody, as in the adaptations of Meyerbeer and Wagner (*Robert der Teuxel,* 1833; *Tannhäuser,* 1857; and *Lohengrin,* 1859), may often be a question of the status and familiarity of the original; in these works, Nestroy relies upon the audience's knowledge of, or at least about, the target chosen. In other plays, the original may be superseded: works such as *Die verhängnisvolle Faschingsnacht* (produced 1839; The Fateful Carnival Night, based on a little known play by Karl von Holtei) and *Judith und Holofernes* (produced 1849; Judith and Holofernes), the classic parody of the bombast and sexual mystification of Friedrich Hebbel's biblical drama *Judith* (1840), have come to stand as outstanding works of comic theater in their own right.

By the mid-1830s, the magic play was discarded, and Nestroy's *Sprachspiel* was now rooted firmly in the *Lokalstück,* or comedy of local life. But that shift to greater "realism" brought with it a dilemma that confronts Nestroy's drama from that point on. His drama, of necessity, responded to changes in the composition of his audience and its taste: a movement away from the old blending of estates toward a new bourgeois public that sought its own image on the stage. Repeated demands from the critics for a more elevated and morally instructive portrayal of the people reflect the new orthodoxy, which found its ideal in the sentimental *Lebensbild* (picture of life) developed by Friedrich Kaiser. Such demands were coupled with allegations that saw crude innuendo and cynicism in the ambiguities of Nestroy's acting and wordplay. The comment of Julius Seidlitz in 1837, that Nestroy was the "Napoléon of baseness," was to pursue him, echoed in a variety of forms, well beyond the grave and derives essentially from the inability to distinguish the satirist from his fiction. Clearly, the moralistic "truth to life" expected of Nestroy is quite incompatible with the satiric ambivalence that is the core of his comedy. The struggle to maintain that necessary principle of satiric negation is reflected, too, in the record of Nestroy's dealings with the censor, where his scheme to fool a sophisticated system of precensorship—submitting a doctored script to the authorities and then reintroducing potentially contentious elements in the performance—was not always sufficient to evade reprimands and penalties for risqué improvisation. The social and political dimension of his middle-class critics' fear of the satirist's mask also finds striking expression in C.L. Costenoble's 1837 comparison of Nestroy's acting to the "ferment of the mob," with its readiness to "plunder and kill at times of revolution." Given the need to observe what was prescribed as moral and political propriety, together with the ongoing pressure with each new play to achieve lasting commercial success, Nestroy was, in fact, uniquely successful in maintaining the favor of both the authorities and the public. From the mid-1830s, his comedies, which, in contrast to other writers, included resounding successes staged throughout his career, dominated the company's repertoire, and a very large majority of the roles that he performed were his own. Even with some plays of little wit or originality, the sheer comic force of his tall, angular figure on the stage, supported by his opposite in Werner Scholz, was enough to win over his audience.

Nevertheless, it is difficult to speak of a clear path of progression in Nestroy's work. The critical acclaim of *Zu ebener Erde und erster Stock* (produced 1835; Upstairs, Downstairs), a social drama of rich and poor, makes it the first and favorite in a line of plays that reveal the complexity of his position. Although after a number of failures in a more hybrid mode he reverted to the

Posse mit Gesang (farce with song), Nestroy still continued to experiment with elements of social realism, where satiric word-play often rests uneasily side by side with earnest rhetoric. That uncertainty of focus characterizes the substantial pre-revolutionary dramas of the 1840s such as *Der Unbedeutende* (produced 1846; The Unimportant Man) and *Der Schützling* (produced 1847; The Protégé), with their emphatic tone of social critique, as well as the ironic resignation of such major postrevolutionary works as *Mein Freund* (1851; My Friend) and *Kampl* (1852). In the classic farces of the earlier 1840s, however, from *Der Färber und sein Zwillingsbruder* (produced 1840; The Dyer and His Twin Brother) and *Der Talisman* (produced 1840; *The Talisman*) to *Das Mädl aus der Vorstadt* (produced 1841; The Girl from the Suburbs), *Einen Jux will er sich machen* (produced 1842; translated as *The Merchant of Yonkers, The Matchmaker,* and *On the Razzle*), *Liebesgeschichten und Heiratssachen* (produced 1843; *Love Affairs and Wedding Bells*), and *Der Zerrissene* (produced 1844; *A Man Full of Nothing*), the integrity of his satiric farce is preserved and heightened. These plays' dramatic structures and dialogue are informed by a coherent comic vision and a linguistic virtuosity that give full rein to the analytic-satiric commentaries of the Nestroy role, the raisonneur in whose songs and monologues Nestroy's fusion of corrosive intellect and "combinatory phantasy" (Rommel) finds fullest expression. At the same time, it is in the central protagonists in these plays—Kilian Blau, Titus Feuerfuchs, Schnoferl, Weinberl, Nebel, and Lips—that Nestroy achieves some of his most searching depictions of the problematic situation of the word- and role-player, whose rhetorical strategies can lead to predicaments where the manipulator is manipulated. Here, the intrigue advances to a point from which the comedy barely retrieves its happy end—a dilemma to which the strain of resignation and pathos in Nestroy's "darker" comedies can also be traced. At the close of the 1840s, the satiric spirit returns, most freely in the Hebbel parody, with its ridicule of military, or any other, heroics, and in the farce of revolutionary Vienna, *Freiheit in Krähwinkel* (produced 1848; *Liberty Comes to Krähwinkel*), where, although the mood is undoubtedly one of celebration at the collapse of a repressive order, the phrases of both "reactionaries" and "progressives" are exposed to the scrutiny of Nestroy's *Sprachspiel.*

These plays and others associated with the 1848 revolution—the "political hangover" (Mautner) of *Lady und Schneider* (produced 1849; Lady and Tailor), with its portrayal of the unscrupulous political agitator Hyginus Heugeig'n; the somber tones of *Der alte Mann mit der jungen Frau* (1849; The Old Man with the Young Wife), which was not performed for another century, with its sympathetic picture of the victims of repression; and the grotesque farce of cosmic revolution and metaphysical protest, *Höllenangst* (1849; Hellish Fear), with its celebrated denunciation of all government, heavenly and earthly—have been compared by critics as examples of the conflicting positions taken up by Nestroy "for" and "against" the revolution, which were, indeed, cited at the time as evidence of political opportunism. But this is again to mistake the satirist for his subject. In the final flourishing of his *Sprachspiel,* in the one-act *Frühere Verhältnisse* (*As You Were*) and *Häuptling Abendwind* (Chief Evening Breeze; both produced 1862), Nestroy dramatizes both the neuroses of the parvenu in a class-bound society and the aspirations to civilization and culture of a (thoroughly Viennese) South Seas primi-

tive. Here again, as in the *Zauberspiele,* the classic farces and the revolutionary plays, the breadth and variety of social and political comment is rooted in the wealth of dramatic situations and roles portrayed. Nestroy reveals his world through his characters: their pronouncements on reality on both sides of the footlights bear the mark of their subjective perspective. If we can speak of a Nestroyan creed at all, it would be what was attributed to another great satirist of language, Lichtenberg: namely, a "doctrine of scattered occasions" (J.P. Stern), occasions of insight that arise out of the ambiguities of our engagement with words. Nestroy's language consciousness, is not, of course, without social and political significance, but that is realized in the multifarious fictions of his stage.

Only after the pioneering dedication of Kraus and Rommel, and the transformation of social and cultural values in our own time, has the depth of Nestroy's farce been widely recognized. Academically, his work has finally emerged from the shadow of outdated, normative aesthetics. Continuing research, the production of a comprehensive critical edition, and the activities of the International Nestroy Society, with its periodical *Nestroyana,* have helped to consolidate and disseminate appreciation. On the German-language stage Nestroy became, at one point, the fourth most performed playwright—after Brecht, Shakespeare, and Molière. He remains one of the very few dramatists of the 19th century whose work combines intellectual and imaginative substance with theatrical effectiveness, not by the communication of doctrine but by making us participate in the comedy of its language.

ANTHONY COULSON

See also Zauberstücke

Biography

Born in Vienna, Austria, 7 December 1801. Law student at the University of Vienna, 1817–21; stage debut as bass singer (Sarastro in Mozart's *Die Zauberflöte*), Kärntnertor Court Opera, Vienna, 1822; actor and singer with the German Theater of Amsterdam, 1823–25, the Nationaltheater in Brünn (now Brno, Czech Republic), 1825–26, and theaters in Graz and Pressburg, 1826–28, with guest appearances in Vienna; withdrew from operatic roles; comic actor and writer with Karl Carl's theater company, based at the Theater an der Wien (from 1845, at the Theater in der Leopoldstadt, later renamed the Carl-Theater), 1831–54; director and manager of the company, 1854–60; leading comic actor on Vienna's commercial stage, 1830s–50s; appearing in his own plays; tours and guest appearances in Germany and Central Europe. Died 25 May 1862.

Selected Works

Collections

Gesammelte Werke, edited by Vincenz Chiavacci and Ludwig Ganghofer, 12 vols., 1890–91
Sämtliche Werke, edited by Fritz Brukner and Otto Rommel, 15 vols., 1924–30
Gesammelte Werke, edited by Otto Rommel, 6 vols., 1948–49
Komödien, edited by F.H. Mautner, 1970
Sämtliche Werke, edited by Jürgen Hein and Johann Hüttner, 1977–

Plays

Die Verbannung aus dem Zauberreiche; oder, Dreissig Jahre aus dem Leben eines Lumpen (produced 1828), in *Sämtliche Werke,* vol. 1, 1924

Der gefühlvolle Kerkermeister; oder, Adelheid, die verfolgte Wittib (produced 1832), in *Gesammelte Werke*, 1890–91

Nagerl und Handschuh; oder, Die Schicksale der Familie Maxenpfutsch (produced 1832), in *Gesammelte Werke*, 1890–91

Der konfuse Zauberer; oder, Treue und Flatterhaftigkeit (produced 1832), in *Gesammelte Werke*, 1890–91; adapted by Kurt Kraus, 1925

Der böse Geist Lumpazivagabundus; oder, Das liederliche Kleeblatt (produced 1833), 1835

Robert der Teuxel (produced 1833), in *Gesammelte Werke*, 1890–91

Die Familien Zwirn, Knieriem und Leim; oder, Der Welt-Untergangs-Tag (produced 1834), in *Gesammelte Werke*, 1890–91

Weder Lorbeerbaum noch Bettelstab (produced 1835), in *Gesammelte Werke*, 1890–90

Zu ebener Erde und erster Stock; oder, Die Launen des Glückes (produced 1835), 1838

Die beiden Nachtwandler; oder, Das Notwendige und das Überflüssige (produced 1836), in *Gesammelte Werke*, 1890–91; as *Der Notwendige und das Überflüssige*, adapted by Karl Kraus, 1920

Eine Wohnung ist zu vermieten in der Stadt . . . (produced 1837), in *Gesammelte Werke*, 1890–91

Das Haus der Temperamente (produced 1837); as *The House of Humors*, translated by Robert Harrison and Katharina Wilson, in *Three Viennese Comedies*, 1986

Glück, Missbrauch und Rückkehr; oder, Das Geheimnis des Grauen Hauses (from a novel by Paul de Kock) (produced 1838), 1845

Gegen Torheit gibt es keine Mittel (produced 1838), in *Gesammelte Werke*, 1890–91

Die verhängnisvolle Faschingsnacht (produced 1839), 1842

Der Färber und sein Zwillingsbruder (produced 1840), in *Gesammelte Werke*, 1890–91

Der Talisman (produced 1840), 1843; as *The Talisman*, translated by Max Knight and Joseph Fabry, in *Three Comedies*, 1967; translated by Robert Harrison and Katharina Wilson, in *Three Viennese Comedies*, 1986

Das Mädl aus der Vorstadt; oder, Ehrlich währt am längsten (produced 1841), 1845

Einen Jux will er sich machen (produced 1842), 1844; as *The Merchant of Yonkers,* translated and adapted by Thorton Wilder, 1939; as *The Matchmaker*, 1954; as *On the Razzle*, translated and adapted by Tom Stoppard, 1981

Die Papiere des Teufels; oder, Der Zufall (produced 1842), in *Gesammelte Werke*, 1890–91

Liebesgeschichten und Heiratssachen (produced 1843), in *Gesammelte Werke*, 1890–91; as *Love Affairs and Wedding Bells,* translated by Max Knight and Joseph Fabry, in *Three Comedies*, 1967

Nur Ruhe! (produced 1843), in *Gesammelte Werke*, 1890–91

Eisenbahnheiraten; oder, Wien, Neustadt, Brünn, (produced 1844), in *Gesammelte Werke*, 1890–91

Der Zerrissene (produced 1844), 1845; as *A Man full of Nothing,* translated by Max Knight and Joseph Fabry, in *Three Comedies*, 1967

Unverhofft (from a play by J.-F.-A. Bayard and Philippe Dumanoir) (produced 1845), 1848

Der Unbedeutende (produced 1846), 1849

Der Schützling (produced 1847), in *Gesammelte Werke*, 1890–91

Die schlimmen Buben in der Schule (produced 1847), in *Gesammelte Werke*, 1890–91

Die Anverwandten (from a novel by Charles Dickens) (produced 1848)

Freiheit in Krähwinkel (produced 1848), 1849; as *Liberty Comes to Krähwinkel,* translated by Sybil and Colin Welch, 1961

Lady und Schneider (produced 1849), in *Gesammelte Werke*, 1890–91

Judith und Holofernes (from a play by Friedrich Hebbel) (produced 1849), in *Gesammelte Werke*, 1890–91; as *Judith and Holofernes,* translated by Robert Harrison and Katharina Wilson, in *Three Viennese Comedies*, 1986

Höllenangst, in *Gesammelte Werke*, 1890–91

Mein Freund (produced 1851), 1851

Kampl; oder, Das Mädchen mit den Millionen und die Näherin (produced 1852), 1852

Heimliches Geld, heimliche Liebe (produced 1853), in *Gesammelte Werke*, 1890–91

Theaterg'schichten durch Liebe, Intrige, Geld und Dummheit (produced 1854), 1854

Umsonst (produced 1857)

Tannhäuser (from the libretto by Richard Wagner) (produced 1857), 1857

Frühere Verhältnisse (produced 1862), in *Gesammelte Werke*, 1890–91; as *As You Were*, translated and adapted by Geoffrey Skelton, 1997

Häuptling Abendwind; oder, Das greuliche Festmahl (from an operetta by Jacques Offenbach) (produced 1862), in *Sämtliche Werke*, vol. 14, 1930

Der alte Mann mit der jungen Frau (produced in revised version, as *Der Flüchtling*, 1890; original version produced 1948), in *Gesammelte Werke*, 1890–91

Three Comedies (includes *A Man full of Nothing; The Talisman; Love Affairs and Wedding Bells*), translated and adapted by Max Knight and Joseph Fabry, 1967

Three Viennese Comedies (includes *The Talisman; Judith and Holofernes; The House of Humours*), translated by Robert Harrison and Katharina Wilson, 1986

Other

Gesammelte Briefe und Revolutionsdokumente (1831–1862), edited by Fritz Brukner, 1938

Unbekannte Couplets von Johann Nestroy, edited by Otto Rommel, *Jahrbuch der Gesellschaft für Wiener Theaterforschung* (1951–52)

Briefe, edited by Walter Obermaier, 1977

Further Reading

Brill, Siegfried, *Die Komödie der Sprache: Untersuchungen zum Werke Johann Nestroys*, Nuremberg: Carl, 1967

Diehl, Siegfried, *Zauberei und Satire im Frühwerk Nestroys*, Bad Homburg: Gehlen, 1969

Hein, Jürgen, *Das Wiener Volkstheater: Raimund und Nestroy*, Darmstadt: Wissenschaftliche Buchgesellschaft, 1978

———, *Johann Nestroy*, Stuttgart: Metzler, 1990

Hillach, Ansgar, *Die Dramatisierung des komischen Dialogs: Figur und Rolle bei Nestroy*, Munich: Fink, 1967

Kraus, Karl, *Nestroy und die Nachwelt*, Vienna: Jahoda und Siegel, 1912; Frankfurt: Suhrkamp, 1975

Mackenzie, John R.P., "Political Satire in Nestroy's *Freiheit in Krähwinkel*," *Modern Language Review* 75 (1980)

Mautner, Franz Heinrich, *Nestroy*, Heidelberg: Stiehm, 1974

Nestroyana, Vienna: Internationale Nestroy-Gesellschaft, 1979–

Rommel, Otto, "Johann Nestroy: Ein Beitrag zur Geschichte der Wiener Volkskomik," in *Johann Nestroy: Sämtliche Werke*, edited by Fritz Brukner and Otto Rommel, vol. 15, Vienna: Schroll, 1924

———, "Johann Nestroy, der Satiriker auf der Altwiener Komödienbühne," in *Johann Nestroy: Gesammelte Werke*, vol. 1, Vienna: Schroll, 1948

Yates, W.E., *Nestroy: Satire and Parody in Viennese Popular Comedy*, Cambridge: Cambridge University Press, 1972

———, *Nestroy and the Critics*, Columbia, South Carolina: Camden House, 1994

Yates, W.E., and John R.P. McKenzie, editors, *Viennese Popular Theatre: A Symposium—Das Wiener Volkstheater: Ein Symposium*, Exeter: University of Exeter, 1985

Neue Sachlichkeit

The term *Neue Sachlichkeit* (New Objectivity) is commonly used to refer to the cultural climate in Germany between the stabilization of the economy in 1924 and the advent of National Socialism in 1933. It gained currency after being used as the title of an art exhibition held in Mannheim in 1925, which aimed, in the words of its organizer Georg Friedrich Hartlaub, "to unite representative works by artists who, during the last ten years, have been neither impressionistically diffuse nor expressionistically abstract." As it was applied to the visual arts, then, the term did not denote one particular style but described a broad trend that encompassed the mythical depictions of Max Beckmann, the social satire of George Grosz, the doll-like figures of Georg Schrimpf, the wryly aggressive portraits of Otto Dix and Rudolf Schlichter, a variety of depersonalized representations of industrial machinery and architecture, and the obsessively clinical studies of Christian Schad. The reasons why Neue Sachlichkeit caught on as a general descriptive term for the culture of the 1920s relate both to developments in design and architecture that go back to around 1900 and to the public mood of the Weimar period. In the former context, the term was associated with the elimination of ornamentation, the utilitarian application of modern materials and rational design concepts, and the improvement of housing and working conditions for an industrialized society. Such thinking, which was promoted by the Werkbund association, and after 1924 by the Bauhaus, made its greatest impact during the course of the 1920s.

The application of the term to literary writing is more problematic. A programmatic commitment to *Sachlichkeit* in the sense of a down-to-earth appraisal of material realities can be found as early as 1919 in the writings of authors who were eager to break with the idealistic fervor and introspective pathos of Expressionism (e.g., Brecht, Feuchtwanger, and Oskar Maria Graf). A similar attitude can be found in the editorial policy of cultural journals that were either newly founded or renamed in the wake of World War I (*Die Weltbühne, Das Tagebuch, Der Querschnitt,* and *Die literarische Welt*). These journals' common impulse was to create opportunities for open-minded discussions of contemporary social and political developments in an international perspective; a narrower concern with literary and cultural issues had previously characterized such journals. The trend toward reportage and essay writing was further encouraged by a strong public interest in travelogues and documentary articles, as German readers sought to overcome the isolation they had experienced during World War I and to adapt to a period of rapid technological change. The fascination with factual information and the power of technology was shared during the 1920s by the liberal and conservative press, which provided many young writers with early professional experience, and by writers associated with the communist movement (notably Johannes R. Becher and Egon Erwin Kisch). Evidence that Neue Sachlichkeit had come to denote a vague sense that the world was being driven forward into a new era by a combination of technological development and a functionalist approach to providing for human needs, as well as by the impact of political mass movements, was apparent from the public responses to the heavily technologized theater productions of Erwin Piscator in the later 1920s. This sense was also synthesized within the domain of popular entertainment by works such as the revue *Es liegt in der Luft* (There's Something in the Air) of 1928, the theme song of which alluded explicitly to these trends. But the serious criticism of such attitudes by intellectuals and literary authors also set in around that time.

Brecht, whose fascination with the momentum of technological change and the subordination of the individual to the demands of the collective is apparent in his play *Mann ist Mann* (1926), satirized such thinking in 1928 in a poem about 700 intellectuals venerating an oil tank. In the same year, independent Marxist commentators began to analyze contemporary trends in terms of the commodification of human productivity. Anthologies of prose writing published around 1930 (*Fazit,* edited by Ernst Glaeser, and *24 neue Erzähler,* edited by Hermann Kesten) were received both as representative of the aspirations of young authors to precise sociological inquiry into the nature of the postwar age and as symptomatic of their retreat from issues of an emotional or spiritual nature. Joseph Roth, who had been publicly associated with a documentary approach to narrative since the publication of *Die Flucht ohne Ende* (1927; Flight without End), denounced the general trend of Neue Sachlichkeit in a major essay of 1930, arguing the need for rounded narrative presentations (*Gestaltung*) as vehicles for the deeper understanding of human experience. Within the communist movement, too, Georg Lukács attacked the shallowness of a documentary style of writing and advocated the conventions of traditional realist narrative in a series of articles in *Die Linkskurve* in 1932; these writings mark the beginning of his campaign against modernist literary experiments.

For many years, scholarly understanding of what Neue Sachlichkeit meant was dominated by the heritage of Marxist sociological analysis, exemplified in the writings of Ernst Bloch, Walter Benjamin, Theodor W. Adorno, and Siegfried Kracauer, where the term was categorically associated with a retreat on the part of middle-class intellectuals from ideological commitment and with a cynical pursuit of short-term self-interest. Since the 1980s, however, research has begun to focus more precisely upon the way in which the discourse of Neue Sachlichkeit relates to longer-term cultural trends in the 20th century and upon how, and in what terms, the rising generation of authors after 1918 were developing critical perspectives on the issues of their day rather than uncritically reflecting them. A stance of undeluded unsentimentality may be said to constitute a conventional mannerism in much of the writing of male authors whose formative years had coincided with World War I and who experienced severe intellectual disillusionment during the Weimar years (e.g., Ernst Glaeser, Erich Kästner, and Hermann Kesten). A more differentiated picture, however, is now emerging of the achievement, within the historical constraints of the time, of such writers as Hans Fallada, Marieluise Fleißer, Ödön von Horváth, and Irmgard Keun.

DAVID MIDGLEY

See also Die Moderne; Weimar Republic

Further Reading

Becker, Sabina, and Christoph Weiß, editors, *Neue Sachlichkeit im Roman: Neue Interpretationen zum Roman der Weimarer Republik,* Stuttgart: Metzler, 1995

Hermand, Jost, "*Neue Sachlichkeit:* Ideology, Lifestyle, or Artistic

Movement?," in *Dancing on the Volcano: Essays on the Culture of the Weimar Republic*, edited by Thomas W. Kniesche and Stephen Brockmann, Columbia, South Carolina: Camden House, 1994

Hirdina, Karin, *Pathos der Sachlichkeit: Funktionalismus und Fortschritt ästhetischer Kultur*, Berlin: Dietz, 1981

Lethen, Helmut, *Neue Sachlichkeit, 1924–1933: Studien zur Literatur des "Weißen Sozialismus,"* Stuttgart: Metzler, 1970

———, "Neue Sachlichkeit," in *Weimarer Republik—Drittes Reich: Avantgardismus, Parteilichkeit, Exil, 1918–1945*, Deutsche Literatur: Eine Sozialgeschichte, vol. 9, edited by Horst Albert Glaser, Reinbek bei Hamburg: Rowohlt, 1983

Lindner, Martin, *Leben in der Krise: Zeitromane der neuen Sachlichkeit und die intellektuelle Mentalität der klassischen Moderne*, Stuttgart: Metzler, 1994

Mayer, Dieter, *Die Epoche der Weimarer Republik*, Geschichte der deutschen Literatur vom 18. Jahrhundert bis zur Gegenwart, edited by Viktor Zmegac, vol. 3, Königstein: Athenäum, 1984

Petersen, Klaus, "'Neue Sachlichkeit': Stilbegriff, Epochenbezeichnung oder Gruppenphänomen?" *Deutsche Vierteljahrsschrift* 56 (1982)

Schmied, Wieland, *Neue Sachlichkeit und Magischer Realismus in Deutschland, 1918–1933*, Hannover: Fackelträger, 1969

Trommler, Frank, " Technik, Avantgarde, Sachlichkeit: Versuch einer historischen Zuordnung," in *Literatur in einer industriellen Kultur*, edited by Götz Großklaus and Eberhard Lämmert, Stuttgart: Cotta, 1989

Willett, John, *The New Sobriety: Art and Politics in the Weimar Period, 1917–1933*, London: Thames and Hudson, 1978

Neue Subjektivität

The term *Neue Subjektivität* (New Subjectivity), which affords no easy definition, is associated with developments in German literature in the 1970s, which are usually seen as a reaction to the excessive politicization of writing in the previous decade. When the "death of literature" was being proclaimed during the heady days of the 1968 student rebellion, it was inevitable that there would be some kind of reaction. As early as 1970, Martin Walser, who at that time was championing directly sociocritical writing, complained about a new mood that was concerned with the personal rather than the political, he signaled out for criticism writing that evoked dreams, visions, and ecstasy, particularly if these states were induced by the use of drugs. It was, however, the new mood that prevailed. Looking back on the previous decade in 1980, Michael Rutschky spoke, in the title of his essay, of *Erfahrungshunger* (1980; Hunger for Experience). It is the emphasis on personal experience and feeling that provides a defining element of what became known as New Subjectivity.

The paradigm shift in the 1970s can be linked to the different political atmosphere of the period. Whereas the events of 1968 and the accession of Willy Brandt to the chancellorship in 1969 of West Germany engendered a mood of optimism, the 1970s were a decade of economic crisis and general retrenchment, as encapsulated in the word *Tendenzwende* (change of direction), which was used to mark a return to more conservative values in society. It was a time to take stock and to search for identity, particularly for those who had been associated with student politics, especially when certain activists turned to political terrorism and brought left-wing politics into discredit.

This does not mean that the more subjective literature of the 1970s is free of politics. It is certainly incorrect to see it simply as a return to the apolitical German tradition of inwardness. In this literature, the political and the personal often come together, with the personal asserting itself against the abstract and the theoretical. This is certainly the case in Peter Schneider's *Lenz* (1973), where the eponymous hero, whose name recalls the unhappy 18th-century dramatist, feels increasingly estranged from political debate in Berlin and, in the time-honored fashion, finds greater fulfillment in Italy. The first page of the book immediately, if not very subtly, underlines this alienation by recalling how Lenz has turned his picture of Marx on its head. Another novel, which shows in an altogether more subtle way the limits of 1960s political activism, is Nicolas Born's *Die erdabgewandte Seite der Geschichte* (1976; The Dark Side of the Story). As he takes part in demonstrations on 1 May, the first-person narrator can only feel contempt for those with direct answers to life's problems.

The literature of New Subjectivity did not restrict itself to confronting the most recent past. It is also marked by a whole series of *Vaterbücher* (father books) in which the protagonist seeks clarity about his own background. This theme, too, has a marked political dimension, particularly if the father was compromised by his role in National Socialism. This is the case in Peter Härtling's *Nachgetragene Liebe* (1980; Love, Retrospective), Christoph Meckel's *Suchbild* (1980; Picture Puzzle), and, in the most noted work at the time, Bernward Vesper's *Die Reise* (1977; The Trip), which, as the narrator struggles to establish clarity about his own identity, not only deals with the author's relationship to his father, the Nazi poet Will Vesper, but also with his own political activities. It was not only men who sought clarity about their fathers. Elisabeth Plessen's impressive novel *Mitteilung an den Adel* (1976; Message to the Aristocracy), which is undoubtedly autobiographical, describes the attempt by a young woman of aristocratic background to come to terms with the traditional, authoritarian values of her father as she drives to his funeral.

Writing by women about their experiences is a feature of the literature of the 1970s. Having been consigned to a largely marginal role in the political upheavals of the 1960s, they, too, sought to express their identity as the feminist movement became an increasingly significant feature of West German society. Against this background, Karin Struck achieved instant success with her novel *Klassenliebe* (1973; Class Love), which relates the tribulations of a young woman caught between her lower-class background and the intellectual circles in which she is beginning to move. Now, much of the writing appears simplistic, much more so than the writing in Verena Stefan's *Häutungen* (1975; *Shedding*), the text that was received at the time as a seminal feminist work. The first-person narrator in Stefan's novel, who is clearly based on the author herself, experiences no warmth in her relationships with men and turns to women in her search for greater happiness. Although this is not unproblematic, her sense of well-being improves. She also seeks in her writing to create a language that will reflect the female condition.

Established writers also turned to personal themes in the 1970s. Max Frisch, in his 1975 story *Montauk,* uses the framework of a brief affair with an American for what appear to be direct reflections on his own life and, specifically, his experiences with women. What superficially seems to be pure subjectivity, however, is in many respects a carefully crafted piece of fiction that does not easily fit within the category of New Subjectivity. The same can be said for Ingeborg Bachmann's 1971 *Malina,* which, although concerned with the position of women, bears no resemblance to confessional autobiography. Equally, the writings of Botho Strauß and Peter Handke, despite, especially in the latter case, clear autobiographical elements, seem aesthetically far removed from the kind of work described above.

This is not to belittle everything that can be most easily subsumed within the category New Subjectivity. The texts at their best are not merely a reflection of a particular historical context in the development of German literature and society. They opened up new fields of experience to writing and, in the case of the female authors, helped to liberate women's writing from the largely peripheral position it had previously occupied in the public consciousness.

STUART PARKES

See also Peter Handke

Further Reading

Bullivant, Keith, *Realism Today,* Leamington Spa and New York: Berg, 1987; distributed in U.S. by St. Martin's Press

Kreuzer, Helmut, "Neue Subjektivität: Zur Literatur der siebziger Jahre in der Bundesrepublik Deutschland," in *Deutsche Gegenwartsliteratur,* edited by Manfred Durzak, Stuttgart: Reclam, 1981

McGowan, Moray, "Neue Subjektivität," in *After the "Death of Literature,"* edited by Keith Bullivant, Oxford, New York, and Munich: Berg, 1989; distributed in U.S. and U.K. by St. Martin's Press

Rapisadra, Cettina, "Women's Writing 1968–80," in *Postwar Women's Writing in German,* edited by Chris Weedon, Providence, Rhode Island and Oxford: Berghahn Books, 1997

Schlösser, Hermann, "Subjektivität und Autobiographie," in *Gegenwartsliteratur seit 1968,* edited by Klaus Briegleb and Sigrid Weigel, Munich: Deutscher Taschenbuchverlag, 1992

Schnell, Ralf, *Die Literatur der Bundesrepublik,* Stuttgart: Metzler, 1986

Das Nibelungenlied ca. 1200

With its 35 manuscripts, 11 of which are complete or virtually complete, the *Nibelungenlied* was one of the most popular works known to the aristocracy of the Middle High German *Blütezeit* (Classical Period, ca. 1170–1250). It shares with most other "heroic epics" an anonymous author, a strophic form, and a penchant for depicting mass battle scenes set against an epic landscape (in contrast to medieval romance's preference for individual jousts). Yet the "spirit" of the *Nibelungenlied*—succinctly stated in the second-to-last strophe, namely, that all joy turns to sorrow in the end—sets it distinctly apart from the numerous works that comprise both the historical and fairy-tale Dietrich epics of the German Middle Ages and from the other German "heroic epic" that was composed within the following 40 years, *Kudrun,* which concludes with a series of marriages symbolizing renewal, fecundity, and continuity through succeeding generations. In this respect, the *Nibelungenlied* can hardly be considered "representative" of extant medieval German heroic epic; there is nothing that approximates it in the same way, for example, that Hartmann von Aue's *Erec* or *Iwein* might be said to fit the same generic mold as Ulrich von Zatzikhoven's *Lanzelet* or, for that matter (and despite its greater subtlety and depth), Wolfram von Eschenbach's *Parzival.* The works that constitute the Dietrich cycle, as well as *Kudrun,* lack the "epic tragedy" that characterizes the *Nibelungenlied* and that justifies its being re-garded as a "unicum" among the non-romance works of the period. It is small wonder that Harold Bloom includes it as the sole German "heroic epic" among his recommended readings in *The Western Canon* (1994).

The *Nibelungenlied* is a tale of joy, sorrow, arrogance, power, love, treachery, and revenge, which is spread over 2,379 strophes (manuscript B) and divided into 39 *âventiuren* (chapters). The first 19 *âventiuren* relate the story of Siegfried, prince and later king of the Netherlands (and the otherworldly Nibelungenland), although the epic opens, significantly, with a chapter devoted to Kriemhild and her kinsmen in Worms, capital of Burgundy. Siegfried's arrival at Worms, punctuated by his unwarranted claims on Burgundian lands, creates, from the outset, tensions between himself and this royal family, which are exacerbated rather than alleviated by his marriage to the Burgundian princess, Kriemhild. His efforts to become a true friend to her brother and king, Gunther, are precluded by his own imprudent words and deeds. Siegfried acts against his better judgment to procure the amazon-like Icelandic queen, Brünhild, for the hopelessly outmatched Gunther (thereby receiving the latter's sister, Kriemhild, in return). He consequently becomes inextricably tangled in a web of deception that eventually leads to the compromising of Burgundian honor by his spouse and, subsequently, his own death at the hands of Hagen. Siegfried's murder, coupled with the theft of Kriemhild's treasure (also by Hagen), sets the stage for the second part of the *Nibelungenlied,* encompassing *âventiuren* 20 through 39.

In the second part, the plot revolves around Kriemhild's quest for revenge against Hagen, which she pursues at all costs. Deprived of her major source of power (the Nibelungen hoard) by Hagen, she reluctantly agrees to marry Etzel (Attila) after receiving assurance from his revered and renowned liege man, Rüdiger of Pöchlarn, that he will avenge any wrong done to her. Individual tragedy—the murder of Siegfried—ultimately culminates in collective destruction as the Burgundians, following (against Hagen's advice) an invitation by Etzel to come to Hungary, are annihilated (at the instigation of Kriemhild) by Hunnish forces who are themselves decimated in the final conflagration. All of Kriemhild's family perish—Gunther is beheaded on her orders—and a captured, defenseless Hagen dies by her hand. She, in turn, is hacked to death by one of her own allies, Hildebrand, who is repulsed at the sight of a magnificent warrior slain by a woman turned she-devil.

The major manuscripts of the *Nibelungenlied,* A (Munich), B (St. Gall), and C (Donaueschingen), have been the subject of considerable dispute among scholars for much of the almost two and a half centuries that have passed since the physician Jacob Hermann Obereit literally lifted the *Nibelungenlied* from the dust of obscurity in Hohenems/Vorarlberg. For several generations of scholars, manuscript B has been considered the most "reliable" in terms of its proximity to the archetype, although more recently greater attention has been accorded the Donaueschingen variant, with at least one scholar (Joachim Heinzle) calling for a break from the fixation with manuscript B. Apart from matters of manuscript affiliation with respect to a lost archetype, there is a clear difference between C and the other variants with regard to thematic accentuation and, perhaps, authorial intentionality. Manuscript C, along with the *Klage* (the first commentary on the *Nibelungenlied,* dating from approximately 1200 and appended to virtually all of the complete manuscripts), casts Kriemhild in a remarkably positive light when compared to other versions.

While the *Nibelungenlied* was initially received with scorn by Friedrich II of Prussia and representatives of the Enlightenment, the epic was seen by Goethe as constituting an integral element in the education of the nation. It was revered by the Romanticists in the early 19th century, and the dramatist Friedrich Hebbel used it as the basis for one of his most successful and psychologically intriguing plays (*Die Nibelungen,* 1855–60), which enjoyed critical acclaim from both audiences and scholars alike throughout the late 19th and well into the 20th century. Nibelungen themes, although they are more the ones that are found in the Norse analogues than in the German *Nibelungenlied* itself, inspired Wagner to compose his majestic and itself "epic" *Ring des Nibelungen* (1854–74). Popular editions of the work flourished at the turn of the century both within and without Germany, the epic became a standard part of school curricula, and its content has inspired artists, sculptors, musicians, and writers (although never of the stature of Hebbel) to capture in more "modern" garb the highly charged drama of the medieval original. Its reception was not confined to the literary sphere. Particular ideas and ideals, especially the binary concepts of loyalty/honor and treachery/dishonor that are so integral to the *Nibelungenlied,* were applied to the spheres of politics and military achievements and expectations. In a speech to officers of the *Wehrmacht* at the Reich Ministry for Aviation on 30 January 1943, Hermann Göring compared the struggle of German troops at Stalingrad to the "Kampf der Nibelungen"; the comparison could already have been extended to include the demise of von Paulus's Sixth Army. Intriguingly, the last unit established within the élite Waffen-SS (Combat SS) of the German armed forces was the 38th SS Grenadier Division "Nibelungen," formed in March 1945, two months before the end of the war in Europe. Hans Helmut Kirst's novel, *Die Nacht der Generale* (1962; *The Night of the Generals*), which was translated into English in 1963 and released as a film in 1967 with Peter O'Toole in the leading role, fictionalizes the role of the "Nibelungen" division—which in reality did not exceed regimental strength—under the command of the notorious General Tanz. Most postwar approaches to the Nibelungen theme, particularly in literary works, have de-emphasized the heroic and more often than not have used the topic as a basis for a critical or parodic treatment of the concepts of loyalty and honor; to little effect, however, as it is clearly the *Nibelungenlied* and not its detractors that has withstood the test of time.

WINDER McCONNELL

See also Middle High German; Richard Wagner

Editions

First edition: *Chriemhilden Rache, und die Klage; zwey Heldengedichte aus dem schwäbischen Zeitpuncte. Sammt Fragmenten aus dem Gedichte von den Nibelungen und aus dem Josaphat . . . ,* Zurich: Orell, 1757 (partial edition); *Der Nibelungen Liet: Ein Rittergedicht aus dem XIII. oder XIV. Jahrhundert. Zum ersten Male aus der Handschrift abgedruckt,* Berlin: Spencer, 1782 (first complete edition, the first part based on manuscript A and the second part on manuscript C)

Critical editions: *Die Nibelunge Not,* edited by Karl Lachmann, Berlin: Reimer, 1826 (manuscript A); *Das Nibelungenlied,* edited by Ursula Hennig, Tübingen: Niemeyer, 1977 (manuscript C); *Das Nibelungenlied,* edited by Siegfried Grosse, after the editions by Karl Bartsch and Helmut de Boor, Stuttgart: Reclam, 1997 (manuscript B)

Translation: *The Nibelungenlied,* translated by A.T. Hatto, New York: Penguin, 1969

Further Reading

Andersson, Theodore M., *A Preface to the "Nibelungenlied,"* Stanford, California: Stanford University Press, 1987

Ehrismann, Otfrid, *"Nibelungenlied:" Epoche — Werk — Wirkung,* Munich: Beck, 1987

Härd, John Evert, *Das Nibelungenepos: Wertung und Wirkung von der Romantik bis zur Gegenwart,* translated by Christine Palm, Tübingen: Francke, 1996

Haug, Walter, "Montage und Motif im *Nibelungenlied,"* in *"Nibelungenlied und Klage: Sage und Geschichte, Struktur und Gattung. Passauer Nibelungengespräche 1985,* edited by Fritz Peter Knapp, Heidelberg: Winter, 1987

Heinzle, Joachim, "The Manuscripts of the *Nibelungenlied,"* in *Companion to the "Nibelungenlied,"* edited by Winder McConnell, Columbus, South Carolina: Camden House, 1998

Hoffmann, Werner, *Das Nibelungenlied,* 6th edition, Stuttgart: Metzler, 1992

McConnell, Winder, *The Nibelungenlied,* Boston: Twayne, 1984

Friedrich Nicolai 1733–1811

Friedrich Nicolai first appeared on the German cultural scene in the early 1750s. Initially establishing himself as a literary critic in Berlin, he later achieved prominence and financial success through his activities as a bookseller, publisher, editor, and author. As a champion of the Enlightenment in Germany, Nicolai advocated a program of national improvement through reasoned debate, social engagement, religious tolerance, and didactic art. His publications, which ranged from original novels to literary journals to historical and philosophical essays, did much to encourage the spread of progressive, middle-class ideology in Germany. Although originally viewed as an innovator, Nicolai's outspoken criticism of late 18th-century social and cultural developments led him to appear increasingly reactionary to a new generation of intellectuals. His later years were marked by hostile confrontations with opponents and a declining influence on German cultural life.

Nicolai's early critical works signaled a new phase in efforts by the emergent middle class to establish a German literary tradition worthy of international acclaim. After an initial essay in 1753 defending Milton's *Paradise Lost* against false accusations of plagiarism, Nicolai made his first substantive contribution to this project with his *Briefe über den itzigen Zustand der schönen Wissenschaften in Deutschland* (1755; Letters on the Current State of the Fine Arts in Germany). Taking as his starting point the controversies between J.C. Gottsched's intellectual clique in Leipzig and the Zurich group around J.J. Bodmer, Nicolai offered his reflections on the failure of recent German literature to realize its potential. Refusing allegiance to either of these two schools, he instead faulted their self-indulgent sectarianism as one cause of the mediocrity of much German writing. What German authors lacked, according to Nicolai, was genius, and he felt this deficiency was exacerbated by insufficient exposure to "the world." Only through the spread of candid, nonpartisan criticism (*Kritik*), he argued, could one hope to remedy the situation.

The *Briefe* established the 22-year-old Nicolai as a member of the critical vanguard and led him to important friendships with G.E. Lessing and Moses Mendelssohn. The fruits of their collaboration can be seen in the *Bibliothek der schönen Wissenschaften und der freyen Künste* (1756–59; Library of the Fine and Liberal Arts), a journal of book reviews, critical essays, and original works edited by Nicolai and containing contributions from all three. More lasting in their impact were the *Briefe, die neueste Litteratur betreffend* (1759–1765; Letters Concerning the Most Recent Literature), the first publication of the Nicolai press after Friedrich assumed control in 1758. Initially conceived as an extension of the three friends' debates on literary topics, these letters offered weekly book reviews under the guise of a correspondence with an officer wounded in what is now known as the Seven Years' War. The epistolary character of the reviews allowed the authors to adopt a familiar, conversational tone, thereby demonstrating just the sort of popular engagement with art that they felt was so important for the cultivation of good taste in Germany.

Nicolai's crowning achievement in his tireless quest to improve German letters was the publication of the review journal *Allgemeine deutsche Bibliothek* (*ADB*; Universal German Library). The journal appeared continuously from 1765 until 1806, although the threat of Prussian censorship forced Nicolai to give up ownership between 1792 and 1800. A rapid expansion in the publishing industry meant that the *ADB* was unable to keep its promise of a comprehensive review of all new books appearing in German; nonetheless, during its 40 years of existence, over 400 contributors reviewed some 80,000 books on virtually all aspects of intellectual life. The significance of the *ADB* as an instrument of national cultural integration should not be underestimated. Nicolai himself, who already in the *Briefe* of 1755 had remarked on the absence of a German cultural center that was comparable to Paris or London, viewed the journal as a kind of textual surrogate for an actual capital city.

Beginning in the 1770s, Nicolai expanded his activities as an author to include biography, philosophy, history, and original literary works. Whatever the field of endeavor, however, his operative category remained that of *Kritik*. Between 1773 and 1776, he published the three-volume *Das Leben und die Meinungen des Herrn Magisters Sebaldus Nothanker* (*The Life and Opinions of Master Sebaldus Nothanker*), the first of several satires aimed at societal elements that he perceived as threats to enlightened progress. The main target of this popular tale of a hapless country cleric is religious intolerance in all its guises, but the novel criticizes other contemporary cultural phenomena as well, from literary *Empfindsamkeit* to the German publishing industry. As a cultural artifact, the work is also remarkable for its detailed depiction of late 18th-century Berlin. Nicolai had become a citizen of the city in 1762 and did much to enhance Berlin's (and the Prussian King Friedrich II's) reputation in Germany and in Europe as a whole. His early critical, editorial, and publishing projects helped put Berlin on the literary map, and he also wrote and published three editions of a mammoth historical and statistical volume on the city entitled *Beschreibung der königlichen Residenzstädte Berlin und Potsdam* (1769; Description of the Royal Cities Berlin and Potsdam).

Nicolai's other satires proved far less successful with the general public. Moreover, his lengthy polemics against perceived regression in the cultural sphere provoked the wrath of an emergent intellectual avant-garde. Firmly committed to an art and philosophy with immediate social utility, he could only regard with suspicion the claims of aesthetic and intellectual autonomy voiced by representatives of new movements: first the Sturm und Drang and later German Classicism, German Romanticism, and German Idealism. For authors in these movements, Nicolai came to embody the Berlin literary establishment and was considered a shallow philistine beholden to an overly rationalistic concept of Enlightenment. Whereas they saw in esoteric art an alternative to a flawed reality, Nicolai remained committed to art in the service of that reality. Reflecting his position as a political conservative who was well integrated into existing society, Nicolai's works called for self-improvement and social assimilation rather than for any radical criticism of the status quo.

A long series of attacks and (often vicious) counterattacks was initiated in 1775 with the publication of Nicolai's *Freuden des jungen Werthers* (Joys of Young Werther), a parody of Goethe's epistolary novel *Die Leiden des jungen Werthers* (1774; translated as *The Sorrows of Young Werther* and *The Sufferings of Young Werther*). Hypothesizing as his starting point the failure of Werther's suicide attempt and an ensuing marriage to Lotte, Nicolai sought to demonstrate the impracticality of the protagonist's extreme views and the appeal of a modest bourgeois life. The alleged excesses of the Sturm und Drang also constituted the target of *Eyn feyner kleyner Almanach* (1777–78; A Fine Little Almanac). Through this collection of authentic, occasionally obscene folk songs, introduced in archaic German by a satirical 16th-century narrator, Nicolai hoped to counter claims that the genre could serve as a model for modern poetry. A 16-year hiatus from literary production followed the *Almanach,* during which time Nicolai continued his critical forays into the public sphere with a variety of other publications. In addition to completing two expanded editions of his Berlin book in 1779 and 1786, he wrote 8 of the 12 volumes of his colossal—and highly polemical—travel journal *Beschreibung einer Reise durch Deutschland und die Schweiz, im Jahre 1781* (1783–96; Description of a Journey through Germany and Switzerland in 1781). Nicolai conceived the work as an attempt to improve relations among diverse German-speaking regions. His negative remarks on the practices of southern German Catholics, however, antagonized such prominent intellectuals as C. Garve and J.K. Lavater, who did not share his views. The *Reisebeschreibung* led to other hostilities as well: a critical review of Friedrich Schiller's *Die Horen* in volume 11 of the journal (1796) prompted Goethe and Schiller to heap scorn on Nicolai in their collection "Xenien."

In 1794, Nicolai returned to literature with another satire entitled *Geschichte eines dicken Mannes worin drey Heurathen und drey Körbe nebst viel Liebe* (Story of a Fat Man including Three Marriages and Three Rejections Together with Much Love). Here, he sought to discredit Kantian philosophy by parodying its esoteric terminology and by demonstrating the impracticality of its ivory-tower abstractions. The attack on the Kantians continued in the anonymously published *Leben und Meinungen Sempronius Gundibert's eines deutschen Philosophen* (1798; Life and Opinions of Sempronius Gundibert, a German Philosopher), a work that also derided the early-Romantic circle around Johann Gottlieb Fichte, Ludwig Tieck, and the brothers Friedrich and Wilhelm Schlegel. The latter group served as the focus of Nicolai's final, also anonymously published satire, *Vertraute Briefe von Adelheid an ihre Freundinn Julie S*** (1799; Confidential Letters from Adelheid B** to Her Friend Julie S**). Described by scholars as both an "anti-Lucinde" and an "anti-Werther," this epistolary novel recounts the relationship between the widowed Adelheid B** and her young brother-in-law Gustav. The female protagonist, first a mentor to Gustav and then the object of his affections, serves as Nicolai's mouthpiece throughout the work. The targets of her criticism are by now familiar: egotism, obscurantism, and an overreliance on starry-eyed speculation; these qualities are most strikingly embodied in the novel by the Friedrich Schlegel caricature Doctor Pandolfo.

Nicolai's criticisms of his opponents, although not without some merit, revealed an increasing inability to submit his own position to that same impartial criticism that he had argued for so convincingly in the 1750s and 1760s. Moreover, his accusations of cliquishness and esotericism rang a bit hollow given Nicolai's own memberships in a variety of open and secret societies, including the Berlin Monday Club, the Freemasons, the Illuminati, and the exclusive and influential Berlin Wednesday Society.

If Nicolai was fighting a rearguard action in the literary sphere, his projects as a historian and demographer were more forward-looking. In addition to the *Reisebeschreibung* and his investigations of Berlin and Prussia, he published volumes on the origins and history of the Knights Templars, the Rosicrucians, and the Freemasons, as well as works on the history of culture and language. As was the case with his satires, Nicolai viewed these projects as a means to advance his critical agenda of public enlightenment, particularly vis-à-vis all forms of religious orthodoxy. Nonetheless, he adhered in his historical representations to strict standards of objectivity. His emphasis on society and culture rather than high politics, his use of statistics and archival research, his insistence on causality over simple chronology, and his belief in the need for historically sensitive judgments all point to his participation in the development of a progressive historiography that emerged in Germany in the latter half of the 18th century.

Given the canonization of Classicism and Romanticism in German literary studies, it is not surprising that most literary and cultural historians until recently adhered to the view of Nicolai proffered by his opponents. There were a few notable early exceptions; Heinrich Heine, for example, presents in his *Zur Geschichte der Religion und der Philosophie in Deutschland* (1835; Religion and Philosophy in Germany: A Fragment) a characteristically ironic but still balanced consideration of the author's accomplishments. Since the mid-1970s, a general trend toward cultural studies has led to increased interest in Nicolai, with a concomitant expansion of the field of inquiry to include his activities as a publisher, editor, historian, cultural critic, and public intellectual. As a key player in the drama of the German Enlightenment, he remains a productive figure for intellectual historians of this period, particularly for those interested in the sociology of culture, Enlightenment historiography, and the genealogy of modern urbanism.

MATTHEW ERLIN

Biography

Born in Berlin, 18 March 1733. Apprenticeship with bookseller in Frankfurt an der Oder, 1749-51; returned to Berlin to join family publishing business, 1752; left business for a brief period to work as a freelance author, 1757; took over family press upon death of eldest brother, 1758; edited numerous journals, including *Bibliothek der schönen Wissenschaften und der freyen Künste,* 1756–59, *Briefe, die neueste Literattur betreffend,* 1759–65, *Allgemeine deutsche Bibliothek/Neue allgemeine deutsche Bibliothek,* 1765–1806, and *Neue Berlinische Monatsschrift,* 1799–1810. Elected to the Münchener Akademie, 1781; elected to the Berliner Akademie, 1798. Died in Berlin, 8 January 1811.

Selected Works

Collections

Gesammelte Werke, edited by Bernhard Fabian and Marie-Luise Spiekermann, 20 vols., 1985–97

"*Kritik ist überall, zumal in Deutschland, nötig*": Satiren und Schriften zur Literatur, edited by Wolfgang Albrecht, 1987

Sämmtliche Werke, Briefe, Dokumente: Kritische Ausgabe mit Kommentar, edited by P.M Mitchell, Hans-Gert Roloff, and Erhard Weidl, 1991–

Fiction

Das Leben und die Meinungen des Herrn Magister Sebaldus Nothanker, 1773–76; as *The Life and Opinions of Sebaldus Nothanker,* translated by Thomas Dutton 1798; (abridged) as *The Life and*

Opinions of Master Sebaldus Nothanker, translated by John R. Russell, 1997

Freuden des jungen Werthers, Leiden und Freuden Werthers des Mannes: Voran und zuletzt ein Gespräch, 1775

Geschichte eines dicken Mannes worin drey Heurathen und drey Körbe nebst viel Liebe, 1794

Leben und Meinungen Sempronius Gundibert's eines deutschen Philosophen. Nebst zwey Urkunden der neuesten deutschen Philosophie, 1798

*Vertraute Briefe von Adelheid B** an ihre Freundinn Julie S***, 1799

Criticism/Essays

Untersuchung ob Milton sein Verlohrnes Paradies aus neuern lateinischen Schrifstellern ausgeschrieben habe, 1753

Briefe über den itzigen Zustand der schönen Wissenschaften in Deutschland, 1755

Abhandlung vom Trauerspiele, 1757

Versuch über die Beschuldigungen welche dem Tempelherrenorden gemacht worden, und über dessen Geheimniß; nebst einem Anhange über das Entstehen der Freymaurergesellschaft, 1782

Nachricht von der wahren Beschaffenheit des Instituts der Jesuiten, 1785

Patriotische Phantasien eines Kameralisten, 1790

Beispiel einer Erscheinung mehrerer Phantasmen nebst einigen erläuternden Anmerkungen, 1799

Über meine gelehrte Bildung, über meine Kenntniß der kritischen Philosophie und meine Schriften dieselbe betreffend, und über die Herren Kant, J.B. Erhard und Fichte, 1799

Über den Gebrauch der falschen Haare und Perrucken in alten und neuern Zeiten, 1801

Über die Art wie vermittelst des transscendentalen Idealismus ein wirklich existirendes Wesen aus Principien konstruirt werden kann. Nebst merkwürdigen Proben der Wahrheitsliebe, reifen Überlegung, Bescheidenheit, Urbanität und gutgelaunten Großmuth des Stifters der neuesten Philosophie, 1801

Einige Bemerkungen über den Ursprung und die Geschichte der Rosenkreuzer und Freymaurer, veranlaßt durch die sogenannte historisch-kritische Untersuchung des Herrn Hofraths Buhle über diesen Gegenstand, 1806

Philosophische Abhandlungen, 1808

Other

Beschreibung der königlichen Residenzstädte Berlin und Potsdam und aller daselbst befindlichen Merkwürdigkeiten. Nebst einem Anhange, enthaltend die Leben aller Künstler, die seit Churfürst Friedrich Willhelms des Großen Zeiten in Berlin gelebet haben, oder deren Kunstwerke daselbst befindlich sind, 1769; revised 1779; revised 1786

Eyn feyner kleyner Almanach vol schönerr echterr liblicherr Volckslieder, lustigerr Reyen, vnndt kleglicherr Mordgeschichte, gesungen von Gabriel Wunderlich weyl. Benkelsengernn zu Dessaw,

herausgegeben von Daniel Seuberlich, Schusternn tzu Ritzmück ann der Elbe, 1777–78

Beschreibung einer Reise durch Deutschland und die Schweiz, im Jahre 1781. Nebst Bemerkungen über Gelehrsamkeit, Industrie, Religion und Sitten, 1783–96

Anekdoten von König Friedrich II. von Preussen, und von einigen Personen, die um Ihn waren. Nebst Berichtigungen einiger schon gedruckten Anekdoten, 1788–92

Further Reading

Albrecht, Wolfgang, "Friedrich Nicolais Kontroverse mit den Klassikern und Frühromantikern (1796–1802)," in *Debatten und Kontroversen: Literarische Auseinandersetzungen am Ende des 18. Jahrhunderts*, vol. 2, edited by Hans-Dietrich Dahnke and Bernd Leistner, Berlin: Aufbau, 1989

Berghahn, Klaus L., "Maßlose Kritik: Friedrich Nicolai als Kritiker und Opfer der Weimarer Klassiker," *Zeitschrift für Germanistik* 8, no. 1 (1987)

Craig, Charlotte M., "Friedrich Nicolai and the Occult," in *Subversive Sublimities: Undercurrents of the German Enlightenment*, edited by Eitel Timm, Columbia, South Carolina: Camden House, 1992

Fabian, Bernhard, editor, *Friedrich Nicolai, 1733–1811: Essays zum 250. Geburtstag*, Berlin: Nicolaische Verlagsbuchhandlung, 1983

Laan, James M. van der, "Friedrich Nicolai and Johann Jakob Dusch: A Study in Eighteenth-Century Criticism," *Seminar* 28, no. 2 (1992)

Mollenhauer, Peter, *Friedrich Nicolais Satiren: Ein Beitrag zur Kulturgeschichte des 18. Jahrhunderts*, Amsterdam: Benjamin, 1977

———, "Friedrich Nicolai: Catalyst of the Prussian Enlightenment," *Schatzkammer der deutschen Sprachlehre, Dichtung und Geschichte* 10, no. 2 (1984)

Möller, Horst, *Aufklärung in Preußen: Der Verleger, Publizist, und Geschichtsschreiber Friedrich Nicolai*, Berlin: Colloquium, 1974

Schneider, Ute, *Friedrich Nicolais Allgemeine Deutsche Bibliothek als Integrationsmedium der Gelehrtenrepublik*, Wiesbaden: Harrassowitz, 1995

Schulte-Sasse, Jochen, "Friedrich Nicolai," in *Deutsche Dichter des 18. Jahrhunderts: Ihr Leben und Werk*, edited by Benno von Wiese, Berlin: Schmidt, 1977

Selwyn, Pamela, "A *Philosophe* in the *Comptoir*: The Bookseller-Publisher Friedrich Nicolai, 1733–1811," in *Histoires du livre: Nouvelles orientations: Actes du colloque du 6 et 7 septembre 1990, Göttingen*, edited by Hans Erich Bödeker, Paris: IMEC Éditions, 1995

Sichelschmidt, Gustav, *Friedrich Nicolai: Geschichte seines Lebens*, Herford: Nicolai, 1971

Wolf, Norbert Christian, "Blumauer gegen Nicolai, Wien gegen Berlin: Die polemischen Strategien in der Kontroverse um Nicolais *Reisebeschreibung* als Funktion unterschiedlicher Öffentlichkeitstypen," *Internationales Archiv für Sozialgeschichte der deutschen Literatur* 21, no. 2 (1996)

Friedrich Wilhelm Nietzsche 1844–1900

The fact that Nietzsche is nowadays routinely bracketed together with thinkers such as Darwin, Einstein, Freud, and Marx as one of the "makers of the 20th century" testifies to a perception of his continuing importance a century after his death, and more than a century since the untimely end of his intellectual career. Yet of all these figures, his status as "founding father" is the most problematic: far from seeking to establish a school of followers to defend an orthodoxy, he contented himself with a handful of readers and correctly anticipated that his "explosive" thinking would in any event be disastrously misinterpreted. Far from claiming that his doctrine was the sole scientific truth, he rejected the very concepts of "impersonal" scientific inquiry and "objective" truth for the majority of his career. The one notion that he did put forward latterly as a fundamental explanatory principle and that might have achieved axiomatic status, "der Wille zur Macht" (the will to power), became rapidly debased by its erroneous association with social Darwinism and, subsequently, Nazism. As a consequence, his reputation was rehabilitated in the postwar period largely through its marginalization and a focus on other—if in many respects equally controversial—aspects of his copious and polyvalent literary-philosophical output.

Nietzsche's published writings are conventionally divided into "early" (pre-1878), "middle" (1878–82), and "late" (1883–89) periods, although many of the current debates in Nietzsche scholarship center on the extent to which such divisions can be strictly maintained—in particular, whether Nietzsche ever managed to free himself from his Romantic inheritance and "overcome" metaphysics in the manner that he himself claimed. He began his career as a precociously brilliant academic classicist, securing the chair in Classical Philology at the University of Basel in Switzerland at the age of 24 in 1869. The two decisive early influences on Nietzsche's intellectual development were his encounters with the philosophy of Arthur Schopenhauer and the music of Richard Wagner, to which he became "converted" in 1865 and 1868, respectively. From Schopenhauer he derived a conviction of the primacy of (post-Kantian) aesthetics in philosophical inquiry, a preoccupation with music as the highest art form, and a general existential pessimism. Wagner—who by this stage had himself embraced Schopenhauerianism in *Tristan und Isolde* (1865) and was at the peak of his creative powers—Nietzsche came to know personally and adopt as a spiritual mentor cum father figure.

These two "extracurricular" interests are clearly reflected in Nietzsche's first book, *Die Geburt der Tragödie aus dem Geiste der Musik* (1872; *The Birth of Tragedy out of the Spirit of Music*), a wide-ranging essay in cultural history that goes far beyond its ostensible remit. Here, Nietzsche starts by proclaiming a fundamental tension between two antagonistic "artistic drives in nature" that find expression in human creativity: the "Dionysian" reality of a senseless, chaotic metaphysical ground to existence and the "Apollonian" veil of beautiful appearance and order drawn over that reality (respectively associated with the states of intoxication and dreaming, and paradigmatically expressed in music and the visual arts). It was the miraculous achievement of the ancient Greeks, Nietzsche argues, to recognize and reconcile the two in the art form of tragic drama, which reached its pinnacle with Aeschylus and Sophocles but declined and was ultimately "killed off" by Euripidean psychologism and, especially, the Socratic privileging of scientific rationality over myth. The new Socratic rationality, according to Nietzsche, led to the triumph of "theoretical man" and an extended period of degenerate "Alexandrian culture." Leaping over millennia of cultural history, Nietzsche hails Wagner as a second Aeschylus who, by fashioning the *Gesamtkunstwerk* on mythical themes, is single-handedly bringing about the rebirth of tragic drama and thereby ushering in a new golden age for the German spirit. Nietzsche's first book was a succès de scandale: it established his reputation as one of the foremost proselytizers for the Wagnerian cause, but at the same time its boldly speculative thesis and "unscholarly" style prompted protests from more staid professional colleagues and wrecked his chances of academic respectability from the outset. Unabashed, he continued to stray beyond the bounds of his discipline, and over the next four years he published a series of four provocative essays in cultural criticism under the collective title *Unzeitgemäße Betrachtungen* (1873–76; *Untimely Meditations*): two iconoclastic broadsides against current trends in "rationalist" theology and historiography, and two further eulogies on his personal heroes, Schopenhauer and Wagner.

By the mid-1870s, however, Nietzsche had outgrown both his nationalism (in disillusionment at the founding of the German Reich in 1871) and his attachment to his two chosen mentors. His next book, *Menschliches, Allzumenschliches: Ein Buch für freie Geister* (1878; *Human, All Too Human: A Book for Free Spirits*), reflects a profound reassessment of his philosophical position. Dedicated to a "free-thinking" Enlightenment Frenchman (Voltaire), the work inverts Nietzsche's previous hierarchy of values, downgrading artistic achievement and debunking metaphysical speculation in the name of a new philosophical methodology that draws instead on techniques of historical and scientific analysis. In a new spirit of ruthless skepticism, Nietzsche argues that abstract "eternal verities" about human nature in particular must be subjected to close critical scrutiny, unmasked, and ultimately displaced by the "little unpretentious truths" that a more disabused psychological realism affords. The inspiration of the French *moralistes* can be seen not only in the subject matter but also in the style of the book, for its texture is altogether more open and "experimental" than Nietzsche's previous discursive essays. Single numbered paragraphs, more or less closely linked and ranging in length from the briefest of aphoristic *aperçus* to more sustained reflections of a few pages, are grouped thematically into sections. This becomes Nietzsche's characteristic style in most of his remaining works.

In 1879, after several periods of leave occasioned by ill health, Nietzsche finally resigned his chair in Basel and for another decade was free to roam Switzerland, Italy, and France (as far as possible avoiding Germany) on a university pension. He was frequently laid low by blinding headaches and nausea, yet he still published a book each year. His works of the period 1878–82 form a closely related group reflecting the new "psychological turn" in his thinking, and they are often referred to collectively as the "free spirit trilogy": *Human, All Too Human* itself—including the two "supplements" that would later become its book 2, *Vermischte Meinungen und Sprüche* (1879; *Assorted Opinions and Maxims*) and *Der Wanderer und sein Schatten* (1880; *The Wanderer and His Shadow*)—*Morgenröte: Gedanken über die moralischen Vorurteile* (1881; *Daybreak: Thoughts on the Prejudices of Morality*), and *Die fröhliche Wissenschaft* (1882; expanded edition 1887; *The Gay Science*). The last takes the project of "demythologization" to its logical conclusion with the pronouncement (from the mouth of a "madman") that "God is dead."

In the summer of 1881, Nietzsche discovered the village of Sils-Maria in the Upper Engadine region of southeast Switzerland and returned there each summer from 1883 to 1888, for during his first stay he experienced the epiphanic moment that convinced him of the "eternal return" (*ewige Wiederkehr/Wiederkunft*) of all things. This idea is introduced in the penultimate paragraph of (the first edition of) *The Gay Science,* and the paragraph immediately following introduces the figure of Zarathustra, whose "most abyssal" idea it will become at the climax of Nietzsche's next and still best-known work, *Also sprach Zarathustra: Ein Buch für Alle und Keinen* (1883–92; *Thus Spoke Zarathustra: A Book for Everyone and No One*). It was typical of Nietzsche to emerge from an extended period of critical thinking (which corresponded to a sense of increasing isolation in his personal life, culminating in the crisis of his failed romance with Lou Andreas-Salomé) in affirmative mode, wearing another new "mask" and promoting a parabolic new mythology couched in the form of an epic, mock-biblical prose poem in four books. Nietzsche's new mouthpiece is a parodic version of the historical Zoroaster, who is ironically enlisted to preach the "overcoming" of existing moral systems, the "self-overcoming" (*Selbstüberwindung*) of man in anticipation of the advent of the "overman" or "superman" (*Übermensch*) who will "redeem" the earth.

In 1884, Nietzsche began amassing notes in preparation for what was to be his magnum opus, and to which he gave various provisional titles, including *Der Wille zur Macht* (*The Will to Power*), the one ultimately chosen for a posthumous collection coedited by his sister, Elisabeth Förster-Nietzsche. Yet Nietzsche himself abandoned the project in August 1888, and by this time he had in any case drawn extensively on these notes for the two works published next after *Zarathustra*—*Jenseits von Gut und Böse: Vorspiel einer Philosophie der Zukunft* (1885; *Beyond Good and Evil: Prelude to a Philosophy of the Future*) and *Zur Genealogie der Moral: Eine Streitschrift* (1887; *On the Genealogy of Morals: A Polemic*). The former returns to the style of the "free spirit" period and many of the same preoccupations, especially the critique of moral and religious systems. It also brings to the fore two major new themes: the philosophy of power itself and the relativistic epistemology of "perspectivism." The *Genealogy,* a series of three linked essays presented "by way of clarification and supplement" to the previous book, elaborates its "immoralism" and develops the emphasis on historical explanation proposed already in *Human, All Too Human,* charting the creeping corruption of spiritual health brought about by the moralization of value judgments. The first essay argues that the aboriginal "master morality" (*Herrenmoral*) of "good" and "bad" was superseded by a "slave morality" (*Sklavenmoral*) of "good" and "evil," the Judaeo-Christian morality of "resentment"; the second explores the development of the "guilty conscience" through the internalization (*Verinnerlichung*) of punishment; and the third, an anatomy of "nihilism," analyzes various cases of the sickness that arises when "life" turns against itself in paradoxical pursuit of the "ascetic ideal": the artist (Wagner), the philosopher (Schopenhauer), the priest, the scientist, and the historian.

Nietzsche's late conception of philosophy as a kind of psychophysiological, "medi-cynical" diagnostics finds its fullest expression in the "open letter" *Der Fall Wagner: Ein Musikanten-Problem* (1888; *The Case of Wagner*), an analysis of the "decadence" of his former mentor-turned-archantagonist. The abandonment of the *Will to Power* project that summer led to an outpouring of further short works, which were produced in remarkably quick succession over the autumn and winter: *Götzen-Dämmerung; oder, Wie man mit dem Hammer philosophiert* (1889; *Twilight of the Idols; or, How to Philosophize with a Hammer*), a synoptic overview of his mature philosophical positions; *Der Antichrist: Fluch auf das Christentum* (1895; *The Antichrist: Curse on Christianity*), the most caustic of his polemics; *Ecce homo: Wie man wird, was man ist* (1908; *Ecce Homo: How One Becomes What One Is*), a fascinatingly eccentric autobiography; *Nietzsche contra Wagner: Aktenstücke eines Psychologen* (1895; *Nietzsche contra Wagner: Out of the Files of a Psychologist*), a lightly edited collection of previously published passages; and *Dionysos-Dithyramben* (1892; *Dithyrambs of Dionysus*), an anthology of poems that brought to a close Nietzsche's annus mirabilis. In Turin, on 3 January 1889, he collapsed into a syphilitic insanity from which he failed to recover before his death, in Weimar, on 25 August 1900.

The impact of Nietzsche's philosophy was immediate and intense: already by the time of his death his ideas had been adopted (and were being fought over) throughout Europe and beyond, across the social and political spectrum, and in all areas of cultural expression. The Nietzsche vogue was especially marked in Germany itself (despite Nietzsche's own fulminations against his compatriots), where an engagement with the writings of this superlative philosophical stylist (especially *Zarathustra*) proved de rigueur for the literary avant-garde in particular, from the naturalists through the "George-Kreis," "Kosmiker," and Expressionists to the "high modernist" prose writers of the interwar period. Relatively superficial early reactions such as a fascination with the iconic figure of the *Übermensch* and imitations of "Zarathustran" style gave way to more nuanced (and critical) appreciations of Nietzschean aesthetic and ethical doctrines by writers such as Hermann Broch, Heinrich and Thomas Mann, and Robert Musil. Although the Nietzschean impulse in German letters noticeably declined after the National Socialists appropriated him as their spiritual forebear, his thinking has reemerged as a powerful stimulus in contemporary ethical and political philosophy, while the widespread influence of the work of French Nietzsche-inspired thinkers such as Gilles Deleuze, Jacques Derrida, and Michel Foucault has ensured that versions of Nietzscheanism have passed into the mainstream of contemporary critical debate, especially in the U.S. academy.

DUNCAN LARGE

See also Richard Wagner; Wagner, Parsifal: Wagner/Nietzsche Debate; Weimar

Biography

Born in Röcken, 15 October 1844. Studied theology and classical philology at Bonn University, 1864–65; studied classical philology at Leipzig University, 1865–69; military service, 1867–68; met Richard Wagner in Leipzig, 1868; appointed to chair of classical philology, Basel University, 1869; Ph.D., 1869; renounced Prussian citizenship, 1869; volunteer in army medical service, 1870; sick leave from Basel, 1871–72 and 1876–77; retired from teaching, 1879; frequent travel to Genoa, Venice, Sils-Maria, Nice, and Turin, 1879–89; suffered mental illness, 1889–1900, in Jena and Weimar. Died 25 August 1900.

Selected Works

Collections

Werke [Grossoktavausgabe], edited by Elisabeth Förster-Nietzsche, 15 vols., 1894–1904; 2nd edition, 19 vols., 1901–13
The Complete Works, various translators, edited by Oscar Levy, 18 vols., 1909–11
Gesammelte Werke [Musarionausgabe], edited by Richard Oehler et al., 23 vols., 1920–29
Werke: Kritische Gesamtausgabe, edited by Giorgio Colli and Mazzino Montinari, 1967–

Briefwechsel: Kritische Gesamtausgabe, edited by Giorgio Colli and Mazzino Montinaro, 16 vols., 1975–84

The Complete Works, various translators, edited by Ernst Behler, 1994–

Philosophical Works

Die Geburt der Tragödie aus dem Geiste der Musik, 1872; as *Die Geburt der Tragödie; oder, Griechentum und Pessimismus,* 1886; as *The Birth of Tragedy,* translated by William A. Haussmann, 1909; translated by Francis Golffing, 1956; translated by Walter Kaufmann, 1967; translated by Shaun Whiteside, 1993; translated by Ronald Speirs, 1999

Die Philosophie im tragischen Zeitalter der Griechen, 1873; as *Philosophy in the Tragic Age of the Greeks,* translated by Marianne Cowan, 1962

Unzeitgemäße Betrachtungen, 4 vols., 1873–76; as *Thoughts Out of Season,* translated by Anthony M. Ludovici, 1909; as *Untimely Meditations,* translated by R.J. Hollingdale, 1983; as *Unfashionable Observations,* translated by Richard T. Gray, 1995
Vol. 1, *David Strauss, der Bekenner und der Schriftsteller,* 1873
Vol. 2, *Vom Nutzen und Nachteil der Historie für das Leben,* 1874; as *The Use and Abuse of History,* translated by Adrian Collins, 1949; as *On the Advantage and Disadvantage of History for Life,* translated by Peter Preuss, 1980
Vol. 3, *Schopenhauer als Erzieher,* 1874; as *Schopenhauer as Educator,* translated by James W. Hillesheim and Malcolm R. Simpson, 1965
Vol. 4, *Richard Wagner in Bayreuth,* 1876

Menschliches, Allzumenschliches: Ein Buch für freie Geister, vol. 1, 1878; *Vermischte Meinungen und Sprüche,* vol. 2/1, 1879; *Der Wanderer und sein Schatten,* vol. 2/2, 1880; complete edition, 1886; as *Human, All Too Human: A Book for Free Spirits,* translated by Alexander Harvey, 1908; vol. 1 translated by Helen Zimmern, 1909, vol. 2 translated by Paul V. Cohn, 1911; translated by Marion Faber and Stephen Lehmann, 1984; translated by R.J. Hollingdale, 1986; vol. 1 translated by Gary Handwerk, 1997

Morgenröte: Gedanken über die moralischen Vorurteile, 1881; as *The Dawn of Day,* translated by Johanna Volz, 1903; translated by J.M. Kennedy, 1911; as *Daybreak: Thoughts on the Prejudices of Morality,* translated by R.J. Hollingdale, 1982

Die fröhliche Wissenschaft, 1882; revised edition, including book 5, 1887; as *The Joyful Wisdom,* translated by Thomas Common, 1910; as *The Gay Science,* translated by Walter Kaufmann, 1974

Also sprach Zarathustra: Ein Buch für Alle und Keinen, vols. 1–3, 1883–92; as *Thus Spake Zarathustra,* translated by Alexander Tille, in *Works of Friedrich Nietzsche,* vol. 8, 1896; translated by Thomas Common, in *The Complete Works of Friedrich Nietzsche,* vol. 4, 1898; as *Thus Spoke Zarathustra,* translated by Walter Kaufmann, in *The Portable Nietzsche,* 1954; translated by R.J. Hollingdale, 1969

Jenseits von Gut und Böse: Vorspiel einer Philosophie der Zukunft, 1885; as *Beyond Good and Evil: Prelude to a Philosophy of the Future,* translated by Helen Zimmern, 1907; translated by Marianne Cowan, 1955; translated by Walter Kaufmann, 1966; translated by R.J. Hollingdale, 1973; translated by Marion Faber, 1998

Zur Genealogie der Moral, 1887; as *A Genealogy of Morals,* translated by William A. Haussmann, 1897; as *The Genealogy of Morals,* translated by Horace B. Samuel, 1910; translated by Francis Golffing, 1956; as *On the Genealogy of Morals,* translated by Walter Kaufmann and R.J. Hollingdale, 1967; translated by Douglas Smith, 1996; as *On the Genealogy of Morality,* translated by Carol Diethe, 1994; translated by Maudemarie Clark and Alan Swensen, 1998

Der Fall Wagner: Ein Musikanten-Problem, 1888; as *The Case of Wagner,* translated by Thomas Common, 1896; translated by Anthony M. Ludovici, 1910; translated by Walter Kaufmann, 1967

Götzendämmerung; oder, Wie man mit dem Hammer philosophiert, 1889; as *Twilight of the Idols,* translated by Thomas Common, 1896; translated by Anthony M. Ludovici, 1911; translated by Walter

Kaufmann, 1954; translated by R.J. Hollingdale, 1968; translated by Richard Polt, 1997; translated by Duncan Large, 1998

Der Antichrist: Fluch auf das Christentum, 1895; as *The Antichrist,* translated by Thomas Common, 1896; translated by Anthony M. Ludovici, 1911; translated by H.L. Mencken, 1920; translated by P.R. Stephensen, 1928; translated by Walter Kaufmann, 1954; as *The Anti-Christ,* translated by R.J. Hollingdale, 1968

Nietzsche contra Wagner: Aktenstücke eines Psychologen, 1895; as *Nietzsche contra Wagner,* translated by Thomas Common, 1896; translated by Anthony M. Ludovici, 1910; translated by Walter Kaufmann, 1954

Der Wille zur Macht, edited by Peter Gast and Elisabeth Förster-Nietzsche, 1901; 2nd expanded edition, 1906; as *The Will to Power,* translated by Anthony M. Ludovici, 1909–10; translated by R.J. Hollingdale and Walter Kaufmann, 1968

Ecce homo: Wie man wird, was man ist, edited by Raoul Richter, 1908; as *Ecce Homo: How One Becomes What One Is,* translated by Anthony M. Ludovici, 1927; translated by Clifton P. Fadiman, 1927; translated by Walter Kaufmann, 1967; translated by R.J. Hollingdale, 1979

The Portable Nietzsche, edited by Walter Kaufmann, 1954

Philosophy and Truth: Selections from Nietzsche's Notebooks of the Early 1870s, edited by Daniel Breazeale, 1979

Friedrich Nietzsche on Rhetoric and Language, edited by Sander L. Gilman et al., 1989

Poetry

Dionysos-Dithyramben, 1892; as *Dithyrambs of Dionysus,* translated by R.J. Hollingdale, 1984

Letters

Selected Letters of Friedrich Nietzsche, edited by Christopher Middleton, 1969

Further Reading

Allison, David B., editor, *The New Nietzsche: Contemporary Styles of Interpretation,* New York: Dell, 1977; 2nd edition, Cambridge, Massachusetts, and London: MIT Press, 1985

Aschheim, Steven E., *The Nietzsche Legacy in Germany, 1890–1990,* Berkeley, Los Angeles, and London: University of California Press, 1992

Hayman, Ronald, *Nietzsche: A Critical Life,* London: Weidenfeld and Nicolson, and New York: Oxford University Press, 1980

Hillebrand, Bruno, editor, *Nietzsche und die deutsche Literatur,* 2 vols., Tübingen: Niemeyer, 1978

Hollingdale, R.J., *Nietzsche: The Man and His Philosophy,* Baton Rouge: Louisiana State University Press, and London: Routledge and Kegan Paul, 1965

Kaufmann, Walter, *Nietzsche: Philosopher, Psychologist, Antichrist,* Cleveland: World, 1950; 4th edition, Princeton, New Jersey: Princeton University Press, 1974

Krummel, Richard Frank, *Nietzsche und der deutsche Geist,* 3 vols., Berlin and New York: de Gruyter, 1974–98

Magnus, Bernd, and Kathleen M. Higgins, editors, *The Cambridge Companion to Nietzsche,* Cambridge and New York: Cambridge University Press, 1996

Nehamas, Alexander, *Nietzsche: Life as Literature,* Cambridge, Massachusetts, and London: Harvard University Press, 1985

Pasley, Malcolm, editor, *Nietzsche: Imagery and Thought,* London: Methuen, and Berkeley: University of California Press, 1978

Pütz, Peter, *Friedrich Nietzsche,* Stuttgart: Metzler, 1967; 2nd edition, 1975

Reichert, Herbert William, *Friedrich Nietzsche's Impact on Modern German Literature: Five Essays,* Chapel Hill: University of North Carolina Press, 1975

Reichert, Herbert William, and Karl Schlechta, editors, *International Nietzsche Bibliography*, Chapel Hill: University of North Carolina Press, 1960; revised edition, 1968

Schacht, Richard, *Nietzsche*, London and New York: Routledge and Kegan Paul, 1983

Sedgwick, Peter R., editor, *Nietzsche: A Critical Reader*, Oxford and Cambridge, Massachusetts: Blackwell, 1995

Solomon, Robert C., and Kathleen M. Higgins, editors, *Reading Nietzsche*, New York and Oxford: Oxford University Press, 1988

Stern, J.P., *A Study of Nietzsche*, Cambridge and New York: Cambridge University Press, 1979

Also sprach Zarathustra 1883–1892

Essay by Friedrich Wilhelm Nietzsche

Subtitled *Ein Buch für Alle und Keinen* (A Book for All and None), Nietzsche wrote what was to become his most popular work in four spells of creative activity beginning in 1882, the year in which he met Lou Andreas-Salomé in Rome in April. He spent three precious weeks with Andreas-Salomé in August, until their friendship was wrecked through a series of misunderstandings coupled with the active interference of Nietzsche's sister Elisabeth. Part 1 of *Also sprach Zarathustra* (*Thus Spoke Zarathustra*) was completed by mid-February 1883, part 2 by July 1883, part 3 by January 1884, and part 4 by February 1885, although the latter was not in print until it was published privately in 1892. The foundation of the central character of Zarathustra had been laid in *Die fröhliche Wissenschaft* (1881; *The Gay Science*), as had the concept of eternal return, underpinned by the central declaration that God is dead.

The feature that makes *Thus Spoke Zarathustra* unique in Nietzsche's oeuvre is its style: the work is written with an ecstatic flourish. Nietzsche makes frequent use of dithyrambs, often in passages that he actually calls *songs*, although the formal use of poetry is reserved for later in the book (at the end of part 3 and extensively in part 4). The rationale behind the work, that of life affirmation, is fully in keeping with the style and can be termed Dionysian in spirit, although there is no actual mention of Dionysus. The reason for Zarathustra's exultant joy is his knowledge of freedom, a freedom that comes from the acknowledgment that God is dead and that therefore there is no judgmental higher being to whom a debt must be paid. The man who can realize the truth of this will laugh and lift his legs high in joyful dancing. But Zarathustra teaches more than this: he foresees a time when the *Übermensch* will accept the responsibility for creating his own morality. Although Nietzsche, via Zarathustra, makes it clear that the circumstances under which the *Übermensch* could emerge do not yet exist, he describes the qualities such a person might possess. These qualities, which include hardness and virile courage, deliberately pose a direct challenge to the traditional Christian qualities of meekness and humility. Nietzsche holds that man is full of a resentment (which he terms *ressentiment*) inculcated by a morality that denies the instincts; for this reason, man himself is "something that must be overcome."

Although there are notorious passages in which Zarathustra extols martial qualities and insists on male supremacy ("The man's happiness is: I will. The woman's happiness is: he will"),

the real point that Nietzsche makes is that the *Übermensch* creates his very existence through willpower. The underlying theme of *Thus Spoke Zarathustra* makes constant reference to the will to power, which is described as being a force that works through all living things. Although Nietzsche returns to this theme later, as in his next work, *Jenseits von Gut und Böse* (1885; *Beyond Good and Evil*), it is never again dealt with as cogently as in *Thus Spoke Zarathustra*. Admirers of *Der Wille zur Macht* (1901; *The Will to Power*), the work that Nietzsche's sister compiled from her brother's unpublished notes after his death, are unlikely to agree with this assessment, since this particular book has been a mainstay of authors engaged in poststructuralist theory (such as Michel Foucault). The concept of eternal return, which Nietzsche hardly mentions after *Thus Spoke Zarathustra*, is closely allied to both the notion of the will to power and the *Übermensch*, since the entire creativity of the *Übermensch* relies on him being prepared to will the return of every second of his life. "All 'It was' is a fragment, a riddle, a dreadful chance—until the creative will says to it: 'But I willed it thus!'"

Niezsche's works did not achieve a wide readership until the mid-1890s. Toward the end of the century, two of his works became cult books: one was *Thus Spoke Zarathustra* and the other was *Die Geburt der Tragödie* (1872; *The Birth of Tragedy*), a work in which Dionysus is described as a metaphor for man's instinctual life (or at least such was the construction put on it). Early admirers of Nietzsche thus fell into two camps: those who felt themselves Zarathustran—the majority—and those who felt themselves Dionysian. It is impossible to overstate the worldwide cultural phenomenon that *Thus Spoke Zarathustra* had become by the early part of the 20th century. However, Nietzsche enthusiasts were not always careful readers and tended to impose their own interpretations on the work. Thus, writers and artists in the emerging modernist movements, such as German Expressionism, tended to merge Zarathustran belligerence with Freudian theories, such as the Oedipus complex.

Zarathustra's putative bellicosity was also a factor in the popularity enjoyed by *Thus Spoke Zarathustra* in Germany during the war years. Soldiers were able to buy a very cheap edition for their rucksacks (they were not provided with free copies, as legend would suggest: the print runs were insufficient). During the interwar years, *Thus Spoke Zarathustra* was somewhat less popular, with intellectuals such as the Frenchman Julien Benda accusing Nietzsche of complicity "after the fact" in the fervor that had encouraged Germany to go to war. Antiwar books such as Erich Maria Remarque's best-seller *Im Westen nichts Neues* (1929; *All Quiet on the Western Front*) placed Nietzsche's work somewhat in the shade, although Remarque himself was an eager Nietzschean, as was Carl Gustav Jung, whose notes for the seminar he gave on *Thus Spoke Zarathustra* make up a weighty tome.

The real damage to Nietzsche's reputation came during the Third Reich, when Hitler adopted the rhetoric of the will to power even though he probably had no true understanding of what Nietzsche meant by the term. After World War II, the rehabilitation of Nietzsche's reputation was begun by Walter Kaufmann, and new translations of Nietzsche's works have been prolific in recent years. With the emphasis on style, which has been a feature of postmodernism, *Thus Spoke Zarathustra* has again become a cult book. The translations of the term *Übermensch*—"superman" and "overman"—have been gendered in

English and have served to reinforce the perception, common from the outset, that Zarathustra is synonymous with male chauvinism. However, it must be stated that many scholarly women have, for the last century, felt themselves included in the term *Übermensch* when used in the original, and they have construed the liberating potential of the term as applicable to them as well as to men. This does not mean that there have not been feminists who, during the past century, have taken exception to the tone of Nietzsche's remarks, not just in *Thus Spoke Zarathustra,* but elsewhere, where he targets his attack at emancipated and scholarly women. In *Thus Spoke Zarathustra,* the misogyny found in the first and second parts is more general and has been assumed to have been inspired by Nietzsche's hurt feelings after the collapse of his hopes of forming a lasting friendship with Lou Andreas-Salomé.

Carol A. Diethe

Editions

First edition: *Also sprach Zarathustra: Ein Buch für Alle und keinen,* vols. 1–3, Chemnitz: Schmeitzner, 1883–85; vol. 4 printed privately, 1892

Critical editions: in *Werke in drei Bänden,* edited by Karl Schlechta, vol. 1, Munich: Hanser, 1954; in *Werke: Kritische Gesamtausgabe,* edited by Giorgio Colli and Mazzino Montinari, vol. 6/1, Berlin: de Gruyter, 1967–70; in *Sämtliche Werke: Kritische Studienausgabe,* edited by Giorgio Colli and Mazzino Montinari, vol. 4, Berlin: de Gruyter, 1967–77, revised edition, 1988

Translations: *Thus Spake Zarathustra,* translated by Alexander Tille, in *Works of Friedrich Nietzsche,* vol. 8, London: Henry, and New York: Macmillan, 1896; translated by Thomas Common, in *The Complete Works of Friedrich Nietzsche,* edited by Oscar Levy, vol. 4, Edinburgh: Foulis, 1909; *Thus Spoke Zarathustra,* translated by Walter Kaufmann, in *The Portable Nietzsche,* New York: Viking, 1954; translated by R.J. Hollingdale, Harmondsworth and New York: Penguin, 1969

Further Reading

Bennholdt-Thomsen, Anke, *Nietzsches "Also sprach Zarathustra" als literarisches Phänomen: Eine Revision,* Frankfurt: Athenäum, 1974

Cousineau, Robert Henri, *Zarathustra and the Ethical Ideal,* Amsterdam and Philadelphia, Pennsylvania: Benjamins, 1991

Duhamel, Roland, *Nietzsches Zarathustra: Mystiker des Nihilismus: Eine Interpretation von Friedrich Nietzsches "Also sprach Zarathustra—Ein Buch für alle und keinen,"* Würzburg: Königshausen und Neumann, 1991

Goicoechea, David, editor, *The Great Year of Zarathustra (1881–1981),* Lanham, Maryland: University Press of America, 1983

Happ, Winfried, *Nietzsches Zarathustra als moderne Tragödie,* Frankfurt, Bern, and New York: Lang, 1984

Higgins, Kathleen M., *Nietzsche's Zarathustra,* Philadelphia, Pennsylvania: Temple University Press, 1987

Jung, Carl Gustav, *Nietzsche's Zarathustra: Notes of the Seminar Given 1934–39,* 2 vols., edited by James L. Jarrett, Princeton, New Jersey: Princeton University Press, 1988

Lampert, Laurence, *Nietzsche's Teaching: An Interpretation of "Thus Spoke Zarathustra,"* New Haven, Connecticut: Yale University Press, 1987

Pieper, Annemarie, *"Ein Seil geknüpft zwischen Tier und Übermensch": Philosophische Erläuterungen zu Nietzsches erstem Zarathustra,* Stuttgart: Klett-Cotta, 1990

Rosen, Stanley, *The Mask of Enlightenment: Nietzsche's Zarathustra,* Cambridge and New York: Cambridge University Press, 1995

Thumfart, Stefan, *Der Leib in Nietzsches Zarathustra,* Frankfurt and New York: Lang, 1995

Whitlock, Greg, *Returning to Sils Maria: A Commentary to Nietzsche's "Also sprach Zarathustra,"* New York: Lang, 1990

1950s

The 1950s may be defined as the period of the emergence of two German literatures; while characteristics of late 1940s literary life continued into the 1950s, divergent new directions of postwar literature became more prominent. The West German economic miracle, started by Marshall Plan aid and the currency reform of 1948, became apparent by 1950; with the continued confiscation of plants from the GDR by the Soviet Union, the economic gulf of east and west opened. The Cold War and rearmament prevailed. The split of the German PEN center into East and West organizations in 1951 was also a sign of the times. In West Germany, the emptiness of postwar reality and its unsatisfactory filling by growing affluence were major themes; between 1959 and 1961, new subjects (the Third Reich) and types (proletarian writing) came to prominence. In the East, the communist state enforced an official line of socialist realism, and it was the loosening of this around 1961 that showed a certain maturity. The contemporaneous Berlin Wall underlined the existence of two Germanies. The 1960s continued many trends of the 1950s as well.

East Germany underwent a series of social and economic upheavals, including progressive nationalization and collectivization, and recovered prosperity only slowly. The state was everywhere in public and personal life, encouraging women to work and enforcing Marxist tenets in every area of education; there was a highly directed literary life: homology of all discourses came with the official control of publishing, theater, and the press. The German literary tradition was fostered wherever its proponents were at all socially progressive; established antifascist writers and the canon accepted in the Soviet Union were added. The reception of modern classics such as Kafka and even critical Westerners such as Wolfgang Koeppen, however, was largely prevented. Authors had broadly to accept the official ideology and socialist realist style; critical or independent approaches were rarely allowed public airing. Some useful institutions such as the periodical *Sinn und Form* flourished, but the government was always ready to intervene in cultural affairs; the end of Stalinism brought little relief. The tone was set by those who returned from exile, including J.R. Becher (Kulturminister, 1954–58), Anna Seghers, Friedrich Wolf, Willi Bredel, and others—socialist realists or proven antifascists all.

The literary scene of the West was much more diverse, with more writers, a larger public, a plurality of perspectives fostered by the official ideology of liberal civil society, more publishing and performing outlets, and close links with Austria and German-speaking Switzerland. Political, economic, and social contexts and pressures were complex and included the psychology of a nation destroyed in 1945 and quickly recovering through individual enterprise, which in turn became a creed among workers as well as bourgeois; changes in class and family structures; and new mentalities within the postwar generation. Many people held politics in suspicion, as the slogans *ohne mich* (leave me out of it) and *totaler Ideologieverdacht* (global suspicion of ideologies) indicate. The Western allies established an unfamiliar, democratic—albeit restorative and conservative (*keine Experimente* [no experiments])—state and neoliberal socioeconomic order that was welded to the Western bloc and much influenced by the United States. Consumerism, new media, demographic movement, accelerated transport, and improved working conditions and leisure altered horizons.

The 1950s were in many ways backward looking: the more obvious manifestations of Nazism were discredited, and so people looked back to see what older traditions were still useful. But many conservative-minded people who flourished under Hitler still set the agenda in publishing, education, and other cultural institutions. Literary prizes were still awarded to old nationalists, notably Ernst Jünger. Proletarian literature was almost excluded from mainstream publishing. Newspaper critics such as Friedrich Sieburg concentrated on work in classically privileged genres and from conservative publishers, despising writing that dealt with postwar problems or political decision making. Conservative cultural and critical discourses, as in Arnold Gehlen's *Urmensch und Spätkultur* (1958; Primeval Man and Late Culture) and Hans Sedlmayr's *Verlust der Mitte* (1948; Loss of the Center), were influential. Many writers and critics sought an independent world of art, an autonomy of the creative mind, and looked on realistic literature, let alone political commitment, with suspicion; abstraction, fantasy, and magic realism were on their agenda. International styles fused into a vague classical modernity, with an ambiguous view of literary commitment: merely writing a poem was an act of criticism, so a writer did not need to be overtly political. Subjectivism rooted in postwar psychological insecurity echoed this apolitical attitude. Kafka, much read and viewed as the modernist writer par excellence, was interpreted as a metaphysical writer rather than a social critic.

But subjectivism also issued in rebellious attitudes: Sartre's combination of existentialism and political commitment attracted many. Another influential idiosyncratic Marxist was Ernst Bloch, who produced *Das Prinzip Hoffnung* (1954–56; *The Principle of Hope*). There also was a wave of discovering writing that was not available during the Third Reich, from Dos Passos and Hemingway through Kafka and Joyce to Sartre and Camus. German writing became international, its multiplicity of voices a microcosm of world literature. Writers tried to shock people out of their complacency, show the shakiness of their world, provoke argument, and criticize the increasing materialism in the Germany of the economic miracle, bureaucracy, philistinism, taboos, the mass society, and diminished individuality. Nonconformity meant questioning values, and language satire was rife, matching younger authors' desire to purify a language perverted by Nazism. *Gesinnungsästhetik* was born, a cult of the well-meaning and well-expressed. *Gruppe 47* summed up the progressive attitudes of the time, demanding a social but not clumsily proletarian attitude, skepticism toward language, and autonomy. It brought together open-minded critics and gave young writers access to them.

Nonconformist writers remained sidelined through their opposition to the restoration mentality; they were powerless against the social, political, and economic machine. Hans Magnus Enzensberger later claimed that literary culture took the place of political culture in postwar Germany: it was expected to demonstrate a rejection of Nazism and a commitment to democracy and social reform—but the more it turned to these functions, the less influence or connection it had with the political field. The media could digest any literary form and content without the real world thereby being altered; so authors turned to more direct action in the 1960s. Authors in the 1950s generally saw themselves as part of the world of Geist, apart from the political class and from the workers. Even left-wingers did not feel moved, for instance, to revive the overtly socialist writing or documentary experiments of the 1920s.

Taschenbücher--paperbacks—revolutionized reading habits and attitudes toward literature. The sheer quantity of books produced hid the fact that authors found it hard to make a living when publishers had all the power. Writers and recipients gave more attention to the growing mediums of radio, television (although intellectuals disdained it), and film. Fresh markets appeared for essayistic work, newspaper feuilletons, printed or broadcast features, and the like. Journalistic genres sometimes rose to literary standards, although reportage did not flourish as in the 1920s. Literary diaries combining several genres, notably Max Frisch's *Tagebuch 1946–1949* (1950; *Sketchbook 1946–1949*), were generally underrated.

The dominant theme of the period was perhaps identity. Buffeted by war, political upheaval, the loss of traditional values, the disruption of life plans, the threat of atomic war, and the end of all human life, writers reflected general spiritual miseries, asking: Who am I, what am I doing here, what constitutes my selfhood? The first "complete" edition of Robert Musil's *Der Mann ohne Eigenschaften* (1952; *The Man without Qualities*) links back to 1920s modernism. Frisch defined the postwar crisis of identity in *Stiller* (1954; *I'm Not Stiller*), whose protagonist takes the claim not to be the man who disappeared some years previously to untenable lengths. An even more radical text, Peter Weiss's *Der Schatten des Körpers des Kutschers* (1960; The Shadow of the Body of the Coachman), completed in 1952, long found no publisher. Germany's flirtation with the theater of the absurd in Grass and Wolfgang Hildesheimer had no lasting effects; Hildesheimer seemed only to repeat the experience of the individual's inadequacy in an arbitrarily arranged world, where things were not as they seemed.

Many theories about how Nazism had managed to take control were floated after 1945, although the population at large was unwilling to deal with its own role. In East Germany, fascism was equated with capitalism. To attack Nazism was thus also to attack the West, whose democracy was seen as a disguised neofascism, and to affirm communism. Franz Fühmann brought a fresh note to World War II narratives in *Kameraden* (1955; Comrades). Erwin Strittmatter's picaresque *Der Wundertäter* (1957; The Miracle Worker) started the revision of the common image of the *Wehrmacht* soldier as a victim who had no part in cold-blooded murders, and Bruno Apitz's concentration camp novel *Nackt unter Wölfen* (1958; Naked among Wolves) drew upon personal suffering.

In autobiographical writing in the West, Alfred Andersch in *Die Kirschen der Freiheit* (1952; The Cherries of Freedom), Margarete Buber-Neumann in *Als Gefangene bei Stalin und Hitler* (1952; Imprisoned by Stalin and Hitler), and others added fresh aspects to the reckoning with Nazism seen in the earlier memoirs of Ernst Wiechert and others. Paul Celan's heavily encrypted poems of mourning after the Shoah became required reading for intellectuals; they are now seen as the major lyric oeuvre of this period, with their sophisticated critique of language and their political implications. In prose literature, after forerunners such as Albrecht Goes's much-read *Das Brandopfer* (1954; *The Burnt Offering*), a period of *Vergangenheitsbewältigung* (coming to terms with the past) started with Andersch's *Sansibar* (1957; Flight to Afar). The annus mirabilis, 1959, brought Heinrich Böll's *Billard um halbzehn* (*Billiards at Half Past Nine*), whose distinction between lambs and buffaloes, the innocent and the unscrupulous, entered into the language. Its success, however, was overshadowed by that of Günter Grass's *Die Blechtrommel* (1959; The Tin Drum), with its detailed, imaginative reconstruction of Nazism's takeover in Danzig. The major dramatic treatment, although in abstract parable form, was Frisch's *Andorra* (1961; Andorra).

Contemporary social questions gained prominence in narrative with Böll's *Und sagte kein einziges Wort* (1953; *Acquainted with the Night*), *Haus ohne Hüter* (1954; *The Unguarded House*), and *Das Brot der frühen Jahre* (1955; *The Bread of Our Early Years*), and the experimental trilogy—ahead of its time in its criticism and in its techniques—of Wolfgang Koeppen. Through the 1950s and early 1960s, the novel became an indispensable commentary on the preoccupations of Western people. Martin Walser commenced his major portrayals of the *Wirtschaftswunder,* notably in *Halbzeit* (1960; Half-Time), the study of an ambitious but inadequate salesman. Gerd Gaiser's *Schlußball* (1958; The Last Dance of the Season) was another snapshot popular at the time. The year 1959 saw Uwe Johnson's *Mutmaßungen über Jakob* (*Speculations about Jakob*), with which the disillusioned Easterner moved West, broaching the question of the division of Germany in its personal repercussions. The same year Stefan Heym, another dissident, but one who stayed in the East, completed *Der Tag X* (X Day), which was on the 1953 revolt, and which was published belatedly in West Germany as *5 Tage im Juni* (1974; Five Days in June).

The East German novel largely dealt with the world of work, frequently postwar reconstruction, but also socialist struggles of the recent past. Bredel's *Die Enkel* (1953; The Grandchildren), Seghers's *Die Entscheidung* (1959; The Decision), and Erik Neutsch's *Spur der Steine* (1964; Track of the Stones) are of at least historical interest. Of authors dealing with the modernization of rural life, the individual voice is that of Strittmatter, who wrote the plays *Katzgraben* (1953; Katzgraben), *Tinko* (1954;

Tinko), and *Ole Bienkopp* (1963; Ole Bienkopp). When the Bitterfeld Way was instituted in 1959, underscoring the social aim of literature, an unintended effect was to make writers more confident of their subjective approach to everyday reality—hence the so-called *Ankunftsliteratur* (Arrival literature) (see Christa Wolf, *Der geteilte Himmel* [1963; The Divided Sky]; Brigitte Reimann, *Ankunft im Alltag* [1961; Arrival in the Everyday] and *Die Geschwister* [1963; Siblings]). On the stage, Heiner Müller in *Der Lohndrücker* (1957; The Wage Reducer) took a cool view of early socialist reality. His lively comedy *Die Umsiedlerin* (1956–61; The New Arrival, revised as *Die Bauern* [1964; The Peasants]) fell afoul of officialdom. A comedy with a more harmonious note, *Frau Flinz* (1961; Frau Flinz) by Helmut Baierl, had great success. Peter Hacks's two plays on the industrial reality of the East, *Die Sorgen und die Macht* (1959; Cares and Power) and *Moritz Tassow* (completed in 1961, but performed and published only 1965; Moritz Tassow) met with official incomprehension and were condemned after prolonged controversy: the humor was too sophisticated, and functionaries discovered breaches of socialist realist rules.

The 1950s saw itself as a lyric decade. A few critical literary cabarets existed: the *Kom(m)ödchen* in Düsseldorf, the *Schmiere* in Frankfurt, and the *Brettl vorm Kopf* in Vienna with its satirical writers Carl Merz, Helmut Qualtinger, and Georg Kreisler. Hans Magnus Enzensberger sought an operative effect in his much-discussed early verse; Peter Rühmkorf started to write politically tinged lyrics in a parlando style. At the other end of the spectrum, nature poetry was a dominant school, often connected with the so-called magic realism that used natural phenomena as the doorway to a realm of metaphysics and meaning, often also paired with cultural, critical, and personal themes. Still read, apart from Wilhelm Lehmann and Heinz Piontek, are mainly those poets who straddled the divide of public, social-critical and private, ivory-tower poetry in the so-called *öffentliches Gedicht* (public poem), showing social awareness without specific political commitment. These poets included Günter Eich, Karl Krolow, and Ingeborg Bachmann; the last of these writers blended feminine sensitivity and an awareness of the dangers of modern society. Today, Bertolt Brecht's *Buckower Elegien* (1953; Buckow Elegies) and other poems of the 1950s, which are personal, nature-orientated, and political, are viewed as very important; their contemporary publication was haphazard and the author's poetic reputation rested on *Hundert Gedichte* (1951; A Hundred Poems).

Gottfried Benn's *Statische Gedichte* (1948; Poems of Statics), followed by *Destillationen* (1953; Distillations) and *Aprèslude* (1955; Aprèslude), with their quasi-existentialistic nihilism, insistence on the autonomy of artistic creation, and slangy expression influenced many and brought a more bracing climate to poetry. Nelly Sachs and Hans Arp also brought the modernist tradition into the postwar era. Generally, the conservative poets, especially the nature lyricists who were fashionable at the time, are now neglected, and their anti-ideological facade is suspected of hiding reactionary attitudes. Bachmann, Celan, Christine Lavant, and Ilse Aichinger show the strength of lyric in Austria. Of poets from the Bukowina active at this time, although disregarded by the world of letters, Alfred Gong and Rose Ausländer are the most important. In East Germany, traditionalism, conformism, and concessions to popular taste reigned. Personal expression was largely repressed. Huchel, Brecht, and Johannes

Bobrowski, lyricists of modernity and originality, remained marginal. A few poets tried to introduce realism, but publishing chances were slim. Günter Bruno Fuchs introduced mourning for Nazi murders with the collection *Zigeunertrommel* (1956; Gypsies' Drum) and made a name for himself with apparently lightweight but formally and politically advanced verses: *Trinkermeditationen* (1962; Drinker's Meditations).

German fiction shows many styles: the *Entwicklungsroman* (development novel) of the German bourgeois-realist tradition, montage, sparse narration copied from American models, symbolic modes, and free association and other psychology-based techniques. Although often proclaimed dead because the crisis of modernity was perceived to make narration and characterization untenable, the novel was the leading literary genre of postwar Germany. Older, conservative writers, often of abstract and symbolic style, still led the field: Ernst Jünger, Heimito von Doderer, and Werner Bergengruen, with *Der letzte Rittmeister* (stories, 1952; The Last Captain of Horse). Thomas Mann, Elisabeth Langgässer, and Hermann Hesse continued to be influential—Mann in East Germany as well. Some such elders were highly traditional; even the modernists among them still showed an old-fashioned attitude toward the role of the creative writer in a bourgeois world—thus, their work fit the restorative tendencies of the Adenauer years' politics. Some, however, never returned permanently from exile and were disregarded (e.g., Alfred Döblin).

Younger writers who continued the high abstractions of the older school (Edzard Schaper, Reinhold Schneider) have not worn well. Surrealism was practiced by Hans Erich Nossack; myth, discredited by misuse under Hitler, was reexplored by Walter Jens in *Das Testament des Odysseus* (1957; Odysseus's Testament). The short story, after the apparent unpretentiousness of the immediate postwar period, as in Böll's collection *Wanderer, kommst du nach Spa . . .* (1950; Traveller, If You Come to Spa . . .), struck a fantastic vein that was mined by the Austrians, the Swiss, and the Jewish returners from exile: Friedrich Dürrenmatt (*Der Tunnel* [1952; The Tunnel]), Aichinger (*Spiegelgeschichte* [1952; Mirror Story]), and Hildesheimer (*Lieblose Legenden* [1952; Loveless Legends]). Against this background, Wolfdietrich Schnurre's stories in *Eine Rechnung, die nicht aufgeht* (1958; A Sum That Won't Come Out), which minutely depict Germany's recent past, seem old-fashioned.

The stage was generally conservative. Theatergoers considered themselves an elite in dark suits and evening gowns. The survival of Gustaf Gründgens, Göring's favorite, as an influential director is indicative. The serious theaters concentrated on the classics: Sophocles, Shakespeare, Lessing, and the rest; they also focused upon modern classics such as Gerhart Hauptmann and, to some extent, the imported absurdists, Beckett and Ionesco. It became a commonplace to lament the shortage of new German plays between the successes of Zuckmayer and Borchert in the late 1940s and the documentary wave of the 1960s. Two Swiss, Frisch and Dürrenmatt, were the dramatists of the decade. With his wide-ranging public and private themes, Frisch exemplifies the characteristic 1950s style, which includes a model or parable without a lesson except what the recipient provides, civic conscience, attacks on hypocrisy and ideology made by a critique of language, and the underlying pessimism about the chance of improving anything. Dürrenmatt exposed the pitfalls of idealism harshly in well-made artificial plays that drifted toward endings no less tragic for being ridiculous.

The East German stage was also fond of going back to the classics. Faust turned from national figure to progressive and popular hero. For the rest, bureaucracy and inertia ruled, as Brecht, East Germany's main divergent literary voice, complained. Although the most brilliant dramatist and practitioner, with the Berliner Ensemble, he was marginalized and disregarded, and he wrote little; instead, Stanislavsky was officially promoted, without inspiring new writing. The official rejection of Brecht's opera *Das Verhör des Lukullus* (*The Trial of Lucullus*) with Paul Dessau's music (1951) set the tone. Shortage of new plays led to the institution of drama competitions—satirized in the prizewinning *Shakespeare dringend gesucht* of Heinar Kipphardt (1953; Shakespeare Urgently Required), who in 1959 moved, disillusioned, to the West. Hacks moved the other way in 1955, bringing *Die Schlacht bei Lobositz* (1955; The Battle of Lobositz), a leftward view of an 18th-century war, relevant, he hoped, to West German rearmament.

In West Germany, radio play thrived, a lifesaver for some authors who made much more money from broadcasting than from publishers. Literary *Hörspiel* tended to be abstract, bland, and tailored to the publicly owned, publicly accountable medium. The annual award of the *Hörspielpreis der Kriegsblinden* (War-Blinded Men's Radio Play Prize) established the genre institutionally and encouraged more innovation. The acknowledged master was Eich, who combined social commentary, exoticism, surprising technical effects, and a metaphysical, even tragic frame of mind. Fred von Hoerschelmann wrote *Die verschlossene Tür* (1952; The Locked Door) and *Das Schiff Esperanza* (1953; The Ship Esperanza), with its bitter portrayal of the treachery of the older generation; other authors who tried their hand include Aichinger, Frisch, Böll, and Bachmann. Bachmann wrote *Die Zikaden* (1955; The Cicadas) and *Der gute Gott von Manhattan* (1958; The Good God of Manhattan), where the evocation of a utopia of pure self-absorbed love serves to criticize a society that destroys the beautiful and absolute). *Hörspiel* starts to move toward realism with Dieter Wellershoff's *Der Minotaurus* (1960; The Minotaur).

The nonconforming decade also was an era of experimentalism. In the novel, there were Arno Schmidt's experimental novels, frequently with some eccentric at odds with society, at their center. The *Wiener Gruppe* (Vienna Group), formed in 1951 (Hans Carl Artmann, Konrad Bayer, Gerhard Rühm, Andreas Okopenko, Oswald Wiener, and others), self-consciously opposing the dominant conservatism of Austrian literary life, radicalized the conception of poetry. Artmann particularly insisted upon play, liberation from grammar, triviality, and freedom to engage in pastiche. A school of concrete poetry emerged as well.

Many scriptwriters and directors active under Hitler still worked in German film. A large proportion of films (and of television drama) in the period were based on existing literary work. Despite the popularity of some topical films, German film really only emerged in 1962 when young directors including Alexander Kluge and Edgar Reitz proclaimed the *Junger Deutscher Film* (Young German Film); Volker Schlöndorff's *Der junge Törleß* (1966; Young Törless) and Kluge's *Abschied von gestern* (1966; Farewell to Yesterday) demonstrated how Germany caught up with the state of the art.

Literary high culture had little penetration below the *Bildungsbürgertum* (cultivated middle class); mass-produced formulaic *Trivialliteratur* (popular writing) without intellectual or ethical rigor prevailed. Types of trivial literature aimed at specific readerships flourished. From best-seller novels at the top end of the scale, the range went down to pulp fiction. In the former group, there were pretensions to quality; new themes (war, identity, and adolescence) and techniques (documentary, ironized narrators) appeared some years after their emergence in the higher literature. The author's name—Heinz Konsalik, Johannes Mario Simmel, Hans Hellmut Kirst, or Hugo Hartung—guaranteed digestible, intelligent leisure reading; but the nonconformity and questioning characteristic of higher *Dichtung* (fine literature) was absent.

Mass-produced narratives in flimsy brochure forms, modeled on American dime novels, included detective, science fiction, western, war (*Landserhefte*), horror, romance, *Heimat* (local), nobility, doctor, and family stories. It is estimated that about 37 percent of the literate population in the 1950s regularly read pulp; through these works, readers met a world in which West Germany was to become great again through efficiency and peaceful competition, World War III would be winnable (technological progress as a force for good is not questioned), women would find happiness in love matches and motherhood (never facing questions of abortion or contraception), and all social disharmonies could be solved within the nuclear family. Conservatism (not to say reactionary persistence in discredited genres such as blood and soil literature) ruled, present-day problems of the urban world where the readers lived were not addressed; but however exotic the settings, the family structures in these works reflect the lower-middle-class ideals of the mid-century German.

For many readers who insisted on factuality and distrusted imagination, the place of literature was taken by *Sachbuch*, the work of scientific popularization, which frequently rendered its content digestible by including adventures about discoveries and scientists. After C.W. Ceram's *Götter Gräber und Gelehrten* (1949; *Gods, Graves, and Scholars*), Werner Keller and Robert Jungk were highly successful. Children's literature scarcely liberated itself from the commonplaces of proto and neofascism; positions of respect both among writers and in publishing and education were occupied by old Nazis. Role models for girls tended to be old-fashioned paragons of virtue, piety, and sentimentality. A certain unwillingness to produce war stories ended with the introduction of general conscription in 1956, after which boys, too, could enjoy old values—soldierliness and heroism. The best books on the youth market were often translations.

ALFRED D. WHITE

See also Stunde Null

Further Reading

Balzer, Bernd, et al., *Die deutschsprachige Literatur in der Bundesrepublik Deutschland: Vorgeschichte und Entwicklungstendenzen,* Munich: Iudicium, 1988

Barner, Wilfried, editor, *Geschichte der deutschen Literatur von 1945 bis zur Gegenwart,* Munich: Beck, 1994

Berg, Jan, et al., *Sozialgeschichte der deutschen Literatur von 1918 bis zur Gegenwart,* Frankfurt: Fischer Taschenbuch, 1981

Bullivant, Keith, editor, *The Modern German Novel,* Leamington Spa, UK and New York: Berg, 1987; distributed in U.S. by St. Martin's Press

Dictionary of Literary Biography, vols. 56, 69, 75, 124, Detroit, Michigan: Gale Research, 1987, 1988, 1992

Fischer, Ludwig, editor, *Literatur in der Bundesrepublik Deutschland bis 1967,* Munich: Hanser, 1986

Hermand, Jost, *Kultur im Wiederaufbau: Die Bundesrepublik Deutschland 1945–1965,* Munich: Nymphenburger, 1986

Peitsch, Helmut, "Towards a History of *Vergangenheitsbewältigung*: East and West German War Novels of the 1950s," *Monatshefte* 87 (1995)

Schnell, Ralf, *Die Literatur der Bundesrepublik: Autoren, Geschichte, Literaturbetrieb,* Stuttgart: Metzler, 1986; revised as: *Geschichte der deutschsprachigen Literatur seit 1945,* Stuttgart: Metzler, 1993

Novalis 1772–1801

The literary pseudonym "Novalis" was adopted by the Saxon aristocrat Friedrich von Hardenberg in part by way of a coded reference to his family estate but more as an act of symbolic self-definition: it means "he who clears new ground for cultivation," the writer who, in Novalis's words, practices "literarische Sämereien" (literary seed-sowings). Novalis was a member of the Early Romantic group of writers centered in Jena and active between 1795 and 1801. Born into a Pietist family, a religious tradition that influenced him throughout his life, he encountered the prevailing culture of the Enlightenment while a student, reading Kant and at the same time embracing the idealistic humanism of Schiller. After an intensive study of the subjective epistemology of Fichte, Novalis became one of the most important and influential proponents of Romanticism, advocating a poetic transformation of the human spirit and the adoption of a new religiosity. Such steps were for Novalis of a missionary and indirectly political character; they would effect a regeneration of society and lead to a new golden age.

For over 150 years after his death, Novalis was held to be the most Romantic of all Romantics in a popular and trivializing sense: the unworldly dreamer who sentimentally longed for a flower of unsurpassable beauty, the poet whose mysterious devotion to his dead child fiancée led him into a cult of death. Even engravings of Novalis were adjusted in the 19th century to conform with this image of ethereal introversion. Early editors of his work unintentionally gave rise to a further misrepresentation. Novalis's Romantic friends Ludwig Tieck and Friedrich Schlegel began a tradition of interspersing his published aphorisms with arresting jottings culled from his notebooks. The result was a farrago, however stimulating, in which his ideas were torn from their context. His thoughts on poetic theory and narrative technique could then be interpreted as prescient anticipations of modernist literary practice, as happened initially with the French symbolists, with Nerval and Maeterlinck, then in German literature with Hofmannsthal, Benn, and Musil. In the 1920s, Hermann Hesse adopted Novalis as a precursor of neo-Romantic mysticism, the priest of an alternative culture set against the technological rationalism of the 20th century. With the rediscovery of Hesse himself in the 1960s, particularly in the United States, Novalis became a cult figure among initiates of "flower power" and hippie culture. The emphasis in this context on Novalis's blue flower as a symbol of unworldly alternative values provoked a counterreaction from the campus radicals of the anti-authoritarian movement in Germany in 1968: Romanticism was to be overthrown by Marxism, the blue flower by red revolution. The latest fictional treatment of Novalis, a historical novel by Penelope Fitzgerald published in 1995, offers a more neutral and factually based account of his relationship with his dying fiancée, but continues the myth in its title, *The Blue Flower*.

Novalis had written poetry since 1788 and made an initial draft of *Hymnen an die Nacht* (*Hymns to the Night*) in 1797, but his first published works were collections of aphorisms: *Blütenstaub* (*Pollen*) and *Glauben und Liebe* (*Faith and Love*), both of which appeared in 1798. *Blütenstaub* was published in the journal *Das Athenäum,* edited by the Schlegel brothers. It consists of something over a hundred "fragments," varying between a single sentence and two or three paragraphs, each containing a terse or epigrammatic observation, what Novalis called "Texte zum Denken" (texts for thought). They concentrate, in the light of Novalis's recent engagement with Fichte's philosophy, on the necessity to transcend empirical phenomena in order to seek absolute truth. Thus, the very first "fragment" runs, with a typical play on words: "Wir suchen überall das Unbedingte, und finden nur Dinge" (We seek the absolute everywhere and find only things). The absolute is, however, not to be found in the external world, but in the recesses of the human spirit. The spiritual task for each individual is therefore to gain access to his or her "transcendental self" in addition to the material self, to be not only the ego but also the "ego of the ego" (Ich des Ichs). The search for a transformed existence does not take us, as might be supposed, into the physical heights or depths, but into the self: "Nach innen geht der geheimnisvolle Weg. In uns oder nirgends ist die Ewigkeit" (The mysterious path leads inwards. Eternity is in us or nowhere). Finding eternity or the absolute in ourselves enables us, so Novalis believes in Fichtean and indirectly Kantian fashion, to transform the empirical world and thus—his own religious addition—to redeem it. These convictions inform all of Novalis's subsequent work. They underlie his celebrated definition of the Romantic approach to experience in a further fragment dating from 1797: "Die Welt muß romantisiert werden. So findet man den ursprünglichen Sinn wieder . . . Indem ich dem Gemeinen einen hohen Sinn, dem Gewöhnlichen ein geheimnisvolles Ansehn, dem Bekannten die Würde des Unbekannten, dem Endlichen einen unendlichen Schein gebe, so romantisiere ich es" (The world must be romanticized. Thus the original meaning of things can be rediscovered . . . By giving to the ordinary a superior meaning, to the usual a mysterious look, to the known the dignity of the unknown, to the finite the appearance of the infinite, I romanticize it).

After the French Revolution, a debate arose in Germany between republicans and monarchists, a controversy that was intensified by the continuing crisis in France in the 1790s. The "fragments" in *Glauben und Liebe* and its sequel, *Politische Aphorismen* (*Political Aphorisms*) represent Novalis's contribution to this ideological debate. Reacting against utilitarian views of the state and against what he saw as the depravity of 18th century courts, he imagined the ideal state as a family. In this enlightened and humane community, moral and spiritual leadership is provided by the king and queen as parental figures. On the other hand, every citizen is "thronfähig"—that is, has the potential to ascend the throne and achieve representative status. Novalis's perfect state thus combines, he maintains, the best of both the monarchical and republican forms of government, monarchy offering "mature age" and republicanism "blooming youth." Novalis named King Friedrich Wilhelm III and his young queen Luise, who had acceded to the Prussian throne in 1797, as models for his enlightened monarchy. Following the publication of *Glauben und Liebe* in 1798 in the *Jahrbücher der Preußischen Monarchie,* however, the king was displeased, and *Political Aphorisms* fell victim to the censor.

Similar problems beset Novalis's next venture into political thought, the essay or address he entitled *Europa* (Europe). His Romantic associates in Jena, to whom he read it aloud in 1799, judged it controversial and referred it to Goethe, who advised against publication, so that it did not appear until 1826, under the title *Die Christenheit oder Europa* (*Christendom or Europe*). This essay has been persistently misread, most recently by Marxists in the GDR, as a counterrevolutionary tract and a plea for renewed domination of Europe by the Catholic Church. Its essence lies, however, in a poetic conception of the state, as in *Glauben und Liebe,* presented by Novalis as a countermodel to mechanistic and narrowly constitutional theories of government. In the turmoil of the post-revolutionary years, Novalis believes that political stability and permanent European peace cannot be achieved by a political solution, but only by the restoration of a religiously unified community on the pattern of the papacy in the Middle Ages. He retraces the history of Europe from the Middle Ages to the French Revolution and interprets it as a process in which "the sense of the sacred" was increasingly usurped by skepticism, political self-interest, commercialism, and ultimately by rationalism and deism in the 18th century. Yet in the French Revolution and its aftermath, he sees cause for hope: in the subsequent anarchy there are signs that "the sense of the sacred" is reasserting itself, not least in the new religious awareness proclaimed in Friedrich Schleiermacher's *Reden über die Religion,* which had just appeared. The Catholic papacy may well be finished after Napoleon's conquests in Italy, but Novalis envisions the institution of a "neue, dauerhaftere Kirche" (new, more enduring church) to replace it and ensure a Europe again united by religion. What had opened apparently as a historical essay becomes in the end a hymnic celebration of European harmony as a metaphorical act of holy communion.

Such semi-mystic conceptions recur in Novalis's two groups of poems, the *Geistliche Lieder* (1802; *Sacred Songs*) and *Hymnen an die Nacht* (1800). The *Geistliche Lieder* are devotional poems based on traditional forms of congregational worship but are at the same time marked by Pietistic notions of an intimate or even erotic relationship between Christ and the worshipper. Similar ideas pervade the *Hymnen an die Nacht,* but this cycle of six poems is influenced also by Novalis's personal experiences and by Romantic philosophy. The *Hymnen* focus on the relationship between material reality and the transcendental, the finite and infinite, day and night. Day is dismissed as the sphere of mortality restricted by time and space, and the speaker in the poems commits himself to night as the equivalent of eternity, uninterrupted by time divisions. The autobiographical experience reflected in the third hymn, the death of a beloved, is no more than one starting point, albeit of great intensity, for this train of thought. At the graveside the realization is achieved that the physical demise of the beloved in fact opens up the possibility of everlasting union in the hereafter. Death is therefore not an end and a cause for despair but a release—in the metaphor of the fourth hymn, a route through a range of mountains—into a timeless and boundless realm of love. This revaluation of death leads to a modified view of reality: the real world can be tolerated and even enjoyed in the knowledge that death will bring salvation. The fifth hymn shows that such convictions accord with the Christian message of the salvation of mankind through Christ's death. A parallel emerges between the dead beloved and Christ; both are intermediaries whose death opens the way to eternity. The *Hymnen* are characterized by a dense body of interrelated metaphor and by great linguistic fervor, making them one of the most striking bodies of poetry in German Romantic literature.

Novalis had not completed his novel *Heinrich von Ofterdingen* when he died. We possess the first part and the opening sections of the second. The novel portrays the educational journey of the medieval poet Heinrich von Ofterdingen from Eisenach to Augsburg and his spiritual and artistic development along the way, but the real theme of the novel is the power of poetry to redeem the world. In becoming a poet and experiencing phenomena poetically, Heinrich fulfills his mission to transform reality. Novalis wrote that the novel depicts "Übergangsjahre vom Unendlichen zum Endlichen" (transition years from the infinite to the finite), the invasion of infinity into the finite historical dimension. Heinrich's development occurs in part through a series of instructive encounters with representative individuals: merchants, an Arab slave girl, knights, a miner, a hermit, and, above all, the poet Klingsohr. Such a procedure owes much to the bildungsroman tradition, which culminated in Goethe's *Wilhelm Meisters Lehrjahre* (1795–96; *Wilhelm Meister's Apprenticeship*), a novel with which Novalis entered into an intense love-hate relationship. Yet *Heinrich von Ofterdingen* is structured even more by a series of dreams, recollections of the past, and premonitions of the future. Such experiences serve to dissolve present time, indeed temporality altogether, so that in the end Heinrich leaves historical reality behind and enters into the continuum of past and future that is eternity. "Der Roman soll allmählich in Märchen übergehen" (I intend that the novel should gradually evolve into fairy tale), Novalis wrote to Friedrich Schlegel about *Heinrich von Ofterdingen*, and the dominance of fairy-tale conditions increases throughout the novel, so that the last chapter of the first part is devoted exclusively to a fairy tale narrated by Klingsohr, while the opening of the second part finds Heinrich transposed into a supernatural sphere in which plants and stones communicate with mankind. Klingsohr's fairy tale itself, an eclectic combination of elements from various mythologies and from speculative natural science, reiterates in symbolic form the themes of the novel as a whole:

the allegorical figures of fable and eros, poetry and love, release the human world from the tyranny of the unfeeling "clerk," pedantic rationalism.

The dream of the blue flower in *Heinrich von Ofterdingen* is thus not mere sentimentality but a vision in erotic form of heightened human sensitivity, the first of a series of experiences in which the imagination transfigures imperfect empirical reality. Novalis's grief over the death of Sophie von Kühn is in reality complemented and relativized by a range of literary, philosophical, religious, and scientific influences which feed into his work. His thought, far from being divorced from the material world, engages ideologically with the French Revolution in order to construct a utopian or millennialist view of an impending golden age. Such critical revisions have been possible since the 1960s due to a determined effort by scholars both to uncover and demystify the facts of Novalis's life as Friedrich von Hardenberg and to re-edit his writings so as to produce reliable texts not only of his published works but also of his private notes. The critical edition originated by Kluckhohn and Samuel and completed in 1998 has laid the foundation for still further demythologising of Novalis and his work.

RICHARD LITTLEJOHNS

See also Romanticism

Biography
Born in Oberwiederstedt, Thuringia, 2 May 1772. Studied at the University of Jena, 1790–91, the University of Leipzig, 1791–93, and the University of Wittenberg, 1793–94; law degree, 1794; studied at the school of mining, Freiberg, 1797–99; administrative assistant in the Kreisamt, Tennstedt, 1794–95; administrative assistant, 1796–97, and administrator, 1797–99, in Saxon salt mines, Weissenfels. Died in Weissenfels, 25 March 1801.

Selected Works

Collections
Schriften, edited by Ludwig Tieck and Friedrich Schlegel, 2 vols., 1802
Schriften, edited by Ernst Heilborn, 3 vols., 1901
Schriften, edited by Jakob Minor, 4 vols., 1907
Schriften, edited by Paul Kluckhohn and Richard Samuel, 4 vols., 1929; 2nd edition, 4 vols., 1960–75; 3rd edition, 6 vols., 1977–98
Novalis Werke, edited by Gerhard Schulz, 1969
Werke, Tagebücher, und Briefe Friedrich von Hardenbergs, edited by Hans-Joachim Mähl and Richard Samuel, 3 vols., 1978–87
Pollen and Fragments: Selected Poetry and Prose, translated by Arthur Versluis, 1989
Pollen; Faith and Love; Political Aphorisms; Christianity or Europe, in *The Early Political Writings of the German Romantics*, edited and translated by Frederick C. Beiser, 1996

Poetry
Hymnen an die Nacht, 1800; as *Hymns to the Night* (bilingual edition), translated by Mabel Cotterell, 1948; translated by Charles E. Passage, 1960; translated by Dick Higgins, 1984
Geistliche Lieder, 1802; as *Devotional Songs*, edited by Bernard Pick, 1910; as *Sacred Songs*, translated by Eileen Hutchins, 1956

Fiction
Heinrich von Ofterdingen, 1802; as *Henry von Ofterdingen*, translated by Palmer Hilty, 1964

Further Reading

Frye, Lawrence O., "Spatial Imagery in Novalis's *Hymnen an die Nacht*," *Deutsche Vierteljahresschrift für Literaturwissenschaft und Geistesgeschichte* 41 (1967)

Hamburger, Michael, *Reason and Energy: Studies in German Literature*, London: Routledge, and New York: Grove Press, 1957; revised edition, London: Weidenfeld and Nicolson, 1970

Haywood, Bruce, *Novalis, the Veil of Imagery: A Study of the Poetic Works of Friedrich von Hardenberg, 1772–1801*, Cambridge, Massachusetts: Harvard University Press, 1959

Hiebel, Friedrich, *Novalis: German Poet, European Thinker, Christian Mystic*, Chapel Hill: University of North Carolina Press, 1954; 2nd revised edition, 1959

Kuzniar, Alice A., *Delayed Endings: Nonclosure in Novalis and Hölderlin*, Athens: University of Georgia Press, 1987

Mähl, Hans-Joachim, *Die Idee des goldenen Zeitalters im Werk des Novalis: Studien zur Wesenbestimmung der frühromantischen Utopie und zu ihren ideengeschichtlichen Voraussetzungen*, Heidelberg: Winter, 1965

Malsch, Wilfried, *"Europa": Poetische Rede des Novalis: Deutung der französischen Revolution und Reflexion auf die Poesie in der Geschichte*, Stuttgart: Metzler, 1965

Neubauer, John, *Novalis*, Boston: Twayne, 1980

O'Brien, William Arctander, *Novalis: Signs of Revolution*, Durham, North Carolina: Duke University Press, 1995

Saul, Nicholas, *History and Poetry in Novalis and in the Tradition of the German Enlightenment*, London: Institute of Germanic Studies, University of London, and Atlantic Highlands, New Jersey: Humanities Press, 1984

Schulz, Gerhard, *Novalis in Selbstzeugnissen und Bilddokumenten*, Reinbek bei Hamburg: Rowohlt, 1969

Uerlings, Herbert, *Friedrich von Hardenberg, genannt Novalis: Werk und Forschung*, Stuttgart: Metzler, 1991

Novel *see* Bildungsroman; Epistolary Novel; Novella; War Novels

Novella

Originally a diminutive of the Latin adjective *novus, novella* appeared in the writings of Cicero and Virgil to describe a young plant or animal. For Ovid the word meant "something new," and in the Byzantine Empire of the sixth century, it acquired a legal meaning as an addendum to or expansion of a law in the Justinian Code. By the 12th century, *novella* had a literary meaning in Italy as a prose account of a newsworthy event. With Boccaccio's *Decameron* of 1353, a collection of 100 novellas, the word came to mean an account that could be true or fictional, new or simply unusual. In English, the novella is a story with a compact and pointed plot.

German writers became acquainted with the novella in the late 15th century, when they read translations of Boccaccio's *Decameron*, but the term (in German, *Novelle*) was not widely used until at least 1820. *Decameron* was an important influence because of the narrative framework for its 100 novellas. A group of ten Florentine citizens who have fled to the hills of Fiesole to escape the plague of 1348 tell the stories over a ten-day period. The most influential writer in Germany in the 19th century, Johann Wolfgang von Goethe, published an early example of novella form with *Unterhaltungen deutscher Ausgewanderten* (1795; *Conversations of German Refugees*), although he did not give it that label. His narrative clearly reflects the influence of Boccaccio in its structure and content, however. Goethe's framework is the French Revolution, which forces an aristocratic family to leave its home. On the journey to safety, each person tells a story.

In the Boccaccio and Goethe texts, the realistic "frame story" (*Rahmenerzählung*) gives the subsidiary stories a cohesion, a cyclical structure, and a real-life reason for their existence. The inner novellas are a mixture of anecdotes, tales, and even ghost stories. Boccaccio's tone is playful, sensual, and entertaining. Goethe added to the entertainment value of his novellas a moralizing aim: to show how, with reason and self-possession, one can overcome the lawlessness of a dispossessed society in the wake of war or other calamity. The didacticism of his narrative had a strong influence on the genre in Germany. Heinrich von Kleist, whose eight novellas are often described as the culmination of the form in Germany, also had a moralistic goal.

The popularity of the novella form in the 19th century is perhaps due to the writer's ability to express a truth or provide a lesson in an aesthetic context; this latter facet of the form has venerable ancestors. Some theorists, in fact, claim that myths, tales, and even 15th-century pranks (*Schwänke*) are early German novellas. They report something new and unusual, and they are instructive—an aspect of narration that goes back to the time of Aristotle and the exemplum, an anecdote meant to exemplify a moral principle. By including such anecdotes in *Conversations of German Refugees*, Goethe forges a link with Aristotle as well as Boccaccio. Another ancestor of the novella, the Indian "frame" narrative *Panschatantra* (300 B.C.), also contains moralizing anecdotes, which were meant to teach the king's sons about life.

Goethe defined the novella as an unheard-of occurrence. His *Novelle* (1828; *Novella*) is an account of a carnival lion who is freed from its cage by a fire in the market place and who threatens a princess. The young son of the lion's owner saves the princess by leading the lion into another cage as he plays his flute and sings. Neither the boy nor the princess is of central interest to the story; it is the event that matters, and the event is so unusual that the reader is compelled to think about what it means.

A single striking and realistically oriented event that embodies a message is the distinguishing feature of the German novella. This much of the form has been generally accepted by literary theorists and critics since the mid–19th century. Other features—a *Wendepunkt* (turning point), identified by Ludwig Tieck at the beginning of the 19th century, and the *Falkentheorie* (falcon theory) of Paul Heyse—are disputed. So, too, is the notion that a novella must have a frame.

The frame of Goethe's *Novella* is the omniscient narrator, who intrudes now and then to address the reader; for example, he tells us "Let us thank the diligent artist." Some theorists maintain that frame narration is essential, but many novellas do not have a frame. The omniscient narrator never addresses the reader in Kleist's novellas, written between 1807 and 1811. Two of the most renowned contemporary examples of the genre, Thomas Mann's *Der Tod in Venedig* (1913; *Death in Venice*) and Franz Kafka's *Die Verwandlung* (1916; *The Metamorphosis*), have no intrusive narrator.

Annette von Droste-Hülshoff's only novella, *Die Judenbuche* (1842; *The Jew's Beech*) has a modest frame narrator whose only personal remark appears in the last paragraph. Theodor Storm, who published over 50 novellas, employed a memory framework (*Erinnerungsrahmen*) that was frequently emulated: a story that begins in the present, shifts to the past, and returns at the end to the present. In *Immensee* (1851; *Immensee*) an elderly man recalls his youthful love for Elisabeth, who slipped away from him to marry another man. *Die schwarze Spinne* (1842; *The Black Spider*) by Jeremias Gotthelf; *Der arme Spielmann* (1847; *The Poor Musician*) by Franz Grillparzer; *Bergkristall* (1845; *Rock Crystal*), by Adalbert Stifter; and *Die Leiden eines Knaben* (1883; *The Sufferings of a Boy*) by Conrad Ferdinand Meyer are only a few of the similar frame stories.

Gottfried Keller invented a Swiss village blessed with rich natural resources and published two volumes of novellas about the odd experiences of its genial, well-to-do, but irresponsible inhabitants when, for example, an outsider enters the community or an insider is forced to leave. The tone of the narrator of *Die Leute von Seldwyla* (1856, 1874; *The People of Seldwyla*) is comic and gently ironic as he offers a moral evaluation of the frivolity and unrighteousness of the Seldwylers. In these novellas the village itself may be considered the frame. In Keller's later collection, *Züricher Novellen* (1876, 1878; *Zurich Novellas*), it is his native city that frames the critique of contemporary social mores. Keller also provides both a "turning point" and a "falcon."

In the novella the disputed "turning point" is the moment when a striking event occurs that effects a change in the narrative. In Goethe's *Novella* it is the lion's response to music, which leads to a happy and nonviolent conclusion. In Mann's *Death in Venice* the turning point occurs when Aschenbach sees Tadzio, the beautiful Polish boy who becomes the object of his obsession. Kafka presents the turning point of *The Metamorphosis* in the first line of the story ("When Gregor Samsa woke up one morning from unsettling dreams, he found himself changed in his bed into a monstrous vermin"—Corngold translation). Not all critics believe a turning point is necessary, while others note that this device occurs in drama and novels as well. In general, however, the idea of a turning point is more widely accepted than the "falcon theory," which numerous critics have derided.

Paul Heyse, a prolific writer of novellas and winner of the Nobel Prize for Literature in 1910, outlined his theory of the novella in the preface to a collection of German novellas that he edited in 1871. Influenced by the works of Goethe and Tieck, he declared that the novella should be simple, individualistic, deal with social and ethical problems of the time, and have a central event with a strong silhouette that includes something specific to distinguish this type of story from all others. By "silhouette" he meant a plot structure that can be summarized in a single sentence. To illustrate something specific, he cited one of the *Decameron* stories. A young man spends his fortune trying to win the love of a lady and is left, finally, with only his prized falcon. One day the lady, a widow, visits him to ask if she might have his falcon for her son, who has become ill from coveting the bird. The young man, who does not immediately know the reason for her visit, has his beloved falcon killed to provide a banquet for his guest. When the lady later realizes the sacrifice the young man made for her, she consents to marry him. The silhouette of this story might be, "A young man who gives up his beloved falcon for love wins the lady's hand because of his sacrifice."

Heyse felt that the writer of a novella should continually ask himself, "Where is the falcon?" Critics who accept his theory interpret the falcon as a concrete object, or a *Dingsymbol* (symbolic thing), or a leitmotif. In Goethe's *Novella* the falcon is the lion; in Grillparzer's *The Poor Musician* it is a violin. The title of a novella sometimes identifies the falcon, for instance, Droste-Hülshoff's beech tree.

The length of a novella varies. The longest is Otto Ludwig's *Zwischen Himmel und Erde* (1856; *Between Heaven and Earth*), which is over 200 pages long. Kleist's *Das Bettelweib von Locarno* (1810; *The Beggar Woman of Locarno*) covers less than three pages. Tieck, who wrote more than 40 novellas, favored a size between 20,000 and 40,000 words.

The novella's popularity in Germany in the 19th century resulted from its ability to reflect the issues of the time, since its focus is events and not character development. In the early 19th century, the novella gave the Romantics the opportunity to attempt to bridge the gap between the objective world and the poetic, subjective one. The fairy-tale novella (*Märchennovelle*) dominates the period, its union of realism and fantasy exemplified by Tieck's *Der blonde Eckbert* (1796; *Blonde Eckbert*) at the beginning and Joseph Freiherr von Eichendorff's *Aus dem Leben eines Taugenichts* (1826; *Memoirs of a Good-for-Nothing*) at its end. In the Biedermeier period (1820–50) the novella provided an effective vehicle for portraying man's need of religious faith to battle evil. Gotthelf's *The Black Spider* is a significant contribution. From 1850 to 1890, the period of Realism, a growing feeling of isolation and determinism—the sense that one is a victim of social, psychological, or physical drives, or an imperfect genetic inheritance—led to an increased interest in reading. The structure of novellas of this period mirrors the isolation of the reader, for instead of a frame in which people tell stories to each other, there is a single narrator who tells a story about someone else. Grillparzer's *The Poor Musician* and numerous Storm novellas are witness to the social fragmentation of the time.

From 1890 to 1945 the novella declined in importance; its closed structure seemed no longer suitable for times of spiritual relativism, economic struggles, and war. Writers preferred the open-endedness of the short story. Those who employed the novella form turned to the past—for example, Agnes Miegel, whose *Geschichten aus Altpreußen* (1926; Stories of Old Prussia) recount events from the Middle Ages to the 18th century. Since 1945 narratives by Christa Wolf, Stefan Zweig, Günter Grass, Martin Walser, and others have revived the form. These narratives adhere to the now characteristic pattern for a novella: its central interest is an unusual, realistic event within a compact frame structure of medium length and a small cast of characters who are not developed. There is one or more "turning point," leading each time to a sudden change in the action of the story, often with a twist of fate. A central symbol or leitmotif informs the narrative, which is overtly objective and covertly subjective.

PATRICIA H. STANLEY

Further Reading

Aust, Hugo, *Novelle,* Stuttgart: Metzler, 1990

Bennett, Edwin Keppel, *A History of the German Novelle from Goethe to Thomas Mann,* Cambridge: Cambridge University Press, 1934; 2nd edition as *A History of the German Novelle,* revised and continued by H.M. Waidson, 1961

Clements, Robert John, and Joseph Gibaldi, *Anatomy of the Novella: The European Tale Collection from Boccaccio and Chaucer to Cervantes,* New York: New York University Press, 1977

Ellis, John M. *Narration in the German Novelle,* London and New York: Cambridge University Press, 1974

Himmel, Hellmuth, *Geschichte der deutschen Novelle,* Bern: Francke, 1963

Leibowitz, Judith, *Narrative Purpose in the Novella,* The Hague: Mouton, 1974

Paine, J.H.E., *Theory and Criticism of the Novella,* Bonn: Bouvier, 1979

Paulin, Roger, *The Brief Compass: The Nineteenth-Century German Novelle,* Oxford and New York: Clarendon Press, 1985

Polheim, Karl Konrad, editor, *Theorie und Kritik der deutschen Novelle von Wieland bis Musil,* Tübingen: Niemeyer, 1970

Remak, Henry H.H. *Structural Elements of the German Novella from Goethe to Thomas Mann,* New York: Lang, 1996

Sammons, Jeffrey L., editor, *German Novellas of Realism,* New York: Continuum, 1989

Silz, Walter, *Realism and Reality: Studies in the German Novelle of Poetic Realism,* Chapel Hill: University of North Carolina Press, 1954

Springer, Mary Doyle, *Forms of the Modern Novella,* Chicago: University of Chicago Press, 1975; London: University of Chicago Press, 1976

Swales, Martin, *The German Novelle,* Princeton, New Jersey: Princeton University Press, 1977

Weing, Siegfried, *The German Novella: Two Centuries of Criticism,* Columbia, South Carolina: Camden House, 1994

Wiese, Benno von, *Novelle,* Stuttgart: Metzler, 1963

O

Old High German

The term *Old High German* (OHG) is used as a label for the very earliest period in German language and literature. It covers historical, geographical, and linguistic elements, and similar to most of our knowledge of this period, it contains much that is inexact or only partially recorded for future generations. The word *old* is used to cover everything from the first, unrecorded beginnings of German through the middle of the 11th century. The early part of this period—roughly from the end of the Roman Empire in A.D. 476—is also known, somewhat unfairly, as "the Dark Ages," a time when Europe was divided into meandering and warring tribes, each with its own dialect and shifting allegiances. In this period, Latin was the dominant language of scholarship, the Christian Church was the guardian of all written knowledge, and the earliest surviving Germanic texts are mostly scraps of Bible translation, commentary, or other functional pieces. There is not much in the way of pure literature until the time of the great king and emperor Charlemagne (from the year 780).

This middle part of the period, covering the ninth century, is sometimes called, rather ambitiously, "the Carolingian Renaissance," because like the later, more illustrious Renaissance, there existed a newfound belief in education and a great admiration for the classical Greek and especially Latin traditions. Writers of all kinds, both in Latin and in German, flourished in the ninth century under Charlemagne's generous patronage. After his death, however, Charlemagne's empire was broken up, and his territories were parceled out among his descendants. In the religious and political upheaval that followed, there was less enthusiasm for learning. The last part of the OHG period, from about 900 to about 1050, is characterized by the continued production of Latin texts, but very few texts in the vernacular.

The word *high* derives from a geographical feature: the mountains of central Europe. This is in contrast to the so-called low countries of the north, who had their own set of dialects, which later developed into separate languages such as Dutch, Swedish, Danish, and English. The linguistic boundaries of what we have come to call German are also quite flexible: there was no such thing as Germany, and the authors of the period saw themselves as members of much smaller tribal or regional units. A number of linguistic features—such as changes in particular sounds over time—were drawn from the many variations of early manuscripts, and philologists have used these changes to define the boundaries of OHG. The cultural dominance of the Franks has also reinforced the status of Frankish, in its many dialects, as the most typical example of OHG, although of course Bavarian, Alemannic, and other variations are also included.

The major works in OHG include Otfrid's *Evangelienbuch* (860–70), the *Ludwigslied* (881), and the *Muspilli, Georgslied,* and *Petruslied* (all late ninth century), all of which are much influenced by Christian ideas. Additionally, there are echoes of pre-Christian ideas in the *Hildebrandslied* (mid-ninth century) and in the many fascinating fragments of charms, oaths, phrase lists, and political texts that have survived. By far the majority of the material, however, is religious translation and commentary, often recorded alongside the Latin original.

One of the most interesting issues in this period is the struggle of the emerging Frankish nation to achieve a cultural identity against the overwhelming superiority of the dominant Latin-based Christian tradition. Charlemagne had led the Franks to a position of political power—his empire at its greatest stretched from Spain in the west almost to the Russian steppes in the east. He could himself barely write the letters of the alphabet, but he gathered around him the best scholars of his day, including several Irish and British monks, because he was aware that the great civilizations of the past ruled as much by their mastery of the pen as by their skill with the sword. Diplomatic skills, resources management, and a guaranteed place of honor in the history books are matters that require an educated workforce. Charlemagne struck a strategic alliance with the Christian Church that allowed both the church and the Frankish state to develop their separate agendas across central Europe. The history of German relations with successive church leaders from this period onward revolves around the tension between different kinds of power: spiritual influence, political influence, and the need to secure sufficient labor, materials, and wealth.

The decision of a few brave souls to write in their own first language can be seen in this context as a form of support for the Frankish cause or even as a resistance to the Latin-speaking church hierarchy. Some 19th- and early 20th-century scholars were tempted to read into works of this period such as the *Ludwigslied* and even parts of the *Evangelienbuch* a kind of proto-nationalism—the first steps on the way to the German domination of Europe. The evidence, however, shows a tentative, modest coming of age—a natural expression of a very basic human need to speak in everyday rhythms instead of the formal Latin prose of the day.

Old High German was in no way a threat to the dominance of Latin. It was not until the time of Martin Luther and the printing press some 600 years later that the church lost its almost absolute sway over the composition and preservation of substantial written texts. What we see in OHG is the authentic voice of humble scholars, most of them practicing monks, who sought to serve the ends of both church and state by copying Latin sacred texts, translating them, interpreting them, and occasionally daring to paraphrase and reformulate them in the local dialect. While we suspect that there was a lively indigenous and secular culture of literary composition, it was confined to oral forms and has not been preserved in the monastic libraries. Old High German may not have many original works that have the stature of *Beowulf* in the English tradition, but it has significantly more material than any of the Celtic languages. We owe much to the work of the scribes and authors of this period: their imitation of Latin styles and their choice of topics illustrate their piety more than any personal or national ambition, and their legacy is a conscientious record of the first phases in the development of German language, literature, and culture.

LINDA ARCHIBALD

See also German Language; Middle High German

Further Reading

Assion, Peter, *Altdeutsche Fachliteratur,* Berlin: Schmidt, 1973

Bostock, John Knight, *A Handbook on Old High German Literature,* revised by K.C. King and D.R. McLintock, Oxford: Clarendon Press, 1976

Fleckenstein, Josef, *Early Medieval Germany,* translated by Bernard S. Smith, Amsterdam: North Holland, 1978; distributed in U.S. and Canada by Elsevier North-Holland

Godman, Peter, *Poets and Emperors: Frankish Politics and Carolingian Poetry,* Oxford: Clarendon Press, and New York: Oxford University Press, 1986

Groseclose, J. Sidney, and Brian O. Murdoch, *Die althochdeutschen poetischen Denkmäler,* Stuttgart: Metzler, 1976

Kartschoke, Dieter, *Geschichte der deutschen Literatur im frühen Mittelalter,* Munich: Deutscher Taschenbuch, 1990

McKitterick, Rosamond, *The Frankish Kingdoms under the Carolingians, 751–987,* New York and London: Longman, 1983

——, *The Carolingians and the Written Word,* Cambridge and New York: Cambridge University Press, 1989

Murdoch, Brian, *Old High German Literature,* Boston: Twayne, 1983

Reuter, Timothy, *Germany in the Early Middle Ages,* London and New York: Longman, 1991

Sonderegger, Stefan, *Althochdeutsche Sprache und Literatur: Eine Einführung in das älteste Deutsch, Darstellung und Grammatik,* Berlin and New York: de Gruyter, 1974

Wehrli, Max, *Geschichte der deutschen Literatur vom frühen Mittelalter bis zum Ende des 16. Jahrhunderts,* 2nd edition, Stuttgart: Reclam, 1984

Wipf, Karl A., editor and translator, *Althochdeutsche poetische Texte,* Stuttgart: Reclam, 1992

Martin Opitz 1597–1639

Martin Opitz has been called the father of German literature, and although this reputation does not rest on his poetic talent, it is certainly the case that he had a tremendous impact on the development of German literature during the 17th century and thereafter. He was celebrated and revered by his contemporaries as a national hero for his efforts to put German literature on the path that would lead it to a place alongside the national literatures of Italy, France, England, Spain, and Holland. Other poets trained in the humanistic tradition shared Opitz's desire for a refined German literature, but because their attempts to adapt the forms and content of the classical poetic tradition to the German language were experimental and unsystematic, these poets remained isolated in their endeavors. In contrast, Opitz was able to formulate clear rules and give examples that others could then follow.

The work with which Opitz established his reputation was his *Buch von der deutschen Poeterey* (1624; Book of German Poetry), in which he set down rules for a complete reform of German poetry. This verse reform must be viewed in the context of European Renaissance literature if we are to understand what motivated Opitz and why his reform was so successful. Following the Italian Renaissance, poets throughout northern Europe increasingly emphasized the virtues of their national languages, but the introduction of sophisticated classical meters, verse

forms, and ideas into these languages was a slow process. In France, England, and Holland, poets were able to accomplish this by the end of the 16th century, but this was not the case in Germany. There, poets who were capable of writing polished neo-Latin verse continued to favor in German verse the use of *Knittelvers,* an indigenous metrical line of four stresses with between 7 and 15 syllables. For centuries, poets such as Hans Sachs in Nuremberg had used such doggerel successfully for popular works, but it proved to be inadequate for polished lyric poetry. For such poetry, new rules of versification as well as new poetic forms were needed.

Through his study and appreciation of foreign literatures (most notably the Dutch), Opitz recognized that significant prosodic changes were needed to elevate German poetry. Whereas educated German poets would soon recognize that verse ictus and natural word stress should coincide in metrically regular lines, popular German poets were accustomed to writing metrically irregular lines. Opitz rejected this traditional versification and codified the metrical rules necessary to create a new German poetry. However, his reform did not simply modify accepted poetic theory. It was a fundamental conceptual change in the way in which humanistic German poets viewed poetry in that it introduced not only sophisticated meters and forms but also an awareness of new potential for poetic language and structure. In this way, Opitz expanded the variety of meters in German poetry and at the same time opened new poetic forms and genres to his fellow poets. In the process, he also elevated the status of poets themselves.

In the seventh chapter of his poetic treatise, Opitz described in detail the characteristics of various verse forms, especially those of alexandrine verse: a line of six metrical feet (usually iambic) with either 12 syllables (with masculine rhyme) or 13 (with feminine rhyme). The speed with which German poets began to write alexandrine verse is an important measure of the acceptance of the new rules. Although isolated examples of rudimentary German alexandrines had appeared at least a quarter of a century before the verse reform, it is generally agreed that Opitz is the person who deserves credit as the creator of this verse form in German. He gave clear examples of polished German alexandrines, encouraged the use of feminine rhyme and enjambment, and emphasized the need for a caesura with masculine stress after the sixth syllable. Many examples of well-crafted alexandrine verse in his own poems appeared in his collection *Martini Opitii Acht Bücher, Deutscher Poematum* (1625; Martin Opitz's Eight Books of German Poetry). By the early 1630s, the alexandrine was widely used in broadsheet verse and in occasional poems, and it ultimately became the standard metrical line for 17th-century German poets. It retained its popularity until poets such as Klopstock and Goethe in the following century rejected it for freer, more personal forms of poetic expression.

In keeping with his desire to elevate German literature, Opitz translated several works into German to demonstrate that the German language was as capable of sophisticated poetic expression as other languages. As he argued in the eighth chapter of his poetic treatise:

> It is good practice for us to undertake occasionally to translate something by the Greek and Latin poets, for in so doing we learn about the meaning and splendor of words, the wealth of figures of speech, and the ability to invent them ourselves.

Early in his career, Opitz translated poems by Daniel Heinsius, who had a significant influence on his verse reform. From classical literature he translated Seneca's *Trojan Women* (1625), distichs attributed to Cato the Elder (1629), and Sophocles's *Antigone* (1636). He also translated several biblical works, as well as works by modern authors such as John Barclay's *Argenis* (1626), Jean Puget de la Serre's *The Sweet Thoughts of Death* (1626), and Hugo Grotius's *The Truth of the Christian Religion* (1631).

In addition to these translations, Opitz composed new types of works that served as examples for other poets. In 1627 he wrote the first German opera libretto, *Dafne* (after Ottavio Rinuccini's opera of the same name), for Heinrich Schütz's music. More important, Opitz's prose eclogue *Schäfferey von der Nimfen Hercinie* (1630; Pastoral of the Nymph Hercinia) served as the model for the many pastorals written in German in the 17th century.

By the time of his premature death in 1639, Opitz could view with satisfaction the success of the poetic revolution he had begun less than two decades earlier. The rules that he had succinctly formulated and the examples he had given of sophisticated, learned poetry had taken firm root and were to in-

fluence the development of German literature over the next century and a half. It is thus with justification that Opitz can be called the father of German literature.

JOHN ROGER PAAS

See also Annolied

Biography

Born in Bunzlau (Silesia), 23 December 1597. Educated in Breslau, 1614–16, and at Beuthen, 1617; studied at Heidelberg, 1619, but forced to flee the advancing Catholic army, 1620; traveled to Holland and Denmark, 1620; employed as tutor at Weissenburg Latin Academy in Transylvania, 1622–23; returned to Silesia, 1623; crowned poet laureate by Emperor Ferdinand II, 1625; entered the service of the Catholic Count Karl Hannibal von Dohna, 1626; ennobled by Emperor Ferdinand II, 1627; admitted to the Fruchtbringende Gesellschaft (Fruit-Bringing Society), a prestigious literary society, 1629; entered the service of the dukes of Liegnitz and Brieg, 1633; employed by the Swedish general Johann Baner, 1634; forced to flee to Poland, 1635; employed by King Ladislaus IV of Poland as royal historiographer, 1636. Died (of the plague) in Danzig, 20 August 1639.

Selected Works

Aristarchus sive De Contemptu Linguae Teutonicae, 1617
Lob deß Feldtlebens, 1623
Zlatna; oder, Von Rhue des Gemütes, 1623
Buch von der deutschen Poeterey, 1624
Martini Opicii Teutsche Pöemata und Aristarchus Wieder die verachtung Teutscher Sprach, 1624
Martini Opitti Acht Bücher, Deutscher Poematum, 1625
Dafne, 1627
Martini Opitii Deütscher Pöematum Erster Theil, 1628
Martini Opitii Deütscher Pöematum Anderer Theil, 1628
Viel Gut, 1629
Schäfferey von der Nimfen Hercinie, 1630
Trost Gedichte in Widerwertigkeit deß Kriegs, 1633
Judith, 1635
Martini Opitii Deutsche Pöematum, 2 vols., 1637
Martini Opitii Geistliche Pöemata, 1638
Martini Opitii Weltliche Pöematia, Das Erste Theil, 1638

Further Reading

Becker-Cantarino, Barbara, "Martin Opitz," in *German Baroque Writers, 1580–1660*, Dictionary of Literary Biography, edited by James Hardin, vol. 164, Detroit, Michigan and London: Gale Research, 1996

Becker-Cantarino, Barbara, and Jörg Fechner, editors, *Opitz und seine Welt: Festschrift für George Schulz-Behrend*, Amsterdam and Atlanta, Georgia: Rodopi, 1990

Garber, Klaus, *Martin Opitz, der "Vater der deutschen Dichtung": Eine kritische Studie zur Wissenschaftsgeschichte der Germanistik*, Stuttgart: Metzler, 1976

Gellinek, Janis Little, *Die weltliche Lyrik des Martin Opitz*, Bern and Munich: Francke, 1973

Hacken, Richard D., *The Religious Thought of Martin Opitz as the Determinant of his Poetic Theory and Practice*, Stuttgart: Heinz, 1976

Schulz-Behrend, George, "On Editing Opitz," *Modern Language Notes* 77 (1962)

Szyrocki, Marian, *Martin Opitz*, Berlin: Rütten und Loening, 1956; 2nd edition, Munich: Beck, 1974

Ulmer, Bernhard, *Martin Opitz*, New York: Twayne, 1971

Aras Ören 1939–

In the 1970s, Aras Ören was one of the first Turkish-German writers to gain critical recognition. His work, written in Turkish but translated and directed equally at a German readership, is set largely in Berlin (where he has lived since 1969 and worked as a radio journalist since 1974). In the poems and stories of the 1970s and 1980s, the social experience of labor and other migrants, and its psychological consequences, are central themes. But Ören locates them within European working-class experience as a whole, arguing for a commonality between his migrant figures (predominantly but not exclusively Turkish) and the native Germans that outweighs their different stages of historical development. The story *Bitte, nix Polizei* (1981; *Please, No Police*), embeds an illegal immigrant's fear of officialdom in a mosaic of working-class experience, German as much as Turkish. Especially in the "Berlin Trilogy" of longer poems—*Was will Niyazi in der Naunynstraße?* (1973; What Does Niyazi Want in the Naunynstraße?), *Der kurze Traum aus Kagithane* (1974; The Brief Dream from Kagithane), and *Die Fremde ist auch ein Haus* (1980; The Alien Place, Too, Is a House)—the Berlin district of Kreuzberg, once a German proletarian quarter and now the largest Turkish settlement outside Turkey, manifests the "blutende Wunde" ("bleeding wound") of European history: a continuum of class and ethnic exploitation. This exploitation links Niyazi, laborer from Istanbul; Frau Kutzer, proletarian German widow; Horst Schmidt, bohemian potter; Kazim Akkaya, Anatolian peasant; and Emine, rebellious second-generation migrant.

The everyday details, class-struggle rhetoric and characteristic *wir* (we) perspective with which the narrator affirms his solidarity with migrant labor experience are balanced by consciously literary syntax and imagery. Moreover, Ören's image of "Europa" displays more than a one-way exploitation. The inequalities of labor migration generate economic, demographic, and cultural dialectics which eventually transform the colonizing as well as colonized society. By, for example, offering rural Turks the chance to escape semifeudal conditions, the city (be it Istanbul or Berlin) promises migrants the potential to become active subjects. Yet through marginalization and exclusion, it also frustrates this promise. Disappointment in turn generates new transformative energies: Turkish children like Emine cannot reconcile the "consumer chaos" of the German city with the values invoked within their family. Like an Expressionist observing the early-20th-century city, Ören sees this dialectic throwing up "NEUE MENSCHEN" (NEW HUMAN BEINGS). Ören's conception of Europe never wholly loses this visionary element, though he becomes increasingly skeptical as the Marxist project of the 1970s fades.

Privatexil (1977; Private Exile) already signals abandonment of the poet's self-image as a privileged educator. Turkish-German identity (itself a complex, fluctuating amalgam, not a fixed unity) is neither Turkish nor German, though it draws elements from both. Instead, it stands independently like a bridge resting on neither bank. Ören's later volumes only apparently contradict this when they invoke more explicitly German and Turkish poetic traditions (the latter previously rejected by Ören as decayed and dishonest, a rejection typical of modernist poetry in Turkey itself) without abandoning critical awareness of migrant experience's material causes: *Deutschland, ein*

türkisches Märchen (1978; Germany, a Turkish Fairytale), echoing Heinrich Heine, and possibly Wolf Biermann, and *Mitten in der Odyssee* (1980; In the Midst of the Odyssee). The existential restlessness that migration unleashes is explored in poetry such as *Gefühllosigkeiten. Reisen von Berlin nach Berlin* (1986; *Unfeelingnesses. Journeys from Berlin to Berlin*) or *Dazwischen* (1987; *In Between*). The central theme of Turkish-German experience remains, but now the poems are generally shorter, more epigrammatic, more metaphoric, exploring complex cultural histories rather than simple dichotomies. The poem "Ach Du, Goethe, der Alltag ist schwer" (Say, Goethe, Everday Life Is Hard) in *Das Wrack: Second-hand Bilder* (1986; The Wreck: Second-hand Images), confronts Goethe's *Italian Journey* and *Roman Elegies* with the narrator's contemporary experience in Italy. Goethe is finally consigned to a museum "on a far-off planet," not because he belongs to an alien cultural tradition for Ören (who, as an educated urban Turk, knows occidental culture very well), but because technological change, mass tourism, pollution, and media-dominated "secondhand images" render Goethe and his Italy alien and unattainable. *Wie die Spree in den Bosporus fließt* (1991; As the Spree Flows into the Bosporus), Ören's exchange of letter poems with the Berlin writer Peter Schneider, presents the cities less as polar opposites than as twin places of complex interchange in European metropolitan culture.

The novel *Eine verspätete Abrechnung* (1988; The Delayed Reckoning), though retaining an essentially Marxist perspective on migrant experience, explores the semi-autobiographical narrator's tangled cultural roots and widens the sociological panorama of Turkish life in Germany to include the growing self-made middle class. *Berlin Savignyplatz* (1995) recycles figures and motifs from *Bitte nix Polizei* in a novel of narratological self-awareness against the background of a multicultural *bohème* surprised by the fall of the Berlin Wall. *Unerwarteter Besuch* (1997; Unexpected Visit) develops the narrative experiment further: memories of relationships and experiences from the narrator's past in divided Berlin are interwoven into a web of narrative levels and subplots which strings together the two halves of the city, the various ethnic groups, male and female, past and present. *Granatapfelblüte* (1998; Pomegranate Blossom) abandons Berlin for the Turkish resort of Side; but "Europa" is not escaped so easily: the love affair between the Turkish narrator and the German tourist against the background of the classical ruins, Europe's roots in Asia Minor, becomes a parable of the complex relationship between Turkey and Europe.

The novels since *Berlin Savignyplatz* each carry the subtitle *Auf der Suche nach der gegenwärtigen Zeit* (In Search of the Present Time). Interweaving reflexive, relatively plotless ruminations on multiple narrative levels, they are an extended, and sometimes for the reader rather wearisome, attempt to assert a place in the European (including, of course, the Turkish) modernist tradition, after the exhaustion of the political project within which Ören's work of the 1970s and 1980s was predominantly seen.

MORAY MCGOWAN

Biography

Born in Bebek-Istanbul, Turkey, 1939. Moved in the 1960s to Germany and settled in Berlin; editor-in-chief for Turkish affairs, German broadcasting company SFB, since 1974; one of the first Turkish migrant writers of poetry and prose works to receive major recognition in Germany.

Selected Works

Poetry

Was will Niyazi in der Naunynstraße, translated from Turkish by H. Achmed Schmiede and Johannes Schenk, 1973

Der kurze Traum aus Kagithane: Ein Poem, translated from Turkish by H. Achmed Schmiede, 1974

Privatexil: Gedichte, translated from Turkish by Gisela Kraft, 1977

Deutschland, ein türkisches Märchen: Gedichte, translated from Turkish by Gisela Kraft, 1978

Mitten in der Odyssee: Gedichte, translated from Turkish by Gisela Kraft, 1980

Die Fremde ist auch ein Haus: Berlin-Poem, translated from Turkish by Gisela Kraft, 1980

Gefühllosigkeiten; Reisen von Berlin nach Berlin: Gedichte, translated from Turkish by Helga Daĝyeli-Bohne, Yildirim Daĝyeli, and Yüksel Pazarkaya, 1986

Paradies kaputt: Erzählungen, translated from Turkish by Helga Daĝyeli-Bohne, Yildirim Daĝyeli, and Petra Kappert, 1986

Das Wrack: Second-hand Bilder: Gedichte, translated from Turkish by Helga Daĝyeli-Bohne and Yildirim Daĝyeli, 1986

Dazwischen: Gedichte, translated from Turkish by Helga Daĝyeli-Bohne and Yildirim Daĝyeli, 1987

Wie die Spree in den Bosporus fließt: Briefe zwischen Istanbul und Berlin 1990/1991, with Peter Schneider, 1991

Prose

Bitte, nix Polizei: Kriminalerzählung; as Please, No Police, translated from Turkish by Cornelius Bischoff, 1981

Der Gastkonsument und andere Erzählungen in fremden Sprachen, translated from Turkish by Helga Daĝyeli-Bohne and Yildirim Daĝyeli, 1982

Manege: Erzählung, translated from Turkish by Helga Daĝyeli-Bohne and Yildirim Daĝyeli, 1983

Eine verspätete Abrechnung; oder, Der Aufstieg der Gundogdus: Roman, translated from Turkish by Zafer Senocak and Eva Hund, 1988

Berlin Savignyplatz, translated from Turkish by Deniz Göktürk, 1995

Unerwarteter Besuch, translated from Turkish by Deniz Göktürk, 1997

Granatapfelblüte, translated from Turkish by Eva Hund and Zafer Senocak, 1998

Sehnsucht nach Hollywood, translated from Turkish by Deniz Göktürk, 1999

Further Reading

Chiellino, Carmine, *Am Ufer der Fremde: Literatur und Arbeitsmigration,* Stuttgart: Metzler, 1995

Gott, Gil Michael, "Migration, Ethnicization and Germany's New Ethnic Minority Literature," Ph.D. diss., University of California, Berkeley, 1994

Kassouf, Susan, "'Wir haben ihnen Romanautoren gesandt': Aras Ören's *Eine verspätete Abrechnung* and Güney Dal's *Der enthaarte Affe,*" in *The Germanic Mosaic: Cultural and Linguistic Diversity in Society,* edited by Carol Aisha Blackshire-Belay, Westport, Connecticut: Greenwood Press, 1994

McGowan, Moray, "'Bosporus fließt in mir': Europa-Bilder und Brückenmetaphern bei Aras Ören und Zehra Çirak," in *Brücken zwischen Zivilisationen,* edited by Hans-Peter Waldhoff, Dursun Tan, and Elçin Kürsat-Ahlers, Frankfurt: Verlag für Interkulturelle Kommunikation, 1997

Rösch, Heidi, *Migrationsliteratur im interkulturellen Kontext,* Frankfurt: Verlag für Interkulturelle Kommunikation, 1992

Sölçün, Sargut, *Sein und Nichtsein: Zur Literatur in der multikulturellen Gesellschaft,* Bielefeld: Aisthesis, 1992

Veteto-Conrad, Marilya, *Finding a Voice: Identity and the Works of German-Language Turkish Writers in the Federal Republic of Germany to 1990,* New York: Lang, 1996

Orléans, Elisabeth Charlotte d', *see* Liselotte von der Pfalz

Oswald von Wolkenstein ca. 1376–1445

Oswald von Wolkenstein was born into an aristocratic family in the Southern Tyrol, an area that, as a nodal point on major trade routes between northern Italian cities and the southern part of the Holy Roman Empire, experienced in the later Middle Ages a significant growth in its economic and cultural importance. The works of Oswald themselves, while both highly individual and demonstrably indebted to specifically German traditions, nevertheless reflect in certain respects (perhaps especially musical ones) the significant influence exerted by Italy on 15th-century Tyrolean culture.

Some 132 poems by Oswald have been preserved, almost all of them with musical notation. Remarkably, 126 of these appear in one or both of two parchment manuscripts written at his own instigation—one of many features of his life and works that bespeak an arguably modern desire to be known to and appreciated by posterity.

Oswald's oeuvre is significant not least for its diversity. He wrote love lyrics of various kinds (including several in dialogue form), religious lyrics (which evince a particular predilection for the Blessed Virgin), and, especially in later life, moral-didactic songs of a relatively conventional character. Moreover, a number of his songs, above all *Der mai mit lieber zal* (May, with Charming Chatter), in which the sounds of the countryside in spring are recorded with extraordinary vividness, reflect an interest in the natural world for its own sake, which has been held by many critics to be strikingly unmedieval.

Oswald's favorite subject, however, was himself. Whether motivated by the increased importance attached to individual experience in contemporary humanist thought, by a craving for self-assertion and recognition resulting from the loss of an eye (probably in a childhood accident), or by a combination of these and other factors, Oswald articulates his own emotions and experiences with a degree of directness and subjectivity unprecedented in German literature. A number of poems, of which the best known are *Es fügt sich* (ca. 1416; It Came to Pass) and *Durch Barbarei, Arabia* (ca. 1426–27; Through Barbary, Arabia), have been categorized by scholars as autobiographical; and many poems on other themes are markedly self-revelatory.

It would be naive, however, to accept everything that Oswald writes about himself entirely at face value. As scholars such as Ulrich Müller have demonstrated, even in those songs that are most heavily autobiographical, Oswald is apt to describe his experiences in a decidedly stylized way. The 112-line poem *Es fügt sich,* for example, tells us much that is plausible about his travels, achievements, vicissitudes, and feelings, and very little that contradicts what we know of his life from historical documents. It does this, however, in a way that owes much to several literary traditions. The song as a whole has affinities with the so-called *Alterslied,* in which an aging man looks back ruefully over his earlier life; and in the course of his song Oswald at least implicitly casts himself in conventional literary roles as diverse as a knight in the service of a lady, a pilgrim, an amorous cleric, a merchant, and a fool.

Such an indebtedness to traditional forms and motifs, along with an urge to renew, modify, combine, and at times parody these forms and motifs, is, indeed, one of the most striking and pervasive features of Oswald's oeuvre. A case in point is his treatment of the dawn song, in which a knight and lady are awoken in a courtly setting, conventionally by a watchman, after an illicit night together. Approximately half of Oswald's 12 dawn songs remain securely within this tradition, although they introduce occasional formal or thematic innovations; others combine dawn-song elements with those from the Marian or dance-song traditions; and three depart radically from the traditional model. *Wol auf und wacht* (Come, Awake) is a religious dawn song, in which Oswald casts himself as a watchman warning against sin and its consequences; *Stand auff, Maredel* (Get up, Maredel), set in a farmhouse, is a vituperative early morning dialogue between the farmer's wife and a maid who is reluctant to leave her peasant lover; and *Ain tunkle varb* (A Dark Color) parodies or reverses many standard dawn-song motifs in presenting the poet alone in bed yearning frustratedly for his wife.

Oswald's music similarly combines traditional with innovative elements. Most of his songs are monophonic and reproduce or adapt melodic structures common in the work of earlier poets. There is some evidence, however, to suggest that he envisaged a more intrinsic link between the words and melodies of his songs than had most of his predecessors; certainly relatively few of his melodies appear to have been intended for use with more than one set of words. Of arguably greater historical significance was Oswald's espousal of polyphony. Only 39 of his songs are polyphonic, and at least a third of these are demonstrably based on French or Italian models. Nevertheless, building on the precedent set by the 14th-century Mönch von Salzburg, he became the first German poet to compose a substantial number of vernacular polyphonic songs, and the first also to base his choice of monophony or polyphony on the songs' subject matter. For Oswald, polyphony is largely reserved for love lyrics and songs describing a specific scene or atmosphere, whereas monophony is employed for religious, didactic, autobiographical, and other songs in which the precise communication of the words is of paramount importance.

Perhaps in part because of his idiosyncratic originality, Oswald appears to have exerted very little influence on later 15th-century poets. Since his "rediscovery" by the Tyrolean priest Beda Weber in the 1840s, however, and especially over the last 40 years, he has been the subject of considerable scholarly interest. Moreover, in recent decades he has become known to a wider public, at least in the German-speaking world. This development is no doubt attributable to several factors: the popularizing efforts of various scholars, a widely read biography by Dieter Kühn, numerous recordings of Oswald's songs, and, not least, several translations of his work into New High German (particularly important given the sometimes impenetrable nature of Oswald's language, with its coinages, dialect forms, and admixture of foreign words). Above all, however, Oswald's songs themselves possess a vigor, variety, individuality, and (in certain respects) modernity, which enable them to be readily appreciated by those not otherwise conversant with 15th-century culture.

NIGEL HARRIS

See also Minnesang

Biography

Born in South Tyrol between 1376 and 1378. Second of three sons of important local landowner; left home in boyhood, probably as squire to an itinerant knight; wandered throughout Europe; returned on death of father, 1400; married Margarethe von Schwangau, 1417; fathered seven children; lengthy inheritance dispute with brothers, settled only in 1427, when family lands divided between them; devoted much of life to protecting and extending his own possessions, but also active further afield; close links with cathedral at Brixen and priory at Neustift; 1415–19, and again 1431–34, employed in various capacities by Emperor Sigismund III, notably at Councils of Constance and Basle and Diets of Nürnberg and Ulm; adviser and representative of Count Heinrich von Görz, from 1434. Died in Meran, 1445.

Selected Works

Poetry
Die Lieder Oswalds von Wolkenstein, edited by Karl Kurt Klein et al., 1962; 2nd edition, 1975, 3rd edition, 1988

Lieder, edited by Burghart Wachinger, 1977

Lieder, translated into modern German by Klaus J. Schönmetzler, 1979; translated by Wernfried Hofmeister, 1989

Further Reading

Baasch, Karin, and Helmuth Nürnberger, *Oswald von Wolkenstein,* Reinbek bei Hamburg: Rowohlt, 1986

Jones, George F., "Fact and Fancy in Oswald von Wolkenstein's Songs," in *Studies in Honor of Tatiana Fotitch,* edited by Josep M. Sola-Solé et al., Washington, D.C.: Catholic University of America Press, 1972

——, *Oswald von Wolkenstein,* New York: Twayne, 1973

Joschko, Dirk, *Oswald von Wolkenstein: Eine Monographie zu Person, Werk, und Forschungsgeschichte,* Göppingen: Kümmerle, 1985

Kühn, Dieter, *Ich Wolkenstein: Eine Biographie,* Frankfurt: Insel, 1977

Müller, Ulrich, *"Dichtung" und "Wahrheit" in den Liedern Oswalds von Wolkenstein: Die autobiographischen Lieder von den Reisen,* Göppingen: Kümmerle, 1968

Müller, Ulrich, editor, *Oswald von Wolkenstein,* Darmstadt: Wissenschaftliche Buchgesellschaft, 1980

Robertshaw, Alan, *Oswald von Wolkenstein: The Myth and the Man,* Göppingen: Kümmerle, 1977

Röll, Walter, *Oswald von Wolkenstein,* Darmstadt: Wissenschaftliche Buchgesellschaft, 1981

Schwob, Anton, *Oswald von Wolkenstein: Eine Biographie,* Bozen: Athesia, 1977

Otfrid von Weißenburg ca. 800–ca. 871

Otfrid von Weißenburg is the best known of the very early writers of German. His *Evangelienbuch* (863–71; Gospel Book) is the earliest surviving complete literary work in German. It is also, as far as we know, the first German work to use rhyme as a consistent literary feature in a period when the metrical forms of Latin and the alliterative form of Germanic languages prevailed.

Otfrid spoke a dialect of Old High German called South Rhenish Franconian. He devoted his life to teaching young monks and preparing manuscripts on a variety of religious subjects. There are traces of Otfrid's handwriting in many Weißenburg manuscripts, often in the margins, which suggests that he was in charge of the monastery's library, organizing the work of copyists, correcting and annotating the finished products, and no doubt training scribes in the skills of their trade. His gospel text was the distillation of all his experiences as a monk, a scholar, and a teacher; it was written at the end of his life as a study aid for future generations.

This great original work, the *Evangelienbuch,* has been much studied, although more for its linguistic and structural features than for its literary merit. It is composed of 7,104 lines that are arranged in pairs and collected into five books. Each book is divided into chapters, but there is no consistent pattern in the number, length, or content of these chapters—despite attempts by Ernst and others to derive complex numerological designs based on chapter lengths. Appended to the work is a collection of four dedicatory letters, three in the same rhyming long-line form, and one in Latin prose. Thanks to these additions, we have an unusually detailed record of the author's own personal motivation in writing this early work.

The *Evangelienbuch* is preserved in four manuscripts, only one of which is complete. This is the illustrated version "V," which is beautifully laid out with red enlarged initials and has a clear, orderly script known as "Carolingian minuscule." The chapter headings are all in Latin, serving as a ready reference tool and often as a link back to the Latin Gospels from which

the subject matter derives. Most of the chapters are narrative accounts of events or parables from the life of Christ. Occasionally, Otfrid inserts a follow-up chapter entitled "Spiritaliter" (spiritual meaning) or "Moraliter" (moral meaning), which explains the symbolism of the preceding chapter, usually with some exhortation to the reader. For example, a long chapter on the seamless robe explains how it represents the undivided fellowship and love of the Church. Most of the work is a retelling of the Gospel—not a direct translation but a free, and somewhat repetitive reworking of the text. The passages of explanation are mostly adapted from famous Christian commentators such as Augustine or Gregory the Great.

The work's tone throughout is didactic, and the layout implies that it was intended to be read and studied, although the presence of a few musical notes and our knowledge of the daily monastic routine would both suggest that it was also read aloud or even chanted for listeners' edification. Otfrid makes it clear, both in the text of the work and in the introductory letters, that he is keen for his readers or listeners to understand both the surface meaning and the deeper implications of the Christian scriptures. This is the main motivation behind his somewhat radical decision to write in his native language rather than Latin. He says in the Latin letter to Liutbert that his book is for those who are frightened by the difficulty of Latin. It is a humble, human version of the perfect, divine Gospels. His work reflects (and makes much reference to) the five human senses, and in typical number symbolism, five has connotations of unevenness, while four represents foursquare completeness. Otfrid admits that his own language, which he calls "frenkisgon" (Frankish), is untamed and even barbaric, because it does not follow the neat rules of Latin. He says that he has subjected it to the discipline of rhyme in order to make it worthy of its noble subject. The measured syllables and innovative end rhyme of his new long-line couplets are, similar to the strict daily routine of the Benedictine monastic rule, a polishing and purifying process.

In this Christian context of obedience and collective service, individual experimentation was not much encouraged. Otfrid is careful to surround his argument with formulaic humility and flattery of the addressee. Further, the three verse letters of introduction contain elaborate acrostic devices: the first, last, and, incredibly, the middle letters of the rhyming pairs form a cryptic message, which is also the title to each piece. It is as if Otfrid is determined to show off his command of Latin and his skill in rhetorical embellishments in order to fend off criticism that he may have written his work in German because he was not competent in the more scholarly Latin-based traditions of the Church.

Otfrid is remembered mainly for his important contribution to our knowledge of the very earliest stages in the emergence of German as a language. Compilers of dictionaries and historical grammars find in him an authoritative source of material not least because his work, unlike so many early fragments, is free composition rather than direct translation. Literary scholars have concentrated on Otfrid's comments on literary theory and his deliberate creation of a new poetic form. There has been much debate, and no clear conclusion, on the origins of his ideas, with reference to classical and early Christian Latin, Germanic, and also possibly Celtic influences. Few scholars have been able to appreciate the true literary merits of the work as a whole. Judged by the standards of the heroic epic (or compared, say, with the *Heliand*), Otfrid's text is disjointed and burdened by too much commentary and stylistic repetition. There are, however, passages of great lyrical beauty and crisscrossing ideas about the nature and value of teaching, of brotherly love, and of man's lonely exile from the presence of God, which together make Otfrid the first great writer in the canon of German literature.

LINDA ARCHIBALD

Biography

Date of birth unknown; probably ca. 800. Entered the monastery at Weißenburg (now called Wissembourg, in Alsace) in 807; became a monk there before 820; traveled to Fulda to learn from the great teacher Hrabanus Maurus, some time between 820 and 840; there he met the tow monks Hartmuot Werinbert of St. Gall, to whom he dedicated one of his introductory letters; returned to Weißenburg to continue his work as a priest and monk, specializing in teaching and looking after the monastery's manuscript collection; there is little surviving evidence to suggest any illustrious achievements, apart from the *Evangelienbuch*, but scholars including Kleiber and Haubrichs have found evidence of Otfrid's careful handwriting on several Weißenburg manuscripts; marginal comments and corrections suggest that he was in charge of collecting samples of new works from sister monasteries, and having them copied. Date of death unknown, probably ca. 871.

Selected Works

Poetry

Evangelienbuch; Otfrids Evangelienbuch, edited by Oskar Erdmann, 1882; revised and edited by Ludwig Wolff, 1973; *Christi Leben und Lehre besungen von Otfrid*, translated into modern German by Johann Kelle, 1870; *Otfrids Evangelienbuch aus dem Altdeutschen frei übersetzt*, translated into modern German by Richard Fromme, 1928; *Otfrid von Weißenburg: Evangelienbuch*, selection of extracts translated into modern German by Gisela Vollmann-Profe, 1987

Further Reading

Archibald, Linda, "The Seamless Robe and Related Imagery in Otfrid von Weißenburg's Evangelienbuch," in *"Mit regulu bithuungan": neue Arbeiten zur althochdeutschen Poesie und Sprache*, Göppingen: Kuemmerle, 1989

Belkin, Johanna, and Jürgen Meier, *Bibliographie zu Otfrid von Weißenburg und zur altsächsischen Bibeldichtung*, Berlin: Schmidt, 1975

Ernst, Ulrich, *Der Liber Evangeliorum Otfrids von Weißenburg: Literarästhetik und Verstechnik im Lichte der Tradition*, Cologne: Böhlau, 1975

Hartmann, Reinildis, *Allegorisches Woerterbuch zu Otfrieds von Weißenburg Evangeliendichtung*, Munich: Fink, 1975

Haubrichs, Wolfgang, "Otfrids St. Galler Studienfreunde," *Amsterdamer Beiträge zur älteren Germanistik* 4 (1973)

Hellgardt, Ernst, *Die exegetischen Quellen von Otfrids Evangelienbuch*, Tübingen: Niemeyer, 1981

Kleiber, Wolfgang, *Otfrid von Weissenburg: Untersuchungen zur handschriftlichen Überlieferung und Studien zum Aufbau des Evangelienbuches*, Bern and Munich: Francke, 1971

Kleiber, Wolfgang, editor, *Otfrid von Weißenburg*, Wege der Forschung 419, Darmstadt: Wissenschaftliche Buchgesellschaft, 1978

Roberts, Michael, *Biblical Epic and Rhetorical Paraphrase in Late Antiquity*, Liverpool: Cairns, 1985

Vollmann-Profe, Gisela, *Kommentar zu Otfrids Evanglienbuch*, Bonn: Habelt, 1976

Aysel Özakin 1942–

Before she chose exile in Germany in 1981, Aysel Özakin was already an acclaimed author in Turkey, her country of origin. There, she is predominantly perceived as a feminist writer who displays a great sensitivity for social hierarchies. Her work concentrates on gender conflicts and describes them in connection with categories such as class, culture, and generational differences. Her narratives concentrate on the representation of emotions and behavior rather than actions. Her protagonists, however, are representative of social groups, and their internal worlds are determined by social conditions and processes.

The main focus of Özakin's writing is on the situation of city-bred women who struggle to liberate themselves from the limitations of cultural tradition. The author constructs typical biographies of city women to explore the manifold strategies of emancipation.

In her novel *Glaube, Liebe, Aircondition* (1991; *Faith, Lust, and Air Conditioning*), the author presents two models of female liberation. The first-person narrator is a woman who grows up in an urban, working-class environment. As a young girl she learns the typical tricks that women of her age use to circumvent moral restrictions. By seemingly adapting to society's moral conventions, she avoids marriage and gains access to education, which for her is the prerequisite for social advancement and economic independence. The second protagonist of Özakin's novel is the daughter of a rich estate owner who grows up in a rural area. She marries the man of her choice, but breaks out of her marriage while she is already pregnant. She moves from the small town to the big city, where she registers at university and has many affairs. Being a divorced woman and a single mother who claims her sexual freedom, she is soon branded an outsider and dies in a mysterious way. Her death documents the failure of an unconventional strategy of identity formation. By contrast, the first-person narrator's way to emancipation, which is based on a pretended conformity to the precepts of society, is much more successful.

Özakin's writing suggests that many Turkish city women who strive for sexual freedom are in reality submitting to the oriental myth of the superior Western world. They study European languages and try to copy elements of a Western lifestyle. Traditional moral standards and forms of expression, including the Arabic language, are downgraded as uncivilized. Many of Özakin's protagonists, in fact, emigrate to European cities to be able to live according to so-called Western values. Like Dina, a character in Özakin's novel *Die blaue Maske* (1989; *The Blue Mask*), however, they often fail: in many cases the Western values they have adopted are turned against them. They are confronted with Eurocentric stereotypes of the Orient, and they are discriminated against or even excluded from many areas of social life. The Turkish women who have rejected their cultural traditions and substituted them with Western values are left in a state of severe disorientation. In the case of Özakin's protagonist Dina, this experience leads to a mental breakdown.

Özakin herself encountered this traumatic feeling of rootlessness when she went into exile in Germany: her contact to her home land was interrupted, and the prejudices of the German population prevented her from getting a firm footing in the new society. Suddenly she was confronted with the stereotype of the Turkish labor migrant: the poor, uneducated, and helpless Anatolian peasant. In her 1986 article "Ali hinter den Spiegeln" (Ali behind the Mirrors), Özakin accuses Günther Wallraff of fostering this image in his book *Ganz unten* (1985; *Lowest of the Low*) in order to provoke readers' pity. From her point of view, pity is a means of stabilizing cultural dominance. By approaching ethnic minorities with pity, members of the German public categorize them as inferior groups and at the same time purify themselves from historical guilt.

Although Özakin expresses a strong solidarity with the Anatolian peasants who are categorized by the German stereotype, she repeatedly emphasizes that she has nothing in common with them. To her they seem much more alien than the foreign intellectuals she meets during international conferences. The great distance between her and the people of rural Anatolia becomes evident in her early narrative *Die kalten Nächte der Kleinstadt* (1974; The Cold Nights of the Small Town; translated into German and published in Germany in 1990). It focuses on the situation of the people in a small town whose lives are radically transformed by the establishment of a factory nearby. The description of the factory, with its phallic chimney rising into the sky, lets the beginning of industrialization in Anatolia appear like a violent act of conquest with sexual connotations. Özakin compares the people in the town to the minerals that are treated in the factory: they are raw material turned into objects that are useful to society. Özakin's metaphor of the mineral illustrates the exploitation of the Anatolian people but at the same time discriminates against them. It repeats the Western cliché of the naturalness of peasants and denies them a social identity. Özakin's collection of narratives *Soll ich hier alt werden?* (1982; Am I to Grow Old Here?) gives an account of the author's first direct encounter with Turkish labor migrants in Germany and reveals her prejudices in the face of this group: she expresses compassion but also amazement and sometimes even disgust.

Despite the author's aversion to the Turkish labor migrants in Germany, the *Gastarbeiter* image has always influenced the German public's perception of Özakin's literary work. On the one hand, she has been celebrated as the "other Turkish woman," the Turkish woman without a head scarf. On the other hand, she has been accused of being too European: the links of her writing to Western feminism have been seen as too close. Her works did not express the typical Oriental perspective that German critics expected from a Turkish author. In addition, many other Turkish intellectuals in Germany reproached her for not addressing the concerns of the Turkish immigrants clearly enough.

The author who perceives her writing as cosmopolitan rather than Turkish saw herself deprived of all her literary achievements. Her cycle of poems *Du bist willkommen* (1985; You Are Welcome) and her autobiographic novel *Die Leidenschaft der Anderen* (1983; The Passion of the Others) give evidence of her search for a new place as a Turk, a woman, and a writer in the Western world. In 1990 Özakin emigrated to the United Kingdom to escape the limitations she experienced in Germany.

SABINE FISCHER

Biography

Born in Urfa, Turkey, 7 September 1942. Studied French and educational theory in Ankara; worked as a lecturer in French, Istanbul; started publishing prose in the 1970s; published 3 novels and 2 narratives that were widely read by a Turkish readership; accepted an invitation by the *Literary Colloquium* to come to Berlin, 1981; decided to stay in the Federal Republic of Germany because of the political conditions in Turkey after the military coup; lived in Berlin and Hamburg; emigrated to the United Kingdom in 1990. Sabahattin-Ali-Award, 1974. Currently lives in Helston, Cornwall.

Selected Works

Novels
Die Leidenschaft der Anderen, 1983
Die blaue Maske, 1989

Faith, Lust, and Air Conditioning, 1991; as *Glaube, Liebe, Aircondition,* translated by Cornelia Holfelder-von der Tann, 1991

Poetry
Du bist willkommen, 1985

Other
Soll ich hier alt werden? (narratives), 1982
Ali hinter den Spiegeln (essay), 1986
Die kalten Nächte der Kleinstadt (narratives), 1990

Further Reading

Rösch, Heidi, *Migrationsliteratur im interkulturellen Kontext: Eine didaktische Studie zur Literatur von Aras Ören, Aysel Özakin, Franco Biondi, und Rafik Schami,* Frankfurt: Interkulturelle Kommunikation, 1992

Wierschke, Annette, *Schreiben als Selbstbehauptung: Kulturkonflikt und Identität in den Werken von Aysel Özakin, Alev Tekinay, und Emine Sevgi Özdamar,* Frankfurt: Interkulturelle Kommunikation, 1996

Emine Sevgi Özdamar 1946–

Today, the Turkish minority is the largest ethnic minority in Germany, and Turkish women predominate among female migrant writers. The variety of their lifestyles and literary expression mirrors the diversity within this ethnic community. At the end of the 1970s, Turkish migrant women became a popular subject of research for social scientists in the Federal Republic of Germany. A large number of studies were published that created a stereotype of the Turkish woman as an uneducated peasant who was the helpless victim of poverty, male dominance, and Islamic fundamentalism. This image added to the much more traditional one of the beautiful, mysterious, and seductive oriental woman—and to exotic images of the Orient in general. In the face of these powerful representations, many Turkish women immigrants have felt the need to explore their past in order both to rediscover the origins of their own personal development and to create their own female cultural history of the Orient as a reaction to the dominant discourse.

In her novel *Das Leben ist eine Karawanserei* (Life is a Caravanserai), published in 1992, E.S. Özdamar portrays a family saga over three generations from the perspective of the daughter figure. The family history is described as an ongoing journey that starts with the grandfather's emigration from the Caucasus to Turkey and ends with the daughter's labor emigration to Germany. Özdamar presents Turkey as a multicultural society in a state of transition. The narrator's personal development is marked by constant changes of place and numerous encounters with people of different social and ethnic backgrounds. On her journey she picks up tales, prayers, and superstitious sayings in Arabic, Turkish, and Kurdish, as well as U.S. films and comics, which became popular in Turkey in the 1950s and 1960s. At the novel's conclusion, the narrator takes all these valuable ideas and items to Germany as her "luggage." Özdamar describes her family history as a "carpet made of stories" to show that history is made up of numerous texts and that identities are predominantly based on language. In addition, the metaphor of the carpet is linked to the image of the fairy-tale Orient. As the author points out, her novel is intended to preserve the memory of a culture that—as a result of Atatürk's radical reforms—has largely disappeared, and for which Western stereotypes have been substituted.

In her latest novel, *Die Brücke vom goldenen Horn* (1998; The Bridge of the Golden Horn), Özdamar continues her recollection of memories. She narrates the arrival of a young Turkish woman in Berlin at the end of the 1960s; her integration into the world of the labor immigrants; her brief return to Istanbul, which at the time is a city shaken by riots; and her final detachment from her parents. The novel picks up some of the themes that dominated the literature of ethnic minorities in its early stages: life in the hostel, the situation at the workplace, homesickness, and the struggle with the German language. Now, in the period of transition from labor migration to de facto immigration in Germany, the author documents these experiences anew to save them from falling into oblivion.

While Germany changes into a multiethnic society and definitions of collective identities dissolve, many members of ethnic minorities regard the revival of cultural traditions as a positive way of reorientation. Özdamar deals with this strategy of identity formation in her narratives *Mutterzunge* (1990; *Mother Tongue*) and *Großvaterzunge* (1990; Grandfather Tongue). Her protagonist, a young Turkish woman who has been living in Berlin for many years, experiences the loss of her native language and notices her emotional alienation from her native country. To restore her cultural roots, she elects to learn Arabic, her grandfather's language, which had once been forbidden by Atatürk, and falls in love with her teacher. This involvement with her cultural roots confronts her with an ambivalent part of her past. Arabic, the language of her childhood and her love, also represents the Ottoman Empire and is connected to many different forms of oppression. During 40 days of ritualistic seclusion, the narrator lets this lost, problematic part of her cultural-historical identity take possession of her body and soul again.

The voluntary subordination of a modern Turkish woman to an archaic oppressive culture represents a model of identity formation that radically turns away from Western feminist ideas of emancipation. With this model, Özdamar deliberately confronts her German readership with its own traditional anti-Islamic prejudices, which have surfaced again in current debates on Islamic fundamentalism. The author undermines these stereotypes by introducing elements of grotesque exaggeration into her narratives, and this means of writing also reveals her love for the theater.

Özdamar has written two plays, which focus on the life of labor migrants in Germany. *Karagöz in Alamania* (1982; Black Eye in Germany) portrays the roguish character of a traditional Oriental shadow play within the setting of contemporary Germany and clothes him in the garments of a *Gastarbeiter*. *Kel-*

oglan in Alamania (1991; Keloglan in Germany), which has not been staged as of yet, also makes use of the masquerade to deconstruct stereotypes of Turkish women. Özdamar's protagonist is a Turkish singer who works as a cleaning woman in a German theater. While cleaning the stage, she regularly puts on the worn-out wig of "Madame Butterfly" and sings arias from Puccini's opera. For a little while, the Turkish cleaner can be identified with the Oriental woman who is the embodiment of female suffering under the yoke of Western patriarchy. However, this perception is destroyed whenever the protagonist puts down her mask.

Özdamar's plays have been perceived as "too alien." Her narrative *Großvaterzunge* has provoked attacks from the German public because of the reactionary model of identity formation it seemed to present. Her novel *Das Leben ist eine Karawanserei*, however, received the prestigious Ingeborg Bachmann Prize in 1991 even before it was published. Today, it is the most reviewed text by an immigrant author in German-speaking Europe. As the novel draws on images such as the carpet and the caravanserai, it is often praised for bringing the Oriental myth back to life, introducing it to German literature, and—by doing so—enriching it. Nonetheless, many immigrant writers in Germany accused Özdamar of provoking this perception in order to sell her book. The differences in perception of Özdamar's work is symptomatic of the situation of ethnic minority writing in Germany as a whole. It shows how difficult it is for these writers to create literary models of identity formation that cannot be excluded from or absorbed by powerful discourses on cultural and sexual difference.

SABINE FISCHER

Biography

Born in Malaty, Turkey, 20 August 1946. Attended Drama School in Istanbul, 1967–70; assistant director under Benno Besson and Matthias Langhoff at the Ostberliner Volksbühne, 1976; engagements and appearances at various theaters, including the Théâtre de la Ville and the Comédie Française, Paris, and the Bochumer Schauspielhaus, Kammerspiele München, Frankfurter Schauspielhaus, and the Freie Volksbühne, Berlin; starred in several films, including *Yasemin,* directed by Hark Bohm, and *Happy Birthday, Türke,* directed by Doris Dörrie; wrote first play under commission from Bochumer Schauspielhaus and directed its premiere at Frankfurter Schauspielhaus, 1986. Ingeborg Bachmann Prize, 1991; Walter Hasenclever Prize, 1993.

Selected Works

Plays
Karagöz in Alamania, 1982
Keloglan in Alamania, 1991

Novels
Das Leben ist eine Karawanserei, 1992
Die Brücke vom goldenen Horn, 1998

Narratives
Mutterzunge, 1990; as *Mother Tongue,* translated by Craig Thomas, 1994
Großvaterzunge, 1990

Further Reading

Horrocks, David, and Eva Kolinsky, editors, *Turkish Culture in Germany Today,* Providence, Rhode Island: Berghahn Books, 1996
Müller, Regula, "Ich war Mädchen, war ich Sultanin: Weitgeöffnete Augen betrachten türkische Frauengeschichte(n)," in *Denn du tanzt auf einem Seil: Positionen deutschsprachiger MigrantInnenliteratur,* edited by Sabine Fischer and Moray McGowan, Tübingen: Stauffenburg, 1997
Neubert, Inge, "Searching for Intercultural Communication: Emine Sevgi Özdamar, a Turkish Woman Writer in Germany," in *Postwar Women's Writing in German: Feminist Critical Approaches,* edited by Chris Weedon, Oxford and Providence, Rhode Island: Berghahn Books, 1997
Pfister, Eva, "Ein Roman wie ein Teppich gewebt aus unendlichen Geschichten," *Börsenblatt des Deutschen Buchhandels* (8 April 1993)
Wierschke, Annette, *Schreiben als Selbstbehauptung: Kulturkonflikt und Identität in den Werken von Aysel Özakin, Alev Tekinay, und Emine Sevgi Özdamar,* Frankfurt: Verlag für Interkulturelle Kommunikation, 1996

P

Pfalz, Liselotte von der, *see* Liselotte von der Pfalz

Philosophy and Literature

The relationship between philosophy and literature will be examined here in terms of how individual works of literature reflect the influence of a particular philosophical movement or philosopher. The primary focus will be on ideas that find expression in literary works.

If by philosophy we mean a relatively autonomous system of freedom of inquiry and expression of criticism, then the medieval period would, for the most part, have to be excluded. Philosophy, properly speaking, begins with its emancipation from theology. Scholasticism had as its ultimate goal the confirmation of Christian dogma. Our survey cannot in good conscience begin with Luther, since he was not a philosopher in the sense defined above but primarily a theologian with a decidedly anti-intellectual bent; his characterization of reason as "the Devil's Whore" is well-known. In his *Lectures on Romans* (1515–16), he saw his mission as a protest *against* philosophy, and he even referred to Aristotle as "the stinking philosopher." Luther's standpoint had consequences for the philosophy of religion rather than for the philosophy of literature.

The appropriate starting point for a consideration of how philosophy clearly influences literature is the Enlightenment, or, in German, *Aufklärung,* the roots of which reach back into the early 17th century in the philosophy of Descartes and, later in the century, in that of Leibniz. The German Enlightenment should not be regarded as a passing episode in the intellectual history of Germany. It is true that its rationalist philosophy was replaced as the dominant mode of thinking by the subjectivity and fascination with the irrational associated with Romanticism, but its rationalistic principles were to emerge again periodically, most notably during the period of materialism and later in naturalism. The German Enlightenment was by no means as liberal as the French Enlightenment, especially in the domain of politi-

cal reform. There were, however, two areas in which it was strong and made a significant impact: its position on orthodox religion and its views regarding moral conduct.

For the first half of the 18th century, the influence of Christian Wolff (1679–1754) was most far-reaching. Wolff followed the rationalistic assumption that, just as mathematics starts from axioms, philosophic thought should start from axioms that are native to reason and are true independently of experience and Christian revelation. These axioms are self-evident. Good increases our perfection and evil diminishes it. Virtue (*Tugend*) is the most certain source of happiness. Christian Fürchtegott Gellert (1715–69) expressed these views in his *Leben der schwedischen Gräfin von G.* (1747, 1748; Life of the Swedish Countess of G.), which is perhaps the most representative novel of the German Enlightenment. Several motifs of the movement are in evidence in this work. For instance, the novel is exemplary in providing a model for dealing with the blows of fate. The countess loses her beloved husband, whom she presumes dead, then experiences his sudden return after having married another; as if that were not enough, she finally discovers that her children have become involved unwittingly in incest. All of this is accepted with a stoicism founded on an unbending faith in reason and a conduct guided by the notion of virtue.

As the very term *Aufklärung* itself implies, education played a central role in the Enlightenment. The early scenes in Gellert's novel are devoted to the education of the 16-year-old countess by her male cousin. Reflecting on this educational process in retrospect, the countess's thoughts on the relationship between religion and reason and also on the role of virtue are noteworthy:

> My cousin did not structure my education according to the principles of a profound philosophical system. By no

means. He taught me religion in a manner that was very rational, and he convinced me of the great advantages of virtue. . . . And it was because of these concepts that I have never regarded virtue as a burden, but rather as a most pleasant traveling companion that makes our journey through the world easier.

Leibniz's idea of "the best of all possible worlds" led to the representation of nature as an embodiment of the perfection of the all-wise divine Creator and to songs praising God in the nine volumes of poems by Heinrich Barthold Brockes (1680–1747), which were published under the title *Irdisches Vergnügen in Gott, bestehend in physikalisch und moralischen Gedichten* (1721–48; Earthly Delight in God, Consisting of Natural and Moral Poems). His poems alternate between meticulously detailed descriptions of natural phenomena and moralizing reflections on the goodness of God as revealed in *this* world:

Let yourself be moved by this example, dearest reader,
Give honor to God who ordered this world so rationally,
and adorned so beautifully as to delight you almost to
rapture.
Let us intone a joyous song of praise.

Immanuel Kant (1724–1804) saw attacks on religious intolerance as one of the best avenues for increasing enlightenment, and Gotthold Ephraim Lessing's *Nathan der Weise* (1779; *Nathan the Wise*) is the crowning achievement of that aim. Here, religious tolerance is expressed symbolically when it is revealed that the representatives of the three major religions, Christianity, Judaism, and Mohammedanism, are in fact members of one family. Hence, all men are brothers in their search for perfection and virtue.

Attacks against the arid rationalism of the Enlightenment came early in Germany. Goethe's *Die Leiden des jungen Werthers* (1774; translated as *The Sorrows of Werther* and *The Sufferings of Young Werther*) was prototypical for the rising generation of young Romantics. Werther consistently champions feeling and passion over cold and calculating reason, most poignantly in his debate with Albert in which he sympathizes with the suicide against Albert's view that suicide is a sign of weakness and the ignominious loss of rational control over one's life. The sight of a natural garden as opposed to the customary geometrically designed gardens of the nobility elicits Werther's enthusiastic praise: "The garden is simple, and one feels as soon as one enters that it was planned not by a scientific gardener but by an impressionable soul that wanted here to take its pleasure."

The Romantic and pre-Romantic attacks against the Enlightenment were not only directed against the dominance of reason but also against what were considered to be its deleterious effects on literature. Looking at the literature of the Enlightenment as a whole, it must be said that, aside from the works of Lessing and Wieland, the period gave rise to some of the most uninspired writing since the Protestant Reformation. The reason is not difficult to see: the primary aim of the Enlightenment was to educate and teach moral lessons. That accounts for the popularity of the fable as a genre. In sum, the literature of the Enlightenment was far more philosophical and didactic than it was artistic.

Romanticism arose as a counterforce to the staid literature and culture of rationalism. It is instructive to read Ludwig

Tiecks's preface, written in 1813, to the second edition of his novel *William Lovell*, which was originally published in 1796:

The early youth of the author coincided with those years which, not only in Germany but in most of the cultured world, witnessed the slumber if not the death of the sensibility for the beautiful, the elevated and the mysterious. The shallow zeal of the Enlightenment had gained control and sought to present the sacred as an empty dream; indifference to religion was called free thought; and the concept of the fatherland, which was on the edge of extinction, was replaced by cosmopolitanism. Instead of philosophy there was popular conversation. Even poetry itself had died. In a battle against these prevalent currents the author sought to make Nature, Art, and Faith indigenous once again.

The philosophy of Johann Gottlieb Fichte (1762–1814) is an important key to understanding the literature of German Romanticism. For Fichte, the source of all reality was the ego, the self, which both perceives and creates its own world and thus gains sovereignty. Fichte's epistemology seems to be nothing more than a celebration of pure subjectivity. It also contains the germ of Romantic irony, a reflection upon the act of consciousness itself, whereby the author views both the self and the work critically and has the freedom to engage in playful manipulation or even destruction of illusion, as illustrated most clearly in the role of the audience in Tieck's *Der gestiefelte Kater* (1797; Puss in Boots), which also ridicules the utilitarianism of the *Aufklärung* and much of the lyric poetry of Heinrich Heine.

Tieck's *William Lovell* embodies a number of major Romantic motifs: the sharp awareness of generational conflict, the extreme subjectivism of Fichte, which borders on solipsism, and the antithesis of calculating reason and feeling. In a letter to Eduard Burton, Lovell writes:

I fear that my father regards my happiness from a completely different point of view . . . he assesses and measures relationships at the palace with the yardstick of reason . . . alas, Eduard, he is *calculating* my happiness instead of, as I would wish, *feeling* it.

In a conversation with Lovell, his friend Balder expounds on the inefficacy of reason, with distinct echoes of Kant's *Kritik der reinen Vernunft* (1781; *Critique of Pure Reason*):

O William, What do we mean by "reason"? Many persons have already gone insane worshiping their reason . . . our faculty of reason which comes from heaven is able to roam only on earth; no one has yet been able through reason to arrive at the truth about eternity, immortality, God, and the destiny of the world. We have strayed with our reason into a prison, whining for freedom, screaming for daylight, pounding on iron doors which are forever shut and hearing only a hollow echo.

Lovell writes a letter to Rosa in which the imprint of Fichte is distinct:

With an air of triumph I stand above everything—above life with its joys and sorrows, I look down with proud contempt into the turmoil of the world. The free person bears the stamp of caprice released from all bonds, I roar ahead like a windstorm, tearing down forests and soaring over mountains with a loud and wild howl. . . . We are our own lawgivers as well as our own subjects: with the intoxication of youth let us reel toward the evening sunset and become immersed in its glow.

For the Romantics, the real world was not to be reached by a plodding empiricism and cold reason but by mystical experience or intuition. The real world was spiritual in nature, not material. In the 1830s, however, this orientation to the world was to change drastically. Materialist philosophy reversed the Romantic view: the real world, in fact, life in general, was matter. It denied the existence of pure spirit that is independent of a material substrate. Therefore, there is no God, incorporeal soul, or spirit. Atheistic materialism received its impetus from at least three primary sources: the legacy of the Enlightenment tradition, the rise of natural science, and the effort to undermine the philosophy of the divine right of kings, which had been used for centuries to legitimate political power and abuse. Atheistic materialism, according to Marx, was no longer satisfied with describing and understanding the world; it wanted to change it.

Karl Gutzkow's *Wally die Zweiflerin* (Wally the Doubter) was published in 1835. As the title of the work suggests, the main problem has to do with religious doubts that plague Wally, the heroine. The following passage shows her conflict-ridden state of mind:

To doubt the existence of God would be to deny my present state of mind. Would I have this trouble if there really were no God? Atheism has always ended up by itself becoming a religion. . . . We are supposed to fear and love God. We are often born into the most miserable circumstances. Life is a constant struggle with matter. No one has a right to criticize me for thinking that the acceptance of the belief in the existence of God is based on a wholly political and legal agreement between the people and the state. We will always be subject to anthropomorphic ideas. Christianity lends support to this habit. The notion of a craftsman on a throne high above us is a need which our fantasy will always indulge.

Five years later, Ludwig Feuerbach's *Das Wesen der Religion* (1840; *The Essence of Religion*) was to say essentially the same thing, but with greater assurance. The main line of his thought is that God did not create man; rather, man created God out of an innate need to believe in something higher than himself. After the idea of God was created in fantasy, it was projected out into the heavens, where it took on an independent existence.

Modern theories of determinism were inspired mainly by the development of physical science, particularly in the 17th and 18th centuries. The rise of science, beginning in the 1840s, undermined metaphysical causes and called into question the autonomous status that had been attributed to the mind and the will. Under the influence of positivistic science, literature began to adopt the habits of close observation and to focus more on the concrete aspects of the world. Naturalism was born. Emile Zola (1840–1902) equated the work of literature with a scientific experiment, arguing that in nature there is embedded a causal nexus of which the writer is an objective recorder. This recording aims at a photographic and phonographic reproduction of reality, which calls its artistic quality into question. But writers such as Gerhart Hauptmann and Thomas Mann, for whom naturalism was a kind of artistic preparatory school, left behind some powerful and significant productions that, while capturing the rigorous determinism of the movement, also pointed to the more fertile domains of literary artistry that subsequently came into fruition.

Erich Heller convincingly demonstrates that Thomas Mann's first novel, *Buddenbrooks* (1901; *Buddenbrooks: The Decline of a Family*), is a work with naturalistic elements but is also a philosophical novel in the sense that it bears the imprint of Arthur Schopenhauer's thought in *Die Welt als Wille und Vorstellung* (1819; *The World as Will and Idea*). The conflict is between the world that is a will willing itself without sense or reason and the mind of man. The dramatic opposition, which can be traced through four generations, turns on that of Schopenhauer's philosophy with elements also of Nietzsche's thought and the music of Richard Wagner. The fate of the family progresses with a relentless logic and determinism. In each generation the drama and conflict are reenacted through the gradual refinements of consciousness. The essential Schopenhauerian plot is that the will comes to know itself and, astonished at its own activities, begins to inquire into its own character. The result in those whose will is vulnerable, such as Thomas Buddenbrook, is the awareness of the vanity of all its labors and the illusoriness of its freedom. The will yields to introspection, which brings about erosion. Yet the will in the case of Thomas seeks to employ all moral resources as a counterforce, which results in oscillating between Nietzsche's affirmation of the will and Schopenhauer's moral denial of it. For Thomas, the businessman with a conscience, and his son, Hanno, the introspective and sensitive artist-to-be, the end is exhaustion, surrender, and death.

Existentialist philosophy, by contrast, rejected the rigorous determinism of the turn of the century. It also marked a turning away from the traditional philosophic approach to such fields as metaphysics, ethics, aesthetics, and axiology. Owing in large part to the impetus of the experiences of World War II and its aftermath, it was in France, in particular, where existentialism showed a concern with how man can survive in, and adjust to, a changing world. In Germany, the presence of existentialist themes in the work of Wolfgang Borchert has been noted. Such themes include universal existential guilt, the search for the ultimate meaning of human existence, authentic existence versus "das Man" (the anonymous member of the crowd), and *Angst* as the original revelation of freedom. The plot of Borchert's play *Draussen vor der Tür* (1947; *The Man Outside*) can be favorably compared with Albert Camus's thoughts in his essay "Absurdity and Suicide" (1942). Camus focuses first on the discovery of the absurd: the yawning chasm between the human nostalgia for meaningfulness and reasonableness of existence and the unreasonable silence of the world. Camus, however, is particularly interested in the *consequences* of this discovery. Will they lead to suicide, which is a surrender to the absurd, a confession that life is too much? Or will they lead to a revolt, confronting absurdity in implacable opposition and unremitting struggle?

Borchert's protagonist Beckmann vacillates throughout the play between these poles: remaining alive in spite of the obscene absurdity of a world populated by such types as the Colonel, the Cabaret Director, and Frau Kramer, and despite the availability of the escapist solution of suicide by drowning. Returning home from the war, Beckmann discovers the absurd: he finds another man in bed with his wife and learns that his one-year-old son has been killed in the bombing.

Beckmann cries out in distress, but both human and divine ears are deaf. Beckmann is confronted with what Camus calls the "benign indifference" of the universe. The conclusion of the play remains open. Beckmann asks urgent questions, but he receives no answer. The universe has become mute and benignly indifferent. In the unreasonable silence of an absurd world, he will receive no answer. He will have to rely on himself. The mind, Camus says, when it reaches its limits, must make a judgment and choose its conclusions. Beckmann stands in that waterless desert where thought has reached its limits. He will have to choose between life and death.

DON NELSON

See also Aesthetics

Further Reading
Beiser, Frederick C., *Enlightenment, Revolution, and Romanticism*, Cambridge, Massachusetts: Harvard University Press, 1992
Edwards, Paul, editor, *The Encyclopedia of Philosophy*, 8 vols., New York: Macmillan, 1967
Gellert, Christian, *Werke*, edited by Gottfried Honnefelder, 2 vols., Frankfurt: Insel, 1979
Heller, Erich, *The Ironic German: A Study of Thomas Mann*, Boston: Little, Brown, 1958
Nelson, Donald, "To Live or Not to Live: Notes on Archetypes and the Absurd in Borchert's *Draussen vor der Tür*," *German Quarterly* (May 1975)
Pascal, Roy, *From Naturalism to Expressionism*, New York: Basic Books, 1973
Paulin, Roger, *Ludwig Tieck: A Literary Biography*, Oxford: Clarendon Press, and New York: Oxford University Press, 1985

Popular Literature

With the advent of cultural studies and postmodern theories, heralded by Leslie Fiedler's battle cry to "cross the border—close that gap" between so-called highbrow and lowbrow literatures and cultures, the English term *popular literature* (the German correlatives are *Populärliteratur* or *Unterhaltungsliteratur*) has surpassed if not totally replaced the terms *Schundliteratur* (trash literature) or *Trivialliteratur*. German literary scholars have hotly debated the parameters and definitions of class- and gender-related differences between literary productions and habits of reception since the early 1960s. While some have guarded the classical literary canon and its bourgeois tradition with thinly disguised and self-serving mechanisms of quality control, others have solely focused on Marxist, sociological, and ideology-critical approaches to literature—according to R. Schenda's credo, "the reading material of the dominated class is the dominant literature" (Bayer). By contrast, the newer term *popular literature* promises to allow for a "plurality of methods" (Petzold and Späth) intent on discovering the specific interrelations between literature, mass production, distribution, and consumption.

Since the term *popular* has generally been linked to the technical ability to reproduce cultural products mechanically, the phrase *popular literature* describes literature from the beginning of printing onward, but especially the dramatic increase in literary productions after 1765. Today, the phrase is equally applicable to the phenomenon of international best-sellers as to *Serienliteratur* (serial literature), *Heftromane* (threepenny novels), genre fiction (including thrillers, romances, science fiction, fantasy, and war books), and television and film novels. The adjective "popular" thus not only delineates the common taste of a majority of people but also always connotes accessibility and "of the populace"—the people's choice. While it is true that popular publications by female and male authors, whether writing under their own name or pseudonyms (such as Utta Danella, Johannes Mario Simmel, or Hans Bemmann) or contracted per volume by one of the many international series, tend to reinforce existing social, racial, and political prejudices and dichotomies, it is just as true that many examples of popular fiction instead criticize the very assumptions on which the status quo is based.

During the years of waning aristocratic power and beyond, "popular" held the threat of democracy, even anarchy. In the 18th century in Germany, several interconnected factors created an increase in literature production, reception, and purchases, among them the advance of scientific positivism paired with philosophical Enlightenment, general schooling, social and geographic mobility, more leisure time for the middle class, newspaper and magazine circulation, the appearance of book clubs, public libraries, and the move toward a national literature. The modern novel could be called the single most important contributor to the promotion of popular fiction. As Tony Tanner so adequately put it, the modern novel has been embroiled in adulterous activities from the beginning, filching material from myths and neighboring genres such as letters, poetry, and drama and developing a narratology of seduction, incest, and betrayal. Because the reading of novels was soon widespread, the act of reading in private was associated with addiction (Langenbucher) and sinful fantasies (wanting to lead a better life than the one God granted) and was imbued with sexual overtones (voyeurism), whether the actual content perused was morally uplifting or, indeed, erotically or politically charged. Due to the simultaneous rise in female and "common" readerships and authorship beginning in the late 18th century, which ran counter to the period's stylization of the individual male artist as social outsider and to the perception of artistic creation as a sacrifice of conventional life, the conflation of popular and trivial indeed bears the stamp of critical chauvinism.

In the age of colonialism and orientalism, the figure of woman became a projection not just of sexual but also of racial fantasies and anxieties, especially regarding impurity and hybridity. By definition, mass culture in this age was based on reproductions: pirated copies, hybrid forms such as the postcard, or the serialized novel in the *Gartenlaube* (summer house). According to Andreas Huyssen, "the gendering of mass culture as feminine and inferior has its primary place in the late 19th century, even though the underlying dichotomy did not lose its power until quite recently." Because "trivialization" is defined as the process by which "once valid and valued objects or forms drift into the common, the general, resulting in a superficiality of content and a one-dimensionality of form" (Bayer), this definition has crucial implications whenever and wherever women enter the public sphere. When popular literature is seen as verging on *Kitsch* (Ludwig Giesc, 1960), this idea is more often than not demonstrated by pointing to the literary products of women writers such as Ida Hahn-Hahn (1805–80), Eugenie Marlitt (1825–87), Hedwig Courths-Mahler (1867–1950), and Vicki Baum (1888–1960).

As Jochen Schulte-Sasse points out, "ideas of aesthetic value regarding *Kitsch* . . . were developed during the Goethe age by Goethe and Schiller themselves in their discourse on trivial literature." What is voiced in terms of a decrease in variance, however, appears as a mode of purity control. That adaptations and stylistic mixes create new forms and are largely responsible for innovating genres, not to mention literature as such, is ignored. In the 20th century, the modernist foible for clean, straight lines and high functionality, while itself exemplifying a cultural reaction to Biedermeier ostentatiousness, did not allow for any type of adulteration. Despite the awareness raised by current feminist, postmodern, post-Marxist, postcolonial, and queer scholarship, thematic and formal bricolages, unless realistically representing the chaos of modern life, are still viewed with skepticism from the modernist vantage point of a resilient avant-gardism.

Contemporary women authors such as Svende Merian in *Der Tod des Märchenprinzen* (1980; The Death of the Fairy Prince), Elfriede Jelinek in *Krankheit, oder moderne Frauen* (1987; Sickness, or Modern Women), and Marlene Streeruwitz in her picture serial *Lisa* (1995–97), as well as filmmakers Doris Dorrie in her comedies and Monika Treut in *Die Jungfrauenmaschine* (1988; Virgin Machine), have not only leveled their own brand of genre-critical parodies at the conflation of women with romance and the trivial but they have also created a postmodern form of popular fiction. In addition, in a relatively recent development, postfeminist popular novels exemplified by Hera Lind's *Das Superweib* (1994; Superwoman) and the thriller author Ingrid Noll's *Der Hahn ist tot* (1991; The Rooster Is Dead) actually couch values such as motherhood, sacrifice, emotional strength, heterosexual bonding rituals, and physical beauty in the language of emancipation and lifestyle choices reminiscent of politically conscious and "correct" feminist thought and action.

While the term *popular* appears more neutral than its predecessors *trivial* or *entertaining*, it tends to mask the difficulty in accounting for taste and popularity trends within and across class, race, gender, and nationality lines. Is a book popular simply because thousands of people buy it? Is the desire to buy equal to the desire to read? What makes some works and authors steady sellers, such as Karl May's adventure novels, Johannes Mario Simmel's spy novels, or Utta Danella's romances, and others such as Patrick Süskind's *Das Parfüm* (1985; *Perfume*) instant best-sellers? Is the book design, its advertisement, or its sale price a diagnosis for popularity? How does one account for the popularity of English and Scandinavian titles in translation (Peter Hoeg's and Hannah Erickson's novels in particular)? And is it simply an effect of the normalization of globalization that lies behind the phenomenon that German readers and cinemagoers sometimes do not even realize that they are consuming a translated title, despite the foreign scenery and different names? What is the role of literary and journalistic criticism for popular literature and film? What has and will continue to change as the electronic information age is altering print culture as we know it?

SUNKA SIMON

See also Children's Literature; Fairy Tales

Further Reading

Ashley, Bob, editor, *The Study of Popular Fiction: A Source Book*, London: Pinter, and Philadelphia: University of Pennsylvania Press, 1989

Bayer, Dorothee, *Der triviale Familien- und Liebesroman im 20. Jahrhundert*, Tübingen: Tübinger Vereinigung für Volkskunde, 1971

Beaujean, Marion, *Der Trivialroman in der zweiten Hälfte des 18. Jahrhunderts: Die Ursprünge des modernen Romans*, Bonn: Bouvier, 1964

Bürger, Christa, *Textanalyse als Ideologiekritik: Zur Rezeption zeitgenössischer Unterhaltungsliteratur*, Frankfurt: Athenäum, 1973

Burger, Heinz Otto, editor, *Studien zur Trivialliteratur*, Frankfurt: Klostermann, 1976

Domagalski, Peter, *Trivialliteratur*, Freiburg: Herder, 1981

Fiedler, Leslie, "Cross the Border—Close That Gap: Post-Modernism," in *American Literature since 1900*, edited by Marcus Cunliffe, London: Barrie and Jenkins, 1975

Geyer-Ryan, Helga, *Der andere Roman: Versuch über die verdrängte Ästhetik des Populären*, Wilhelmshafen: Heinrichshofen, 1983

Greiner, Martin, *Die Entstehung der modernen Unterhaltungsliteratur*, Reinbek bei Hamburg: Rowohlt, 1964

Hienger, Jörg, et al., editors, *Unterhaltungsliteratur: Zu ihrer Theorie und Verteidigung*, Göttingen: Vandenhoeck und Ruprecht, 1976

Humm, Peter, et al., *Popular Fictions: Essays in Literature and History*, London and New York: Methuen, 1986

Huyssen, Andreas, *After the Great Divide: Modernism, Mass Culture, Postmodernism*, Bloomington: Indiana University Press, 1986

Klein, Albert, and Heinz Hecker, *Trivialliteratur*, Opladen: Westdeutscher Verlag, 1977

Langenbucher, Wolfgang, *Der aktuelle Unterhaltungsroman*, Bonn: Bouvier, 1964

Lowenthal, Leo, *Literature, Popular Culture, and Society*, Englewood Cliffs, New Jersey: Prentice Hall, and Palo Alto, California: Pacific Books, 1961

Müller-Seidel, Walter, *Probleme der literarischen Wertung: Über die Wissenschaftlichkeit eines unwissenschaftlichen Themas*, Stuttgart: Metzler, 1965

Neuburg, Victor E., *Popular Literature: A History and Guide from the Beginning of Printing to the Year 1897*, London and Totowa, New Jersey: Woburn Press, 1977

Nusser, Peter, *Romane für die Unterschicht,* Stuttgart: Metzler, 1976; 5th edition, 1981

Pawling, Christopher, editor, *Popular Fiction and Social Change,* London: Macmillan, and New York: St. Martin's Press, 1984

Petzold, Dieter, and Eberhard Späth, editors, *Unterhaltungsliteratur,* Erlangen: Universitätsbund Erlangen-Nürnberg, 1990

Rucktäschel, Annemarie, and Hans Dieter Zimmermann, editors, *Trivialliteratur,* Munich: Fink: 1976

Schulte-Sasse, Jochen, *Die Kritik an der Trivialliteratur seit der Aufklärung,* Munich: Fink, 1971

Skreb, Zdenko, and Uwe Baur, editors, *Erzählgattungen der Trivialliteratur,* Innsbruck: Institut für Germanistik, 1984

Postmodernism

The idea of postmodernism has been pursued by different interpretative communities in different ways since the 1960s. At the end of the century, the discursive event that once determined the course of artistic practices—predominantly those in the United States—has become a Babel of cultural and socio-political discourses, in part as a result of the impact of poststructuralist positions. A micrological account of this history—with specific reference to the German reception of postmodern perspectives—can better illuminate the complex intertextuality of the various initiatives than a macrological survey.

The term is documented in several early usages, from Rudolf Pannwitz's "postmodern man" (1917) to Arnold Toynbee's similarly pessimistic view of a postmodern age (1947). In the 1960s, the concept of the postmodern became the shibboleth of literary and academic circles in the United States that were disillusioned with the l'art pour l'art program of aesthetic modernism. Their pursuit of rupture was aided by developments in the New York art scene, where the canonization of Abstract Expressionism was countered by a new generation of artists, the pop artists, who were committed to bridging the gap between high and low culture. Leslie Fiedler's quasi-manifesto, "Cross the Border—Close the Gap," which appeared in the December 1969 issue of *Playboy,* is characteristic of the populist agenda that informed both academic inquiry and creative writers alike. Susan Sontag's essays "Against Interpretation" and "Notes on Camp" were also important in shaping a new sensibility that defined itself against the high culture productions embraced by the New Criticism. The postmodern movement in American prose writing is documented by the 1998 *Norton Anthology of Postmodern American Fiction.* Important members of this movement were Paul Auster, John Barth, Donald Barthelme, Raymond Carver, Robert Coover, Raymond Federman, Thomas Pynchon, and Kurt Vonnegut. The most seminal theoretical proponent of a new type of literary text in the 1970s and early 1980s was Ihab Hassan, who influenced Americanists in many parts of the world, especially in Western Europe. He pleaded for a postmodern aesthetic of antiform and play—disjunctive, open, collage—and for a literature of the absurd (considered modern in Europe).

The German reception of these developments began with Fiedler's problematic delivery of a paper preceding the above essay, with the added subtitle "A Case for Postmodernism," in Freiburg in 1968. A politically engaged Martin Walser and critics such as Reinhard Baumgart mistook Fiedler's casual remarks for the constitutive postmodernist program of Americanists. Their negative reception—positive only in the case of the writer Rolf Dieter Brinkmann—marks the beginning of a long-lasting negative reception of the concept of the postmodern in the German intellectual community, which crystallized in terms such as "postmoderne Beliebigkeit" (postmodern arbitrariness) or "Anything Goes" (Feyerabend). This crystallization, however, ignored the politicized and democratizing nature of the antimodernist commitment within this U.S. movement.

An essay by Frankfurt School philosopher Jürgen Habermas, "Modernity—An Unfinished Project," which he gave as a speech upon accepting the Adorno Prize in 1980, significantly shaped German understanding of postmodernism in the 1980s. The brilliant polemic, much reprinted in English, suffers from two strata of misunderstanding that nonetheless structured the German horizon of knowledge with regard to postmodernism. Habermas decisively dismissed the new postmodern style in architecture that had just been programmatically displayed at the Venice Biennale. Unlike practicing architects or architectural historians, the philosopher did not see the postmodern style in architecture as a reaction against the purist, anti-historical functionalism of Bauhaus-type modernism, which had lost its utopian edge in the corporate idiom of the "international style." The new architecture did not present a challenge to modernity as an epoch, as Habermas claimed, but aimed at commercially reintegrating historical styles into contemporary building technology. Postmodern architecture was theorized by the architect Robert Venturi (*Complexity and Contradiction in Architecture,* 1966) and by the architectural historian Charles Jencks (in many publications, beginning with *The Language of Post-Modern Architecture* [1977]). Artistically ambitious architects ceased to build in the postmodern idiom by the early 1990s, while watered-down versions continued in general building practices in the United States and elsewhere. As the architects pursued their new directions (e.g., "Deconstruction"), postmodern architecture was historicized as a style period.

Habermas's attack on postmodernism of 1980 (and later) further equated the concept with poststructuralist positions, in particular those of Michel Foucault and Jacques Derrida, that in his view presented a radical critique of enlightenment ideals and embraced irrationality and neo-conservativism. Although "Vernunftkritik" was upgraded by philosophers such as Wolfgang Welsch, drawing on the theory of Jean-Francois Lyotard,

German cultural discourse continued to associate the postmodern with a lack of ethical direction and to characterize it as a threat to modernity. Claims that "Postmoderne," having barely existed in the first place, was dead could be found in a *Merkur* theme issue in 1998.

Such a hostile climate of reception is not typical of other interpretive communities. In Anglophone countries in particular, artistic practices as different as architectural discourse, art, and literature participated in complex and differentiated critiques of aesthetic modernism. This early phase of the movement encouraged pluralist and hybrid tendencies, which later merged with the decentering, self-reflexive, and deconstructing directives of poststructuralist theory. The notion of the postmodern became a cultural dominant that was gradually infused with positive and politicized signification. Many fields now turned to poststructuralist theory in order to critique ("deconstruct") the belief system of their respective disciplines—sociology, anthropology, and the "new" art history, among others. At the same time, in the second half of the 1990s, the New York physicist Alan Sokal strongly rejected a "postmodern" approach to the sciences.

Many concepts of poststructuralist critical theory have spread beyond academic circles into general cultural discourse. In his pioneering study *La condition postmoderne* (1979; *The Postmodern Condition*), Lyotard introduced the notion of "grand narratives," referring to the great ideological projects in history as master discourses that are susceptible to radical questioning. The concept functions to open up ideological constellations in different ways than predominantly progress-oriented modern perspectives did. Other important themes of the postmodern debate generated by the trope of the master narrative are the "crisis of knowledge," the "crisis of representation," the simulacrum as the hyperreal (Jean Baudrillard), and the "decentered subject" (Jacques Lacan et al.). The transformation of thought that undermined essentialism—including Foucault's discourse analysis as cultural critique—paved the way for a Marxist-poststructuralist merger most prominently represented by Fredric Jameson. His essay, "Postmodernism; or, The Cultural Logic of Late Capitalism," first published in *New Left Review* in 1984 (produced as a full-length book in 1991), provided the Anglophone community with a politicized perspective on postmodernism beyond the left-right opposition.

At the end of the 1990s, cross-cultural agreements and applications abound. These are not unrelated to concepts in literature that Americanists and comparatists established in the 1980s as markers of postmodern fiction. Narrative auto-reflexivity and meta-fictional irony are the outstanding structural features of the most prominent genre of postmodern literature, the novel and prose writing. Texts by John Barth from the 1960s or Italo Calvino's *If, on a winter's night a traveller* (1979) are considered exemplars of postmodern autoreflexivity. Günter Grass's ironic reflection on the making of a novel today at the beginning of *The Tin Drum* (1959) was classified by Americanists as a postmodern move, a notion that Germanists considered problematic. In German post-1945 critical discourse, narrative self-reflexivity was considered characteristic of high-modernist German literature, of a strand that began, roughly, with Rilke's *The Notebooks of Malte Laurids Brigge* (1910) and continued with Broch and Musil. One may speak of "Ungleichzeitigkeit des Gleichzeitigen," the non-simultaneity of the contemporaneous, which is characteristic of the meandering flow of "traveling" theory and postmodern naming. Postmodern writing, however, radicalizes the device of narrative autoreflexivity, which permits critics to subsume selected works of German literature under the new heading. Some of the Austrian and German authors frequently considered postmodern in some aspects and from different perspectives are Thomas Bernhard, Peter Handke, Elfriede Jelinek, Heiner Müller, Hanns-Josef Ortheil, Christoph Ransmayr, Botho Strauss, and Patrick Süskind.

A genuine innovation in postmodern prose writing is "double-coding." The term was coined in 1978 by Jencks to define postmodern architecture as a combination of modern techniques with architectural signs directed toward the user. In literature, this concept denotes the two-tier structure of novels that function on the surface as a popular genre, such as the detective novel, and as sophisticated critical commentary on a second, allegorical level. The exemplar of postmodern double-coding is Umberto Eco's *The Name of the Rose* (1980). Süskind's *Das Parfum* (1985; *Perfume*) is the first work in German to use the device. It became so popular that it graced the shelves of U.S. supermarkets. The "story of a murderer" (the novel's subtitle) is narrated as a thriller that, on a level invisible to the uninitiated reader, critiques the German literary canon in numerous pastiches.

Stylistic trends that can be discerned in most contemporary art forms are the conflation of genres, intertextuality, and pastiche structuration (registered negatively by Jameson). These trends can be seen as corresponding to a general tendency toward hybridity, which the philosopher Cornel West also discerns in contemporary social practices. Postmodern American poetry typically merges high modernist language, often borrowings, with contemporary clichés and media trivia (e.g., John Ashbery), whereas German poets such as Dirk von Petersdorff make poems about contemporary theory paradigms. Postmodern conflation may denote the juxtaposition of heterogeneous language styles, as is typical of Heiner Müller's hyper-Expressionist idiom, or it may be found in the shape of asynchronies in Christoph Ransmayr's *Die letzte Welt* (1988; *The Last World*). In this novel, scenes playing in ancient Rome and in Ovid's exile at the Black Sea, where the writer Cotta is searching for "the book," are narrated in a seemingly traditional poetic realism that is shot through with signs of 20th-century media culture. The asynchronic juncture works as an allegory for the contemporary writer's plea for the literary as "the last world" (alternate interpretations involve "the last world" as an apocalypse).

Performance styles in genres ranging from operas (including those arranged by Robert Wilson) to MTV use pastiche structuration and quotation to make visible the intertextual movement of culture. Popular and "elitist" signs can be found side by side in a variety of productions. Artistically ambitious films such as those by Peter Greenaway that pastiche famous old-masterly paintings, David Lynch's *Blue Velvet*, or the hybrid films of Ulrike Ottinger all make quotation and "referencing" a constituent of their style, which co-produces their story.

Whereas the shapes of aesthetic postmodernism can be observed as relatively concrete phenomena, postmodern culture and its socio-political dissemination, which involves a potentially global scope, are considerably more difficult to assess. This discursive event is ongoing. Whether postmodernism or postmodernity will shape up to an epoch born out of the crisis of modernity cannot be determined at the end of the 20th century. For the time being, it is a cultural dominant whose varied impulses are spreading like the invisible roots of a rhizome. The concept of the postmodern is bound to continue to exist in displacements and transformations as it moves from theoretical contexts to social practices.

INGEBORG HOESTEREY

See also Avant-Garde; Die Moderne

Further Reading

Bertens, Hans, *The Idea of the Postmodern,* London: Routledge, 1995

Calinescu, Matei, and Douwe Fokkema, editors, *Exploring Postmodernism,* Amsterdam and Philadelphia, Pennsylvania: Benjamins, 1987

Fokkema, Douwe, and Hans Bertens, editors, *Approaching Postmodernism,* Amsterdam and Philadelphia, Pennsylvania: Benjamins, 1986

Habermas, Jürgen, "Modernity: An Incomplete Project," translated by Seyla Benhabib, in *The Anti-Aesthetic: Essays on Postmodern Culture,* edited by Hal Foster, Port Townsend, Washington: Bay Press, 1983

Hassan, Ihab, *The Dismemberment of Orpheus: Towards a Postmodern Literature,* New York: Oxford University Press, 1971

Hoesterey, Ingeborg, editor, *Zeitgeist in Babel: The Postmodernist Controversy,* Bloomington: Indiana University Press, 1991

Huyssen, Andreas, and Klaus Scherpe, *Postmoderne: Zeichen eines kulturellen Wandels,* Reinbek bei Hamburg: Rowohlt Taschenbuch, 1986

Jameson, Fredric, *Postmodernism, Or, The Cultural Logic of Late Capitalism,* Durham, North Carolina: Duke University Press, and London: Verso, 1991

Lützeler, Paul Michael, editor, *Spätmoderne und Postmoderne: Beiträge zur deutschsprachigen Gegenwartsliteratur,* Frankfurt: Fischer Taschenbuch, 1991

Lyotard, Jean Francois, *The Postmodern Condition: A Report on Knowledge,* Minneapolis: University of Minnesota Press, and Manchester: Manchester University Press, 1984

Welsch, Wolfgang, *Unsere postmoderne Moderne,* Weinheim: VHC-Acta humaniora, 1987

Prague

Prague (population approximately 1.25 million), the capital of the Czech Republic, is situated in Central Europe, often referred to as the "heart of Europe." It has become a major gateway to Eastern Europe after the 1989 "Velvet Revolution" removed the Iron Curtain and the communist government and re-established an independent democratic state. The city's development has been shaped by the multiethnic traditions of its Czech, Italian, Jewish, German, and most recently, American residents. Its long history as a European intellectual and cultural center, overshadowed by Habsburg imperialism, then by Nazism, and finally by Communism, is now being revived in the context of democracy and a free-market economy.

The origin of Prague is most closely associated with the myth of Libussa (Libuše), founding mother of the Přemyslid dynasty. She married Přemysl, the plowman, in order to satisfy her people's request for a male ruler. The city's name, *Praha,* from *prah,* meaning "threshold," stems from one of her prophesies in which she foretold the future glory of the city, to be built where they would find a man carving a threshold in the middle of the forest, but reminded people at the same time that even great lords have to stoop before a low threshold. Libussa is known as the founder of Prague's ancient fortress, *Vyšehrad* (founded in 717; since 1869 including the national cemetery), and her legend inspired writers and musicians, among them Clemens Brentano (1778–1842), who wrote the drama *Die Gründung Prags* (1812, The Founding of Prague), and Franz Grillparzer (1791–1872), who reinterpreted the Czech myth in his play *Libussa* (1874). But it was Bedřich Smetana's (1824–84) festive opera *Libuše* (1872) that became a symbol of Czech history and national iden-

tity. It was first performed at the opening of the National Theater in 1881 and is now presented every year on the Czech National Holiday, 28 October, while its famous *Libuše* fanfare is used at state ceremonies and on the Czech radio.

The Přemyslid dynasty ruled Bohemia for over four hundred years, until the late 13th century. Duke Václav (ruling 924–29 or –35), also known as St. Wenceslas, became Bohemia's patron saint. In 1212, the Golden Bull of Sicily endorsed the royal status of Bohemia's ruler, making him one of the electors of the Holy Roman Empire and thus increasing Bohemia's political influence in Europe.

The dynasty's most powerful ruler, Přemysl Otakar II (1253–78), the "king of iron and gold," further strengthened Bohemia's position through his military exploits in Austria. His life and death were dramatized by Grillparzer in *König Ottokars Glück und Ende* (1825; The Fortune and Fall of King Otakar).

The height of Prague's status as a medieval commercial and cultural center came during the "Golden Age" under Charles IV (1316–78), when the city became capital of the Holy Roman Empire. A descendant of both the Přemyslid and the Luxembourg dynasties, Charles joined his Bohemian heritage with the refined traditions of Western civilization and his desire for European unity. In 1356, he proclaimed the Golden Bull, the Holy Roman Empire's first written legal code. Crowned as Holy Roman Emperor in 1355, he chose Prague as his imperial capital and, more than anyone else until the 19th century, shaped its character as a European metropolis. He rebuilt the ancient seat of the Přemyslid rulers, *Vyšehrad,* as well as the newer castle complex *Hradčany.* He employed one of the best architects of the time, Peter Parler, to erect the Gothic Cathedral of Saint Vitus on *Hradčany* and the "Stone Bridge," or "Prague Bridge," known since 1870 as Charles Bridge. Charles's generous support lead to the establishment of Prague's New Town: new monasteries, parish churches, and markets, one of which is now named Charles Square. He was also responsible for Prague's elevation to archbishopric, and in 1348 he founded Prague University. Under his reign, Prague, then with about 40,000 inhabitants, experienced a flourishing of its economy, its crafts, its arts (architecture and painting), and its scholarship.

The 1380 plague epidemic, the 1389 pogrom against the Jewish inhabitants, and the buildup of social, national, and religious tensions during and after the reign of Charles IV all resulted in a decline in prosperity and power. In 1415, religious reformer Jan Hus who had protested the practice of papal indulgences and the church's self-enrichment, was burnt at the stake after the Council of Konstanz declared him a heretic. Hus, rector of Prague University, also had reformed the Czech language and elevated its status. His violent death made him a national hero and provoked the Hussite Revolution (1415–22), which led to the first defenestration in Prague (1419) and, after many wars (1419–36), to a weakening of the Catholic Church and the Bohemian royalty, an exodus of Germans from Prague, and a "Czechization of the burgher state" (Sayer, 1998).

During the Renaissance, Prague experienced another period of prosperity under Emperor Rudolf II (1552–1612), famous for his patronage of the arts and sciences. He attracted an international group of painters, jewelers, stonecutters, musicians, poets, physicians and scientists to his court, among them the astronomers Tycho de Brahe (1546–1601) and Johannes Kepler (1571–1630). It was also a golden age for Prague's Jewish community, whose most prominent scholar, Rabbi Löw (1512–1609), is remembered primarily as the creator of the legendary Golem. The story of the Golem, popularized later by Expressionist filmmaker Paul Wegener (1874–1948) and novelist Gustav Meyrink (1868–1932), contributed much to the persistent view of Prague as a city populated by alchemists, occultists, and eerie ghosts, and to the creation of the legend of "mystical" or "magic" Prague.

After Rudolf II's death, religious and national tensions came to a head in the 1618 Rising of the Protestant Bohemian Estates. A second defenestration in Prague to protest the suppression of religious freedom by Habsburg rulers triggered the Thirty Years' War. The 1620 Battle of *Bílá hora* (White Mountain) on the outskirts of Prague brought defeat to the Protestants and final victory to the Counter Reformation. For modern Czech history, the result was devastating: over the next three centuries, the Kingdom of Bohemia became a provincial backwater of the Habsburg Empire. Prague was no longer the seat of power and lost its Protestant nobility, burgher estates, and intelligentsia. Much of its Czech culture vanished, and German replaced Czech as the official language and language of high culture. Italian Baroque architecture, blooming during this time of re-Catholicization, added another style to the city's appearance and the well-known statuary to Charles Bridge. Wolfgang Amadeus Mozart's (1756–91) visits to Prague between 1787 and 1791, including one for the world premiere of his *Don Giovanni* at Prague's Estates Theater, have been fictionalized in Eduard Mörike's (1804–75) novella *Mozart auf der Reise nach Prag* (1855; *Mozart on His Way to Prague*).

By 1650, the number of inhabitants had declined to 26,000. During the "dark times" of the 17th and 18th centuries, the city fell victim to a Saxon invasion (1631), Swedish attacks (1639 and 1648), and a Prussian siege (1744). The 19th century was characterized by the Czech National Revival and industrialization. What later became the Czech national anthem, *Kde domov můj?* (Where Is My Home?), was first played in the Estates Theater in 1834. The 1848 uprising of the people of Prague against Austrian troops revolved around the national question. Prague witnessed the establishment of cultural institutions such as the National Museum (1818, present building 1885) and the National Theater (*Národní divadlo,* 1881). Czech newspapers and periodicals such as the cultural magazine *Zlata Praha* (Golden Prague, 1884–1929) were started. The Czech language was revived with the publication of grammars and dictionaries, and in 1882 it was introduced as a second language of instruction at Prague University, where only German had been used since 1784. The percentage of Germans in Prague declined from 60 percent in 1848 to 6 percent in 1910. This new strong Czech identity was clearly manifested in the 1895 Czechoslavic Ethnographic Exhibition.

Czech literature came alive in Prague in the 19th century with the patriotic poems of romantic writer Karel Hynek Mácha (1810–36) and the folktales of Božena Němcová (1820–62), as well as her influential novel *Babička* (1855; *Granny*). František Palacký (1798–1876) became known as the "Father of the Nation," and his *History of the Czech Nation* was published first in German (1836) and then in Czech (1848). Alois Jirásek (1851–1930) taught in Prague, and his popular historical novels and stories became part of the Czech literary canon, as did the lyrics and stories of Prague poet Jan Neruda (1834–91) and the works of Svatopluk Čech (1846–1908).

During the time of the Revival, Prague also became a center for Czech music, which often incorporated patriotic and folk elements. Bedřich Smetana (1824–84) composed on Czech themes in his operas *The Bartered Bride* (1866) and *Libuše* (1872) and his symphonic poem *Má vlast* (1879; My Fatherland). Antonín Dvořák (1841–1904) is known for his *Slavonic Dances* (1878 and 1886) and his Ninth Symphony, "From the New World" (1893). The Czech Philharmonic Orchestra was established in 1894. Gustav Mahler (1860–1911), who was born in Bohemia, conducted performances in Prague. In the 20th century, composers Leoš Janáček (1854–1928) and Bohuslav Martinů (1890–1959) were both professors of music in Prague. The city's strong musical tradition lives on in the annual Prague Spring International Music Festival (since 1946).

Industrialization in the second half of the 19th century, especially after 1880, profoundly changed the urban landscape and social structure of Prague. Large factories, banks, and insurance companies opened, and the city's suburbs expanded. In the name of urban modernization, the city government razed the old Jewish quarter of the city.

At the fin de siècle and into the early 20th century, Prague experienced a cultural shift toward European international modernism. Impulses from Paris, Vienna, Symbolism, and German *Jugendstil* (1894–1914) shaped the Prague Secession (1897–1910), whose art nouveau can be found in building facades and in Prague's cubist architecture (1910–20). Czech poster art blurred the boundary between high art and commerce. The leading representative of the Prague Secession, Alfons

Mucha (1860–1939), is known both for his decorative, sensual posters (created mostly in Paris) and his grand *Slavic Epic* (20 monumental pictures on Slavic mythology, painted in Prague).

Intellectual life flourished in Prague's many literary cafés, such as Café *Arco,* a meeting place for a group of German-speaking intellectuals, who became known through the writings of Max Brod (1884–1968) as the Prague Circle. Besides Brod, its numerous members included Expressionist writers Franz Werfel (1890–1945), Paul Kornfeld (1889–1942), and Ernst Weiss (1882–1940), as well as Paul Leppin (1878–1945) and the "roving reporter" Egon Erwin Kisch (1885–1948), who wrote social criticism. Also part of the group was the gifted Czech journalist Milena Jésenská (1896–1944), who is known mainly through her love letters from Franz Kafka (*Briefe an Milena,* 1920–23, published 1952; *Letters to Milena*). Kafka (1883–1924) is undeniably the most famous figure of the Prague German Literature authors, and his novels *Der Prozeß* (1914–15, published 1925; *The Trial*) and *Das Schloß* (1922, published 1926; *The Castle*) as well as his famous story *Die Verwandlung* (1912, published 1915; *The Metamorphosis*) have entered the canon of world literature. Kafka lived in Prague almost all his life, yet he wrote very little about the city itself, with the exception of his stories *Beschreibung eines Kampfes* (1902–10, published 1936; *Description of a Struggle*) and *Das Stadtwappen* (1920, published 1931; *The City Coat of Arms*). Recent research, however, has traced much of the dark, haunting quality of the Kafkaesque back to his difficult position of double exclusion: as a member of Prague's German minority as well as the Jewish minority. One of the greatest poets writing in German, Rainer Maria Rilke (1875–1926), was also from Prague. He left the city in 1896, but wrote *Zwei Prager Geschichten* (1899; *Two Prague Stories*) and poems alluding to Prague.

The literary scene in Prague in the early 20th century also produced a strong literature in the Czech language. Národní Kavárna (National Café) was the meeting place of the avant-garde group Devětsil, founded by Karel Teige (1900–51), and also of the Prague Linguistic Circle, whose founder Roman Jakobson (1896–1982) was a precursor of structuralism. Karel Capek (1890–1938) invented the word "robot" in his play, *R.U.R.* (1921). Jaroslav Hašek (1883–1923) achieved international renown with his satirical novel *The Good Soldier Švejk and His Fortunes in the World War* (1920–23), whose picaresque hero sabotages the military bureaucracy of the late Austro-Hungarian monarchy. The novel inspired Bertolt Brecht's (1898–1956) comedy *Schweyk im zweiten Weltkrieg* (1944; *Schweyk in the Second World War*). The poet Jaroslav Seifert (1901–86) was the first Czech writer to receive the Nobel Prize (1984).

The end of World War I brought the collapse of the Austro-Hungarian Empire and, on 28 October 1918, the declaration of the independent republic of Czechoslovakia, with Tomáš G. Masaryk (1850–1937) as its president. Prague became the national capital, and in 1922 the metropolitan region, with 700,000 citizens, was the sixth-largest city in Europe. In the 1920s and 1930s, Czechoslovakia ranked among the world's 10 leading industrial countries. The Munich Agreement of 30 September 1938 handed over parts of the republic to Hitler, and in 1939 German troops marched into Prague and made it the capital of the German Protectorate of Bohemia and Moravia. The 1942 assassination of Reichsprotektor Reinhard Heydrich by the Czechoslovak resistance movement led to the razing of the whole village of Lidice. Prague's multiethnic and multinational population was changed forever by the destruction of its 1,000-year-old Jewish community during the Holocaust and the deportation of its German inhabitants after 1945.

Under Communist rule from 1948 to 1989, Prague once more was condemned to subsist in the shadow of a colonial oppressor. Behind the Iron Curtain, it became isolated from Western Europe and lost its cosmopolitan atmosphere. The liberalizing reforms of the Prague Spring of 1968 under the leadership of Alexander Dubček were cruelly crushed by the Soviet invasion on 21 August 1968. The self-immolation of students Jan Palach and Jan Zajíc in Wenceslas Square in January 1969 marked the climax of mass protests against Soviet oppression. The "normalization" period of the 1970s and 1980s further hastened Prague's economic and cultural decline, except for its vibrant theater tradition, especially the black light theater of the *Laterna Magica,* and the puppet and marionette theater. Literature split into three distinct traditions: "official" authors, such as Bohumil Hrabal (1914–97); banned, underground *samizdat* writers, such as Ludvík Vakulík (1926–) and the famous playwright Václav Havel (1936–); and exiled authors, such as Arnošt Lustig (1926–), Pavel Kohout (1928–), Josef Skvorecký (1924–), Milan Kundera (1929–), and Libuše Moníková (1946–98). Moníková's texts, all written in German, have become an integral part of contemporary German literature. The dissidents who stayed behind after 1968 created the document *Charter 77* in defense of basic human and civic rights, and suffered repression and imprisonment for signing it. Among the 1,886 signators were philosopher Jan Patočka (1907–77) and Václav Havel. Only *perestroika,* initiated by Russian leader Mikhail Gorbachev, ended the Cold War and prepared the way for the "Velvet Revolution" of 1989, which catapulted Václav Havel into the office of president of the new democratic state. In 1993, however, Czechoslovakia seperated into two independent Czech and Slovak republics, reducing the size of the country of which Prague is the national capital.

Since 1989 Prague has once more become a bustling European metropolis. Its "old world charm" is attractive to tourists and its business opportunities to a new community of international residents. Westernization is the latest in a long series of dramatic changes to permanently alter the city's character.

HELGA G. BRAUNBECK

Further Reading

Brod, Max, *Der Prager Kreis,* Stuttgart: Kohlhammer, 1966
Demetz, Peter, *Böhmische Sonne, mährischer Mond: Essays und Erinnerungen,* Vienna: Deuticke, 1996
———, *Prague in Black and Gold: Scenes from the Life of a European City,* New York: Hill and Wang, 1997
Fiala-Fürst, Ingeborg, *Der Beitrag der Prager deutschen Literatur zum deutschen literarischen Expressionismus: Relevante Topoi ausgewählter Werke,* St. Ingbert: Röhrig Universitätsverlag, 1996
Garton Ash, Timothy, *We the People: The Revolution of '89 as Witnessed in Warsaw, Budapest, Berlin, and Prague,* Cambridge: Granta Books, 1990; as *The Magic Lantern: The Revolution of '89 Witnessed in Warsaw, Budapest, Berlin, and Prague,* New York: Random House, 1990
Hoensch, Jörg K., *Geschichte Böhmens: Von der slavischen Landnahme bis ins 20. Jahrhundert,* Munich: Beck, 1987; 2nd revised edition, 1992

MacDonald, Callum, and Jan Kaplan, *Prague in the Shadow of the Swastika: A History of the German Occupation 1939–1945,* London: Quartet Books, 1995

Měšťan, Antonín, *Geschichte der tschechischen Literatur im 19. und 20. Jahrhundert,* Cologne: Böhlau, 1984

Moníková, Libuše, *Prager Fenster: Essays,* Munich: Hanser, 1994

Mühlberger, Josef, *Geschichte der deutschen Literatur in Böhmen: 1900–1939,* Munich: Langen-Müller, 1981

Musil, Jiří, editor, *The End of Czechoslovakia,* Budapest and New York: Central European University Press, 1995

Novák, Arne, *Czech Literature,* edited by William E. Harkins, translated by Peter Kussi, Ann Arbor: Michigan Slavic Publications, 1976

Prague, New York: Knopf, 1994

Ripellino, Angelo Maria, *Praga Magica,* Torino: Einaudi, 1973; as *Magic Prague,* edited by Michael Heim, translated by David Newton Marinelli, Berkeley: University of California Press, 1994

Sayer, Derek, *The Coasts of Bohemia: A Czech History,* Princeton, New Jersey: Princeton University Press, 1998

Schamschula, Walter, *Geschichte der tschechischen Literatur,* Cologne: Böhlau, vol. 1, 1990; vol. 2, 1996

Wagenbach, Klaus, *Kafkas Prag: Ein Reiselesebuch,* Berlin: Wagenbach, 1993; as *Kafka's Prague: A Travel Reader,* translated by Shaun Whiteside, Woodstock, New York: Overlook Press, 1996

Wheaton, Bernard, and Zdeněk Kavan, *The Velvet Revolution: Czechoslovakia, 1988–1991,* Boulder, Colorado: Westview Press, 1992

Williams, Kieran, *The Prague Spring and Its Aftermath: Czechoslovak Politics, 1968–1970,* Cambridge and New York: Cambridge University Press, 1997

Wittlich, Petr, *Prague: Fin de Siècle,* translated by Maev de la Guardia, Paris: Flammarion, 1992

R

Wilhelm Raabe 1831–1910

Wilhelm Raabe's writing career spanned almost the entire era of German Realism and extended into the period of Naturalism. However, he came to be quite detached from these movements, in time virtually ignoring his German contemporaries and their literary theories while allowing his own work to be influenced by English novels, especially those of Charles Dickens (for empathic representation of the trials and sorrows of ordinary people) and William Makepeace Thackeray (for sardonic social commentary and dubiously reliable first-person narrators). While his contemporaries demanded the suppression of the narrative voice and a transparency of style, Raabe did just the opposite, complicating the narrative perspective in a variety of ways and foregrounding fictionality. His German contemporaries decided that he just did not know how to tell stories, but they admired his spirit and came to revere him not as a literary artist but as an oracle of bourgeois wisdom, forming a cult around him that served as a kind of fame from the latter part of his life into the Nazi period but then became a burden for his reputation because of its nationalist and fascist complicities. This was not, in any case, what he wanted; he strove to reconcile his distinctive narrative imagination with his ambition to be acknowledged as a major writer of the German nation, and in his own eyes, he never succeeded.

Raabe's first novel, *Die Chronik der Sperlingsgasse* (1857; The Chronicle of Sparrow Alley), a layered narrative of reminiscence, attracted enough respectful attention to encourage him to pursue a vocation of writing stories, novellas, and novels. In his first phase, much of his writing tried to accommodate the then popular modes of historical fiction and the bildungsroman; critics follow him in dismissing these works as immature, but some show promise, such as the exposé of religious fanaticism, *Der heilige Born* (1861; The Holy Spring), or the socially critical *Die Leute aus dem Walde* (1863; The People from the Forest).

In 1862 he moved from Berlin to Stuttgart in the hope of finding a livelier literary and intellectual environment. There he attempted, among numerous works, three ambitious, increasingly dark novels: *Der Hungerpastor* (1864; The Hunger-Pastor), *Abu Telfan; oder, Die Heimkehr vom Mondgebirge* (1868: *Abu Telfan; or, The Return from the Mountains of the Moon*), and *Der Schüdderump* (1870; the title is an untranslatable designation of a cart for the disposal of the corpses of plague victims). At first all were indifferently received, but *The Hunger-Pastor* gradually became his best-known work. Unfortunately, it is modeled to some extent on the best-seller of the time, Gustav Freytag's *Soll und Haben* (1855; *Debit and Credit*), and Raabe unwisely and uncharacteristically replicated Freytag's pejorative characterization of a contrasting Jewish figure, which long burdened Raabe with an unjust odium of anti-Semitism. More suggestive of Raabe's future were a little-noticed work, *Drei Federn* (1865; Three Pens), in which the same story is narrated from three points of view in six segments, and a realistic retelling of a fairy tale, *Die Hämelschen Kinder* (1863; The Pied Piper of Hamelin).

Having become both professionally and politically uncomfortable in Stuttgart, he moved to Brunswick in 1870, where he remained for the rest of his life. But even before then, he had begun to listen to his own voice rather than to those of others, and he produced a steady stream of inventive works, many with unreliable narrators or shifting perspectives. In one unusual story (*Im Siegeskranze* [1866; In the Victory Wreath]), he experimented with a female narrator who releases the madwoman in the attic against the will of her family. Among his other resources were queries of ideological assumptions, social-psychological studies, and wit ranging from kindly humor to raucous comedy. Outstanding among the late works are two pacifist and antiheroic historical novels dealing with the Seven Years' War, *Das Odfeld* (1889; The Odin Field) and *Hastenbeck* (1899), and two social novels regarded today as the pinnacle of his career: *Stopfkuchen* (1891; *Tubby Schaumann*) and *Die Akten des Vogelsangs* (1896; The Documents of the Birdsong). After the appearance of his last novel, *Hastenbeck,* Raabe asserted that he was not suited to be a 20th-century author and designated himself as "writer, ret." Privately, however, he worked on a final, obliquely autobiographical novel, *Altershausen,* a fragment published posthumously in 1911.

The task of modern criticism has been to free Raabe from the grip of the antiliterary and anti-intellectual cult that established his reputation. Although he has been little translated into English, there have been pioneering efforts from British, Canadian, and American scholars who, when they encountered him, recognized a major novelist of the Victorian age. These studies have harmonized with a substantial body of contemporary German scholarship that has transformed and enriched our understanding of his artistic achievement.

JEFFREY L. SAMMONS

Biography

Born in Eschershausen, 8 September 1831. Apprenticed to a book dealer in Magdeburg, 1849–53; audited courses at the University of Berlin, 1854–56; freelance author from 1856; grantee of the Schiller Foundation from 1886. Bavarian Order of Maximilian, 1899; honorary doctorates from the universities of Göttingen and Tübingen, 1901, and Berlin, 1910. Died in Brunswick, 15 November 1910.

Selected Works

Collections

Sämtliche Werke, edited by Karl Hoppe, et al., 25 vols., 1951–94
Werke in Auswahl, edited by Hans-Werner Peter, 9 vols., 1981
Werke in Einzelausgaben, edited by Hans-Jürgen Schrader, 10 vols., 1985

Fiction

Die Chronik der Sperlingsgasse, 1857
Ein Frühling, 1857; revised, 1872
Halb Mähr, halb mehr! Erzählungen, Skizzen, und Reime, 1859
Die Kinder von Finkenrode, 1859
Der heilige Born, 2 vols., 1861
Nach dem großen Kriege, 1861
Unseres Herrgotts Canzlei, 2 vols., 1862
Verworrenes Leben: Novellen und Skizzen, 1862
Die Leute aus dem Walde, ihre Sterne, Wege und Schicksale, 3 vols., 1863
Der Hungerpastor, 1864; as *The Hunger-Pastor,* translated by Arnold Congdon, 2 vols., 1885
Drei Federn, 1865
Ferne Stimmen, 1865; excerpt from *Die schwarze Galeere* as *How the "Black Galley" Took the "Andrea Doria,"* translated by Gertrude M. Cross, in *Great Sea Stories of All Nations,* edited by Henry Major Tomlinson, 1930
Abu Telfan; oder, Die Heimkehr vom Mondgebirge, 3 vols., 1868; as *Abu Telfan; or, The Return from the Mountains of the Moon,* translated by Sophie Delffs, 1882
Der Regenbogen: Sieben Erzählungen, 1869; *Elsa von der Tanne* as *Elsa of the Forest,* in *Elsa von der Tanne,* translated by James C. O'Flaherty and Janet K. King, 1972; *Keltische Knochen* and *Sankt Thomas* as *Celtic Bones* and *St. Thomas,* translated by John E. Woods, in *German Novellas of Realism,* vol. 2, edited by Jeffrey L. Sammons, 1989
Der Schüdderump, 3 vols., 1870
Der Dräumling, 1872
Christoph Pechlin: Eine internationale Liebesgeschichte, 2 vols., 1873
Deutscher Mondschein: Vier Erzählungen, 1873
Meister Autor; oder, Die Geschichten vom versunkenen Garten, 1874
Horacker, 1876; translated by John E. Woods, in *Wilhelm Raabe: Novels,* 1983
Krähenfelder Geschichten, 3 vols., 1879

Wunnigel, 1879
Alte Nester, 1880
Deutscher Adel, 1880
Das Horn von Wanza, 1881
Fabian und Sebastian, 1882
Prinzessin Fisch, 1883
Pfisters Mühle: Ein Sommerferienheft, 1884
Villa Schönow, 1884
Unruhige Gäste: Ein Roman aus dem Saekulum, 1886
Im alten Eisen, 1887
Der Lar: Eine Oster-, Pfingst-, Weihnachts- und Neujahrsgeschichte, 1889
Das Odfeld, 1889
Stopfkuchen: Eine See- und Mordgeschichte, 1891; as *Tubby Schaumann,* translated by Barker Fairley and John E. Woods, in *Wilhelm Raabe: Novels,* 1983
Gutmanns Reisen, 1892
Kloster Lugau, 1894
Die Akten des Vogelsangs, 1896
Hastenbeck, 1899
Altershausen, edited by Paul Wasserfall, 1911

Further Reading

Daemmrich, Horst S., *Wilhelm Raabe,* Boston: Twayne, 1981
Denkler, Horst S., *Neues über Wilhelm Raabe: Zehn Annäherungsversuche an einen verkannten Schriftsteller,* Tübingen: Niemeyer, 1988
———, *Wilhelm Raabe: Legende, Leben, Literatur,* Tübingen: Niemeyer, 1989
Di Maio, Irene Stocksieker, *The Multiple Perspective: Wilhelm Raabe's Third-Person Narratives of the Braunschweig Period,* Amsterdam: Benjamins, 1981
Fairley, Barker, *Wilhelm Raabe: An Introduction to His Novels,* Oxford: Clarendon Press, 1961; as *Wilhelm Raabe: Eine Deutung seiner Romane,* Munich: Beck, 1961
Goedsche, Charlotte L., *Narrative Structure in Wilhelm Raabe's "Die Chronik der Sperlingsgasse,"* New York: P. Lang, 1989
Helmers, Hermann, editor, *Raabe in neuer Sicht,* Stuttgart and Berlin: Kohlhammer, 1968
Lensing, Leo A., *Narrative Structure and the Reader in Wilhelm Raabe's "Im alten Eisen,"* Bern and Las Vegas, Nevada: P. Lang, 1977
Lensing, Leo A., and Hans-Werner Peter, editors, *Wilhelm Raabe: Studien zu seinem Leben und Werk,* Braunschweig: PP-Verlag, 1981
Sammons, Jeffrey L., *Wilhelm Raabe: The Fiction of the Alternative Community,* Princeton, New Jersey: Princeton University Press, 1987
———, *The Shifting Fortunes of Wilhelm Raabe: A History of Criticism as a Cautionary Tale,* Columbia, South Carolina: Camden House, 1992
Vormweg, Uwe, *Wilhelm Raabe: Die historischen Romane und Erzählungen,* Paderborn: Igel, 1993

Doron Rabinovici 1961–

Doron Rabinovici has recently emerged as a strong voice in a new scene of young Viennese Jewish writers, including Robert Schindel and Robert Menasse, whose fiction reflects themes that stem from contemporary Jewish life in Vienna. Although the topic of growing up Jewish in post-Holocaust Europe has been a relatively popular subject of literature for well over a decade, particularly among Jewish writers in Germany, Rabinovici's fiction differs not only because the language, scenes, and characters are portrayed in a specifically Viennese setting but because the background that accompanies many of his stories is bound to the circumstances of an Austrian postwar society working through its past. Although this is by far not the only subject with which his work is concerned (imaginary and often surreal themes of the criminal underworld, complex love relationships, and the effects of technology on everyday life are also well represented), it is his unsentimental and insightful characterizations of Jewish life in Vienna, portrayed in a simple, clear style and with a humorous and ironic tone, that resonate most strongly from his work.

Rabinovici's debut, *Papirnik* (1994), is a collection of ten short stories, most of which concern Jewish characters as they negotiate life, love, and religious and cultural identity in contemporary Vienna. Both the prologue and epilogue of this work concern an imaginary character, Papirnik, whose body consists solely of books. Although both stories are filled with puns and other word games (when asked to describe him, his lover, Lola, replies "Er war vielseitig" [He was multifaceted]), by the end of the book Papirnik has been burned throughout, and only Lola is left with his memory, for only she has "read" him. Set within such a framework, reminiscent undoubtedly of the book burnings by the Nazis, the remaining eight stories reflect back on a heritage of Jewish writers censored by Nazis. The tone of this first work is set from tension-filled relationships, along with bizarre and humorous cases of mistaken identity, but it also encompasses more mundane, yet never sentimental, love triangles between Jewish and non-Jewish characters. Such stories emphasize that issues of identity depend not only upon how the characters view themselves, but also on how others view them. The flexible defining boundaries between Jews and non-Jews, for example, are shown through the characters' interchangeable use of languages such as Austrian dialect, Hebrew, and Yiddish, as well as through playing upon stereotypes of appearance such as the Jewish nose. Although various issues of Austrian, Israeli, and even American national identity are raised, most of the Jewish characters have an ironic, and therefore complex, attachment to the city of Vienna. This is hinted at through references to the famous monument for the victims of the plague (*Pestsäule*) or to a favorite café located directly across from a large statue of Karl Lueger, a former mayor of Vienna well-known for his anti-Semitic remarks. *Papirnik* thus captures much of the complexity of present day anti-Semitism, for every anti-Semitic statement uttered by a Viennese character is usually followed by an equally racist response from a Jewish character, and any would-be philo-Semite sooner or later touts an underhanded, if subconscious, anti-Semitic remark.

Although presented in a lighthearted manner, Rabinovici's writing covers much of the complex and painful ground of what it means to identify with a country, a city, and a language from which one's parents had been driven. In addition to dealing with Austrians who, for the most part, seem content to adhere to the official, illusory postwar government stance that Austria was the first country to fall victim to National Socialism, Rabinovici's characters cannot escape the ghosts of their parents' pasts, who, having survived the horrors of the concentration camps, often choose to remain just as silent as their non-Jewish compatriots about the years between 1933 and 1945. Rabinovici's second work, *Suche nach M: Roman in zwölf Episoden* (1997; The Search for M: Novel in Twelve Episodes), is an even deeper exploration of Jewish cultural and religious identity, including the way in which these issues are inseparable from those of Zionism,

patriotism, and national identity in general. The story traces two generations of a Jewish family in Austria, following couples who survived concentration camps and then concentrating on the effects of their silence about the past on their children, one of whom relocates to Israel searching for criminals as a member of the secret service, while the other remains in Vienna and develops an obsessive guilt complex without having ever committed any immoral deed. Each of the 12 episodes of the book are devoted to a single character, all of whom are intertwined, by the end, in one imaginative mystery.

In addition to writing fiction, Rabinovici has also published widely in German and Austrian newspapers, using these fora to express his opinions in often controversial political essays. Born in 1961 in Tel-Aviv to parents of Eastern-European Jewish descent, one of whom survived a concentration camp, but having lived since 1964 in Vienna, Rabinovici's own background seems to mirror the lives of many of the characters in his fiction. His name usually sparks a strong reaction among those who know his work, both within and outside the members of the Jewish community of Vienna. Although he is not very well known outside German-speaking countries, in Germany and Austria his books have received some of the highest critical acclaims, including favorable reviews in newspapers such as the *Süddeutsche Zeitung*. His work is also important in light of the fact that present-day Austria, at a time when many countries in both Eastern and Western Europe are trying to define their place in a newly defined Europe, stands at the geographical midpoint of this redefinition. In addition, most recently, the Austrian government has shown signs of changing its attitude toward the official stance of silence about the past that characterized the postwar years until the mid-1990s. A possible step forward in publicly acknowledging responsibility for the past has been evidenced by the government's willingness to compensate Austrian victims of the Holocaust and to investigate former Jewish ownership of valuable artworks in Austrian museums. Such moves render the writing of Rabinovici a timely and accurate reflection of the complicated and rapidly changing atmosphere of national, religious, and cultural identity in present-day Vienna.

LISA SILVERMAN

Biography

Born in Tel Aviv, Israel, 2 December 1961. Moved with family to Vienna, Austria, 1964; studied medicine, psychology, ethnology, and history at the University of Vienna; dissertation on "Examples of Paralysis: The Reaction of Vienna's Israelite Cultural Community to National Social Persecution from 1938–1945"; founder of Vienna's Middle Eastern Peace Movement, Schalom Aschaw-Peace Now; freelance historian and journalist; publishes frequently in Austria's daily *Der Standard* and the weekly *Profil*. Curtius Foundation Prize, 1997. Currently lives in Vienna.

Selected Works

Papirnik: Stories, 1994
Suche nach M: Roman in zwölf Episoden, 1997

Further Reading

Deleuze, Gilles, and Félix Guattari, "What Is a Minor Literature?" in *Reading Kafka: Prague, Politics, and the Fin de Siècle*, edited by Mark Anderson, New York: Schocken Books, 1989
Geyer, Michael, and Miriam Hansen, "German-Jewish Memory and

National Consciousness," in *Holocaust Remembrance: The Shapes of Memory*, edited by Geoffrey H. Hartmann, Oxford and Cambridge, Massachusetts: Blackwell, 1994

Gilman, Sander L., *Jews in Today's German Culture*, Bloomington: Indiana University Press, 1995

Gilman, Sander L., and Karen Remmler, editors, *Reemerging Jewish Culture in Germany: Life and Literature since 1989*, New York: New York University Press, 1994

Konzett, Matthias, "The Politics of Recognition in Contemporary Austrian Jewish Literature," *Monatshefte* 90, no. 1 (1998)

Pauley, Bruce F., *From Prejudice to Persecution: A History of Austrian Anti-Semitism*, Chapel Hill: University of North Carolina Press, 1992

Christoph Ransmayr 1954–

In 1988, Christoph Ransmayr was enthusiastically embraced as the new superstar of German-Austrian literary writing at the world-famous Frankfurt Book Fair. His two novels, *Die Schrecken des Eises und der Finsternis* (1984; *The Terrors of Ice and Darkness*) and *Die letzte Welt* (1988; *The Last World*) were considered "blue chips" of contemporary literature and brought him fame and fortune. In 1995, Ransmayr published his third novel, *Morbus Kitahara* (*The Dog King*). His three novels are translated into all major foreign languages and can be found on many bestseller lists. In August 1997, Ransmayr gave the opening speech at the Salzburg Festival entitled "Die dritte Luft oder Eine Bühne am Meer" (1997; The Third Air or the Stage at the Sea). In the same year, his collection of essays, speeches, and short stories was published under the title *Der Weg nach Surabaya* (1997; The Way to Surabaya).

Ransmayr's work has been awarded numerous national and international honors, such as the Anton-Wildgans-Preis in 1988, the Großer Literaturpreis der Bayerischen Akademie der Schönen Künste in 1992, Franz-Kafka-Preis for Literature in 1995, the Franz-Nabl-Preis of the city of Graz in 1996, as well as the prestigious European "Prix Aristeion," a literary honor he shared with Salman Rushdie in 1996. A year later, Ransmayr received the Solothurner Literaturpreis. Furthermore, a rendition of *The Last World* was published in the distinguished "Oldenbourg Interpretations" series in 1992. This superior study inducted Ransmayr into an elite circle of authors and poets, including Goethe, Schiller, Thomas Mann, Dürrenmatt, and Böll, which prompted some scholars to speculate that Ransmayr might be considered a "new classic."

The author's first novel, *The Terrors of Ice and Darkness*, emerged from a journalistic assignment to write about the once spectacular but long-forgotten Austro-Hungarian expedition to the North Pole between 1872 to 1874 under the leadership of Captain Carl Weyprecht and the explorer and cartographer Julius Payer. Ransmayr's studies of the logbooks and pictures he unearthed stimulated him to investigate further the personal motivations of the crew for sailing into the remote areas of the Arctic waters and to study the traumatic experiences of the expedition members. His novel seems to bring the dramatic voyage back to life, yet it is an intriguing blend of reality and fiction. Ransmayr skillfully interweaves three strands of narratives: the factual accounts of the Austro-Hungarian Weyprecht/Payer expedition; the writings of the fictional character, Josef Mazzini, a Viennese eccentric of Italian descent who wants to relive the experience of exploring the world of ice and darkness; and the experiences of the first-person narrator who reconstructs Mazzini's journey to the Arctic Circle by examining his sketches and diary entries in an attempt to find some answers to his traceless disappearance on Spitsbergen, a group of ice-covered islands north of Norway. The author conjoins his narrative and the narrator's own reflections about the age of exploration and discovery with pieces of factual information, such as portraits of the members of the Austro-Hungarian expedition, excerpts from their diaries and logbooks, and old lithographs of the polar world. In addition, the reader finds encyclopedic information about previous adventures and quotes from commentaries on these heroic endeavors. Thus, Ransmayr is able to shed light on the driving ambition to venture into uncharted territories while defying death and destruction.

The Last World, like Ransmayr's first novel, was a commissioned work. The author was asked to write a prose translation of Ovid's *Metamorphosis*. However, Ransmayr's novel takes on a form of its own. The ancient Ovidian text functions as its paradigm and source, and provides the temporal and spatial realm for the plot. The palimpsest structure of Ransmayr's *Die letzte Welt* determines the relationship of both texts to each other. The central figure in Ransmayr's novel is Cotta, a senator and respected citizen of Rome, and a former friend of Publius Ovidius Naso, who had been expelled from Rome to live in exile. Naso had been gone for 11 years, and rumors of his death reached the gates of Rome. Cotta, in order to find the truth, travels to the gray iron town of Tomi on the Black Sea, which lies at the outskirts of ancient civilization. Cotta's journey repeats Naso's experiences: the transformation of identity, the metamorphosis of truth into illusion, of reality into myth. Like Cotta, the reader is continually confronted with elements of temporal and spatial *Verfremdung* (alienation) such as the rusty bus stop in Tomi, or the trucks rolling through the town, the microphone, the binoculars, and names of places such as Accademia Dante. Even though both novels hail the arts and the world of myths, Ovid's text leads the reader towards a world of enlightenment in which apocalyptic visions of the past cannot endanger the present time.

Ransmayr's novel, on the other hand, ends with the mythical image of Cotta's ascent of Mount Olympus, the symbol of the cradle of western civilization.

Ransmayr's third novel, *The Dog King,* projects a fantastic and cruel world of deindustrialized Germany-Austria as the Allies' punishment for Germany's crimes committed against humanity during World War II. The land and its people are condemned to a barbaric agrarian and barter culture saturated with fear and feelings of guilt. The novel displays another world of mythic intensity. Here, Ransmayr intertwines Greek and Germanic mythology and postwar American cultural icons with fragments of the devastating historical reality of the war and the fictional lives of Ambras, the Dog King; of Bering, the blacksmith and bodyguard who suffers from the rare eye disease "Morbus Kitahara," which gradually darkens the vision; and of Lily, the amazon huntress who can kill and heal.

Ransmayr's novels are studies of loneliness and human suffering. His characters are bleeding; they lick their wounds. They build "walls" for protection and thus, create empty and lonesome spaces. They search for happiness but find only desolation and barrenness. Ransmayr's literature can be read as western *Zivilisationskritik.* His novels display harsh criticism of post–World War II civilization with its unrelenting machinery of progress, its ferocious materialistic consumption, and its ruthless struggle for success, recognition, and dominance. Nevertheless, the author rejects the idea that literature could settle the score for the moral failures of today's society.

Scholars are divided in their opinions whether Ransmayr's novels can or should be read as examples of postmodern writing—where sign leads to sign but not to exhaustive signification. Nevertheless, Ransmayr's phenomenal success does seem to indicate that the author has touched the nerve of our time. Our preoccupation with past events, the thematizing of apocalyptic destruction, and our preference for the refined and cultured have been prevalent during the past decade. His literature reflects our *zeitgeist,* and thus Ransmayr's novels convey a multitude of ideas for cultural, anthropological, philosophical, and text-theoretical thought and interpretations.

MARGARETE LAMB-FAFFELBERGER

Biography

Born in Wels, Austria, 20 March 1954. Studied philosophy and ethnology at the University of Vienna, 1972–78; cultural editor of the monthly *Monatszeitschrift,* 1978–82; freelance contributor to various journals, such as *Transatlantik, Merian,* and *Geo;* full-time writer since 1982. Großer Literaturpreis der Bayerischen Akademie der Schönen Künste, 1992; Kafka Prize, 1995; Europäischer Literaturpreis "Prix Aristeion," 1996; his novel *Die letzte Welt,* 1988, became an international bestseller. Currently lives in Dublin, Ireland.

Selected Works

Novels and Essay Collections

Strahlender Untergang, 1982
Die Schrecken des Eises und der Finsternis, 1984; as *The Terrors of Ice and Darkness,* translated by John E. Woods, 1991
Im blinden Winkel: Nachrichten aus Mitteleuropa, 1985
Die letzte Welt, 1988; as *The Last World,* translated by John E. Woods, 1990
Morbus Kitahara, 1995; as *The Dog King,* translated by John E. Woods, 1997
Der Weg nach Surabaya, 1997
Die dritte Luft; oder, Eine Bühne am Meer: Rede zur Eröffnung der Salzburger Festspiele, 1997

Further Reading

Bartsch, Kurt, "Dialog mit Antike und Mythos: Christoph Ransmayrs Ovid-Roman *Die letzte Welt,*" *Modern Austrian Literature* 23, nos. 3–4 (1990)
Epple, Thomas, *Christoph Ransmayr, Die letzte Welt: Interpretation,* Munich: Oldenbourg, 1992
Gehlhoff, Esther Felicitas, *Wirklichkeit hat ihren eigenen Ort: Lesarten und Aspekte zum Verständnis des Romans Die letzte Welt von Christoph Ransmayr,* Paderborn: Schöningh, 1999
Glei, Reinhold, "Ovid in den Zeiten der Postmoderne: Bemerkungen zu Christoph Ransmayrs Roman *Die letzte Welt,*" *Poetica: Zeitschrift für Sprach-und Literaturwissenschaft* 26, nos. 3–4 (1994)
Habers, Henk, "Die Erfindung der Wirklichkeit: Zu Christoph Ransmayrs *Die letzte Welt,*" *German Quarterly* 67, no. 1 (1994)
Kiel, Martin, *Nexus: Postmoderne Mythenbilder—Vexierbilder zwischen Spiel und Erkenntnis: Mit einem Kommentar zu Christoph Ransmayrs "Die letzte Welt,"* Frankfurt and New York: Lang, 1996
Lamb-Faffelberger, Margarete, "Christoph Ransmayr's *Die Schrecken des Eises und der Finsternis:* Interweaving Fact and Fiction into a Postmodern Narrative," in *Modern Austrian Literature: Interpretations and Insights,* edited by Paul Dvorak, Riverside, California: Ariadne Press, 1999
Landa, Jutta, "Fractured Vision in Christoph Ransmayr's *Morbus Kitahara,*" *German Quarterly* 71, no. 2 (1998)
Scheck, Ulrich, "Katastrophen und Texte: Zu Christoph Ransmayrs *Die Schrecken des Eises und der Finsternis und Die letzte Welt,*" in *Hinter dem schwarzen Vorhang: Die Katastrophe und die epische Tradition: Festschrift für Antony Riley,* edited by Friedrich Gaede, Patrick O'Neill, and Ulrich Scheck, Tübingen: Francke, 1994

Realism

Historically, German Realism is associated with the work of writers and artists in German-speaking cultures from the beginnings of the industrial capitalism in the 1840s to the achievement of the "small German solution" (Prussian leadership of a united Germany, excluding Austria and the Habsburg Empire) to the German problem in 1871 and the resultant *Gründerzeit* of the 1880s and 1890s. Initially seen as a European-wide reaction to Romanticism, realism is now commonly thought to describe literary and other artistic productions that conveyed to readers or viewers a mimetic reproduction of social realities, in some cases so that such realities might be better understood and perhaps changed. Realism also was closely connected to social undertakings that sought to further the cause of the German middle class in its endeavor to wrest control of the means of production from the aristocratic and patrician classes and to establish a bourgeois organization of society and culture. Socialist Realism, the official aesthetic of Soviet and East European communist cultures, is a derivative of this earlier European movement.

The "German form of realism" (Sagarra) is generally thought to have differed from other European realisms by virtue of the delayed German relationship to the emergence of the capitalist means of production in Europe. Michael Winkler, however, points out:

> In historical terms, however, and as a movement, poetic r[ealism] is concomitant with the full emergence of bourgeois culture by 1840. In German countries, this development was given a characteristic turn by the fact that the revolutions of 1848 were unsuccessful. They mark a turning-point also for literature and introduce the new era of *poetischer Realismus* (1849–70).

Realism, in German countries, has thus become associated with theories of German particularity that have been contradicted in the past several decades by numerous scholars (e.g., El, Hull) who have persuasively demonstrated the full accession of German society and culture to its European context, with numerous local and regional distinctions but without any German *Sonderweg* (Germany's different development from other European countries).

The term *poetic realism* is most associated with several major writers of the German form of realism between 1840 and 1890, including several prominent writers from what is also referred to in Austria and other southern German-speaking areas as the Biedermeier period, which describes the decades between the Congress of Vienna (1815) and the revolutions of 1831 and 1848. Poetic realism suggests a flight into the aesthetic rather than the political when the irreversible nature of capitalist forms of social relations was finally acknowledged. The novella, the favorite form of the poetic realists, ensured the isolation of the narrative's ideological thrust from direct engagement or interaction with the reader by its exquisitely complex form of the story within a story and its reliance on consummate artistic realization. Scholars of German literature have usually relied on works by the poetic rather than the social realists in shaping the canon of German literature, thereby contributing to the perception of German realist writing as generally nonpolitical and as embracing a version of the *Sonderweg* theory of German cultural and political development.

Among the more socially interventionist writers, however, Gustav Freytag's (1816–95) novel *Soll und Haben* (1855; *Debit and Credit*) depicts the economic processes by which the feudal and patrician classes and their ownership of the means of production were dispossessed by the new bourgeois class and its adherents. Typical, too, of some of the period's thinking was the novel's inveterate anti-Semitism, which associates the entrepreneurial class with Jews, linking the villains of Christian ideology from the German and European Middle Ages to the modern

fears of economic ruin. Friedrich Spielhagen's (1829–1911) works, by contrast, especially the great novels of bourgeois liberalism such as *Problematische Naturen* (1861–62; *Problematic Characters*) and *Hammer und Amboß* (1869; *Hammer and Anvil*), engage in a literary political action that was rare in German artistic life. In his powerful diatribes against Bismarck as the representative of the forces that combined the old-fashioned feudal aristocracy with the techno-greed of the newly rich middle class, Spielhagen, until the end of his life a very successful and influential writer and liberal intellectual, set the tone for what in German countries might have become a public literary art for the middle classes, one that combined literature with social engagement. Unread nowadays in large part due to the highly mannered writing style and the seeming naïveté of his psychological characterizations, his works were widely acclaimed in their time and contributed to the rise of the social democratic movement within both the liberal bourgeoisie and the highly literate German working classes.

Wilhelm Raabe's (1831–1910) novels and stories achieved a greater degree of literary fame in the aftermath of their writer's lifetime. His first published work, *Die Chronik der Sperlingsgasse* (1857; *The Chronicle of Sperling Alley*), documents the political, social, and economic conditions of urban life in Prussia's capital, Berlin, while at the same time indulging in the sort of nostalgia for precapitalist community formation that is found in Charles Dickens's (1812–70) *A Christmas Carol* (1843). Raabe's subsequent work found less receptive audiences even as his art reached more and more mature levels. In *Der Hungerpastor* (1864; *The Famine Pastor*), subsequent works such as *Abu Tefan; oder, Die Heimkehr vom Mondgebirg*e (1868; *Abu Telfan; or, The Return from the Mountains of the Moon*), and his later work *Stopfkuchen: Eine See- und Mordgeschichte* (1891; *Stopfkuchen: A Tale of the Sea and of Murder*), he focuses instead on the effects of the new economic relations upon the social relations among ordinary middle-class people. His writing is subtle, often very humorous, and conveys an elegiac sense of loss with an appreciation of individual character and psychology.

In this respect, his work resembles that of the Swiss writer Gottfried Keller (1819–90), whose formative years were spent in Berlin, where he met and thereafter remained on close terms with both Paul Heyse (1830–1914) and Theodor Storm (1817–88). Keller's best-known works are his stories *Die Leute von Seldwyla* (1856–74; *Seldwyla Stories*), in which he depicts the social relations of rural and small-town residents, often with biting irony, as in *Die Drei Gerechten Kammacher* (1856; *The Three Honest Combmakers*), or with sentimentality combined with bitter psychological realism, as in his best-known work, *Romeo und Julia auf dem Dorfe* (1856; *A Village Romeo and Juliet*). His novel *Der grüne Heinrich* (1853–55; *Green Henry*) is one of the best examples of German Realism's attempts to combine the older literary form of the bildungsroman with the subject of bourgeois social and economic relations.

The German writer, Theodor Storm, who, similar to Stifter and Keller, was a civil servant as well as a writer, achieved instant success with his first published short story or novella, *Immensee* (1849). His later works, especially *Der Schimmelreiter* (1888; *The Rider on the White Horse*), have secured for him a lasting place in the German and European literary canons. Within German Realism, he has a reputation as a writer who well understood the ruinous effect of capitalism on the social relations of the economically disadvantaged populations of Germany's nonurban, nonbourgeois population.

The Austrian writer Adalbert Stifter (1805–68) began his literary career relatively late in life, having first been a landscape artist and a private tutor to the wealthy nobles of pre-1848 Vienna. His most famous writings are the cycle of stories that were collected (and extensively reworked from their original journal publications) under the title *Bunte Steine* (1853; *Colored Stones*). Stifter's epic work *Der Nachsommer* (1857; *Indian Summer*) is a demonstration of the particular interest shared by many of the poetic realists concerning the combination of the aesthetic with the ethical import of literature; this interest helped to create a reputation for German literature well into the 20th century as primarily philosophical rather than narratological in intention.

While the novels of Theodor Fontane (1819–98) comprise the last major texts of German Realism that look more often backward than forward into history and social relations, they are also read for their more English or French narrative focus. Unlike the works of Keller, Storm, or Stifter, Fontane's writings, which he began to compose only after a long career as a journalist, emphasize the psychology of the ruling class and the new middle class rather than the latter's aesthetic aspirations. From his early novel of Prussian aristocratic manners, *Schach von Wuthenow* (1883), to his German novel of adultery, *Effie Briest* (1895), and his last works on contemporary Prussian-German life in the new capital of Germany, Berlin, *Die Poggenpuhls* (1896) and *Der Stechlin* (1899), Fontane's writings emphasize the narrative style of storytelling and character development, which differentiates his work from the aesthetic and ethical concerns of his realist precursors.

The Swiss writer Conrad Ferdinand Meyer (1825–98), whose novella *Der Heilige* (1880; *The Saint*) established his literary reputation, dealt with historical themes. He presents works in which the writer's carefully maintained narrative objectivity allows an apparently dispassionately critical evaluation of personal psychologies and historical events. Subsequent novellas, his preferred literary form, include *Die Hochzeit des Mönchs* (1884; *The Monk's Marriage*), *Die Versuchung des Pescara* (1887; *The Temptation of Pescara*), and *Angela Borgia* (1891). In all of these works, a historical theme combines with narrative distance to allow a strict framework within which moral and ethical issues can be examined.

Other important writers associated in German-speaking culture with realism were Fritz Reuter (1810–74), Klaus Groth (1819–99), who wrote in the *Plattdeutsch* or Northern German regional dialectic, Emanuel Geibel (1815–84), and Paul Heyse (1830–1914), whose novella *L'Arrabiata* (1855) achieved widespread popularity. Other important writers include Otto Ludwig (1813–15) and Willibald Alexis (1798–1871), whose historical novel *Die Hosen des Herrn von Bredow* (1846–48; *The Trousers of Milord Bredow*) treated Brandenburg-Prussian historical themes with satire and humor. Friedrich Hebbel (1813–63) was the most famous of the mid-19th-century German dramatists, and in works such as *Judith* (1840), *Maria Magdalena* (1844), *Herodes und Mariamne* (1850), and *Agnes Bernauer* (1852), he dealt with biblical and epic themes of German history in which moral and political predicaments of his own time, including the roles of social class and women, were examined. Hebbel, an exception to the prose domination of the German Realist era, was undoubtedly the most prominent dramatic author of mid-19th-century Germany. Both Eduard Mörike and Annette von Droste-Hülshoff are also considered to be among the earliest and most poetic of the German Realist writers. The Austrian writer Maria von Ebner-Eschenbach is also one of the most interesting of the period's authors of prose fiction.

With the exception of the more socially engaged work of Freytag and Spielhagen or critics of German Realist writing such as Karl Marx, German-language authors in the period also rarely emulated the artistic self-confidence about the role of the writer and artist in capitalist society that characterizes English literature by Dickens and others. Keller's ironic portrayals of the psychology of individuals caught up in a community of greed and economic transformation is rarely tempered by the deus ex machina or "happy endings" of Dickens's most successful novels.

But the production of literature in this first great epoch of capitalist dominance of economic and social relations was in Germany rapidly overcome by those economic relations. Prose works, which comprise virtually the entire corpus of realist literature, were usually serialized initially in journals and later published as separate volumes. Authors began to play a role as producers of commodities for a particular market niche, which interested those who sought control of the market and of the ideology of citizens or subjects of capitalist state formations. The split between the literary community and the larger civil society influenced the organization of the canon of German-language literature in the 19th and 20th centuries.

Scholars discern a precarious situation for German-language writers responding to this commodification of artistic production, particularly literary production. Most of what are now considered to be the great exponents of German literary realism were decidedly unsuccessful in the expanding arena of capitalist literary relations, especially in their later and more mature works. Several such as Spielhagen and, later, Fontane, however, did achieve popular literary fame and even reaped some financial rewards from their art.

Within this dichotomous realism existed two literary cultures, both supported by the new forms of literary and artistic production. The one was socially engaged, and the other was reflective or nostalgic, conveying already that elegiac sense of loss that, in subsequent literary manifestations following World War II, would become typical of European and even of some U.S. high culture. In the selection of the canon of German Realist writing, the critics and scholars responsible for the process have regularly opted to include the poetic realists rather than the more critical social realists, but this choice has given further credibility to critics who challenge theories of German particularism.

Similar to other forms of European realism, German Realism is a literary articulation of writers' experiences of the new economic, social, and cultural relations of capitalism. It differs from French, English, Russian, and U.S. realism only in its greater degree of emphasis on the aesthetic and ethical implications of the social changes on society and, particularly, on literature and art. More than the other European forms of this movement, German Realism expresses the perilous position of words and texts in the coming pancommodification of all production, including literary production.

DUNCAN SMITH

See also Naturalism; Socialist Realism

Further Reading

Bernd, Clifford A., *German Poetic Realism,* Boston: Twayne, 1980

Boyle, Nicholas, and Martin Swales, *Realism in European Literature,* Cambridge: Cambridge University Press, 1986

Blackbourn, David, and Geoff Eley, *The Peculiarities of German History: Bourgeois Society and Politics in Nineteenth-Century Germany,* Oxford and New York: Oxford University Press, 1984

Demetz, Peter, *Marx, Engels, und die Dichter,* Stuttgart: Deutsche Verlags-Anstalt, 1959; as *Marx, Engels, and the Poets: Origins of Marxist Literary Criticism,* Chicago: University of Chicago Press, 1967

Holub, Robert, *Reflections on Realism: Paradox, Norm, and Ideology in Nineteenth-Century German Prose,* Detroit, Michigan: Wayne State University Press, 1991

Hull, Isabel V., *Sexuality, State, and Civil Society in Germany, 1700–1815,* Ithaca, New York and London: Cornell University Press, 1996

Lukács, Georg, *Deutsche Realisten des 19. Jahrhunderts,* Bern: Francke, 1951; as *German Realists in the Nineteenth Century,* Cambridge, Massachusetts: MIT Press, 1993

Mullen, Inga E., *German Realism in the United States: The American Reception of Meyer, Storm, Raabe, Keller, and Fontane,* New York: Lang, 1988

Nochlin, Linda, *Realism,* New York: Penguin, 1971

Sagarra, Eda, *Tradition and Revolution: German Literature and Society, 1830–1890,* New York: Basic Books, 1971

Sammons, Jeffrey L., editor, *German Novellas of Realism,* The German Library, vol. 37–38, New York: Continuum, 1988–89

Silz, Walter, *Realism and Reality: Studies in the German Novelle of Poetic Realism,* Chapel Hill: University of North Carolina Press, 1954; New York: AMS Press, 1979

Stern, J.P., *Re-Interpretations: Seven Studies in Nineteenth-Century German Literature,* New York: Basic Books, and London: Thames and Hudson, 1964

———, *On Realism,* London and Boston: Routledge and Kegan Paul, 1973

Swales, Martin, *Studies of German Prose Fiction in the Age of European Realism,* Studies in German Language and Literature, vol. 16, Lewiston, New York: Mellen Press, 1995

———, *Epochenbuch Realismus: Romane und Erzählungen, Grundlagen der Germanistik,* edited by Werner Besch and Hartmut Steinecke, vol. 32, Berlin: Schmidt, 1997

Winkler, Michael, "Realism," in *The New Princeton Encyclopedia of Poetry and Poetics,* edited by Alex Preminger and T.V.F. Brogan, Princeton, New Jersey: Princeton University Press, 1993

Regensburg, Konrad von, *see* Konrad von Regensburg

Gerlind Reinshagen 1926–

Gerlind Reinshagen is one of the first women dramatists who gained a foothold on the German stage after World War II. Her success is remarkable because even now not many women writers see their plays staged in German-speaking countries. In the early 1970s, the women's movement drew attention to other overlooked writers as well, and the works of dramatists such as Marieluise Fleißer and Else Lasker-Schüler, who had written already in the first part of the 20th century, were rediscovered and staged.

Most of Reinshagen's plays display a crass realism but at the same time establish a contrast and depth by switching to Expressionist language and surreal images. Without moralizing, she draws attention to social and cultural problems of the post–World War II period. Many of her plays critically explore a society dominated by the *Wirtschaftswunder* (economic miracle), and some of them probe uniquely into the fascist past. The existential displacement of individual people and their attempts to cope with an environment that no longer provides security are the fabrics that stimulated interest for her plays on stage. The writer later on (from the late 1980s) began to write prose as well, and she published a considerable number of novels that are critically acclaimed for their stylistic achievements and for the exposure of submerged realities. Her roots as a writer are connected with the literary movement of the late 1960s that reacted against political and societal tendencies in Germany. The unkept promises of this postwar era lend a melancholy to all her writings.

Reinshagen's first theater play, *Doppelkopf* (1968; Double Head), which includes strong criticism of a system that promotes capitalist profiteering and the exploitation of people who do not participate in the new materialistic trend, drew the attention of the notable theater director Claus Peyman, who staged the play the same year. Other plays touch on controversial themes that had not been broached on stage previously: for instance, fascist tendencies in everyday life are made visible through family behavior in a first play of a trilogy, *Sonntagskinder* (1982; Sunday's Children). In the course of the trilogy (*Sonntagskinder, Frühlingsfest* [Spring Celebration], *Tanz Marie* [Dance Marie]), the author traces the lives of the members of a middle-class family from 1939 until the 1980s. She pursues the consequences of World War II, showing the protagonists distancing themselves from normal society and even their desperate route to suicide. Then, long before it became fashionable, *Himmel und Erde* (1974; Heaven and Earth) thematizes cancer. Similarly remarkable is Reinshagen's avant-garde style in her virtually postmodern play, *Leben und Tod der Marilyn Monroe* (1971; Life and Death of Marilyn Monroe), in which she stages the body politics and the construction of a myth through the example of a multiple Marilyn Monroe. The play is an anatomy of the commodity woman when it exists within the power circle of the male gaze. In this early play she experiments with a new version of the Greek chorus, which she increasingly uses later in order to insert the contradictory voice of the people. Reinshagen's plays attempt to allow the individual human being a utopia within an inhuman environment to help them survive. *Die fremde Tochter* (1988; The Estranged Daughter) and *Die Feuerblume* (1988; Fire Flower) tackle issues regarding demagoguery and the end of the world through atomic war.

In numerous essays and interviews, as well as in her plays *Die Clownin* (1985; The Female Clown) and *Kann das Theater noch aus der Rolle fallen? oder, Die halbwegs emanzipierte Mariann* (1972; Can the Theater Transcend Its Role? or, The Partially Emancipated Mariann), the author addresses the question of art and the viability of theater as a location for communal experience. For her, the theater is to be a house of language. The text should remain the basis of the stage rather than those visual extremes presented by the Regisseur Theater (director's theater) in vogue in Germany even now, where directors tend to impart personal stamps upon plays through nonverbal elements and outrageous distortions.

A clear continuity can be observed in Reinshagen's works. Some of her novels, which she published in the 1980s, include figures from earlier plays and prose, although in slightly different configuration. With a rhythmically controlled, but strong and unaffected language, known primarily from her plays, she is able to provide subtle contours to previously unarticulated border areas of human experience. She realizes in her novels what she recognizes as the basis of her writing: stories must be kept alive if mankind is to exist in the future—*narramus fabulas, ergo sumus* (we tell tales, therefore we exist). Reinshagen's dramatic talent is evident even in her novels. For instance, in *Jäger am Rand der Nacht* (1993; Hunter at the Margins of Night) a list of characters stands at the beginning, and all of the novels employ extended dialogues and monologues. Both in her plays and in her novels, the protagonists experience existential crises. In her novel *Die flüchtige Braut* (1984; The Evasive Bride), the narrator reflects on his life and says on the first page: "[Es] war . . . ihm vorgekommen, als sei er plötzlich aus seinem eigenen Leben, seiner Existenz herausgetreten" (It seemed to him as if he had stepped out of his own life, his own existence). In *Rovinato; oder, Die Seele des Geschäfts* (1981; Rovinato; or, The Soul of the Business), she focuses on lower-level employees of the business world, as she had already done in her play *Prinz Eisenherz* (1982; Prince Iron Heart). This is an unusual picaresque novel since the protagonist does his roving mainly in or close to the office building. Despite her adherence to utopian thinking, most of Reinshagen's stories end disastrously. In her novel *Am großen Stern* (1996; At the Big Star), a middle-aged single man is attempting to educate a homeless 12-year-old girl he adopts from Russia. The traditional studies of the great writers and thinkers prescribed to the child, however, fail due to the daily realities of the modern city, including emotional, exotic, erotic entanglements, which mix and contribute to a catastrophic end. A new novel, including a series of modern "Göttergespräche" (dialogues with gods), will be published in 2000.

In scholarly discussion, Gerlind Reinshagen is best known for her plays. German and British stages continue to show her work. A new play, *Die Grüne Tür: Medea bleibt* (The Green Door: Medea Stays Put), had its world premiere in Dresden in February 1999.

HELGA W. KRAFT

Biography

Born in Königsberg (then Prussia), 10 May 1926. Staatsexamen (equivalent of master's degree) in pharmacy, University of Brunswick, 1949; worked in pharmacy for a number of years; studied at the Hochschule der Künste, Berlin, 1953, 1956; worked on radio plays, 1956–1966; playwright and novelist, 1966–. Currently lives in Berlin.

Selected Works

Collections

Gesammelte Stücke (includes *Doppelkopf, Leben und Tod der Marilyn Monroe, Kann das Theater noch aus seiner Rolle fallen; oder, Die halbwegs emanzipierte Mariann, Himmel und Erde, Sonntagskinder, Das Frühlingsfest, Tanz, Marie!, Eisenherz, Die Clownin*), 1986
Drei Wünsche frei. Chorische Stücke (includes, in addition to some plays published in *Gesammelte Stücke, Feuerblume, Die fremde Tochter, Drei Wünsche frei*), 1993
Die grüne Tür. Chorische Stücke (includes, in addition to some plays published in *Gesammelte Stücke, Die grüne Tür. Medea bleibt*), 1999

Plays

Die Clownin, 1985
Tanz Marie! 1987
Die Feuerblume, 1988
Drei Wünsche frei. Chorische Stücke, 1992
Die grüne Tür: Medea bleibt, 1998

Novels

Rovinato; oder, Die Seele des Geschäfts, 1981
Zwölf Nächte, 1989
Die flüchtige Braut, 1984
Jäger am Rand der Nacht, 1993
Am großen Stern, 1996

Further Reading

Bossinade, Johanna, "Haus und Front: Bilder des Faschismus in der Literatur von Exil und Gegenwartsautorinnen, Am Beispiel Anna Seghers, Irmgard Keun, Christa Wolf, und Gerlind Reinshagen," *Neophilologus* 70, no. 93 (1986)

Herzog, Madeleine, *Ich bin-nicht ich: Subjektivität, Gesellschaft, und Geschlechterordnung in Gerlind Reinshagens dramatischen Werk*, Bielefeld: Aisthesis, 1995

Kraft, Helga, *Ein Haus aus Sprache: Dramatikerinnen und das andere Theater*, Stuttgart: Metzler, 1996

Reinshagen, Gerlind, "Utopian Subjectivism," in *Exiles, Eccentrics, Activists: Women in Contemporary Theater*, edited by Katrin Sieg, Ann Arbor: University of Michigan Press, 1994

Sieg, Katrin, "The Representation of Fascism in Gerlind Reinshagen's *Sunday's Children*," *Theatre Studies* 31, no. 44 (1991)

Reiseliteratur *see* Travel Literature

Religion and Literature

All Western literatures have been greatly influenced by a strong religious tradition, but none more so than German literature. Throughout the Middle Ages and through the Renaissance and the Enlightenment into the modern age, German writers reflected the religious triumphs and tensions of their day. Most of the writings by German speakers of the first millennium consciously promote Christian beliefs and practices. Most of the writings throughout the second millennium struggle with the Judeo-Christian tradition, whether to explore some of its inner conflicts or to spring out of its confines into a world without God, without faith, and with only humankind and its achievements to believe in. It remains to be seen whether the third millennium will be any different, but it is more than likely that German literature will continue to focus, as ever, on humankind's place in the universe, on moral and personal issues, and on the individual human being's search for something beyond the material world.

From the beginning of recorded German history, the Christian Church was an overwhelming presence, and the monks and priests were the mediators of all learning. Their ideas, concerns, and Christian literary models dominated all writing activities. The indigenous pre-Christian artistic tradition was passed on in oral form. All we have left is a collection of tantalizing fragments: runes and charms and old legends of Nordic and Celtic gods. Old Norse and Old English texts carry references to this, and these shadows are picked up and reworked by medieval German authors. The tales of the Nibelungen in all their various versions remind us of a distant barbarian world of epic warriors and capricious gods, quite similar in tone to the works of the great Greek and Latin classical epic poets. Magic was very much a part of this world, and Celtic influences can be discerned too in the reverence for trees and wells.

The first flowering of German literature started around the year 800, when the great emperor Charlemagne was crowned and the early missionaries had established a flourishing network of monasteries throughout his realm. The monasteries took care of preparing, storing, and copying the favorite manuscripts of the day and notably also the education of the young. The choice of early learning materials heavily influenced the thought processes of future lords, diplomats, merchants, and teachers. And so it was that the forms and imagery of the Psalms, the Liturgy, and the Gospels were imprinted on German language and culture. In this early period almost everything can be categorized as Christian writing, and there is a wealth of material intended for use in churches, such as hymns, homilies, and paraphrases, modeled on Latin forms. Favorite literary themes of this age are saints' lives or tales of adventure recounted with a strong undercurrent of Christian doctrine. The purpose of these earliest works was to promote the faith—to teach basic doctrines, encourage good behavior, and further the work of the Church. Even when the content of the stories is secular or even tends toward the early Germanic pantheistic worldview, a heavy overlay of Christian morality makes sure that the values of the Church are promoted.

As more writers turned to German rather than the formal Latin of their sacred texts, they developed literary forms that reflected their Christianized sensibility. The second great flowering in German literature was the period of the High Middle Ages, from about 1100, when warring heroes gave way to the gentler tones of Minnesang or the lyrical beauty of Arthurian romance. The knight's loyal service to king and country or the poet's wooing of a noble lady owes much to Christian ideas of worship and devotion. German states were surrounded on all sides by other developing countries, and German literature borrowed freely from its neighbors, whether from the Irish and British in the ninth century or from the French in later eras. The 12th century was a time of large-scale crusades to the Holy Land, and issues such as the baron's need for stirring songs to entertain the troops are often found in both long and short pieces of this period. The moral code in the romances is reflected in allegorical or symbolic language so that the unlettered audience can follow the plot and understand the point of the story. This literary skill of telling a surface story with a deeper meaning behind it is inspired by the teaching methods of the Old Testament and the Gospels. It is a basic principle of Christian doctrine that the sacred texts can be interpreted to reveal hidden moral and spiritual messages. Miraculous events occur, mythical creatures such as unicorns and dragons appear, and authors weave Christian elements into the story. Wolfram von Eschenbach's *Parzival* (ca. 1210; *Parsifal*) presents the whole chivalric code of medieval German feudal society, and the focus of all the action is a supposed Christian relic called the Holy Grail. The hero in such tales is depicted as a pilgrim on the road to heaven or a soldier in a holy war. The knight's clothing or armor was a clue to his role in the story, just as in a modern Western the good guy wears a white hat and the bad guy a black one, and of course the readers and listeners are supposed to identify with the good characters.

By the middle of the 15th century, a certain amount of prosperity and the emergence of ever-larger towns created a literate middle class that was eager for reading material and able to debate some of the current political, social, and religious issues of their time. It was a practical advance, however, that changed forever the Church's position of control over the production of written materials, namely, the invention of the printing press. Martin Luther (1483–1546) translated the Bible, and like the King James Version in England, this feat gave to the German language a new coherence. Its spelling became the standard for High German, and its poetic rhythms imprinted themselves on poets and authors across German-speaking areas. However, the same cannot be said for Martin Luther's own writings. The waves of Reformation and Counter Reformation were strongest of all in German-speaking countries, and the 16th century brought a spate of extremely bitter polemic texts. The dramas and pamphlets of this period are thinly disguised attacks on the doctrines or even the leading personalities of the opposite camp. Hans Sachs (1494–1576) is known for his *Fastnachtsspiele* (*Shrovetide Plays*), and this was an especially popular dramatic form, although they had moved on from their original purpose as overtly Christian festivals to become broader and more literary in their approach. They were designed to appeal to a diverse audience, some of whom would have little or no education. The themes are ostensibly religious, including terrifying visions of hell and biting satirical portraits of some sin or other, but the real struggle is for power over the minds of men and women and a political desire to unite communities under a common banner. Modern community drama and television farces owe much to this tradition.

In contrast to this rather public religiosity is also a strand of mystical writing that draws the reader inward to a more personal religious experience. We find this in medieval authors such as Hildegard von Bingen (1098–1179) and Meister Eckhart (ca. 1260–1328), but in later years this impulse takes on a more philosophical and less overtly Christian flavor. Writers of the 17th century, such as Andreas Gryphius (1616–64) and Angelus Silesius (1624–77), adopt a rather wordy approach, but they present undogmatic homilies and allegories in quite complex literary patterns. Their appeal to the inner self in reflective poetry owes much to the early humanists (Erasmus, 1466–1536), but this Baroque period also continues the tradition of interminable dramas with heavy moral undertones. One author, Hans Jakob Christoffel von Grimmelshausen (1622–76), wrote a highly influential narrative called *Abentheurliche Simplicissimus* (1668; *The Adventurous Simplicissimus*), which used a novelistic approach to illustrate the interplay of deeply religious ideas in the life of its main character. This was an early example of a writer who used religious ideas as part of a more complex worldview, presenting fiction as a way of allowing the individual reader to work through personal, moral, and religious issues.

A further and, some would say, the greatest flowering of German literature occurs in the 18th century. The English author E.M. Butler noted a deep-seated impulse in German literature that she traced to this period. In 1935 she wrote, "For the Germans cherish a hopeless passion for the absolute, under whatever name and whatever guise they imagine it." At the beginning of the century, the discovery and transportation to Western Europe of large quantities of classical Greek artifacts encouraged a renewed enthusiasm for classical ideas. During this period, writers reflected on the meaning of life, on beauty, on art, and on human nature, all in a deeply philosophical mode. Christian ideas are infused with a new kind of rationalism, and writers struggle to work out in their characters the great unanswered questions of existence. The middle part of the century, from about 1748 until 1788, is given the name Sturm und Drang (Storm and Stress), and it produced German literature's greatest figure: Johann Wolfgang von Goethe (1749–1832). It was a time when extremes were fashionable and writers experimented with new forms and wild emotions. Goethe himself made great swings from pantheistic longings imitating Greek poetry to rationalist philosophy, high drama, and narrative fiction. Focus returned to the individual and his pilgrimage through life to a final revelation. The novelistic form was developed further by Goethe and was, at the time, a new kind of writing. Goethe has often been compared with Shakespeare, and in his long and prolific life he produced a number of world classic works. The comparison is not, however, completely justified. Whereas Shakespeare is loved for his urbane and yet tender all-encompassing worldview, Goethe leaves us with a number of flashes of genius embedded in much that is confused, obscure, or contradictory. The famous *Faust* (1808 and 1832) reworks the medieval tale of the artist who sells his soul to the devil. Medieval authors have no compunction about sending Faust to hell, but in Goethe's version the Faust figure is saved at the last minute. Scholars have debated endlessly what the work means. Goethe's Faust figure is a pitiful character, but his Mephistopheles (the character who represents the devil) is by far the more engaging. What then becomes of the Christian morality of the original myth? For Goethe, religion provides the material, the questions, but it certainly does not provide the answers. These must be worked out in a character's tortuous, difficult life or disguised in a deceptively light lyrical poem or a deeply complex rational argument. Goethe was able to appreciate the enormous importance of an emerging scientific approach, but his insistence on pursuing multiple careers, beliefs, and perspectives means that he belongs much more to the Renaissance tradition of wide-ranging exploration than to the truly modern tendency to ever-increasing specialization and compartmentalization.

From the time of Goethe onward, German literature returns again and again to religion for its central themes and for its store of imagery, but more often than not it leads away from the narrow path of mainstream beliefs. An important figure in this century was Gotthold Ephraim Lessing (1729–81), whose play

Nathan der Weise (1779; *Nathan the Wise*) carried a recommendation of tolerance for different religious beliefs. It is interesting that the Nazis banned this work because they feared its persuasive power. The latter part of the century was characterized by a swing back and forth between two of the most powerful forces in German literary history: Classicism and Romanticism. Friedrich Gottlieb Klopstock (1724–1803) romanticized the figure of the poet, giving him a quasi-religious mystical power. Meanwhile, German philosophers were rethinking the ethical content of their faith, and their writings begin to separate inwardness and spirituality from the outward manifestation of organized religion. Immanuel Kant (1724–1804) tried to find a pure and abstract system of ethics that was self-evident truth rather than religious doctrine, whereas Friedrich Schleiermacher (1768–1834) emphasized the inner processes of the individual rather than the outward forms of religion. In their different ways these thinkers had an enormous effect on poets, dramatists, and novelists. Writers found in these ideas whole new approaches to their craft, and a period of experimentation and innovation followed. The modern scientific age produced spectacular advances, so much so that Ludwig Feuerbach (1804–72) began to postulate a world in which reason and science was everything and in which humankind's own ability and striving for evermore knowledge could replace dependence on faith in a divine being.

It must not be forgotten that alongside the dominant Christian tradition there had been, at least since the 15th century, an important parallel tradition of the Jews. At first this was contained within the Yiddish language, which used German grammar and mostly German vocabulary but was written in the Hebrew script. Yiddish speakers could enjoy the literature of both cultures, but Yiddish literature was hidden from the German speakers because of its written form. The tradition is influenced, of course, by the Talmud and by writers from both eastern and western Jewish communities, and yet it shares many features with German literature: the inwardness, the spirituality, and the seeking for moral guidance. One common theme to both traditions is the social setting for much of this material. Small villages and ordinary people were often featured, and there is a strong emphasis on community and mutual aid. Given the marginal place of Jewish communities in the German-speaking areas and repeated persecution, it is not surprising that Jewish writers were especially fond of this subject matter. Not until the 19th century did Jewish consciousness have a major effect on the much larger German literary scene. Throughout the 19th century, a number of Jewish authors wrote very popular works in German (Arthur Schnitzler, 1862–1931; Hugo von Hofmannsthal, 1874–1929). In other fields, thinkers from a European Jewish background, such as Sigmund Freud (1856–1939), were rewriting the history of modern ideas. The certainties of previous centuries were coming under threat. The theories of psychoanalysis suggested that good and evil were to be found within, and the old mythical-allegorical method was applied to every aspect of human experience.

The great philosopher-poet Friedrich Nietzsche (1844–1900) finally declared that God is dead, and a wave of decadence swept across the European artistic scene. Some, such as the great lyrical poet Rainer Maria Rilke (1875–1926) and the Jewish poet Else Lasker-Schüler (1869–1945), sought refuge in a simpler kind of paganism or primitivism that rejected organized religious expression and turned within to the individual's search for the divine wherever it can be found. However, the greatest of the writers from the Jewish tradition was undoubtedly Franz Kafka (1883–1924), whose tales of nameless guilt and alienation epitomize the fate of early 20th-century humankind—dimly aware of a distant and awesome authority but unable to find a way of making contact with it or working out how to deal with it.

Two very different men from disciplines outside literature were near contemporaries and very strong influences on the literature of the 20th century: Karl Marx (1818–83) and Richard Wagner (1813–83). Marx's ideas on the nature of human society fundamentally challenged the Judeo-Christian foundations of Western Europe. Richard Wagner, in the field of music, transcended narrow boundaries of genre to reintroduce the mythical, the romantic, and some would say excessively emotional dimension to German culture. Neither of these men could have known how much others would make of their views and what deep political and religious (or antireligious) use would be made of their work.

At the start of the 20th century, Thomas Mann (1875–1955), more than most, was able to reflect on the intellectual currents of the day and fashion literary works of uncommon depth and sophistication. His works refuse the old simplistic presentation of specific symbols and hidden meanings, preferring to give ambiguous hints and a very complex moral landscape. Mann's *Doktor Faustus* (1947; *Doctor Faustus*) and his reworking of Christian stories involving such Old Testament figures as Joseph or the medieval Pope Gregorius are not allegories showing the main character's path between good and evil choices and the consequences of that action. Rather, they are psychological explorations that are imbued with Schopenhauer's sense of worship and yet also Nietzsche's triumphant nihilism. Just as in neighboring countries Marcel Proust (1871–1922) and James Joyce (1882–1941) were producing stream-of-consciousness novels to find an expression of psychological processes, so in the German tradition new forms were invented to deal with new ideas. Mann continued the strong German novel tradition but developed a distinctive ironic narrator, casting doubt on the motivations of the characters or the significance of events but never giving the whole picture. Just as an omniscient God is unfashionable in society, so in Mann's work there is a refusal to play this role.

The poets Stefan George (1868–1933) and Rilke looked to the French symbolist movement for inspiration, while in drama, Bertolt Brecht (1898–1956) found a way to transform contemporary theater by involving the audience much more than had previously been the practice.

The Sturm und Drang of Germany's literary history continued through two world wars and the cataclysmic effect of National Socialism. In the years immediately following World War II, a period of reflection ensued, and in some writers, notably Heinrich Böll (1917–85), there is a return to life-affirming Christian values. Hermann Hesse (1877–1962) was, like Brecht, attracted to the gentle, reflective religions of the East, and his enigmatic novels *Siddhartha* (1922; *Siddhartha*) and *Das Glasperlenspiel* (1943; *The Glass Bead Game*) were world classics. They were especially popular in the English-speaking world in the 1960s.

German literature of the later 20th century is overshadowed by the events of World War II. In the absence of a loving God, the themes of existentialism and despair prevail. The awful events of the Holocaust are repeatedly the subject of literary composition. For example, Paul Celan (1920–70) tries to make sense of this colossal evil in carefully controlled poetry, but the legacy of such a past is impossible to overcome. The division of Germany into communist East and capitalist West and its subsequent reunification again have been sources of conflict and stress. Documentary-style writings appear to be designed to step back from the emotional and moral extremes of the subject matter to allow the author a space in which to write. Overtly religious works are rare in modern German literature, but modern authors cannot escape the religious foundations on which their craft is built.

LINDA ARCHIBALD

See also Biblical Drama; Jesuit Drama

Further Reading

Butler, E.M., *The Tyranny of Greece over Germany,* Cambridge: Cambridge University Press, and New York: Macmillan, 1935

Grenzmann, Wilhelm, *Dichtung und Glaube: Probleme und Gestalten der deutschen Gegenwartsliteratur,* Frankfurt: Athenäum, 1950; 4th edition, 1960

Grimm, Gunter, and Hans-Peter Bayerdorfer, editors, *Im Zeichen Hiobs: Jüdische Schriftsteller und deutsche Literatur im 20. Jahrhundert,* Königstein: Athenäum, 1985

Guthke, Karl Siegfried, *Die mythologie der entgötterten Welt: Ein literarisches Thema von der Aufklärung bis zur Gegenwart,* Göttingen: Vandenhoeck und Ruprecht, 1971

Hamburger, Michael, *From Prophecy to Exorcism: The Premises of Modern German Literature,* London: Longmans, 1965

Heller, Erich, *The Disinherited Mind: Essays in Modern German Literature and Thought,* Philadelphia, Pennsylvania: Dufour and Saifer, 1952; 3rd edition, London: Bowes and Bowes, 1971

Reichert, Herbert William, *Friedrich Nietzsche's Impact on Modern German Literature: Five Essays,* Chapel Hill: University of North Carolina Press, 1975

Salm, Peter, *Pinpoint of Eternity: European Literature in Search of the All-Encompassing Moment,* Lanham, Maryland and London: University Press of America, 1986

Erich Maria Remarque 1898–1970

Remarque is a product of his own experience of World War I, which prompted him, after some false starts in literature, to write what remains one of the best-known war novels of all time, *Im Westen nichts Neues* (1929; *All Quiet on the Western Front*). It became not only a best-seller, but a model for other antiwar books. The publication of this work is an important literary event in world literature, but it also gave rise to a series of controversies and misunderstandings. The novel records the war through the eyes of a 19-year-old soldier who sees, but does not understand, life and death in the trenches, behind the lines, on leave, and in a military hospital. He reaches a point of resignation in which his innate will to live takes over from any conscious efforts, but ironically, he himself is killed in the last weeks of the war.

The work clearly appealed to those who had fought and felt themselves a betrayed generation. The deceptively straightforward episodic narrative style, which was part of the appeal, led to criticism of the work as trivial, and many critics overlooked not only the careful structuring of the work but also the fact that the young narrator is entirely consistent in his role and is not Remarque. The pacifist message also led to a backlash from those who wanted to see the war as a great testing, and there were numerous anti-Remarque publications, although others (not just in Germany) imitated the work.

Some stories published in English in 1930–31 (such as *The Enemy,* published more than 60 years later in German as *Der Feind*) expand upon *All Quiet on the Western Front*. The U.S. film of the book was disrupted by the Nazis, and Remarque's continued association with the film world (many of his novels have been filmed and he appeared in some) contributed to the

view of him as a less serious writer. Far more accurate is his designation in a biography as a "chronicler of the twentieth century," although there is no denying the readability and popularity of his novels.

Der Weg zurück (1931; *The Road Back*) shows events immediately after the war in the chaos of Germany. This work not only counters the erroneous view of *All Quiet* as a hymn to military comradeship by showing its rapid deterioration, but also warns against a new militarism. *Drei Kameraden* (1938; *Three Comrades*) carried on this theme in an even more pessimistic novel concerning the fate of a group of friends (and the girlfriend of one of them) in the period of struggle following the war. Even the love affair is destroyed by illness and death in the economic wilderness, and Remarque stresses often the temporary nature of human relationships.

Remarque's next novels chronicle exile from Nazi Germany. *Liebe deinen Nächsten* (1941; *Flotsam*) depicts the plight of refugees trying to establish themselves in a reluctant host country. *Arc de Triomphe* (1946; *Arch of Triumph*) focuses on a single refugee figure in Paris at the very beginning of the war, culminating in the despair following the fall of France. Remarque himself spent the war in exile, but in two further novels he tried to come to terms with the new light in which Germany now had to see itself: as the nation that had permitted the concentration camps and the Nazi regime. *Der Funke Leben* (1952; *Spark of Life*) takes up a permanent theme of Remarque's, the inextinguishable will to go on living even in the worst circumstances, be it in the trenches or, as here, in the concentration camps. The work was a brave one, and because of Remarque's talent for making things real, it is a moving one. The problem of Germany itself was tackled in *Zeit zu leben und Zeit zu sterben* (1954; *A Time to Love and a Time to Die*). The English version represented for some years Remarque's full text because the German had been cut. World War II could not be seen simply as an outside evil imposed on a generation, and this is the lesson learned by the young German soldier at its center. Again, the work is realistic, and it does condemn war (especially bombing) as such, but its hero is at the end not a passive one, but instead makes an active gesture against the regime. He is killed, but he has made his point. As elsewhere, a love story (hence the English title) counterpoints the other themes and may even provide for the continuation of the spark of life.

Of the last novels, *Der schwarze Obelisk* (1956; *The Black Obelisk*) draws on Remarque's early life and shows us the years of inflation in Germany. Although the title refers to a grave monument, the theme is again the gradual movement toward an awareness of the spark of life. *Der Himmel kennt keine Günstlinge* (1961; *Heaven Has No Favorites*) returns to the theme of car racing used in *Three Comrades*, with other material from a novel published in a magazine in 1927–28, but although there are elements of the (doomed) pursuit of life that are found in so many of the works, the novel is not especially successful. *Die Nacht von Lissabon* (1962; *The Night in Lisbon*) picks up the theme of exile and of refugees escaping from the Nazis in 1942, stressing again the combination of the tragedy imposed on people by a random fate and that imposed by other human beings. The last (posthumously published and probably unrevised) work, *Schatten im Paradies* (1971; *Shadows in Paradise*) is again a work of exile and has autobiographic elements in a central character exiled in the United States who is aware that the Nazis were not outsiders but were Germans accepted by other Germans.

Remarque chronicles the darker aspects of the 20th century, trying to come to terms first with World War I and then with a war for which he was aware of Germany's responsibility. And yet he is himself a refugee who would not return to live in Germany. Many of the novels stress the often unconscious spark of life, but Remarque is aware of fate and of the transience of human relationships; the struggle is an uphill one, and his novels come to the gradual awareness that the enemy is not political in the narrowest sense, nor some outside force, but is mankind itself.

BRIAN MURDOCH

See also War Novels

Biography

Born in Osnabrück, 22 June 1898. Studied at a Catholic teacher's seminary, Osnabrück, 1915–16; military service in the German army, 1916–18; wounded in action; teacher in Lohne and other places near Osnabrück, 1919–20; worked as an advertising copywriter, Hannover, 1920–25; wrote for various newspapers and journals; editor of *Sport im Bild*, Berlin, 1925; in Switzerland and Osnabrück, 1929–32; residence in Porto Ronco, Switzerland, from 1932; books banned and burned, 1933; German citizenship taken away, 1938; close friendship with Marlene Dietrich; exile in the United States, 1939; in Hollywood, 1939–42, and New York, from 1942; Remarque's sister, Elfriede Scholz, executed by Nazis in 1943; became a U.S. citizen, 1947; married Paulette Goddard, 1958; lived in New York and Porto Ronco, 1948–62; thereafter, only in Switzerland; visits to Germany and Italy. Great Order of Merit, Federal Republic of Germany, 1967; member, German Academy for Language and Literature, 1968. Died 25 September 1970.

Selected Works

Fiction

Note: some of Remarque's novels appeared in English translation prior to the German edition

Die Traumbude, 1920
Station am Horizont, 1927–28 (published in the magazine *Sport im Bild*)
Im Westen nichts Neues, 1929; as *All Quiet on the Western Front*, translated by A.W. Wheen, 1929; translated by Brian Murdoch, 1994
The Enemy (and other stories), translated by A.W. Wheen in *Collier's*, 1930–31; translated into German by Barbara von Bechtolsheim as *Der Feind*, 1993
Der Weg zurück, 1931; as *The Road Back*, translated by A.W. Wheen, 1931
Drei Kameraden, 1938 as *Three Comrades*, translated by A.W. Wheen, 1937
Liebe deinen Nächsten, 1941; as *Flotsam*, translated by Denver Lindley, 1941
Arc de Triomphe, 1946; as *Arch of Triumph*, translated by Walter Sorrell and Denver Lindley, 1945
Der Funke Leben, 1952; as *Spark of Life*, translated by James Stern, 1952
Zeit zu leben und Zeit zu sterben, 1954; as *A Time to Love and a Time to Die*, translated by Denver Lindley, 1954; uncensored German version, 1989
Der schwarze Obelisk, 1956; as *The Black Obelisk*, translated by Denver Lindley, 1957
Der Himmel kennt keine Günstlinge, 1961; as *Heaven Has No Favorites*, translated by Richard and Clara Winston, 1961
Die Nacht von Lissabon, 1962; as *The Night in Lisbon*, translated by Ralph Manheim, 1964
Schatten im Paradies, 1971; as *Shadows in Paradise*, translated by Ralph Manheim, 1972

Plays

Die letzte Station (produced 1956; produced as a radio play, 1958), 1958; as *Full Circle*, translated by Peter Stone, 1973
Die Heimkehr des Enoch J. Jones (produced 1988)

Further Reading

Antkowiak, Alfred, *Erich Maria Remarque: Leben und Werk*, Berlin: Volk und Wissen, 1977; West Berlin: Verlag das europäische Buch, 1983
Barker, Christine R., and R.W. Last, *Erich Maria Remarque*, London: Wolff, and New York: Barnes and Noble, 1979
Baumer, Franz, *E.M. Remarque*, Berlin: Colloquium, 1976
Erich Maria Remarque Jahrbuch, Osnabrück: Erich Maria Remarque Gesellschaft, 1991–
Firda, Richard Arthur, *Erich Maria Remarque: A Thematic Analysis of His Novels*, Bern and New York: Lang, 1988
Murdoch, Brian, et al., editors, *Remarque against War*, Glasgow: Scottish Papers in Germanic Studies, 1998
Owen, C.R., *Erich Maria Remarque: A Critical Bio-Bibliography*, Amsterdam: Rodopi, 1984
Schneider, Thomas, *Erich Maria Remarque: Ein Chronist des 20. Jahrhunderts*, Bramsche: Rasch, 1991
Schrader, Bärbel, editor, *Der Fall Remarque*, Leipzig: Reclam, 1992
Taylor, Harley U., *Erich Maria Remarque: A Literary and Film Biography*, Bern and New York: Lang, 1989
Wagener, Hans, *Understanding Erich Maria Remarque*, Columbia: University of South Carolina Press, 1991
Westphalen, Tilman, editor, *Erich Maria Remarque: Bibliographie*, Osnabrück: Universität Osnabrück, 1988
———, editor, *Erich Maria Remarque 1898-1970*, Bramsche: Rasch, 1988

Restoration

The Restoration period is framed between 1815 (the reorganization of Europe after the Napoleonic years started in 1814 by the Congress of Vienna had finally come to fruition) and the March Revolution of 1848. Some critics use the term to denote a shorter period, ending with the July Revolution of 1830, and there is some debate as to whether the so-called Rhine crisis of 1840 does not mark the beginning of a separate period. The term *Vormärz* is often attached to the shorter period preceding 1848. The period is, of course, not defined from literary events. While some periods of literature and culture may define themselves autonomously, the Restoration period—similar to *Nachkriegsliteratur* (post-1945 literature) or the Weimar Republic—uses the outer frame of political history to find its cohesion, but even fixed historical dates do not guarantee identity. As the events of 1989 showed, German history is made up of controversial restarts, and 1815 is no exception, so that the concept of restoration itself—while it usefully defines the reactionary nature of the post-1815 climate—is at best questionable. Certainly, the shape of the German territories that emerged from the end of the Napoleonic wars was greatly different to that existing before those wars, both in the number of separate states (by 1815, the number was reduced to 39) and in the bureaucratic efficiency and ensuing economic modernization of the large states. Quite apart from political pressures, the need for economic modernization would lead ultimately to the end of the ancien régime, and the emergence of the Custom Unions from 1834 can be seen as early stages on the road to the German unification of 1871. The features of pre-1815 that could be restored were limited to the principle of particularism (with the effect of frustrating the hopes for national unity that emerged in the final years of the Napoleonic period) and to the mechanisms with which absolute rulers attempted to hold back the spirit of revolution and change. In the so-called Karlsbad Decrees, these measures were greatly sharpened in response to the assassination of a well-known reactionary, the conservative writer and politician Kotzebue, by the student Karl Ludwig Sand. Despite the fact that all the progressives of the period condemned the murder, this act was interpreted as a systematic threat to all existing order. The fear of the French Revolution of 1789 was more than a recoil from the excesses of the Terror, and the German Confederation became little more than the framework within which Austria (under the direction of Chancellor Metternich) and Prussia attempted to block nationalism and liberalism, the twin streams that had been the more solid legacy of the French Revolution and the Napoleonic period. Whatever else might be blocked, however, the rise of the middle class seemed unstoppable.

The year 1815 does not represent any kind of literary caesura, therefore, but lands uncomfortably in late Romanticism, 17 years before the death of Goethe. The subdivisions of literary history in these years appear remote from the real currents of historical development, and the treatment of the period in literary history has never been free from the dominant political concerns of the day, whether in ignoring its radical strand as an aberration in an affirmative literary history or in welcoming the period as the birth years of German socialism. In the Third Reich, historians emphasized only its national tendencies (the former German national anthem, Hoffmann von Fallersleben's *Deutschlandslied* [1841], is a characteristic product of the years after the Rhine crisis) and—turning their backs on the work of writers who did not fit into its racist canon—left a highly partial view of the period. The classifications that have been attempted more recently include the concept of *Biedermeierzeit* (Biedermeier era), a term made popular at the turn of the 20th century by art historians and subsequently by Friedrich Sengle's monumental work of that title (1971).

Sengle's work falls, somewhat accidentally, at an important moment in the development of interest in this period. To the literary historians of the generation of 1968, the Restoration period offered evidence of important and sympathetic developments. The first emergence of a modern political consciousness in writers dates from this time, and for the historians of the 1970s, the thrust of the period is prerevolutionary—the sun of the coming revolution is for them stronger than the shadow of restoration. Within a wider historical dimension, the period has given rise to important discussions concerning the failure of Germany in these years to develop a middle-class political sphere, that "bürgerliche Öffentlichkeit," whose origins the philosopher Jürgen Habermas posited in the Enlightenment. For examining the social and political structures within which the heritage of the Enlightenment might have established itself in Germany—which are, of course, crucial to a full understanding of literary history—Sengle's work seemed significantly remote. Further, for all of its extraordinary depth of scholarship and understanding of the material culture of the time, it represented a conservative voice in a field increasingly organized by the New Left and by the more traditional concepts used in the literary scholarship of the GDR. Sengle's reading of the period attempts to preserve a sense of the interplay between the idealism of the previous age and the greater commitment to reality of the scientific age and thus to combine in one epochal concept features of the late classical period and late romanticism (the creative rather than the theoretical work, for a large amount of the oeuvre of E.T.A. Hoffmann, Eichendorff, Lenau, and Mörike was in fact produced in the Restoration period), and early forms of poetic realism. Its philosophy would be a conservative Hegelianism, with a strong religious element emanating from Schleiermacher that expressed itself, among other things, in pietism. Such harmonizing summaries, however, are less persuasive than that famously propounded by Heinrich Heine in the late 1820s, when he spoke of the *Kunstperiode* that had begun "at Goethe's cradle" and would come to an end with his death. Over the last 30 years, critics have tended to emphasize Heine's thesis concerning German developments. The accidents of biographical dates in Austria, on the other hand, have made it possible for literary historians to see greater unity in this period; indeed, some critics write of the whole period as "the Age of Grillparzer"—Grillparzer's life (1791–1872) representing a continuity that bridges the political caesura. In German literary history, the significant dates are 1831 (the death of Hegel) and 1832 (the death of Goethe), with the July revolution of 1830 unmistakably marking the end of the *Kunstperiode* still more strongly, even if its political implications for Germany took the more limited form of the Hambacher Fest (1832) and minor episodes of civic unrest.

Such arguments have little time for epochal continuity and emphasize the increasing radicalism of the period after 1830.

The redirection of philosophy away from mere interpretation, which is contained in Marx's celebrated 11th Feuerbach thesis, is shown more widely than in the philosophical circles of the young Hegelians (Bruno Bauer, Max Stirner, Moses Hess, and Ludwig Feuerbach himself) or the literary-political activism of the Young Germans. The period after 1830 was marked by an ever more widely held sense that political and social problems required some answer from writers, regardless of their political stance, and that a retreat into inwardness was no longer adequate. The famous remarks of Heine that are scattered through these years express something more than the personal stance of a professional radical: they may genuinely be interpreted as the spirit of the age. When he announced his commitment to "Emancipation" as a historical goal, Heine meant by this not only political emancipation (referring to the universally acceptable examples of Ireland and Greece, as well as the more problematic cases such as Poland) and the emancipation of the Jews or women (issues that could be identified as belonging to a clear radical agenda). He also had in mind what was called, in the typical catchphrase of the time, the "emancipation of prose," which prepared the ground for the realism of the later part of the century. Heine's reference, however, was to something still more widespread: an acceptance of the given reality of human experience, with or without transcendence, and the subsequent emphasis on the importance of the human facilities and senses. It would be hard by the end of this period to find writers who were not in support of these aims. Indeed, it is noticeable that in Gerhard Plumpe's recent (1995) application of system theory to the periodicization of these years—an approach that, by its very nature, excludes extraliterary reference of the kind that has been discussed here—the shift from Romanticism to realism is based entirely on a turn toward reality perceived from the turn of the century in religious and, subsequently, in aesthetic discourse.

The Restoration period is marked by a rapid and seemingly boundless expansion of the apparatus of literary culture, a growth in literacy and publishing, and the accelerated spread of newspapers and periodicals. This expansion implied a spread of popular forms of writing, not only of the modern forms of "high" literature, which by this time had been made available to other sections of society than those who had been the focus of literary life in the late 18th century, but of more popular forms as well, from mass-market fiction to almanacs and calendars. These radical changes in literary life involved a major relocation of writing within society—including such factors as the professionalization of the writer as a class, the acceptability of more socially engaged types of writing such as journalism, and the ending of a type of elitism that had separated literature—both in its production and reception—from social action or the writer from the public. Most notably, the Young German group of writers emerged as the first examples of writers making their living entirely within the literature market—a process that stood in marked contrast to the summary way in which the German Confederation announced its ban on these writers in 1835. Only recently, however, have historians been in a position to assess the central importance of literary clubs for the intellectual culture of this period. Once again, the period is characterized by the conflict between modernization and more archaic social forms, between an increasing freedom of thought and the mechanisms of repression.

While the literary scene showed the marks of profound change, the Restoration period was a time when the universities flourished in the fields of natural science and, preeminently, in philology and history. The identification of German literature with the emergence of national identity had been started earlier—by Herder and Fichte, among others—and after 1815 it showed itself in the emergence of professional literary histories. In addition, the Grimm brothers in particular, both as lexicographers and as collectors of German legends and fairy tales, belong to a process that consolidated national identity through cultural activity. Here, too, it is unclear to what extent these processes were political movements or merely furnished a substitute for the reforming political activity from which intellectuals were barred. The famous case of the "Göttinger Sieben" (seven renowned professors of the University of Göttingen were summarily dismissed from their posts by the King of Hannover in 1837) again highlighted the conflict between the modernization of the states and the resistance to the ideas inevitably brought by modernization.

Exploring this period can take place through individual works—there is no shortage of significant works, including *Faust: 2 Teil* (1825), Büchner's (1813–37) posthumously published *Woyzeck,* Heine's *Deutschland: Ein Wintermärchen* (1844; Germany: A Winter's Tale), or the work of Annette von Droste-Hülshoff (1797–1848), but such an approach is perhaps less rewarding than for other periods. Indeed, the period is more often criticized (both by contemporaries and by subsequent historians) for its inability to produce works that show the forms of literary modernity associated with contemporary French or English Realism. Despite the increasing interest in French and English culture, German writers similar to Balzac or Dickens were slow to replace established literary models in Germany. Apart from the continued influence of Sir Walter Scott (his principal imitator was Willibald Alexis [1798–1871]), the legacy of the 18th century was the bildungsroman, in which the hero's encounter with society—rather than providing the action of the novel, as it does in Balzac and other realists—tended to lie outside the novel, which concerned itself with the lengthy period of self-discovery by the hero. The genre was decisively continued into the Restoration period by Karl Immermann (1796–1840). Perhaps Karl Gutzkow (1811–78) was the first to break radically with that tradition, but his major novels lie outside the Restoration period. The success of the *Novelle* genre, in which the Restoration period produced numerous masterpieces, also acted as a disincentive to the growth of the novel. Drama flourished, although from the names associated with this period, only Büchner remains in the repertoire. Again, the situation was different in Austria, where Grillparzer, Ferdinand Raimund (1790–1836), and Johann Nestroy (1801–62) are still firmly established in the theater. One should not ignore the major operatic tradition that was established in both Austria and Germany during these years. In recent years, despite its stature, the work of Friedrich Hebbel (1813–63) has dated. Shifts in taste have affected the reception of his work much more adversely than, for instance, that of Ibsen, whose work is otherwise foreshadowed in so many aspects of the *bürgerliches Trauerspiel* (middle-class tragedy) with which Hebbel's early work (e.g., *Maria Magdalene* [1844]) is associated.

In general, it may well be that the more fascinating impulses of this period come less from individual literary works than from aspects of the social and intellectual experiences of writers, which did not always find their expression in major works but are reflected in diaries, essays, journalistic sketches, and newspaper articles. While the first wave of interest in this period was concerned with the rediscovery of writers and themes that have traditionally been neglected in German literary history, recent research has focused strongly on more ephemeral texts. The tension and excitement produced by the currents of modernization that swept Europe found expression not merely in political and social unrest but in less contentious, if not less exciting ways: at the end of the period stood not only the elaborated forms of socialism and its practical consequence, revolution, but the technical accomplishments celebrated in the Great Exhibition, not to mention the emergence of the great cities. Another important feature of the age is the interest generated by travel, not merely the type of pilgrimage to the sites of Western civilization epitomized by Goethe's *Italienische Reise* (1816–17; translated as *Travels in Italy* and *Italian Journey*), but travel for other reasons, to places whose charms were practical rather than aesthetic. Travel became an obsession. The exploration of the United States—Charles Sealsfield (Karl Postl: 1793–1864) is the best known German writer on the United States—was much more than a cultural experience. Hard economic necessity drove many Germans to emigration both during this period and in the wake of the failed revolution, no less decisively than the political exile that placed Börne and Heine in Paris. So travel writing became on the one hand more political; on the other hand, as railways started to change the rhythms of rural life, travel also became a symptom of a new age that was less marked by political ideology: the railways, mobility, and the increasing pace of life became understood as the direct voice of history. As a result of these changes, the period is marked, perhaps most notably, by its shifting sense of time: the emergence of a dynamic of history.

The activation of a sense of history is a paradoxical achievement for an age misleadingly entitled the Age of Restoration.

HUGH RIDLEY

See also Napoleonic Era

Further Reading

Conze, Werner, editor, *Staat und Gesellschaft im deutschen Vormärz,* Stuttgart: Klett, 1970

Hermand, Jost, editor, *Das Junge Deutschland: Texte und Dokumente,* Stuttgart: Reclam, 1966

Hermand, Jost, and Manfred Windfuhr, editors, *Zur Literatur der Restaurationsepoche, 1815–1848,* Stuttgart: Metzler, 1970

Hohendahl, Peter Uwe, *Literarische Kultur im Zeitalter des Liberalismus, 1830–1870,* Munich: Beck, 1985

Koselleck, Reinhart, *Kritik und Krise: Eine Studie zur Pathogenese der bürgerlichen Welt,* Freiburg: Alber, 1959; 2nd edition, Frankfurt: Suhrkamp, 1976

Lauster, Martina, editor, *Deutschland und der europäische Zeitgeist: Kosmopolitische Dimensionen in der Literatur des Vormärz,* Bielefeld: Aisthesis, 1994

Plumpe, Gerhard, *Epochen moderner Literatur: Ein systemtheoretischer Entwurf,* Opladen: Westdeutscher Verlag, 1995

Sagarra, Eda, *Tradition and Revolution in Germany: German Literature and Society, 1830–1890,* London: Weidenfeld and Nicolson, and New York: Basic Books, 1971

Sengle, Friedrich, *Biedermeierzeit: Deutsche Literatur im Spannungsfeld zwischen Restauration und Revolution, 1815=1848,* 3 vols., Stuttgart: Metzler, 1971=1980

Stein, Peter, *Epochenproblem Vormärz, 1815–1848,* Stuttgart: Metzler, 1974

Wülfing, Wulf, et al., editors, *Handbuch literarisch-kultureller Vereine, Gruppen, und Bünde, 1825–1933,* Stuttgart: Metzler, 1998

Reuental, Neidhart von, *see* Neidhart von Reuental

Richter, Johann Paul Friedrich, *see* Jean Paul (Johann Paul Friedrich Richter)

Rainer Maria Rilke 1875–1926

Rilke turned suffering into verse and verse into praise of life. His poetic work is an intensely personal achievement that demands equally personal responses—often refused by readers who criticize the rational element in a poet's work, find it wanting, and do not tolerate the irrational that sometimes appears in outlandish garb. Rilke was preoccupied with the occult and ready to believe in ghosts—one of whom dictated poems in Italian to him. (But he described such experiences as relevant only if integrated with one's total existence.) Accounts of his candlelit recitations in rose-scented rooms harmed his later reputation in an age that believes, with Brecht (who had no time for Rilke), that a poem should be able to stand daylight.

Rilke suffered as the sensitive outsider who finds few kindred spirits, the introvert who cannot settle to relationships, the neurotic rubbed raw by practicalities and modern life (seen in the 1899–1900 story *Ewald Tragy*, published in 1929), and the mystic unsatisfied by conventional religion. He cultivated suffering and heightened his mental state by shutting himself away alone rather than seeking relief in company or psychoanalysis. Obstinately, he followed his feelings even into deep unhappiness. This spiritual masochism gave us a series of poems that encapsulate some characteristic troubles of 20th-century man.

Allusive, elliptical, and demanding—often with irregular structures and meters, a wide idiosyncratic vocabulary, and extended metaphors—the poems call for intellectual effort. In Rilke's rarefied state, he does not write to be understood. The reader has to follow the poet's pilgrimage step by step, ending on the bare mountain of the heart where words and feelings are long left behind.

Yet extreme subjectivity does not exclude acceptance and fine observation of the empirical world and of other personalities. Rilke finds it self-evident that the poet, although isolated from the human in his sublime suffering and without satisfactory knowledge of the divine, has a necessary function in expressing the things of this world, raising them at least to potential divinity by praising their beauty.

His parental household gave Rilke no deep culture; he felt little in common with his parents. Much has been made of his Catholic background and of the way in which his mother brought him up as a girl until he was six and his father sent him off to military cadet institutions when he was ten. Particularly in Mährisch-Weißkirchen (where a little later Musil followed him), bullied and isolated, Rilke developed a vivid inner life. But none of this explains the peculiarity of his life's work.

He never forgot or disowned anything in his life: in later life he could recover vividly the embarrassment of his telling a bully that he suffered meekly because Jesus had done so, or remember when his daydream of being a brave cavalry officer was interrupted when his horse was startled by a dog. Disparate past experiences were always present to him, producing the characteristic startling referential leaps in his poems. He compares himself to a flower that, having opened too widely to the sunlight, cannot close when cold night surrounds it, but unhappily (yet greedily) takes in every unpleasant impression. Somewhere deep down is a real life of poetic expression; squeezed in between, as he wrote to Lou Andreas-Salomé, are "the actual dwellings of healthy feeling."

He was also a hard, single-minded worker. As a student he assiduously cultivated career-furthering contacts with influential authors and publishers; he also published five collections of (mainly derivative and self-indulgent) verse in the impressionist mode from 1894 to 1898 and wrote stories with fashionable social themes. When secretary to the sculptor Auguste Rodin, he took to sitting at a desk for a given time to produce a poem, rather than waiting for fragile inspiration. He was an inveterate letter writer. In his pursuit of productive loneliness, he shamelessly exploited the hospitality that he solicited from a circle of benevolent rich and noble women (and some men), whose country houses he would borrow, often forbidding them to come near, offering as a reward some reflected fame (an offer fulfilled, notably in the quasi-dedication of the *Duineser Elegien* [1923; *Duino Elegies*] to Princess Marie von Thurn und Taxis-Hohenlohe). None of his friends seem to have found this odd or arrogant.

An oddly romantic view of military experience informed the work that was most popular in his lifetime and well beyond, the miniature epic *Die Weise von Liebe und Tod des Cornets Christoph Rilke* (1899; translated as *The Story of the Love and Death of Cornet Christopher Rilke*, *The Tale of the Love and Death of Cornet Christopher Rilke*, *The Lay of the Love and Death of Cornet Christoph Rilke*, and *The Cornet*), an energetic account—"in language and rhythm of almost unearthly beauty" (B.J. Morse)—of the erotic awakening and the death in battle of a young member of his ancestral family in 1664. Yet by 1898 he saw his path—a poem runs:

This is my battle:
dedicated by longings
to explore every day.
Then, strong and broad,
with a thousand rootlets
to grasp deep into life—
and through suffering
to ripen far out of life,
far out of time!

Similar to all of his generation, he fell under Nietzsche's spell. Poems of the late 1890s invoke visions of Christ denying his false doctrine or show the poet at one with the universe, demolishing the barrier between I and Non-I. A more sophisticated aesthetic version of Nietzscheanism comes in the poems of the *Buch vom mönchischen Leben* (part of *Das Stunden-Buch*, 1905; Book of the Monkish Life): God is not dead, but in a way takes the place of the superman, evolving, being worked at by generations of artists.

Lou Andreas-Salomé, to whom Nietzsche had once proposed marriage, was Rilke's lover for a time. After a journey east with her, he fell in love with a poetic image of Russia: illimitable spaces, mystic peasants, and icons. To many, this infatuation (disregarding the obvious explosive social inequalities) seemed a one-sided pose, but he was just taking from experience what served his development. The next experience came from living in the artistic colony in Worpswede near Bremen, where he soaked up then-current painterly ideas of the relationship between the contemplation and reproduction of external objects. Phenomenological and vitalistic thought of the time denied the possibility of absolute knowledge, stressing the roles of intuition, the patterns of experience, and the unconscious generalizations by which our minds build a knowledge of the universe. From these ideas, Rilke built a technique of surrounding the object with the subjective, giving a quirky poetic likeness.

He developed esoteric ideas about the soul of the virgin (the virgin *female*—for his part, he was naturally promiscuous and had been sexually active since his teens). He also walked around Hamburg with a deep red rose pressed into one eye, looking like the complete decadent (although the tactile aesthetic experience and the symbolic image-connection of eye and rose are both serious parts of his poetic universe; the connection is evoked in several poems and his auto-epitaph).

Separating from Lou, who appears to have thought he was at risk of syphilis (but eventually became a maternal friend and later wrote a book on him), Rilke married Clara Westhoff, a Worpswede artist he had previously venerated as a virginal soul. She had a daughter seven months later. Rilke, however, could not afford to support a family; his father withdrew his allowance when Rilke refused, predictably, to earn his living in a bank in Prague. As a consequence, Clara mainly lived with her well-to-do parents; Rilke went to Paris to write a commissioned monograph on Rodin. He then travelled around in search of cheap lodgings, free hospitality, and quietude. He soon found that Paris—although (or because) he found it a depressing abyss—was the only place where he could work; eventually, his publisher Anton Kippenberg (Insel-Verlag) paid regular advances on royalties to enable Rilke to live there. The marriage became a friendship carried on by letters and occasional short breaks together; Rilke sometimes had Kippenberg send Clara money.

By going to Paris, Rilke abandoned the German literary scene; despite Expressionist features around 1914, the rest of his work is impossible to incorporate in any specific German-ism or movement. Another aspect of Rilke's alienation from literary trends was his openness to visual, rather than verbal, aesthetic experiences. Later in life he approached French literature, admiring Valéry and translating French poetry.

His first really satisfying verse collection was *Das Stunden-Buch* (1905; translated as *Poems from the Book of Hours* and *The Book of Hours*), which incorporated the cycles *Buch von der Pilgerschaft* (Book of Pilgrimage) and *Buch von der Armut und vom Tode* (Book of Poverty and of Death) as well as that on monastic life. He saw value in dignified rural poverty, but then Paris overwhelmed him with its rush and money-grubbing, the hospitals, and the mass dying of people in the metropolis. He opposed this scene to the idea of the "eigener Tod" (personal death). Individuality was to be the elite artist's hallmark even in death: a theme of *Die Aufzeichnungen des Malte Laurids Brigge* (1910; translated as *Journal of My Other Self, The Notebook of Malte Laurids Brigge*, and *The Notebooks of Malte Laurids Brigge*).

Another Parisian experience was the work of Rodin, his friend, adviser, and onetime employer, and *Neue Gedichte* (1907–8; New Poems) show Rodin's influence. They work on three levels: object, type, and symbol. In these poems, Rilke seeks a formal representational equivalent for something in the real world, but this representation, in turn, is also a type of other things and possibly a symbol of another layer of inward experience reached by contemplation of the object. Strict stylization raises the object from reality and gives it the permanence of art. Thus, in "The Panther," the exact image of the caged animal is suffused with a philosophy of willpower and hints at analogies with the frustrations of human life—all in 12 exquisitely shaped lines. Hermann Pongs, a pioneering academic critic of Rilke's work, named such poems *Dinggedichte* (thing poems).

After 1910 came a period in which Rilke moved around to various noble residences and grand hotels. Increasingly, he traveled first class, but still attracted generosity: in 1914, Ludwig Wittgenstein anonymously donated 20,000 Austrian Crowns. In 1912, Rilke began the *Duino Elegies*, writing more whenever he could concentrate sufficiently and reject the temptations of normality and sexual love.

His early enthusiasm for World War I soon gave way to depression. Mistakenly found fit for active service, he was for a short, traumatic period an Austrian infantryman; then, he lived a shadowy life in a military records office until he was demobilized, when he moved to Munich, fighting the misery of being unable to understand the evil of the war, unable to offer any comfort, and unable to settle to the *Elegies*. He consoled himself with women, especially Lulu Albert-Lazard; she painted his portrait—he had "unfathomable eyes," as she said, a strangely Chinese moustache and weak chin. France being too costly when the war ended, he went to Switzerland where, after a period in Berg am Irchel during which he worked daily at being astonished by natural things, he settled in the castle of Muzot, a 13th-century tower in the Rhone valley. Here, early in 1922, he suddenly finished the elegies and wrote the *Sonette an Orpheus* (1923; *Sonnets to Orpheus*). These poems satisfied his ambitions, fusing elegiac and hymnic elements and transposing the world into poetic forms; this success assured him that life was still worth living in the rootless 20th century, that the tensions and insecurities of modern life were soluble, and that death and time were not only the great enemies.

His last years were spent in fear of illness—he was always sickly, even spending his honeymoon in a sanatorium—and he also had a preoccupation with spiritualism. He met his fitting end after scratching himself while picking a rose; the wound failed to heal and was a first in a series of ailments. Eventually, acute leukemia was diagnosed.

Increasingly popular in his lifetime, Rilke's poems became the object of critical study in Germany even before his death, in France in the 1920s, and in Britain by the 1930s. In Germany after 1945, as is seen in Hans Egon Holthusen's influential essays, a mood of existential despair made them relevant to a fresh generation, and they were thought the equal of Eliot's. The literature on Rilke is among the most extensive on any 20th-century writer. Several volumes of his correspondence, notably his letters with Lou Andreas-Salomé, have been published. Numerous translations into other languages show the international appeal of the poems. But their eccentricity and lack of social concern have closed them to left-wing critics and readers, who are unable to see what Rilke does for the workers.

ALFRED D. WHITE

Biography

Born in Prague, Austro-Hungarian Empire, 4 December 1875. Traveled throughout Europe; at a painters' colony at Worpswede, 1901–2; associated with Rodin in Paris, 1902–3, 1905–6; lived in Denmark, Sweden, Italy, and France, 1896–1914; lived in Munich, 1914–19, except for a term served in the military records office, Vienna, 1916; lived in Switzerland, 1919–26; supported by various patrons, including Princess Marie von Thurn und Taxis, from 1910; lived in Chateau de Muzot, Switzerland, from 1921. Died 29 December 1926.

Selected Works

Collections

Selected Works, translated by G. Craig Houston and J.B. Leishman, 2 vols., 1954–60
Sämtliche Werke, edited by the Rilke-Archiv in cooperation with Ruth Sieber-Rilke and Ernst Zinn, 7 vols., 1955–97; revised edition, 1980
Werke, edited by Horst Nalewski, 3 vols., 1978
The Best of Rilke (bilingual edition), translated by Walter Arndt, 1989

Poetry

Leben und Lieder, 1894
Larenopfer, 1896

Traumgekrönt, 1897

Advent, 1898

Mir zur Feier, 1899; revised edition, as *Die frühen Gedichte*, 1909

Die Weise von Liebe und Tod des Cornets Christoph Rilke, 1899; edited by Walter Simon, 1974; as *The Story of the Love and Death of Cornet Christopher Rilke*, translated by B.J. Morse, 1927; as *The Tale of the Love and Death of Cornet Christopher Rilke*, translated by M.D. Herter Norton, 1932; as *The Lay of the Love and Death of Cornet Christoph Rilke*, translated by Leslie Phillips and Stefan Schimarski, 1948; translated by M.D. Herter Norton, 1959; translated by Stephen Mitchell, 1983; as *The Cornet*, translated by Constantine FitzGibbon, 1958

Das Buch der Bilder, 1902; revised edition, 1906; translated in part as *The Voices*, by Robert Bly, 1977; as *The Book of Images*, translated by Edward Snow, 1991

Das Stunden-Buch, 1905; as *Poems from the Book of Hours*, translated by Babette Deutsch, 1941; as *The Book of Hours*, translated by A.L. Peck, 1961

Neue Gedichte, 2 vols., 1907–8; as *New Poems*, translated by J.B. Leishman, 1964; as *New Poems (1907)*, 1985, and *New Poems (1908): The Other Part*, 1987, both translated by Edward Snow; as *New Poems* [bilingual edition], translated by Stephen Cohn, 1992

Requiem, 1909

Das Marien-Leben, 1913; as *The Life of the Virgin Mary*, translated by R.G.L. Barrett, 1921; translated by C.F. MacIntyre, 1947; translated by Stephen Spender, 1951; translated by N.K. Cruickshank, 1952

Fünf Gesänge, 1915

Duineser Elegien, 1923; as *Duineser Elegien: Elegies from the Castle of Duino*, translated by Vita and Edward Sackville-West, 1931; as *Duino Elegies*, translated by J.B. Leishman and Stephen Spender (bilingual edition), 1939; revised edition, 1948, 1963; translated by Nora Wydenbruck, 1948; translated by Harry Behn, 1957; translated by C.F. MacIntyre, 1961; translated by Stephen Garmey and Jay Wilson, 1972; translated by Elaine E. Boney, 1975; translated by David Young, 1978; translated by Stephen Mitchell, in *The Selected Poetry of Rainer Maria Rilke*, 1982; translated by Stephen Cohn, 1989; translated by David Young, 1993

Die Sonette an Orpheus, 1923; as *Sonnets to Orpheus*, translated by J.B. Leishman, 1936; translated by M.D. Herter Norton, 1942; translated by A. Poulin, Jr., in *Duino Elegies and Sonnets to Orpheus*, 1977; translated by David Young, 1987; translated by Leslie Norris and Alan Keel, 1989

Späte Gedichte, 1934; as *Late Poems*, translated by J.B. Leishman, 1938

Requiem and Other Poems, translated by J.B. Leishman, 1935

Fifty Selected Poems, translated by C.F. MacIntyre, 1940

Selected Poems, translated by J.B. Leishman, 1941

Thirty-One Poems, translated by Ludwig Lewisohn, 1946

Poems 1906–1926, translated by J.B. Leishman, 1957

Angel Songs, translated by Rhoda Coghill, 1958

Poems, edited and translated by G.W. McKay, 1965

Visions of Christ: A Posthumous Cycle of Poems, edited by Siegfried Mandel, translated by Aaron Kramer, 1967

Selected Poems, edited by Frank M. Fowler, 1969

Holding Out: Poems, translated by Rika Lesser, 1975; new edition as *Rilke: Between Roots*, 1986

Possibility of Being: A Selection of Poems, translated by J.B. Leishman, 1977

The Rose and the Windows, translated by A. Poulin, Jr., 1979

Selected Poems, translated by Robert Bly, 1981

Requiem for a Woman and Selected Lyric Poems, translated by Andy Gaus, 1981

An Unofficial Rilke: Poems 1912–1926 (bilingual edition), edited and translated by Michael Hamburger, 1981

Selected Poetry (bilingual edition), edited and translated by Stephen Mitchell, 1982

The Unknown Rilke: Selected Poems, translated by Franz Wright, 1983; enlarged edition, 1990

Rainer Maria Rilke: Translations from His Poetry, by Albert Ernest Flemming, 1983

The Migration of Powers: The French Poems, translated by A. Poulin, Jr., 1985

Plays

Im Frühfrost (produced 1897), in *Aus der Frühzeit*, 1921; as *Early Frost*, translated by Klaus Phillips and John Locke, in *Nine Plays*, 1979

Ohne Gegenwart, 1898; as *Not Present*, translated by Klaus Phillips and John Locke, in *Nine Plays*, 1979

Die weisse Fürstin, 1899; revised version, in *Die frühen Gedichte*, 1909; as *The White Princess*, translated by Klaus Phillips and John Locke, in *Nine Plays*, 1979

Das tägliche Leben (produced 1901), 1902; as *Everyday Life*, translated by Klaus Phillips and John Locke, in *Nine Plays*, 1979

Nine Plays, translated by Klaus Phillips and John Locke, 1979

Fiction

Am Leben hin, 1898

Zwei Prager Geschichten, 1899; as *Two Stories of Prague: King Bohush; The Siblings*, translated by Angela Esterhammer, 1994

Vom lieben Gott und Anderes, 1900; revised edition, as *Geschichten vom lieben Gott*, 1904; as *Stories of God*, translated by Nora Purtscher-Wydenbruck and M.D. Herter Norton, 1932

Die Letzten, 1902

Die Aufzeichnungen des Malte Laurids Brigge, 1910; as *Journal of My Other Self*, translated by John Linton, 1930; as *The Notebook of Malte Laurids Brigge*, translated by Linton, 1930; as *The Notebooks of Malte Laurids Brigge*, translated by Stephen Mitchell, 1983

Ewald Tragy, 1929; translated by Lola Gruenthal, 1958

Other

Worpswede, 1903

Auguste Rodin, 1903; revised edition, 1907; as *August Rodin*, translated by Jesse Lemont and Hans Trausil, 1919; as *Rodin*, translated by Robert D. Firmage, 1979

Aus der Frühzeit: Vers, Prosa, Drama 1894–1899, edited by Fritz Adolf Hünich, 1921

Briefe an Auguste Rodin, 1928

Briefe an einen jungen Dichter, 1929; as *Letters to a Young Poet*, translated by M.D. Herter Norton, 1934; translated by K.W. Maurer, 1943; translated by Reginald Snell, 1945; translated by Stephen Mitchell, 1984

Briefe und Tagebücher, edited by Ruth Sieber-Rilke and Carl Sieber, 7 vols., 1929–37; revised edition of *Briefe*, as *Gesammelte Briefe*, 6 vols., 1936–39

Briefe an eine junge Frau, edited by Carl Sieber, 1931; as *Letters to a Young Woman*, translated by K.W. Maurer, 1945

Tagebücher aus der Frühzeit, edited by Ruth Sieber-Rilke and Carl Sieber, 1942

Letters 1892–1926, translated by Jane Bannard Greene and M.D. Herder Norton, 2 vols., 1945

Selected Letters, 1902–1926, translated by R.F.C. Hull, 1946

Freundschaft mit Rilke, by Elya Maria Nevar, 1946

La Dernière Amitié: Lettres à Madame Eloui Bey, edited by Edmond Jaloux, 1949; as *Rainer Maria Rilke: His Last Friendship: Unpublished Letters to Mrs. Eloui Bey*, translated by William H. Kennedy, 1952

Briefe an Gräfin Sizzo 1921–1926, edited by Ingeborg Schnack, 1950; revised edition, 1977

Briefwechsel in Gedichten, with Erika Mitterer, 1950; as *Correspondence in Verse*, translated by N.K. Cruickschank, 1953

Briefwechsel, with Benvenuta, edited by Magda von Hattingberg, 1954;

as *Letters to Benvenuta*, translated by Heinz Norden, 1951; as *Rilke and Benvenuta: An Intimate Correspondence*, translated by Joel Agee, 1987

Briefwechsel, with Marie von Thurn und Taxis, edited by Ernest Zinn, 2 vols., 1951; as *The Letters of Rainer Maria Rilke and Princess Marie von Thurn and Taxis*, translated by Nora Wydenbruck, 1958

Briefe über Cézanne, edited by Clara Rilke, 1952; as *Letters on Cézanne*, translated by Joel Agee, 1985

Briefwechsel, with Lou Andreas-Salomé, edited by Ernst Pfeiffer, 1952; revised edition, 1975

Correspondance 1909–1926, with André Gide, edited by Renée Lang, 1952

Briefe an Frau Gudi Nölke, edited by Paul Obermüller, 1953; as *Letters to Frau Gudi Nölke during His Life in Switzerland*, translated by Violet M. Macdonald, 1955

Briefwechsel, with Katharina Kippenberg, edited by Bettina von Bomhard, 1954

Lettres françaises à merline, 1919–1922, 1950; as *Letters to Merline, 1919–1922*, translated by Violet M. Macdonald, 1951; translated by Jesse Browner, 1989

Rilke, Gide, et Verhaeren: Correspondance inédite, edited by C. Bronne, 1955

Lettres milanaises 1921–1926, edited by Renée Lang, 1956

Briefwechsel, with Inga Junghanns, edited by Wolfgang Herwig, 1959

Selected Letters, edited by Harry T. Moore, 1960

Briefe an Sidonie Nadherny von Borutin, edited by Bernhard Blume, 1973

Rilke on Love and Other Difficulties, edited by John J.L. Mood, 1975

Briefwechsel 1910–1925, with Helene von Nostitz, edited by Oswalt von Nostitz, 1976

Gesammelte Erinnerungen, 1926–1956, edited by Klaus E. Bohnenkamp, 1976

Briefe an Nanny Wunderly-Volkart, edited by Niklaus Bigler and Rätus Luck, 2 vols., 1977

Briefwechsel 1899–1925, with Hugo von Hofmannsthal, edited by Rudolf Hirsch and Ingeborg Schnack, 1978

Where Silence Reigns: Selected Prose, translated by G. Craig Houston, 1978

Briefe an Axel Juncker, edited by Renate Scharffenberg, 1979

Briefwechsel, with Rolf Freiherr von Ungern-Sternberg, edited by Konrad Kratzsch, 1980

Maria Cvetaeva, Boris Pasternak, Rainer Maria Rilke: Lettere 1926, edited by Yevgeny Pasternak, Yelena Pasternak, and Konstantin M. Azadovsky, 1980; as *Letters, Summer 1926*, translated by Margaret Wettlin and Walter Arndt, 1985

Briefwechsel, with Anita Forrer, edited by Madga Kérényi, 1982

Rodin and Other Prose Pieces, translated by G. Craig Houston, 1986

Schweizer Vortragsweise, 1919, edited by Rätus Luck, 1986

Rilke und Russland: Briefe, Erinnerungen, Gedichte, edited by Konstantin Asadowski, 1986

Briefe an Ernst Norlind, edited by Paul Åström, 1986

Die Briefe an Karl und Elisabeth von der Heydt, 1905–1922, edited by Ingeborg Schnack and Renate Scharffenberg, 1986

Briefwechsel, with Regina Ullmann and Ellen Delp, edited by Walter Simon, 1987

Briefwechsel mit den Brüdern Reinhart, 1919–1926, edited by Rätus Luck and Hudo Sarbarch, 1988

Briefe und Dokumente, with Stefan Zweig, edited by Donald A. Prater, 1988

Briefe an Tora Vega Holmström, edited by Birgit Rausing and Paul Åström, 1989

Translations

Elizabeth Barrett Browning, *Sonette nach dem Portugisischen*, 1908

Maurice de Guérin, *Der Kentauer*, 1911

Die Liebe der Magdalena, 1912

Marianna Alcoforado, *Portugiesische Briefe*, 1913

André Gide, *Die Rückkehr des verlorenen Sohnes*, 1914

Louise Labé, *Die vierundzwanzig Sonette der Louïze Labé*, 1918

Paul Valéry, *Gedichte*, 1925

Further Reading

Brodsky, Patricia Pollock, *Rainer Maria Rilke*, Boston: Twayne, 1988

Casey, Timothy J., *Rainer Maria Rilke: A Centenary Essay*, London: Macmillan, and New York: Barnes and Noble, 1976

Leppmann, Wolfgang, *Rilke: Sein Leben, seine Welt, sein Werk*, Berne: Scherz, 1981; revised edition, 1993

Nalewski, Horst, editor, *Rilke: Leben, Werk und Zeit in Texten und Bildern*, Frankfurt: Insel, 1992

Prater, Donald, *A Ringing Glass: The Life of Rainer Maria Rilke*, Oxford: Clarendon Press, and New York: Oxford University Press, 1986

Sanford, John, *Landscape and Landscape Imagery in Rilke*, London: Institute of Germanic Studies, University of London, 1980

Schnack, Ingeborg, *Über Rainer Maria Rilke: Aufsätze*, Frankfurt: Insel, 1996

Schnack, Ingeborg, editor, *Rilkes Leben und Werk im Bild*, Wiesbaden: Insel, 1956

———, editor, *Rainer Maria Rilke: Chronik seines Lebens und seines Werkes, 1875–1926*, Frankfurt: Insel, 1975; 2nd edition, 1990

Stahl, August, *Rilke: Kommentar zum lyrischen Werk*, Munich: Winkler, 1978

Die Aufzeichnungen des Malte Laurids Brigge 1910

Novel by Rainer Maria Rilke

Die Aufzeichnungen des Malte Laurids Brigge (*The Notebooks of Malte Laurids Brigge*) is Rainer Maria Rilke's most famous narrative work. This eponymous novel records the first-person reflections of a young Dane living in Paris early in the 20th century. As an aspiring writer, Malte Laurids Brigge discovers that he must learn to see—in a metaphorical as well as literal sense—in order to learn to write. He spends a good deal of time attempting to master his childhood and adolescent experiences and memories in order to collect a coherent self that can make sense of experience and create narrative from it.

Rilke's short novel, which draws to some extent on his own letters and experiences, greatly influenced the French existentialists (among many others); Sartre's *La Nausée* is particularly indebted to it. Visual artists also admire the work; Ben Shahn created a series of lithographs (issued posthumously in 1974) from passages in *Malte*. Rilke's text was first interpreted as a largely autobiographical piece (as the title of the earliest translation into English, *Journal of My Other Self* [1930] indicates). Later critics emphasized the book's confusing structure and argued as to whether it could be classified as a novel of personal development or a novel about the progression toward becoming a true artist. Critics have also focused on *Malte* as an urban novel that reveals the assaults of modern, industrial society on the individual. More recently, the book has been analyzed from a psychological perspective, with an emphasis on Malte's fragmented personality and his attempt to create an integrated self.

The novel's structure reveals a chaotic, nonlinear surface that disrupts any sense of chronological order or causality. As the word *Aufzeichnungen* (sketches or notebooks) of the title indicates, the narrative appears to be a number of incomplete notes or sketches. The text begins almost in mid-sentence, as though we are eavesdropping on ruminations in midstream. To complicate matters, the novel's first-person narrator, Malte, is an idiosyncratic, psychologically troubled young man who seeks shock treatments, which raises issues of his reliability as a narrator.

This apparently chaotic surface, however, contains a more coherent structure of repeated images, which are linked to the novel's primary themes. Rather than following a chronological plot, Rilke repeats and varies key images. *Malte,* therefore, must be read in the way in which one reads a poem rather than the manner in which one normally reads a novel; it is what Ralph Freedman calls a "lyrical novel."

Images such as faces and costumes repeat throughout the text and connect to Rilke's investigation of identity, of finding a genuine self not imposed by the outer world and its expectations. Such images in the first part of the novel are mirrored in the second part. For example, being trapped in a costume that takes over his identity becomes a moment of existential crisis for Malte as a child in part 1, just as it does for the false Czar Dimitri in part 2—or just as being imprisoned in an imposed identity forces the prodigal son to flee in the novel's closing section. Or again, in part 1, Rilke depicts a woman who sits with her face cradled in her hands and, startled, looks up too quickly, leaving her face in her cupped hands and revealing what Rilke calls "the inside of a face," an unprotected vulnerable self with its identity torn away. This passage is mirrored in part 2 by the duke, who dies in battle on an icy pond and has his face torn away when he is rolled over for identification. The loss of a face, of a protective identity, represents a repeated moment of trauma on both the personal and historical levels.

These examples also reveal a progression in the text from Malte's concentration on first-person, personal memoirs in part 1 to his emphasis on third-person, historical narrative in part 2. (A comparison of the opening paragraphs of parts 1 and 2 reveals this shift.) This progression allows Rilke to move what might seem a very idiosyncratic character to a more general and universal context by demonstrating that Malte's most personal and seemingly singular experiences have parallels in history. Thus, a very personal identity finds support and validation on a larger stage.

This possibility becomes crucial in order for Malte to find stability, for he is a character who is cut off from all the usual means of defining himself. As a Dane in Paris, Malte is outside of his homeland, away from his family and ancestral inheritance, and cut off even from his own language. He feels isolated and assaulted by the rushing noise and power of a modern urban center where even death seems factory-like. Malte must find a stable self in the modern city. To do so, Malte explores his own memories to find a personal identity and then explores the narrative of history to establish a broader support for that identity.

Malte's personal background rests on two opposing but complementary forces. His mystical, irrational, and emotional mother provides a hypersensitivity to objects, life, and the otherworldly realm of ghosts. His controlled, rational, and disciplined father provides the form and order to structure experience and to give it shape. Both of these are necessary to create the artist. Thomas Mann suggests a very similar scheme in many of his narratives and might define these as the Dionysian and Apollonian aspects of the artist.

Malte explores his own background by creating vivid images. These seem disjointed in the narrative but are ordered by a model of the development of consciousness that Rilke derives from Heinrich von Kleist's *Über das Marionettentheater* (1810; *On Puppetshows*). Kleist suggests that consciousness moves through a cycle that begins with nonconscious objects, runs through animals to children to fully self-conscious humans, and then goes beyond the self-conscious to lovers, artists, saints, and, finally, all-conscious angels and God. The nonconscious and all-conscious realms can comfortably interact, as Rilke demonstrates in his striking image of an old man feeding birds, who, if he were so still as to become a doll, could lure the angels to feed from his hand. But self-conscious humans constitute the most troubled part of the cycle by being isolated by their own self-consciousness. Humans must first strive to attain a coherent self, a stable identity. Then, trapped by their own self-consciousness, adult humans must find a way to move beyond it to participate in the super-conscious realm of the angels.

In part 1 of the novel, Malte explores positions earlier in this cycle of consciousness. He examines objects, things, animals, and his own childhood. In part 2, by exploring historical narrative and love, Malte seeks to move beyond his personal self-consciousness to a larger sphere. Malte does not complete this movement in the novel, but rather gestures toward it and, as the novel closes, the all-conscious realm of God. Rilke believed that writing *Malte* would also trigger his breakthrough to that larger realm of consciousness and spark his finest work. Ironically, *Malte* was followed instead by a period of a dozen years of relatively meager publications that was finally broken by a flood of poetic achievement in 1922, when Rilke completed both his *Duineser Elegien* (1923; *Duino Elegies*) and his *Die Sonette an Orpheus* (1923; *Sonnets to Orpheus*) in which he completed the cycle of consciousness he envisioned through the creation of art.

The final section in *Malte*, often read as a key to the volume as a whole, replays many of the text's themes. In this section Malte retells the story "Der verlorene Sohn" (The Prodigal Son). Unlike the biblical version, however, Malte's protagonist leaves home not to spend his wealth but rather to avoid being trapped in an identity dictated by the expectations and "love" of those around him. Similar to Malte, he leaves to search for his own identity. When the prodigal son has found a stable identity within himself, he returns home with the understanding that his self is now his own and cannot be harmed by his loved ones. He closes by seeking to move beyond this self-conscious state toward a unity with the all-conscious condition of God.

This final tale by Malte also counters his earlier lament that no one knows how to narrate any longer in our modern, fragmented, urban world. As the novel closes, the fact that Malte is able to produce a coherent, structured story may indicate that he is progressing toward his goal of learning to see and learning to write—in short, toward his goal of becoming an artist.

KATHLEEN L. KOMAR

Editions

First edition: *Die Aufzeichnungen des Malte Laurids Brigge*, Leipzig: Insel-Verlag, 1910

Critical edition: in *Sämtliche Werke*, edited by the Rilke-Archiv in cooperation with Ruth Sieber-Rilke and Ernst Zinn, vol. 6, Frankfurt: Insel Verlag, 1966

Translations: There are several translations of Rilke's *The Notebooks of Malte Laurids Brigge*. Among the best (both bearing this title) are those by M.D. Herter Norton, New York: Norton, 1949; and by Stephen Mitchell, New York: Random House, 1983

Further Reading

Bradley, Brigitte L., *Zu Rilkes Malte Laurids Brigge,* Bern: Francke, 1980

Engelhardt, Hartmut, editor, *Materialien zu Rainer Maria Rilke: Die Aufzeichnungen des Malte Laurids Brigge,* Frankfurt: Suhrkamp, 1974

Freedman, Ralph, *The Lyrical Novel,* Princeton, New Jersey: Princeton University Press, 1963

Liu, Huiru, *Suche nach Zusammenhang: Rainer Maria Rilkes "Die Aufzeichnungen des Malte Laurids Brigge,"* Frankfurt and New York: Lang, 1994

Loock, Wilhelm, *Rainer Maria Rilke: Die Aufzeichnungen des Malte Laurids Brigge,* Munich: Oldenbourg, 1971

Lyon, Laurence Gill, "Related Images in *Malte Laurids Brigge* and *La Nausée,*" *Comparative Literature* 30 (1978)

Shahn, Ben, *For the Sake of a Single Verse . . . : From The Notebooks of Malte Laurids Brigge by Rainer Maria Rilke,* New York: Potter, 1974

Sokel, Walter H., "Zwischen Existenz und Weltinnenraum: Zum Prozeß der Ent-Ichung im Malte Laurids Brigge," in *Rilke Heute: Beziehungen und Wirkungen,* edited by Ingeborg H. Solbrig and Joachim W. Storck, Frankfurt: Suhrkamp, 1975

Stephens, Anthony B., *Rilkes Malte Laurids Brigge: Strukturanalyse des erzählerischen Bewußtseins,* Bern and Frankfurt: Lang, 1974

Ziolkowski, Theodore, *Dimensions of the Modern Novel: German Texts and European Contexts,* Princeton, New Jersey: Princeton University Press, 1969

Duineser Elegien 1923

Collection of Poems by Rainer Maria Rilke

Written between 1912 and 1922, Rainer Maria Rilke's *Duineser Elegien* (1923; *Duino Elegies*) represent the apogee of his poetic career and constitute one of German literature's best-known cycles of poems. Rilke's fame is worldwide, and his work has been translated into scores of languages. Earlier in this century, critics associated Rilke with the existentialists; by the 1980s and 1990s, he became an icon of New Age thinkers, spiritual leaders, popular psychologists, and even film directors, particularly in the United States. Rilke's ten elegies, begun in the castle of Duino, are a response to the isolation of individual human consciousness and the pressures, so strongly felt by writers and artists between the two world wars, of a dehumanized technological world.

At a time when Albert Einstein's theory of relativity (1905) undermined temporal and spatial stability as well as causality, Sigmund Freud's *Die Traumdeutung* (1900; *The Interpretation of Dreams*) implied that the world of conscious control was underpinned by a less controllable force, and World War I threatened to end the common social forms of European culture (as Thomas Mann argues in *The Magic Mountain*), artists and writers felt compelled to seek new methods and structures with which to realize their visions. Between 1905 and 1915, the Fauves, the Cubists, and the Expressionists emerged in the realm of painting; T.S. Eliot began "Prufrock" in 1910; Kafka began *Der Prozeß* and James Joyce began *Ulysses* in 1914. Rilke's ele-gies, begun amid this turmoil, seek to understand the ways in which art can function in an increasingly chaotic world in which universal ordering principles and absolutes had crumbled.

The *Duino Elegies* explore humanity's longing for transcendence in a world that seemed to reject it. In the course of this quest, Rilke learns that the poet's true calling is not to the divine realm but rather back to the humanly possible world, transformed by human consciousness and given duration in poetic language. The *Duino Elegies* open with a call to the angelic realm but close with a gesture that returns poet and reader to the fertile earth. The poems begin by aspiring upward; they end by falling, happily, back to the earth to engender a new poetic understanding. The poet's proper task becomes transforming ("Verwandlung") objects and the earthly through language.

Rilke's *Duino Elegies* are elegiac in tone, often lamenting unities lost, but they also echo the traditional form of the elegy (i.e., the elegiac distich, which consists of a line of dactylic hexameter followed by a line of dactylic pentameter). Rilke's meter is predominantly dactylic, and he sometimes produces perfect elegiac distichs. Thematically, Rilke explores the angelic and human realms. He moves from an early focus on the divine realm and humanity's separation from it to a series of reflections and retractions—until he arrives back in the realm of the humanly possible. His journey of self-conscious reflections becomes an exploration not only of his individual role but of the poet's role in general; the cycle dramatizes the construction of a poetics as well as an ontology.

Being a cosmopolite and traveler, Rilke had a literary context much broader than the Austro-Hungarian Empire and Germany. He was influenced by the cultures of Russia, Scandinavia, and France, as well as by a range of fellow German-speaking authors. About 1911, shortly before beginning the *Duino Elegies,* Rilke studied such major German poets as Goethe, Hölderlin, and Heinrich von Kleist. Hölderlin in particular became crucial to Rilke's interest in classical poetic forms and to his development of a model of consciousness that moves from the nonconscious state of objects through man's troubled and isolated self-conscious position to an all-conscious state of the angels. This model closely parallels Kleist's theory of consciousness as presented in *Über das Marionettentheater* (1810; *On Puppetshows*) and becomes a working model for Rilke's ruminations in the *Elegies.* By linking the two ends of the model, the nonconscious realm and the all-conscious realm, Rilke finds a task for the poet—transforming the physical world into the invisible by the power of his poetic consciousness.

In the first elegy, Rilke contemplates how to approach the transcendent realm represented by the angels. How can man, limited by his self-conscious state, attain the angels' realm of all-encompassing superconsciousness? He proposes several models for escaping the self-conscious state: first, children and those who die young, who are not yet trapped in self-consciousness; second, the hero, who bypasses paralyzing self-consciousness to move directly into action; and finally, lovers, particularly unrequited lovers, who have moved beyond isolated consciousness toward a larger unity with another consciousness (the beloved) or with consciousness at large if the love is unrequited.

As the elegies progress, however, each of these categories falls short of the ultimate goal of transcendence. Children grow up. Heroes are too unique to represent a general strategy for those who are already burdened with self-consciousness. Lovers frequently have the "misfortune" of being loved in return or the distractions of sexual urgency (explored in Elegy III) or future expectations.

After spending the majority of the first six elegies exploring the limits of these models of possible access to the transcendent realm, Rilke in the seventh elegy comes to understand that it is not the grand gesture of hero or lover that ameliorates self-consciousness but rather the small, familiar interaction of our isolated consciousness with objects in the world.

In the seventh and ninth elegies, the poetic speaker reverses the entire direction of his activity. What had been an attempt to call or woo the angels in the opening lines becomes a celebration of the human condition, a praise of man's world to the angels. The speaker stops pursuing transcendence and turns rather to the process of transforming the physical world within his consciousness. The poet realizes that one can escape solipsism by participating in the physical world and transforming it through his own consciousness.

Once the poet recognizes that he has the power of rescuing objects from time and decay by transforming them from within, his task becomes one of praising and accomplishing such transformations. The poet now can reveal to the angel what the angelic realm cannot perceive because the angel's all-encompassing consciousness cannot recognize the physical world's discrete divisions and boundaries. The poet ceases his attempt to join the angels and accomplishes, because of his human limits, something that they could not.

The poet discovers that he can sing the living, the physical and limited world, that "Hiersein ist herrlich" (Being here [in this physical world] is magnificent). According to the poet, human culture, architecture, religion, music, and art, the transformation of the physical world by human consciousness, has always had the power to create a kind of human transcendence. The finite world becomes the task of the poet and his gift to the angels. Rilke substitutes a realizable and fruitful poetic project for a futile one.

In the *Duino Elegies*, Rilke comes to realize that a pure poetic voice will grow beyond the personal and, therefore, will outgrow wooing the angel. He realizes that interaction with the world of objects and physicality, and not flight or pleading, will produce protection from solipsism. The poet thus radically shifts his focus from the transcendent realm to the earthly realm, to "Hiersein." He steps away from the realm of the angels and back to the realm of man. This enables him to affirm human existence even to the angels and moves him much closer to a geocentric and anthropocentric poetics. The final three elegies reaffirm this epiphany.

The *Duino Elegies* begin as an attempt to storm the transcendent realm and escape the limits of the physical world. After testing a number of strategies for transcendence, Rilke comes in the seventh and, more conclusively, in the ninth elegy to realize that the beyond is not his proper sphere, that the idea of transcendence itself is a distracting trap. The poet turns finally to the world and to the consciousness he had sought to escape. By making the two interact, he creates a form more permanent than either, the aesthetic form. These elegies record the course of Rilke's journey to a modern poetics.

KATHLEEN L. KOMAR

Editions

First edition: *Duineser Elegien*, Leipzig: Insel Verlag, 1923
Critical editions: *Sämtliche Werke*, edited by the Rilke-Archiv in cooperation with Ruth Sieber-Rilke and Ernst Zinn, 7 vols., Frankfurt: Insel Verlag, 1955–97
Translations: There are several translations of Rilke's *Duineser Elegien*. Of these, the most faithful to the original German and best annotated are those by J.B. Leishman and Stephen Spender, *Duino Elegies* (bilingual edition), New York: Norton, 1939; revised edition, 1948, 1963; and by Stephen Mitchell, *The Selected Poetry of Rainer Maria Rilke*, New York: Random House, 1982; see also the translation by C.F. MacIntyre, *Duino Elegies* (bilingual edition), Berkeley: University of California Press, 1961

Further Reading

Baron, Frank, et al., editors, *Rilke: The Alchemy of Alienation*, Lawrence: Regents Press of Kansas, 1980
Fiedler, Theodore, "Rilke at the Movies," in *Rilke-Rezeptionen: Rilke Reconsidered*, edited by Sigrid Bauschinger et al., Tübingen: Francke, 1995
Freedman, Ralph, *Life of a Poet: Rainer Maria Rilke*, New York: Farrar, Straus, and Giroux, 1996
Fülleborn, Ulrich, and Manfred Engel, editors, *Materialien zu Rainer Maria Rilkes "Duineser Elegien,"* Frankfurt: Suhrkamp, 1980
Komar, Kathleen L., *Transcending Angels: Rainer Maria Rilke's Duino Elegies*, Lincoln: University of Nebraska Press, 1987
——, "Rilke: Metaphysics in a New Age," in *Rilke-Rezeptionen: Rilke Reconsidered*, edited by Sigrid Bauschinger et al., Tübingen: Francke, 1995
Steiner, Jacob, *Rilkes Duineser Elegien*, Bern: Francke, 1962; 2nd edition, 1969
Ziolkowski, Theodore, *The Classical German Elegy 1795–1950*, Guildford and Princeton, New Jersey: Princeton University Press, 1980

Die Sonette an Orpheus 1923
Collection of Poems by Rainer Maria Rilke

Rilke's *Die Sonette an Orpheus* (1923; *Sonnets to Orpheus*) began as a stroke of serendipity. While he was struggling to complete his *Duineser Elegien* (1923; *Duino Elegies*), a project that had extended over a period of 12 years, Rilke suddenly found himself writing a series of sonnets. Between 2 and 5 February 1922, 25 sonnets poured forth; another, subsequently inserted into this first sequence, was written on 13 February; and from 15 to 23 February, a second set of 29 sonnets emerged. After the agonizing efforts to complete his *Duino Elegies*, this rich spurt of production so astonished Rilke that he believed the sonnets had been "dictated."

Inscribed with the dedication, "written as a grave-marker for Wera Ouckama Knoop," the sonnets commemorate a ballet dancer who had died at the age of 19. In this sense, they form part of the mourning exercise of which the *Duino Elegies* was the most conspicuous manifestation. They also hark back to Rilke's double *Requiem* of 1908, which consists of *Für eine Freundin* (For a Friend), composed in memory of the artist Paula Modersohn-Becker, and *Für Wolf Graf von Kalkreuth* (For Count Wolf von Kalkreuth). In selecting Orpheus as the addressee of his sonnet sequence, however, Rilke was placing these personal acts of mourning and remembrance into a larger, mythic context. This, too, was a context he had explored before, notably in his long poem *Orpheus; Eurydike; Hermes* (composed in 1904 and published in the first volume of his *Neue Gedichte* [*New Poems*] in 1907).

The *Sonnets to Orpheus* create a new version of the Orpheus myth. The poet whose song had charmed first the god of the underworld and then the animals and trees of the earth is reinterpreted as a poetic forerunner whose song continues to subsist, unheard, in nature itself. In so reinventing the ancient myth, Rilke recurs to a Romantic conception of poetry as the voice of nature, which is able to be heard and translated into human language by the poet alone. In the *Sonnets to Orpheus,* the ancient singer with the lyre is felt primarily as a kind of vibration in nature: his song is silence rather than sound. Orpheus is seen as belonging to "two realms at once," that of the living and that of the dead; "he comes and goes," and he is "metamorphosed" into manifold natural phenomena such as a rose, the wind, and the aroma of ripe fruit. Orpheus thus becomes a link between the tangible and the intangible, the imagined and the actual: his former existence and continued subsistence in nature makes possible the transference of reality into poetic language; it also makes possible the transformation of mourning into praise. This new conception of Orpheus connects with a figure that underlies Rilke's poetry from at least the *New Poems* on: the notion of inversion or reversal. In accordance with this idea, Rilke includes a poem about mirrors in the second sequence of *Sonnets to Orpheus.*

The poems in *Sonnets to Orpheus* are in fact rather uneven in quality. At their best, however, they represent an extraordinary linguistic and formal innovation. While each of these sonnets has 14 lines, many of them use nontraditional metrical schemes, including short-line forms adapted from the mystical chorus at the end of Goethe's *Faust II.* The *volta,* or turning point, in many of the sonnets is ingeniously placed, often across an enjambment or in the gap marked by a dash. Some of the imagery is almost surrealist, notably in the opening sonnet of the first sequence, where Orpheus's song is described as a "high tree in the ear." The motifs treated in the sequence range widely, from topics more conventionally associated with the god of poetry or themes of death and mourning to more loosely related ideas. The unicorn ("oh, this is the animal that does not exist") stands in for the power of the imagination, an entirely new constellation of stars called the "Rider" elaborates the notion of unity in duality, and the rose with its multiple petals represents the inexhaustible nature of poetic creativity. As wind or breath (in the sense of *pneuma*), Orpheus is at once an "invisible poem" and a "counterweight in which I rhythmically happen." Since Orpheus has already enacted the loss of Eurydice and the transformation of that loss into mourning song, he makes it possible for the modern poet to take a more positive approach to death, decay, and loss. "Be ahead of all parting," the speaker enjoins both the reader and himself, "as if it were behind you like the winter that is just departing." The dead young ballerina Wera Ouckama Knoop becomes a reiteration of Orpheus, a figure who, like the mythic god, also "comes and goes," manifesting the continued presence of the creative spirit. At the end of *Sonnets to Orpheus,*

the complete reversal of mourning—and all other earthly phenomena—takes place as the speaker says: "To the silent earth declare: I flow. / To the rapid water speak: I am."

For some time, the scholarship on *Sonnets to Orpheus* was locked in a quasi-philosophical mode. Rilke's later poetry was seen as a closed system of thought that required certain linguistic or discursive keys to be understood before the poem could be interpreted correctly. Although the *Duino Elegies* often have been read as advice manuals, the *Sonnets to Orpheus* have not suffered as much as some of Rilke's other work; nonetheless, the hortative structures of certain sonnets have laid them open to this kind of reading. In German-language scholarship of the 1970s, a deep skepticism set in about the social relevance and truth values of Rilke's poetry; although the *Sonnets* were not the primary butt of this critique, they were regarded as overly aesthetic and grandiloquent. Among many American readers, by contrast, Rilke remains something of a cult figure. In the scholarly world, however, there has been a return in recent years to a more sober approach to Rilke's work. The new annotated edition edited by Manfred Engel and others sets Rilke more clearly within the context of the early 20th century. Rilke's complex relationship to modernism in general has begun to be probed in several volumes of recent essays on his poetry. The results of this new approach have only begun to emerge in the scholarship as a whole.

JUDITH RYAN

Editions

First edition: *Die Sonette an Orpheus,* Leipzig: Insel, 1923

Critical editions: in *Sämtliche Werke,* vol. 1, edited by the Rilke-Archiv in cooperation with Ruth Sieber-Rilke and Ernst Zinn, Frankfurt: Insel Verlag, 1955; in *Werke: Kommentierte Ausgabe in vier Bänden,* vol. 2, edited by Manfred Engel et al., Frankfurt: Insel, 1996

Translations: *Sonnets to Orpheus,* edited and translated by M.D. Herter Norton, New York: Norton, 1942; *Duino Elegies and Sonnets to Orpheus,* translated by A. Poulin, Jr., Boston: Houghton Mifflin, 1977

Further Reading

Martens, Lorna, *Shadow Lines: Austrian Literature from Freud to Kafka,* Lincoln: University of Nebraska Press, 1996

Mörchen, Hermann, *Rilkes Sonette an Orpheus,* Stuttgart: Kohlhammer, 1958

Parry, Idris, "Space and Time in Rilke's Orpheus Sonnets," *Modern Language Review* 58 (1963)

Ryan, Judith, *Rilke, Modernism, and Poetic Tradition,* Cambridge: Cambridge University Press, 1999

Segal, Charles, *Orpheus: The Myth of the Poet,* Baltimore, Maryland: Johns Hopkins University Press, 1989

Sprengel, Peter, "Orphische Dialektik: Zu Rilkes Sonett 'Sei allem Abschied voran' (Sonette an Orpheus II, 13)," in *Gedichte und Interpretationen,* vol. 5, edited by Harald Hartung, Stuttgart: Reclam, 1983

Johann Rist 1607–1667

Johann Rist was a prolific and well-known literary figure during the Baroque period in Germany. Dramatist, poet of secular love songs as well as devotional songs, and writer of colloquies, he was also the hub of a wide circle of poets and musicians. He lived during the Thirty Years' War, a time of terrible suffering, economic chaos, and political change. Similar to most of his contemporaries, Rist was adversely affected by the intermittent warfare that intruded in a most terrifying manner into everyday existence; his home was looted and destroyed several times. He held the widely shared attitude that destruction and suffering were signs of divine judgment against the moral decay of the times and of a call to repentance. The period was a time when the moral decay deplored by Rist and others was countered by a revival of lay piety. This revival moved away from orthodox Lutheran liturgical expression toward private and small-group devotional practices, which often tended toward an intense emotionality and even mysticism. In spite of his position in the Lutheran ministry, Rist contributed enormous numbers of texts—primarily devotional song texts—to the cause of private devotional exercises.

The literary Baroque period is defined largely by the language and verse reforms of the 17th century, beginning with the foundation in 1617 of the Fruchtbringende Gesellschaft (The Fruit-Bearing Society), the first and most important of the societies that were established to foster the usage of a cleansed and elevated German language, and by the publication in 1624 of Martin Opitz's *Buch von der Deutschen Poeterey* (Book of German Poetics). Rist participated in such efforts not only as a member of the Fruchtbringende Gesellschaft but also by writing a satire on the misuse of German, *Rettung der Edlen Teütschen Hauptsprache* (1642; Rescue of the Noble German Language), and by founding his own language society, the Elbschwanenorden (The Order of the Swans of the River Elbe). He fostered the efforts both of vocal music composers and of other poets. Visitors to his parsonage and correspondents included many of the famous poets and musicians of the day, among them Martin Opitz and Heinrich Schütz.

Rist's more than 650 devotional songs dominate his oeuvre. The most important collections are the five volumes of his *Himlische Lieder* (1641–42; Heavenly Songs) and the *Neuer Himlischer Lieder Sonderbahres Buch* (1651; Special Book of New Heavenly Songs). More than 100 of his songs, mostly from these two collections, entered hymnals and other compilations of devotional song texts during the 17th century. Crucial to the popularity of Rist's works was his partnership with a number of important Hamburg composers whose original settings of his song texts helped them to stand out from among the hundreds of rivals. As is clear from the prefaces, Rist worked closely with the composers in order to assure that the musical settings helped clarify the presentation of the texts, thus contributing to the development of a special aesthetic for musical settings of poetic texts.

Rist's secular lyrical poetry, mostly consisting of pastoral love songs, was equally popular. Two lyric song cycles, complete with music, were published: *Galathee* (1642) and *Florabella* (1651). Their verse forms were emulated and their melodies were borrowed repeatedly by his contemporaries. The fact that a first line of a Rist song itself sufficed to identify a melody demonstrates how well known these works were. He also wrote a great deal of poetry for special occasions, much of which was published in *Neüer Teütscher Parnass* (1652; New German Parnassus).

Rist's surviving dramatic and theatrical works, which include three peace masques, a prose tragedy, and a sing-ballet, are of considerable interest for any history of the theater. With the exception of the ballet, each incorporates comic characters, some of whom speak in dialect. The three masques on the topics of war and peace—*Irenomachia* (1630), *Das Friedewünschende Teutschland* (1647; Peace-Wishing Germany), and *Das Friedejauchzende Teutschland* (1653; Peace-Celebrating Germany)—use public performance to satirize contemporary morals and fashions, employing both personifications and stereotyped characters for this purpose. The two later masques incorporate numerous songs, published complete with simple but memorable melodies. The tragedy *Perseus* (1635) portrays the horrible deeds and downfall of the tyrant Perseus, who is driven to suicide by the ghosts of those he had persecuted, but the play's serious scenes and speeches are interspersed with coarsely comic ones, including some in dialect. The sing-ballet *Die Triumphirende Liebe* (1653; Love Triumphant), created for the occasion of a court wedding, is an allegorical presentation of the triumph of the virtues over the vices in a series of "entrées" accompanied by verse texts, some of which include melodies.

The colloquies that Rist wrote (one for each of the first six months of the year, hence, the commonly used designation *Monatsgespräche*) have garnered considerable attention in recent decades, in part due to their accessibility in the critical edition. The title of each begins with *Das Aller Edelste* (The Most Noble)—for example, *Das Aller Edelste Nass der gantzen Welt* (The Most Noble Fluid in the Entire World). They appeared essentially annually beginning in 1663; the sixth was published in the year following Rist's death. Each contains a fictitious debate on the topic in the title among Rist and three fellow members of the Elbschwanenorden, who are depicted as sitting in his garden at the parsonage.

The reception of Rist's poetic oeuvre has varied considerably over time. The devotional songs have had the most continuous republication, and 12 of his songs still appear in the Lutheran hymnal today, including "O Ewigkeit, du Donnerwort" ("Oh Eternity, Word Like Thunder") and "Werde munter, mein Gemüte" ("Become Cheerful, My Spirit"). Even the devotional songs were under assault early in the 18th century, however, when Baroque literature in general was lambasted as tasteless and many 17th-century devotional texts were castigated as lacking heartfelt religiosity. A notable exception was Johann Sebastian Bach's use of the hymn "O Ewigkeit, du Donnerwort" for a cantata (BWV 20). The dramatic texts experienced a revival of interest in the late 19th century, primarily due to their dialect scenes and patriotic political sentiments, and another revival followed their publication in the critical edition that began to appear in 1967, the 300th anniversary of Rist's death. The lack of a critical edition of the lyric and devotional poetry to date has hindered treatment of this vast portion of Rist's oeuvre, although literary scholars and hymnologists have written dissertations on portions of this work and articles on individual songs.

JUDITH P. AIKIN

Biography

Born in Ottensen, near Hamburg, 1607. Studied theology at Rinteln and Rostock universities; tutor in Heide, 1633; pastor at Wedel, northwest of Hamburg, 1635; member of Die Fruchtbringende Gesellschaft, 1647; received a patent of nobility, 1653; founded the Elbschwanenorden in Hamburg, 1660. Died in Wedel, near Hamburg, 1667.

Selected Works

Collections

Sämtliche Werke, edited by E. Mannack, 10 vols., 1967–

Plays

Irenomachia, 1630
Perseus, 1635
Das Friedewünschende Teutschland, 1647
Das Friedejauchzende Teutschland, 1653

Poetry

Musa Teutonica, 1634
Poetischer Lust-Garte, 1638
Himlische Lieder, 5 vols., 1641–42; *Neüer Himlischer Lieder Sonderbahres Buch*, 1651
Galathee, 1642
Florabella, 1651
Neüer Teütscher Parnass, 1652

Treatises

Rettung der Edlen Teütschen Hauptsprache, 1642

Colloquies

Das alleredelste Nass der gantzen Welt, 1663
Das alleredelste Leben der gantzen Welt, 1663
Die alleredelste Tohrheit der gantzen Welt, 1664
Die alleredelste Belustigung, 1666
Die alleredelste Erfindung der gantzen Welt, 1667
Die alleredelste Zeit-Verkürtzung der gantzen Welt, 1668

Further Reading

Aikin, Judith, "Baroque," in *A Concise History of German Literature to 1900*, edited by Kim Vivian, Columbia, South Carolina: Camden House, 1992

Bepler, Jill, "Johann Rist," in *Dictionary of Literary Biography*, vol. 4: *German Baroque Writers, 1580–1600*, edited by James Hardin, Detroit, Michigan, Washington, D.C., and London: Gale Research, 1996

Krabbe, Wilhelm, *Johann Rist und das deutsche Lied: Ein Beitrag zur Geschichte der Vokalmusik des 17. Jahrhunderts*, Bonn: Broch und Schwarzinger, 1910

Mannack, Eberhard, "Johann Rists 'Perseus' und das Drama des Barock," *Daphnis* 1 (1972)

———, *Johann Rist: Gelehrter, Organisator, und Poet des Barock*, Munich: Gesellschaft der Bibliophilen, 1988

Schade, Richard E., "Baroque Biography: Johann Rist's Self-Concept," *German Quarterly* 51 (1978)

Thomas, Richard Hinton, *Poetry and Song in the German Baroque*, Oxford: Clarendon Press, 1963

Romance, Arthurian, *see* Arthurian Romance

Romantic Irony *see* Irony, Romantic

Romanticism

It was during the middle phases of German Romanticism that the study of German literature as an academic discipline originated. In part as a response to French occupation of Germany under Napoleon, as an attempt to preserve a distinctively German cultural identity from extinction, Romantic writers and scholars began from around 1805 to edit and publish German literary texts from the Middle Ages to the 18th century. Thus, Jacob and Wilhelm Grimm recorded and published German fairy tales, while Ludwig Tieck edited medieval *Minnelieder* (courtly love songs). Given these patriotic origins, it is understandable that from the middle of the 19th century, after a brief phase of denigration of Romanticism during its final phases by liberal and early socialist critics such as Heinrich Heine and Arnold Ruge, German literary history began to celebrate Romanticism as a specifically German phenomenon. It was held to be part of the "deutsche Bewegung" (German movement), the ascent of German culture to preeminence in Europe, and was regarded as one of the main constituents of the triumphant *Goethezeit* (Age of Goethe).

For over a century, Romanticism was interpreted as a characteristically German reaction against an arid, mechanistic rationalism and intellectualism emanating primarily from France. Romanticism, so it was asserted, was irrational in nature and placed an emphasis on primitive feelings and intuitions, on the life of the soul, on what was proudly termed *deutsche Innerlichkeit* (German inwardness). Even after the collapse of the Third Reich, this view of Romanticism remained generally intact in Germany; the close textual criticism of the 1950s produced much subtle exegesis of Romantic works without challenging the accepted ideological bias.

Since the 1960s, this traditional view of German Romanticism has been discredited in a number of ways. First, it has been recognized that Romanticism is not by any means an exclusively German movement, but is rather part of a shift in consciousness on a European scale: comparatist studies have shown that certain themes and attitudes recur in all "Romanticisms" (a plural first coined by Arthur Lovejoy), Romanticism everywhere developing out of a shared pre-Romanticism derived not least from Rousseau in France. Second, critics have pointed out that German Romanticism is politically diverse, encompassing not only conservative and nationalistic viewpoints but also what Helmut Schanze in 1967 termed "die andere Romantik" (the other Romanticism), a line of progressive and emancipatory thought stretching from the republicanism of the young Friedrich Schlegel in the 1790s to the irreverent social criticism of E.T.A. Hoffmann in the 1810s. Moreover, this "other Romanticism" had its roots in 18th century libertarian rationalism, so that in particular the first phases of Romanticism in Germany represented a continuation of the Enlightenment, not the negation of it. The nationalistic interpretation of German Romanticism, so it was now appreciated, had overemphasized and exalted precisely those reactionary tendencies in the German consciousness that had led in time to fascism. In the light of these new insights, it became important not only to see German Romanticism as part of a European tradition and in its concrete historical and social context, but also to reexamine the biographies of Romantic authors and reedit their works in order to remove the ideological mystification and distortion perpetrated by generations of sentimentalizing apologists. Recent decades have therefore seen a process of "Entromantisierung der Romantik" (Deromanticising Romanticism), as it was termed by Hans-Joachim Mähl.

There has, however, been no need to discard the traditional categorization of Romantic writers in Germany into two groups. Between 1795 and 1800 a coterie of Early Romantics was active briefly but intensively in Jena and Berlin. Some of the Late or "High" Romantics, a more diffuse grouping, were based in Heidelberg between 1805 and 1808, while others were dispersed around Germany, some of them continuing to publish until the 1830s and even 1840s. The Early Romantics adhered to the values of the enlightened humanism in which they had been brought up (most of them were born around 1770) and asserted an idealism in which faith in the principles of the French Revolution was never entirely compromised. Their humanism and historical optimism were a heritage that they shared with Weimar Classicism, which was at its height in the same five-year period, so that in Germany the conventional antithesis between romanticism and classicism is not as pronounced as some Romantics themselves later tried to suggest. The Late Romantics, following Napoleon's seizure of power and French military expansion, suffered a disillusionment and turned away from utopianism and millennialism, often taking refuge in the organic continuity of history and nationhood, in German folk culture, and in religion of a Catholic or even superstitious rather than chiliastic character.

The Early Romantics, based in Prussia and Saxony, were sheltered from the upheavals of the age by the military neutrality of North Germany for a decade after the Peace of Basle in 1795. The output of the Jena group, centered around the brothers Schlegel, was predominantly cerebral in character and rarely lyrical or sentimental in a conventionally romantic way. They particularly cultivated the aphorism, or *Fragment* as they termed the genre, the cryptic or epigrammatic *aperçu* expressed in a few sentences. It served to pillory the more pedantic assumptions of the cultural establishment while avoiding the compromising definitiveness of full exposition. August Wilhelm Schlegel (1767–1845) made his name as a reviewer and as a translator, initially of Shakespeare and later of Spanish and Italian literature, and lectured influentially on the history of European culture. Friedrich Schlegel (1772–1829), having produced important studies of Greek literature, turned from 1796 onwards to the development of innovative literary theory, producing the first definitions of the term *romantic* in its modern sense, and then in 1799 attempted to put his ideas into practice in the experimental novel *Lucinde*.

An important feature of the literary activity of the Early Romantics was their emphasis on collaborative thought and production. Working from a concept of *Geselligkeit* (sociability) which they derived in part from the model of the contemporary Berlin literary salons, they sought intellectual interaction through conversation or correspondence and termed such exchanges "Symphilosophie" and "Sympoesie"; that is, "joint" philosophy and poetry. Such aspirations, combined with the difficulty of finding outlets for unorthodox ideas and forms of expression, led the Schlegels to found and edit their own journal, *Das Athenäum* (1798–1800). For this collective enterprise, they recruited most of the Romantic circle around them, most significantly Novalis (Friedrich von Hardenberg; 1772–1801), an occasional visitor to Jena. Within the *Athenäum* too the emphasis was on collaborative communication: multiauthored collections of "fragments" and Friedrich Schlegel's own *Gespräch über die Poesie* (1800; *Conversation on Poetry*), in which a group of acquaintances regale each other with discourses and essays on literature and subject them to critical discussion. Two of the subjects covered in the *Athenäum* deserve special mention. First is the theory of the novel, in which it is argued that the future for the novel form lies in abandoning conventional linear narration and adopting a subjective, digressive, and open mode of narrative which can encompass poetry, dialogue, and other forms. Second is a bold concept of irony, what came to be known as Romantic Irony, encompassing all types of self-contradiction and self-referentiality that may indicate a capacity to think dialectically. Most famously, in one of the "fragments" in the

Athenäum, Friedrich Schlegel attempted a definition of romantic literature: it is "progressive Universalpoesie" (progressive universal poetry), a comprehensive poetic experience which is infinitely evolving and never complete. In the *Conversation on Poetry,* he varies the definition: the romantic consists of "sentimentalen Stoff in einer fantastischen Form" (sentimental content in a fantastic form), a phrase which may be interpreted as "content of a spiritual or metaphysical kind presented in a form governed by the imagination."

Novalis's principal contributions to the *Athenäum* were his *Hymnen an die Nacht* (1800; *Hymns to the Night*) and his own collection of "fragments" entitled *Blütenstaub* (1798; *Pollen*). The *Hymnen* are a cycle of intense poems expressing in semi-mystical imagery a vision of eternity as a realm of love for which the human being, trapped in finite imperfection, can only long. In his unfinished novel *Heinrich von Ofterdingen* (1802), Novalis created an allegorical account of the vatic mission of the creative artist to redeem civilization. Similarly utopian visions of a regenerate community inform *Die Christenheit; oder, Europa* (1826; *Christendom; or, Europe*), a hymnic essay which Novalis read out at a gathering of Romantic writers in Jena in 1799 but which was deemed so controversial that it remained unpublished until 1826. Here Novalis argued that political and military discord in Europe could only be ended by a universal recovery of Christian faith, which would act as the basis for a community of nations akin to the Middle Ages united under the papacy. In this essay, Novalis drew inspiration expressly from the *Reden über die Religion* (1799; *Addresses on Religion*) of the Romantic theologian Friedrich Schleiermacher in Berlin, to whose work he was introduced by Friedrich Schlegel following Schlegel's move from Jena to Berlin in 1797. *Addresses on Religion* attempts a rehabilitation of religion in a post-rationalist age by redefining it: religion is not about theological doctrine or moral prescriptions; it is any conception of existence that transcends the merely empirical. Thus all Early Romantic aspirations to spiritual totality, what they termed "transcendental philosophy," were identified as fundamentally religious. The way was open for the religious revival that became a central feature of German Romanticism.

In Berlin, Schlegel also encountered two other Early Romantics who were far less intellectual and theoretical than the Jena group: Ludwig Tieck (1773–1853) and Wilhelm Heinrich Wackenroder (1773–98). Tieck's Romantic comedies *Der gestiefelte Kater* (1797; *Puss in Boots*) and *Die verkehrte Welt* (1798; *The Topsy-Turvy World*) use fairy-tale plots whimsically to satirize the contemporary literary and theatrical scene. Tieck's major contribution to Early Romanticism, however, arose from his friendship with Wackenroder. In 1797 they jointly published the *Herzensergießungen eines kunstliebenden Klosterbruders* (*Effusions of an Art-Loving Friar*), a collection of brief hagiographic biographies of Renaissance artists interspersed with essays meditating on the significance of art. In the essays, Wackenroder, the principal author of *Effusions,* proclaims a fundamentally humanist aesthetic derived from his Enlightenment background: all forms of art, primitive and sophisticated, classical and Gothic, are equally valid expressions of the human creative impulse. The sections on individual artists are more Romantic in implication and more open to misunderstanding. They appear to suggest that the only valid art is a manifestation of Christian faith. In fact, the religious perspective of the fictional narrator, the friar, is a metaphor for the belief that art conveys spiritual truth rather than reflecting physical reality. In this context Wackenroder introduced the concept of the hieroglyph, which was to become widespread in Romanticism and which encapsulates the Romantic view of symbolism enunciated by the Schlegel brothers and found everywhere in Romantic theory, for instance in Shelley's *Defence of Poetry.* Art and poetry are the "hieroglyphic," encoded expression of the evanescent glimpses of the absolute vouchsafed to the visionary few, "intimations of immortality" which would otherwise remain inaccessible to limited mortals.

Wackenroder died in 1798, Novalis in 1801. The Early Romantic coterie disintegrated. Tieck and the Schlegels went their separate paths, although they continued to publish, remained in occasional contact, and, in their different ways, influenced the second generation of Romantics. The Late Romantics now turned away from abstract theorizing and moved to the pursuit of poetry and imaginative literature. However, in typically Romantic fashion, they confronted these imagined worlds with a social reality which they could hardly respect but equally could not discount.

Clemens Brentano (1778–1842), a lyric poet of exquisite but agonized sensibility, and Achim von Arnim (1781–1831), principally remembered as an historical novelist, constituted the nucleus of the Heidelberg Romantics. Between 1805 and 1808, they together published a comprehensive anthology of German folk poetry in two volumes under the improbable title *Des Knaben Wunderhorn* (*The Boy's Miraculous Post-Horn*). In collecting and sensitively editing the vigorous verse of a mainly oral tradition, they gave new impetus to the German lyric in the 19th century, especially to the poetry of the later Romantic Joseph von Eichendorff (1789–1857), who himself was a student in Heidelberg in this period. At a time when the Rhineland had long been under French domination and Napoleon's empire was extending ever further eastward into Germany, such ostensibly antiquarian research represented an act of cultural nationalism. These motives also inspired the maverick Joseph Görres (1776–1848), who moved to Heidelberg in 1806 and joined Brentano and Arnim not only in their editorial activity but in their antirationalist polemics. In 1807 he published *Die teutschen Volksbücher* (*The German Chapbooks*)—the "t" in the German title was a deliberate archaism—in which he summarized and interpreted German legends such as Till Eulenspiegel.

With the Heidelberg writers, German Romanticism had now taken a decidedly conservative turn, cultivating history and tradition. It was to be a fateful and specifically German development, for in France and Britain, by contrast, Romantic writers after 1800 tended to be liberal and modernist in outlook. As early as 1806, the Romantic philosopher Johann Gottlieb Fichte (1762–1814) had delivered a series of lectures in Berlin under the title *Reden an die deutsche Nation* (*Addresses to the German Nation*), in which he counterposed the notion of the "Volk" (the folk community) to the French revolutionary concept of the nation state and at the same time proclaimed the unique historical mission of the Germans. Thus, in Germany the Romantic reaction against France, the country identified with liberal reform, led in the 19th century to an ominous rejection of democratic and cosmopolitan Western thought.

The search for traditional certitudes in a destabilized age, coupled with the loss of faith in the humanistic and utopian visions of Early Romanticism, also led a number of German Romantics to turn to Catholicism in the first decades of the 19th century. Both Brentano, whose conversion was formalized in 1817, and

Görres became Catholic propagandists in the 1830s and 1840s. Friedrich Schlegel moved to Vienna in 1808 and simultaneously converted to Catholicism, later propounding the Christian monarchist ideology of the Restoration. Conservative Catholicism found a far more subtle exponent in Joseph von Eichendorff, whose novels, stories, and lyrical poetry from the 1810s through to 1840 contain complex tensions between religion and poetry and also a richly ambiguous view of nature. Eichendorff's novel *Ahnung und Gegenwart* (1815; *Premonition and Present*) presents a caustic picture of pretentious German provincial life in the late Napoleonic epoch. As a countermodel, he offered the idyll of rural, itinerant, and carefree existence based on unobtrusive religious conviction which was to become his hallmark, especially in the tale *Aus dem Leben eines Taugenichts* (1826; *Extracts from the Life of a Good-for-Nothing*). In his verse, Eichendorff extols the wonder of nature as an expression of the divine and an antidote to profane modern civilization, yet at the same time, he shies away from the potentially godless pantheism inherent in such adulation of nature. With similar ambivalence, he proclaims the value of poetry in a utilitarian age, yet fears the equally godless seductions of aestheticism.

The reactionary Germany of the Restoration epoch encountered its most sarcastic Romantic critic in the lawyer and musician Ernst Theodor Amadeus Hoffmann (1776–1822). In his modern fairy tales, most notably *Der goldne Topf* (1813; *The Golden Pot*) and *Klein Zaches* (1819; *Little Zaches,* the tale of the malevolent freak Zaches who rises to political eminence), he created a typically painful Romantic duality: on the one hand the complacency of the bourgeoisie and the corruption of the ruling aristocracy, on the other a poetic world which embodies mythical fairy bliss but which is itself relativized as elusive and ambiguous. The historical optimism of the Early Romantics had disappeared. In the *Kreisleriana* (1810–13; *Tales of Kreisler*), a series of satirical skits and musical anecdotes, and the ingeniously constructed novel *Lebensansichten des Katers Murr* (1822; *Life and Opinions of the Tomcat Murr*), Hoffmann painted an at times hilarious but at times distressing portrait of the isolation of the inspired Romantic artist in an insufferable society. Hoffmann's disorientation is manifest too in his alarming tales of neurosis and derangement, such as *Der Sandmann* (1816) and *Das Fräulein von Scuderi* (1818), and his "Gothic" horror novel *Die Elixiere des Teufels* (1815–16: *The Devil's Elixirs*). The increasing emphasis on contemporary reality in Hoffmann's later work is mirrored in the novella *Peter Schlemihl* (1814) by his friend Adelbert von Chamisso (1781–1838) and in differing ways in the short stories of Brentano and Tieck which appeared up until the 1830s. Romanticism was evolving into early realism, while also coming under direct attack with the advent of the liberal Junges Deutschland movement (Young Germany) in 1830.

What the Early and Late Romantics in Germany shared with each other and with Romantics elsewhere in Europe was an alienation from contemporary reality in its increasingly urban, industrial, and commercial form, in the Marxist view from developing capitalism. Their craving for humane alternative values led all of them into a dualistic view of human experience: on the one hand material reality, on the other a more significant or "higher" existence located either inside the human spirit or in visions of an idyllic past or regenerate future. This dualism was at times a cause for despair, at times a source of stimulating tension, at times the basis of self-irony or black humor. While the Early Romantics in Germany remained confident that their visions were positive and eventually realizable, their Late Romantic counterparts became aware of the potentially delusory or even damaging nature of the subjective alternatives in which they nevertheless continued to believe. The dismissal of social reality was perceived as a dubious procedure by a second generation which had been abruptly confronted with *realpolitik*.

In *Die Romantische Schule* (1833; *The Romantic School*), Heine denounced Romanticism as the latest expression of a tradition of spiritualism that served the purposes of political reaction by diverting attention from material reality and its social injustice. Yet both the dismissal of Romanticism by Heine and later leftist critics such as Georg Lukàcs, and the conservative adulation of it in the late 19th century and the first half of the 20th, are reductivist. In Germany and elsewhere, it represented nothing less than the breakthrough of European culture into individualistic and therefore divided modern consciousness, an intellectual emancipation which was bound to produce a wide spectrum of opposing ideologies. Nowhere was this variety and contradictoriness more apparent than in German Romanticism.

RICHARD LITTLEJOHNS

Further Reading

Berlin, Isaiah, *The Roots of Romanticism,* edited by Henry Hardy, Princeton, New Jersey: Princeton University Press, and London: Chatto and Windus, 1999

Hughes, Glyn Tegai, *Romantic German Literature,* London: Arnold, and New York: Holmes and Meier, 1979

Menhennet, Alan, *The Romantic Movement,* London: Croom Helm, and Totowa, New Jersey: Barnes and Noble, 1981

Peter, Klaus, editor, *Romantikforschung seit 1945,* Königstein: Hain, 1980

Prang, Helmut, editor, *Begriffsbestimmung der Romantik,* Darmstadt: Wissenschaftliche Buchgesellschaft, 1968

Prawer, Siegbert, editor, *The Romantic Period in Germany: Essays by Members of the London University Institute of Germanic Studies,* London: Weidenfeld and Nicholson, and New York: Schocken Books, 1970

Saul, Nicholas, "Aesthetic Humanism: German Literature, 1790–1830," in *The Cambridge History of German Literature,* edited by Helen Watanabe-O'Kelly, Cambridge and New York: Cambridge University Press, 1997

Schanze, Helmut, editor, *Romantik-Handbuch,* Stuttgart: Kröner, 1994

Ziolkowski, Theodore, *German Romanticism and Its Institutions,* Princeton, New Jersey: Princeton University Press, 1990

Gerhard Roth 1942–

By the mid-1980s, Gerhard Roth had established himself as one of Austria's most demanding new novelists. A writer primarily of prose fiction, he also tried his hand at experimental stage and radio plays at the start of his career. More recently, he has shown an interest in television, contributing scripts that use material from his own novels. His variegated and rather idiosyncratic oeuvre resists classification according to thematic or stylistic consistencies. Its most original parts reveal a generational pre-occupation, if not obsession, with the abiding virulence of a fascist mentality in his native country. Roth shares Thomas Bernhard's aggressiveness, for example, in his relentless inquiries into the sources and expressions of violence, but he is less given to satirical invective and insistent exaggerations.

As a social critic Roth has encountered his share of "patriotic" hostility. He has also received a measure of feigned indifference from a public that has an almost compulsive need to acknowledge only the "positive" side of its cultural and political traditions and its more recent societal compromises. Anything negative, Roth has come to be convinced, is being buried under a pretense of idyllic *gemütlichkeit* (comfort). His response to this collective silence (and to periodic outbursts of exculpatory righteousness) is an unflinching determination to confront his adversaries with the facts and stringencies of rational arguments. While Roth is by temperament an individualist with a capacity for ascetic solitariness, he has also become a public (although not an iconic) figure who has participated directly in cultural and political controversies. His journalism, consisting mostly of polemical essays and self-analytical interviews, is thus the inevitable by-product of his sense of civic responsibility.

Roth has pointed to three principal impulses that inform the particular subjectivity of his style. The first is his pictorial imagination and its grounding in a profusion of visual images. In the process of writing, such images expand incessantly until they assume an existence independent of rational coherence. Often they accumulate hypertrophically and form seemingly uncontrolled clusters of raw material. The second involves his fascination with schizophrenia and with mental states that produce associative perceptions of reality and that defy the predictability of "normal," rational behavior. The third comprises the unabated persistence of childhood fears, anxieties, and early insecurities and traumas, which make his fiction, especially when it retrieves the impact and long-term effects of war experiences, as much an autobiographical as a "political" exploration.

Roth started writing in 1967. He had broken off his medical studies and was employed as a programmer at the Center for Statistics in his hometown of Graz. In Graz, Alfred Kolleritsch edited the journal *manuskripte* and guided a group of young writers (among them Peter Handke, G.F. Jonke, Helmut Eisendle, and Wolfgang Bauer) who were known as *Forum Stadtpark*. Roth's life as a husband and father of three children had by then become an intense struggle, which balanced many conflicting needs and obligations. His artistic response to these pressures and strains was a sequence of experimental prose texts, notably five mini-novels (*Kurzromane*), whose titles and "plots" allude to popular genres of realistic fiction. His method was to demolish conventional mimetic techniques and subvert them radically. For instance, the narrative progression that is re-

tained in his first book, *Die Autobiographie des Albert Einstein* (1972; *The Autobiography of Albert Einstein*), adds up to no more than the protocol of a paranoid schizophrenic's perceptions. This character fails to detect, from the time of his existence as a fetus until his death, any system in the infinite mass of scientific data, empirical facts, and private observations that constantly bombard his senses and his brain. Such random accumulation of perception produces a collage of arbitrary prismatic constellations that nonetheless suggest the emergence of a fundamentally new, albeit illogical picture of reality—as the revolutionary world view of a self-conscious but demented intelligence.

This cerebral solipsism permits but few variations on its basic mode and material, for it rigorously abstains from storytelling. To get out of this self-imposed impasse, Roth constructed his next three novels around standard, although differently focused, fictional devices. In *Der grosse Horizont* (1974; The Great Horizon), for example, he used the motifs and techniques of the detective novel to provide a plot and authentic locales for the portrayal of psychopathological conflicts. His protagonist Daniel Haid, a recently divorced hypochondriac from Vienna, even imagines himself as the fictional Philip Marlowe (of Raymond Chandler's books) as he roams through New York and other American cities in search of a new identity. These travels, much like those of the village teacher Nagl's Italian *Winterreise* (1978; Winter Journey)—this character's existential despair expresses itself both as sexual ferocity and a numbed indifference to the world outside of him—may be read as tersely antiromantic refutations of the bourgeois bildungsroman.

Roth's depictions of deranged characters and their perceptions, however, rely entirely on a single third-person narrator whose credibility as an objective observer is never in doubt. He tells of near fatal estrangements with the intense but dispassionate reliability of a clinician's report. This technique is retained in *Der stille Ozean* (1980; *The Calm Ocean*), the story of a physician, Ascher, who has sought refuge in a poor mountain village. What he experiences as a slowly accepted outsider and what he hears when his neighbors talk evolve into the picture of a desperate and brutal but also resourcefully humane life that is constantly beset by poverty and violence.

It is in this world that Roth also situated his most ambitious novel, *Land-läufiger Tod* (1984; The Customary Way to Die). The narrative structure of this voluminous phantasmagoria is defined by its controlling brain, that of the mute schizophrenic Franz Lindner, which is analogous to the "flying cells" of a swarm of bees: it forms a composite being without a fixed body, yet is guided by the sum of instincts connate in every single part of it. The voices in his head thus create a far-reaching topography of the surreal imagination and historical experience that encompasses both the microcosm of life in a rural society and a maze of purely mental landscapes. The aesthetic risk inherent in such an attempt—to replace a decrepit order with the creative chaos of a new vision, "to rewrite the Bible"—is the inevitable arbitrariness of its inventions, which can easily turn into oddities and then multiply with the monotonous compulsion that they are meant to supersede.

But Roth had developed here a narrative style of precise observations and illogical associations, which he adapted to evoke another disjointed world, the Vienna of a murderous maniac who becomes an attorney, and of his pursuer, the morally frustrated intellectual judge Sonnenberg, the principal character of *Der Untersuchungsrichter* (1988; The Investigator). Most recently, however, Roth has turned to a slightly ironic realism in two intricately plotted and fast-paced crime novels that make effective use of what constitutes the genre's popular appeal: the linkage of the mysterious and the plausible with the expectation of ultimate justice.

MICHAEL WINKLER

Biography

Born in Graz, Styria, Austria, in 1942. Studied medicine at the University of Graz, 1961–67; worked as a computer programmer, 1967–77; several trips to the United States, 1972–81; belongs to the artistic and literary circle of the Forum Stadtpark, Graz, and its literary magazine *manuskripte*; member of the Grazer Autorenversammlung, 1973–78; writes Archives of Silence (*Archive des Schweigens*), seven volumes, 1978–91; freelance writer, since 1977, with residences in Graz, Hamburg, and, most recently, Vienna.

Selected Works

Prose

Die Autobiographie des Albert Einstein, 1972; as *The Autobiography of Albert Einstein*, translated by Malcolm Green, 1992
Der grosse Horizont: Roman, 1974
Ein neuer Morgen: Roman, 1976
Winterreise: Roman, 1978; as *Winterreise*, translated by Joachim Neugroschel, 1980
Menschen Bilder Marionetten: Prosa Kurzromane Stücke, 1979
Der stille Ozean: Roman, in *Die Archive des Schweigens*, vol. 2, 1980
Die schönen Bilder beim Trabrennen, 1982
Dorfchronik zum "Landläufigen Tod," 1984
Landläufiger Tod: Roman, in *Die Archive des Schweigens*, vol. 3, illustrated by Günter Brus, 1984
Am Abgrund: Roman, in *Archive des Schweigens*, vol. 4, illustrated by G. Brus, 1986
Der Untersuchungsrichter: Die Geschichte eines Entwurfs: Roman, in *Die Archive des Schweigens*, vol. 5, 1988
Über Bienen. Mit Fotos von Franz Killmeyer. Essays, 1989
Im tiefen Österreich: Bild/Textband, in *Die Archive des Schweigens*, vol. 1, 1990
Die Geschichte der Dunkelheit: Ein Bericht, in *Die Archive des Schweigens*, vol. 6, 1991
Eine Reise in das Innere von Wien: Essays, in *Die Archive des Schweigens*, vol. 7, photography by F. Killmeyer and Chr. de Grancy, 1991

Die Archive des Schweigens. Sieben Bände, 1992
Das doppelköpfige Österreich: Essays, Polemiken, Interviews, edited by Kristina Pfoser-Schewig, 1995
Der See: Roman, 1995
Der Plan: Roman, 1998

Plays

Lichtenberg (produced 1973), 1973
Sehnsucht (produced 1977), 1977
Dämmerung (produced 1978)
Erinnerungen an die Menschheit (produced 1985), 1985
Fremd in Wien (produced 1993)

Films

Der große Horizont: TV-Film, directed by Peter Lehner and Gerhard Roth (produced 1976)
Der stille Ozean, directed by F.X. Schwarzenberger (produced 1983)
Landläufiger Tod: TV-Film in zwei Teilen. 1. Teil: "Mikrokosmos," 2. Teil: "Am Abgrund," directed by Michael Schottenberg (produced 1991)
Das Geheimnis: TV-Film, directed by Michael Schottenberg (produced 1993)
Geschäfte: TV-Film, directed by Michael Schottenberg (produced 1994)
Eine Reise in das Innere von Wien: TV-Dokumentation, directed by Jan Schütte (produced 1995)
Schnellschuß: TV-Film, directed by Thomas Roth (produced 1995)
Der See: TV-Film, directed by Thomas Roth (produced 1997)

Further Reading

Baltl, Marianne, and Christian Ehetreiber, *Gerhard Roth*, Graz: Droschl, 1995
Ensberg, Peter, "The Theme of Insanity and Its Effects on Form and Style in the Work of Gerhard Roth," *Modern Austrian Literature* 24, no. 3/4 (1991)
Federico, Joseph, *Confronting Modernity: Rationality, Science, and Communication in German Literature of the 1980s*, Columbia, South Carolina: Camden House, 1992
Osterle, Heinz D., "The Lost Utopia: New Images of America in German Literature," *German Quarterly* 54, no. 4 (1981)
Ryan, Simon C., *Gerhard Roth and the Graz Literary Revival: The Emergence of an Austrian Author*, Ph.D. dissertation, Cambridge University, 1990
Schreckenberger, Helga, and Peter Ensberg, *Gerhard Roth: Kunst als Auflehnung gegen das Sein*, Tübingen: Stauffenburg, 1994
Schütte, Uwe, *Auf der Spur der Vergessenen: Gerhard Roth und seine Archive des Schweigens*, Vienna: Böhlau, 1997
Wittstock, Uwe, editor, *Gerhard Roth: Materialien zu "Die Archive des Schweigens,"* Frankfurt: Fischer Taschenbuch, 1992

Joseph Roth 1894–1939

The writing career of Joseph Roth exemplifies in acute forms the tensions experienced by central European intellectuals in the period between the world wars: tensions between traditional conceptions of literary writing and economic practicalities, between inherited conceptions of community and the rationalizing processes of a Western model of modernity, between humane idealism and personal despair.

Roth established himself as a journalist in the period immediately following World War I, reporting—often in a spirit of revolutionary fervor—on the political and social upheavals in Eastern Europe and in the German-speaking world. His first novel, *Das Spinnennetz* (1923; The Spider's Web), which was published in a Viennese workers' newspaper, remains fragmentary because serialization was halted by the news of Hitler's Munich putsch. It tells of a young man's rise to power and influence aided by the antidemocratic and anti-Semitic prejudices he shares with others, and of how the climate of mutual manipulation in the early 1920s makes life in its entirety come to resemble a "web" of machination and double-dealing suspended above a void. This depiction of aggressive nihilism is complemented by the tragicomic plot of *Die Rebellion* (1924; The Rebellion), in which the protagonist cleaves to the heroic patriotism for which he has fought and lost a leg in the war, is subjected to a series of mishaps which make him the victim of denunciation and imprisonment, and responds by abandoning himself to cosmic despair. Taken together, these two early works give a vivid picture of a world from which any sense of fundamental value and legitimizing authority has been peremptorily removed.

In other novels of the 1920s, Roth continued to depict the effects of postwar disruption on the lives of the younger generation returning from the war, combining close attention to the detail of personal circumstances with a fuller sense of the symbolic significance of such detail. The hotel he describes in *Hotel Savoy* (1924), with its seven stories stratified according to the wealth and status of the clientele, is like an emblematic chunk of Western civilization set down in a Polish provincial town. It provides temporary accommodation for a variety of figures who are searching in the postwar world for vestiges of a past life, or for intimations of a future one, and who are destined to be disappointed in both respects. *Die Flucht ohne Ende* (1927; *Flight without End*) traces the experiences of an Austrian soldier who confronts the fragility of personal identity as he makes his way back from captivity in Siberia. His sense of dislocation becomes all the more intense when he reaches the West and finds himself paralyzed by the sense of his own superfluity and alienated from what now appear to him as the mechanical laws of bourgeois society. It was this work that led Roth's name to be associated with the vogue for documentary writing in the 1920s because he claimed in the preface to be reporting the authentic experience of a personal friend rather than creating a fiction. By 1930, however, Roth was firmly distancing himself—in his essay "Schluss mit der 'Neuen Sachlichkeit'" (Let's Put a Stop to "New Objectivity")—from any such naive reliance on factual veracity as a criterion for the value of literary writing. *Zipper und sein Vater* (1928; *Zipper and His Father*), which is again narrated as if from a position of personal acquaintance, contrasts the unsettled and aimless life of a young war veteran from Vienna with the self-assured, if socially limited, outlook of his father.

As a much sought-after writer of feuilleton articles in the 1920s, Roth simultaneously continued to report on contemporary events as indications of a general cultural malaise in Western Europe. His articles on Jewish migration from Eastern Europe, which were published in book form under the title *Juden auf Wanderschaft* (1927; Migrating Jews), display his distaste for the way in which Western assumptions about national identity and socioeconomic organization have been imposed on the ethnically mixed communities of Eastern Europe. At the same time, he maintains the stance of the investigative journalist seeking to expose and challenge the effects of stereotyping within those Eastern European communities as well as in the West. Roth's sense of the inherent value of traditional Judaic beliefs and practices is most intensely apparent in the novel *Hiob* (1930; *Job*), which adopts the narrative structure of the biblical legend while telling of experiences that are very much those of

the 20th century. Here his East European Jewish protagonist, Mendel Singer, stoically endures the various afflictions visited upon his wife and children until those sufferings are eventually dispelled, as if by a miracle, when the family is reunited in New York.

Radetzkymarsch (1932; *The Radetzky March*), the work for which Joseph Roth is most commonly remembered, recalls the measured life style of the prewar Hapsburg Empire, with its peculiar combination of precarious multiethnic equilibrium, bureaucratic correctness, and hedonistic sensuality. But it also depicts that society as burdened with the consciousness of its own impending demise. The first chapter shows a political myth being created out of the spirit of self-delusion: at the battle of Solferino in 1859, a young lieutenant saves the life of the still younger Emperor by pulling him to the ground just in time to avoid an enemy bullet, and the incident is subsequently stylized into an act of extravagant military bravery. Through his account of the descendants of this "hero of Solferino," Roth shows a world in which, from one generation to another, all sense of purpose drains away from the preservation of inherited practices until the last member of the family finds a meaningless death in the opening skirmishes of World War I. A Spenglerian vision of European culture in decline is an inescapable feature of Roth's novels, but it is accompanied by a passionate commitment to the assiduous recording of the personal and cultural experiences of loss.

The works that Roth completed after fleeing from the Nazis in 1933 continue to display this distinctive mixture of cultural pessimism and laconic defiance. The title figure of *Tarabas* (1934), which is based on a story from a Ukrainian newspaper, is a ruthless military commander who develops the potential for becoming a pentitent and a holy fool of the kind familiar from Russian literature. Roth's *Die hundert Tage* (1936; *The Story of the Hundred Days*) shows us a Napoleon who renounces the aspiration to power after learning to recognize his own human frailty. *Das falsche Gewicht* (1937; *Weights and Measures*) tells of a weights-and-measures inspector in the borderlands of the Tsarist Empire who experiences both intense emotional disappointments and the emptiness of a life dedicated wholeheartedly to duty, and who ends up imagining that he will be prosecuted for "false weights" in heaven, as he has prosecuted others on earth. *Die Kapuzinergruft* (1938; *The Emperor's Tomb*), which is a sequel to *Radetzkymarsch,* shows Roth responding to the National Socialist takeover in Austria with an expression of true nostalgia for the Hapsburg dynasty. *Die Legende vom heiligen Trinker* (1939; *The Legend of the Holy Drinker*), finally, conveys a self-ironic impression of Roth's own condition in his last years, presenting the inveterate alcoholic as a disheveled but pure emblem of a kind of honor which can ultimately find refuge only in God's mercy. Roth's peculiar achievement as a writer was to make the acute observation of sensory experience into a medium for conveying an intense sense of cultural and existential crisis.

DAVID MIDGLEY

See also Austria: Late Habsburg Literature in Vienna

Biography

Born in Brody, Galicia, Austria (now the Ukraine), 2 September 1894. Studied at the University Lemberg, Vienna, 1913; studied German literature at the University of Vienna, 1914–16; served in the Austrian army, 1916–18; claimed to have spent months in Russian captivity as a prisoner of war; journalist in Vienna, 1919–23; staff member, Berlin, 1923–25, and cultural correspondent, Paris, 1925, Soviet Union, 1926, Albania, 1927, and Poland, 1928, for the *Frankfurter Zeitung;* moved to Paris to escape the Nazi regime, 1933, where he lived the remainder of his life; traveled to Poland, 1933 and 1937, on a PEN lecture tour. Died in Paris, 27 May 1939.

Selected Works

Novels

Das Spinnennetz, 1923 (serialized); 1967 (book form); as *The Spider's Web,* translated by John Hoare, with *Zipper and His Father,* 1988

Hotel Savoy, 1924; translated by John Hoare, in *Hotel Savoy; Fallmerayer the Stationmaster; The Bust of the Emperor,* 1986

Die Rebellion, 1924

April: Die Geschichte einer Liebe, 1925

Der blinde Spiegel, 1925

Die Flucht ohne Ende, 1927; as *Flight without End,* translated by Ida Zeitlin, 1930; translated by David Le Vay and Beatrice Musgrave, 1977

Zipper und sein Vater, 1928; as *Zipper and His Father,* translated by John Hoare, with *The Spider's Web,* 1988

Rechts und Links, 1929; as *Right and Left,* translated by Michael Hofmann, 1991

Hiob: Roman eines einfachen Mannes, 1930; as *Job: The Story of a Simple Man,* translated by Dorothy Thompson, 1931

Radetzkymarsch, 1932; as *The Radetzky March,* translated by Geoffrey Dunlop, 1933; translated by Eva Tucker, 1974; translated by Joachim Neugroschel, 1995

Tarabas: Ein Gast auf dieser Erde, 1934; as *Tarabas: A Guest on Earth,* 1934; translated by Winifred Katzin, 1987

Le Buste de l'Empereur (in French), 1934; as *Die Büste des Kaisers,* 1964; as *The Bust of the Emperor,* translated by John Hoare, in *Hotel Savoy; Fallmerayer the Stationmaster; The Bust of the Emperor,* 1986

Der Antichrist, 1934; as *Antichrist,* translated by Moray Firth, 1935

Die hundert Tage, 1936; as *The Ballad of the Hundred Days,* translated by Moray Firth, 1936; as *The Story of the Hundred Days,* 1936

Beichte eines Mörders, erzählt in einer Nacht, 1936; as *Confession of a Murderer, Told in One Night,* translated by Desmond L. Vesey, 1938

Das falsche Gewicht, 1937; as *Weights and Measures,* translated by David Le Vay, 1982

Die Kapuzinergruft, 1938; as *The Emperor's Tomb,* translated by John Hoare, 1984

Die Geschichte von der 1002. Nacht, 1939; as *The Tale of the 1002nd Night,* translated by Michael Hofmann, 1998

Die Legende vom heiligen Trinker, 1939; as *The Legend of the Holy Drinker,* translated by Michael Hofmann, 1989

Der Leviathan, 1940

Romane, Erzählungen, Aufsätze, 1964

Der stumme Prophet, 1966; as *The Silent Prophet,* translated by David Le Vay, 1979

Die Erzählungen, 1973

Further Reading

Bronsen, David, *Joseph Roth: Eine Biographie,* Cologne: Kiepenheuer and Witsch, 1974

Bronsen, David, editor, *Joseph Roth und die Tradition: Aufsatz- und Materialiensammlung,* Darmstadt: Agora, 1975

Chambers, Helen, editor, *Co-existent Contradictions: Joseph Roth in Retrospect: Papers of the 1989 Joseph Roth Symposium at Leeds University,* Riverside, California: Ariadne Press, 1991

Heizmann, Jürgen, *Joseph Roth und die Ästhetik der Neuen Sachlichkeit,* Heidelberg: Mattes, 1990

Henze, Volke, *Jüdischer Kulturpessimismus und das Bild des Alten Österreich im Werk Stefan Zweigs und Joseph Roths,* Heidelberg: Winter, 1988

Kessler, Michael, and Fritz Hackert, editors, *Joseph Roth: Interpretation, Kritik, Rezeption,* Tübingen: Stauffenburg, 1990

Magris, Claudio, *Weit von wo: Verlorene Welt des Ostjudentums,* Vienna: Europaverlag, 1974

Müller-Funk, Wolfgang, *Joseph Roth,* Munich: Beck, 1989

Nürnberger, Helmuth, *Joseph Roth: In Selbstzeugnissen und Bilddokumenten,* Reinbek bei Hamburg: Rowohlt, 1981

Shaked, Gershon, "Wie jüdisch ist ein jüdisch-deutscher Roman? Über Joseph Roths *Hiob: Roman eines einfachen Mannes,*" in *Juden in der deutschen Literatur: Ein deutsch-israelisches Symposion,* edited by Stéphane Moses and Albrecht Schöne, Frankfurt: Suhrkamp, 1986

Siegel, Rainer-Joachim, *Joseph Roth, Bibliographie,* Morsum/Sylt: Cicero, 1995

Steinmann, Esther, *Von der Würde des Unscheinbaren: Sinnerfahrung bei Joseph Roth,* Tübingen: Niemeyer, 1984

Trommler, Frank, *Roman und Wirklichkeit: Eine Ortsbestimmung am Beispiel von Musil, Broch, Roth, Doderer und Gütersloh,* Stuttgart: Kohlhammer, 1966

Radetzkymarsch 1932
Novel by Joseph Roth

Joseph Roth's novel *Radetzkymarsch* (*The Radetzky March*) is a prime example of that literary construction of Austrian cultural identity to which Claudio Magris has given the name "Habsburg myth" and which seemed to acquire an enhanced potency after 1918, when the Habsburg Empire had ceased to exist as a reality. Whereas the cultural atmosphere of that lost cosmopolitan empire was treated with nostalgia by Franz Werfel (*Barbara; oder, Die Frömmigkeit* [1929; translated as *The Pure in Heart* and *The Hidden Child*]) and with irony by Robert Musil (*Der Mann ohne Eigenschaften* [1930–43; *The Man Without Qualities*]), the tone of Roth's depiction is one of sharply etched melancholy. His narrative frequently lingers over the description of a measured prewar lifestyle with its peculiar combination of precarious multiethnic equilibrium, bureaucratic correctness, and hedonistic sensuality, but he presents both the characters and the Austrian state apparatus as imbued with the consciousness of their own impending demise.

The story begins with the battle of Solferino, which is remembered by historians as marking the effective loss of Austrian influence in Italy and which is recalled later in the novel as the moment when the rot set in. In Roth's narrative it also marks the creation of a political legend out of the stuff of self-delusion. In this battle of 1859, a Slovenian lieutenant saves the life of the young Emperor Franz Joseph by pulling him to the ground just in time to avoid an enemy bullet. He is subsequently dismayed to find that the incident has been stylized by patriotic wishful thinking into an act of extravagant military bravery. The descendants of this "hero of Solferino," the Trotta family, are destined to live with an ambiguous legacy: on the one hand they are the beneficiaries of recurrent imperial favors, but by the same token their lives become inextricably linked with an increasingly ossified imperial order. Not only does it appear to be an open secret among high-ranking army officers and civil servants that Austro-Hungary cannot long hold together against the strains of its internal ethnic and social tensions, and that it is bound to lose any war it is compelled to fight, there are also more palpable intimations of decay that accompany the lives of the Trottas themselves. Young Carl Joseph, the grandson of the "hero of Solferino," experiences his sexual initiation at the hands of a married woman, only to find that she dies soon afterward in childbirth (a childbirth for which he is by implication responsible).

During the early stages of Carl Joseph's army service he develops a bond of fellowship with the Jewish regimental doctor, with whom he shares a sense of emptiness, a sense of not belonging, and an awareness of the "call" of his ancestors; the doctor, however, is soon killed in a duel provoked by a malicious insinuation about the nature of Carl Joseph's relationship with the doctor's estranged wife. In the figures of Carl Joseph and his father (a district commissioner of the Empire), Roth depicts a way of life that, from one generation to another, has seen all sense of purpose drained away from the preservation of inherited practices. Carl Joseph himself eventually finds the "meaningless" death he has anticipated through an act of quiet defiance and implicit humanity in the opening phase of World War I: he fetches water for his troops from a well that he knows to be under enemy fire.

What lends Roth's narrative its peculiar vividness is the precise attention it brings to sensory detail, which is a general characteristic of the author's writing. The poignancy and sensuous experience of Carl Joseph's relationship with Frau Slama is evoked through the bitter aftertaste of the raspberry juice he has previously shared with her and which he now shares with her widower before his love letters are returned to him—very correctly and without apparent animus. The close association of loyalty and frailty is brought home by a moment of physical description when the old emperor comes face to face with Carl Joseph and mistakes him for the son, rather than the grandson, of the "hero of Solferino"; what follows is a description of the droplet that has formed on the emperor's nose, the tension that builds up among the assembled troops as they watch that droplet gather, and their relief when it finally falls. The text concludes, indeed, with an image that suggests the continuing presence of the past in the domain of sensory experience: after the Trotta family and their emperor have passed away, a solitary figure sits in a coffeehouse, bereft of his companion, but still going through the motions of a routine chess game, with the incessant autumn rain falling outside.

The hollowness of the old regime is blended, in Roth's depiction of it, with the tender reconstruction of Habsburg Austria's Catholic outlook and humanity. The resulting ambiguities have ensured that *The Radetzky March* has remained an object of controversy in the critical literature. The ideological criticism of the 1970s, of which the *Text und Kritik* volume of 1974 is a clear example, interpreted the backward-looking perspective of the work as apologetic, regressive, and politically pessimistic. Others have seen the intimations of social and political unrest in the novel—Carl Joseph's company is deployed in the suppression of a strike among rural workers, and ethnic conflicts show signs of erupting within his father's district—as evidence of a critical

intention and the evocation of a new social order emerging from the old (Manger). The dignity that *The Radetzky March* confers upon a lost world has been seen as preserving a "magical" hope in the supranationalism of the Habsburg Empire (Müller-Funk), and the undeludedness with which it commemorates that world has led Magris to describe the work as an epic rather than an elegy. The sense in which *The Radetzky March* reflected the character of its time has probably never been more accurately summarized than in Ludwig Marcuse's review of the original publication. Marcuse recognized Carl Joseph as a desperate man whose nobility of bearing preserves him from cynicism and characterized the narrative as one simultaneously imbued with the coldness of nihilism and the goodness of humanity.

DAVID MIDGLEY

Editions

First edition: *Radetzkymarsch*, Berlin: Kiepenheuer, 1932
Critical edition: in *Werke*, vol. 5, edited by Fritz Hackert, Cologne: Kiepenheuer und Witsch, 1990
Translations: *The Radetzky March*, translated by Geoffrey Dunlop, New York: Viking Press, 1933; translated by Eva Tucker (based on Dunlop's translation), London and New York: Penguin, 1974; translated by Joachim Neugroschel, Woodstock, New York: Overlook Press, 1995

Further Reading

Bronsen, David, "Das literarische Bild der Auflösung in *Radetzkymarsch*," in *Joseph Roth: Werk und Wirkung*, edited by Bernd M. Kraske, Bonn: Bouvier, 1988
Hackert, Fritz, "Joseph Roth: *Radetzkymarsch*," in *Deutsche Romane des 20. Jahrhunderts: Neue Interpretationen*, edited by Paul Michael Lützeler, Königstein: Athenäum, 1983
Henze, Volker, *Jüdischer Kulturpessimismus und das Bild des alten Österreich im Werk Stefan Zweigs und Joseph Roths*, Heidelberg: Winter, 1988
Magris, Claudio, *Der habsburgische Mythos in der österreichischen Literatur*, Salzburg: Müller, 1966
Manger, Philip, "*The Radetzky March*: Joseph Roth and the Habsburg Myth," in *The Viennese Enlightenment*, edited by Mark Francis, London: Croom Helm, 1985
Marcuse, Ludwig, "Radetzkymarsch," in *Wie alt kann Aktuelles sein?* Zurich: Diogenes, and New York: St. Martin's Press, 1989
Menhennet, Alan, "Flight of a 'Broken Eagle': Joseph Roth's *Radetzkymarsch*," *New German Studies* 11 (1983)
Müller, Klaus-Detlef, "Joseph Roth: *Radetzkymarsch*, ein historischer Roman," in *Romane des 20. Jahrhunderts*, Stuttgart: Reclam, 1993
Reidel-Schrewe, Ursula, "Im Niemandsland zwischen Indikativ und Konjunktiv: Joseph Roths *Radetzkymarsch*," *Modern Austrian Literature* 24, no. 1 (1991)
Scheible, Hartmut, *Joseph Roth: Mit einem Essay über Gustave Flaubert*, Stuttgart: Kohlhammer, 1971
Steinmann, Esther, *Von der Würde des Unscheinbaren: Sinnerfahrung bei Joseph Roth*, Tübingen: Niemeyer, 1984
Trommler, Frank, *Roman und Wirklichkeit: Eine Ortsbestimmung am Beispiel von Musil, Broch, Roth, Doderer und Gütersloh*, Stuttgart: Kohlhammer, 1966
Wörsching, Martha, "Die rückwärts gewandte Utopie: Sozialpsychologische Anmerkungen zu Joseph Roths Roman *Radetzkymarsch*," in *Joseph Roth* [special issue of *Text und Kritik*], edited by Heinz Ludwig Arnold, Munich: Boorberg, 1974

Rudolf von Ems ca. late 12th Century–ca. 1254

Rudolf von Ems is one of the most prominent Middle High German writers of verse-couplet narrative poetry of the "postclassical" period (1220–90). This was an era in which German poets, for the first time, could look back on an established literary tradition in their own vernacular, and an era that saw vernacular works being composed in ever greater numbers, as well as the growth of literacy among lay people and the development of material conditions more propitious to the codification of vernacular texts in manuscript books. Rudolf may be viewed as a figurehead for the authorial self-consciousness that marks out the literary production of his day, and his works feature a whole series of passages in which he gives expression to two impulses: first, a keen awareness of belonging to the generation of poets who were heirs to the "masters" of the past (Heinrich von Veldeke, Hartmann von Aue, Gottfried von Straßburg, and Wolfram von Eschenbach); and second, a preoccupation with recording his own name, often in conjunction with details of the broader circumstances of composition, in the prologues, digressions, and epilogues of the literary texts themselves. Rudolf's close association with Latin traditions of literacy also becomes apparent in this context, especially from his repeated employment of the self-referential acrostic (RVODOLF) that clearly presupposes some kind of readership.

Rudolf's own "narratorial" comments lead us to believe that he was the author of six works, five of which survive (his working of the St. Eustachius legend is lost). The early narratives, the freely composed fictional work *Der guote Gêrhart* (Good Gerhard; for all questions of dating, see the following biography) and the widely attested saint's life *Barlaam und Josaphat,* are dominated in their respective structure by dialogues of one kind or another. In *Der guote Gêrhart,* this takes the form of an extended story-within-a-story as the eponymous hero, a merchant of Cologne, relates his life of exemplary humility to the German emperor, whose own praiseworthy deeds are flawed by conceit. Similarly, a substantial part of the tale of Barlaam the hermit's conversion of the Indian prince, Josaphat, consists of direct exchanges between the master and the pupil on points of Christian doctrine. The doctrinal aspect of *Barlaam und Josaphat* betrays the monastic origins of the story material, although Rudolf's primary audience would appear to be of a different type (lay nobility?), as suggested by the poet's striking integration of a mock dialogue between himself and his heart in defense of women and *minne.*

In the course of the latter part of his career, Rudolf made a formal transition from continuous narrative to subdividing his works into booklike sections. This latinate model may have seemed particularly appropriate for the overtly historiographical text *Alexander,* but it was also brought to bear on the composition of the courtly romance *Willehalm von Orlens,* Rudolf's third complete work. In this work, the practice of attributing an individual prologue to each subsection allows Rudolf to articulate, programmatically and at regular intervals, the ethos that informs this "sentimental" tale of the love affair between the titular hero and Princess Amelie of England, alongside its portrayal of virtually every aspect of courtly ceremony and etiquette. The same format is exploited systematically in *Alexander,* with repeated reference to Rudolf's own poetic activity, to reflect on the themes of fortune (*saelde*) and the problematic relationship between merit and reward. In spite of Rudolf's apparent pretensions to composing the definitive account of Alexander the Great in German, this work remained a fragment, albeit one of some 20,000 lines. In Rudolf's most ambitious project of all, the *Weltchronik* (The Chronicle of the World), the subdivision of the (incomplete) text corresponds to the established paradigm in Christian historiography of the six world ages (*aetates mundi*); the poet's ultimate aim is to present the conjunction of salvation and secular history in the figure of his royal patron, Conrad IV of Hohenstaufen.

The sheer quantity of "complete" manuscripts transmitting Rudolf's *Barlaam und Josaphat* (14), *Willehalm von Orlens* (19), and *Weltchronik* (25) permits us to suppose that these three texts enjoyed relatively high levels of success as medieval literary works. The most vivid illustration of Rudolf's authorial status in the later Middle Ages, however, is provided by the numerous author portraits that are a feature of the transmission of *Willehalm von Orlens, Alexander,* and *Weltchronik.* It should be noted that no other German vernacular author of the 12th and 13th centuries is privileged to this extent in this way. In terms of modern reception, Rudolf was for a long time regarded as the archetypal "postclassical" epigone whose compositions were stylistically accomplished but entirely bereft of the literary quality of his "classical" predecessors. This opinion prevailed until the late 1960s when the first serious attempts were made to analyze Rudolf in his own right and to highlight his concern with the workings of history (Brackert) and his place in a tradition of historiographical romance extending back to late antiquity (von Ertzdorff). More recently, interpretations of Rudolf's works, especially *Willehalm von Orlens,* have played an important role in the debate surrounding the possibilities of vernacular literary theory in the 13th century.

SEBASTIAN COXON

Biography

Date of birth unknown; ca. late 12th century. Self-designation in *Willehalm von Orlens* as *Ain dienest man ze Muntfort* and identification as *Rudolf von Ense* in the "first continuation" of the *Weltchronik* suggest that he was a lowly relation of the lords of Hohenems (southeast of Lake Constance); his ability to rework Latin sources betrays a clerical education; references in his works to patrons who were attested elsewhere provide a rudimentary chronological framework for most of his texts; prominent individuals at the Hohenstaufen court of Conrad IV named as the patrons of *Willehalm von Orlens;* Conrad IV himself commissioned the *Weltchronik* prior to his fateful expedition to Italy (d. 1254); unknown whether Rudolf accompanied Conrad IV and died in his service, as the "first continuator" of the *Weltchronik* apparently believed.

Selected Works

Alexander, edited by Viktor Junk, 2 vols., 1928–29
Barlaam und Josaphat, edited by Franz Pfeiffer, 1843
Der guote Gêrhart, edited by John A. Asher, 1962; 3rd revised edition, 1989
Weltchronik, edited by Gustav Ehrismann, 1915
Willehalm von Orlens, edited by Victor Junk, 1905

Further Reading

Brackert, Helmut, *Rudolf von Ems: Dichtung und Geschichte*, Heidelberg: Winter Universitätsverlag, 1968

Bumke, Joachim, *Mäzene im Mittelalter: Die Gönner und Auftraggeber der höfischen Literatur in Deutschland, 1150–1300*, Munich: Beck, 1979

Calomino, Salvatore, *From Verse to Prose: The Barlaam and Josaphat Legend in Fifteenth-Century Germany*, Potomac, Maryland: Scripta Humanistica, 1990

Green, Dennis, "On the Primary Reception of the Works of Rudolf von Ems," *Zeitschrift für deutsches Altertum* 115, no. 3 (1986)

Haug, Walter, *Literaturtheorie im deutschen Mittelalter: Von den Anfängen bis zum Ende des 13. Jahrhunderts*, Darmstadt: Wissenschaftliche Buchgesellschaft, 1985; 2nd revised edition, 1992

Heinzle, Joachim, *Wandlungen und Neuansätze im 13. Jahrhundert*, Geschichte der deutschen Literatur von den Anfängen bis zum Beginn der Neuzeit, edited by Joachim Heinzle, vol. II/2, Königstein: Athenäum, 1984; 2nd revised edition, Tübingen: Niemeyer, 1994

Jaurant, Danielle, *Rudolfs "Weltchronik" als offene Form: Überlieferungsstruktur und Wirkungsgeschichte*, Tübingen: Francke, 1995

Palmer, Nigel F., "Kapitel und Buch: Zu den Gliederungsprinzipien mittelalterlicher Bücher," *Frühmittelalterliche Studien* 23, no. 1 (1989)

———, "The High and Later Middle Ages (1100–1450)," in *The Cambridge History of German Literature*, edited by Helen Watanabe-O'Kelly, Cambridge and New York: Cambridge University Press, 1997

von Ertzdorff, Xenja, *Rudolf von Ems: Untersuchungen zum höfischen Roman im 13. Jahrhundert*, Munich: Fink, 1967

Wachinger, Burghart, "Autorschaft und Überlieferung," in *Autorentypen*, edited by Walter Haug and Burghart Wachinger, Tübingen: Niemeyer, 1991

Wisbey, Roy, *Das Alexanderbild Rudolfs von Ems*, Berlin: Schmidt, 1966

Wyss, Ulrich, "Rudolfs von Ems *Barlaam und Josaphat* zwischen Legende und Roman," in *Probleme mittelhochdeutscher Erzählformen: Marburger Colloquium 1969*, edited by Peter F. Ganz and Werner Schröder, Berlin: Schmidt, 1972

Zöller, Sonja, *Kaiser, Kaufmann, und die Macht des Geldes: Gerhard Unmaze von Köln als Finanzier der Reichspolitik und der "Gute Gerhard" des Rudolf von Ems*, Munich: Fink, 1993

Der Ruf

The influential postwar journal *Der Ruf* came into existence on 1 March 1945 in a U.S. prisoner camp at Fort Kearney, Rhode Island. Directly under the control of the U.S. military authorities, the journal was originally intended to form part of the U.S. government's reeducation program for German prisoners of war. The journal appeared twice monthly under the editorship of Gustav René Hocke and Curt Vinz, who were joined by Alfred Andersch and Hans-Werner Richter later that year.

The intention of the Americans had been to produce a neutral, nonpolitical journal with a claim to objectivity. The *Ruf*, however, soon adopted a clear editorial stance; in particular, it sought to establish a link between the prisoners and their homeland. This involved an examination of 12 years of National Socialist rule, discussions of Germany's postwar reconstruction and the vexed question of the collective guilt of the German people, and proposals for an independent socialist Germany in the future. Inevitably, such emphases were viewed with extreme displeasure by the authorities, and it was not long before serious disagreements surfaced. With the accelerating repatriation of German prisoners, however, the journal's readership quickly diminished, and the last issue of the U.S. *Ruf* appeared on 1 April 1946.

This was not the demise of the *Ruf,* for it now appeared in a reincarnation, its second, more important phase. The first issue of the journal to be printed in Germany (1 August 1946) was under the aegis of the Nymphenburger Verlagshandlung in Munich, which had been granted a publishing license by the U.S. occupying forces. The journal was designed to continue the political and cultural aims of the U.S. *Ruf*, but it was accommodated to fit the new German circumstances. This last claim was disputed years later in self-contradictory statements by Hans-Werner Richter. More important, however, the journal was to appeal to a democratic elite of young people, as the journal's subtitle clearly indicates: "Unabhängige Blätter der jungen Generation" (Independent Journal of the Young Generation). This young audience covered the ages between 18 and 35 and thus consisted primarily of former participants in World War II.

Under the editorship of Andersch and Richter, the journal became a virtual oppositional paper, especially after its eighth issue, which listed Germany's main postwar tasks. In particular, the *Ruf*'s political program entailed opposing nationalism and advocating the reintegration of Germany into democratic societies. It urged a united Europe along socialist lines and opposed the reestablishment of political parties that carried with them the old, discredited principles and ideologies of the Weimar Republic. The postwar period was seen as a chance to start afresh, and it was the young generation that would be the means of achieving these aims. Through a process of self-determination, Germany was to decide its own future political shape in an embryonic democracy. At this time, the *Ruf* had a large readership and a considerable effect; there was even talk of establishing a *Ruf* party. While the *Ruf*'s aims may have been worthwhile, they were not realistic given the prevailing political circumstances, which were already witnessing a cooling of the relationship between the United States and Russia. Moreover, there was a certain idealistic naiveté in the belief that there existed a homogeneous, young generation that shared similar ideals.

The U.S. authorities had grown increasingly alarmed by what they called the "nationalistic" and "nihilistic" tendencies of the journal, and Andersch and Richter were forced into resigning from the editorship of the *Ruf* in dubious circumstances. The official reasons were irreconcilable differences between the editors, the contributors, and the license holder, Nymphenburg. In April 1947, Erich Kuby became the journal's provisional editor.

The development of Kuby's *Ruf* has to be seen within the context of a changing, international political world. Although basically following his predecessors' line, Kuby altered the tone of his criticism of the Allies, but not the focus of his attack. He dealt sharply with the problems of denazification, especially the methods adopted by the Americans; nor did he shrink from constantly reminding the Americans of their responsibilities, as a newly emerged superpower, toward the Germans. His calls for the self-determination of the Germans and a united Germany produced problems for him, and as an upholder of German neutrality he was intellectually and morally unable to support Western political ideals in the *Ruf*. Nymphenburg now alleged that the *Ruf* had become directionless and needed a new path to follow. By the end of 1947, Kuby had left the *Ruf*.

Kuby was replaced by W. von Cube, who had already achieved a journalistic reputation and wanted to change the *Ruf* radically. It no longer became a journal for the young generation but followed a conservative, anticommunist, and Christian humanist direction, which was based on Western ideology. In 1948, however, the German currency reform had a profound effect on publishing. The *Ruf* lost readers and much of its advertising, and Nymphenburg sold the journal to the Mannheimer Morgen, a German newspaper. The deal in October 1948 marked the ultimate demise of the *Ruf*, for none of its former contributors were now represented. The last issue was in March 1949.

Even though the *Ruf* had always remained a U.S. project concerned with carrying out the reeducation program of the U.S. government, it nonetheless filled an important gap in an historical situation and was a typical product of its time. Ultimately, the journal was destined to disappear when Germany's postwar political direction and restoration were determined by Cold War politics. The editors had been oblivious to the wider political scene and never really came to terms with the political reality of postwar Germany. There was a gap between their initial hopes and the manner in which these aspirations were fulfilled. *Der Ruf*, however, provides us with an insight into people's hopes and fears and contributes to an understanding of events at that time.

PETER PROCHNIK

See also Alfred Andersch; Gruppe 47

Further Reading

Burns, Rob, and Wilfried van der Will, *Protest and Democracy in West Germany: Extra-Parliamentary Opposition and the Democratic Agenda,* London: Macmillan, and New York: St. Martin's Press, 1988

Lehnert, Herbert, "Die Gruppe 47: Ihre Anfänge und ihre Gründungsmitglieder," in *Die deutsche Literatur der Gegenwart: Aspekte und Tendenzen,* edited by Manfred Durzak, Stuttgart: Reclam, 1971

Pross, Harry, *Literatur und Politik: Geschichte und Programme der politisch-literarischen Zeitschriften im deutschen Sprachgebiet seit 1870,* Olten: Walter, 1963

Richter, Hans Werner, editor, *Almanach der Gruppe 47, 1947–1962,* Reinbek bei Hamburg: Rowohlt, 1962

Vaillant, Jérôme, *Der Ruf: Unabhängige Blätter der jungen Generation (1945–1949): Eine Zeitschrift zwischen Illusion und Anpassung,* Munich, New York, and Paris: Saur, 1978

Wehdeking, Volker, *Der Nullpunkt: Über die Konstituiering der deutschen Nachkriegsliteratur (1945–1948) in den amerikanischen Kriegsgefangenenlagern,* Stuttgart: Metzler, 1971

Widmer, Urs, *1945 oder die "Neue Sprache": Studien zur Prosa der "Jungen Generation,"* Düsseldorf: Pädagogischer Verlag Schwann, 1966

Williams, Rhys W., et al., editors, *German Writers and the Cold War, 1945–61,* Manchester and New York: Manchester University Press, 1992; distributed exclusively in the U.S. by St. Martin's Press

S

Hans Sachs 1494–1576

Hans Sachs is the best known and by far the most productive German author of the 16th century. Blessed with both industry and longevity, he composed over 6,000 works in his 81 years, an especially astonishing output considering that his primary profession was that of shoemaker. Sachs crafted rhymes and shoes with the same economy of effort, but his direct, didactic approach to literature has occasionally led scholars to dismiss his works as pedantic exercises of a petit bourgeois mind. Sachs was nonetheless, perhaps, the most popular author of his day, and he remains the undisputed master of *Meister(ge)sang* (meister-singing) and the carnival play. To deny his works' literary quality is to misunderstand the interests and cultural significance of the 16th-century bourgeoisie in Nuremberg, a leading center of trade and the author's lifelong home. Through his adaptations of biblical, classical, and Renaissance literature, Sachs popularized humanist ideals and learning like no other contemporary German author.

Just as guild tradition guided his progression from apprentice to master shoemaker, Sachs's development and subsequent ethos as a writer were rooted in the guild-like practices of meister-singing. Meistersingers composed their songs according to established metrical rules, performing them in public competitions before four *Merker* (judges, or "markers"), who declared the singer whose composition violated the fewest rules as the winner. To become a meistersinger, one had to compose a new *Ton* (song) with a unique meter, rhyme, and melody. Instructed by the Nuremberg meistersinger Lienhard Nunnenbeck, Sachs learned this art during the years 1509–11 while apprenticing in shoemaking. During his subsequent travels as journeyman, he seems to have chosen towns known for their meistersinger guilds. He wrote his first meistersongs ca. 1513, including the highly successful *Silberweise*, and, in 1514, he organized his first meistersinger competition (*Singschule*) in Munich. Upon his return to Nuremberg in 1516, he was accepted into the local guild and soon became its leading member. His milestones in the service of the Nuremberg guild include his collection of songs by Hans Folz and other local singers (ca. 1517; next to the Colmar manuscript [ca. 1460], the most important source for pre-Reformation *Meistersang*), the *Schulzettel* of 1540 (a compilation of the Nuremberg meistersinging statutes, or *Tabulatur*, which became a model for other guilds), and the *Gemerkbüchlein*, which contains *Singschule* minutes from 1555–61 (the first in a series of record books documenting Nuremberg competitions through 1689).

That we are so well-informed concerning Sachs's literary activities is in no small part due to the author's own detailed records of his prodigious production. He entered each of his works, with date of completion, in a total of 34 manuscript volumes (16 for his meistersongs and 18 for his other writings). He further compiled a *Generalregister* listing the beginning verse of each work, and in the 1550s, he began work on a five-volume edition of his collected works (minus his meistersongs, which—as guild rules dictated—could not be printed). The volumes appeared in 1558, 1560, 1561, and, posthumously, in 1578 and 1579. By far the most important source for Sachs's production, however, is the *Summa all meiner Gedicht* (1567; The Sum of My Writings), in which the author proudly took stock of his life and works to date.

The generic categories most often used to describe Sachs's oeuvre are taken from the *Summa*. The meistersongs, which Sachs numbers at 4,275, treat predominantly biblical themes (performed during the so-called *Hauptsingen* [main singing]), but also contain "weltlich Histori" (secular stories) taken from classical and medieval sources (performed during *Freisingen* [free singing]). In addition, Sachs mentions 73 songs that did not follow the strophic structure of *Meistersang*, including hymns, courtship songs, and other "Gassenhawr" (hits). After the songs, roughly 1,700 "Sprüch" (*Spruchgedichte*, or sententious poems) form the next largest body of work. Their content is highly heterogeneous; the genre seems to have been a convenient catch-all for *Knittelvers* (doggerel) versifications of encomia, disputations, fables, and fabliaux. Two hundred and eight plays follow, which the author subdivides into "Comedi" (happy ending), "Tragedi" (sad ending), and "kurtzweilige Spil" (*Fastnachtspiele*, or carnival plays); we know from council records that many of these plays were performed either in Nuremberg's secularized St. Martha's church or in the former Dominican monastery. Although Sachs touches upon his carnival plays in only one line of the *Summa*—compared to 55 lines for his meistersongs—their lively dialogue makes them his best known works today, along with the *Ständebuch* (1568; *Book of Trades*), in which Sachs composed four rhymed couplets for each of the 114 woodcuts of contemporary estates and professions designed by Swiss artist Jost Amman.

The *Summa* also refers to seven prose dialogues; of these, four were written in the cause of the Protestant Reformation and amply demonstrate that Sachs was by no means an apolitical author. Indeed, the author's early Reformation writings were highly successful, especially the poem *Die Wittembergisch Nachtigall* (1523; The Wittenberg Nightingale), an allegory of Martin Luther as the herald of the light-bringing gospel, which went through seven editions in its first year of publication. When Sachs collaborated with the local pastor Andreas Osiander on an anti-papal pamphlet entitled *Eine wunderliche Weissagung von dem Papsttum* (1527; A Wondrous Prophecy Concerning the Papacy), however, the city censor, concerned that the work might damage the Nuremberg's delicate relations with Emperor Charles V and Catholic trading partners, confiscated the tract and advised Sachs "das er seins handtwerks und schüechmachens warte" (that he attend to his trade and shoemaking). Sachs composed only meistersongs for the next three years; when he did return to publishing, he avoided direct commentary on contemporary issues by couching his criticism in allegories and dreams. Nonetheless, denominational diplomacy again led the council to suppress the performance of Sachs's carnival play *Der Abt im Wildbad* (The Abbot at the Spa) in January of 1551. Even following his death, Sachs's writings had political potential: on 20 November 1576, the day after the author's passing, the council confiscated the *Gespräch von der Himmelfahrt des Markgrafen Albrechts anno 1557* (Dialogue on the Ascension of Margrave Albrecht in the Year 1557) from his estate. Although the satire existed only in manuscript form, the councilors feared that Sachs's derision of Albrecht Alcibiades (Margrave of Brandenburg-Kulmbach), who had laid siege to Nuremberg in 1552 and had died in 1557 following a two-year exile as an outlaw, could cause the city difficulty. Luckily, this and other impounded works survive in transcriptions.

The reception of Sachs's writings has largely depended on subsequent generations' assessment of popular literature. The court-oriented, classically schooled authors of the Baroque had little but ridicule for the craftsman-poet. Andreas Gryphius's *Absurda Comica. Oder Herr Peter Squentz* (1658; Absurd Comedy, or Mr. Peter Squentz) or Gottfried Wilhelm Sacer's *Reime dich oder ich fresse dich* (1673; Rhyme or I'll Eat You) are delightful, if exaggerated, satires of Sachs's doggerel. By the 200th anniversary of his death, however, Sachs was again in vogue, thanks to the post-Enlightenment reevaluation of *Volksliteratur* that began under Johann Gottfried Herder and extended into the Romantic period. Christoph Martin Wieland featured Sachs in the April 1776 edition of his literary journal *Teutscher Merkur* (German Mercury), to which Johann Wolfgang von Goethe contributed the poem *Erklärung eines alten Holzschnittes vorstellend Hans Sachsens poetische Sendung* (Elucidation of an Old Woodcut Portraying the Poetic Calling of Hans Sachs). Goethe's attraction to Sachs's "Poesie des Tages" (poetry of the day) also led to the composition of several short plays in "Hans Sachsische" style— as Goethe relates in the 18th book of his autobiography *Aus meinem Leben: Dichtung und Wahrheit* (1811–33; Poetry and Truth)—and to productions of Sachs's carnival play *Das Narrenschneiden* (1536; The Foolectomy) in Weimar in 1777 and 1778. In the 19th century, some 20 plays and operas romanticized Sachs as a populist hero, culminating in his apotheosis as a "true" German poet in Richard Wagner's *Die Meistersinger von Nürnberg* (1862; The Meistersinger of Nuremberg). Since 1945, scholars have worked to free the author and his oeuvre from nationalistic and moralistic clichés, focusing instead on the social and cultural context of his writings.

GLENN EHRSTINE

See also Mastersingers

Biography
Born in Nuremberg, 5 November 1494. Apprentice shoemaker, instruction in meistersinging, 1509–11; journeyman in Passau, Munich, Frankfurt, Cologne, and elsewhere, 1511–16; master cobbler and member of the meistersinging guild, Nuremberg, 1516. Died in Nuremberg, 19 January 1576.

Selected Works

Collections
Werke, edited by Adalbert von Keller and Demund Goetze, 26 vols., 1870–1908
Dichtungen von Hans Sachs, edited by Karl Goedeke and Julius Tittmann, 3 vols., 1870–71
Sämtliche Fastnachtspiele, edited by Edmund Goetze, 7 vols., 1880–87
Sämtliche Fabeln und Schwänke von Hans Sachs, edited by Edmund Goetze and Carl Drescher, 6 vols., 1893–1913
Die Prosadialoge von Hans Sachs, edited by Ingeborg Spriewald, 1970
The Early Meisterlieder of Hans Sachs, edited by Frances H. Ellis, 1974
Werke in zwei Bänden, edited by Reinhard Hahn, 2 vols., 1992
Werke in der Reihenfolge ihrer Enstehung, edited by Wolfgang F. Michael and Roger A. Crockett, 3 vols., 1996

Plays
Das Hofgesinde Veneris, 1517
Lucretia, 1527
Henno, 1531
Das Narrenschneiden, 1536
Hecastus, 1549
Der fahrende Schüler im Paradies, 1550; as *The Travelling Scholar*, translated by W. Leighton, in *Merry Tales and Three Shrovetide Plays*, 1910; as *The Wandering Scholar*, translated by E.U. Ouless, in *Seven Shrovetide Plays*, 1930; as *The Scholar Bound for Paradise*, translated by B.Q. Morgan, in *Three Shrovetide Comedies*, 1937; as *The Travelling Scholar in Paradise*, translated by R. Aylett, in *Translations of the Carnival Comedies of Hans Sachs*, 1994
Das heiße Eisen, 1551; as *The Hot Iron*, translated by W. Leighton, 1910; as *The Red Hot Poker*, translated by R. Aylett, 1994
Das Kälberbrüten, 1551; as *The Calf-Hatching*, translated by R.W. Listerman, in *Nine Carnival Plays by Hans Sachs*, 1990
Der böse Rauch, 1551; as *Evil Fumes*, translated by R. Aylett, 1994
Judith, 1551
Die ungleichen Kinder Evä, 1553; as *The Children of Eve*, translated by E.U. Ouless, 1930
Der Roßdieb zu Fünsing, 1553; as *The Horse Thief*, translated by W. Leighton, 1910
Herr Tristant mit der schönen Königin Isalden, 1553; edited by Danielle Buschinger and Wolfgang Spiewok, 1993
Der Krämerskorb, 1554; as *The Merchant's Basket*, translated by B.Q. Morgan, 1937
Der verlorene Sohn, 1556
Der hürnen Seufried, 1557; edited by Edmund Goetze, 2nd edition, 1967
Der gantz Passio nach dem Text der vier Evangelisten, 1558
Das jüngste Gericht, 1558
Hester, 1559

Poems and Songs

Ein Buhlscheidlied, 1513
Die Wittembergisch Nachtigall, 1523
Das Schlaueraffenland, 1530
Lobspruch der Stadt Nürnberg, 1530
Ein Epitaphium; oder, Klagred ob der leich D. Mart. Lutheri, 1546
Der Wunderliche Traum, von meiner abgeschiden lieben Gemahel,
    Künegund Sächsin, 1560
Das künstlich Frauenlob, 1562
Summa all meiner Gedicht, 1567

Other

Disputation zwischen einem Chorherren und Schuhmacher, 1524
Eine wunderliche Weissagung von dem Papsttum, 1527
Eigentliche Beschreibung aller Stände auf Erden [Das Ständebuch],
    1568; as *The Book of Trades,* edited by Benjamin A. Rifkin, 1973

Further Reading

Balzer, Bernd, *Bürgerliche Reformationspropaganda: Die Flugschriften des Hans Sachs in den Jahren 1523–1525,* Stuttgart: Metzler, 1973

Berger, Willy R., *Hans Sachs: Schuhmacher und Poet,* Frankfurt: Societäts Verlag, 1994

Bernstein, Eckhard, *Hans Sachs: Mit Selbstzeugnissen und Bilddokumenten,* Reinbek bei Hamburg: Rowohlt, 1993

——, "Hans Sachs," in *German Writers of the Renaissance and Reformation, 1280–1580,* edited by James Hardin and Max Reinhart, vol. 179, Dictionary of Literary Biography, Detroit, Michigan: Gale Research, 1997

Brunner, Horst, et al., editors, *Hans Sachs und Nürnberg,* Nuremberg: Verein für Geschichte der Stadt Nürnberg, 1976

Cramer, Thomas, and Erika Kartschoke, editors, *Hans Sachs: Studien zur frühbürgerlichen Literatur im 16. Jahrhundert,* Bern and Las Vegas, Nevada: Lang, 1978

Füssel, Stephan, editor, *Hans Sachs im Schnittpunkt von Antike und Neuzeit: Akten des interdisziplinären Symposions vom 23./24. September 1994 in Nürnberg,* Nuremberg: Carl, 1995

Geiger, Eugen, *Der Meistergesang des Hans Sachs: Literarhistorische Untersuchung,* Bern: Francke, 1956

Genée, Rudolf, *Hans Sachs und seine Zeit,* Leipzig: Weber, 1894

Hahn, Reinhard, "Hans Sachs," in *Deutsche Dichter der frühen Neuzeit, 1450–1600,* edited by Stephan Füssel, Berlin: Schmidt, 1993

Könneker, Barbara, *Hans Sachs,* Stuttgart: Metzler, 1971

——, *Die deutsche Literatur der Reformationszeit: Kommentar zu einer Epoche,* Munich: Winkler, 1975

Merzbacher, Dieter, editor, *500 Jahre Hans Sachs: Handwerker, Dichter, Stadtbürger,* Ausstellungskataloge der Herzog-August-Bibliothek 72, Wiesbaden: Harrassowitz, 1994

Otten, Franz, *Mit hilff gottes zw tichten: Got zw lob und zw auspreittung seines heilsamen wort: Untersuchungen zur Reformationsdichtung des Hans Sachs,* Göppingen: Kümmerle, 1993

Schade, Richard E., *Studies in Early German Comedy, 1500–1650,* Columbia, South Carolina: Camden House, 1988

Spriewald, Ingeborg, *Literatur zwischen Hören und Lesen: Wandel von Funktion und Rezeption im späten Mittelalter: Fallstudien zu Beheim, Folz, und Sachs,* Berlin: Aufbau, 1990

Taylor, Archer, *The Literary History of Meistergesang,* New York: Modern Language Association of America, and London: Oxford University Press, 1936

Willers, Joahnnes Karl Wilhelm, editor, *Hans Sachs und die Meistersinger in ihrer Zeit,* Nuremberg: Germanisches Nationalmuseum, 1981

Nelly Sachs 1891–1970

The works of Nelly Sachs are unique in German postwar letters. Though a poet and dramatist since age 17, Sachs did not publish her first collection of poems until age 55, blossoming to her full potential at an even more advanced age. In the 1960s, she became the single most celebrated lyrical voice in Germany, and her works were translated into 17 languages.

The literary singularity of Nelly Sachs's work is due to a number of factors. Before escaping from Nazi Berlin to Sweden in May 1940, Sachs had hardly made a critical impact on the literary scene with her poetry. Once in Stockholm, the years of fear and terror and the anxiety of exile, with its challenges of a foreign language, loneliness, and feeling of utter abandonment, are transformed into a belated but powerful new literary beginning. In capturing the unspeakable, Sachs's formerly conventional, romantic poetic language turns hard yet transparent, as in her first and most famous poem, "O die Schornsteine" (1946; O the Chimneys):

> O the chimneys
> on the ingeniously conceived apartments of death
> when Israel's body
> evaporated

> dissolved in smoke
> through the air. . . .
> o the chimneys!
> freedom paths
> for Jeremiah's and Job's dust.

The first line of this poem also became the title of the first collection of Sachs's poetry available in English, which also included her best known verse play, *Eli: Ein Mysterienspiel vom Leiden Israels* (1951; *Eli: A Mystery Play of the Sufferings of Israel*).

During the 1910s, while the revolutionary and heated debates of the German avant-garde took place only blocks away from Sachs's home in the Berliner Neopathetische Cabarett, the beautiful but extremely shy Nelly Sachs lived in total seclusion in her father's villa in the fashionable Tiergarten district, finding her inspiration in the mysticism of the German Romantics, especially Tieck and Novalis. Almost all of the thoughts Sachs developed throughout her poetic oeuvre were already present during this early study of the Romantics, whose major influence was the German philosopher Jakob Böhme, whose source of inspiration, in turn, had been the *Sohar,* Book of Creation. Nelly Sachs once described the *Sohar* as a book "in which the mysticism of the whole world meets." It is this all-embracing mysticism which sees nature as eternal creation out of destruction, as transformation of death into new life, which gave her the strength in her exile to survive the Nazi horrors. Sachs repeatedly expressed the view that "death has been my teacher." In this mysticism, beyond any religious affiliation—both her parents were very cultured, nonreligious, assimilated Jews—she seeks an explanation, a worldview, in which her fate could be understood as not totally nonsensical. Thus, with her native language as only companion (her mother died in 1950), Nelly Sachs derived the strength to write out of the consciousness that she—saved at the very last minute from persecution and death—could give voice to those irrevocably silenced, while struggling against her own suffocation. Key concepts of her poetry are, therefore, the letter and language as God's word:

> People of the earth
> do not destroy the universe of the words
> do not cut up with the knives of hatred
> the tone, born at the same time as breathing.

She also invokes the theme of creation and transformation, most often found in the recurring metaphors of dust, stone, and the butterfly, "the most visible sign of transformation:" "The sick butterfly / will soon again know the ocean - / this stone / with the inscription of the fly / gave itself into my hand - / Instead of homeland / I hold the transformations of the world."

When the Association of Swedish Poets honored her with the Literature Prize for her pioneering translation of modern Swedish poetry in 1957, Sachs's time of isolation was over. In that same year, she published her lyrical cycle *Und niemand weiss weiter* (And Nobody Knows How It Will Continue) in Germany. A dream had come true for Nelly Sachs: to be recognized in and by the country of her birth and in whose language she thought, felt, and wrote. Earlier that year, four of her poems had appeared in *Texte und Zeichen,* whose editor was Alfred Andersch, founder also of the Radio-Essay of the South German Radio, which performed her play *Eli.* Suddenly, the exiled German voice in the North became a lighthouse for the young avant-garde poets who were starting to question the involvement of their parents' generation with the recent past. Sachs became their symbol of atonement. Writers such as Hans Magnus Enzensberger, Alfred Andersch, and Peter Hamm traveled to Sweden to pay their respects to the poet. Despite her utterly contradictory feelings, Sachs was delighted and they became friends. The honors followed each other in quick succession. In 1959 the poet received the Cultural Prize of German Industry. In 1960 the Droste Prize followed and, in 1961, the Literary Prize of the city of Dortmund, given by a foundation that will forever be linked to the poet's name. In 1965, Sachs was awarded the prestigious Peace Prize of the German book trade, and in 1966, she received the International Nobel Prize for Literature along with the Israeli writer S.Y. Agnon. She felt very ambivalent about this prize, for in her opinion it pushed her and her work back into the unambiguous Jewish position, which according to her own understanding she had left behind with a poetry that aimed at the universal. Thus she commented that Agnon represented the country Israel, whereas "I represent the tragedy of the Jewish people."

The 1960s witnessed the triumphant culmination of Sachs' career. Her reception in the German-speaking countries was nothing but stunning. At almost 80 years old, the fragile, white-haired poet had become an idol, a cult figure of humanity and atonement to the postwar generation. Not only was she widely read and worshipped in both academic and non-academic circles, but she was also invited to perform readings of her poetry in all the major cities throughout the German-speaking countries. These readings became major cultural events, a sort of pilgrimage to worship this delicate person with the powerful voice that had given expression to the unspeakable horrors perpetrated on an entire people. Tragically, however, the irreconcilable conflicting feelings of joy and grief sapped her delicate physical constitution, and her last years were darkened by long hospital stays.

After her heyday in the 1960s and with her death in 1970, this wave of enthusiasm declined as abruptly as it had started. One possible explanation might be that the underlying mystic dimension of her oeuvre is less appealing to today's generation. Nevertheless, selections of Sachs's poems are a standard feature in German poetic anthologies. Since the 1980s, a few doctoral dissertations in Germany and one in the United States have reignited an academic interest in this poet.

INCA RUMOLD

Biography

Born in Berlin, 10 December 1891. At age 15, began a correspondence with the Swedish poet Selma Lageröf, who was ultimately of the utmost importance in obtaining a visa for the writer during her persecution and exile. Jewish refugee in Stockholm, Sweden, 1940, where she took up residence as a writer and translator; she settled in Sweden in the postwar era while publishing in Germany and gaining widening recognition. Nobel Prize for Literature (with S.Y. Agnon), 1966. Died 12 May 1970.

Selected Works

Collections
Gedichte, edited by Hilde Domin, 1977
O the Chimneys: Selected Poems, Including the Verse Play Eli, translated by Michael Hamburger, et al., 1967
The Seeker, and Other Poems, translated by Ruth Mead, et al., 1970

Poetry
In den Wohnungen des Todes, 1947
Sternverdunkelung, 1949
Und niemand weiss weiter, 1957
Flucht und Verwandlung, 1959
Fahrt ins Staublose, 1961
Ausgewählte Gedichte, 1963
Späte Gedichte, 1965
Suche nach Lebenden, edited by Margaretha and Bengt Holmqvist, 1971
Teile dich Nacht: Die letzten Gedichte, edited by Margaretha and Bengt Holmqvist, 1971

Plays
Eli: Ein Mysterienspiel vom Leiden Israels, 1951; as *Eli: A Mystery Play of the Sufferings of Israel,* in *O the Chimneys,* translated by Michael Hamburger, et al., 1967

Zeichen im Sand: Die szenischen Dichtungen der Nelly Sachs, 1962
Verzauberung: Späte szenische Dichtungen, 1970

Other
Briefe der Nelly Sachs, edited by Ruth Dinesen and Helmut Müssener, 1984

Further Reading
Bahr, Ehrhard, *Nelly Sachs*, Munich: Beck, 1980
Berendsohn, Walter, *Nelly Sachs: Einführung in das Werk der Dichterin jüdischen Schicksals*, Darmstadt: Agora, 1974
Cervantes, Eleonore, *Strukturbezüge in der Lyrik von Nelly Sachs*, Bern: Lang, 1982
Dinesen, Ruth, *Nelly Sachs: Eine Biographie*, Frankfurt: Suhrkamp, 1992

Falkenstein, Henning, *Nelly Sachs*, Berlin: Colloquium, 1984
Holmquist, Bengt, "Die Sprache der Sehnsucht," in *Das Buch der Nelly Sachs*, Frankfurt: Suhrkamp, 1968
Bahti, Timothy, and Marilyn Sibley Fries, editors, *Jewish Writers, German Literature: The Uneasy Examples of Nelly Sachs and Walter Benjamin*, Ann Arbor: University of Michigan Press, 1995
Kersten, Paul, *Die Metaphorik in der Lyrik von Nelly Sachs*, Hamburg: Ludke, 1970
Lagercrantz, Olof, *Versuch über die Lyrik der Nelly Sachs*, Frankfurt: Suhrkamp, 1967
"Nelly Sachs," *Text und Kritik* 23 (July 1969)
Nelly Sachs zu Ehren: Zum 75. Geburtstag 1966, Gedichte, Beiträge, Bibliographie, Frankfurt: Suhrkamp, 1966
Ostmeier, Dorothee, *Sprache des Dramas, Drama der Sprache: zur Poetik der Nelly Sachs*, Tübingen: Niemeyer, 1997

Salons

We still cannot say exactly how the story began. Compared with other countries, literary salons in Germany made a belated appearance; nor is it clear whether they can be situated in a tradition of salons in other parts of Europe. In Italy we find salons as early as the Renaissance. In 17th-century France intellectuals gathered in the houses of higher nobility in order to debate literary and theoretical issues. There was nothing comparable in Germany at those times. It was only 100 years later that social events occurred in some small towns that might be regarded as predecessors of the salons. The "Weimarer Musenhof," for example, initiated by the Duchess Anna Amalia von Sachsen-Weimar (1739–1807), was an assembly for reading and conversation that was restricted to the nobility. In the late 18th century something similar, yet at the same time absolutely different, appeared in Berlin: Jewish families opened their doors to scholars, writers, and artists. Moses Mendelssohn (1729–86) invited people to discuss philosophy and literature in particular, but also music and art. The banker Salomon (1760–1806), together with his wife, the harpsichordist Sara Levy (1761–1854), gathered those who were particularly interested in music. Markus (1747–1803) and Henriette Herz (1764–1847) established two types of society at their house: private lectures and experiments were held in the rooms of the philosopher and doctor, while in Henriette's rooms debates concentrated on literature.

It was under the auspices of a man—sometimes famous, sometimes rich—that these Jewish families, who for centuries had lived mostly isolated from the Christian-dominated society, developed these emerging social forms. Unmarried or divorced Jewish women, however, were also responsible for the extraordinary flourishing of what are retrospectively called the "Berlin salons." The main figure in this regard was Rahel Levin Varnhagen (1771–1833). Dorothea (1763–1839), born Brendel Mendelssohn, who in 1804 married Friedrich Schlegel, and her younger sister Henriette Mendelssohn (1768–1831), who later worked as a governess in Vienna and Paris, were other prominent *salonnières*. To them can be added, among others, the sisters Sophie von Grotthuß and Mariane von Eybenberg, born Sara (1763–1828) and Mariane Meyer (1770–1812) into a banker's family, as well as Esther Gad (later Lucie Domeier [1767–1834]), who came from Breslau to Berlin in 1800. Collectively, these young women were responsible for an entire chapter of German literary history.

Compared to literary salons in Berlin after 1806, the meetings in the last decade of the 19th century brought together a heterogeneous group of people: noblewomen and noblemen, diplomats, young intellectuals, writers, and actresses. Surveying the phenomenon from a distance, Rahel Levin defined this special conviviality in a letter from December 1819: "The whole constellation of beauty, gracefulness, coquetry, inclination, wittiness, elegance, cordiality, the drive to develop ideas and thoughts; honest seriousness, uninhibited gatherings and meetings, good tempered jest, has been dispersed."

We see here the elements of an extraordinary cultural experiment being precisely assembled. No special interest brought the guests together; they instead had a mixture of often irreconcilable wishes, desires, and thoughts. Salons were a site of knowledge where everything that aroused passionate attention was reflected upon: politics, theater, literature, music, and philosophy. The echoes of salon conversations that came down to us in letters and autobiographical sketches show debates characterized by remarkably fluid shifts from one field of knowledge to another. At the center of the salons' literary interest stood one particular author: Johann Wolfgang von Goethe. It is not too much to claim that his significance for his contemporaries was established in these settings.

Despite the idealized tenor of earlier histories of the salons, current research has come to recognize that they do not present a simple, happy image of Christian and Jewish harmony. Letters and billets show how pervasive anti-Jewish and anti-Semitic attitudes remained even among those who visited the salons on a regular basis: Wilhelm von Humboldt in 1804 did not refrain from calling his friends "Jewish rabble" (*Judenpack*), and Karl Gustav von Brinckmann, a Swedish diplomat at the Prussian court, talked in 1805 of an "expectoration of vulgarity that dominated her [Rahel Levin's] company during this winter."

It was only in the 1820s that the word *salon* came to mean more than a particular room, but also a social event. The women around 1800 had called their meetings "Geselligkeit" (sociability), "Gesellschaft" (society), or "unser Kreis" (our circle). From the very beginning the word *salon* carried a double meaning: on the one hand, a rather nostalgic gesture toward a lost culture, but on the other hand, mocking disparagement. In the poem "Sie saßen und tranken am Theetisch," for example, Heinrich Heine ridiculed as sentimental and mendacious the conversations around the aesthetic tea tables in Prussia's capital. Fanny Lewald (1811–89), who came to Berlin in 1839, wrote in her autobiography that the glory days of the salon had already long ago vanished. At the very moment when the salons were being defined, they appeared to have come to an end. Now, "all gatherings are Dinés or Assemblées," Rahel Levin Varnhagen wrote in 1819, and "all discussions" are "a pale confusion of notions" (*fade Begriffsverwirrung*). After the decline of "formless" conviviality, it was much easier to distinguish different types of salons. Among those were ones whose conversations concentrated on literature. But discussions on literature in private homes now also bore the seal of a new restriction. After the foundation of the modern university in Berlin in 1810, debates on theoretical problems were delegated to the academic world. And there, women had no voice.

Despite these restrictions, whose force only grew in times of increasing political reaction, many women continued to open their houses to visitors. Especially in the 1840s, Bettina von Arnim (1785–1859) tried to cross the boundaries between literature and politics not only in her own writing but also by bringing together in her residence writers and those who were later engaged in the 1848 revolution. But the inclusion of democratic sympathizers in these gatherings, however, ruptured the conviviality into two antagonistic camps. Bettina's daughters preferred the aristocratic visitors, who were strictly against any social and political reform in Prussia. The two salons at the Arnims' residence show, therefore, how strongly rivalries and interfered with the conviviality of hostesses and guests. Some habitués of the salons still tried to mediate between the different sides—and not only in the Arnim family. By the turn of the century, however, the social situation no longer permitted the unfettered conviviality of the early salons. In rich bourgeois families, where the political orientations were reliably antidemocratic, something like a formalized salon tradition could continue. Elsewhere, less traditional groups gathered into programmtic *Bünde* or leagues. This development, in turn, did not leave the salons unaffected, which now at times began to take on their own programmatic character. The meetings hosted by Hedwig Dohm (1833–1919), for ex-

ample, favored women authors who were engaged in the women's movement, among them Ellen Key and Lily Braun. In addition to literary discussion, then, Dohm's salon functioned as a center of networking for particular purposes.

While some of the later salons gained new and important roles in the visual arts—mediating French Impressionist painting into Germany, for example—they were steadily losing influence on the production and distribution of literature. Clearly, Bettina von Arnim's socially engaged literature had depended on the friends and guests at her salon. For authors of the so-called realistic literature and subsequent literary movements, however, this was not the case. Although both Theodor Storm and Gottfried Keller visited salons during their Berlin sojourns, among them the house of Lina Duncker (1825–85), wife of the publisher Franz Duncker, these conversations and debates in the context of an open house had no discernible effect on their work.

What took place at the salon of Sabine Lepsius (1864–1942) can be seen as marking the definitive end of the salon. Sabine Lepsius was a close friend of Stefan George, and at her house in Berlin he read his poems to a carefully selected group of people. Only those who participated in the admiring atmosphere could count on further invitations to these exclusive events. Such extreme exclusivity contradicts the culture of a salon, which is premised on at least a balance between exclusion and openness. But when Sabine Lepsius wrote an epitaph for the salons in 1913 ("Über das Aussterben der 'Salons,'" in *März*), she did not consider this problem. At the center of her argumentation is the vanishing art of conversation. Instead of a culture of communal talk, self-representation took over, and salons were transformed into stages for vanity. From this perspective, the long life of salons in Germany could be seen as evidence of the political weakness of the middle-class.

Traces of the intellectual heritage of the salon can be found in new social gatherings and not in self-consciously literary salons. The assemblies convened at the house of Gertrud and Georg Simmel in Berlin, or at the house of Marianne and Max Weber in Heidelberg, were not called salons but rather, "jour fixe." People came together on evenings at the Simmels' house when the work of the day was done, or on Sunday afternoons in Heidelberg, when the university was closed. As the cultural philosopher Margarete Susman, a regular guest at the Simmel house, wrote in her autobiography, "Conversation took shape there in such a way that no one could impose his idiosyncrasies, problems, or needs; it was a form that, liberated from all weightiness, floated in an atmosphere of spirituality, affection, and tact." Here, it is not the "inner self" on parade; rather, idiosyncrasies are so strongly de-emphasized that genuine individuality is able to appear. Only when those present ignore the personal do they become a community that, collectively, gives rise to something new.

BARBARA HAHN

See also Rahel Levin Varnhagen

Further Reading

Busch-Salmen, Gabriele, et al., *Der Weimarer Musenhof: Dichtung, Musik und Tanz, Gartenkunst, Geselligkeit, Malerei*, Stuttgart: Metzler, 1998
Drewitz, Ingeborg, *Berliner Salons: Gesellschaft und Literatur zwischen Aufklärung und Industriezeitalter*, Berlin: Haude und Spener, 1965
Hertz, Deborah, *Jewish High Society in Old Regime Berlin*, New Haven, Connecticut, and London: Yale University Press, 1988

Schultz, Hartwig, editor, *Salons der Romantik: Beiträge eines Wiepersdorfer Kolloquiums zu Theorie und Geschichte des Salons*, Berlin and New York: de Gruyter, 1997

Seibert, Peter, "Der literarische Salon: Ein Forschungsüberblick," *Internationales Archiv für Sozialgeschichte der deutschen Literatur* (1992)

——, *Der literarische Salon: Literatur und Geselligkeit zwischen Aufklärung und Vormärz*, Stuttgart: Metzler, 1993

Susman, Margarete, *Frauen der Romantik*, Jena: Diedrichs, 1929; Frankfurt: Insel, 1996

Wilhelmy, Petra, *Der Berliner Salon im 19. Jahrhundert: 1780–1914*, Berlin and New York: de Gruyter, 1989

Sangspruchdichtung

The word *Spruch* (utterance, saying, proverb) occurs in the manuscripts to designate works by der Teichner and other late-medieval poets, but apparently without any precise form being intended; *Rede* (speech) is used in a similar way. Hans Sachs spoke of *Spruchdichtung* (proverbial or sentential poetry) to refer to his own writings generally, and Goethe used the same terminology for some of his epigrammatic and wisdom poetry. The scholarly appropriation of these words as generic terms for a category of medieval German lyric, however, is a 19th-century caprice that has proved utterly unhelpful. The poetry in question was intended to be sung, not spoken, and was not proverbial, although it could be moralizing. A convention that is increasingly popular, although not new, is to expand the word to *Sangspruch* (sung *Spruch*), thus retaining the term but acknowledging the problems. Sometimes this is contrasted with *Sprechspruch* (spoken *Spruch*), referring to poems such as those in Freidank's collection *Bescheidenheit* (Understanding), which were not intended to be sung, and other didactic pieces of a nonlyrical nature that are better accommodated under such categories as *maere* (tale) or *bîspel* (exemplum, exemplary moral story) and, therefore, will not be discussed here. Even *Sangspruch*, however, says little about the actual nature of the form. A more useful term might be "functional songs," for the one common element in these works is that they address a problem that is immediately relevant to the poet or seek to further a specific aim.

Sangspruchdichtung is often defined negatively: in the realm of medieval lyrics, a *Sangspruch* is anything that does not fall into the categories *Lied*—as do Minnesang and *Kreuzlyrik* (love songs and crusading poetry)—or *Leich* (lay). Into this dustbin category fall political and satirical songs; gnomic and moralizing pieces; commentaries on religious, social, and literary matters; and petitions and requests, some of them representing poetry of a very high standard. Traditionally, critics have considered the *Sangspruch* to differ formally from other Middle High German lyric poetry, in that it is fundamentally a single-strophe piece. When several strophes are found to have the same formal structure, these are then understood to be separate songs with the same tune. When such groups of *Sangsprüche* also show similarities of theme and language, however, it is clear that the dogmatic view of the independent strophe cannot be applied unconditionally; at the very least, we must speak in such cases of a cycle of *Sangsprüche*. The opposing view, that these are in fact multistrophic songs revealing a formal unity precisely like that of Minnesang, has been espoused since the 1960s, and there is much to be said for a middle view, which differentiates various degrees of strophic independence. This has necessitated a reopening of the debate on the definition and delineation of the form. All attempts to find formal or thematic uniformity run into difficulties, and it may be that, in the last analysis, *Sangspruchdichtung* must be judged an arbitrary assembly of lyrics, which have the commonality of defying other categorizations. The fact remains, however, that a series of poets specialized in *Sangsprüche*, covering the full range of thematic possibilities and often writing nothing else. This would indicate that the poets themselves had at least a loose sense of the unity of the form.

The Middle High German *Sangsprüche* are known mainly through the Heidelberg (C, D) and Jena (J) manuscripts, the magnificent 14th-century collections of lyrics that are also our major sources for Minnesang. They were produced for performance at court and later also in the higher circles of urban society. The principle early witness (late 12th century) is a collection attributed in the manuscripts to a certain Spervogel. This is generally regarded as the work of two separate poets, now known as Herger (Pseudo-Spervogel) and (the real or younger) Spervogel. Herger was a professional singer, not of noble birth, and this seems to be the pattern for most of his successors. The form was next taken up by Walther von der Vogelweide, who produced at least 13 new *Sangspruch*-melodies. Walther's songs have received vastly more scholarly attention than those of any other Middle High German poet, and there is no doubt that the modern awareness of *Sangsprüche* is heavily dependent on him. The fashion for *Sangsprüche* continued to flourish throughout the 13th century; significant later contributors were Reinmar von Zweter, Bruder Wernher, der Marner, Konrad von Würzburg, Heinrich von Meissen (Frauenlob), and the possibly Jewish Süßkind von Trimberg. The *Sangspruch* on fragile happiness (*das gläserne Glück*) attributed to Gottfried von Straßburg is, however, now universally regarded as not genuine. The high point in the production of *Sangsprüche* was roughly contemporaneous with that of Minnesang; a decline set in after the mid–13th century, although some authorities see a line of continuity between works in this period and those by the mastersingers of the 14th and 15th centuries.

The thematic variety of the *Sangsprüche* makes them particularly interesting as historical witnesses, for they tell us far more than other lyrical forms about the everyday reality of the poets and about their attitudes to social and political questions. In a short account we can do little more than hint at the richness of the tradition. The religious *Sangsprüche* are typically songs of praise for the Creator, the Trinity, and the Virgin Mary—Frauenlob may have his epithet from his poems on Mary—and prayers such as those of der Marner; other reflections include Herger on the torments of Hell and Süßkind on death and the soul. The gnomic-didactic *Sangsprüche* vary from brief maxims to longer discussions on an astounding range of topics; we have Spervogel on truth, faithfulness, and friendship, Walther on raising children and corporal punishment, and Reinmar von Zweter on jousting and drunkenness. Some convey spiritual values, others worldly, as in Herger's animal fables. *Sangsprüche* advocating courtly virtues often focus on such key words as *êre* (honor), *milte* (generosity), and *mâze* (moderation). *Minne* (courtly love) also arises, as when Konrad expounds upon the correct expression of love; here, the thematic boundary with Minnesang is fluid. One topic of great interest in a feudal society was the discussion of nobility of birth versus nobility of character, and this is treated by Reinmar von Zweter and Süßkind. There is also moral instruction for women and praises for good wives. Best known among the political *Sangsprüche* are Walther's poems in the service of successive emperors, and against Rome, but we should not forget Frauenlob's polemic against the Franciscans. The social issues of riches and poverty are frequently raised, sometimes linked to the problematic question of the artist and the patron; we can follow Walther's repeated petitions for financial security and his delight when these are rewarded: "ich hân mîn lêhen" (I have my feoff). Other motifs include Süßkind on freedom of thought, Konrad on artistic merit, and Walther on Gerhard Atze, the rogue who had shot the poet's horse because, he claimed, it had bitten off his finger.

GRAEME DUNPHY

See also Minnesang

Further Reading

Blank, Walter, et al., *Mittelhochdeutsche Spruchdichtung, früher Meistersang: Der Codex Palatinus Germanicus 350 der Universitatsbibliothek Heidelberg*, Wiesbaden: Reichert, 1974

Brunner, Horst, "Sangspruchdichtung," in *Die Musik in Geschichte und Gegenwart: Allgemeine Enzyklopädie der Musik*, 8 vols., edited by Ludwig Finscher, Kassel and New York: Bärenreiter, 1994

Moser, Hugo, editor, *Mittelhochdeutsche Spruchdichtung*, Darmstadt: Wissenschaftliche Buchgesellschaft, 1972

Müller, Ulrich, "Walthers Sangspruchdichtung," in *Walther von der Vogelweide: Epoche, Werk, Wirkung*, edited by Horst Brunner and Sigrid Neureiter-Lackner, Munich: Beck, 1996

Nix, Matthias, *Untersuchungen zur Funktion der politischen Spruchdichtung Walthers von der Vogelweide*, Göppingen: Kümmerle, 1993

Petzsch, Christoph, "Mittelhochdeutsch spruch: Eine Vortragsart," *Deutsche Vierteljahrsschrift* 60 (1986)

Sowinski, Bernhard, *Lehrhafte Dichtung des Mittelalters*, Stuttgart: Metzler, 1971

Spechtler, Franz-Viktor, "Strophen und Varianten: Zur Sangspruchlyrik des 13. Jahrhunderts am Beispiel des Bruder Wernher," in *Spectrum Medii Aevi: Essays in Early German Literature in Honor of George Fenwick Jones*, edited by William C. McDonald, Göppingen: Kümmerle, 1983

Tervooren, Helmut, "Spruchdichtung, mittelhochdeutsche," in *Reallexikon der deutschen Literaturgeschichte*, edited by Klaus Kanzog and Achim Masser, vol. 4, Berlin: de Gruyter, 1955; 2nd edition, 1984

———, *Sangspruchdichtung*, Stuttgart: Metzler, 1995

Wachinger, Burghart, *Sängerkrieg: Untersuchungen zur Spruchdichtung des 13. Jahrhunderts*, Munich: Beck, 1973

Satire

In 1945 Edgar Johnson pointed out that whoever studies satire is confronted with the paradox that almost everybody recognizes satire but hardly anybody knows exactly what it is. One difficulty in defining *satire* arises because the term is ambiguous. It is both a historical genre and a tone, ethos, or mode that transgresses genre boundaries. Attempts to define *satire* by tracing the meaning of the word etymologically have added to the confusion. It is nowadays agreed that the term *satire* is derived from the Latin *satura* or *lanx satura* (medley, full or mixed dish) and that it is not, as was often believed in early modern times, related to the Greek satyr plays, a faulty derivation first propounded by Diomedes in the fourth century A.D. In order to encompass the spectrum of what ought to be considered satire, however, one needs to acknowledge that there was a Greek type of satire that preceded the Roman's verse satire. Usually referred to as Menippean satire (Menippus, ca. third century B.C.), it is characterized by prose style and little emphasis on a specific form.

The Menippean tradition was introduced by Varro (116–27 B.C.) to the Roman world. Varronian satire stood in sharp contrast with the developing Roman verse satire, the *satura*, which was first introduced by Lucilius (180–102 B.C.) and reached its height with Horace (65–8 B.C.), Persius (A.D. 34–63) and Juvenal (ca. A.D. 58–140). The *satura* has a fairly clear formal definition as verse-satire written in hexameter, and it was claimed as an original Roman invention by Quintilian (ca. A.D. 35–ca.100) in his famous statement "satura quidem tota nostra est" (*satura* [satire] belongs to us [Romans] alone).

The distinction between satire as a historical genre on the one hand and satire as an ethos on the other hand is thus too broad because it does not differentiate between the formally nonspecific Menippean satire and the Roman verse satire. Moreover, because the term *Menippean satire* is quite broad, it was soon stretched to encompass all satire that did not meet the strict genre criteria of formal verse satire in the Lucilian tradition. This has made it almost impossible to differentiate clearly between the definition of the Menippean satire as a historical manifestation of a genre and satire as an ethos.

Currently there is no strict and generally accepted definition for satire as an ethos: every attempt to define satire in this manner makes it possible—as Edgar Johnson claims—to recognize satire by naming a few essential elements, then adding long but rather vague lists of other characteristics. However, almost everyone agrees that humor in the form of wit, whimsy, irony, parody, and so on is one of the main ingredients of satire and that humor, other than for example in comedy, is not an end in itself but rather a means to aim at an extraliterary target considered undesirable and perceived as a deviation from a norm to which an author reacts with indignation. This norm or ideal is usually not expressed directly; there is, however, the assumption that a reader, listener, or viewer will automatically decode the satirical message in such a way that the implicit norm reveals itself as a logical consequence of the follies that are being portrayed.

The concept of a *verkehrte Welt* (the world put upside down/topsy-turvy) has been a popular means to convey indirectly a corrective, and Lazarowicz even goes so far as to define the concept of a *verkehrte Welt* as an integral component of satire. Other critics consider this definition too narrow, and even Brummack's newer and by far more open and flexible definition that satire is "ästhetisch sozialisierte Aggression" (aesthetically socialized aggression) is still rejected by Arntzen as being too restrictive because it does not specifically take into consideration the moral component of satire. Arntzen insists that satire is not "in Verse gehüllte Entrüstung" (indignation wrapped in verse/literature) but that it is rather "Vers *aus* Entrüstung" (verse/literature *arising from* indignation); that is, someone's initial reaction to an undesirable reality should be regarded as the creative source for satire. Only a few people, however, are willing and able to use this creative source and channel it into literary production in order to promote or inhibit change in the extraliterary world.

Satirical tone is primarily dependent on the author's degree of outrage and can range from derisive laughter to open aggression and anger, which some critics try to translate as a polarity between "laughing satire" and "punitive satire." But not only the author's perspective is of relevance; the recipient's point of view and his/her sociohistorical context is of equal importance. Independent of an author's intention, the same satire that may trigger derisive laughter in one person can lead to bewilderment and consternation in another. The classic example of decoding a satire in a way that was completely unintended by the author is the staging of Brecht's *Heilige Johanna der Schlachthöfe* (1959; *Saint Joan of the Stockyards*) in Zurich, where an ultrabourgeois audience applauded a Marxist and anticapitalist play. This hints at the difficulty that modern satire in particular faces: highly dependent on interpretation, satire is particularly unstable, and if there exists no generally accepted ideal or norm that links author and recipient, the satirical message might get lost. Weidauer, Larrau, and Morris-Keitel correctly point out that satire lives from negativity, but that this is also its weak point:

> The combination of aggression and indignation with the pleasurable sensation of laughter makes for a touchy balance. The negativity can spur critical consciousness or numb its audience into mocking everything without reflection. . . . The balance between affirmative laughter and destructive mockery rests on that elusive third element of satire: the ideal.

This difficulty is connected with the current debate whether it is harder today than ever before to write or produce satire, a question that was the focus of an interdisciplinary colloquium on satire in literature, film, and television that took place in Copenhagen in 1995. With this newest debate, satire seems to have become less definable than ever before. While in 1945 Edgar Johnson still thought that it would be reasonable to assume that everyone is able to recognize satire, we have now entered an era where social changes and changes in the media landscape make it necessary to treat this assumption with caution. The focus of attention in this most recent debate concerning the status of satire at the end of the 20th century is not really on whether it is still possible to write satire. The crucial point seems to be whether it is still possible to recognize satire as something that is distinct from humor, as something that uses humor not as an end in itself but as a means that is intended to raise a critical consciousness and to bring about or inhibit extraliterary change.

Written text is not the only medium though which a satirical message can be conveyed. Visual forms of satire can be found side-by-side or in combination with text-based satire in the form of caricatures or cartoons beginning with late medieval times. From the late 19th century, one also needs to take into consideration the development of musical cabaret, film (even though only very few films in their entirety qualify as satire), and an even more recent phenomenon, satirical television shows with or without an audience present.

From the Middle Ages through the Baroque, *ordo*—a social system with fixed roles that was considered God-given and did not allow for vertical mobility—was the unnamed norm expressed in most satirical works. While Heinrich von Melk (second half of the 12th century) must be regarded as the first German satirist, the best-known satirical texts from this period are the *Tierepos* (animal fable) *Reynke de Vos* (1498) and its different adaptions, Heinrich Wittenwiler's *Ring* (ca. 1400; *Ring*), texts by Neidhart von Reuental (early 13th century), and Sebastian Brant's *Narrenschiff* (1494; *Ship of Fools*), which in turn became the source for the satirical texts of Thomas Murner (1475–1537).

The 16th century was labeled the satirical era of German literature by some critics. Changes brought by the Reformation prompted many to engage in satirical production; as compared to medieval times, the spectrum of what was being expressed through satire widened tremendously, and satire became one of the most popular means to explore the social and religious conflicts of the time. Some of the most influential satires from this period are Ulrich von Hutten's *Gespräch Büchlein* (1521; Conversation Booklet; first published in Latin in 1520), the *Epistolae obscurorum virorum* or *Dunkelmännerbriefe* (1515–17; *Letters of Obscure Men*, a collection of fictitious letters in which humanist authors scorn the narrow-mindedness of their opponents), Thomas Murner's *Von dem grossen Lutherischen Narren* (1522; On the Great Lutheran Fool), Friedrich Dedekind and Caspar Scheidt's *Grobianus* (1549–51; Ruffianism), and Johann Fischart's *Geschichtklitterung* (1575; Perversion of History). In addition to these longer works, a vast number of satirical pamphlets appeared during this period.

For a long time it was believed that only a few influential satires were written during the 17th century, but Arntzen has proven the opposite by focusing on satirical productions that had been ignored primarily due to a too restrictive definition of satire. Arntzen not only elucidates the connections between satire and the early picaro novel but also discusses satire in the context of comedy and in relation to the formation of the *Wanderbühne* (touring theater). During the 17th century, satires were written in verse and prose. The satirical novel became quite popular toward the end of the century, and its major representatives were Christian Weise, Johannes Riemer, Johann Beer, and

Hans Jacob Christoffel von Grimmelshausen, who wrote the most widely known satire of this period, *Simplicissimus Teutsch* (1668; *The Adventures of Simplicissimus*).

As the guiding norm for the production of satire, *ordo* was eventually replaced by *ratio* as the principle that should guide every action. As long as *ordo* had been considered the guiding principle of all human existence, satirists had scorned any actions that were geared toward leaving a predefined role or any form of vertical mobility; when it was replaced by *ratio,* most satirists began to condemn human actions that were not guided by reason. As a result, the focus of all satirical production during the 18th century is clearly didactic, and Brummack even goes so far as to claim that the main tenor of the majority of novels written during the Enlightenment is satirical-humoristic (*satirisch-humoristisch*). Some of the better-known authors that need to be mentioned in this context are Christian Ludwig Liscow, Albrecht von Haller, Ludwig von Heß, Georg Christoph Lichtenberg (aphorism), Johann Gottfried Seume, Adolph von Knigge, Christoph Martin Wieland, Johann Karl Wezel, and Gottlieb von Hippel. During the early Enlightenment period, two women authors, Sidonia Hedwig Zäunemann and Christiana Mariane Ziegler, also wrote satires and thus have to be regarded as the first female satirists in German literary history. In this period there also arose a highly specialized form of satire: travel-satire.

Up to the end of the Enlightenment, universal validity was attributed to either *ordo* or *ratio,* and both defined a specific worldview that was given precedence over everything. Toward the end of the 18th century, universalist worldviews were more and more replaced by individualist thinking, and satirical writing changed accordingly: where it so far mainly had targeted deviations from norms that were established by a universalist worldview, it turned against anything that hindered the new ideal in the era of Romanticism—individualism. In consequence, the philistine whose intellectual inflexibility was scorned became a popular target of satire up to the mid–19th century. Such use of satirical elements is common to authors as different as the German Romantics and the Young Germans.

The time around 1800 also marks an important change in direction with regard to criticism and the theory of satire in German literature. Before the mid–18th century, satire had been measured mainly against Roman verse satire. Gottsched then defined the poetic value of comical elements based on their usefulness for a greater purpose (e.g., morals, norms). During the era of Romanticism, the definition of satire as a means to endorse one specific worldview using strict forms became the basis for declaring satire as only of secondary aesthetical and poetic value. Hegel reinforced this view by declaring in his *Vorlesungen über die Ästhetik II* (1927; *Aesthetics: Lectures on Fine Art*) that satire was too inflexible to make room for a real dialectics that could lead from the undesirable to a larger truth. According to Könneker, all of these views shaped the perception of satire in West Germany up to the early 1960s, and these assessments and value judgments help explain why it became fairly unpopular for authors to label their works as satires from the era of Romanticism onward and why in the context of criticism it became more common to refer to the satirical elements in these works as irony or humor.

From a modern standpoint that applies a more flexible definition of satire as an ethos, the term *satire* is reintroduced to discuss the literary production of many of the late 18th- to mid-19th-century authors, including Jean Paul, Tieck, Brentano, Eichendorff, Heine, Hoffmann, Immermann, Gutzkow, Börne, Grabbe, Weerth, Platen, Nestroy, and Gotthelf. Their novels, novellas, comedies, fairy tales, epic poems, and travel literature are usually texts in which satirical elements are amalgamated with fantastic, poetic, or idyllic elements.

While satirical production flourished up to the mid–19th century, it then declined—with Keller and Fontane (*Frau Jenny Treibel,* 1892; *Jenny Treibel*) being the exceptions—before it picked up again more aggressively with authors such as Hauptmann, Wedekind, Sternheim, Heinrich Mann, Musil, Brecht, Kafka, Tucholsky, Kästner, Marieluise Fleißer, and Karl Kraus, the most influential German satirist of the early 20th century.

During the late 19th century, several satirical journals came into existence (e.g., *Simplicissimus, Kladderadatsch*). This put new emphasis on the visual representation of satire just as the development of musical cabaret incorporated music into satirical performances.

In his article "Zur Frage der Satire," Georg Lukács attributes a positive function to satire as long as it supports the "progressive class" in overcoming an unwanted social order. In contrast, Adorno, disillusioned by the Third Reich, points out in his aphorism "Juvenals Irrtum" ("Juvenal's Error") in *Minima Moralia* (1951; *Minima Moralia*) that it has become difficult—if not impossible—in a totalitarian society to write satire.

After World War II, the theoretical discussion of satire in East Germany was from the beginning rooted in Lukács's work on satire and focused on the possibility of using satire as a means to support the struggle against imperialism (*programmatisch-anti-imperialistische Kampfsatire*) and to further socialist awareness (*innersozialistisch-erzieherische Satire*). Both aspects can be found, for example, in Wolf Biermann's works.

In West Germany, many impulses from research on satire in the Anglo-American countries led to a new theoretical discussion of satire in the 1950s and 1960s, one of the most influential theorists being Northrop Frye. Several anthologies of *satirische Kleinformen* (satirical short texts) were published during the 1960s, showing a growing interest in satirical writing for entertainment purposes. Some of the major authors who use satire or satirical elements in larger works are Heinrich Böll, Hans Magnus Enzensberger, Martin Walser, Gisela Elsner, C.F. Delius, Arno Schmidt, Christa Reinig, Irmtraud Morgner, Elfriede Jelinek, Şinasi Dikmen, and Osman Engin.

Sigrid Weigel coined the expression *shuddering laughter* in order to describe a common female reaction to satires written by women. She describes this form of laughter more as a borderline case between crying and laughing and explains it as a gender-specific laughter that always includes knowledge about one's own marginalization and the acknowledgment of one's own role as a victim who is trapped through social rituals, images, and expectations.

Looking beyond literature to film, many German movies contain satirical elements, but only very few—above all Kurt Hoffmann's *Wir Wunderkinder* (1958; Aren't We Wonderful) and Wolfgang Staudte's *Der Untertan* (1951; The Loyal Subject)—can in their entirety be regarded as satires. Satire, however, seems to become ever more popular in television shows, and recent developments indicate that satirical cabaret is experiencing a renaissance. At the same time, political satire in the form of cartoons or caricatures has become an integral component of most daily newspapers and political journals.

STEFANIE OHNESORG

See also Irony, Romantic

Further Reading

Allen, Ann Taylor, *Satire and Society in Wilhelmine German: Kladderadatsch und Simplicissimus 1890–1914*, Lexington: University Press of Kentucky, 1984

Arntzen, Helmut, *Satire in der deutschen Literatur: Geschichte und Theorie*, vol. 1, *Vom 12. bis zum 17. Jahrhundert*, Darmstadt: Wissenschaftliche Buchgesellschaft, 1989

Arntzen, Helmut, editor, *Deutsche Satire des 20. Jahrhunderts*, Heidelberg: Rothe, 1964

Braese, Stephan, *Das teure Experiment: Satire und NS-Faschismus*, Opladen: Westdeutscher Verlag, 1996

Brummack, Jürgen, "Zu Begriff und Theorie der Satire," *Deutsche Vierteljahrsschrift für Literaturwissenschaft und Geistesgeschichte* 45 (May 1971)

——, "Satire," in *Reallexikon der deutschen Literaturgeschichte*, 2nd edition, Berlin: de Gruyter, 1977

——, *Satirische Dichtung: Studien zu Friedrich Schlegel, Tieck, Jean Paul, und Heine*, Munich: Fink, 1979

Coupe, W.A., *German Political Satires from the Reformation to the Second World War*, 6 vols., White Plains, New York: Kraus International Publications, 1985–93

Ekmann, Bjørn, editor, *Die Schwierigkeit, Satire (noch) zu schreiben: Kopenhagener Kolloquium 3.–4. März 1995*, Copenhagen: Fink, 1996

Fabian, Bernhard, editor, *Satura: Ein Kompendium moderner Studien zur Satire*, Hildesheim: Olms, 1975

Feinäugle, Norbert, editor, *Satirische Texte: Für die Sekundarstufe*, Stuttgart: Reclam, 1976

Fletcher, M.D., *Contemporary Political Satire: Narrative Strategies in the Post-Modern Context*, Lanham, Maryland: University Press of America, 1987

Frye, Northrop, *Anatomy of Criticism: Four Essays*, Princeton, New Jersey: Princeton University Press, 1957

Gaier, Ulrich, *Satire: Studien zu Neidhart, Wittenwiler, Brant und zur satirischen Schreibart*, Tübingen: Niemeyer, 1967

Grimm, Reinhold, and Jost Hermand, editors, *Laughter Unlimited: Essays on Humor, Satire, and the Comic*, Madison: University of Wisconsin Press, 1988

Grimm, Reinhold, and Walter Hinck, editors, *Zwischen Satire und Utopie: Zur Komiktheorie und zur Geschichte der europäischen Komödie*, Frankfurt: Suhrkamp, 1982

Heidemann-Nebelin, Klaudia, *Rotkäppchen erlegt den Wolf: Marieluise Fleißer, Christa Reinig, und Elfriede Jelinek als satirische Schriftstellerinnen*, Bonn: Holos, 1994

Herzog, G.H., and Ehrhardt Heinold, editors, *Scherz beiseite: Die Anthologie der deutschsprachigen Prosa-Satire von 1900 bis zur Gegenwart*, Munich: Scherz, 1966

Jacobs, Jürgen, *Prosa der Aufklärung: Moralische Wochenschriften, Autobiographie, Satire, Roman: Kommentar zu einer Epoche*, Munich: Winkler, 1976

Johnson, Edgar, editor, *A Treasury of Satire*, New York: Simon and Schuster, 1945

Klein, Ulrich, *Die deutschsprachige Reisesatire des 18. Jahrhunderts*, Heidelberg: Winter, 1997

Kneip, Birgit, *Zwischen Angriff und Verteidigung: Satirische Schreibweise in der deutschen Erzähl- und Dokumentationsprosa 1945–75*, Frankfurt: Lang, 1993

Könneker, Barbara, *Satire im 16. Jahrhundert: Epoche, Werke, Wirkung*, Munich: Beck, 1991

Lazarowicz, Klaus, *Verkehrte Welt: Vorstudien zu einer Geschichte der deutschen Satire*, Tübingen: Niemeyer, 1963

Lukács, Georg, "Zur Frage der Satire," *Internationale Literatur* 2, no. 4–5 (1932)

Preisendanz, Wolfgang, and Rainer Warning, editors, *Das Komische*, Munich: Finck, 1976

Rehm, Walter, "Satirischer Roman," in *Reallexikon der deutschen Literaturgeschichte*, 2nd edition, Berlin: de Gruyter, 1977

Rothe, Norbert, editor, *Frühe sozialistische satirische Prosa*, Berlin: Akademie-Verlag 1981

Schmidt, Josef, *Lestern, lesen, und lesen hören: Kommunikationsstudien zur deutschen Prosasatire der Reformationszeit*, Bern: Lang, 1977

Seibert, Regine, *Satirische Empirie: Literarische Struktur und geschichtlicher Wandel der Satire in der Spätaufklärung*, Würzburg: Königshausen und Neumann, 1981

Tauscher, Rolf, *Literarische Satire des Exils gegen Nationalsozialismus und Hitlerdeutschland: Von F.G. Alexan bis Paul Westheim*, Hamburg: Verlag Dr. Kovac, 1992

Vormweg, Heinrich, editor, *Hieb und Stich: Deutsche Satire in 300 Jahren*, Cologne: Kiepenheuer und Witsch, 1968

Wedel, Mathias, "Zur Satiredebatte in den sechziger Jahren: Eine Studie zur Entfaltung einer zeitgemäßen Satireauffassung," *Weimarer Beiträge* 33, no. 5 (1987)

Weigel, Sigrid, *Die Stimme der Medusa: Schreibweisen in der Gegenwartsliteratur von Frauen*, Dülmen-Hiddingsel: Tende, 1987

Wilhelm, Frank, *Literarische Satire in der SBZ/DDR 1945–1961: Autoren, institutionelle Rahmenbedingungen und kulturpolitische Leitlinien*, Hamburg: Kovac, 1998

Rafik Schami 1946–

Syrian born Rafik Schami rates as one of the leading figures of German *Gastarbeiterliteratur* (guest worker literature) or *Migrantenliteratur* (migrant literature). Invited to help with the rebuilding of Germany, *Arbeitsmigranten* (migrant workers) from Mediterranean countries—mainly Turkey—began to arrive in 1960, and by 1968 their numbers were over 150,000. A distinctive migrant literature began to emerge in significant quantities in the late 1970s. Schami's importance lies in both his own writing and his role as a facilitator for other writers: in 1980, he cofounded the literary groups Südwind (South Wind) and Po-LiKunst (Polinationaler Literatur- und Kunstverein [Polynational Literary and Art Society]), which aimed at fostering the work of nonnative German authors.

Typical themes of migrant literature are conditions in the homeland and life as an alien in Germany. Both of these are to be found in Schami's works, but unlike many migrant writings in

German, they never degenerate into a lament on the difficulties of the foreign worker or an exposé of German xenophobia. Rather, they seek gently to draw from the reader a sympathy and tolerance for cultural diversity. Mostly they are set in Damascus, and occasionally in Malula, the Aramaic village from which the author's family originated. The works describe life in the Arab world for the benefit of the Western reader, providing factual information and offering insights into many aspects of daily life. In doing so, they quietly undermine all kinds of prejudice. The short novel *Eine Hand voller Sterne* (1987; *A Handful of Stars*), which contains many autobiographical elements, is a good example of this. It takes the form of the diary of a Damascan youth, following his progress through school, work, and family life, and featuring the themes of friendship and first love in a difficult situation of social conflict. Without ever appearing didactic, it educates the reader to an awareness of the richness of life in a foreign culture. Important here is the differentiating presentation of the Arab world, which mitigates against the homogeneity of Western perceptions. Like the author, the diary writer stands in the Christian-Aramaic tradition: not all Arabs are Muslims. Cultural diversity in Syria is a key theme in the book; for example, the riddle of the "madman" can only be solved by the cooperation of all the communities in Damascus. The story "Nuh, mein Freund" (My Friend Nuh) in the collection *Der Fliegenmelker* (1985; The Fly Milker), moreover, deals with the young man's discovery of his affection for the Kurdish minority.

If the fiction set in Syria presents a positive view of Arab family and social structures, it frequently contains critical comments on Damascan politics, corruption, censorship, and issues of civil and human rights. It was because of these problems that Schami himself left Syria and was unable to return. *A Handful of Stars* is again a good example, charting as it does the growing political awareness of the boy as he discovers journalism as a form of civil resistance. The story "Als der Angstmacher Angst bekam" (When the Fear-Maker Became Afraid) in *Der Fliegenmelker* takes a malicious delight in the downfall of a government informer, a stock figure in Schami's Damascan fiction. Other texts speak of the fear of police brutality, skepticism vis-à-vis government propaganda, and disillusionment as a series of coups fail to bring political change.

By contrast, Schami has a generally positive view of Germany. In interviews and speeches he warns against undercurrents of intolerance but speaks optimistically of the Germans as a people who are well-placed, precisely because of their history, to embrace foreign elements. Some stories dealing generally with intolerance and injustice could certainly be read in the context of migrant workers in Germany. One commentator interprets the title story of *Das letzte Wort der Wanderratte* (1984; The Itinerant Rat's Last Word) in this way: rats symbolize the guest workers, humans symbolize the Germans, and the massacre of Hamelin rats symbolizes the Holocaust. The interpretation is possible but not necessary. Similarly, the title story of *Das Schaf im Wolfpelz* (1982; Sheep in Wolf's Clothing) and many others that very obviously contain a social moral could certainly be taken to address the situation in Germany, but they could be equally applicable to the situation in Syria or elsewhere. The story "Vampire lieben Knoblauch" (Vampires Love Garlic) in *Das letzte Wort der Wanderratte* tells how Günter with his crucifix and Ali with his crescent are equally helpless victims of the predator, Dracula; it is a mistake to seek anti-German polemics in Schami's writing. His sharpest criticism is directed against the principle of assimilation, with its implication that outsiders settling in Germany should abandon their own cultural identity. In the story "Als der Meister auftrat" (When the Master Entered) in *Das letzte Wort der Wanderratte,* the migrant worker Hassan has himself transformed into a Siegfried, only to discover that the deception is untenable. The magician who sells him his German skin is named Gnussapna—an inversion of *Anpassung,* assimilation. As an alternative the story speaks of bridge building, the disarming of prejudices in both communities. Against the pressure for ethnic minorities to become invisible, Schami champions the concept of a boldly multicultural society, which, indeed, was the basic ideal of the PoLiKunst movement. A fine expression of the importance of coexistence is the parable "Der Wald und das Streichholz" (The Forest and the Matchstick) in *Der Fliegenmelker:* if the pines and the olives each hope the match will burn the others, it will burn them all.

The overriding characteristic of Schami's style is its affinity to the oral tradition of Arabic storytelling: one could speak of his integration of Arabic and German narrative traditions. Most of his books are collections of stories, and the novels abound in echoes of the *Arabian Nights,* even in the titles of *Erzähler der Nacht* (1989; *Damascus Nights*) or *Der ehrliche Lügner* (1992; The Honest Liar), which is subtitled *Roman von tausendeiner Lüge* (Novel of 1001 Lies). Both of these works are structured as a series of inserted stories presented orally by protagonists within a narrative framework. *Damascus Nights* in particular is a story about storytelling. *Vom Zauber der Zunge* (1991; On the Magic of the Tongue) gives an account of the background to *Damascus Nights.* As a child, Schami began telling stories to his friends on the streets of Damascus, and his promotional appearances are less public readings than free retellings of his works. Storytellers are favorite protagonists. One consequence of this is that Schami's target audience is extremely fluid: while some of his works are clearly published as children's literature (picture books, cassettes), the distinction between youth, young adult, and adult literature is not easily made; traditional storytelling addresses the entire community at once. The interplay of truth and fiction, always difficult concepts, is also a recurring theme in Schami's writings. *Der ehrliche Lügner* opens with the words: "My name is Sadik, but not even that is certain." Elsewhere we are told that the important thing is not whether stories are true, but rather that we live with them (*A Handful of Stars*). Although elements from fairy-tale worlds may appear in these stories, they are always rooted in daily life. Schami has made a distinction between *Illusion* and *Phantasie* (illusion and vision). Illusion is an unachievable dream, distorting the world to something impossible, whereas vision is the imaginative construction of achievable goals; rooted in reality, it indicates something for which we can strive, but this reality means that we also accept the other possibility, that there may not be a happy ending. Asked by an interviewer whether literature is an escape from reality, Schami answers, yes: but one that enables the reader to return to reality better equipped.

GRAEME DUNPHY

Biography
Born in Damascus, Syria, 23 June 1946. Schooling and university study (diploma in chemistry) in Damascus; wrote stories in Arabic, 1965–; cofounder and editor of the wall news-sheet *Al-Muntalak* in the old quarter of the city, 1964–70; moved to Heidelberg and financed further studies by typical guest-worker jobs (factories, building sites,

restaurants), 1971; began to learn German; doctorate in chemistry, 1979; began career in chemical industry; cofounder of the literary group *Südwind* and the PoLiKunst movement, 1980; full-time author from 1982. Adelbert von Chamisso Prize, 1993; Hermann Hesse Prize, 1994; Hans-Erich-Nossack-Preis der deutschen Wirtschaft, 1997. Currently lives in Kirchheimbolanden.

Selected Works

Fiction
Andere Märchen, 1978
Das Schaf im Wolfpelz: Märchen und Fabeln, 1982
Luki: Die Abenteuer eines kleinen Vogels, 1983
Das letzte Wort der Wanderratte: Märchen, Fabeln, und phantastische Geschichten, 1984
Der erste Ritt durchs Nadelöhr: Noch mehr Märchen, Fabeln und phantastische Geschichten, 1985
Der Fliegenmelker: Geschichten aus Damaskus, 1985
Weshalb darf Babs wieder lachen? 1985
Bobo und Susa: Als der Elefant sich in eine Maus verliebte, 1986
Eine Hand voller Sterne, 1987; as *A Handful of Stars*, translated by Rika Lesser, 1990
Malula: Märchen und Märchenhaftes aus meinem Dorf, 1987
Die Sehnsucht fährt schwarz: Geschichten aus der Fremde, 1988
Erzähler der Nacht, 1989; as *Damascus Nights*, translated by Philip Böhm, 1993
Der Löwe Benilo, 1989
Der fliegende Baum: Die schönsten Märchen, Fabeln und phantastischen Geschichten, 1991
Der ehrliche Lügner, 1992
Das ist kein Papagei, 1994
Fatima und der Traumdieb, 1995; as *Fatima and the Dream Thief*, translated by Anthea Bell, 1996
Reise zwischen Nacht und Morgen, 1995
Der Schnabelsteher, 1995; as *The Crow Who Stood on His Beak*, translated by Anthea Bell, 1996
Loblied und andere Olivenkerne, 1996
Gesammelte Olivenkerne, 1997
Milad: Von einem, der auszog, um einundzwanzig Tage satt zu werden, 1997

Play
Als die Puppen aus der reihe tanzten, 1987

Radio Plays
Der Kameltreiber von Heidelberg, 1986
Verrückt zu sein ist gar nicht so einfach, 1987
Der Wunderkasten, 1990

Scholarly Writing
Vom Zauber der Zunge: Reden gegen das Verstummen, 1991
Der brennende Eisberg: Eine Rede, ihre Geschichte und noch mehr, 1994
Zeiten des Erzählens, edited by Erich Jooß, 1994
Damals dort und heute hier, edited by Erich Jooß, 1998

Further Reading
Deeken, Annette, "Der listige Hakawati: Über den orientalischen Märchenerzähler Rafik Schami," *Deutschunterricht* 48 (1995)
Foraci, Franco, "Das Wort ist die letzte Freiheit, über die wir verfügen: Ein Gespräch mit dem syrischen Erzähler und Literaten Rafik Schami," *Diskussion Deutsch* 26 (1995)
Kahlil, Iman Osman, "Rafik Schami's Fantasy and Fairy Tales," *International Fiction Review* 17, no. 2 (1990)
———, "Narrative Strategies as Cultural Vehicles: On Rafik Schami's Novel *Erzähler der Nacht*," in *The Germanic Mosaic: Cultural and Linguistic Diversity in Society*, edited by Carol Blackshire-Belay, Westport, Connecticut: Greenwood Press, 1994
———, "Zum Konzept der Multikulturalität im Werk Rafik Schamis," *Monatshefte* 86, no. 2 (1994)
Kinerney, Donna, "The Stories of Rafik Schami as Reflections of His Psychopolitical Program," in *The Germanic Mosaic: Cultural and Linguistic Diversity in Society*, edited by Carol Blackshire-Belay, Westport, Connecticut: Greenwood Press, 1994
Rösch, Heidi, *Migrationsliteratur im interkulturellen Kontext: Eine didaktische Studie zur Literatur von Aras Ören, Aysel Özakin, Franco Biondi, und Rafik Schami*, Frankfurt: Verlag für interkulturelle Kommunikation, 1992
———, "Interkultureller Unterricht mit Rafik Schamis *Eine Hand voller Sterne*," *Diskussion Deutsch* 26 (1995)

Scheffler, Johannes, *see* Angelus Silesius (Johannes Scheffler)

Friedrich Wilhelm Joseph von Schelling 1775–1854

Together with Fichte, Schelling is one of the main philosophers of post-Kantian Idealism. His most important contribution is his claim that transcendental idealism culminates in a theory of art. In Schelling, we witness a major shift in German philosophy from epistemology and ethics to aesthetics.

At the Tübinger Stift, Schelling met both Hölderlin and Hegel, with whom he collaborated in producing one of the foundational manifestos of Romanticism, *Das älteste Systemprogramm des deutschen Idealismus* (ca.1796; The Oldest Systematic Program of German Idealism). The authors of this document claimed:

We must have a new mythology, but this mythology must be in the service of the Ideas, it must be a mythology of Reason. . . . Mythology must become philosophical in order to make the people rational, and philosophy must become mythological in order to make the philosophers sensible [*sinnlich*].

Following his appointment at Jena University, he became part of the early Romantic circle there, meeting the Schlegel brothers, Tieck, and Novalis, and in 1803 he married Caroline von Schlegel.

Arguing along Fichtean and then anti-Fichtean lines, but always attempting to overcome the dualism of Kantianism, Schelling's early work can best be understood in summary form in terms of the two ways in which it describes itself. First, it is a *Naturphilosophie* that attempts to restore to nature to its rightful place after Fichte's (and his own) emphasis on the Kantian role of the human ego in constituting reality. Spread over nature, Schelling detects "a veil of melancholy" (*Schwermut*), as nature strives to become wholly present to itself in the way that man is (or should be). Second, his philosophy is an *Identitätsphilosophie*, because self-consciousness, albeit at different levels, is present in both subjective (man) and objective nature (the natural world). This position provides the basis for the speculative theology of Schelling's later period.

Schelling's treatment of one concept in particular serves as an indication of his significance. Whereas Kant had restricted human knowledge to two sources (sensory intuition [organized by the a priori] and reason), Schelling explored a third, unmediated source of knowledge that Kant had defined but declared (humanly) impossible, "intellektuelle Anschauung" ("intellectual intuition"). In his *Philosophische Briefe über Dogmatismus und Kritizismus* (1795; Philosophical Letters on Dogmatism and Criticism), Schelling speaks of "a secret, marvelous faculty within all of us to withdraw from temporal change into our innermost self stripped of all that accrued to it and there, under the form of immutability, to behold the eternal in us." Yet Schelling, too, appears to place such intuition beyond our limits when he says: "Were I to engage upon intellectual intuition, I would cease to live; I would go out of time into eternity." By 1809, however, intellectual intuition had become part of Schelling's theory of art. In his *System des transzendentalen Idealismus* (1800; *System of Transcendental Idealism*), he claims that "aesthetic intuition is intellectual intuition become objective," and the importance that Schelling came to attach to art becomes clear in two further pronouncements: "Beauty is the infinite represented in finite terms" and "Art is the sole true and eternal organon and at the same time document of philosophy." Equally, the link between art and mythology that characterizes his later work is evident from his claim in *Philosophie der Kunst* (1802–3; *Philosophy of Art*) that we do not need a mythology of reason, but that "mythology is absolute poetry."

It was, in part, this late definition of the aesthetic that earned Schelling the hostility of Goethe who, despite his earlier appreciation of Schelling's respect for nature, spoke of Schelling's "Zweizüngigkeit" (forked tongue) to convey his suspicion of his later philosophical maneuvers. Even more trenchantly, Hegel—who had provided a careful analysis of the positions of Fichte and Schelling in his *Differenz des Fichteschen und Schellingschen Systems der Philosophie* (1801; *The Difference Between Fichte's and Schelling's System of Philosophy*)—made his famous condemnation of Schelling's concept of the Absolute in his own *Phänomenologie des Geistes* (1807; *Phenomenology of Spirit*): "the night in which all cows are black." Schelling's lectures in Berlin were attended by, among others, Kierkegaard, Arnold Ruge, Engels, and Bakunin, none of whom was impressed. A constant theme in Schelling's work was the suspicion of the state, which appeared as early as his rejection of political philosophy in the "Oldest Systematic Program" and was continued in the dismissive discussion in lecture 24 of his lectures on the *Philosophie der Mythologie* (1842; Philosophy of Mythology). Indeed, after the death of Caroline in 1809, there is a marked shift in Schelling's work away from the problems of *Identitätsphilosophie* and *Naturphilosophie* toward religion, mythology, and mysticism (in these later works, he draws greatly on the German mystic Jacob Böhme and the Roman Catholic theologian Franz von Baader), and it is largely these works that have earned him his bad reputation. Yet rather than simply trying to turn back the Kantian clock, Schelling's work also anticipates many later themes of German philosophy, and Schellingian themes reemerge in Schopenhauer, Tillich, Jung, and existentialism. Of his reception in this century, Heidegger's lectures on Schelling's *Abhandlung über das Wesen der menschlichen Freiheit* (1936; published 1971; *Schelling's Treatise on the Essence of Human Freedom*) are the most notable, and Jaspers's 1955 book was a major contribution to understanding Schelling, as was Jürgen Habermas's 1954 *Habilitationsschrift* on Schelling's theory of history. The last 15 years have seen detailed discussions of his work by Manfred Frank and Andrew Bowie, as well as by the Slovenian philosopher Slavoj Žižek, so it is no exaggeration to speak of a renaissance of interest in Schelling's work.

PAUL BISHOP

See also Mythology; Romanticism

Biography
Born in Leonberg, Württemberg, 27 January 1775. Studied philosophy and theology, Tübingen University, 1790–95, and mathematics and natural sciences, Leipzig University, 1796–98; made Extraordinary Professor in Jena (at the recommendation of Goethe), 1798; subsequent academic posts at Würzburg, 1803–6, Erlangen, 1820–27, Munich, 1827–41, and Berlin, 1841–52; no university activity, 1806–20, but a member of the Academy of Sciences in Munich, 1806, and general secretary of the Academy of the Plastic Arts, 1808. Died in Bad Ragaz, Switzerland, 20 August 1854.

Selected Works
Philosophische Briefe über Dogmatismus und Kritizismus, 1795
Ideen zu einer Philosophie der Natur, 1797; as *Ideas for a Philosophy of Nature*, translated by Errol E. Harris and Peter Heath, 1988
Von der Weltseele, 1798
Erster Entwurf eines Systems der Naturphilosophie, 1799
System des transzendentalen Idealismus, 1800; as *System of Transcendental Idealism*, translated by Peter Heath, 1978
Darstellung meines Systems im Ganzen, 1801
Philosophie und Religion, 1804
Philosophie der Kunst, 1802–03; as *Philosophy of Art*, translated by Douglas W. Stott, 1989
Philosophische Untersuchungen über das Wesen der menschlichen Freiheit, 1809; as *Schelling: Of Human Freedom*, 1936

Philosophie der Mythologie, 1842
Philosophie der Offenbarung, 1854

Further Reading

Beach, Edward Allen, *The Potencies of God(s): Schelling's Philosophy of Mythology,* Albany: State University of New York Press, 1994

Bowie, Andrew, *Schelling and Modern European Philosophy: An Introduction,* London and New York: Routledge, 1993

Copleston, Frederick, *Fichte to Hegel,* A History of Philosophy, vol. 7, Westminster, Maryland: Newman Press, 1963

Esposito, Joseph L., *Schelling's Idealism and Philosophy of Nature,* Lewisburg, Pennsylvania: Bucknell University Press, and London: Associated University Presses, 1977

Frank, Manfred, *Eine Einführung in Schellings Philosophie,* Frankfurt: Suhrkamp, 1985

Hegel, Georg Friedrich Wilhelm, *Difference between Fichte's and Schelling's System of Philosophy,* translated by Walter Cerf and H.S. Harris, Albany: State University of New York Press, 1977

Heidegger, Martin, *Schelling's Treatise on the Essence of Human Freedom,* translated by Joan Stambaugh, Athens and London: Ohio University Press, 1985

Jaspers, Karl, *Schelling: Größe und Verhängnis,* Munich: Piper, 1955

Kirchhoff, Jochen, *Friedrich Wilhelm Joseph von Schelling mit Selbstzeugnissen und Bilddokumenten,* Reinbek bei Hamburg: Rowohlt, 1982

Roberts, Julian, "Schelling," in *German Philosophy: An Introduction,* Cambridge: Polity Press, 1988

Wetz, Franz Josef, *Friedrich W.J. Schelling zur Einführung,* Hamburg: Junius, 1996

White, Alan, *Schelling: An Introduction to the System of Freedom,* New Haven, Connecticut and London: Yale University Press, 1983

Žižek, Slavoj, *The Indivisible Remainder: An Essay on Schelling and Related Matters,* London and New York: Verso, 1996

———, *The Abyss of Freedom,* Ann Arbor: University of Michigan Press, 1997 [with text of Schelling's *Die Weltalter,* translated by Judith Norman as *Ages of the World*]

Friedrich von Schiller 1759–1805

Friedrich Schiller, considered by some the greatest playwright of German literature, until relatively recently maintained a perennial place on the German stage second only to Shakespeare's. Even today his dramas are found near the top of the list of the most frequently performed plays in Germany. The common language remains full of tags from Schiller's dramas, ballad verse, and philosophical poems, sometimes playfully applied, for he is doubtless the most parodied writer in the German language. For a century he remained an icon for the German people for a somewhat abstract but nonetheless powerful concept of freedom. The celebration of his centennial in 1859 was the largest spontaneous movement of civilians in the history of the German nation up to that time, involving hundreds of thousands and quite possibly millions of people in cities and towns all over Germany and around the world, from St. Petersburg to San Francisco.

Schiller was the son of an army captain who in 1775 was put in charge of the orchards of Duke Karl Eugen of Württemberg, a task that, with a characteristic tendency toward knowledge and self-improvement (which was inherited by his son), he discharged with honor. If the boy and his family had been left to their own devices, Schiller undoubtedly would have passed through the remarkable hierarchy of educational institutions in Württemberg, culminating in the prestigious Protestant seminary, the Tübinger Stift. It was the system that in his time educated Hegel, Hölderlin, Schelling, Mörike, and David Friedrich Strauss. Instead, at the age of 13 he was forced into a peculiar school devised by the duke to create a cadre of educated officials loyal to the duke alone; thus, the pupils were never let out of the school for any reason. From age 13 to 21, Schiller was cut off from his family and any friends other than his schoolmates. Although the school provided a good education, it was a traumatic environment that marked his personality for the rest of his life, leaving him with a bitter feeling that his full human potential

had been blighted and a hatred of tyranny that developed into pessimism about the moral possibilities of any exercise of power.

As a boy, Schiller had dreamed of becoming a pastor, but Karl Eugen, a Catholic ruler of a Protestant state, had no use for the disruptive discipline of theology and did not offer it in his school. Schiller began to study law but did poorly out of lack of interest; when a medical faculty was introduced, he switched to that subject, but he was never to overestimate his medical knowledge or skills as a physician. When his first medical dissertation was rejected for criticizing authorities, he was obliged to remain in the school for another year, fueling the rage that motivated his first drama, *Die Räuber* (1781; *The Robbers*), a violently social-critical tragedy of hostile brothers. It was the last important work of the Sturm und Drang, introducing Schiller's lifelong themes: the moral corruption of power, and the necessary but fragile and often dysfunctional relationship between fathers and sons.

The Robbers promptly got young Schiller into trouble. After leaving school he was a lowly medical corpsman in a regiment of invalids in Stuttgart; when he went without leave to attend performances of his play in Mannheim, Karl Eugen put him under arrest for two weeks and forbade him to write any more "comedies." In September 1782 he took the opportunity of a court reception to flee Stuttgart. For the next several years, his life was very difficult and unsettled. In 1785 he accepted the hospitality of an admirer in Dresden, Gottfried Körner, who became his best friend, and his career did not fare badly. *The Robbers* was enthusiastically received; the first reviewer expressed the hope that a German Shakespeare had appeared, and Schiller achieved a contract with the Mannheim theater for three dramas.

The first of these commissioned plays was *Die Verschwörung des Fiesko zu Genua: Eine republikanische Tragödie* (1783; *Fiesco; or, The Genoese Conspiracy*), concerning a rebellion against the rule of Andrea Doria; it continues Schiller's themes but is confused on the issue of power and is generally regarded as the weakest of his dramas. His next effort, a bourgeois tragedy, was more successful. He wanted to call it *Luise Miller,* but the actor August Wilhelm Iffland, in order to make it more commercial, renamed it *Kabale und Liebe* (1784; *Intrigue and Love*). It was inspired by a fashion imported from England but executed with greater skeptical intelligence, for the impetuous and progressive lover who seeks to emancipate the middle-class girl is in fact locked into his ruthless, aristocratic mental habits, as she is in her own way imprisoned by her naïveté. The third of the contractual dramas, *Don Carlos* (1787), was to give Schiller an immense amount of trouble. He conceived it as a "family portrait in a princely house," joining bourgeois sentiment and family concern to the tragic impact of a fall from a high place; Carlos broods on the loss of his fiancée to his father, the terrifying King Philip II of Spain, but Carlos comes to be displaced in the action by his confidant, Marquis Posa, a visionary of freedom. Then the concept is bent again as Posa becomes ruthless and manipulatory in his effort to exercise power over events and people. For years the play expanded while Schiller revised and abridged it without solving its problems. Despite its flaws, it retains memorable force; the line that Posa fires at the king, almost exactly at the center of the drama, "Give freedom of thought," continued to echo into the Nazi period.

Schiller's problems with *Don Carlos,* however, persuaded him that he was not educated to the forefront of modern thought, and he entered into a decade of historical and philosophical studies. His historical works, which led to a professorship at the University of Jena in 1788, are not as much read today as they were in the past, but the two major ones, *Die Geschichte des Abfalls der vereinigten Niederlande von der spanischen Regierung* (1788; *The History of the Defection of the United Netherlands from the Spanish Empire*) and *Geschichte des dreißigjährigen Krieges* (1793; *The History of the Thirty Years' War in Germany*), though both incomplete, show in their crispness and their often sour view of human affairs that Schiller was neither naive nor idealistic about the ways of the world. The philosophical writings are primarily about aesthetics and are much engaged with the model of Kant, but their real subject is the achievement of human freedom through the experience of art as an alternative to the terror of the French Revolution. The three most important of them are *Über Anmut und Würde* (1793; *On Grace and Dignity*), *Über die ästhetische Erziehung des Menschen in einer Reihe von Briefe* (1795; *On the Aesthetic Education of Man, in a Series of Letters*), and *Über naive und sentimentalische Dichtung* (1795–96; *On the Naive and Sentimental in Literature*).

On the Naive and Sentimental in Literature is read by some interpreters as Schiller's effort to distinguish his mode of poetic creativity, stressfully bridging modern alienation, from Goethe's natural, effortless, timelessly Greek genius. The bond between Schiller and Goethe evolved cautiously; in 1794 they came to recognize their shared aspirations in antagonism to their immediate literary and cultural environment, and they began to exchange thoughts and projects, criticism and suggestions. The relationship was not without subliminal incongruities and stresses that intermittently rose to the surface, and there is some evidence that, toward the end of his life, Schiller was looking for a way to emancipate himself from the affiliation. Nevertheless, it was a mutually enriching and supportive relationship; the approximately 1,000 letters they exchanged constitute one of the great correspondences of world literature.

Schiller came to be uncertain whether his philosophical inquiries were achieving what he had hoped they would and developed a longing to return to primary creativity. What is remarkable about this last phase of his career is its experimental nature: none of the dramas resembles any other, and each confronts a new task, chosen not because it seemed to recommend itself for dramatic treatment but because it presented difficulties. He began with the most plausible German successor to Shakespeare, the three-part *Wallenstein: Wallensteins Lager* (1789; *Wallenstein's Camp*), *Die Piccolomini* (1799; *The Piccolominis*), and *Wallensteins Tod* (1799; *The Death of Wallenstein*). This is not a trilogy, as it is sometimes called, but a single ten-act tragedy with a dramatic prologue. Its intricate inquiry into the inscrutability of historical circumstance and the psychology of power presents a proud and ambitious man whose disingenuousness has become so internalized that he can no longer read his own motives.

Schiller followed the sprawling epic theater of *Wallenstein* with his most architectonic drama, modeled on the well-made plays of French classicism, *Maria Stuart* (1801; *Mary Stuart*), in which, contrary to expectations for a Protestant playwright, the imprisoned Catholic queen achieves more moral freedom than the Protestant Queen Elizabeth on the throne. *Die Jungfrau von Orleans* (1801; translated as *The Maid of Orleans* and *Joan of Arc*) is subtitled *A Romantic Tragedy,* but it could be understood as an antiromantic tragedy, so thoroughly is Joan of Arc puppetized and dehumanized by a transcendental imperative devoid of grace. Schiller then attempted a competition with ancient Greek tragedy, complete with chorus, in *Die Braut von Messina* (1803; *The Bride of Messina*). It is the most poetic of his dramas, but with its operative family curse, it became contaminated with the Gothic fate-tragedy mode of the time and has been regarded by many observers as a noble failure. There followed Schiller's only nontragic drama, the strangely double-plotted *Wilhelm Tell* (1804; *William Tell*), which enacts a morally justified revolution while implying the impossibility of such a revolution in the modern world. Its subtleties and enigmas ignored, it became a popular pageant for decades; although Schiller had never seen Switzerland, it permanently defined the Swiss image of William Tell, his crossbow, and his shooting of an apple placed on his son's head.

Schiller, whose health was never strong, died at the height of his powers; he had reached the second act of a new work, *Demetrius* (posthumously published 1815), the story of the false czar Dmitri, which was also the subject of Pushkin's poem and Mussorgsky's opera *Boris Godunov*. Another inquiry into the psychology of power, it has been thought that it might have been his greatest drama. For the rest of the century and beyond, he remained, even more than Goethe, the national poet of the German people. But his reputation was international: he was particularly influential in Russia, and in Italy Giuseppe Verdi made operas of four of his dramas (there have been more than two dozen other operas based on Schiller's works, including Gioacchino Rossini's *Guillaume Tell,* with its unforgettable overture). However, his identification with the German nation and its claims to cultural superiority became a burden on his reputation in modern times. On the whole, his works were resistant to intensive efforts at co-optation by the Nazis, and his standing remained unquestioned in East Germany as one of the guarantors of its humanistic inheritance. But in the West there came to be skepticism about Schiller's political legacy, due to his horrified rejection of the French Revolution and the implication that aesthetic education must balance and moderate the spirit before political purposes might be humanely pursued, as well as his sententiousness and austere moralism, not least in sexual matters. His plays came to be performed parodistically, aggressively against the grain. But after the 1970s the intensity of this tormented relationship to the past began to recede, and Schiller has become less its object. The crucial Nationalausgabe (1943–, National Edition), begun at an unpropitious time in the middle of World War II, has been nearing its completion, and the Deutsche Schillergesellschaft (German Schiller Society) is allied with the central archive of German literature in Marbach and publishes an ample yearbook (*Jahrbuch der deutschen Schillergesellschaft*) that is one of the finest of German scholarly periodicals. Schiller continues to live on the stage, in fresh literary and philosophical study, and in the cultural memory.

JEFFREY L. SAMMONS

See also Die Horen; Weimar

Biography

Born in Marbach am Neckar, Duchy of Württemberg, 10 November 1759. Forced into military academy of Duke Karl Eugen of Württemberg, 1773; studied law and medicine, 1773–80; regimental surgeon, 1780; fled Württemberg in 1782 as a result of the Duke's displeasure with his writing; contract to write for the Nationaltheater, Mannheim, 1783–84; editor, *Rheinische Thalia*, later *Thalia* and *Neue Thalia*, 1785–93, *Die Horen*, 1795–97, and *Musen-Almanach*, 1797–1800; member of the Körner circle, Leipzig and then Dresden; in Weimar, 1787; with Goethe's influence, became professor of history, University of Jena, 1789–91; in Weimar after 1799; several of his plays produced under Goethe's direction at the court theater. Died in Weimar, 9 May 1805.

Selected Works

Collections

Works, 7 vols., 1897–1903
Schillers Werke: Nationalausgabe, edited by Julius Petersen, Gerhard Fricke et al., 1943–
Sämtliche Werke, edited by Gerhard Fricke, Herbert G. Göpfert, and Herbert Stubenrauch, 5 vols., 1958–59
Werke und Briefe, edited by Klaus Harro Hilzinger et al., 1988–

Plays

Die Räuber (produced 1782), 1781; as *The Robbers*, translated by A.F. Tytler, 1792; translated by F.J. Lamport, with *Wallenstein*, 1979; edited by Alan C. Leidner in *Sturm und Drang*, 1992; translated by Robert David Macdonald, 1995
Die Verschwörung des Fiesko zu Genua (produced 1784), 1783; as *Fiesco; or, The Genoese Conspiracy*, translated by G.H. Noehden and J. Stoddart, 1796
Kabale und Liebe (produced 1784), 1784; edited by Elizabeth M. Wilkinson and Leonard A. Willoughby, 1944; as *Cabal and Love*, 1795; as *The Minister*, translated by M.G. Lewis, 1798; as *The Harper's Daughter*, 1813; as *Love and Intrigue*, translated by Frederick Rolf, 1962; as *Intrigue and Love*, translated by Charles E. Passage, 1971; translated by Johanna Setzer and Elaine Gottesman, 1978; translated by A. Leslie and Jeanne W. Willson in *Plays*, edited by Walter Hinderer, 1983

Don Carlos (produced 1787), 1787; translated by G.H. Noehden and J. Stoddart, 1798; translated by James Kirkup in *Classic Theatre 2*, edited by Eric Bentley, 1959; translated by Charles E. Passage, 1959; translated by James Maxwell, 1987; translated by Robert David Macdonald, 1995; translated by Hillary Collier Sy-Quia, with *Mary Stuart*, 1996
Wallenstein: Wallensteins Lager, Die Piccolomini, Wallensteins Tod (produced 1798–99), 1798–99; as *Wallenstein*, translated by S.T. Coleridge, 1800; translated by Charles E. Passage, 1958; translated by F.J. Lamport, with *The Robbers*, 1979; edited by Walter Hinderer, with *Mary Stuart*, 1991
Maria Stuart (produced 1800), 1801; as *Mary Stuart*, translated by J.C. Mellish, 1801; translated by Stephen Spender, 1959; translated by F.J. Lamport, in *Five German Tragedies*, 1969; translated by Robert David Macdonald, 1987; edited by Walter Hinderer, with *Wallenstein*, 1991; translated by Hillary Collier Sy-Quia, with *Mary Stuart*, 1996
Die Jungfrau von Orleans (produced 1801), 1801; as *The Maid of Orleans*, translated by J.E. Drinkwater, 1835; translated by Charles E. Passage, 1961; as *Joan of Arc*, translated by Robert David Macdonald, 1987
Die Braut von Messina (produced 1803), 1803; as *The Bride of Messina*, translated by G. Irvine, 1837; translated by A. Lodge, 1841; translated by E. Allfrey, 1876; translated by Charles E. Passage, 1962
Wilhelm Tell (produced 1804), 1804; as *William Tell*, translated by R.L. Pearsall, 1825; translated by Sidney E. Kaplan, 1954; translated by Gilbert T. Jordan, 1964; translated by John Prudhoe, 1970; translated by William E. Mainland, 1972
Demetrius (fragment; produced 1890), 1815

Fiction

Der Verbrecher aus Infamie, 1786; as *Der Verbrecher aus verlorener Ehre*, 1792; as *The Dishonoured Irreclaimable*, translated by R. Holcroft, in *Tales from the German*, 1826
Der Geisterseher (fragment), 1789; as *The Ghost Seer; or, Apparitionist*, 1795; as *The Armenian; or, The Ghost-Seer*, translated by W. Render, 1800; as *The Ghost-Seer*, translated by Henry G. Bohn, 1992
Spiel des Schicksals, 1789

Poetry

Anthologie auf das Jahr 1782, 1782
Gedichte, 2 vols., 1800–1803
Lyrical Ballads, translated by Anne Trelawy Gibbons, 1838
The Minor Poems, translated by J.H. Merivale, 1844
The Poems and Ballads, translated by Edward Bulwer Lytton, 1844
The Poems of Schiller Complete, translated by E.A. Bowring, 1856
Selected Poems, edited by Frank M. Fowler, 1969

Other

Die Geschichte des Abfalls der vereinigten Niederlande von der spanischen Regierung, 1788; as *History of the Rise and Progress of the Belgian Republic*, translated by T. Horne, 1807; as *The History of the Defection of the United Netherlands from the Spanish Empire*, translated by E.B. Eastwick, 1844; as *The Revolt of the Netherlands*, translated by A.J.W. Morrison and L. Dora Schmitz, 1897
Geschichte des dreißigjährigen Krieges, 1793; as *The History of the Thirty Years War in Germany*, translated by Captain Blaquiere, 1799; translated by A.J.W. Morrison, 1899
Über Anmut und Würde, 1793
Über die ästhetische Erziehung des Menschen in einer Reihe von Briefe, in *Die Horen*, 1795; as *Upon the Aesthetic Culture of Man*, in *Philosophical and Aesthetic Letters and Essays*, 1845; as *On the Aesthetic Education of Man, in a Series of Letters*, translated by Reginald Snell, 1954; edited and translated by Elizabeth M. Wilkinson and L.A. Willoughby, 1967

Über naive und sentimentalische Dichtung, in *Die Horen*, 1795–96; as *On Simple and Sentimental Poetry*, in *Essays Aesthetical and Philosophical*, 1884; as *Naive and Sentimental Poetry*, translated by Julius A. Elias, 1966 (also published in *German Aesthetic and Literary Criticism: Winckelmann, Lessing, Hamann, Herder, Schiller, and Goethe*, edited by H.B. Nisbet, Cambridge and New York: Cambridge University Press, 1985); as *On the Naive and Sentimental in Literature*, translated by Helen Watanabe-O'Kelly, 1981

Correspondence between Goethe and Schiller, 1794–1805, translated by George H. Calvert, 1845; translated by L. Dora Schmitz, 1877–79; translated by Lieselotte Dieckmann, 1994

Correspondence of Schiller with Körner, translated by Leonard Simpson, 1849

Friedrich Schiller: Medicine, Psychology, and Literature, translated by Kenneth Dewhurst and Nigel Reeves, 1978

Further Reading

Berghahn, Klaus L., *Schiller: Ansichten eines Idealisten*, Frankfurt: Athenäum, 1986

Graham, Ilse, *Schiller's Drama: Talent and Integrity*, New York: Barnes and Noble, and London: Methuen, 1974

Guthke, Karl S., *Schillers Dramen: Idealismus und Skepsis*, Tübingen: Francke, 1994

Hinderer, Walter, editor, *Schillers Dramen: Neue Interpretationen*, Stuttgart: Reclam, 1979

Kerry, S.S., *Schiller's Writings on Aesthetics*, Manchester: Manchester University Press, and New York: Barnes and Noble, 1961

Koopmann, Helmut, *Friedrich Schiller*, 2 vols., Stuttgart: Metzler: 1966; 2nd edition, 1977

Sammons, Jeffrey L., "Friedrich von Schiller (1759–1805)," in *European Writers: The Romantic Century*, edited by Jacques Barzun and George Stade, vol. 5, *Johann Wolfgang von Goethe to Alexander Pushkin*, New York: Scribner, 1985

Sharpe, Lesley, *Schiller and the Historical Character*, London and New York: Oxford University Press, 1982

——, *Schiller's Aesthetic Essays: Two Centuries of Criticism*, Columbia, South Carolina: Camden House, 1995

Staiger, Emil, *Friedrich Schiller*, Zurich: Atlantis, 1967

Ugrinsky, Alexej, editor, *Friedrich von Schiller and Drama of Human Existence*, New York: Greenwood Press, 1988

Wiese, Benno von, *Friedrich Schiller*, Stuttgart: Metzler, 1959; 4th edition, 1978

Kabale und Liebe 1784

Play by Friedrich von Schiller

Kabale und Liebe (*Intrigue and Love*) was Friedrich Schiller's third play. His only attempt at domestic tragedy (*bürgerliches Trauerspiel*), it became a landmark of the genre and has remained one of his most frequently performed plays. Its vivid characters, swift-moving action, and climactic confrontations are characteristic of Schiller's dramatic technique, while the rhetoric, which arguably strains credibility in some scenes, points to a dramatist who would in his next play (*Don Carlos*) find his natural home in the world of historical verse tragedy.

The play shows the influence of previous examples of German domestic tragedy, in particular that of Gotthold Ephraim Lessing's *Emilia Galotti* (1772). Indeed, Schiller's first title for the play was *Luise Millerin*. In both plays, the heroine's moral consciousness is central to the tragedy, a strong contrast exists between the sexual license of the court and the uprightness of the heroine, a father attempts unsuccessfully to protect his daughter, a mother's social ambitions play a part in the catastrophe, a court intrigue is devised to entrap the heroine, and the ruler's mistress has a prominent role.

Written about a decade after the main works of the Sturm and Drang, the radical avant-garde literary movement of the early 1770s, the play bears the mark of that period of literary history in its move away from an adherence to classical conventions to a greater social realism and freedom of dramatic form. It is written in a vigorous prose that gives each character his or her peculiarities of speech such as contemporary slang or words borrowed from the French. The action, although streamlined and swift and not replicating the more experimentally open form of Schiller's first play *Die Räuber* (1781; *The Robbers*), takes place in a variety of locations and is based on the strong contrast between court and non-aristocratic milieus. Comic elements are introduced, as in the person of the foppish, vain Hofmarschall von Kalb, in whom the morals and manners of the court are satirized.

Intrigue and Love has done much to encourage the view that Schiller was a young social revolutionary, denouncing injustice and princely abuses of the kind rife in his native Württemberg; Schiller's radicalism is exemplified in his portrayal of the President and suggested by what we learn of the unseen Duke. The famous scene in which Lady Milford discovers that her jewels were bought by the sale of the Duke's subjects as soldiers to America usually had to be cut in performance, as it was for the première. Ferdinand's and Lady Milford's denunciations of the moral bankruptcy of the court and the President's disdain for those beneath him reflect a criticism of aristocratic values and abuses heard elsewhere in Schiller's early work. In this play he also takes up a popular theme of domestic tragedy, that of a young woman finding herself the object of desire of a man far above her in rank. Unlike many aristocratic men in domestic tragedy, however, Ferdinand rejects the values he was brought up in and wishes not to seduce Luise, but to marry her. Yet although the idealistic love of Ferdinand and Luise is defeated by the intrigues of the court, as the play's title suggests, Schiller shows that the lovers are pulled apart not only by opposition from without but by deeply rooted differences in character and attitude that become apparent as external pressure is brought to bear on them. After the President's first failed attempt in act 2 to put an end to the relationship by intimidation, Luise, whose inclination is to accept suffering as her due, renounces Ferdinand, claiming that their duty is to their parents and that their love oversteps the God-given order. Ferdinand, who (realistically) judges that they should flee in order to start a new life, is enraged by Luise's passivity and begins to show signs (act 3, scene 7) of the irrational and violent behavior that eventually leads him to destroy Luise and himself. Although this view has been disputed, critics see Luise's passive acceptance of suffering and Ferdinand's imperious arrogation to himself of the right to judge and destroy her as rooted in their internalization of social attitudes that were typical of the middle class and the aristocracy. On a deeper level, the play can be seen as exploring an irreconcilable conflict regarding the nature of the claims of love itself.

Wurm's intrigue against the lovers is based on psychological manipulation. He calculates that Luise will not break her oath of silence and that Ferdinand's jealous nature will be outraged when he discovers Luise to have been trifling with him. He does not foresee that Ferdinand will kill Luise and then himself.

Wurm is thus typical of the Schillerian intriguer (Octavio in *Wallenstein* is another) who cannot control the intrigue once it is unleashed and who loses what he hoped to gain (Luise's hand). He does so because he underestimates Ferdinand's extremism. The characterization of Ferdinand shows Schiller's continuing fascination—after Karl Moor of *The Robbers*—with the contradictions within the idealist figure, who sees himself at odds with a degenerate world but whose extremism and imperiousness destroys all that he holds most dear. As a result of renewed critical interest in recent years in Schiller's medical writings, Ferdinand's violent physical reactions (see the stage directions to act 3, scene 7) have been interpreted as demonstrating the playwright's fascination with the interdependence of mind and body in extreme states. Although he is a mouthpiece for the longing for a better world, Ferdinand's lack of inner composure suggests that Schiller's undoubted sympathy with the humanitarian aspirations of his age was tempered with a skepticism regarding the ability of the most idealistic to put such ideals into practice.

The play provoked strongly contrasting reactions when it was first performed, from enthusiasm—especially among the young—to appalled rejection of the play's alleged tastelessness, melodrama, and weaknesses of plot. Nevertheless, it continued to be performed. In the 1960s the play's note of social and political criticism made it particularly popular; this trend, however, gave way to renewed emphasis on Ferdinand's egoism and the failure of communication between the doomed lovers.

LESLEY SHARPE

Editions

First edition: *Kabale und Liebe,* Mannheim: Schwan, 1784
Critical editions: *Kabale und Liebe,* edited by Elizabeth M. Wilkinson and Leonard A. Willoughby, Oxford: Blackwell, 1944; 6th edition, Oxford: Oxford University Press, 1964 [contains excellent introduction in English]; in *Schillers Werke: Nationalausgabe,* vol. 5, edited by Heinz Otto Burger and Walter Höllerer, Weimar: Hermann Böhlaus Nachfolger, 1957
Translation: *Intrigue and Love,* translated by Charles E. Passage, New York: Ungar, 1971

Further Reading

Auerbach, Erich, "Miller the Musician," in *Mimesis: The Representation of Reality in Western Literature,* Princeton, New Jersey: Princeton University Press, 1953
Dewhurst, Kenneth, and Nigel Reeves, *Friedrich Schiller: Medicine, Psychology, and Literature,* Oxford: Sandford, 1978
Graham, Ilse A., "Passions and Possessions in Schiller's *Kabale und Liebe,*" *German Life and Letters* new series 6 (1952–53)
Guthke, Karl S., "*Kabale und Liebe,*" in *Schillers Dramen: Neue Interpretationen,* edited by Walter Hinderer, Stuttgart: Reclam, 1979
Heitner, Robert R., "*Luise Millerin* and the Shock Motif in Schiller's Early Dramas," *Germanic Review* 41 (1966)
Sharpe, Lesley, *Friedrich Schiller: Drama, Thought, and Politics,* Cambridge and New York: Cambridge University Press, 1991

Die Räuber 1781

Play by Friedrich von Schiller

Schiller's first play, *Die Räuber* (*The Robbers*), is normally regarded as a late manifestation of Sturm und Drang, also called the *Geniezeit* (the genius period), a literary movement in Germany during the 1770s that took Rousseau's cult of feeling to apoplectic extremes by celebrating the man of passion and power (*der Kraftmensch,* Müller's "grosser Kerl") who releases the force of his personality into the world without regard for law or decorum. The *Stürmer* deplored both the suffocating narrowness of the German principalities as well as the materialistic routine of typical middle-class ambitions. They longed for a more impressive social context in which to deploy their talents and energies. Instead of the formality of French classical literary models, where a character is an "ice-cold spectator of his own rage," as Schiller put it in his "Suppressed Preface" to *The Robbers,* they preferred the dramatic exuberance and greater class inclusivity of Shakespeare.

Schiller wrote *The Robbers* while he was a medical student at the military academy of Duke Karl Eugen of Württemberg. The Karlsschule's discipline and rigidity along with the authoritarian paternalism of Schiller's patron provided a microcosm of the world against which Schiller's generation was in revolt. The audience's reaction to the play at its premiere in Mannheim on 13 January 1782 was astonishing: an eyewitness spoke of clenched fists, hoarse cries, rolling eyes, tearful strangers embracing, and women staggering toward the exits; the theater resembled a madhouse. Schiller had had to publish his play at his own expense and to go absent without leave to see it performed. For these efforts he was sternly reproved, put under a two-week house arrest, and told to confine his interests to medicine. Schiller took advantage of official festivities in honor of foreign visitors to flee Württemberg for the neighboring Palatinate. Some indication of the play's impact on Schiller's reputation can still be seen in Goethe's remote formality during Schiller's first meeting with him in September 1788. Goethe supposedly disapproved of the play, but jealousy can hardly be ruled out; its public reception had been greater than anything Goethe had written since *Werther.*

The operatic plot of *The Robbers* involves a conflict between two sons of Count Maximilian von Moor. Karl is the first born: he is handsome, charismatic, and engaged to his lovely cousin, Amalia von Edelreich. The younger Franz, embittered by the inequities of primogeniture and by his own physical ugliness, schemes to have Karl disowned and to seize Amalia for himself. While away at university in Leipzig, Karl has been involved in high-spirited shenanigans and has incurred debts. Some of his acquaintances such as Spiegelberg are actual career criminals. Karl has written to his father to apologize for outrageous past behavior and is on the point of freeing himself from this dubious element and returning home. He is confident of Old Moor's forgiveness. The resentful Franz intercepts the letter, producing another from an "informant," which makes Karl out to be a satanic reprobate. Old Moor allows Franz to represent his paternal displeasure with the prodigal's behavior, and Franz seizes the occasion to burn his brother's bridges to the family. The proud and rebellious Karl plunges into a life of crime and terror to punish the whole paternal order, which he believes has rejected him. He slaughters the rich and privileged along with the lawyers who protect them, appropriating their money for the benefit of orphans and poor students. He strangles reactionary priests with his bare hands. Franz's Machiavellian cunning, by contrast, outpaces his emotional development and makes him an Enlightenment *philosophe* and materialist, although one ultimately unable to ignore his conscience.

In his published "Preface," Schiller seems worried that his play could be misunderstood as an apology for evil. But the rich texture of his allusions subvert the seductions of an energetic plot. Karl wants to believe that robbery and murder are justified in class warfare and revolution, that the violence of his robber band is sanctified by the purity of his intentions. Similarly, Kant argues in the *Grundlegung zur Metaphysik der Sitten* (1785; *Groundwork of the Metaphysics of Morals*) that the moral worth of an action lies more in the will of the actor than in the action's effect in the world. Karl, however, is stricken by the sufferings of his innocent victims. He feels scarred by crimes he did not intend to commit. At first, Spiegelberg's innate criminality seems designed to contrast with Karl's, which is brought about by circumstance. But Schiller shows in Spiegelberg's remarkable pantomime during Karl's reading of Franz's duplicitous letter that as long as you cry "Your purse or your life!" you are a thief, however pure your will. In the allusions to Jacob and Esau and their struggles over Isaac's birthright and blessing, Franz would seem to play the role of Jacob, since he misleads his father and usurps what does not belong to him. It is the disguised Karl who steals Old Moor's blessing, however, although it belongs to him by right. Similarly, Franz plots to murder his father by shock (*Schreck*) and orders Karl poisoned, but it is Karl who actually manages both patricide and fratricide, shocking Old Moor to death and driving the terrorized Franz to suicide. Karl's nobility causes as much sociopathic mayhem as do Franz's cynical machinations.

The play's sharp distinctions between villain and hero are deliberately illusory. Schiller's investment in the character of Spiegelberg encourages expectations of a Judas-like betrayal of Karl. Spiegelberg, who seduces citizens into crime and rapes nuns, is jealous of Karl's leadership and launches ineffectual plots to murder him. But Karl is unable to dissociate himself from his band's worst depredations, namely, Schufterle's tossing a baby into the fire during a raid. Karl even murders Amalia when his band wants to recruit her for their collective erotic recreation. His every act of leadership is entangled in vainglory, as his band points out when he surrenders himself to justice. In his pride he is a fit parallel to Milton's Satan, a character whom Karl, in one of Schiller's variants for act I, scene ii, recommends to Spiegelberg, the parodic image of Karl, as Satan is of Christ.

DAN LATIMER

Editions
First edition: *Die Räuber: Ein Schauspiel*, Frankfurt and Leipzig: privately printed, 1781
Critical editions: in *Schillers Werke: Nationalausgabe*, vol. 3, edited by Herbert Stubenrauch, Weimar: Böhlau, 1953–; in *Sämtliche Werke*, edited by Gerhard Fricke et al., Munich: Hanser Verlag, 1958–59
Translations: *The Robbers*, translated by A.F. Tytler, London: Robinsons, 1792; *The Robbers* (published with *Wallenstein*), translated and with an introduction by F.J. Lamport, Harmondsworth and New York: Penguin, 1979

Further Reading
Gilman, Sander, *The Case of Sigmund Freud*, Baltimore, Maryland: Johns Hopkins University Press, 1993
Graham, Ilse, *Schiller's Drama: Talent and Integrity*, New York: Barnes and Noble, and London: Methuen, 1974
Praz, Mario, *La carne, la morte e il diabolo nella letterutura romantica*, Milan: Soc. editrice "La Cultura," 1930; as *The Romantic Agony*, translated by Angus Davidson, Cleveland, Ohio: World Publishing, 1933
Sharpe, Lesley, *Friedrich Schiller: Drama, Thought, and Politics*, Cambridge and New York: Cambridge University Press, 1991

Über die ästhetische Erziehung des Menschen in einer Reihe von Briefen 1795

Essay by Friedrich von Schiller

Friedrich Schiller's *Über die ästhetische Erziehung des Menschen in einer Reihe von Briefen* (1795; *On the Aesthetic Education of Man, in a Series of Letters*) is a seminal theoretical work of German classicism. It comprises the period's most elaborate conception of the aesthetic education of man.

Schiller developed his ideas on the historical and political potential of art in ten letters, which he wrote in 1793 and early 1794 to the Danish crown prince Friedrich Christian of Holstein-Augustenburg, who had awarded him a three-year stipend in 1791. This first version, the so-called *Augustenburger Briefe* (Augustenburg Letters), was in part a discursive extrapolation of ideas Schiller had already advanced in his poem "Die Künstler" (1789; "The Artists") and in the essay *Über Anmut und Würde* (1793; On Loveliness and Dignity). During the second part of 1794, Schiller rewrote and extended the letters to 27 and developed his ideas into a programmatic analysis of the historical potential of art. The work was published in his journal *Die Horen* in 1795. The discussion of the beneficial influence of taste on morals that Schiller had forwarded in the letter of 3 December 1793 was published separately under the title *Über den moralischen Nutzen ästhetischer Sitten* (1796; On the Moral Use of Aesthetic Manners). Other theoretical concerns were further treated in *Über die notwendigen Grenzen beim Gebrauch schöner Fromen* (1800; On the Necessary Limits in the Use of Beautiful Forms) and *Über naive und sentimentalische Dichtung* (1795–96; On the Naive and Sentimental in Literature).

Schiller took the excesses of the French Revolution as proof that humanity was not yet ready for the political realization of the moral state of freedom and individual rights. Enlightenment rationality had been successful in finding the principles of true humanity, but it could not be implemented simply by a rational decree or by force. Rather, political change could be successful only if those citizens who attempted to build a moral state had themselves already attained a high level of moral integrity. However, how could the citizens of an immoral world attain the necessary degree of morality? This is the central question that informs Schiller's analysis of contemporary culture and his speculations on the role that art could play for the betterment of humanity.

Schiller's aesthetic analysis departs from Kant's *Critique of Judgment* (1790). As in Kant's anthropological approach, the aesthetic experience is understood as a free and purposeless (autonomous) interplay of cognitive faculties. However, Schiller introduces a different terminology (partly borrowed from Fichte). Kant's dualism of reason and imagination is replaced by the dualism of a formal impulse (ruled by reason) and a sensual impulse (ruled by the sensation of the material world). Beauty is defined as an equilibrium existing between reality and form—an ideal that can never be fully realized. The object of the sensual impulse is life, and the object of the formal impulse is the idea. The equilibrium of life and idea can be realized only in a third impulse, the impulse of play, which thus can be termed a living form that appears as beauty. The impulse of play completes man's being: "he is wholly man only where he plays" (letter 15).

Onto this "transcendental method" (letter 10), Schiller superimposes an idealist philosophy of history to investigate the historical potential of art. Although modern humans have developed the possibilities of rationality and reason in unprecedented ways, they have lost the naive totality of a mythological, aesthetic existence that is represented by classical Greece. For post-Enlightenment humanity, no way leads back to such a naive harmony where the individual could at any time represent the whole of society and sensuality and reason formed one totality. Modern humans are fragmented:

> We see not only single subjects, but whole classes of men develop only one portion of their faculties. . . . Chained to the whole as a single little fragment, man now confines himself to a fragmentary development; listening only to the monotonous noise of the wheel which he is perpetually revolving, he never develops the harmony of his being, and instead of impressing upon his nature the image of humanity, he contents himself with exhibiting in his person the imprint of his business or science. (letter 6)

This is where the impulse of play becomes important. Humans and society must undergo an aesthetic education to once again experience the totality of their harmonized human potential. Schiller's analysis of beauty and the fate of modern humanity, combined with an idealist teleology of history, develops into a programmatic theory of cultural politics: "For it is through beauty that we are led to freedom" (letter 2). The aesthetic education of humanity and the realization of the aesthetic state can thus be seen as the preparation of the moral state. It is precisely the autonomy of art that allows humans (regardless of the political form they are subjected to) to experience, practice, and internalize freedom, equality, and harmony in "the joyous empire of play and appearance" (letter 27). The cultural-political formula thus is that the state of aesthetic appearance as "living form" is the practical presupposition for the development of the moral state, as beauty is the forecast of a harmonized humanity, a "symbol of the realization of humanity's destiny" (letter 14).

However, Schiller emphasizes an important weakness in the contemporary teleological philosophy of history that had already been problematized by Kant. Teleological concepts of history seem to require that generations of humans labor for the Enlightenment project of realizing true humanity without hope of achieving this state in their own lifetime:

> We would have been the servants of humanity, we would have been their slaves for a few thousand years. . . . Can it be man's destiny to neglect himself by attending to any one end? . . . It must be given unto us to restore by a higher art the integrity of our forces which the mechanism of the actual has destroyed. (letter 6)

Seen from this vantage point, the harmony and freedom of the impulse of play provides the alienated and fragmented individual with a separate autonomous realm of experiencing harmonized totality in his own individual life. Compensating humans for the societal and cognitive alienation in their actual life situations becomes a goal in itself, notwithstanding any hope for humanity's ultimate destiny. Therefore, Schiller's "living form" of aesthetic appearance has two potentials: it can be therapy in the service of humanity's emancipation, and it can compensate for an alienated and one-dimensional life, making it bearable:

> In the aesthetic state everything, even a common tool, enjoys the privilege of free citizenship as fully as the noblest element of this republic; here the understanding, which elsewhere subjects the submissive mass to its ends with a despotic force, has to interrogate the substance it intends to mold concerning its destiny. Here, in the empire of aesthetic forms, the ideal of equality is realized, which the enthusiastic worshipper would like to see ingrafted upon real life. (letter 27)

The first potential of Schiller's theory, aesthetic emancipation, was most prominently adopted in the sociological and aesthetic theory of Herbert Marcuse. The second potential, aesthetic compensation for an immoral world, was criticized by Friedrich Engels (among others) but was politically embraced by Joseph Goebbels. To this day, no scholarly consensus exists on the most appropriate interpretation of Schiller's state of aesthetic appearance. I would submit that this double potential of aesthetic education speaks for the realism of Schiller's theory, as there can be no question, in our times of avant-gardism turning into mass culture, that the political potential of art is indeed twofold, and the interdependencies of its contradictory political effects are still not well understood. It is, therefore, no coincidence that the weaker parts of Schiller's theory are already entangled in attempting to analyze this complex interdependency. This goes, for example, for his dialectics of temporal art, which fulfills the lower needs of the consumer and therefore increases one's immorality, and high art, which is conceived by a genius who, while remaining a contemporary, is no product of his time and finds inspiration in the eternal truth of immortal ideas and forms. It holds also true for Schiller's dualisms of the savage and the barbarian (letter 4), the uncivilized classes that are slaves of their immediate impulses and the civilized classes that have lost any sense of compassion, the differentiation of society into sensual men and spiritual men, and so on. All dualisms are ultimately resolved in the synthesis of the impulse of play that, because of its potential for harmonized unity, at times seems to act as an antidote to whatever shortcoming and one-sidedness Schiller's binary analysis could diagnose in modern humanity and society.

The *Letters* are no easy reading, and the reception among Schiller's contemporaries was mixed and controversial. Positive reactions came, for example, from Goethe, Körner, W.v. Humboldt, Kant, and Hegel. Negative reactions came, for example, from Klopstock, Herder, Nicolai, Jean Paul, and the Romantics, notwithstanding that their literary theory (most evident in the *Systemprogramm*) can hardly be conceived without Schiller's influence. More important than these individual voices of praise or critique is the implicit role that Schiller's theory has played in the further development of 19th- and 20th-century theory of cultural politics. Some of the work's core concerns and theoretical concepts—such as alienation, autonomy, play, and the aesthetical state—have remained significant to this very day. (For a detailed analysis of the reception and influence, see Wilkinson and Willoughby.)

BERND FISCHER

See also Aesthetics

Editions

First edition: *Über die ästhetische Erziehung des Menschen in einer Reihe von Briefen*, in *Die Horen*, Tübingen: Cotta, 1795

Critical edition: in *Friedrich Schiller: Theoretische Schriften*, edited by Rolf-Peter Janz, Frankfurt: Deutscher Klassiker Verlag, 1992

Translation: *On the Aesthetic Education of Man, in a Series of Letters*, edited and translated by Elizabeth M. Wilkinson and L.A. Willoughby, Oxford: Clarendon Press, 1967

Further Reading

Berghahn, Klaus L., *Schiller: Ansichten eines Idealisten*, Frankfurt: Athenäum, 1986

Bolten, Jürgen, "Zum werk- und denkgeschichtlichen Kontext der Briefe *Über die ästhetische Erziehung des Menschen*," in *Schillers Briefe über die ästhetische Erziehung*, edited by Jürgen Bolten, Frankfurt: Suhrkamp, 1984

Düsing, Wolfgang, *Friedrich Schiller: Über die ästhetische Erziehung des Menschen in einer Reihe von Briefen: Text, Materialien, Kommentar*, Munich: Hanser, 1981

Hempel, Charles Julius, editor, *Schiller's Complete Works*, Philadelphia, Pennsylvania: I. Kohler, 1861

Kontje, Todd Curtis, *Constructing Reality: A Rhetorical Analysis of Friedrich Schiller's Letters on the Aesthetic Education of Man*, New York: Lang, 1987

Ueding, Gert, *Schillers Rhetorik: Idealistische Wirkungsästhetik und rhetorische Tradition*, Tübingen: Niemeyer, 1971

Wilkinson, Elizabeth M., and Leonard Ashley Willoughby, *Schillers ästhetische Erziehung des Menschen: Eine Einführung*, Munich: Beck, 1977

Über naive und sentimentalische Dichtung 1795–1796

Essay by Friedrich von Schiller

Über naive und sentimentalische Dichtung (translated as *Naive and Sentimental Poetry* and *On the Naive and Sentimental in Literature*) is a classic statement of the problem of the modern writer's divided consciousness. It was written at the end of the phase in Friedrich Schiller's life lasting from 1788 to 1796, during which he turned away from creative writing and devoted himself to history, aesthetics, and criticism, and it shows him ready again to take up creative work. In part an exploration of his own kind of poetic consciousness, the essay was also prompted by his developing friendship with Goethe, in whom he saw a different kind of poetic consciousness, one more characteristic of a past age.

On the Naive and Sentimental in Literature marks an important transition in criticism as well as in Schiller's career. It gathers up many of the critical debates of the 18th century (on the naive, on genius, and on the status of genres) and gives decisive impetus to the development of new critical perspectives of the 19th century and beyond. The naive, a subject much written about in the later 18th century, is the quality of unreflectiveness perceived by sophisticated people in those in whom feeling and reason are still one. Complementary to the naive is what Schiller calls the *sentimentalisch,* a term he has coined for the self-reflexiveness of the modern, divided consciousness. He uses these complementary concepts to reopen and change completely a long-standing critical debate, the "Querelle des Anciens et des Modernes," which had raged intermittently for a century on the subject of the relative status of ancient and modern literature. This was a prominent issue in Schiller's mind for two main reasons. First, he was a writer in a language and within a culture that was struggling to establish its credentials as having a great literature of European stature. Yet, in a revolutionary age in which all norms were being challenged, the old criteria of judgment were breaking down, and emphasis was shifting away from poetic attributes to the psyche of the poet. Second, Schiller perceived himself as a "sentimental" writer with a characteristically modern consciousness and was concerned to achieve theoretical clarity about the nature of literature in the modern world and thus about his own calling as a poet.

Schiller places his discussion of poetry within a historical framework characteristic of his thought but also of that of several prominent contemporaries, including Herder, Kant, and Hegel, who see humankind as being on a journey from an original unity through division to an ultimate recovery of unity, but on a higher plane that incorporates the experience and advantages gained on the journey. The naive is associated with the first stage of human development, the "sentimental" with the second, until the two can be reunited in a higher unity. The goal, however, recedes into infinity and can be approached only by gradual degrees. Thus, although expressing his admiration for and belief in the perfection of naive poetry, Schiller's essay decisively vindicates the modern by giving positive value to experimentation in art in pursuit of an infinite goal.

For the naive poet, there is no gulf or tension between the world as it is and the world as it should be or, to use Schiller's terms, between nature and the ideal. Thus, the naive poet never interposes his personality or reactions between the reader and the work. The "sentimental" poet, the product of a more corrupt world, always experiences a tension between the world as it is and the world as it should be and thus can adopt a variety of standpoints to his material. These "modes of feeling" (*Empfindungsweisen*) are satiric (where the poet emphasizes the inadequacies of the real), elegaic (where he treats the ideal as lost and a subject of regret), or idyllic (where the real and the ideal are presented as one). Schiller consciously uses these terms in new senses and does so to free the discussion of modern literature from the old hierarchy of genres associated with the classical tradition. Although it is clear that Schiller regards the work of the naive poet with awe and envy, he nevertheless succeeds in vindicating the "sentimental" poet, whose work he credits with being capable of greater complexity and intellectual content.

The interpretation of Schiller's essay is hampered by his shifting use of terminology and his tendency to use familiar terms (such as *satire* and *elegy*) with new meanings. In the early part of the essay, *nature* has anti-urban, Rousseauian connotations. Later in the argument, *nature* means external reality as perceived by the naive poet. Later still, in the discussion of "sentimental" poetry, *nature* means nature as idea. These shifts of meaning suggest that Schiller wrote the essay in a less planned way than some of his other theoretical works, and it fascinates less as a result of its overall argument than by virtue of remarkable moments and insights: the striking two paragraphs contrasting tragedy and comedy, the comparison of Homer and Ariosto, the practical criticism of the work of prominent contemporaries, the attempt to free poetics from the dominance of genre, and the insight that the future of poetry lies in constant experimentation and of striving toward an infinite goal. This last insight was hugely influential in German Romantic criticism, especially that of Friedrich Schlegel.

Schiller ends his treatise with a discussion of the two psychological types underlying the naive and the "sentimental" poet: the realist and the idealist. His comments, especially those on the dangers inherent in the idealist type, who claims to love humanity but tends to despise and ride roughshod over actual human beings, suggest his response to the course taken by French Revolution and illuminate his own plays, especially his presentation of Max and Octavio Piccolomini in *Wallenstein* (1798–99). His analysis of realist and idealist was commented on by Carl Gustav Jung in *Psychological Types* (1921) as anticipating Jung's types: the extrovert and the introvert.

LESLEY SHARPE

Editions

First edition: *Über naive und sentimentalische Dichtung*, in *Die Horen*, vol. 4, Tübingen: Cotta, 1795; vol. 5, 1796

Critical edition: in *Schillers Werke: Nationalausgabe*, vol. 20, *Philosophische Schriften 1*, edited by Benno von Wiese and Helmut Koopmann, Weimar: Hermann Böhlaus Nachfolger, 1962

Translations: *Naive and Sentimental Poetry*, translated with introduction and notes by Julius A. Elias, New York: Ungar, 1966 (also published in *German Aesthetic and Literary Criticism: Winckelmann, Lessing, Hamann, Herder, Schiller, and Goethe*, edited by H.B. Nisbet, Cambridge and New York: Cambridge University Press, 1985); *On the Naive and Sentimental in Literature*, translated by Helen Watanabe-O'Kelly, Manchester: Carcanet, 1981

Further Reading

Abrams, Meyer H., *Natural Supernaturalism: Tradition and Revolution in Romantic Literature*, New York: Norton, and London: Oxford University Press, 1971

Jauss, Hans Robert, "Fr. Schlegels und Fr. Schillers Replik auf die 'Querelle des Anciens et des Modernes'," in *Europäische Aufklärung: Herbert Dieckmann zum 60. Geburtstag*, edited by Hugo Friedrich and Fritz Schalk, Munich: Fink, 1967

Lovejoy, Arthur O., "Schiller and the Genesis of German Romanticism," *Modern Language Notes* 35 (1922)

Lukács, Georg, "Schiller's Theory of Modern Literature," in *Goethe and His Age*, translated by Robert Anchor, London: Merlin, 1968

Pugh, David Vaughan, *Dialectic of Love: Platonism in Schiller's Aesthetics*, Montreal and Buffalo, New York: McGill-Queen's University Press, 1996

Sayce, Olive, "Das Problem der Vieldeutigkeit in Schillers ästhetischer Terminologie," *Jahrbuch der Deutschen Schillergesellschaft* 6 (1962)

Sharpe, Lesley, *Schiller's Aesthetic Essays: Two Centuries of Criticism*, Columbia, South Carolina: Camden House, 1995

Wellek, René, *The Later Eighteenth Century*, A History of Modern Criticism, vol. 1, London: Cape, 1955

Robert Schindel 1944–

Robert Schindel was known mainly as a Viennese poet to literary insiders until his transnational success brought about by his novel *Gebürtig* (1992; *Born Where?*). His success coincided with a revival of Jewish literature in Germany and Austria and has made him one of the outstanding exponents of emerging ethnic literatures in the 1990s. However, it should be kept in mind that Schindel's treatment of ethnicity is highly nuanced, much like that found in his contemporaries Elfriede Jelinek and Doron Rabinovici. No easy definitions of ethnicity and Jewish identity can be found throughout the highly plurivocal novel *Born Where?* Instead, Schindel's novel foregrounds the multiplicities of negotiations in which subjective and cultural identities are formed. Unlike the more explicitly ethnic Jewish novels of Raphael Seligmann, Barbara Honigmann, and Esther Dischereit, Schindel draws on the cosmopolitan setting of Vienna in which collective definitions are at best tentative and exploratory.

Reflecting, nevertheless, a provocative and distinctly Jewish point of view, the novel takes a highly critical view of Austria's dubious normalization, belying a climate of enforced harmonized consensus: "Your fathers have pushed our people into the ovens, your mothers have prayed the rosary and the sons generously want to incorporate us, disregard the past, and, untarnished, want to be the victims themselves." Yet, even in light of this denial of the past, Schindel emphasizes the possibility of cultural rebirth to the extent that it involves a genuine engagement with history affecting the present. With a sympathetic perspective, Schindel's multiplot novel shows most of his characters (Jewish and non-Jewish) struggling for more viable forms of cultural identity in which difference and commonality can coexist and in which the past is acknowledged but is not necessarily the single determining avenue to Jewish identity: "Is it permissible for our Jews to remain occasionally dead or must their bones and ashes always remain sharpened?"

The centrality of social and cultural codependence is emphasized by the twin characters Sascha Graffito and Danny Demant, who are symbiotically connected to each other as passive observer-narrator and acting character, respectively, thus producing together a narratively enframed life or story. This symbiotic model subsequently plays itself out in a series of other paired characters whose lives intersect with Danny and Sascha's. At the outset, the novel depicts patterns of interaction typical of Austria's amnesiac society: "He emphasized his Jewish heritage; she said that she could do little with that, she wasn't interested in politics." The work further highlights generational conflicts between survivors and their descendants, such as Emmanuel Katz, who becomes the indirect victim of his mother's traumatic memory, or Susanne Ressel, who questions her father's fond memories of communist activism and comradeship during the Spanish civil war. Eventually, however, the novel presents more positive transformations, such as the public outing of a repressed

Jewish identity (Katz and Adel) or a hidden Nazi past (Konrad Sachs), the commitment to confront once again a traumatic past as a witness in a Nazi trial (Gebirtig), and the approximation of the Shoah experience, albeit highly ironized, as stand-ins in a Holocaust movie set.

The novel's flippant tone, admittedly not without its own problems, resists a sanctimonious quality that lately has become a cliché in the treatment of the Holocaust, turning critical reflection into iconic reverence for events claimed to be beyond human comprehension. Like his German colleague Maxim Biller, Schindel attempts to break this spell of unquestioning awe and reticence by means of irreverent satire to allow for a continued inquiry into Jewish history and identity. In addition, Schindel's more easygoing cosmopolitan perspective, critically grounded in distinct regional settings, does not attempt to globalize or universalize its thematic of various cultural encounters between Jews and non-Jews. Indeed, each of the novel's encounters produces a unique negotiation of Jewish identity from within uniquely interpreted cultural settings. Schindel's collection of short stories Nacht der Harlekine (1994; Night of the Harlekins) underscores such a regional emphasis in its grotesquely Viennese and regionally colored characters and language.

In Schindel's Born Where?, seemingly stable cultural boundaries are likewise qualified by various peripheral and centrifugal topographical movements away from and toward Vienna as the novel's main locale as well as by linguistic and regional differences. His novel thus foregrounds a multicontextual (rather than multicultural) negotiation of identity that occurs on many levels of discourse and not merely on the level of bipolar oppositions between typified ethnic, national, or regional identities. Renewing the significance of Jewish identity and its public visibility, Schindel ultimately manages to avoid a facile pluralism and a dogmatic politics of identity obliging every Jew to be Jewish in the same manner. Because Jewishness, as Schindel realizes, overlaps with other private and public identities, it recedes or presses into the foreground in accordance with changing subject positions influenced by age, gender, generation, community, region, and language. Its visibility, although desirable in Austria's all-too-homogeneous cultural landscape, cannot be reduced to any single strategy or form of public disclosure.

In a follow-up collection of public lectures, Gott schütz uns vor den guten Menschen (1995; God Protect Us from the Good People), Schindel continues his work of cultural memory that runs from his poetry of the 1980s through his prose works of the 1990s. Exploring his own biography as the son of a mother who had survived Auschwitz and a father executed at Dachau, Schindel delves into his communist family background that, on closer analysis, betrays disturbing anti-Semitic tendencies in its abstract universalization of humanity and freedom that cancels out any specific ethnic identity. For Schindel, however, the recovery of his Jewish heritage in a maze of overlapping ideologies of nationhood, assimilation, and political orientation does not imply a mere return to the religious traditions of Judaism. As the child of atheist Jews, he is cut off from this tradition and views himself more linked to a modern diasporic tradition of European Jews interested in the restoration of a context of solidarity with other oppressed groups and individuals suffering from displacement. The work of Schindel, it can be said, revives and reinvents this dynamic tradition of transnational and postideological concerns, reflecting the shift from inherited traditions of Judaism to a post-Shoah construction of secular Jewishness.

MATTHIAS KONZETT

Biography
Born in Vienna, 1944. Son of deported Jewish parents; survived the Holocaust in a hideout near Vienna; pursued a philosophy degree, specializing in Kant and Hegel, but interrupted his studies and became politically active in the late 1960s; founder of the literary journal Hundsblume; became known as a poet and drew wider public attention with his best-selling novel Gebürtig, 1992. Currently lives in Vienna.

Selected Works

Poetry
Ohneland: Gedichte vom Holz der Paradeiserbäume: 1979–1984, 1986
Geier sind pünktliche Tiere: Gedichte, 1987
Im Herzen die Krätze: Gedichte, 1988
Ein Feuerchen im Hintennach: Gedichte: 1986–1991, 1992

Prose
Gebürtig: Roman, 1992; as Born Where? translated by Michael Roloff, 1995
Nacht der Harlekine: Erzählungen, 1994
Gott schütz uns vor den guten Menschen: Jüdisches Gedächtnis—Auskunfstbüro der Angst, 1995

Further Reading
Bormann, Alexander von, "Die Dinge, die Menschen—Auge und Herz: Zu Gedichten von Bernd Wagner und Robert Schindel," Die Horen 34, no. 1 (1989)
Kernmeyer, Hildgeard, "Gebürtig Ohneland: Robert Schindel: Auf der Suche nach der verlorenen Identität," Modern Austrian Literature 27, no. 3–4 (1994)
Konzett, Matthias, "The Politics of Recognition in Contemporary Austrian Jewish Literature," Monatshefte 90, no. 1 (1998)
Posthofen, Renate, "Erinnerte Geschichte(n): Robert Schindel's Roman Gebürtig," Modern Austrian Literature 27, no. 3–4 (1994)
Sanford, Gerlinde Ulm, "Zaubernahen, Immernie, Frostesonnen, Nullerei: Zu Robert Schindel's Liebliedern und ähnlichen Gebilden," Modern Austrian Literature 27, no. 3–4 (1994)
Spork, Ingrid, "1992 Robert Schindel's Novel Gebürtig Continues the Development of Jewish Writing after the Shoah," in Yale Companion to Jewish Writing and Thought in German Culture, edited by Sander L. Gilman and Jack Zipes, New Haven, Connecticut: Yale University Press, 1997

Schlaf, Johannes, *see* Arno Holz and Johannes Schlaf

August Wilhelm Schlegel 1767–1845

A.W. Schlegel was one of the leading exponents of German Romanticism, especially Early Romanticism. His poetic and translation skills were stimulated under the guidance of Heyne and Bürger at the University of Göttingen, which resulted in his first publications in 1788 and 1792. At Schiller's suggestion, A.W. Schlegel moved to Jena in 1796, where he became associated with the circle of Romantics whose "presiding spirit" was his brother Friedrich (1772–1829).

Early Romanticism was preoccupied with establishing its radically new weltanschauung (i.e., its philosophy of life, society, political, religious, and cultural considerations, and literary criticism). Representatives of the Early Romantic school, however, were less productive as poets than their later counterparts. The central organ for the dissemination of the Romantics' critical and philosophical ideas was *Das Athenäum* (1798–1800), a periodical edited by the Schlegel brothers. In this journal, which also contained essays, poems, and aphorisms, the program and theories of the movement were promulgated.

The most subjective and individualistic phase of the Romantic movement, Early Romanticism, acknowledged no literary restraints or established forms and indulged in emotionalism. It also had a predilection toward imaginative, fantastic, extravagant, and irrational elements, as well as obscure and chaotic aspects and fragments; a preoccupation with the past, particularly a glorification of the Middle Ages; and a vehement opposition to some of the most stringent viewpoints of the Enlightenment. An all-pervasive force of remarkable depth, Romanticism—against the backdrop of the Napoleonic era and its consequences—was by no means a purely aesthetic affair. Its extraordinary vitality touched every facet of culture and learning.

A.W. Schlegel's strength lay in criticism and translating. Thanks to his profound linguistic knowledge and his exquisite feeling for idiom and versification, he succeeded in rendering into German works by Dante, Petrarch, Horace Walpole, and, most prominently, Shakespeare. While German audiences had received an introduction to Shakespeare's dramatic works through the efforts of Lessing, the Sturm und Drang movement, Eschenburg, and Wieland's prose versions (none of which could do justice to the original meters), A.W. Schlegel produced excellent metric translations in irregular blank verse of 16 of Shakespeare's plays between 1797 and 1801. An additional edition in 1810 also featured 13 plays translated by Dorothea Tieck and her husband, Wolf Heinrich von Baudissin. This monumental work is known as the "Schlegel-Tieck" translation and is probably the most frequently used version on the German stage.

A.W. Schlegel sought to transfer faithfully the text and scenes from Shakespeare's time to his own time; he was aware of the original rhetorical conventions while remaining sensitive to an audience whose standards of propriety might be intolerant of Elizabethan bawdiness. His concern with fidelity extends to reproducing delicate nuances, figurative language, and word plays. Vastly superior to his predecessors' efforts, his translations succeed in reproducing related sound patterns and preserving the original image. Following Herder's example, A.W. Schlegel declined the method of ameliorating the text, as practiced in classicism. While figuring prominently in casting Shakespeare as a "naturalized" author, A.W. Schlegel was aware of the somewhat muted effect. Other masterful translations from Italian, Portuguese, and Spanish appeared in 1804, after the first volume of his rendering of Calderon's plays, collectively entitled *Spanisches Theater*. Critical editions with Latin translations of the *Bhagavad-Gita* (1823) and the *Ramayana* (1823–46) followed; he also was credited with inaugurating Sanskrit studies in Germany.

As a literary critic, lecturer, and teacher at the Universities of Jena and Bonn, A.W. Schlegel made important theoretical contributions. His aesthetic theories are reflected chiefly in his *Vorlesungen über schöne Litteratur und Kunst* (1801–4; *Lectures on Literature and Art*), his outstanding compendium of literary theory and criticism, and the *Vorlesungen über dramatische Kunst und Litteratur* (1809–11; *Lectures on Dramatic Art and Literatur*), a veritable textbook regarding the central concepts of tragedy and comedy, definitions of antiquity and modernity, and theories concerning the origins of poetry, the relationship of nature and art, and of theory, history, and criticism. His ideas focus mainly on the juxtaposition of the classical and the Romantic, or on modern concepts of literature and art—for A.W. Schlegel, the classical deals individually with diverse genres, while the modern favors an intimate blend of nature and art, poetry and prose. Seeking to overcome the chasm between classical and Romantic concepts, he advocates a synthesis of the theory, history, and criticism of the fine arts and sciences and argues that this synthesis should include manifestations of individual and social lifestyles. He rejects the Aristotelian system of antiquated, authoritarian rules, which ignore problems pertaining to modern national literatures.

A.W. Schlegel is critical also of Kant's *Kritik der ästhetischen Urteilskraft* (1792; *Critique of Judgment*), with its analysis and dialectic of aesthetic criticism, and with its sharp division between the beautiful and the good. A.W. Schlegel also takes exception to Kant's tendency to subjugate purely aesthetic values to intellectual and moral values, including the concept of the sublime. He thus deplores Kant's relegating the issue of good taste to a category where the existence of pure aesthetics is rendered problematic altogether.

A.W. Schlegel's aesthetic theories are grounded in his conception of the organic unity of all arts. According to Schlegel, poetry is the most comprehensive art because language is the medium of expression. History teaches what has been accomplished, and theory shows us what is yet to be done. Having laid the foundation of modern Romantic criticism, A.W. Schlegel emerged as a pioneer in the area of comparative literature. In accordance with Herder's and Friedrich Schlegel's concept, A.W. Schlegel pled the case of integrating aesthetically sophisticated, universalized poetry into world literature as an organic entity. The concept of a "progressive universal poetry," which is rooted in Friedrich Schlegel's "Gespräch über die Poesie" (1800; Conversations about Poetry) and *Athenäum* Fragment 116 (1798), is to include all poetic elements and to establish the connection between philosophy and rhetoric. To A.W. Schlegel, criticism suggests skill in judging works of art through free, sensitive reflection, which manifests the critic's personal independence. This viewpoint is based on Fichte's *Wissenschaftslehre* (1797; *Theory of Science*), as is the concept of Romantic irony, which allows the narrator to assume a position detached from the narrative, an important ingredient particularly in literary products in the fantastic genre such as the fairy tale.

A.W. Schlegel's significant accomplishments as philologist, translator, historically oriented literary-critical comparatist, and innovator of world format contributed to his prominence as an aesthetic and cultural force of consequence within the Romantic movement and beyond.

CHARLOTTE M. CRAIG

See also Athenäum

Biography

Born in Hannover, 5 September 1767. Brother of Friedrich Schlegel; son of J.A. Schlegel, pastor and writer, and nephew of J.E. Schlegel, playwright and critic. Studied at Göttingen University, 1786–91; private tutor in Amsterdam, 1791–95; in Jena, 1795, where he contributed to Schiller's journal *Die Horen*, 1796–1800; lectured at Jena University, 1796–98, and became professor there, 1798–1801; reviewer for *Jenaer Allgemeine Literaturzeitung*, 1796–1801; cofounded and co-edited with his brother, Friedrich Schlegel, the journal *Das Athenäum*, 1798–1800, a publication supporting the romantic literary movement; translated 17 plays of Shakespeare; series of lectures in Berlin on the romantic movement, 1801–4; accompanied Madame de Staël on trips throughout Germany, Italy, France, Sweden, and Russia, 1804–8; gave a series of lectures on drama in Vienna, 1808; worked as a French-speaking propagandist for the prince of Sweden and General Bernadotte, 1812–14; with Madame de Staël, 1815; professor of art history and literature at Bonn University, from 1818; founding editor of the journal *Indische Bibliothek*, 1823–30. Died in Bonn, 12 May 1845.

Selected Works

Collections

Sämtliche Werke, edited by E. Böcking, 26 vols., 1846–48
Kritische Schriften und Briefe, edited by Edgar Lohner, 7 vols., 1962–74
Kritische Ausgabe der Vorlesungen, edited by Ernst Behler, 1989–

Nonfiction

Ehrenpforte und Triumphbogen für den Theaterpräsidenten von Kotzebue, 1801
Vorlesungen über schöne Literatur und Kunst, 1801–4; edited by Jakob Minor, 1884

Comparaison entre la Phèdre de Racine et celle d'Euripide, 1807
Vorlesungen über dramatische Kunst und Literatur, 1809–11; edited by Giovanni V. Amoretti, 1923; as *A Course of Lectures on Dramatic Art and Literature*, translated by John Black, 1815; revised edition translated by A.J.W. Morrison, 1846
Werke, 1812–17
Betrachtungen über die Politik der dänischen Regierung, 1813
Réflexions sur l'état actuel de la Norvège, 1814
Tableau de l'état politique et moral de l'Empire français en 1813, 1814
Lettre aux éditeurs de la bibliothèque italienne, sur les chevaux de bronze de Venise, 1816
Rezension von Niebuhrs Römischer Geschichte, 1816
Le couronnement de la Sainte Vierge, et les miracles de Saint-Dominique, 1817
Observations sur la langue et la littérature provençales, 1818
Vorlesungen über Theorie und Geschichte der bildenden Künste, 1827
Berichtigung einiger Missdeutungen, 1828
Kritische Schriften, 1828; edited by Emil Staiger, 1963
Réflexions sur l'étude des langues asiatiques adressées à Sir James Mackintosh, suivies d'une lettre à M. Horace Hayman Wilson, 1832
Essais littéraires et historiques, 1842
Oeuvres de M. Auguste-Guillaume de Schlegel écrites en français, edited by Eduard Böcking, 1846
Briefwechsel zwischen Wilhelm von Humboldt und August Wilhelm Schlegel, edited by Albert Leitzmann, 1908
Briefwechsel A.W. von Schlegel, Christian Lassen, edited by W. Kirfel, 1914
August Wilhelm Schlegels Briefwechsel mit seinen Heidelberger Verlegern, edited by Erich Jenisch, 1922
August Wilhelm und Friedrich Schlegel im Briefwechsel mit Schiller und Goethe, edited by Josef Körner and Ernst Wieneke, 1926
Briefe von und an Friedrich und Dorothea Schlegel, edited by Josef Körner, 1926
Briefe von und an August Wilhelm Schlegel, edited by Josef Körner, 1930

Translations

Calderón, *Spanisches Theater*, 1803–9
Blumensträusse italienischer, spanischer und portugiesischer Poesie, 1804
Bhagavad-Gita, 1823
with Christian Lassen, *Hitopadesas, id est, Institutio salutarius*, 1829–31
Ramayana, 4 vols., 1829–46
Joachim Rendorp, *Geheime Nachrichten zur Aufklärung der Vorfälle während des letzten Kriegs zwischen England und Holland*, 1793
William Shakespeare, *Dramatische Werke*, 9 vols., 1797–1819
Horace Walpole, *Historische, literarische und unterhaltende Schriften*, 1800
Albertine Necker de Saussure, *Über den Charakter und die Schriften der Frau von Staël*, 1820

Edited Works

Johann Gottlieb Fichte, *Friedrich Nicolais Leben und Sonderbare Meinungen*, 1801
Wilhelm von Schütz, *Lacrimas: Ein Schauspiel*, 1804
Friedrich de la Motte-Fouqué, *Dramatische Spiele*, 1804
Dépeches et lettres interceptées par des partis détachés de l'armée combinée du nord de l'Allemagne, 1814
Madame de Staël, *Considérations sur les événements principaux de la révolution française, ouvrage posthume, publié par M. le Duc de Broglie et M. le Baron de Staël*, 1818
Sophie Bernhardi, *Flore und Blanchefleur: Romantisches Gedicht in zwölf Gesängen*, 1822
Verzeichnis einer von Eduard Alton hinterlassenen Gemäldesammlung, 1840

Poetry
Gedichte, 1800
Rom, 1805
Poetische Werke, 1811

Play
Ion (adaptation of Euripides) (produced 1802), 1803

Further Reading

Atkinson, Margaret Edith, *August Wilhelm Schlegel as a Translator of Shakespeare,* Oxford: Blackwell, and Brooklyn, New York: Haskell House, 1958

Bernays, Michael, *Zur Entstehungsgeschichte des Schlegelschen Shakespeare,* Leipzig: Hirzel, 1872

Besenbeck, Alfred, *Kunstanschauung und Kunstlehre August Wilhelm Schlegels,* Berlin: Ebering, 1930

Craig, Charlotte M., "A.W. Schlegel's Rendering of Shakespearean Wordplays," *Michigan Germanic Studies* 15, no. 2 (1989)

Evans, B. Ifor, *The Language of Shakespeare's Plays,* London: Methuen, and Bloomington: Indiana University Press, 1952

Gebhardt, Peter, *A.W. Schlegel's Shakespeare-Übersetzung: Untersuchungen zu seinem Übersetzungsverfahren am Beispiel des Hamlet,* Palaestra 257, Göttingen: Vandenhoeck und Ruprecht, 1970

Joachimi-Dege, Marie, *Deutsche Shakespeare Probleme im XVIII: Jahrhundert und im Zeitalter der Romantik,* Leipzig: Haessel, 1907; reprint, Hildesheim: Gerstenberg, 1976

Jolles, Frank, editor, *A.W. Schlegel's Sommernachtstraum in der ersten Fassung vom Jahre 1789,* Palaestra 244, Göttingen: Vandenhoeck und Ruprecht, 1967

Kökeritz, Helge, *Shakespeare's Pronunciation,* New Haven, Connecticut: Yale University Press, 1953

Lazenby, Marion Candler, *The Influence of Wieland and Eschenburg on Schlegel's Shakespeare Translation,* Ph.D. dissertation, Johns Hopkins University, 1941

Leitzmann, Albert, "Aus Briefen der Brüder Schlegel an Brinckmann," *Euphorion* 3 (1896)

Lohner, Edgar, *August Wilhelm Schlegel: Kritische Schriften und Briefe,* 2 vols., Stuttgart: Kohlhammer, 1962, 1963

Schenk-Lenzen, Ulrike, *Das ungleiche Verhältnis von Kunst und Kritik: Zur Literaturkritik August Wilhelm Schlegels,* Würzburg: Königshausen und Neumann, 1991

Caroline Schlegel 1763–1809

Caroline Michaelis Böhmer Schlegel Schelling is one of the most popular and controversial literary figures of early Romanticism. The conflicting views of her held by her contemporaries persist. They can be found in numerous novels and biographies, which are more concerned with recycling scandals than with Caroline Schlegel as an author. Literary history has tended to idealise her life, portraying her as the "Queen of Romanticism," or the "soul of the Goethe cult," limiting her to the role of attractive Muse to men such as August Wilhelm and Friedrich Schlegel.

In the 1970s, West German critics interpreted early Romantic sociability as a form of cultural revolution, a precursor to Paris 68. East German critics stressed Caroline Schlegel's affinity with the Mainz revolution in order to integrate early Romanticism into the German Democratic Republic's cultural tradition as a precursor to the writings of Clara Zetkin.

Feminist critics elevated the early Romantic woman—with her "instinctive inclination towards independence"—into a role model, rejecting the later Caroline, wife of Schelling. Even 19th-century literary critics such as Ricarda Huch relied in their idealisation of Caroline Schlegel on polarizing demon images of other women, such as Dorothea Veit Schlegel or Therese Forster Huber. In all cases Schlegel functions as a screen on which her biographers project their imagination. They read her letters selectively, as documents of her life, and fill the sometimes large gaps in the source materials with their own ideals. Historical norms of genre are disregarded when Schlegel's letters are identified with confessional texts of the late 20th century. Despite her popularity, interpretations of Caroline Schlegel's texts which do not rely on biography are still in their infancy. Schlegel herself sought "in vain for a mirror which does not reflect me in distorted way." The importance of her letters to friends has been recognised only recently.

Caroline Schlegel belonged to the privileged exceptional women of the late 18th century. A daughter of Louise Philippine Antoinette (née Schröder) and the wealthy orientalist and theologian Johann David Michaelis, she enjoyed an excellent private education. Visitors to her parents' house in Göttingen included Lessing, Lichtenberg, and Goethe. Her youthful wish for independence was sacrificed to gender conventions. At the age of 21, she married the son of her neighbor, the physician Wilhelm Böhmer. The couple moved to the Harz. Her husband died unexpectedly when she was pregnant with their third child. Her son died a few days after birth, followed a bare year later by her younger daughter.

In 1792 she and her remaining daughter, Auguste, moved to Mainz, where she experienced the occupation of Mainz by French revolutionary troops in October 1792. Of the more than 300 letters that Schlegel is thought to have written in Mainz, only ten remain. Among those lost are her letters to Georg Forster in Paris. The surviving letters show no evidence of particular involvement in Mainz politics. Her sympathy with the revolutionary events can be read indirectly from Friedrich Schlegel's letters, when he wished "she had left public affairs to the men." Two weeks after the Mainz Republic was declared, Caroline and Auguste fled the besieged town with the writer Meta Forkel. On the way to Frankfurt, mother and daughter were taken prisoner by Prussian troops and spent the next three months in prison in Königstein and Kronberg. Her contemporaries saw the women's involvement in Jacobin politics as a strong provocation. Her acquaintance with Forster was interpreted as high treason. Pregnant by one of the French occupying officers, she planned suicide. Her letters to August Wilhelm Schlegel (a scholar and poet and Friedrich's brother), who was trying to bring about her release and who provided her with poison, are lost. Her younger brother obtained her release from the Prussian king. In the Saxon town of Lucka she bore her fourth child, Julius Krantz, under a false name.

After her marriage to August Schlegel and her move to Jena, her house became the focal point of early Romantic sociability. Guests included among others Ludwig and Amalie Tieck, Novalis, Clemens Brentano, and Schelling. Friedrich Schlegel and his partner, Dorothea Veit, lived in the house along with her son. The Jena circle dissolved as early as 1800. Auguste died from dysentery at age 15 and her mother never got over her distress. With the support of Goethe and Herder, she divorced August Wilhelm and married Schelling, whom she followed to Würzburg and later to Munich. In 1809 she died from the same illness that had killed her daughter.

Caroline Schlegel's literary texts include among others the "design for a novel," an ironic poem about Fichte's *Wissenschaftslehre* (1794), and her hidden contribution to the translation of Shakespeare published under her husband's name. Numerous reviews appeared anonymously in the *Athenaeum* (1798–1800), the key periodical of the early Romantics. Between 1796 and 1799 August Schlegel published over 300 reviews in the Jena *Allgemeine Literatur-Zeitung*, an unknown number of which had been written by Caroline. She was the anonymous co-author of "Ueber Shakespeares Romeo und Julia" (1797; "Of Shakespeare's Romeo and Juliet"), published in Schiller's *Horen* (1797), and of "Die Gemälde. Gespräch. In Dresden 1798," published in the *Athenaeum* (1799).

The most important part of her legacy, however, is her numerous letters. Even her contemporaries praised Caroline Schlegel as epistolary writer. About 400 letters remain, encompassing nearly all stages of her life from 1778 onwards. More than half of them are addressed to her lifelong friend Luise Gotter. At the end of the 18th century the letter became an important semi-public genre which enabled women to transcend the limits of the private sphere. Here a variety of styles and constructions of identity could be tried out on a range of addressees. If the idea of emancipation propagated by early Romantic men was hardly realized, the self assured 'I' in Caroline Schlegel's letters—"let people talk; I prefer to rely on myself"—is far removed from the inner conflict betrayed by her Jewish contemporaries Dorothea Veit Schlegel and Rahel Levin. Caroline Schlegel's letters report on everyday life and politics and take part in discussions about works of contemporary literature and literary life. The variety of content is matched by a similar variety in levels of style. One of the most striking features of this polyphony is irony. Her very conscious use of the epistolary form can be seen in the thoroughly dialogical structure of her texts. Research on the genre of epistolary writing has still much to discover about this remarkable author.

FRANZISKA MEYER
TRANSLATED BY CHRIS WEEDON

Biography

Born in Göttingen, 2 September 1763. Studied language and literature with her father, Johann David Michaelis; married and moved to Clausthal-Zellerfeld, 1784; lived with her step brother in Marburg, 1789–91; moved to Mainz, 1792; fled Mainz, and imprisoned in the fortress Königstein, near Frankfurt, 1793; met F. Schlegel, 1793; lived in Gotha and Brunswick, 1794–95; married August Wilhelm Schlegel and moved to Jena, 1796; divorced Schlegel, 1801; married Friedrich Wilhelm Joseph von Schelling and moved to Würzburg, 1803; moved to Munich, 1806. Died in Maulbronn, 7 September 1809.

Selected Works

Collections of Letters

Caroline: Briefe an ihre Geschwister, ihre Tochter Auguste, die Familie Gotter, F.L.W. Meyer, A.W. und Fr. Schlegel, J. Schelling u.a. nebst Briefen von A.W. und Fr. Schlegel, edited by Georg Waitz, 1871
Caroline. Briefe aus der Frühromantik. Nach Georg Waitz vermehrt herausgegeben, edited by Erich Schmidt, 1913
Caroline und Dorothea in Briefen, edited by Ernst Wieneke, 1914
Krisenjahre der Frühromantik. Briefe aus dem Schlegelkreis, edited by Josef Körner, 1936
Frauen der Goethezeit in ihren Briefen, edited by Günter Jäckel, 1964
Frauenbriefe der Romantik, edited by Katja Behrens, 1981
"Caroline Schlegel: Selected Letters," translated by Janice Murray, in *Bitter Healing: German Women Writers 1700–1830*, edited by Jeannine Blackwell and Suzanne Zantop, 1990

Further Reading

Baader, Meike, "'Frau Eigensinn': Caroline Schlegel-Schelling. Revolution und die Idee persönlicher Freiheit," in *Frauen, Literatur, Revolution*, edited by Helga Grubitzsch et al., Pfaffenweiler: Centaurus, 1992
Bürger, Christa, *Leben Schreiben: Die Klassik, die Romantik, und der Ort der Frauen*, Stuttgart: Metzler, 1990
Damm, Sigrid, "Introduction," in *Begegnung mit Caroline: Briefe von Caroline Michaelis-Böhmer-Schlegel-Schelling*, Leipzig: Reclam, 1979
Dischner, Gisela, *Caroline und der Jenaer Kreis: Ein Leben zwischen bürgerlicher Vereinzelung und romantischer Geselligkeit*, Berlin: Wagenbach, 1979
Ebrecht, Angelika, et al., editors, *Brieftheorie des 18. Jahrhunderts: Texte, Kommentare, Essays*, Stuttgart: Metzler, 1990
Friedrichsmeyer, Sara, "Caroline Schlegel-Schelling: 'A Good Woman, and No Heroine,'" in *In the Shadow of Olympus: German Women Writers around 1800*, edited by Katherine R. Goodman and Edith Waldstein, Albany: State University of New York Press, 1992
Hoffmann-Axthelm, Inge, *"Geisterfamilie": Studien zur Geselligkeit der Frühromantik*, Frankfurt: Akademische Verlagsanstalt, 1973
Huch, Ricarda, *Die Romantik*, Leipzig: Haessel, 1899–1902
Kleßmann, Eckart, *Caroline: Das Leben der Caroline Michaelis-Böhmer-Schlegel-Schelling 1763–1809*, Munich: List, 1975
Meyer, Franziska, "'Nur nicht eine Minute Schwärmerey': Caroline Schlegel-Schellings Freundschaft mit Luise Stieler-Gotter," *Querelles: Jahrbuch für Frauenforschung*, vol. 3, Freundschaft im Gespräch, edited by Sabine Eickenrodt and Cettina Rapisarda, Stuttgart: Metzler, 1998
Oellers, Norbert, "Caroline Schelling," *Deutsche Dichter der Romantik: Ihr Leben und Werk*, edited by Benno von Wiese, Berlin: Schmidt, 1971
Ritchie, Gisela F., *Caroline Schlegel-Schelling in Wahrheit und Dichtung*, Bonn: Bouvier, 1968
Struzyk, Brigitte, *Caroline unterm Freiheitsbaum*, Darmstadt: Luchterhand, 1988
Susman, Margarete, "Caroline," in *Frauen der Romantik*, Jena: Diederichs, 1929

Dorothea Schlegel 1764–1839

Together with Rahel Levin and Henriette Herz, Dorothea Mendelssohn Veit Schlegel was one of the best-known Jewish women of her time. She was one of the most productive literary figures of the age. Literary history has largely overlooked the contribution that she made to Romantic literature, preferring to see her in purely biographical terms as either the daughter of Moses Mendelssohn or the nurturing wife of Friedrich Schlegel. Her biographers were more interested in her quarrel with her sister-in-law Caroline Schlegel than in engaging with her literary work and, most especially, her extensive correspondence. Nor was she welcome to feminist literary criticism of the 1970s as a paradigm of the emancipated, independent woman. In the late 1980s, however, a new focus developed, which centered on the complex historical problems relating to the literary activity of emancipated Jewish women. Two biographies have now appeared, as has Dorothea's only novel, *Florentin* (1801), in new editions in both German and English. Previously, the importance of *Florentin* had been recognized only by a few. Theodor Storm saw in it "the only work produced by the Romantics, which without being ridiculous one may mention alongside *Wilhelm Meister*"; Rudolf Haym's view in his altogether pioneering *Romantische Schule* (1870), that the novel "far outstrips Tieck's *Sternbald*, Novalis's *Heinrich von Ofterdingen*, or even Friedrich Schlegel's *Lucinde*," also found no echo. It was rather Dorothea's manner of life, the numerous transgressions of the Jew, woman, and writer, that challenged posterity, as it had her contemporaries. Her conversion to Christianity did not protect her against anti-Semitic attacks by her opponents, who included Caroline Schlegel, Karoline von Humboldt, and Jean Paul.

Dorothea, whose original given name was Brendel, was born in Berlin to Fromet Gugenheim and the famous Jewish Enlightenment philosopher Moses Mendelssohn. She was fortunate to undergo an exceptional private education, and from early youth was able to share in the late Enlightenment debates that took place in her parents' hospitable house. In obedience to religious tradition, her father betrothed her at the age of 14 to the banker Simon Veit who was ten years her senior; "her young life withered in the bud," remembered her childhood friend Henriette Herz. She bore four children, of whom Johannes (Jonas) and Philipp Veit survived. They were later to find fame as members of the Nazarene School of painters. In 1787, together with Henriette Herz, Alexander and Wilhelm von Humboldt, her sister Henriette, and Karoline von Dacheröden (subsequently von Humboldt), among others, she founded a secret society, the Tugendbund (League of Virtue). At the same time, following a custom of her father's, she ran a small reading club in her own home between 1783 and 1798. As a regular guest at Herz's literary salons she took part in Berlin's late Enlightenment salon culture, which coincided with the initial period of early Romanticism. Having in the meanwhile adopted the name of Dorothea, she encountered Friedrich Schlegel at the Herz salon and divorced Simon Veit in 1799.

This radical departure, one not made by many middle-class Jewish women, meant much more than the surrender of financial security. She also lost the "general privilege" accorded to "recognized protected Jews" and, worst of all, the right to bring up her two sons. Money worries were to beset her for the rest of her life. As a divorced, Jewish, female intellectual, who was deprived of all rights and "living in sin" with Friedrich, she was to discover that it was not only religious tolerance that had its limits. Her flouting of traditional values meant a breach with many members of her family. The appearance of Friedrich's novel *Lucinde* (1799) compromised her publicly and also aroused the anti-Semitic spite of her contemporaries, who attributed the "improper" and "unfeminine" qualities of the heroine to Dorothea's own origins. In the real world, the early Romantic aspirations toward a reversal of traditional relations between the sexes had their limits. Thus, when the couple together with her son Philipp moved to Jena and took up residence in Caroline and August Wilhelm Schlegel's house, the focal point of early Romantic sociability, Friedrich's friend Novalis urged that "the proper seal be set on this state of affairs."

Dorothea's most creative period was 1799–1808. In Jena, she wrote articles for the *Athenaeum* (1798–1800), the key periodical of the early Romantics, including her important 1800 review of Friedrich Wilhelm Basilius Ramdohr's "Ramdohrs Erzählungen" (Ramdohr's Tales). Moreover, it was not long before she began work on *Florentin*, which appeared anonymously in 1801 with Friedrich as its editor.

The eponymous hero is an Italian nobleman "in search of his destiny." In the castle of a count, whose life he has saved, he recounts the earlier events of his life: novice in a monastery, then lover of a woman whom he lost to a cardinal. Having now fallen in love with the count's daughter, he leaves the castle on her wedding day. It may be that he will go to America. It may be that the bride's aunt will be found to be his mother.

Drafts for a continuation of the fragmentary text, found among Dorothea's papers, were published posthumously under the title "Camilla" (1965). Now that *Florentin* is no longer excluded from the history of the German novel on account of the conventionality of its central motifs, critical comparisons of the novel to classical and Romantic novels by male authors have been replaced by questions as to the significance of the writer's sex: those who wish to see Dorothea as the daughter of Mendelssohn emphasize its Enlightenment aspects. Others argue over the hero's masculinity, which they read as either conventional or subversive. Others again speak of a necessarily fragmentary text, which reflects the historical and biographical uncertainty of the authorial voice.

Following the dissolution of the early Romantic circle, Dorothea followed Friedrich to Napoleonic Paris; there she produced essays, poems, and reviews for Friedrich's periodical *Europa* (1803–5), including "Discourse on the Latest Novels by Frenchwomen" (1803). She also entered into a close collaboration with Helmina von Chézy, the granddaughter of Anna Louisa Karsch. The two translated and adapted medieval French and German epics, all of which appeared under Friedrich's name. Dorothea is the author, among other works, of *Die Geschichte des Zauberers Merlin* (1804; *History of Merlin the Magician*) and *Lothar und Maller: Eine Rittergeschichte* (1805; *Lothar and Maller: A Knightly Tale*). Her labors secured a livelihood for Friedrich and herself.

In order to be able to remarry, she became a Protestant. Four years later the couple converted to Catholicism. Plans to continue

Florentin went unrealized. Great success, however, attended Dorothea's translation of Madame de Staël's novel *Corinne; ou, l'Italie* (*Corinna; oder, Italien*, 1807–8), which remains the standard translation; once again it was published under Friedrich's name. After Friedrich took service as an official under Metternich, the Schlegels spent the last few years of the Napoleonic era and the ensuing period of reaction in anti-Napoleonic Vienna and later in Frankfurt. In Vienna, Dorothea came to know, among others, Fanny (Itzig) Arnstein and the writer Karoline Pichler. She spent two years with her sons in the German artists' colony in Rome, while Friedrich's letters from Germany told of pogroms and the so-called Hepp Hepp attacks (1819). Her circle of friends included Ester Gad Bernard, Friedrich Schleiermacher, and Karoline Paulus; she maintained lifelong friendships and correspondences with Henriette Herz and Rahel Levin Varnhagen. After the death of Friedrich (1829), she moved to Frankfurt to be with her sons, and, by ensuring the posthumous appearance of many of her husband's works, she laid the foundation for his lasting fame.

FRANZISKA MEYER
TRANSLATED BY ELEONORE BREUNING

Biography

Born in Berlin, 24 August 1764. Daughter of Fromet Gugenheim and Moses Mendelssohn; received instruction in philosophy, religion, languages, and literature from her father; engagement to Simon Veit, 1778; married 1783; gave birth to Jonas (Johannes), 1790, and Philipp Veit, 1793; met Friedrich Schlegel, 1797; divorced Veit, joined the early Romantic circle in Jena, 1799; moved to Paris, 1802; converted to Protestantism, married F. Schlegel in Paris, moved to Cologne, 1804; converted to Catholicism, 1808; moved to Vienna, 1809; moved to Frankfurt, 1816; lived in Rome, 1818–20; lived in Vienna, 1820–29; upon the death of her husband moved via Dresden to Frankfurt, 1831–32. Died in Frankfurt, 3 August 1839.

Selected Works

Collections of Letters

Dorothea v. Schlegel geb. Mendelssohn, und deren Söhne Johannes und Philipp Veit. Briefwechsel im Auftrage der Familie Veit, 2 vols., edited by Johann M. Raich, 1881
Briefe von Dorothea Schlegel an Friedrich Schleiermacher, edited by Heinrich Meissner and Erich Schmidt, 1913
Briefe von Dorothea und Friedrich Schlegel an die Familie Paulus, edited by Rudolf Unger, 1913
Caroline und Dorothea Schlegel in Briefen, edited by Ernst Wieneke, 1914
Der Briefwechsel Friedrich und Dorothea Schlegels 1818–1820 während Dorotheas Aufenthalt in Rom, edited by Heinrich Finke, 1923
Briefe von und an Friedrich und Dorothea Schlegel, collected and annotated by Josef Körner, 1926

Briefe von und an Friedrich und Dorothea Schlegel, in *Kritische Friedrich-Schlegel-Ausgabe, Dritte Abteilung*, edited by Ernst Behler et al., 10 vols., 1980–85
Frauenbriefe der Romantik, edited by Katja Behrens, 1981
"Dorothea Schlegel: Selected Letters," translated by Lorely French, in *Bitter Healing: German Woman Writers from 1700 to 1830*, edited by Jeanine Blackwell and Susanne Zantop, 1990
Correspondence: The Berlin and Jena Years (1764–1802), translated by Edwina Lawler and Ruth Richardson, forthcoming

Fiction

Florentin, edited by Friedrich Schlegel, 1801; translated by Edwina Lawler and Ruth Richardson, 1988
"Camilla. Eine unbekannte Fortsetzung von Dorothea Schlegels *Florentin*," edited by Hans Eichner, 1965; as *Camilla: A Novella*, translated by Edwina Lawler, 1990

Translations

Geschichte der Jungfrau von Orleans: Aus altfranzösischen Quellen, mit einem Anhange aus Hume's Geschichte von England, edited by Friedrich Schlegel, 1802
Geschichte der Margaretha von Valois, Gemahlin Heinrichs IV., von ihr selbst beschrieben, 1803
Die Geschichte des Zauberers Merlin, 1804
Lothar und Maller: Eine Rittergeschichte, edited by Friedrich Schlegel, 1805
Madame de Staël, *Corinna; oder, Italien*, edited by Friedrich Schlegel, 4 vols., 1807–8

Further Reading

Deibel, Franz, *Dorothea Schlegel als Schriftstellerin im Zusammenhang mit der romantischen Schule*, Berlin: Mayer und Müller, 1905; reprint, New York: Johnson Reprint, 1970
Frank, Heike, ". . . die Disharmonie, die mit mir geboren ward, und mich nie verlassen wird . . .": Das Leben der Brendel/Dorothea Mendelssohn-Veit-Schlegel (1764–1839)*, Frankfurt and New York: Lang, 1988
Helfer, Martha-B., "Dorothea Veit-Schlegel's *Florentin*: Constructing a Feminist Romantic Aesthetic," *German Quarterly* 69 (1996)
Hibbert, J., "Dorothea Schlegel's *Florentin* and the Precarious Idyll," *German Life and Letters* 30 (1977)
Stephan, Inge, "Weibliche und männliche Autorschaft: Zum *Florentin* von Dorothea Schlegel und zur *Lucinde* von Friedrich Schlegel," in *"Wen kümmert's, wer spricht": Zur Literatur und Kulturgeschichte von Frauen aus Ost und West*, edited by Inge Stephan, et al., Cologne: Böhlau, 1991
Stern, Carola, "Ich möchte mir Flügel wünschen": Das Leben der Dorothea Schlegel*, Reinbek bei Hamburg: Rowohlt, 1990
Susman, Margarete, "Dorothea," in *Frauen der Romantik*, Jena: Diederichs, 1929
Thornton, Karin Stuebben, "Enlightenment and Romanticism in the Work of Dorothea Schlegel," *German Quarterly* 34 (1966)
Weissberg, Liliane, "The Master's Theme and Some Variations: Dorothea Schlegel's *Florentin* as Bildungsroman," *Michigan Germanic Studies* 13, no. 2 (1987)

Friedrich Schlegel 1772–1829

Friedrich Schlegel lives on in literary history as the theoretical leader of a group of young intellectuals, which in the 1790s became known as the Jena or Early Romantic "group"; it included his older brother August Wilhelm, Ludwig Tieck, Wilhelm Heinrich Wackenroder, Friedrich von Hardenberg (Novalis), and Friedrich Schleiermacher. Initial contact between the group members occurred at Jena in 1796; but when the Schlegel brothers founded the literary journal *Athenäum* in 1798, and when Friedrich defined "Romantic poetry" as "progressive universal poetry" in the fragment collection published in the second issue of the journal during its inaugural year, he named a European literary movement that was in the process of overcoming its inherited neoclassicist legacy. The "school" was ephemeral and short-lived: when Novalis died in 1801 and Schlegel left Jena soon thereafter, the Early Romantic moment was over; yet from a contemporary perspective, it foreshadowed many developments of our literary modernity.

Friedrich Schlegel was born in Hannover in 1772. He was the youngest child of a prominent family of Protestant clerics, state officials, poets, and literary critics. While August Wilhelm, five years his elder, showed promising talent in the Gymnasium and began his studies in Göttingen in 1786, the melancholy and defiant youngest son, Friedrich, was viewed as a problem child in need of discipline and was shipped off to Leipzig at age 15 for an apprenticeship in banking. Friedrich's hatred of this yoke and his begging to be allowed to study like his successful brother were perhaps predictable, but as a condition of university study, he had to acquire a Gymnasium education on his own, which he proceeded to do—an effort that included a surprising, ravenous acquisition of the classical languages.

Given his amazing facility with languages, he decided in 1794 to master the entire classical Greek legacy. He made a name as a classical scholar with his first essays on Greek themes and never lost his interest in Greek writers, primarily Plato; his attribution to Athenian Greece of a progressive, republican cultural life is related to his admiration for the ideals of the French Revolution. He also turned his attention to modern literature, however; his first important work was his programmatic study *Über das Studium der griechischen Poesie* (written in 1795, published 1797; On the Study of Greek Literature). In this work, he defended classical literature against modern or "interesting" literature, although he gave the latter the most attention and heralded Goethe's appearance as a "new dawn" of the modern.

In 1796 he came to Jena, where he worked further on his *Geschichte der Poesie der Griechen und Römer* (1798; History of the Literature of the Greeks and Romans), heard Fichte, and wrote his first modern literary essays on Jacobi, Lessing, and Georg Forster. These essays not only founded Romantic criticism but are also regarded as the basis for what become postwar literary "New Criticism." For such critics, the work is an autonomous creation and not mimesis, and the critic, conversant with the totality of an author's work, must react to it aesthetically and be sensitive to the immediate impression made by the work as a whole yet able to analyze or, in Lessing's words, "doubting with admiration and admiring with doubt."

With the establishment of the *Athenäum*, the Romantic movement found its decisive voice. At the end of the second 1798 issue of the journal, an issue that had opened with his stimulating fragments, Schlegel achieved the apotheosis of his critical activity with his groundbreaking, multilayered essay *Über Goethes Meister* (On Goethe's Meister). It is the merit of the greatest German literary critic of this century, Walter Benjamin, to have identified in his 1920 dissertation the central element—the mechanism of philosophical reflection—that Schlegel had acquired in his reading of Fichte and that he both attributed to Goethe's novel and employed in his own creation of Romantic art criticism.

In tandem with Novalis, Schlegel also developed a theory of Romantic poetry ("Poesie" in the broadest sense) that is surprising in its modernity (Lacoue-Labarthe and Nancy). Abolishing the hoary distinction between philosophy and literature, and between poetry and prose, they elevated such forms as the fragment, the essay or speech, and the dialogue ("symphilosophy"), resulting in a theory of the novel (previously regarded with suspicion) as a form capable of encapsulating all the others and of providing an indirect, allegorical representation of a totality that can only be approached, never achieved. With regard to literary content, Schlegel's most famous contribution is surely the theory of irony developed in the fragments, which employs Fichtean philosophy to take the ancient rhetorical device in new directions. One famous fragment (238) stresses the intimate connection with post-Kantian idealist philosophy by calling for and defining "transcendental poetry," a literature that consistently reflects the conditions of its own production; although born in idealist philosophy, this description is also surprising for its modernity. In 1799 he published the novel that was apparently intended to demonstrate his theories; *Lucinde* (*Lucinda*), while autobiographically tinged and formally innovative, is perhaps more noteworthy for its apparently progressive depiction of women and sensuality, for which it and its author were decried as "immoral."

The final year of the journal (1800) brought Schegel's *Gespräch über die Poesie* (*Dialogue on Poetry*), modeled on the *Symposium* and featuring reflections on the novel and a call for a "new mythology," a totality that would unify the dissonant modern cultural situation. The journal ends with Schlegel's critical "swan song," *Über die Unverständlichkeit* (*On Incomprehensibility*), a labyrinthine play on irony and indirection. Although the Early Romantic moment ends here, Schlegel also delivered lectures on transcendental philosophy in Jena (1800–1) that have recently gained renewed attention.

Schlegel left Jena for Paris and then Cologne, where he continued his editorial and philosophical activities, started a new journal entitled *Europa*, and became interested in other literatures and languages, including Sanskrit. This last interest led to his pathbreaking book *Über die Sprache and Weisheit der Indier* (1808; "On the Language and Wisdom of the Indians"). That same year, he and his wife Dorothea (daughter of Moses Mendelssohn) converted to Catholicism—after his novel *Lucinde,* this was the second event in his life that lived in infamy. With his move to Vienna and employment in Metternich's regime, he became a tireless, conservative Catholic publicist, presenting lectures on world literature and philosophy before a large royal audience. Although an attempt to rediscover the Catholic

Schlegel was one impetus for the publication of the splendid critical edition, this attempt has clearly failed, and it is the Friedrich Schlegel of 1796–1801 that justifies his inclusion here.

MICHAEL T. JONES

See also Athenäum

Biography

Born in Hanover, Germany, 10 March 1772. Brother of August Wilhelm Schlegel; son of J.A. Schlegel, pastor and writer, and nephew of J.E. Schlegel, playwright and critic. Studied at Göttingen University, 1790–91, and Leipzig University, 1791–94. Apprentice to a banker, Leipzig, 1788; in Dresden, 1794, and Berlin, 1797; contributor to *Deutschland*, Berlin, 1797, and *Der Teutsche Merkur*; cofounded and co-edited with his brother, August Wilhelm Schlegel, the journal *Das Athenäum*, 1798–1800, a publication supporting the romantic literary movement; lecturer, Jena University, 1800–1801; in Paris, 1802–4; founding editor of the journal *Europa*, 1803–5; married the writer Dorothea Veit, 1804; in Cologne, 1804–7; became a Roman Catholic, 1808; in Vienna, 1808; with the Austrian diplomatic service, 1809; service in the Austrian army, 1809–10; editor of the army newspaper, *Österreichische Zeitung*; lectures on modern history, 1811; cofounder and editor of *Deutsches Museum*, 1812–13; appointed to the Austrian delegation to the Bundestag, Frankfurt, 1815–18; in Vienna, 1818; editor of the journal *Concordia*, 1820–23. Died 12 January 1829.

Selected Works

Collections

Sämtliche Werke, 10 vols., 1822–25; 2nd edition, 15 vols., 1846
Kritische Friedrich-Schlegel-Ausgabe, edited by Ernst Behler et al., 1958–

Nonfiction

Die Griechen und Römer, 1797
Geschichte der Poesie der Griechen und Römer, 1798
Gespräch über die Poesie, 1800; as *Dialogue on Poetry*, translated by Ernst Behler and Roman Struc, 1968
Über die Sprache und Weisheit der Indier, 1808; as "On the Language and Wisdom of the Indians," translated by E.J. Millington in *The Aesthetic and Miscellaneous Works of Friedrich Schlegel*, 1849
Über die Neuere Geschichte (lectures), 1810; translated by Lyndsey Purcell and R.H. Whitelock, in *A Course of Lectures on Modern History*, 1849
Geschichte der alten und neuen Literatur, 1812; as *Lectures on the History of Literature, Ancient and Modern*, translated by H.G. Bohn et al., 1859
Die drei ersten Vorlesungen über die Philosophie des Lebens, 1827
Philosophie des Lebens (lectures), 1827; as *The Philosophy of Life and Philosophy of Language*, translated by A.J.W. Morrison, 1847
Philosophie der Geschichte (lectures), 1828; as *The Philosophy of History*, translated by James Burton Robertson, 1835
Philosophische Vorlesungen inbesondere über Philosophie der Sprache und des Wortes, 1830; as *The Philosophy of Life and Philosophy of Language*, translated by A.J.W. Morrison, 1847
Briefe an seinen Bruder August Wilhelm, edited by O.F. Walzel, 1890
Krisenjahre der Frühromantik: Briefe aus dem Schlegelkreis, edited by J. Körner, 1936–58
Literary Notebooks 1797–1801, edited by Hans Eichner, 1957

Edited Works

Dorothea Schlegel, *Florentin*, 1801
Gotthold Ephraim Lessing, *Lessings Gedanken und Meinungen aus dessen Schriften*, 1804

Novel

Lucinde, 1799; edited by K.K. Polhein, 1964; as *Lucinda*, translated by Paul Bernard Thomas, in *The German Classics of the Nineteenth and Twentieth Centuries*, vol. 4, 1913; as *Lucinde*, translated by Peter Firchow, in *Friedrich Schlegel's Lucinde and the Fragments*, 1971

Play

Alarcos, 1802

Poetry

Gedichte, 1809

Further Reading

Behler, Ernst, *Friedrich Schlegel in Selbstzeugnissen und Bilddokumenten*, Reinbek bei Hamburg: Rowohlt, 1966
———, *German Romantic Literary Theory*, Cambridge and New York: Cambridge University Press, 1993
Benjamin, Walter, *Der Begriff der Kunstkritik in der deutschen Romantik*, Bern: Francke, 1920; as "The Concept of Criticism in German Romanticism," in *Selected Writings*, vol. 1, Cambridge, Massachusetts, and London: Harvard University Press, 1996
Bowie, Andrew, *From Romanticism to Critical Theory: The Philosophy of German Literary Theory*, London and New York: Routledge, 1997
Brown, Marshall, *The Shape of German Romanticism*, Ithaca, New York: Cornell University Press, 1979
Eichner, Hans, *Friedrich Schlegel*, New York: Twayne, 1970
Frank, Manfred, *Einführung in die frühromantische Ästhetik*, Frankfurt: Suhrkamp, 1989
Lacoue-Labarthe, Philippe, and Jean-Luc Nancy, *The Literary Absolute: The Theory of Literature in German Romanticism*, Albany: State University of New York Press, 1988
Menninghaus, Winfried, *Unendliche Verdopplung: Die frühromantische Grundlegung der Kunsttheorie im Begriff absoluter Selbstreflexion*, Frankfurt: Suhrkamp, 1987
Peter, Klaus, *Friedrich Schlegel*, Stuttgart: Metzler, 1978
Pikulik, Lothar, *Frühromantik: Epoche, Werke, Wirkung*, Munich: Beck, 1992
Schanze, Helmut, editor, *Friedrich Schlegel und die Kunsttheorie seiner Zeit*, Darmstadt: Wissenschaftliche Buchgesellschaft, 1985
Schulte-Sasse, Jochen, editor, *Theory as Practice: A Critical Anthology of Early German Romantic Writings*, Minneapolis: University of Minnesota Press, 1997
Seyhan, Azade, *Representation and Its Discontents: The Critical Legacy of German Romanticism*, Berkeley: University of California Press, 1992

Gespräch über die Poesie 1800
Essay by Friedrich Schlegel

Friedrich Schlegel's *Gespräch über die Poesie* (*Dialogue on Poetry*) appeared in the third volume of *Athenäum*, the literary and critical journal he edited with his brother August Wilhelm, which was the organ of the circle of early Romantic writers and thinkers associated with the university town of Jena. The *Dialogue* is the most ambitious expression of early Romantic thinking about aesthetics, extending earlier contributions such as the *Athenäum* fragments (1798), Schlegel's *Ideen* (1799; *Ideas*), and Novalis's *Blütenstaub* (1798; *Pollen*). In the *Dialogue*, Schlegel reflects on the status of literature in modern culture and thus responds to questions bequeathed to the Romantic generation by

Kant's *Kritik der Urteilskraft* (1790; *Critique of Judgment*). The *Athenäum* met with widespread interest in literary circles and was seen to make new and radical claims for its authors. Subsequently, however, Schlegel's *Athenäum* essay "Über die Unverständlichkeit" (1800; On Incomprehensibility) indicates a failure by his readers to engage with the subtlety of Romantic thinking.

The *Dialogue* consists of an introduction followed by four talks interspersed with conversational exchanges among a group of friends. "Epochen der Dichtkunst" (Epochs of Literature) is discussed by Andrea, who is identified with August Wilhelm Schlegel; a "Rede über die Mythologie" (Talk on Mythology) is given by Ludoviko, identified with the philosopher Schelling; "Brief über den Roman" (Letter on the Novel) is by Antonio, identified as Friedrich Schlegel himself; and "Versuch über den verschiedenen Stil in Goethes früheren und späteren Werken" (Essay on the Different Styles in Goethe's Earlier and Later Works) is by Marcus, who represents Tieck. The other participants in this symposium represent Dorothea Veit, who subsequently married Friedrich (Camilla), Caroline Schlegel-Schelling (Amalia—August Wilhelm's name for her), and Novalis (Lothario). The *Dialogue* thus stages the collaborative form of thinking ("symphilosophy") promoted by Friedrich in the Jena circle, but the lecture style also points to the growing academic interest in literature associated with the work of the Schlegel brothers.

More than a framework for a series of reflections on topics of contemporary literary interest, the dialogue form of the *Dialogue* raises the question of literary genre and claims for itself the status of Plato's dialogues (such as the *Republic* and *Symposium*). Each of the major contributions in the text is cast in a different form—academic lecture, talk, letter, or essay—while the social context is presented first in a novelistic way and then as dramatic dialogue. In this way, the work also reemphasizes the mutually dependent and supplementary pattern of the *Athenäum* fragments, stressing the contrasts of *ganz verschiedene Ansichten* (quite different opinions) and *Vielseitigkeit* (many-sidedness). The sequence of the texts, their focal topics, and their formal properties all indicate a careful calculation by Schlegel. The *Dialogue* moves from the generality of antiquity to a specific modern author via a conjuring of a universal mythical principle and a discussion of a specific modern genre (the novel). There is a further symmetry in the essentially *historical* accounts of "Epochen der Dichtkunst" and the "Versuch," in contrast to the rhetorical or persuasive force of the "Rede" and "Brief."

"Epochen" seeks a secure foundation for the development of literature in its historical evolution since antiquity. Roman literature is particularly significant because it provides a model for everything in Europe that succeeded Greek culture. Since Goethe, Andrea claims, Germany has the opportunity, not to imitate that Greek originality, but to create it anew in native terms. "Rede über die Mythologie" points out that modern literature lacks the sort of unifying focus that myth provided for antiquity. Here, too, a restoration is thought possible, and is glimpsed in contemporary physics and in the aspiration of idealism to the absolute (*das Höchste*); these ideas draw on Spinoza as an instance of the expressivity of the whole through a part. Ultimately, the very idea of meaning and the possibility of giving form in literary creativity (*bilden*) seem to be the substance of the proposed new mythology. The novel is suggested as the most fully realized form of such a myth of the meaning of the whole (*die Bedeutung des Ganzen*), and the "Brief über den Roman" is dedicated to this novel genre.

The "Brief" is addressed to Amalia, proposing to educate her taste in novels. This means rejecting certain popular authors such as Fielding and promoting instead Sterne, Jean Paul, and Diderot, who can equal Cervantes or Shakespeare. These are all instances of the "sentimental"—writing in which a spirit of love appears to hover over the whole, as the principle that draws the material together into a higher unity. The novel is the definitive *Romantic* book (*Ein Roman ist ein romantisches Buch*) because it is uniquely capable of making this higher unity operative and apparent in every detail. The model for such a claim is shown, in Marcus's "Versuch," to be Goethe's *Wilhelm Meisters Lehrjahre* (1795–96; *Wilhelm Meister's Apprenticeship*). This novel is the groundbreaking climax of Goethe's development from the enthusiasm and energy of *Götz von Berlichingen*, through the reflective harmony of *Torquato Tasso*, to the balanced objectivity of *Hermann und Dorothea*. Goethe's modern and progressive novel promises to fulfill the highest task of literature, the harmony of the classical and Romantic.

This is one of three aspects particularly praised by Schlegel, each of which is also a feature of the *Dialogue* itself. Schlegel's text, too, echoes Plato's dialogues: like Plato, Schlegel also presents his own views prismatically (*in verschiedene Strahlen gebrochen*) through the medium of different characters, and his work is constantly doubled by the effect of irony. The self-reference has been particularly emphasized in connection with the "Brief über den Roman," which has been interpreted as a Romantic theory of the novel that illuminates Schlegel's own *Lucinde*. More recently, the "Rede" has gained greater prominence as an account of Schlegel's myth of irony. The fullest analysis, by Lacoue-Labarthe and Nancy, concentrates on the failed symmetry of the *Dialogue*. Following Blanchot's suggestions, the absence of Lothario's poetic contribution is read as indicating, by its own definition, the insufficiency of both Romanticism and the work in the *Dialogue*.

ANTHONY PHELAN

Editions

First edition: *Gespräch über die Poesie*, in *Athenäum*, vol. 3, Berlin: 1800; reprint, Darmstadt: Wissenschaftliche Buchgesellschaft, 1960
Critical edition: *Kritische Friedrich-Schlegel-Ausgabe*, vol. 2, edited by Ernst Behler, Munich: Schöningh, 1958; in Friedrich Schlegel, *Schriften zur Literatur*, edited by Wolfdietrich Rasch, Munich: Deutsche Taschenbuch-Verlag, 1972
Translation: *Dialogue on Poetry*, translated by Ernst Behler and Roman Struc, University Park: Pennnsylvania State University Press, 1968

Further Reading

Blanchot, Maurice, "The Athenaeum," translated by Deborah Esch and Ian Balfour, *Studies in Romanticism* 22 (1983)
Eichner, Hans, "Friedrich Schlegel's Theory of Romantic Poetry," *PMLA* 71 (1956)
Lacoue-Labarthe, Philippe, and Jean-Luc Nancy, *L'Absolu littéraire*, Paris: Éditions du Seuil, 1978; as *The Literary Absolute*, translated by Philip Barnard and Cheryl Lester, Albany: State University of New York Press, 1988
Newmark, Kevin, "*L'absolu littéraire*: Friedrich Schlegel and the Myth of Irony," *Modern Language Notes* 107 (1992)
Szondi, Peter, "Friedrich Schlegel and Romantic Irony," and "Friedrich Schlegel's Theory of Poetical Genres," in *On Textual Understanding, and Other Essays*, translated by Harvey Mendelsohn, Minneapolis: University of Minnesota Press, 1986

Kritische Fragmente 1797

Essay by Friedrich Schlegel

Shortly after completing the manuscript of his 127 *Kritische Fragmente* (*Critical Fragments*) in 1797, Friedrich Schlegel wrote to Novalis on 26 September that he had just sent a few pages of a "critical Chamfortade" into the world. But whereas Chamfort's maxims reflect the kind of self-contained completion Schlegel signaled in his Fragment 206 of the *Athenäum*—that a fragment should be just like a little work of art wrapped within itself like a hedgehog—this purported ideal was often undercut by the philosophical content of Schlegel's *Lyceum* fragments. The fragment in early Romantic theory may indeed relate to a totality, but it is precisely the skepticism with regard to the representation of that totality that informs and characterizes many of these fragments, as Manfred Frank has shown. Totality has the function of a regulative idea or—as Ernst Behler has illustrated—constitutes that elusive goal of attainability in humankind's progressive approximation toward perfectibility in the tension of part and whole, fragment and system, and the impossibility of complete and perfect communication. Walter Benjamin characterized the intellectual attitude emerging from the Romantic fragments of Friedrich Schlegel and Novalis as an infinite process of self-reflective thinking extending to all spheres of human endeavor. Indeed, one is not amiss in regarding the Romantic critical fragment as the vehicle for transporting Romantic language skepticism—the oscillating hovering above irreconcilable poles of thought and endless self-reflective analysis—to the 20th-century stylistic phenomena of writers such as Nietzsche, Thomas Mann, Heidegger, and Derrida.

Following his intensive study of Greek literature in *Über das Studium der griechischen Poesie* (1797; On the Study of Greek Literature) and juxtaposing characteristics of antiquity to the modern, Schlegel concluded that the task of his generation was to link the ancient and the modern in a productive tension, an alternating pulsation that denoted irony and wit. While Greek poetry had attained the highest beauty, this was a "relative maximum," Schlegel claims, one congenial to its age, whereas the "absolute maximum" can never emerge in any history or era. "Art is infinitely perfectible, and an absolute maximum is not possible in its continuous development: but yet a limited, relative maximum, an insurmountable fixed proximum." The problem of poetry was now to combine the essentially modern with the essentially ancient, an achievement already begun by Goethe in the new *Kunstperiode*. Yet, as Ernst Behler (1993) notes, only with the publication of these 127 literary fragments can we speak of the "hour of birth of a new literary genre in which form and content correspond."

These critical fragments divulge literary concerns ranging from the antinomies of art and nature, the classical and the modern, to the concept of poetry itself, the novel, the role of the author, wit, and critique, but at their core lies the phenomenon of irony. Indeed, irony is seen here as that mode of comprehension and communication that marks both ancient and modern poetry and that provides the only tenable means of communicating the antagonistic, irreconcilable forces of poetry and life that constitute the Romantic turn. Irony is not merely the style, but the content of what literature should be and do. The poet is to rise to the reflection of the second power, transform it artistically, reflect upon his poetic mission, and incorporate such reflection with his artistic production, achieving not merely poetry, but the poetry of poetry. In Fragment 7, Schlegel faults his own earlier study of Greek literature as totally lacking in irony and provides a corrective antidote to such mannerism in Fragment 28: "the sense (for a specific art, science, a person, etc.) is divided spirit; self-restriction, thus a result of self-creation and self-destruction." Elaborating the process of such irony in Fragment 37, Schlegel refers to the distance an author must have from his subject to write well, a withdrawal from initial enthusiasm to the stance of self-possession. Self-restriction and control is necessary and paramount not only for the creative artist, but for any human being, for if one does not exert self-control, then the world will enforce it, whereby one becomes a knave. Then, too, such restraint belies the writer's infinite power. There are ancient and modern poems that breathe the divine aura of irony, Schlegel contends in Fragment 42, elevating it above one's own art, virtue, or genius. Fragment 48 denotes irony as the form of paradox, everything that is both good and great, and in Fragment 108, Schlegel betrays his debt to a Socratic irony in which all is jest and earnestness, everything candidly open and at the same time deeply disguised. Emerging from the union of the art of life and scientific intellect, in the meeting of perfected natural and artistic philosophy, this irony contains and inspires a feeling for the indissoluble agon of the unrestricted and the restricted, the impossibility and the necessity of a complete communication. In a series of clever formulations, wit is described as that spirit both dividing and uniting genius (7), a witty idea that is likened to a decomposing of intellectual material that had to have been intimately mixed a moment earlier, an electrical current jolting sociability (34), indeed, "an explosion of bound intellect" (90).

An educated person must be able to attune himself philosophically or philologically, critically or poetically, historically or rhetorically, ancient or modern at whim, and at any time and to any degree (55), and an artist is formed not by artistic works, but rather by sense, enthusiasm, and drive (63). In a now famous formulation, Schlegel describes the critic as a reader who ruminates (27) and later remarks that a critical judgment that is not itself a work of art in content, depiction, or beautiful form has no civil rights in the aesthetic realm (117). Whoever were to aptly characterize Goethe's *Wilhelm Meister,* Schlegel notes in Fragment 120, would thereby state what poetry should be and could then happily sit on his laurels and retire. While Schlegel was to hang up his critical bow and arrow only after the devastating reception of his own novel *Lucinde* (1799) a few years later, his review of Goethe's *Wilhelm Meister,* locating its modernity in the aura of irony it exudes, remains a masterpiece of literary interpretation. Other examples of the required ironic mode permeate fragments dealing with the classical-modern dichotomy (7, 14, 20, 39, 44, 60, 84), as well as those heralding the novel as the new vehicle for modern poetic sensibility, or as constituting the Socratic dialogues of modern times (26). Many an excellent novel forms an encyclopedia of the entire intellectual life of a genial individual, Schlegel claims, and while any educated person who continues to learn holds a novel within, it is not necessary to write it down (78). The infinite progressivity of irony, life, and art is condensed in Schlegel's query as to whether it would not be superfluous for an artist who has not become a new person to write more than one novel (89).

The critical discernment, poetic sensibility, and historical sense for the interrelated productivity of ancient and modern forms emanating from these 127 critical fragments mark not only a crucial turning point in theoretical reflections about writers and literature but about evolving humanity and human endeavors in the art of living. It is not surprising that contemporary and postmodern critics have found fertile ground for their own reflections in these seminal fragments, as well as in those formulated later in the *Athenäum* in the spirit of a *Symphilosophie* of fragmentary contributions from within the Jena circle of the Schlegel brothers.

DIANA IPSEN BEHLER

See also Irony, Romantic

Editions

First edition: in *Sämtliche Werke,* 10 vols., Vienna: Mayer, 1822–25
Critical edition: in *Kritische Friedrich-Schlegel-Ausgabe,* vol. 2, edited by Hans Eichner, Munich: Schöningh, 1967
Translation: *Critical Fragments,* translated by Peter Firchow, in *Friedrich Schlegel's Lucinde and the Fragments,* Minneapolis: University of Minnesota Press, 1971

Further Reading

Behler, Ernst, *Die Zeitschriften der Brüder Schlegel,* Darmstadt: Wissenschaftliche Buchgesellschaft, 1983
——, *Studien zur Romantik und zur idealistischen Philosophie,* Paderborn: Schöningh, 1988
——, *Irony and the Discourse of Modernity,* Seattle: University of Washington Press, 1990
——, *German Romantic Literary Theory,* Cambridge and New York: Cambridge University Press, 1993
Benjamin, Walter, *Der Begriff der Kunstkritik in der deutschen Romantik,* Bern: Francke, 1920; as "The Concept of Criticism in German Romanticism," in *Selected Writings,* vol. 1, Cambridge, Massachusetts, and London: Harvard University Press, 1996
Blanchot, Maurice, *L'entretien infini,* Paris: Gallimard, 1969
Frank, Manfred, "Das 'fragmentarische Universum' der Romantik," in *Fragment und Totalität,* edited by Lucien Dällenbach, Frankfurt: Suhrkamp, 1984

Lucinde 1799

Novel by Friedrich Schlegel

For reasons both formal and thematic, Friedrich Schlegel's only novel was an object of controversy at the time of publication, and in varying ways it has remained so ever since. *Lucinde* was unorthodox formally because its use of digression and nonlinear narration is at variance with the structural traditions of the bildungsroman and did not offer the mimetic realism that came to be expected of the novel in the 19th century. Thematically, the novel caused controversy because its treatment of gender and sexual behavior challenged and offended against bourgeois morality, while in recent decades it has incurred additional odium on the grounds of sexism. Schiller described *Lucinde* in a letter to Goethe as "der Gipfel moderner Unform und Unnatur" (the height of modern formlessness and unnaturalness). Progressive writers, by contrast, have frequently praised its libertarian

stance on sex, education, and the function of work. At the same time, they have welcomed its innovative narrative strategies: both Friedrich Schleiermacher in his *Vertraute Briefe über Friedrich Schlegels "Lucinde"* (1800; Confidential Letters on Friedrich Schlegel's "Lucinde") and later Karl Gutzkow wrote passionately in its defense.

Lucinde, however, was never the manifesto of female emancipation for which feminists and liberal reformers so long mistook it. It is more a self-indulgent and largely autobiographical portrayal of its author's personal development and his self-discovery through increasingly sophisticated relationships with a succession of women. In the course of this portrayal Schlegel expresses views on sex and marriage that were contentious at the time; the novel advocates candor and freedom in sexual conduct but comes out in the end for a form of permanent and exclusive cohabitation. Marriage is not an institution involving a ceremony but an "ewige Einheit und Verbindung unsrer Geister" (everlasting unity and union of our spirits), in which the woman acts neither as sex object nor as platonic soul mate but instead performs the functions simultaneously of "zärtlichste Geliebte . . . beste Gesellschaft . . . und vollkommene Freundin" (most amorous beloved . . . best companion . . . and perfect friend). Yet this very functionality, however idealistically it is described, denies women their independence and confines them to the status of private mentors for men. The women encountered by Julius, the autobiographical hero of the novel, are presented only as the catalysts of his own maturation and fulfillment. Elsewhere in the novel Schlegel asserts that women are more intuitively sensual than men and are as uncorrupted by society as children; as a consequence, they can educate their male partners in uninhibited sexuality and emotional intimacy. Modern feminists have justifiably pointed out that such a view amounts to a condescending idealization, which only reinforces traditional gender stereotyping. Certainly, Schlegel presents women as the intellectual and spiritual equals of men, but he does not suggest any changes in traditional gender roles or endorse any form of legal or economic equality for women.

The image of the plant is prominent in *Lucinde* and embodies the central theme of the text, namely, the belief that human behavior should be organic and spontaneous rather than planned and directed at some objective. Thus, particularly in the section "Idylle über den Müßiggang" (Idyll on Indolence), the novel opposes utilitarianism and the bourgeois work ethic and instead advocates a reflective, intuitive, and imaginative lifestyle. In education the emphasis is on the free growth of the individual. Sexual conduct, too, should be based upon spontaneity and naturalness; sexual partners should discard inhibition and convention in glorious self-expression and fulfill the divine destiny of all life forms to mate and reproduce. In all respects, ideal behavior is "ein reines Vegetieren" (pure plant-like existence or pure vegetating), the ambiguity being intentional and provocative. Social libertarianism thus becomes part of a "religion," as Schlegel termed it, of primitive naturalness.

Lucinde itself is expressly intended as a literary manifestation of such free organic development, and it deliberately flouts rational order so as to proceed by association, whimsy, and fantasy. The short novel consists of 13 heterogeneous sections arranged in what is repeatedly termed "reizende Verwirrung" (charming confusion). The unity of the text thus lies not in an unfolding plot and coherent structure but in the body of ideas and attitudes that it reiterates in varying forms, ranging from letter and dialogue to allegory and character sketch. Only the longest and central section, the "Lehrjahre der Männlichkeit" (Apprenticeship in Manhood), resorts to a linear, third-person narration, which describes the instructive but never entirely satisfactory relationships experienced by Julius before he meets his ideal partner, the Lucinde of the title. Her name perhaps indicates that her role is to bring light into Julius's life: she shows him that in Schlegel's conception of marriage the partners fulfill all of each other's needs completely and so render infidelity superfluous. Schlegel does not hesitate to refer explicitly to sexual activity; for instance, he extols the pleasures of reversing conventional sexual positions and the innocence of the infant that exposes itself. He does not, however, altogether avoid prurience in his depictions. He insists on the virtues of levity and frivolity in flirtation and sexual banter, both of which he defends, but his own wit sometimes descends into unsubtle innuendo.

Such candor about sex was not new at the time: it had been featured in the salacious rococo novels of the 18th century. In part, Schlegel's target was precisely the hypocrisy of those who read such novels while preaching prudery and condoning the dreariest conventional marriages. What was new in *Lucinde* and what scandalized his contemporaries was the honesty and directness with which Schlegel tried to write about sex; he did not intend to titillate but to suggest more permissive attitudes to sexuality in contemporary society. Indeed, as his critics well knew, he was putting such attitudes into practice himself, for he was living with a married woman nine years his senior, Dorothea Veit, who provided the barely disguised model for Lucinde. In later life, following his marriage to Dorothea and his conversion to Catholicism, Schlegel regretted the frankness and provocation of *Lucinde* and withheld it from his collected works. Leaving aside such ephemeral controversies, however, *Lucinde* remains important as both a vehicle for the Romantic ideals of spontaneity and creativity and a narrative experiment that prefigures the 20th-century novel. On literary merit alone it would not have survived.

RICHARD LITTLEJOHNS

Editions

First edition: *Lucinde*, Berlin: Fröhlich, 1799

Critical edition: *Kritische Friedrich Schlegel-Ausgabe*, vol. 5, edited by Hans Eichner, Munich, Paderborn, and Vienna: Schöningh, 1962

Translation: *Friedrich Schlegel's "Lucinde" and the Fragments*, translated with an introduction by Peter Firchow, Minneapolis: University of Minnesota Press, and London: Oxford University Press, 1971

Further Reading

Becker-Cantarino, Baerbel, "Schlegels *Lucinde*: Zum Frauenbild der Frühromantik," *Colloquia Germanica* 10 (1976–77)

Blackall, Eric A., *The Novels of the German Romantics*, Ithaca, New York, and London: Cornell University Press, 1983

Eichner, Hans, *Friedrich Schlegel*, New York: Twayne, 1970

Firchow, Peter, editor and translator, *Friedrich Schlegel's "Lucinde" and the Fragments*, Minneapolis: University of Minnesota Press, and London: Oxford University Press, 1971

Higonnet, Margaret R., "Writing from the Feminine: *Lucinde* and *Adolphe*," *Annales Benjamin Constant* 5 (1985)

Kluckhohn, Paul, *Die Auffassung der Liebe in der Literatur des 18. Jahrhunderts und in der deutschen Romantik*, Halle: Niemeyer, 1922

Littlejohns, Richard, "The 'Bekenntnisse eines Ungeschickten': A Re-Examination of Emancipatory Ideas in Friedrich Schlegel's *Lucinde*," *Modern Language Review* 72 (1977)

Neubauer, John, "Time, Character, and Narrative Strategy in *Tristram Shandy* and *Lucinde*," in *Literary Theory and Criticism*, edited by Joseph Strelka, Bern and New York: Lang, 1984

Friedrich Daniel Ernst Schleiermacher 1768–1834

For the paradigm shift that marks the transition from the Enlightenment to Romanticism, Friedrich Schleiermacher was the chief architect of the new theology. As his counterparts in literature and in philosophy demonstrated the limitations of rationalist aesthetics and of critical philosophy through their affirmation of the imagination and subjectivity, respectively, so did Schleiermacher similarly dismantle rationalist theology. Against the deism that presupposed compatibility between reason and divinity, Schleiermacher advocated a religion of individual inner feeling and intuition. Yet Schleiermacher was not only an opponent of the rationalist intellectuals. His first important text, *Über die Religion: Reden an die Gebildeten unter ihren Verächtern* (1799; *On Religion: Speeches to its Cultured Despisers*), was directed toward his fellow Romantic idealists. Ever conscious of his vocation as clergyman, Schleiermacher combined strong subjective argumentation with a powerful emotional appeal to attract his Romantic friends to religion. As they esteemed art, individuality, and the imagination, they should likewise cherish religion, for, understood as a source of knowledge and as a means toward greater self-fulfillment, it, too, conveyed a sense of the infinite, not merely moral precepts. The radical nature of Schleiermacher's argument for a seemingly pantheistic, impersonal divinity, the ultimate ground of one's individuality, was reflected in the bitter condemnation of these claims by his fellow theologians, even by the progressive F.S.G. Sack.

Schleiermacher's influence on the cultural climate of the age extended far beyond the theological domain. A man of enormous versatility, Schleiermacher made valuable contributions to Romantic sensibilities, the academic world, the church, and, indeed, his nation. An active participant in the salon culture of Berlin, in particular at the home of Henriette Herz, Schleiermacher composed poetry and wrote entries for the Romantic journal *Das Athenäum*. Perhaps his most important literary contribution was the anonymously published *Vertraute Briefe über Friedrich Schlegels Lucinde* (1800; Confidential Letters on Friedrich Schlegel's Lucinde). While defending his friend's novel, Schleiermacher objected to the underlying assumption that the love it portrayed—the union of the spiritual with the sensuous—resulted from the inevitable workings of an absolute entity; this assumption, in Schleiermacher's view, too severely limited human agency. Schleiermacher's interest in literary matters was likewise manifested in his translation of the Platonic dialogues. The translations and the commentary, which is still of use to scholars today, have led many to consider him the founder of Platonic scholarship. His hermeneutics, which sought to understand the dialogues in their historical development, has also attracted the interest of 20th-century philosophers and theologians.

While Schleiermacher's philosophical interests were ultimately secondary to his theological interests, his *Monologen* (1800; *Schleiermacher's Soliloquies*) marked a departure from the Enlightenment intellectual tradition in both form and content. The lyrical reflections of the *Monologen* intimately linked philosophy with literature. Philosophy no longer consisted of formal, didactic theses abstracted from human life; rather, its new literary form made philosophy accessible to the reading public and reflective of the ambiguity of life itself. In the *Monologen* Schleiermacher proposed an individuality different from the Kantian universalism; morality was no longer grounded on an obligation to a universal moral law but on individual inner development. In general, against the Kantian dualism (phenomenal and noumenal selves) and the unconditionality of rational choice, Schleiermacher set his own belief in cultural ethics, namely, that choice was determined by one's situation in life, especially by one's own previous thoughts and experiences.

In contrast to some of his fellow Romantics, Schleiermacher, throughout his life, was much more conscious of the necessity of practical individual integration into society. As he sought philosophically to reconcile freedom and spirit with necessity and nature, so he insisted on the compatibility of individual desire and communal responsibility. This sense of the indispensability of individual interaction with the community is evident in his political thinking. An early enthusiast of the emancipatory aspirations of the French Revolution, Schleiermacher altered his view as the Jacobin terrorism denied societal legitimacy. The primacy of community in his thought as well as his own political self-consciousness are also clear both in patriotic sermons delivered during his tenure as a professor in French-occupied Halle (1806) and in his clandestine meetings with political reformers there.

Schleiermacher's emphasis on the practical life continued when he settled in Berlin (1809). As he administered to the spiritual needs of his fellow citizens as pastor of the Trinity Church, he also helped outline the organization and philosophy of the new university and later became the dean of its theology faculty. During the Wars of Liberation, Schleiermacher spoke out for the unification of Germany through a victory over the French. He blessed soldiers and participated in a militia. But when the promised constitution and political reforms failed to become reality, Schleiermacher voiced his criticism of the government, in particular his objection to the king's handling of the war. For his protest he was removed from his position in the Department of Education, reprimanded by the king, and carefully monitored in his clerical and academic activities. The rebellious and progressive spirit of his thinking can also be seen in his support of the theologian Wilhelm Martin De Wette, who had sought to console the mother of Karl Sand, the executed assassin of August von Kotzebue.

Among theologians Schleiermacher is best remembered for the delineation of his dogmatics in his *Der christliche Glaube* (1821–22, 1830–31; *The Christian Faith*). "Unsurpassed in Christian theological literature" (Gerrish), *The Christian Faith* lays the groundwork for a new "Glaubenslehre" or dogmatics by again underscoring the essentially intuitive and communal nature of religious experience. Unrelated to the intellect, this immediate feeling of Christian "religiousness" starts from personal experience and reveals the utter dependence of our being and our activity on something else, "das Woher des Abhängigkeitsgefühls." In its subjectivity, historicity, and intellectual rigor, Schleiermacher's new dogmatics reflects the changed weltanschauung of his age.

For his wide-ranging practical accomplishments and for his contributions to the intellectual and cultural life of Prussia, Schleiermacher enjoyed enormous public acclaim, even if the crown was frequently skeptical of his views. That thousands of his countrymen observed his funeral procession in 1834 is further testimony to his cultural importance. Scholarship has likewise shown its respect for the diversity of his intellectual legacy. In a pivotal biography of Schleiermacher, Dilthey accentuated Schleiermacher's proximity to *Lebensphilosophie*. In the early part of the 20th century (1925–55), Schleiermacher was criticized by some theologians (K. Barth) for having connected religion too intimately with culture. Later scholarship on Schleiermacher has concerned itself with the theologian's relationship to Romanticism. Kluckholm contended that Schleiermacher was deeply indebted to the Romantic worldview, while Redeker claimed that Schleiermacher's Romanticism was only a temporary phase. More recently, Crouter observed that Schleiermacher, while sharing much with the Romantics, including the notions of the incompleteness of the finite and the final inexpressibility of reality, differs with the Romantic identity philosophy (spirit = nature) by affirming a necessary separation between the two. While Schleiermacher's involvement with the Romantic movement continues to attract scholarly attention (Dyrness), his contribution to hermeneutics has also been the subject of study (Gmunden, Rajan). In addition, his theory of translation and his association with the feminine (Ellison) have likewise drawn the interest of scholars.

EDWARD T. LARKIN

See also Hermeneutics

Biography

Born in Breslau, 21 November 1768. Studied at the University of Halle, 1787–89; passed the theological examination in Berlin, 1790; position as house tutor with the Dohna family, East Prussia, 1790–93; ordained as a Protestant minister, 1794; pastor of Charité Hospital, Berlin, 1796; court preacher at Stolpe in Pomerania, 1802; extraordinary professor of theology, University in Halle, 1804; fled Napoléon's army, 1807; settled in Berlin, 1809; designed the new University of Berlin and became pastor of Dreifaltigkeitskirche (Trinity Church); appointed to the theological faculty, University of Berlin, 1810; dean of theology faculty, University of Berlin. Died 12 February 1834.

Selected Works

Über die Religion: Reden an die Gebildten unter ihren Verächtern, 1799
Monologen: Eine Neujahrsgabe, 1800
Vertraute Briefe über Friedrich Schlegels Lucinde, 1800
Die Weihnachtsfeier, 1806
Gelegentliche Gedanken über Universitäten im deutschen Sinn: Nebst einem Anhang über eine neu zu errichtende, 1808
Der christliche Glaube nach den Grundsätzen der evangelischen Kirche im Zusammenhange dargestellt, 1821–22, 1830–31

Further Reading

Barth, Karl, *Protestant Thought*, New York: Harper, and London: SCM Press, 1959

Clements, Keith, *Friedrich Schleiermacher: Pioneer of Modern Theology,* London and San Francisco: Collins, 1987

Crouter, Richard, "Introduction," in *On Religion,* by Friedrich Schleiermacher, Cambridge: Cambridge University Press, 1988

Dierkes, Hans, "Friedrich Schlegels *Lucinde,* Schleiermacher, and Kirkegaard," *Deutsche Vierteljahresschrift* 57 (1983)

Dilthey, Wilhelm, *Leben Schleiermachers,* Berlin: Reimer, 1870; Berlin: de Gruyter, 1970

Dyrness, William A., "Caspar David Friedrich: The Aesthetic Expression of Schleiermacher's Romantic Faith," *Christian Scholar's Review* 14, no. 4 (1985)

Ellison, Julie, *Delicate Subjects: Romanticism, Gender, and the Ethics of Understanding,* Ithaca, New York: Cornell University Press, 1990

Fallon, Daniel, "Friedrich Schleiermacher and the Idea of the University: Berlin 1810–1817," in *The German University: A Heroic ideal in Conflict with the Modern World,* Boulder: Colorado Associated University Press, 1980

Frank, Manfred, "The Text and Its Style: Schleiermacher's Hermeneutic Theory of Language," *Boundary* 11 (1983)

Gemunden, Gerd, *Die hermeneutische Wende: Diszipline und Sprachlosigkeit nach 1800,* New York: Lang, 1990

Gerrish, Brian Albert, *A Prince of the Church: Schleiermacher and the Beginnings of Modern Theology,* Philadelphia, Pennsylvania: Fortress Press, and London: SCM Press, 1984

———, "Friedrich Schleiermacher," in *Nineteenth-Century Religious Thought in the West,* edited by Ninian Smart, 3 vols., Cambridge University Press, 1985

Rajan, Tilottama, "Is there a Romantic Ideology? Some Thoughts on Schleiermacher's Hermeneutic and Textual Criticism," *Text: Transactions of the Society for Textual Scholarship* 4 (1988)

Redeker, Martin, *Friedrich Schleiermacher: Leben und Werk,* Berlin: de Gruyter, 1968; as *Schleiermacher: Life and Thought,* translated by John Wallhausser, Philadelphia, Pennsylvania: Fortress Press, 1973

Arno Schmidt 1914–1979

One of postwar Germany's most esoteric and reclusive literary figures, Arno Schmidt also ranks among the most prolific and engaging writers of the period. In his early stories and novels, he charts with great stylistic virtuosity and psychological perspicacity the fortunes of Germany from the Nazi period and World War II into the era of the Cold War and the Federal Republic's Phoenix-like economic recovery. His later works, four dialogue novels comprising together more than 2,000 oversize 12-by-17-inch pages of evocative, sensual, and oftentimes unnavigable prose, were composed largely under the aegis of Sigmund Freud and James Joyce and are even more experimental in nature than the already unconventionally playful and intertextually charged early prose. While in German literary histories Schmidt is sometimes treated as a pretentious enfant terrible and negligible solipsist, his work has been surprisingly influential for the generation of writers born during and shortly after World War II and coming into their own in the 1960s and 1970s. Schmidt's most tangible impact is undoubtedly that upon Rolf Dieter Brinkmann. Other younger authors who have expressed either their admiration for or their indebtedness to Schmidt are Jurek Becker, Christoph Hein, Peter Rühmkorf, and Hans Wollschläger.

Born on the eve of World War I into a petit-bourgeois family in Hamburg, Schmidt graduated from high school in the very year that the Nazis took control of Germany. Thereby cut off from the major intellectual and literary developments that followed Expressionism outside of Germany, he first entered the labor force and, during the war, was forced to serve in the German army. A dissident in thought but (as far as we know) never in action, Schmidt came out of the Nazi period and his wartime experiences embittered, resentful, and irate. In his prose and radio essays on German literature, Schmidt typically employs his narrators or speakers—more often than not mirror images of the author himself—to vent his anger over and flaunt his opposition to the rampant militarism, political chauvinism, and religious

hypocrisy that, in his view, characterized the newly founded Federal Republic.

Schmidt is best known for his early prose works, all of which provide fascinatingly detailed and realistic portraits of everyday life under Nazi rule and during the postwar period. The earliest published story, *Leviathan* (1949; *Leviathan*), depicts the demise of the Nazi empire as seen from the perspective of a recalcitrant German officer and philosophical nihilist. *Aus dem Leben eines Fauns* (1953; *Scenes from the Life of a Faun*) follows the life of a petty German bureaucrat and nonactivist inner émigré from the outbreak of World War II to the final catastrophe in 1945, impressively captured at the close of the story in the image of an all-engulfing explosion at a rural munitions factory. The two short stories *Brand's Haide* (1951; *Brand's Heath*) and *Die Umsiedler* (1953; *The Displaced*) relate the fortunes and vicissitudes of various forced transplantees in the immediate postwar period. Seemingly more ethereal and intimate, yet interspersed with many a sinister memento of the recent violent past, the short love story *Seelandschaft mit Pocahontas* (1955; *Lake Scenery with Pocahontas*) uses the Pocahontas myth as a backdrop to illustrate the first steps of middle-class Germans toward economic recovery; it was for this story that a lawsuit—soon after dismissed—was brought against Schmidt for blasphemy and pornography. The enigmatic subtitle of *Das steinerne Herz* (1956; *The Stony Heart*), "Ein historischer Roman aus dem Jahre 1954" (Historical Novel from Anno Domini 1954), alludes to the figural underlaying of its contemporary plot with the tragic love affair between the princess of Ahlden and Count Königsmarck; *The Stony Heart* has been credited as one of the earliest West German novels to take on the thorny issue of a divided Germany without pontificating against the East. Set after World War III, the hilariously satirical novel *Die Gelehrtenrepublik* (1957; translated as *The Egghead Republic* and *Republica Intelligentsia*) features a love affair between its American narrator and a mutant centaur. *Kaff auch Mare Crisium* (1960; *B/Moondocks*), finally, is a dual action narrative: spending a couple of days in the country with his girlfriend, the novel's late 1950s protagonist conjures up in conversation his version of life in an American lunar colony after the atomic holocaust.

The prelude to his late work is the short-story collection *Kühe in Halbtrauer* (1964; *Country Matters*); here Schmidt pays homage to James Joyce, whose mythological referencing (*Ulysses*) and linguistic experimentalism (*Finnegans Wake*) Schmidt reenacts most masterfully in "Caliban über Setebos" (Caliban upon Setebos), his shrewd rewriting of the classical Orpheus myth. After exorcising Joyce's oppressive but nonetheless productive influence through the weighty exorbitance of *Zettels Traum* (1970; *Zettel's Dream*)—1,300 oversize pages that cover one day in the life of the fictitious writer and Poe-connoisseur Daniel Pagenstecher—Schmidt again comes into his own, writing two wonderfully capricious and carnivalesque typescript novels, both rich in intertextual allusion and erotic diversion, *Die Schule der Atheisten* (1972; The School of Atheists) and *Abend mit Goldrand* (1975; *Evening Edged in Gold*).

Schmidt's reputation as rogue elephant of West German literature rests not on his stories and novels alone; he was also an industrious, if oftentimes notoriously disrespectful, literary critic. His numerous radio essays helped spawn renewed interest in such important 18th-century figures as Christoph Martin Wieland and Johann Gottfried Schnabel. He wrote a 700-page biography of the Romantic author Friedrich de la Motte Fouqué and the first major Freudian analysis of the writer Karl May. Schmidt is also known for excellent translations of works by Wilkie Collins, Edward Bulwer Lytton, James Fenimore Cooper, William Faulkner, and Edgar Allan Poe.

While Schmidt initially presented himself as a latter day Jacobin, his late works show signs of his disillusionment with mainstream politics—left or right—and his growing detachment from contemporary society. Because of Schmidt's own waywardness and elitism, Schmidt criticism has, more than is the case with other authors, been unduly faulted for exhibiting the same idiosyncrasies; still, today a peculiar aura is attached to the community of Schmidt devotees. While Schmidt criticism has not always remained aloof from uncritical idolatry, recent scholarship has witnessed a steady increase in theoretical sophistication and methodological resourcefulness.

ROBERT K. WENINGER

Biography

Born in Hamburg-Hamm, 18 January 1914. Lived in Lauban and Greiffenberg, Silesia, 1928–45; worked as an accountant for a textile firm, 1934–40; drafted into the German army, 1940; taken prisoner by the British and released, 1945; relocated to Cordingen, Lower Saxony, and then to Gau-Bickelheim, Kastel, and Darmstadt; worked as a freelance writer; settled in Bargfeld, Lower Saxony, 1958. Fontane Prize, 1964 (laudatio by Günter Grass); Frankfurt Goethe Prize, 1973. Died 3 June 1979.

Selected Works

Collections
Bargfelder Ausgabe, 1985–
Collected Early Fiction 1949–1964, 4 vols., translated by John E. Woods, 1994–97

Fiction
Leviathan, 1949; as *Leviathan*, translated by John E. Woods, 1994
Brand's Haide, 1951; as *Brand's Heath*, translated by John E. Woods, 1994
Aus dem Leben eines Fauns, 1953; as *Scenes from the Life of a Faun*, translated by John E. Woods, 1983
Seelandschaft mit Pocahontas, 1955; as *Lake Scenery with Pocahontas*, translated by John E. Woods, 1996
Das steinerne Herz, 1956; as *The Stony Heart*, translated by John E. Woods, 1997
Die Gelehrtenrepublik, 1957; as *The Egghead Republic*, translated by Michael Horovitz, 1979; as *Republica Intelligentsia*, translated by John E. Woods, 1994
Kaff auch Mare Crisium, 1960; as *B/Moondocks*, translated by John E. Woods, 1997
Kühe in Halbtrauer, 1964; as *Country Matters*, translated by John E. Woods, 1996
Zettels Traum, 1970
Die Schule der Atheisten: Novellen-Comödie in 6 Aufzügen, 1972
Abend mit Goldrand: Eine MärchenPosse. 55 Bilder aus der Lä/Endlichkeit für Gönner der VerschreibKunst, 1975; as *Evening Edged in Gold: A FairytalefArse / 55 Scenes from the Coun/untryside for Patrons of Erra/ota*, translated by John E. Woods, 1980
Julia, oder die Gemälde: Scenen aus dem Novecento, 1983

Critical Writings
Fouqué und einige seiner Zeitgenossen: Biografischer Versuch, 1958
Dya Na Sore: Gespräche in einer Bibliothek, 1958
Belphegor: Nachrichten von Büchern und Menschen, 1961
Sitara und der Weg dorthin: Eine Studie über Wesen, Werk und Wirkung Karl May's, 1963
Die Ritter vom Geist: Von vergessenen Kollegen, 1965
Der Triton mit dem Sonnenschirm: Großbritannische Gemütsergetzungen, 1969
Deutsches Elend: 13 Erklärungen zur Lage der Nationen, 1984
Der Platz, an dem ich schreibe: 17 Erklärungen zum Handwerk des Schriftstellers, 1993

Further Reading

Albrecht, Wolfgang, *Arno Schmidt*, Stuttgart and Weimar: Metzler, 1998
Arnold, Heinz Ludwig, editor, *Arno Schmidt*, Munich: Edition Text und Kritik, 1968; 4th edition, 1986
Drews, Jörg, and Hans-Michael Bock, editors, *Der Solipsist in der Heide: Materialien zum Werk Arno Schmidts*, Munich: Edition Text und Kritik, 1974
Eisenhauer, Gregor, *"Die Rache Yorix": Arno Schmidts Poetik des gelehrten Witzes und der humoristischen Gerichtsbarkeit*, Tübingen: Niemeyer, 1992
Martynkewicz, Wolfgang, *Selbstinszenierung: Untersuchungen zum psychosozialen Habitus Arno Schmidts*, Munich: Edition Text und Kritik, 1991
———, *Arno Schmidt*, Reinbek: Rowohlt, 1992
Menke, Timm, editor, *Arno Schmidt am Pazifik: Deutsch-amerikanische Blicke auf sein Werk*, Munich: Edition Text und Kritik, 1992
Minden, M.R., *Arno Schmidt: A Critical Study of His Prose*, Cambridge and New York: Cambridge University Press, 1982
Schneider, Michael, *Bilanzen des Scheiterns: Raum, Wirklichkeit, und Subjekt in Arno Schmidts Werken*, Frankfurt: Bangert und Metzler, 1984
Weninger, Robert, *Arno Schmidt-Bibliographie: Ein Verzeichnis der wissenschaftlichen Sekundärliteratur nach Titeln und Themen*, Munich: Edition Text und Kritik, 1995
———, *Framing a Novelist: Arno Schmidt Criticism 1970–1994*, Columbia, South Carolina: Camden House, 1995

Peter Schneider 1940–

Peter Schneider belongs to the last identifiable generation of (West) German writers who were born during World War II, marked in their 20s by the student revolt, and emerged in the shadow of the *Gruppe 47*. After the premature deaths of Rolf Dieter Brinkmann, Bernward Vesper, and Nicolas Born, Schneider is one of this generation's greatest representatives, along with F.C. Delius and Uwe Timm. Since *Lenz* (1973), his classic tale of disillusionment with the dogmatic, worker-oriented strand of the student movement, Schneider's career documents the maturing of a restlessly creative and politically motivated author, who gradually came to articulate the views of a liberal establishment he had once derided. Schneider has lived mainly from his pen after making his name as an essayist, commentator, and the author of prose fiction, screenplays, and drama. He has always written for a wide readership and engaged with topical issues, including terrorism, the legacy of the Nazi past, racism, and the division and subsequent reunification of Germany; sometimes he reacts to current debates, but more often he initiates them. He has a canny eye for sales, most notoriously illustrated by *Vati* (1987; Daddy), which was based on the true search of the son of the Auschwitz doctor, Josef Mengele. Schneider was accused of lifting the story verbatim from a popular magazine, but his revealing encounter of the generations would not have been received with such opprobrium had it not touched a raw nerve. Schneider made clear that the perpetrators of the Holocaust had been human beings, not monsters, who led otherwise unexceptional lives and who were linked still, by ties of blood if nothing else, with the Germans 40 years after 1945. While 1960s radicals, the *Achtundsechziger*, would not have accepted that the Nazis had anything remotely to do with them and expressed their distance in terms of ideology, the central figure of *Vati* recognizes the emotional impracticability of that position, recalling how his student friends had ritualistically but unconvincingly denounced their own fathers.

Lenz is often said to articulate the 1968 experience, perhaps mainly because the classic account of the student movement and its short-term failure was never quite written—in spite of so many attempts. Schneider in fact does both more and less than give literary form to this experience, which shaped the mental outlook of a generation of West Germans. His focus is limited to an intensely intellectual activist, who undergoes a nervous breakdown caused, so he believes, by the discrepancies between Maoist revolutionary theory and his personal everyday life. He regains emotional equilibrium after a journey to Italy, where the political situation seems far more mature and the pace of life far less frenetic, which teaches him that he has to think things through for himself and that contradictions between theory and reality are a fact of life. *Lenz* is a deeply traditional German narrative, a mini-bildungsroman (novel of education), borrowing motifs from both Büchner's tale of the same title and Goethe's seminal *Italienische Reise* (*Italian Journey*). A knowledge of literary tradition enhances the enjoyment of Schneider's texts: *Paarungen* (1992; *Couplings*) makes multiple use of Romantic tropes adapted from the tales of E.T.A. Hoffmann, and several stories in *Die Wette* (1978; The Wager) rework themes treated first by Ernest Hemingway and Max Frisch.

In the election campaign of 1965, when the Christian Democratic Union's Ludwig Erhard fought off a challenge from the Social Democrats' Willy Brandt, Schneider joined the *Wahlkontor Deutscher Schriftsteller* (Election Office of German Writers), which was set up by the novelist-cum-party activist Günter Grass in order to enable aspiring writers to help SPD politicians with formulating speeches and slogans. After Brandt, who lost the election, entered a grand coalition with the CDU the following year, Schneider, similar to other *Wahlkontor* veterans such as Gudrun Ensslin and her boyfriend Bernward Vesper, no longer supported the party during the next elections in 1969. Yet *Lenz* contains a sympathetic portrait of Grass, who appears as "the Patron," indicating that Schneider himself was edging back to the mainstream. He subsequently accompanied Grass on visits to East Berlin to meet GDR writers during the 1970s; they also mounted joint protests against the stationing of new missiles on German soil in the 1980s and both made German division and reunification a major theme of essays and literary publications. Schneider's *Der Mauerspringer* (1982; *The Wall Jumper*) and Grass's *Ein weites Feld* (1995; Too Far Afield) are two of the most significant attempts by West Germans to understand life on the other side of the Berlin Wall.

Schneider's next work after *Lenz* was . . . *schon bist du ein Verfassungsfeind* (1975; . . . Already You're an Enemy of the Constitution), which documents how a school teacher's career is cut short by Brandt's notorious *Radikalenerlaß* (Radicals' Decree), which was intended to combat left-wing terrorism. This, too, met a public need and became a steady seller for Klaus Wagenbach's cult left-wing *Rotbuch-Verlag*. Schneider continued with this general theme for *Messer im Kopf* (1979; Knife in the Head), a film screenplay, in which he draws on his friendship with the student leader, Rudi Dutschke, before turning to new subjects in the following decade. It is with *Der Mauerspringer*, a collection of essays, autobiographical sketches, and stories, that he breaks new ground, disproving the view, expressed forcibly during the debate triggered by *Vati*, that he made literary capital out of topical subjects—the GDR was hardly fashionable at the time. As Schneider had lived in West Berlin since 1961, the year the wall was built, he was well placed to depict the interaction, or lack of it, between the two Germanies. His expertise also fed into an internationally best-selling travelogue, *Extreme Mittellage* (1990; The German Comedy), which reflects on reactions from a grass roots perspective on the vexed German Question in the year of unification. German-German relations play a role, too, in Schneider's most substantial literary publication, and his first novel, *Paarungen* (1992), set in West Berlin during the 1980s, which once more focuses on the '68 generation, now liberal professionals beset by mid-life crises and relationship turmoil. A thought-provoking social and moral comedy, the novel indicates the range of a literary talent that Schneider all too rarely exploited to the full until the 1990s. Its sequel, *Eduards Heimkehr* (1999; Edward's Return), is a witty and engaging comedy of manners set against the backdrop of the new Germany.

JULIAN PREECE

Biography

Born in Lübeck, 21 April 1940. Studied German literature, history, and philosophy at the universities of Freiburg, Munich, and Berlin; settled in West Berlin, 1961; first review published 1964; member of Election Office of German Writers, 1965; active in the German student movement, 1967–71; friend of Rudi Dutschke; worked in a factory job; graduated, 1972; because of his political leanings, initially not admitted to the teaching profession; eventually opted to become a freelance writer once the teaching ban had been lifted in 1976; frequent visiting lecturer in the United States.

Selected Works

Essays and Letters
Ansprachen, Reden, Notizen, Gedichte, 1970
Atempause: Versuch meine Gedanken über Literatur und Kunst zu ordnen, 1977
Die Botschaft des Pferdekopfs und andere Essays aus einem friedlichen Jahrzehnt, 1981
Ratte tot . . . ein Briefwechsel (with Peter Jürgen Boock), 1985
Deutsche Ängste. Sieben Essays, 1988
Extreme Mittellage: Eine Reise durch das deutsche Nationalgefühl, 1990; as *The German Comedy: Scenes of Life after the Wall,* translated by Philip Boehm and Leigh Hafrey, 1991
Wie die Spree in den Bosporus fließt: Briefe zwischen Istanbul und Berlin 1990/1991 (with Aras Ören), 1991

Fiction
Lenz, 1973
. . . schon bist du ein Verfassungsfeind: Das unerwartete Anschwellen der Personalakte des Lehrers Kleff, 1975
Die Wette. Erzählungen, 1978
Messer im Kopf: Drehbuch (film directed by Reinhard Hauff), 1979

Der Mauerspringer, 1982; as *The Wall Jumper,* translated by Leigh Hafrey, 1983
Vati. Erzählung, 1987
Leyla und Medjnun: Märchen für Musik (with Aras Ören), 1992
Paarungen, 1992; as *Couplings,* translated by Philip Boehm, 1996
Eduards Heimkehr, 1999

Drama
Alte und neue Szenen zum Thema "Radikale," in *Theaterstücke zum Radikalenerlaß: Texte, Bilder, und Dokumente,* 1978
Totoloque: Das Geiseldrama von Mexico-Tnochtitan. Stück in drei Sprachen, 1985

Further Reading
Goodbody, Axel, "Walls in the Mind: Peter Schneider and the German Question in the 1980s," *Quinquereme* 13 (1990–91)
Höfer, Adolf, "Vater-Sohn-Konflikte in moderner Dichtung: Symptome einer Verharmlosung des Faschismus am Beispiel von Peter Schneiders Erzählung *Vati,"* *literatur für leser* 1 (1994)
Pender, Malcolm, "Historical Awareness and Peter Schneider's *Lenz,"* *German Life and Letters* 37, no. 2 (1984)
Riordan, Colin, "Introduction," in *Peter Schneider: Vati,* Manchester: Manchester University Press, 1993
Riordan, Colin, editor, *Peter Schneider,* Cardiff: University of Wales Press, 1995
Schneider, Michael, "Die Linke und die Neue Sensibilität," in *Die lange Wut zum langen Marsch,* Reinbek bei Hamburg: Rowohlt, 1975

Arthur Schnitzler 1862–1931

Arthur Schnitzler is one of the most important authors of the Austrian fin de siècle period (1890–1925), which was a time of great achievements in the fields of literature, art, architecture, music, and psychology. Most of the artists and scientists lived in Vienna, the capital of the disintegrating Austrian Empire, which was ruled by the last Habsburg emperor, Franz Joseph (1830–1916).

Schnitzler established his reputation as a writer with *Anatol* (1893), a cycle of seven one-act plays offering various character-facets of a bachelor who prefers to stay in his illusory world rather than live in reality. In Schnitzler's later productions, the world of dreams and reality, or *Schein* and *Sein,* intermingle. This is the case in his one-act play *Der grüne Kakadu* (1899; *The Green Cockatoo*), a play that the censors closed down after only a few performances. It is set in a tavern at the beginning of the French Revolution in Paris of 1789, where actors perform impromptu stagings for members of their aristocratic clientele, who are unable to distinguish between illusion and historical reality. In *Paracelsus* (1899; *Paracelsus*), the title character uses hypnosis to show to Cyprian that underneath his wife's unquestioned faithfulness there exist unspoken, subconscious erotic desires. This play ends with the often-quoted lines: "There flow together dream and waking time, / Truth and deception. Certainty is nowhere. / Nothing we know of others, of ourselves no more; / We always play—and wise is he who knows." Schnitzler shows

the same confusing blending of the world of the theater and the real world in his marionette-play *Zum Grossen Wurstel: Burleske in einem Akt* (1905; The Great Pierrot: Burlesque in One Act), in which he satirizes his own characters and plays.

A mixture of illusion and reality is also present in his one-act play *Die Frau mit dem Dolche* (1902; *The Woman with the Dagger*), which in addition contains the element of eternal recurrence. Themes concerning the omnipotence of thought can be found in his narrative "Das Schicksal des Freiherrn von Leisenbogh" (1904; "The Fate of the Baron of Leisenbogh"), his mystery novelette "Das Tagebuch der Redegonda" (1911; "Redegonda's Diary"), and "Die Weissagung" (1905; "The Prophecy"); in these works, readers find themselves in the twilight zone of unfamiliar territory, unable to orient themselves in their routine existence, which is limited by time and space. A masterpiece is Schnitzler's *Traumnovelle* (1926; *Rhapsody: A Dream Novel*), in which a husband and his wife live out their unfulfilled erotic desires—he at a secret party and she in her dream, which parallels her husband's adventure in almost every detail. In all of these works, the reader is left with the baffling question of what is truth and what is merely appearance. Some critics interpret Schnitzler as a determinist who shows the individual living and acting in a predetermined world. They refer primarily to his short parable "Die dreifache Warnung" (1911; "The Triple Warning"), in which they see the negation of free will. This nihilistic interpretation is challenged by contemporary Schnitzler research, which focuses upon his posthumously published literary works, especially his collection *Aphorismen und Betrachtungen* (1967; From Book of Aphorisms and Considerations), his diaries, and his numerous correspondence. All of these writings show Schnitzler's preoccupation with, and ultimate rejection of, determinism; he believed that it would eliminate individual responsibility and the freedom of creativity.

Schnitzler portrayed the dual nature of his Viennese society by revealing the human weaknesses and the subconscious, underlying motives of his characters. His endeavor is thus similar to that of Sigmund Freud: both were physicians and psychologists who lived at the same time in the same city and both diagnosed the dual nature of man, Freud with psychoanalysis and Schnitzler in his poetic work. Schnitzler very seldom compromised, and he was not afraid to criticize his bourgeois contemporaries for their pretensions and moral cowardice. Evidence for his unmasking technique can be seen in *Leutnant Gustl* (1901; translated as *None but the Brave* and *Lieutenant Gustl*) and *Reigen* (1903; *Hands Around: A Cycle of Ten Dialogues*). *Lieutenant Gustl*, considered by many critics as the towering masterpiece of Schnitzler's prose narrative production, is written in the style of the interior monologue, which was used before him by Edouard Dujardin in his short story "Les Lauriers sont coupés." Gustl puts himself into a situation where he, according to the military code of honor, has to commit suicide. He lacks the courage to do so, and Schnitzler lays bare how his inner thought process interprets the events around him, exposing thereby not only his own unflattering self but also the hypocritical value system of society.

Hands Around, probably the most controversial play Schnitzler wrote, is a round dance in which the characters, whose positions on the social scale range from a prostitute to an aristocrat, are doubly linked by sex. This play has often been compared to a dance of death, a form that has a long literary and cultural tradition in Austria; the form's significance at Schnitzler's time was that many people died of syphilis, for which there was then no cure. Schnitzler's interest was not to show the sexual act, which he indicated in his written play by dashes, but the hypocritical use or misuse of language before and after the act. The reception of this play was very stormy. When it was performed in Berlin in 1920 and 1921 in Vienna, a scandal, initiated by nationalistic and other anti-Semitic organizations, broke loose. Schnitzler subsequently withdrew his permission to have this play performed in Europe, and only after Schnitzler's son Heinrich lifted the ban on 1 January 1982 could it be seen again on the European stages. The 1950 French film version by Max Ophuls (*La Ronde*), a generally acknowledged masterpiece, was also banned in New York State, and it was not until 1954 that the U.S. Supreme Court overturned the ban.

While the turn of the century was a time of economic boom and significant cultural and scientific achievements, it also was one of rising anti-Semitism. During the 1870s and 1880s, emancipated and assimilated Jews had gained power and influence under Austrian Liberalism; between the 1860s and 1890s, they held positions in high finance, the professions, and the liberal press, at a time when the press was the only mass medium. By 1900, however, the political power of the liberals came to an end with the election of the anti-Semitic Karl Lueger as mayor of Vienna. Leon Botstein has formulated the atmosphere of the Jewish situation in 1990 Vienna as follows:

Anti-Semitism emerged as a virulent racist prejudice, justified by political ideology directed at eradicating the ills of capitalism, liberalism and modernity. The successful identification, in Viennese politics, of the Jews with these presumed sources of all social, moral and political evil provided an explosive political formula that would serve later as a model for the Nazis.

Arthur Schnitzler, who was Jewish himself, was keenly aware of the spreading anti-Semitism, and this topic occurred frequently in his poetic work, diaries, and letters. In his novel *Der Weg ins Freie* (1908; *The Road into the Open*), he describes the problems facing the Jewish intellectuals at that time: whether to assimilate or to adhere to the Jewish faith and customs, and how to respond to the anti-Semitic ressentiment of the Austrians, which was often hidden underneath their masks of gaiety. For the Jews there was no easy answer, and the title of the novel is ironical since there is no road to the open.

The Jewish question is also treated in his most powerful social play, *Professor Bernhardi* (1912; *Professor Bernhardi*). The title character, the director of a hospital, refuses a priest, who is called in by a Catholic nurse, access to a dying young woman who is in a state of euphoria and who is not aware of her condition. Bernhardi, a highly successful Jewish physician, is the target of anti-Semitic prejudices, fueled by attacks made upon him by the Catholic Church. Censors, who considered this work to be inflammatory, did not give permission to have it performed in 1913; it was staged only after the disintegration of the monarchy in 1918, but it has been shown repeatedly all over Europe and in the United States since then.

One of the recurring themes in Schnitzler's plays and narratives is the coexistence of different value systems; this idea is similar to Nietzsche's perspectivism, which argues that a human being is not an *individuum* but a *dividuum*. In this sense Schnitzler lets the title character in his *Casanovas Heimfahrt* (1918; *Casanova's Homecoming*) say: "Had he not learned a thousand times that in the soul of all truly vital persons, discrepant and even apparently hostile elements may coexist in perfect harmony." This is echoed in Schnitzler's posthumously published autobiography *Jugend in Wien* (1968; *My Youth in Vienna*): "Feelings and understanding may sleep under the same roof, but they run their own completely separate households in the human soul." In one of his often performed plays, *Das weite Land* (1911; *Undiscovered Country*), Friedrich Horeiter asks the hotel director Aigner why he had cheated on his wife. Aigner's answer is:

Why have I betrayed her? . . . Haven't you ever thought what a strange uncharted country is human behavior? So many contradictions find room in us—love and deceit . . . loyalty and betrayal . . . worshipping one woman, yet longing for another, or several others. We try to bring order into our lives as best as we can; but that very order has something unnatural about it. The natural condition is always chaos. Yes, Hofreiter, the soul . . . is an undiscovered country as the poet once said . . . .

Genia, Hofreiter's wife, whose faithfulness gives her unfaithful husband a guilty conscience, subsequently has a short-lived affair, and Hofreiter duels with her young lover and kills him. Schnitzler shows here the hypocritical nature of the duel, which often was carried out for personal reasons under the guise of preserving honor.

The absurdity of the duel is also depicted in his play *Fink und Fliederbusch* (1917). One journalist, writing under two different names for a conservative paper as well as a liberal one, challenges his alter ego to a fictitious duel. This situation portrays not only the emptiness of the prevailing honor code but also attacks the members of the media who use their power for the purpose of influencing popular opinion.

One of Schnitzler's best-known types is the *süße Mädel*, the so-called sweet girl, "a loving and frivolous young thing from the outskirts [of Vienna] who, during the flower of her youth, seeks pleasurable experience with the young men of better social class and then, in maturity, marries a workman—a good man" (Urbach). Her great attraction is that she is readily sexually accessible—one cannot get involved in a duel in such a relationship—and she does not make great demands on the young man to whom she belongs for a limited time. Christine in *Liebelei* (1895; *Light-O'-Love*) is considered a *süße Mädel* by her two-timing lover Fritz; she knows of the impermanence of her relationship, but this does not prevent her from falling in love with him. He betrays this love by having an affair with a married woman and, having been found out, gets killed in a duel with the husband, while Christine very likely will end her own life.

Women at Schnitzler's time had very little opportunity to construct and live their own existence. This is shown in the life of Therese, the title character in his novel *Therese: Chronik eines Frauenlebens* (1928; *Theresa: The Chronicle of a Woman's Life*). Her experiences are described in a rather episodic way, showing her in a variety of situations. Her social position is that of governess, but people treat her more like a maid or a *süße Mädel*, an easily accessible sex object. Schnitzler offers here a look behind the scenes of bourgeois respectability and illustrates the fragile nature of the morally disintegrating society.

Schnitzler's works are written for a specific time, but they are also timeless. He wrote in and for the period of the Austro-Hungarian monarchy and the First Republic, describing the attitudes, beliefs, prejudices, and political and social conditions of his time. In this sense he is a chronicler of his era, and his oeuvre can be read as an expression of a given sociohistorical era, not only by academics, but also by the general public. Schnitzler, however, is also describing our own *fin de siècle*, since he masterfully illuminates the conflicting nature of the multifaceted self. He is one of the most esteemed writers in Austria, and his plays are continuously performed not only on Austrian stages but all over Europe, as well as the United States. A large number of his works have been turned into films, others are shown on television, and some prose works have been dramatized for the same purpose. The many books, articles, feuilletons, magazine articles, monographs, and dissertations written about him and his literary productions testify to his status as an eminent writer who will be of interest to people of all ages and social classes.

GERD K. SCHNEIDER

See also Austria: Late Habsburg Literature in Vienna; Jung Wien

Biography

Born in Vienna, Austria, 15 May 1862. Medical student at the University of Vienna, 1879–85, M.D. 1885; medical intern, 1885–88; assistant at Allgemeine Poliklinik, 1888–93; private practice from 1893. Bauernfeld Prize, 1899, 1903; Grillparzer Prize, 1908; Raimund Prize, 1914; Vienna Volkstheater Prize, 1920. Died 21 October 1931.

Selected Works

Collections

Gesammelte Werke, 7 vols., 1912; enlarged edition, 9 vols., 1922
Gesammelte Werke, edited by Robert O. Weiss, 5 vols., 1961–67
Plays and Stories, edited and translated by Egon Schwarz, 1982
Illusion and Reality: Plays and Stories, translated by Paul F. Dvorak, 1986
Three Late Plays, translated by G.J. Weinberger, 1992
Paracelsus and Other One-Act Plays, translated by G.J. Weinberger, 1995
The Final Plays, translated by G.J. Weinberger, 1996

Plays

Anatol (seven one-act plays produced as a cycle, 1910), 1893; as *Anatol*, translated by Frank Marcus, 1982
Liebelei (produced 1895), 1896; as *Light-O'-Love*, translated by Bayard Quincy Morgan, *The Drama*, August 1912; as *The Game of Love*, translated by Carl Mueller in *Masterpieces of the Modern Central European Theatre*, edited by Robert W. Corrigan, 1967; as *Love Games*, translated by Charles Osborne, in *The Round Dance and Other Plays*, 1982; as *Flirtations*, translated by Arthur S. Wensinger and Clinton J. Atkinson, in *Plays and Stories*, 1982; as *Dalliance*, translated and adapted by Tom Stoppard, 1986
Der grüne Kakadu, Paracelsus, Die Gefährtin, 1899; as *The Green Cockatoo*, translated by G.J. Weinberger, in *Paracelsus and Other One-Act Plays*, 1995
Reigen (scenes 4–6 produced 1903; complete production in Budapest, in Hungarian, 1912; in German, 1920), 1903; as *Hands Around: A Cycle of Ten Dialogues* ("Authorized" translation), 1920; as *La Ronde*, translated by Eric Bentley, in *From the Modern Repertoire*, 1955; translated by Hans Weigert and Patricia Newhall, in *Masters of the Modern Drama*, edited by Haskell M. Bock and Robert G. Shedd, 1962; translated by Carl Mueller, in *Masterpieces of the Modern Central European Theatre*, edited by Robert W. Corrigan, 1967; translated by Sue Davies and adapted by John Barton, 1982; as *Dance of Love*, 1965; as *The Round Dance*, translated by Charles Osborne, in *The Round Dance and Other Plays*, 1982
Der Einsame Weg (produced 1904), 1904; as *The Lonely Way*, translated by Edwin Björkman, 1904; as *The Lonely Road*, 1985
Die Verwandlung des Pierrot, 1908; as *The Transformation of Pierrot*, translated by G.J. Weinberger, in *Paracelsus and Other One-Act Plays*, 1995
Komtesse Mizzi; oder, Der Familentag (produced 1909), 1909; as *Countess Mizzie; or, the Family Reunion*, translated by Edwin Björkman and revised by Caroline Wellbery, in *Plays and Stories*, edited by Egon Schwarz, 1982
Der Schleier der Pierrette, music by Ernst von Dohnányi (produced 1910), 1910; as *The Veil of Pierrette*, translated by G.J. Weinberger, in *Paracelsus and Other One-Act Plays*, 1995
Das weite Land (produced 1911), 1911; as *Undiscovered Country*, translated by Tom Stoppard, 1980
Professor Bernhardi (produced 1912), 1912; edited by Martin Swales, 1972; translated by Louis Borell and Ronald Adam, in *Famous Plays of 1936*, 1936
Komödie der Verführung (produced 1924), 1924; as *Seduction Comedy*, translated by G.J. Weinberger, in *Three Late Plays*, 1992
Der Gang zum Weiher (produced 1931), 1926; as *The Way to the Pond*, translated by G.J. Weinberger, in *Three Late Plays*, 1992
Im Spiel der Sommerlüfte (produced 1929), 1930; as *In the Play of Summer Breezes*, translated by G.J. Weinberger, in *The Final Plays*, 1996

Fiction

Sterben, 1895; as "Dying," translated by Harry Zohn, in *The Little Comedy and Other Stories*, 1977

Der Blinde Geronimo und sein Bruder, 1900; as *The Blind Man's Brother*, translated by Bernard Muddiman, 1913; as *Blind Geronimo and His Brother*, translated by Harry Steinhauer, 1961

Leutnant Gustl, 1901; as *None but the Brave*, translated by Richard L. Simon, 1926; as *Lieutenant Gustl*, translated by Richard L. Simon, 1993

Der Weg ins Freie, 1908; as *The Road into the Open*, translated by Roger Byers, 1923

Der Tod des Junggesellen, 1908; as "The Bachelor's Death," translated by Richard and Clara Winston, in *German Stories and Tales*, 1954

Casanovas Heimfahrt, 1918; as *Casanova's Homecoming*, translated by Eden and Cedar Paul, 1921

Fräulein Else, 1924; translated by Robert A. Simon, 1925; translated by F.H. Lyon, 1925

Die Frau des Richters, 1925; as "The Judge's Wife," translated by Peter Bauland, in *The Little Comedy and Other Stories*, 1977

Traumnovelle, 1926; as "Fridolin and Albertine," translated by Erich Posselt, in *Vanity Fair*, October 1926; as *Rhapsody: A Dream Novel*, translated by Otto P. Schinnerer, 1927

Spiel im Morgengrauen, 1926; as *Daybreak*, translated by William A. Drake, 1927

Flucht in die Finsternis, 1931; as *Flight into Darkness*, translated by William A. Drake, 1931

Further Reading

Arnold, Heinz L., editor, *Arthur Schnitzler*, Munich: Edition Text und Kritik, 1998

Fliedl, Konstanze, *Arthur Schnitzler: Poetik der Erinnerung*, Vienna: Böhlau, 1997

Botstein, Leon, "The Jews of Vienna in the Age of Franz Joseph," *New York Times Book Review* (14 January 1990)

Janz, Rolf-Peter, and Klaus Laermann, *Arthur Schnitzler: Zur Diagnose des Wiener Bürgertums im Fin de Siècle*, Stuttgart: Metzler, 1977

Lindken, Hans-Ulrich, *Arthur Schnitzler: Aspekte und Akzente, Materialien zu Leben und Werk*, Frankfurt and New York: Lang, 1984

Liptzin, Solomon, *Arthur Schnitzler*, Riverside, California: Ariadne Press, 1932; revised edition, 1995

Perlmann, Michaela L., *Arthur Schnitzler*, Stuttgart: Metzler, 1987

Rey, William H., *Arthur Schnitzler: Die späte Prosa als Gipfel seines Schaffens*, Berlin: Schmidt, 1968

Scheible, Hartmut, editor, *Arthur Schnitzler mit Selbstbildnissen und Bilddokumenten*, Reinbek bei Hamburg: Rowohlt, 1976; revised edition, 1994

Schneider, Gerd K., *Die Rezeption von Arthur Schnitzlers "Reigen," 1897–1994*, Riverside, California: Ariadne Press, 1995

Schnitzler, Heinrich, et al., *Arthur Schnitzler: Sein Leben, sein Werk, seine Zeit*, Frankfurt: Fischer, 1981

Schnitzler, Olga, *Spiegelbild der Freundschaft*, Salzburg: Residenz, 1962

Schorske, Carl E., "Politics and the Psyche," in *Fin de Siècle Vienna: Politics and Culture*, New York: Vintage, 1981

Swales, Martin, *Arthur Schnitzler: A Critical Study*, Oxford: Clarendon Press, 1971

Tax, Petrus W., and Richard H. Lawson, editors, *Arthur Schnitzler and His Age: Intellectual and Artistic Currents*, Bonn: Bouvier, 1984

Urbach, Reinhard, *Arthur Schnitzler*, Velber bei Hannover: Friedrich, 1968

——, *Schnitzler Kommentar zu den erzählenden Schriften und dramatischen Werken*, Munich: Winkler, 1974

Wagner, Renate, *Arthur Schnitzler: Eine Biographie*, Vienna and New York: Molden, 1981

Weinzierl, Ulrich, *Arthur Schnitzler: Lieben, Träumen, Sterben*, Frankfurt: Fischer, 1994

Fräulein Else 1924
Novella by Arthur Schnitzler

Arthur Schnitzler wrote two novellas in the interior monologue style: *Leutnant Gustl* (1901; translated as *None but the Brave* and *Lieutenant Gustl*) and *Fräulein Else*. In the latter work he shows the psychological dilemma of a 19-year-old, beautiful, virginal woman who is asked by her mother to obtain 30,000 gulden (later increased to 50,000) from the rich art dealer Dorsday to save her father, a Viennese lawyer of questionable reputation, from going to jail. Dorsday, a friend of the family also residing at the same spa, is willing to give her the money provided she allows him to see her naked body for 15 minutes. Else, torn between dutiful, filial love for her father and her own sexual desires, between the pleasure she experiences when men look at her and the shame she feels at the same time, finds a solution to her problem by covering her naked body with only a coat, which she lets slip while she walks down the hotel steps to the vestibule, showing herself naked to Dorsday as well as to the other hotel guests. She then loses consciousness and is carried to her room, where she ends her life by taking a fatal dose of Veronal. Dying, she experiences a vision of uniting with the entire world, including her father.

There are primarily three modes of interpreting this work: the oldest one is based on the Freudian model, a more modern one considers Else a victim of society, and the third one focuses on the musical notations that appear in the text. In the psychoanalytic, or Freudian, reading Else is a hysterical autoerotic neurotic, a narcissistic exhibitionist deriving pleasure from seeing her own beautiful body. Her libido is not only returned to her own ego but also attaches itself to her father, whom she desires. Else, according to this approach, suffers from the Electra complex, and Dorsday is a father surrogate. In her death she achieves the desired sexual union with her father. This perspective is founded on Schnitzler's professional status as a psychologist, a contemporary of Freud, whom he met a few times.

The Freudian interpretation was felt by some scholars to be too one-sided; it considered neither the rich inner life of the heroine nor the author's criticism of the fin de siècle bourgeois society of Imperial Vienna. Else not only has strong sexual desires, but at the same time she feels guilty and shameful about them. Also, Dorsday (as Rey points out) can be understood as a representative of the late-bourgeois capitalistic society, which lives according to the market forces of supply and demand; to Dorsday, everything has a price and can be bought, including Else. Else, by baring herself, fulfills her part of the bargain so that Dorsday will pay the required amount for her father's legal liberation; she exhibits herself, however, on her own terms. Else, who stands alone and has no one in whom to confide, exposes not only herself but, at the same time, the superficial hypocritical value system of society, which she feels is to blame for her death: "The murderers!—They're all murderers. . . . They all murdered me and say nothing about it. They'll say, 'She committed suicide.' All of you killed me. All of you killed me. All of you. All of you."

At the dramatic high point of this novella, Else's tension-filled moments before and during the act of disrobing, a pianist plays excerpts from Robert Schumann's piano cycle *Carnaval: Scènes mignonnes sur quatre notes,* opus 9, and three musical notations appear in the text (they are missing from the first publication). Schnitzler assumed that his audience was able to "read" the musical score; Schumann himself had integrated verbal and musical language by inserting into the musical score of *Carnaval* the four notes of the title to be read: *ASCH,* the hometown of Schumann's love Ernestine von Fricken and also the only musical letters contained in his own name. The inclusion of the musical score in *Fräulein Else* shows both the psychological tension of the heroine and the unmasking of society. The music reveals the inner life of Else more subtly than words could accomplish; by "reading" the increasing frequency of the natural sign, the simultaneous legato and staccato, and the crescendo and decrescendo markings, the conflicting emotional forces of Else are more subtly underscored than words could achieve. The title of the piano work can be associated with hiding one's true face: *carnaval* is a masked ball, and Else wears a mask that hides her true feelings from the outside world. At the end the masks are taken off: Else's coat falls when she hears excerpts from *Reconnaissance* ("recognition"), as Schumann had titled this segment.

Fräulein Else, filmed in 1929 with Elisabeth Bergner in the title role, is a masterpiece within the works of this Viennese author. Because Schnitzler was a writer and a physician-psychologist, residing in Vienna at the same time as Freud, this first-person narrative can be read as a psychoanalytic case study. Indeed, in the United States, one critic referred to this work as a study in "morbid psychology." The novella can also be interpreted as a condemnation of a society in which illusion is more important than reality and truth, and where old traditional humanistic values have been replaced with capitalistic ones. The parallels existing between the music and the written text can be used to support both approaches.

GERD K. SCHNEIDER

Editions
First edition: *Fräulein Else,* Berlin: Paul Zsolnay, 1924
Translation: *Fräulein Else: A Novel,* translated by Robert A. Simon, New York: Simon and Schuster, 1925

Further Reading
Aurnhammer, Achim, "Selig, wer in Träumen stirbt: Das literarisierte Leben und Sterben von *Fräulein Else,*" *Euphorion* 77 (1983)
Bareikis, Robert, "Arthur Schnitzler's *Fräulein Else*: A Freudian Novelle?" *Literature and Psychology* 19, no. 1 (1969)
Buhler, Arnim-Thomas, *Arthur Schnitzlers "Fräulein Else": Ansätze zu einer psychoanalytischen Interpretation,* Wetzlar: Kletsmeier, 1995
Green, Jonathan D., "Music in Literature: Arthur Schnitzler's *Fräulein Else,*" in *Collage,* edited by Jeannine Parisier Plottel, New York: New York Literary Forum, 1983
Hoppe, Klaus D., "Psychoanalytic Remarks on Schnitzler's *Fräulein Else,*" *Journal of the International Arthur Schnitzler Research Association* 3, no. 1 (1964)
Huber, Martin, "Optische Musikzitate als Psychogramm in Arthur Schnitzlers *Fräulein Else,*" in *Text und Musik: Musikalische Zeichen im narrativen und ideologischen Funktionszusammenhang ausgewählter Erzähltexte des 20. Jahrhunderts,* Frankfurt and New York: Lang, 1992
Lerch-Schumacher, Barbara, "'Ich bin nicht mütterlich': Zur Psychopoetik der Hysterie in Schnitzlers *Fräulein Else,*" *Text und Kritik: Arthur Schnitzler,* no. 138/139 (April 1998)
Neuse, Werner, "'Erlebte Rede' und 'Innerer Monolog' in den erzählenden Schriften Arthur Schnitzlers," *Publications of the Modern Language Association of America* 49 (1934)
Oswald, Victor A., Jr., and Veronica Pinter Mindess, "Schnitzler's *Fräulein Else* and the Psychoanalytic Theory of Neuroses," *Germanic Review* 26, no. 4 (1951)
Raymond, Cathy, "Masked in Music: Hidden Meaning in Schnitzler's *Fräulein Else,*" *Monatshefte* 85, no. 2 (1993)
Rey, William H., "*Fräulein Else,*" in *Arthur Schnitzler: Die späte Prosa als Gipfel seines Schaffens,* Berlin: Schmidt, 1968
Schmidt-Dengler, Wendolin, "Inflation der Werte und Gefühle: Zu A. Schnitzlers *Fräulein Else,*" in *Akten des Internationalen Symposiums "Arthur Schnitzler und seine Zeit,"* edited by Giuseppe Farese, Berne and New York: Lang, 1985
Schneider, Gerd K., "Ton- und Schriftsprache in Schnitzler's *Fräulein Else,*" *Modern Austrian Literature* 2, no. 3 (1969)

Professor Bernhardi 1912
Play by Arthur Schnitzler

Professor Bernhardi revealed Arthur Schnitzler to be at the height of his dramatic powers, capable of producing a full-length play in addition to using the vignette principle of construction with which he had established his reputation and notoriety in such earlier works as *Liebelei* (1896; *Light-O'-Love*), *Reigen* (1903; *Hands Around*), and the one-act play *Anatol* (1893).

In *Professor Bernhardi,* a minor incident provides the catalyst for a merciless exposure of the hypocrisy and corruption of the Habsburg monarchy in Vienna at the beginning of the 20th century. Professor Bernhardi, the director and driving force behind a successful private clinic, tries to prevent a Roman Catholic priest from visiting a dying patient. She is the victim of an illegal abortion, but in a state of drug-induced euphoria she is unaware of either her condition or her imminent death. Bernhardi is motivated simply by the wish to spare his patient the anguish that the priest's presence and his inevitable insistence on confession and repentance would cause. The dying, abandoned girl is of no social status and her death unavoidable, so her run-of-the-mill fate is apparently of no particular consequence. Yet Bernhardi is Jewish, and thus the incident rapidly develops into a major political scandal. Conservative and anti-Semitic parties within Austria seize upon the perceived insult to the Catholic Church, regarding it as an assault upon Christian society and as further evidence of Jewish erosion of Catholic and Austrian values.

Bernhardi's initial insouciance makes light of the affair, but the pace of events, timed with the dramatic assuredness of a writer at his best, soon takes the incident out of Bernhardi's control and exposes him to the charge of political naïveté. The clinic's board of patrons resigns, the incident is the subject of hostile questions in Parliament, and the press and senior political figures are drawn into the issue.

Once the financial future of the clinic becomes threatened by the withdrawal of patronage, even Bernhardi's closest medical colleagues break rank along political and religious lines. Schnitzler's mastery of stagecraft is demonstrated in the way in which he introduces and establishes the characters of the host of medical men around Bernhardi. (The rivalries and the anti-Semitism within the medical profession were keenly understood by Schnitzler from his own medical days and from the treatment of his father, whose personal experience as a doctor of professional animosity and jealousy provided much of the material for the play.) The large cast of fellow doctors is delineated not so much by any action they take as by their language. It is ironic that Schnitzler should have received harsh critical treatment from Karl Kraus, for Schnitzler possesses Kraus's unfailing ear for the hollowness of language in the hands of demagogues. Humane language quickly gives way, as the tension rises, to grotesque rhetorical contortions. Empty phrases, the mindless shibboleths of the popular press and convoluted expressions of nationalist fervor, fail to disguise naked racism and gut prejudices. The nature of language is explored most tellingly in the unctuous figure of Professor Flint, the minister of education, whose political flexibility acts as a foil to Bernhardi's dogged but unpolitical resolve. Initially a declared supporter of Bernhardi, Flint apparently changes side halfway through his own address to Parliament on the affair.

Bernhardi is too disgusted by his opponents to wish to challenge them at a political level, and even when he is sentenced to a short term of imprisonment for insulting religion, he rejects the possibility of an appeal. His position initially suggests a nobility and incorruptibility of character, as does his refusal to follow the advice to appoint, as a placating gesture, a Christian but less talented doctor to his clinic in preference to a far more talented Jew. It is only when we appreciate this focus on Bernhardi's character—rather than on his situation—that we can understand Schnitzler's designation of the play as a comedy. At first sight, there is little to laugh about. Anti-Semitism, bigotry, corruption, and political connivance, as well as the fate of the girl, which triggers off the whole course of events, are deadly serious matters, yet it was not Schnitzler's primary purpose, as he told a correspondent, to write a political play (*Tendenzstück*); instead, he wanted to offer a comedy of character. Bernhardi is not a truly tragic figure, because his well-developed sense of irony holds him back from complete commitment to his own argument. It is this inconsistency, this disdain about fully entering the arena for the cause he espouses—a trait to be found in many of Hofmannsthal's characters—that renders him comic. But it also suggests the flaw in Schnitzler's genius. He offers in *Professor Bernhardi* two currencies, and an audience must choose the one in which it wishes to deal. It can see the play in its social context, with Bernhardi as the victim of clerical intriguing and as "a kind of medical Dreyfus," to quote one of the characters. By contrast, the audience can also see the play as the dilemma of the individual who is dragged down into a corrupt world for which he is ill-prepared, despite his best intentions to do good.

The play is firmly established in the repertoire of the contemporary German and Austrian stage. With hindsight, an audience can appreciate the ultimate and dreadful fulfilment of the anti-Semitism articulated in the play. In its construction, it is deeply indebted to classical Greek drama. The principal events take place offstage: the death of the girl, the resignation of the clinic's patrons, the uproar in Parliament, the court scene, Bernhard's guilty sentence, and his triumphant release from prison are all reported rather than shown. The play's history was as turbulent as the reception of Schnitzler's erotic plays. *Professor Bernhardi* fell victim to the censors within the Austrian Empire, and productions in Vienna and Bratislava were banned. Its first performance was in Berlin in 1912, where the play's alleged anti-Catholic stance would not have been uncongenial to a Prussian audience. The first Austrian performance had to wait until the collapse of the monarchy in 1918.

ANTHONY BUSHELL

Editions

First edition: in *Die Theaterstücke*, Band 1–4, Berlin: Fischer, 1912
Critical editions: *Gesammelte Werke: Die dramatischen Werke*, Band II, Frankfurt am Main: Fischer Verlag, 1962; edited by Martin Swales, Oxford and New York: Pergamon, 1972
Translation: *Professor Bernhardi*, translated by Louis Borell and Ronald Adam, in *Famous Plays of 1936*, London: Gollancz, 1936

Further Reading

Blickle, Peter, "Die Einlösung subversiven Wirkungspotentials: Die Theaterskandale um Arthur Schnitzlers *Professor Bernhardi* und Rolf Hochhuths *Stellvertreter*," *New German Review* 10 (1994)
Melchinger, Siegfried, "Das Jüdische in *Professor Bernhardi*," *Theater heute* 5, no. 12 (1964)
Urbach, Reinhard, *Arthur Schnitzler*, Velber bei Hannover: Friedrich, 1968
Williams, Cedric E., *The Broken Eagle: The Politics of Austrian Literature from Empire to Anschluss*, London: Elek, and New York: Barnes and Noble, 1974
Yates, W.E., "The Tendentious Reception of *Professor Bernhardi*: Documentation in Schnitzler's Collection of Press Cuttings," *Austrian Studies* 1 (1990)

Arnold Franz Walter Schoenberg 1874–1951

Best known as a composer, Arnold Schoenberg also wrote technical treatises on music; published and unpublished essays, mostly on music, but also on public issues, including Jewish affairs; and lyric and dramatic texts for music, as well as a play.

Schoenberg's prose is marked by witty wordplays, puns, metaphors, aphorisms, and tones ranging from the polemical and the dryly ironic to the impassioned and the exalted. After emigrating to the United States in 1933, he began speaking and writing in

English. Like most Viennese intellectuals of the time, Schoenberg admired Karl Kraus's vigorous and precise German. A selection of Schoenberg's essays, *Style and Idea,* appeared a year before his death; the second edition (1975) is greatly enlarged.

Schoenberg's lyric and dramatic texts exhibit the evolution of his thinking and art. A poem by Richard Dehmel furnished the program for *Verklärte Nacht* (1899; Transfigured Night), as did a play by Maurice Maeterlinck for *Pelleas und Melisande* (1903). The *Gurrelieder* set texts written in 1869–70 by Jens Peter Jacobsen. All three texts are tales of love, jealousy, and death in an evocative natural setting. After 1907, Schoenberg associated with Expressionist artists who carried these themes and emotions to an extreme. Personal experience supported his aesthetic evolution. In 1908, his wife eloped with his friend, the painter Richard Gerstl. She eventually returned, and, shortly after, Gerstl committed suicide. The trauma lent a powerful concreteness to the compelling force of Schoenberg's artistic ideas. At his suggestion, the poet and doctor Marie Pappenheim supplied the text for his musical monodrama *Erwartung* (1909; Expectation). It presents an intense and multilayered emotional instant in the form of the interior monologue of a woman who wanders into a forest seeking her lover but comes across his bloody corpse.

Fragmentary, quickly changing, intense, and obsessive emotions mark Oskar Kokoschka's short drama *Mörder, Hoffnung der Frauen* (1909; Murderer, Hope of Women). But Schoenberg insisted that an independent path led him to his own drama, *Die glückliche Hand* (1910; The Golden Touch). Instead of the emotional experience of a hysterical woman, it presents the emotional experience of the creative man. In 1911, Schoenberg began corresponding with the painter Wassily Kandinsky, and was thus recognized as part of the international movement of Expressionism. But he was already moving to a new phase by seeing in the torments of the individual soul the symptoms of wider cultural realities. In 1912–14, he made notes for a vast symphony that would draw on Balzac's Swedenborgian novella *Seraphita* and the late plays of August Strindberg. In a quest for the meaning of life, the work would record the "insufficiency of the bourgeois God" in a "death-dance of principles" and would culminate in a modern form of prayer and a faith fit for the skeptical "disillusioned one." In this oratorio, "modern man, having passed through materialism, socialism, and anarchy and, despite having been an atheist, still having in him some residue of ancient faith . . . wrestles with God . . . and finally succeeds in finding God and becoming religious. Learning to pray!" Much of this material was incorporated into *Die Jakobsleiter* (1917; Jacob's Ladder), for which he never finished the music.

Schoenberg thus participated in the religious quest of his era, which was shared by thinkers as diverse as Martin Buber and Ludwig Wittgenstein. His quest took a decisive turn in 1922, when he went with his family for a summer vacation near Salzburg and was told that Jews were not welcome. Like Freud, he responded to anti-Semitism by reconnecting with his Jewish tradition. He came to the view that the Jews' identity lies in their having been chosen to preserve "a singular Idea," namely, that God is "unrepresentable" (unvorstellbar).

In a prescient play, *Der biblische Weg* (composed 1926–27; *The Biblical Way*), he explored the tension between this religious idea and the political and social realities of refounding a state for the Jews. He took up the same theme in the libretto for his unfinished opera *Moses und Aron* (1928), in which the one who grasps the idea (Moses) clashes with the one who tries to express and communicate it to the people (Aron). He restated this tension in later works, notably a series of "Modern Psalms," which were left unfinished at his death. The tension, however, cannot be resolved. The idea demands expression, but every expression risks idolatry and materialism. Schoenberg insisted that modern man's experience must be expressed in modern, not traditional language. His style in these works reflects the intellectual nature of the theme, but it is grasped so intently, so much with every drop of his artistic life's blood, that it releases an astonishing dramatic and emotional power.

Interpreters of Viennese modernism such as Carl Schorske, Alan Janik, and Stephen Toulmin see here an example of the force that drove innovation in many cultural fields from 1890–1940: namely, the quest to develop, as much by logical extension as by abrupt innovation, new means of representation suited to diagnosing and then responding to the forms and pressures of modern life that rendered outmoded a traditional way of life and its associated artistic conventions and styles of representation. Schoenberg, however, insisted that modern man faces not just a cultural but a spiritual and, specifically, religious crisis, which he can understand and resolve only if he follows "the biblical way."

Schoenberg's music is the most influential in the century, but his views about art and the religious crisis at the core of modernity are still neglected. This is due in part to the long delay in the appearance of his most important works. *Moses und Aron* was first performed in 1954, and *The Biblical Way* was first published in 1994. In Thomas Mann's novel *Doktor Faustus,* the central character is a composer whose music is described in terms that evoke Schoenberg. The composer was infuriated at the use Mann made of his ideas and blamed his former student, Theodor Adorno (Wiesengrund), for having misinterpreted him to Mann. Schoenberg was eventually reconciled with Mann, but never with Adorno—ironically enough, since Schoenberg's music is the central example for Adorno of how art can resist assimilation to the oppressive structures of capitalist bourgeois life.

DONALD MARSHALL

See also Der Blaue Reiter

Biography
Born in Vienna, Austria, 13 September 1874. Baptized in a Protestant sect, 1889; service in the Austrian army, 1915; composition teacher at the Stern Conservatory, Berlin, 1902–3, 1911–14; cofounder with Alexander von Zemlinsky, of the Vereinigung Schaffender Tonkünstler, Vienna, 1904; founder of the Verein für musikalische Privataufführungen, 1918; composition teacher at the Prussian Academy of Arts, Berlin, 1926–33; returned to Jewish faith and emigrated to the United States, 1933–34; taught composition at the Malkin Conservatory, Boston, Massachusetts, 1933; private teaching in Hollywood, California, 1934–36; lecturer, University of Southern California, Los Angeles, 1935; naturalized citizen of the United States, 1941; professor of composition, University of California, Los Angeles, 1936–44. President of the International Mahler League, 1920–21; honorary president, Israel Academy of Music, 1951. Died in Los Angeles, California, 13 July 1951.

Selected Works

Treatise, Essays, and Literary Works
Harmonielehre, 1911; revised edition, 1921; abridged version as

Theory of Harmony, 1948; complete version, translated by Roy E. Carter, 1978

Der biblische Weg (written 1926–27); as *The Biblical Way,* translated by Moshe Lazar, *Journal of the Arnold Schoenberg Institute* 17, vols. 1–2, 1994

Schöpferische Konfessionen, 1921; edited by Willi Reich, 1964

Style and Idea, 1950; enlarged edition, 1975

Texts for Music

Die glückliche Hand (one-act drama, 1910), op. 18; translated as *The Fortunate Hand*

Die Jakobsleiter (oratorio, 1917)

"Unertrinnbar," "Du sollst nicht, du musst," in *Four Pieces for Mixed Chorus* (1925), op. 27

"Am Scheideweg," "Vielseitigkeit," "Der neue Klassizismus," in *Three Satires* (1925), op. 28

Moses und Aron (libretto for opera, 1928)

"Hemmung," "Das Gesetz," "Ausdrucksweise," "Glück," "Landesknechte," "Verbundenheit," in *Six Pieces for Male Chorus A Cappella* (1929–30), op. 35

Kol Nidre (English text adapted from traditional prayer, 1938), op. 39

A Survivor from Warsaw (based on a report by a survivor, 1947), op. 46

Moderner Psalm (1950), op. 50c

Von Heute auf Morgen (in collaboration with Gertrud Schoenberg, 1929), op. 32

Further Reading

Christensen, Jean, and Jesper Christensen, *From Arnold Schoenberg's Literary Legacy: A Catalog of Neglected Items,* Warren, Michigan: Harmonie Park Press, 1988

Janik, Allan, and Stephen Toulmin, *Wittgenstein's Vienna,* New York: Simon and Schuster, and London: Weidenfeld and Nicolson, 1973

Journal of the Arnold Schoenberg Institute (1976–)

Kallir, Jane, *Arnold Schoenberg's Vienna,* New York: Rizzoli, 1984

Reich, Willi, *Arnold Schoenberg: A Critical Biography,* translated by Leo Black, Harlow: Longman, 1971

Ringer, Alexander L., *Arnold Schoenberg: The Composer as Jew,* Oxford: Clarendon Press, 1990

Rosen, Charles, *Arnold Schoenberg,* New York: Viking Press, 1975

Rufer, Josef, *Das Werk Arnold Schoenbergs,* Kassel: Barenreiter, 1959; as *The Works of Arnold Schoenberg: A Catalogue of His Compositions, Writings, and Paintings,* translated by Dika Newlin, New York: Glencoe, 1962

Schorske, Carl E., *Fin-de-Siècle Vienna: Politics and Culture,* New York: Knopf, 1979

Smith, Joan Allen, *Schoenberg and His Circle: A Viennese Portrait,* New York: Schirmer Books, and London: Collier Macmillan, 1986

Stuckenschmidt, H.H., *Arnold Schoenberg,* Zurich: Atlantis, 1957; as *Schoenberg: His Life, World, and Work,* translated by Humphrey Searle, New York: Schirmer Books, 1977

Kurt Schwitters 1887–1948

Although he is known in North America primarily as a visual artist, Kurt Schwitters produced a substantial body of literary work. Schwitters's creative output is best considered as a single oeuvre. Indeed, it is not always easy to distinguish his literary work from his visual art. Much of his poetry is primarily visual or aural in impact, and some of his paper collages incorporate extensive textual material. Schwitters himself applied the term *Merz* to his entire output. A coinage derived from the middle syllable of the word *Kommerzbank* (appearing in one of his collages), *Merz* refers to Schwitters's particular approach to collage, using the discarded material and verbal trivia of everyday life to create works of visual and literary art.

Early in his career, Schwitters was closely associated with Herwarth Walden's Sturm group. His works were exhibited in the Sturm Gallery, and a number of his poems and prose works were published in the journal *Der Sturm.* Schwitters's early poetry falls clearly within the Expressionist tradition. It is strongly influenced by August Stramm: it displays the same compression of language and the same privileging of certain grammatical forms (such as verbs in the infinitive).

Beginning in 1919, Schwitters maintained a close association with members of the international Dada movement. Although he was never formally part of the Berlin Dada group, and according to some accounts was actually rejected for membership in the Club Dada because he and his art were too "bourgeois," Schwitters's visual and literary art show such a strong kinship with Dada that his *Merz* is generally considered the Hanover branch of the movement. Schwitters took part in Dada tours of Germany, Czechoslovakia, and the Netherlands with such artists and writers as Raoul Hausmann, Hannah Höch, and Theo van Doesburg. The journal *Merz,* which Schwitters edited from 1923 to 1932, published works by Doesburg, Hans Arp, Tristan Tzara, and other Dadaists in addition to his own writings and drawings.

Central to Schwitters's *Merz* writings is his collage technique. Just as any object from the physical realm might be incorporated into his paper collages or three-dimensional constructions, so anything from the realm of language might become material for his literature. Proverbs and banal sayings, fragments of advertisements and political pronouncements, signs posted in public places, and even numerals became material from which Schwitters crafted his literary works.

Of all Schwitters's literary output, it was the poem "An Anna Blume" (1919; translated by Schwitters as "Anna Blossom Has Wheels") that had the strongest public impact during the author's lifetime. This parody of a love poem was itself the object of countless parodies in the 1920s, and was translated into more languages than any other work by Schwitters. Anna Blume, like Cervantes's Dulcinea, is a woman ordinary to the point of banality who is elevated to near divinity by absurdly exaggerated praise. Her character recurs in many of Schwitters's works, a number of which were collected in volumes such as *Anna Blume: Dichtungen* (1919) and *Die Blume Anna* (1922).

Schwitters's visual and sound poetry was a major precursor of the concrete poetry of the 1960s and later. As early as 1919,

Schwitters created poems composed entirely of fragments of words, sequences of numerals, isolated syllables, letters arranged for purely visual effect, or even, in one instance, a single lower-case "i" (with instructions for reading aloud). One of his sources of income was his work in the advertising industry, where his innovative use of typography had a significant influence; Schwitters extended this experimental typography to his visual poetry and prose. Schwitters's most significant effort in the realm of aural literature was his *Ursonate* (1932). Basing his work on a few one-line phonetic poems by Raoul Hausmann, Schwitters developed this scanty material into one of the most extensive pieces of sound poetry ever created. Written in a rigorous sonata form in four movements and lasting about 30 minutes when read aloud, the *Ursonate* essentially erases the distinction between poetry and music.

Just as he pointedly undercut distinctions among literature, music, and visual art, Schwitters subverted the distinctions among the literary genres, so it is not always possible to distinguish his poetry from his prose fiction. For example, Schwitters's first major prose story, "Der Zwiebel" (1919; "The Onion"), is designated as "Merzgedicht 8" ("Merz Poem 8"). Like much of his prose, "The Onion" belongs to the tradition of the grotesque. The narrator tells the story of his own gruesome (and apparently voluntary) execution at the hands of a butcher, and his subsequent miraculous rebirth/reassembly. The story ends with the death of the king who had ordered the protagonist's slaughter—one of many references to the revolutionary events occurring in Germany at this time. Similarly set in a revolutionary context, "Ursachen und Beginn der grossen glorreichen Revolution in Revon" (1922; "Revolution: Causes and Outbreak of the Great and Glorious Revolution in Revon") is the longest surviving chapter of the fragmentary novel *Franz Müllers Drahtfrühling* (Franz Müller's Wire Spring). As in several of Schwitters's other works, this fragment depicts cataclysmic events resulting from absurdly trivial causes—the mere fact of a man standing immobile and an art critic commenting on this leads to a violent but ludicrous uprising in Revon (Hanover). Schwitters's fiction often satirizes single-minded characters obsessed with seemingly trivial phenomena. The protagonist of his longest prose work, the novella *Auguste Bolte: Ein Lebertran* (1923; *Augusta Bolte: A Liver Extract*), is fixated on two innocuous facts: she sees ten people walking in the same direction and she notices that some of the words in Schwitters's story rhyme. She sets out on a search for an explanation of the first phenomenon by developing a rigorous system for following the ten pedestrians, who divide into ever-smaller groups, pushing Auguste's method beyond the point of absurdity with increasingly disastrous yet hilarious results. Schwitters saw Auguste Bolte as a personification of the art critic, a figure who plays a major role in his fiction and essays of the 1920s. Much of this work is, like *Auguste Bolte*, highly self-referential; there are frequent allusions to a work's status as literature and to the author's other works. The use of eclectic typography in some of the fiction makes it a visual as well as a literary experience for the reader. In the fairy tale *Die Scheuche* (1925; The Scarecrow), created in collaboration with Doesburg and Kate Steinitz, the letters on the page actually become characters in the story.

Schwitters also left a substantial corpus of discursive prose writings on art, literature, and theater, as well as short plays and dramatic fragments. His conception of a *Merztheater* that would combine all art forms was consistent with the ideal of the *Gesamtkunstwerk* (total art work) advocated by some of his contemporaries; however, the Nazi takeover and the subsequent war prevented Schwitters from realizing these ideas in any major way. During his exile, Schwitters produced a body of work in English and even a few pieces in Norwegian. While his mastery of English was not strong, it was adequate to create literary collages that displayed his characteristic humor while poignantly reflecting the sorrow of exile and permanent separation from his wife, who had stayed behind in Germany. Schwitters's last major literary project was a collection of sound poems and pieces in English, *Pin* (1962), produced in collaboration with his former Dada colleague Raoul Hausmann, who by this time was writing in French and English.

Apart from the Anna Blume poems, Schwitters's literary works had little impact during his lifetime. However, his experiments with language, with the visual aspects of the printed word, and with dissolving distinctions among different art forms were influential in the 1960s and 1970s not only in the German-speaking world but also among members of the literary avant-garde throughout Europe, the United States, and Latin America. And in the waning years of the German Democratic Republic, Schwitters's seemingly apolitical sound poetry was read aloud to jazz accompaniment as a form of protest against the regime. A poem such as "Wand" (1922, "Wall"), with its sustained repetition of that single word, took on clearly political overtones in the context of post-1961 East Berlin.

TIMOTHY SHIPE

See also Dadaism

Biography

Born in Hannover, 20 June 1887. Studied art at the Kunstgewerbeschule, Hannover, 1908–9, and the Königliche Kunstakademie, Dresden, 1909–14; military service, March–June 1917; studied architecture at the Technische Hochschule Hannover, 1918–19; association with Herwarth Walden's Sturm group and with the international Dada movement, 1918–26; exhibited paintings and collages in the *Sturm* Gallery and other venues in Germany and abroad from 1918; edited and published the Journal *Merz*, 1923–32; worked on the *Merzbau*, a monumental installation piece in his house in Hannover, 1923–36; cofounded the advertising and design group Ring Neuer Werbegestalter and the artists' group Die Abstrakten Hannover, 1927; exile in Norway, 1937–40; held in internment camp for enemy aliens on Isle of Man, 1940–41; residence in London, 1941–45, and in Ambleside, Westmoreland, 1945–48. Died in Kendal, England, 8 January 1948.

Selected Works

Collections

Das literarische Werk, edited by Friedhelm Lach, 5 vols., 1973–81

Books

Anna Blume: Dichtungen, 1919; expanded edition, 1922
Memoiren Anna Blumes in Bleie: Eine leichtfassliche Methode zur Erlernung des Wahnsinns für Jederman, 1922
Die Blume Anna: Die neue Anna Blume, 1923
Auguste Bolte: Ein Lebertran, 1923; as *Augusta Bolte: A Liver Extract*, translated by Pierre Joris in *PPPPPP: Poems, Performance Pieces, Proses, Plays, Poetics*, 1993
Hahnepeter (with Kate Steinitz), 1924

Die Märchen vom Paradies (with Kate Steinitz), 1924
Die Scheuche (with Kate Steinitz and Theo van Doesburg), 1925
Die neue Gestaltung in der Typographie, 1926
Erstes Veilchenheft: Eine kleine Sammlung von Merz-Dichtungen aller Art, 1931
Ursonate, 1932
Pin (with Raoul Hausmann), 1962
Wir spielen, bis uns der Tod abholt: Briefe aus fünf Jahrzehnten, edited by Ernst Nündel, 1975
Kurt Schwitters und die "andere" Schweiz: Unveröffentlichte Briefe aus dem Exil, edited by Gerhard Schaub, 1998

Further Reading

Elderfield, John, *Kurt Schwitters*, London and New York: Thames and Hudson, 1985

Henzler, Harald, *Literatur an der Grenze zum Spiel: Eine Untersuchung zu Robert Walser, Hugo Ball, und Kurt Schwitters*, Würzburg: Königshausen und Neumann, 1992

Homayr, Ralph, *Montage als Kunstform: Zum literarischen Werk von Kurt Schwitters*, Opladen: Westdeutscher, 1991

Imm, Karsten, *Absurd und Grotesk: Zum Erzählwerk von Wilhelm Busch und Kurt Schwitters*, Bielefeld: Aisthesis, 1994

Kurt Schwitters Almanach, Hannover: Postskriptum, 1982–91 (annual)

Lach, Friedhelm, *Der Merz Künstler Kurt Schwitters*, Cologne: DuMont Schauberg, 1971

Last, Rex William, *German Dadaist Literature: Kurt Schwitters, Hugo Ball, Hans Arp*, New York: Twayne, 1973

Nündel, Ernst, *Kurt Schwitters: Mit Selbstzeugnissen und Bilddokumenten*, Reinbek bei Hamburg: Rowohlt, 1992

Scheffer, Bernd, *Anfänge experimenteller Literatur: Das literarische Werk von Kurt Schwitters*, Bonn: Bouvier, 1978

Schmalenbach, Werner, *Kurt Schwitters*, New York: Abrams, and London: Thames and Hudson, 1970

Spengemann, Christof, *Die Wahrheit über Anna Blume: Kritik der Kunst, Kritik der Kritik, Kritik der Zeit*, Hannover: Zweemann, 1920

Webster, Gwendolen, *Kurt Merz Schwitters: A Biographical Study*, Cardiff: University of Wales Press, 1997

Webster, Michael, *Reading Visual Poetry after Futurism: Marinetti, Apollinaire, Schwitters, Cummings*, New York: Lang, 1995

Winkelmann, Judith, *Abstraktion als stilbildendes Prinzip in der Lyrik von Hans Arp und Kurt Schwitters*, Frankfurt: Lang, 1995

Charles Sealsfield 1793–1864

At the height of his literary productivity (1833–1843), Charles Sealsfield was celebrated in both Europe and the United States as the other great unknown realist after Scott. His true identity (Karl Postl, a runaway monk of the Prague Order of the Holy Cross) remained a mystery until his death. Some critics connected to the literary movement of the Young Germans went so far as to praise him as the greatest living U.S. author. It is true that, at least for part of this period, Sealsfield was one of the most widely read contemporary authors writing in the German language.

Sealsfield's remarkable, but short-lived success—after the failed revolution of 1848 he fell back into oblivion—can be attributed to both his unique imagination of the U.S. republic and his distinctive writing style. In spite of his liberal thematic and topical borrowing from U.S. and European authors, Sealsfield's prose had hardly any precursors in Europe or the United States. While he does not fulfill the genre expectations we commonly associate with realism, his narrations about an outspokenly democratic frontier society remained sufficiently connected to historical, geographic, and demographic facts. Many of Sealsfield's works fictionalize Jacksonian political populism with its ideology of an expansionist democracy and Manifest Destiny. Today, Sealsfield's language appears more Baroque and cliché-ridden than realistic, but, for his contemporary readers, it must have provided an echo of the authentic voices of the U.S. hodgepodge of races, nationalities, mentalities, rhetorics, and dialects. Many of Sealsfield's novels seem to break with any structural constraints, and their excessive use of lengthy, interlocking first-person narrations can, at times, be utterly confusing. His images are often laden with pantheistic or apocalyptic symbolism. The language can be rough and unpolished, hyperbolic and crudely comical. Sealsfield described the open and panoramic form of his novels as democratic: the people had become the hero. This does not, however, mean that he always offers a multi-perspectival portrait of competing strata within society. Often the author harkens back to crude generalizations of nationalities and races; the new men of the new republic are also personified as larger than life heroes who have ominous theories of race and history. Sealsfield's narrators and characters tend to be opinionated, prejudiced, and violent in advancing their cause. They defend Indian removal, slavery, radical agriculturalism, anti-Catholicism, and anti-European sentiments. In Sealsfield's novels, the promise of freedom and opportunity unfolds in a world that must have seemed intriguingly foreign and dangerously "real" to the contemporary reader.

Today, only one of his works, *Das Cajütenbuch; oder, Nationale Charakteristiken* (1841; *The Cabin Book; or, National Characteristics*), is still available in a paperback edition, and only one excerpt from this novel (usually entitled *The Prairie on the Jacinto*) is still being read as an example of the 19th-century U.S. adventure story. Indeed, this is how Sealsfield's work was already seen in the later part of the 19th century. Early 20th-century scholarship picked up on the novels' racism and Arianism as an ideological basis for Western dominance and imperialism. During the 1940s, German scholarship stressed Sealsfield's later skepticism toward the future of the U.S. republic. Post–World War II scholarship has largely been occupied with reassessing biographical and bibliographical facts, as well as with questions of literary-historical and ideological affiliation: U.S., German, Austrian, or Swiss; European Biedermeier or U.S. plantation novel? The current consensus suggests that, with regard to themes and ideology, Sealsfield's novels must be seen within the context of the U.S. novel, even though the European literary influences and spiritual roots for some fundamental structures of his philosophical and historical speculation can hardly be neglected.

Sealsfield's first novel *The Indian Chief; or, Tokeah and the White Rose* (1829), expanded and revised in 1833 in German as *Der Legitime und die Republikaner* (The Legitimist and the Republicans), seems at first glance to ride the wave of successful U.S. and European Indian novels, which concentrated thematically on the figure of the noble savage and the tragic plight of a doomed civilization. While Sealsfield does employ these devices, there can be no question as to who acts in the name of history, as the title already indicates. The Indians are equated with the legitimist party of the old European aristocracy, hanging on to their entitlements and ways of life. The U.S. frontier and Jacksonian politics represent the face of republicanism, the irreversible future, as Jackson himself declares in a fictional confrontation with the Indian chief Tokeah.

The *Lebensbilder aus der westlichen Hemisphäre* (1834–37; Images of Life From the Western Hemisphere), a cycle of five more or less connected novels, form the core of Sealsfield's oeuvre. Two novels deal with George Howard's conversion from a fashionable New York dandy to a Louisiana planter and Ralph Doughby's transformation from a rough Kentuckian to a southern Jacksonian. The next two novels bear the title *Pflanzerleben* (Plantation Life) and offer a panorama of the life and debates on Louisiana plantations. At stake is the cultural and ideological confrontation between the established French (respectively Creole) planters and the Anglo-Saxon newcomers, whose claim of superior work ethics and politics the novel ultimately supports. The fifth novel tells the story of *Nathan der Squatter-Regulator* (1837; Nathan, the Squatter-Regulator). In the footsteps of Daniel Boone and Timothy Flint, this patriarchal hero of the U.S. frontier incarnates Sealsfield's imagination of frontier democracy and liberty. He takes the land that he needs from those he considers inferior but handles affairs among his equals in a fundamentally democratic fashion. After the Louisiana Purchase, he moves on to the new frontier, Texas.

This is where Sealsfield's best-known novel, *The Cabin Book*, takes place, which, accordingly, is sometimes seen as the true ending of the cycle. The central figure, the Alkalde, resembles Nathan Strong in many ways; his unscrupulous vision of a frontier republic made up of Anglo-Saxon farmers and planters, supposed heirs to a mythological Norman heritage, has been seen as Sealsfield's ultimate political message.

Sealsfield's utopian vision of the frontier is not transplanted into Mexico. *Der Virey und die Aristokraten, oder, Mexiko im Jahre 1812* (1835; The Virey and the Aristocrats; or, Mexico in the year 1812) follows the contemporary ideological sentiment that Mexico was too politically backward to bring its own revolution to a successful conclusion. At the same time, the political backwardness depicted in the novel can be read as a commentary on the politics of the Holy Alliance in the Old World. Seals-

field considered his last novel, *Süden und Norden* (1842; *North and South; or, Scenes and Adventures in Mexico*), his most poetic. Four travelers from the United States experience an identity crisis in Catholic Mexico. Here, Sealsfield moves further in conflating landscapes and psychology, and the political and ideological moral seems to remain unresolved.

The fragmentary character of *Die Deutsch-amerikanischen Wahlverwandtschaften* (1839; German-American Elective Affinities) does not fulfill what the title promises. Instead, the book bears testimony to Sealsfield's increasing skepticism toward the future of the U.S. republic as well as to his unchanged criticism of German political affairs.

BERND FISCHER

Biography
Born Karl Anton Postl in Poppitz, near Znaim, Moravia, 3 March 1793. Joined the Order of the Holy Cross with the Red Star, Prague; as a young monk, quickly rose to become secretary of the grand master of the order; vanished in 1823 without a trace; traveled to the United States, where he probably acquired a passport under the name Charles Sealsfield; spent 1826 and 1827 in France, Germany, and England, and published a political travel account of the United States in German and English and a political treatise on Austria in English; returned to the United States in 1827 and worked as a journalist; contributed to a French newspaper in New York, supporting the Bonapartist cause; settled in Switzerland in 1830 and began publishing a series of novels on the United States in German; returned to the United States in 1837 for several months and again from 1853–59. Died in Solothurn, Switzerland, 26 May 1864.

Selected Works

Collections
Sämtliche Werke, edited by Karl J.R. Arndt et al., 1975–

Novel
Das Kajütenbuch; oder, Nationale Charakteristiken, edited by Alexander Ritter, 1982

Further Reading
Brancaforte, Charlotte L., editor, *The Life and Works of Charles Sealsfield (Karl Postl), 1793–1864*, Madison, Wisconsin: Max Kade Institute, 1993
Grünzweig, Walter, *Das demokratische Kanaan: Charles Sealsfields Amerika im Kontext amerikanischer Literatur und Ideologie*, Munich: Fink, 1987
Sammons, Jeffrey L., "Charles Sealsfield's *Images of Life from Both Hemispheres*: A New Aquisition," *Yale University Library Gazette* 64, no. 1–2 (1989)
———, "Charles Sealsfield: A Case of Non-Canonicity," in *Autoren Damals und Heute: Literaturgeschichtliche Beispiele veränderter Wirkungshorizonte*, edited by Gerhard Peter Knapp, Amsterdam and Atlanta, Georgia: Rodopi, 1991
Schnitzler, Günter, *Erfahrung und Bild: Die dichterische Wirklichkeit des Charles Sealsfield (Karl Postl)*, Freiburg: Rombach, 1988
Schüppen, Franz, editor, *Neue Sealsfield-Studien: Amerika und Europa in der Biedermeierzeit*, Stuttgart: M and P, 1995
Strelka, Joseph P., editor, *Zwischen Louisiana und Solothurn: Zum Werk des Österreich-Amerikaners Charles Sealsfield*, Bern: Lang, 1997

W.G. Sebald 1944–

W.G. Sebald is both a literary scholar and the author of narrative prose and poetry. In his first published work of fiction, *Nach der Natur* (1988; Natural), for which he was awarded the Fedor-Malchow Literary Prize in 1991, Sebald explores the nature of memory and of dream. His formal devices—Sebald describes himself as a writer of prose, not a novelist—initially caused some frustration among literary critics, and early reviews of this first work and subsequent nonscholarly works suggest that Sebald's docu-fiction fits none of the traditional categories of literature. Markus R. Weber notes that "even when Sebald does not appear in the mask of the first-person narrator, he nonetheless brings in historical persons, minor historical figures, and literary characters as protagonists, documents biography and cultural history, and picks up available texts of various genres."

In his 1990 book *Schwindel, Gefühle* (Vertigo, Emotions), Sebald integrates visual representations into the printed text, which function to document and question the authenticity of the narrative. The narrative relationship to reality is thus made suspect, and the relationship of the reader to the text itself is also rendered complex, for it is no longer based upon a sure knowledge of what happens in the "story" but only upon what happens in the text itself.

With his next book, *Die Ausgewanderten* (1992; *The Emigrants*), Sebald achieved an international reputation. Translated into English by Michael Hulse, the work was favorably reviewed in both England and the United States, and the author made his first reading tour of the latter country in 1997.

The Emigrants consists of four separate stories united by the theme of emigration from Germany around the historical period of the Third Reich. Once again, the author combines biography, autobiography, historical persons, and photographs with a fictional narrative, and this combination gave rise to a feeling among critics and readers that Sebald was somehow dealing with a Holocaust-related theme rather than with the theme of loss and sorrow and, ultimately, of melancholy.

Each of the protagonists of the four stories is a man who is immersed in sadness, in a melancholy whose origins lie not only in the fact of emigration, the term Sebald prefers to *exile*, but perhaps in the reasons for that emigration. Those reasons are in part connected to the history of Germany in the 1930s and 1940s, the years of National Socialism, and a pervasive awareness of the incurable harm done to these people by more than a century of European and German experiments with ethnic and racial nationalisms. The personal histories of each of the four central characters of the stories echoes this historical dysthymia. The first character, Dr. Henry Selwyn, leaves Lithuania in 1899 at the age of seven and eventually becomes a doctor in England. In his old age, when the narrator meets him, Selwyn is at last experiencing the homesickness that pervades both his story and the entire collection of stories. His suicide, which brings to an end this first story, sets the dominant tone of despair and resignation that Sebald works to accommodate with his language, which can be placed in the tradition of German-language writers from Hölderlin to Celan. The photographic portrait of a helmeted German soldier, which appears in the story of Paul Bereyter, a dedicated school teacher who remains in Germany but kills himself in 1984, suggests the fatal connections to the more recent German past. Ambrose Adelwarth, the great uncle of the narrator of the third story, becomes the butler and confidante of a wealthy Jewish employer in New York. After the latter's death, Ambrose enters the same sanitarium to which his former employer was once committed in order to die while stoically enduring all attempts by the institution's chief psychiatrist to restore him to mental health. The painter Max Ferber, the subject of the fourth story, has, similar to Sebald himself, found a new home in England, but he returns to Germany as a soldier in the British army toward the end of World War II. It is through Ferber that Sebald gives expression to the function of art in a world of constant and annihilating change.

> It had also been of the greatest importance to him, Ferber once remarked casually, that nothing should change at his place of work, that everything should remain as it was, as he had arranged it, and that nothing further should be added but the debris generated by painting and the dust that continually fell and which, as he was coming to realize, he loved more than anything else in the world.

It is this same dust to which Ambrose Adelwarth's assisting psychiatrist, Dr. Abramsky, refers when he longs for the destruction of the sanitarium by the beetles that gnaw perpetually at the failing wooden structure. It is Sebald's elegant use of the German language, which combines a seemingly archaic style, a fascination with detail, and a poetic realism, that links him to a long line of Austrian writers from Handke, Bernhard, Musil, and Hofmannsthal to Stifter. The constant questioning of memory, of its integrity and its validity, is joined to a text that is nevertheless based on history and memory. This unresolvable contradiction forms the dynamic of the text, which flows at times with an extraordinary gracefulness.

Sebald's more recent literary works include *Die Ringe des Saturn* (1995; *The Rings of Saturn*), which purports to be a travelogue of a journey by the narrator through the English county of Suffolk. The title once again alludes to the planet that in astrology is thought to govern melancholia, while its rings, gases, dust, and fragments of formerly more solid objects are suggestive of the accumulated materials of memory that limit human consciousness. This work is more clearly related to a tradition of writing about and from within melancholia, which reaches back to Rousseau (Weber).

Sebald's most recent work, *Luftkrieg und Literatur* (1999; Aerial Warfare and Literature), is a published version of a series of lectures delivered by the author that raised the question among German and Austrian writers as to why they had not yet dealt with the aerial bombardments of German and Austrian cities. The controversy that surrounded this politically incorrect posture—German-language writing has often handled the German destruction of other European cities and has spoken often of the guilt associated with these acts of warfare—has led in some circles to a rethinking of the questions raised in the 1950s by Alexander and Margarete Mitscherlich in their work *Die Unfähigkeit zu Trauern* (1957; *The Inability to Mourn*); it has also affirmed the author's significance for contemporary German letters.

The writer's world-weariness and melancholia, which is uncharacteristic of the safe objectivity of postmodernist writing, seems directly connected to the legacy of the art of resigned but ever graceful despair that characterizes much of the literature of German-language, Austro-Hungarian, and later Austrian writers in the decades before and after World War I. Yet Sebald's writing betrays no nostalgia for any past, Austrian, European, or otherwise. In essays such as the aforementioned *Luftkrieg und Literatur,* he intervenes directly into the larger political and social issues of both present-day Germany and Austria, as well as into the practical or ethical role of literature in society. In his scholarly essays and analyses, including those contained in the 1991 volume *Unheimliche Heimat: Essays zur österreichischen Literatur* (1991; Uncomfortable Homeland: Essays on Austrian Literature), Sebald not only explores the canonical works of Austrian writers but also portrays more immediately the peculiarities of the writers themselves—Stifter's uncontrollable appetites for food and drink, for example, or the way in which he makes writers characters in his own prose writing.

Sebald's work is aesthetically masterful, in its content and in its narrative style elegiac, and yet often despite the overriding theme of melancholy still capable of the social intervention that literature, reading, and writing convey.

DUNCAN SMITH

Biography

Born in Wertach, Allgäu, in 1944. School teacher in St. Gallen, Switzerland; eventually moved to Manchester, England, where he worked as a lecturer at the university; teaches modern German literature at the University of East Anglia, Norwich, since 1970; his works comprise both scientific studies on literature and literary works; his recent novel *The Emigrants* was enthusiastically received in the Unites States, which Sebald visited on a lecture tour in 1997.

Selected Works

Essays and Critical Writings

Der Mythos der Zerstörung im Werk Döblins, 1980
Die Beschreibung des Unglücks: Zur österreichischen Literatur von Stifter bis Handke, 1985
editor, *A Radical Stage: Theatre in Germany in the 1970s and 1980s,* 1988

"Austrian Studies—Texte des Expressionismus—Der Beitrag judischer Autoren zur osterreichischen Avantgarde," *Journal of European Studies* 19, no. 76 (1989)
Schwindel, Gefühle, 1990
Unheimliche Heimat: Essays zur österreichischen Literatur, 1991
Luftkrieg und Literatur, 1999

Fiction

Nach der Natur: Ein Elementargedicht, 1988
Die Ausgewanderten; Vier lange Erzählungen, 1992; as *The Emigrants,* translated by Michael Hulse, 1996
Die Ringe des Saturn: Eine englische Wallfahrt, 1995; as *The Rings of Saturn,* translated by Michael Hulse, 1988

Further Reading

Aciman, Andre, "In the Crevasse," *Commentary* 103, no. 6 (1997)
Annan, Gabriele, "Ghosts," *New York Review of Books* 44, no. 14 (1997)
Anonymous, "The Emigrants," *New Yorker* 73, no. 3 (1997)
Brady, Philip, "Ghosts of the Present," *Times Literary Supplement* 4867 (1996)
Chalmers, Martin, "Angels of History," *New Statesman (1996)* 9, no. 411 (1996)
Detering, Heinrich, "Große Literatur für kleine Zeiten," *Frankfurter Allgemeine Zeitung* (17 November 1992)
Howell-Jones, Gareth, "A Doubting Pilgrim's Happy Progress," *Spectator* 280, no. 8860 (1998)
Malin, Irving, "The Emigrants," *Review of Contemporary Fiction* 17, no. 1 (1997)
Ozick, Cynthia, "The Posthumous Sublime," *New Republic* 215, no. 25 (1996)
Reiter, Andrea, "Unheimliche Heimat: Essays zur österreichischen Literatur by W.G.," in *Austrian Studies,* edited by Brian Keith-Smith, *Modern Language Review,* 88 (Pt. 3)
Rundell, Richard J., "A Radical Stage: Theatre in Germany in the 1970s and 1980s edited by W.G. Sebald / The Battle: Plays, Prose, Poems by Heiner Müller edited and translated by Carl Weber / Explosion of a Memory edited and translated by Carl Weber," *Theatre Journal* 43, no. 21 (1993)
Swales, Martin, "W.G. Sebald: *Die Beschreibung des Unglücks,*" *Modern Language Review,* no. 1 (1987)
Vourvoulias, Bill, "The Loss World," *Village Voice* 42, no. 2 (1997)
Wolff, Larry, "When Memory Speaks," *New York Times Book Review* 7, 19, no. 1 (1997)

Anna Seghers 1900–1983

Anna Seghers ranks with Thomas Mann, Kafka, and Brecht as one of the great modernists of the 20th century. Similar to Mann, she developed a narrative manner and style that both acknowledged and superseded the aesthetic tenets of European realism. Similar to Kafka, she was a storyteller steeped in Jewish lore who unremittingly pursued the themes of injustice, suffering, and redemption in her work. Similar to Brecht and the avant-gardists, she espoused the theory of an enlightened popular or folk art, and in this spirit she chronicled the myriad upheavals of her time. Seghers is compared by the broad reach of

her style and subject matter to both Virginia Woolf and Nadine Gordimer and by her stature as a woman author and intellectual of her culture and era to Simone de Beauvoir.

Although her work tends to be categorized in political or ideological terms—she is best-known as an antifascist writer—the aesthetic design underlying her prose reveals a decidedly mythic trajectory. As Hans Mayer fittingly observed, "All the world in Anna Seghers is at once *mythic* world." Reminiscent of Joseph Conrad, Seghers embedded her prose in a vast topography of myth, a metanarrative, as it were, from which myriad landscapes and seascapes unfold (the Rhineland, the Carpathian Mountains, the edge of the Mediterranean, the mountains and plains of Mexico, and the Caribbean Sea). The mythic continuity of the waterway, of the forests and surrounding terrain, links the characters and their often tragic fates within the works—and from one work to the next. Similar to Conrad, and before him Balzac, Seghers endowed her narratives with a seemingly arbitrary recurrence of mythic topographies, characterizations, and names (Marie, Anna, Johann, etc.) that form a loose but thoroughly composed epic arrangement when the oeuvre is viewed as a whole. The underlying mythic-cyclical structure, as well as her storytelling in the tradition of *The Thousand and One Nights* and *Decamerone,* goes unnoticed by those who read the texts solely for their mimetic value against the backdrop of German history. To be sure, Seghers saw herself as a chronicler of her time, but one might well compare her conception of her narrative oeuvre to that of Balzac's in his *Comédie humaine,* a work to which she can be said to have added the chiliastic-tragic parameters of her own century. As Siegfried Kracauer already noted in 1932, her preferred narrative form was the "martyr chronicle"; or as Walter Benjamin observed six years later, she wrote about "martyrs in the literal sense of the word (martyr, in Greek: the witness)," and thus offered us stories that do not so much await "the *reader*" as "the *listener.*"

Anna Seghers's pen name combines the names of the first-century Hebrew prophetess Hannah and the 17th-century Dutch landscape painter-engraver Hercules Seghers. Her study of portraiture in her dissertation *Jude und Judentum im Werke Rembrandts* (1924; Jews and Judaism in the Works of Rembrandt) reveals the aesthetic principles that guided her own narrative work. The influence of the Dutch masters is evident in such early narratives as *Grubetsch* (1927) and *Aufstand der Fischer von St. Barbara* (1928; The Revolt of the Fishermen), and in the remarkable physiognomies and land- and seascapes that pervade her entire oeuvre. She was the quintessential pictorial writer whose prose conveys meaning by the sequencing of images rather than the movement of dialogue or psychological introspection. Raised in the liberal traditions of Judaism and the Enlightenment, she was decisively influenced in her writing by the philosophical ideas of the young Georg Lukács, Karl Mannheim, Béla Balázs, and other members of the Budapest Sunday Circle, which also included her husband László Radványi.

During her 13-year exile in France and Mexico, she was an active essayist and speaker on behalf of the antifascist movement. The novels of this period foreground a recurring theme—the failed uprising and flight into the diaspora—inspired by contemporary events and the legacies of the Jewish Christians and other radical first-century groups. Some of these widely acclaimed works are *Das Siebte Kreuz* (1942; The Seventh Cross), about the resistance within Germany, since translated into over 40 languages; *Transit,* an eloquent first-person account of the plight of European Jews trapped at the edge of the Mediterranean in 1940–41; and *Die Toten bleiben jung* (1949; The Dead Stay Young), an epic cross-section of everyday German life within the framework of history from the 1919 murders of Luxembourg and Liebknecht to the collapse of the Third Reich in 1945. Seghers also experimented with shorter forms so as to grapple with the disturbing historical events attending the fascist-antifascist paradigm. The radio play *Der Prozeß der Jeanne d'Arc zu Rouen 1431* (1937; The Trial of Jeanne d'Arc at Rouen in 1431) is a critique of the German and Soviet show trials, while the allegorical texts "Sagen von Artemis" (1938; Legends of Artemis) and "Die schönsten Sagen vom Räuber Woynok" (1938; The Handsomest Tales of Woynok the Brigand) address the larger problematic of Stalin's purges of left-wing—to a large extent Jewish—internationalists. In response to the Holocaust and the deportation of her mother, she wrote *Der Ausflug der toten Mädchen* (1946; The Excursion of the Dead Girls), *Post ins gelobte Land* (1946; Post to the Promised Land), and *Das Ende* (1946).

After the war Seghers settled in the eastern part of Germany. Inspired by the literacy campaigns of the Mexican muralists, she wrote about the postwar era with the aim of reeducating a generation of Germans raised under National Socialism. Narrative cycles such as *Friedensgeschichten* (1953; Peace Stories) and *Die Kraft der Schwachen* (1965; The Power of the Weak) are compelling testimonies to the extraordinary conditions of everyday life under fascism and the transition to socialism. Her Latin American novellas and stories (1948–80) reveal a remarkable sensitivity to the impact of colonialism on the historical struggles of Indians, Blacks, and European Jews. As president of the Writers Union for 25 years, she encouraged progressive developments in literature and the arts, and she had an especially favorable influence on the work of younger writers, notably Heiner Müller and Christa Wolf. Since her death in 1983, literary texts, letters, and other materials have been released, which shed fascinating new light on this extraordinary German-Jewish woman writer whose postwar reception was marked by Cold War controversies and whose ultimate significance within the history of modern literature was yet to be fully recognized.

HELEN FEHERVARY

See also German Democratic Republic

Biography

Born in Mainz, 19 November 1900. Studied philosophy, history, sinology, and art history at the University of Heidelberg, 1920–24; Ph.D. in art history, 1924; escaped to France via Switzerland, March 1933; residence in Paris suburb of Bellevue; co-editor of the Prague-based *Neue Deutsche Blätter,* 1933–35; travel to Austria following workers' uprising, 1934, and Belgium (Borinage), 1935; active participation in Schutzverband Deutscher Schriftsteller; major speeches at the International Writers Conferences for the Defense of Culture, Paris, 1935, Valencia/Madrid, 1937, and Paris, 1938; in Mexico City, July 1941; returned to Berlin via New York, Stockholm, Paris, and Mainz, 1947; addressed First Congress of German Writers, 1947; frequent trips to Paris; trip to the Soviet Union, 1948; addressed the World Peace Council, Paris, 1949; trip to China, 1951; president of the German Writers' Union, 1952–78; participation in Soviet writers' congresses, 1954, 1967. Kleist Prize, 1928; Büchner Prize, Darmstadt, 1947; Stalin Peace Prize, 1951; GDR National Prize, 1951, 1959, 1971; honorary doctorate, University of Jena, 1959, University of Mainz, 1977; World Peace Council Prize, 1975. Died in Dorotheenfriedhof, Berlin, 3 June 1983.

Selected Works

Collections
Der Bienenstock: Ausgewählte Erzählungen, 2 vols., 1953
Glauben an Irdisches: Essays aus vier Jahrzehnten, edited by Christa Wolf, 1969
Über Kunstwerk und Wirklichkeit, 4 vols., edited by Sigrid Bock, 1970–79

Werke, 10 vols., 1977
Gesammelte Werke in Einzelausgaben, 14 vols., 1977–80
Die Macht der Worte: Reden, Schriften, Briefe, 1979
Woher sie kommen, wohin sie gehen: Essays aus vier Jahrzehnten,
    edited by Manfred Behn, 1980
Erzählungen 1924–1980, 6 vols., edited by Sonja Hilzinger, 1994
Textkritische und kommentierte Werkausgabe, edited by Helen
    Fehervary and Bernhard Spies, 2000–

Novels

Die Gefährten, 1932
Der Kopflohn, 1933; as *A Price on His Head*, translated by Eva Wulff,
    1960
Der Weg durch den Februar, 1935
Die Rettung, 1937
Das siebte Kreuz, 1942; as *The Seventh Cross*, translated by James A.
    Galston, 1942
Transit, 1948; as *Transit*, translated by James A. Galston, 1944
Die Toten bleiben jung, 1949; as *The Dead Stay Young*, translated by
    James A. Galston, 1950
Die Entscheidung, 1959
Das Vertrauen, 1968

Novellas, Longer Narratives

Aufstand der Fischer von St. Barbara, 1928; as *The Revolt of the
    Fishermen*, translated by Margaret Goldsmith, 1929; as *Revolt of the
    Fishermen of Santa Barbara*, translated by Jack and Renate Mitchell,
    1960
Der letzte Weg des Koloman Wallisch, 1934
Der Ausflug der toten Mädchen, und andere Erzählungen (includes *Post
    ins gelobte Land*; *Das Ende*), 1946; enlarged edition (includes *Die
    Saboteure*; *Das Obdach*), 1948; *Der Ausflug der toten Mädchen* as
    The Outing of the Dead Girls, translated by Michael Bullock, 1968;
    as *The Excursion of the Dead Girls*, translated by Elisabeth Rütschi
    Herrmann and Edna H. Spitz, in *German Women Writiers of the
    Twentieth Century*, 1978
Die Hochzeit von Haiti: Zwei Novellen (includes *Wiedereinführung der
    der Sklaverei in Guadalupe*), 1949
Der Mann und sein Name, 1952
Das Licht auf dem Galgen, 1961
Das wirkliche Blau, 1967; as *Benito's Blue*, translated by Joan Becker,
    in *Benito's Blue and Nine Other Stories*, 1973
Überfahrt, 1971
Sagen von Unirdischen, 1973
Die Reisebegegnung, 1973; as *Encounter*, translated by Joan Becker, in
    Benito's Blue and Nine Other Stories, 1973
Steinzeit, 1975
Der gerechte Richter, 1990

Stories, Shorter Narratives

Die Toten auf der Insel Djal, 1924
Die Wellblech-Hütte, 1929
Auf dem Weg zur amerikanischen Botschaft, und andere Erzählungen
    (includes *Die Ziegler*; *Grubetsch*; *Bauern von Hruschowo*), 1930
Der Führerschein, 1932
Die schönsten Sagen vom Räuber Woynok, 1938
Sagen von Artemis, 1938
Reise ins elfte Reich, 1939
Der sogenannte Rendel, 1940
Das Obdach, 1941–42; as *Shelter*, translated by Joan Becker, in *They
    Lived to See It: A Collection of Short Stories*, 1963
Die drei Bäume, 1946
Das Argonautenschiff, 1949
Friedensgeschichten, 1953
Vierzig Jahre der Margarete Wolf, 1957
Die Kraft der Schwachen: Neun Erzählungen (includes *Agathe
    Schweigert*; *Der Führer*; *Der Prophet*; *Das Schilfrohr*; *Wiedersehen*;

Das Duell; *Susi*; *Tuomas beschenkt die Halbinsel Sorsa*; *Die
    Heimkehr des verloreren Volkes*), 1965; translations by Joan Becker,
    in *Benito's Blue and Nine Other Stories* (includes *Agathe Schweigert*
    [*Agathe Schweigert*]; *Der Führer* [*The Guide*]; *Der Prophet* [*The
    Prophet*]; *Das Schilfrohr* [*The Reed*]; *Das Duell* [*The Duel*], 1973
Zwei Denkmäler, 1968
Drei Frauen aus Haiti (Das Versteck, Der Schlüssel, Die Trennung),
    1980
Frauen und Kinder in der Emigration, 1985

Radio Plays

Der Prozeß der Jeanne d'Arc zu Rouen 1431 (broadcast 1937), 1937;
    expanded by Seghers, Brecht, and Benno Besson for a Berliner
    Ensemble theater production, 1952; as *The Trial of Joan of Arc at
    Rouen, 1431*, translated by Ralph Manheim and Wolfgang
    Sauerlander, in Bertolt Brecht, *Collected Plays*, vol. 9, 1972
Die Stiefel, 1969
Ein ganz langweiliges Zimmer (broadcast 1938), 1973

Further Reading

Albrecht, Friedrich, *Die Erzählerin Anna Seghers, 1926–1932*, Berlin:
    Rütten und Loening, 1965
Wagner, Frank, et al., editors, *Anna Seghers: Eine Biographie in
    Bildern*, Berlin: Aufbau, 1994
Argonautenschiff: Jahrbuch der Anna-Seghers-Gesellschaft, Berlin:
    Aufbau, 1992–
Batt, Kurt, *Anna Seghers: Versuch über Entwicklung und Werke*,
    Leipzig: Reclam, 1973
Benjamin, Walter, "Eine Chronik der deutschen Arbeitslosen: Zu Anna
    Seghers Roman *Die Rettung*," in *Gesammelte Schriften*, vol. 3, edited
    by Hella Tiedemann-Bartels, Frankfurt: Suhrkamp, 1980
Brandes, Ute, *Anna Seghers*, Berlin: Colloquium, 1992
Einhorn, Barbara, "1947: Anna Seghers Returns to Germany from
    Exile and Makes Her Home in East Berlin," in *Yale Companion to
    Jewish Writing and Thought in German Culture, 1096–1996*, edited
    by Sander L. Gilman and Jack Zipes, New Haven, Connecticut and
    London: Yale University Press, 1997
Haas, Erika, *Ideologie und Mythos: Studien zur Erzählstruktur und
    Sprache im Werk von Anna Seghers*, Stuttgart: Heinz, 1975
Mayer, Hans, "Anna Seghers," in *Der Widerruf: Über Deutsche und
    Juden*, Frankfurt: Suhrkamp, 1994
Rilla, Paul, "Die Erzählerin Anna Seghers," *Sinn und Form* 6 (1950)
Romero, Christiane Zehl, *Anna Seghers: mit Selbstzeugnissen und
    Bilddokumenten*, Reinbek bei Hamburg: Rowohlt, 1993
Stephan, Alexander, *Anna Seghers im Exil: Essays, Texte, Dokumente*,
    Bonn: Bouvier, 1993
Text und Kritik 38 (1973 and 1982) [two special issues devoted to
    Anna Seghers]
Wagner, Frank, *"Der Kurs auf die Realität": Das epische Werk von
    Anna Seghers (1935–1943)*, Berlin: Akademie-Verlag, 1975
Weimarer Beiträge (1990)
Wallace, Ian, editor, *Anna Seghers in Perspective*, Amsterdam: Rodomi,
    1998
Wolf, Christa, essays in *Die Dimension des Autors*, vol. 1, Berlin:
    Aufbau, 1986

Das siebte Kreuz 1942

Novel by Anna Seghers

Anna Seghers's most renowned work, *Das siebte Kreuz* (1942;
The Seventh Cross) is internationally acclaimed as an eloquent

testimony to the human spirit of resistance and as the great anti-fascist novel of its time. Set in the mid-1930s in the environs of the author's native Mainz, the novel's plot is organized around the escape of seven political prisoners from a concentration camp and the recapture and deaths of all but one, Georg Heisler, who eventually boards a Rhine freighter bound for Holland. The novel's enduring characterizations, however, are also the more-or-less anonymous members of the organized resistance who figure in the background and make possible the "small triumph" of Heisler's escape, and an entire palette of characters who unwittingly display the "unassailable and inviolable" qualities that abet his survival—including a Jewish physician who risks much to treat the wounded man, a carnival seamstress who offers a change of clothes and money, and a cathedral priest who burns the evidence of Heisler's camp clothes. The brutal storm trooper Zillich is first portrayed in Seghers's *Der Kopflohn* (1934; *A Price on His Head*) and reappears as a death camp guard in *Das Ende* (1946; The End); other characters reappear in *Die Saboteure* (1948; The Saboteurs) and *Vierzig Jahre der Margarete Wolf* (1957; Forty Years in the Life of Margarete Wolf).

As a literary work, one written at the height of the realism debates of the 1930s, the novel employs modernist techniques—epic-montage structure, inner monologue, cyclical storytelling, and mythic allusion—without relinquishing either historical authenticity or the author's commitment to her political vision. The aesthetic conception is also consistent with those of Seghers's other works, which foreground the tragic-mythic theme of the failed uprising and the subsequent flight into the diaspora. The device of framing the main events of the plot within another temporal dimension of collective memory—in this case, the messianic time of concentration-camp inmates huddled as witnesses around a fire made from the seven crosses—is typical of Seghers's cyclical-chronicle prose style. Equally characteristic are the stunning visual sequences such as the first chapter's panoramic view of the Rhine valley at dawn from the edge of the lower Taunus range, where, as Carl Zuckmayer observed, "the shepherd stands as if drawn by Dürer." Similarly, at the end of the novel, through Georg Heisler's eyes, we see the view across the Rhine of Mainz's great Romanesque cathedral, and between its spires the figure of St. Martin "bending down from his horse to share his cloak with the beggar."

The history of the manuscript attests to the extraordinary conditions of antifascist exile at the time. Seghers wrote the novel in Paris in 1938–39. It was based on her familiarity with the Mainz-Frankfurt-Höchst area in which she was raised and on her extensive knowledge of political conditions in that region from both personal and documented sources. She also relied on first-person accounts from former inmates who had escaped from concentration camps such as Osthofen, which was located south of Mainz (depicted in the novel as "Westhofen"). After the novel's completion in the spring of 1939, the Moscow-based journal *Internationale Literatur* published several chapters, but terminated its installments after the Hitler-Stalin pact. The onset of the war limited the chances of European publication (and the author's own survival!), and in the winter of 1939–40 she sent three manuscript copies of the novel for safekeeping to friends who had fled to the United States. When the German army occupied Paris she was forced underground and still had two copies in her possession: one was burned by her 14-year-old son and a friend before the Gestapo raided her apartment; another went to an acquaintance who hid it in a footlocker while preparing the

French translation. A New York manuscript was offered to Boston's Little, Brown and Co., which published a slightly abridged English translation in September 1942. From her exile in Mexico, Seghers had little control over the alterations and rights that were sold. As a Book-of-the-Month Club selection, the novel became a bestseller. The U.S. reception emphasized the fugitive/chase aspects of the plot rather than the work's portrayal of political resistance, as indicated by reviews of the novel, its nationwide newspaper syndication as a comic-strip, its Armed Forces edition (which was used for recruiting), and the 1944 film by Fred Zinnemann, starring Spencer Tracy, Hume Cronin, Jessica Tandy, and, in minor roles, Alexander Granach and Helene Weigel. (Otto Preminger's plans for a Broadway production went unrealized.) The German version of the novel first appeared in Mexico in late 1942 and sold out within weeks. The English translation was republished in Canada and England, and within five years the novel appeared in Portuguese, Spanish, Swedish, Dutch, French, Russian, Norwegian, and Danish. To date it has been published in over 40 languages.

The novel's tribute to the antifascist (largely, but not only, German Communist Party) political resistance *within* Germany during the Third Reich raises crucial issues about the era of National Socialism, which have been widely debated since the onset of the cold war. In East Germany, the novel was singled out from the start as a classic of antifascist writing (often to the detriment of the author's less explicitly antifascist works). GDR adaptations include a 1955 radio play, a series of art works, a never-produced 1965 filmscript, and a successful 1981 theater production. In a country of 17 million people, the novel was familiar to every schoolchild and became Aufbau Verlag's top-selling modern German novel, with over a million copies sold. The novel's western reception was more uneven. Like other returning exiles, Seghers was initially celebrated as an antifascist author, and the city of Darmstadt awarded her its prestigious Büchner Prize in 1947. Her internationally acclaimed novel was quickly made available in German to a wide spectrum of postwar readers—by Querido in Amsterdam, Aufbau in East Berlin, Desch in Munich, Rowohlt in Homburg, and the Büchergilde Gutenberg in Zurich. After the German division, however, Western acclamation ceased. When Luchterhand Verlag announced a West German edition in 1962, protest and controversy ensued. Only since the advent of exile research in the 1970s have Western critics accorded the novel serious scholarly attention. (Albeit the 1987 republication of *The Seventh Cross* by Monthly Review Press in the United States went largely unnoticed.) Heralding the revival of interest in Seghers in post-unification Germany, in 1990 the president of the West German Akademie der Künste, Walter Jens, paid tribute to her as an author whose work "combines justice with compassion" and serves as testimony that "Goethe's Germany was not preserved in the Reichskanzlei, but in the barracks of Buchenwald." Not insignificantly, the tribute evokes the legacy of *The Seventh Cross*.

HELEN FEHERVARY

Editions

First edition: *Das siebte Kreuz. Roman aus Hitlerdeutschland*, Mexico City: Editorial "El libro libre," 1942
Critical edition: *Das siebte Kreuz*, vol. 4 in *Textkritisch durchgesehen, kommentierte Werkausgabe*, edited by Helen Fehervary, Berlin: Aufbau, 2000–

Translation: *The Seventh Cross*, translated by James A. Galston, Boston: Little Brown, 1942; reprint, New York: Monthly Review Press, 1987 (foreword by Kurt Vonnegut, afterword by Dorothy Rosenberg)

Further Reading

Beicken, Peter, "Anna Seghers: *Das siebte Kreuz*," in *Deutsche Romane des 20. Jahrhunderts*, edited by Paul Michael Lützeler, Königstein: Athenäum, 1983

Hilzinger, Sonja, editor, *"Das siebte Kreuz" von Anna Seghers: Texte, Daten, Bilder,* Frankfurt: Luchterhand, 1990

Naumann, Uwe, *Anna Seghers, "Das siebte Kreuz": Materialien,* Stuttgart: Klett, 1981

Rosenberg, Dorothy, "Afterword," in *The Seventh Cross*, by Anna Seghers, translated by James A. Galston, New York: Monthly Review Press, 1987

Schlenstedt, Dieter, "Beispiel einer Rezeptionsvorgabe: Anna Seghers' Roman *Das siebte Kreuz*," in *Gesellschaft-Literatur-Lesen: Literaturrezeption in theoretischer Sicht,* edited by Manfred Naumann, Berlin: Aufbau, 1973

Schwarz, Egon, "Lese- und Lebenserfahrung mit Anna Seghers: 40 Jahre Lektüre *Das siebte Kreuz*," *Text und Kritik* 38 (1982)

Spies, Bernhard, *Anna Seghers: Das siebte Kreuz*, Frankfurt: Diesterweg, 1993

Stephan, Alexander, *Anna Seghers, "Das siebte Kreuz": Welt und Wirkung eines Romans*, Berlin: Aufbau, 1997

Wagner, Frank, "*Das siebte Kreuz*: Antifaschistische Widerstandsaktion und Bestandsaufnahme der Menschlichkeit," in "*... der Kurs auf die Realität*": *Das epische Werk von Anna Seghers (1935–43)*, Berlin: Akademie, 1975

Walter, Hans-Albert, "Eine deutsche Chronik: Das Romanwerk von Anna Seghers aus den Jahren des Exils," in *Exil und Rückkehr*, edited by Anton Maria Keim, Mainz: Schmidt, 1986

Wolf, Christa, "Das siebte Kreuz," in *Die Dimension des Autors*, Berlin: Aufbau, 1986

Zafer Şenocak 1961–

In the past decade, Zafer Şenocak has emerged as one of the most innovative German intellectuals and writers, aiming in his works beyond the ethnic position of older writers such as Aras Ören and Aysel Özakin, or contemporaries such as Sevgi Özdamar. Inserting himself much more boldly into German culture and its aesthetic traditions, he questions the boundaries that are all too neatly drawn between minority and mainstream writers. The present catchphrase of multiculturalism in Germany, Şenocak's work suggests, is no more than an invention in which liberal-minded citizens congratulate themselves for granting minority cultures their separate space, while avoiding any contaminating contact with them. Şenocak's work counters such rhetoric of multiculturalism with an irreverent and satirical perspective, thereby avoiding the often cliché-ridden treatment and discussion of German Turkish identity.

As a poet following in the tradition of Ingeborg Bachmann and Günther Eich, Şenocak initially experimented in a lyrical and subjective mode. The phenomenon of cultural displacement is grasped in an existential, surreal-Expressionist manner in such volumes of poetry as *Elektrisches Blau* (1983; Electric Blue), *Flammentropfen* (1985; Drops of Flames), *Das senkrechte Meer* (1991; The Vertical Ocean), and *Fernwehanstalten* (1994; Broadcasting Stations of Desire). Alongside these works, Şenocak published a series of critical essays in various German dailies such as *Süddeutsche Zeitung*, *Tageszeitung*, and *Berliner Tagesspiegel* that challenge prevalent stereotypes pertaining to Turkish culture in Germany. *War Hitler Araber?* (1994; Was Hitler an Arab?), a collection of feuilleton essays, responds to the Gulf War and its xenophobic specter of an anti-Western Islamic conspiracy. *Atlas des tropischen Deutschlands* (1993; A Map of Tropical Germany) attacks among other things the notion that Turks must forever remain a proletarian migrant culture in Germany, and attests to a growing critical awareness of the one-dimensionality of mainstream discourses on minorities.

More recently, Şenocak has found in his prose writings the perfect medium for his critical talent. In these writings, he challenges the sanctimonious expectations that are brought to so-called minority causes. These sometimes well-meant approaches quickly end up reifying the image of the Turkish resident in cliché scenarios of cultural and linguistic illiteracy, socio-economic dependence, and religious fundamentalism conflicting with Western secular values. As an alternative to these scenarios, Şenocak takes up the genre of the detective story, which German Turkish writers such as Ören and Jakob Arjouni had converted into a paradigmatic narrative depicting the search for ethnic and cultural identity. In his story collection *Der Mann im Unterhemd* (1995; The Man in His Undershirt), Şenocak all but eliminates the sociological residues of his precursors to gain a fresh and unorthodox insight into the complexity of German Turkish identity. The story "Fliegen" ("Flying"), for example, evokes the detective genre merely as a cliché convention wherein a detective who investigates "multicultural" crimes enters into a futile search for criminal clues tarnished by cultural stereotypes. The search for a young woman who has presumably been abducted by Islamic fundamentalists ends on a farcical and anticlimactic note, when the detective discovers that she faked her abduction in order to become an airline stewardess. The story parodies predictable responses to Turkish culture on the part of German readers. A further target of Şenocak's subversive humor is the pious discourse of intercultural hermeneutics by which the "foreign otherness" of an immigrant culture can be experienced through "Betroffenheit," a form of empathetic intersubjectivity. Şenocak questions this naive concept of intercultural empathy in his depiction of uncomfortable and problematic encounters with *das Fremde* (the foreign, the other) in which the foreign resists domestication and instead disrupts the routine of German native habits. Şenocak's prose frequently launches into pornographic episodes that haunt the reader with his or her own stereotypes pertaining to the hypersexuality attributed to a Mediterranean or Oriental culture. The encounter with Turkish culture is far from accessible and is not served ready-made for intercultural consumption but evokes visceral fears of threat and invasion.

Die Prairie (1997; The Prairie) extends Şenocak 's critical perspective in a more humorous fashion, parodying the author's own complicit role in a culture that markets identity and multiculturalism. Sascha, the narrator, is a second-rate "intercultural" writer rushing from one liaison to the other in which women serve him mainly for sexual gratification. In between these adventures, he takes up writing assignments for German journals and newspapers. Because of his Turkish background, Sascha is asked to write an essay about the Fatwa against Salman Rushdie. He copies the information from various handbooks and satisfies in spite of many transcription mistakes an uncritical public demand for "authentic" comment on Islamic matters. Şenocak's novel marks a new stage in German ethnic literature with its critique of its own commodity value on the literary market. Not surprisingly, the figure of Sascha eventually makes himself independent from the author's control and disappears into the romantic myth of the American prairie. The novel ends on the author's apology for not being able to deliver to the reader the expected closures and redemptive images of his Turkish German hero.

In his most recent novel, *Gefährliche Verwandtschaft* (1999; Dangerous Relation), Şenocak continues his story about Sascha Muhteschem but pays greater attention to the hero's origins. Born to a German Jewish mother and a Turkish father, Sascha now exhibits a more crucial border position in the cultural negotiation of conflicting identities and legacies. After the death of his parents in a car accident, Sascha inherits the diaries of his Turkish grandfather written between 1916 and 1936, an era that saw the demise of the Ottoman Empire and the emergence of modern Turkey, and resolves to write his first novel. Since he cannot read the Cyrillic the diaries were written in, he sets out to reconstruct his family genealogy from memory and imagination in order to uncover the reasons behind the mysterious suicide of his grandfather. This approach contrasts with that of his German girlfriend Marie, who is putting together a purely factual documentary film on Talat Pascha, a Turkish political figure responsible for the deportation of hundreds of thousands of Armenians and their ensuing genocide.

The novel, moving between fact and fiction, shows the complexity of German-Turkish relations both in the past and the present. Sascha's maternal Jewish grandfather, for example, finds asylum with his in-laws in Turkey during the Nazi era. This individual history is complemented by historical accounts of friendly Muslim-Jewish relations during the Ottoman era and Turkey's former alliance with the German Empire. These multicultural configurations and legacies seem negated by the genocidal history of both countries and by their present uneasy relationship with one another. The novel also documents in the figure of Sascha's paternal grandfather a thoroughly Western and secular Turkish tradition that is frequently unrecognized by Europeans who view Turkey as a so-called Oriental country outside the sphere of European culture. Sascha's own position within Germany as an assimilated Turkish resident throws further light on the limitations of liberalism and its multicultural categories that provide for oppressed but not assimilated cultural minorities. Unlike his fellow writers, Sascha fails to benefit from his Jewish origins in an era of philo-Semitism and is likewise not perceived as a genuine Turkish German writer since he lacks the proper migrant labor background.

Şenocak shows how philanthropic stereotypes in the end fall short of accepting Turkish German residents on an equal footing but prefer them in positions that require paternalistic care from German society. This impasse in cross-cultural relations is underscored by the novel's ending, in which Sascha discovers the true cause of his grandfather's suicide after his diaries are deciphered and translated by a multilingual expert. Upon receiving a letter from his former Armenian lover from her exile in Paris, Sascha's grandfather ends his life, as he is about to accompany the Turkish team to the Olympic Games of 1936 in Berlin. The novel, with its ironic overlapping of conflicting interests and identities, provides a sober perspective for the realistic implementation of multiculturalism in Germany, one in which immigrant generations will have been superseded by thoroughly acculturated German Turkish citizens who have yet to be given full cultural recognition. Şenocak's strength lies in his vision of a radically democratic Germany where citizens encounter one another on equal economic, social, and cultural footing. Will mainstream German society be able to accept the Turkish German citizen competing with "white" Germans at all levels? Will it have space for assimilated and well-educated Turks who break with cultural stereotypes of the migrant laborer (a Turk is not supposed to attend the Opera—"Ein Türke geht nicht in die Oper"), speak standard German, and display intimate knowledge of German culture? Şenocak's work provides a litmus test for the sincerity of multiculturalism and liberalism in the Europe of the new century.

Matthias Konzett

Biography

Born in Ankara, Turkey, 1961. Moved to Munich, 1970; studied German literature, politics, and philosophy; writes feuilleton essays and critical commentary in major German newspapers, including *Süddeutsche Zeitung* and *Tageszeitung;* founder and co-editor of the transnational literary journal *Sirene;* writer-in-residence at Miami University, Ohio, 1996, as well as at the Lion Feuchtwanger Society, Villa Aurora, Los Angeles, and the Massachusetts Institute of Technology, where he was also the 1997 Max-Kade Distinguished Visiting Professor. Adelbert von Chamisso Förderpreis, 1988. His works have been translated into Turkish, English, French, Dutch, and Hebrew. Currently lives in Berlin (since 1990).

Selected Works

Poetry
Elektrisches Blau: Gedichte, 1983
Verkauf der Morgenstimmungen am Markt: Gedichte, 1983
Flammentropfen: Gedichte, 1985
Ritual der Jugend.: Gedichte, 1987
Das senkrechte Meer: Gedichte, 1991
Fernwehanstalten: Gedichte, 1994

Novels
Die Prairie, 1997
Gefährliche Verwandtschaft, 1999

Other
Atlas des tropischen Deutschland: Essays, 1993
War Hitler Araber? IrreFührungen an den Rand Europas: Essays, 1994
Der Mann im Unterhemd: Prosa, 1995

Further Reading

Adelson, Leslie, "Migrants' Literature or German Literature?" in *Writing New Identities: Gender, Nation, and Immigration in Contemporary Europe*, edited by Gisela Brinker-Gabler and Sidonie Smith, Minneapolis: University of Minnesota Press, 1997

Amirsedghi, Nasrin, and Thomas Bleicher, editors, *Literatur der Migration*, Mainz: Kinzelbach, 1997

Blackshire-Belay, Carol Aisha, editor, *The Germanic Mosaic: Cultural and Linguistic Diversity in Society*, Westport, Connecticut: Greenwood Press, 1994

Fischer, Sabine, and Moray McGowan, editors, *Denn du tanzt auf einem Seil: Positionen deutschsprachiger Migrant Innenliteratur*, Tübingen: Stauffenberg, 1997

Horrocks, David, and Eva Kolinsky, editors, *Turkish Culture in German Society Today*, Providence, Rhode Island: Berghahn Books, 1996

Leggewie, Claus, and Zafer Senocak, editors, *Deutsche Türken: Das Ende der Geduld*, Reinbeck bei Hamburg: Rowohlt, 1993

Rösch, Heidi, *Migrationsliteratur im interkulturellen Kontext: Eine didaktische Studie zur Literatur von Aras Ören, Aysel Özakin, Franco Biondi, und Rafik Schami*, Frankfurt: Verlag für interkulturelle Kommunikation, 1992

Sen, Faruk, and Andreas Goldberg, editors, *Türken in Deutschland: Leben zwischen zwei Kulturen*, Munich: Beck, 1994

Suhr, Heidrun, "Ausländerliteratur: Minority Literature in the Federal Republic of Germany," *New German Critique* 46 (1989)

Shoah Literature *see* Holocaust (Shoah) Literature

Angelus Silesius (Johannes Scheffler) 1624–1677

Born in the year in which Martin Opitz published his celebrated *Buch von der deutschen Poeterey* (Manual of German Poetry), which in many ways set the canon of orthodoxy for German Baroque writers, Scheffler was very much the literary child of his age. He was born in Breslau, in Silesia, the literary heartland of 17th-century Germany, and his work exhibits many of the features traditionally associated with the Baroque. Similar to many of his contemporaries, he is something of a literary split personality, capable of the most intense and sustained passion in his longer works, as well as the most rigorous intellectualism in the epigrammatic brevity of an Alexandrine couplet. Like the rest of his age, he loved to express himself in paradoxes and antitheses and, in his longer poems, exhibits a characteristically Baroque predilection for sustained metaphors, oxymoron, accumulation, synonymity, and parallelism.

In an age characterized by bitter religious wars and controversies, Scheffler was himself a controversial figure and noted polemicist. At the age of 29, he formally rejected the Lutheran faith, in which he had grown up, in favor of Roman Catholicism; he marked this step with a change of name to Angelus Silesius (The Silesian Messenger). Six years later he abandoned the profession of medicine and took orders. Thereafter, he devoted himself passionately to the service of the Counter Reformation in his native Silesia. His *Ecclesiologia oder Kirchenbeschreibung* (1677; Ecclesiologia or Church Description) is a collection of numerous polemical works that, with their exposure of Protestant "errors," constituted a handy manual for generations of polemically minded Catholic preachers. There was, however, nothing opportunistic about Scheffler's conversion, and, again

with the best representatives of his age, he is characterized by the earnestness and intensity of his search for God. His two great works of 1657, the *Geistreiche Sinn- und Schlußreime* (Witty/Spiritual Epigrams and Rhymes; the second edition in 1675 is entitled *Cherubinischer Wandersmann*, The Cherubic Pilgrim) and the *Heilige Seelen-Lust* (Holy Pleasure of the Soul), both testify to the earnestness of this search.

Scheffler had early contact with the world of contemporary literature through his teacher in Breslau, Christoph Köler, who was a friend and biographer of Opitz and also a poet in his own right. The decisive influence in Scheffler's development, however, came while he was serving as physician to Duke Sylvius Nimrod von Württemberg in Öls. Here, he was drawn into the circle around Abraham von Frankenberg, editor and biographer of Jakob Böhme, who introduced him to the great representatives of the mystical tradition, including Tauler, Eckhart, Weigel, Berhard of Clairvaux, and Gertrud the Great. It was the reformulation of many of the traditional concepts of mysticism in German verse of great power and intensity that was to constitute the essence of Scheffler's works.

The *Heilige Seelen-Lust* and the *Geistreiche Sinn- und Schlußreime* exemplify, respectively, the two great branches of the mystical tradition, the *seraphic*, or emotional approach to God, and the *cherubinic*, or intellectual approach to God. The *Heilige Seelen-Lust* looks back ultimately to the Song of Songs and the bride-mysticism of Bernard of Clairvaux. In a way that had been anticipated by Johannes Khuen and Friedrich von Spee but that was now given unparalleled emotional intensity, Scheffler here sings of the love of the Christian soul for the Godhead made flesh in Christ. The characteristic device is *Kontrafaktur*—the parodic use of the situations, imagery, and emotive vocabulary of the secular Petrarchian love lyric or pastoral—which helps express the love of the soul for her heavenly bridegroom. The result, with its plethora of nightingales, shepherds, bees, and roses and with its overt eroticism, is often not to the taste of the modern reader. Less strikingly characteristic, but equally important for Scheffler, are the lyrics in which he celebrates the "real presence" of God on earth in his Christmas hymns. Not surprisingly, perhaps, it is the less obviously mystically inspired hymns such as "'Mir nach', spricht Christus, unser Held" that have retained a place in Catholic hymnnals.

While the *Heilige Seelen-Lust* expresses the emotional yearning of the soul for the *unio mystica*, the *Cherubinischer Wandersmann* is concerned with a philosophical examination of the necessity and consequences of the mystic marriage and resulting *deificatio*. In over 1,600 Alexandrine couplets, the latter work distills many of the central concerns of mystic thought into pithy and often perplexing epigrams. The two lines of the Alexandrine couplet, each with its caesura, were ideally suited to the Baroque love of antithesis and paradox and the predilection for the surprising *pointe*. Both Frankenberg and the Silesian mystic Daniel von Czepko had used the form, but it was Scheffler who brought it to new heights of aesthetic and intellectual brilliance. The necessity of union with God and the consequences of that union are conveyed in strikingly bold images, frequent wordplays, arresting metaphors, and also in unadorned, relentless logic, which, for the scrupulous modern reader, can seem to border on the blasphemous in their expression of the ineffable by means of a paradox. Theologians such as Arnold and Tersteegen drew inspiration from the *Cherubinischer Wandersmann* for their own hymns and prayers, and philosophers such as Leibniz, Schopenhauer, and Hegel found much to ponder in it as well, but modern audiences have largely

lost the taste for mystical paradoxes—Rilke's successful use of them in the *Stundenbuch* notwithstanding. The appearance of familiar words that are used in a special sense constitutes a further barrier to modern readers. These readers' lack of comprehension does not, of course, alter the fact the Angelus Silesius is arguably the greatest mystical poet in the German language.

W.A. COUPE

Biography
Born in Breslau, Silesia, 25 December 1624. Studied medicine at Leyden and Padua; court physician to Duke Sylvius Nimrod von Öls; under the influence of Abraham von Frankenberg, long-standing interest in mysticism; converted to Roman Catholicism, 1653, taking Holy Orders, 1661; wrote anti-Protestant polemics and verse embodying a wide range of mystical experience and thought. Died in Breslau, 9 July 1677.

Selected Works

Collections
Sämtliche Poetische Schriften und eine Auswahl aus seinen Streitschriften, 2 vols., edited by G. Ellinger, n.d.
Angelus Silesius: Cherubinischer Wandersmann, edited by G. Ellinger, 1895
Angelus Silesius: Heilige Seelenlust; oder, Geistliche Hirtenlieder der in ihren Jesum verliebten Psyche, edited by G. Ellinger, 1901
Angelus Silestius: Sämtliche Poetische Werke in drei Bänden, 3rd edition, edited by H.L. Held, 1949–52

Further Reading
Ellinger, Georg, *Angelus Silesius: Ein Lebensbild*, Breslau: Korn, 1927
Gnädiger, Louise, "Angelus Silesius," in *Deutsche Dichter des 17. Jahrhunderts: Ihr Leben und Werk*, edited by H. Steinhagen and B. von Wiese, Berlin: Schmidt, 1984
Sammons, Jeffrey L., *Angelus Silesius*, New York: Twayne, 1967

Socialist Realism

The theory and practice of socialist realism is an illustration of the overt intrusion of politics into the production of art. The tenets of socialist realism were formulated in 1934 at a conference of the Soviet Writers Congress held in Kharkov, Russia, which had the deliberate intention of setting out a method of artistic production that would reflect and underpin the paramount importance of communist ideology. It is quite distinct from the social realism of the great middle-class European novelists of the 19th century—among them Dickens, Flaubert, Balzac, Tolstoy, and Zola—who thematized the massive social and political changes of their times in realistic prose and subject matter. It is also different from the critical realism of the post-1945 wave of German writers such as Böll, Grass, Koeppen, and Walser, whose liberalism voiced vigorous protest against the bourgeois

capitalist society they lived in without demanding fundamental revolutionary political change.

The proclamation at Kharkov of socialist realism as the officially sanctioned method of art was promulgated by Maxim Gorky and the literary theorist Zhdanov, and it enshrined the Stalinist clampdown on the imaginative, ebullient, and somewhat anarchic art of the early years of the revolutionary Soviet Union. After Lenin's death in 1924, both the avant-garde and the popular "Proletkult" (Proletarian Culture) were brought to heel within the confines of party thinking, and innovation and experiment were frowned upon. Writers and artists were to be organized along the correct lines in conformity with prescriptive dogma, and their work was expected to incorporate objective depiction (the truth), historical specificity (realism), and ideological instruction (party adherence). The official decree ran: "Socialist realism is the basic method of Soviet literature and literary criticism, and requires of the artist a faithful, historically concrete representation of reality in its revolutionary development." One consequence of these directives was the prevalence in socialist realist writings of the themes of collective work in factory and farm, the heroic figure of the worker building a serene future, and the all-embracing wisdom of the Communist Party. While serious attempts were made to portray and elucidate the deeper historical context of the new order in the Soviet Union, all too often slavish obedience to the directives of socialist realism resulted in trivial works of superficial, bathetic naturalism.

The debate about a communist method of writing came to prominence in East Germany after its isolation from the West in 1945, especially because its political and cultural leaders had largely been trained in Moscow and looked to the Soviet Union for their models. As in the early stages of the Soviet Union, a period of relative freedom and experiment in art in East Germany was quickly suppressed by the political functionaries, who asserted a prescriptive authority in all areas. Cultural policies were strictly controlled from the effectively one-party political center, which announced socialist realism to be the one and only method of writing in the newly founded GDR. A virulent campaign to outlaw formalism and cosmopolitanism was launched in 1951, culminating in March of that year at the Fifth Plenum of the Central Committee of the SED (Socialist Unity Party) with a concerted attack on Brecht's opera *Das Verhör des Lukullus* (1951; *The Trial of Lucullus*) and the music of Paul Dessau. The rejection of decadence, aestheticism, modernism, experiment, and novelty, perhaps intensified by the fear of individual subjectivism, was programmatically decreed at the Plenum in the document *Der Kampf gegen den Formalismus in der Kunst und Literatur für eine fortschrittliche deutsche Kultur* (1951; *The Struggle against Formalism in Art and Literature, and for a Progressive German Culture*). This document imposed the dead hand of bureaucratic directives in its official adoption of socialist realism on the Soviet model as the only perspective for writing in the young socialist republic. The theoreticians and cultural functionaries Wilhelm Girnus and Hans Koch led the subsequent centralization of all artistic production, and institutes were set up to control literature, art, radio, film, and publishing within the rigid limits enunciated by Koch: "In the context of a socialist society it is inevitable and necessary to develop the method of socialist realism into the prime, definitive, all-embracing and in the end sole method of artistic creativity."

In the GDR, the programmatic insistence on the official definition of socialist realism led to a stifling of the lively debates on realism that went back to the earlier controversies between the theoretician Georg Lukács, Brecht, and Anna Seghers. Literary production was now only measured by authors' adherence to the formulaic tenets of socialist realism promulgated by cultural politicians. Five principal guidelines had to be followed to create a "socialist" work and to gain permission to publish. The first guideline was that an author had to reproduce reality by incorporating the objective laws governing any particular historical process in such a way that the intricate mechanisms of social and political development that gave rise to a situation became evident. These objective laws could only be perceived by keeping to the party line (Parteilichkeit), so belief in Marxist-Leninist ideol-

ogy was the second requisite. Third, the scenes and characters, although individual and particular, should also be "typical" as representatives of a group or class or should articulate the essential social constellation. Fourth, as every work inherently celebrated the inevitable movement of history toward the ultimate supremacy of socialism, its protagonists could only be depicted as positive heroes in a process that was imbued with optimism and pointed forward to a harmonious future—the state of "concrete Utopia" postulated by Ernst Bloch. There would, of course, be difficulties in developing the perfect society, and these were not to be blurred or glossed over; but they were to be seen as the resolvable, non-antagonistic problems of socialism, not the brutally destructive contradictions of capitalism. Fifth and last, as the express aim of socialist realism was to convert and educate the people to Marxist thinking, simplicity of form and language was essential to achieve wide reception and to be accessible to readers hitherto unfamiliar with literature.

The impact of socialist realism on writing in East Germany, however, was to stultify the creative imagination, resulting in largely formulaic works by mediocre writers that affirmed the ruling ideology (a worthy exception is perhaps Eduard Claudius's *Menschen an unsrer Seite* [1951; People at Our Side], which was elevated to exemplary status). The dissatisfaction voiced by many writers and artists at the restrictive dictates imposed on them induced the authorities to hold a massive conference in 1959 at Bitterfeld, which attempted to find ways of bridging the perceived gap between workers of the hand and those of the brain. This attempt to bring art and the people (Kunst und Volk) closer together found a practical outlet in the so-called Bitterfelder Weg (The Bitterfeld Path), which consciously encouraged writers to enter the factories for firsthand experience and suggested that workers try their hand at writing.

Such regulation was ultimately unsuccessful, and despite the efforts of talented authors such as Brigitte Reimann, Herbert Nachbar, Hermann Kant, and the veteran Anna Seghers to implement the method of socialist realism, the East German writers who made their mark internationally—Christa Wolf, Heiner Müller, Volker Braun, and others—ignored the constraints demanded by hard-line theorists such as Kurt Hager and Klaus Gysi and produced imaginative works of great depth and texture that nonetheless succeeded in dealing with the realities of the GDR both realistically and symbolically. With the abrupt disintegration of the East German state at the end of the Cold War, socialist realism became discredited as well.

ARRIGO V. SUBIOTTO

See also Der Bitterfelder Weg; Documentary Literature; German Democratic Republic

Further Reading

Chung, Hilary, and Michael Falchikov, editors, *In the Party Spirit: Socialist Realism and Literary Practice in the Soviet Union, East Germany, and China*, Amsterdam and Atlanta, Georgia: Rodopi, 1996

Pracht, Erwin, and Werner Neubert, *Sozialistischer Realismus: Positionen, Probleme, Perspektiven*, Berlin: Dietz, 1970

Robin, Régine, *Socialist Realism: An Impossible Aesthetic*, Stanford, California: Stanford University Press, 1992

Scriven, Michael, and Dennis Tate, editors, *European Socialist Realism*, Oxford and New York: Berg, 1988

Song of the Nibelungs *see* Nibelungenlied

Martin Sperr 1944–

Martin Sperr belongs to a group of authors, among them Wolfgang Bauer, Rainer Werner Fassbinder, and Franz Xaver Kroetz, who in the late 1960s sought to revitalize German theater by breaking with traditional models and reviving the *Volksstück* (folk play). Drawing on the works of Ödön von Horváth and Marieluise Fleißer from the 1920s and 1930s, they injected a new social realism into this form. This realism paralleled the growing politicization of the West German theater and society in the late 1960s, which culminated in the student protest movement of 1968 and APO (extra-parliamentary opposition), and which reflected the widening popularity of the critical philosophy of the Frankfurt School.

Sperr came to prominence in 1966 with his play *Jagdszenen aus Niederbayern,* which was first published in 1971 under the title *Jagd auf Außenseiter: Jagdszenen aus Niederbayern* (Hunting Outsiders: Hunting Scenes from Lower Bavaria), the first of the plays that make up his *Bayrische Trilogie* (1972; Bavarian Trilogy). The play, set in 1949, the year of the currency reform that laid the foundation for West Gemany's postwar economic success, reveals what Sperr sees as the social foundations of the Federal Republic. As the full title suggests, these hunting scenes are not depictions of bucolic pursuits in some rural idyll, as one might find in the traditional *Volksstück.* The human quarry are the victims of the petty-minded intolerance of a village community whose collective psychology is that of unreconstructed fascism. These victims include Protestant Silesian refugees; a mentally disturbed youth who commits suicide to escape being placed in an institution for family convenience; and the homosexual Abram, who seeks to conform by establishing a liaison with a local girl, but then murders her when he discovers she is pregnant. The predominant feature of this society is the dysfunctional nature of personal and familial relations, which are subordinate to the authoritarian control of economic, moral, and legal social determinants. The community's hypocritical self-congratulation at its "purification" through the expulsion of the supposedly sexually deviant and the destruction of the assumed genetically inferior reveals a repressive authoritarianism and an explicit fascist nostalgia in the expression of a need for a new Hitler to counter those who deviate from the societal norm.

The first play of the trilogy illustrates the characteristic features of the new *Volksstück:* a restricted, localized social setting; characters from the common people; and the use of regional dialect. Through this closed regional community a microcosm of contemporary society is offered. As Sperr stresses, although the setting is regional, the inner processes of these communities are intended as paradigms for the whole of the Federal Republic.

The familiarity of the regional setting is also used to expose the grotesque reality of the social structures within it, as the seemingly ordinary, familiar, and protective local community is dissected to expose the authoritarian structures behind it and the repressive mechanisms that control society.

In the second play of the trilogy, *Landshuter Erzählungen* (1967; *Tales from Landshut*)—the title suggests romanticized anecdotes in the tradition of the *Heimatroman* (folkloric novel)—the location shifts from rural village to small town. The social setting also moves from the class of agricultural laborers to entrepreneurial middle-class people who exhibit explicit racist and neo-Nazi sentiments. Set in 1958, the play's historical location is the West German economic miracle. What emerges from the play, however, is not the official image of a social market economy or an industrial democracy but the ruthless struggle of monopoly capitalism, as the heads of two local family construction firms vie for market supremacy and the elimination of their rival. Organized labor is shown to be manipulated by self-seeking opportunistic leaders whose claimed advances for their fellow workers are simply more effective means of exploitation. All personal relations are of an economic order: the daughter's engagement to the rival's son is a financial and business strategy, and the "solution" to the capitalist struggle is patricide, allowing the two firms to be merged through the children's marriage.

These themes are intensified in the third play of the trilogy, *Münchner Freiheit* (1970; Munich Freedom), where the location is moved from the small town to Munich, the Bavarian metropolis, and from the small entrepreneur to national and, subsequently, international business, while the chronological setting is contemporaneous with the play's writing in 1969. Sperr's criticism here is directed at the manipulative practices of big business and the collusion of politicians. Local communities are destroyed at the hands of businesspeople whose meglomaniac dreams of total technological control ride roughshod over individual rights. Ranged against the powerful business lobby and politicians are the protesting students. Sperr does not, however, see any hope in this radicalized youth. Their "emancipation" is no more than posturing self-indulgence, and they are ridiculed as chanters of clichéd political slogans; they function as a channel of impotent, but legitimized protest. As in the other plays, personal relations are grotesquely distorted and subordinated to ruthless self-interest.

The trilogy found a mixed critical reception. The response to the first play was generally positive, but the response was less favorable toward the second, and the third was treated with open hostility and judged a perversion of the social reality of the then contemporary Federal Republic. The criticism itself confirms Sperr's view of society. The first play was seen as no more than a criticism of regional prejudice. The remaining two plays could not be interpreted in this way, and critics were not prepared to accept them as valid social comments.

Sperr's artistic creativity suffered a setback as a consequence of a traffic accident in 1972, after which he created no works comparable to the trenchantly critical originality of the trilogy. The plays that follow the trilogy, *Der Räuber, Mathias Kneißl, Koralle Meier,* and *Die Spitzeder,* which feature an eponymous bandit, a prostitute, and a fraud, respectively, deal with historical, picaresque anti-heroes whose fates reflect the same gloomy theme of social and economic determinism as the more celebrated plays.

MALCOLM READ

Biography
Born in Steinberg, Bavaria, 14 September 1944. Attended a vocational school in Munich and worked in various professions before studying drama at the Max Reinhardt Seminar in Vienna; from 1966, worked as actor and playwright; career interrupted in 1972 after suffering from a brain hemorrhage.

Selected Works

Plays
Landshuter Erzählungen, 1967; as *Tales from Landshut,* translated by Anthony Vivis, 1969
Koralle Meier, 1970
Die Kunst der Zähmung (based on Shakespeare), 1970
Der Räuber Mathias Kneißl, 1970
Münchner Freiheit, 1970
Jagd auf Außenseiter. Jagdszenen aus Niederbayern, 1971
Bayrische Trilogie, 1972
Die Spitzeder, 1977

Further Reading
Anton, Bernd, "Ein bayerischer Dichter: Zum Theater Martin Sperrs," in *Studien zur Dramatik in der Bundesrepublik Deutschland,* edited by Gerhard Kluge, Amsterdam: Rodopi, 1983
Dornbacher, Rolf, "Martin Sperr: Jagdszenen aus Niederbayern," in *Das deutsche Drama vom Expressionismus bis zur Gegenwart,* edited by Manfred Brauneck, Bamberg: Buchner, 1970
Ganschow, Uta, "Martin Sperr, *Landshuter Erzählungen,*" in *Von Lessing bis Kroetz,* edited by Jan Berg, Kronberg: Scriptor, 1975
Müller, Gerd, "Das Volksstück der Gegenwart: Martin Sperr und Franz Xaver Kroetz," in *Das Volksstück von Raimund bis Kroetz,* Munich: Oldenburg, 1979

Spruchdichtung *see* Sangspruchdichtung

Verena Stefan 1947–

Verena Stefan made an impact with the publication in Germany of her first book, *Häutungen* (1975; *Shedding*), by the newly founded feminist press in Munich, Frauenoffensive. The book not only established the author but also enabled the publishing house to produce many further publications by women writers and thus to contribute significantly to the development of feminist thinking and writing in West Germany. A Swiss national, Verena Stefan had moved to Berlin in 1968, where she was active in the women's movement, including the campaign to legalize abortion. Since *Shedding,* she has published further books, as well as numerous articles, reviews, and translations.

Shedding bears the hallmarks of radical feminist thinking of the mid-1970s and echoes ideas developed in the United States, Britain, and France. Translated in 1978, it is also one of the few German feminist texts from that period to have had an impact in English-speaking countries. Subjective and authentic in style, the largely first-person narrative tells the story of a woman named Veruschka, who moves from a hostile environment where she is harassed and exploited by men, or at times subservient to a male lover, to a lesbian separatist lifestyle, which enables her to develop positive attitudes toward both her own body and her creative and intellectual potential. At the time of publication, many readers identified with Veruschka's situation, a response evoked by the book's strong adherence to the principle of the time that "the personal is political."

Above all, in contrast to the issues of race and class, which had formed the focus of the male-dominated political left of the 1960s, the book prioritizes gender: "Sexism runs deeper than racism or than class struggle." Stefan's approach, however, was quickly perceived to be problematic even by feminist sympathizers. The emphasis on the female body and the traditionally taboo subjects of sexuality and menstruation appeared to some to be counterproductive and to trap women in precisely the essentialist rhetoric that they were trying to escape; in particular, the book's argument that "woman equals nature" and its Freudian counterpart "anatomy is destiny" had historically been used to "prove" women's alleged weakness, inferiority, or irrationality.

In the introduction to the book, Stefan defends her attempt to reclaim nature imagery for women, declaring it to be part of her intention to transform the misogynist language used to describe women's bodies and their sexuality. Employing autobiographical strategies as a "Darstellungsform" (form of representation) and changing the male-defined language hitherto used to represent women's bodies and sexuality, Stefan attempts to show the possibility of self-determination for women. Her stylistic innovation is evident in her departures from conventional usage, including her use of small letters for nouns, except proper names; some compound nouns are also written as separate words, creating an alienation effect. At times, this technique draws attention to the etymology of misogynist terminology such as the euphemistic "unter leib" (lower body, for female genitalia) or highlights terms that suggest physical restrictions placed on women through their clothing, such as "büsten halter" (breast holder, for bra). Stefan also associates images from nature with Veruschka's increasingly positive perception of her own body. The title metaphor *Häutungen* has proved problematic and ambivalent, although the English title *Shedding* emphasizes the positive aspects of casting off the past. More important than the literal exactness of the nature imagery, however, is the evolution of the narrative from the first person to the third person, as Veruschka evolves into Cloe, a writer. Reflecting finally on her newly released creativity, Cloe concludes the narrative with the self-confident assertion, "I am my own woman."

Mit füssen mit flügeln (1980; With Winged Heels), a collection of poems and graphics inspired by matriarchal cultures, especially that of ancient Crete, pursues the theme of woman and nature. Nature and intellect are perceived by Stefan as polarized forces that she seeks to reconcile: "To observe the changing seasons, and become familiar with plants and animals, was just as important as reading books about archaeology and mythology."

A similar concern is apparent in the later work *Wortgetreu ich träume* (1987; Literally Dreaming). The narrative, in eight sections, depicts encounters with women in the rural community where the narrator and her woman lover settle and establish their own living area, which in turn becomes a spatial metaphor for women's creative shaping of their environment. The external, natural world, more important here than in *Shedding*, is endangered by "progress," prompting the narrator at times to list imperiled natural species, as if her words made it possible to retain their substance. Thus, following the mention of a "nuclear accident," she lists the names of wild flowers facing annihilation. Here again, the author strives to overcome and reconcile the competing claims of nature and intellectual activity, a goal succinctly articulated in the words "Die Bäume lieben wie die Buchstaben" (to love the trees like letters on the page).

Es ist reich gewesen (1993; A Full Life) is the biography of the author's mother, written after her death. As it was with Peter Handke (*Wunschloses Unglück* [1972; *A Sorrow beyond Dreams*]) and Brigitte Schwaiger (*Lange Abwesenheit* [1980; Long Absence]), the death of a parent here acts as the trigger for an examination of the life of the individual within the political and social context of their time, but Stefan's book is also a subjective account in which the author reflects upon her own life.

While this theme tends to be associated with the writing of New Subjectivity, the literary rehabilitation of the mother-daughter relationship in particular became important in the wake of the feminist movement, especially since it allowed the prioritizing of gender to span generations.

In *Rauh, wild und frei: Mädchengestalten in der Literatur* (1997; Rough, Wild and Free: Young Girls in Literature), Stefan adopts an analytical approach, showing how writers from different linguistic and cultural backgrounds have provided positive images of young women in their fiction. For Stefan, the importance of girls is revealed by the fact that they are still free, physically and emotionally, and have the potential for activities that are closed off when they reach womanhood. Stefan concludes that the writers succeed in giving girls a strong presence and "bringing them into focus."

JULIET WIGMORE

Biography

Born in Bern, Switzerland, 3 October 1947. Moved to Berlin, 1968; trained as a physiotherapist; active in the feminist group Brot Rosen, which campaigned to abolish the section of the law that outlawed abortion, 1972–74; professional writer, translator, and lecturer in creative writing, 1977– . Ehrengabe des Kantons Bern, 1977. Lives in Munich and near Montreal, Canada.

Selected Works

Fiction

Häutungen, 1975; as *Shedding*, translated by Johanna Steigleder Moore and Beth E. Weckmüller, 1978
Wortgetreu ich träume, 1987; as *Literally Dreaming*, translated by Johanna Albert and Tobe Levin, 1994

Memoir

Es ist reich gewesen, 1993

Essays

Rauh, wild, und frei: Mädchengestalten in der Literatur, 1997

Poetry

mit füssen mit flügeln, 1980

Further Reading

Brügmann, Margret, *Amazonen der Literatur: Studien zur deutschsprachigen Frauenliteratur der 70er Jahre*, Amsterdam: Rodopi, 1986
Classen, Brigitte, and Gabriele Goettle, "'Häutungen'—eine Verwechslung von Anemone und Amazone," in *Die Überwindung der Sprachlosigkeit*, edited by Gabriele Dietze, Frankfurt, Darmstadt, and Neuwied: Luchterhand, 1979; 2nd edition, Darmstadt: Luchterhand, 1981
Clausen, Jeanette, "Our Language, Our Selves: Verena Stefan's Critique of Patriarchal Language," in *Beyond the Eternal Feminine*, edited by Susan Cocalis and Kay Goodman, Stuttgart: Hans-Dieter Heinz, 1982
Dangel, Elsbeth, "Übergang und Ankunft: Positionen neuerer Frauenliteratur," *Jahrbuch für internationaler Germanistik* 22, no. 2 (1990)
Frederiksen, Elke, "Verena Stefan," in *Neue Literatur der Frauen: Deutschsprachige Autorinnen der Gegenwart*, edited by Heinz Puknus, Munich: Beck, 1980

Leal, Joanne, "The Politics of 'Innerlichkeit': Karin Struck's *Klassenliebe* and Verena Stefan's *Häutungen*," *German Life and Letters* 50, no. 4 (1997)

Richter-Schröder, Karin, *Frauenliteratur und weibliche Identität*, Frankfurt: A. Hain, 1986

Schmidt, Ricarda, *Westdeutsche Frauenliteratur in den 70er Jahren*, Frankfurt: R.G. Fischer, 1982; 2nd edition, 1990

Tubach, Sally Patterson, "Verena Stefan's *Häutungen:* Homoeroticism and Feminism," in *Beyond the Eternal Feminine*, edited by Susan Cocalis and Kay Goodman, Stuttgart: Hans-Dieter Heinz, 1982

Carl Sternheim 1878–1942

After an inauspicious literary beginning, Sternheim achieved a breakthrough to a new and distinctive comic form with *Die Hose* (1911; translated as *A Pair of Drawers*, *The Underpants*, and *The Bloomers*). The impetus for his new comic mode derived from a productive misreading of Molière's comedy *George Dandin*. For Sternheim, Dandin is a hero: having attempted to assimilate to a higher social class through marriage, Dandin recognizes the error of his ambition. Molière, Sternheim insisted, was motivated by a desire to preserve the vitality of his own bourgeois class by ridiculing its attempts to assimilate into the aristocracy. Sternheim sided with the central comic character, seeing his obsession not as ridiculous, but as an exaggeration of qualities (such as brutal realism) that are essential to his survival. Small wonder, then, that Sternheim reserved his highest praise for Molière's Alceste, whose misanthropic rejection of prevailing social values Sternheim viewed as highly positive. In a post-Nietzschean world the refusal to conform to the "mentality of the herd" becomes positively heroic. Idiosyncratic as his interpretation of Molière is, it supplied Sternheim with a blueprint for his own comedies.

Theobald Maske in *The Bloomers* was the first of a long line of "bourgeois heroes." His behavior is dominated by his concern with his position as a minor civil servant. When his wife, Luise, loses her knickers in public, he fears that the extraordinary incident will draw attention to him and threaten his secure position and the pension that awaits him. The incident is witnessed by two bystanders, the would-be poet Scarron and the Wagnerian barber Mandelstam. Both apply to rent the vacant room in Theobald's flat, hoping that they might seduce Luise, who is aided and abetted in her romantic dreams by Fräulein Deuter. An audience nurtured on French classical comedy would have no difficulty in recognizing the comic constellation. Theobald, with his obsessive fear of scandal and his brutal materialism, has all the rigidity of character of Molière's central comic figures and seems destined to be cuckolded. The comedy, however, confounds the expectations of Scarron and Mandelstam (and those of the audience). Far from being defeated by the comic action, Theobald's obsessive realism triumphs over the delusions of the ideology-ridden minor characters. While in Molière's comedy the central comic figure is defeated and society itself vindicated at the end of the play, in Sternheim's brand of comedy it is society, represented by all the minor characters, that is defeated and the "bourgeois hero" who is vindicated. The audience finds itself laughing not *at* Theobald, but *with* Theobald at the minor characters who constitute society. The laughter that the play originally directs at Theobald proves to be misplaced; the audience is forced to concede that it has been laughing at itself, at its own cultural assumptions, and it is this that constitutes the shock of recognition that Sternheim's comedies provide.

In his next three comedies, *Die Kassette* (1912; *The Strongbox*), *Bürger Schippel* (1913; *Paul Schippel Esq.*), and *Der Snob* (1914; translated as *A Place in the World* and *The Snob*), Sternheim once again adapted Molière's comedies for his own ends. *Die Kassette* offers a reworking of *L'Avare*: in Molière's comedy Harpagon fails in his attempt to impose his rigid order on the other characters, while in *The Strongbox* it is materialism, in the shape of the cash box, that prevails, drawing all the characters into its orbit. In *Paul Schippel Esq.*, Sternheim takes a most unlikely candidate for acceptance into the bourgeoisie and demonstrates his rapid assimilation. In this function Schippel is a typical Sternheim hero: dynamic and vital, he serves to expose the intellectual feebleness of an ideology-ridden society. But Schippel is also a comic figure: he can curse the bourgeoisie with one breath and willingly prostitute his talent as a singer with the next. The ambiguity is characteristic of Sternheim's comic manner. Schippel's vitality and materialism unmask bourgeois pretensions and ensure his success, but he is sidetracked into a make-believe world. Self-delusion in French classical comedy points away from society, but in Sternheim's world it is bourgeois society that is deluded; hence, Schippel's self-delusion leads to his social integration. In *The Snob*, Sternheim produces a modern version of *Le bourgeois gentilhomme*: similar to Monsieur Jourdain, Christian Maske is obsessed with the outward trappings of aristocratic life. But if he retains the comic features of the social climber, his efforts (unlike Monsieur Jourdain's) are crowned with success, as he pensions off his now dispensable mistress and marries Count Palen's daughter. The audience, expecting to laugh at Christian's expense, finds that it is he who has the last laugh. Bourgeois society (including that represented by the audience's values) is no match for the ruthless dynamism of Sternheim's hero.

The outbreak of war in 1914 marked a turning point in Sternheim's fortunes. He was widely regarded as an opponent of the war, and his work was banned from performance. He responded by adapting the work of others: a play by Flaubert, another by the 18th-century German writer F.M. Klinger, Molière's *L'Avare*, Prévost's *Manon Lescaut*, a Maupassant story, and material found in the work of Diderot. That French literature, in the main, supplied the models was in itself a provocative political act on Sternheim's part at a time of unprecedented jingoistic nationalism. He also adapted his "bourgeois hero" to the changed situation, producing a series of plays championing a radical individualism, which finds it expression in a wholesale rejection of European society. While the prewar heroes could fulfill themselves in and through society, characters such as Ständer in the political play *Tabula rasa* (1916) turn their backs on Europe and contemplate a regression to a primitive idyll set in the South Seas. Sternheim's postwar work—*Der entfesselte Zeitgenosse* (1920; Modern Man Unchained), *Der Nebbich* (1922; The Nonentity), *Das Fossil* (1925; The Fossil), *Oskar Wilde* (1925), and *Die Schule von Uznach* (1926; Uznach School)—never reached the level of his prewar work. While he is best known as a dramatist, Sternheim also published short stories, collected under the title *Chronik von des 20. Jahrhunderts Beginn* (1918; Chronicle of the Beginning of the 20th Century), the novel *Europa* (1919–20), and an autobiography, *Vorkriegseuropa im Gleichnis meines Lebens* (1936; Pre-War Europe as a Parable of My Life). The linguistic distortion and density of his prose style, derived from his theory that language should be pared down to essentials in order to grasp a hidden "essence," render Sternheim's prose works, especially in their later reworked editions, difficult to access.

Comedy traditionally deals in aberrations from current social norms; Sternheim's brand of comedy operates in a world in which social norms are portrayed as spurious. For Sternheim, social conventions merely mask materialistic power struggles; linguistic conventions have petrified into cliché. He presents society, not from the perspective of social normality, but from that of the outsider. Aberrations from the norm are seen as heroic, and only incidentally comic; they constitute a kind of perverse ideal, measured against which society is shown to be enfeebled and debilitated. A comic vision that takes as its starting point an individualistic and misanthropic materialism is calculated to challenge the received ideas and values of an audience familiar with the cultural tradition. It is this sociocritical reversal of traditional comedy that constitutes Sternheim's startling originality.

RHYS W. WILLIAMS

Biography

Born in Leipzig, 1 April 1878. Studied at the universities of Munich, Göttingen, Leipzig, and Berlin, 1897–1901; worked as a freelance writer; in Munich, 1903; in Italy, 1905–6; co-editor of the journal *Hyperion*, 1908–12; in Brussels, 1912–13, 1917, and settled there in 1930; in Harzburg, 1914, Königstein, 1916, Switzerland, 1918–22, and Dresden, 1923; his works were banned by the Nazi regime. Died 3 November 1942.

Collections

Aus dem bürgerlichen Heldenleben, 2 vols., edited by Friedrich Eisenlohr, 2 vols., 1947; additional 2 vols. as *Das dramatische Werk*, 1948
Gesammelte Werke, 6 vols., edited by Fritz Hofmann, 1963–68
Gesamtwerk, 10 vols., edited by Wilhelm Emrich, 1963–76

Plays

Der Heiland, 1898
Judas Ischarioth, 1901
Auf Krugdorf (produced 1902), 1902

Vom König und der Königin (produced as *Die Königin*, 1929), 1905
Ulrich und Brigitte, 1907
Don Juan (produced 1910), 1909
Die Hose (produced as *Der Reise*, 1911), 1911; as *A Pair of Drawers*, in *Translation*, vols., 6–9, 1927; as *The Underpants*, translated by Eric Bentley, in *Modern Theatre 6*, edited by Eric Bentley, 1960; as *The Bloomers*, translated by M.A. McHaffie, in *Scenes from the Heroic Life of the Middle Classes*, edited by J.M. Ritchie, 1970
Die Kassette (produced 1911), 1912; as *The Strongbox*, translated by Maurice Edwards and Valerie Reich, in *An Anthology of German Expressionist Drama*, edited by Walter H. Sokel, 1963
Bürger Schippel (produced 1913), 1913; as *Paul Schippel Esq.*, translated by M.A.L. Brown, in *Scenes from the Heroic Life of the Middle Classes*, edited by J.M. Ritchie, 1970
Der Kandidat, from the play by Flaubert (produced 1915), 1914
Der Snob (produced 1914), 1914; as *A Place in the World*, translated by Barrett H. Clark and Winifred Katzin, in *Eight European Plays*, edited by Winifred Katzin, 1927; as *The Snob*, translated by Eric Bentley, in *From the Modern Repertoire*, 1949; also translated by J.M. Ritchie and J.D. Stowell, in *Scenes from the Heroic Life of the Middle Classes*, edited by J.M. Ritchie, 1970; translated by Marion Andre, 1984
1913 (produced 1919), 1915; translated as *1913* by J.M. Ritchie, in *Scenes from the Heroic Life of the Middle Classes*, edited by J.M. Ritchie, 1970
Das leidende Weib (from a play by F.M. Klinger) (produced 1916), 1915
Der Scharmante (produced 1915), 1915
Der Geizige (from a play by Molière) (produced 1917), 1916
Tabula rasa (produced 1919), 1916
Perleberg (produced 1917)
Die Marquise von Arcis (from a play by Diderot), 1918; as *The Mask of Virtue*, translated by Ashley Dukes, in *Famous Plays of 1935*, 1935
Der entfesselte Zeitgenosse (produced 1921), 1920
Manon Lescaut (from the novel by Abbé Prévost) (produced 1921), 1921
Der Nebbich (produced 1922), 1922
Der Abenteurer, 1922
Das Fossil (produced 1923); in *Die Aktion*, vol. 13, 1925; as *The Fossil*, translated by J.M. Ritchie, in *Scenes from the Heroic Life of the Middle Classes*, edited by J.M. Ritchie, 1970
Oskar Wilde, 1925
Die Schule von Uznach; oder, Neue Sachlichkeit (produced 1926), 1926
Die Väter; oder, Knock Out, 1928
John Pierpont Morgan (produced 1930), 1930
Aut Caesar aut nihil, 1930
Scenes from the Heroic Life of the Middle Classes: Five Plays (includes *The Bloomers*; *Paul Schippel Esq.*; *The Snob*; *1913*; *The Fossil*), edited by J.M Ritchie, 1970

Fiction

Busekow, 1914; translated by Eugene Jolas, in *Transition*, vol. 1, 1927
Napoleon (stories), 1915
Meta, 1916
Schuhlin, 1916
Die drei Erzählungen, 1916
Mädchen (stories), 1917; revised edition, 1926
Posinsky, 1917
Chronik von des 20. Jahrhunderts Beginn (stories), 2 vols., 1918
Ulrike, 1918
Vier Novellen: Neue Folge der Chronik vom Beginn des zwanzigsten Jahrhunderts. 1918, 1918
Europa, 2 vols., 1919–20
Fairfax, 1921; as *Fairfax*, translated by Alfred B. Kuttner, 1923
Libussa, des Kaisers Leibross, 1922

Poetry
Fanale! 1901

Other
Prosa, 1918
Die Deutsche Revolution, 1919
Berlin; oder, Juste milieu (essays), 1920
Tasso; oder, Kunst des Juste milieu: Ein Wink für die Jugend (essays), 1921
Gauguin und van Gogh (essays), 1924
Lutetia: Berichte über europäische Politik, Kunst, und Volksleben 1926 (essays), 1926
Kleiner Katechismus für das Jahr 1930–31, 1930
Vorkriegseuropa im Gleichnis meines Lebens (autobiography), 1936

Further Reading

Billetta, Rudolf, editor, *Sternheim-Kompendium: Carl Sternheim, Werk, Weg, Wirkung*, Wiesbaden: Steiner, 1975

Dedner, Burghard, *Carl Sternheim*, Boston: Twayne, 1982
Durzak, Manfred, *Das expressionistische Drama: Carl Sternheim—Georg Kaiser*, Munich: Nymphenburg, 1978
Emrich, Wilhelm, "Die Komödie Carl Sternheims," in *Der deutsche Expressionismus: Formen und Gestalten*, edited by Hans Steffen, Göttingen: Vandenhoeck and Ruprecht, 1965
Karasek, Hellmuth, *Carl Sternheim*, Velber bei Hannover: Friedrich, 1965
Linke, Manfred, *Carl Sternheim in Selbstzeugnissen und Bilddokumenten*, Reinbek bei Hamburg: Rowohlt, 1979
Rogal, Andreas, and Donald Sturges, editors, *Carl Sternheim 1878–1942: The London Symposium*, London: Institute of Germanic Studies, 1992; as *Carl Sternheim 1878–1942: Londoner Symposium*, Stuttgart: Heinz, 1995
Sebald, Winfried Georg, *Carl Sternheim: Kritiker und Opfer der Wilhelminischen Ära*, Stuttgart: Kohlhammer, 1969
Wendler, Wolfgang, *Carl Sternheim: Weltvorstellung und Kunstprinzipien*, Frankfurt: Athenäum, 1966
Williams, Rhys W., *Carl Sternheim: A Critical Study*, Bern: Lang, 1982

Adalbert Stifter 1805–1868

Although Adalbert Stifter's contribution to 19th-century German writing has never been doubted, the nature of that contribution remains contentious. He is still relatively unknown outside the German-speaking world—not least because he is commonly seen in terms of that peculiarly German type of "bourgeois realism" which is so different from that of contemporary French or English authors (e.g., Flaubert or Dickens). Stifter styled himself the heir to German classicism; when it first appeared in print, his fiction was judged purely in terms of conventional social values: a review of *Bunte Steine* (1853; Colored Stones) gushed about characters such as the "poor, child-like priest" (*Kalkstein* [1848; Limestone]) who harmlessly lived out their modest lives. The same years, however, also saw Hebbel's notorious attacks on Stifter's "triviality"; the former sardonically claimed that an inventory would make more interesting reading than *Der Nachsommer* (1857; Indian Summer).

But love him or loathe him, no one then questioned what Stifter represented: he was the high priest of post-classical, Biedermeier values (tranquillity, unambiguous normality, the organic bond between man and nature, the Happy Family and community, and the transcendent nature of "things," *die Dinge*). In the closing decades of the 19th century, however, the true complexity of his work became more apparent when Nietzsche vaunted *Indian Summer* as one of only two German novels that deserved to be read more than once. The notion of Stifter as a simple "flowers-and-insects" poet was finally exploded in the 20th century, especially by Thomas Mann. Mann perceived dark forces beneath the smug surface of Stifter's fiction: he spoke of its "inclination to the excessive, elemental, catastrophic, pathological" and called Stifter "one of the most remarkable, profound, secretly bold and strangely exciting writers in world literature." It is this tension between an unruffled surface and the volcanic stirrings and ructions underneath that makes Stifter's writing so powerful and fascinating to modern readers. Stifter tended to see himself as harking back to Goethe (in one of his more immodest moments, he compared his correspondence with his publisher to that between Goethe and Schiller); seen from our postmodern vantage point, he seems far more the precursor of Franz Kafka.

The first volume of *Studien* (1844–50) demonstrates Stifter's debt to German Romanticism, in particular Jean Paul. We find its trademarks everywhere: beautiful, swooning maidens; love-struck youths; ruined castles; and paradisal nature untouched by humans. Nonetheless, Romantic posturing aside, these early stories demonstrate *in nuce* all the characteristics of Stifter's finest writing, both in content and style. *Der Condor* (1840; The Condor), for instance, displays Stifter's first and arguably most arresting treatment of dual perspective. Stifter claimed to be deeply Christian and, accordingly, insisted that the world is a coherent, unambiguous whole that can be perceived as such by humans who have the "right perspective"—but *Der Condor* is one of many texts that suggest otherwise. Cornelia rises above the clouds in her hot-air balloon, whereupon the familiar, God-given earth appears to her suddenly as cold and alien. Stricken with fear, she looks above her for reassurance; but heaven has ceased to exist, and she sees only a black abyss extending "without measure and without end." The poise that Stifter achieves in this first published work between contrary perspectives—that which reveals measure, order, and stability and that which reveals the measureless, the orderless, and the unfathomable—proves to be typical of his entire oeuvre. It is certainly central to *Der Hochwald* (1844; The High Forest), one of his finest stories, which is, alas, still little appreciated. Here, the paramount theme is that of man's relationship with nature. Stifter, firmly grounded in the Catholic, Baroque tradition of Austria, as well as the classical legacy of the 18th century, perceived nature as a divine agency that operates according to moral laws. Moreover, in the preface to *Bunte Steine,* he asserts that the same laws govern human conduct. He was also a contemporary of Darwin, however, and *Der Hochwald* offers in truth an almost Darwinian view of nature: it is an amoral, autonomous entity that blithely carries on its cycle of death and renewal. Humans, by contrast, have lost whatever oneness they might have had with nature. They alone have to make moral choices and, in Stifter's vision, one false step—particularly if it involves sexuality—condemns them (if they are really lucky) to a lifetime's hard labor in the cause of atonement. The indifference of nature to the plight of humans is a theme that recurs obsessively in Stifter's fiction. *Abdias* (1843) is particularly illuminating here, not least because it reflects the concerns of an age straddled between traditional religious beliefs and explanations and those of the new "science" (Stifter was in this respect a living embodiment of his age: a pious Catholic peasant who nonetheless made painstaking attempts at scientific inquiry and had ambitions to become professor of physics at the University of Vienna). Right at the beginning, the narrator poses the eternal question: "Warum nun dieses?" Why do things happen? Why is it that some individuals suffer a deluge of extreme misfortune while others become the target of equally extreme good fortune? (The same question is repeated almost verbatim in Kafka's *Das Schloss* [1926; *The Castle*]). In *Der Hochwald,* the trigger is clearly sexual transgression—but in *Abdias,* the "crime" lies beyond definition, in the realm of the existential. Man has always sought to comprehend such incomprehensibility by supposing that some metaphysical or godly design lies behind the apparently random visitations of fortune and misfortune. Through the narrator in *Abdias,* however, Stifter offers a radically different, "scientific" explanation: he argues that there is no such thing as "Fate," but instead an infinite "chain of cause and effect" that man's reason is capable of tracing right through to the (implicitly divine) hand that controls it. This seems a comforting and confident vision—but two things are striking as the narrator goes on to elaborate it. One is that the promised understanding will be achieved only at some unimaginably remote point in the future (to borrow a proto-absurdist phrase from *Indian Summer:* "when the human race has ceased to exist" [!]; again, this is starkly prefigurative of Kafka). The second, and more disturbing, is the outcome that Stifter posits. Mankind *will* one day understand the chain of cause and effect—but what he will find is grim indeed: seemingly random catastrophes are in truth the result of "Verschulden," of human fault and failure (the implications of this for Stifter himself are particularly horrendous, given that his adopted daughter ran away and drowned herself in the Danube). In this respect, Stifter is part of a German cultural phenomenon that goes back to Goethe, Schiller, Kleist, and Büchner and that also continues into the 20th century: an obsession with guilt, besmirchment, and wrongdoing and a concomitant anguished fixation upon who or what is responsible.

This vain attempt to fathom the unfathomable is also reflected to great effect by Stifter's narrative technique. The poet Eichendorff praised his eschewing of modern experimentation; indeed, Stifter's calm, laconic style creates an impression of tranquil objectivity and simplicity, of a life lived in accordance with the "sanftes Gesetz" (gentle law) famously postulated in the *Bunte Steine* preface. This simplicity, however, is deceptive. The intro-

ductory paragraph of *Turmalin* (1853; *Tourmaline*), for example, claims that we are going to find a cautionary tale with an unambiguous moral, but the whole story is riddled with subjunctives, uncertain conjectures, and hypotheses, which are again reminiscent of Kafka, and the narrative switches between three narrators, none of whom even witnessed all the recounted events. Similarly, *Limestone* is apparently going to be a "simple tale," but it slides from narrator to narrator to narrator, leaving the reader completely in the dark about the central character, the priest. *Limestone* is particularly fascinating, not least because its reception illustrates the wild divergence of opinion concerning Stifter. It is still sometimes given to children in Germany and Austria as a confirmation present. This may not be surprising: after all, the narrator does tell us that the story contains "nothing unusual" and goes on to recount the story of the good, self-sacrificing priest who helps the local children to cross the flooded fields, saves his pennies to build them a new school, and ensures that his linen is whiter than white. There is far more to this story, however, than meets the eye: beneath the surface, the priest is a shame-ridden fetishist attempting to compensate for his one grievous lapse, namely, his attempt to seduce the half-child, half-woman next door. This, of course, is never directly stated; instead, a web of beautifully subtle symbolism coupled with Stifter's masterful narrative technique intimates the truth with wonderful obliqueness. *Tourmaline, Granit* (1853; *Granite*), and *Katzensilber* (1853; *Mica*) deal principally with another of Stifter's prime concerns, the Happy Family—but all three (similar to so many of his stories) surreptitiously suggest only the ways in which family life is rooted in violence, cruelty, and hypocrisy. In *Bergkristall* (1853; *Rock Crystal*), Stifter's ambivalent stance toward nature recurs: Is nature the agent of God, or scientifically explicable matter? When the children are lost on the mountain on Christmas Eve, Sanna claims to have seen Jesus—but the narrator suggests that a "world beyond" simply does not exist ("Aber es gab kein Jenseits").

After *Bunte Steine,* Stifter, suffering both from hypochondria and real ill health, unhappily married, and loathing his day job, began work on *Indian Summer.* Its surface undoubtedly owes much to German classicism: the work is pervaded by notions of harmony, totality, and wholeness, and Stifter tirelessly trumpets the morally edifying function of aesthetics. Despite this surface, however, the underlying feeling is one of resignation, meaninglessness, and overwhelming sadness in the face of a life in which real love and vital passion have been forcibly stifled. *Indian Summer* is generally viewed as the archetypal Biedermeier bildungsroman. Indeed, it reflects many of the concerns of the age (the importance of collections; the interest in horticulture; the attempts to classify, systematize and measure nature; and the descriptions in lavish detail of pieces of furniture), as well as Stifter's own development as a writer from the subjectivity of the early *Studien* to a more objective style. It would nevertheless be wrong to approach it simply as a bildungsroman. It is true that the main story concerns Heinrich Drendorf's journey from boyhood to manhood; the character, however, barely changes in 800 pages (he undergoes no trials, is never faced with any moral choices, slips into his mentor Freiherr von Risach's way of life, and marries the daughter of Risach's erstwhile love). Moreover, even Stifter admitted that Heinrich's development was not the central theme of the novel. He characteristically did not reveal what was central, but the reader can piece together an alternative story: that of the passionate love and painful renunciation once experienced by Risach and his young tutee, Mathilde. This story takes up relatively little space in the narrative, but the power of Stifter's writing here in all its "classical" simplicity and objectivity means that *Indian Summer* becomes a story of bleak austerity, missed opportunities, and silent grief; of "what a summer it might have been, if it had been a summer at all."

Indian Summer is the point at which interest in Stifter largely dwindles away. Even during his lifetime, his publisher refused to publish the story *Der fromme Spruch* (1867; The Incantation) on the grounds that the style was so boringly, embarrassingly repetitious. It is a fact that Stifter's later writing is astonishingly repetitious: *Der Kuss von Sentze* (1866; The Kiss of Sentze), *Nachkommenschaften* (1864; Descendants), and *Winterbriefe aus Kirchschlag* (1866; Winter Letters from Kirchschlag) are prime examples. His vocabulary is far more restricted than in his early stories (he principally uses only verbs such as "to go," "to be," "to have," "to say," and "to ask"), long phrases are connected with a simple "and then . . . ", and the dialogue invariably consists of repetition of what has already been said. This development in style is particularly well demonstrated by comparing the versions of *Die Mappe meines Urgrossvaters* (1870; The Portfolio of My Great-Grandfather). The early version is flowery and overblown, both in language and in sentiment, whereas the manifold repetitions and circumlocutions in the unfinished novel lead us to the edge of 20th-century absurdism. This is even more marked in *Witiko* (1865–67; also unfinished; Witiko), which, despite being one of the greatest, most extraordinary achievements in German literature, is more often than not ignored or disparaged. This so-called historical novel has no plot to speak of, yet in terms of style, it is Stifter's extreme masterpiece—one seemingly far removed from *Der Condor* and the other early works, but differing from it only in mode, not in its essential burden. *Witiko* is quite devoid of the kind of paraphernalia in *Der Condor* and the other early works; indeed, it is devoid of anything save its mesmeric, litaneutical style. The vision of the abyss, of a world falling apart, however, is even more drastic than that in *Der Condor* because Stifter attempts to stifle it completely—and by trying to stifle it, expresses it all the more emphatically. Beneath the surface of Biedermeier stuffiness is a vision of fracture, emptiness, and meaninglessness more radical than that of any other 19th-century author and, indeed, of any 20th-century author, precisely because there is such a disjuncture between text and subtext. Stifter simply leaves the future behind.

No doubt this narrative technique bears some relation to Stifter's own increasing mania to list in repetitive detail every single minute he spent painting, and his obsession with *Mein Befinden* (The State of My Health), the diary he kept before his suicide, in which he records his ailments and describes the color and consistency of his feces. However, this narrative technique goes far beyond such "psychobiography": it is an unwittingly modern linguistic/stylistic attempt to hold together a world that is about to collapse. Why, then, is Stifter's reputation largely still that of a provincial writer? Partly because he has little to say about urban life, and, moreover, the few comments that he does make are unambiguously hostile. Instead, he retreats, in the tradition of all German conservative culture, to the apparent solidity and integrity of the surroundings where he grew up. But even here he cannot escape the conflicts of his age, the fear that perhaps there is no ultimate meaning and that all events are attributable to a "letzte Unvernunft des Seins" (ultimate unreason of being). Stifter was indeed a Biedermeier backwoodsman; but at the same time, he magisterially transcended not only the limitations of his personal background and horizons but also the artistic conventions and fashions of his age, and he voiced a profoundly modern vision that even now has yet to be truly appreciated.

HELENA RAGG-KIRKBY

See also Biedermeier Period

Biography

Born in Oberplan, Bohemia, Austria (now Horní Plraná, Czech Republic), 23 October 1805. Studied law at the University of Vienna, 1828–30; personal tutor (physics and mathematics) to Metternich's son, Vienna, 1843–46; school inspector, Linz, 1850–65; art critic for the *Linzer Zeitung*, 1852–57; curator, Monuments for Upper Austria, 1853; vice president, Linzer Kunstverein. Member of the order of Franz Joseph, 1854; Ritterkreuz des Weissen Falkenordens, 1867. Died (suicide) 28 January 1868.

Selected Works

Collections

Sämtliche Werke, edited by August Sauer, Franz Hüller, Kamill Eben, Gustav Wilhelm, et al., 25 vols., 1901–79
Werke, edited by Gustav Wilhelm, 5 vols., 1926
Gesammelte Werke, edited by Max Stefl, 6 vols., 1939–54
Werke, edited by Magda Gerken and Josef Thanner, 5 vols., 1949–54
Werke, edited by Max Stefl, 9 vols., 1950–60
Gesammelte Werke, edited by Konrad Steffen, 14 vols., 1962
Werke und Briefe: Historisch-kritische Gesamtasugabe, edited by Alfred Doppler and Wolfgang Frühwald, 1978–

Fiction

Der Condor, 1840
Julius: Eine Erzählung: Erstausgabe nach der Handschrift, edited by Franz Hüller, n.d.
Studien (stories), 6 vols., 1844–50; enlarged edition, 1855
Bunte Steine: Ein Festgeschenk (stories), 1853
Der Nachsommer, 3 vols., 1857; as *Indian Summer,* translated by Wendell Frye, 1985
Witiko, 1865–67
Erzählungen, edited by Johannes Aprent, 2 vols., 1869
Die Mappe meines Urgrossvaters (final version), 1870
Erzählungen in der Urfassung, edited by Max Stefl, 3 vols., 1950–52
Limestone and Other Stories, translated by David Luke, 1968
Brigitta (includes *Abdias; Limestone; The Forest Path*), translated by Helen Watanabe-O'Kelly, 1990

Other

Briefe, edited by Johannes Aprent, 3 vols., 1869
Stifter: Sein Leben in Selbstzeugnissen, Briefen, und Berichten, edited by Karl Privat, 1946
Jungendbriefe (1822–1839), edited by Gustav Wilhelm, 1954
Leben und Werk in Briefen und Dokumenten, edited by K.G. Fischer, 1962
Briefwechsel, edited by Josef Buchowiecki, 1965
"Die kleinen Dinge schreien drein": 59 Briefe, edited by Werner Welzig, 1991

Edited Work

with Johannes Aprent, *Lesebuch zur Förderung humaner Bildung,* 1854

Further Reading

Blackall, Eric A., *Adalbert Stifter: A Critical Study*, Cambridge: Cambridge University Press, 1948

Haines, Brigid, *Dialogue and Narrative Design in the Works of Adalbert Stifter*, London: Modern Humanities Research Association for the Institute of Germanic Studies, University of London, 1991

Hein, Alois Raimund, *Adalbert Stifter: Sein Leben und seine Werke*, Vienna: Krieg, 1952

Kaiser, Michael, *Adalbert Stifter: Eine literaturpsychologische Untersuchung seiner Erzählungen*, Bonn: Bouvier, 1971

Lunding, Erik Peter, *Adalbert Stifter: Mit einem Anhang über Kierkegaard und die existentielle Wissenschaft*, Copenhagen: Nyt nordisk forlag, 1946

Mason, Eve, *Stifter: "Bunte Steine,"* London and Wolfeboro, New Hampshire: Grant and Cutler, 1986

Preisendanz, Wolfgang, "Die Erzählfunktion der Naturdarstellung bei Stifter," *Wirkendes Wort* 16 (1966)

Ragg-Kirkby, Helena, "Stifter's *Witiko* and the Absurd," in *The Biedermeier and Beyond: Selected Papers from the Symposium Held at St. Peter's College, Oxford, from 19–21 September 1997*, edited by Ian F. Roe and John Warren, Berlin: Lang, 1999

Reddick, John, "Tiger und Tugend in Stifters *Kalkstein*: Eine Polemik," *Zeitschrift für deutsche Philologie* 95 (1976)

———, "Mystification, Perspectivism, and Symbolism in Stifter's *Der Hochwald*," in *Adalbert Stifter heute: Londoner Symposium 1983*, edited by Johann Lachinger et al., Linz: Adalbert-Stifter-Institut des Landes Oberösterreich, 1985

———, "The Wild Beyond: Symbolic Journeyings in the Stories of Adalbert Stifter," *Oxford German Studies* 20/21 (1991–2)

Reed, T.J., "The *Goethezeit* and Its Aftermath," in *Germany: A Companion to German Studies*, London: Methuen, and New York: Barnes and Noble, 1972

Roedl, Urban, *Adalbert Stifter in Selbstzeugnissen und Bilddokumenten*, Reinbek bei Hamburg: Rowohlt, 1965

Swales, Martin, and Erika Swales, *Adalbert Stifter: A Critical Study*, Cambridge and New York: Cambridge University Press, 1984

Der Nachsommer 1857
Novel by Adalbert Stifter

Adalbert Stifter's original three-volume *Erzählung*, or tale, *Der Nachsommer* (1857; *Indian Summer*), often referred to as a bildungsroman, elicited from archenemy and contemporary dramatist Friedrich Hebbel (1813–63) the remark that he would give the crown of Poland to anyone who could truthfully claim to have read all of the book. Since the crown of Poland was in fact at that time no longer available, the promise could not have been kept in any case, but the biting criticism of this Stifter masterpiece would be remembered as much, perhaps, as the work itself by all but the most fervent admirers of Stifter's writing.

The journeys of the work's protagonist, Heinrich Drendorf, the son of a well-to-do Viennese merchant family, into the mountainous landscape west of the city is the central story of this slow-moving epic narrative. On one of these journeys, Heinrich comes upon an impressive estate that belongs to a retired Habsburg civil servant of high rank whose name is Her von Risach, otherwise referred to by the narrator, Drendorf, as *"mein Gastfreund"* (my host). This strange figure, clad in eccentric and self-made apparel suitable to his many occupations in retirement, greets the young man and invites him to stay awhile in the house, a spacious building covered in roses and overlooking a carefully cultivated landscape lying somewhere between the foothills of the western mountains and the plains, which extend eastward toward Vienna.

The remainder of the tale—another 600 or so pages in some editions—concerns the ways in which Heinrich's relationship with his host and mentor, his host's wife, and his host's daughter lead to the young man's ethical and aesthetic education or, more properly, *Bildung*, in that all encompassing sense in which the term was used in 18th- and early 19th-century German writing.

At the conclusion of the epic, Heinrich has married von Risach's daughter and lives in harmony among his new and his original family members, withdrawn from the banal world of business and politics and immersed in the universality of the arts.

The great Austrian poet and dramatist Hugo von Hofmannsthal wrote in his essay on *Indian Summer* that this work was closely related to Goethe's *Wilhelm Meister* and bound Austrian literature to German literary traditions more intimately than any other work. The epic shares with Goethe's famous work the same breadth of scope and the quiet intensity of aesthetic and social engagement. Each of its three books, bearing distinct headings and subdivided into sections with their own titles, are tightly related to the others in formal textual arrangements that are nonetheless belied by the expansiveness of the story. Yet in these books the entire scope of a grand bourgeois experience of life is encompassed, including the fruition of mentoring relationships between fathers and their sons, the poverty of the allegedly grand world of masculine nation-state power, and finally the perpetuation of bourgeois values through moral and aesthetic unions of men and women in marriages that form the most appropriate and most necessary of bonds within bourgeois communities. Within this grand design, architecturally reinforced by the text's elaborate if diffuse appearing structures—its division into books and sections, and its elaborate syntactical structures—there yet lingers behind the marble staircase and the endless rosebushes the seeds of its subversion. These seeds are always present—Stifter formulated this idea elsewhere in that telling phrase *die fürchterliche Wende der Dinge* (the awesome twist of material fate)—and comprise the awesome twists of material fate that cannot ever be entirely banished from even the most exquisitely crafted life or the most carefully contrived textual structures. The formal structure of *Indian Summer*, perceived by many readers and even some critics as "weighty" or even "solemnly ponderous," is meant not to conceal Stifter's wise insight in this and all his works but rather to accommodate the stresses that awareness of these awesome twists of material fate place upon Risach and Heinrich and their companions and upon the readers of this novel. The looseness of the narrative and the ponderous bulk of the epic structures are carefully crafted architectural devices that are meant to accommodate stresses without concealing the ever present fault lines. If the novel resembles, in Hofmannsthal's opinion, Goethe's *Wilhelm Meister*, it also incorporates elements of Goethe's less famous work, *Die Wahlverwandtschaften* (1809; *Elective Affinities*), that novel of catastrophe within the most refined of all erotic relationships, the bourgeois marriage and family. Stifter conveys the essence of both these works, their contents and messages, and their superb textual architecture in *Indian Summer*, which rightly deserves the respect and even awe it still inspires today among its small but devoted group of readers.

This extensive work of literature and educational philosophy—Stifter was one of the foremost if largely unrecognized pedagogical theorists of his time in Europe—was for the author an attempt at summing-up his own ethical and aesthetic aspirations. This effort followed his earlier considerable literary success as the author of novellas and short stories, which were serialized in a major literary magazine and later issued separately in book form. It was also the beginning of a long decline of the author's popularity with the wider reading public. Although Hebbel's personal attacks (and those of later writers, such as Arno Schmidt) on Stifter may have been unjustified, there is certainly truth to the implied assertion that this book and the subsequent epic, *Witiko* (1865–67), were decidedly difficult to access for even the well-educated reading public.

There was little critical acclaim for *Indian Summer* when it appeared. It was supported chiefly by Stifter's ever loyal publisher, Heckenast in Pest (now Budapest), who remained a steadfast if often bewildered proponent of his most famous writer. Nonetheless, *Indian Summer* became a "classic," part of the canon of German literature that still determines the reading lists of graduate students preparing for doctoral examinations in German Studies; moreover, it is still honored by Stifter adherents in the several Stifter societies in Europe.

The book has been translated by Wendell Frye under the title of *Indian Summer* (1985), paradoxically both a misleading and accurate English translation of the title, for although there is no hint of the late-season Indian attacks on settlers that gave rise, supposedly, to this term in American English, the ever-present sense of threat in Stifter's work is not entirely banished from this supposed idyll. *Die fürchterliche Wende der Dinge* (the awesome twist of material fate), the more telling citation from Stifter's own work about the nature of reality as he perceived it, lurks in *Indian Summer* in every thunderclap and every ascent or descent of the famous marble staircase that leads to both the inspirational statue of the semi-nude girl and the mentor's private gallery. This perception of reality also parallels the frequent and sudden onsets of disaster that pervade most of Stifter's writings. In *Indian Summer,* it is the very overwhelming affirmation of harmony that somehow does not conceal the potential for tragedy, which that same harmony has only ever pushed to the periphery of authorial or reader consciousness. It is that quality of Stifter's writing in *Indian Summer* and elsewhere that was missed by critics from Hebbel to Arno Schmidt, but was discovered by writers such as Hofmannsthal, Nietzsche, and Thomas Mann, and then emulated by such recent Austrian authors as Peter Handke and Thomas Bernhard and the German W.G. Sebald.

The work is also the inspiration for a recent film, *The Marble Staircase* (1998) made by Roger Mayer, Duncan Smith, and David Udris. The film uses a montage of images and sound tracks to emulate the ways in which the literary work uses language and imagery to conceal and yet to reveal its elegiac heart.

If Mann's ironic comment on the fate of *Death in Venice* protagonist Gustav Aschenbach's works, namely that they had become so famous that they were not a mandatory part of the school curriculum, is insightful about Stifter's place in the canon of German literature, it is also true that these same works, including *Indian Summer,* are increasingly read and reread as examples of that attempt to conceal with language what the writer and the reader nevertheless know to be true, that lightning strikes the just and the unjust (*Abdias* [1843]), that good people plunge to their deaths from high bridges (*Die Mappe meines Urgrossvaters* [1841–65; The Notebooks of My Great Grandfather]), that good deeds are often unrewarded (*Kalkstein* [1848; Limestone]), and that the mysteries of life include the fact of despair (*Hagestolz* [1845; The Old Bachelor], *Turmalin* [1853; Tourmaline]). In *Indian Summer,* although these tribulations are absent, their very absence strikes the reader familiar with Stifter's work at least as an ominous indication of their powerful presence in this work as well. For the persistent and dedicated reader, this work, like the entirety of Stifter's literary work, is also an example of some of the most beautiful German-language writing ever.

DUNCAN SMITH

Editions

First edition: *Der Nachsommer*, 3 vols., Pest: Heckenast, 1857
Critical edition: in *Werke und Briefe: Historische-kritische Gesamtausgabe*, edited by Alfred Doppler and Wolfgang Frühwald, vol. 4, Stuttgart: Kohlhammer, 1997–
Translation: *Indian Summer*, translated by Wendell Frye, New York: Lang, 1985

Further Reading

Bruford, W.H., *The German Tradition of Self-Cultivation: Bildung from Humboldt to Thomas Mann*, London and New York: Cambridge University Press, 1975
Haines, Brigid, *Dialogue and Narrative Design in the Works of Adalbert Stifter,* London: Modern Humanities Research Association for the Institute of Germanic Studies, University of London, 1991
Klieneberger, H.R., *The Novel in England and Germany: A Comparative Study,* London: Wolff, 1981
Marshall, Susan, "Men Dream While Women Struggle: Educational Paradigms in the Bildungsroman," Ph.D. dissertation, University of California, Riverside, 1995
Sjögren, Cristine Oertel, *The Marble Statue as Idea: Collected Essay on Adalbert Stifter's "Der Nachsommer,"* Chapel Hill: University of North Carolina Press, 1972
Swales, Martin, and Erika Swales, *Adalbert Stifter: A Critical Study,* Cambridge and New York: Cambridge University Press, 1984
Van Zuylen, Marina, *Difficulty as an Aesthetic Principle: Realism and Unreadability in Stifter, Melville, and Flaubert,* Tübingen: Narr, 1994

Theodor Storm 1817–1888

There was a time in Germany when Storm was one of the most canonical figures on the compulsory reading lists at universities and in schools. This was true equally in foreign countries, where Storm was immensely popular in numerous translations or where his texts were edited time and time again for school and university use in the original. Halfway through Storm's literary career, his novella *Immensee* (1849; translated as *Immensee* and *Immen Lake*) had already been edited 30 times; by 1915 this work was available in its 79th edition. At the other end of his writing career, *Der Schimmelreiter* (1888; translated as *The Rider on the White Horse, The White Horseman,* and *The White Horse Rider*) has now been translated into 14 languages. In fact, the 20th century saw a situation where, in the United States and the United Kingdom, protests were voiced against the never-ending flood of editions of *Immensee*. It was also claimed that the Chinese communist leader Mao Zedong ranked this little work among his ten most favorite books.

Things have changed over the last two decades, however. Whereas 1971 still witnessed six editions of Storm's collected works in Germany, there has been only a trickle of published primary and secondary works since. Storm's works have also lost their status as compulsory reading in any literature course at secondary and tertiary education level. This seems to indicate that Storm is no longer perceived as having to contribute anything to today's postmodern zeitgeist, despite valiant attempts by literary critics to establish him as a precursor of existentialism or as an important literary social historian and critic of his times. Storm as a writer of novellas who never produced a novel has suffered the same fate as the other writers of novellas of the 19th century in German-speaking countries. Apart from his poem "Die graue Stadt am Meer" (The Grey Town on the Sea), Storm's poetry has remained relatively unknown and has generally not met with the appreciation that it deserves even today. Even film versions of his novellas, notably of *The White Horse Rider,* have not stood the test of time and are at best regarded nowadays as documents enunciating the prevalent ideology of their respective periods.

It can be agreed that in many ways Storm has been the victim of his own reception, something that he himself became aware of in his later life. He himself believed that he was not a successful writer. In his lifetime, the success of *Immensee* was never to be repeated. From time to time, publishers rejected his novellas for publication, notably *Von jenseits des Meeres* (1865; From Beyond the Sea) and *Bulemanns Haus* (1864; Bulemann's House). Most important, however, he suffered from what he perceived as a lack of public acclaim and peer appreciation. Contemporary writers such as Spielhagen and Geibel, who are virtually forgotten in the 20th century, enjoyed considerably more praise from the political classes, literary critics, and readers at large. Essentially, Storm was decried by leading critics such as Franz Mehring and the great novelist Theodor Fontane as the epitome of a provincial regional writer (*Heimatdichter*). Fontane was full of praise for Storm the lyric poet but coined the phrase *Husumerei* for Storm the novella writer: Husum was Storm's birthplace and stood in stark contrast to Fontane's metropolitan Berlin. The result was that Storm, who fundamentally rejected Prussianism, was ignored both by the ideological establishment and by the literary avant-garde. Storm was adopted instead by the petite bourgeoisie and hailed as the *Heimatdichter* who wrote sentimentally about the confines of the home and the melancholy retreat into the provincial. Storm himself attempted to break out of this reception corset by proclaiming that he was not a "poet of the *Gartenlaube*"—the leading magazine of sentimental kitsch literature. Storm also became a staunch anti-Prussian agitator after his enforced exile in Berlin from 1853 to 1864. His novella *Drau(en im Heidedorf* (1871; Out There in the Village on the Heath) marks the turning point in his novella writings. In this novella, a young rebellious farmer attempts to break away from the confines of his birth and the morality and traditional values of the village community. The focal point of this rebellion is his love for an outsider, a Slovak woman, who is rejected and hated by the villagers. This theme of rejection of and rebellion against the value system of parochial communities receives stark treatment in his 1882 novella *Hans und Heinz Kirch*. By this time, Storm had left Husum and had taken early retirement from his legal occupation. It is ironic that even today the tourist industry of Husum utilizes Storm for its own purposes—when the writer himself on many occasions criticized the restricted outlook of this small North German town's citizens. His novellas after 1871 castigate the limited views of small town and village society, and the tyranny of public opinion in such communities. In his second-to-last and longest novella, *The White Horse Rider,* he puts the Faustian figure of Hauke Haien in opposition to the narrow-minded obstinacy of a farming community.

Despite Storm's own shift toward becoming a realist writer, however, the reception history of Storm's work bears witness to the fact that this North German has continued to be classified as a provincial *Heimatdichter* of bittersweet melancholy and resignation. Three of the six 1971 collected-works editions squarely put Storm into this category. They make this judgment despite Thomas Mann's statement in his collection of essays *Nobility of the Mind (Adel des Geistes)*, in which this greatest of German novelists rejects the image of Storm as a parochial writer and accords to Storm's language "the absolute global dignity of poetry." It has to be said, however, that, if one contrasts the limited landscapes of Storm's writings, his people, and their experiences with the momentous historical event of the times and the writings of his comparatively gigantic literary contemporaries, then Storm only appears as a precision toolmaker and not as an engineer of the soul. For comparative purposes, one only has to think of Ibsen, Dostoyevski, Zola, Wagner, Nietzsche, Strindberg, Tolstoy, Henry James, Mark Twain, and many others.

Ironically, at the same time that younger critics from the early 1970s onward have made great and perceptive efforts to change Storm's reception history by emphasizing the socially critical impact of Storm's writings (Peter Goldammer) or the fundamentally existential nature of his works (Wolfgang Heybey), Storm's star has faded. It can now be assumed that he will be (wrongly) reduced to a historical figure of Poetic Realism, a literary school celebrating the retreat from harsh public life, the growth of technology, and the advance of industry, and desperately clinging to the concept of a *Heile Welt* (a world in harmony). This literature of the threatened idyllic is the category into which Storm has already been put and where he (unfortunately) will remain.

                                                    J.K.A. THOMANECK

Biography

Born in Husum, Schleswig-Holstein, 14 September 1817. Law student at Kiel and Berlin Universities, 1837–42; practiced law in Husum, 1843–53; in exile in Potsdam during Danish occupation, 1853; in the Prussian civil service, Potsdam, 1853–56; magistrate in Heiligenstadt, 1856; legal and administrative officer, 1864, and judge, 1874, Husum. Died 4 July 1888.

Selected Works

Collections

Gesammelte Schriften, 10 vols., 1877–89
Gedichte, edited by Hans Heitmann, 1943
Sämtliche Werke, edited by Peter Goldammer, 4 vols., 1956
Werke, edited by Gottfried Honnefelder, 2 vols., 1975
Sämtliche Werke, edited by Karl Ernst Laage and Dieter Lohmeier, 4 vols., 1987–88

Fiction

Immensee, 1849; translated by Helene Clark, 1863; translated by Irma Ann Heath, 1902; translated by Charles C. Bubb, 1909; translated by C.W. Bell, 1919; translated by Matthew Taylor Mellon, 1937; translated by E.W. Triess, 1941; translated by Ronald Taylor, 1966; as *Immen Lake*, translated by M. Briton, 1981
Ein grünes Blatt (stories), 1853
Im Sonnenschein, 1854
Hinzelmeier, 1857
Auf dem Staatshof, 1859
In der Sommer-Mondnacht (stories), 1860
Drei Novellen, 1861
Im Schloss, 1862
Auf der Universität, 1863; as *Lenore*, 1865
Zwei Weihnachtsidyllen (stories), 1865
Drei Märchen, 1866; as *Geschichten aus der Tonne*, 2nd edition, 1873
Eine Malerarbeit, 1867
In St. Jürgen, 1867
Von jenseits des Meeres, 1867
Zerstreute Kapitel, 1873
Pole Poppenspäler and *Waldwinkel*, 1874
Viola tricolor, 1874; translated by Bayard Quincy Morgan, 1956
Psyche, 1875
Ein stiller Musikant, 1875
Aquis submersus, 1876; translated by James Millar, 1910; as *Beneath the Flood*, translated by Geoffrey Skelton, 1962
Carsten Curator, 1878; translated by Frieda M. Voigt, 1956
Renate, 1878; translated by James Millar, 1909
Eekenhof and *Im Brauer-Hause*, 1879; *Eekenhof*, translated by James Millar, 1905
Zur Wald-und-Wasserfreude, 1879
Die Söhne des Senators, 1880; as *The Senator's Sons*, translated by E.M. Huggard, 1947
Der Herr Etatsrath, 1881
Hans und Heinz Kirch, 1882
Schweigen, 1883
Zwei Novellen, 1883
Zur Chronik von Grieshuus, 1884; as *A Chapter in the History of Grieshuus*, translated by James Millar, 1905
Ein Fest auf Haderslevhuus, 1885; revised, 1889; as *A Festival at Haderslevhuus*, translated by James Millar, 1909

Bötjer Basch, 1886
Vor Zeiten, 1886
Bei kleinen Leuten (stories), 1887
Ein Bekenntnis, 1887
Ein Doppelgänger, 1887
Es waren zwei Königskinder, 1888
Der Schimmelreiter, 1888; numerous translations including as *The Rider on the White Horse*, 1915; as *The White Horseman*, translated by Geoffrey Skelton, 1962; as *The White Horse Rider*, translated by Stella Humphries, 1966

Poetry

Liederbuch dreier Freunde, 1843
Gedichte, 1852

Other

Der Briefwechsel zwischen Theodor Storm und Gottfried Keller, edited by Albert Köster, 1904
Briefe an Friedrich Eggers, edited by Hans Wolfgang Seidel, 1911
Briefe an seine Frau, edited by Gertrud Storm, 4 vols., 1915–17
Briefwechsel zwishen Theodor Storm und Eduard Mörike, edited by Hanns Wolfgang Rath, 1919
Theodor Storms Briefe an seinen Freund Georg Lorenzen 1879 bis 1882, edited by C. Höfer, 1923
Blätter der Freundschaft: Aus dem Briefwechsel zwischen Theodor Storm und Ludwig Pietsch, edited by V. Pauls, 1939
Storm als Erzieher: Seine Briefe an Ada Christen, edited by O. Katann, 1948
Garten meiner Jugend (autobiography), edited by Frank Schnass, 1950
Der Weg wie weit (autobiography), edited by Frank Schnass, 1951
Bittersüsser Lebenstrank (autobiography), edited by Frank Schnass, 1952
Der Briefwechsel zwischen Theodor Storm und Gottfried Keller, edited by Peter Goldammer, 1960
Briefwechsel mit Theodor Mommsen, edited by H.E. Teitge, 1966
Theodore Storm und Iwan Turgenjew: Persönlichkeit und literarische Beziehungen, Einflüsse, Briefe, Bilder, edited by K.E. Laage, 1967
Theodor Storm—Emil Kuh, Briefwechsel, edited by E. Streitfeld, 1985

Further Reading

Bernd, Clifford A., *Theodor Storm's Craft of Fiction*, Chapel Hill: University of North Carolina Press, 1963
Goldammer, Peter, *Theodor Storm: Eine Einführung in Leben und Werk*, Leipzig: Reclam, 1968
Rogers, Terence John, *Techniques of Solipsism: A Study of Theodor Storm's Narrative Fiction*, Cambridge: Modern Humanities Research Association, 1970
Stuckert, Franz, *Theodor Storm: Der Dichter in seinem Werk*, Tübingen: Niemeyer, 1940; 3rd edition, 1966

Der Schimmelreiter 1888

Novella by Theodor Storm

Der Schimmelreiter (*The White Horse Rider*) is Theodor Storm's last novella of the more than 50 that he wrote during his lifetime, and it is considered by many to be his finest and most popular work. From his correspondence with family members, friends, critics and publishers, and from entries in his journal, we are well informed about the genesis and development of the work.

As early as the spring of 1885, Storm had made plans for the novella, but he did not begin the actual writing until the summer of 1886. The composition was interrupted by a serious bout with cancer and by the completion of the novella *Ein Bekenntnis* (1887; A Confession). When friends and family members finally deceived him by telling him that his illness was not cancer and, consequently, not life threatening, Storm's serious depression changed to a positive mood, and he completed the manuscript in February 1888. He sent it to his publisher, Elwin Paetel, who printed it in April and May 1888 in his journal *Deutsche Rundschau*, and a few months later in book form in Berlin. Storm, indeed, died of cancer on 4 July 1888; thus, we owe his most popular novella to an act of kind deception.

Long before Storm began writing *The White Horse Rider*, he researched historical documents, volumes about dike maintenance and construction, as well as ancient tales and legends about ghosts, apparitions, and supernatural events. Karl Ernst Laage in his *Sylter Novelle, Der Schimmelreiter* reports that Storm kept two chronicles in his library that date back to the 17th and 18th centuries: M. Antoni Heimreich's *Erneuerte Nordfriesische Chronick* (1669) and J. Laß's *Sammlung einiger Husumischer Nachrichten* (1750). Both chronicle devastating North Sea hurricanes that resulted in the breaching of the dikes, the subsequent flooding of large sections of land, and the substantial loss of life, events that all play a major role in Storm's novella. Heimreich also gives an account of "ein groß geschmeiß einer sonderlichen art von fliegen" (large vermin-like strange kinds of flies) falling like snow from the sky, violent hail storms, "ein sonderbahres blutzeichen" (strange blood images), and five pea-sized human skulls that a county clerk discovers in his washbasin. These details, as well as some others, Storm incorporated in his story. Hans Momsen, a noted mathematician and constructor of diverse implementations, may have served as one of the models for the main character, Hauke Haien.

In various collections of legends and folk tales, Storm found sources of inspiration for other details such as the superstition that a living being—in the folk tales, the child of a gypsy woman; in *The White Horse Rider*, a small dog—must be buried alive in a dike so that the structure will not be breached by the raging, threatening sea. Obviously, the tale of a mysterious apparition, the *Schimmelreiter*, a man on a white horse who appears before imminent danger from storms to warn the villagers, left an indelible impression on Storm's mind. Critics generally classify Storm and his writings as part of poetic realism, a literary movement prevalent in Germany during the mid- to late 19th century. In the case of *The White Horse Rider*, the villagers' opposition to Hauke's projects, the tender love story, the cruel, untamed sea that relentlessly threatens civilization, and the depiction of the North German landscape are related in a realistic fashion, while the supernatural elements are characteristic remnants of Romanticism.

In his youth, Hauke Haien occupies himself with mathematical formulas and the drawing of various dike configurations in the search for the ideal dike, which becomes the driving force in his life. When he is hired as "Kleinknecht" by the dikegrave Tede Volkerts, he begins to manage Tede's books and to advise him on his responsibilities regarding the maintenance and improvement of the dikes. After Volkerts's death, and against the opposition of many of the villagers, notably Ole Peters, but with the essential support of Volkerts's daughter, Elke, Hauke is appointed dikegrave. He is now in a position to realize his main project: the construction of a radically designed dike, behind which new land is cultivated.

Elke Volkerts, an engaging, somewhat emancipated woman and Hauke's only faithful friend to the end, is a definitive support and vital influence in Hauke's life. Again and again, she intervenes on his behalf at crucial moments in his career. She persuades her father to let Hauke keep the books and appoint him "Großknecht," a significant step in his growth. During the crucial election process, when Hauke's candidacy for the position of dikegrave is in doubt because his land holdings are too small, she announces that she will marry him and turn over all of her father's substantial property to him. Hauke, consequently, is appointed the new dikegrave. Without Elke's consistent encouragement and support, Hauke would not have succeeded in bringing his projects to fruition. In the end, when the old dike breaks and the catastrophe is imminent, she, in a last desperate effort, sacrifices her life to come to his aid. Hauke, unable to save her and his daughter from the raging sea, forces his white mare into the breach and drowns. Ever since that ominous event, the *Schimmelreiter* reportedly appears on the dike, warning the villages along the coast of impending danger.

Storm skillfully places the actual story inside a triple frame that serves as an important stylistic element. In the opening paragraph, someone, conceivably Storm himself, reports having read, as a boy, the events that are to be related. The second frame is formed by a traveler, who is compelled by a hurricane to spend the night in a country inn. On the dike, a dark figure on a spectral white horse rushes past him several times in eerie silence. The traveler hears neither the horse's hoofbeat nor its snorting. In the inn, he tells his strange encounter to the assembled guests, who are convinced that it was the *Schimmelreiter*. The inner frame is formed by the village schoolmaster, the actual narrator, who, upon the traveler's request, tells the story proper. The next morning, the traveler continues his journey. Walter Silz, in his excellent analysis of *The White Horse Rider*, explains the function of the frames and the reason for the several interruptions of the account by the narrator.

Storm's masterpiece has intrigued readers for more than a century and will undoubtedly continue to fascinate and entertain audiences for decades to come.

HANS-WILHELM KELLING

Editions

First edition: *Der Schimmelreiter*, in *Deutsche Rundschau* 55 (April/May 1888); *Der Schimmelreiter*, Berlin: Elwin Paetel, 1888
Translation: as *The White Horse Rider*, translated by Stella Humphries, London and Glasgow: Blackie, 1966

Further Reading

Artiss, David S., "Bird Motif and Myth in Theodor Storm's *Schimmelreiter*," *Seminar* 4 (1968)
Barz, Paul, *Der wahre Schimmelreiter: Die Geschichte einer Landschaft und ihres Dichters Theodor Storm*, Hamburg: Kabel, 1982
Blankennagel, John C., "Tragic Guilt in Storm's *Schimmelreiter*," *German Quarterly* 25 (1952)
Burchard, Annemarie, "Theodor Storm's *Schimmelreiter*: Ein Mythos im Werden," *Antaios* 2 (1961)
Ellis, J.M., "Narration in Storm's *Der Schimmelreiter*," *Germanic Review* 44 (1969)

Eversberg, G., et al., *Erläuterungen zu Theodor Storm "Der Schimmelreiter,"* Hollfeld: Bange, 1983

Freund, Winfried, *Theodor Storm "Der Schimmelreiter": Glanz und Elend des Bürgers,* Paderborn: Schoningh, 1984

Frühwald, Wolfgang, "Hauke Haien, der Rechner: Mythos und Technikglaube in Theodor Storm's Novelle *Der Schimmelreiter,*" *Literaturwissenschaft und Geistesgeschichte* (1981)

Heine, Thomas, *"Der Schimmelreiter:* An Analysis of the Narrative Structure," *German Quarterly* 55 (1982)

Hermand, Jost, "Hauke Haien: Kritik oder Ideal des gründerzeitlichen Übermenschen," *Wirkendes Wort* 15 (1965)

Hildebrand, Klaus, *Theodor Storm "Der Schimmelreiter": Interpretation,* Munich, 1990

Holander, Reimer Kay, *Theodor Storm: "Der Schimmelreiter": Kommentar und Dokumentation, Dichtung und Wirklichkeit,* Berlin: Ullstein, 1976

Laage, Karl Ernst, "Der ursprüngliche Schluß der Stormschen 'Schimmelreiter'-Novelle," *Euphorion* 73 (1979)

Lange, Ilse, "Volksaberglaube und paranormales Geschehen in einigen Szenen des *Schimmelreiter,*" *Schriften* 24 (1975)

Silz, Walter, "Theodor Storm's *Schimmelreiter,*" *Publications of the Modern Language Assocation* 61 (1946)

Wagener, H., *Theodor Storm: "Der Schimmelreiter," Erläuterungen und Dokumente,* Stuttgart: Reclam, 1976

Weinreich, Gerd, *Theodor Storm: "Der Schimmelreiter,"* Frankfurt: Diesterweg, 1988

White, Alfred D., "Society, Progress, and Reaction in *Der Schimmelreiter,*" *New German Studies* 12 (1984)

Wittmann, Lothar, "Theodor Storm: *Der Schimmelreiter,*" in *Deutsche Novellen des 19. Jahrhunderts,* Frankfurt: Diesterweg, 1961

Woesler, Maria, "Der Rahmen im *Schimmelreiter,*" *Zeitschrift für Deutschkunde* 54 (1940)

Zimorski, W., *Theodor Storm: "Der Schimmelreiter,"* Hollfeld, 1986

Storm and Stress *see* Sturm und Drang

Straßburg, Gottfried von, *see* Gottfried von Straßburg

Botho Strauß 1944–

Botho Strauß emerged in the 1960s as critic for the theater journal *Theater heute.* In an influential essay, *Versuch, ästhetische und politische Ereignisse zusammenzudenken* (1970; Attempt at Thinking Aesthetical and Political Events Together), he presents himself as a leftist intellectual well versed in Frankfurt School theory. At the same time, he insists that a politically effective theater cannot just mimic revolutionary events on the streets but has to follow its own laws and be guided by its own history. In the middle of the student revolt, Strauß prefers a constructive rather than a naturalistic approach and thus applauds Peter Handke's self-reflexive "Theater-Theater" and Peter Stein's production of Goethe's *Tasso,* with its mirroring and contrasting arrangements and dialogues.

As this influential essay in *Theater heute* suggests, Strauß's work is rich with intertextual references, which range from the Greek classics to the latest advances in theoretical physics. These subtexts make understanding his work at the same time difficult and enlightening. They require readers who dig up the diachronic material to contrast a symbol, allegory, or myth with its usage in literary history. Not surprisingly, Strauß was often re-proached for his elitism and aestheticism. By contrast, scholars have also emphasized the historical rootedness of the subjectivity that legitimizes the work of memory Strauß performs in his texts; his archaeological sensitivity also recalls the discursive work associated with Michel Foucault's concept of "archeology."

Strauß's texts of the 1970s were labeled—similar to those of Peter Handke—as an expression of New Subjectivity, in which the coming to terms with one's own identity and the inability to understand an "other" is central. His early plays present an "aesthetics of loss." The loss of identity that borders on madness corresponds with the loss of a plausible plotline. Strauß's dramaturgical trademarks from his earliest play, *Die Hypochonder* (1972; *The Hypochondriacs*), are the mysteriousness of his protagonists and his vexing play with identity, time, and reality. It is impossible to determine whether the murder in this mystery was real or imagined, and it is left open in *Bekannte Gesichter, gemischte Gefühle* (1974; Well-Known Faces, Mixed Feelings) whether the confused relationships among a group of contemporary people will ever get disentangled and whether their feelings will be defrosted. In *Trilogie des Wiedersehens* (1976; *Three*

Acts of Recognition), the missing plotline is substituted entirely by the logic of visitors meeting, separating, and meeting again by chance, at which time they exchange empty, phraselike conversations, thus mirroring contemporary society. *Groß und klein* (1978; *Big and Little*) brought a breakthrough to German stages. Its central protagonist, Lotte, tries in vain to establish any kind of human contact. Strauß's later success as the most-often played German contemporary playwright is largely due to his ability to transform ideas into theatrical symbols or gestures; it begins with Lotte in the phone booth or in front of the voice com—scenes that capture the total absence of what these new media promise: communication. Lotte's failed attempt at transcending contemporary profaneness or smallness by talking to God or the realm of mythology is written into the play's title and introduces a gnostic element that persists throughout Strauß's later work. The contrast between big and little will continue to serve Strauß as a central theme.

The "subjective" conflicts of the 1970s, which were mainly played out among alienated couples or singles, were subsequently translated into a more comprehensive inability to grasp the inexplicable or "the other." When he has the protagonists of his later plays display a severe loss of memory, Strauß is thus fully in line with a renaissance of myth reception in the literature, culture, and philosophy of the 1980s. He counteracts this loss by making the mythological transparent in everyday life. In *Kalldewey, Farce* (1981), the mythical realm breaks into the play as an allusion to the Orpheus myth and points to the protagonists' conflict as the age-old battle between the sexes. And even after they undergo therapy, they wait for the mysterious, Dionysian Kalldewey to come back. The gods come back in *Der Park* (1983; *The Park*), an adaptation of Shakespeare's *A Midsummer Night's Dream*. But the project of having myth and art work on modernity, or of awaking godlike sensuality and nobleness in the contemporary sleepwalkers, fails: while Oberon transforms into his modern-day counterpart, he has an accident, henceforth called "Mittenzwei" (split-in-two). Since there is no intellectual capacity to receive anything from the beyond, the protagonists live through myth's dark sides without being able to distance themselves from it. Hence, myth returns as ideology (i.e., as Helen's racism). No catharsis is offered either in *Die Fremdenführerin* (1986; *The Tourist Guide*). When love strikes a teacher and his tourist guide on classical ground, here in Greece, the outcome is either animalistic regression (Kristine) or diabolical transcendence (Martin as Pan). It is thus fitting when a critic places Strauß's text within the tradition of negative theology and diagnoses the principle of erotic transcendence as his most important theme. A dramaturgical consequence of these scenarios of expected but never occurring transcendence are Strauß's famous in-between places, which function as places of transition and passage, of waiting and expectation—from the exhibition hall in *Three Acts of Recognition* and the hallway in *Kalldewey, Farce* to the thresholds in *Sieben Türen* (1988; *Seven Doors*) and in *Die Zeit und das Zimmer* (1988; *Time and the Room*).

With *Besucher* (1988; *Visitors*), a play about the conception and realization of a theater play, Strauß's transition from a theater of loss (that allegorically mourns its lost origin in myth and cult) to a theater of presence begins. Orientated at the scientific revolutions in chaos research, Strauß's plays in the 1990s perform what they deal with and present an unexpected, emerging event instead of re-presenting it. Within the autopoetic undertaking of *Besucher*, the fragile reality of language is in the center; theater presents itself as a powerful realm of constant innovation opposite the stagnating reality that it complements. It tries to have its constructed audience perform a eucharistic part in its magical cult, its visions and images. *Schlußchor* (1991; Final Chorus), Strauß's postunification piece, presents the unified Germany as a society unable to conceive of the revolutionary event. The symbolic beginning scene shows the event as a photographic negative, as representation, while the mythological second part presents the possibility of experiencing an absolute moment. *Das Gleichgewicht* (1993; Equilibrium) continues such hidden comment on a united society whose all-too-comfortable balance, which does not seem to allow for change, has fatal consequences.

Similar to his plays, Strauß's prose texts of the 1970s were read as cynical diagnoses of decay (*Rumor* [1980; *Tumult*]). The loss of the self and its annihilation depicted in *Theorie der Drohung* (1975; Theory of Threat), *Die Widmung* (1977; *Devotion*) was criticized as negative-Romanticism. While the negativity of his early prose texts was largely a heritage of modernity, their negation also followed Adorno's *Negative Dialektik*, which already critiqued dialectical thinking as unable to grasp the nonidentical. Strauß's hypochondriacs, madmen, outsiders, and homeless people, however, are also an aesthetic answer to this philosophy of non-identity. Furthermore, the formal fragmentation of Strauß's prose approaches his central theme, the contrast between big and little, by offering (with reference to a paragraph with the same title in Adorno's *Minima Moralia*) detailed penetration of the panorama of German life in small and microscopic scenes (*Paare, Passanten* [1981; *Couples, Passersby*]): "das im Entwischen Erwischte" (that what can be grasped while it escapes) is the kind of paradoxical realism that makes the rootlessness of its working conditions a poetological consequence.

Similar to his plays, his prose texts also reflect the conditions of their own medium: writing as an erotic process of annihilation. Strauß's reception of structuralist and poststructuralist theories on the process of writing is evident. The question "bin ich ein Buch?" (am I a book?) from his earliest prose *Marlenes Schwester* (1975; Marlene's Sister) and the main thread in *Theorie der Drohung*, "was ich auch schreibe, es schreibt über mich" (whatever I write, it writes about me), both trace the annihilation process an author suffers while writing. *Devotion* finds a more theoretical formulation: "nun läuft die Schrift. Es gibt kein Entkommen mehr" (now writing flows. There is no longer an escape). Life is only possible as secondhand experience, and so the writer commits forced plagiarism and perceives himself as "Nullperson, als Durchgangsstation aller möglichen Literatur" (nonentity and a passageway for all types of literature). These insights into the reversal of subject and object in language, and of language and citation as the master of the subject, lead to Strauß's explicit renunciation of dialectics in *Couples, Passersby*—"ohne Dialektik denken wir auf Anhieb dümmer. Aber es muß sein, ohne sie" (without dialectics we immediately think sillier. But we have to do without it). Thus, Strauß's postmodern phase begins. *Fragmente der Undeutlichkeit* (1989; Fragments of Imprecision) is the ultimate consequence of Strauß's poststructuralist insight into the power of the text over its "author." It presents the writer as "Umräumer" (rearranger) of an already existing work. At this point, Strauß's writing becomes more and more allegorical, for allegory as form means a loss—the nonbeing of what it is nonetheless talking about. Strauß's postmodernism also gives a new reading of modernism. It alludes to its themes and styles (i.e., Rilke and Hofmannsthal in *Der junge Mann* [1984; *The Young Man*]) by presenting them as lost and by distancing his postmodern condition from their modernism. Similarly, self-reflexivity and irony, the Romantic tools of expressing the autonomy of an artwork, still serve Strauß to create an autonomy within which—as he stated in his Büchner Prize acceptance speech (1989), "jeder Schaffensakt Überlieferung, jede Progression Rückbindung wäre" (every act of creation would be tradition, every progression retrospection). Imitating a cybernetic biology, *The Young Man* tries to perform memory work by creating such "Schaltkreise zwischen Einst und Jetzt" (circuits between then and now). They compensate for the complete loss of memory in German society, of mythological and historical depth, by reinscribing symbolic knowledge: "denn ohne Mythe und Metapher ist unser zentrales Organ, der Herzkopf . . . nicht angeschlossen an die Ordnung des Lebendigen" (for without myth and metaphor our central organ, the heart-head . . . is not connected to the order of the living). *Beginnlosigkeit: Reflexionen über Fleck und Linie* (1992; Absence of Origin: Reflections on Spot and Line), as closely as it develops its chaotic form, which is oriented at the nonlinear structures of chaos and steady state theories in physics, also attempts to create a mystical communion to grasp the unexplainable, the unexpected, and the emergent.

The texts of the late 1980s and 1990s thus shift toward a more outspoken conserving-conservative attitude, which goes against the democratization of life and the all-encompassing "totalitarianism" of television. *Tumult* and *The Young Man* in particular make the ever-growing loss of memory responsible for the latent continuity of fascism in German society. According to *Niemand anderes* (1987; Nobody Else), the rationalizations and negativity of Germany's satirical intelligence have not only not prevented the reemergence of dark forces such as neo-Nazis but also cannot offer intellectual orientation to escape the feeling of emptiness. After unification, a new debate about what terms such as *left* and *right* still meant followed as a reaction to some prominent leftist intellectuals' (e.g., Enzensberger, Heiner Müller, and Martin Walser) political shift to the right. As long as Strauß's conservatism was still expressed on stage or through debating protagonists in his prose, his critics focused on his "hopelessly Romantic" attitude and secluded existence, and on detecting the politics behind the seemingly unpolitical. They called him nationalistic after his identification of himself as German in his prose poem *Diese Erinnerung an einen, der nur einen Tag zu Gast war* (1985; This Memory of Someone Who Was a Guest for One Day Only). Expressing his heretic views about a necessary "Gegenaufklärung" (counterenlightenment) in an essay in the weekly *Der Spiegel* titled *Anschwellender Bocksgesang* (1993; Growing/Rising Tragedy), however, caused a scandal during which Strauß was labeled a representative of the New Right in Germany, called a fascist, or put in a camp with the Conservative Revolution of the 1920s. His reaction was a flight back to Greek antiquity (*Ithaka* [1996]) on the one hand; on the other hand, he radicalized Adorno's critique of rationality to a point where his work became—as *Fragmente der Undeutlichkeit*

had called it—"untranslatable" for political readings, or "einschweigbar" (capable of being made silent). When language forgets its communicability, it may happen that one can see an abrupt, inconceivable beauty emerge again and offer a home as in the work of an elected affinity, Robinson Jeffers, to whom Strauß pays tribute in *Jeffers-Akt I & II* (1998), the scenic version of some of his poems (*Mara*, 1998), or *Der Kuß des Vergessens* (1998; Kiss of Forgetting).

Strauß's most recent texts seem to come full circle with where the critics had left him on the height of his fame, before his fall from grace: *Wohnen, Dämmern, Lügen* (1994; Living Glimmering Lying) and, even more so, *Die Fehler des Kopisten* (1997; The Errors of the Copyist) seem to copy *Couples, Passersby* in their unpretentious, witty diagnosis of contemporary society. The difference is that in the latter text not so many passersby remain to be observed. By contrast, it focuses mainly on nature in the "Uckermark" (a quiet area in Brandenburg where Strauß moved from Berlin with his family.) The literary models for this most autobiographical account, cited by the critics with some uneasiness, range from Rousseau to Flaubert to Jünger. The emphatic descriptions, sometimes celebrations, of his new home and the long reflective walks with his son suggest that he has arrived in a *hortus conclusus* and is producing a new form of mature work.

SIGRID BERKA

Biography

Born in Naumburg/Saale, 2 December 1944. Studied German languages and literatures, history of theater, and sociology at the universities of Cologne and Munich; editor of *Theater Heute*, 1967–70; dramatic adviser for Schaubühne am Halleschen Ufer theater company, 1970–75; lived in Berlin most of his life. Hannover Dramatists' Prize, 1974; Villa Massimo grant, 1976; Schiller Prize, 1977; German Records Prize, 1980; Bavarian Academy of Fine Arts Prize, 1981; Mülheim Dramatists' Prize, 1982; Jean Paul Prize, 1987; Büchner Prize, 1989. Currently lives in the Uckermark, a remote area in Brandenburg.

Selected Works

Plays

Die Hypochonder (produced Hamburg, 1972), 1979; as *The Hypochondriacs* (produced 1992)
Bekannte Gesichter, gemischte Gefühle (produced 1975), 1974
Trilogie des Wiedersehens (produced 1977), 1976; as *Three Acts of Recognition*, in *West Coast Plays*, vol. 8, 1981
Groß und klein: Szenen (produced 1978), 1978; as *Big and Little: Scenes* (produced 1979), translated by Anne Catteneo, 1979; as *Great and Small* (produced 1983)
Kalldewey, Farce (produced 1982), 1981
Der Park (produced 1984), 1983; as *The Park* (produced 1988), translated by Tinch Minter and Anthony Vivis, 1988
Die Fremdenführerin (produced 1985), 1986; as *The Tourist Guide* (produced 1987), 1987
Sieben Türen: Bagatellen, 1988; as *Seven Doors* (produced 1992)
Besucher, 1988
Die Zeit und das Zimmer, 1988
Fragmente der Undeutlichkeit (includes *Jeffers-Akt I & II*; *Sigé*), 1989
Schlußchor (produced 1991), 1991
Angelas Kleider, 1991
Theaterstücke, 2 vols., 1991 (vol. 1 includes *Die Hypochonder*; *Bekannte Gesichter, gemischte Gefühle*; *Das Sparschwein*, by Eugène Labiche, translated and produced by Strauß; *Sommergäste*, by

Maxim Gorky, rewritten by Strauß and Peter Stein; *Trilogie des Wiedersehens*; *Gross und klein*; vol. 2 includes *Kalldewey*; *Der Park*; *Die Fremdenführerin*; *Molière's Misanthrop*, translated by Strauß; *Besucher*; *Die Zeit und das Zimmer*; *Sieben Türen*; *Schlußchor*; *Angelas Kleider*)
Das Gleichgewicht, 1993
Ithaka: Schauspiel nach den Heimkehr-Gesängen der Odyssee, 1996
Die Ähnlichen: Moral Interludes, 1998
Der Kuß des Vergessens: Vivarium rot, 1998
Jeffers-Akt I und II, 1998

Fiction

Schützenehre, 1974–75
Marlenes Schwester (collection), 1975
Die Widmung, 1977; as *Devotion*, translated by Sophie Wilkins, 1979
Rumor, 1980; as *Tumult*, translated by Michael Hulse, 1984
Paare, Passanten, 1981; as *Couples, Passersby*, translated by Roslyn Theobald, 1996
Der junge Mann: Roman, 1984; as *The Young Man*, translated by Roslyn Theobald, 1995
Niemand anderes, 1987
Über Liebe: Geschichten und Bruckstücke, 1989
Fragmente der Undeutlichkeit, 1989

Poetry

Diese Erinnerung an einen, der nur einen Tag zu Gast war: Gedicht, 1985

Other

Versuch, ästhetische und politische Ereignisse zusammenzudenken: Texte über Theater, 1967–1986, 1987
Kongress: Die Kette der Demütigungen, 1989
Beginnlosigkeit: Reflexionen über Fleck und Linie, 1992
Anschwellender Bocksgesang, in *Der Spiegel*, vol. 6, 1993; 2nd edition, in *Der Pfahl: Jahrbuch aus dem Niemandsland zwischen Kunst und Wissenschaft VII*, 1993
Wohnen, Dämmern, Lügen, 1994
Die Fehler des Kopisten, 1997

Translations

Molière, *Molières Misanthrop*, 1987
Eugène Labiche, *Das Sparschwein*, 1981

Edited Works

Peer Gynt, ein Schauspiel aus dem neunzehnten Jahrhundert, with Ellen Hammer and Karl Ernst Herrmann, 1971
Moses Mendelssohn, *Briefwechsel*, 1974

Further Reading

Adelson, Leslie, *Crisis of Subjectivity: Botho Strauß's Challenge to West German Prose of the 1970's*, Amsterdam: Rodopi, 1984
Bauer, Karin, "Gegenwartskritik und nostalgische Rückgriffe: Die Abdankung der Frau als Objekt männlichen Begehrens und die Erotisierung der Kindfrau in Botho Strauß' *Paare, Passanten*," *German Quarterly* 69, no. 2 (1996)
Berka, Sigrid, *Mythos-Theorie und Allegorik bei Botho Strauß*, Vienna: Passagen, 1991
Frederico, Joseph, "German Identity and the Politics of Postmodernity: A Reading of Botho Strauß's *Der junge Mann*," *German Quarterly* 66, no. 3 (1993)
Herwig, Henriette, *Verwünschte Beziehungen, verwebte Bezüge: Zerfall und Verwandlung des Dialogs bei Botho Strauß*, Tübingen: Stauffenburg, 1986
Kaußen, Helga, *Kunst ist nicht für alle da: Zur Ästhetik der Verweigerung im Werk von Botho Strauß*, Aachen: Alano, 1991

McGowan, Moray, "Botho Strauß," in *The Modern German Novel*, edited by Keith Bullivant, Leamington Spa and New York: Berg, 1987

Dramas

Botho Strauß is one of Germany's most critically acclaimed and influential authors and cultural critics, but he is also one of the most enigmatic and controversial. Avoiding publicity and shunning performances of his dramas, Strauß leads the life of a recluse in Berlin. Hailed by Marcel Reich-Ranicki as the representative author of the 1968 student generation, Strauß enjoys a literary reputation that developed in the mid-1970s after the publication of his well-received drama, *Trilogie des Wiedersehens* (1976; *Three Acts of Recognition*), which German critics voted play of the year in 1977. The drama earned Strauß several awards, including the Förderpreis des Schillerpreises, and cemented his position as one of Germany's leading playwrights. The play, organized around an art exhibition, portrays several former 1960s radicals who seem to have forgotten their ideals and the issues that seemed so important to them just a few years prior and who are now mired in indecision and social confusion. The German television station ZDF broadcasted the play.

Strauß began his career as a dramatic advisor at the Schaubühne in Berlin, where he worked from 1970 to 1974. His first two dramas, *Die Hypochonder* (1979; The Hypochondriacs) and *Bekannte Gesichter, gemischte Gefühle* (1974; Well-Known Faces, Mixed Feelings), are overly gloomy and contain characters who appear despondent, incapable of action, and stymied by society. Influenced by the failure of the student revolutions of the late 1960s to effect long-lasting social change and informed by French structuralist and poststructuralist theory—Michel Foucault in particular—Strauß suggests that individuals are defined by social, political, and economic structures. Severed from history and haunted by a loss of subjectivity due to the mass media and technology, his characters search for meaning and purpose, but they continually find disappointment, alienation, and further confusion. Although critics labeled his works as typical of the *Neue Subjektivität* or *Neue Innerlichkeit* trends, Strauß's work tends to defy categorization.

Continuing the critical success and popularity of *Trilogie des Wiedersehens*, Strauß's next three dramas, *Groß und klein: Szenen* (1978; *Big and Little: Scenes*), *Kalldewey, Farce* (1981; Kalldewey, Farce), and *Der Park* (1983; *The Park*), explore in further detail themes of alienation, loss of subjectivity, and the failure of language as a means of communication. In *Big and Little: Scenes*, a ten-scene *Stationsdrama*, the protagonist Lotte encounters individuals who are locked in their own world of isolation. Lotte exhibits a mood of diachronic longing and a desire to reestablish a vibrant relationship with history and traditions, a relationship that has been destroyed by modern media and technology. She raises theological and epistemological questions about salvation and existence only to find a general sense of helplessness and disinterest. In 1980, the drama was broadcast on television. In *Kalldewey, Farce*, intersubjective relationships are shown to be untenable due to societal, technical, and personal oppression. *The Park*, which incorporates aspects of Shakespeare's *A Midsummer Night's Dream*, thematizes artistic production, salvation, and repression. Oberon and Titania's mission to return beauty to earth is met with contempt by society, and they are ultimately stripped of their otherworldly powers. Each of these dramas underscores Strauß's rejection of the Frankfurt School, its negative dialect, and Adorno's notion of aesthetic autonomy in favor of a postmodern view of a plurality of meanings. Proceeding from the standpoint that all meaning and signs are suspect, Strauß forces the reader to confront the drama's language and its set of signifiers. The drama *Die Fremdenführerin* (1986; *The Tourist Guide*) continues Strauß's interest in mythology and the possibilities a modern mythology may present. Desiring to flee the world and uncover each other's secrets, Martin and Kristine return to Olympia. When Kristine leaves him, she appears as a mythological allusion. This adaptation of the Orpheus and Eurydice myth finds expression in several of Strauß's works.

Besucher (1988; Visitors) is a collection of three plays, each exploring the tenuous relationship between the individual and modern society, as well as the individual's perception of and relationship to time and history, a topic that pervades most of Strauß's dramatic and prose works. In the title play *Besucher,* a play within a play, Strauß merges the perspective of a play to be performed and the text itself, thus forcing the reader to differentiate between them. The two textual perspectives correspond to the artistic perspectives of the two main characters, a famous actor in favor of realistic acting and a young, avant-garde actor who wishes to transcend realism. *Die Zeit und das Zimmer* (1988; Time and the Room) and *Sieben Türen* (1988; Seven Doors) are reminiscent of *Big and Little: Scenes* and, especially, the prose work *Paare, Passanten* (1981; *Couples, Passersby*). In *Die Zeit und das Zimmer,* two men observe from their apartment window strangers walking below. As they comment upon them, they begin to substitute these stories for their own history, but ultimately their lives are shown to be filled with desperation and an unarticulated sense of loss and emptiness. In *Sieben Türen,* a play consisting of 11 vignettes, Strauß suggests that the abilities to express personal freedom, make decisions, and enjoy life are products of societal control and a definition of the individual that prohibits a sincere expression of the self. In 1987, Strauß published his collected essays on the theater in *Versuch, ästhetische und politische Ereignisse zusammenzudenken: Texte über Theater, 1967–1986* (1987; Essays on the Combination of Aesthetic and Political Events).

Since the unification of Germany in 1990, Strauß has been keenly interested in the issues raised by the 40 years of separation undergone by the two German cultures. In 1991, he published two works that treat on a metaphorical level the difficulties the unified Germany will have in overcoming the problems history, and in a larger sense, two competing economic and ontological views, have placed on it. In *Angelas Kleider* (1991; Angela's Clothes), a mother continually purchases new clothes in order to disguise her young daughter, only to find her ugliness more pronounced. Criticizing how Germany was unified, Strauß suggests that a unified Germany must undergo a renewed *Vergangenheitsbewältigung* (coming to terms with the past) and come to terms with disparate histories. In *Schlußchor* (1991; Final Chorus), Strauß uses the leitmotif of a mirror to suggest that each character, as well as the reader, must reflect on his or her position in the public sphere (German society) and the private sphere (interpersonal relationships). Male figures such as

the architect Lorenz, who symbolizes West Germany, are shown as dominating personalities who fail to recognize women as autonomous beings. In the end, Anita von Schastorf, a woman and symbol of the weaker East Germany, asserts her individuality and kills an eagle, a longtime symbol of Germany. These dramas led to renewed criticism that Strauß is a postmodern melancholic and cultural pessimist.

Since his essay *Anschwellender Bocksgesang* (1993; Growing/Rising Tragedy) in the German weekly *Der Spiegel,* Strauß has been associated with the growing right-wing extremism among German intellectuals and authors and denounced for his supposed reactionary tendencies. In *Das Gleichgewicht* (1993; Equilibrium), the bourgeois Groth returns home from a year's absence and tests the loyalty of his younger wife, Lily. Groth suspects that Lily, who had led a double life as a faithful wife and punk rocker on the Berlin *S-Bahn,* has had an affair with a pop singer. The Odysseus and Penelope myth also serves as the basis for one of Strauß's most recent dramas, *Ithaka* (1996; Ithaca), which is a dramatization of the last ten books of Homer's *Odyssey.* Upon returning home, Odysseus refrains from killing those who had conspired against him during his absence, but Athena persuades him to act and assert his legitimate power. In this drama of little action, Strauß criticizes contemporary political culture, in which special interest groups and political parties seem more concerned about their agenda than with the welfare of the state. *Ithaka* is also a crass warning for strong-armed politicians or irresponsible leaders who manipulate a weak government for private gain.

GREGORY H. WOLF

Editions

First editions:

Bekannte Gesichter, gemischte Gefühle: Komödie, Frankfurt: Verlag der Autoren, 1974
Trilogie des Widersehens: Theaterstücke, Munich and Vienna: Hanser, 1976
Groß und klein: Szenen, Munich and Vienna: Hanser, 1978
Die Hypochonder; Bekannte Gesichter, gemischte Gefühle: 2 Theaterstücke, Munich and Vienna: Hanser, 1979
Kalldewey, Farce, Munich: Hanser, 1981
Der Park: Schauspiel, Munich: Hanser, 1983
Die Fremdenführerin: Stück in 2 Akten, Munich: Hanser, 1986
Besucher: Drei Stücke, Munich: Hanser, 1988
Angelas Kleider: Nachtstück in zwei Teilen, Munich: Hanser, 1991
Schlußchor: Drei Akte, Munich: Hanser, 1991
Das Gleichgewicht: Ein Stück in drei Akten, Munich: Hanser, 1993
Ithaka: Ein Schauspiel nach den Heimkehr-Gesängen der Odyssee, Munich: Hanser, 1996

Translations:

Big and Little: Scenes (Groß und klein: Szenen), translated by Anne Cattaneo, New York: Farrar, Straus, and Giroux, 1979
Three Acts of Recognition (Trilogie des Widersehens), in *West Coast Plays,* vol. 8, Berkeley, California: California Theatre Council, 1981
The Park (Der Park Schauspiel), translated by Tinch Minter and Anthony Vivis, Sheffield: Sheffield Academic Press, 1988

Further Reading

Adelson, Leslie, *Crisis of Subjectivity: Botho Strauß' Challenge to West German Prose of the 1970's,* Amsterdam: Rodopi, 1984
Arnold, Heinz Ludwig, editor, *Botho Strauß,* Munich: Text und Kritik, 1984

Berka, Sigrid, *Mythos-Theorie und Allegorik bei Botho Strauß*, Vienna: Passagen, 1991

Kapitza, Ursula, *Bewußtseinsspiele: Drama und Dramaturgie bei Botho Strauß*, Frankfurt and New York: Lang, 1987

Kazubko, Katrin, *Spielformen des Dramas bei Botho Strauß*, Hildesheim and New York: Olms, 1990

McGowan, Moray, *"Neue Subjektivität,"* in *After the "Death of Literature": West German Writing of the 1970s*, edited by Keith Bullivant, Oxford: Berg, 1988

Radix, Michael, editor, *Strauß Lesen*, Munich: Hanser, 1987

Sandhack, Monika, *Jenseits des Rätsels: Versuch einer Spurensicherung im dramatischen Werk von Botho Strauß*, Frankfurt and New York: Lang, 1986

Anschwellender Bocksgesang 1993

Essay by Botho Strauß

Botho Strauß's essay *Anschwellender Bocksgesang* (Growing/Rising Tragedy) was published in the German weekly *Der Spiegel*, an unusual place for a writer who had never before published an outspoken political pamphlet. Due to its provocative argumentation, it caused—two years after the notorious Christa Wolf scandal—a new literary debate. The essay was taken as a signifier for a mood swing in the cultural scenery of the 1990s: authors who had represented a long-standing leftist or liberal tradition, such as Hans Magnus Enzensberger, Peter Schneider, Martin Walser, and Heiner Müller, suddenly seemed to have shifted toward a conservative rightist consensus. Trying to cope with the sudden reversal of what should be considered "left" or "right," critics accused Strauß of propagating reactionary paradigms of the Conservative Revolution of the 1920s, which was linked with thinkers and writers such as Spengler, Heidegger, and Jünger. He was even called a "noble fascist."

What had caused this outrage? *Anschwellender Bocksgesang* regards the free and enlightened German welfare society as stuck in a dangerous *Gleichgewicht* (steady-state/equilibrium). It is threatened in its core by its pure economical orientation, its diminishing capacity to change itself, its loss of positive values and norms, and by the overpowering and all-encompassing telecratic regime of the modern television-influenced society. Strauß sees the hostility against foreigners and the revival of neo-Nazism as direct effects of the purely negative, critical energy of leftist intellectuals (with whom he used to align himself in the 1960s and 70s). In Strauß's view, their mainly negative attitudes toward institutions such as the church, the military, and, in short, any kind of authority, has left a nihilistic void—now filled with right-wing extremism—leaving the postwar generation without an orientation at all, without stabilizing convictions or religious beliefs for which this society—in case of a crisis—would be willing to stand up or even fight. "Der Liberale ist nicht liberal durch sich selbst, sondern . . . als Gegner des Anti-liberalismus." (The liberal is not liberal through himself, but . . . as an opponent of anti-liberalism.)

As some critics recognized, Strauß here follows through with a radicalized version of Adorno's *The Dialectic of Enlightenment*, a philosophy that had been in the background of Strauß's writings in the 1980s, and which—contrary to the arguments of some literary scholars—he never really left behind. While his writings in this sense have always focused on that which escapes the enlightened mind—by evoking the mysterious, unexplainable, unexpectedly emergent—the *Spiegel* essay is a failed attempt at translating his genuinely conservative aesthetics, displayed in his texts in allegorical, hermetical, or ironic fashion, into a clear political lingo. Strauß's mysterious self-identification in *Bocksgesang* as *ein Rechter in der Richte* (a right/right-wing person in the right setting/adjusting position/direction) was thus taken as a political rather than as an aesthetic credo. In another context, Strauß's postscript to the 1990 German translation of George Steiner's 1989 *Real Presences* (*Von Realer Gegenwart*) clarifies that what he calls "reactionary" thinking is really imminently progressive: The reactionary is precisely not, as political denunciation has it, the one who delays or the one who incorrigibly regresses—on the contrary, he progresses if concerned with bringing back something forgotten into memory. According to Steiner, each great work of art proceeds in exactly the same way and, hence, is in a temporary sense "reactionary"; it fights against forgetfulness in each era.

Strauß senses the breakdown of a society whose telecratic "totalitarianism" does not allow for a rebellion by its members, who are unable to grasp any kind of unenlightened past, historical progress, or mythical time. His countermodel is—again—an aesthetic one: Greek tragedy (to which the title *Bocksgesang* alludes), which still provides for the means of experiencing dawning catastrophes and for coping with suffering. The only way to achieve a fundamental change in attitudes, in his view, is to withdraw into the position of the "Einzelgänger" (loner, hermit) in order to contribute to such a change of mind.

While few critics acknowledged the truth of Strauß's societal analysis, they also thought it dangerous to mix aesthetic and political discourses in the way that Strauß had done. They argued that he went too far in his analysis of the "totalitarian character" of modern media society, with its talk shows in which the most intimate details of a person's life were "moderated" down to an endless public *Gerede* (rumor). And last, but not least, they denounced Strauß's argumentation, which stipulated right-wing violence as a direct outcome (or the Janus head) of 1968's generation of father-haters, as too simplistic.

The debate flared up again after Strauß allowed his essay to be published in a collection of right-wing essays, *Die selbstbewußte Nation: Anschwellender Bocksgesang und weitere Beiträge zu einer deutschen Debatte* (1994; The Self-Confident Nation: Growing/Rising Tragedy and More Contributions on a German Debate), one of which promoted the German's right to claim a home of their own due to the genuine German heritage of *metaphysische Unbehaustheit* (metaphysical homelessness). As a consequence, the author of this particular essay, Gerd Bergfleth, opted against the notion of Germany as an immigration country or a multicultural society. If one reads Strauß's reference in *Bocksgesang* to René Girard's book *Das Heilige und die Gewalt* (originally published in French, 1992; *Violence and the Sacred*), which postulates that the source of violence in premodern cultures was a *Gleichgewicht* (steady state/equilibrium) that prevented them from changing, against the decidedly political nature of a claim like Bergfleth's, it is easy to understand some critics' concern about *Bocksgesang* promoting violence. Strauß's unwise decision to have his text, which he sees as politically unusable, published within such a dubious context, made some of his defenders reconsider their position. And, given the correspondences between Strauß's argumentation and the antiliberal and anti-enlightened positions during the Conservative Revolution, the appropriateness and up-to-datedness of an old argument—namely, that the fall of the Weimar Republic was partially due to such positions—became evident.

SIGRID BERKA

Editions

First edition: *Anschwellender Bockgsgesang*, in *Der Spiegel* 6 (1993); 2nd edition in *Der Pfahl: Jahrbuch aus dem Niemandsland zwischen Kunst und Wissenschaft VII*, Munich: Maathes und Seitz, 1993

Further Reading

Berka, Sigrid, "Das Werk von Botho Strauß und die 'Bocksgesang'-Debatte," *Weimarer Beiträge* 2 (1994)

Harbers, Henk, "Botho Strauß' *Bocksgesang* oder Wie die Literatur im Essay ihr Gleichgewicht verliert," *Amsterdamer Beiträge zur neueren Germanistik* 38/39 (1995)

Wolting, Stephan, "Wer wird denn einen Essayisten loben?" in *Schreiben und Übersetzen: Theorie allenfalls als Versuch einer Rechenschaft*, edited by Wilhelm Gossmann and Christoph Hollender, Tübingen: Narr, 1994

Marlene Streeruwitz 1950–

Marlene Streeruwitz established herself as a shooting star among contemporary playwrights with *New York. New York.* (1993). After five years, some German stages took on the challenge of performing her provocative plays; *Waikiki. Beach.* (Cologne, 1992), and then *New York. New York.* (Munich, 1993), with great success. Violence in everyday life, especially violence against women, is a common theme in Streeruwitz's plays as well as her prose, as in *Frühstück und Gewalt: Prosa und Szenen* (1997; Breakfast and Violence: Prose and Scenes).

In her plays, the unity of place is kept throughout, but the exotic titles stand in ironic contrast to the fact that these places—be it a subterranean toilet or a run-down building frequented by the mayor of the city and his lover—can clearly be found in the middle of Vienna. They stand in for "die Welt als Möglichkeit" (the world as possibility), as Streeruwitz remarked in her recent *Sein. Und Schein. Und Erscheinen. Tübinger Poetikvorlesungen* (1997; Being. And Seeming. And Appearing. Tübingen Poetics Lecture). The passageways or through-stations beyond hope in her plays channel through figures pieced together by quotations, clichés, and secondhand gestures. Streeruwitz's dramaturgy is that of the *Regietheater,* which breaks up the text and style by inserting now highly symbolic, now quite arbitrary parallel scenes that allude to the dramatic tradition of the Western world (from Shakespeare to Ibsen, Maeterlinck, Hofmannsthal, and Horvath). In addition, in *Bagnacavallo.* (1995) and *Elysian Park.* (1993), Streeruwitz borrows from Edward Bond the technique of eliminating any inside information, of leaving both audience and protagonists in the dark about the direction of the action. The typically elliptic utterances add to the suppression of clarifying information.

Streeruwitz uses a similar rhetorical device in her first novel, *Verführungen. 3. Folge. Frauenjahre.* (1996; Seductions. 3. Series. Women's Years.), where the flow of speech is blocked by a notorious punctuation mark, the period, which allows only for a furor of main clauses. This is at the same time an extreme form of parataxis, a very modern heritage, as it is a decidedly antimetaphysical gesture. The marker of the end (of a sentence) interferes with linear thinking, with the promise of historical progress. In addition, the dot as *Würgemal* (strangulation mark), as well as frequent breaks and silences, helps say *das Unsagbare* (the unspeakable). *Verführungen* exemplifies Streeruwitz's "Poetik des Banalen. Eine Poetik des Schweigens" (poetics of the banal, a poetics of silence) by making the (hitherto unspeakable/ unpoetic) everyday life of a single mother with two daughters the subject of literature. *Lisa's Liebe. Roman* (1997; Lisa's Love. Novel) takes up the project of the banal by only seemingly parodying the trivial novel. The mixture of text, photo material, ads, obituaries, and news clips creates the unassuming atmosphere of a young woman's life that is beyond any sensations. Streeruwitz's prose is an attempt to arrive at a description of a woman's life that is nonpatriarchal and develops a "poetics of decolonization" (*Können. Mögen. Dürfen. Sollen. Wollen. Müssen. Lassen.* [1998; Can. Like. May. Should. Want. Must. Let.]). It grows out of a work of mourning: to sketch what is yet unthinkable.

In contrast, the penetrating brutality of *New York. New York.* and the dismantling of political intrigue, decaying hedonism, and unmatched (male) egoism in *Waikiki. Beach.* seem like a sensationalistic presentation of a world governed by disillusionment and hopelessness. *New York. New York.*'s Ms. Horvath, who reigns absolutely in the underworld of a pissoir, is resigned about her ability to interfere with violence—despite the diagnostic power her last name promises (alluding to the work of Ödon von Horvath) and unlike the Promethean character locked up in one of her toilets. And Michael and Rudolf, lover and husband of Helene in *Waikiki. Beach.*, cover up Helene's murder and love affair for political reasons. Within the world of Streeruwitz's dramas, the destruction of morals and ethics is reflected in the destruction of the grammatical structures. The rhetorical device of a sudden break, called "aposiopesis," is the consequence of Streeruwitz's dream of a theater without catharsis, in which the theatrical figures do not resolve a conflict but just appear and disappear again. *Sloan Square.* (1992), which contrasts the life of modern day family conflicts with those of antiquity (in Goethe's *Iphigenia*), makes clear that tragedy and its way of conflict resolution is no longer possible today. No ship or other means of transportation is in sight that could reunite family members or lead to victory.

> Ms. Fischer We are waiting for the subway/underground.
> Ms. Marenzi: To Victoria.
> Ms. Fischer: But none is coming.

Whereas redemption could still be the solution of classical drama, Streeruwitz calls for a "theater as the last place of liberation." It requires the cooperation of the audience in an anarchical search for happiness, emphasizing a formal solution of the problem of transforming time into presence. Heavily indebted to Adorno's concept of "constellation" from *Ästhetische Theorie*, which advertises a formal utopia in artworks that create "das Andere" (the Other) out of "das Immergleiche" (Ever-the-Same), Streeruwitz writes in "Passion. Devoir. Kontingenz. Und keine Zeit." (Passion. Devoir. Contingency. And No Time):

> Spontaneous accessibility has to condense this presence. The senses can also be addressed in a senseless way. Even at the cost of becoming entertaining. The whole broken to pieces and have it become another. Fleeing from the scientification of our life contexts through pleasure.

This form of a formal utopia is directed against Austria's deep-seated culture of hope. In an exemplary way, *Tolmezzo: Eine symphonische Dichtung*. (1994; Tolmezzo: A Symphonic Poetry) deconstructs, in the tradition of Austrian language skepticism, language's potential to express "ein Anderes" (an Other) as "Die durch den Indikativ hergestellte Versprechung auf ein real mögliches Ganzes eine Lüge durch das Begraben des Konjunktives im Indikativ" (the promise of an actually possible whole implied in the indicative forms a lie through the burial of the subjunctive in the indicative mode). The function of the theater would thus be to reintroduce the subjunctive mode, to open up possible worlds without filling in an actual reality.

While the potential for a formal utopia remained largely unrecognized in reviews about her plays, critics focused on the scenes of horror and violence, which made Streeruwitz in their view the same kind of "Nestbeschmutzerin" (one who befouls her nest) as Thomas Bernhard and Elfriede Jelinek before her. They suggested that Streeruwitz (like Jelinek) was looking for a scandal to achieve a breakthrough. Nonetheless, she has become one of the most performed dramatists on German stages. *Ocean Drive*. (1994) presented an exception in this respect: the stage production could not convey the play's humor and ambitious postmodern structure, although the inherent mixture of slapstick scenes, high and pop culture, and kitsch and cliché would have lent itself to a fast-paced, funny production. It would also have been a good example of Streeruwitz's concept of literature, which, according to her Tübingen poetics lectures, extends to all texts that can be read or heard.

SIGRID BERKA

Biography

Born in Baden bei Wien, Austria, 28 June 1950. Studied law, Slavic languages and literatures, and art history; freelance writer, playwright, journalist, and stage director; her plays have been performed at Kölner Schauspielhaus, Deutsches Theater und Kammerspiel, Berlin, and Schauspielhaus, Vienna. Würdigungspreis für Literatur des österreichischen Bundeskanzlesamts, 1996; Mara-Cassens-Preis, 1997;

honorary lectures on poetics at the University of Tübingen, 1995/96, and at the University of Frankfurt, 1997–98. Currently lives in Vienna.

Selected Works

Plays
Waikiki. Beach. Sloane Square. Zwei Stücke, 1992
New York. New York. Elysian Park. Zwei Stücke, 1993
Ocean Drive: Ein Stück, 1994
Tolmezzo: Eine symphonische Dichtung, 1994
Bagnacavallo. Brahmsplatz. Zwei Stücke, 1995

Prose
Verführungen. 3. Folge. Frauenjahre. Roman, 1996
Lisas Liebe: Roman, 1997

Radio Plays
Der Paravent (produced 1987)
Alkmene (produced 1989)
Kaiserklamm und Kirchenwirt (produced 1989)
Urlaub (produced 1989)
Schubertring (produced 1990)
Yocasta, You'd Better Leave (produced 1990)

Essays
"'Helb auer mischon!' Schwarzenegger for Burgtheater," *Frankfurter Rundschau*, 29 February 1992
"Passion. Devoir. Kontingenz. Und keine Zeit," *Theater heute* yearbook (1992)
"Der Lustmörder. Eine Stütze der Gesellschaft," *Spectaculum 59* (1995)
"Tu Infelix Austria Cogita," *Der Standard* [Vienna], 28 April 1995
Sein. Und Schein. Und Erscheinen. Tübinger Poetikvorlesungen, 1997
Frühstück und Gewalt: Prosa und Szenen, edited by Marlene Streeruwitz and Jürgen Wertheimer, 1997
"Über Verachtung. Rede zur Verleitung des Würdigungspreises für Literatur," 1997

Further Reading

Becker, Barbara von, "Weniger als die Welt wollen wir nicht," *Süddeutsche Zeitung* 27 (January 1993)
Berka, Sigrid, "The (Non)Position of Woman in Marlene Streeruwitz's Work," in *After Postmodernism: Austrian Literature and Film in Transition*, edited by Willy Riemer, Riverside, California: Ariadne Press, 1999
Fischer, Ulrich, "Debüt einer Dramatikerin aus A in D," *Freitag*, 21 August 1992
Gjestvang, Ingrid-L., "Which 'Reality'? Images of Technology in Marlene Streeruwitz's Waikiki Beach," in *The Image of Technology in Literature, the Media, and Society*, edited by Will Wright and Steve Kaplan, Pueblo, Colorado: Society for the Interdisciplinary Study of Social Imagery, 1994
Merschmeier, Michael, "Horvath in der Unterwelt," *Theater heute* 3 (1993)
Möhrmann, Renate, "Frauenjahre, 3. Folge: Ein Frauenroman, Aber ein wirklicher, Von Marlene Streeruwitz," *EMMA* 3 (1996)

Stunde Null

The term *Stunde Null* (zero hour) refers to a historical moment after the collapse of the German Reich in 1945. Its meaning is derived from the imaginary moment at midnight, when the previous day is over and the new day has not started. The analogy is used to signify the undefined and open time span between two historical periods, the Third Reich and the creation of two German states in 1949. Its meaning refers to a break in the historical continuity, a few weeks following the capitulation of the German army in May 1945 (captured in Edgar Reitz's film *Stunde Null*, 1976) or the years prior to the currency reform of 1948, and it has been used, without reference to a specific time frame, to signify a specific state of mind characterized by indeterminacy and potentiality.

Stunde Null has also been interpreted in more dramatic ways: such as an existentialist or religious moment of awakening, as a last reflex of 30 years of apocalyptic warfare (1914–45), or as a period of collective denial and loss of reality. The term was introduced at the time and is representative of the experience and self-image of a generation deeply affected by the collapse of the German state and society. In political and literary history, the concept of *Stunde Null* was never fully accepted. Around 1970, a controversy emerged about the continuity or discontinuity in German history, and literary scholars questioned the adequacy of the term. New evidence had been gathered to support an interpretation that stressed continuities, rather than the previous emphasis placed on a complete break associated with the end of the political institutions of the Reich. Rather than viewing the years 1933 and 1945 as caesuras in the history of literature, scholars now proposed a specific literary periodization. It was argued that decisive changes in the history of ideas and literature were not synchronous with changes in politics, and that the years 1930 and 1960 were of much greater significance. As a consequence, the *Stunde Null* became insignificant for the conception of literary history.

The debate resurfaced after 1989, when the collapse of the German Democratic Republic gave rise to a comparison of the respective ends of two states and the associated turning points in German political, social, and intellectual history. Questions raised then focused on the role of the intelligentsia in maintaining totalitarian systems and in overthrowing them, and more generally, on the role of literature for historical change. Also, questions of guilt, moral implications, and shame were now raised. The importance of the Holocaust for the conception of a *Stunde Null* had been marginal. This was now changing, and looking back at 1945 from a different angle provided new insights into collective behavior. New interpretations of familiar sources, as well as the discovery of new evidence, including visual material such as photography and film, supported the hypothesis that there was no marked break in collective attitudes and perceptions in 1945.

The collapse of the German Reich has no parallel in modern European history. The military defeat was complete (the Allies invented the term *unconditional surrender*). The entire territory was occupied by the victorious powers; the government and local administrations ceased to exist, and the sovereignty of the nation state was assumed by the military commanders of the four zones of occupation. National Socialism as the pervasive state ideology disappeared overnight. Most cities were in ruins. Public transportation, the postal services, and the infrastructure had collapsed, and in some areas water, gas, and electricity supplies were discontinued. Life was thrown back, it was said at the time, to Stone Age conditions. Soldiers returning home, released camp survivors and prisoners of war, 5 million refugees from eastern German provinces, and uncounted women and children who had fled the cities and now returned to their ruined homes created a massive movement of unsettled people. It was a society in flux, literally and metaphorically. In some cities and industrialized areas, political grass-roots movements emerged but soon disappeared, and the organization of political life and the everyday remained in the hands of the occupying forces.

These were the conditions that gave rise to the perception of a total disintegration of public and private life, summarized in the feeling of a zero hour of existence. Not dissimilar to the situation at the end of World War I, when the theory of a lost generation emerged, now too a young generation felt the need for an unconditional new beginning. For committed intellectuals, the *Stunde Null* was identical with hope, expressed in vague and emotional rather than concrete political terms of a revolution. Among the many periodicals of these years, *Der Ruf* (Hans Werner Richter, Alfred Andersch) and *Frankfurter Hefte* (Walter Dirks, Eugen Kogon) most consistently gave expression to an ethical socialism and socialist Catholicism. *Stunde Null* refers to an experience significant for the three western zones of occupation, later the Federal Republic of Germany. It has been interpreted as the origin of that society's climate of disillusionment and skepticism. The programmatic distance between its intelligentsia and, specifically, the *Gruppe 47* and the new state and society can be traced back to a disappointment in the unfulfilled promise of a new beginning at a *Stunde Null*. Compared with the great expectations expressed in the *Stunde Null* image of the immediate postwar period, the political and social reality appeared to be a mere restoration.

Stunde Null was of no importance for Swiss and Austrian literature and had little significance for the literary history of the later German Democratic Republic. After 1945, Austrian writers preferred to define the country between 1938 and 1945 as an occupied territory and wanted to connect the present with the years prior to the *Anschluß*. There was no room for a zero hour in this concept of a specific Austrian literary history. In a similar way, the GDR divided German history into two and defined itself as the heir to the socialist, humanist, and democratic tradition in German history. The year 1945 was celebrated as liberation from fascism, making it possible to tie in with the progressive tradition and to establish a continuity in one part of the divided German nation. The *Stunde Null* was essential for the creation of a specific self-image of the emerging Federal Republic and was also an elementary reference point for separating German literary history into four distinct histories (Swiss, Austrian, East German, and West German).

Stunde Null had its own aesthetics, built upon negativity and rejection of the past. Its approach to the literary tradition was that of clear-cutting (*Kahlschlag*) and propagation of a language of the ruins (*Trümmerliteratur*). After it had been contaminated by National Socialist ideology, language needed purification.

Literary language had to be reduced to the bare minimum of linguistic structures, to short and simple sentences and concrete nouns avoiding all attributes suspected of arousing emotions or heroism, or of carrying political or military symbolism. As Storz, Stemberger, and Süßkind wrote in *Aus dem Wörterbuch des Unmenschen*, "das Wörterbuch des Unmenschen" (the dictionary of the monsters), had to be destroyed and a new and true language invented. Literary traditions, it was felt, had been corrupted by ideological abuse, and the aim of the young generation was to liberate literature from conventional forms implicated in the disastrous history of the 20th century. Günter Eich's poem *Inventur* (1948; *Stocktaking*) has been read as paradigmatic for this reductionist approach to language. "Young thought" (*das junge Denken*), a "new connection between thinking and living," and "humanist socialism" became key words for the emerging *Kahlschlag* literature. The period of ruins needed a literature made of rubble, and young authors, among them Wolfgang Weyrauch, Arno Schmidt, Heinrich Böll, Horst Koeppen, and Alfred Andersch, were invested in this attempt to detach writing from the past and respond to the indeterminacy of the situation by destroying contexts and fragmenting literature. This literature has been read as a symptom of exhaustion, apathy, and demoralization. It has also been interpreted as the initiation of a genuine German literature of modernity that emerged ten years after the dreams of a zero hour.

BERND HÜPPAUF

See also Federal Republic of Germany; 1950s

Further Reading

Barnouw, Dagmar, *Germany 1945: Views of War and Violence*, Bloomington: Indiana University Press, 1996

Erhard, Walter, and Dirk Niefanger, editors, *Zwei Wendezeiten. Blicke auf die deutsche Literatur 1945 und 1989*, Tübingen: Niemeyer, 1997

Hüppauf, Bernd, editor, *"Die Mühen der Ebenen": Kontinuität und Wandel in der deutschen Literatur und Gesellschaft 1945–1949*, Heidelberg: Winter, 1981

Schäfer, Hans Dieter, "Die nichtfaschistische Literatur der 'jungen Generation' im nationalsozialistischen Deutschland," in *Die deutsche Literatur im Dritten Reich: Themen, Traditionen, Wirkungen*, edited by Horst Denkler and Karl Prümm, Stuttgart: Reclam, 1976

——, "Zur Periodisierung der deutschen Literatur seit 1930," in *Nachkriegsliteratur*, edited by Nicolas Born and Jürgen Manthey, Reinbek: Rowohlt, 1977

Scheichl, Sigurd Paul, *Weder Kahlschlag noch Stunde Null. Besonderheiten des Voraussetzungssystems der Literatur in Österreich 1945 und 1966. Kontroversen, alte und neue*, vol. 10, Vier deutsche Literaturen? Literatur seit 1945, edited by Albrecht Schöne et al., Tübingen: Niemeyer, 1986

Trommler, Frank, "Der Nullpunkt 1945 und seine Verbindlichkeit für die Literaturgeschichte. Basis," *Jahrbuch für deutsche Gegenwartsliteratur* 1 (1970)

——, "Nachkriegsliteratur: Eine neue deutsche Literatur?" in *Nachkriegsliteratur*, edited by Nicolas Born and Jürgen Manthey, Reinbek: Rowohlt, 1977

Vormweg, Heinrich, "Deutsche Literatur 1945–60. Keine Stunde Null," in *Deutsche Gegenwartsliteratur: Ausgangspositionen und aktuelle Entwicklungen*, edited by Manfred Durzak, Stuttgart: Reclam, 1981

Sturm und Drang

According to literary historians, Sturm und Drang (Storm and Stress) began with the publication of Johann Gottfried Herder's *Fragmente* (Fragments) in 1767 and ended in 1785, the beginning of Weimar classicism. The zenith of the movement is generally placed between the publication of Johann Wolfgang von Goethe's drama *Götz von Berlichingen mit der eisernen Hand* (1773; *Götz of Berlichingen with the Iron Hand*) and Friedrich von Schiller's drama *Die Räuber* (1781; *The Robbers*).

As the German expression of European pre-Romanticism, the roots of Sturm und Drang go back at least as far as the Swiss writers and theorists Johann Jakob Bodmer and Johann Jakob Breitinger. In works such as Bodmer's *Critische Abhandlung von dem Wunderbaren in der Poesie* (1740; Critical Treatise on the Marvelous in Poetry) and Breitinger's *Critische Dichtkunst* (1740; Critical Art of Poetry), these two Swiss thinkers called attention to the imagination and advocated a freer, more original use of language than the Enlightenment aesthetic allowed. Their writings were an early challenge to traditional aesthetic norms.

Aesthetically, Sturm und Drang represents a rejection of classicism, particularly the French models, which had been advocated by the influential Johann Christoph Gottsched. His views had considerable influence during the first half of the 18th century. Rather than imitate French drama, Gottsched's opponents preferred Shakespeare, who had found an early advocate in Germany in Johann Elias Schlegel. They also began to look toward Teutonic rather than Greek mythology in their search for material, and they discovered the German Middle Ages. These stratagems can also be explained by a growing European consciousness of national literatures. Further, the emotions, de-emphasized during the Enlightenment, were to be a factor in their new literature. Thus, the poet Friedrich Gottlieb Klopstock and his stirring lyrics were greatly admired by the later group of writers who are more narrowly defined as *Stürmer und Dränger*. The new subjectivism also took its cue from Pietism and sentimentality, expressed particularly in Sophie von La Roche's internationally successful novel *Geschichte des Fräuleins von Sternheim* (1771; *The History of Lady Sophia Sternheim*).

A group of poets who defined themselves according to the newly emerging aesthetic were loosely united as the Göttinger Hain. Most prominent among them was Gottfried August Bürger, whose masterpiece, the poem "Lenore" (1774), introduces Gothic elements into his examination of love and death. A turn to the folkloric, a preoccupation shared by the later Romantics, is evident in Bürger's poem and in the poetry of his contemporaries. Johann Gottfried Herder published a collections of international folk songs, *Stimmen der Völder in Liedern* (Voices of the People in Songs) in 1778–79. The most successful novel written during this period was Goethe's *Die Leiden des jungen Werthers* (1774; translated as *The Sorrows of Werter* and *The Sufferings of Young Werther*). It extolled individualism and self-expression and challenged religious and societal norms with Werther's essentially exonerated suicide. The novel, translated into many languages, was popular throughout Europe. Today, outside of Germany, it is read not as a Strum und Drang novel but as a Romantic novel.

Herder and Johann Georg Hamann were the two theorists admired by the *Stürmer und Dränger*. Hamann's nonlinear, often fragmentary style and innovative language became a model for the new generation of writers, while Herder's philosophy of history, especially his contention that art is the product of the historical moment, profoundly affected Sturm und Drang aesthetics. For instance, it allowed Goethe to proclaim Gothic architecture superior to classical architecture in his comments on the Strasbourg cathedral, "Von deutscher Baukunst" (1771; On German Architecture). Jakob Michael Reinhold Lenz's *Anmerkungen übers Theater* (1774; Observations on the Theater) became the movement's manifesto for their dramas, which are Sturm und Drang's most significant achievements. Echoing Jean-Jacques Rousseau and Edward Young, the new generation of writers proclaimed a return to nature and feeling. Young's *Conjectures on Original Composition* (1759), in which he acclaims the creative genius and points to Homer and Shakespeare as examples, was eagerly adopted by young German writers. The young dramatists were also influenced by Sebastien Mercier and his argument that drama should serve political ends. An early drama experimenting with the new aesthetic was Heinrich Wilhelm von Gerstenberg's *Ugolino* (1768).

Sturm und Drang derived its provocative name from a drama by Friedrich Maximilian Klinger, originally called *Der Wirrwarr* (1777; The Confusion). Contemporary critics of Sturm und Drang regarded the new dramas being written as just that and rejected them on aesthetic grounds, but their criticism often could not disguise their moral objections. The young writers were rebels. They rejected all barriers and authority, arguing for political, individual, erotic, and social freedom. Among their most eloquent supporters was Christian Daniel Schubart, particularly in his role as editor of the journal *Deutsche Chronik* (German Chronicle). He lived in the same part of Germany, Baden-Württemberg, in which Schiller wrote *The Robbers* to protest the policies of the ruler, Karl Eugen. *The Robbers* continues to be one of the most performed plays on the German stage and is particularly poignant during oppressive times. Two other well-known dramas of the period are Schiller's *Kabale und Liebe* (1784; Intrigue and Love) and Heinrich Leopold Wagner's *Die Kindsmörderin* (1776; The Childmurderess).

Noticeably few women wrote during this period of upheaval, protest, and plans for social reform. Most of their attempts at self-expression, the central component of the new aesthetic, failed, a phenomenon that has caused them to be described as "the silent generation." One explanation is that, while male writers creatively expressed frustration and aggression in literature, societal pressure caused these feelings—when they were experienced by the young generation of women—to be turned inward, resulting in depression rather than in literature. An exception may be Marianne Ehrmann, who, although writing until the 1790s, used Sturm und Drang techniques and shared Sturm und Drang goals and beliefs.

The male writers of the 1770s vented their protest against authority and tradition by creating surprising new characters for the stage. Theirs was the age of Promethean rebellion; they wanted action, and their hero was the *Kraftmensch*, Götz, or Karl Moor in *Die Räuber*, the larger-than-life individual who rejects all barriers and limits. Some scholars consider Sturm und Drang's explosiveness and stress on individualism to be an outgrowth of the Enlightenment, while others regard Germany's lack of national unity and desire for identity as the cause. The plays are strangely ambiguous, however, for the erstwhile rebels fail in their mission and succumb to order by the end of the drama. One explanation for this phenomenon is that the plays express the dramatists' desire to reconcile spontaneity and accountability.

Interestingly, Sturm und Drang also produced a second type of dramatic character, a passive and often melancholy victim of her or his personality and environment. The most prominent writer associated with this strategy is Lenz, whose *Der Hofmeister* (1774; The Tutor) and *Die Soldaten* (1776; The Soldiers) are today regarded as prototypes of modern German drama. His characters accept responsibility for their actions and, taking inspiration from Pietism, have a tendency toward inwardness. These two plays are relevant today and have been adapted (Bertolt Brecht's 1950 drama *Der Hofmeister*) and re-created (Alois Zimmermann's opera *Die Soldaten* [1958–60]).

HELGA STIPA MADLAND

See also Romanticism

Further Reading

Auerbach, Erich, "Miller the Musician," in *Mimesis: The Representation of Reality in Western Literature*, translated by Willard R. Trask, Princeton, New Jersey: Princeton University Press, 1953

Blackall, Eric A., "The Language of Sturm und Drang," in *Stil- und Formprobleme in der Literatur*, edited by Paul Böckmann, Heidelberg: Winter, 1959

Blunden, Allen, "J.M.R. Lenz," in *Literary Essays*, German Men of Letters, edited by Alex Natan and Brian Keith-Smith, vol. 6, London: Wolff, 1972

Bruford, Walter Horace, *Germany in the Eighteenth Century: The Social Background of the Literary Revival*, Cambridge: Cambridge University Press, 1934

Ergang, Robert Reinhold, "Möser and the Rise of National Thought in Germany," *Journal of Modern History* 5 (1993)

Huyssen, Andreas, *Drama des Sturm und Drang*, Munich: Winkler, 1980

Kieffer, Bruce, *The Storm and Stress of Language: Linguistic Catastrophe in the Early works of Goethe, Lenz, Klinger, and Schiller*, University Park: Pennsylvania State University Press, 1986

Kistler, Mark O., *Drama of the Storm and Stress*, New York: Twayne, 1969

Köpke, Wulf, *Johann Gottfried Herder*, Boston: Twayne, 1987

Leidner, Alan C., "A Titan in Extenuating Circumstances: Sturm und Drang and the *Kraftmensch*," *PMLA* 104, no. 2 (1989)

——, *The Impatient Muse: Germany and the Sturm und Drang*, Chapel Hill: University of North Carolina Press, 1994

Madland, Helga Stipa, *Non-Aristotelian Drama in Eighteenth-Century Germany and Its Modernity: J.M.R. Lenz*, Bern: Lang, 1982

——, "Gender and the German Literary Canon: Marianne Ehrmann's Infanticide Fiction," *Monatshefte* 84, no. 4 (1992)

McInnes, Edward, "The Sturm und Drang and the Development of Social Drama," *Deutsche Vielteljahrsschrift* 46 (1972)

O'Flaherty, James C., *Johann Georg Hamann*, Boston: Twayne, 1979

Osborne, John, *J.M.R. Lenz: The Renunciation of Heroism*, Göttingen: Vandenhoeck und Ruprecht, 1975

Pascal, Roy, *The German Sturm und Drang*, New York: Philosophical Library, and Manchester: Manchester University Press, 1953

Prokop, Ulrike, "Die Einsamkeit der Imagination: Geschlechter konflikt und literarische Produktion um 1770," in *Deutsche Literatur von Frauen*, edited by Gisela Brinker-Gabler, vol. 1, Munich: Beck, 1988

Ryder, Frank, "Toward a Revaluation of Goethe's *Götz*: Features of Recurrence," *PMLA* 77 (1962)

Schmidt, Henry J., "The Language of Confinement: Gerstenberg's *Ugolino* and Klinger's *Sturm und Drang*," *Lessing Yearbook* 11 (1979)

Stockmeyer, Clara, *Soziale Probleme im Drama des Sturmes und Dranges*, Hildesheim: Gerstenberg, 1922; reprint, 1974

Vincent, Deirdre, *Werther's Goethe and the Game of Literary Creativity*, Toronto and Buffalo, New York: University of Toronto Press, 1992

Whiton, John, "Faith and the Devil in H.L. Wagner's *Die Kindermörderin*," *Lessing Yearbook* 16 (1984)

Patrick Süskind 1949–

One of the most celebrated younger writers in contemporary German literature, Patrick Süskind's success rests on a remarkably slender body of works. His literary debut, the monodrama *Der Kontrabaß* (premiered 1981; *The Double Bass*), quickly became the darling of the German stage in the 1980s. It was followed in 1985 by the widely acclaimed best-selling novel *Das Parfum: Die Geschichte eines Mörders* (*Perfume: The Story of a Murderer*), which sold millions of copies internationally. Collaborations with filmmaker Helmut Dietl on scripts for the television series *Monaco Franze* (1983) and *Kir Royal* (1986) added to Süskind's public visibility. Less glamorous than his previous writings, his short prose works, *Die Taube* (1987; *The Pigeon*) and *Die Geschichte von Herrn Sommer* (1991; *The Story of Mr. Sommer*), have not attained the same popularity. Süskind's notoriety stands in sharp contrast to his secretive personal life. An ascetic recluse who rejects public recognition and only rarely and ironically comments on his writings, Süskind is a postmodern Diogenes. Changing style and genre with each successive publication, Süskind's authorial identity and intentions are similarly elusive. His characters, as reclusive as their author, are misanthropic outsiders who shun others while harboring secret desires for love and acceptance. A parabolic mirror of the postmodern condition, Süskind appeals both to mass audiences seeking well-crafted entertainment and to intellectuals who sense in his writings playful revisions of important philosophical and psychological problems that are clothed in a parodic style that in turn deconstructs the seriousness of traditional German literature.

His first work, the hugely successful stage play *The Double Bass*, is a grotesquely comical one-man show featuring a paranoid musician whose frustrated desire for recognition fuels aggressively anti-social fantasies. He perceives his chosen instrument, the awkward double bass, as a metaphor for his human fate: like his bass, he considers himself socially inept; like his bass, which never gets a solo part, he must always remain unnoticed in the background. As an emotional compensation for this neglect, he indulges in fantasies of aesthetic terrorism—such as disrupting musical performances—which would put him, albeit negatively, in the spotlight. The bassist's feelings of self-loathing, narcissistic rage, and grandiose fantasies of self-aggrandizement apparently resonated deeply with the large audiences that flocked to this play.

Perfume: The Story of a Murderer presents a different kind of frustrated artist, whose murderous desires are not limited to the realm of fantasy. Set in 18th-century France, Süskind's tale parodies the historical novel and tells the story of Jean-Baptiste Grenouille, an emotionally and physically abused orphan whose superhuman sense of smell leads him on a quest for the lost origin of his identity. A genius of odors who has no personal scent, Grenouille is obsessed with "essences," especially his own human essence or identity, which he hopes to create artificially by murdering virginal maidens, whose personal odors he extracts and blends to concoct an ultimate perfume that forces those who smell it to love its wearer unconditionally. Despite his hatred of fellow humans, from whom he recoils in disgust, the mad perfumer is driven by an almost erotic lust for the affection and attention of others. The novel has been read variously as an allegory of the fascist mind, as an indictment of enlightenment rationality, or simply as a clever, postmodern pastiche that cynically serves the reader titillating but derivative kitsch. As every critic has noted, *Perfume* invites and sustains a seemingly unlimited game of source hunting. The novel's rich intertextuality draws on canonical literature from the 18th century to the present, borrowing so much from precursor texts that it seems to function almost exclusively as a parody of previous works. Read as a self-conscious parody of the *Künstlerroman* (novel of the artist), the theme of creativity and the correlative problem of artistic originality assume central importance in the novel. While allegorically depicting the rise of the genius myth from the Enlightenment and Romantic periods to its culmination in modernism, however, the novel's pervasive imitation of dead styles also challenges the traditional belief in the original artist-proprietor, redefining the creative act as a blending of pre-existing materials into a hybrid style that is without a source in individual authorial identity.

Similar to the evil genius of *Perfume*, the protagonist of *The Pigeon* is a recluse whose emotionally impoverished adult life has been preprogrammed by a childhood trauma. By contrast to Grenouille, however, Jonathan Noel is a law-abiding, timid man whose clockwork existence is circumscribed by his tiny bachelor's flat and a meaningless job as a doorman for a Paris bank. With a practically nonexistent plot, the story parodies the dramatic tension expected of the traditional novella, while detailed descriptions of the doorman's daily routines underscore the deadening uniformity of his life. Noel's mechanical performance of his monotonous job duties and his paranoiac avoidance of human relationships result from a childhood abandonment trauma that causes his ostensible attachment disorder. His occupation—*Wachmann* (watchman)—signifies the vigilant mistrust that isolates him and reduces his life to a kind of protracted deathwatch, while also mirroring his persecution complex. His rigid order disrupted by a pigeon nesting outside of his door, which he cannot confront presumably because it occurs outside the immutable order of his solipsistic universe, Noel flees to a hotel room, where in a revelatory dream he relives the trauma of his childhood abandonment and realizes that without meaningful human relationships his existence is intolerable. Characteristically, Süskind's portrait of psychic disorder is not explicitly psychoanalytic. Similar to the fictional characters themselves, whose emotional truths appear to them only as dreams that compel them to act, Süskind's reader is offered a suggestive, Kafkaesque allegory and left to puzzle with its implications.

The Story of Mr. Sommer features yet another recluse, whose explicit clinical diagnosis as claustrophobic departs from Süskind's usual reluctance to categorize his characters psychologically. Although the story's murky thematic concerns seem focused on the title figure, who unwittingly prevents the narrator's suicide, the text consists mainly of the first-person reminiscences of a young boy growing up in the Adenauer years. Written as a kind of children's tale for adults (featuring abundant drawings by the French artist Sempe), the story digresses self-consciously, emulating the wandering thought patterns of a child in the throes of self-discovery. The withdrawal into minimal space so common of Süskind's figures is here reversed: Mr. Sommer's alleged claustrophobia forces him to wander ceaselessly through the open landscapes around Lake Starnberg (where Süskind grew up). Terrified by the presence of others, Mr. Sommer must stay in motion, never stopping or saying a word, except for the fateful utterance: "Why don't you just leave me in peace?" The final scene depicts Mr. Sommer marching into the lake in an act of self-destruction reminiscent of the death of King Ludwig II,

who also perished mysteriously in Lake Starnberg. Those looking either for facile interpretive solutions to Süskind's mysterious texts or for clues to the enigmatic author's identity may do well to read Mr. Sommer's words as the final plea of the vanishing postmodern writing subject: "Why don't you just leave me in peace?"

JEFFREY ADAMS

Biography
Born in Ambach, 26 March 1949. Studied at the universities of Munich and Aix-en-Provence; scriptwriter for television for 10 years. Gutenberg Prize, 1987 (not accepted). Currently lives in Munich, Paris, France, and Montolieu, France.

Fiction
Das Parfum: Die Geschichte eines Mörders, 1985; as *Perfume: The Story of a Murderer*, 1986
Die Taube, 1987; as *The Pigeon*, 1988
Die Geschichte von Herrn Sommer, 1991; as *The Story of Mr. Sommer*, 1992

Plays
Der Kontrabaß (produced 1981), 1983; as *The Double Bass*, 1987
Monaco Franze: Der ewige Stenz (television series), with Helmut Dietl, 1983
Kir Royal (television series), with Helmut Dietl, 1986

Further Reading
Butterfield, Bradley, "Enlightenment's Other in Patrick Süskind's *Das Parfum*: Adorno and the Ineffable Utopia of Modern Art," *Comparative Literature Studies* 32, no. 3 (1995)
Donahue, Neil H., "Scents and Insensibility: Patrick Süskind's New Historical Critique of 'Die Neue Sensibilität' in *Das Parfum*," *Modern Language Studies* 22, no. 3 (Summer 1992)
Grey, Richard T., "The Dialectic of 'Enscentment': Patrick Süskind's *Das Parfum* as Critical History of Enlightenment Culture," *Publications of the Modern Language Association* 108 (1993)
Ryan, Judith, "The Problem of Pastiche: Patrick Süskind's *Das Parfum*," *German Quarterly* 63, no. 3/4 (1990)

Switzerland

Switzerland is the name given in English to a country whose complex political and religious history and demographic and linguistic structure have led to its being described as a Europe in miniature. The official Latin name of Switzerland is *Confoederatio Helvetica* or, in German, *Schweizerische Eidgenossenschaft*, and from the beginning of its independent existence as a political entity, it has relied on and developed its federal structure. The essentially democratic and decentralized nature of its political institutions, therefore, has actually made Switzerland a notable exception to the general Western European model of the "nation state," and it is not surprising that, in the 19th century, it reminded German visitors of the old *Reich*, the Holy Roman Empire, that Napoléon had dismantled. Since the emergence of the European Community or Union, Switzerland, which is not a

member, may thus be said to be both forward-looking and backward-looking: it offers a pattern to be imitated but is unlikely, as things stand, to participate in Europe's moves toward federalization.

A distinct Swiss tradition in German-language literature can be traced back to *Die Alpen* (1732; The Alps), a poem by the great 18th-century Bernese scientist, neurologist, and botanist Albrecht von Haller. *Die Alpen* opened up a new landscape in European literature and at the same time transmitted a moral discourse inherited from antiquity and from German humanism both to Jean-Jacques Rousseau and the German classicism of Friedrich von Schiller. Haller's depiction of the happy, well-ordered Alpine community may have been primarily intended as a satirical comment on the state of modern society in his day, but it also contributed significantly to the development of the Swiss self-image, which is central to Swiss literature. That self-image is an integral facet of the national identity of the composite and therefore artificial country whose inhabitants call themselves "Swiss" and who are as recognizable to each other as they are to their French, German, Austrian, and Italian neighbors because of the similarities possessed by all those who call themselves by this term. The literary expression of this self-image, however, is also conditioned by Switzerland's multilingualism (its four official national languages are German, French, Italian, and Romansh). For its German-speaking population of almost 4 million—some two-thirds of the country's total population—this literary expression is further complicated by the coexistence in Switzerland to this day of a "correct" written language (known as *Schriftdeutsch*) and a plethora of high Alemannic dialects, which reflect in linguistic terms the geographical and political diversity of "German-speaking" Switzerland.

For all Swiss Germans, dialect is the normal means of linguistic expression, although by its very nature it is rooted in a specific locality. Swiss literature in German reflects this state of affairs. The rich 200-year-old tradition of Swiss-German dialect writing is essentially regional and often parochial; even successful and talented dialect authors such as Bern's favorite historical novelist, Rudolf von Tavel (1860–1934), have failed to become nationally, let alone internationally significant. For Swiss writers, diglossia is a fact of life, and their ability to get a hearing or hold their own in a book market of some 100 million German-speakers depends on many factors, especially the ability to handle writing a language they seldom speak. Language divides the Swiss, and their unity has been achieved and preserved in the face of a linguistic plurality that is as profound as it is potentially divisive. Switzerland's religious divisions since the 16th-century Reformation are equally profound, but they do not correspond to its linguistic divisions. What is of considerable interest, however, is that central Switzerland, the German-speaking historical nucleus of the Swiss Confederation (and hence known in German as *die Urschweiz*), has remained loyal to Roman Catholicism but has made only a relatively slight contribution to Switzerland's literature in German. Indeed, that literature, unlike those of neighboring Austria and Bavaria, may be described as broadly Protestant in its underlying value system and general outlook on the world.

Switzerland has always had to depend on the good will of its neighbors. The secession of the nuclear Swiss Confederation from the Holy Roman Empire took place in the Middle Ages, but its long-standing de facto independence, like that of the Netherlands, was not formally recognized by Europe's other nations until the Treaty of Westphalia in 1648. Switzerland's independence is closely bound up with the principle of neutrality. This was recognized by the great powers at the Congress of Vienna in 1815, and the country's neutrality was responsible for Switzerland's immunity during the Franco-Prussian War and World War I, both of which placed severe strains on the relationship between the country's German-speaking and French-speaking inhabitants, and during World War II, when Switzerland found itself surrounded, an island in a Nazi-dominated Europe. Ever since the Napoleonic Wars, relations between Switzerland's component linguistic communities have come under stress during periods of European and world conflict. These tensions, and the ambiguities of the country's stance and policy during World War I, loom large in *Schweizerspiegel* (1938;

Swiss Mirror), an impressive novel by the Lucerne novelist Meinrad Inglin (1893–1971), which gives a panoramic account of life in Zurich during and after the war. Meanwhile, another major novel, *Die grosse Unruhe* (1939; The Great Unrest), by the Zurich novelist and poet Albin Zollinger (1895–1941) captures the uneasiness that pervaded Swiss and, indeed, European society during the 1930s. The compromises, tensions, and half-truths that marked Swiss government and commercial policy during World War II, although increasingly scrutinized and hotly debated in the final years of the 20th century, have not yet shown themselves to be the stuff of great literature except, perhaps, in *Die Hinterlassenschaft* (1965; The Legacy), a novel centered on Swiss immigration policy during the Nazi period and written and published by Walter Matthias Diggelmann (1927–79), and, by implication, in Max Frisch's theatrically effective but controversial drama *Andorra*, premiered in Zurich in 1961. Paradoxically, the impulse of Frisch and many younger Swiss writers to debunk the idealizing aspects of Switzerland's self-image points to both that image's ambiguity and its remarkable resilience and longevity.

The origins of Switzerland as a political entity date back to 1291, when a rudimentary German-speaking independent state was founded in and around the present canton of Schwyz, which gave its name to "die Schweiz": in Swiss German both names are pronounced the same. In 1291, its founding fathers are said to have bound themselves together by a solemn oath—the *Rütli-Schwur*—into an *Eidgenossenschaft,* or federation for mutual help and defense. The effective and subtle dramatization of this foundation myth by a non-Swiss, Friedrich von Schiller, in his last completed play, *Wilhelm Tell* (1804), is the key landmark in its literary consolidation, while the 700th anniversary in 1991 of the legendary events Schiller brought to literary life, which Frisch had already attempted to demythologize in his spoof schoolbook *Wilhelm Tell für die Schule* (1971), led to a wave of self-searching. This impulse, in turn, was soon given extra stimulus by a spate of claims and revelations about Switzerland's conduct, and especially that of its financial institutions, during World War II. So far, these blows to the national image and the Swiss psyche have not produced any really significant literary effect. The same, however, cannot be said of an earlier landmark in Switzerland's modern evolution: the ratification in 1848 of its revised federal constitution. This was one of the few long-term successes of the European "year of revolutions," and it established Switzerland as a model of democratic government in a central European region that had earned itself a reputation as a hotbed of anarchy and given the word *putsch* to the political vocabulary. The Switzerland that emerged from 1848 and its recent experience of civil war (the so-called *Sonderbundkrieg* of 1847, in which the Catholic cantons attempted to secede from the Confederation and create a federation of their own) became a constitutional federal state characterized by the very opposites of political instability and social disorder.

From the point of view of literature in the wider European sense, something much more important had been taking place. This was the Romantic discovery of Switzerland. This phenomenon was of no great importance to Switzerland's own literature during the period known throughout Europe as the Romantic Age, but it owed its origins to two Swiss writers: Albrecht von Haller (1708–77) and the Zurich painter and engraver Salomon Gessner (1730–88). The publication in 1732 of Haller's *Die Alpen* and that of Gessner's internationally acclaimed *Idylls* in

1756 had wide repercussions for the sensibility of 18th-century Europe. Haller's evocation of a naturally moral rural community in a sublime, untamed alpine setting, and its presentation in satirical contrast to the manners and life of corrupt society on the plains below, can be seen as an anticipation of Rousseau's philosophy of natural innocence, which the Geneva-born French thinker propounded in *Emile* and *Du contrat social,* the seminal educational and political writings that he published in the early 1760s. The *Idylls,* the main contribution in German to the 18th-century bucolic tradition, were admired by Goethe, and Gessner's delicate word paintings left their mark on *Die Leiden des jungen Werthers* (1774: *The Sorrows of Young Werther*); thus, they prepared the way for the new responsiveness to landscape and the delights of rural simplicity, and these attitudes became the vogue among the leisured classes in Europe during the final decades of the *ancien régime.*

In 1775, Goethe paid the first of his three visits to Switzerland (the other two followed in 1779 and 1797). His enthusiasm for its sights and scenes was soon being echoed by other foreign travelers. Readers all over Europe were already responding to the scenery of Lake Geneva, for this was the setting of Rousseau's emotive novel *Julie; ou, La Nouvelle Héloïse* (1761; *Julie; or, The New Eloise*) in this area. Authors such as Samuel Rogers relished and reported the delights Swiss mountains had to offer, while others brooded amid the sublime grandeur of its peaks, most notably Byron in the "Swiss" sections of Canto III of *Childe Harold's Pilgrimage* (1812–14). Evocations of alpine landscape can also be found in Byron's "Faustian" poetic drama, *Manfred* (1817).

Swiss literature was remarkably unaffected by these aesthetic responses to alpine scenery. Mountains did not figure in the pastoral landscape created by the Swiss Theocritus, Gessner, but he peopled it with shepherds and shepherdesses who, despite their anacreontic names, owed much to the peasantry of canton Zurich and had their feet firmly on its soil. As rococo idealization gave way to realism in the 19th century, Swiss writers increasingly concentrated their attention on the lives of the peasantry and ordinary folk in the rural communities and small towns of the *Mittelland,* the broad swath of relatively flat land between the Alps and the Jura where most of the Swiss-German population live. Although it is seldom read today, *Lienhard und Gertrud* (1781–87), the long novel about peasant life that Johann Heinrich Pestalozzi wrote for peasants themselves to read, was a decisive landmark in Switzerland's literary development. Its blend of didactic purpose and a homely anecdotal narrative style set the pattern for what proved to be the dominant strand in the Swiss novel to the present day. Unlike the German bildungsroman and its various 19th-century variations, which focus on the development of the central character, the German-language novel in Switzerland has always left its readers in no doubt that what interests the novelist most is the real world that the characters inhabit.

This tendency is already clearly visible in *Der Bauernspiegel* (1836; *The Mirror of the Peasantry*), the semiautobiographical novel that started the literary career of the author who called himself Jeremias Gotthelf, a name he shared with its semi-fictitious protagonist. Its publication marked the discovery of the peasantry as the natural subject matter for a specifically Swiss literature in German. Gotthelf's novels are firmly set in and around the Emmental, a rich agricultural region to the north and east of Bern, and, ever since, one of the most obvious character-

istics of narrative literature in Switzerland has been that it is highly localized. Familiar topographies are evoked and settings are frequently explicit; even when they are given "invented" names, as in the *Novellen* that constitute Gottfried Keller's *Die Leute von Seldwyla* (1856; The People of Seldwyla), readers and reviewers were generally quick to guess where they purportedly take place. As Keller pointed out with a chuckle in his foreword to the second volume of this collection (1873–74), many an Alemannic backwater was quick to proclaim itself to be the original of "Seldwyla," a place remarkable as much for its parochial pettiness and silliness as for its rural charm.

What to outsiders may seem a fatal narrowness of range and vision is generally seen by Swiss authors as a fact of life and, therefore, as an aesthetic challenge. Once a Swiss writer leaves home ground, the "Swissness" that distinguishes him or her from the writers of Austria and Germany is drastically reduced. Solutions can be found. Rudolf Jakob Humm's semiautobiographical masterpiece *Die Inseln* (1936; The Islands) pieces together a mosaic of memories of a childhood in Italy, which float like partially submerged islands in the sea of the subconscious. Frisch's *Homo Faber* (1957) takes its modern Swiss protagonist, an average 20th-century engineer, to Central America and Greece in a not entirely successful attempt to discover a reality that lies outside his neat calculations and stereotypical expectations. Few Swiss German writers have succeeded in producing first-rank works that are set outside their usual home territory. One exception, however, was Johann David Wyss (1743–1818), the author of one of the great classics of children's literature, *The Swiss Family Robinson* (1812–14), which is set on an unlikely yet, to the boyhood imagination, entirely credible desert island, and which combines a characteristically Swiss flair for practical pedagogy with sublimated escapism and a longing for adventure. The book reminds us that, during the first half of the 19th century, Swiss emigrants left what was then a relatively poor preindustrial rural economy to set up home in North and South America, Australia, and elsewhere. Another exception may well be Friedrich Glauser (1896–1938), who based some of his novels on his experiences as a French foreign legionary and who is now hailed, half a century after his death, as the outstanding German-language crime novelist. It is perhaps significant that no major Swiss literary work is set in Germany or Austria, with the exception of Frisch's postwar drama *Als der Krieg zu Ende war* (1949; When the War was Over), which takes place in occupied Berlin.

Gotthelf was the first of the three great prose writers whose work represents the golden age of Switzerland's 19th-century German literature. Between 1836 and his death in 1854, he wrote 12 novels and a large number of stories, some realistic and contemporary in theme and setting, others set in a more distant and imaginary past, but all drawing on the particular landscape of the Emmental and its indigenous peasant culture. The Zurich author and lyric poet Gottfried Keller (1819–90) was deeply aware of his great predecessor's powerful example, but he adopted a lighter, more-distanced tone in *Die Leute von Selwyla* and in his two subsequent collections of *Novellen, Züricher Novellen* (1878; Zurich Tales) and *Das Sinngedicht* (1882; The Epigram). These, together with the great semiautobiographical novel, *Der grüne Heinrich* (1854–55, revised version 1879–80; Green Henry), on which he worked for most of his creative life, earned Keller the rare distinction among discerning contemporaries throughout the German-speaking world as the finest living writer of German and gave him a degree of genuine popularity rare among authors of classic status in the German cultural area. Conrad Ferdinand Meyer (1825–98), the third great 19th-century Swiss writer, was also Zurich born and bred, but he introduced to Swiss literature new notes of restiveness and dissatisfaction with the present, which are implicit in his choice of other times and places for the majority of the historical *Novellen* that made his reputation as a writer of prose fiction. Meyer anticipates later writers by sometimes using as his narrator a Swiss who finds himself witnessing momentous historical events outside his own small country: a good example is Hans, the Zurich-born crossbow maker at the English court in *Der Heilige* (1879; The Saint), who at close hand, but not always with full comprehension, observes the ups and downs of the turbulent relationship between Thomas à Becket and King Henry II. Meyer's *Jürg Jenatsch* (1876) is Switzerland's major contribution to the historical novel in German. This work depicts the violence, intrigue, and conflicts of loyalties associated with an alpine trade route during the Thirty Years' War.

Meyer's subject in this novel was well chosen. Historically and economically, Switzerland has owed much to the trade routes that linked the commercial centers of North Italy to Germany and northern Europe, and in the late Middle Ages the country's control of the major passes brought prosperity to cities such as Lucerne, Zurich, and Basel. Basel joined the Confederation in 1502, bringing access to northern Europe's major waterway, the Rhine. At the time of the novel's publication, the passes were being moved into the modern era by the arrival of the railways: the St. Gotthard railway opened in 1882. The railways also brought mass tourism with them. This factor added further dimensions to Switzerland's image, and authors seized the opportunity to exploit the narrative potential of new developments such as the construction of the Simplon Tunnel in 1896–1905 and the building and commercial success of large hotels (e.g., *Der König der Bernina*, a best-selling "hotel" novel by Jakob Christoph Heer [1900]). It was left to a Swiss woman writer, Johanna Spyri (1829–1901), to revive the Swiss national image by giving it an alpine dimension in the two parts of her world-famous children's novel *Heidi* (1880–81). This novel captured the imaginations of generations of children with its reinvigorating saga of family roots rediscovered, social prejudices set aside, and health regained high up in the open air of the Alps. By 1924, another aspect of tourism, the Swiss sanitarium, provided the subject and setting for a major work of German and world literature. Thomas Mann's analysis of contemporary culture, *Der Zauberberg*, was partly based on his visit to a sanitarium at the health resort of Davos in 1912.

The cities of Bern and Zurich have played a central role throughout the course of Swiss literary history. From the biting satire of Niklas Manuel's Reformation dramas in the 1520s to the disturbing postwar dramas of Friedrich Dürrenmatt (1921–90), Bernese literature has been characterized by its authors' compulsion to confront the flaws in the moral makeup of society and in the personalities of their central characters. By contrast, most of Zurich's foremost writers, from Pestalozzi, the great educational pioneer in the late 18th century, to the postwar dramatist and novelist Max Frisch (1911–91), have displayed a rationalistic and often strongly pedagogic outlook on the world around them. Where Bern castigates, Zurich edifies: but what the literature of both cities has shared throughout the centuries

is an eye for pictorial description and an unquenchable sense of humor. The profoundest humorist among Switzerland's 20th-century writers, and its finest German stylist, is Robert Walser (1878–1956), who came from the partly German-speaking, partly French-speaking town of Biel/Bienne in the canton of Bern, but who possessed an exceptional command of German in a wide range of registers. Walser's deeper seriousness prevents his sardonic and satirical humor from being superficial or dated. Thus, although Walser's three early novels are as essentially autobiographical as Keller's *Der grüne Heinrich* and Gotthelf's *Bauernspiegel*, his ironic sense of self gives them an objective distance that enhances their modernity and their deeper qualities. The spate of shorter prose works he went on to produce throughout his creative life are unique in range and resonance, in sharpness of perception and observation, and in their ability to communicate a uniquely unmistakable voice. These qualities account for Walser's pervasive influence on 20th-century Swiss writers such as Gerhard Meier (1917–) and for the high esteem in which his work in now held. Walser's withdrawal from active participation in literary life in 1933 and his silence during the Nazi and postwar years have fascinated scholars and writers—as has the decipherment of the notebooks he went on keeping in minute handwriting—and have made him the most problematic Swiss writer of the 20th century.

In 1929, the publication of *Geisteserbe der Schweiz* (Switzerland's Intellectual Legacy), an anthology of excerpts ranging from writings by Gessner and Pestalozzi to pieces by many later writers, compiled by Eduard Korrodi, was a landmark in 20th-century Switzerland's acceptance of its cultural tradition and the "Swissness" of its literature. The mood of confidence that it created helped the German-speaking Swiss to survive the tensions and anxieties of the Nazi period and war years (it was reprinted in 1943). Korrodi showed that the country's majority German-speaking population did, indeed, have its own separate culture and tradition. It may therefore be seen as a major element in the neutral Switzerland's *Landesverteidigung*, or self-defense during the war. A less gratifying yet equally telling milestone in the country's postwar development was the publication in 1963 of *Unbehagen im Kleinstaat* (1963), a study by the Zurich literature professor Karl Schmid (1907–74) of some of the Swiss writers who, unlike Keller and Gotthelf, felt ill at ease and marginalized in a society that was essentially materialistic, narrow in outlook, and uninterested in the arts. Meyer, Frisch, and Jakob Schaffner, a talented half-Swiss, half-German writer who had become a Nazi sympathizer and had been killed in an air raid on Strasbourg (then annexed to Germany, in 1944), were three examples Schmid used, along with the Basel Renaissance art historian Jakob Burckhardt (1818–97) and his French-language contemporary, the inward-looking diarist and essayist Henri Frédéric Amiel (1821–81). The appearance of Schmid's study and the debate it unleashed both called into question much of what Swiss opinion had long held dear and had taken for granted, which in turn contributed to the development of a malaise that has been endemic in Swiss intellectual circles ever since. Two important collections of essays appeared in 1978, which complemented Schmid's work but also set the record straight. *Bürgerlichkeit und Unbürgerlichkeit in der Literatur der Deutschen Schweiz*, a volume put together by Werner Kohlschmid, also included commentary on Schaffner but had the merit of redrawing attention to Inglin and Zollinger, whose work had been marginalized because they had not yet been included in the unofficial canon of "great Swiss writers." It also reminded readers that lyric poetry, and drama, too, are part of Switzerland's literature, even if excellence in both has tended to be sporadic, and that Haller and his *Versuch schweizerischer Gedichten* (1732; An Essay in Swiss Poems), generally acknowledged to contain the finest poetry of its period in German, was not alone. *Die Dichter und ihre Heimat* by Arthur Häny not only treated poetry but argued that the relationships of writers to their homeland or to the landscape and townscape in which they lived or grew up was an integral part of their imaginative worlds and, therefore, of their creativity.

Poetry has had a fluctuating history in Switzerland. The early 14th-century collection of Middle High German love poetry, made in Zurich and known as the Manesse manuscript, suggests a long tradition, but with few exceptions—such as Johann Wilhelm Simler (1605–72), whose rather unexciting collection of religious and occasional verse was published in Zurich in 1648—little or no poetry, and none of any great distinction was written by Swiss Germans until the 18th century. With Johann Martin Usteri (1763–1827), a notable author of unassuming folksong-like lyrics such as "Freut euch des Lebens," and Johann Gaudenz von Salis-Seewis (1762–1834), whose nostalgic poetical recollections of his homeland, written in revolutionary Paris, are an interesting treatment of the town/countryside topos, a modern lyrical tradition slowly began to take shape in Switzerland. This new tradition displayed less independence of style, subject matter, and outlook than the rich Swiss prose tradition, but in the 19th century, it achieved a recognizable Swiss voice, especially in Gottfried Keller's occasional verse for public and patriotic occasions, which displays an infectious bravado, and in the verbal rhythms of Conrad Ferdinand Meyer's often almost symbolist poems. Less well known is their contemporary, Heinrich Leuthold (1827–79), whose personal voice was submerged by the poetry of Platen, Geibel, and their admirers precisely because he set out to shun any lingering touches of "helveticism." In 1919, the Swiss poet Carl Spitteler (1845–1924) was awarded the Nobel Prize for Literature because his voice was powerful enough, in his pseudo-epic *Olympischer Frühling* (1905; Olympian Spring), to be heard above the rest. At the outbreak of World War I, *Unser Schweizer Standpunkt* (1915; Our Swiss Standpoint), Spitteler's published 1914 speech advocating reconciliation between the French-speaking and German-speaking Switzerland, made a major literary contribution to the nation's integrity and self-understanding as well as to its survival in the 20th century.

Whether German-speaking Switzerland has produced a poet of comparable stature since Spitteler is not evident; yet, as the poems of Kurt Marti and Gerhard Meier show, poetry is not dead. In 1953, Erika Burkhart's first collection revealed that Switzerland, a country not noted for its women writers apart from Johanna Spyri, had produced one of the most original and distinctive lyric voices of the later 20th century. Burkhart views nature from an intensely personal angle, but she shares the general anxiety of Western society about its well-being and future. By focusing on nature and childhood, she has rediscovered two of the constant and intertwined threads that run through Swiss literature, while her wish to inform and warn perpetuates a cast of mind central to the Swiss cultural tradition. Burkhart demonstrates that Switzerland's failure to produce a woman writer of

the first rank does not mean that it has never produced any women authors. From Jeremias Gotthelf's daughter, Marie Walden (1834–90), to Maria Waser (1878–1939) and Cécile Ines Loos (1883–1959) in the first half of the 20th century and on to contemporary authors such as Erika Pedretti and Maja Beutler, women have contributed significantly to the modern Swiss literary achievement.

During World War II, Zurich provided a haven for exiled German writers and its theater performed plays forbidden on the German stage. After the war, and for the first time in its literary history, Swiss dramatists became almost synonymous with German dramatic literature. Between 1956 and 1961, the Zurich premieres of *Der Besuch der alten Dame* (The Visit of the Old Lady) and *Die Physiker* (The Physicists) by the Bernese playwright Friedrich Dürrenmatt and of *Biedermann und die Brandstifter* (Biedermann and the Arsonists) and *Andorra* by the Zurich-born Max Frisch brought the two authors to the attention of an international audience that no other Swiss writer had enjoyed in the 20th century. Their bold confrontations with the hang-ups and anxieties of their generation have been Switzerland's main contribution to 20th-century world literature. In Frisch, the country had a writer whose plays, novels, and essays articulated the anxieties of his contemporaries far beyond its own frontiers, while in Dürrenmatt, it can fairly claim to have had a writer of international importance, whose fragmented oeuvre exposed the interactions of guilt and complicity, the price of prosperity, and the modern dread of nuclear destruction.

The deaths of Dürrenmatt and Frisch in quick succession in 1990 and 1991 relegated Swiss literature in German to the sidelines once again. None of its many other postwar writers was able to establish a comparable place in the consciousness of readers within the German-speaking world, let alone beyond it. The major contemporary authors, from Gerhard Meier, Peter Bichsel, and E.Y. Meyer to Hugo Loetscher and Kurt Marti, have been left to pick up the pieces and ask themselves the question: Where does Swiss literature go from here? It is a question regularly discussed at the *Solothurner Literaturtage*, a literary forum and workshop that has brought the German-language writers of Switzerland together for the last 20 years in the small cantonal capital of Solothurn. Left out of a European federation shaped on its own model and unsettled by self-searching, crises of conscience, and recriminations about its role during the Hitler era, yet largely dependent on publishers and readers in the German Federal Republic (and in France and Italy) for the royalties of its writers, Switzerland's national literary future is as uncertain as it is challenging.

PETER SKRINE

See also Zurich

Further Reading

Acker, Robert, and Marianne Burkhard, editors, *Blick auf die Schweiz: Zur Frage der Eigenständigkeit der Schweizer Literatur seit 1970*, Amsterdam: Rodopi, 1987

Baechtold, Jacob, *Geschichte der deutschen Literatur in der Schweiz*, Frauenfeld: Huber, 1892; 2nd edition, 1919

Burkhard, Marianne, and Gerd Labroisse, *Zur Literatur der deutschsprachigen Schweiz*, Amsterdam: Rodopi, 1979

Butler, Michael, and Malcolm Pender, editors, *Rejection and Emancipation: Writing in German-Speaking Switzerland, 1945–1990*, Oxford and New York: Berg, 1991

Faesi, Robert, *Gestalten und Wandlungen schweizerischer Dichtung,* Zurich: Amalthea-Verlag, 1922

Flood, John, editor, *Modern Swiss Literature: Unity and Diversity,* London: Wolff, and New York: St. Martin's Press, 1985

Fringeli, Dieter, *Von Spitteler zu Muschg: Literatur der deutschen Schweiz seit 1900,* Basel: Reinhardt, 1975

Kohlschmidt, Werner, editor, *Bürgerlichkeit und Unbürgerlichkeit in der Literatur der Deutschen Schweiz,* Bern: Francke, 1978

Korrodi, Eduard, *Geisteserbe der Schweiz,* Erlenbach-Zurich: Rentsch, 1929; 2nd edition 1943

Mörikofer, Johann Caspar, *Die schweizerische Literatur des achtzehnten Jahrhunderts,* Leipzig: Hirzel, 1861

Natan, Alex, *Swiss Men of Letters,* London: Wolff, 1970

Pezold, Klaus, and Hannelore Prosche, editors, *Geschichte der deutschsprachigen Schweizer Literatur im 20. Jahrhundert,* Berlin: Volk und Wissen, 1991

Schmid, Karl, *Unbehagen im Kleinstaat,* Zurich: Artemis, 1963; 3rd edition, 1977

Steinberg, Jonathan, *Why Switzerland?* Cambridge and New York: Cambridge University Press, 1976; 2nd edition, 1996

Stump, Doris, et al., *Deutschsprachige Schriftstellerinnen in der Schweiz 1700–1945,* Zurich: Limmat Verlag, 1994

Walzer, Pierre Olivier, *Lexikon der Schweizer Literaturen,* Basel: Lenos Verlag, 1991

T

George Tabori 1914–

George (György) Tabori, a novelist, essayist, translator, dramatist, stage director, and radio play and film scriptwriter, was born in Hungary and has lived and worked in Germany, Austria, England, Bulgaria, Turkey, the Middle East, and the United States. Today, Tabori lives in Vienna, Austria. He possesses a British passport, but he breaks with all concepts of a "national" writer. He is a global citizen who feels more comfortable with a transnational, transcultural identity. This cosmopolitan heritage is reflected in his writing. After his breakthrough as stage director in 1984 (with Samuel Beckett's *Waiting for Godot*), and as playwright in 1987 with *Mein Kampf*, Tabori emerged in the early 1990s as one of the major contemporary dramatists and stage directors in German theater. The major reception of his work has taken place in Germany and Austria, even though Tabori writes in English and his work for German-speaking audiences is published in translation.

During his time in the United States, Tabori wrote film scripts for Alfred Hitchcock (1953; *I Confess*), Anthony Asquith (1954; *The Young Lovers*), and Anatole Litvak (1959; *The Journey*), among others. He met Bertolt Brecht, who deeply influenced his interest in drama. Tabori's oeuvre has been variously categorized as existentialist, theater of the absurd (Tabori has repeatedly staged Beckett), psychological literature, and Holocaust literature. Tabori's background in Austro-Hungarian German-Jewish culture and the experience of the Shoah have profoundly shaped his work. Translating this history into theater has been his major theme.

In the 1940s, he began his career as a novelist. *Beneath the Stone the Scorpion*, published in London in 1945 and a bestseller in the United States, deals with literary memory and offers an unconventional portrayal of a German officer during World War II. His second novel, *Companions of the Left Hand* (1946), was included in the Armed Services Editions. In *Original Sin* (1947), Tristan Manasse recounts the death of his wife, Adela, whom, as the reader finds out through a long process of first-person narration, he murdered. But was it brutal murder or was it a redemption from a humiliating, depressing, empty life? Tabori's early novels express a clear existentialist influence and deal with the challenge of personal freedom. "Is the murderer of a murderer a murderer?" is the theme of *The Caravan Passes* (1951). The plot takes place at the crossroads of Europe and the Orient at the end of colonialism; this setting is common in Tabori's early work and is influenced by his own biography.

The novels confront the reader with motifs, themes, and literary techniques that also became part of his numerous later plays: flashbacks, stream of consciousness, memory and recall, the present and the past, illness and death, victim and violence, and the representation of conflicting truths. His novels, as well as his plays, often choose a setting at the intersection of different cultures, religions, and values. The confrontation with different value systems leads inevitably to a discussion of moral and ethical behavior. In Tabori's plays, the motif of competing truth systems is omnipresent.

The Cannibals (premiered in New York in 1968) represents an experiment in approaching and showing the unrepresentable and unimaginable horror of Auschwitz. Tabori reanalyzes the victim-perpetrator dichotomy by presenting the very thin line that determines when humans become oppressors or oppressed. Concentration camp prisoner Puffi is murdered by his starving fellow inmates because he possesses a piece of bread. The inmates gradually come to realize that the fresh meat of their comrade could save them from starvation. While the cook prepares the meal, the others tell stories of their lives, and the stage becomes the place for the scenic imitation of memory. They then plan to murder the guards and to escape. But "Onkel," a dignified old man (modeled on Tabori's father, who was murdered in Auschwitz), considers this plan morally unacceptable. In the end, the prison commandant Schreckinger gives the order to eat the human soup, but only two inmates do. The others refuse to eat the flesh of their comrade and die in the gas chamber.

For Tabori, inherited tradition leads to active reappropriation. Parallel to *The Cannibals*, which was written in memory of his father, he memorialized his mother in his 1979 play *Münchner Kammerspiele* (*My Mother's Courage*). This play, which portrays the mother's deportation as a misunderstanding with a happy end, began as a story, was later broadcast as a radio play, and was then filmed by director Michael Verhoeven (Bundesfilmpreis, 1996). This technique of reworking a story into a radio play and then a stage production is very common with Tabori. For him, it is not the final stage product that is important, it is the entire process of production, die *Erarbeitung*. In order to replicate this process, he has preferred to work with his own group of actors and his own theater team (Wiener Kreis and Bremer Theaterlabor, among others), as he himself had been part of Lee Strasberg's New York Actor's Studio.

In 1987, Tabori directed the premiere of his play *Mein Kampf*. A farce filled with black humor and rhetorical acrobatics, the piece is shockingly eloquent in portraying the absurdity and horrors of Nazi ideology. Tabori imagines an acquaintance between Jewish protagonist Schlomo Herzl and aspiring artist Adolf Hitler in an asylum for homeless men. Schlomo takes care of the psychologically unstable Hitler, gives him advice on demagogy and outer appearance (Hitler's beard), and becomes the target of Hitler's hysterical attacks and the first object of his anti-Semitism and brutality.

Tabori's writing and adaptations resist categorization. Nonetheless, one might speak of "biographical plays" (*The Cannibals, My Mother's Courage,* and *Peepshow*), "Holocaust plays" (*Shylock Improvisationen, Jubiläum* [1983], *Mein Kampf, Nathans Tod* [1991], and *Die Ballade vom Wiener Schnitzel* [1996]), and plays about theater (*Babylon-Blues* [1991], *Goldberg Variationen* [1991]), although the lines between the categories are fluid. Tabori furthermore very successfully demonstrates the connections between the horrors of the Nazi period and the growing potential for violence toward minorities within our contemporary societies, especially within multicultural settings (*Demonstration, Jubiläum, Weisman und Rotgesicht* [1990], and *Nathans Tod*).

BARBARA FISCHER

Biography

Born in Budapest, Hungary, 1914. Emigrated to London, 1935, where he worked as journalist and translator; in Turkey, Bulgaria, and the Middle East, 1939; moved to the United States, 1947; worked in theater and film productions; collaborated with Alfred Hitchcock, Elia Kazan, and Bertolt Brecht; returned to Europe, 1971, and directed his own plays as well as those of other playwrights in Bremen, Munich, Bochum, and Berlin; settled in Vienna, 1987, where he staged plays at the Burgtheater and Akademietheater. Bundesverdienstkreuz, 1979; Theater Prize, Berlin, 1988; Büchner Prize, 1992.

Selected Works

Collections
Theaterstücke, 2 vols., 1994

Fiction
Beneath the Stone the Scorpion, 1945
Companions of the Left Hand, 1946
Original Sin, 1947
The Caravan Passes, 1951
The Journey, 1958
The Good One, 1960
Son of a Bitch, 1981
Meine Kämpfe, 1986

Selected Plays and Stage Productions
Flight into Egypt, 1952
The Emperor's Clothes, 1953
Brouhaha, 1958
Brecht on Brecht: An Improvisation, 1967
The Niggerlovers, 1967
The Cannibals, 1968
Pinkville, 1971
Clowns, 1972
Demonstration, 1972
The 25th Hour, 1977
My Mother's Courage, 1979
Der Voyeur, 1982
Jubiläum, 1983
Peepshow, 1984
Mein Kampf, 1987
Weisman und Rotgesicht: Ein jüdischer Western, 1990
Der Babylon-Blues oder wie man glücklich wird, ohne sich zu verausgaben, 1991
Die Goldberg-Variationen, 1991
Nathans Tod, 1991
Requiem für einen Spion, 1993
Die Massenmörderin und ihre Freunde, 1995
Die Ballade vom Wiener Schnitzel, 1996
Die letzte Nacht im September, 1997

Other
Unterammergau oder Die guten Deutschen (essays and plays), 1981
Betrachtungen über das Feigenblatt. Handbuch für Verliebte und Verrückte (essays), 1991

Further Readings

Bayerdörfer, Hans-Peter, and Jörg Schönert, editors, *Theater gegen das Vergessen: Bühnenarbeit und Drama bei George Tabori,* Tübingen: Niemeyer, 1997

Feinberg-Jütte, Anat, "The Task Is Not to Reproduce the External Form, but to Find the Subtext: George Tabori's Productions of Samuel Beckett's Texts," *Journal of Beckett Studies,* no. 1/2 (1992)

Gronius, Jörg W., and Wend Kässens, *Tabori,* Frankfurt: Athenäum, 1989

Marshall, Brenda K. DeVore, *A Semiotic Phenomenology of Directing,* Carbondale: Southern Illinois University, 1988

Ohngemach, Gundula, *George Tabori,* Frankfurt: Fischer, 1989

Radtke, Peter, *M wie Tabori: Erfahrungen eines behinderten Schauspielers,* Zürich: Pendo, 1987

Strümpel, Jan, editor, *George Tabori,* Munich: Edition Text und Kritik, 1997

Uberman, Iwona, *Auschwitz im Theater der "Peinlichkeit": George Taboris Holocaust-Stücke im Rahmen der Theatergeschichte seit dem Ende der 60er Jahre,* Munich: Dissertationsverlag NG-Kopierladen, 1995

Welker, Andrea, editor, *George Tabori: Dem Gedächtnis, der Trauer, und dem Lachen gewidmet: Portraits,* Vienna: Bibliothek der Provinz, 1994

Welker, Andrea, and Tina Berger, editors, *Ich wollte meine Tochter läge tot zu meinen Füßen und hätte Juwelen in den Ohren: Improvisationen über Shakespeares Shylock: Dokumentation einer Theaterarbeit,* Munich: Hanser, 1979

Yoko Tawada 1960–

The Japanese woman writer Yoko Tawada, who has lived in Hamburg since 1982, formulated the basis of her literary career in her essay "Erzähler ohne Seelen" (1996; Narrators without Souls). In this essay, she writes about visiting Hamburg's Museum of Ethnology, where she becomes motivated to develop a "fictional ethnology." She describes the doll of a shaman, who is exhibited in a showcase. The shaman is surrounded by prose texts and photos, which explain the life of his ethnic community. His voice comes out of a cassette. In Tawada's opinion, the real—potentially dangerous—foreigner is replaced (and eliminated) by a domesticated replica. This fiction takes root in the heads of the observers, while the authentic culture is irretrievably lost. According to Tawada, therefore, the explanations in the museum do not really contribute to understanding the cultural "other," but rather only confirm what is in the imagination of the visitors. Tawada counters this pseudoethnic ethnology with a consciously fictional one. She invests her characters with an artificial Japanese perspective, before whose eyes she has a created European world.

Through her work, the writer portrays the process by which her female protagonists draw closer toward foreigners, who are held to be extremely different. She concentrates on the processes of perception that play a role during the discovery and exploration of a foreign culture and ultimately influence integration into that culture. For Tawada, stereotypical works of fiction can hinder the process of contacting a foreign culture. By contrast, hardened boundaries can also be dissolved by the imagination. In all her texts, Tawada emphasizes the dream's creative powers, which undermine static ideas about the other. The energy of the dream also flows into her writing style, with which she has tried to break down the structure of everyday speech.

As a 19 year old, Tawada traveled to Europe for the first time on the Trans-Siberian railway. This journey is seen in the German speaking-public as the central event of her writing career and private life. In *Wo Europa anfängt* (1991; Where Europe Starts), her first narrative written directly in German, the writer makes reference to this journey.

In keeping with many other writers of non-German origin living in Germany, Tawada uses the journey as a metaphor in order to clarify the fundamentally distressing life experiences involved in changing cultural contexts. She represents the journey of her female protagonist as a process of initiation, and the protagonist's departure is described as the severing of the umbilical cord. For the author, the departure signifies an abrupt break with her original historical, geographical, and cultural identity.

The journey from Asia to Europe leads unavoidably to a confrontation with the relationship between continents, which is weighted down with conflict. The protagonist traces her parents' dreams of Europe and engages intensively with legends in which European fantasies about the discovery and conquest of Asia are revealed. Right from the start, the protagonist questions the distinction between her own self and the other. On the long journey, which at first leads across the shapeless expanse of water and then through the monotonous landscape of Siberia, the distinction is completely blurred. The question about the geographical beginning of Europe can no longer be answered with certainty, and the protagonist's personal biography also suddenly appears as a work of fiction. The traveler falls into a dream, devoid of images, from which she awakes only on her arrival. Because of this reverie, she can not authentically reproduce her travel experiences. Instead, she quotes from a report, which she compiled before her journey, and from a diary that she kept afterward: the journey on the Trans-Siberian railway becomes pure invention.

In her travel story *Das Leipzig des Lichts und der Gelatine* (1991; The Leipzig of Light and Gelatine), Tawada counters the strength of dreams to dissolve boundaries with the power of prejudice to erect them. This time, the journey is from Berlin to Leipzig and takes place just after the fall of the Berlin Wall. For quite a while, however, the protagonist cannot begin her journey because her movement is hindered by her fear of the otherness of the East. As the text suggests, imaginary boundaries become much more effective in a time when real boundaries are dissolving.

The interplay between the dissolution and the establishment of boundaries continues when Tawada's artificial foreigners try to find out about everyday life in West German towns. In both *Rothenburg ob der Tauber: Ein deutsches Rätsel* (1996; Rothenburg ob der Tauber: A German Riddle) and *Talisman* (1996; Talisman), the female protagonists are thrown into a foreign culture that has a signifying system they do not understand. Mysterious signs such as the pieces of metal hanging from women's ears, for example, tempt them to form their own interpretations. While attempting to uncover the secrets of the foreign environment, they develop great creative energies. Since they do not know what significance is attached to these signs in the foreign society, they fall back on their own signifying systems. Their interpretations bring a dreamlike world into being, in which toys come to life, roads turn into snakes, and *Brezeln* (pretzels) are components of a secret language. In conversations with the natives, however, the foreigners are unable to assert themselves using their new interpretations of the environment. The natives react with incomprehension and point out the foreigners' deficiencies. They will not admit the possibility that the foreigners' creative interpretations open up the traditional conventions with which they ascribe meaning.

The body of the exotic woman as a sign that is overloaded with meanings is the focus of Tawada's short novel *Das Bad* (1989; The Bath). Her protagonist, a young Japanese woman, is transformed into a screen for the projections of others as she looks into the mirror. Her body is covered again and again with images of exotic femininity, which reveal the hidden wishes and anxieties of European men. The continuous metamorphoses experienced by the young woman prevent these images from defining her identity, however. Through her transformations, she repeatedly brings about that moment in which one image has dissolved and the next has not yet appeared. For this short moment the screen is blank.

Tawada reserves a special place among signifying systems for written language. For example, foreign characters have a strong visual attraction to the female protagonist of the story *Bilderrätsel ohne Bilder* (1987; Picture Puzzle without Pictures). The longing for mysterious characters eventually motivates the protagonist to travel to Europe. Like her protagonist, Tawada herself also regards the intensive study of foreign characters as an opportunity to free herself from the conventions of her native language. As she remarks in her essay "Von der Muttersprache zur Sprachmutter" (1996; From the Mother Tongue to the Mother of Language), in one's native tongue, words are too closely bound up with particular meanings, and so there is scarcely any room left for authorial creativity. Words in a foreign language, however, can be considered separately from their meanings and tempt the author to play with them. In her dreamlike texts, Tawada releases the words of the German language from their connections and puts them together in new combinations. She transforms images into writing and characters into images. Thus, she demonstrates to her German-speaking readership the arbitrariness intrinsic to every production of meaning.

SABINE FISCHER

Biography
Born in Tokyo, Japan, 23 March 1960. Studied European literature (especially Russian literature) in Tokyo; in Hamburg, 1979; M.A. in contemporary German Literature, Hamburg University, 1991. Literature Prize, City of Hamburg, 1990; Akutagawa-Sho, Japan, 1993; Lessing Prize, Hamburg, 1994. Writes and publishes in both German and Japanese. Currently lives in Hamburg (since 1982).

Selected Works

Poetry and Prose
Wo Europa anfängt, 1991
Nur da wo du bist da ist nichts, 1997

Novels
Das Bad, 1989
Ein Gast, 1993

Plays
Die Kranichmaske, die bei Nacht strahlt, 1993
Aber die Mandarinen müssen heute abend noch geraubt werden, 1997
Orpheus und Izanagi (for theater and radio), 1998

Narratives
Das Leipzig des Lichts und der Gelatine, 1991
Tintenfisch aus Reisen, 1994

Essays
Rothenburg ob der Tauber: Ein deutsches Rätsel, 1996
Talisman, 1996
Verwandlungen: Tübinger Poetik Vorlesungen, 1998
Spielzeug und Sprachmagie in der europäischen Literatur, 1999

Further Reading

Fischer, Sabine, "Verschwinden ist schön: Zu Yoko Tawadas Kurzroman *Ein Bad*," in *Denn du tanzt auf einem Seil: Positionen deutschsprachiger MigrantInnenliteratur*, edited by Moray McGowan and Sabine Fischer, Tübingen: Stauffenburg, 1997
——, "Die Welt ist voller Stimmen und Blicke," *Materialien Deutsch als Fremdsprache* 46 (1997)
Grond, Walter, "Das Deutschland Yoko Tawadas," in *Stimmen: Ein Roman als Konzept*, Graz: Droschl, 1992
Weigel, Sigrid, "Transsibirische Metamorphosen: Laudatio auf Yoko Tawada zur Verleihung des Adalbert-von-Chamisso-Preises 1996," *Frauen in der Literaturwissenschaft: Rundbrief* 49 (December 1996)

Ludwig Tieck 1773–1853

Ludwig Tieck was both an initiator and a representative figure: his career shaped and mirrored the German Romantic movement from its beginnings in the Enlightenment to its succession by Realism. Tieck's earliest writings—written-to-order contributions to works of popular literature—demonstrate his talent in writing quickly and adapting to any variety of styles: this ability remained characteristic and has often been used in evidence against him. The corpus of work Tieck produced in the course of his career is immense; some is no longer considered part of the literary canon, a great deal is derivative, yet so much was innovative and inspirational.

The early Romantic movement, it is often claimed, was born with the publication of *Herzensergießungen eines kunstliebenden Klosterbruders* (1796; *Outpourings of an Art-Loving Friar*). This joint venture, with Wilhelm Heinrich Wackenroder, inspired a new way of appreciating art as a divine force (which could also be demonic) and of approaching art with emotion rather than with rationality. *Phantasien über die Kunst* (1799; *Fantasies on Art for Friends of Art*) was published by Tieck after Wackenroder's death in the same spirit, and Tieck's first novel, *Franz Sternbalds Wanderungen* (1798; Franz Sternbald's Wanderings), represents a culmination of the theme, establishing stock Romantic motifs, such as the artist-protagonist as wanderer, music as the ultimate (because least mimetic) art form, and

the sensuous and dangerous appeal of the South represented by Italy. Recent scholarship has put a new, more differentiated light on the (re)discovery of nationalism, Catholicism, and the Middle Ages, then so uncritically revered by younger artists and writers and so summarily despised by Goethe.

However, the pious wonder of the art-loving friar and the apprentice artist was only one side of the early Tieck, who depicted fin de siècle world weariness and nihilism in *Abdallah* (1795) and *William Lovell* (1795–96). In the latter, Tieck reinterpreted the 18th-century epistolary novel and the bildungsroman by means of the Gothic novel tradition and contemporary Kantian philosophy, reducing man to marionette, alone in a world beyond his grasp, unable to understand himself or communicate with others. Tieck expresses profound loneliness and disorientation in this novel (feelings shared by many of his contemporaries), but critics, such as Heinrich Heine, were quick to pick up hints of posturing, a general feeling of falseness—signs that the young author was testing his powers of describing emotion rather than expressing those truly felt.

Another strand to Tieck's creative powers can be found in the novel *Peter Lebrecht* (1795–96), written in the tradition of Laurence Sterne, and in his dramatic work. The theater played a central role in Tieck's oeuvre, and he was considered an absolute authority in his later days in Dresden. At the beginning of his career, he parodied the "play-within-the-play" scenario in *Der gestiefelte Kater* (1797; *Puss in Boots*), multiplying the number of levels on which the play operates to include the audience and the poet himself. This self-reflexivity was a pioneering venture in Romantic irony and chaos and influential as a forerunner of the anti-illusionist theater. His *Kaiser Octavianus* (1804) contains the much-quoted reference to "mondbeglänzte Zaubernacht" (magical moonlit night), describing Romantic atmosphere. By this point, Tieck was a cult author for the younger generation of his contemporaries with such ideas quickly becoming common property. For a century afterward, they were considered clever but insincere. Now critics are reevaluating the cliché of Tieck's clichés.

Tieck experimented with the fairy tale and edited (under the pseudonym Peter Leberecht) a pseudo-collection titled *Volksmärchen* (1797; Folk Tales). In these works, dream and reality, the supernatural and the everyday, are intertwined in a new and confusing way, and dream often becomes a nightmare, as in *Der blonde Eckbert* (1797; *Fair-Haired Eckbert*), which inspired other writers and remains a key text of the Romantic period.

In the period 1812–16, Tieck published the collection of novellas *Phantasus* (*Tales from the Phantas*), integrating previously published work with new works. In his later years, he was to develop this narrative situation (reminiscent of the Romantic salon) to its limit and beyond in his "conversation novellas," in which characters of the upper classes meet and discuss contemporary issues, often without much reason, and mainly with no real plot action, for example, in *Die Gesellschaft auf dem Lande* (1825; The Social Gathering in the Country).

Tieck's gravitation toward longer prose works as well as toward Realism can also be observed in the historical novellas *Der Aufruhr in den Cevennen* (1826; *The Rebellion in the Cevennes*), *Hexen-Sabbath* (1831; Witches' Sabbath), and *Der junge Tischlermeister* (1836; The Young Master Joiner), none of which achieve the same freshness as the best early works.

In the debate on novella theory, Tieck is remembered and still relevant for his insistence on *Wendepunkte*, turning points that determine the action unexpectedly yet inevitably. These could be supernatural events (typical of the early period of Romanticism) or events outside the social sphere (typical of later Romanticism and Realism).

Tieck's repertoire included the more exact literary sciences of editing and translating; however, his work bears witness to their creative and imaginative scope within Romanticism. His lifelong fascination with the works of Shakespeare culminated in his completion of A.W. Schlegel's translation of Shakespeare's works in collaboration with his daughter Sophie and Wolf von Baudissin in the years 1825–33. It made Shakespeare accessible and popular in Germany and is still widely quoted and highly regarded. Collaboration and friendship with the painter Phillip Otto Runge bore fruit in the form of *Minnelieder aus dem schwäbischen Zeitalter* (1803; Courtly Love Songs from the Swabian Epoch), a new edition of Germany's medieval poetry, with the same intercultural and imaginative slant. Tieck also edited works by important Romantic authors, such as Novalis and Heinrich von Kleist.

The decline in quality and quantity of Tieck's later output has led to the comment that he lived too long. However, whereas his friends Wackenroder and Novalis died romantically young, Tieck's survival gives insight into German Romanticism in its widest parameters.

SHEILA JANET DICKSON

See also Romanticism; Wilhelm Heinrich Wackenroder

Biography

Born in Berlin, 31 May 1773. Theology student, Halle University, 1792; studied English literature at the University of Göttingen, 1792; in Nuremberg with Wilhelm Heinrich Wackenroder, 1793; worked for Christoph Friedrich Nicolai, publisher in Berlin, as a writer for *Straussfedern*, 1794–97; associated with the Jena Romantics; traveled between Berlin, Dresden, and Hamburg, 1799–1801; in Ziebingen, near Frankfurt, 1802–19; met Samuel Taylor Coleridge in England, 1817; literary historian and editor for the Dresden theater, 1819–41; dramaturge and stage director, Berlin, 1841–53. Died 28 April 1853.

Selected Works

Collections
Sämtliche Werke, 12 vols., 1799
Sämtliche Werke, 30 vols., 1817–24
Schriften, 28 vols., 1828–54
Novellen, 7 vols., 1823–28; enlarged edition as *Gesammelte Novellen*, 14 vols., 1835–42
Kritische Schriften, 4 vols., 1848–52
Werke, edited by Marianne Thalmann, 4 vols., 1963–66
Schriften, edited by Manfred Frank et al., 1985–
Schriften, edited by Achim Hölter, 1991

Fiction
Abdallah, 1795
Peter Lebrecht: Eine Geschichte ohne Abentheuerlichkeiten, 1795–96
William Lovell, 1795–96
Volksmärchen (under the pseudonym Peter Leberecht; includes *Der blonde Eckbert*), 3 vols., 1797; *Der blonde Eckbert* as *Fair-Haired Eckbert*, in *German Literary Fairy Tales*, translated by Thomas Carlyle, 1983
Almansur, 1798
Franz Sternbalds Wanderungen, 1798
Romantische Dichtungen, 1799–1800
Phantasus: Eine Sammlung von Märchen, Erzählungen, Schauspielen und Novellen, 3 vols., 1812–16; as *Tales from the Phantas*, translated by Julius Hare et al., 1848
Die Gemälde, 1822; as *The Pictures*, translated by G. Cunningham, in *Foreign Tales and Traditions*, 1829
Die Verlobung, 1823
Der Geheimnißvolle, 1823
Musikalische Leiden und Freuden, 1824
Die Reisenden, 1824
Die Gesellschaft auf dem Lande, 1825
Der Aufruhr in den Cevennen, 1826; as *The Rebellion in the Cevennes*, translated by Madame Burette, 1845
Der Alte vom Berge, und die Gesellschaft auf dem Lande: zwei Novellen, 1828; *Der Alte vom Berge*; as *The Old Man of the Mountain*, translated by J.C. Hare, 1831
Der Schutzgeist, 1835
Der junge Tischlermeister, 1836
Wunderlichkeiten, 1837
Die Klausenburg, 1837
Des Lebens Überfluß, 1839
Vittoria Accorombona, 1840; as *The Roman Matron; or, Vittoria Accorombona*, 1845

Plays
Ritter Blaubart (produced 1835), 1797
Die sieben Weiber des Blaubart, 1797
Der gestiefelte Kater (produced 1844), 1797; as *Puss in Boots*, translated by Lillie Winter, in *The German Classics of the Nineteenth and Twentieth Centuries*, vol. 4, edited by Kuno Francke and W.G. Howard, 1914; translated by Gerald Gillespie, 1974

Die verkehrte Welt, 1798

Prinz Zerbino; oder, Die Reise nach dem guten Geschmack, 1799

Leben und Tod der Heiligen Genoveva, 1800

Das Ungeheuer und der verzauberte Wald: Ein musikalisches Märchen in vier Aufzügen, 1800

Kaiser Octavianus, 1804

Die Sommernacht: Eine Jugenddichtung (fragment), 1851; as *The Midsummer Night; or, Shakespeare and the Fairies*, translated by Mary C. Rumsey, 1854

Poetry

Gedichte, 3 vols., 1821–23

Gedichte, 1841

Other

Herzensergießungen eines kunstliebenden Klosterbruders, with Wilhelm Heinrich Wackenroder, 1796; as *Outpourings of an Art-Loving Friar*, translated by Edward Mornin, 1975

Phantasien über die Kunst, für Freunde der Kunst, with Wilhelm Heinrich Wackenroder, 1799; as *Fantasies on Art for Friends of Arts*, translated by Mary Hurst Shubert, in *Confessions and Fantasies*, 1971

Dramaturgische Blätter, 3 vols., 1826–52

Tieck and Solger: The Complete Correspondence, edited by Percy Matenko, 1933

Letters of Ludwig Tieck Hitherto Unpublished 1792–1853, edited by Edwin H. Zeydel et al., 1937

Translations

William Shakespeare, *Der Sturm: Ein Schauspiel*, 1796

Miguel de Cervantes Saavedra, *Leben und Thaten des scharfsinnigen Edlen Don Quixote von La Mancha*, 1799–1800

and editor, *Alt-Englisches Theater; oder, Supplement zum Shakespear*, 2 vols., 1811

William Shakespeare, *Dramatische Werke*, 1825–33

Leben und Begebenheiten des Escudero Marcus Obregon; oder, Autobiographie des Spanischen Dichters Vicente Espinel, 1827

William Shakespeare, *Vier Schauspiele von Shakespeare*, 1836

Edited Works

Minnelieder aus dem schwäbischen Zeitalter, 1803

Ulrich von Lichtenstein, *Frauendienst; oder, Geschichte und Liebe des Ritters und Sängers*, 1812

Heinrich Kleist, *Hinterlassene Schriften*, 1821

Shakespeares Vorschule, 1823–29

Heinrich Kleist, *Gesammelte Schriften*, 1826

Karl Ferdinand Solger, *Schriften und Briefwechsel*, with Friedrich von Raumer, 1826

J.M.R. Lenz, *Gesammelte Schriften*, 1828

Johann Gottfried Schnabel, *Die Insel Felsenburg; oder, Wunderliche Fata einiger Seefahrer: Eine Geschichte aus dem Anfange des achtzehnten Jahrhunderts*, 6 vols., 1828

Novalis, *Gesammelte Schriften*, with Friedrich Schlegel, 5th edition, 1837

Franz Berthold, *Gesammelte Novellen*, 1842

Karl Förster, *Gedichte*, 1843

Johann Wolfgang Goethe, *Ältestes Liederbuch*, 1844

Novalis, *Novalis Schriften: Dritter Theil*, with Eduard von Bülow, 1846

Further Reading

Crisman, William, *The Crises of "Language and Dead Signs" in Ludwig Tieck's Prose Fiction*, Columbia, South Carolina: Camden House, 1996

Immerwahr, Raymond M., *The Esthetic Intent of Tieck's Fantastic Comedy*, St. Louis, Missouri: Washington University Press, 1953

Jost, Walter, "Stilkrise der deutschen Shakespeare-Übersetzung," *Deutsche Vierteljahrsschrift* 35 (1961)

Lillyman, William J., *Reality's Dark Dream: The Narrative Fiction of Ludwig Tieck*, Berlin and New York: de Gruyter, 1978

Lüdeke, H., "Zur Tieck'schen Shakespeare-Übersetzung," *Jahrbuch der deutschen Schillergesellschaft* 55 (1919)

Paulin, Roger, *Ludwig Tieck: A Literary Biography*, Oxford: Clarendon Press, and New York: Oxford University Press, 1985; translated as *Ludwig Tieck: Eine litterarische Biographie*, Munich: Beck, 1988

——, *Ludwig Tieck*, Stuttgart: Metzler, 1987

Pikulik, Lothar, *Romantik als Ungenügen an der Normalität: Am Beispiel Tiecks, Hoffmanns, Eichendorffs*, Frankfurt: Suhrkamp, 1979

Rath, Wolfgang, *Ludwig Tieck: Das vergessene Genie: Studien zu seinem Erzählwerk*, Paderborn: Schöningh, 1996

Ribbat, Ernst, *Ludwig Tieck: Studien zur Konzeption und Praxis romantischer Poesie*, Kronberg: Athenäum, 1978

Schmitz, Walter, editor, *Ludwig Tieck: Literaturprogramm und Lebensinszenierung im Kontext seiner Zeit*, Tübingen: Niemeyer, 1997

Sullivan, Heather I., *The Intercontextuality of Self and Nature in Ludwig Tieck's Early Works*, New York: Lang, 1997

Trainer, James, *Ludwig Tieck: From Gothic to Romantic*, The Hague: Mouton, 1964

Wesollek, Peter, *Ludwig Tieck, oder, Der Weltumsegler seines Innern: Anmerkungen zur Thematik des Wunderbaren in Tiecks Erzählwerk*, Wiesbaden: Steiner, 1984

Zybura, Marek, *Ludwig Tieck als Übersetzer und Herausgeber: Zur frühromantischen Idee einer deutschen Weltliteratur*, Heidelberg: Winter, 1994

Der blonde Eckbert 1797

Novella by Ludwig Tieck

Ludwig Tieck's novella *Der blonde Eckbert* (1797; *Fair-Haired Eckbert*) has been a riddle to its readers ever since its appearance. Published in a collection of fairy tales by different authors, the novella borrows neither form nor plot from any known text and begins a new genre, the literary fairy tale (*romantische Kunstmärchen*), a genre to which Tieck himself contributed many more texts in his later *Phantasus* (1812–16; *Tales from the Phantas*) collection. The "unintelligibility" of the story rests on a déjà vu at its center. Bertha, the wife of the knight Eckbert, recounts her childhood to her husband's friend Walther. In her story, after she runs away from her parents, she finds a new home and substitute family at an old woman's house in a remote forest. There she lives in seclusion with a dog and a magical bird whose eggs contain jewels and who repeatedly sings his song of *Waldeinsamkeit* (loneliness in the woods). Dreaming of finding a prince, she again runs away, taking only the bird, whom she will later kill. When Bertha is done telling her story, Walther comments on it by referring to the dog's name, the very name Bertha had not been able to remember and a name that, besides Bertha, only the old woman could have known. The shock of hearing again the forgotten name and Walther's impossible knowledge of it lead to Bertha's fatal illness and Eckbert's murder of Walther.

Not only do Eckbert and Bertha experience a déjà vu, but the whole text is marked by a pattern of four repetitions: a person somewhat irresponsibly runs away from a family, or substitute family (perhaps killing the members), and after some time wandering through forests finds a new family. In this second family, however, the suppressed first family returns in the form of names, ghosts, or similarities. Each time, money and possessions cause jealousy and suspicion, thereby provoking the person to run away. In this pattern of repetition, the different characters of the text are condensed into two: the "bert"-character who leaves his or her family (Eck*bert* and *Bertha*) and the "alter"-character who is abandoned or murdered (Bertha's *Elter*n [parents], W*alther,* and the *Alte* [old woman]). The repetition of these two characters under different disguises, as well as the pattern's four repetitions, makes it impossible for the "bert"-character to recognize the *alter*ity of the "alter"-character. This paranoid circularity reaches its ultimate climax at the end of the story when Eckbert suddenly appears in the forest where the old woman lives and learns from her that Bertha had actually been his sister. She concludes: "See how injustice punishes itself! No one but I was Walther." Eckbert responds, just before he collapses, apparently dying: "In what frightful solitude have I passed my life!"

It has been argued that Eckbert and Bertha are haunted by their pasts because they never completed it, never mourned their losses, and never admitted their guilt. Thus, Ernst Bloch suggests that the shocking return of the suppressed in Tieck's novella figures as a return of the uncompleted: "Then, the shock would be a placeholder for each sudden return to a self which did not—or not completely—turn out as it had meant to" (Bloch).

While the novella has split its readers between harsh critics, who condemn its mere effect-oriented populism (Gundolf), and enthusiastic proponents (the Schlegels, Arno Schmidt), even the most extreme reactions to the text respond to the crisis of understanding the story. Thus, it is no coincidence that the birth of modern literary criticism (F. and A.W. Schlegel) and hermeneutics (Schleiermacher) took place not only at that time but also in Tieck's circle of friends—all of whom were close to Jena Romanticism. At this time, the relationship between reader and text was called into question, which resulted in the institutionalization of a discipline that could potentially secure the meaning of texts. Perhaps the only text preceding *Fair-Haired Eckbert* that puzzles the reader in a similar way is Goethe's *Das Märchen* (1795; *The Fairy-Tale,* which is part of *Unterhaltungen deutscher Ausge-*

wanderten [*Conversations of German Refugees*]), a piece that shares its fairy-tale scenario.

The riddle *Fair-Haired Eckbert* poses to its readers can be seen in light of the way in which the text itself deals with riddles. Several times one of the characters unveils a secret of his or her life, and each time the result is a betrayal or loss. The old woman is betrayed by Bertha when she explains the magic of the bird to her. Bertha dies after telling Walther her story, and Eckbert loses his new friend Hugo after telling him of his secret. Thus, the story itself avoids its characters' mistakes by not giving away its secret. The very intensive discussion of the story in the 1970s and 1980s reflects basic conceptual changes of cultural periodization (e.g., "Romanticism"), genre, and the status of reading. It has been shown that the story is less a novella or fairy tale but rather the prototype of the modern novel, for it combines various genres and uses a psychological twist that pathologizes the protagonists by means of ambiguities and incest.

FRITZ BREITHAUPT

Editions

First edition: in *Volksmärchen,* vol. 1, Berlin: Carl August Nicolai, 1797 (published under the pseudonym Peter Leberecht)
Critical edition: in *Schriften,* edited by Manfred Frank, vol. 6, Frankfurt: Deutscher Klassiker Verlag, 1985
Translation: *Fair-Haired Eckbert,* in *German Literary Fairy Tales,* translated by Thomas Carlyle, edited by Frank G. Ryder and Robert M. Browning, New York: Continuum, 1983

Further Reading

Bloch, Ernst, "Bilder des déjà vu," in *Gesamtausgabe, Literarische Aufsätze,* vol. 9, Frankfurt: Suhrkamp, 1959
Greiner, Bernhard, "Patho-logie des Erzählens: Tiecks Entwurf der Dichtung im *Blonden Eckbert,*" *Deutschunterricht* 39, no. 1 (1987)
Rath, Wolfgang, *Ludwig Tieck: Das vergessene Genie: Studien zu einem Erzählwerk,* Paderborn: Schöningh, 1996
Schlaffer, Heinz, "Ein formtheoretischer Versuch über Tiecks *Blonden Eckbert,*" in *Ludwig Tieck,* edited by Wulf Segebrecht, Darmstadt: Wissenschaftliche Buchgesellschaft, 1976
Tatar, Maria, "Unholy Alliances: Narrative Ambiguity in Tieck's *Der blonde Eckbert,*" *Modern Language Notes* 102 (1987)

Ernst Toller 1893–1939

The life and work of Ernst Toller are of key importance in understanding those turbulent areas where the culture and politics of Weimar Germany met. His plays and political writing, along with the reactions they provoked and the social insights they enshrine, highlight some of the destructive tensions of this era. Hounded by the right for his socialist affiliations, he was the first victim of Goebbels's campaign against Jewish writers. He was also the target of vituperative smears from the German Communist Party for his efforts to assert a brand of moral and political conviction that steered clear of party ideology. In short, Ernst

Toller offers depressing evidence of what befell German intellectuals in the interwar years who attempted to pick their way between the fateful rigidity of right and left and to make a stand for ethical and humanitarian values.

Time and the wide availability of Brecht's plays have taught us to think of Bertolt Brecht as the most celebrated German dramatist of the 1920s and 1930s. In fact, in May 1939, when he hanged himself in a New York hotel, this accolade would more properly have belonged to Toller. His international fame rests largely on the works—translated into 27 languages—that he wrote while in prison between 1919 and 1924. His first play, *Die Wandlung* (1919; *Transfiguration*)—arguably the definitive Expressionist drama—was completed some months before his incarceration on a spurious charge of high treason in July 1919. Over the following five years, he produced four more plays, three collections of poems, and a considerable volume of correspondence, later published as *Briefe aus dem Gefängnis* (1935; translated as *Letters from Prison* and *Look Through the Bars*). Born of the psychological need for a lifeline to the outside world, this burst of creativity was accompanied by a decline in the fervor of his revolutionary aspirations. In *Transfiguration*, a work of autobiography in heightened and stylized form, the fate of the hero, Friedrich, is clearly meant to have exemplary significance: a single life remolded to a new awareness will have miraculous and messianic effect. But despite what Toller and other Expressionist dramatists may have maintained, a stage is not a political arena. What art proposes with conviction may seldom be smoothly translated into political reality. The heady conclusion of *Transfiguration* and its proclamation of revolution leaves audiences and readers with uneasy reservations about the practicalities of implementation. As Toller was to discover to his cost, the abstract ethic trumpeted so insistently in his play could find little resonance in the social and political upheavals in Germany during the immediate post–World War I period.

After the sanguine heights of *Transfiguration*, Toller's writing is marked by an inexorable and escalating strain of despondency. *Masse-Mensch* (1922; *Masses and Man*) reflects both the bitter experiences associated with his involvement in the short-lived and chaotic Bavarian Soviet Republic and the irreconcilable clash between his own vision of social revolution, inspired by the ideas of Kurt Eisner and Gustav Landauer, and the ruthlessness of communist orthodoxy. In *Die Maschinenstürmer* (1922; *The Machine Wreckers*), he uses the Luddite riots of 1811 to 1816 to give a dispiriting view of the class struggle, and *Der deutsche Hinkemann* (1923; *Brokenbow*) is a harrowing depiction of an ex-soldier made impotent by a war wound who is forced to earn his living in a fairground booth biting off the heads of live mice and rats. The raw cynicism of the play was clearly intended to reflect conditions in Weimar Germany, and it attracted unfavorable attention from right-wing groups who disrupted the Dresden production in January 1924.

Toller's disillusionment came to suffuse his view of Germany and the Germans, and, by implication, his understanding of the human condition. Looking back in his autobiography, *Eine Jugend in Deutschland* (1933; *I Was a German*), he wrote: "Have the German people learnt the lesson of these fateful times? . . . No, in fifteen years they have forgotten everything and learnt nothing."

A fascinating exception to the somber dramas that Toller wrote in prison is the comedy *Der entfesselte Wotan* (1923; *Wotan Unbound*), a satire on the genesis of a political dictatorship, which was written well before Hitler's abortive Munich beer hall putsch of 1923. This hilarious account of a dreamy and indecisive barber transformed into a petty tyrant with the help of ruthless aristocratic and financial interests is not only astonishingly prophetic but also uncannily anticipates the comic method adopted by Charlie Chaplin in *The Great Dictator*.

The two most important plays that Toller wrote after being released from prison return to a somber mode, constituting further gloomy comments on the failure of his early hopes and ambitions. In Toller's partly autobiographical *Hoppla, wir leben!* (1927; *Hoppla!*)—his collaboration with the highly innovative director Erwin Piscator made the 1927 production one of the Berlin theatrical events of the 1920s—he dramatizes the problems of readjustment that confront an erstwhile revolutionary released from prison into a society he now barely recognizes. *Feuer aus den Kesseln* (1930; *Draw the Fires!*) is a robust examination of the Kiel naval mutiny of 1918 and the trial of its ringleaders.

For some critics, the Expressionist excesses that tinge much of Toller's dramatic work diminish his contribution to the political debates in Germany between the wars. This, however, is to fail to distinguish between what he wrote for the theater and his political journalism. While his plays embody personal visions—initially of utopia, ultimately of despair—his writing on the vital issues of the day reveals a shrewd political mind at work. The intelligent and rhetorically powerful speeches and essays written over 20 years on a wide variety of subjects—the iniquitous state of Bavarian justice, Hitler, theater censorship, pacifism, and his travels in the Soviet Union or the United States—are always impressive. We should also not forget that he was one of the few among Weimar Germany's intellectuals to test his political principles in office (during the ill-fated Bavarian Soviet Republic of 1919) and that he was one of the very first to recognize the dangers of Nazism, against which, to the end of his days, he spoke out persistently and persuasively.

MARTIN KANE

Biography

Born in Samotschin (now Szamocin, Poland), 1 December 1893. Law student at the University of Grenoble, France, 1912–14, University of Munich, 1914–17, University of Heidelberg, 1917–18; in the army during World War I; discharged from army due to mental breakdown, 1916; co-organized munitions workers' strike, Munich, 1918; arrested and convicted of treason; active in anti-war politics; associated with the Communist government in Bavaria; candidate for the newly formed Independent Social Democratic Party of Germany (USPD), Bavaria, 1919, and chairman, USPD, 1919; section commander of the Red army during the Bavarian uprising; arrested and sentenced to five years imprisonment, 1919–24; lectured on antifascist causes in Europe, the Soviet Union, and the United States in the 1920s and 1930s; exiled from Germany, 1933; in Switzerland, France, and England, 1933–35; in Portugal and Spain, 1936; in the United States, 1936; screenwriter for Metro-Goldwyn-Mayer, 1936–38; activist for pro-Republican intervention in the Spanish Civil War in the United States, France, England, and Sweden, 1938. Died (suicide) 22 May 1939.

Selected Works

Collections
Ausgewählte Schriften, 1959
Prosa, Briefe, Dramen, Gedichte, 1961
Gesammelte Werke, edited by John M. Spalek and Wolfgang Frühwald, 5 vols., 1978

Plays
Die Wandlung: Das Ringen eines Menschen (produced 1919), 1919; as *Transfiguration*, translated by Edward Crankshaw, in *Seven Plays*, 1935
Masse-Mensch (produced 1920), 1922; as *Masses and Man*, translated by Vera Mendel, 1923; as *Man and the Masses*, translated by Louis Untermeyer, 1924
Die Maschinenstürmer (produced 1922), 1922; as *The Machine Wreckers*, translated by Ashley Dukes, 1923

Der deutsche Hinkemann (produced 1923), 1923; as *Hinkemann,* 1924; as *Brokenbrow,* translated by Vera Mendel, 1926

Der entfesselte Wotan (produced 1924), 1923

Die Rache des verhöhnten Liebhabers; oder, Frauenlist und Männerlist (puppet show), 1925

Hoppla, wir leben! (produced 1927), 1927; as *Hoppla!* translated by Herman Ould, 1928

Feuer aus den Kesseln (produced 1930), 1930; as *Draw the Fires!* translated by Edward Crankshaw, 1934 (also published in *Seven Plays,* 1935)

Wunder in Amerika, with Hermann Kesten (produced 1934), 1931; as *Mary Baker Eddy; or, Miracle in America,* translated by Edward Crankshaw in *Seven Plays,* 1935

Die blinde Göttin, 1933; as *The Blind Goddess,* translated by Edward Crankshaw, 1934

Seven Plays, translated by Edward Crankshaw, 1935

Nie wieder Friede! 1936; as *No More Peace! A Thoughtful Comedy,* translated by Edward Crankshaw, 1937

Pastor Hall, 1938; translated by Stephen Spender and Hugh Hunt, 1939

Berlin—letzte Ausgabe! (radio play), in *Frühe sozialistische Hörspiele,* edited by Stefan Bodo Würffel, 1982

Poetry

Der Tag des Proletariats, 1920
Gedichte der Gefangenen: Ein Sonettenkreis, 1921
Vormorgen, 1924
Weltliche Passion, 1934

Other

Das Schwalbenbuch, 1924; as *The Swallow Book,* translated by Ashley Dukes, 1924

Deutsche Revolution, 1925

Justiz, 1927

Quer Durch: Reisebilder und Reden, 1930; translated in part as *Which World Which Way?* by Herman Ould, 1931

Nationalsozialismus (radio broadcast), 1930

Eine Jugend in Deutschland (autobiography), 1933; as *I Was a German,* translated by Edward Crankshaw, 1934

Briefe aus dem Gefängnis, 1935; as *Letters from Prison* (includes *The Swallow Book*), translated by R. Ellis Roberts, 1936 (also published as *Look Through the Bars,* 1937)

Further Reading

Benson, Renate, *German Expressionist Drama: Ernst Toller and Georg Kaiser,* London: Macmillan, and New York: Grove Press, 1984

Bütow, Thomas, *Der Konflikt zwischen Revolution und Pazifismus im Werk Ernst Tollers: Mit einem Dokumentarischen Anhang, Essayistische Werke Tollers, Briefe von und über Toller,* Hamburg: Ludke, 1975

Dove, Richard, *Revolutionary Socialism in the Work of Ernst Toller,* New York: Lang, 1986

———, *He Was a German: A Biography of Ernst Toller,* London: Libris, 1990

Frühwald, Wolfgang, and John M. Spalek, editors, *Der Fall Toller: Kommentar und Materialien,* Munich: Hanser, 1979

Grunow-Erdmann, Cordula, *Die Dramen Ernst Tollers im Kontext ihrer Zeit,* Heidelberg: Winter, 1994

Haar, Carel ter, *Ernst Toller: Appell oder Resignation,* Munich: Tuduv, 1977

Hermand, Jost, editor, *Zu Ernst Toller: Drama und Engagement,* Stuttgart: Klett, 1981

Kändler, Klaus, *Drama und Klassenkampf,* Berlin: Aufbau, 1970

Kane, Martin, *Weimar Germany and the Limits of Political Art: A Study of the Work of George Grosz and Ernst Toller,* Tayport, Fife: Hutton Press, 1987

Ossar, Michael, *Anarchism in the Dramas of Ernst Toller: The Realm of Necessity and the Realm of Freedom,* Albany: State University of New York Press, 1980

Pittock, Malcolm, *Ernst Toller,* Boston: Twayne, 1979

Rothe, Wolfgang, *Ernst Toller: In Selbstzeugnissen und Bilddokumenten,* Reinbek bei Hamburg: Rowohlt, 1983

Spalek, John M., *Ernst Toller and His Critics: A Bibliography,* Charlottesville: University of Virginia Press, 1968

Masse-Mensch 1922

Play by Ernst Toller

Ernst Toller wrote *Masse-Mensch* (*Masses and Man*), his second and most famous play, during three days of creative frenzy in the Bavarian jail of Eichstätt, followed by a year spent revising the text. A restricted production, by and for trade unionists, opened at the Nürnberg Stadttheater on 15 November 1920 and was banned after four performances. The first production for the general public, directed by Jürgen Fehling, opened at the Berlin Volksbühne on 29 September 1921 and became one of the greatest theatrical hits of Expressionism, in part owing to Fehling's spectacular use of light, sound, and spatial effects. Productions in New York and London followed in 1924, but there have been no notable revivals since.

Toller's first play, *Die Wandlung* (1919; *Transfiguration*), written in 1917–18, drew upon his experiences as a soldier in World War I. *Masses and Man* reflects his leading role in the short-lived Bavarian Soviet Republic of 1918 and his imprisonment for high treason. The central figure—called "the Woman" or "Sonja Irene L."—is modeled on Sarah Sonja Lerch, a conservative academic's left-wing wife who was arrested for organizing a strike of ammunition workers in Munich; she then committed suicide in prison. She also, however, stands for Toller, with whom she shares the predicament of any pacifist caught up in violence. Her antagonist—called "the Nameless"—impersonates Eugen Leviné, the communist opponent of Toller and his Independent Social-Democratic Party; at the same time, the character embodies the principle of violent revolution. Thus, *Masses and Man* examines the dilemmas inherent in all political engagement and, ultimately, in the human condition itself.

The action is set in an unspecified country and era. A war is raging, and the Woman prepares to call a nonviolent strike. Although her state-employed husband threatens to divorce her, she remains firm, accusing the state of oppressing the people. At a mass meeting of workers, she reluctantly assents to the Nameless's demand for a bloody revolution. When she tries to prevent the murder of hostages, the workers condemn her as a bourgeois traitor, but the government troops, crushing the uprising, arrest her as the ringleader. Finally, she refuses to escape from prison at the cost of a warder's life, and is executed. While these events are portrayed in four moderately realistic scenes, three symbolic "dream pictures" underline their hidden psychological and political significance: a grotesque caricature of the stock exchange reveals the inhumanity of the capitalist system, the transformation of a guard's face into that of his condemned prisoner demonstrates the common humanity of killer and victim, and the Woman's confinement in a cage haunted by headless shadows illustrates her sense of guilt.

The play is a prime example of the Expressionist style. The seven episodes form a loosely structured *Stationendrama,* each representing a stage in the development of the heroine. The irregular verse is marked by deliberate distortions of traditional grammar, pointed dialectical exchanges, and the innovative use of impassioned choral speaking. The characters are abstract types, epitomizing social functions or attitudes. The indeterminacy of time and place gives an impression of universality. All these features arise from the Expressionists' desire to convey not the material appearance of things but visions of their spiritual essence.

When Toller wrote *Transfiguration* he still believed in the possibility of social and political renewal through moral regeneration. By the time he wrote *Masses and Man,* however, he had already had to choose between the two evils he describes in his autobiography, *Eine Jugend in Deutschland* (1933; *I Was a German*): "Must a man who acts become guilty, for ever and ever! Or if he is not willing to become guilty, be destroyed?" In his own life, he chose the guilt of a revolutionary leader who "used violence and called for violence." In *Masses and Man,* as he explained in a letter to a friend, he explored the "insoluble contradiction" through the confrontation of the individual and the masses, carrying it to its bitter conclusion: "The ethical man: living solely according to his own principles. The political man: fighter for social forms which are the prerequisite of a better life for others . . . even if he violates his own principles. If the ethical man becomes a political man, what tragic road is spared him?"

Like Toller himself, the Woman suffers from an inner conflict between Kantian and Marxist positions. While she pleads for a nonviolent strike she is able to preserve her ethical purity, but she then does not have any prospect of alleviating the misery of the masses. When she consents to the Nameless's call for revolution, her human compassion ironically makes her an accessory to inhuman political actions. The Nameless, for his part, personifies the masses who long for a truly human existence but, owing to the inhumanity of the system, can only resort to inhuman behavior. By adopting violent means the revolution defeats its own humanitarian ends even before the reactionary state physically terminates it.

Toller tries to solve the insoluble by making the Woman understand and then atone for her guilt. Facing the devastation, she recognizes that both she and the masses are "guiltlessly guilty" because they committed violence—albeit for reasons beyond their control. When she decides to sacrifice herself for the warder, her own sense of liberation merges with a utopian image of the masses turning into "free people, freely working together"; and, at the moment of her execution, two prisoners stop looting her belongings, as their conscience awakens. Despite this idealistic ending, however, the play bears witness to the fading of Toller's Expressionist belief in a "new mankind."

The heroine's moral rehabilitation at the point of death echoes the classical German tragedy of Friedrich Schiller, while the inevitability of her guilt recalls the fatalistic tragedy of the Greeks and the deterministic tragedy of the major German realist Georg Büchner. Thus, *Masses and Man* proves a worthy successor to great dramatic traditions. Its failure to find a lasting place in the theatrical repertory was perhaps due to Toller's inability to deliver his "raw confession" with the necessary "objectivity of art"—as he admitted to Fehling. The quality of his later works, with the possible exception of *Die Maschinenstürmer* (1922; *The Machine Wreckers*) and *Der deutsche Hinkemann* (1924; *Brokenbow*), never came close to that of his first two plays.

LADISLAUS LÖB

Editions

First edition: *Masse-Mensch,* Potsdam: Kiepenheuer, 1922
Critical edition: *Masse-Mensch,* edited by John M. Spalek and Wolfgang Frühwald, in *Gesammelte Werke,* vol. 2, Munich: Hanser, 1978
Translation: *Masses and Man,* translated by Vera Mendel, London: Nonesuch, 1923

Further Reading

Altenhofer, Rosemarie, "Nachwort," in *Ernst Toller: "Masse Mensch,"* Stuttgart: Reclam, 1979
Benson, Renate, *German Expressionist Drama: Ernst Toller and Georg Kaiser,* London: Macmillan, and New York: Grove Press, 1984
Davies, Cecil, *The Plays of Ernst Toller: A Revaluation,* Amsterdam: Harwood, 1996
Dove, Richard, *Revolutionary Socialism in the Work of Ernst Toller,* New York: Lang, 1986
Frühwald, Wolfgang, and John M. Spalek, *Der Fall Toller: Kommentar und Materialien,* Munich: Hanser, 1979
Knellessen, Friedrich Wolfgang, *Agitation auf der Bühne: Das politische Theater der Weimarer Republik,* Emsdetten: Lechte, 1970
Mennemeier, Franz Norbert, "Das idealistische Proletarierdrama: Ernst Tollers Weg vom Aktionsstück zur Tragödie," *Der Deutschunterricht* 24, no. 2 (1972)
Patterson, Michael, *The Revolution in German Theatre, 1900–1933,* London and Boston: Routledge, 1981
Ritchie, J.M., *German Expressionist Drama,* Boston: Twayne, 1976
Rothe, Wolfgang, *Ernst Toller: In Selbstzeugnissen und Bilddokumenten,* Reinbek bei Hamburg: Rowohlt, 1983
Sokel, Walter, *The Writer in Extremis: Expressionism in Twentieth-Century German Literature,* Stanford, California: Stanford University Press, 1959

Friedrich Torberg 1908–1979

Friedrich Torberg, born Friedrich Ephraim Kantor in Vienna/Alsergrund, was one of the three children of Alfred Kantor, a liquor merchant from Prague, and his wife Therese, née Berg. In elementary school, Torberg began to write poems that expressed patriotism and the pride of being a Jew. Both sentiments reflect the complete trust that middle-class Jews had in the Austrian-Jewish symbiosis in the early 20th century. Torberg continued to identify himself as a modern urban Jew and a son of the Habsburg Empire, whose past glory he celebrated in nostalgic and satirical tales about Jewish Austro-Hungary and its coffeehouse culture in *Die Tante Jolesch; oder, Der Untergang des Abendlandes in Anekdoten* (1975; Aunt Jolesch; or, The Demise of the Occident Told in Anecdotes) and *Die Erben der Tante Jolesch* (1978; The Heirs of Aunt Jolesch). Torberg began to fight against anti-Semitism when he was still a student at the predominantly Jewish Wasagasse *Gymnasium*. Torberg was a successful sportsman and a soccer and water polo player; sports activities were an integral part of the Jewish-Maccabean identity that he embraced. Torberg was a fan of the Viennese HAKOAH soccer team and a member of the Jewish sports club Hagibor in Prague. In the strongly autobiographical novel *Die Mannschaft: Roman eines Sport-Lebens* (1977; The Team: A Novel about a Life Devoted to Sport), Torberg thematizes this aspect of his life.

In 1922, the Kantors moved back to Prague, and Torberg came in conflict with the authoritarian educational system, which was devoid of the democratic spirit of "Red Vienna." From 1926 on, he wrote poetry for the journal *Jung-Juda*. His quick wit and the aplomb with which he discussed topical issues, however, were better suited for journalistic writing and narrative prose. Torberg's first novel, *Der Schüler Gerber hat absolviert* (1930; The Examination), which ends with the youthful protagonist's suicide, brings to the foreground difficulties Torberg had to face at the time of his high school graduation in 1928. The work is intended as a moral outcry against a rigid, outdated pedagogy. One year later, Torberg was engaged by a major daily paper, the *Prager Tagblatt*. His contributions included short stories, reviews, and reports on sports events. His fiction was often criticized for being sentimental, bordering on the trivial. Critics have also pointed out that Torberg's romantic, self-involved stories *Und glauben, es wäre die Liebe* (1932; And Believe It Is Love) and *Abschied* (1937; Last Farewell) seem out of keeping with the time at which they were written, an era of major social and political crises.

In the 1930s, however, Torberg performed in the cabaret Literatur am Naschmarkt and collaborated under the pseudonym Prokop with Peter Preses and the socialist satirist Jura Soyfer. An outspoken anti-Nazi, he took a public stand against the opportunism with which the Austrian PEN reacted to Hitler's rise to power and the persecution of oppositional intellectuals. He publicly condemned Thomas Mann and Gottfried Benn for their conciliatory attitude toward Germany. Despite his connections to the leftist scene and the *Arbeiter-Zeitung*, Torberg, convinced that communist activists slavishly followed directions from Moscow, repudiated intellectuals such as Brecht and Feuchtwanger and everyone he suspected of being a "Fellow Traveler." His rejection of what he conceived as totalitarianism continued in the Second Republic. He was on friendly terms with prominent representatives of the Social Democratic Party (SPÖ), (namely, Bruno Kreisky and Christian Broda) and considered anyone he suspected of communist proclivities his enemy.

Torberg's career is closely connected with the avant-garde of the interwar period, and he was a major player among Austrian exiles. He was in close contact with intellectuals, writers, and actors from Prague, Vienna, and Budapest, such as Anton Kuh, Alfred Polgar, Ernst Polak, Hermann Broch, Fritz von Herzmanovsky-Orlando, Alma Mahler-Werfel, Joseph Roth, Hilde Spiel, Marlene Dietrich, and Erich Maria Remarque. Torberg's posthumously published novel *Auch das war Wien* (1984; This Too Was Vienna) sketches the world of a Viennese-Praguer journalist at the time of the Nazi takeover. In his characteristic reportage style, Torberg evokes the demise of the diverse culture in which he lived. He shows the brittleness of relationships, revealing the opportunism of some and the heart-rending but ultimately futile loyalty of others. For Torberg, 1938 was the end of the civilization with which he identified; the only unquestionable identity left to him was his Jewishness.

In 1938, Torberg emigrated to Switzerland; many of his family members and associates whom he tried to rescue, including the cabaret performer Fritz Grünbaum, perished in Nazi concentration camps. He was appalled by the pro-Nazi sentiments in Switzerland and moved on to France, where he wrote for *Die Österreichische Post*, an exile journal published under the auspices of the *Legitimisten*, Austrian monarchists supporting the cause of Otto von Habsburg. Torberg had few connections with German exiles. In 1939, he joined the Czech exile army. Under the designation of an "Outstanding German Anti-Nazi Writer," which he shared with authors such as Heinrich Mann, Leonhard Frank, Alfred Neumann, and Alfred Döblin, Torberg ended up in the United States after a narrow escape from France. The works he started writing at that time deal with the Jewish experience; persecuted by the Nazis, his protagonists try to deal with a reality foreign to them, as in, for example, *Mein ist die Rache* (1943; Revenge Is Mine). *Hier bin ich, mein Vater* (1948; Here I Am, My Father) thematizes both generational and political conflicts. The central issue in this work is the topic of Jewish ethics in the larger context of National Socialism and the Holocaust. The suspenseful novel about a man who becomes a Nazi spy after assuming that his betrayal of other Jews will save his father from deportation was published in Stockholm but was not made available in Germany. In an intricate network of plots and characters, *Die zweite Begegnung* (1950; The Encounter) probes into a variety of issues, including communism, homosexuality, and postwar politics.

In New York, Torberg came in contact with Austrian exiles connected with the American-German weekly *Aufbau* and the cabarets run by Viennese singers and songwriters such as Hermann Leopoldi, Armin Berg, and Hans Kolitscher. Torberg's hopes to land a movie career in Hollywood, however, came to naught. With dismay, he noticed that certain segments of American society were receptive to radical ideologies, both Nazi and communist. Through these experiences, he came to identify his own mission: to provide an intellectual continuity between pre-Nazi Austria and the Austria of the much-awaited future postwar and to help shape a new Austrian identity. In 1950, Torberg prepared for his return to Austria. Together with a few close associates and the support of the CIA, which had an interest in introducing Western programs into postwar Europe, he founded the Congress for Cultural Freedom. In 1951, he returned to Vienna, where he wrote for the *Wiener Kurier* and the radio station *Rot-Weiß-Rot*, articulating uncompromising pro-Western sentiments. In 1954, he founded the cultural-political journal *Forum*. Through these activities and connections with personalities such as the publisher Gottfried Bermann-Fischer, Torberg quickly became a central figure in postwar Austria, where he played an active and often controversial role.

Torberg's most important contribution to postwar culture was keeping alive the legacy of German-Jewish culture and Vienna Jewry. He reintroduced Jewish concerns into Austrian literature and became a model and mentor of the post-Shoah generation of Viennese Jews, such as Ruth Beckermann and Robert Schindel, who searched for ways to express their point of view as post-Shoah Jewish intellectuals. Torberg's novella *Golems Wiederkehr* (1968; Golem's Return), despite its Holocaust setting, projects confidence about the continuity of Central European Jewish life. Set in a distant future when the Nazis have long been forgotten, it shows Jewish culture emerging victorious. Conversely, *Süskind von Trimberg* (1972), a novel about a German-speaking troubadour, is set in the Middle Ages. Certain weaknesses notwithstanding, these works, but most of all the cultural information, the decidedly Jewish point of view, and the brilliant satire in *Die Tante Jolesch,* place Torberg at the forefront of post-Shoah Austrian Jewish writing.

DAGMAR C.G. LORENZ

Biography

Born in Vienna-Alsergrund, 16 September 1908. Family relocated to Prague, 1922; poetry published in *Jung-Juda,* 1926; journalist for *Prager Tagblatt;* 1929; performer in the cabaret *Literatur am Naschmarkt,* 1930s; collaboration with satirists Peter Preses and Jura Soyfer; association with *Arbeiter-Zeitung,* Vienna; exile in Czechoslovakia, Switzerland, and France, 1938; volunteer in Czech army, 1939; escape to United States via Spain and Portugal, 1940; exile in Los Angeles; in New York, 1944; wrote for the *Aufbau;* return to Austria, honorary professorate, 1951; editor of the monthly *Forum,* 1954. Austrian State Prize, 1979. Died in Vienna, 10 November 1979.

Selected Works

Collections
Gesammelte Werke, 1948
Almanach: das vierundsechzigste Jahr: 1886–1950, 1950
Wien oder der Unterschied, 1998

Novels
Der Schüler Gerber hat absolviert, 1930; as *The Examination,* 1932
Hier bin ich, mein Vater, 1948
Die zweite Begegnung, 1950
Süsskind von Trimberg, 1972
Die Mannschaft: Roman eines Sport-Lebens, 1977
Auch das war Wien, 1984

Novellas
Mein ist die Rache, 1943
Nichts ist leichter als das, 1956
Golems Wiederkehr, 1981
Der letzte Ritt des Jockeys Matteo, edited by David Axmann and Marietta Torberg, 1987

Satires and Essays
Mit der Zeit - gegen die Zeit, 1965
Mensch, Maier! sagte der Lord : kleines kritisches Welttheater, 1975

Die Tante Jolesch oder Der Untergang des Abendlandes in Anekdoten, 1975
Die Erben der Tante Jolesch, 1978
Wo der Barthel die Milch holt, 1981
Auch Nichtraucher müssen sterben, 1985

Letters
Kaffeehaus war überall: Briefwechsel mit Käuzen und Originalen, 1982
In diesem Sinne— : Briefe an Freunde und Zeitgenossen, 1988
Eine tolle, tolle Zeit : Briefe und Dokumente aus den Jahren der Flucht 1938-1945: Zürich, Frankreich, Portugal, Amerika, edited by David Axmann and Marietta Torberg, 1989
Liebste Freundin und Alma: Briefwechsel mit Alma Mahler-Werfel: nebst einigen Briefen an Franz Werfel, ergänzt durch zwei Aufsätze, edited by David Axmann, 1990
Pegasus im Joch: Briefwechsel mit Verlegern und Redakteuren, 1991
Voreingenommen wie ich bin: von Dichtern, Denkern, und Autoren, 1991

Poetry
Lebenslied, 1958

Film
38 Vienna before the Fall, directed by Wolfgang Glück, 1989

Further Reading

Axmann, David, editor, *Und Lächeln ist das Erbteil meines Stammes: Erinnerung an Friedrich Torberg,* Vienna: Edition Atelier, 1988
Beckermann, Ruth, "1938: During the Austrian Anschluss to the Third Reich, Friedrich Torberg Escapes from Prague, First to Zurich and Then to Paris," in *Yale Companion to Jewish Writing and Thought in German Culture, 1096–1996,* edited by Sander L. Gilman and Jack Zipes, London and New Haven, Connecticut: Yale University Press, 1997
Glück, Wolfgang, director, *38: Vienna before the Fall,* Wayzata, Minnesota: Crocus Entertainment, 1988 [Feature film based on *Auch das war Wien*]
Hackel, Franz-Heinrich, *Zur Sprachkunst Friedrich Torbergs, Parodie, Witz, Anekdote: Mit einem Anhang unbekannter Arbeiten aus der Frühzeit Torbergs,* Frankfurt and New York: Lang, 1984
Rupp, Gerhard, "'Nichts mehr wahrnehmen, nichts erkennen in zeitlosem Nebel?' Schüler reagieren auf die Schulkritik des 'Schüler Gerber' (1929) von Friedrich Torberg," *Der Deutschunterricht* 41, no. 4 (1989)
Strelka, Joseph, editor, *Der Weg war schon das Ziel: Festschrift für Friedrich Torberg zum 70. Geburtstag,* Munich: Langen Müller, 1978
Tichy, Frank, *Friedrich Torberg: Ein Leben in Widersprüchen,* Vienna: O. Müller, 1995
Zohn, Harry, "*. . . ich bin ein Sohn der deutschen Sprache nur . . .*": *Jüdisches Erbe in der österreichischen Literatur,* Vienna: Amalthea, 1986

Total Art Work *see* Gesamtkunstwerk

Georg Trakl 1887–1914

Critical readers of Georg Trakl have in general fluctuated between seeing his poetry either as extreme and unique or as derivative; his plays and prose are rarely discussed. American poets such as Robert Bly praise Trakl for reflecting the living world, abandoning the dying "sublime" tradition of Goethe, Hölderlin, George, Hofmannsthal, and Rilke. Symbolist poets (Arthur Rimbaud) and Expressionists (Albert Ehrenstein, Else Lasker-Schüler, Herwarth Walden, and Karl Kraus) influenced Trakl strongly. Comparing his early "St. Peters Friedhof" (1909; "St. Peter's Cemetery") and "Die schöne Stadt" (1911; "The Beautiful City") shows how his style matured under the influence of Klammer's translation of Rimbaud into German (1907). Synesthesia comes to displace conventional descriptions through a tighter syntax and eloquent pauses, producing an expressive force and musicality unique among Austrian writers at the time. The four-line stanza becomes Trakl's preferred prosodic medium, as it imposes limits that concentrate his exquisite imagery.

Trakl's contact with Expressionism derived strongly from his friendships with the painters Oskar Kokoschka and Max von Esterle and the architect Adolf Loos. Trakl also appreciated Egon Schiele's work. Kokoschka asserts that when he knew him, Trakl painted in addition to writing. Kokoschka also credits Trakl with inspiring his famous painting *Die Windsbraut* (1914; The Bride of the Wind), claiming that they painted it together. Some verses of Trakl's late "Die Nacht" (1914; "The Night") refer to colors and motifs in that painting. By 1914, writing poems with an emphatically visual technique had become one of Trakl's artistic goals. At this time in his career, long unrhymed lines in the manner of Hölderlin prevailed. His paratactic style yielded to hypotactic structures that the reader's eye follows like a painter's brush on canvas.

Traditional themes and motifs dominate in Trakl's early poetry; he remained close to nature, preferring symbolic subjects such as the earth, village life, farmers, servant girls, or fountains to expressly political or social questions. The poems by Trakl that Kurt Pinthus included in his anthology *Menschheitsdämmerung* (1920; *Twilight of Humanity*) reveal how the poet identified himself with the agonies of a world gone mad. In a related vein, Christian interpretations by critics such as Ludwig von Ficker and Eduard Lachmann, which deal with the poet's symbols and mystical allusions, long dominated Trakl scholarship. His conception of himself as a medieval monk and his hope that poetry could redeem men from sin suggested such interpretive approaches.

More recently, investigators see little more than Trakl's psychopathology in his works. From often stereotypical points of view on "genius" and "madness," the late poems in particular are cited as language constructs of psychopathological processes (including drug dependency and incest) that led to the poet's self-destruction. Because the changes in Trakl's brief life were so drastic and strongly affected his work, it is important to articulate its critical phases. Four brief periods emerge: the first range is 1906–12, the second from "De Profundis" to "Helian" in 1912–13, the third is characterized by "Sebastian im Traum" (in the cycle *Sebastian im Traum*, 1914; "Sebastian in Dream"), and the fourth is exemplified by "Traum und Umnachtung" (1914; "Dream and Derangement"). Trakl's development might also be seen as his movement from the "objective" toward the "demonic image" (Lindenberger). Trakl's writings from all four periods reveal a highly conscious effort of a self to come to terms with its world. The moral convictions that he expresses in his writings and his strong artistic control deny that psychopathology is the only possible key to his work. Trakl's earliest ideas and his urgent appeal to mankind as a whole are coherently present even in his latest texts. The horror of modern warfare led Trakl to despair and death, but certainly not to doubt his art.

Even in his last poem, "Grodek" (a town in Galicia), written in the fall of 1914, Trakl expressed the torment of the living at the thought of the misery awaiting those generations to inherit this 20th century, the "ungebornen Enkel" (unborn grandchildren). Without peace, life cannot exist on this planet "unter Sternen" (under stars), which appears determined only to destroy itself in endless global warfare. Trakl longed for a new Eden or Arcadia, where the painful dualities of male and female, silence and language would be absent. He felt that he himself had lost his battle against the terror of the world and the hell in his own soul and saw no reason to continue living. Yet his poetry points to an enduring and redeeming mystery of existence, to our universe as an ever-growing "Baum der Gnaden" (tree of grace).

Trying with varying success to fulfill his roles as student, pharmacist, and soldier, Trakl could see himself only as a *poète maudit*, afflicted with a talent with which he could not make a profession. His plays *Der Totentag* (1906; Day of the Dead) and *Fata Morgana* (1906), composed in the style of Ibsen and Maeterlinck, aroused the revulsion of the critics and failed utterly; the young playwright destroyed the manuscripts of both plays. *Blaubart: Ein Puppenspiel* (1909–10; Bluebeard: A Puppet Play), which remained unfinished, includes a gruesome murder scene, and its subtitle heightens the sense of pitiless cruelty in relations between the sexes. Trakl seemed to live chiefly in a private world of visions, alternately tormented and ecstatic, that gave him a uniquely distanced outlook on "the world." At a poetry reading organized by the journal *Der Brenner*, Trakl spoke so softly that the audience could barely hear him. In 1914, Kurt Wolff accepted his poems *Sebastian im Traum* for publication, and Ludwig Wittgenstein planned to give him financial support; these first signs of imminent public recognition, however, came too late. Rilke grasped the essence of Trakl's poetry and its modernity when he wrote: "Even he who was closest to him receives these images and insights like someone excluded; for Trakl's experience transpires as though in mirror images and occupies an entire space that cannot be entered, like the space within a mirror. (Who could he have been?)" Trakl's uncanny experimentation with the language of the unconscious, his dangerous ventures into otherwise inaccessible domains, endow his poetry, unlike that of most of the other Expressionists, with lasting validity.

ERIKA A. METZGER

See also Expressionism

Biography

Born in Salzburg, Austria, 3 February 1887. Apprenticed at a pharmacy in Salzburg, 1905–8; studied at the University of Vienna, 1908–10, and received a pharmacy degree; in the military, Vienna, 1910–11, 1914; pharmacist in Salzburg, 1911; worked a number of short-term jobs as a military pharmacist; regular writer for *Der Brenner*, 1912–14. Died 3 November 1914.

Selected Works

Collections

Gesamtausgabe, edited by Wolfgang Schneditz, 3 vols., 1948–59
Dichtungen und Briefe, edited by Walther Killy and Hans Szklenar, 2 vols., 1969
Werke, Entwürfe, Briefe, edited by Hans-Georg Kemper and Frank Rainer Max, 1984
Die Dichtungen, edited by Walther Killy, 1988

Poetry

Gedichte, 1913
Sebastian im Traum, 1914
Die Dichtungen, edited by Karl Röck, 1918
Aus goldenem Kelch: Die Jugenddichtungen, edited by Erhard Buschbeck, 1939
Decline: Twelve Poems, translated by Michael Hamburger, 1952
Twenty Poems (bilingual edition), translated by James Wright and Robert Bly, 1961
Selected Poems, edited by Christopher Middleton, translated by Robert Grenier et al., 1968
Poems, translated by Lucia Getsi, 1973
Autumn Sonata: Selected Poems, translated by Daniel Simko, 1989

Other

Erinnerung an Trakl: Zeugnisse und Briefe, edited by Ludwig von Ficker, 1926; 3rd edition, 1966

Georg Trakl: A Profile (poetry and letters), edited by Frank Graziano, 1983

Further Reading

Basil, Otto, *Georg Trakl in Selbstzeugnissen und Bilddokumenten*, Reinbek bei Hamburg: Rowohlt, 1965
Csuri, Karoly, editor, *Zyklische Kompositionsformen in Georg Trakls Dichtung: Szegeder Symposion*, Tübingen: Niemeyer, 1996
Detsch, Richard, *Georg Trakl and the Brenner Circle*, New York: Lang, 1991
Grimm, Reinhold, "Georg Trakls Verhältnis zu Rimbaud," in *Zur Lyrik-Diskussion*, compiled by Reinhold Grimm, Darmstadt: Wissenschaftliche Buchgesellschaft, 1966
Hamburger, Michael, *Reason and Energy: Studies in German Literature*, London: Routledge and Kegan Paul, and New York: Grove Press, 1957
Lindenberger, Herbert, *Georg Trakl*, New York: Twayne, 1971
Ritzer, Walter, *Neue Trakl-Bibliographie*, Salzburg: Müller, 1983
Saas, Christa, *Georg Trakl*, Stuttgart: Metzler, 1974
Schneditz, Wolfgang, editor, *Georg Trakl in Zeugnissen der Freunde*, Salzburg: Pallas, 1951
Sharp, Francis Michael, *The Poet's Madness*, Ithaca, New York: Cornell University Press, 1981
Sokel, Walter, *The Writer in Extremis: Expressionism in Twentieth Century German Literature*, Stanford, California: Stanford University Press, 1959
Strelka, Joseph, editor, *Internationales Georg Trakl-Symposium*, Albany, N.Y., Bern and New York: Lang, 1984
Williams, Eric, editor, *The Dark Flutes of Fall: Critical Essays on Georg Trakl*, Columbia, South Carolina: Camden House, 1991

Travel Literature

There is no universally accepted definition of travel literature. Both the motives for travel and the reasons for documenting travel experiences shape the genre and leave a vast range of possibilities with regard to content and form. Looking at existing definitions, it becomes quite obvious that they differ tremendously depending on whether "travel" or "literature" is treated as the genre's guiding element. Some critics insist that travel literature needs to be related to real travel. But even with this limitation, their definitions still embrace a vast spectrum of possibilities, ranging from statistical data and books with instructions on how to travel (*Apodemiken*) to outbursts of emotions triggered by the travel experience. Yet others even include accounts of imaginary voyages and/or texts that are constructed around the metaphor of "life as a voyage." The resulting openness leaves room for almost limitless possibilities. The heterogeneity of the texts that can be subsumed under the heading travel literature makes it close to impossible to oversee and manage the genre, and it becomes nearly impossible to differentiate between "literature" and "travel literature."

Most critics, nevertheless, prefer a rather broad definition of the genre and introduce subcategories in order to group and analyze travel texts with common features. The decisive elements

can be the form, content, destination, time frame, intentions and mind-set of the traveler, means of transportation, circumstances surrounding travel, questions of real versus imagined travel, or a combination of any of these elements. This results in categories such as travel and expedition (*Expedition; Forschungsreise*), the educational journey (*Bildungsreise*), Robinsonade (*Robinsonade*), pilgrimages (*Pilgerreisen*), travel to the Near East (*Orientreise*), medieval travel (*Reisen des Mittelalters*), female travel (*Frauenreise*), the sentimental journey (*empfindsame Reise*), trips into exile (*Exilreise*), utopian travel (*Utopia-Reise*), adventure and conquest (*Abenteuer- und Eroberungsreise*), travel satire (*Reisesatire*), travel diary (*Reisetagebuch*), and so forth.

Especially before 1980, however, there were also numerous attempts to move in exactly the opposite direction—establishing a hierarchy within the genre by singling out a "classical canon" of travel literature. Interestingly enough, sometimes not even the travel texts themselves were considered the most important factor that defined their ranking: what mattered more was the reputation that a travel writer had already gained from his/her literary production that was not related to travel. While it cannot be denied that authors such as Lichtenberg, Goethe, Heine, Eichendorff, Seume, Laube, Börne, Fontane, Hauptmann, and

Böll made important contributions to German travel literature, any attempt to define a core of German travel literature solely based on the overall reputation of an author (in itself a highly problematic criterion) clearly reflects an outdated, all too narrow concept of what ought to be considered as "literature." Consequently, recent research in the field of travel writing hardly operates within such a limited and normative framework. In fact, many modern studies focus on works by travel writers whose texts are primarily considered valuable sources for interdisciplinary research that links sociohistorical and literary studies; many of these travel texts would hardly be included in the pre-1980s "classical canon" of travel literature.

With this shift in attitude, four areas in particular received major attention during the last 15 years: travel writing by women, *Revolutionstourismus* (accounts of travelers who depict the events of the French revolutions), travelogues that were written during the Enlightenment period, and travel texts that can serve as source material in the context of colonial and postcolonial studies.

It needs to be pointed out that in the case of travel literature it would be misleading to explain this trend toward interdisciplinary research solely as a logical and necessary response to recent shifts and developments within the field of literary studies in general. Looking at research that focuses on travel literature from a historical point of view clearly illustrates that the attempt to incorporate it into one specific academic discipline was already considered problematic during the last century. Up to the late 18th century, travel literature, the description of countries and people, was hardly ever dealt with as "literature"; it was first and foremost considered to be valuable source material within the academic field of history (geography, statistics, ethnology, and political science were still treated as major subdisciplines within history). Five mainly independent developments subsequently unhooked travel literature from any single academic discipline. First, during the 19th century, geography, sociology, and ethnology developed into independent academic disciplines and designed distinct scientific instruments. Within each of these disciplines, travel texts that contained relevant factual information continued to be regarded as a valuable basis for research. Second, Lawrence Sterne's highly imitated and impressionistic account of his trip to France and Italy, *Sentimental Journey* (1768), influenced not only the production but also the reception of travel writing and prompted interest in travel writing within the field of literary studies. Third, with the improvement of streets and means of transportation, travel became easier and less dangerous. More and more people developed an interest in traveling themselves; as a result, organized tourism developed during the 19th century. Fourth, many 19th-century travelers felt obliged to cater to the needs of the ever-growing reading public. An almost insatiable appetite for sensationalist and/or exotic accounts of foreign worlds made travelogues easy to publish, and by the mid 19th-century the literary market was flooded with travel accounts. Fifth, and last, as readers were confronted by a vast array of travelogues that differed tremendously in aesthetic quality, interest in travel literature within the field of literary studies dwindled again.

Such attitudes hardly changed for more than 100 years: travel literature simply floated in between disciplines. No discipline was interested in the study of travel literature *per se;* within literary studies, travel literature as a genre received marginal recognition at best. Other disciplines approached the field even less

systematically and exploited nothing but the factual information of selected texts.

Within the field of *Germanistik,* only in the 1970s did critics start to approach individual subgenres of travel literature in a more systematic way. When critics slowly gave up a strictly normative definition of "literature" and utilized interdisciplinary, cross-disciplinary, and multidisciplinary approaches, the former "stepchild" of the discipline suddenly received an unprecedented amount of attention: travel literature seemed to be an ideal starting point to venture into interdisciplinary research.

In the context of this new popularity, it soon became clear that "travel literature" had never been approached systematically within *Germanistik;* there existed neither a reliable description of the history of the genre from the beginnings to the present (*Gattungsgeschichte*) nor a systematic attempt to outline major directions of research related to travel literature. The first attempt to fill this void was made by Peter Brenner in 1990 when he published *Der Reisebericht in der deutschen Literatur (Travelogues in German Literature).* The subtitle *Ein Forschungsüberblick als Vorstudie zu einer Gattungsgeschichte* (An Overview of Existing Research for a Yet to Be Written History of the Genre) suggests that a reliable history of the genre, a comprehensive evaluation of travel literature within its social and cultural context, still needs to be written. In his survey, Brenner limits himself to a systematic presentation of research conducted between 1970 and 1990 that is related to German travel literature from late medieval times to the present; he, however, does not himself analyze and interpret the travel texts. Unfortunately, he almost completely excludes research on travel literature by women, thereby neglecting an area that has received major attention during the last two decades. Future attempts to write histories of the genre need to correct this exclusion.

STEFANIE OHNESORG

Further Reading

Bausinger, Hermann, et al., editors, *Reisekultur: Von der Pilgerfahrt zum modernen Tourismus,* Munich: Beck, 1991

Blackwell, Jeannine, "An Island of Her Own: Heroines of the German Robinsonades from 1720 to 1800," *German Quarterly* 56, no.1 (1985)

Bleicher, Thomas, "Einleitung: Literarisches Reisen als literaturwissenschaftliches Ziel," *Komparatistische Hefte* 3 (1981)

Brenner, Peter J., *Der Reisebericht in der deutschen Literatur: Ein Forschungsüberblick als Vorstudie zu einer Gattungsgeschichte,* Tübingen: Niemeyer, 1990

——, *Reisen in die Neue Welt: Die Erfahrung Nordamerikas in deutschen Reise- und Auswandererberichten des 19. Jahrhunderts,* Tübingen: Niemeyer, 1991

Brenner, Peter J., editor, *Der Reisebericht: Die Entwicklung einer Gattung in der deutschen Literatur,* Frankfurt: Suhrkamp, 1989

——, editor, *Reisekultur in Deutschland: Von der Weimarer Republik zum "Dritten Reich,"* Tübingen: Niemeyer, 1997

Bürgi, Andreas, *Weltvermesser: Die Wandlung des Reiseberichts in der Spätaufklärung,* Bonn: Bouvier, 1989

Cole, Garold L., "The Travel Account as a Social Document; A Survey of Recent Journal Articles," *Exploration* (Journal of the Modern Language Association Special Session on the Literature of Exploration and Travel) 7 (1979)

Enzensberger, Hans Magnus, "Eine Theorie des Tourismus," in *Einzelheiten,* Frankfurt: Suhrkamp, 1962 [translated by Gerd Gemünden and Kenn Johnson as "A Theory of Tourism," *New German Critique* 68 (1996)]

Felden, Tamara, *Frauen Reisen: Zur literarischen Repräsentation weiblicher Geschlechterrollenerfahrung im 19. Jahrhundert,* New York: Lang, 1993

Fohrmann, Jürgen, *Abenteuer und Bürgertum: Zur Geschichte der deutschen Robinsonade im 18. Jahrhurdert,* Stuttgart: Metzler, 1981

Fuchs, Anne, et al., editors, *Reisen im Diskurs: Modelle der literaischen Fremderfahrung von den Pilgerberichten bis zur Postmoderne: Tagungsakten des internationalen Symposions zur Reiseliteratur, University College Dublin vom 10.-12. März 1994,* Heidelberg: Winter, 1995

Gemünden, Gerd, "Introduction to Enzensberger's 'A Theory of Tourism,'" *New German Critique* 68 (Spring–Summer 1996)

Graf, Johannes, *"Die notwendige Reise": Reisen und Reiseliteratur junger Autoren während des Nationalsozialismus,* Stuttgart: M and P, 1995

Griep, Wolfgang, and Annegret Pelz, *Frauen reisen: Ein bibliographisches Verzeichnis deutschsprachiger Frauenreisen 1700 bis 1810,* Bremen: Temmen, 1995

Griep, Wolfgang, editor, *Reiseliteratur und Geographica in der Eutiner Landesbibliothek,* 2 vols., Heide: Westholsteinische Verlagsanstalt Boyens, 1990

———, editor, *Sehen und Beschreiben: Europäische Reisen im 18. und frühen 19. Jahrhundert,* Heide: Westholsteinische Verlagsanstalt Boyens, 1991

Griep, Wolfgang, and Hans-Wolf Jäger, editors, *Reise und soziale Realität am Ende des 18. Jahrhunderts,* Heidelberg: Winter, 1983

———, editors, *Reisen im 18. Jahrhundert: Neue Untersuchungen,* Heidelberg: Winter, 1986

Höhle, Thomas, editor, *Reiseliteratur im Umfeld der französischen Revolution,* Halle: Martin-Luther-Universität Halle-Wittenberg, 1987

Jäger, Hans-Wolf, editor, *Europäisches Reisen im Zeitalter der Aufklärung,* Heidelberg: Winter, 1992

Jedamski, Doris, et al., editors, *"Und tät' das Reisen wählen!" Frauenreisen-Reisefrauen,* Zurich: eFeF, 1994

Klein, Ulrich, *Die deutschsprachige Reisesatire des 18. Jahrhunderts,* Heidelberg: Winter, 1997

Krasnobaev, B.I., et al., editors, *Reisen und Reisebeschreibungen im 18. und 19. Jahrhundert als Quellen der Kulturbeziehungsforschung,* Berlin: Camen, 1980

Kraus Worley, Linda, "Through Others' Eyes: Narratives of German Women Traveling in Nineteenth-Century America," *Yearbook of German-American Studies* 21 (1986)

Krusche, Dietrich, *Reisen: Verabredung mit der Fremde,* Weinheim: Quadriga, 1989

Kutter, Uli, "Apodemiken und Reisehandbücher: Bemerkungen und ein bibliographischer Versuch zu einer vernachlässigten Literaturgattung," *Das achtzehnte Jahrhundert* 4 (1980)

Lüdtke, Helga, "Grenzen überschreiten—Die Faszination der Fremde: Frauen-Reise-Literatur in Vergangenheit und Gegenwart," *Buch und Bibliothek* 47, no. 7–8 (July–August 1995)

Mączak, Antoni, and Hans Jürgen Teuteberg, editors, *Reiseberichte als Quellen europäischer Kulturgeschichte: Aufgaben und Möglichkeiten der historischen Reiseforschung,* Wolfenbüttel: Herzog August Bibliothek, 1982

Maler, Anselm, editor, *Galerie der Welt: Ethnographisches Erzählen im 19. Jahrhundert,* Stuttgart: Belser, 1988

———, editor, *Exotische Welt in populären Lektüren,* Tübingen: Niemeyer, 1990

Ohler, Norbert, *Reisen im Mittelalter,* Munich: Artemis, 1986; translated by Caroline Hillier as *The Medieval Traveller,* Woodbridge, Suffolk: Boydell, 1989; Rochester, New York: Boydell, 1995

Ohnesorg, Stefanie, *Mit Kompaß, Kutsche und Kamel: (Rück-)Einbindung der Frau in die Geschichte des Reisens und der Reiseliteratur,* St. Ingbert: Röhrig Universtiätsverlag, 1996

Paßmann, Uwe, *Orte fern, das Leben: Die Fremde als Fluchtpunkt des Denkens deutsch-europäische Literatur bis 1820,* Würzburg: Königshausen and Neumann, 1989

Pelz, Annegret, *Reisen durch die eigene Fremde: Reiseliteratur von Frauen als autogeographische Schriften,* Cologne: Böhlau, 1993

Piechotta, Hans Joachim, editor, *Reise und Utopie: Zur Literatur der Spätaufklärung,* Frankfurt: Suhrkamp, 1976

Potts, Lydia, editor, *Aufbruch und Abenteuer: Frauen-Reisen um die Welt ab 1785,* Berlin: Orlanda, 1988

Scheitler, Irmgard, *Gattung und Geschlecht: Reisebeschreibungen deutscher Frauen 1780–1850,* Tübingen: Niemeyer, 1999

Schivelbusch, Wolfgang, *Geschichte der Eisenbahnreise: Zur Industrialisierung von Raum und Zeit im 19. Jahrhundert,* Munich: Hanser, 1977; translated by Anselm Hollo as *The Railway Journey: Trains and Travel in the 19th Century,* New York: Urizen Books, 1979; Oxford: Blackwell, 1980

———, "Railroad Space and Railroad Time," *New German Critique* 14 (1978)

Stewart, William E., *Die Reisebeschreibung und ihre Theorie im Deutschland des 18. Jahrhunderts,* Bonn: Bouvier, 1978

Strack, Thomas, *Exotische Erfahrung und Intersubjektivität: Reiseberichte im 17. und 18. Jahrhundert: Genregeschichtliche Untersuchung zu Adam Olearius, Hans Egede, Georg Forster,* Paderborn: Igel Verlag Wissenschaft, 1994

Wuthenow, Ralph-Rainer, *Die erfahrene Welt: Europäische Reiseliteratur im Zeitalter der Aufklärung,* Frankfurt: Insel, 1980

Kurt Tucholsky 1890–1935

Tucholsky was the most prominent of the left-wing, but non-party journalists of Weimar Germany. His main platform was Siegfried Jacobsohn's Berlin weekly *Die Weltbühne,* which was well respected despite its small circulation. Tucholsky's work, much of which was republished in his own time in anthology form, ranges from political polemic through satires of contemporary society, reviews of books and plays, lyric poetry, cabaret songs, and short stories to a play written in collaboration with Walter Hasenclever. The range, stylistic accessibility, and occasional humor of his work, alongside his image as representative of the "other," anti-Nazi Germany have earned his writings a postwar renaissance, with over 5 million copies sold in German and translations into 32 languages.

Tucholsky emerged from war service in December 1918 as a convinced critic of the German Officer Corps, which in his view represented the outdated "spirit of Prussianism" and had abused its privileges. In common with Carl von Ossietzky, Kurt Hiller, and other "Aktivisten," Tucholsky in 1919 supported a nonviolent "geistige Revolution"; he believed that intellectuals should put their insight in the service of humanitarian values and democratic reform.

Becoming disillusioned with the Social Democrats for what he saw as their half-hearted response to the Revolution and their willingness to allow the country's traditional elites to retain their power, he campaigned for the dismissal of army minister Gustav Noske, the self-styled "bloodhound" whose Freikorps had brutally suppressed left-wing risings. The minister was forced to resign in March 1920, after being betrayed by his protégés during the abortive putsch by Kapp and Lüttwitz. Tucholsky responded by joining the USPD (Independent Socialist Party) and writing for its daily *Die Freiheit* until the party was dissolved in 1922. As an active critic of German militarism, he helped to found pacifist organizations such as the Friedensbund der Kriegsteilnehmer, and he delivered speeches and recited his own antiwar poems at the "Nie wieder Krieg!" demonstrations of the early 1920s. In 1922 he assisted the Social Democratic Interior Minister Köster in organizing a celebration of the democratic constitution. This effort gives the lie to allegations from SPD sympathizers that he was negative and impractical in his approach. His optimism, however, was shaken by a wave of political assassinations carried out by right-wing officers and usually condoned by judges appointed under the imperial regime and sharing the social standing and prejudices of the killers. During the hyperinflation of 1923, a combination of despair and financial straits drove Tucholsky temporarily to abandon his literary career and to take up a post in a Berlin bank.

As the threat to democracy and the economy receded in 1924, however, Tucholsky, a fluent French speaker from his schooldays at the Französisches Gymnasium in Berlin, took the opportunity to move to Paris and contribute articles on French life to both *Die Weltbühne* and the liberal *Vossische Zeitung*. The threat of a new Franco-German war concerned him, even at a time when Foreign Minister Stresemann, whom he distrusted, was planning a rapprochement through the Locarno Treaty. In March 1925, Tucholsky forecast in *Die Weltbühne* in detail the steps by which Germany would reconquer Eastern Europe—the militarization of society, *Anschluß* with Austria, the exploitation of the German-speaking minority in Czechoslovakia, and a temporary alliance with the Soviet Union to carve up Poland. He also foresaw that the aggressive policy would create an anti-German coalition "from Caledonia to California" and lead to a military defeat more disastrous than 1918.

Disillusioned with events at home—after a majority of his compatriots elected as president the monarchist former commander-in-chief von Hindenburg—and worried by the fascist victory in Italy, Tucholsky sought new allies. As a member of the nonparty *Deutsche Linke,* he campaigned in the referendum to expropriate Germany's former royal houses in 1926; as a pacifist, he warned against his country's generals, advocated the creation of the United States of Europe as the best way of pre-

serving peace, and enraged conservatives of his own time (and even government ministers today) with the blunt assertion "Soldaten sind Mörder!" (Since 1989 pacifists have quoted this message in spoken or written form. They were tried for slandering the *Bundeswehr,* but they were generally acquitted on the grounds of freedom of speech. The Kohl government tried to introduce a special law to protect the army's honor from further criticism.)

After trying to democratize the German bourgeoisie in *Ulk* and preaching to converted left-wingers in *Die Freiheit* and to pacifists in journals such as *Die Menschheit* and *Das andere Deutschland,* Tucholsky made a final attempt to write for a wide audience by publishing propaganda poems in the *Arbeiter Illustrierte Zeitung,* which was run by the communist MP and media boss, Willi Münzenberg. He also collaborated with John Heartfield in the ironically entitled satirical anthology *Deutschland, Deutschland über alles* (1929), which attacked the survival of Wilhelminian values in the supposedly democratic Republic. This later earned Tucholsky, courtesy of Golo Mann, the title of a "grave-digger of the Republic." This exaggerates Tucholsky's importance and also represents a travesty of history: the Republic was destroyed by the Nazis, his bitterest enemies. But the attempt to ally himself with the communists, whom he briefly regarded as the last effective progressive force in German society, was doomed, as much through the dogmatism of the KPD as through Tucholsky's refusal to abandon his critical faculties on behalf of the Moscow-inspired party line.

Tucholsky was already a sick and depressed man when the Nazis began their march to power. Apart from writing satirical poems against the SA and Goebbels, he underestimated the strength conferred by the mass movement and the effectiveness of its leader, believing that Hitler was less of a threat than his Nationalist allies, the DNVP, whom he had been fighting throughout the Republic. Nevertheless, Tucholsky was high on the Nazi hate list: anthologies of his work were ceremonially burned in the Berlin auto-da-fé of May 1933, and he was deprived of his citizenship a few months later. Although living outside Germany, Tucholsky was hit by the confiscation of his bank account; this was especially damaging since he had no ambition to contribute to the ineffective exile press and, in any case, was prohibited by Swedish law from earning a living there. Weakened by illness and near-constant headaches, he took an overdose and died in a hospital in Gothenburg in December 1935.

IAN KING

See also Satire

Biography

Born in Berlin, 9 January 1890. Studied law at Berlin University from 1909; doctor of law, 1915; first journalistic articles in *Ulk,* the satirical supplement of the liberal *Berliner Tageblatt,* 1907, the Social Democratic *Vorwärts,* 1911–14, and *Die Schaubühne,* from 1913 (renamed *Die Weltbühne,* 1918); military service on the eastern front, first as sapper, 1915, then as editor of the air force newspaper *Der Flieger,* in Courland, 1916–17; in the military police in occupied Romania, 1918; returned to Berlin, December 1918, and edited *Ulk* through February, 1920; main contributor to *Die Weltbühne,* which he edited between December 1926 and May 1927; member of USPD and contributor to *Die Freiheit,* 1920–22; Paris correspondent of the liberal *Vossische Zeitung,* from 1924; also wrote for *Arbeiter Illustrierte Zeitung;* cabaret songs and texts for Max Reinhardt's *Schall und*

Rauch, 1919, and for Rudolf Nelson and Friedrich Hollaender and others throughout the 1920s; in Paris, 1924–29, with intermittent visits to Germany and Scandinavia; in Sweden, 1929–32, Zurich, 1932–33, and Sweden, 1933–35; gave up writing for publication in January 1933. Died (probable suicide), 21 December 1935.

Selected Works

Collections

Gesammelte Werke in 10 Bänden, edited by Mary Gerold-Tucholsky and Fritz Joachim Raddatz, 1975
Gedichte, 1983
Germany? Germany! The Kurt Tucholsky Reader, translated by Harry Zohn et al., 1990
Gesamtausgabe Texte und Briefe, edited by Antje Bonitz et al., 1996–

Fiction

Rheinsberg, 1912
Ein Pyrenäenbuch, 1926
Deutschland, Deutschland über alles, 1929; edited by Fritz Joachim Raddatz, 1973; as *Deutschland, Deutschland über alles*, translated by Anne Halley, 1972
Schloß Gripsholm, 1931; as *Castle Gripsholm, a Summer Story*, translated by Michael Hofmann, 1988

Play

Christoph Kolumbus; oder, Die Entdeckung Amerikas (with Walter Hasenclever), 1985

Further Reading

Bemmann, Helga, *Kurt Tucholsky: Ein Lebensbild*, Berlin: Verlag der Nation, 1990
Grenville, Bryan P., *Kurt Tucholsky: The Ironic Sentimentalist*, London: Wolff, and Atlantic Highlands, New Jersey: Humanities Press, 1981
Hepp, Michael, *Kurt Tucholsky: Biographische Annäherungen*, Reinbek bei Hamburg: Rowohlt, 1993
King, William John, *Kurt Tucholsky als politischer Publizist*, Frankfurt and Bern: Lang, 1983
Poor, Harold L., *Kurt Tucholsky and the Ordeal of Germany, 1914–1935*, New York: Scribner, 1968
Porombka, Beate, *Verspäteter Aufklärer oder Pionier einer neuen Aufklärung?: Kurt Tucholsky*, Frankfurt and New York: Lang, 1990
Raddatz, Fritz Joachim, *Tucholsky ein Pseudonym*, Reinbek bei Hamburg: Rowohlt, 1989

Deutschland, Deutschland über alles 1929

Satire by Kurt Tucholsky

Satire is by its very nature a controversial pursuit and literary form, and it has been the fate of many satirists to be misunderstood and maligned by those who expect from a practitioner of "total satire" unerring tact, taste, fairness, and political right-mindedness. Berlin-born Kurt Tucholsky, along with the very dissimilar Viennese Karl Kraus one of the foremost satirists of the 20th century, is no exception. The picture book that he published in 1929 may not be his best work, but its mordant depiction of the Weimar Republic and its unwholesome legacy of the imperial period, as well as the threat of the fascist mind, certainly make it his most aggressive and possibly his most charac-

teristic publication. For many decades this book, more than Tucholsky's voluminous output as a whole, has served as a touchstone or litmus test for artistic, ideological, political, and sociological attitudes. Fifty thousand copies were sold within a year of its publication by a firm owned by the communist Willi Münzenberg, but, once again, this success illustrated the satirist's old complaint that his works were widely read but ineffectual. Today copies of the first edition are prized collector's items. It is interesting to note that, while the first German postwar edition of 1964 garnered negative reviews and the East German printing of 1964 led critics to equate Bonn with Weimar, the book has been regarded as a modern classic for the past 25 years. The inexpensive facsimile reprints issued since 1973 by the satirist's longtime publisher Rowohlt contain annotations inspired by the U.S. edition of 1972.

In this book, an exemplar of the anti-coffee-table variety (in the first edition subtitled "A Picturebook by Kurt Tucholsky and Many Photographers. Mounted by John Heartfield"), the satirist graphically catches Germany and holds it in suspended animation, as it were, at a time of political and economic instability and social disintegration, a few years before the philistinism and brutality rampant in public life made the country ripe for a vicious dictatorship. In retrospect, it is evident that this book illustrates or foreshadows many ingredients of the witch's brew of Nazism. Tucholsky's main satiric targets are there: a state organized along nationalistic and militaristic lines, the injustices of an antiquated and insensitive legal system, the German brand of Babbitry and other deeply rooted flaws in the German national character, and human stupidity and cupidity in their miriad guises.

Tucholsky's unsparing portrait of *homo teutonicus* had a long gestation period. As early as 1912, the young satirist had called for more muckraking photos with contrasts and juxtapositions but little text, and in a later essay he envisaged a fighting periodical illustrated along these lines. In John Heartfield, born in Berlin as Helmut Herzfeld but bearing an English name as a protest against German chauvinism during World War I, he found an ideal partner in his quest for what Marcel Belvianes has described as a "sociology of the photograph." Heartfield, the foremost master of photomontage, was known as the "Monteur-Dada." In their totality, these pictures constitute the photographic equivalent of the powerful graphic art of George Grosz and Käthe Kollwitz. As for the text, much of Tucholsky's short prose and poetry included in the book had previously appeared in *Die Weltbühne* and other periodicals and newspapers. Lacking any consistent ideological thrust, the nondoctrinaire satirist intermingled the tragic with the trivial to produce a cross-section of German life that constitutes a strange mixture of involvement and alienation, a reformer's zeal and a contemptuous withdrawal. Weary of pointlessly poking about the roots of the German oak tree, as he once put it, the ailing, deracinated, and desperate satirist sought and found "the truest of all democracies, the democracy of death" in Sweden, a cold country in more ways than one, shortly before his 46th birthday.

The most controversial photomontage in the book is the trenchant depiction of eight military leaders with the caption "Tiere sehen dich an" (Animals Looking at You), the title of a popular book of photographs by Paul Eipper. Harboring a *Haßliebe* (love-hatred) for his native land in the manner of Heinrich Heine, Tucholsky poignantly wrote in his concluding essay,

"Heimat" (Homeland): "Because we love Germany, we have the right to hate it."

It would not be difficult to compile a catalog of institutions to which and individuals to whom Tucholsky may be said to have been "unfair." A case in point is the Breslau Germanist A.H. Hoffmann von Fallersleben, whose "foolish line from a big-mouth poem . . . which a really demented Republic chose for its national anthem" provided the title of the book and its cover art. In his "Song of the Germans" (1841), the patriotic professor urged his compatriots to place the idea of a Germany united in brotherhood above separatism and factional strife, but the German rejection of such idealism and the horrendous misapplication of the poet's message justified the satirist's approach.

With some notable exceptions, *Deutschland, Deutschland über alles* has come in for critical condemnation. In the year of its publication, Tucholsky dealt with the animadversions of the critic Herbert Ihering, who deplored the decline of polemics and satire in his time, accused Tucholsky of repeating himself, and felt that he should be fighting in Germany, not in France, Switzerland, or Sweden. "Tucho" admitted that his book was somewhat anachronistic and pointed to the difficulty of using photos to illustrate psychic situations. Later the satirist became more defensive and described his book as "much too mild." Its lack of timeliness was noted by the American historian Harold Poor, who wrote that, while Tucholsky ostensibly concerned himself with Weimar culture, his criticism really harked back to the abuses of the old imperial regime and its culture. The most balanced and useful account may be found in Hans-Joachim Becker's book. Stefan Salter, who left his native Germany to become a leading American book designer, writes in his autobiography *From Cover to Cover* (1969):

> I have seen many picture books in my life . . . but never before or since such an impressive one as *Deutschland, Deutschland über alles*. This was the book which made it abundantly clear to me, a young man who knew nothing about politics or economics, that there was trouble brewing. . . . What impressed me most about the book were the photographs, the photomontages, and the way the text ran with the illustrations. Dramatic statements were made not only by the text or illustrations but by the way they were laid out. It was a great textbook of our time, teaching important lessons which few people were willing to learn. It was like the handwriting on the wall, and it sent me away forever and in ample time.

The German-born critic Ernst Pawel found the picture book "ahead of its time in avant-garde vulgarity," and the German-born historian Walter Laqueur regarded this "caricature of Weimar Germany" as a primary cause of a disturbingly disrespectful "Tucholsky Syndrome" in the United States. The American historian Gordon Craig called Tucholsky the greatest German satirist since Heinrich Heine but believed that this "atrabilious collection of essays did more to weaken the cause of democracy in Germany than to help it." With a youthful faith in "the other Germany," Erika and Klaus Mann wrote in 1939 that the book was part of the satirist's "unremitting truculent warfare with the nature of the German people." Referring to "Herr Wendriner," Tucholsky's series of monologues by an unsympathetically depicted German-Jewish type, Gershom Scholem, who had left Berlin for Jerusalem at an early age, passed the harsh judgment that Tucholsky was "one of the most gifted and most offensive Jewish anti-Semites."

HARRY ZOHN

Editions

First edition: *Deutschland, Deutschland über alles,* Berlin: Neuer Deutscher Verlag, 1929
Critical edition: edited by Fritz Joachim Raddatz, Reinbek bei Hamburg: Rowohlt, 1973
Translation: *Deutschland, Deutschland über alles,* translated by Anne Halley, edited by Harry Zohn, Amherst: University of Massachusetts Press, 1972

Further Reading

Becker, Hans-Joachim Paul, *Mit geballter Faust: Kurt Tucholskys "Deutschland, Deutschland über alles,"* Bonn: Bouvier, 1978
Bemmann, Helga, *Kurt Tucholsky: Ein Lebensbild,* Berlin: Verlag der Nation, 1990
Deák, István, *Weimar Germany's Left-Wing Intellectuals: A Political History of the Weltbühne and Its Circle,* Berkeley: University of California Press, 1968
Hepp, Michael, *Kurt Tucholsky: Biographische Annäherungen,* Reinbek bei Hamburg: Rowohlt, 1993
King, William John, *Kurt Tucholsky als politischer Publizist,* Frankfurt and Bern: Lang, 1983
Meyer, Jochen, editor, *"Entlaufene Bürger": Kurt Tucholsky und die Seinen,* Marbach: Deutsche Schillergesellschaft, 1990
Poor, Harold L., *Kurt Tucholsky and the Ordeal of Germany, 1914–1935,* New York: Scribner, 1968
Schulz, Klaus Peter, *Kurt Tucholsky in Selbstzeugnissen und Bilddokumenten,* Hamburg: Rowohlt, 1959; 23rd edition, 1992
Soldenhoff, Richard von, editor, *Kurt Tucholsky 1890–1935: Ein Lebensbild,* Berlin: Quadriga, 1985
Wessling, Berndt Wilhelm, *Tucholsky: Ein deutsches Ärgernis,* Gerlingen: Bleicher, 1985
Zohn, Harry, editor, *Germany? Germany! The Kurt Tucholsky Reader,* Manchester: Carcanet, 1990
Zwerenz, Gerhard, *Kurt Tucholsky: Biographie eines guten Deutschen,* Munich: Bertelsmann, 1979

U

Universities

The oldest university on the territory of today's Federal Republic of Germany is Heidelberg, which was founded in 1386. It is not normally regarded as the oldest German university, however; that honor is accorded, on the basis of what at the time was seen as constituting the geographical entity of Germany, to the University of Prague, which dates from 1348.

To understand the contemporary German university, it is necessary to go back to the creation of the Humboldt University in Berlin in 1810. This foundation formed part of the reforms that helped to reestablish the state of Prussia following its humiliation by Napoléon. Wilhelm von Humboldt, the Prussian state official responsible for education in the years 1809 and 1810, laid down the principles of the new institution in his memorandum "Über die innere und äußere Organisation der höheren wissenschaftlichen Anstalten in Berlin" (On the Internal and External Organization of Institutions of Higher Education in Berlin), which contains many of the ideas associated with German universities that are still relevant today.

Of major importance is the ideal of the unity of teaching and research (*Einheit von Forschung und Lehre*), whereby professors should teach in the area of their research expertise. Equally significant is the principle of academic freedom, by which Humboldt sought to protect universities from state interference. Students continue to have the freedom to determine the length of their studies, although the current average of around seven years before graduation has as much to do with academic and financial constraints as with the exercise of freedom. They also have the right to enter the university on the basis of having passed the *Abitur,* the school-leaving examination introduced by Humboldt for pupils of the *Gymnasium* (grammar school). This right, however, is nowadays restricted in a number of subject areas; for example, medical sciences, by the system of *numerus clausus,* restrict the number of students accepted to the number of places available. Since 1973, this system has been administered by the Zentrale Vergabestelle für Studienplätze (Central Admissions Agency for University Places).

Despite the freedoms traditionally enjoyed by German universities, there have always been close links with the state. Humboldt himself believed that professorial appointments should be in the hands of the state, and to this day professors enjoy the privileged status of public servant (*Beamter*). Moreover, the normal leaving qualification in such areas as the humanities and law remains the *Staatsexamen* (state examination), the first hurdle on the way to achieving *Beamter* status as, for example, a teacher or state lawyer. Given this tradition, it is not surprising that a private university sector has hardly developed in Germany, with the best-known institution, Witten-Herdecke, dating only from 1981–82.

Insistence on traditional Humboldtian ideals was particularly pronounced immediately after World War II. Despite the liberal principles referred to above, German universities had tended to be hotbeds of nationalism, both in the late 19th century and during the Third Reich. The (admittedly brief) tenure by the philosopher Heidegger as the rector at the University of Freiburg and the apparently pro-Nazi sentiments he then expressed are frequently seen as epitomizing German academia's capitulation before Hitler. After 1945, control of universities passed to the federal states (*Länder*) as part of the policy of preventing the central control of such sensitive areas as education and broadcasting. This has largely remained the case despite some amendments to the constitution, including the establishment of a federal ministry covering higher education by the Brandt government in 1969 and the passing of a number of framework laws for higher education (*Hochschulrahmengesetz*) from 1976 onward.

The creation of the new ministry was part of the reactions to the first major crisis in higher education in the Federal Republic, the student movement of the late 1960s. In 1964 a distinguished teacher, Georg Picht, had proclaimed an impending "educational catastrophe" (*Bildungskatastrophe*), by which he meant a lack of educated personnel to meet future challenges. University expansion became the order of the day, something the Humboldtian model, which was designed for a small elite, was ill-equipped to cope with. Students began to protest against what were seen as outdated university structures, with the slogan "Unter den Talaren Muff von tausend Jahren" (Beneath the gowns the fustiness of 1,000 years) gaining widespread currency. A major demand was the democratization of decision making under a system of *Drittelparität* (three-way parity) in which professors, other academic staff, and students and nonacademic staff would have equal decision-making powers. This idea was quickly challenged and was deemed illegal with a court verdict of 1973, which restored power to the professoriat. Nevertheless, there were lasting changes at that time. Other institutions of higher education such as *Technische Hochschulen,* which had grown up in the 19th century to teach scientific and technological disciplines that had no place within the Humboldtian ideal of "Bildung," that is, a largely theoretical education with no overt application, expanded and generally adopted the title "Universität." *Fachhochschulen* offering more applied courses but with less of a research role were established, while many *Pädagogische Hochschulen* (teacher training colleges) were incorporated into universities. Combining a university and *Fachhochschule* to form a *Gesamthochschule* (comprehensive university) has not proved popular, although a few such institutions exist.

Since the 1970s, there have been periodic bursts of student unrest at German universities, which are just one sign of continuing difficulties. Despite increasing public expenditure on higher education (DM 26.1 billion in 1993), one major problem German universities undoubtedly face is underfunding. There are frequent media reports of buildings in disrepair, library cutbacks, or a lack of modern equipment such as computers. For the individual student the great problem is overcrowding. The increase in the number of university students from 239,000 in 1960 to 1,394,000 in 1994 has frequently led to crammed lecture theaters. The first hurdle for new students is understanding the requirements of the system, not least because of a lack of academic counseling. Academic freedom often means that students must "sink or swim," while professors devote their time to research and are rarely available for consultation. Some students also face financial difficulties. There are systems of financial support, in particular what is always referred to as *Bafög*—a shortened form of *Bundesausbildungsförderungsgesetz* (federal law for the support of training). Since the 1980s this support has tended to be in the form of loans rather than grants, which may be one reason why many students take on jobs to support themselves during their studies. This, in turn, along with overcrowding, undoubtedly contributes to the extended periods of study at universities and to the frequently lamented state of affairs that Germany has the oldest graduates and—although this cannot be blamed on the universities—the youngest pensioners. Many do not graduate at all, with dropout rates in some arts subjects reaching 80 percent in at least one state.

During their time at university, students put together a program of studies in accordance with their institution's examination requirements. They begin with a *Grundstudium* (basic studies), which should last around two to three years. Once the intermediary examination (*Zwischenprüfung*) has been passed, the main period of study (*Hauptstudium*) begins. Usually at least two subjects are studied, with successful participation in seminars being marked by the acquisition of a certificate (*Schein*). Once the required number has been gained and a larger piece of work (*Examensarbeit*) has been completed, the final examination, in which there is usually a significant oral component, can be undertaken. Once students have gained their award—besides the *Staatsexamen,* these include the *Diplom* (followed by reference to the subject) or *Magister*—they face another factor that casts a shadow over universities: increased graduate unemployment, although the rate remains low in comparison with other social groups.

Progress can be equally difficult for the aspiring academic. On completion of a doctorate, (s)he may find a position in the "Mittelbau" (middle stratum), where jobs are often only based on limited contracts; there are no real equivalent to lecturers in

Britain or assistant professors in the United States. The aim of less experienced academics must be to gain—in the time-honored German tradition—a second doctorate (*Habilitation*), which, although now not mandatory, is still usually needed to gain a chair at a university and the freedoms this brings. Previously appointments were made on the basis of a "call" (*Ruf*) to a suitable candidate; now positions tend to be openly advertised.

A variety of solutions have been offered to solve the current malaise at German universities. The panacea of a large injection of public funds is unlikely to be forthcoming, as both state and federal governments see other major priorities and can point to the need for universities to put their own houses in order. One contentious area is academic quality. There has generally been little sense of hierarchy among institutions, with students choosing where to study on the basis of proximity or by the related question of which federal state they inhabit. Especially since the media have started compiling ranking lists of universities in recent years, however, there are now increasing demands for greater competition between institutions and some forms of quality audits. Complaints about declining standards, not least in research where references have been made to a decrease in the number of Nobel laureates, have multiplied over the years. A general agreement, however, exists about the need for universities to enjoy greater freedom from state government bureaucracy and for students to be able to study for shorter periods. Budgetary autonomy is being introduced in some states, while the introduction of degrees at a bachelor level and penalties for dilatory students have been seen as ways of reducing time spent at university.

Many of these proposals were contained in a new *Hochschulrahmengesetz,* which was passed in the final months of the Kohl government. The law also made possible the introduction of another frequently canvassed way of overcoming the financial crisis afflicting universities: the introduction of tuition fees. These were abolished in the early 1970s, but, as Chancellor Schröder is on record as saying that this step made his own legal studies possible, it is unlikely that his government will allow their reintroduction.

Unlike some of the other difficulties facing Germany, the problems of German universities cannot easily be linked with unification. The GDR's system of higher education was tightly structured, with the number of graduates in any discipline being linked to the state's needs in that area. For example, the vast majority of students of English were simultaneously trained as teachers, the principal area of employment for English graduates. This meant tight controls on entry to university, with factors other than academic attainment playing a part. Willingness to undertake three years military service helped the cause of males, while females, too, were increasingly expected to engage in paramilitary training. The number of students in the GDR declined between 1970 and 1989, although it must be remembered there were many opportunities for part-time study in the GDR.

The influence of state ideology naturally made itself felt in GDR universities, with Marxism-Leninism being a compulsory subject since 1951. Its influence was also felt across the curriculum. For example, sociology was only taught beginning in 1963–64; before then, it was considered a "bourgeois" subject. Where the GDR had a good record was in the number of female students, who in 1985 reached 50 percent of the total and were less concentrated in traditional "female" subjects than in the West, where from the 1970s women comprised up to 45 percent of student numbers, a figure that has not changed significantly since unification. In both states the number of women professors was very low, although here, too, the GDR had a small advantage. This has been maintained since unification, with 11 percent of the professoriat in the East being women in 1994 as opposed to 6 percent in the West. That women are now awarded around 30 percent of doctorates means that the current situation should change in the future.

Unification led to a complete overhaul of GDR universities in terms of both curriculum and personnel. The process of *Abwicklung*, a word literally meaning "unwinding," used to describe the reshaping of Eastern institutions, was carried out particularly strenuously in the universities. This meant the dismissal of staff seen as closely associated with the GDR state and its ideology. In most cases they were replaced by West Germans. Nevertheless, Eastern universities are still distinctive in that student numbers remain smaller, something that, along with a greater commitment among staff, has attracted comers from the West. To this extent, the Eastern universities may provide something of a model for the future.

Of the other German-speaking countries, long periods of study (five to six years) are also normal in Austria. Here, however, there is no *numerus clausus*, and higher education is orga-nized at the federal level. Switzerland is distinguished by a system in which universities tend to specialize in a limited number of subject areas. The major centers for scientific and technical subjects are the two institutes of technology, which, unlike the ten universities, are federal institutions.

STUART PARKES

See also Wilhelm von Humboldt

Further Reading

Arbeitsgruppe Bildungsbericht am Max-Planck-Institut für Bildungsfragen, *Das Bildungswesen in der Bundesrepublik Deutschland*, Reinbek bei Hamburg: Rowohlt, 1994

Ash, Mitchell G., *German Universities, Past and Future: Crisis or Renewal?* Providence, Rhode Island: Berghahn Books, 1997

Daxner, Michael, *Ist die Uni noch zu retten? Zehn Vorschläge und eine Vision*, Reinbek bei Hamburg: Rowohlt, 1996

Führ, Christoph, *Deutsches Bildungswesen seit 1945*, Bonn: Inter Nationes, 1996

Klemm, Klaus, et al., *Bildungsplanung in den neuen Bundesländern*, Weinheim: Juventa, 1992

MacKinnon, Donald, et al., *Education in Western Europe: Facts and Figures*, London: Hodder and Stoughton, 1997

Utopianism

Utopianism is a kind of thinking guided by ideals or desires toward the realization of the best possible society. Because it seeks to transcend present realities, it is usually critical or negative. Were it ever to be satisfied, as Karl Mannheim noted, it would turn into ideology. Utopia is often equated with Shangri-la or Paradise or some other fanciful place. In fact, utopia is no place at all (Gk. *ou* + *topos*, "no place"). The island to which Thomas More gave this name in 1516 was an idea, stimulated by the 15th-century rediscovery of Plato (*Republic*) and necessitated by the failure of humanists to provide solutions to the unprecedented social and moral problems accompanying the rise of the early modern state. German utopias have been alternately praised as humanitarian, ridiculed as unrealistic, or condemned as totalitarian from the 17th-century Rosicrucians to the 19th-century Social Democrats to the post–World War II scientific establishment.

Utopia is a secular vision. More's *Utopia* scandalized the Church because it dared to propose an ideal society predicated solely on human agency without benefit of divine revelation. Utopia shares theology's view of a fallen world populated by sinful human beings but answers by regulating human behavior through prudent laws and institutions. This concern was the link between utopia and the emerging early modern sovereign state, with the accompanying debate over how to achieve the best society. Utopia in early modern Europe had many names—*Antangil* (anonymous, Paris, 1616), *Christianopolis* (Johann Andreae, 1619), *Città del Sole* (Tommaso Campanella, 1620), *New Atlantis* (Francis Bacon, 1627), and *Oceana* (James Harrington, 1656)—but only one purpose, namely, the idealization of society. Utopianism differed from the other major discourses on social idealization (moralism and millennialism) not only by its secular view but also by the thoroughness with which it engineered controls on human behavior. This organizational rigor could be weighted more toward absolutist constraints or decentralized power sharing, depending on whether the model rested on an essentially pessimistic or optimistic anthropology. The totalizing utopias of Campanella (state as mirror of cosmic mechanics), Andreae (state as factory), and Bacon (state as scientific laboratory), together with the absolutist doctrines of Niccolò Machiavelli, Jean Bodin, and Thomas Hobbes, demonstrate profound doubts about the ability of human beings to manufacture their happiness unassisted. By contrast, Arcadian utopias, such as Joshua Barnes's *Gerania* (1675), together with the political writings deriving from natural law, such as Johannes Althusius's *Politica* (1603), Hugo Grotius's *De iure belli ac pacis* (1625), or Samuel Pufendorf's *De iure naturae et gentium* (1672), emphasize the natural inclination or need of humans to seek social cooperation and harmony. Christian anthropological constructs around 1700 differed mainly on the question of whether a prelapsarian state of perfection could be regained. Heinrich von Ahlefeldt believed it possible on the basis of his study of ancient utopian writings (*De fictis rebuspublicis* [1704]); Leibniz considered sinful conditions a necessary part of the divine theodicy (*Essais de théodicée* [1710]).

Utopianism was not described systematically before the mid-19th century. Prior to that time, it existed simply as a mode of thought in loose imitation of More, referring to some vague place or country, and was frequently disguised as moral satire or political theory; the cosmopolitan humanist Erasmus described himself as a "civis Utopiensis" (citizen of Utopia). It provides the allegorical key to interpreting Baroque pastoral writings, especially prose eclogue (Martin Opitz's *Hercinie* [1630]; Johann Hellwig's *Die Nymphe Noris* [1650]). In 1735 the aesthetician Alexander Baumgartner used the term as part of a tripartite poetic classification: *figmenta vera, figmenta heterocosmica, figmenta utopica. Utopica* are not strictly utopian but rather unpoetic (because inorganic) elements that are to be purged from literary works; utopia itself belongs more to the second category, *heterocosmica* (unusual but possible features). Elsewhere in the 18th century, utopia was the equivalent of *Schlaraffenland* (fairy-tale land) and continued to be so defined into the 19th century (e.g., in the 1809 *Brockhaus* dictionary). Kant dismissed the idea of utopia as chimerical, preferring the concept of the ideal as a heuristic for envisioning ultimate conditions.

The socialist movements in France and Germany during the 1830s and 1840s charged the concept of utopia politically, as an idea oriented to the future. This development had literary implications, beginning with Robert von Mohl's use of utopia in 1845 as a modern historical category in his typology of the *Staatsroman* (novel of state). Wilhelm Schulz's investigation into precursors of "communistic" and "socialistic" utopian writings yielded an index of utopias from More to the present. However, it was mainly as a symptomatic term of political consciousness that the term flourished after midcentury. Theodor Mundt applied *Utopismus* polemically to typify an earlier, immature stage of socialism—a value judgment that Marx and Engels would borrow in distinguishing true socialism or communism from mere utopianism. In 1848 Marx wrote, "Der deutsche Kommunismus ist der entschiedenste Gegner alles Utopismus" (German communism is decisively opposed to all forms of utopianism), by which he meant that utopianism could not lead to social progress and productivity. Until the end of the century, conservatives and socialists alike would inveigh against the other side's "utopian" social ideas, and socialists themselves attacked one another's programs as unscientific and illusionary (e.g., Marx's mockery of the Social Democrats' platform of a classless education).

Around the turn of the 20th century, utopianism entered the vocabulary of historians to characterize recurrent trends, typically misunderstood as fanciful, that in fact contained the seeds of progress. Gustav Landauer recognized the revolutionary potential of *Utopien* to overthrow historically retarding periods of *Topien*, an insight that anticipated Mannheim's distinction between utopia and ideology. The terrors of the two world wars and the fearful totalitarian regimes around the world, modeled in part on utopian social engineering, led to almost universal censure of utopianism. Ernst Bloch's insistence, however, on a positive, "concrete" utopia, as opposed to the "abstract" (ideological) utopia, did much to rehabilitate utopia as a legitimate and humane approach to social progress. Bloch's concrete utopia (also called "hope") begins with the most intimate aspirations of individuals for a better world but recognizes the necessity of working within and through present realities. Other thinkers are less sanguine. Theodor Adorno finds aesthetic utopian moments or fragments buried here and there, such as in music, and Gert Ueding identifies literature as the chief carrier of a redemptive utopianism. Some postmodern social theorists see in the "utopia of an ideal communication community" (Habermas) a measure of our alienation from this standard and a sign that human striving has led not to utopia but to dystopia, its opposite.

MAX REINHART

Further Reading

Bloch, Ernst, *Geist der Utopie*, Munich: Duncker and Humblot, 1918; 2nd edition, Berlin: Cassirer, 1923; reprint, Frankfurt: Suhrkamp, 1973

———, *Das Prinzip Hoffnung*, 3 vols., Berlin: Aufbau-Verlag, 1953–54; as *The Principle of Hope*, 3 vols., translated by Neville Plaice et al., Oxford: Blackwell, and Cambridge, Massachusetts: MIT Press, 1986

Davis, J.C., "Utopianism," in *The Cambridge History of Political Thought 1450–1700*, edited by J.H. Burns and Mark Goldie, Cambridge and New York: Cambridge University Press, 1991

Habermas, Jürgen, *Theorie des kommunikativen Handelns*, Frankfurt: Suhrkamp, 1981; as *The Theory of Communicative Action*, translated by Thomas McCarthy, Boston: Beacon Press, and London: Heinemann, 1984

Hölscher, Lucian, "Utopie," in *Geschichtliche Grundbegriffe*, edited by Otto Brunner et al., Stuttgart: Klett, 1972–97

Kumar, Krishan, *Utopia and Anti-Utopia in Modern Times*, Oxford: Blackwell, 1986; New York: Blackwell, 1987

Levitas, Ruth, *The Concept of Utopia*, Syracuse, New York: Syracuse University Press, and London: Allan, 1990

Liebersohn, Harry, *Fate and Utopia in German Sociology, 1870–1923*, Cambridge, Massachusetts: MIT Press, 1988

Mannheim, Karl, *Ideologie und Utopie*, Bonn: Cohen, 1929; 8th edition, Frankfurt: Klostermann, 1995; translated by Louis Wirth and Edward Shils, London: Paul, Trench, Trubner, and New York: Harcourt, Brace, 1936; new edition, San Diego, California: Harcourt Brace Jovanovich, 1985

Marcuse, Herbert, *Das Ende der Utopie*, Berlin: Maikowski, 1967

Pippen, Robert B., et al., *Marcuse: Critical Theory and the Promise of Utopia*, South Hadley, Massachusetts: Bergin and Garvey, and Houndmills, Basingstoke, Hampshire: Macmillan, 1988

Pizer, John, "Jameson's *Adorno*, or, the Persistence of the Utopian," in *New German Critique* 58 (1993)

Ricoeur, Paul, *Lectures on Ideology and Utopia*, edited by George H. Taylor, New York: Columbia University Press, 1986

Siebers, Tobin, editor, *Heterotopia: Postmodern Utopia and the Body Politic*, Ann Arbor: University of Michigan Press, 1994

Stockinger, Ludwig, *Ficta Respublica: Gattungsgeschichtliche Untersuchungen zur utopischen Erzählung in der deutschen Literatur des frühen 18. Jahrhunderts*, Tübingen: Niemeyer, 1981

Ueding, Gert, *Literatur ist Utopie*, Frankfurt: Suhrkamp, 1978

Voßkamp, Wilhelm, editor, *Utopieforschung: Interdisziplinäre Studien zur neuzeitlichen Utopie*, 3 vols., Stuttgart: Metzler, 1982

Winter, Michael, "Staatstheorien und Utopien," in *Zwischen Gegenreformation und Frühaufklärung: Späthumanismus, Barock 1572–1740*, edited by Harald Steinhagen, Reinbek bei Hamburg: Rowohlt, 1985

V

Karl Valentin 1882–1948

Previously ignored by most German studies literary reference works, Bavarian Karl Valentin is increasingly recognized as a unique comic writer-performer, whose multimedia artistry elevated him beyond the Munich *Volkssänger* milieu from which he emerged at the turn of the century. Appearing initially on the *Kleinkabarettbühne* pub-cabaret stage as a stand-up comedian, he also pioneered the silent screen in Germany with early performances such as his 1912 *Bayerischer Landgendarm*—a Bavarian equivalent of the "keystone cop"—and was billed as Germany's Charlie Chaplin. "Valentiniaden" (performances of his own material) also were featured regularly in radio broadcasts during the 1930s. In this period, many filmed versions of *Szenen* were also produced, and Valentin appeared in several full-length films, but unlike his rival *Volkshumorist* Weiß Ferdl, he was never won over to the Nazi cause despite attempts to woo him. Valentin's scripts were also published regularly.

Valentin's dexterous physical slapstick reflects his preoccupation with *die Tücke des Objekts* (things that have a will of their own), and his linguistic acrobatics, which often defy translation, also display the scurrilous brooding humor of vaudeville and film star W.C. Fields. Valentin's sideways view of the world (*vertrackte Logik*) and his long gangling physique, accentuated by elongated boots and false nose, contributed to comic stage performances that were applauded by contemporaries such as Bertolt Brecht, Kurt Tucholsky, and Thomas Mann and by audiences extending beyond local boundaries during his guest appearances, among others, at the prestigious Berlin KaDeKo (*Kabaret der Komiker*). The essence of Valentin's electrifying stage presence was also captured exquisitely in Lion Feuchtwanger's 1930 novel *Erfolg* (*Success*), set in Munich, in which he portrays a cabaret performance of *Der Komiker Hierl und sein Volk* (The Comedian Hierl and His Audience); the performer is clearly recognizable as Valentin.

Teaming up in 1913 with comedienne Liesl Karlstadt, the perfect foil, Valentin developed a repertoire of monologues, dialogues, and sketches in a partnership akin to that of American contemporaries Laurel and Hardy; one was unthinkable without the other. Many sketches such as the 1934 *Der Firmling* (Candidate for Confirmation) and the 1936 *Die Erbschaft* (The Inheritance) focused on working-class impoverishment and are rightly regarded as social satires. Interspersed with *Pointen* (stinging punch lines), they also reflect Valentin's preoccupation with the inherently ambiguous nature of communication per se (and the resultant potential for conflict). Valentin's drunken war veteran in *Der Firmling*, for example, senses the reluctance of the snooty waiter in the *feines Weinlokal* (posh restaurant) to serve him and his son Pepperl. In the communication "duel" that ensues, however, the veteran triumphs during the confusion over the phrase "einfache Doppelportion für zwei" (a single double portion for two). In the 1940 telephone conversation *Buchbinder Wanninger* (Bookbinder Wanninger), however, the simple craftsman's inability to articulate suggests an individual powerless against a faceless corporate communication hierarchy. His unsuccessful bid to elicit payment for services rendered ends in linguistic frustration—"Saubande! Dreckade!" (Bastards! Scum of the earth!).

Valentin's professional life spanned four periods: the Wilhelmine era, the Weimar era, the Nazi dictatorship, and the *Aufbau* period of reconstruction after the end of World War II. With the Reichssender München, he recorded a substantial number of radio broadcasts, which avoided the sycophancy of politically correct humor otherwise required by a politically aligned cultural world. His 1926 *Zwangsvorstellungen* (Compelling Performances), for example, republished during the Nazi period, considers tongue-in-cheek the merits of enforced theater attendance, while in the 1938 monologue *Vereinsrede* (Club Speech), he satirizes political speech making of the day in a delivery reminiscent of Goebbels. Surprisingly, this thinly veiled attack on the Nazi party (referred to by Valentin as the "club") escaped the censor.

Valentin was unwilling to be pressed into the service of the Nazi regime, however, and by 1941, his days as a *Kulturschaffender* ("approved" artist) were numbered. He lived his final years under the U.S. occupation of southern Germany, and he then returned sporadically to radio broadcasting, having received his *Persilschein* (certification of non-Nazi allegiance). Postwar *Radio München* scripts such as the 1946 *Der ewige Friede; oder, Zwei Frauen über die Atombombe* (Eternal Peace; or, Two Women on the Atomic Bomb), the 1946 *Kalorienmangel/Das Nichts* (Calorie Deficit/The Void), and the 1947 *Vater und Sohn über den Krieg* (Father and Son on War) point convincingly to Valentin's growing politicization. Black humor in response to the grim *Stunde Null* (Zero Hour) aftermath of defeat appears to have been unacceptable to listeners reluctant to examine the past (*Vergangenheitsbewältigung*). Poor audience ratings and programming policy led to a return to his *Kleinkabarettbühne* origins and to "safe" material. Commercial exploitation of his work after his death reflected similar "sanitizing" of his work.

Very much a cult figure in Germany in recent years, his influence on contemporary performers is exemplified by 1970s humorist Loriot's *Die Nudelkrise* (The Noodle Crisis), which employs techniques similar to Valentin's to attack political rhetoric. Valentin's 40-odd films continue to run in repertoire cinemas and have been presented by the London National Film Theatre. His work has also been staged by English, French, and Italian theater companies. Academic recognition has increased since the 1970s, and a major retrospective exhibition was mounted by the Münchner Stadtmuseum in 1982, the centenary year of his birth. Although research has been hampered by continued legal restrictions surrounding Valentin's *Nachlass* (literary estate), published and unpublished works have been brought together in a recent eight-volume edition by Bachmaier and Faust. Recordings previously released as LPs are now being reissued as CDs.

MURRAY HILL

See also Cabaret; Munich

Biography

Born in Munich, 4 June 1882. Trained as a *Salonhumorist* (stand-up comedian) at the *Varietéschule*, Munich; performed on the Munich *Gaststätte*/variety hall circuit, later in more discriminating cabarets; partnership with Liesl Karlstadt, from 1913; early involvement in film and radio broadcasting, substantial commercial sound recordings, and footage of *Valentiniaden* (performances of his own material) produced; his satirical observations became increasingly politicized, and he was a victim of *Gleichschaltung* under the Nazis; his black humor during the post–World War II American occupation was at odds with broadcasting policies; returned to the Munich cabaret with resounding success. Died in Planegg, 9 February 1948.

Selected Works

Collections

Original-Vorträge von Karl Valentin, 1918–20
Allerlei Blödsinn: Original Vorträge, 1919
Karl Valentin: Original Vorträge, 1926
Brilliantfeuerwerk, 1938
Valentiniaden, 1940
Karl Valentins Lachkabinett [Munich edition], edited by Gerhard Pallmann, 1950
Karl Valentins Panoptikum [Munich edition], edited by Gerhard Pallmann, 1952
Alles von Karl Valentin [Munich edition], edited by Michael Schulte, 1978

Sämtliche Werke [Munich edition], 8 vols., edited by Helmut Bachmaier and Manfred Faust, 1995–98

Recordings

Karl Valentin: Die alten Rittersleut, Teldec, 1962
Karl Valentin-Liesl Karlstadt, Polydor, 1965
Karl Valentin: Das große Erinnerungsalbum, Teldec, 1972; Bogner, 1998
Unvergessen: Karl Valentin und Liesl Karlstadt, Ariola, 1974
Karl Valentin und Liesl Karlstadt: Die alte Welle, Ariola, 1977
Karl Valentin: Sein unvollständiges Gesamtwerk mit und ohne Liesl Karlstadt, Ariola, 1982
Karl Valentins Lachmusäum, Ariola, 1987
Karl Valentin: Geschichten aus der Nachkriegszeit, Hörverlag, 1995
Werkausgabe, TR-Verlagsunion, 1997–98

Films

Der neue Schreibtisch, 1913
Der Sonderling, 1929
Die verkaufte Braut. Im Photoatelier, Orchesterprobe, 1932
Der Theaterbesuch. Im Schallplattenladen, der verhexte Scheinwerfer, So ein Theater, Der Firmling, Der Zithervirtuose, 1934
Kirschen in Nachbarsgarten, 1935
Musik zu zweien. Ein verhängnisvolles Geigensolo. Donner, Blitz und Sonnenschein, Die Erbschaft, 1936

Further Reading

Appignanesi, Lisa, *The Cabaret*, London: Studio Vista, 1975; New York: Universe Books, 1976; revised edition, New York: Grove Press, 1984
Bauer, Richard, and Christoph Stölzl, editors, *Karl Valentin: Volkssänger? DADAist?* Munich: Wolf, 1982
Hill, Murray, "Thinking Sideways: Language, Object, and Karl Valentin (1882–1948)," *New German Studies* 8 (1980)
———, "'Mit Original-Vorträgen, Soli und Gesang': Some Notes on Karl Valentin," *New German Studies* 10 (1982)
———, "Interpretations and Misinterpretations of Karl Valentin (1882–1948)," Ph.D. dissertation, Stirling University, 1983
———, "Karl Valentin in the Third Reich: No Laughing Matter," *German Life and Letters* 36 (1983)
Keller, Roland, *Karl Valentin und seine Filme*, Munich: Heyne, 1996
Pemsel, Klaus, *Karl Valentin im Umfeld der Münchner Volksbühnen und Varietés*, Munich: Wilhelm Unverhau, 1981
Sackett, Robert Eben, *Popular Entertainment, Class, and Politics in Munich, 1900–1923*, Cambridge, Massachusetts: Harvard University Press, 1982
Schulte, Michael, *Karl Valentin*, Reinbek bei Hamburg: Rowohlt, 1968
———, *Karl Valentin: Eine Biographie*, Munich: Piper, 1998
Schulte, Michael, and Peter Syr, editors, *Karl Valentins Filme*, Munich and Zurich: Piper, 1978; 2nd edition, 1989
Schwimmer, Helmut, *Karl Valentin: Eine Analyse seines Werks mit einem Curriculum und Modellen für den Deutschunterricht*, Munich: Oldenbourg, 1977

Rahel Levin Varnhagen 1771–1833

What is perhaps most astonishing about Rahel Levin Varnhagen is her creation of a new practice of writing. She was not the only woman who concentrated on epistolary writing; but from the outset she was aware of the particular implications of letter writing and worked to establish a network of people who would self-consciously engage in this as a common enterprise. In contrast to the notions of authorship that appeared in Europe around 1800, which anchored writing in the exceptional individual, here a heterogeneous group of people was producing something together. And yet a break with established genres always brings its own risks. Authors who write books can be relatively confident that their work will be preserved in libraries. Those who write letters, on the other hand, are prey to all the vicissitudes of their dispersal. Sooner or later, letters tend to get lost. A historical vulnerability is built into the form, and so Varnhagen had to develop a strategy that prevented these texts from disappearing. Already in her early 20s she collected and kept all the letters that she received. Before she left for Paris in 1800, she asked a friend not only to tend to this collection, should she die, but also to try to retrieve from their various addressees all the letters that she had herself written. This is a sign of how extremely seriously she took this particular form of writing and collecting.

Her new strategy forced her to confront another problem, since she wanted to preserve all this ephemeral material but was also concerned with publishing it. As early as 1812, she began a long series of epistolary publications in different journals, following two contradictory organizational principles. The first project was a dialogue in which she was engaged together with the man she would later marry, Karl August Varnhagen. From their correspondence, they selected those remarks that concerned the poet Goethe's work, and these they arranged as a montage. Later publications show a different structure: in these, it is only Rahel Levin Varnhagen who talks. The replies are not part of the printed dialog.

Another ambitious enterprise undertaken by the couple would wait for publication until a few months after Rahel Varnhagen's death—*Rahel: Ein Buch des Andenkens für ihre Freunde* (1834; Rahel: A Commemoration for her friends). In the summer of 1833, Karl August Varnhagen published a one-volume edition; a year later he had collected so many of his late wife's letters that he was able to expand the edition into three volumes. In 1836, Karl August Varhagen also brought to print a collection of letters to his wife. But the Varnhagens also had edited Rahel's correspondences: during Rahel's lifetime her letters to and from David Veit, Alexander von der Marwitz, and Rebecca Friedländer were prepared for publication. Thus, many books were planned, and only some of them would appear during the second half of the 19th century. But the *Sammlung Varnhagen,* the collection of manuscripts Rahel Levin Varnhagen had started as a young woman, contains much more, including letters from famous countesses, her unknown cook, important politicians, and unestablished writers. She was in contact with more than 300 people, and her archive contains about 6,000 letters. Everybody is found there: actresses and philosophers, acculturated Jewish women, and young intellectuals. We also find diaries, not written in the style of a journal, but rather *Denktagebücher,* or "diaries of thought," and—last but not least—another expanded version of the *Buch des Andenkens* in a manuscript of almost 5,000 pages. This archive could be seen as Varnhagen's "work," but how does one read an archive?

What we find in these letters and aphorisms is as exiting as the story of their creation and transmission. Varnhagen thought in a way that cannot be easily integrated into given genre categories. It is clear that she was never drawn to narrative or poetic writing. Hers was a special kind of thinking that did not move within disciplinary boundaries and established fields of knowledge. "I do not have a stored up stock of thoughts," she once wrote. A special moment, a conversation, a book, or anything else might serve as the source of her productivity. And so she developed an entire world of insights into philosophy and music, literature, and politics. Since what was relevant to her was not the results of thinking, but the movement of thoughts, her friendships and convivial gatherings were of greatest importance to her. Both were seen as political and philosophical enterprises.

Rahel Levin Varnhagen was the first Jewish woman to establish herself as an important intellectual and political figure in a German culture dominated by Christianity. She used her excluded status as a chance: "One is not free if one must represent something in the bourgeois society, a spouse, the wife of a civil servant etc." she wrote to Pauline Wiesel, also an outcast, but for different reasons.

Only recently has this unusual "work" been understood to have theoretical relevance. In former times it was biography that kept her name alive. Letters were felt to come directly from the heart of the writer, and only biography seemed to be able to arrange the fragments of letters and those of a life into a whole. This is why the theoretical richness of Rahel Levin Varnhagen's "work" still awaits discovery. But for new ways of reading, one also will need new ways of editing this writing: annotated editions can show the complex network she has woven. The Edition Rahel Levin Varnhagen follows the structure of the archive, and even when Varnhagen's letters have not survived, it presents exclusively the dialogic form.

Barbara Hahn

See also Salons

Biography
Born in Berlin, 19 May 1771. Acquaintance with Dorothea Schlegel and Alexander and Wilhelm von Humboldt in the 1790s; met Goethe in Karlsbad, 1795; travel to Paris, 1800–1801; first publication of her letters, 1812; married a diplomat and lived in Vienna, Frankfurt, and Karlsruhe; due to her husband's loss of his diplomatic post and for political reasons, returned to Berlin, 1819; met Heine and Hegel. Died in Berlin, 7 March 1833.

Selected Works

Collections of Letters
Rahel: Ein Buch des Andenkens für ihre Freunde, edited by Karl August Varnhagen, 4 vols., 1833–34
Galerie von Bildnissen aus Rahel's Umgang und Briefwechsel, edited by Karl August Varnhagen, 2 vols., 1836
Briefwechsel zwischen Rahel und David Veit, edited by Ludmilla Assing, 2 vols., 1861

Briefwechsel zwischen Varnhagen und Rahel, edited by Ludmilla Assing, 6 vols., 1874–75

Aus Rahel's Herzensleben: Briefe und Tagebuchblätter, edited by Ludmilla Assing, 1877

Rahel und Alexander von der Marwitz in ihren Briefen: Ein Bild aus der Zeit der Romantiker, edited by Heinrich Meissner, 1925

Rahel-Bibliothek. Rahel Varnhagen. Gesammelte Werke, edited by Konrad Feilchenfeldt et al., 10 vols., 1983

Rahels erste Liebe: Rahel Levin und Karl Graf von Finckenstein in ihren Briefen, edited by Günter de Bruyn, 1985

Briefe an eine Freundin: Rahel Varnhagen an Rebecca Friedländer, edited by Deborah Hertz, 1988

Edition Rahel Levin Varnhagen, edited by Barbara Hahn and Ursula Isselstein, 6 vols., 1997–

Further Reading

Arendt, Hannah, *Rahel Varnhagen: The Life of a Jewess,* translated by Richard and Clara Winston, edited by Liliane Weissberg, Baltimore, Maryland and London: Johns Hopkins University Press, 1997

Hahn, Barbara, *"Antworten Sie mir": Rahel Levin Varnhagens Briefwechsel,* Basel: Stroemfeld/Roter Stern, 1990

Isselstein, Ursula, *Studien zu Rahel Levin Varnhagen: Der Text aus meinem beleidigten Herzen,* Torino: Tirrenia, 1993

Tewarson, Heidi Thomann, *Rahel Varnhagen: The Life and Work of a German Jewish Intellectual,* Lincoln: University of Nebraska Press, 1998

Veldeke, Heinrich von, *see* Heinrich von Veldeke

Vienna

Vienna (with slightly over 1.6 million inhabitants, including some 100,000 foreign workers) is the capital of Austria and home to 20 percent of the country's population. The city is both the republic's smallest federal state (Bundesland)—its mayor serves also in the capacity of governor (Landeshauptmann)—and an independent community with its own statutes. It is administered by a *Stadtsenat* (a mayor, two vice mayors, and 14 councilmen), which is elected by a Council (Gemeinderat) of 100 members. Such facts by themselves suggest that Vienna, which is divided now into 23 districts (Gemeindebezirke), is the center of Austria's government services. In 1979, Vienna gained worldwide prominence as the third United Nations Organization City (after New York and Geneva). Four glass towers with a large convention complex and a new business/residential area—outside of the historic part of town but in close enough proximity for all to see—highlight the city's more recent distinction as a venue for international conferences. It is a recognition, however, that was acquired at some cost to Austrian pride in the cohesion of Vienna's architectural beauty. For what defines the city's self-image are the traditions of her imperial past, of which a very few survive as an active element of public life. Most of these traditions have instead been transfigured by nostalgic idealizations—a visible and often spectacularly imposing heritage that is preserved, most notably, in more than 60 museums and other cultural institutions.

There is, of course, nothing typically Austrian in this tendency to look for reassurance to a cultural past that is both distant and near enough to encourage its very selective memorialization. But the success of such restorative conservatism was virtually inevitable in an impoverished country and in its only metropolitan center—Vienna had been Europe's fourth largest city in 1910—after both had been severely diminished by the terms of the Peace Treaty of Trianon (1918) and, following the *Staatsvertrag* (State Treaty) of 1955, were eager to accommodate to the status of formal neutrality. Especially the rebuilding of Vienna after the extensive destructions of 1944–45 and, later, the very cautious modernization of the inner city were designed to suggest an unbroken continuity, one that connects the present "modern" city with the era of its most impressive grandeur at the end of the 19th century. Such adherence to historical precept and to the return of the past as visible presence gave expression to the nation's old/new self-invented mission, that of being a mediator between cultures, religions, social ideologies, and military ambitions. It invoked a revival of the traditional *humanitas Austriaca,* after the lamentable aberration of Nazism, to serve again as a cultured and gently equalizing force in the heart of *Mitteleuropa,* practicing tolerance and avoiding all extremes.

The complementary suspicion of anything radical or even just markedly different and inventive (and the attendant pleasure at its recognition abroad) has riled Vienna's critics throughout at least its more recent history. They have come to see their city more and more as an oversized archive, if not as a labyrinth of evasions, suggestive silences, smooth reparations, and self-perpetuating palaver that is all sentimental, superficial, and thus condemned to a mediocrity that seeks refuge in heavily subsidized cultural festivals (the annual *Wiener Festwochen* in May/June, for example). Meanwhile, the city cannot support a newspaper of more than regional importance. Tourists from Europe and overseas, however, have made Vienna a favorite destination, due also, no doubt, to both the absence of large

concentrations of old industry even in the poorer outlying suburbs and the preponderance of beautiful parks and woods and,
in general, a variously pleasant countryside.

The beginnings of Vienna's modern history go back to the late
17th century. Before that, the city, although it had been the principal residence of the Habsburgs since 1276, was little more than
a heavily fortified administrative and military outpost on the
Empire's eastern frontier. It was only after the defeat of a huge
Turkish army in 1683 by forces under Rüdiger von Starnhem-
berg, who repelled a siege of two months with the help of German and Polish troops, that this situation changed significantly.
Most of Hungary and, between 1718 and 1739, large territories
in the Balkans (including the northern parts of Bosnia and Ser-
bia, with Belgrade) were now added to Habsburg control. This
offset serious losses in the West, which, during the next 50 years,
removed Austria from its traditional sphere of influence: Charles
VI, in 1714, was forced to relinquish his Iberian possessions and,
in 1735, Sicily and Naples to the Spanish Bourbons; Maria
Theresia (1740–80) had to cede, in 1748, the dukedoms of
Parma and Piacenza to them; and, in 1763, most of the prosperous province of Silesia went to her Prussian rival Frederick II
(1740–86) after the Seven Years' War. Austria's subsequent com-
pensations were disproportionate: Galicia after the First Polish
Partition of 1772 and the Bukovina in 1775.

Relief from the Turkish threat consolidated the political
power of the ruling dynasty, who had been Holy Roman Emperors since 1558; it also reinforced the influence of the prominent
aristocratic families through their control of the city's commercial expansion and their ambitious building program. The
grandiose Baroque palaces of the Lobkowitzes, Liechtensteins,
Batthyany-Schönborns, Daun-Kinskys, and the Schwarzenbergs
opened the formerly cramped confines of the historical center
and came to dominate its new appearance, none more lavishly
than the Baroque *Stadtpalais* (built by J.B. Fischer von Erlach)
and the Belvedere Palace (by J.L. von Hildebrandt, 1713–23) of
Eugene, Prince of Savoy-Carignan (1663–1736), from 1707 the
Imperial Field Marshal. After his successes against the Turks,
Eugene became a generous patron of the arts and sciences who
corresponded with Leibniz, Voltaire, and Montesquieu, among
many others, and who assembled a highly respected library. His
personal wealth appears to have exceeded that of the imperial
family whose construction of a summer residence at Schönbrunn
(1696–1711, after designs by Fischer von Erlach and with various changes and additions until 1780), proved to be ruinous.
Such activities, including the more humble proceedings of the
Academy of Arts (founded in 1707), were solely for the benefit
of the ruling elite, the feudal absolutists, who, by the middle of
the century, conversed and preferred their opera performances to
be in Italian and French, used Latin in their dealings with the
Church and the Hungarians, and conducted business in Greek,
Italian, French, Yiddish, and German (they wrote the last with a
very liberal admixture of foreign terms). To protect the "native"
idiom, Joseph II, co-regent from 1765, reform-minded, and intent on using his bureaucracy as the vanguard of administrative
efficiency, had to decree, in 1776, that at least the performances
of the Court Theater had to be given in German.

Of course, none of this was of immediate consequence to the
rest of Vienna's population, now numbering close to 200,000.
The populace did share, however, a predilection for theatrical
shows. The most popular show was a distinctive type of comedy
that had stock characters borrowed from the commedia dell'arte
and that was fond of improvisations; it also included pantomime
as well as musical and ballet numbers, magic and other illusions,
and, often, fanciful mythological and fairy-tale stories. The origin of this Viennese *Volkstheater* can be traced to 1712, when
J.A. Stranitzky bought a hall at the Kärntnertor (Carinthian
Gate) and made it a permanent theater for troupes of actors and
entertainers. The language in which these plays mixed sentiment
with hilarity, usually around underdog figures such as Hanswurst, Kasperl, or Bernadon, was the local dialect, and it was
employed most effectively in scenarios of, for example, A.
Bäuerle, J.A. Gleich, and K. Meisl. The potential of these performances for political subversion and aggressive satire, although
more suspected by government censors than practiced on stage,
nonetheless resulted, in 1752, in a prohibition of speaking ex-
temporaneously on stage, and this ban was renewed several
times until 1854. By then, the refined conversational idiom of
the Viennese bourgeoisie and aristocracy ("Schönbrunnerisch")
had taken over, replacing the cruder and more drastic effects of
dialect, although not at the expense of ridiculing allusions to the
foibles of the high and mighty.

Vienna (and virtually all of Austria) had been reconverted to
Catholicism during the Jesuit Counter Reformation under
Leopold I (1658–1705), which was a rigorously determined
process that included the especially harsh suppression of Protestantism in Hungary and the expulsion of all Jews from Vienna in
1670. In 1740, only 12 Jewish families were allowed to live regularly within the city walls. In 1780, their number increased to
53; ten years later, although they were restricted for the next
quarter of a century by some 600 regulations issued from the
State Chancellor's office, a total of 840 Jewish individuals
resided in Vienna. Most of them were rich. The *Toleranzpatent*
of Joseph II, signed in 1781 to offer legal protection and the benefits of at least partial emancipation, proved to be of some efficacy for Vienna's cultural life. There were a very small number
of intellectually prominent Jews, among them Joseph von Son-
nenfels (1732–1817), the grandson of a Grand Rabbi in Berlin
and the guiding light of the "Wiener Deutsche Gesellschaft," and
Fanny von Arnstein (1758–1818), an intelligent Prussophile
whose salon was a major attraction during the Congress of Vienna, even though her political preferences irked many of her
competitors. She was a knowledgeable patron of the arts, especially of music, a generous philanthropist, and the hostess of
many intellectuals, a role in which her daughter Henriette
Pereira-Arnstein also excelled. But contacts between Jews and
Christians were almost always private and did not extend beyond the small circles of the very prosperous merchants and
bankers, the social leaders of the high bourgeoisie.

While Vienna, around 1800, was the center of Europe's musical culture, it did not have a distinctive literary life or a truly
progressive intellectual atmosphere. To be sure, the official policy of promoting the ideals of the Enlightenment was systematically enforced by administrative decree in the Austro-Bohemian
Erblande, the dynasty's hereditary domains. But it was strongly
resisted in Hungary and elsewhere. And while it produced some
beneficial results, any expression of critical independence was
quickly destroyed by the massive intervention of the censors,
whose authority was upheld by official fears of revolutionary
upheavals. Their power was quickly expanded when Austria suffered a series of disastrous defeats at the hands of Napoleon.

Even minimal expressions of dissent were stifled with increasing ruthlessness from 1810 until 1848, when Metternich served as chancellor. As early as 1814, Vienna's police chief Count Sedlnitzky could boast that the city has been sealed off from the rest of Europe behind a "Chinese wall" of supervision and repressions. The Congress that in 1814–15 restored the continent to the principles of dynastic legitimacy and returned the old ruling elites to their hereditary privileges had no reason whatsoever to be apprehensive about signs and arguments that might indicate political dissatisfaction. The grand assemblage of diplomats and their entourage could pursue their business in an atmosphere of festive elegance and of military as well as theatrical spectacles.

At the same time, the court under Francis II (1792–1835; but from 1806 ruling just as Francis I of Austria, and thus without the Habsburgs' universal claim) made an effort to propagate the virtues of petit-bourgeois respectability and even of folksy homeliness. This was meant to vindicate a traditionalist sense of national identity that emphasized regional and ethnic distinctiveness rather than a reliance on the unifying potential of political freedom, economic success, and cultural prestige. Vienna, in fact, had become the last major refuge for conservative Romantics whose search for a transcendent order, spiritual wholeness, and traditional values found congenial reassurances in the culture of an urbane Catholic organicism. Encounters with the realities of modern secularism that proved to be unavoidable produced a retrospective and mostly evasive literature, one of forced conciliations and sentimental appeals. Only in its most subtle and most precariously self-conscious examples—in the mature works of Franz Grillparzer (1791–1872) and Adalbert Stifter (1805–68)—was this longing for harmony and compensatory sublimations countered by the disorienting recognition that all life is profoundly unstable and constantly fluctuating, and that literature should be an uncompromising engagement as much with destructive psychological impulses as with the hostile forces in nature, society, and history. Where this confrontation did take place, it engendered writing of the highest refinement in apparently conventional modes, and in a style that gains its persuasive impact from the nuanced interplay and unobtrusive tensions of ultimately irremediable contradictions.

But this blending of traditional aesthetic principles and an acutely modern consciousness, which locates these writers' work at the cusp of epochal changes, went largely unappreciated in its time. Most readers preferred a straightforward and descriptive realism with a slightly melancholy but ultimately optimistic attitude. To use poetry for the propagation of political viewpoints was considered almost blasphemous: a collection such as Anastasius Grün's *Spaziergänge eines Wiener Poeten* (Strolls of a Viennese Poet), published anonymously in 1831, and the weekly *Sonntagsblätter für heimatliche Interessen* (Sunday Pages for our Country's Interests), edited by Ludwig August Frankl from 1842 and for a decade the only lively organ of political debate in Vienna, were remarkable more as local exceptions and did not have much international stature.

Virtually all discussions of political and artistic issues had to be kept private; they took place in the drawing rooms of the bourgeoisie or in coffeehouses. The *Kaffeehaus* especially, offering the intimate comforts of home without its distractions, served as the appropriate venue where artists, writers, journalists ("the maladjusted and dissatisfied *raisonneurs*, life's misfits"),

and politicians and businesspeople met to further their professional contacts and interests and to find intellectual stimulation. Its relaxed atmosphere encouraged deliberative and witty conversations rather than the more boisterous attitudes seen at fraternal associations or political clubs. No coffeehouse habitué, most definitely not the daily guests (*Stammgäste*), was obligated to consume more than suited his need to see and be seen; a large selection of newspapers and journals was available, usually also a billiard room. Discreet familiarity and observant skepticism prevailed, as did a courteous demeanor that was never free of jealousy and *médisance* (slander) but more often provided the pleasures of amiable companionship rather than those of controversy. The German expressionist Karl Otten stated, with customary pathos, that the coffeehouse was for his generation what the Athenian agora had meant for Socrates. The Viennese feuilleton writer Alfred Polgar, perhaps more perceptively, saw it "as a kind of organization for the disorganized" who experienced it as the only place in their lives "where 'people without a center of gravity' are able to live . . . and where no one, therefore, need fear to be bested by somebody else's weight," and where one could espouse "any *Weltanschauung* without first taking a good look at the world."

For 50 years, from 1847 until its demolition in 1897, the most prominent among these cultural market places was the Café Griensteidl, prestigiously located in the old Palais Herberstein, which was around the corner from the imperial residences. Nearly every Viennese writer with whatever claim to distinction at one time or the other made it his public home: from Grillparzer and Heinrich Laube (1806–84), the playwright and, from 1849 until 1867, the director of the *Hofburgtheater* (court theaters), to the "Young Vienna" group of the 1890s (comprising such diverse talents as Hermann Bahr, Arthur Schnitzler, Richard Beer-Hofmann, Felix Salten, Ferdinand von Baumgarten, Viktor Leon, Ferry Beraton, and Hugo von Hofmannsthal), whose doings the critic Karl Kraus, himself a regular visitor there, lampooned in a satirical piece of 1896 titled "Die demolierte Literatur" (Demolished Literature). Griensteidl's successor, until 1918, as the preferred "Schriftstellerschwemme" (writers' watering place) was Café Central and, during the interwar years, Café Herrenhof (which Musil, Broch, Werfel, and J. Roth frequented). Journalists met at the Rebhuhn and at haunts such as the Colosseum, the Museum, or the Moser.

It is symptomatic that in other countries of continental Europe, the epithet "young" (as in *la jeune France, la giovane Italia, das Junge Deutschland*) had attached itself to movements of politically radicalized writers, including journalists and social theorists, who drew their inspiration and rhetoric from the revolution of July 1830 in France. "Young Vienna," on the contrary, is associated with the modernist attitudes of fin de siècle authors whom popular estimation, if it took cognizance of them at all, identified with decadent immoralism, artificiality, and the elitist postures of a highly idiosyncratic subjectivity. They appeared to be an anachronism and an anomaly even in their youth, cultivating an aura of worldly-wise resignation and ostensibly avoiding engagements with "social questions," especially with the many problems that beset industrial mass societies. And this was at a time when bourgeois Vienna had attained its greatest prosperity. And, indeed, Viennese high culture during its culmination around 1900, and its literature in particular, which had not gone through a naturalist phase and did not subsequently contribute significantly to the experimental upheavals of Expressionism, was an often precarious response to barely acknowledged societal contradictions, to a sense of accelerating decline and disorientation—without naming any contemporary facts and factors directly.

The ultimate cause of this intellectual malaise may be found in the realization, vaguely felt and hardly ever confronted head-on, that Vienna itself had become a glorious anachronism, the site of a "joyous apocalypse." The traumatic shock of 30 October 1848, when masses of bourgeois revolutionaries surrendered only after a bombardment of the inner city, was an abiding reminder of the need for drastic reforms. Instead of such reforms, however, the court, especially during the centralist Era of Liberalism (1859–79), expanded the rituals of symbolic politics, while the municipality embarked on a spectacular construction program. The ten dominant buildings of the *Ringstrasse,* which, from 1857, replaced the inner city walls and include museums, the Parliament, City Hall, the Palace of Justice, and the University, are of grandiose dimensions and eclectically imitate Greek, Gothic, and Renaissance paradigms. The project, which was completed by the end of the golden era of the 1880s, further isolated the centers of power and government from the bourgeois populace of the suburbs. It also did nothing to alleviate a catastrophic shortage of affordable housing, a problem that remained unaddressed until the late 1920s, when "Red Vienna" was governed by an absolute majority of Social Democrats under mayor K. Seitz.

But the new boulevard, some three miles long and generously lined by avenues of trees, was a magnificent venue for grand parades, the citizens' way of participating in politics. Most noteworthy were those of 1879, arranged by the painter Hans Makart to celebrate the imperial couple's silver anniversary, and the Corpus Christi Procession of 1898, with the Christian Social Karl Lueger, mayor from 1895 until 1910, leading the way. His official appointment in 1897, which had been deferred twice by order of the emperor, Francis Joseph (1848–1916), came at a time when the conduct of national politics was mired in scandal and corruption and was paralyzed by a constitutional impasse over questions of regional prerogatives and the official status of German as a language. Lueger, by contrast, presided over an efficient and socially minded municipal administration. But his party also knew how to exploit an often virulent anti-Semitism that pitted its own "healthy folkish beliefs" against the "gout juif," as exemplified in the internationalist liberalism of the dominant newspapers (*Wiener Allgemeine Zeitung, Neue freie Presse, Die Zeit,* and *Neues Wiener Tagblatt*), and in the "degeneracy" of modernist intellectualism. Both "aberrations" were attributed to the "pernicious ubiquity" of Jews and the resultant ethnic and cultural imbalance: in 1900, 147,000 Jews lived in the inner districts among a total population of approximately 1,662,000, of whom 1,386,000 were of Austro-German descent, 103,000 were of Czech-Slovak descent, and 133,000 were of Hungarian descent.

In reality, the patronage of the wealthy Jewish banking and merchant families, while not ungenerous to innovative individualists, favored the established institutions of high culture: museums, orchestras, theaters, and the various reorientations in philosophy and the arts that took place beyond the interests of the general public. The public taste, by contrast, found its perfect expression in the music (some 140 waltzes and such operettas as *Die Fledermaus* of 1874 and *The Gypsy Baron* of 1885) of the younger Johann Strauss (1825–99) and his equally successful brother Eduard (1835–1916). The experiments of Arnold Schönberg with free atonality (since 1907), his 12-tone technique (after 1920), and its adaptations by Webern, Berg, Wellesz, and H. Eisler; Ernst Mach's empiriocritical philosophy of scientific cognition and the logical positivism of his disciples (the "Vienna Circle" around M. Schlick, R. Carnap, and K. Gödel); and the various trends in psychoanalysis (Krafft-Ebing, Freud and Breuer, A. Adler, and V.E. Frankl)—all these revolutionary breakthroughs of exceptional minds did fascinate and unsettle a few alert writers and thinkers, but in their time they were given little professional recognition and had no influence on the dominant culture.

The two decades between World War I and World War II, a time both of democratic reforms and, finally, of authoritarian rule under the Dollfussian mayor R. Schmitz (1934–38), may paradigmatically be characterized by two events that also had a significant impact on literature: the burning of the Palace of Justice by irate workers on 15 July 1927, and the uprising of the working-class Republican Protective League (11–16 February 1934), whose suppression by military forces was followed by a ban of all political parties, the constitutional establishment of Christian fascism, and (on 13 March 1938) Hitler's annexation of Austria, the *Anschluss.* The precarious social and intellectual life of this era informs the great epochal novel and its analytical companion piece, the philosophical essay, as represented by the compendious narratives of Musil, Broch, and Heimito von Doderer (1896–1966) and by such contradictory talents as Fritz von Herzmanovsky-Orlando (1877–1954), George Saiko (1892–1962), Franz Werfel, Joseph Roth, Karl Kraus, and Elias Canetti.

Postwar Vienna is the background for the film classic *The Third Man* (1949, Carol Reed), starring Orson Welles, which portrays the city in ruins and fraught with corruption. Analogous to the political situation, the film's hero is asked to turn in his former friend to authorities for conducting a black market business in rare pharmaceuticals, a practice that takes its toll on countless innocent victims. Vienna, adopting the myth of Austria's annexation, failed to turn in its war criminals and soon lapsed into historical amnesia. Not until the 1950 did signs of cultural production appear that broke with the consensus of silence. The avant-garde Wiener Gruppe, with its formal and Dadaist literary experiments, soon gave way to the more radical Wiener Aktionisten, who in performances staged victimization through body art involving bandaging and mutilation, thus drawing the public's attention by means of shock to its repressed history. Ingeborg Bachmann addressed the city's complicity and dubious remembrance in her story "Among Murderers and Madmen" (1961). In the 1960s, Vienna slowly regained its international standing through its painters (Fuchs, Hausner, Hutter, Brauer), known as the phantastic realists. Soon its literature followed by conquering the German book and international markets in the works of Ingeborg Bachmann, Thomas Bernhard, and Elfriede Jelinek. In film, the works of Valie Export and Michael Haneke, and in architecture, the work of Hans Hollein, have received international attention. In the 1990s, Vienna also witnessed a revival of Jewish literature in the works of Georg Tabori, Robert Menasse, Robert Schindel, Doron Rabonivici, and Elfriede Jelinek. With its massive restoration of public buildings, Vienna has of late also recovered its modern architectural tradition as found in the works of Otto Wagner, Adolf Loos, Max Fabiani, and Oskar Marmorek. Amid European integration and the opening of the Iron Curtain, Vienna is quickly becoming the multicultural metropolis that it was at the beginning of the 20th century.

MICHAEL WINKLER

See also Austria: Late Habsburg Literature in Vienna; Jung Wien

Further Reading
Bauer, Roger, *Die Welt als Reich Gottes: Grundlagen und Wandlungen einer österreichischen Lebensform*, Vienna: Europaverlag, 1974
Beller, Steven, *Vienna and the Jews, 1867–1938: A Cultural History*, Cambridge and New York: Cambridge University Press, 1989
Boyer, John W., *Culture and Political Crisis in Vienna: Christian Socialism in Power, 1897–1918*, Chicago: University of Chicago Press, 1995
Bridge, Francis R., *The Habsburg Monarchy among the Great Powers, 1815–1918*, New York: Berg, 1990
Broch, Hermann, *Hugo von Hofmannsthal and His Time: The European Imagination, 1860–1920*, edited and translated by Michael P. Steinberg, Chicago: University of Chicago Press, 1984
Bruckmüller, Ernst, *Sozialgeschichte Österreichs*, Vienna: Herold, 1985
Crankshaw, Edward, *Vienna: The Image of a Culture in Decline*, London: Macmillan, 1938
Hamann, Brigitte, *Hitler's Vienna: A Dictator's Apprenticeship*, translated by Thomas Thornton, New York: Oxford University Press, 1999
Janik, Allan, and Stephen Toulmin, *Wittgenstein's Vienna*, New York: Simon and Schuster, 1973
Johnston, William M., *The Austrian Mind: An Intellectual and Social History, 1848–1938*, Berkeley: University of California Press, 1972
Kann, Robert, *A Study in Austrian Intellectual History: From Late Baroque to Romanticism*, New York: Praeger, and London: Thames and Hudson, 1960
Macartney, Carlile Aylmer, *The Habsburg Empire, 1790–1918*, London: Weidenfeld and Nicholson, 1968; corrected edition, 1971
McCagg, William O., *A History of Habsburg Jews, 1670–1918*, Bloomington: Indiana University Press, 1989
McGrath, William J., *Dionysian Art and Populist Politics in Austria*, New Haven, Connecticut: Yale University Press, 1974
Rumpler, Helmut, *Eine Chance für Mitteleuropa: Bürgerliche Emanzipation und Staatsverfall in der Habsburgermonarchie*, Vienna: Ueberreuter, 1994
Schorske, Carl E., *Fin-de-Siècle Vienna: Politics and Culture*, New York: Knopf, 1980
Sedgwick, Henry Dwight, *Vienna: The Biography of a Bygone City*, Indianapolis, Indiana: Bobbs-Merrill, 1939
Wagner-Rieger, Renate, *Wiens Architektur im 19. Jahrhundert*, Vienna: Österreichischer Bundesverlag, 1970
Wagner-Rieger, Renate, editor, *Die Wiener Ringstrasse: Bild einer Epoche: Die Erweiterung der inneren Stadt Wien unter Kaiser Franz Joseph*, 8 vols., Vienna: Böhlau, 1969–81

Vogelweide, Walther von der, *see* Walther von der Vogelweide

Vormärz

The term *Vormärz* (meaning "pre-March" and referring to the March Revolution of 1848) is sometimes used by critics in preference to more generic, politically less focused terms such as *Restoration* or *Biedermeier* to denote the whole period from 1815 to 1848, or at least that from 1830 to 1848. For these critics, the anticipated revolution—with its failures and achievements, all of which have left an indelible mark on the subsequent course of German history—offers the focal point of the currents of the period. It represents the goal of the liberal strand represented by those close to the Young Germans (who may be regarded as the inheritors of the French July Revolution in 1830). The year 1848 was also a crisis point for the strong currents of German nationalism that had come clearly to the fore after the

Rhine crisis. The repressive machinery of the German states also means that the concept *Vormärz* must include the writers in exile in Paris, notably Heinrich Heine and Ludwig Börne. Other historians prefer to use the term to denote the period from 1840 to 1848. The Rhine crisis of 1840 has its monument in Nikolaus Becker's poem "Der deutsche Rhein" (1840; The German Rhine), which insists that the French are not to have the Rhine just as long as there are Germans to defend it. Following this crisis, a popular wave of political nationalism came to expression in German literature and caused the more serious, long-term revolutionary writers in Germany such as Heine himself to look askance at developments in Germany and to question the sincerity and poetic seriousness of this new literature.

In the course of the decade of the 1840s, political and social unrest was becoming more evident in Germany, and in 1844 the short-lived weavers' revolt took place in Silesia. This was the inspiration of the naturalist Gerhard Hauptmann's celebrated play *Die Weber* (1893; The Weavers) and Heine's haunting poem "Die schlesischen Weber" (The Silesian Weavers), perhaps the most famous political poem in the German language. The revolt threw into question the legitimacy and capacity for survival of the entire system. Heine was not alone in seeing the event as challenging the pillars of the whole society: namely, God, the king ("the king of the rich"), and the fatherland. The insistent refrain of his poem drives this point home: the weavers declare that they are weaving the burial shroud for Germany herself. In a much quoted letter to Karl Gutzkow in 1836, Georg Büchner had criticized the Young Germans for their idealistic conviction that *ideas*--in particular, progressive ones—could change the course of history: the weavers' revolt (which Büchner did not live to experience) reinforced his argument and gave credence to Marx's view that economic realities were the driving force of social change and that ideas were a byproduct of social and economic conditions. Büchner himself had examined the "fatalism" of history in his French Revolution drama *Dantons Tod* (1835; Danton's Death), while *Woyzeck* (published 1879; produced 1913; translated as *Wozzeck* and *Woyzed*) looked at the emotional and personal desperation experienced by the inarticulate lower classes. It was the novel, however, that would focus most strongly on the social problems of the day.

The emergence of a strong social novel at this time was in part a response to the example of Eugène Sue's best-selling novel *Les Mystères de Paris* (1842; The Mysteries of Paris), itself wittily criticized by Marx and Engels in *Die Heilige Familie* (1844; The Holy Family). The German social novel was also partly influenced by the emerging English social novel, and following the weaver's revolt, these novels disseminated a harrowing picture of the negative features of economic progress: the inhumanity of industrial work practices and pauperization on the land. Although its forms might be inappropriate to the new subject matter, the German social novel focused attention on the incompatibility between a traditional aesthetic of the novel and a more politically aware understanding of the function and appeal of literature—a conflict of values to which Theodor Fontane's critical writings at this time bear ample testimony. The failure of novelists such as Ernst Willkomm and Georg Weerth, whose principal works fall in this period, to establish themselves in the canon of German literature is thus evidence less of shortcomings in their creative ability (this was the judgment of Friedrich Sengle on this whole genre) than, more significantly, of their inability to replace the received aesthetic wisdom of the German idealistic tradition. There is no doubt that the aesthetic positions stemming from German classicism and Romanticism persisted in German literary history well into the 20th century and prevented a full appreciation of the literary work of this period. For as long as literature is defined according to these codes, works of this period that describe the early stages of industrialization in Germany will remain neglected. Willkomm's *Eisen, Gold, und Geist* (1843; Iron, Gold, and Spirit) and *Weisse Sclaven* (1845; White Slaves), or Weerth's uncompleted novel fragment, *Fragment eines Romans* (dating from the early 1840s but first published in 1968) do not deserve this neglect. It may be that the ideological-

ly motivated canonization of Weerth as, in Engel's phrase, "the first poet of the German proletariat" was hardly more successful in ensuring his place in the pantheon of German literature, but it should be recognized that it is only in German literary history, with its ideological and aesthetic commitment to the canon and its constantly politicized encounter with history, that texts of this kind have been so seriously neglected. This neglect suggests the importance of comparative, interdisciplinary work on this period. Without the efforts of critics in the 1960s and 1970s—in part through the publication of anthologies—this field would have remained forgotten.

Together with the social novel, one other kind of literature, *Tendenzpoesie* (political poetry), came into its own during these years, both in Germany and Austria, where the work of writers such as Anastasius Grün had a familiarly ambiguous status: while enjoying popularity if not critical acclaim, these writers' relationship to the state remained troubled. The issues raised in this type of writing are not only those that Heine explicitly discusses in his own poetry—in particular, in the humorous verse epic *Atta Troll* (1843), which satirizes *Tendenzpoesie* through the activities of a politically conscious bear and in so doing questions the sincerity, effectiveness, and style of this form of literature. The still more central issue of politically committed literature was discussed most notably in the famous debate in verse in 1841–42 between two of the major poets of the mid-century, Georg Herwegh and Ferdinand Freiligrath. Their debate concerned the two possible positions for poetry in the modern age: on the timeless battlements of poetry above the tides of partisan political passion ("auf einer höhern Warte, / Als auf den Zinnen der Partei" [in a more elevated position than on the battlements of one party]), or, as Herwegh argued, on the side of the oppressed, a position that—without reference to a particular political party—Herwegh affirmatively called *Partei*: "Partei! Partei! Wer sollte sie nicht nehmen, / Die noch die Mutter aller Siege war" (To be partisan, to take sides—that is what all should do, for partisanship is the mother of all victories). While Herwegh remained faithful to his position and was one of the few writers explicitly to attack the foundation of the German Empire in 1871, Freiligrath—after a period of cooperation with the Bund der Kommunisten (the Communist League) and a close personal friendship with Karl Marx—distanced himself decisively from all forms of political activity. For years German literary historians did little to illuminate these issues, although they were central in the debates in the Social Democratic Party at the turn of the century and again in the Weimar Republic. The process of rediscovery of the *Vormärz* reestablished the relevance of this period to the situation of the generation of 1968 and to the self-understanding of the two postwar German literatures. The one was trying to continue the traditions of socialist poetry from the *Vormärz,* while the other was critical of committed positions yet looking to create in West Germany a socially aware literature that could contribute to the rehabilitation of German literature after the fascist period. Despite its occasionally anachronistic style, *Vormärz* is the setting for some of the most stimulating literary debates of the century and as such is constantly accessible to the modern reader.

HUGH RIDLEY

See also Das Junge Deutschland

Further Reading

Conze, Werner, editor, *Staat und Gesellschaft im deutschen Vormärz 1815–1848*, Stuttgart: Klett, 1962; 3rd edition, 1978

Hermand, Jost, editor, *Der deutsche Vormärz: Texte und Dokumente*, Stuttgart: Reclam, 1967

Koopmann, Helmut, and Martina Lauster, editors, *Vormärzliteratur in europäischer Perspektive I: Öffentlichkeit und nationale Identität*, Bielefeld: Aisthesis, 1996

Lauster, Martina, and Günter Oesterle, editors, *Vormärzliteratur in europäischer Perspektive II: Politische Revolution, Industrielle Revolution, Ästhetische Revolution*, Bielefeld: Aisthesis, 1996

Sengle, Friedrich, *Biedermeierzeit: Deutsche Literatur im Spannungsfeld zwischen Restauration und Revolution 1815–1848*, Stuttgart: Metzler, 1971–80

Stein, Peter, *Epochenproblem Vormärz: 1815–1848*, Stuttgart: Metzler, 1974

Johann Heinrich Voß 1751–1826

Goethe's younger contemporary Johann Heinrich Voß was famous in his lifetime and for many years after his death in 1826 for his verse translation of Homer's epics. The choice of the hexameter as peculiarly appropriate to the genius of the German language helped establish his *Odüssee* (1781; *Odyssey*) and *Ilias* (1793; *Iliad*) as classics of German literature in their own right. Equally noted in his time for his rediscovery of the classical idyll in modern form, his dialect poem in *Plattdeutsch* ("low German"), and his polemics, Voß was a typical product of the didactic and dialogic culture of late Enlightenment Germany. In a letter to Goethe (20 April 1826) following her husband's death, Ernestine Voß wrote that the best part of their family life had been their lively conversations.

As a young man, together with the other poets who styled themselves the *Göttinger Hain*, Voß versified, wrote for, planned, and edited journals for a livelihood. His career as a writer (an interesting case study in itself) exemplifies the key role played by the social forms of the North German Enlightenment and also by the tangible material support its more fortunate members were ready to offer to someone of his obscure and impoverished origins. Thus H.C. Boie, editor of the *Göttinger Musenalmanach*, modeled on the Paris *Alamanach des Muses*, actually invited the poor tutor, on the basis of poems Voß had sent him, to be his guest at Göttingen in 1772. Boie also supported him from 1772–74 at university and passed on to him the editorship of the almanac so that Voß could marry Boie's sister in 1777. In 1782, another friend, Friedrich Count Stolberg, secured Voß a post as school principal at Eutin.

Voß's early satiric idylls in the tradition of Theocritus are characterized by the politicization of his literary discourse. Like Salomon Geßner before him (and Ebner-Eschenbach in her best-known story, *Er laßt die Hand küssen* [1886; He Kisses Her Hand]), he knew that ancient classical texts might be read politically. In his attack on serfdom in *Die Leibeigenen* (1775; The Serfs) and *Die Entrechteten* (1776; Those Deprived of Their Rights), the choice of idealized peasants, as contrasted with wicked or stupid noblemen, belongs at the heart of Sturm und Drang writers' empathy with the common people and their belief in the capacity of literature to bring about change and progress. The same principle is at work in Voß's dialect poetry in *Plattdeutsch*, a pioneering achievement often overlooked today.

Even more influential were his verse idylls of family life. *Der siebzigste Geburtstag* (1781; The Seventieth Birthday), with its hero, Pastor Grünau, spawned a whole host of imitators well into the 19th century to write "idylls from clerical life." *Luise* (1795; *Louisa*) had an even greater impact. First published in the *Voßische Musenalmanach* for 1783–84 and in Wieland's widely read *Teutsche Merkur* in 1784, it was constantly reprinted. Goethe praised it warmly and even wrote to Schiller in 1798 that it helped inspire his own most popular work, *Hermann und Dorothea*: "Such was my delight in *Louisa* that it led me to try my hand at the genre, it led me to *Hermann*." Voß's idylls of family life were popular precisely because they gave those forced to live a frugal middle-class existence a sense of their own worth. His contribution to this self-conscious ritualization of family life is arguably his most enduring achievement, admired and imitated by Biedermeier writers. They included the Swabian poets and, more importantly, Eduard Mörike. Voß, it could be argued, helped institutionalize the German ritual celebration of birthdays and other intimate festivals, of present-giving, of receiving visitors to the home, while regarding the guest rather than the host as the benefactor. Nationalist propaganda in the later 19th century would exploit Voß's idylls as examples of "typically German values," to be played off against the decadence of Germany's neighbors. Later still, Marxist propaganda rediscovered his satiric idylls and promoted them in the German Democratic Republic as alleged evidence of an enduring revolutionary peasant tradition.

Voß's mastery of metrics won tributes from many writers, among them August Wilhelm Schlegel and Wilhelm von Humboldt. But he had little understanding of rhythm, and Clemens Brentano—whose *Knaben Wunderhorn* Voß had attacked relentlessly—locates him firmly among the Philistines in his *Geschichte der Philister vor, in und nach der Geschichte* (1811; History of the Philistines before, in, and after History). A natural polemicist, Voß became dogmatic in old age, and Goethe and Schiller parted company with him over his purist views on translation.

Perhaps Heine, provocative but penetrating, came closest to the man when he suggested that Voß reminded him of "old one-eyed Wotan himself become a schoolmaster at Ottersdorf . . . bashing his verse into place with Thor's hammer." But then, Heine went on, there was someone else whom Voß resembled even more: Martin Luther himself.

EDA SAGARRA

Biography

Born in Sommersdorf bei Waren, 20 February 1751. Became private tutor out of material need, unable to study, 1769–72; helped by H.C. Boie to study theology and philology at Göttingen, from 1772; joined Hainbund in Göttingen, 1772; met Klopstock in Hamburg, 1774; edited *Göttinger Musenalmanach*, 1775; began translation of Homer's *Odyssey*, 1776; publication appeared 1781; became headmaster of school at Ottendorf, 1778; headmaster at Eutlin, 1782–1802; moved to Jena, 1802; translated Homer, Ovid (1798), Horace (1806), Shakespeare (1818–29), Aristophanes (1821), Propertius (1830); pensioned in Heidelberg, 1805–26. Died in Heidelberg, 29 March 1826.

Selected Works

Collections

Sämmtliche poetische Werke, edited by Abraham Voß, 1835
Ausgewählte Werke, edited by Adrian Hummel, 1996

Poetry

Der siebzigste Geburtstag, 1781
Gedichte, 2 vols., 1785–95
Luise: Ein ländliches Gedicht in drei Idyllen, 1795; as *Louisa*, translated by James Cochrane, 1852
Die Leibeigenen, 1775
Die Freigelassenen, 1776
Hymnus an die Freiheit, Nach der Melodie der Marsellaise, 1792
Die Erleichterten, 1800
Idyllen, 1801

Other

Mythologische Briefe, 2 vols., 1794; 2nd enlarged edition, 5 vols., 1827–34

Wie ward Fritz Stolberg ein Unfreier? 1819
Antisymbolik, 2 vols., 1824–26

Translations

Homer, *Homers Odüssee*, 1781 (translation of *The Odyssey*)
Homer, *Werke*, 4 vols., 1793 (translations of *The Odyssey* and *The Iliad*)
Ovid, *Verwandlungen nach Publius Ovidius Naso*, 2 vols., 1798 (translation of selections from *Metamorphoses*)
Horace, *Werke*, 2 vols., 1806 (translations of *Odes, Epodes, Satires,* and *Epistles*)
William Shakespeare, *Schauspiele*, 9 vols. 1818–29 (translations of Shakespeare's plays)
Aristophanes, *Aristofanes*, 3 vols., 1821 (translations of Aristophanes's plays)
Sextus Propertius, *Werke*, 1830 (translations of elegies)

Letters

Briefe von Johann Heinrich Voß, edited by Abraham Voß, 4 vols., 1829–33

Further Reading

Häntzschel, Günter, *Johann Heinrich Voß: Seine Homer-Übersetzungen als sprachschöpferische Leistung*, Munich: Beck, 1977
Schneider, H.J., "Johann Heinrich Voß," in *Deutsche Dichter des 18. Jahrhunderts: Ihr Leben und Werk*, edited by Benno von Wiese, Berlin: Schmidt, 1977
Voß, E. Theodor, "Nachwort," in reprint of *Idyllen*, by Johann Heinrich Voß, Heidelberg: Schneider, 1968
——, "Johann Heinrich Voß," in *Literaturlexikon: Autoren und Werke deutscher Sprache*, vol. 12, Gütersloh: Bertelsmann Lexikon, 1992

W

Wilhelm Heinrich Wackenroder 1773–1798

In 1796, there appeared an unusual text that was to set the standards by which the nature of art, of the artist, and of viewing art were delineated for Romanticism. Wilhelm Heinrich Wackenroder's *Herzensergießungen eines kunstliebenden Klosterbruders* (translated as *Confessions from the Heart of an Art-Loving Friar* and as *Outpourings of an Art-Loving Friar*) was edited and published anonymously by Ludwig Tieck, who added the preface and 4 of his own essays to the 13 others by his close friend. It is clear, however, that Wackenroder's texts form the core of the work. In 1799, *Phantasien über die Kunst, für Freunde der Kunst* (*Fantasies on Art for Friends of Art*) appeared, again with Tieck as editor. Here, 9 of the 21 essays are by Wackenroder, the rest by Tieck. There is some controversy as to authorship of a couple of the essays, since Tieck's own statements are contradictory in a few cases and since he and Wackenroder shared many ideas about art. It is also possible that Tieck, when editing his friend's essays, made some changes. Most critics have accepted Richard Alewyn's conclusions as to authorship.

Wackenroder's essays are based on extensive studies of art history in Berlin and at various universities, as well as on visits to museums and to cities such as Erlangen, Nürnberg, and Bamberg. In both works, he has as his narrator an artist who withdrew to a cloister when he realized that his talent was so much inferior to that of a Raphael or Michelangelo.

A good part of the *Outpourings* consists of portraits of Renaissance artists, mostly painters. Raphael, because of his Christian piety, his receiving divine inspiration, and his living in harmony with the world, is the perfect artist. He is the model against which all other artists are measured—each one of them falling short of the ideal to a greater or lesser degree. There are the almost perfect—Michelangelo, Leonardo da Vinci, and Dürer—and there is Francesco Francia, who fails both as a human being and as an artist.

The final section of *Outpourings*, entitled "Das merkwürdige Leben des Tonkünstlers Joseph Berglinger" ("The Remarkable Musical Life of the Composer Joseph Berglinger"), can be considered a novella in its own right. The piece belongs to the genre of the biography of a fictitious artist. It is clearly the most interesting part of the book and has had a great impact on later authors. Berglinger's achievements as well as his shortcomings are best seen in relation to the artists portrayed in the work's previous sections. His life is told by his intimate friend, the friar, who tells the story in two parts; the first one ends when Berglinger runs away from home, where he is at odds with his father, to the episcopal residence. The second part deals with his successes as a composer of sacred music and as a conductor. Soon, however, he becomes more and more despondent as he realizes that his audiences take his music as entertainment, not as a spiritual experience that lifts the soul to God, as Berglinger himself does. Toward the end of his life, there is a moment when he notices that his music has had the intended effect. He is then able to compose his masterpiece for the Easter festival. Soon after the performance, he falls ill and dies.

Berlinger was happiest as a young man when he was lifted to spiritual raptures while listening to music, especially religious music. Once he achieves fame, however, doubts about his calling and his role in society torture his mind. Should he not have become a physician like his father and tended to the poor and sick? Is he justified to cater to the taste of the rich and is he not worshiping an idol? He is unable to resolve the dilemma, but the narrator hopes that an environment as friendly to art as it was during the Renaissance will one day prevail again and that then divinely inspired artists will come to the fore.

There are two sections in the *Fantasies on Art* that are of special interest. In one of them, the narrator reflects on Berglinger's fate and observes that inspiration is ultimately incomprehensible; all we can do is to venerate great art. The other section is entitled "Ein wunderbares morgenländisches Märchen von einem nackten Heiligen" (Wondrous Oriental Tale of a Naked Saint). It deals with the existential fear of the passing of time by a crazed man who is cured by the song of two lovers who praise the beauty of the night.

It is significant that Wackenroder places music and musicians at the center of the post-Renaissance essays. Music uses a language that does not have obvious correlatives in real life and thus became for the Romantics the highest art form. In his writings, Wackenroder criticizes the attempts by Enlightenment critics to approach art rationally and to deny the essential unity of art and religion. Rather, he stresses such aspects as enthusiasm, faith, and inspiration. He was well acquainted with Giorgio Vasari's biographies of artists. Also of importance for Wackenroder's aesthetics was Johann Gottfried Herder's emphasis on the creative genius. Later Romantics, such as E.T.A. Hoffmann with his eccentric musician Johannes Kreisler and other artist figures, were to elaborate on the Berglinger theme. Thomas Mann gave the dilemma facing the modern artist its fullest depiction in *Doctor Faustus* (1947).

CHRISTOPH E. SCHWEITZER

See also Romanticism; Ludwig Tieck

Biography

Born in Berlin, 13 July 1773. Studied music and art together with his friend Ludwig Tieck, but his father wanted him to become a lawyer; Wackenroder and Tieck spent a semester at the University of Erlangen, 1793, taking frequent trips to Nürnberg, the home of Albrecht Dürer, and to the art gallery at the castle in Pommersfelden, where the "Pommersfelder Madonna," believed to be a work by Raphael, was housed; Wackenroder went to Bamberg by himself and was greatly impressed by the celebration of a Catholic feast in the cathedral; after a year of study in Göttingen, returned to Berlin to work as a legal clerk while at the same time finishing the short essays that Tieck was to publish as *Outpourings* in 1796. Died 13 February 1798.

Selected Works

Collections
Sämtliche Werke und Briefe, edited by Silvio Vietta and Richard Littlejohns, 2 vols., 1991

Essays
Herzensergießungen eines kunstliebenden Kosterbruders, with Ludwig Tieck, 1796; edited by R. Benz, 1961; as *Confessions and Fantasies*, edited and translated by Mary Hurst Schubert, 1971; as *Outpourings of an Art-Loving Friar*, translated by Edward Mornin, 1975; *Phantasien über die Kunst, für Freunde der Kunst*, with Tieck, 1799; as *Confessions and Fantasies*, edited and translated by Mary Hurst Schubert, 1971

Further Reading
Alewyn, Richard, "Wackenroders Anteil," *Germanic Review* 19, no. 1 (1944)
Bollacher, Martin, "Wilhelm Heinrich Wackenroder: *Herzensergießungen eines kunstliebenden Klosterbruders* (1796–97)," in *Romane und Erzählungen der deutschen Romantik: Neue Interpretationen*, edited by Paul Michael Lützeler, Stuttgart: Reclam, 1981
Ellis, John, *Joseph Berglinger in Perspective*, Bern: Lang, 1985
Kemper, Dirk, *Sprache der Dichtung: Wilhelm Heinrich Wackenroder im Kontext der Spätaufklärung*, Stuttgart: Metzler, 1993
Littlejohns, Richard, *Wackenroder-Studien: Gesammelte Aufsätze zur Biographie und Rezeption des Romantikers*, Frankfurt and New York: Lang, 1987
Sudhof, Siegfried, "Wilhelm Heinrich Wackenroder," in *Deutsche Dichter der Romantik*, edited by Benno von Wiese, Berlin: E. Schmidt, 1971; 2nd edition, 1983

Richard Wagner 1813–1883

Richard Wagner's life was framed by the "Battle of the Nations" (Leipzig, 1813), which liberated the divided German states from Napoléon, and by the rapid growth of a single Germany following Bismarck's unification in 1871. The deliberately Germanic image Wagner fostered made him into a leading figure of the drive for a national identity that fueled German culture and politics during the 19th century. A composer, playwright, essayist, and political and cultural luminary, he was a controversial figure during his own lifetime, provoking a mixture of sensation and scandal wherever he went. Wagner was a master of self-promotion, a cult figure who created his own dynasty and festival that continue to honor his memory. While audiences the world over pack opera houses performing his creations, Wagner's life, work, and lingering influence remain the subject of intellectual debate in diverse fields—musicology, history, and German studies—a debate made all the more complex because of the Third Reich's appropriation of his works and ideology.

Wagner's impact on literature, as well as an evaluation of his literary merit, is impossible without a discussion of his music and his place in music history. This comes in part from his own desire to integrate the two arts but most of all because it was through his musical style that he exerted the greatest influence on Western culture.

Born during the era of Romanticism, Wagner was especially drawn to two of its essential notions: the desire to revive and reconnect to the "truly German" and a quasi-religious belief in the transcendent and redemptive power of music. The most signifi-

cant musical influence on Wagner was Ludwig van Beethoven, whose nine symphonies, especially, represented a decisive break with the classicism of Haydn and Mozart. Beethoven transformed music into a mode of intense personal expression, composing works that conveyed an emotion and dynamism that often shocked his audiences. Almost single-handedly, he formulated musical Romanticism and elevated the status of the composer to that of *Originalgenie* (original genius). For Romantic authors such as E.T.A. Hoffmann, Beethoven's music was a revelation, and music as such became a portal to transcendence, capable of conveying a meaning more essential than language. The problem for composers following Beethoven was that his daring yet successful experiments with form and harmony had set a benchmark of originality that seemed impossible to meet, much less exceed.

One form relatively untouched by Beethoven was opera, which, in the early decades of the 19th century, continued largely to be the realm of the Italians and the French. Wagner circumvented the problems of following Beethoven by deciding to develop a new German operatic form, often referred to as "music drama," that could become a source of national pride by exemplifying German intellectual and emotional depth and superiority over Franco-Italian (*welsche*) superficiality. In a series of theoretical essays, *Die Kunst und die Revolution* (1849; *Art and Revolution*), *Das Kunstwerk der Zukunft* (1849; *Artwork of the Future*), *Oper und Drama* (1851; *Opera and Drama*), and *Eine Mitteilung an meine Freunde* (1851; *A Communication to My*

Friends), Wagner introduced his concepts of *Gesamtkunstwerk* (total artwork) and *Grundmotiv* (fundamental motif), also called *melodische Momente* (melodic elements), which later commentators referred to as *leitmotif,* a term that Wagner never used. Influenced by Feuerbach and by the revived interest in classical Greece as espoused by Winckelmann, Goethe, and Schiller of the Weimar period, Wagner proclaimed that his compositions would reunite the now-separated arts, making them of equal value and importance in the newly synthesized "total artwork"—the artwork of the future. Furthermore, and in the spirit of the Greeks, these works were to be performed in a communal setting, a concept also at the heart of Wagner's festival theater in Bayreuth, opened in 1876. The leitmotif constituted brief and recognizable musical ideas often representing a character, object, emotion, or idea that would be woven into the fabric of the drama and, through repetition, subtle musical variation, and transformation, would gain in significance as the drama progressed, functioning as a "subtext" to the story. Analysis and interpretation of Wagner's mature works frequently focus on his use and development of the leitmotifs and their relationship to the sung text and stage directions, although such interpretations are often guilty of oversimplification, for example, mistakenly associating leitmotifs with one exclusive "meaning."

As a composer, Wagner, together with his older and initially more successful colleague Franz Liszt, belonged to the avant-garde, which was responsible mainly for initiating the transition from musical Romanticism to modernism, characterized most blatantly by the move to atonality. Many consider this move to have been first suggested in the destabilized sense of tonality evident in the prelude to Wagner's *Tristan und Isolde* (1865). Wagner also created a distinctive orchestral sound by increasing its size, introducing new instruments especially in the brass, and by combining the instruments in original and innovative ways. Using these means, Wagner was able to achieve a wide variety of musical-emotional effects, such as a sensuously languid lyricism, which he built into erotically suggestive climaxes, or music of a vital warlike heroism. Perhaps most daring and influential of all was his way of suspending rhythmic, melodic, and harmonic movement, which ordinarily propels music forward, depriving the listener of a sense of time. The effect of this timelessness has been described as narcotic and psychologically self-absorbing. Beyond the profound impact of his style on music history, Wagner's innovations found their echo in the modernist literary movements of fin de siècle Europe, starting with the French symbolists and in the diverse works of authors such as Proust, Joyce, and Thomas Mann.

As an author, Wagner was equally prolific. He wrote the texts of his music dramas and published essays on topics ranging from aesthetics to politics. After his early and only moderately successful operas, including *Das Liebesverbot* (1836) and *Rienzi* (1842), Wagner produced *Der fliegende Holländer* (1843; *The Flying Dutchman*), *Tannhäuser* (1845), and *Lohengrin* (1850), which increasingly bear his mature stamp. The preoccupation with themes from Germanic mythology came to dominate, especially in the case of the 17-hour tetralogy *Der Ring des Nibelungen* (begun 1851, completed 1876; *The Ring of the Nibelungs*), derived from an assortment of Nordic sagas. Wagner's text even emulates the formulaic and alliterative *Stabreim* convention from the epic tradition, although Germanists have tended to deem Wagner's texts as second-rate because they apparently lack

sophistication. The mythical component of Wagner's works serves to mask more complex layers of meaning. The *Ring,* read as an allegory of modernity, is a critique of capitalism and budding industrialization. Autobiographical allusions also abound, such as the mystery surrounding Lohengrin's lineage, reflective of Wagner's own uncertainty about his real father, or the theme of *Tristan und Isolde,* which reflects the hopeless passion Wagner shared with the married Mathilde Wesendonck.

The gestation period for many of Wagner's dramas often exceeded a decade and in the case of *Die Meistersinger von Nürnberg* (1868; *The Mastersingers of Nuremberg*), lasted over 20 years. For Germanists, *The Mastersingers* is among Wagner's most interesting works. The result of extensive research, and using Gervinus's *Geschichte der poetischen National-Literatur der Deutschen* (1840–44) as its basis, the opera makes a national hero of the early modern cobbler and master poet Hans Sachs. The opera has also been understood as a hymn to Germany that lauds the Protestant work ethic, instilled and guarded by the guild system, and that celebrates Nuremberg as both geographically and spiritually the heart of Germany. The opera presents Wagner's aesthetic image of himself as a lone figure fighting against the conservative musical establishment of 19th-century Europe. This is humorously portrayed in the conflict between the wise Hans Sachs and Beckmesser, a caricature of the famous critic Eduard Hanslick, who opposed Wagner and advocated instead the music of Robert Schumann and Johannes Brahms.

Beginning around 1864, the patronage of King Ludwig II of Bavaria helped alleviate the chronic financial difficulties that had plagued Wagner and that had often forced him to flee debtors. In 1872 he moved to Bayreuth and laid the foundation stone for his new home, the Villa Wahnfried, as well as for the Festspielhaus (festival theater), which opened in 1876, conceived expressly and exclusively for the performance of his works, especially the *Ring* and even more his last opera, *Parsifal* (1882). With sporadic interruptions only, the Bayreuth summer festival has been held ever since and constitutes the longest-running tradition on the German stage.

The staunch and self-consciously German element in much of Wagner's political, cultural, and artistic efforts, especially when considered together with his essays—for example, *Das Judentum in der Musik* (1850; *Judaism in Music*) and *Was ist deutsch?* (1865; *What Is German?*), which articulate a nationalistic and anti-Semitic agenda—constitute the most problematic part of the Wagner legacy. This agenda found support with the founding in 1878 of the journal *Bayreuther Blätter*, edited by Hans von Wolzogen, an early Wagnerite and committed nationalist. Anti-Semitism was openly preached by Wagner's family, especially by his second wife, Cosima—daughter of Franz Liszt and married originally to conductor and Wagner enthusiast Hans von Bülow—who headed the Wagner dynasty after 1883, making Bayreuth a Wagner shrine. Wagner's son-in-law and early biographer, Houston Stewart Chamberlain, was a proto-Nazi, and Wagner's daughter-in-law, Winifred, personally welcomed Hitler to Bayreuth.

The ongoing controversial reaction to Wagner found its first and most eloquent expression in Friedrich Nietzsche, initially a profound admirer and close friend who paid homage to Wagner's new aesthetic conception in *Die Geburt der Tragödie aus dem Geiste der Musik* (1871; *The Birth of Tragedy*) by extolling the narcotic, ecstatic (*rauschhafte*), Dionysian quality of his music. This was followed by the essay "Richard Wagner in Bayreuth" (1876), the fourth of his *Unzeitgemäße Betrachtungen* (*Untimely Meditations*), in which Nietzsche places Wagner on par with Luther and Goethe as the most significant embodiments of the German spirit. The personal break with Wagner began in 1877 and deepened in 1878 when he received a draft of Wagner's libretto to *Parsifal,* which Nietzsche rejected as a return to a limited and weak Catholicism, anathema to what he felt Wagner's preceding works had advocated. *Der Fall Wagner* (1888; *The Case of Wagner*) crystallizes Nietzsche's critique of Wagner, the "irresistible" embodiment of "sickly" "decadent" modernity, whose orchestral sound he compares to the "sirocco." The motif of the "sirocco" is taken up by Thomas Mann in *Der Tod in Venedig* (1912; *Death in Venice*). The novella, read as a metaphor for Wagner's impact on European culture, depicts Venice—the city where Wagner died—overcome by a cholera epidemic carried there by a "sirocco," robbing protagonist Gustav von Aschenbach of the will to live. Mann's earlier novella *Tristan* (1903) re-creates in prose the love duet from the second act of Wagner's opera and similarly fuses the eroticism, sickness, and abdication from life that Nietzsche had already observed. Mann also penned a series of essays on Wagner, culminating with *Leiden und Größe Richard Wagners* (1933; *Suffering and Greatness of Richard Wagner*), which precipitated a Nazi backlash and forced Mann into exile until the end of the war.

The postwar period has seen efforts to depoliticize Wagner, especially evident in Wieland Wagner's (his grandson) bare stagings at Bayreuth. However, the consequences of anti-Semitism in Germany and Wagner's debatable responsibility in fanning its flames have led several critics (e.g., Adorno, Rose, and Weiner) to reexamine his music dramas in an effort to uncover an anti-Semitic subtext there also, although some (e.g., Barenboim, Borchmeyer, and Vaget) argue with equal vigor that such a reading is unsupportable. The controversial filmmaker Hans Jürgen Syberberg has attempted to take on the rich complexity of Wagner's legacy in his *Hitler: Ein Film aus Deutschland* (1977; *Our Hitler*) and in *Winifred Wagner und die Geschichte des Hauses Wahnfried 1914–1975* (Winifred Wagner and the History of House Wahnfried).

Wagner is inexorably bound up with the vicissitudes of modern German history. His defenders argue for guiltless enjoyment of his sublime works, separating them from his disturbing words and abrasive personality, a defense made all the more difficult because it was Wagner himself who originally strove to connect music, words, and ideas in the total artwork of the future.

NICHOLAS VAZSONYI

Biography

Born in Leipzig, 1813. Studied music at Leipzig University; choir master at Würzburg, 1833; conductor, Magdeburg, 1834–36; conductor, Riga, 1837; in London, 1839, and Paris, 1840; Hofkapellmeister, Dresden opera, 1843; involved in the Saxony revolt, 1849; in Zurich, 1849–59; in London, 1855; in Paris, 1861, for a production of his opera *Tannhäuser;* in Munich under the patronage of King Ludwig II, 1865; premiere of his operas *Tristan und Islode,* 1865, and *Die Meistersinger von Nürnberg,* 1868, in Munich; construction begun on a Festspielhaus at Bayreuth designed specifically for his operas, 1872; premiere of his opera cycle *Der Ring des Nibelungen* at the Bayreuth Festspielhaus, 1876; premiere of his opera *Parsifal* at Bayreuth, 1882. Died in Venice, 1883.

Selected Works

Collections
Richard Wagner's Prose Works, translated by W.A. Ellis, 8 vols., 1892–99
Gesamtausgabe, edited by M. Balling, 12 vols., 1907–23
Sämtliche Werke, edited by Carl Dahlhaus, 1970–
Richard Wagners Briefe in Originalausgaben, 17 vols., 1910–12
Sämtliche Briefe, edited by G. Stobel and W. Wolf, 2 vols., 1967–70

Treatises and Essays
(all translated into English in *Richard Wagner's Prose Works*)
Die Kunst und die Revolution, 1849
Das Kunstwerk der Zukunft, 1849
Das Judentum in der Musik, 1850; revised, 1869
Eine Mitteilung an meine Freunde, 1851
Oper und Drama, 1851; revised, 1868
Über Staat und Religion, 1864
Was ist deutsch? 1865
Beethoven, 1870

Music Dramas
Der fliegende Holländer (performed 1843), 1843
Tannhäuser (performed 1845; revised version, performed 1861), 1845
Lohengrin (performed 1850), 1850
Der Ring des Nibelungen (*Das Rheingold, Die Walküre, Siegfried, Götterdämmerung;* complete performance 1876), 1853
Tristan und Isolde (performed 1865), 1859
Die Meistersinger von Nürnberg (performed 1868), 1862
Parsifal (performed 1882), 1877

Autobiography
Mein Leben, edited by M. Gregor-Dellin, 1963; as *My Life,* translated by Andrew Gray, 1983

Further Reading

Adorno, Theodor, *Versuch über Wagner,* Frankfurt: Suhrkamp, 1952; 2nd edition, 1981; as *In Search of Wagner,* translated by Rodney Livingstone, London: NLB, 1981
Borchmeyer, Dieter, *Das Theater Richard Wagners: Idee, Dichtung, Wirkung,* Stuttgart: Reclam, 1982; as *Richard Wagner: Theory and Theatre,* translated by Stewart Spencer, Oxford: Clarendon Press, and New York: Oxford University Press, 1991
Burbidge, Peter, and Richard Sutton, editors, *The Wagner Companion,* London and Boston: Faber, and New York: Cambridge University Press, 1979
Dahlhaus, Carl, *Richard Wagners Musikdramen,* Hildesheim: Friedrich, 1971; 2nd edition, Zurich: Orell Füssli, 1985; as *Richard Wagner's Music Dramas,* translated by Mary Whittall, Cambridge and New York: Cambridge University Press, 1979
Deathridge, John, and Carl Dahlhaus, *The New Grove Wagner,* London: Macmillan, and New York: Norton, 1984
Fischer-Dieskau, Dietrich, *Wagner und Nietzsche,* Stuttgart: Deutsche Verlags-Anstalt, 1974; as *Wagner and Nietzsche,* translated by Joachim Neugroschel, New York: Seabury Press, 1976; London: Sidgwick and Jackson, 1978
Grey, Thomas S., *Wagner's Musical Prose: Texts and Contexts,* Cambridge and New York: Cambridge University Press, 1995
Grimm, Reinhold, and Jost Hermand, editors, *Re-Reading Wagner,* Madison: University of Wisconsin Press, 1993
Levin, David J., *Richard Wagner, Fritz Lang, and the Nibelungen: The Dramaturgy of Disavowal,* Princeton, New Jersey: Princeton University Press, 1998
Müller, Ulrich, and Peter Wapnewski, editors, *Richard Wagner*

Handbuch, Stuttgart: Kröner, 1986; as *Wagner Handbook,* translated by John Deathridge, Cambridge, Massachusetts: Harvard University Press, 1992

Newman, Ernest, *The Life of Richard Wagner,* 4 vols., New York: Knopf, and London and Toronto: Cassell, 1933–46

Nietzsche, Friedrich, *Der Fall Wagner,* Leipzig: Reclam, 1888; new edition, edited by Dieter Borchmeyer, Frankfurt: Insel, 1983

Rose, Paul Lawrence, *Wagner: Race and Revolution,* New Haven, Connecticut: Yale University Press, 1992

Vaget, Hans Rudolf, "*Der Jude im Dorn* oder: Wie antisemitisch sind *Die Meistersinger von Nürnberg?*" *Deutsche Vierteljahrsschrift* 69, no. 2 (1995)

Wapnewski, Peter, *Der traurige Gott: Richard Wagner in seinen Helden,* Munich: Beck, 1978; 2nd edition, 1980

Weiner, Marc A., *Richard Wagner and the Anti-Semitic Imagination,* Lincoln: University of Nebraska Press, 1995

Westernhagen, Curt von, *Richard Wagners Dresdener Bibliothek 1842–1849,* Wiesbaden: Brockhaus, 1966

———, *Wagner,* Zurich and Freiburg: Atlantis-Verlag, 1968; 2nd edition, 1979

Parsifal: Wagner/Nietzsche Debate

Parsifal was Richard Wagner's last opera, premiered at the second Bayreuth Festival on 26 July 1882. Rightly suspecting that he had little longer to live, Wagner had conceived it as the musical and ideological consummation of his life's work, a farewell to the (world) stage. *Parsifal*'s success certainly had the intended effect of setting the seal on Wagner's formidable reputation and securing the fortunes of the Bayreuth enterprise, but through its renunciatory tone and deliberately engineered religious aura, it also confirmed the composer's estrangement from his former disciple, the philosopher Friedrich Nietzsche.

The friendship between the two men had been at its most intense in its earliest years. They first met in November 1868 in Leipzig; Nietzsche moved to Basel the following spring and over the next three years made frequent pilgrimages to the Wagners' residence at Tribschen on Lake Lucerne, where he rapidly established himself as a favored house guest, indeed, a surrogate son. At this time, the two men shared a passion for the culture of the ancient Greeks, the philosophy of Arthur Schopenhauer, German nationalism, and Wagner's genius, enthusiasms that all found their way into Nietzsche's first book, *Die Geburt der Tragödie aus dem Geiste der Musik* (1872; *The Birth of Tragedy out of the Spirit of Music*). From 1874, however, their relationship became increasingly strained as Nietzsche began to chafe under the yoke of subservience Wagner demanded from all his friends. Moreover, Nietzsche grew increasingly disaffected with the more objectionable elements in Wagner's personality, in particular his anti-Semitism and strident nationalistic bigotry. Nietzsche initially suppressed his qualms, but he took almost two years to complete the encomiastic essay *Richard Wagner in Bayreuth,* finally published in July 1876, just in time for the inaugural Bayreuth Festival, which was to prove the watershed in their relationship. Nietzsche remained on the margins of the event and left early, racked by psychosomatic illness and disillusioned with his erstwhile idol over his condescension to popularity; the two met for the last time in Sorrento at the end of October 1876.

By 1877, Wagner was finally clear to embark in earnest on *Parsifal,* which had been on the back burner since he had sketched its first outline 20 years before. As usual, he completed the text of the poem first, in March/April 1877, and sent out copies to his friends at the end of the year; Nietzsche received his on 3 January 1878. Nietzsche would later dramatize the impact of this event, claiming (in *Ecce Homo*) to have been stunned by Wagner's "conversion." Given the length of *Parsifal*'s gestation, however, it in fact came as no surprise, for Nietzsche had long been familiar with the detailed prose sketch Wagner made in August 1865. Nietzsche's initial reaction to the text in its final form was "more Liszt than Wagner, spirit of the Counter-Reformation" (letter to Seydlitz, 4 January 1878). Having earlier championed Wagner (in *The Birth of Tragedy*) for revitalizing pagan myth, Nietzsche was now repelled by a work, subtitled "Ein Bühnenweihfestspiel" (A Stage-Consecration Festival Play), which could scarcely have been more overt in deploying its panoply of Christian (specifically, Roman Catholic) symbolism.

In May 1878, the appearance of Nietzsche's *Menschliches, Allzumenschliches* (*Human, All Too Human*) made public his break from the world that he and Wagner had shared. He mischievously sent two copies to the Wagners in Bayreuth, where the composer became convinced that Nietzsche had taken leave of his senses and in preemptive self-defense published a not-so-covert attack on the philosopher in his article "Public and Popularity" (*Bayreuther Blätter,* August 1878). Yet Wagner's name had been conspicuous by its absence from *Human, All Too Human,* and although there are a few disparaging remarks about the composer and his music in Nietzsche's next works, his criticisms remained relatively restrained until after Wagner's death in February 1883. Book IV of *Also sprach Zarathustra* (written 1885; published 1892; *Thus Spoke Zarathustra*) contains a thinly veiled portrait of the composer in the figure of the Sorcerer who acts out the part of "the penitent of the spirit"; in *Jenseits von Gut und Böse* (1885; *Beyond Good and Evil*), Nietzsche summarily characterizes "what I *object* to in 'late Wagner' and his *Parsifal* music" as "*Rome's faith in all but name!*"

Nietzsche's boycotting of Bayreuth after 1876 ensured that he never actually attended a performance of *Parsifal,* which Wagner forbade to be produced elsewhere, but the philosopher did make a careful study of the score and, in January 1887, finally heard the orchestral Prelude in Monte Carlo. He was profoundly moved by the experience of hearing Wagner's music (and would remain so till the end), but later that year he was back on the offensive in *Zur Genealogie der Moral* (1887; *On the Genealogy of Morals*), citing *Parsifal* as the prime example of an artist's deleterious pursuit of the "ascetic ideal." Failing to convince himself that the opera was intended as a joke, Nietzsche here concludes that it is an artistic lie: he rejects *Parsifal*'s "hatred of sensuality" and glorification of compassion as the worst kind of Christianized Schopenhauerianism, and he sees the figure of Parsifal himself, the "pure fool," as the absolute negation of the (Greek, Enlightenment) spirit of intellectual inquiry.

Nietzsche's animus against Wagner reached its culmination in two brilliant polemics from the final year of his sanity (1888). The first, *Der Fall Wagner: Ein Musikanten-Problem* (1888; *The Case of Wagner*), treats Wagner as a paradigmatic pathology, a symptom in need of diagnosis. Wagner is here denounced as the archetypal "artist of decadence," "the modern artist *par excellence*" whose *Parsifal* is merely his illness writ large. "This Klingsor of all Klingsors" is a histrionic counterfeiter who places music at the service of dramatic gesture; he seduces the unwary with his life-denying concoction and seeks to turn an old man's personal search for "redemption" into a general prescription.

In order to demonstrate that this exuberantly malicious work was no flash in the pan, at the end of 1888 Nietzsche assembled a (lightly edited) collection of his earlier passages in criticism of Wagner, starkly entitled *Nietzsche contra Wagner: Aktenstücke eines Psychologen* (1895; *Nietzsche contra Wagner: Out of the Files of a Psychologist*), which constituted the final act in a remarkable love-hate relationship. For all his vituperation, to the last Nietzsche did not shrink from expressing his gratitude to Wagner: in *The Case of Wagner*, he insisted that "*Other musicians don't count compared to Wagner.*" He could still write even of *Parsifal*: "I admire this work; I wish I had written it myself."

DUNCAN LARGE

See also Friedrich Wilhelm Nietzsche

Further Reading

Beckett, Lucy, *Richard Wagner: Parsifal*, Cambridge and New York: Cambridge University Press, 1981

Borchmeyer, Dieter, "Wagner and Nietzsche," in *Wagner Handbook*, edited by Ulrich Müller and Peter Wapnewski, translated edited by John Deathridge, Cambridge, Massachusetts: Harvard University Press, 1992

Borchmeyer, Dieter, and Jörg Salaquarda, editors, *Nietzsche und Wagner: Stationen einer epochalen Begegnung*, 2 vols., Frankfurt: Insel, 1994

Csampai, Attila, and Dietmar Holland, editors, *Parsifal: Texte, Materialien, Kommentare*, Reinbek bei Hamburg: Rowohlt, 1984

Dahlhaus, Carl, "Parsifal," in *Richard Wagner's Music Dramas*, translated by Mary Whittall, Cambridge and New York: Cambridge University Press, 1979

Fischer-Dieskau, Dietrich, *Wagner und Nietzsche*, Stuttgart: Deutsche Verlags-Anstalt, 1974; as *Wagner and Nietzsche*, translated by Joachim Neugroschel, New York: Seabury Press, 1976

Hollinrake, Roger, *Nietzsche, Wagner, and the Philosophy of Pessimism*, London and Boston: Allen and Unwin, 1982

Montinari, Mazzino, "Nietzsche und Wagner vor hundert Jahren," *Nietzsche Studien* 7 (1978)

Tanner, Michael, "Redemption to the Redeemer," in *Wagner*, London: HarperCollins, and Princeton, New Jersey: Princeton University Press, 1996

Martin Walser 1927–

Along with his near contemporaries Günter Grass and Hans Magnus Enzensberger, Martin Walser belongs to the generation of writers that achieved prominence in the late 1950s and early 1960s and that increasingly came to represent the literature of the Federal Republic. Although he gained the prize of the Gruppe 47 in 1955 for his story "Templones Ende" (Templone's End) from the collection *Ein Flugzeug über dem Haus und andere Geschichten* (1955; An Aeroplane over the House and Other Stories), it was with his first two novels that he truly came to prominence. The first novel, *Ehen in Philippsburg* (1957; *The Gadarene Club*), is principally concerned with the career of Hans Beumann, a young man from the provinces of lowly origins—many of Walser's characters share his South German background—who gradually establishes himself in the world of journalism in metropolitan society, but who compromises with the corrupt and hedonistic values of the world of commerce. Established values, especially those associated with marriage, have been replaced by the desire for success fostered by the German "economic miracle." In contrast to Beumann, a young intellectual, Klaff, who works as a porter, is unwilling to compromise and commits suicide.

Walser's second novel, *Halbzeit* (1960; Half Time), is also largely set in the world of the "economic miracle." It forms the first part of a trilogy centered around the life and times of Anselm Kristlein, the scion of a lower-middle-class family, who has left his university without completing his studies and who has a wife and family to support. Initially, he is working as a salesman, the archetypal profession in a society where material concerns dominate every aspect of life. From this relatively humble position, he is able to rise into the world of advertising—a change symbolized by the exchange of his battered Ford for a new Mercedes. In other ways, however, there is a high price to pay for this material advancement, which takes him into the society of industrialists and their intellectual acolytes. He suffers physically in the form of illness—his strategy of "mimicry" in order to ingratiate himself exacts a premium—while his family life is affected by his extramarital affairs.

Having established himself as a sociocritical novelist, Walser turned to the theater in the early 1960s, when there was a dearth of German plays dealing with contemporary issues. He coined the term *Realismus X* for his attempt to create a kind of drama that would go beyond Brechtian Epic Theater. More specifically, he sought to write a three-part "German chronicle," of which only two plays appeared at this time. *Eiche und Angora* (1962; *The Rabbit Race*) contrasts the survival of the bourgeois Gorbach, who is able to adapt to three types of society—the Third Reich, the pacifistic postwar era, and the Federal Republic during the Cold War—with the inability of the working-class Alois to move with the times. For this failing, Alois was incarcerated under the Nazis as a communist, and the end of the play sees him going to an asylum run by the Catholic Church. Whereas *The Rabbit Race* is a sardonic review of the continuities of German history, the second part of the chronicle, *Der Schwarze Schwan* (1964; The Black Swan), is entirely somber. It deals directly with the amnesia of those directly involved in Nazi crimes. In a manner reminiscent of *Hamlet,* the son of a former SS man tries unsuccessfully to stir the conscience of his father and his associate, before finally taking his own life.

In the early 1950s, Walser had written a number of radio plays. Since his spate of works in the early 1960s, he has continued to write occasionally for the theater, as well as producing television scripts. Because only one of these efforts, *Die Zimmerschlacht* (1967; Home Front), has achieved frequent performance, however, it is fair to say that his reputation rests largely on his prose works. These have dominated his oeuvre since the mid-1960s and the appearance of the second part of the Kristlein trilogy, *Das Einhorn* (1966; The Unicorn). In this work, Kristlein is now working as a writer and is also part of an intellectual scene that is characterized by public discussions of topical issues. When he is commissioned to write a book on love, he himself falls in love with a younger woman of Dutch-Surinamese background, with the latter part of the novel recounting the history of their doomed relationship. The third Kristlein novel, *Der Sturz* (1973; The Fall), is, as the title implies, a story of decline. After both a bewildering set of experiences that mirror his previous life and a period as a manager of a convalescent home, Kristlein sets out on a suicidal winter car journey over the Alps.

Despite the attention he had attracted in literary circles through his earlier works, it was only toward the end of the 1970s, especially following *Ein fliehendes Pferd* (1978; Runaway Horse), that Walser achieved total acceptance by a wider reading public and near universal critical acclaim, including accolades from his former stern critic Marcel Reich-Ranicki. The large number of works that he has written since are dominated by middle-aged male failures from a variety of professions, from chauffeur to teacher to lawyer. Two themes dominate: rivalry and dependence. Whereas Kristlein was initially able to progress in a competitive world, albeit at a price, later characters are invariably outdone by those that they perceive as rivals. In *Das Schwanenhaus* (1980; The Swan Villa), Gottlieb Zürn, a small-time estate agent, hopes to gain the contract to sell an architectural jewel with which he has fallen in love. In the end, he is no match for his smarter rivals, and the art nouveau house will give way to luxury apartments. The theme of dependence dominates *Seelenarbeit* (1979; The Inner Man), whose main character is another member of the Zürn family. He works as the chauffeur to a successful businessman. Their spatial relationship—facing the front, Zürn cannot easily reply to the comments from his employer in the back—epitomizes their respective status. Zürn's lowly status results in a loss of well-being, endless medical tests, and eventual removal from his position. Paradoxically, however, his situation is improved when he is given the even lower status job of a fork-lift truck driver, where he works, however, away from direct contact with his employer.

The failures of Walser's heroes, generally the result of living in a society that places success above all else, affect every aspect of their lives. Attempts to break out inevitably end in failure or help to destroy others, as in the campus novel *Brandung* (1985; Breakers). During a period as a guest lecturer at an American university, Hans Halm becomes hopelessly infatuated with a student, before finally being instrumental in her death by drowning.

He has caused her to break her leg, and, subsequently, she cannot escape from a car when it falls into the sea. Halm conforms to the pattern of the Walserian hero in that he is ineffectual and beset by what amount to neuroses. For such people, the struggle against real or imagined enemies takes on grotesque proportions, as in the appropriately named *Finks Krieg* (1996; Fink's War), where a civil servant allows his conflict with his superior to take over his life.

Walser's literary reputation also rests on his skill as a stylist. Whereas *The Gadarene Club,* in which he broke away from the influence of Kafka, is narrated largely in a traditional, realistic way, the Kristlein trilogy shows the influence of modernism. In the manner of James Joyce's *Ulysses,* much of *Halbzeit* is made up of a narrative of a single day, at times through stream-of-consciousness techniques, while a significant aspect of *The Unicorn,* which, like its predecessor, uses a first-person narrative, is a rejection of Proust's thesis that the past can be recovered through narration. Thereafter, Walser experimented with a number of styles—*Der Sturz* shows in parts his anti-Proustian project by setting a novel in the future—before achieving his definitive style in the 1970s. This new style is based on third-person narration, albeit generally from the perspective of the protagonist, in a clear, yet linguistically brilliant style that captures the tortuous existences of his characters with sympathetic humor. Less positively, the concentration on a single perspective may help to explain why some of Walser's characters, especially female ones, tend to be somewhat two-dimensional.

In addition to being a leading writer, Walser has occupied a central role in the intellectual life of the Federal Republic. Although he satirizes intellectual life in his fiction and is frequently critical in his essays of those who peddle "opinion," he cannot, as he might seem to prefer, be regarded as an outsider—in the manner of his fictional characters. At times, he can be said to have espoused viewpoints that are almost representative of the prevailing intellectual climate at a given time.

Before the 1961 federal election, Walser edited a volume *Die Alternative; oder, Brauchen wir eine neue Regierung?* (The Alternative; or, Do We Need a New Government?), in which writers and intellectuals, including Grass and Enzensberger, pleaded, albeit with limited enthusiasm, for the Social Democrats. When the exercise was repeated four years later, he was not involved, having moved away from the increasingly pragmatic SPD and from the Gruppe 47, many of whose leading figures were increasingly attaching themselves to the party. His new radicalism led him to sympathize with the student protesters of 1968 and, in keeping with the mood of the time, to a temporary abandonment of literary forms in favor of editing the biographies of underprivileged members of society, something he undertook twice. When he began to show support again for a political party, it was the re-formed communist party (DKP). This support found expression in the novel *Die Gallistl'sche Krankheit* (1972; Gallistl's Disease) and in a controversial essay published before the 1972 election.

Walser's support for the DKP was not unconditional. He criticized its lack of a West German identity, a criticism that arguably contains the germ of his most contested political stance: what his detractors see as his German nationalism. From the late 1970s, he began to voice displeasure at the division of Germany. As this state of affairs continued, he increasingly cast Germany into the role of victim, particularly as the Federal Republic had, in his view, already established its democratic credentials. It was therefore not surprising that he rejoiced at German unification. Subsequently, he has blamed those who all too readily accepted the Westernization of Germany for the growth of right-wing extremism. He has also sought to reduce the phenomenon of National Socialism to the personality of Hitler, thus apparently denying any link between that phenomenon and the overall course of German history. Most controversially, in 1998, he both rejected the idea of a Holocaust memorial in Berlin and demanded the right to "look away" when confronted with the horrors of Auschwitz.

Whereas it would be an exaggeration to describe Walser as an unreconstructed nationalist—he has, for example, never denied German guilt—he is open to criticism. For example, in the immensely successful postunification novel *Die Verteidigung der Kindheit* (1991; In Defense of Childhood), he puts forward a positive view of German identity in which he simplistically incorporates the Jewish contribution to German culture, while, by setting much of the novel in Dresden and emphasizing the iniquities of division, he again places the Germans in the role of victims. This novel builds upon the earlier *Dorle und Wolf* (1987; *No Man's Land*), whose main male character spies for the GDR—not because he has any sympathy for communist ideology but because he feels that it is in the interest of equality, and ultimately unity, between the two German states. Both these works show the importance of German themes in Walser's recent work. Nevertheless, both retain the archetypal hero figure. Wolf is a total failure as a spy, while Alfred Dorn in *Die Verteidigung der Kindheit* is a weakling whose all-pervading wish is to recapture his childhood.

The unease that can be felt about some of Walser's political writing should not detract from his literary achievements. He undoubtedly remains a major figure in the literature of the Federal Republic. He owes this status to the consummate artistry with which he portrays what is arguably an almost universal human characteristic: the ability to survive both self-inflicted wounds and life's endless vicissitudes.

STUART PARKES

Biography

Born at Wasserburg, on Lake Constance, 24 March 1927. Studied literature, philosophy, and history at Regensburg and Tübingen, 1946–51; doctorate thesis on Kafka; worked in radio and television in Stuttgart until 1957, when he became a full-time writer; has lived since in his native area in Friedrichshafen and Nußdorf; several periods of residence at American and British universities. Büchner Prize, 1981; Grand Federal Cross of Merit, 1987. Currently lives in Überlingen.

Selected Works

Prose

Ein Flugzeug über dem Haus und andere Geschichten, 1955
Ehen in Philippsburg, 1957; as *The Gadarene Club*, translated by Eva Figes, 1960 (published in the United States as *Marriage in Philippsburg*, 1961)
Halbzeit, 1960
Lügengeschichten, 1964
Das Einhorn, 1966; as *The Unicorn*, translated by Barrie Ellis-Jones, 1971

Fiction, 1970
Die Gallistl'sche Krankheit, 1972
Der Sturz, 1973
Jenseits der Liebe, 1976; as *Beyond All Love*, translated by Judith L. Black, 1982
Ein fliehendes Pferd, 1978; as *Runaway Horse*, translated by Leila Vennewitz, 1980
Seelenarbeit, 1979; as *The Inner Man*, translated by Leila Vennewitz, 1984
Das Schwanenhaus, 1980; as *The Swan Villa*, translated by Leila Vennewitz, 1982
Brief an Lord Liszt, 1982; as *Letter to Lord Liszt*, translated by Leila Vennewitz, 1985
Brandung, 1985; as *Breakers*, translated by Leila Vennewitz, 1987
Meßmers Gedanken, 1985
Dorle und Wolf, 1987; as *No Man's Land*, translated by Leila Vennewitz, 1988
Jagd, 1988
Die Verteidigung der Kindheit, 1991
Ohne einander, 1993
Finks Krieg, 1996
Ein springender Brunnen, 1998

Plays

Der Abstecher, 1961; as *The Detour*, translated by Richard Grunberger in *Plays*, 1963
Eiche und Angora, 1962; as *The Rabbit Race*, translated by Richard Duncan in *Plays*, 1963
Überlebensgroß Herr Krott (produced 1963), 1963
Der Schwarze Schwan (produced 1964), 1964
Die Zimmerschlacht (produced 1967), 1967; as *Home Front* (produced 1971), translated by Michael Roloff in *The Contemporary German Theatre*, 1972
Ein Kinderspiel (produced 1972), 1970
Das Sauspiel (produced 1975), 1975
In Goethes Hand (produced 1982), 1982
Die Ohrfeige (produced 1986), 1986
Das Sofa, 1992
Kaschmir in Parching, 1995

Essays

Erfahrungen und Leseerfahrungen, 1965
Heimatkunde: Aufsätze und Reden, 1968
Aus dem Wortschatz unserer Kämpfe, 1971
Wie und wovon handelt Literatur: Aufsätze und Reden, 1973
Ein Grund zur Freude: 99 Sprüche, 1978
Wer ist ein Schriftsteller? Aufsätze und Reden, 1979
Selbstbewußtsein und Ironie: Frankfurter Vorlesungen, 1981
Versuch, ein Gefühl zu verstehen und andere Versuche, 1982
Liebeserklärungen, 1983
Variationen eines Würgegriffs: Bericht über Trinidad und Tobago, 1985
Geständnis auf Raten, 1986
Heilige Brocken: Aufsätze—Prosa—Gedichte, 1988
Über Deutschland reden, 1988
Auskunft: 22 Gespräche aus 28 Jahren, 1991
Beschreibung einer Form: Versuch über Kafka, 1992
Vormittag eines Schriftstellers, 1994
Zauber und Gegenzauber, 1995

Radio and Television Plays

Tassilo: Die Verteidigung von Friedrichshafen, 1991
Tassilo: Hilfe kommt aus Bregenz, 1991
Tassilo: Das Gespenst von Gattnau, 1991
Tassilo: Zorn einer Göttin, 1991
Tassilo: Lindauer Pietà, 1991
Tassilo: Säntis, 1991

Further Reading

Pilipp, Frank, *The Novels of Martin Walser: A Critical Introduction*, Columbia, South Carolina: Camden House, 1991

Pilipp, Frank, editor, *New Critical Perspectives on Martin Walser*, Columbia, South Carolina: Camden House, 1994

Schlunk, Jürgen E., and Armand E. Singer, editors, *Martin Walser: International Perspectives*, New York: Lang, 1987

Siblewski, Klaus, editor, *Martin Walser*, Frankfurt: Suhrkamp, 1981

Waine, Anthony Edward, *Martin Walser*, Munich: Edition Text und Kritik, 1980

Robert Walser 1878–1956

Robert Walser's beginnings as a young writer at the turn of the 20th century appeared quite auspicious. With the help of Franz Blei, a prominent man of letters who was impressed by Walser's early poems, he established professional contacts in Munich, above all with writers associated with the influential Jugendstil magazine *Die Insel*. Soon after the publication of his first book, *Fritz Kochers Aufsätze* (1904; Fritz Kocher's Compositions), a collection of compositions written by a fictional schoolboy, Walser moved to Berlin and immersed himself in metropolitan life. Through his brother Karl, who had settled there and had become a stage designer under Max Reinhardt, he met, among others, Bruno and Paul Cassirer, Samuel Fischer, Maximilian Harden, Walther Rathenau, Frank Wedekind, and Hugo von Hofmannsthal. In quick succession Bruno Cassirer published his first three, autobiographically inspired novels, all of which play havoc with the traditional 19th-century bildungsroman: *Geschwister Tanner* (1907; The Tanner Siblings), which was enthusiastically received by Christian Morgenstern, then an editor at Cassirer's; *Der Gehülfe* (1908; The Assistant); and *Jakob von Gunten* (1909; *Jakob von Gunten*), which was to become one of Franz Kafka's favorite novels. Furthermore, a bibliophile edition of his poems appeared in 1909, and numerous short prose pieces were accepted by German vanguard newspapers and periodicals (e.g., *Simplicissimus, Neue Rundschau, Die Schaubühne, Pan, Die weißen Blätter*, and *Kunst und Künstler*). These prose pieces were subsequently assembled in three prose collections published by Kurt Wolff, then a leading avant-garde publisher (*Aufsätze* [1914; Essays], *Geschichten* [1914; Stories], and *Kleine Dichtungen* [1914; Sketches]). Walser's Berlin prose received favorable reviews from such critics as Hermann Hesse and Robert Musil.

Following a profound crisis, the exact nature of which remains conjectural, Walser returned to his native Biel. From there, he ventured forth on his famous *Spaziergänge*, walks that led him to the surrounding countryside, villages, and small towns and that inspired the prose sketches he wrote for newspapers and published in 1917 in book form: *Der Spaziergang* (*The Walk*), *Prosastücke* (Pieces in Prose), and *Kleine Prosa* (Short Prose). *Poetenleben* (A Poet's Life) followed in 1918, and *Seeland* (Lake Country) was published in 1919. Back in the province and separated from his German readers during World War I, Walser's Biel publications lack the pert energy of his Berlin texts and are marked by a pastoral, yet ironically refracted tone. To Walser's dismay, contemporary critics and readers increasingly saw in him a writer turned shepherd boy and failed to recognize the fact that the chatty arabesques and "garlands of language" (Walter Benjamin) in his Biel texts provided a critical counterreality to a world at war.

In the early 1920s, following his move to Bern, Walser's prose became more experimental, focusing on the self-referential nature of writing and providing trenchant insights into the commodification of literature by the culture industry. His last novel, *Der "Räuber"-Roman* (1925; The Robber), did not appear until 1972. It was one of over 500 texts that he wrote in pencil in a minuscule script during the Bern years. Walser had developed this "pencil method," as he called it, to overcome writer's block. After Walser's death, most of the microscripts, initially thought to be in secret code, were deciphered thanks to the painstaking labor of a few scholars at the Robert Walser-Archiv in Zurich.

Although he never belonged to a school or movement and only rarely expounded on his aesthetics, Walser, similar to other early 20th-century writers, searched for new forms that would express a radically altered perception of the world. With his contemporaries, he shared, in the early 1900s, a revolt against 19th-century historicism and a repudiation of memory as an organized logical conservation of past experiences. Walser's work of the 1920s and early 1930s approximates the *écriture automatique* of the surrealists. Many texts are structured by homophones and compulsive rhymes, but what appears as nonsense at first sight is in fact a strategy that allows him to subvert conventional patterns of speech. Considering his art of montage, the acrobatics of his puns, the shock effect created by the way in which he challenged good taste, his taboo topics, and his frequent introduction of metaliterary discourse at the expense of plot, Walser is, indeed, as Mark Harman put it, "a quirky one-man avant-garde."

Walser hid behind a myriad of first-person narrators, including page boys and office clerks, children, and women. He also hid behind historical figures, writers, and characters that he lifted out of plays and novels. He once remarked that his entire work is a kind of novel in progress, a "me-book, cut up into countless segments." This observation describes his method of writing, but it says little about the author himself, who eludes readers with his many voices and guises. Since he had lost most of his readership and lived the life of a recluse, especially during the Bern years, Walser wrote both his audience and himself into the text by enacting the act of writing and by interrupting the narrative flow to address some imagined listener or reader.

Robert Walser has ceased to be the "literary rumor" he was called in the 1960s (by Martin Walser, his German namesake). The critical editions of his works are an indication of Walser's growing recognition by the reading public in German-speaking countries. He has attracted attention abroad as well. In Paris, for instance, the 1993 translation of Walser's thorny *Der "Räuber"-Roman* made headlines. In part, the rediscovery of Walser has to do with his influence on Kafka, which was first noted by Robert Musil, and with the influence on recent criticism by Walter Benjamin, who had written a poignant essay on Walser in 1929. Quite a few contemporary writers, recognizing Walser's identity crises and his marginalization as representative of their own condition, have written on him in Walseresque approximations that combine fiction and documentary, essay and hagiography (e.g., E.Y. Meyer, Jürg Amman, Peter Bichsel, Gerd Hoffmann, and Urs Widmer).

Among American artists and writers, Guy Davenport, the Quay Brothers, and the painter Joan Nelson have paid homage to his life and oeuvre. Scholarly criticism since the late 1960s has distanced itself from speculations about Walser's never reliably diagnosed mental illness and has contributed significantly to a fuller understanding of the complexities of his texts. The diversity of topics and interpretive methods, together with the lack of consensus upon just about any aspect of his work and life, corroborates the fair warning Walser gave to his readers: "Nobody has the right to treat me as if he knew me."

TAMARA S. EVANS

Biography

Born in Biel, Switzerland, 8 August 1878. Left school at the age of fourteen and completed his apprenticeship as a bank clerk in 1895; dreams of an acting career shattered by Josef Kainz's blunt criticism; first poems published in a Swiss newspaper in 1898; until 1905 worked mostly in offices, changing jobs and whereabouts countless times; 1905–13 lived in Berlin; enrolled in a school for servants in 1905 and briefly was butler at Dambrau Castle in Upper Silesia; back in Berlin, part-time secretary for the Berlin Secession; after a deep personal crisis, returned to Biel in 1913; in 1921 moved to Bern to work as assistant librarian at the State Archives, a job he quit after six moths; voluntarily entered Waldau, a psychiatric clinic near Bern, in 1929; in 1933, transferal, against his explicit wishes, to a mental institution in Herisau in eastern Switzerland; stopped writing. Died in Herisau, 25 December 1956.

Selected Works

Collections

Das Gesamtwerk [Kossodo edition], edited by Jochen Greven, 13 vols., 1966–75
Das Gesamtwerk [Suhrkamp edition], edited by Jochen Greven, 12 vols., 1978
Briefe, edited by Jörg Schäfer with Robert Mächler, 1979
Sämtliche Werke in Einzelausgaben, edited by Jochen Greven, 20 vols., 1985–86
Aus dem Bleistiftgebiet. Mikrogramme aus den Jahren 1924–1932, edited by Bernhard Echte and Werner Morlang, 7 vols., 1985–

Novels

Geschwister Tanner, 1907
Der Gehülfe, 1908
Jakob von Gunten, 1909; as *Jakob von Gunten,* translated by Christopher Middleton, 1969
Der "Räuber"-Roman, edited by Jochen Greven and Martin Jürgens in vol. 6 of *Das Gesamtwerk,* 1972; as *The Robber,* translated by Susan Bernofsky, forthcoming 2000

Der Räuber [facsimile edition], edited by Bernhard Echte and Werner Morlang, 1986

Other Prose

Fritz Kocher's Aufsätze, 1904
Aufsätze, 1913
Geschichten, 1914
Kleine Dichtungen, 1914
Prosastücke, 1917
Kleine Prosa, 1917
Der Spaziergang, 1917; as *The Walk* in *The Walk and Other Stories,* translated by Christopher Middleton, 1957
Poetenleben, 1918
Seeland, 1919
Die Rose, 1925
Selected Stories, translated by Christopher Middleton and others, 1982
Robert Walser Rediscovered: Stories, Fairy-Tale Plays, and Critical Responses, edited by Mark Harman, 1985
"Masquerade" and Other Stories, translated by Susan Bernofsky with a foreword by William H. Gass, 1990

Plays

Aschenbrödel, 1901; as *Cinderella,* translated by Walter Arndt, 1985
Schneewittchen, 1901; as *Snowwhite,* translated by Walter Arndt, 1985
Komödie, 1919

Poetry

Gedichte, 1909

Further Reading

Avery, George, *Inquiry and Testament: A Study of the Novels and Short Prose of Robert Walser,* Philadelphia: University of Pennsylvania Press, 1968
Bichsel, Peter, "Geschwister Tanner lesen," in *Robert Walser: Pro Helvetia Dossier,* Bern: Zytglogge, 1984
Borchmeyer, Dieter, editor, *Dichtung im Spiegel der Dichtung: Robert Walser und die moderne Poetik,* Frankfurt: Suhrkamp, 1999
Cardinal, Agnes, *The Figure of Paradox in the Works of Robert Walser,* Stuttgart: Hans-Dieter Heinz, 1982
Chiarini, Paolo, and Hans Dieter Zimmermann, editors, *"Immer dicht vor dem Sturze . . .": Zum Werk Robert Walsers,* Frankfurt: Athenäum, 1987
Evans, Tamara, "'A Paul Klee in Prose': Design, Space and Time in the Work of Robert Walser," *German Quarterly* 57 (1984)
Fuchs, Annette, *Dramaturgie des Narrentums: Das Komische in der Prosa Robert Walsers,* Munich: Fink, 1993
Greven, Jochen, *Robert Walser: Figur am Rande, in wechselndem Licht,* Frankfurt: Fischer, 1992
Harman, Mark, editor, *Robert Walser Rediscovered: Stories, Fairy-Tale Plays, and Critical Responses,* Hanover, New Hampshire, and London: University Press of New England, 1985
Hinz, Klaus-Michael, and Thomas Horst, editors, *Robert Walser,* Frankfurt: Suhrkamp, 1991
Kerr, Katharina, editor, *Über Robert Walser,* 3 vols., Frankfurt: Suhrkamp, 1978–79
Mächler, Robert, *Das Leben Robert Walsers,* Frankfurt: Suhrkamp, 1976
Pender, Malcolm, "A Writer's Relationship to Society: Robert Walser's 'Räuber'-Roman," *Modern Language Review* 78 (1983)
Review of Contemporary Fiction 12, no. 1 (1992) [special Robert Walser issue]
Seelig, Carl, *Wanderungen mit Robert Walser,* Frankfurt: Suhrkamp, 1977
Utz, Peter, *Tanz auf den Rändern: Robert Walsers "Jetztzeitstil,"* Frankfurt: Suhrkamp, 1998

Walther von der Vogelweide ca. 1170–ca. 1230

Among the many medieval German lyric poets (minnesingers) of the courtly culture flourishing in the late 12th and early 13th centuries, Walther von der Vogelweide is deservedly the best known. That he was already for his contemporaries and for successive generations of poets an acknowledged master can be inferred from direct evidence such as references to him or quotations from him by poets including Gottfried von Strassburg (*Tristan*), Wolfram von Eschenbach (*Parzival*), Ulrich von Liechtenstein (ca. 1255), and Hugo von Trimberg (around 1300). Further, the probable site of Walther's grave (in Würzburg) was felt significant enough to be already marked and revered some 100 years after his death. His fame is attested by indirect evidence as well: his texts survive in 30 manuscripts, including all the important collections of minnesang, and those manuscripts can be traced to all parts of the German-speaking Empire. Even taking into account that Walther must have traveled far and wide and performed his songs at various courts, the rich diversity and spread of these later manuscripts surely suggest an artist of considerable popularity.

Minnesang poets were also appreciated for their melodies, and it is significant that Gottfried von Strassburg praises Walther's musicianship. A later reference to Walther that compares him with one of his contemporaries even suggests that Walther's fame owed less to his words than to his melodies, at least two of which, the "Wiener Hofton" (Viennese Court Metre, No. 10 in Cormeau's edition) and the "Ottenton" (Otto Metre, No. 4), survived as part of the repertoire of the later meistersingers (15th to 18th centuries). For another song, the "Palästinalied" (Palestine Song, No. 7), the melody survives in full; for two further songs, the melody survives in fragmentary form. In addition, there are six songs that have a similar metrical structure to French songs whose melodies do exist; given that it was common practice for a poet's melodies (and ideas) to be borrowed freely by other poets, it is conceivable that these six Walther songs, which include the famous "Under the lime-tree" (No. 16), may have been sung to the melodies in question, but this is pure speculation. Nevertheless, if medieval songs are to be appreciated in anything like their original context, it is worth remembering that they are, in fact, primarily songs, not poems intended for a reader, and a performance using a genuine medieval melody, even one that cannot be directly linked to Walther, is probably better than treating the songs simply as texts.

The element of performance is an area that has only recently gained the attention that it deserves in scholarly debate. Since records of how songs were performed in Walther's day are almost non-existent, and there is even uncertainty about such things as the degree of musical accompaniment, or whether more than one singer might be involved, it is perhaps understandable that scholars have tended to concentrate on the poetry rather than the potential dramatic impact of the songs in performance. Yet the texts give ample evidence that Walther, perhaps more than some other poets, was aware of his audience, challenging them, cajoling them, indulging in by-play, adopting various personae, and occasionally scoring off rivals or absent enemies. Indeed, it may well have been his value as a performer that assured Walther of further commissions and further opportunities to compose, since unlike many other minnesingers, he seems to have been dependent on his art to provide him with a living. His live appearances would have involved gestures and movements between sections of the public, and these can sometimes be reconstructed from the texts, as when there are words of address that could be sung directly to the audience, or to a part of it.

An awareness of the possibilities of performance has recently led also to new approaches in textual criticism. Traditionally, scholars took the view that discrepancies between the texts preserved in the various manuscripts were generally caused by scribes misreading earlier texts when copying; they also felt that it was the duty of the modern editor to try to "recreate" the poet's original text by eliminating the "errors." It is now accepted by most, however, that there was probably never any single "authentic" original from the poet's own hand; many of the discrepancies may point to variant versions from Walther himself, scribes recording different versions of the song at different performances (performances either by Walther himself, contemporaries, or later singers), or "intertextual" influences at the time when manuscripts were being collected. The idea of writing down a song in a definitive version, with a fixed text and a fixed number and sequence of stanzas, would not have occurred to Walther or anyone else in a culture where, in any case, oral transmission had by no means been supplanted by writing and reading. When manuscripts record a Walther song in versions with different stanza sequences, for example, it is thus legitimate to speculate on the different circumstances of performance involved and on the different dramatic impacts each version may have had. Only recently have modern editions of Walther's songs appeared that are not based on the premise that a single "authentic" version of the text is possible or desirable, but make allowances for variability and even improvisation by the performer (e.g., Schweikle and Cormeau; references in the present article are to Cormeau's edition).

Given Walther's popularity in his own day and the artistry evident in the surviving texts of his songs, it is not surprising that later generations have idealized his image or added to the mythology surrounding his name. Thus, he has been seen variously as one of the "12 old masters" inspiring the later meistersingers, the romantic minstrel alternatively communing with nature and entertaining at imperial courts, and even the prototypical German patriot defending his country's values against popes and foreigners. This last image was fashioned essentially on the basis of a single song (the "Preislied" or Song of Praise, No. 32); elements of this work even eventually found their way into the text of the German national anthem. Suffice it to say that much of the mythology about Walther bore and bears little resemblance to any facts or even probable facts of Walther's career. As with any poet, however, it is important to distinguish between the person and the particular persona he/she may adopt when expressing thoughts in poetry.

What can be deduced about Walther with any certainty can be summarized as follows: he was probably born around 1170, possibly in Austria, since in his songs Austria and the court of Vienna figure more prominently than any other locality. In the 1190s, he composed and performed songs at that court, which also hosted a contemporary, Reinmar; a number of Walther's and Reinmar's songs suggest a period of mutual borrowing and quotation amounting to a rivalry that may or may not have been serious. On the death of Duke Frederick in 1198, Walther had to leave the court— reluctantly, to judge from the note of longing in his later references to it—and it is about this time that he must have begun the career as a political poet, which may have been more successful in securing him material benefits than his minnesang. At various courts, he wrote songs in support of the Emperors Philip of Suabia, Otto of Brunswick, and Frederick II at a time when the Empire was in considerable turmoil. In his later years, Walther received some reward for his long political service, in the form of a fief near Würzburg, where he is assumed to have died by about 1230. The only historical record from his own lifetime is a reference to a payment made to him in a document dated 1203; the usual interpretation is that this is payment for services as a singer, but a recent hypothesis suggests Walther was also an envoy or a messenger, a role that might link him to another "Walther," who was documented to be in the service of the Emperor Otto. Certainly, he appears occasionally in his songs in the persona of a messenger (No. 4, IV; No. 32; No. 84), but other singers did likewise. Walther also adopts the persona of a seer or philosopher in the "Reichstrilogie" (Empire Trilogy, No. 2) and the persona of a pilgrim or crusader in the Palestine Song (No. 7) and the "Alterston" (Song of Old Age, No. 43); such role-playing throws just as little light on the historical Walther as does the role of lover adopted by all minnesinger.

Walther is deservedly known for the tremendous variety of his poetry, both in its forms and its content. For whatever formal education he had, he would have been indebted to the Church, and religion and religiosity permeate many of his songs, some of which have an explicitly spiritual tone, including the "Traveler's Blessing" No. 10, XI; stanzas in praise of God and Mary in Nos. 3, 11, and 54; and partly confessional, partly sermonizing stanzas such as several in No. 10. More particularly, his knowledge of liturgy and spiritual music and literature is obvious from his "Leich" (Lay, No. 1), a remarkable hymn based on the Latin sequence. In his political songs ("Sangsprüche"), however, for which he adapted and raised to new heights a genre traditionally used by itinerant singers to comment on topical events, Walther was inevitably drawn into the power struggle between the papacy and the Emperor. Presumably with the blessing of his patrons, Walther expressed some views on the Church and on the pope that were extremely critical, at times scathingly so. In a song in support of Otto he defies the pope's excommunication of Otto by recalling for the pope's benefit the latter's earlier condemning of all Otto's enemies (No. 4, I). He also imagines the pope gloating at the sight of German money destined for the crusades actually being used for feasting in Rome (No. 12, VIII and IX). Yet Walther also incorporated spiritual ideals constructively, appealing to the audience's sense of God's mysteries in several songs in support of Philip. In his magnificent songs of old age, Walther preaches a spirituality that rises above secular concerns such as courtliness and fashion.

As a love poet, too, Walther set new standards, inviting his audience to rethink some of the basic premises upon which the convention of minnesang was based. Thus, he took up the challenge of an earlier poet who was somewhat disillusioned with the social context (Hartmann von Aue) and suggested that women should be valued for their femininity, a quality not always associated with the traditional subject of love songs, the aristocratic "lady" (No. 25). Many of the songs for which Walther is famous simply ignore the social context entirely, which has given rise to much speculation on the status of the "girls" who figure in them. Walther also questioned the traditional assumption, much championed by Reinmar, that love involved a ritual of endless suffering. Courtly audiences at the end of the 12th century seem to have preferred songs of male lament, but Walther states provocatively that love is only love if it brings joy (No. 44). In the same song, Walther subjects another piece of dogma to scrutiny, the idea that the female should be a distant, unresponsive partner; for Walther, love must be a reciprocal, as well as a joyful, emotion. Yet he could be as analytical and reflective as any of his contemporaries, as is clear from a song such as No. 23, which, although leaving the modern interpreter groping for the precise meaning of some of the terms, seems to be an attempt to find a balance between love's nobler and baser manifestations. Behind many of his ideas one can detect a strong sense of his own worth as a poet and commentator on contemporary culture. Thus, he is one of the few minnesingers to articulate what many of them must have realized about the whole convention; namely, that what minnesingers celebrated in their songs, including the lady's beauty and other qualities, became laudable only through the poets' own artistry.

ROD FISHER

See also Minnesang

Biography

Born in Austria, ca. 1170. Active in the ducal court of Vienna, prior to 1198; worked in courts of southern and central Germany, 1198–1218; received a land grant near Würzburg from Emperor Frederick II, ca. 1215. Died ca. 1230.

Selected Works

Collections
Spruchlyrik, mittelhochdeutsch/neuhochdeutsch, in *Werke: Gesamtausgabe,* vol. 1, edited by Günther Schweikle, 1994
Walther von der Vogelweide: Leich, Lieder, Sangsprüche, edited by Christoph Cormeau et al., 1996

Poetry
I Saw the World: Sixty Poems from Walther von der Vogelweide, translated by Ian G. Colvin, 1938
Poems, translated by Edwin H. Zeydel and Bayard Quincy Morgan, 1952
Gedichte, edited by P. Wapnewski, with modern German translations, 1962
Die Lieder, edited by Friedrich Maurer, 2 vols., 1967, 1974
Leich, Lieder, Sangsprüche, edited by Christoph Cormeau, 1996

Further Reading

Bäuml, Franz, editor, *From Symbol to Mimesis: The Generation of Walther von der Vogelweide,* Göppingen: Kümmerle, 1984
Bein, Thomas, *Walther von der Vogelweide,* Stuttgart: Reclam, 1997
Brunner, Horst, and Sigrid Neureiter-Lackner, *Walther von der Vogelweide: Epoche, Werk, Wirkung,* Munich: Beck, 1996
Edwards, Cyril, "Walther's Third Song of the 'Reichston': ich sach mit mînen ougen," *Forum for Modern Language Studies* 21, no. 2 (1985)
Fisher, Rodney, "Walther von der Vogelweide als Vortragender: Das Mimische und die Strophenfolge seiner Liebeslieder," in *1000 Jahre Österreich im Spiegel seiner Literatur,* edited by August Obermayer, Dunedin: University of Otago, 1997

Hinman, Martha, "Minne in a new mode: Walther and the literary tradition," *Deutsche Vierteljahrsschrift für Literaturwissenschaft und Geistesgeschichte* 48, no. 2 (1974)

Jones, George Fenwick, *Walther von der Vogelweide*, New York: Twayne, 1968

McFarland, Timothy, and Silvia Ranawake, *Walther von der Vogelweide: Twelve Studies*, Oxford: Meeuws, 1982

Rasmussen, Ann, "Representing Woman's Desire: Walther's Woman's Stanzas in *Ich hoere iu sô vil tugende jehen* (L 43,9), *Under den linden* (L 39,11), and *Frô Welt* (L 100,24)," in *Women as*

Protagonists and Poets in the German Middle Ages: An Anthology of Feminist Approaches to Middle High German Literature, edited by Albrecht Classen, Göppingen: Kümmerle, 1991

Sayce, Olive, *The Medieval German Lyric, 1150–1300: The Development of Its Themes and Forms in Their European Context*, Oxford: Clarendon Press, and New York: Oxford University Press, 1982

Wells, David, "Imperial Sanctity and Political Reality: Bible, Liturgy, and the Ambivalence of Symbol in Walther von der Vogelweide's Songs Under Otto IV," *Speculum* 53, no. 3 (1978)

War Novels

The term *war novel* is applied to 20th-century German works in a variety of styles, including not only conventional prose narratives but also works that might otherwise be defined as histories or even memoirs. Such works, all of which are necessarily based to some extent on a historical reality in which men and women had to face death and destruction through mechanized warfare on a scale never before known, represent a wide range of attitudes, from nationalist heroism to pacifist condemnation of war.

German novels concerning World War I interpret the experience of the lost conflict either as a test of the nation's bravery or as a pointless waste of life. Early writings were predictably positive and played down reality in favor of patriotic sentiment, and adventurous memoirs, such as the pilot Gunther Plüschow's *Die Abenteuer des Fliegers von Tsingtau* (1916; *My Escape from Donington Hall*), remained extremely popular after the war. Realistic views of trench warfare did appear in works such as Walter Flex's poeticized, firsthand report *Der Wanderer zwischen beiden Welten* (1917; The Wanderer between Two Worlds), although some, such as Fritz von Unruh's *Opfergang* (1919; *The Way of Sacrifice*), which was written during the battle of Verdun and interprets the war as a release of violent passions, were not allowed to be published until after the war. After 1919, military memoirs predominated, often stressing the adventurous side of the war and sometimes propagating the theory that Germany had been stabbed in the back by socialists and traitors. In literary terms, the most important of these personal works is Ernst Jünger's diary, consciously turned into the novel *In Stahlgewittern* (1920; *The Storm of Steel*), which, while it did not minimize the reality of war, nevertheless presented it as a positive test of the individual.

Toward the end of the 1920s, former soldiers who had come to terms with their experiences tried to make clear the full horrors of the war and question its validity in a new kind of war novel, many of which acquired international fame. The first was Arnold Zweig's *Der Streit um den Sergeanten Grischa* (1927; *The Case of Sergeant Grischa*), a case study of an innocent and illiterate Russian soldier caught up in the inexorable machinery of the German war bureaucracy. *Erziehung vor Verdun* (1935; *Education before Verdun*), a later novel by Zweig, written when he was exiled from Germany by the Nazis, is a fuller indictment of mankind's propensity to wage war.

The most famous of the antiwar novels is Erich Maria Remarque's *Im Westen nichts Neues* (1929; *All Quiet on the Western Front*). Remarque presents the war through the eyes of a young soldier who has gone straight from school to the front and who sees his generation as having been betrayed by those who should know better. The frontline soldiers are victims, aware only that war is something that has happened to them and that has brutalized them. Most are killed, and death is the real enemy, not the Allies. Remarque's message is clearly "no more war," and the vivid writing evoked a sympathetic response in all countries, although it was (mistakenly) praised for stressing the rise of close comradeship. (The sequel, *Der Weg zurück*, [1931; *The Road Back*] makes clear that this comradeship was temporary and artificial, breaking down as Germany descended into divisive turmoil.) *All Quiet* became a model for other antiwar novels: Theodor Plievier's *Des Kaisers Kulis* (1929; *The Kaiser's Coolies*) is its naval equivalent, showing the problems of the ordinary sailor, but it is clearly far more political than Remarque's work, and like many other antiwar novels, it is expressly left-wing.

Many novelists, such as Remarque, Ludwig Renn, Peter Riss, and Ernst Johannsen, drew on their personal war experiences in their fictional writing. Others, such as Edlef Köppen in *Heeresbericht* (1930; *Higher Command*), mixed historical documents with the fictionalized experiences of a central character who gradually becomes aware of the madness of the war as his own sanity crumbles. Some of the antiwar novels of the Weimar Republic were written from different perspectives as well. Alexander Moritz Frey's *Die Pflasterkästen* (1929; *The Crossbearers*) presents the war through the eyes of a noncombatant stretcher bearer, and Adrienne Thomas's *Die Katrin wird Soldat* (1930; translated as *Katrin Becomes a Soldier* and *Cathérine Joins Up*) is the fictitious diary of a volunteer nurse in Alsace-Lorraine. War novels by women are rare. Thomas's central character is caught geographically between France and Germany and sees the men she knows and loves being killed and wounded. Remarque also makes the point that it is the field hospital that shows what war is really like. Yet another perspective is that of Ernst Glaeser's *Jahrgang 1902* (1928; *Class of 1902*), which focuses on a schoolboy at the outbreak of war. The schoolboy's adolescence mirrors the changing response to the war, as seen from the home front, from universal nationalism to disillusion, division, and defeat. The war did not end, of course, with either the armistice or the Treaty of Versailles, and it left deep scars following the revolution of 1919. The political turmoil is clearly presented in Plievier's documentary novel *Der Kaiser ging, die Generäle blieben* (1932; *The Kaiser Goes, the Generals Remain*), while the social aspects are highlighted in works such as Remarque's *The Road Back*.

All Quiet evoked a savage right-wing response, and after the rise of Hitler, pacifist war novels, especially those by Jewish writers such as Zweig, were banned (and burned), and the ensuing ideological realignment tolerated only those novels that stressed the heroism of the German frontline soldier. With the outbreak of a new war in 1939, the Nazis ensured that popular writing again glorified the triumphs in the new conflict. The notion that war could be presented as an adventure did not die out, however, even after 1945, and magazines with war stories of that type—the so-called *Landsershefte*—retained their popularity.

All German war novels written after Germany's defeat in 1945, however, had to take into account a different set of premises than those that applied after World War I. The survivors of the 1914–18 conflict could condemn war as such. German writers after 1945 had to respond somehow to a war that had not only ended in defeat but that had clearly been the responsibility of a German government that had committed atrocities on an unheard-of scale. That it was also a war in which, for the first time, there was no perceptible front and civilians were equally threatened by the new mechanisms of destruction was an additional element, as was the fact that the end of the war—declared *die Stunde Null* in what was soon to be a divided Germany—also marked the start of the atomic era. The potential of the Hiroshima bomb was treated with graphic imagination later in novels of a hypothetical future war, such as Anton-Andreas Guha's *Ende* (1983; *Ende: A Diary of the Third World War*).

The response of many German novelists is summed up in the phrase *Bewältigung der Vergangenheit* (coming to terms with the Nazi past). This took a variety of different forms, and one response was simply to ignore the fact that Germany had been fighting for a Nazi government. What we may still call adventurous war novels often ignored the political side of the war. Gerd Gaiser's *Die sterbende Jagd* (1953; *The Falling Leaf*) shows, for example, an air squadron fighting at the end of the war (rather fewer novels show the beginnings), aware that they will be defeated but convinced of their duty to fight. Other writers in this quasi-heroic style, such as Edwin Erich Dwinger, not only ignored the politics of the war but also stressed the superior bravery of the German soldiers on the Russian front and contributed to the new, cold war between east and west. Another type of popular novel—by Heinz Konsalik and others—used the war simply as a background for human interest stories.

The World War I novelist Plievier, who spent World War II in Russia, documented the struggle between Germany and the Soviets and the victory of the latter in a descriptive if sometimes sensationally written trilogy: *Stalingrad* (1945), *Moskau* (1952), *Berlin* (1954). The universality of the conflict was made clear by writers such as Hans Werner Richter in *Du sollst nicht töten* (1955; *Thou Shalt Not Kill*). Another older writer, Remarque, who lived in the United States throughout the war, made an attempt to understand how Germany could have fought for Nazism. *Zeit zu leben und Zeit zu sterben* (1954; *A Time to Love and a Time to Die*) is initially set on the eastern front and then in Germany late in the war. The central figure, again an ordinary soldier, eventually does face up to his share of responsibility for the toleration of Nazism, although Remarque also indicts modern warfare and the fact that death could come indiscriminately from the skies to civilians and children. His central character learns of the need to resist, allows some Russian prisoners to escape, and is himself killed, perhaps in expiation for Germany's acquiescence to the Nazis. At the time of his death, however, his wife may be pregnant, so there is some hope for a future generation.

Younger men, such as Heinrich Böll, who fought through the war coped with it partly as others had done in World War I, by presenting themselves as a betrayed generation. *Wo warst du, Adam?* (1951; *And Where Were You, Adam?*) shows us a series of (mostly) reluctant soldiers, plus some genuine Nazis, whose psychological backgrounds are explored. There is no attempt to ignore Nazi atrocities, and the extermination camps are portrayed. At the same time, the empathy is for the ordinary soldier and his attempts to stay alive, although the central figure is again killed pointlessly at the very end of the war by one of the Germans' own shells. The overall message is that basically decent people were caught up in the war whether they liked it or not.

The question of what the individual could or should have done is a difficult one. Alfred Andersch offers another response in *Die Kirschen der Freiheit* (1952; *The Cherries of Freedom*), a literary report on his own desertion to the Americans once it had become clear that Germany would be defeated. The work was condemned as self-justificatory, with its questionable portrayal of an inner rejection of Hitler. Certainly it leaves open the idea that if good men remain silent, evil will triumph. Andersch's other war novels explore the same theme, again mixing reality (and documentation) with what might happen, as in his *Winterspelt* (1973; *Winterspelt*). The publication date of *Winterspelt* is an indication that the war was still a literary issue 30 years after its end. Siegfried Lenz, even younger (and drafted at the very end of the war), shows in his novels a more distanced approach to the difficult problem of responsibility, especially in his large novel *Deutschstunde* (1968; *The German Lesson*).

The division of Germany also gave rise to different responses to the war. In the former German Democratic Republic, Anna Seghers, for example, in *Die Toten bleiben jung*, 1949 (*The Dead Stay Young*) focuses on the political resistance by German communists, which itself represents a complete distancing from the Nazi regime. Other writers in the East, however, such as Franz Fühmann, accepted the way in which Germans willingly believed even manifestly untrue Nazi propaganda.

A final stage of German coping is represented by another popular writer, the much-translated Hans Helmut Kirst. His *08/15* trilogy (1954–55; later extended and translated as the "Gunner Asch" books), while apparently critical of Nazism and the war, nevertheless highlights an honest and satisfyingly anti-Nazi rebel who is also a highly effective soldier primarily on the eastern front in defensive rather than attacking positions. Gunner (ultimately Lieutenant) Asch, with whom the reader empathizes, is contrasted with negatively presented Nazis (usually ineffectual as soldiers) and with naive fellow travelers. Kirst does not deny Nazism, but it is rigidly compartmentalized, and as we pursue the individualistic Asch through to the end of the war, the reader is sometimes left wondering how such soldiers could have been defeated.

BRIAN MURDOCH

See also Erich Maria Remarque

Further Reading

Amberger, Waltraud, *Männer, Krieger, Abenteurer,* Frankfurt: R.G. Fischer, 1984; 2nd edition, 1987

Bartz, Thorsten, *Allgegenwärtige Fronten—Sozialistische und linke Kriegsromane in der Weimarer Republik 1918–1933,* Frankfurt: Lang, 1997

Bock, Sigrid, and Manfred Hahn, *Erfahrung Nazideutschland: Romane in Deutschland 1933–1945,* Berlin: Aufbau, 1987

Bostock, John Knight, *Some Well-Known German War-Novels 1914–1930,* Oxford: Blackwell, 1931

Genno, Charles N., and Heinz Wetzel, editors, *The First World War in German Narrative Prose: Essays in Honour of George Wallis Field,* Toronto and Buffalo, New York: University of Toronto Press, 1980

Gollbach, Michael, *Die Wiederkehr des Weltkriegs in der Literatur: Zu den Frontromanen der späten Zwanziger Jahre,* Kronberg: Scriptor, 1978

Klein, Holger, editor, *The First World War in Fiction,* London: Macmillan, 1976; New York: Barnes and Noble, 1978

Klose, Werner, editor, *Deutsche Kriegsliteratur zu zwei Weltkriegen,* Stuttgart: Reclam, 1984

Müller, Hans-Harald, *Der Krieg und die Schriftsteller,* Stuttgart: Metzler, 1986

Pfeifer, Jochen, *Der deutsche Kriegsroman 1945–1960,* Königstein: Scriptor, 1981

Pfeiler, Wilhelm Karl, *War and the German Mind,* New York: Columbia University Press, 1941

Schwarz, Wilhelm J., *War and the Mind of Germany I,* Frankfurt and Bern: Lang, 1975

Stickelberger-Eder, Margrit, *Aufbruch 1914: Kriegsromane der späten Weimarer Republik,* Zurich: Artemis, 1983

Travers, Martin Patrick Anthony, *German Novels on the First World War and Their Ideological Implications, 1918–1933,* Stuttgart: Heinz, 1982

Wagener, Hans, editor, *Gegenwartsliteratur und Drittes Reich,* Stuttgart: Reclam, 1977

——, editor, *Von Böll bis Buchheim: Deutsche Kriegsprosa nach 1945,* Amsterdam and Atlanta, Georgia: Rodopi, 1997

Jakob Wassermann 1873–1934

In 1935, shortly after Jakob Wassermann's death, Thomas Mann described him as a "Weltstar des Romans" (worldwide star of novel writing). In the postwar period, however, Wassermann's literary prominence went into a deep eclipse. Although more recently there has been a significant revival of interest in his works in Germany, only one of his books, *Caspar Hauser; oder die Trägheit des Herzens* (1908; *Caspar Hauser*), remains in print in English at the end of the 20th century. During his lifetime, as Mann's comment indicates, his work was widely read in many languages and enjoyed huge popularity in its German version. With the benefit of hindsight, we can see that the elements that made him so appealing to a contemporary audience also explain his subsequent literary change of fortune. His approach to the novel form derived from his natural talents as a storyteller. The fluidity and ease with which narration came to him permitted him to adapt his manner from 19th-century fiction, but Wassermann never had cause to become self-questioning or self-conscious about his chosen medium, nor did he venture into the self-reflective and self-critical formal experiments of the modern novel. Moreover, the earnestness with which he approached the issues of his time has left him more foreign to subsequent generations than those of his colleagues who framed their artistic vision within a more powerfully aestheticizing distance. Nonetheless, it remains noteworthy that many of his most distinguished contemporaries took his work seriously and set it securely within the significant heritage of its period. Not only did he enjoy the respect of Thomas Mann, but Arthur Schnitzler and Hugo von Hofmannsthal held him in high esteem as well.

The revival of attention in Germany began with the 50th anniversary of Wassermann's death and the organization of an exhibition commemorating his career in 1984. Yet even here, the focus lay initially with his role as a spokesperson for the condition of German Jews rather than with his contributions to the tradition of German literary prose. In this role, the dated quality of his voice does open up an authentic historical perspective. The first of his important books, *Die Juden von Zirndorf* (*The Jews of Zirndorf*), which appeared in 1897, established Wassermann with some conviction as a Jew who refused both assimilation and separation in his relations with German society. The novel begins with a portrayal of the Jewish community of Franconia in the 17th century and the effect of Sabbatai Zevi's ill-fated messianic call. Never before had the Jewish presence been presented with its legitimate place conferred by such deep historical roots in the German landscape, nor with such vital individual quality in that place.

With *Caspar Hauser,* Wassermann achieved a major success in 1908. This novel was based on extensive research into the famous case of a foundling reputed to have been the dispossessed heir to the throne of Baden; according to the author, the theme had been maturing in his mind for many years before he felt sufficient confidence in his judgment to execute it. He conceived the novel as a study of a great injustice perpetrated by a harsh world against a completely innocent party, and he regarded the historical events it retold as an injustice from which the conscience of an entire society would remain poisoned until it acknowledged and then atoned for this wrong. All the brutalities perpetrated against Caspar Hauser are ascribed, ultimately, to the human failing to which Wassermann refers in the title as *Trägheit des Herzens* (inertia of the heart). This idea returns in different aspects throughout his oeuvre. On the one hand, it provides a foundation for his thought, which he is able to vary with some subtlety, but on the other hand, it always reasserts a simple concept of human failings that seems to enthrall his judgment with its narrow certainty.

The secret of Wassermann's particular popularity with a broad bourgeois readership begins to take on some clarity with books such as *Das Gänsemännchen* (*The Goose Man*), published in 1915. As the story of a gifted composer in 19th-century Nürnberg, it foregrounds the burdens that a stupid, uncomprehending, and philistine world imposes on a man of talent and imagination. The narrative also contains frequent points of intersection with motifs from the author's other writings, including characters from previous novels and references to elements of the Caspar Hauser story and to the explorer Stanley, who would be the subject of a biography by Wassermann published in 1932. This interplay would recur right through the author's career, with characters constantly returning in new works. Thus, the reader enters at the author's invitation into a continuous world of interwoven stories. This easy relationship between storyteller and audience, however, belies the moralized critical posture toward the world that Wassermann also adopts. Nonetheless, the aesthetic experience that he offers his reader lets those who take up his books share all too comfortably in the privilege of moral judgment that animates the representation of that world. The moral position that separates the narrator from injustice or narrow-mindedness tends to extend itself to include the reader's position and thus to generate an alibi in the aesthetic compact between them.

The achievement in fiction that marks his greatest impact came in 1928 with *Der Fall Maurizius* (*The Maurizius Case*). In this long account of a son's mistrust of his father and the single-minded pursuit of truth and justice, Wassermann's debt to the Russian novels of the 19th century shows its effect most vividly. This story, too, led to further accounts of its principal characters in 1931 with *Etzel Andergast* (*Doctor Kerkhoven*) and in *Joseph Kerkhovens dritte Existenz* (*Joseph Kerkhoven's Third Existence*), which was still undergoing revisions at the time of the author's death (it was published posthumously in 1934).

Wassermann wrote some light dramas, biographies, and essays. Of his excursions outside fiction, the reflection on German anti-Semitism as he experienced it without doubt remains by far the most significant. Written in 1921, *Mein Weg als Deutscher und Jude* (*My Life as German and Jew*) expresses the defiant demand that Germans acknowledge the rights of a community that has shared German soil with them since the early Middle Ages, and it relates with bitter insistence how far these rights have been denied and the cruel effects this has had on all concerned.

MARCUS BULLOCK

See also Jewish Culture and Literature

Biography

Born in Fürth, near Nuremberg, 10 March 1873. After miserable early years, his fortunes began to improve with his first publications in 1896, which in addition to his literary work included reviews and articles for the *Frankfurter Zeitung*; reputation as a critic and essayist with many prominent journals; visited the United States, 1927, and Egypt, 1928–29; in 1933, *Die neue Rundschau* marked his 60th birthday by devoting most of its March issue to him (those expressing their appreciation of his achievements included Alfred Döblin and Heinrich Mann). Died in Austria, 1 January 1934.

Selected Works

Die Juden von Zirndorf, 1897; as *The Jews of Zirndorf*, translated by Cyrus Brooks, 1933
Die Geschichte der jungen Renate Fuchs, 1900
Der Moloch, 1902
Alexander in Babylon, 1905
Melusine, 1906
Die Schwestern, 1906
Caspar Hauser; oder, die Trägheit des Herzens, 1908; as *Caspar Hauser*, translated by Caroline Newton, 1928
Erwin Reiner, 1910
Der goldene Spiegel, 1911
Die ungleichen Schalen: Fünf einaktige Dramen, 1912
Der Mann von 40 Jahren, 1913
Deutsche Charaktere und Begebenheiten, 1915
Das Gänsemännchen, 1915; as *The Goose Man*, translated by Ludwig Lewisohn and Allen W. Porterfield, 1920
Olivia, 1916
Christian Wahnschaffe, 1918; as *The World's Illusion*, translated by Ludwig Lewisohn, 1920
Der Wendekreis I. Der unbekannte Gast, 1920; as World's Ends, translated by Lewis Galantière, 1927
Mein Weg als Deutscher und Jude, 1921; as *My Life as German and Jew*, translated by S.N. Brainin, 1933
Der Wendekreis II. Oberlins drei Stufen. Sturreganz, 1922; as *Oberlin's Three Stages*, translated by A.W. Porterfield, 1925
Der Wendekreis III. Ulrike Woytich, 1923; as *Gold*, translated by Louise C. Wilcox, 1924
Der Geist des Pilgers, 1923
Deutsche Charaktere und Begebenheiten II, 1924
Der Wendekreis IV. Faber; oder, die verlorenen Jahre, 1924; as *Faber; or, The Lost Years*, translated by Harry Hanson, 1925
Laudin und die Seinen, 1925; as *Wedlock*, translated by Ludwig Lewisohn, 1926
Das Amulett, 1926
Der Aufruhr um den Junker Ernst, 1926; as *The Triumph of Youth*, translated by O.P. Schinnerer, 1927
Lebensdienst, 1928
Der Fall Maurizius, 1928; as *The Maurizius Case*, translated by Caroline Newton, 1929
Hofmannsthal der Freund, 1929
Christoph Columbus, Der Don Quichote des Ozeans, 1929; as *Christopher Columbus, Don Quixote of the Seas*, translated by Eric Sutton, 1930
Etzel Andergast, 1931; as *Doctor Kerkhoven*, translated by Cyrus Brooks, 1932
Lukardis, Schauspiel in drei Akten, 1932
Bula Matari, Das Leben Stanleys, 1932; as *Bula Matari, Stanley, Conqueror of a Continent*, translated by Eden and Cedar Paul, 1934
Selbstbetrachtungen, 1933
Joseph Kerkhovens dritte Existenz, 1934; as *Joseph Kerhoven's Third Existence*, translated by Eden and Cedar Paul, 1934

Further Reading

Corkhill, Allen, "Emancipation and Redemption in Jakob Wassermann's novel *Die Geschichte der jungen Renate Fuchs*," *Seminar* 22 no. 4, (1986)

Garrin, Stephen Howard, *The Concept of Justice in Jakob Wassermann's Trilogy,* Bern and Las Vegas, Nevada: Lang, 1979

Karlweis, Marta, *Jakob Wassermann: Bild, Kampf, und Werk,* Amsterdam: Querido, 1935

Koester, Rudolf, *Jakob Wassermann,* Berlin: Morgenbuch, 1996

Miller, Henry, *Reflections on the Maurizius Case,* Santa Barbara, California: Capra Press, 1974

Rodewald, Dierk, editor, *Jakob Wassermann 1873–1934: Ein Weg als Deutscher und Jude,* Bonn: Bouvier, 1984

Schnetzler, Kaspar, *Der Fall Maurizius: Jakob Wassermanns Kunst des Erzählens,* Bern: Lang, 1968

Wolff, Rudolf, editor, *Jakob Wassermann: Werk und Wirkung,* Bonn: Bouvier, 1987

Frank Wedekind 1864–1918

Frank Wedekind was a member of the talented generation of writers who came onto the literary scene at the end of the 1880s at the height of the German Naturalist movement. Although Wedekind was briefly associated with the Berlin Naturalists around Gerhart Hauptmann in 1888–89, he then based himself in the other center of naturalism in Germany, Munich, in 1889–91. His literary output, including his early masterpiece *Frühlings Erwachen* (1891; *Spring's Awakening*), was written in opposition to that movement. Wedekind rejected naturalism's emphasis on determinism in favor of an individualist *Lebensphilosophie,* which owed much to the philosopher Friedrich Nietzsche. Wedekind has been seen as a forerunner of Expressionism, and while there is undoubtedly some truth in this, it is a categorization that Wedekind himself rejected. Moreover, it was not the Expressionist generation but the young Bertolt Brecht who was most influenced by Wedekind's plays, poems, and, not least, his larger-than-life personality, which Brecht described as his greatest work. Wedekind is thus best viewed as an outsider who resists simple categorization, but it is perhaps precisely for that reason that he is now regarded as one of the most significant figures in the German literary transition from realism to modernism around the turn of the century.

The fictional world of Wedekind's plays is peopled by grotesque, tragicomic characters—if *characters* is the right word, for more often than not his figures are caricatures who often appear to be little more than marionettes in an absurd world. Wedekind's predilection is for outsider figures such as the artist, the swindler, the pimp, and the prostitute—people who were at the margins of the respectable world of bourgeois society that Wedekind never tired of attacking. But that is not to say that these alternative figures embody a viable alternative ideological position, for they, too, are usually destined to fail, as is the case with Lulu and the Marquis of Keith.

Literary success and public notoriety arrived relatively late in Wedekind's life. The radicalism of his challenge to the aesthetic as well as moral norms of Wilhelmine society meant that Wedekind had to wait until 1898 to see any of his plays performed. But it was not until the performance of *Spring's Awakening* in Berlin in 1906, under the direction of Max Reinhardt, that Wedekind achieved the real breakthrough that he craved. In the preceding ten years, Wedekind had worked first as a satirist, then as a cabaret artist. From 1896 to 1899, he was a major contributor to *Simplicissimus,* the leading German satirical magazine of the period, and this allowed him to reach a substantial readership for the first time, but it also brought him an eight-month prison sentence in 1899 for a poem judged to be insulting to the kaiser. Wedekind wrote poetry from an early age, and his poetic oeuvre amounts to nearly 150 poems, mostly on erotic or political themes. As a cabaret artist from 1901 to 1905, Wedekind performed his own poems to a guitar accompaniment, becoming Germany's leading *Bänkelsänger* (ballad singer). The influence of his poetry/songs not only on the young Brecht but also on the post–World War II generation of *Liedermacher* such as Wolf Biermann and Franz-Josef Degenhardt was considerable, but his poetry has received little attention from literary historians.

Following his breakthrough in the theater in 1906, Wedekind concentrated on drama, but he was repeatedly thwarted by ever greater scrutiny from what was an extremely strict censorship regime in Germany in general and Munich in particular. His new plays were regularly banned from the stage, and the situation was exacerbated after the outbreak of World War I, when his plays all but disappeared from the German stage.

Wedekind's plays were quickly rediscovered in the more liberal climate of the 1920s, but it was the plays he wrote before 1906 that were most in vogue (especially *Spring's Awakening,* the Lulu plays, and *Der Marquis von Keith* [1901; The *Marquis of Keith*]); his later plays were largely ignored. This tendency has persisted ever since, so that the later plays have been relatively neglected not only by the stage but also by literary historians. At the same time, the monumental biography of Wedekind by Arthur Kutscher (1922–31) served to reinforce the mythology of Wedekind's scandalous life and to exacerbate the critical tendency to read the plays biographically, which was a detriment to a true appreciation of his plays' radical innovativeness.

Wedekind's works were totally ignored during the Nazi period and were not often staged in the early postwar period either, and certainly not in the GDR. It was not until the 1970s that a Wedekind renaissance occurred as theaters and literary historians rediscovered his work. But it was only in the 1980s that scholars began the task of establishing definitive texts of the plays, which had hitherto been available only in unreliable versions, and which had often been seriously affected by censorship (a major new critical edition of the texts began to appear in 1994). This process has already led to major reevaluations of the better-known plays. Perhaps the most important is Peter Zadek's controversial and highly acclaimed production at the Hamburger Schauspielhaus in February 1988 of the original single-play version of what became the Lulu plays, the so-called *Monstretragödie* or *Monster Tragedy* (the text was subsequently published for the first time in 1990). The production demonstrated that the original precensorship version had lost none of its power to shock and challenge contemporary audiences both morally and aesthetically. The Zadek production of the *Monster Tragedy* was the first of several in Germany, and it also prompted renewed scholarly interest in Wedekind in general and the Lulu plays in particular. It remains to be seen whether this will result in a reevaluation of Wedekind's oeuvre as a whole, including the later plays and the poetry, to say nothing of Wedekind's various, often fragmentary prose works.

KARL LEYDECKER

See also Expressionism

Biography

Born in Hanover, 24 July 1864. Studied at the universities of Lausanne, 1884, Munich, 1884–85, and Zurich, 1888; worked in advertising, 1886–88; secretary for a circus, 1888; worked as a journalist and cabaret artist, performing in several of his own plays; in Paris, London, Zurich, and Berlin; lived primarily in Munich. Died 9 March 1918.

Selected Works

Collections

Gesammelte Werke, edited by A. Kutscher and R. Friedenthal, 9 vols., 1912–21
Ausgewählte Werke, edited by Fritz Strich, 5 vols., 1924
Prosa, Dramen, Verse, edited by Hans-Georg Maier, 2 vols., 1954–60
Werke, edited by Manfred Hahn, 3 vols., 1969
Werke, Kritische Studienausgabe, edited by Elke Austermühl, Rolf Kieser, and Hartmut Vinçon, 8 vols., 1994–

Plays

Der Schnellmaler (produced 1916), 1889
Kinder und Narren, 1891; revised version, *Die junge Welt* (produced 1908), 1897
Frühlings Erwachen (produced 1906), 1891; as *The Awakening of Spring*, translated by Francis J. Ziegler, 1909; as *Spring's Awakening*, translated by S.A. Eliot, in *Tragedies of Sex*, 1923; translated by Frances Fawcett and Stephen Spender, in *Five Tragedies of Sex*, 1952; translated by Eric Bentley in *The Modern Theatre*, vol. 6, 1960; as *Spring Awakening*, translated by Tom Osborn, 1969; also translated by Edward Bond, 1980
Lulu, 1913; as *The Lulu Plays*, translated by C.R. Mueller, 1967; as *Lulu*, 1971
  Der Büchse der Pandora: Eine Monstretragödie (written 1894; produced 1988), 1990
  Der Erdgeist (produced 1898), 1895; as *Erdgeist*, translated by S.A. Eliot, 1914; as *Earth-Spirit*, translated by S.A. Eliot, in *Tragedies of Sex*, 1923; translated by Frances Fawcett and Stephen Spender, in *Five Tragedies of Sex*, 1952
  Die Büchse der Pandora (produced 1904), 1904; as *Pandora's Box*, 1918; translated by Frances Fawcett and Stephen Spender, in *Five Tragedies of Sex*, 1952
Der Kammersänger (produced 1899), 1899; as *Heart of a Tenor*, 1913; as *The Tenor*, translated by André Tridon, 1921
Der Liebestrank (produced 1900), 1899
Der Marquis von Keith (produced 1901), 1901; edited by Wolfgang Hartwig, 1965; as *The Marquis of Keith*, translated by Beatrice Gottlieb, in *From the Modern Repertoire 2*, edited by Eric Bentley,

1957; translated by C.R. Mueller, in *The Modern Theatre*, edited by R.W. Corrigan, 1964
So ist das Leben (produced 1902), 1902; as *König Nicolo*, 1911; as *Such Is Life*, translated by Francis J. Ziegler, 1912
Die Kaiserin von Neufundland (pantomime, produced 1902)
Hidalla; oder, Sein und Haben (produced 1905), 1904; as *Karl Hetmann, der Zwergriese*, in *Gesammelte Werke*, 1913
Totentanz (produced 1906), 1906; as *Tod und Teufel*, 1909; as *Death and Devil*, translated by Frances Fawcett and Stephen Spender, in *Five Tragedies of Sex*, 1952
Musik (produced 1908), 1908
Die Zensur (produced 1909), 1908
Oaha (produced 1911), 1908; as *Till Eulenspiegel*, 1916
Der Stein der Weisen (produced 1911), 1909
In allen Sätteln gerecht, 1910
Mit allen Hunden gehetzt, 1910
In allen Wassern gewaschen, 1910
Schloss Wetterstein (produced 1917), 1912; as *Castle Wetterstein*, translated by Frances Fawcett and Stephen Spender, in *Five Tragedies of Sex*, 1952
Franziska (produced 1912), 1912
Simon; oder, Scham und Eifersucht (produced 1914), 1914
Bismarck (produced 1926), 1916
Überfürchtenichts (produced 1919), 1917
Herakles (produced 1919), 1917
Das Sonnen Spektrum (produced 1922); as *The Solar Spectrum*, translated by D. Faehl and E. Vaughn, in *Tulane Drama Review* 4 (1959)
Tragedies of Sex (includes *Spring's Awakening*; *Earth-Spirit*; *Pandora's Box*; *Damnation!*), translated by S.A. Eliot, 1923
Ein Genussmensch, edited by Fritz Strich, 1924
Five Tragedies of Sex (includes *Earth-Spirit*; *Pandora's Box*; *Castle Wetterstein*; *Death and the Devil*; *Spring's Awakening*), translated by Frances Fawcett and Stephen Spender, 1952; as *The Lulu Plays and Other Sex Tragedies*, 1972

Fiction

Die Fürstin Russalka, 1897
Mine-Haha; oder, Über die körperliche Erziehung der jungen Mädchen, 1901
Feuerwerk, 1905

Poetry

Die vier Jahreszeiten, 1905
Lautenlieder, 1920
Ich hab meine Tante geschlachtet: Lautenlieder und "Simplizissimus"-Gedichte, edited by Manfred Hahn, 1967

Other

Schauspielkunst: Ein Glossarium, 1910
Gesammelte Briefe, edited by Fritz Strich, 2 vols., 1924
Selbstdarstellung, edited by Willi Reich, 1954
Der vermummte Herr: Briefe 1881–1917, edited by Wolfdietrich Rasch, 1967
Die Tagebücher: Ein erotisches Leben, edited by Gerhard Hay, 1986; as *Diary of an Erotic Life*, translated by W.E. Yuill, 1990

Further Reading

Boa, Elizabeth, *The Sexual Circus: Wedekind's Theatre of Subversion*, New York and Oxford and New York: Blackwell, 1987
Jones, Robert A., and Leroy R. Shaw, *Frank Wedekind: A Bibliographical Handbook*, 2 vols., Munich, and New Providence, New Jersey: Saur, 1996
Lewis, Ward B., *The Ironic Dissident: Frank Wedekind in the View of His Critics*, Columbia, South Carolina: Camden House, 1997

Meyer, Michael, *Theaterzensur in München, 1900–1918: Geschichte und Entwicklung der polizeilichen Zensur und des Theaterzensurbeirates unter besonderer Berücksichtigung Frank Wedekinds,* Munich: Kommissionsverlag UNI-Druck, 1982

Vinçon, Hartmut, *Frank Wedekind,* Stuttgart: Metzler, 1987

Frühlings Erwachen 1891

Play by Frank Wedekind

The response to *Frühlings Erwachen* (translated as *The Awakening of Spring, Spring's Awakening,* and *Spring Awakening*) was shock and scandal—reactions that Frank Wedekind's work may still evoke—as well as censorship, a problem that hounded him throughout most of his creative lifetime. Characteristically disposed to treat the urges of the flesh, the author in this play dealt with subjects that flew in the face of prim Wilhelmine morality. Bearing a title metaphorically reflecting the first stirrings of adolescent sexuality, the drama represents copulation, sadomasochism, masturbation, and homosexual love, and it therefore incurred the wrath of the censors. Indeed, it was for this reason that the drama did not see its premiere until 15 years after publication in the production of Max Reinhardt at the Kammerspiele in Berlin in 1906, where Wedekind himself played the role of the Masked Gentleman. The public outrage incited by the dramatist's treatment of taboos was intensified by his social criticism of parents and pedagogues whose authority drove pupils to suicide and whose benightedness and prudery regarding sex education exposed adolescents to risks of pregnancy, abortion, and death.

The nature of the drama puzzled critics and scholars. The figure of the Masked Gentleman suggests allegory; a didactic intent lies behind the illustration of repression in the institutions of family, school, and church; a problem play conveys a tendentious message advocating sexual enlightenment. Traditional coherent dramatic development is replaced by an episodic arrangement of scenes by turns farcical and disturbing, poetic and ironical. The play consists of a diffuse montage of lyrical atmospheric moments as well as literary parody, social satire, and naturalistic family drama. The Aristotelian conventions of empathy and identification, which provide escape for the theatergoer and culminate in emotional catharsis, are abandoned. The Masked Gentleman appears as a deus ex machina in a drama generated by dialogue that is largely unresponsive. Caricature becomes grotesque, and especially so in the scenes of the pedagogical conference and the funeral of Moritz. Subtitled "Ein Kindertragödie" (A Tragedy of Children), the play lacks a central tragic figure and a unified dramatic development. And is it a tragedy, or perhaps a comedy or tragicomedy?

The Masked Gentleman, to whom Wedekind dedicated the work, generates questions himself. Is he to be understood as the devil Mephistopheles, a figure that exerted considerable fascination for the author? Or is he an embodiment of bourgeois society, leading the youthful Melchior to reconciliation with the autocratic patriarchal order? Or does the Masked Gentleman represent affirmation of the vitalistic spirit of life? The connection between the Gentleman and Ilse, the free-loving "Freudenmädchen," although often overlooked by readers as well as directors, is crucial. Ilse incorporates eros and the force of life since the meaning of life is eros. The dictum of the Masked Gentleman regarding morality has gained wide attention, but it may be no more than Wedekind's little mathematical joke, similar to his use of the term *Parallelepipedon* (parallelepipeds), a geometric figure identified by Ilse as the cause of the death of Moritz.

Wedekind was much admired by Bertolt Brecht, who imitated his poetry and ballads. One critic argues that their roles may be perceived as reversed when the dictum regarding morality is described as an "alienation effect," a term generally reserved for Brecht's drama. Such an effect causes the audience to disengage its emotions and observe critically Melchior's grasp at life for survival (Hibberd).

Two short prose tales by Wedekind are often considered as commentaries or companion pieces to *Spring Awakening.* The story "Die Fürstin Russalka" (1897; Princess Russalka) deals with unmarried pregnancy, and its central figure, like Wendla Bergmann, is ignorant of the possibility of conception outside the bonds of matrimony. "Der greise Freier" (1897; The Hoary Suitor) similarly expresses protest against a repressive society, here determined to preserve the propriety and formality of what Gittleman terms "the pre-marital ritual of courtship."

Early criticism was positivistic in that it sought a connection between the author and his work, a demonstration of how experience becomes literature. Emphasis was placed on the author's youth in a Swiss village, where two acquaintances at the *Gymnasium* committed suicide. The withdrawal of censorship during the Weimar Republic led to the discovery of Wedekind by the Expressionists, and he is regarded by some scholars as an early Expressionist. This is, however, not entirely accurate. Breaking with naturalism by his use of the grotesque, Wedekind became a precursor of the Expressionists, sharing with them some attitudes, such as pacifism and antimilitarism, and in *Spring Awakening* treating common themes of sexuality and generational conflict. Stylistically, however, his work demonstrates little of Expressionism.

Wedekind is seen as indebted to the drama of Sturm und Drang, especially as represented by J.M.R. Lenz, because of scenes that are closed in form and language that may be one moment spare and terse and at another flowing and lyrical. Caricature and dialect contribute to lively, grotesque comedy. Among other influences are Christian Friedrich Grabbe and Georg Büchner, especially as manifested in his drama *Woyzeck.*

Although even four decades ago some critics considered *Spring Awakening* dated and no longer capable of shock, the work is still regularly performed and is widely considered Wedekind's best. The English critic Elizabeth Boa accurately summarizes the critical evaluation of the drama when she characterizes it as "a seminal work in the history of modern theater."

WARD B. LEWIS

Editions

First edition: *Frühlings Erwachen,* Zurich: Jean Groß, 1891

Critical editions: in *Gesammelte Werke,* edited by Artur Kutscher and Joachim Friedenthal, vol. 2, Munich: George Müller, 1912

Translations: There are several translations of *Frülings Erwachen,* including *Spring Awakening,* translated by Edward Bond, which appeared as a single title, London: Eyre Methuen, 1980, as well as in the Wedekind anthology *Plays: One,* London: Methuen Drama,

1993. A superior translation is *Spring Awakening* by Ted Hughes, London and Boston: Faber, 1995, which served the Royal Shakespeare Company in its performance at the Pit in the Barbican, London, on 2 August 1995.

Further Reading
Best, Alan D., *Frank Wedekind*, London: Wolff, 1975
Boa, Elizabeth, *The Sexual Circus: Wedekind's Theatre of Subversion*, Oxford and New York: Blackwell, 1987
Dosenheimer, Elise, *Das deutsche soziale Drama von Lessing bis Sternheim*, Konstanz: Südverlag, 1949
Fechter, Paul, *Frank Wedekind: Der Mensch und das Werk*, Jena: Lichtenstein, 1920
Gittleman, Sol, *Frank Wedekind*, New York: Twayne, 1969
Hibberd, John L., "Imaginary Numbers and 'Humor': On Wedekind's *Frühlings Erwachen*," *Modern Language Review* 74 (1979)
Jelavich, Peter, "Wedekind's *Spring Awakening*: The Path to Expressionist Drama," in *Passion and Rebellion: The Expressionist Heritage*, edited by Stephen Erich Bronner and Douglas Kellner, South Hadley, Massachusetts: J.E. Bergin, and London: Croom Helm, 1983
Lewis, Ward B., *The Ironic Dissident: Frank Wedekind in the View of His Critics*, Columbia, South Carolina: Camden House, 1997
Natan, Alex, "Frank Wedekind," in *German Men of Letters*, edited by Alex Natan, vol. 2, London: Wolff, 1963
Rasch, Wolfdietrich, "Sozialkritische Aspekte in Wedekinds dramatischer Dichtung: Sexualität, Kunst, und Gesellschaft," in *Gestaltungsgeschichte und Gesellschaftsgeschichte*, edited by Helmut Kreuzer, Stuttgart: Metzler, 1969
Rothe, Friedrich, *Frank Wedekinds Dramen: Jugendstil und Lebensphilosophie*, Stuttgart: Metzler, 1968
Shaw, Leroy R., *The Playwright and Historical Change*, Madison: University of Wisconsin Press, 1970
Sokel, Walter H., "The Changing Role of Eros in Wedekind's Drama," *German Quarterly* 39, no. 2 (1966)
Spalter, Max, *Brecht's Tradition*, Baltimore, Maryland: Johns Hopkins University Press, 1967
Völker, Klaus, *Frank Wedekind*, Velber bei Hannover: Friedrich, 1965

Weimar

Few German cities can rival Weimar in its claim to cultural pre-eminence. Honored as the European Cultural Capital for 1999, Weimar has long occupied a unique place in German cultural history and in the German cultural psyche; such a position suggests both artistic excellence and, more recently, political self-determination. By virtue of its artistic and humanistic traditions, Weimar has frequently served as the focal point for appeals for the renewal of society. Historically, this small Thuringian town is a reminder of Germany's first significant (if ill-fated) democracy: "Weimar Germany." Yet the important cultural and political achievements of Weimar are not without controversy. It has been pointed out, for example, that many of those who advocated societal transformation through artistic creativity were essentially driven from the town. In short, Weimar has the paradoxical reputation as a city of enlightenment, humanism, and artistic progress, but also of small-mindedness, intransigence, and traditionalism.

First documented as "Wimares" in A.D. 975, Weimar acquired the right to consolidate as a city in 1425. Martin Luther, an occasional visitor to the city, unveiled his political theory in a sermon in 1522 in Weimar, and by 1525, the St. Peter and Paul Church (*Herderkirche*) had become the seat of the Protestant-Lutheran community. The renowned Renaissance painter Lucas Cranach the Elder was the first important artist to take up residence in Weimar when he chose to spend his final years there (1552–53). Weimar experienced the turbulence and deprivation of the Thirty Years' War (1618–48) through the eyes of its celebrated Duke Bernhard, who served as a general on the Protestant side.

Cultural life began to flourish in Weimar when, in 1696, Duke Wilhelm Ernst established an opera in his residence, where pieces were performed in the German language. In 1703, at the age of 17, Johann Sebastian Bach received an appointment as court musician by Duke Johann Ernst, for whom his grandfather had worked 70 years earlier. Bach's duties included playing violin in the Duke's orchestra. But since Bach had been trained as an organist (and, indeed, wrote many fine pieces for the organ in Weimar), he left the city in 1717 when another opportunity presented itself.

While these early cultural and historical developments have found some scholarly interest, researchers have been more intensely drawn to the period known as "Classical Weimar" (1772–1832), perhaps best understood as the fortunate result of the collaboration between a relatively enlightened, culturally minded regime and a collection of outstanding artists. The invitation by the widowed Duchess Anna Amalia in 1772 to Christoph Martin Wieland to become the instructor of her two children, Carl August and Constantin, marks the beginning of this most studied period. A professor of philosophy and history at Erfurt, Wieland intended to educate the middle-class reader to enlightened rationalism with his writings, including his novel, *Agathon*; his influential journal, *Teutscher Merkur*; and his novel, *Der goldene Spiegel*, which had attracted the interest of the Duchess Anna Amalia, and which was aimed at the education of the aristocratic political leadership. In Weimar, he encouraged cultural activities such as amateur theater and roundtable readings at the *Wittumspalais*, which drew from both the bourgeoisie and the aristocracy.

In 1775, the 18-year-old Carl August assumed the throne and promptly invited Johann Wolfgang Goethe, author of the highly successful epistolary novel *Die Leiden des jungen Werthers* and the drama *Götz von Berlichingen*, to Weimar. Coming from cosmopolitan Frankfurt, Goethe found Weimar rather provincial. Through his close personal friendship with Duke Carl August and his service on the Privy Council, Goethe encouraged the continued reform of the absolutist state. Yet his subversive participation in the Free Masons suggests a desire to limit the extent of the political reforms. Meanwhile, his literary writings and scientific experimentation facilitated the transformation of Weimar into an "Athens on the Ilm." In 1776, Goethe was able to convince Carl August to invite Johann Gottfried Herder, the theologian, philosopher, and literary theorist, to Weimar to oversee the school system. In his *Briefe zur Beförderung der Humanität,* Herder articulated the fundamental optimism of the humanistic ideals ("Geist von Weimar") that have come to be associated with Weimar: the organic evolution of a humane society, propelled by artists, that respects the development of the total personality (not just reason).

Goethe's reputation also attracted the dramatist Friedrich Schiller to Weimar. Schiller, whose plays and writings were known throughout Germany, finally settled in Weimar in 1799. In their largely idealized art, Schiller and Goethe propagated the aesthetic ideals of Classical Weimar, chief among which was the necessity and capability of the arts to contribute to the ongoing transformation of existing social and intellectual realities. As longtime superintendent of the theater in Weimar, Goethe aimed to reconcile his and Schiller's artistic and pedagogical interests with popular tastes; despite occasional collisions with the public, the marriage of an elite culture and a popular culture fared reasonably well. Goethe's and Schiller's generally classical aesthetic in literature found a parallel in the architecture of Clemens Coudray, who had come to Weimar in 1816 to create classical buildings, including the Roman House in the park on the Ilm. Recent scholarship on 18th-century Weimar has developed the less-studied aspects of the period: the women who lived in Weimar (Luise von Göchhausen, Christiane Vulpius), less well-known writers of the period (August von Kotzebue, Christian Vulpius), and the economics and the fashion of the period (Friedrich Bertuch's *Landes-Industrie-Comptoir* and his *Journal des Luxus und der Moden*).

Goethe's death in 1832 marked the end of German Classicism, but not the end of efforts to renew society through art. At the height of his international fame, Franz Liszt was invited to Weimar in 1841 to become the *Hofkapellmeister.* Perceiving himself as a cultural heir to Goethe and Schiller and supported by the calls in 1849 to celebrate Goethe's birth, Liszt, in collaboration with the ruling Duke Carl Alexander, developed comprehensive plans for a Goethe Foundation, a *Goethe-Stiftung,* which he then articulated in an 1851 essay, "De la Fondation Goethe à Weimar." Liszt was not merely interested in revering the former cultural icons of Weimar; he wanted to restore Weimar's former international reputation as a proponent of the arts and to transform Weimar into "une nouvelle Athènes." Through an artistic competition, an "Olympiade der Künste," society was to be renewed. The apex of literature under Goethe and Schiller was to be followed by the zenith of Wagner's musical genius, whose *Tannhäuser* was first performed in Weimar in 1849. The Hector Berlioz Week in November 1852, attended by the composer himself, indeed elevated Weimar to the premier city of music, offering, according to one critic, the music of the future. The exhibition and publication of all the arts would, to Liszt's mind, advance the education of humanity. But Weimar's weak economic position as well as larger political factors—the near war between Austria and Prussia—hindered the realization of the project. Moreover, many viewed Liszt, a French-speaking Hungarian, as an unworthy educator of the Germans. In addition to the musical excellence that Liszt envisioned, Duke Carl Alexander also supported a private art school of painters, later

known as the *Weimarer Malerschule,* who incorporated greater realism in the predominant romantic landscape paintings of the period and who also anticipated the German impressionists. These middle decades of the 19th century additionally witnessed the monumentalization of Classical Weimar: monuments to Herder, Wieland, and Goethe and Schiller (Rietschel's famous Goethe/Schiller monument) were all put in place in the 1850s. Weimar also became the home of the great literary societies during this period: the *Deutsche-Schiller Stiftung* (1859), the *Deutsche Shakespeare-Gesellschaft* (1864), the *Deutsche Dante-Gesellschaft* (1865), and, finally, the *Goethe-Gesellschaft* (1885).

Goethe's final testament of 6 January 1831 had provided for his young grandchildren, Walter and Wolfgang, but it also required that his scientific and literary collections remain intact, be made accessible to the public, and become the property of the state of Saxon-Weimar-Eisenach. It was not, however, until his grandchild Walter's will (24 September 1883) that the house on the *Frauenplan* and its collections were given to the state. Under the auspices of the Grand Duchess Sophie, Carl Ruland (1854–1907), the director of the Goethe National Museum, was able to open the museum in 1887. A Goethe Society, which met for the first time on 20–21 June 1885, was founded, and the Goethe Archive, directed by Bernhard Suphan (1845–1911), played a decisive role in the publication of initial volumes of the *Sophienausgabe,* which is still the most complete edition of Goethe's works (1887–1919). It was at this time that a copy of Goethe's "Urfaust," transcribed by Louise von Goechhausen, was discovered. When the Schiller descendants, Ludwig and Alexander von Gleichen-Rußwurm, gave the archive significant portions of Schiller's *Nachlass,* one began to refer to the Goethe and Schiller Archive. A representative building, built under the initiative of Duchess Sophie and dedicated in 1896, added to the splendor to the archive, and it became a repository for other scholarly materials.

At the turn of the century, Weimar, like most of Germany, experienced the transition from the historicism of the *Gründerjahre* to Jugendstil. Still, the arts, this time the fine arts, continued to provide the impulse for an attempted transformation of society. At the center of the renewal process in the new Weimar were the French-born patron of the arts, Count Harry Kessler, and the Belgian *Jugendstil* artist Henry van de Velde. Attracted to Weimar because of its cultural history and because of its growing, educated middle class, Kessler had worked with van de Velde on an illustrated edition of Nietzsche's *Also sprach Zarathustra* and later founded the famous Cranach Press. When he took over the direction of the *Museum für Kunst und Kunstgewerbe* (Museum for Art and Crafts) in 1903, he encouraged highly progressive art, organizing the sensational exhibition of Max Klinger's works and the art of the Impressionists. The year 1903 also marked the founding of the *Deutscher Künstlerbund,* which had connections to the secessionists in Berlin, and which was opposed by Weimar's traditional salon art community. Under Kessler, the *Deutscher Künstlerbund* brought together many famous artists in Weimar, including Lovis Corinth, Auguste Renoir, Paul Cézanne, Wassily Kandinsky, and Auguste Rodin, whose exhibition in 1906, which included several nudes, precipitated the end of this new progressive Weimar. Kessler, who had arranged for Rodin to be awarded an honorary doctorate at the University of Jena, resigned his position in 1906 because of the public attacks on his reputation and because of the hostility to his openness to foreign influence. Van de Velde, who initially had come to Weimar to direct an arts and crafts seminar in order to raise the level of the artisanship in the province, was likewise dismayed at the traditionalism of the Weimar art community. His designs for a new theater (the Dumont Theater) and for the Museum for Art and Crafts were never realized. Similarly, the redesign of the interior of the Grand Ducal Museum was never executed. Like Kessler, van de Velde withdrew from public life to his residence "unter den hohen Pappeln" (under the high poplars) which became a central meeting place for the avantgarde. Kessler's house on Cranach Street, with its white furniture by van de Velde, statues by Aristide Maillol and Auguste Rodin, and paintings by the Impressionists and neoimpressionists Vincent van Gogh and Edvard Munch, was a veritable *Gesamtkunstwerk* of the modern. Rainer Maria Rilke and Hugo von Hoffmannsthal read their poetry in his house. In the ten years of its activity, the new Weimar was a forceful proponent of progressive art on the international scene, even when its activities were unappreciated in Weimar itself.

With the removal of Grand Duke Wilhelm Ernst and the establishment of a provisional republican government in 1919, Walter Gropius, director of the Grand Ducal Saxon School of Arts and Crafts, was able to convince the new political leadership that a union of the fine arts and the crafts was politically and culturally desirable. Hoping that the traditional artistic interest groups of Weimar would join him, Gropius opened the *Staatliches Bauhaus* in 1919 in Weimar. His program called for the combination of the artist and the artisan to realize an artistic community reminiscent of the guilds of the Middle Ages. The Bauhaus sought to diminish the isolation of the artist and to improve the economic condition and social status of the artist and the craftsman. In the words of the Bauhaus Program of 1919, "Wollen, erdenken, erschaffen wir gemeinsam den neuen Bau der Zukunft, der alles in einer Gestalt sein wird: Archtektur und Plastik und Malerei, der aus Millionen Händen steigen wird als kristallenes Sinnbild eines neuen kommenden Glaubens" (Through our wills and our imagination, we shall create the new buildings of the future, which shall contain all art forms—architecture, sculpture, and painting—in a single structure that created by millions of hands, shall become a crystal symbol of the new faith). Lyonel Feiniger's "Kathedrale" served as a fitting symbol of the futuristic aims of the Bauhaus. It suggested not only the intellectual union of the aesthetic with the practical and economical, but also the design of a new society guided by a romantic utopia. The experimental house Am Horn, designed by Georg Muche in 1923 as both a new form of architecture and a demonstration of a new way to live for the common man, further reflected the building notions of the Bauhaus. With the participation of several Bauhaus crafts and workshops, the one-family house am Horn, the only house built in Weimar by the Bauhaus, was essentially without ornamentation and was built according to a functional understanding of space. While it consists primarily of stereometric forms, it is still reminiscent of classical architectural orders: it goes beyond the beauty of the merely functional and represents "a true artwork of the realization of abstract monumental beauty." Another important achievement of Bauhaus art was Gropius' abstract, Expressionistic memorial to the workers who were shot in the Kapp Putsch in March 1920 (*Märzgefallenendenkmal*), which was built in 1922 in the main cemetery of Weimar, and which was later removed

by the Nazis. The impact of the Bauhaus was extended further by the internationally acclaimed exhibition of the Bauhaus Week in 1923, which was attended by thousands of spectators. The program, which consisted of lectures, presentations, exhibitions of music and dance, and stage performances, made some inroads into public acceptability for Bauhaus artists. But the state elections of 1924, which placed in power a coalition of parties, including cultural and political traditionalists, marked the demise of the Bauhaus in Weimar. In September, despite protest from some artistic quarters, the government canceled the contracts of those masters associated with the Bauhaus, and in November, the budget was reduced by half, essentially making further work in Weimar impossible. The institute dissolved itself in April 1925. Gropius's hopes for a social reform under the auspices of the arts could not be realized, for the community's artistic traditionalists and the period's powerful nationalistic factions were not easily reconciled to progressive art forms.

Perhaps nowhere was the discrepancy between Classical Weimar's humanistic spirit and totalitarian power more in evidence than in Nazi Weimar. A nationalistic agenda, however, had been evident in Weimar long before the Nazis came to power in Germany. The Weimar literature professor Adolf Bartels, editor of the journal *Deutsches Schrifttum*, worked consistently to advance a nationalistic cultural ideal that distinguished Jewish from non-Jewish writers. Through Bartels's many writings Weimar came to be known for its anti-Semitism. The year 1928 marked the publication of Paul Schultze-Naumburg's successful book *Kunst und Rasse* (Art and Race), which argued that cultural decline is preceded by racial decline. Schultze-Naumburg, a protégé of Wilhelm Frick, became the director of the Hochschule where Gropius had taught. His inaugural speech made clear his nationalistic aesthetics: he would create German houses, not international houses of glass and steel. With Frick's support, in 1930 he ordered the removal of Oskar Schlemmer's frescos from the walls of the university and took other antimodernist actions, such as removing modern art (by Barlach, Klee, and Dix) from the Schlossmuseum. Against little popular or press resistance, censorship was introduced to the libraries, and some plays were prohibited. By July 1932, the Nazis had attained an absolute majority in the state election. On the occasion of the centennial of Goethe's death in 1932, Thomas Mann remarked on the strange mixture of the Nazi presence in Weimar and the humanistic goals of German Classicism. In 1934, marking the 175th birthday of Schiller, Joseph Goebbels allowed that Schiller no doubt would have been "a great proponent of our revolution." Prof. Julius Petersen, president of the Goethe Society, intoned how Goethe, too, would have lauded the contemporary black and brown shirts just as he had praised the Luetzower Jäger in 1813. Under the Nazis in 1939, Weimar hosted a degenerate art exhibition, similar to that of Munich. During this period, work began on the monumental *Adolf Hitler Platz* (with dimensions of 200 by 350 meters), an architectural symbol of the conquest of the hated "Novembersystem" (the Weimar Republic) that portrayed visually the defeat of the humanistic ideals of German Classicism; fortunately, the events of the war caused the construction to be halted. A review of Weimar cultural history is not complete without mention of its proximity of Buchenwald. As has been written, the way from Frankfurt to Weimar, Goethe's way, passes through this concentration camp. At the urging of SS Group Leader Eicke and Fritz Sauckel, the Gauleiter of Thuringia, who had hoped to gain prestige for Weimar, the concentration camp Buchenwald was opened in 1936, and the first inmates arrived in July 1937.

In the postwar period, Weimar, situated in the eastern part of Germany, experienced firsthand the historical implications of the cold war. While it remains debatable to what extent the humanistic ethos of German Classicism was taken seriously by the political leadership of the GDR, it is clear that the East German government sought to make use of the intellectual and cultural tradition in Weimar in order to move its people toward the formation of a socialist society. Goethe and Schiller were seen as the guarantors of the socialist future of the young state. In a 1965 speech commemorating the bicentennial of Goethe's birth, Johannes R. Becher appealed to this tradition: "Es heisst nicht: zurück zu Goethe, sondern es heisst: vorwärts zu Goethe und mit Goethe vorwärts" (Not back to Goethe, but forward to Goethe, and forward with Goethe). That Buchenwald continued to house prisoners—this time opponents of the socialist regime—suggests that the emancipatory humanistic ideals of German Classicism, praised particularly in the Goethe year of 1949, were not rigorously observed. That Walter Ulbricht dismissed Thomas Mann's letter to him in the summer of 1951, which recounts the injustices of the Waldheim trials, further indicates an erosion of the humanistic ideals. Likewise, the disappearance of the Dante Society and the dissolution of the Shakespeare Society, not to mention the general disregard for the modern, including the Bauhaus and the philosopher Nietzsche, both testify to a restrictive cultural policy. Additionally, the damage to historical buildings and art collections demonstrates how art was to serve material political ends. But along with the instrumentalization of the heritage of German Classicism for socialist political ends, literary scholarship in the GDR was able to historicize and contextualize the *Klassik* in important and useful ways, and cultural production was on occasion able to advance outside of the ideological restrictions, such as the work on the emergence of the Goethe Society.

German Unification and the internet have had a substantial impact on the most recent developments in Weimar's cultural history. In anticipation of the celebration of Weimar as the European Cultural Capital, the 250th anniversary of Goethe's birth, the 70th anniversary of the proclamation of the Weimar Republic, and the tenth anniversary of the "fall of the Wall," buildings of historical and cultural significance have been renovated, including the Duchess Anna Amalia Library, the main building of the Franz Liszt Music College, and the German National Theater. Additionally, many monuments, including those celebrating Lizst and Shakespeare, are being restored. Websites that inform about the innumerable cultural activities pertaining to the European Cultural Capital abound. Yet despite the celebratory, in part self-congratulatory tone that is heard from Weimar, there have, indeed, been voices critical of this most recent period in Weimar culture. The pattern of controversy and cultural appropriation continues to surround Weimar. Rolf Hochhut, in his *Wessis in Weimar* (1993; Westerners in Weimar), offered a bitter indictment of the annexation of East Germany and Weimar by the dominant economic power of West Germany. Enzensberger's *Nieder mit Goethe* (1995; Down with Goethe) confronted the German public's penchant to overlook the reality of Goethe and to acquiesce in an idealized view of the author. More recently, Thomas Schmidt's novel *Weimar; oder, das Ende der Zeit* (1997; Weimar; or, The End of Time) has added to the argument against the takeover by the more powerful economic West the notion that the cultural legacy of Weimar, in particular that of the *Weimarer Klassik,* has been trivialized, and even "Disneyfied," in the preparations for the celebration of Weimar as the European Cultural Capital. Weimar has been and continues to remain a site of deeply contested artistic and political views.

EDWARD T. LARKIN

See also Johann Wolfgang von Goethe; Johann Gottfried Herder; Friedrich von Schiller

Further Reading

Berg, Jan, et al., *Sozialgeschichte der deutschen Literatur von 1918 bis zur Gegenwart,* Frankfurt: Fischer Taschenbuch, 1981

Furness, Raymond, and Malcolm Humble, *A Companion to Twentieth-Century German Literature,* London and New York: Routledge, 1991; 2nd edition, 1997

Grenville, Anthony, *Cockpit of Ideologies: The Literature and Political History of the Weimar Republic,* Bern and New York: Lang, 1995

Taylor, Ronald, *Literature and Society in Germany, 1914–1945,* Brighton: Harvester Press, and Totowa, New Jersey: Barnes and Noble, 1980

Weyergraf, Bernhard, editor, *Literatur der Weimarer Republik 1918–1933,* Munich: Hanser, 1995

Willett, John, *The New Sobriety 1917–1933: Art and Politics in the Weimar Period,* London: Thames and Hudson, 1978; as *Art and Politics in the Weimar Period: The New Sobriety, 1917–1933,* New York: Pantheon Books, 1978

Zmegac, Viktor, editor, *Geschichte der deutschen Literatur vom 18. Jahrhundert bis zur Gegenwart,* vol. 3: 1918–1980, Königstein: Athenäum, 1984

Weimar Republic

World War I—the Weimar Republic's defining experience—brought stress, hunger, and profiteering. The collapse of the Wilhelmine Empire and Wilhelm II's abdication issued in rival power centers. Munich had its chaotic *Räterepublik* (Soviet republic). In Berlin, the Spartacists (forerunners of the KPD, the Communist Party) for a time fought the forces of the inchoate democracy, which became Germany's first venture into really modern political structures, based on moderate conservative, liberal, and social-democrat (SPD) parties. The republic had to sign the catastrophic settlement of Versailles, whose insistence on war guilt and heavy reparations led to popular resentment and economic troubles. Right-wing irredentism threatened until the Hitler putsch of 1923. Endemic inflation culminated in 1923, when France occupied the Ruhr. This inflation demoralized and impoverished the respectable middle classes while enriching profiteers—a disaster in a mature industrial society, as Germany by then was. The following apparent prosperity, based on U.S. loans that enabled capital investment, was balanced by disillusionment with the democratic system. The mood then drifted to the right wing, and political instability and polarization weakened the core parties and strengthened Nazism and Communism. The collapse of the economy from 1929 on completed the mass pauperization, and democracy collapsed into government by presidential decree long before Hitler's appointment as *Reichskanzler*.

Unlike any other epoch of German history, the Weimar Republic forms a literary period. Writers were more aware of public life than before, and their work reflects political and social developments. Germany, united, was the cultural leader of the German-speaking world; there was unprecedented centralization in Berlin, the fresh and irreverent capital of modernity. Much that flowered in the republic, however, was budding in the empire; about half the greatest writers at work were from the old Austro-Hungary. Only some of the most modern-minded writers such as Bertolt Brecht, Heinrich Mann, and the Austrian Robert Musil chose to live in Berlin. Others preferred Berlin's cultural rivals: Munich, Dresden, Frankfurt am Main, and elsewhere. In everyday life, German regions were still very distinct, with dialects, religious divides, and surviving attachments to the old petty statelets. Some writers—largely overlooked by the leading media but with solid provincial readership—stayed in this fertile soil, continually proclaiming that their time would come. Their *Heimat* literature was surprisingly popular with city dwellers, who liked to feel connected with instinct, nobility, and the organic community—although their life was determined by reason, practicality, urban society, and class divisions.

The 1920s were preoccupied with the conflict between tradition and modernity. Tradition meant high literature, organic growth, *Gemeinschaft* (community), religion, dynasties, and serenity; modernity meant journalism, planning or mechanical accretion, *Gesellschaft* (society), fragmentation, democracy, fads such as Esperanto and nudism, and quasi religions and alternative beliefs such as theosophy or psychoanalysis. Commentators noted the acceleration of life, growing anonymity, the decline of the family, and the growth of feelings of *Lebensangst* (fear of survival).

Modernity meant, above all, the influence of the United States, seen as a young, headstrong nation, the home of cutthroat competition and instant obsolescence. Industry rationalized production and concentrated in cartels and trusts. The constitution of the Republic was American-influenced. American literature was translated, jazz and 1920s dances swept the country, Josephine Baker visited, and American films were hits; commentators scanned Berlin's traffic hoping to find it as dense, rudely driven, and dangerous as New York's. As revolution and inflation diminished the traditional sense of the order of society, the way was open for Americanism.

Yet social progress and liberalization seemed fragile accomplishments on a surly and unpredictable base: "dancing on the volcano" (Klaus Mann). Reactionary circles still dominated the law, the military, education, and religion. Censorship, abolished under the constitution, returned gradually; the antipornography law of 1924 was vague enough to allow politically motivated prosecutions of literature. Legal action—even treason trials—

particularly affected left-wing writers such as Carl von Ossietzky, editor of the critical periodical *Die Weltbühne* and scourge of class justice, and Johannes R. Becher. Writers may have wanted to remain apolitical but were forced into public activity: Kurt Tucholsky's satire attacked the army and the law. As National Socialism progressed, it started violent protests at performances of plays and films that it disliked.

Writers first organized themselves in the confusion of 1918: the Politischer Rat geistiger Arbeiter (Political Soviet of Intellectual Workers) in Berlin united Spartacist sympathizers and the left-liberal Heinrich Mann and Musil. Later, the Schutzverband deutscher Schriftsteller (German Writers' Defense League) formed to defend writers' professional and financial interests in the hard postinflation world, the era of the lobbyist. In the Gruppe 1925 (1925 Group), communists and their allies (Becher, Brecht, and Egon Erwin Kisch) met SPD sympathizers (Alfred Döblin). Prussia added a Sektion für Dichtkunst (Literature Section) to its Academy of Arts in 1926; a good debating ground—its democratic aura fostered by Thomas and Heinrich Mann and Döblin and in running conflict with the nationalistic writers led by Erwin Guido Kolbenheyer—it had little institutional influence.

Expressionism's creativity was largely over by 1918: the anthology *Menschheitsdämmerung* (1919; Twilight of Mankind) was more a coffin than a showcase. Activism, Expressionism's politicized wing, thrived briefly in the revolution; Ludwig Rubiner, prophet of a fiery poetic *Geist* and the writer as self-sacrificing leader to a better society, produced the anthology *Kameraden der Menschheit* (1919; Comrades of Mankind). But this political activism was only the individual emotions and aspirations of an intellectual elite writ large. Berlin Dada, thriving amid the upheavals of 1918–19, was more fruitful. It rejected all traditional concepts of art, including Expressionism's dilettante politics; this radicalism paralleled Communist rigor—many Dadaists joined the Left Wing. Dada ended dramatically with the prosecution over the supposedly obscene and insulting antimilitary exhibits at the *Dada-Messe* (Dada Fair) in 1920.

Neue Sachlichkeit (new sobriety), despite differing attitudes among its practitioners and its own inherent ambiguities, reflected the modern side of the Weimar Republic intensely. Its emphasis on surface phenomena, suspicion of emotion, and ambivalence about individual psychology, not to mention its tendency to cynicism, in some sense united authors as diverse as Brecht and Ernst Jünger. Facts seemed safe, but myths and metaphysics appeared unproductive. The detective novel, an inquiry into facts, attained literary respectability; statistics became a normal part of literary texts.

Women were not thought cool enough to master modern life; *Neue Sachlichkeit* was a masculine thing. More broadly, women writers still suffered from inferior education and prejudice in the public arena. Some fought for emancipation, attacking discrimination in the workplace; others took their chances in what was still a man's world. Vicki Baum wrote an international bestseller in *Menschen im Hotel* (1928; Grand Hotel), where she introduced a feminine touch, an emphasis on moments of human contact, into the masculine genre of the novel of disparate lives. Anna Seghers's stories of revolt made a literary sensation but lack an emphasis on what revolution might do for women. A woman's identity was still borrowed; men determined what went, as the lesson of Irmgard Keun's popular novels and

Marieluise Fleißer's plays shows. Yet other writers propagated eternal woman, mother and homemaker. Such images fit Nazism's idea of woman's role; in Ina Seidel's *Das Wunschkind* (1930; *The Wish Child*), the maternal attitude goes with *völkisch* beliefs.

The 1920s saw the rapid development of new media and a shift from a reading to a viewing culture. German film staked its claim to be an art form and not mere entertainment; its Expressionistic style marked its coming-of-age. But the many films on power-obsessed demonic heroes and subservient masses also seem a portent of fascism: from Caligari to Hitler (Siegfried Kracauer). The leading film studio and a growing, influential newspaper empire were concentrated toward the end of the Republic in the hands of Alfred Hugenberg, who supported Hitler, financing him through the industrialists' Herren-Klub. Film influenced literature directly by popularizing close viewing of reality and quick cutting between scenes. Because radio was expanding its audience dramatically, was state-controlled, and was impervious to commercial interests, it too interested writers, particularly left-wingers, until political developments brought programming biases. Innovative sound-plays and journalistic features also appeared.

The written word responded with cheap series of novels and the propagation of best-sellers. Works by authors such as Stefan Zweig and Erich Maria Remarque rubbed shoulders with nationalist potboilers such as Artur Dinter's *Die Sünde wider das Blut* (1918; The Sin against the Blood). Trivial literature, largely within a reactionary ethos, was produced en masse. Book clubs reached a new serious readership; the Büchergilde Gutenberg, a trade union book club with about 80,000 members, encouraged social-democratic oriented authors.

With the end of censorship, avant-garde plays appeared more freely on stage, and an era of theatrical experimentation began. Major directors of the period included Leopold Jeßner, who reduced the stage experience to an abstract and grandiose conflict, and whose trademark was a sweeping staircase for large-scale effects; Jürgen Fehling, with his intellectual and psychological approach, seen in his Sophocles' *Antigone* for the Berlin Volksbühne 1921; and Erich Engel, a member of Brecht's circle, who emphasized epic and clear development of plot, accentuated the social, and produced Wedekind's *Lulu* in Berlin 1926 with Caspar Neher's sets. Erwin Piscator produced plays and revues as communist propaganda in Berlin throughout the decade, importing documentary material in slides and film clips to elucidate the stage action's political message. His production of Ernst Toller's *Hoppla, wir leben!* in 1927 (*Hoppla!*) exemplifies his incorporation of film and audio technology. The return in 1924 of director and impresario Max Reinhardt, an exponent of total theater, and the new social-critical drama after the mid-1920s revivified the stage. Eventually, however, the competitive situation in Berlin theater pushed out the more demanding repertoire, which became a minority pursuit.

The Republic's fatal political fragmentation was mirrored in thought and literature. The division of writers into right-wing, republic-supporting, and communist camps, with their respective theories and institutions, also provides a starting point for classifying novelists—the novel was the most consistently politically charged genre of the time.

The only one of the proponents of restored monarchy, fascism, or corporatism still with canonical reputation is Jünger. But many authors respected and much read at the time sub-scribed to nationalism, Blut und Boden (blood and soil), racism, regionalism, *völkisch* beliefs, anti-Semitism, or conservative revolution: a range of ideologies with wide appeal to capitalists and anticapitalists, peasants and intellectuals. These writers favored extreme conservative parties (from about 1930, Nazism); their philosophers were Hegel and Nietzsche, and their weltanschauung derived scientific underpinning from Darwin and Spencer. Around 1930, right-wing literary circles formed, notably the Nazis' Kampfbund für deutsche Kultur (Fighting Alliance for German Culture).

The conservative revolution was propounded in pure form by Jünger, a member, incidentally, of the Herren-Klub: a mixture of nationalism, oligarchy, and capitalism that emphasized leadership and duty and that glorified war as a means to finding one's self. Bourgeois normality and democracy were rejected for a total and totally functional state of workers and self-sacrificing soldiers. Its roots were in Nietzsche's irrational pseudorevolutionary attitude (Lukács), what was seen as his destructive criticism of all values, and Oswald Spengler's highly influential theory of the rise and decline of civilizations in *Der Untergang des Abendlandes* (1918–22; *The Decline of the West*). Spengler's *Preußentum und Sozialismus* (1920; Prussianness and Socialism) pioneered the connection of right-wing ideas of a total state to the appeal to a commonwealth. Popular World War I literature was also close to conservative revolution: Werner Beumelburg, Ernst von Salomon, and others commonly reached print figures of 150,000 with novels extolling comradeship. The *George-Kreis* is analogous, but George himself kept aloof: his order preferred quasi-sacral imagery and anticivilization rhetoric to the utilitarianism of conservative revolution. Although also independent, Karl Jaspers was influenced by such ideas in his popular *Die geistige Situation der Zeit* (1931; *Man in the Modern Age*), which preached decisionism with no time for democratic consensus.

Of the right-wing novelists, Kolbenheyer was prominent, continuing his novel trilogy *Paracelsus* (1917–26; Paracelsus). His theories saw the author as a true warden of the mystic organic forces of the nation, a quasi-priest of the new *völkisch* religion. Hans Grimm had the great popular success of *Volk ohne Raum* (1926; A People without Space), a plea for colonialism and to give living space for the German workers. Blut und Boden literature flourished generally on a more populist level. Here, the untainted Germanic blood of the countryman and mystical attachment to the ancestral soil were basic; health, respect for tradition, and so on were rural values absent from the ethnically mixed city.

The pillars of the Republic included the decade's major novelists. They were interested in human rights and social justice, suspicious of more specific ideology or belief; their philosophy may come from Kant, Voltaire, and Rousseau. They stressed individualism and truth to one's self. A short catalog can give no idea of their literary significance and only a slight idea of their collective weight in the Weimar context. Important public figures are Thomas Mann, who moved from his initial conservatism to become the Republic's cultural figurehead; Heinrich Mann, the first major writer to support a broad left consensus; and Döblin, whose topical essays treat, among other things, the increasing strains on German Jews. Key issues of the time—Jews in public life, the agricultural crisis, and the white-collar proletariat—appear in the novels of Lion Feuchtwanger, a characteristic figure of the moderate left, and Hans Fallada. A series of war novels, notably those of Arnold Zweig and Remarque, formed the counterpart (although less widely read) to those of the Right wing, showing the reality of war and its ethical problems. Jakob Wassermann and, from his Swiss vantage point, Hermann Hesse concentrated on the development of the individual. From Austria came the long novels of Hermann Broch and Musil, which look critically at the origins of the unhappy Weimar epoch. Stefan Zweig, Joseph Roth, and Franz Werfel, however, were more popular in Germany. Franz Kafka remained an outsider, whose posthumous publications attracted little attention.

Left-wing socialists and communists opposed capitalist liberal democracy (with its vested interests) and hoped to overthrow the Republic. Their philosophy and weltanschauung were from Marx, Engels, and Lenin. Among the leaders of the Munich Räterepublik, characteristically, were writers such as Toller, Erich Mühsam, and Ret Marut. In prison after the collapse of the Soviet, Toller started his series of revolution dramas. Mühsam, despite his many fighting revolutionary lyrics and his proletarian drama *Judas* (1921; Judas), written in prison, was too anarchistic for Communist Party taste. Marut had an odd combination of anarchist, socialist, and individualist theories, propounded with wild enthusiasm; under the pseudonym B. Traven, he later wrote tense social-critical novels, including *Das Totenschiff* (1926; The Death Ship). In more peaceful times, the communist cultural scene was noteworthy for the complex tension between successive aesthetic and political party lines and the individual leanings of practitioners. Many writers stood to the left of communism, following Rosa Luxemburg's spontaneity principle rather than Lenin's harsh reason. Berlin Dadaists, notably George Grosz, artist and poet, and Wieland Herzfelde, publisher of the Rote Roman-Serie (Red Novel Series) and periodicals containing biting verbal and visual satire, could broadly be reckoned here; they saw bourgeois art as a diversion. The avant-garde left's watchword was proletarian culture.

More mainstream voices such as Gertrud Alexander, however, valued the existing bourgeois culture and the classics of the past more highly. Later, the Bund proletarisch-revolutionärer Schriftsteller (League of Proletarian-Revolutionary Writers, founded in 1928; the group was supraparty, but KPD-led), with its influential periodical *Die Linkskurve* (Left Turn), had its internal debates but also generally followed the Moscow line leading toward socialist realism. The party organized socialist writing, encouraging worker-writers to produce workplace reports, novels, autobiographies, and *Sprechchöre* (spoken choruses, performed at party rallies) such as Hans Lorbeer's *Liebknecht, Luxemburg, Lenin* (1927). Press organs were built up. The Internationale Arbeiterhilfe (International Workers' Aid), headed by Willi Münzenberg, founded to disseminate knowledge about the Soviet Union, and active in publishing, film, and applied arts, was an institutional base. Becher, an important literary activist around 1918, became a leading facilitator of communist writing. Espousing, notably in a broadcast discussion with Benn, the idea of committed poetry and desiring only to serve the movement of history, he also wrote his own political poems and a novel on chemical warfare.

The active agitator Franz Jung was the first communist novelist, prolifically producing such works as *Die Eroberung der Maschinen* (1921; The Conquest of the Machines), which pleads for a new kind of solidarity in the machine-dominated modern world. Ludwig Renn in *Krieg* (rejected by publishers in 1924 and published in 1928; War) converted himself to communism, so to speak, by writing on his war experiences. Karl Grünberg's *Brennende Ruhr* (1928; Burning Ruhr) deals with the left-wing struggles in industrial areas after 1918. Willi Bredel describes KPD work in Hamburg in *Maschinenfabrik N und K* (1930; N and K Machine Factory), which drew Georg Lukács's criticism that the proletarian approach was too narrow and did not give the larger picture.

Other genres show less-marked or less-widespread political dissensions. In poetry, for instance, the Right Wing was represented by worker-poets Heinrich Lersch and Karl Bröger, who were already chauvinistic during the war. Rudolf Borchardt perpetuated traditional style and demanded (despite his Jewish descent) a renewal of the idea of the *Volk* and national literature; he also admired Mussolini. Gottfried Benn's nihilism and misanthropy, brilliantly if informally expressed, turned easily to antihumanism; he ended the Republic flirting with Nazism, but his poetic qualities are much more important than his politics. Traditional tones, classicist attitudes, and love of nature themes may mean either unthinking conservatism or reasonable republicanism, as with Oskar Loerke. Overtones of magic realism and attempts to surpass surface beauty to find metaphysical significance in nature were present in the early poems of Peter Huchel and Wilhelm Lehmann.

The lyric of *Neue Sachlichkeit* disregarded literary tradition, immersing itself in modern life. Satirical and leftist political poetry developed greatly. Erich Kästner had success with poems propounding, although rather wearily, humanism and decency in the consumer society. Tucholsky kept up a constant flow of cabaret lyrics. Walter Mehring, pioneer of the genre called Song, founded the Politisches Cabaret and wrote many lyrics exposing the hypocritical pseudodemocracy of the get-rich-quick, protofascist society for Friedrich Hollaender—composer, impresario, and pioneer of the satirical cabaret revue. Yvan Goll's poetry of the time moved from hymnlike Expressionism to slangy nihilism, although he sometimes let revolution inspire him. Rudolf Leonhard in *Spartakus Sonette* (1921; Spartacus Sonnets) and Franz Carl Weiskopf also wrote poetry inspired by the Russian and German revolutions.

The giant of the stage was Gerhart Hauptmann, whose work addresses big questions—life and death, social commitment and religious thought, and reason and mysticism. He used his celebrity to try to make Germany earn its name of *Land der Dichter und Denker*. His 70th birthday in 1932 rivaled the Goethe centenary. Georg Kaiser continued to innovate, following individualistic Expressionist plays with the filmic *Simultanbühne* (multiple stage), ironic comedies, and light explorations of reality and appearance. Ernst Barlach searched for the new man and new world. Hans Henny Jahnn continued his amoralism with *Der Arzt, sein Weib, sein Sohn* (1922; The Doctor, His Wife, His Son). Paradoxically, he also believed in a utopian state that would be led by the creative intellectual, as represented in his novel *Perrudja* (1929; Perrudja). Arnolt Bronnen exemplifies the overtly egocentric postwar generation; he reached a right-wing position from a stance of universal opposition in *Vatermord* (1920; Parricide), a succès de scandale, by way of dramas of technology and topical anti-French feeling. Bronnen was hailed as the leading young dramatist for his *Katalaunische*

Schlacht (1924; Catalaunian Battle), an unadorned representation of World War I. His subsequent oscillation between Nazism and communism cost him general sympathies.

Carl Sternheim, a much-performed repertory playwright of the 1920s, finished his bourgeois cycle; his clipped, cynical tones seem appropriate to the era. The comic writer Carl Zuckmayer, celebrated for *Der fröhliche Weinberg* (1925; The Merry Vineyard), achieved social satire in *Der Hauptmann von Köpenick* (1931; *The Captain of Köpenick*). The drama of social reform is represented by Peter Martin Lampel, whose *Revolte im Erziehungshaus* (1928; Revolt in the Reformatory) actually started a reform of youth custody. Social commitment and a psychological approach are paired in Ferdinand Bruckner's complex, innovative *Krankheit der Jugend* (1926; Sickness of Youth) and *Verbrecher* (1928; translated as *The Criminals* and *Law Breakers*). Ödön von Horváth revivified *Volksstück,* hitherto an earthy and unpretentious kind of play for the undiscerning, and gave it political force by examining topical social problems and attacking the Right Wing. The leading communist playwright, Friedrich Wolf, caused a controversy with his play on the abortion law in its socioeconomic context, *Cyankali* (1929; Cyanide). In addition, Wolf was an early writer of radio plays designed to reach a larger proletarian public; he also became a moving spirit in workers' theater. The young Brecht was a rebel without a cause, rarely sticking to a style or a sentiment; his trek from critical *neusachlich* observation and deconstruction of the individual to social commitment and communism led to his acceptance in Party circles with the *Solidaritätslied* in the film *Kuhle Wampe* (1931).

Factual texts also emerged, claiming equality with creative literature. Reportage, the essay, the sketch, and other journalistic genres often treated subjects that were, so far, closed to higher literature, and they often did so with a committed stance. Responding to Joyce's revolution in the novel, Becher said that if the traditional novel was impossible, the way forward was not experimentalism but reportage, objectivity in a Marxist sense. Ernst Glaeser, celebrated for the antibourgeois novel *Jahrgang 1902* (1928; translated as *Class 1902* and *Class of 1902*), edited the collection *Fazit: Ein Querschnitt durch die deutsche Publizistik (*1929; Summing-Up: A Cross Section of German Reporting) to encourage attention to facts rather than to poesy. Travel writing often included an attempt to gauge Germany's standing in the world after the war was lost. France was a popular destination for nationalists such as Kasimir Edschmid, who wrote *Zauber und Größe des Mittelmeers* (1932; The Magic and Grandeur of the Mediterranean), and Pan-Europeans such as

Tucholsky, who produced *Pyrenäenbuch* (1927; Book of the Pyrenees). A subgenre of reports from the Soviet Union emerged, especially among left-wingers, including Alfons Paquet, Arthur Holitscher, and Kisch. Autobiography thrived: Klaus Mann published his precocious *Kind dieser Zeit* (1932; A Child of Our Time), and Wassermann adopted the telling title *Mein Weg als Deutscher und Jude* (1922; *My Life as German and Jew*).

Most of the achievements of the Weimar Republic were immediately buried after 1933, when the right-wingers had their heyday. The exhumation after 1945 was selective, starting with the conservative and apolitical traditions. During the 1960s, writers exiled after 1933 and some more politically controversial writers were rediscovered, and the similarities of ethos led to more interest in the Weimar period as a whole, bringing even minor writers back into the limelight as representatives of attitudes now once again acceptable. Although today the middle-ground writers are seen as far and away the most important, left-wingers were much admired in the GDR and by the Left in the later years of the Bonn Republic, when communist *Kulturpolitik* was much studied. Most recently, various kinds of postmodernist theory have attempted to claim some aspects of Weimar culture for their own. We have not seen the last reevaluation of the 1920s, a kaleidoscope of concepts of cultural achievement.

ALFRED D. WHITE

See also Berlin; Cabaret; Die Moderne; Neue Sachlichkeit

Further Readings

Berg, Jan, et al., *Sozialgeschichte der deutschen Literatur von 1918 bis zur Gegenwart,* Frankfurt: Fischer Taschenbuch, 1981

Furness, Raymond, and Malcolm Humble, *A Companion to Twentieth-Century German Literature,* London and New York: Routledge, 1991; 2nd edition, 1997

Grenville, Anthony, *Cockpit of Ideologies: The Literature and Political History of the Weimar Republic,* Bern and New York: Lang, 1995

Taylor, Ronald, *Literature and Society in Germany, 1914–1945,* Brighton: Harvester Press, and Totowa, New Jersey: Barnes and Noble, 1980

Weyergraf, Bernhard, editor, *Literatur der Weimarer Republik 1918–1933,* Munich: Hanser, 1995

Willett, John, *The New Sobriety 1917–1933: Art and Politics in the Weimar Period,* London: Thames and Hudson, 1978; as *Art and Politics in the Weimar Period: The New Sobriety, 1917–1933,* New York: Pantheon Books, 1978

Zmegac, Viktor, editor, *Geschichte der deutschen Literatur vom 18. Jahrhundert bis zur Gegenwart,* vol. 3: 1918–80, Königstein: Athenäum, 1984

Otto Weininger 1880–1903

Otto Weininger was an Austrian Jew who aspired to be the most Aryan of Germans. On the day of his high school graduation, he converted to Protestantism. Although he attacked effeminate café society and sought to contain and control all so-called mixed feelings, which he despised, he at the same time came out

for a theory of bisexuality that presupposed the fundamentally mixed sexuality of every individual. It was a theoretical construct for which Wilhelm Fließ claimed ownership, but which ended up under Weininger's signature through Hermann Swoboda, Weininger's friend and Freud's patient, to whom the father of psychoanalysis had explained the notion in a session. Bisexuality was one among many notions Freud and Fließ had discussed and developed in their correspondence, an exchange that provided the transferential frame for Freud's self-analysis. When Weininger's revised dissertation was published in 1903 under the title *Geschlecht und Charakter* and instantly became a bestseller, Fließ was furious with Freud for betraying confidentiality and publicizing to third parties in Vienna the theory of the unconditional bisexuality of all life forms Fließ had developed on his own in Berlin. In the interim, Weininger shot himself only a few months after the appearance of his misogynist epic, which called for the renunciation of sexuality and sexual difference as the only way, ultimately, to redeem the emancipation of women. Joining Daniel Paul Schreber, whose *Denkwürdigkeiten eines Nervenkranken* also appeared in 1903, Weininger thus became a case and one of the prime objects of psychoanalytic study.

Presumably in reaction to his own femininity and Jewish descent, Weininger distilled the equation that the Jew was a woman, and thus subsequently counted Hitler as one of his fans. Jesus Christ was a Jew, too; but he overcame Judaism on his own person. One of Weininger's mentors, the anti-Semite and Wagner fan Houston Stewart Chamberlain, in turn dedicated his *Grundlagen des neunzehnten Jahrhunderts* (1899; *Foundations of the Nineteenth Century*) to Weininger, a racially pure Jew. Although Chamberlain claimed that Jews were incapable of creative genius, he accorded Weininger exceptional status because, as a fellow anti-Semite, and a particularly fervent one at that, he had mercifully surmounted his Jewishness.

Geschlecht und Charakter observes the closed system of paranoid delusions. Unlike Schreber's memoirs, however, it manifests a certain tradition of Western reason, like a manifesto to which others could subscribe by common sense and cause. In his final diary entries, Weininger had to admit to himself that behind his hatred of woman was concealed the hatred of his own sexuality, the original aversion he had not been able to overcome. Then one day he gave his father his worn-out leather glasses case, rented a room in the house in which Beethoven had died 76 years earlier, and there and then shot himself. Stefan Zweig, Karl Kraus, and Ludwig Wittgenstein (14 years old at the time) were among those who attended Weininger's funeral. In a letter written to G.E. Moore on 23 August 1931, Wittgenstein was still impressed by what he referred to as Weininger's "enormous mistake." August Strindberg sent a wreath to be placed on Weininger's grave and composed a eulogy in which he restated the fact of life that a woman was but a rudimentary man. Karl Kraus published the text in his newspaper *Die Fackel*. In a letter to Weininger's friend Artur Gerber, dated 8 December 1903, Strindberg elaborated points of identification between Weininger and himself, such as a high regard for Beethoven. Additional prominent first-generation admirers of the self-declared genius, half a century before Slavoj Zizek, included Heimito von Doderer, Alban Berg, Walter Serner, and Alfred Kubin. In 1982, the French Germanist Jacques Le Rider could write that Weininger was not a genius but a brilliant symptom. The question thus raised concerns about the extent to which, on average, Weininger's psychopathology represented the *Ratio* of his time. A few weeks before his suicide, the already famous 23-year-old author was accused by Paul Julius Moebius, a Leipzig professor, of having plagiarized ideas that he himself had set forth in his own popular book *Über den physi-*

ologischen Schwachsinn des Weibes (1900; On the Physiological Stupidity of Woman).

For years following Weininger's death, Fließ continued to protest the theft of his proper theory. Freud neither granted Fließ exclusive rights to the bisexuality insight nor accepted Fließ's theory, which he concluded was too symmetrical or too biological by half. Karl Kraus was pleased to play the third party in the Fließ property dispute, which he covered in *Die Fackel* largely on Weininger's behalf. Kraus, similar to von Doderer and Ernst Jünger, was invested in Weininger's antifeminist genius theory for the field of resistance it opened wide against psychoanalysis, which was their common object of loathing. Paradoxically, while just another anonymous young graduate student, Weininger had revered Freud as the major inspiration for his work in progress. Freud, in turn, judged Weininger a highly talented but sexually disturbed young philosopher. The nothingness Weininger assigned to woman followed the psychoanalytic theory of castration to the letter while, thereby, reversing it point by point.

After Weininger's suicide in 1903, Friedrich Jodl, Weininger's "doctor father" at the University of Vienna, issued a statement in a Viennese newspaper (*Neues Wiener Journal*, 25 October 1903) identifying the thesis portion of the book as an exceptional achievement. But what Weininger then added on his own, in the year leading to the publication of the thesis-based book, "the second, more deductive section of the book, the part that primarily gave offense," represented work "on which his teachers could not possibly have exercised any direct influence." Indeed, *Geschlecht und Charakter* was a work of crisis: the psychologists who had guided Weininger throughout his university studies, Ernst Mach and Wilhelm Wundt, he then had to abandon or rather demonize, while regrounding his project in an alleged return to Kant. In crisis, Weininger found names for his pain, and they were: "woman," "Jew," "Mach," and "Wundt." Following the publication and instant success of *Geschlecht und Charakter*, which was also the work of his uncontained negative transferences, Weininger shot himself, thereby succumbing to the logic of autocastration his theory and practice of sexual repression had already spelled out.

LAURENCE A. RICKELS

Biography

Born in Vienna, 5 April 1880. Applied for membership in the Philosophical Society of the University of Vienna and began studies at the university, 1898; studied psychology and began work on his doctoral thesis, *Eros und Psyche*, 1900, the title of which was changed to *Geschlect und Charakter* on the recommendation of his adviser, who also recommended that it be published. Died (suicide) in Vienna, 1903.

Selected Works

Psychology

Eros und Psyche: Studien und Briefe, 1899–1902; edited by Hannelore Rodlauer, 1990

Geschlecht und Charakter: Eine prinzipielle Untersuchung, 1903; appendix published as *Anhang: Taschenbuch und Briefe an einen Freund*, edited by Artur Gerber, 1919

Über die letzten Dinge, edited by Moriz Rappaport, 1904

Poetry

"Verse," *Die Fackel* 613, no. 21 (1923)

Further Reading

Harrowitz, Nancy A., and Barbara Hyams, editors, *Jews and Gender: Responses to Otto Weininger*, Philadelphia, Pennsylvania: Temple University Press, 1995

Le Rider, Jacques, *Le cas Otto Weininger: Racines de l'antifeminisme et de l'antisemitisme*, Paris: Presses Universitaires de France, 1982

Rappaport, Moriz, "Vorwort zur zweiten Auflage," in *Über die letzten Dinge*, by Otto Weininger, Vienna and Leipzig: Braumüller, 1907

Swoboda, Hermann, *Otto Weiningers Tod*, Vienna: Deuticke, 1911

Wittgenstein, Ludwig, *Letters to Russell, Keynes, and Moore*, edited by G.H. von Wright, Ithaca, New York: Cornell University Press, 1974

Zweig, Stefan, "Vorbeigehen an einem unauffälligen Menschen: Otto Weininger (1926)," in *Europäisches Erbe*, Frankfurt: Fischer, 1960

Peter Weiss 1916–1982

The son of a Jewish textile manufacturer, Weiss grew up in Berlin and Bremen but emigrated with his parents in 1934 via Prague to England. He spent most of his life in permanent exile, settling in Sweden in 1939, where he was granted citizenship in 1949 and married the stage designer Gunilla Palmstierna. Weiss remained a peripheral—though significant—figure in postwar German culture, expressing his hard-won moral, political, and aesthetic views in several clamorous and often controversial plays during the 1960s and 1970s. Late in life he felt that he was still speaking an unfamiliar language and that he had difficulty expressing himself in German. His physical displacement and mixed blood (Austro-Hungarian on his father's side, Swiss-Alsatian on his mother's) engendered a permanent sense of exclusion ("exile meant finding oneself in a nether world") that intensified his distaste for the nationalistic chauvinism evident everywhere.

Weiss was always acutely aware of his position outside the mainstream of German postwar culture, but he used the uniqueness of his background and the neutrality of his fortuitous Swedish vantage point to cast a detached analytical eye on developments in the Federal Republic. His massive last work, *Die Ästhetik des Widerstands* (1975–81; The Aesthetics of Resistance), was the outcome of his own dialectical and antagonistic relationship with Germany: "I shall try to say something about this country I was born and grew up in, from which I was exiled and to which I never returned, but whose language is the tool I work with."

In his early years Weiss painted, mainly in the surrealist manner, then tried his hand at making experimental documentary films. After 1960, writing became his main concern. His first prose works were characterized by a style of precise, unemotional description, indebted to Kafka and the French *nouveau roman*, through which he attempted to establish autobiographical clarity. *Abschied von den Eltern* (1961; *Leavetaking*) and *Fluchtpunkt* (1962; *Vanishing Point*) record this search for identity against the pressures of family and heritage.

Weiss shot to international prominence in 1964 with the vibrant play *Die Verfolgung und Ermordung Jean Paul Marats, dargestellt durch die Schauspielgruppe des Hospizes zu Charenton unter Anleitung des Herrn de Sade* (1964; *The Persecution and Assassination of Jean-Paul Marat as Performed by the Inmates of the Asylum of Charenton under the Direction of the Marquis de Sade*), a collage of styles and themes influenced by Brecht and Antonin Artaud, which creates a sort of "total theater." Reason and argument, violence and sexuality, and madness and sanity conflict and merge in a fast-moving action in which Marat's defense of collectivism and revolution is opposed to de Sade's assertion of anarchic individualism. The three interacting time levels emphasize the historical significance of the collision between revolution and reaction, conscious reason and instinctive drives. *Marat/Sade* was a play that gripped both the theatrical imagination and the intellect. Peter Brook, speaking of his memorable London production, described how it fulfilled "that time-honoured notion of getting all the elements of the stage to serve the play." As well as incorporating current modes of staging that were revitalizing European drama in the wake of Brecht, Beckett, and Artaud, the play mingles historical events (de Sade's long internment in Charenton, Marat's skin disease, and his assassination by Charlotte Corday) with the bold fiction of a disputatious meeting of de Sade and Marat. This invention enabled Weiss to investigate "the conflict between an individualism taken to extremes and the idea of political and social revolution." Although he situated the drama in an earlier epoch, Weiss saw in de Sade a very modern figure, who passively awaits his own end with self-centered equanimity, an attitude in confrontation with Marat's active pursuit of necessary political ends. Weiss made no secret of his conviction that Marat's was the right and superior standpoint and that Marat should emerge as the moral victor in a "correct" production of the play; he agreed, too, with those who saw it as a political play for its time.

Although Weiss clearly sided with Marat and the revolutionary impetus implicit in his uncompromising view of the need for change, he also shared de Sade's doubts about the means of achieving this end. For Weiss, the ideal socialist order dreamt of by Marat had become the disillusioning reality of the communist state; like Sartre, he rejected this in favor of the "third standpoint." His disappointment perhaps encapsulates the dilemma of the modern intellectual of the Left, who recognizes compelling need for an end to capitalism and colonialism but cannot give up his individual freedom.

Despite his critique of the political leadership in the communist world, Weiss clung to Marxism in his thinking and sought to stimulate his public to political reflection. In 1965, he moved from a subjective, often idiosyncratic approach to his themes to an active desire to educate and influence audiences through objective, factual treatment. That year saw the publication of his programmatic *10 Arbeitspunkte eines Autors in der geteilten Welt* (Ten Working Points of an Author in a Divided World), which opens with the declaration: "Every word I write and publish is political, aiming to reach large groups of people in order to influence them in a particular way." The ten points include an affirmation of his solidarity with the socialist countries of the world and an implicit condemnation of modern Western values. This political philosophy also underlies Weiss's best-known work, *Die Ermittlung* (1965; *The Investigation*), which appeared at this time and touched a raw nerve in German society. This piece—effectively a court scene reenacted on stage—is a chillingly stark dramatization of the lengthy Frankfurt trial of Auschwitz war criminals. The impact of this play is all the more powerful for its restrained documentary style, which was cast in the form of an oratorium in 11 cantos, a structure echoing Dante's *Inferno*. As well as exploiting the resonances of the allusions to Dante and the humanistic values of high Western culture, Weiss manipulated the bald, unemotional legal language of the trial itself—the matter-of-fact, dismissive attitudes of the lawyers and the accused, and the disconcerting anonymity of many survivors—to articulate this somber chapter in German history. From the daily tedium of the long, drawn-out trial—which Weiss partially attended—he raised fact and reportage to a memorable spareness and rigor, creating, along with Paul Celan's poem *Todesfuge* and his own prose description of a visit he made to Auschwitz at this time, *Meine Ortschaft* (1965; My Place), the most moving and controlled evocation to date of the Holocaust theme.

Weiss persisted with his conviction that there was no point in writing unless one intended "to influence or change society," and in the next few years he composed politically agitative works in idiosyncratic dramatic forms that relied essentially on a factual basis. *Gesang vom lusitanischen Popanz* (1967; *Song of the Lusitanian Bogey*), an indictment of Portuguese colonial rule in Angola, sought to expose the oppression of poor lands by rich conquerors and to demonstrate solidarity with the oppressed. Not surprisingly, Weiss contributed to the international polemic on the war in Vietnam with the prime example of his documentary mode, the cumbersomely titled *Diskurs über die Vorgeschichte und den Verlauf des lang andauernden Befreiungskrieges in Viet Nam als Beispiel für die Notwendigkeit des bewaffneten Kampfes der Unterdrückten gegen die Unterdrücker sowie über die Versuche der Vereinigten Staaten von Amerika die Grundlagen der Revolution zu vernichten* (1968; *Discourse on Vietnam*). This work depicts the historical development of Vietnam through centuries of subjection, exploitation, struggle, and deprivation. Similar to other dramas at this time, Weiss supplied a bibliography to the printed version—in this case, 14 pages of historical chronology, some 170 book titles, and dozens of newspapers and journals. His commitment to political theater continued with *Trotzki im Exil* (1970; *Trotsky in Exile*), a rehabilitation of Stalin's dangerous rival, and *Hölderlin* (1971), which muses on the poet's madness as a protest against the betrayal of the ideals of the French Revolution.

Weiss was a leading exponent of the prevailing mode of documentary drama in West Germany in the 1960s—Rolf Hochhuth's *Der Stellvertreter* (1963; *The Representative*) and *Soldaten* (1967; *Soldiers*), and Heinar Kipphardt's *In der Sache J. Robert Oppenheimer* (1964; *In the Matter of J. Robert Oppenheimer*) were comparable plays that also had polemical edges. After the anodyne literature of the 1950s, writers—especially dramatists—began to engage actively in political debates and public controversies. Weiss contributed both his plays and a virtual manifesto in *Notizen zum dokumentarischen Theater* (1968; Notes on the Documentary Theater), in which he delineated the function of this genre as being open protest against the establishment forces who maintained power by trying to keep the public in a stultifying vacuum devoid of information and decision-making. This militant new literature ran parallel with the upheavals generated by the revolts of the student movement in those years.

Paradoxically, the more pugnaciously Weiss committed himself to live political controversies, the more he was attracted to the figure of Dante as an icon of Western civilization. He stated expressly that *The Investigation* took the *Divine Comedy* as its model, although it attempted to place Dante in our time and confront him with contemporary events. Simultaneously, he was meditating an adaptation of Dante's work, which was to be entirely revisionist. His *Vorübung zum dreiteiligen Drama divina commedia* (Preliminary Exercise to the Three-Part Drama Divine Comedy) and *Gespräch über Dante* (Dialogue on Dante) both appeared in 1965. A striking leitmotif of the *Notizbücher* (Notebooks) from 1964 to 1980 is Weiss's preoccupation with Dante and his significance in the post-Holocaust context. In the notebooks, the *Divine Comedy* is drained of all theological and spiritual content—elements absent from the bleak landscape of Auschwitz—for Dante's tight structures of belief and betrayal, reward and punishment, and deed and retribution dissolve in the inexplicability of the technically efficient absurdity that makes a mockery of our vaunted occidental civilization.

Weiss's sustained musing on his Dante material also informs the composition of the monumental opus *Die Ästhetik des Widerstands*, which occupied the last decade of his life. This is in reality a three-volume autobiographical reflection masked as the life of a fictitious working-class narrator, born in 1917, who experiences the events of the Third Reich, the Spanish Civil War, prolonged exile in Czechoslovakia and Stockholm, and the communist diaspora. In effect, Weiss muses here on the history of the European Left, resistance and exile, rigid party loyalty, and individual freedom of choice. This imaginative reconstruction is interwoven with elaborate analyses of great works of art—the Pergamon friezes, Géricault's painting *The Raft of the Medusa*, Picasso's *Guernica*, and Kafka's *The Trial*—to justify a Marxist aesthetic as a necessary element in left-wing resistance, especially during hard times. The *Notizbücher* accompanied the gestation of this impressive work and illuminate Weiss's methods and intentions.

Weiss was a committed Marxist, intellectually and emotionally, who nevertheless pursued his vision of a "third way," rejecting both unreflective subservience to party dictates and right-wing betrayals of the principles of a just society. His uncompromising rectitude earned him vilification from both Right and Left, which reinforced his sense of exile—to the extent that he had no impulse to return to Germany and even felt himself a stranger in the German language.

ARRIGO V. SUBIOTTO

Biography

Born in Nowawes, near Berlin, 8 November 1916. Emigrated with his family to London, 1934; moved to Prague in 1936, where he studied at the art academy; emigrated in 1939 via Switzerland to Sweden; worked initially in father's textile factory and subsequently as a painter; attained Swedish citizenship in 1946; worked in film; originally wrote in Swedish and began publishing literary works in German in the 1960s. Married the artist Gunilla Palmstierna in 1963. Died in Stockholm, 10 May 1982.

Selected Works

Collections

Werke in sechs Bänden [Suhrkamp Edition], edited by Gunilla Palmstierna-Weiss, 1991

Prose

Der Schatten des Körpers des Kutschers, 1960
Abschied von den Eltern, 1961; as *Leavetaking*, translated by Christopher Levenson, 1966; published with *Vanishing Point* as *Exile: A Novel*, translated by E.B. Garside et al., 1968
Fluchtpunkt, 1962; as *Vanishing Point*, translated by Christopher Levenson, 1966; published with *Leavetaking* as *Exile: A Novel*, translated by E.B. Garside et al., 1968
Gespräch der drei Gehenden, 1969; as *The Conversation of the Three Walkers*, translated by S.M. Cupitt, 1972
Notizbücher: 1960–1971, 2 vols., 1982
Notizbücher: 1971–1980, 2 vols., 1981
Die Ästhetik des Widerstands, 3 vols., 1975–81
Rekonvaleszenz, 1991

Plays

Die Verfolgung und Ermordung Jean Paul Marats, dargestellt durch die Schauspielgruppe des Hospizes zu Charenton unter Anleitung des Herrn de Sade: Drama in zwei Akten, 1964; as *The Persecution and Assassination of Jean-Paul Marat as Performed by the Inmates of the Asylum of Charenton under the Direction of the Marquis de Sade*, translated by Geoffrey Skelton, verse adaptation by Adrian Mitchell, 1965
Die Ermittlung: Oratorium in 11 Gesängen, 1965; as *The Investigation: A Play*, translated by Jon Swan and Ulu Grosbard, 1966; as *The Investigation: Oratorio in 11 Cantos*, translated by Alexander Gross, 1966
Diskurs über die Vorgeschichte und den Verlauf des lang andauernden Befreiungskrieges in Viet Nam als Beispiel für die Notwendigkeit des bewaffneten Kampfes der Unterdrückten gegen die Unterdrücker sowie über die Versuche der Vereinigten Staaten von Amerika die Grundlagen der Revolution zu vernichten, 1967; as *Discourse on Vietnam*, translated by Geoffrey Skelton, 1970
Gesang vom lusitanischen Popanz, 1967; as *Song of the Lusitanian Bogey*, translated by Lee Baxandall, 1970
Trotzki im Exil, 1970; as *Trotsky in Exile: A Play*, translated by Geoffrey Skelton, 1972
Hölderlin, 1971
Der neue Prozess: Stück in drei Akten, 1984

Further Reading

Best, Otto F., *Peter Weiss: Vom existentialistischen Drama zum marxistischen Welttheater*, Bern: Francke, 1971
Canaris, Volker, editor, *Über Peter Weiss*, Frankfurt: Suhrkamp, 1970
Cohen, Robert, *Peter Weiss in seiner Zeit: Leben und Werk*, Stuttgart: Metzler, 1992
Gerlach, Rainer, editor, *Peter Weiss*, Frankfurt: Suhrkamp, 1984
Hilton, Ian, *Peter Weiss: A Search for Affinities*, London: Wolff, 1970
Rischbieter, Henning, *Peter Weiss*, Velber: Friedrich, 1967
Vogt, Jochen, *Peter Weiss: Mit Selbstzeugnissen und Bilddokumenten*, Reinbek bei Hamburg: Rowohlt, 1987
Vormweg, Heinrich, *Peter Weiss*, Munich: Beck, 1981

Die Ästhetik des Widerstands 1975–1981
Novel by Peter Weiss

The critical reception of Peter Weiss's major novel *Die Ästhetik des Widerstands* (The Aesthetics of Resistance) has passed through several phases. Initially, the political aspect of the text was emphasized, and the author's left-wing credentials, together with his somewhat misleading statement in an early interview that the novel was a "Wunschautobiographie," helped make it acceptable enough for an East German edition to appear in 1983. Later, the politics were played down, attention being concentrated on aesthetic issues, both those of the text itself and those thematized in the numerous discussions of European art from the ancient Greeks to the avant-garde of the 20th century. Both these approaches have given way to a more measured appreciation of the relationship between politics and aesthetics adumbrated in the novel's title. At the same time, an endless succession of papers and dissertations has illuminated a series of individual aspects, ranging from Weiss's presentation of women through his indebtedness to psychoanalytical theories to the status of surrealism in the text.

The overt political assumptions are given in the novel's story line, which covers the years 1937–45 and tells of the communist resistance to fascism, first in the International Brigades fighting Franco in Spain and later in the clandestine Schulze-Boysen-Harnack group seeking to overthrow Hitler in Germany. The novel is thus yet another example of a literature that seeks to deal with the German past. Coming to a proper understanding of fascism is the precondition for political progress in the present—there can be no progress without a clarification of the past, as Weiss wrote in the notebooks that he kept during the writing of his novel. The evil of fascism is indicated in the horrific detail with which the executions of the resistance fighters are described; fascism could survive for so long because of the connivance of those powers (France, England, and Sweden) that might have held it in check and because of the disunity of the Left and especially the phenomenon of Stalinism. The didactic stance of the novel is embodied in the figure of Lotte Bischoff, a survivor who is determined to become a schoolteacher and ensure that her pupils learn about the past. However, militating against the political tendency of the novel are, on the one hand, the numerous historical parallels in which progress was repeatedly defeated and, on the other, the weight of myth that implies eternal recurrence—a telling detail is the refusal to name either Hitler or Stalin, thus equating and mythologizing both. A strong undercurrent of left-wing melancholy is found in the text, an important motif of which is Albrecht Dürer's woodcut "Melencolia."

Stalin was hostile to the progressive trends in 20th-century art and literature. Thus, on the aesthetic level, one of the text's aims is to reconcile the political with the artistic avant-garde. The discussions of art works deal with the reclaiming of "bourgeois" culture for the proletariat, ranging from the Pergamon altar frieze depicting the struggle of the gods and the Titans discussed by the young working-class communists in the opening section of the novel through Dürer, Courbet, and Géricault to Gaudi and Picasso and from Dante through Goethe to Thomas Mann, Joyce, Kafka, and Brecht. They also reflect the novel's title: To what extent can art be seen as contributing to the struggle against injustice and exploitation? Here, too, the text is more "open" than might have been expected, the dialogic form leaving the debates inconclusive and the final answers up to the reader.

However, the form of Weiss's novel itself is not especially avant-garde. True, it is not an easy work to read. Despite the potential for a gripping plot afforded by the historical background, conventional suspense arises only sporadically and more toward the end as the net closes in on the conspirators. Even visually, Weiss makes no concessions to his readers: although each of the three volumes is divided into two parts, paragraphs run on for several pages at a time, and dialogues are not punctuated as such. At times the surreal breaks through terrifyingly, as in the Holocaust visions of the narrator's mother. One role of the works of art is to add color to the otherwise densely abstract mass of theoretical discussion. Weiss's origins in the visual arts are recalled in echoes of the techniques of abstract painting in his novel: the isolated "stories" might be compared to blobs of bright colors in a mass of gray tones. This said, the underlying structure of Die Ästhetik des Widerstands is that of the traditional German Entwicklungsroman (developmental novel). In the course of the novel and through his encounters with a variety of "mentors," the young narrator overcomes his initial hesitations and joins the Communist Party; at the same time he discovers his true vocation, that of writer, a development signaled by the increasing complexity of his narrative technique. The exegesis of cultural artifacts is part of the tradition, as is the relative facelessness of the narrator himself in contrast to the many memorable figures he encounters, not only his own parents but also Hans Coppi, the ailing Max Hodann, Rosalinde Ossietzky, Brecht, Karin Boye, and Herbert Wehner. It is also a historical novel in the Lukácsian sense: although many of them have become obscure to all but the most sectarian socialists, the characters we encounter actually existed, with the major exception of the narrator and his family, the "mediocre" protagonist juxtaposed with "world-historical" personages.

Die Ästhetik des Widerstands represented the culmination of the career of an author who had always stood on the fringes of the German literary scene and who died only a year after the publication of the final volume. Already unfashionable when the work appeared, the collapse of East European socialism has made it even more so. Nevertheless, its magnificent "epic" qualities, which link it to the great philosophical novels of the earlier part of the 20th century, surely mark it as a milestone in postwar German literature.

J.H. REID

Edition

First edition: Die Ästhetik des Widerstands: Roman, 3 vols., Frankfurt: Suhrkamp, 1975–81

Further Reading

Bommert, Christian, Peter Weiss und der Surrealismus: Poetische Verfahrensweisen in der "Ästhetik des Widerstands," Opladen: Westdeutscher Verlag, 1991

Bond, D.G., "Aesthetics and Politics: Peter Weiss, Die Ästhetik des Widerstands as a Chronicle of Horror," Journal of European Studies 19 (1989)

Dwars, Jens-F., et al., editors, Widerstand wahrnehmen: Dokumente eines Dialogs mit Peter Weiss, Cologne: GNN, 1993

Gerlach, Ingeborg, Die ferne Utopie: Studien zu Peter Weiss' "Ästhetik des Widerstands," Aachen: Fischer, 1991

Götze, Karl-Heinz, Poetik des Abgrunds und Kunst des Widerstands: Grundmuster der Bildwelt von Peter Weiss, Opladen: Westdeutscher Verlag, 1995

Hofmann, Michael, Ästhetische Erfahrung in der historischen Krise: Eine Untersuchung zum Kunst- und Literaturverständnis in Peter Weiss' Roman "Die Ästhetik des Widerstands," Bonn: Bouvier, 1990

Huber, Andreas, Mythos und Utopie: Eine Studie zur "Ästhetik des Widerstands" von Peter Weiss, Heidelberg: Winter, 1990

Kane, Martin, "Culture, Political Power, and the Aesthetics of Resistance: Peter Weiss's Die Ästhetik des Widerstands," in After the "Death of Literature": West German Writing of the 1970s, edited by Keith Bullivant, Oxford and New York: Berg, 1989; distributed in the U.S. by St. Martin's Press

Meyer, Stephan, Kunst als Widerstand: Zum Verhältnis von Erzählen und ästhetischer Reflexion in Peter Weiss' "Die Ästhetik des Widerstands," Tübingen: Niemeyer, 1989

Müller, Jost, Literatur und Politik bei Peter Weiss: Die "Ästhetik des Widerstands" und die Krise des Marxismus, Wiesbaden: Deutscher Universitätsverlag, 1991

Müller, Karl-Josef, Haltlose Reflexion: Über die Grenzen der Kunst in Peter Weiss' Roman "Die Ästhetik des Widerstands," Würzburg: Königshausen und Neumann, 1992

Pischel, Joseph, "Peter-Weiss-Lektüre nach der 'Wende': Noch einmal zum Verhältnis von Kunst und Politik in Die Ästhetik des Widerstands," in Geist und Macht: Writers and the State in the GDR, edited by Axel Goodbody and Dennis Tate, Amsterdam and Atlanta, Georgia: Rodopi, 1992

Poore, Carol, "Mother Earth, Melancholia, and Mnemosyne: Women in Peter Weiss's Die Ästhetik des Widerstands," German Quarterly 58 (1985)

Schulz, Genia, "Die Asthetik des Widerstands": Versionen des Indirekten in Peter Weiss' Roman, Stuttgart: Metzler, 1986

Weiss, Peter, Notizbücher: 1971–1980, Frankfurt: Suhrkamp, 1981

Die Ermittlung 1965

Play by Peter Weiss

Any play that is premiered simultaneously in 17 theaters throughout Germany (both East and West) is guaranteed to make an impact, and that was certainly the case in October 1965 with Peter Weiss's Die Ermittlung (The Investigation). The material with which it dealt was highly topical. Just two months previously, the so-called Frankfurt Auschwitz trial had come to an end with the indictment of 18 of the men who had helped to operate this death camp during World War II. Working from published reports of the trial, Weiss produced a sequence of scenes set in the courtroom with a text that was drawn virtually unaltered from the transcript. In that respect, the play is a prime example of documentary drama, but it is far from impartial in intention. Quite the reverse: in his "Notes on Documentary Theatre," Weiss states that, although this mode of writing "refrains from any invention," it is nevertheless "partisan," because the playwright, while working with authentic material, selects and shapes it in order that social realities that are normally concealed should become visible. The enterprise is, therefore, a highly political one, and this becomes apparent as *The Investigation* proceeds.

The Brechtian, antinaturalistic character of the play is evident from the very beginning with its static presentation and stylized dialogue. Although the formal structure of the trial is retained, Weiss stipulated that no attempt should be made to reproduce either the actual courtroom or the emotional charge that overlaid the original trial. Instead, the actors should be mere "speaking tubes," using bare language to evoke the events of the Holocaust in a distillation of numerous individual experiences. In a further alienating device, Weiss cast his play as an "Oratorio in 11 Cantos" and fashioned the text into free verse, creating a savage contrast between the sacred and poetic resonances of the form and the barbarities with which it deals. In the world of Auschwitz, there was no sense of any higher meaning, let alone of divine justice, just an inexorable progression that is mirrored by the play's succession of scenes, from the loading ramp where the trains arrive to the brutal reality of the camp itself, which is marked by torture and medical experimentation, to the gas chambers and, finally, the crematoria. The division of each canto into three sections may provide an ironic echo of Dante's *Divina Commedia,* but in Auschwitz the inferno is man-made, and the ovens are administered and operated by human beings.

It is some of those human beings who are now on trial, and unlike the witnesses, who remain as anonymous as they were in the camps, the defendants carry their own names. Almost the only stage directions in the play refer to the defendants' dismissive laughter or self-righteous protests in the face of the evidence, a reaction that heightens the shocking effect of the atrocities described. But Weiss makes it clear in a foreword that the purpose is not to indict them again as individuals but rather to present them as "symbols of a system that imposed guilt on many others who never appeared before this court." The "investigation" of the title, therefore, is directed not at individual guilt or innocence, nor even at the nature or extent of the horrors, but above all at the structures that brought them about in the first place, and it is in the explanation offered that the play reveals its ideological colors. Through the words of one of the witnesses who makes no secret of his political convictions, Weiss, echoing Marxist historical interpretations, presents the world of the camp as the extreme outcome of the capitalist ordering of society, one in which the exploiter could exercise his power unhindered and the exploited had to give not just his labor but his very self. In this view, the Holocaust was less a racial phenomenon than a political one, and this interpretation explains why, although the persecution of the Jews as a group is implicit throughout the play, they are never referred to by name. There would be a logic to that approach if it were consistently maintained, but it is significant, and indicative of the play's political agenda, that on two occasions the text specifically highlights the sufferings inflicted in the camp upon Soviet prisoners of war.

Weiss once wrote that, when he dealt with historical themes, his prime interest was in their links with the present, and since *The Investigation* presents a trial in the mid-1960s rather than a dramatic re-creation of Auschwitz itself (as Rolf Hochhuth tried, with dubious success, in *Der Stellvertreter* [1963; *The Representative*]), the focus is as much upon contemporary West Germany as upon the events of 20 years earlier. It is repeatedly pointed out that firms involved in the mechanics of Auschwitz, such as Krupp and IG Farben, are now flourishing again in the Federal Republic and that the defendants have become respected members of West German society. The thrust is obvious: the capitalist Federal Republic is the repository of those same structures and attitudes that, in an earlier incarnation, led to the Third Reich, and if they are not dealt with, they could do the same again. The end of the play underlines the message: finishing in midtrial, it concludes with an impassioned speech from one of the defendants, stressing that all the accused had only done their duty and urging the Federal Republic to concern itself with its regained international status rather than with "charges which should be considered long since past and gone." His codefendants loudly voice their approval.

The deterministic view of human behavior advanced by Peter Weiss is undoubtedly inadequate as an explanation for the Holocaust, but even though *The Investigation* appeared at a time when Marxist ideas enjoyed a wide measure of credibility, its power even then did not derive from the rather shallow political analysis, but from the form. The play may be an uncomfortable hybrid, but the concentrated recitation, in detached and precise detail, of the vilest atrocities is an overwhelming dramatic experience, and *The Investigation* remains for that reason a memorable piece of theater.

PETER J. GRAVES

See also Holocaust (Shoah) Literature

Editions

First edition: *Die Ermittlung: Oratorium in 11 Gesängen,* Frankfurt: Suhrkamp, 1965
Translation: *The Investigation: Oratorio in 11 cantos,* translated by Alexander Gross, London: Boyars, 1966

Further Reading

Bosmajian, Hamida, *Metaphors of Evil: Contemporary German Literature and the Shadow of Nazism,* Iowa City: University of Iowa Press, 1979
Hilton, Ian, *Peter Weiss: A Search for Affinities,* London: Wolff, 1970
Milfull, John, "From Kafka to Brecht: Peter Weiss' Development towards Marxism," *German Life and Letters* 20 (1966/67)
Salloch, Erika, *Peter Weiss' "Die Ermittlung": Zur Struktur des Dokumentartheaters,* Frankfurt: Athenäum, 1972
Vormweg, Heinrich, *Peter Weiss,* Munich: Beck, 1981
Zipes, J.D., "Documentary Drama in Germany: Mending the Circuit," *Germanic Review* 42 (1967)

Weissenburg, Otfrid von, *see* Otfrid von Weissenburg

Franz Werfel 1890–1945

Franz Werfel's first collections of poetry, which appeared shortly before and after World War I, were hailed as the beginning of a new era in literature, known today as Expressionism, and this reception made Werfel one of the most important figures of the new literary movement. During the 1920s he also became successful as a dramatist and even more so as a novelist. When he came to the United States as an exile in 1940, his fame was already firmly established in Germany and the United States, since his novels of the 1920s and 1930s had been received enthusiastically by millions of readers. Although Werfel was unable to market his books in Hitler's Germany, his novel *Das Lied von Bernadette* (1941; *The Song of Bernadette*) became one of the greatest American best-sellers of all time. Werfel scored an amazing Broadway hit with his drama *Jacobowsky und der Oberst* (1944; *Jacobowsky and the Colonel*). Today he is forgotten as an author of lyrical poetry, but he is still recognized as a dramatist for his *Jacobowsky and the Colonel*, one of the few successful German comedies, and, at least in Germany and Austria, a number of his novels still enjoy popularity.

In his first collections of poetry, *Der Weltfreund* (1911; The Philanthropist), *Wir sind* (1913; We Are), and *Einander* (1915; Each Other), Werfel voices a gospel of brotherhood and the love of one's fellow human beings, which soon became the hallmark of Expressionism in German-speaking countries. It was not until, under the influence of the experiences of World War I, *Der Gerichtstag* (1919; Day of Judgment) was published that Werfel's optimism clearly gave way to increasing resignation, which was also confirmed in his later collections of poetry.

His early dramas were typically Expressionist, in particular the metaphysically oriented trilogy *Spiegelmensch: Magische Trilogie* (1920; Mirror Man: Magical Trilogy), a Faustian drama about guilt and the ultimate self-finding of man; *Bocksgesang* (1921; *Goat Song*), a drama about both the intrusion of mythical forces into a rural society and revolution and the ultimate restoration of human togetherness; and *Schweiger* (1922; Schweiger). In all these dramas a spirit of sacrifice and human closeness, of hubris and the ultimate admission of guilt prevails. The message of Werfel's first novel, *Nicht der Mörder, der Ermordete ist schuldig* (1920; Not the Murderer) takes up the theme of patricide and the father-son conflict prevalent in so many German Expressionist dramas.

In his essays of the late 1920s and 1930s, including *Realismus und Innerlichkeit* (1931; Realism and Inwardness), *Können wir ohne Gottesglauben leben?* (1932; Can We Live without Faith in God?), and *Von der reinsten Glückseligkeit des Menschen* (1938; Of Man's True Happiness), Werfel castigates what he calls "abstraction" and, later, "radical realism" and "naturalistic nihilism," stating that the modern world is on the road to soul-lessness and that technology and modern psychology are to blame. In his *Theologumena,* written between 1922 and 1944, he expresses his religious views, his sympathy for Christianity, and his conviction that it is the mission of the Jews to bear negative witness to Christ on earth.

During the 1920s, Werfel gave up the hymnic and ecstatic style of Expressionism in favor of a more factual, sober style close to New Objectivity. His novel *Verdi: Roman der Oper* (1924; *Verdi: A Novel of the Opera*) was perhaps his last work with Expressionist elements. Here he describes how the composer regains his creativity only after he has given up his inner struggle with his competitor, Richard Wagner.

In several novels and novellas, Werfel mourns the demise of the Habsburg Empire. *Der Tod des Kleinbürgers* (1927; *The Man Who Conquered Death*) tells the gripping though ironic story about the dying of a petit bourgeois. His voluminous novel *Barbara; oder, Die Frömmigkeit* (1929; *The Pure in Heart*) is nothing but the reckoning with the past and the ill-effects of the revolutionary spirit of 1918. It is an educational novel about a youth, guided by the simple piety of Barbara, his childhood nursery maid, who at the end finds himself and becomes a ship's doctor.

The conflict between the generations is taken up in Werfel's "Italian novel," *Die Geschwister von Neapel* (1931; *The Pascarella Family*), but it is even more a novel about the end of an era, about the fascist state that wants to control all its citizens' activities and feelings. The powers of godless modernity and the traditional belief in God are also contrasted in *Die vierzig Tage des Musa Dagh* (1933; *The Forty Days of Musa Dagh*). On the one hand, this is a historical novel about a handful of Armenians who under their heroic leader Gabriel fight against an overwhelming Turkish force; on the other hand, it is also a novel about the old, traditional world of belief against the cold, modern one of the Young Turks. Falling away from God is also the theme of *Höret die Stimme* (1937; *Hearken unto the Voice*), a novel about the prophet Jeremiah and the kings of Israel.

Man's relationship to God was time and again Werfel's theme, and as he got older, the religious character of his works became more pronounced. That heaven cannot be bought is demonstrated by the maid Teta in *Der veruntreute Himmel* (1939; *Embezzled Heaven*). In many ways it is a precursor of the novel *The Song of Bernadette*, in which the young Bernadette Soubirous proves the absolute nature of her trust in the lady she has seen by carrying out her orders against the will of her elders. The modern spirit, modern science, and deism are pitted against the simple belief of the country people in the French Pyrenees; humility and obedience win out over arrogant enlightenment and skepticism.

Even in Werfel's posthumously published utopian novel *Stern der Ungeborenen* (1946; *Star of the Unborn*), these two forces are opposed to each other. The world of the Astromentals, which F.W. visits in the year 101,943, is a world in which all basic needs of man have been met, but in which human hubris comes out in man's attempt to circumvent death. The novel is Werfel's final statement against the spirit of modernity, technology, and man's attempt to escape from or to rival God.

Also published posthumously was his novel *Cella; oder, Die Überwinder* (1989; *Cella; or, The Survivors*), a fragment in which Werfel describes the persecution of Jews by the Nazis at the time of the annexation of Austria in 1938. More serious than the exile comedy *Jacobowsky and the Colonel*, a drama about the flight of a Polish colonel and a Jew from the advancing Germans in France in 1940, this realistic novel deals with the types of modern man against which Werfel fought throughout his life.

HANS WAGENER

Biography

Born in Prague, Bohemia (now the Czech Republic), 10 September 1890. Studied at the University of Prague, 1909–10, the University of Leipzig, and the University of Hamburg; volunteer in the Austrian army, 1911–12; on the Russian front during World War I; reader for Kurt Wolff, publishers, Leipzig, 1912–14; cofounder of *Der Jüngste Tag*, 1913–21; freelance writer in Vienna from 1917; member of the Prussian Academy of the Arts, 1926; in Italy, Capri, Locarno, and Ischl in the 1920s; in Palestine, 1925; in the United States, 1935, in France, 1938, Spain, 1940, and, with Heinrich Mann, the United States. Grillparzer Prize, 1926; Austrian Order of Merit for Art and Science, 1937; honorary law degree from the University of California, Los Angeles. Settled in Los Angeles, 1940. Died in Beverly Hills, California, 26 August 1945.

Selected Works

Collections

Gedichte aus den Jahren 1908–1945, edited by Ernst Gottlieb and Felix Guggenheim, 1946
Gesammelte Werke, edited by Adolf D. Klarmann, 14 vols., 1948–75

Plays

Die Versuchung, 1913
Die Troerinnen, adaptation of the play by Euripides (produced 1916), 1915
Der Mittagsgöttin (produced 1925), 1919
Der Besuch aus dem Elysium (produced 1918), 1920
Spiegelmensch (produced 1921), 1920
Bocksgesang (produced 1922), 1921; as *Goat Song*, translated by Ruth Langner, 1926
Schweiger (produced 1923), 1922
Juarez und Maximilian: Dramatische Historie in 3 Phasen und 13 Bildern, 1924; as *Juarez and Maximilian: A Dramatic History in Three Phases and Thirteen Pictures* (produced 1925), translated by Ruth Langner, 1926
Paulus unter den Juden (produced 1926), 1926; as *Paul among the Jews*, translated by Paul P. Levertoff, 1928
Das Reich Gottes in Böhmen (produced 1930), 1930
Der Weg der Verheissung, music by Kurt Weill (produced 1937), 1935; as *The Eternal Road*, translated by Ludwig Lewisohn, 1936
In einer Nacht (produced 1937), 1937
Jacobowsky und der Oberst (produced 1944), 1944; as *Jacobowsky and the Colonel*, translated by Gustave O. Arlt, 1944

Fiction

Der Dschin, 1919
Nicht der Mörder, der Ermordete ist schuldig, 1920

Spielhof, 1920
Verdi: Roman der Oper, 1924; as *Verdi: A Novel of the Opera*, translated by Helen Jessiman, 1925
Der Tod des Kleinbürgers, 1927; as *The Man Who Conquered Death*, translated by Clifton P. Fadiman and William A. Drake, 1927; as *The Death of a Poor Man*, 1927
Geheimnis eines Menschen (stories), 1927
Der Abituriententag: Die Geschichte einer Jugendschuld, 1928; as *Class Reunion*, translated by Whittaker Chambers, 1929
Barbara; oder, Die Frömmigkeit, 1929; as *The Pure in Heart*, translated by Geoffrey Dunlop, 1931; as *The Hidden Child*, 1931
Kleine Verhältnisse, 1931
Die Geschwister von Neapel, 1931; as *The Pascarella Family*, translated by Dorothy F. Tait-Price, 1932
Die vierzig Tage des Musa Dagh, 1933; as *The Forty Days of Musa Dagh*, translated by Geoffrey Dunlop, 1934; as *The Forty Days*, 1934
Höret die Stimme, 1937; as *Hearken unto the Voice*, translated by Moray Firth, 1938; as *Jeremias*, 1956
Twilight of a World (collection), translated by H.T. Lowe-Porter, 1937
Erzählungen aus zwei Welten, edited by Adolf D. Klarmann, 3 vols., 1938–39
Der veruntreute Himmel: Die Geschichte einer Magd, 1939; as *Embezzled Heaven*, translated by Moray Firth, 1940
Eine blaßblaue Frauenschrift, 1941
Das Lied von Bernadette, 1941; as *The Song of Bernadette*, translated by Ludwig Lewisohn, 1942
Die wahre Geschichte vom wiederhergestellten Kreuz, 1942
Stern der Ungeborenen, 1946; as *Star of the Unborn*, translated by Gustave O. Arlt, 1946

Poetry

Der Weltfreund, 1911
Wir sind, 1913
Einander, 1915
Gesänge aus den drei Reichen, 1917
Der Gerichtstag, 1919
Arien, 1923
Beschwörungen, 1923
Gedichte, 1927
Neue Gedichte, 1928
Schlaf und Erwachen, 1935
Gedichte aus dreissig Jahren, 1939
Poems, translated by Edith Abercrombie Snow, 1945
Gedichte aus den Jahren 1908–1945, edited by Ernst Gottlieb and Felix Guggenheim, 1946

Other

Gesammelte Werke, 8 vols., 1927–36
Realismus und Innerlichkeit (essay), 1931
Können wir ohne Gottesglauben leben? (essay), 1932
Reden und Schriften, 1932
Von der reinsten Glückseligkeit des Menschen, 1938
Zwischen Oben und Unten (essays), 1946; as *Between Heaven and Earth*, translated by Maxim Newmark, 1947
Das Franz Werfel Buch, edited by Peter Stephan Jungk, 1986
Gesammelte Werke in Einzelbänden, 1989–

Translations

Ottokar Brezina, *Winde von Mittag nach Mitternacht*, 1920
Giuseppe Verdi and F.M. Piave, *Simone Boccanegra*, 1929
Don Carlos, 1932
Giuseppe Verdi and F.M. Piave, *Die Macht des Schicksals*, 1950

Edited Works

Giuseppe Verdi, *Briefe*, 1926; as *Verdi: The Man in His Letters*, translated by Edward Downes, 1942

Further Reading

Abels, Norbert, *Franz Werfel: Mit Selbstzeugnissen und Bilddokumenten*, Reinbek bei Hamburg: Rowohlt, 1990

Eggers, Frank Joachim, *Ich bin ein Katholik mit jüdischem Gehirn: Modernitätskritik und Religion bei Joseph Roth und Franz Werfel: Untersuchungen zu den erzählerischen Werken*, Frankfurt and New York: Lang, 1996

Foltin, Lore Barbara, editor, *Franz Werfel*, Pittsburgh, Pennsylvania: University of Pittsburgh Press, 1961

Huber, Lothar, editor, *Franz Werfel: An Austrian Writer Reassessed*, Oxford: Berg, 1988; Oxford and New York: Berg, 1989

Jungk, Peter Stephan, *Franz Werfel: Eine Lebensgeschichte*, Frankfurt: S. Fischer, 1987

Michaels, Jennifer E., *Franz Werfel and the Critics*, Columbia, South Carolina: Camden House, 1994

Nehring, Wolfgang, and Hans Wagener, editors, *Franz Werfel im Exil*, Bonn: Bouvier, 1992

Paulsen, Wolfgang, *Franz Werfel: Sein Weg in den Roman*, Tübingen: Francke, 1995

Steiman, Lionel B., *Franz Werfel: The Faith of an Exile: From Prague to Beverly Hills*, Waterloo, Ontario: Wilfrid Laurier University Press, 1985

Strelka, Joseph, and Robert Weigel, editors, *Unser Fahrplan geht von Stern zu Stern: Zu Franz Werfels Stellung und Werk*, Bern and New York: Lang, 1992

Wagener, Hans, *Understanding Franz Werfel*, Columbia: University of South Carolina Press, 1993

Georg (Jörg) Wickram ca. 1500–ca. 1562

The literary reputation of Georg Wickram received endorsements in the 19th century first by Jakob Grimm (1808) and then later by Wilhelm Grimm (1809) in response to a new edition of Wickram's *Der Goldfaden* (1557; *The Golden Thread*) brought out by Clemens Brentano. The significance of these positive evaluations by leading literary figures is all the more striking in view of Jakob Grimm's comment in a letter to a friend, G.F. Benecke (1808), that the name of Wickram was relatively unknown in literary and scholarly circles ("dieser Wickram, über den man in Literaturbüchern vergebens nachschlägt"). In the second half of the 20th century, especially between 1950 and 1970, a renewed interest in Wickram shows up in dissertations and by the inclusion in handbooks of general assessments identifying him as the most significant novelist of the 16th century, father of the middle-class novel. Such assessments reflect the then current trends such as the interest in the representation of historical reality in late medieval writing and the role of the individual in early modern German society. Wickram emerged as a transitional 16th-century figure, who looked to earlier forms and themes of both courtly and popular nature. His skill lay in the adaptation of these aspects to the middle-class world of his contemporaries.

Wickram, an illegitimate child born in Colmar into the respected family of a leading member of the city council, lacked formal education. This did not hinder him from varied occupational activities; he was a dilettante painter, but he also had professional positions as a goldsmith and, later, as a civil servant in the cities of Colmar and Burkheim. His literary activities were equally varied: he continued the Meistersinger tradition established by Hans Sachs, authored *Fastnachtspiele* (Shrovetide Plays) in the manner of Niklaus Manuel and Pamphilus Gengenbach, and, based on his adaptation and expansion of Thomas Murner's *Narrenbeschwörung* (1512; Exorcism of Fools), contributed to the satirical tradition begun by Sebastian Brant.

If the assessments of Wickram as the father of the German novel may be open to challenge, his role as chief representative of the Alsatian Shrovetide Play and his contribution to the thematic transition from medieval romances to novels of social development are noteworthy achievements. Wickram was also the originator of a literary tradition that flourished in the 16th century in Germany: collections of entertaining reading matter for travelers. His collection of stories published as *Das Rollwagenbüchlein* (1555; Stagecoach Stories) stimulated the appearance of eight similar collections by other writers between 1556 and 1603.

Wickram's status as a novelist rests on three works: *Der jungen Knaben Spiegel* (1554; Mirror for Young Boys), *Von guten und bösen Nachbarn* (1556; Of Good and Bad Neighbors), and *The Golden Thread*. *Knaben Spiegel* is illustrative of Wickram's social criticism, his interest in personal and social development, and, given the multiple editions, his literary esteem among his contemporaries. Ostensibly based on true characters, *Knaben Spiegel* brings together the values of the knight Gottlieb, which are representative of values associated with a social class, and the possibilities inherent in individuals, which are represented by Gottlieb's peasant-born adopted son, Fridbert; his natural son, Willibald; their tutor, Felix; and a butcher's son and wastrel companion to Willibald, Lottarius, who is fated to end his days hanging from the gallows. Thematically, *Knaben Spiegel* is indicative of Wickram's other novelistic works in the sense that he concerns himself in each with society and its concrete rewards for meritorious efforts and achievements. The latter may be construed to include demonstrations of strong personal moral and ethical values as well as diligence and goal-oriented work in preparation for and application of professional skills. As the educational attainments of Fridbert, the adopted son, move his peasant origins more and more into the background, fortune leads him into the security and social approval of public service; his tutor Felix becomes a physician. The accompanying personal and social fall of Willibald and his companion in crime, Lottarius, introduces a doubly didactic lesson: the notion that crime does not pay, as shown by Lottarius's execution, and the image of the virtue of a merciful father faced with a prodigal son. The latter image links Wickram's prose writings to his earlier dramatic effort, *Der verlorne Sun* (1540; The Prodigal Son).

Wickram's novels, like his other works, are at the same time representative of the early modern period in Germany and bridges between the humanism of the Renaissance period and the social and moral consciousness of the Reformation and Counter Reformation periods. *Early Modern*, in its current usage, has come to mean a period in which a combined awareness of the values and social structures of an earlier time had begun to blend with varying degrees of harmony with the strivings and idealism of a new age. From a literary perspective, writers realized that old forms and themes did not need to be jettisoned but only to be modified to accommodate new ways of thinking. Social criticism was inherent in this approach, with a strong emphasis on the moral aspect of human actions and interactions. Wickram's figures may lack the multidimensional personalities of modern characters, but they also differ from the flat, fairy-tale-like *Volksbuch* (chap-book) figures found in 16th-century satirical literature.

Elements of constancy and change link Wickram's novels, with lesser degrees of didacticism emerging in *The Golden Thread* than in either *Knaben Spiegel* or *Von guten und bösen Nachbarn*. In each work, however, there is a moral anchor that suggests Wickram's view of contemporary societal figures or types. The "Ritter" Gottlieb (*Knaben Spiegel*), the Count of Merida (*The Golden Thread*), and the merchants Hermanus (*The Golden Thread*) and Robertus (*Von guten und bösen Nachbarn*) are all moral standards against which all other figures are measured. The changing fortunes of the secondary figures represent movements around the moral, ethical centers represented by these older figures. That Wickram's younger males eventually come to respect and emulate their older counterparts underlines the circular, fairy-tale nature of his novel-length tales. The repetitious message of reward and punishment based on the degree of diligence and perseverance behind individual's efforts is a secular program that has its counterpart in the polemical tracts and sermons of the Protestant reformers and writers of the Counter Reformation period.

RICHARD ERNEST WALKER

Biography

Born in Colmar, ca. 1500. Illegitimate son of Colmar municipal official; became citizen and subsequently a minor official in Colmar, 1546; worked as painter and bookseller; literary publications, from 1531; became town clerk of Burkheim, from 1555. Founded school of Meistersinger in Colmar, 1549; modernized the translation by Albrecht von Halberstadt of Ovid's *Metamorphoses*, 1549. Died in Burkheim, ca. 1562.

Selected Works

Collections
Sämtliche Werke, 12 vols., edited by Hans-Georg Roloff, 1967–73

Fiction
Ritter Galmy, 1539
Gabriotto und Reinhart, 1551
Von guten und bösen Nachbarn, 1556
Der jungen Knaben Spiegel, 1554
Der Goldfaden, 1557; as *The Golden Thread,* translated by Pierre Kaufke, 1991

Plays
Der verlorne Sun, 1540
Apostelspiel, 1552

Other
Die zehn Alter dieser Welt, 1531
Tobias, 1550
Von der Trunkenheit, 1555/56
Der Irr Reitend Pilger, 1555/56
Das Rollwagenbüchlein, 1555

Further Reading

Christ, Hannelore, *Literarischer Text und historische Realität: Versuch einer historisch-materialistischen Analyse von Jörg Wickrams "Knabenspiegel" und "Nachbarn" Roman,* Düsseldorf: Bertelsmann Universitätsverlag, 1974

Glaser, Horst Albert, editor, *Deutsche Literatur: Eine Sozialgeschichte, 2: Von der Handschrift zum Buchdruck: Spätmittelalter, Reformation, Humanismus, 1320–1572,* Reinbek bei Hamburg: Rowohlt, 1991

Lancaster, Albert Lake, "The Language of Jörg Wickram's Galmy and a Comparison of It with That of Der jungen Knaben Spiegel," Ph.D. dissertation, University of North Carolina, 1949

Pascal, Roy, and Hannah Priebsch Closs, *German Literature in the Sixteenth and Seventeenth Centuries: Renaissance, Reformation, Baroque,* London: Cresset Press, and New York: Barnes and Noble, 1968

Rapp, Francis, "Les lettres en Alsace à l'époque de l'Humanisme," *Publications de la Société Savante d'Alsace et des régions de l'est* 8 (1962)

Roloff, Hans-Gert, editor, *Sämtliche Werke von Georg Wickram,* Berlin: de Gruyter, 1967–73

Scherer, Wilhelm, *Die Anfänge des deutschen Prosaromans und Jörg Wickram von Colmar,* Strassburg: K.J. Trübner, 1877

Spriewald, Ingeborg, "Jörg Wickram und die Anfänge der realistischen Prosaerzählung in Deutschland," Ph.D. dissertation, Potsdam, 1971

Christoph Martin Wieland 1733–1813

Christoph Martin Wieland is one of the most productive, versatile, learned, and influential authors in the history of German literature. A poet, essayist, novelist, playwright, librettist, editor, translator, professor, public official, and political commentator, he is sometimes called the German Voltaire. Far from exemplifying only the practical reason prescribed during the Enlightenment, however, his life and works also show an enduring concern with moral, social, aesthetic, and religious ideals that link him to the artistic cultures of both the Rococo and Romanticism. With his supple prose and mellifluous poetry, his cultivation of new genres and of the nascent reading public, and his personal presence in "classical" Weimar, this urbane humanist and ironic cosmopolite helped make modern German a literary language.

Although often portrayed as a reclusive bookworm, Wieland led a prominent public life that often affected the tortuous course of his written work. As the son of a Protestant minister and as a precocious schoolboy, he learned ancient languages, pietistic faith, and philosophical skepticism. As the second young protégé of Bodmer in Zurich, he wrote biblical and "seraphic" texts similar to those of the first, Klopstock, and he joined the literary battles of his day by opposing Gottsched and the anacreontic poets. As the municipal clerk in his hometown of Biberach, he witnessed the idiocy of political life in that tiny republic but also welcomed the freer, French air of the aristocratic court at nearby Warthausen. Accordingly, his writing became mundane, satirical, and erotic. As a professor of philosophy at the University of Erfurt and as the personal tutor to the future rulers of Weimar, he realized lifelong ambitions as a pedagogue and a didactic poet. As the editor of *Der teutsche Merkur* (1773–1810; The German Mercury), the most popular literary journal in Germany, he educated his readers by acquainting them with historical as well as current developments in intellectual and political life. As a translator of Shakespeare, Horace, Lucian, and Cicero, he also refined such readers' tastes in foreign literatures. For most of this long career, which lasted six decades, Wieland was a family man who fathered 14 children and was happiest at home with his wife of many years. His first two fiancées, though, had been notable bluestockings: Sophie von La Roche (née Gutermann, the novelist) and Julie Bondeli (a friend of Jean-Jacques Rousseau in Bern). Both women were crucial to his maturation and seem models for his many wise and accomplished female characters. His early disappointments in love and the collapse of his sophomoric religious fervor, moreover, made him sadder but wiser for the rest of his life. Indeed, he was a chastened idealist whose knowledge of human nature often dampened his dreams but whose resulting adherence to a golden mean nonetheless included pursuing happiness and hoping for the best.

The profound ambivalence and cautious optimism apparent in Wieland's life also inform his texts. The two most famous of his many verse tales, for example, seek middle ground between extremes of idealism and sensuality. The title character of his *Musarion; oder, Die Philosophie der Grazien* (1768; *Musarion; or, The Philosophy of the Graces*) uses both her sharp wit and her carnal charms to teach the work's protagonist to avoid silly excesses of sour-grapes Stoicism and Pythagorean pipe dreams. His *Oberon* (1780; *Oberon*), a poem translated by John Quincy

Adams, similarly tells of fidelity tested in ways that prove the human capacity for romantic love and self-denial but that acknowledge the power of sexuality as well. This story of humane ethics was the source of the opera *Oberon* by Carl Maria von Weber. *Alceste* (1773), the text for a *Singspiel* composed by Anton Schweitzer, and the essays that Wieland wrote to explain it likewise show his importance in the history of opera, as does the fact that *Dschinnistan* (1786–89), a collection of fairy tales he edited, was the source of the libretto for Mozart's *The Magic Flute*. Wieland's novels are even more remarkable, for their genre was not taken seriously in Germany before he established its psychological and philosophic credentials. Their style recalls Cervantes, Fielding, Sterne, and Lucian. *Der Sieg der Natur über die Schwärmerey; oder, Die Abentheuer des Don Sylvio von Rosalva* (1764; *Reason Triumphant over Fancy, Exemplified in the Singular Adventures of Don Sylvio of Rosalva*) is a playful variation on the theme of *Don Quixote*, while *Geschichte des Agathon* (1766–67; *The History of Agathon*) is often called the first bildungsroman. Their heroes' dilemmas show how Wieland tried to reconcile both poetic notions and moral ideals with the prosaic and hedonistic ways of the world. *Sokrates mainomenos; oder, Die Dialogen des Diogenes von Sinope* (1770; *Socrates out of His Senses; or, Dialogues of Diogenes of Sinope*) is a critique of Rousseau's social philosophy, whereas *Der goldne Spiegel; oder, Die Könige von Scheschian* (1772; The Golden Mirror; or, The Kings of Scheschian) and *Geschichte des Philosophen Danischmende* (1775; History of the Philosopher Danischmende) are wryly utopian novels about good government. *Die Abderiten* (1774; *The History of the Abderites*) is a comic masterpiece that exposes civic folly. *Geheime Geschichte des Philosophen Peregrinus Proteus* (1791; *Private History of Peregrinus Proteus, the Philosopher*) and *Agathodämon* (1799) both examine religious superstition and belief from rational points of view, while *Aristipp und einige seiner Zeitgenossen* (1800–1802; Aristippus and Several of His Contemporaries) explains ancient Greek philosophy. For *Der teutsche Merkur*, Wieland wrote many articles on numerous topics, most notably the French Revolution. In his most trenchant political analysis, he foresaw the rise of Napoléon. These texts are contained in Wieland's *Sämmtliche Werke* (1794–1811; Collected Works), itself a milestone in the history of German book publishing and intellectual property law.

Wieland's reputation wavered during his lifetime, suffered after his death, and has been restored only in recent years. He is only partly responsible for these shifts in his fame, for his reception is a case study in German cultural history. By changing his tone in the late 1750s from pietistic sentiments and Platonic reveries to a more rational and mildly salacious skepticism, he laid himself open to the same accusation of frivolous immorality that he had once leveled at others. To his early critics, he thus seemed to lack character. In the early 1770s, he enjoyed his greatest celebrity, but he was soon attacked by the angry young men of the Sturm und Drang. They considered his work neither robust nor patriotic enough, jumped up and down on his books, and burned them to light their pipes. The young Goethe was among those who mocked him, but he was soon shamed by Wieland's equanimity. Together with Schiller, however, Goethe chided Wieland anew in the 1790s. At this time, once again, he was also the foil for a new generation of writers who had Romantic ideas about originality and called his liberal use of sources simple plagiarism. A few weeks after his death, Goethe nonetheless delivered a eulogy in which he praised Wieland's "ethical sensualism" and his "moderate, witty joie de vivre," noting that his opinions sometimes changed but that his underlying convictions stayed firm. Moralistic and nationalistic 19th-century critics often dismissed him as a Gallic chameleon who lacked Christian backbone, and his first biographer, J.G. Gruber, defended him against detractors who thought his life and work downright satanic. In doing so Gruber defended the Enlightenment itself. Friedrich Sengle, Wieland's second major biographer, writing after World War II, likewise took issue with Romantic-Christian critics who dismissed Wieland as immoral and un-German. Sengle praised Wieland for renewing the Rococo and achieving a "humoristic classicism," and he offered incisive views of Wieland's complex psyche as well as strong opinions about his texts. Sengle judged Wieland to be merely wise, not great, however, a writer whose metamorphoses never equaled Goethe's sure self-realization and who therefore remained the younger poet's forerunner. More recent studies take Wieland on his own terms by stressing the "balanced dualism" (McCarthy) of his skeptical ideals or by citing his self-reflexive fiction, his involvement of its readers, his anthropological assumptions, or his significance for the dialectics of the Enlightenment and its political, literary, essayistic, cultural, and other historical discourses. Such justified interest in the many philosophical and functional aspects of Wieland's texts should not, however, detract from their remarkable verbal artistry and timeless explorations of existential quandaries.

ELLIS SHOOKMAN

See also Weimar

Biography

Born in Oberholzheim, near Biberach, 5 September 1733. Studied privately in Erfurt and enrolled at the University of Tübingen, 1749–50; lived as a guest of J.J. Bodmer, Zurich, 1752–54; worked as a private tutor, Zurich and Bern, 1754–60; senator and town clerk, Biberach, 1760–69; professor of philosophy, University of Erfurt, 1769–72; private tutor to the sons of Duchess Anna Amalia of Sachsen-Weimar, 1772–74; founding editor and publisher, *Der Teutsche Merkur* and *Der Neue Teutsche Merkur*, 1773–1810. Member, Prussian Academy of Sciences, 1786; Legion of Merit (France), 1808; Cross of Saint Anna (Russia), 1808. Died in Weimar, 20 January 1813.

Selected Works

Collections

Sämmtliche Werke, 45 vols., 1794–1811
Gesammelte Schriften, edited by Bernhard Seuffert et al., 1909–
Briefwechsel, edited by Hans Werner Seiffert and Siegfried Scheibe, 1963–
Werke, edited by Fritz Martini and Hans Werner Seiffert, 5 vols., 1964–68
Werke, edited by Gonthier-Louis Fink et al., 1986–

Poetry

Musarion; oder, Die Philosophie der Grazien, 1768; as *Musarion; or, The Philosophy of the Graces*, translated by Thomas C. Starnes, 1991
Oberon, 1780; translated by William Sotheby, 1798; translated by John Quincy Adams, 1799–1801, and edited by A.B. Faust, 1940

Fiction

Der Sieg der Natur über die Schwärmerey; oder, Die Abentheuer des Don Sylvio von Rosalva, 1764; as *Reason Triumphant over Fancy, Exemplified in the Singular Adventures of Don Sylvio de Rosalva*, 1773; revised version of the 1773 translation as *The Adventures of Don Sylvio*, revised by Ernest A. Baker, 1904
Geschichte des Agathon, 1766–67; revised as *Agathon*, 1773; revised as *Geschichte des Agathon*, 1794; as *The History of Agathon*, translated by John Richardson, 1773
Sokrates mainomenos; oder, Die Dialogen des Diogenes von Sinope, 1770; titled changed to *Nachlass des Diogenes von Sinope*; as *Socrates out of His Senses; or, Dialogues of Diogenes of Sinope*, translated by Mr. Wintersted, 1771
Der goldne Spiegel; oder, Die Könige von Scheschian, 1772
Die Abderiten: Eine sehr wahrscheinliche Geschichte, 1774; expanded as *Geschichte der Abderiten*, 2 vols., 1781; as *The Republic of Fools: Being the History of the State and People of Abdera in Thrace*, translated by Henry Christmas, 1861; in part as *The Case of the Ass's Shadow*, translated by Ellis Shookman, 1992; as *The History of the Abderites*, translated by Max Dufner, 1993
Geschichte des Philosophen Danischmende, 1775
Geheime Geschichte des Philosophen Peregrinus Proteus, 1791; as *Private History of Peregrinus Proteus, the Philosopher*, translated by William Tooke, 1796; in part as *Confessions in Elysium; or, The Adventures of a Platonic Philosopher*, translated by John Battersby Elrington, 1804
Agathodämon, 1799
Aristipp und einige seiner Zeitgenossen, 1800–2

Other

translation of William Shakespeare, *Theatralische Werke*, 8 vols., 1762–66
Alceste (libretto; performed 1773), 1773
Dschinnistan; oder, Auserlesene Feen- und Geister-Märchen, edited with others, 3 vols., 1786–89

Further Reading

Brender, Irmela, *Christoph Martin Wieland*, Reinbek: Rowohlt, 1990
Goethe, Johann Wolfgang, *Wieland's Andenken in der Loge Amalia zu Weimar*, n.p.,1813; reprint, Leipzig: Göschen, 1984
Gruber, Johann Gottfried, *C.M. Wielands Leben*, revised ed., 4 vols., 1827–28; reprint, Hamburg: Hamburger Stiftung zur Förderung von Wissenschaft und Kultur, 1984
Jørgensen, Sven-Aage, et al., *Wieland: Epoche-Werk-Wirkung*, Munich: Beck, 1994
McCarthy, John A., *Christoph Martin Wieland*, Boston: Twayne, 1979
Schaefer, Klaus, *Christoph Martin Wieland*, Stuttgart: Metzler, 1996
Schelle, Hansjörg, editor, *Christoph Martin Wieland*, Darmstadt: Wissenschaftliche Buchgesellschaft, 1981
Sengle, Friedrich, *Wieland*, Stuttgart: Metzler, 1949
Starnes, Thomas C., *Christoph Martin Wieland, Leben und Werk*, 3 vols., Sigmaringen: Thorbecke, 1987
——, "Christoph Martin Wieland," in *German Writers from the Enlightenment to Sturm und Drang, 1720–1764*, Dictionary of Literary Biography, vol. 97, edited by James Hardin and Christoph E. Schweitzer, Detroit: Gale, 1990

Geschichte des Agathon 1766–1767
Novel by Christoph Martin Wieland

Christoph Martin Wieland's *Geschichte des Agathon* is the magnum opus of a major writer. It treats issues of ethics, epistemology, politics, and aesthetics that were considered crucial during the Enlightenment and that preoccupied its author for almost 40 years. Both those issues and the reasons it took him so long to resolve them are implicit in its title. The word "Geschichte" means "history" in the sense of a literary fiction that approximates actual life rather than indulging in romantic flights of fancy; "Agathon," the name of its title character, comes from a Greek adjective meaning "good" in the sense of "virtuous." The empiricism required by such a "history" assumes a skeptical attitude toward human nature, an attitude that is at odds with the moral ideals of virtue and wisdom that Agathon tries to achieve. Wieland's own narrative verisimilitude, that is, seems to preclude the moral lesson that he envisions. He could not overcome this conundrum in the first or second editions of *Agathon,* and did so only in the third, in such a way as to divide scholarly opinion ever since. This same conundrum, however, makes reading his novel an exercise in knowing how, whether, and why to lead a good life.

The events described in the novel show the difficulty of leading such a moral life in the public as well as the private sphere. In the early fourth century B.C., Agathon grows up at the temple of Apollo in Delphi, where he is introduced to the mysteries of Orphic theosophy. After a priest and then a priestess there try to seduce him, he flees to Athens, where he rises to political power before being banished by his unscrupulous rivals. Soon captured by pirates, he then is sold into slavery in Smyrna. His master is Hippias, the renowned sophist, who tries to convince him to abandon his Platonic ideals and to trust in a more hedonistic materialism. When Agathon refuses and remains an incorrigible Platonic enthusiast, Hippias asks the hetaera Danae to prove the power of sensualism by seducing him. She succeeds, but not without being inspired by Agathon's idealism and thus spoiling Hippias's scheme. Hippias then separates them by revealing to Agathon that Danae practices the oldest profession; Agathon then flees again, this time to Syracuse, where he tries to reform the tyrant Dionysius. Just as in Athens, he meets with initial success but is ultimately defeated by his corrupt opponents. Despairing of his high-mindedness and of human nature, Agathon is saved in the end by Archytas, the ruler of the utopian republic of Tarentum, where Agathon reencounters but does not marry Danae; he lives in single retirement instead. Ever clinging to his ideals, he becomes disillusioned, then, growing sadder but wiser as he sees how seldom most people act the way they should.

What Wieland tells is only half the reason why *Agathon* is so significant in the history of the German novel. The other half is how he tells it. Its philosophical disputations about human nature and its political debates about the best form of government are beautifully written. Its acute analyses of its characters' motives, its elaborate and erotic seduction scenes, its many introspective interior monologues, and the long confessions of Agathon and Danae also lend it timeless psychological, sexual, literary, and emotional depth. Throughout the novel, moreover, Wieland addresses his readers in an ironic narrative voice, thereby engaging them in both the novel's moral project and its aesthetic agenda. Above all, he pretends that the source of his story is an ancient manuscript and distances himself from its ostensible Greek editor whenever that story seems too strange or too good to be true. In the first edition of *Agathon,* for example, he attributes the story's happy ending to this editor and thus concedes its improbability. Later revisions, however, omit this ironic concession, apparently advocating the author's moral postulates in earnest. The twists and turns of Wieland's self-conscious nar-

ration, then, parallel the ethical adventures of his hero. That the style, tone, and structure of his novel are therefore no less suggestive or important than its plot helps explain why Gotthold Ephraim Lessing welcomed *Agathon* in 1767 as "the first and only novel for the thinking person of classical taste," as well as why Friedrich von Blanckenburg hailed it in 1774, together with Henry Fielding's *Tom Jones,* as a model modern novel.

There are well over 200 scholarly studies of *Agathon.* Both the methods that they use and the issues that they raise differ greatly, but their authors often weigh the novel's various versions, compare its philosophy to that of Kant, describe Wieland's view of human nature, determine his literary aesthetics, or read the novel as a bildungsroman. The most incisive also note the traits that *Agathon* possesses as a work of fiction. Groß explains its genesis, for example, by arguing that Wieland shifted his intellectual emphasis. According to Groß, the first edition suggests the influence of Montesquieu, Bonnet, and Helvetius's naturalistic concept of "milieu"; the second edition is informed by Shaftesbury's aesthetic moralism; and the third edition illustrates Kantian moral philosophy. Schlagenhaft counters that *Agathon* simply reflects the attitude toward reason and emotion taken by the Enlightenment in general. According to Schindler-Hürlimann, Wieland thought human beings were limited by their circumstances but able to educate themselves to contribute to communal life. Whereas she prefers the existential fragmentariness suggested by the first edition, Buddecke favors the third, arguing that Wieland's notion of personal development was pedagogical rather than political. Much like Buddecke, Hemmerich offers a hermeneutic, close reading of *Agathon,* but he concludes that it is a failure because its moral lesson is unconvincing and its literary aesthetic proves untenable. Oettinger stresses the empiricism of that aesthetic, opposing literary imitation to poetic fantasy, and Thomé traces Wieland's sober taste for empiricism to the natural sciences and their experimental methods. Schrader, by contrast, claims that Wieland's novel links the mimetic and poetic, artistic imitation and illusion, the empirical and the utopian. Swales, Beddow, and von Mücke all examine *Agathon* as a bildungsroman, noting, in turn, the irony with which Wieland treats novelistic conventions, his belief in fictional truth, and the critique of *Bildung* itself supposedly evident in the novel. Frick likes the disavowed and double ending of *Agathon,* finding its self-conscious failure and symptomatic openness signs of a truly philosophic attitude. Erhart maintains that its three editions respond to evolving concerns of the Enlightenment, especially to the dividedness of the modern self, for which Wieland's novel provides therapy in the form of a deconstructive, postmetaphysical, individualistic ethics.

Between 1768 and 1844, *Agathon* was translated into French, English, Dutch, Russian, Italian, Danish, Greek, Serbo-Croatian, Hungarian, and Polish. Such evidence of its international status—added to the urgency of its subject matter, the skill of its narration, and the endurance of its scholarly appeal—leaves no doubt that it belongs in a category whose name is a term coined by Wieland himself: "World Literature."

ELLIS SHOOKMAN

See also Bildungsroman

Editions

First edition: *Geschichte des Agathon,* Frankfurt and Leipzig [actually Zurich: Orell, Geßner], 1766–67; *Agathon,* revised ed., Leipzig:

Weidmann, 1773; *Geschichte des Agathon,* 3rd edition, in
Sämmtliche Werke, vols. 1–3, Leipzig: Göschen, 1794
Critical edition: in *Werke,* vol. 3, edited by Klaus Manger, Frankfurt:
Deutscher Klassiker Verlag, 1986
Translation: *The History of Agathon,* translated by John Richardson,
London: Cadell, 1773

Further Reading

Beddow, Michael, *The Fiction of Humanity: Studies in the
Bildungsroman from Wieland to Thomas Mann,* Cambridge and
New York: Cambridge University Press, 1982
Buddecke, Wolfram, *C.M. Wielands Entwicklungsbegriff und die
Geschichte des Agathon,* Göttingen: Vandenhoeck und Ruprecht,
1966
Erhart, Walter, *Entzweiung und Selbstaufklärung: Christoph Martin
Wielands "Agathon"-Projekt,* Tübingen: Niemeyer, 1991
Frick, Werner, *Providenz und Kontingenz: Untersuchungen zur
Schicksalsthematik im deutschen und europäischen Roman des 17.
und 18. Jahrhunderts,* Tübingen: Niemeyer, 1988
Groß, Erich, *C.M. Wielands "Geschichte des Agathon":
Entstehungsgeschichte,* Berlin: Ebering, 1930

Hemmerich, Gerd, *Christoph Martin Wielands "Geschichte des
Agathon": Eine kritische Werkinterpretation,* Nuremberg: Carl, 1979
Mücke, Dorothea von, *Virtue and the Veil of Illusion: Generic
Innovation and the Pedagogical Project in Eighteenth-Century
Literature,* Stanford, California: Stanford University Press, 1991
Oettinger, Klaus, *Phantasie und Erfahrung: Studien zur Erzählpoetik
Christoph Martin Wielands,* Munich: Fink, 1970
Schindler-Hürlimann, Regine, *Wielands Menschenbild: Eine
Interpretation des Agathon,* Zurich: Atlantis, 1963
Schlagenhaft, Barbara, *Wielands Agathon als Spiegelung aufklärerischer
Vernunft- und Gefühlsproblematik,* Erlangen: Palm and Enke, 1935
Schrader, Monika, *Mimesis und Poiesis: Poetologische Studien zum
Bildungsroman,* Berlin: de Gruyter, 1975
Shookman, Ellis, *Noble Lies, Slant Truths, Necessary Angels: Aspects
of Fictionality in the Novels of Christoph Martin Wieland,* Chapel
Hill: University of North Carolina Press, 1997
Swales, Martin, *The German Bildungsroman from Wieland to Hesse,*
Princeton, New Jersey: Princeton University Press, 1978
Thomé, Horst, *Roman und Naturwissenschaft: Eine Studie zur
Vorgeschichte der deutschen Klassik,* Frankfurt: Lang, 1978

Johann Joachim Winckelmann 1717–1768

Johann Joachim Winckelmann is one of the most significant figures in discussions of the nature of beauty and taste in the 18th century. A classicist by training, he became the foremost art historian and archaeologist of his time, and through his writings he helped to establish the theoretical framework for neoclassicism. In the process Winckelmann revolutionized the study of art. Up until his time there had been an accepted inherent dichotomy in the history of art between the objects themselves and artistic values. The former fell within the purview of collectors, antiquarians, and philologists, whereas the latter were the domain of artists, critics, and theoreticians. For Winckelmann the goal of the history of art became a synthesis of aesthetic understanding with a chronological sense of evolution, all of which was intended to lead to an accurate assessment of stylistic development.

One of the ongoing debates during the 18th century focused on the definition of good taste and its relationship to beauty. While living in Dresden, the electoral capital of Saxony and a city known for its Baroque buildings, Winckelmann addressed this question in his first major work, a pamphlet entitled *Gedanken über die Nachahmung der griechischen Werke in der Malerei und Bildhauerkunst* (1755; *Reflections on the Imitation of Greek Works in Painting and Sculpture*). Sharing with Rousseau a strong distaste for contemporary Rococo culture, which both men despised as overcivilized, unnatural, and effeminate, Winckelmann looked to a past golden age for the universal and timeless ideal to be emulated. Although he had never visited Greece or Italy and had been able to study Greek sculpture only through selected Roman copies, engravings, and secondhand accounts, he was convinced that the origin of good taste was to be found in ancient Greece. For Winckelmann, "The only way . . . to become great or, if this be possible, inimitable, is to imitate the ancients [i.e., the Greeks]." He believed that nature had imperfections, whereas Greek artists had produced works of ideal beauty; thus, the surest way for artists to imitate ideal nature was to use the Greek rules of beauty as a guide. The essence of the Greek masterpieces was a tranquillity, which manifested itself as "a noble simplicity and quiet grandeur, both in posture and expression." This perception of ideal beauty as exemplified in Greek sculpture became widely accepted and helped to shape the aesthetic taste of generations to come. The impact of these ideas was also felt in literary circles; for example, the humanistic thought and restrained style of authors such as Gotthold Ephraim Lessing, Johann Wolfgang von Goethe, Friedrich Schiller, and Johann Gottfried Herder were directly influenced by Winckelmann's writings.

In his approach to art Winckelmann shared the common neoclassical belief that sculpture was the highest form of art. He had an ideal that he projected without questioning onto Greek art, and as a consequence some of his evidence was prejudiced, and at times his reasoning lacked firm scientific foundation. This left Winckelmann open to criticism. Lessing, for example, though sharing his admiration for the Greeks was nonetheless quick to reject Winckelmann's psychological interpretation of Laocoön's sigh in favor of a more accurate aesthetic interpretation. Despite any shortcomings in analysis, Winckelmann, through his insistence on interpreting a work of art within its cultural context, changed the way critics reasoned. It was an approach that resonated with his contemporaries and that was instrumental in establishing the desirability and validity of cultural studies in art as well as in other disciplines.

Around the time that his first work appeared, Winckelmann converted to Catholicism (to facilitate having access to ancient art in Italy) and then moved to Rome. There he had the opportunity to study firsthand such famous works as the *Apollo Belvedere,* the *Laokoon,* and the Belvedere *Torso.* He was also able to experience the rediscovery of stunning ancient works.

Even before he had arrived in Italy, excavations had begun at Herculaneum (1737) and at Pompeii (1748). Winckelmann visited these sites, and in his *Sendschreiben von den Herculanischen Entdeckungen* (1762; Open Letter on the Discoveries at Herculaneum) and *Nachrichten von den neuesten Herculanischen Entdeckungen* (1764; News about the Most Recent Discoveries at Herculaneum), he provided the first scholarly accounts of the excavations. These short works helped to foster the growing interest in ancient art among Europeans.

Through his experience at Herculaneum and Pompeii, Winckelmann also gained a new appreciation for and understanding of ancient art. His initial attraction to Greek art had come through acquaintance with works from the Hellenistic period. During the years of careful study in Italy, however, Winckelmann acquired an unparalleled knowledge of the breadth of ancient art, which allowed him to give meaningful systematic order to the seemingly chaotic collection of ancient works of art. By organizing the material systematically by style and chronologically by period, he was the first scholar to be able to delineate the development of classical styles and to make aesthetic judgments based on this knowledge. Winckelmann was, for example, the first scholar to recognize the difference between classical Greek sculpture and later Hellenistic and Roman copies and to deem the former superior in quality, an opinion still held in scholarly circles. These ideas found expression in his masterpiece, *Geschichte der Kunst des Alterthums* (1764–67; *The History of Ancient Art*), a milestone in art historical research. As he stated in the preface to this work, his intent was "to show the origin, progress, change, and downfall of art, together with the different styles of nations, periods, and artists, and to prove the whole, as far as it is possible, from the ancient monuments now in existence."

One of the ironies of history is that the cultural approach espoused by Winckelmann to establish ancient Greece as the arbiter of good taste is the very approach that led to the rejection of ancient Greece by younger generations of artists and authors. Nonetheless, Winckelmann's basic approach to the study of art and many of the ideas first set down by him are as valid today as they were in his own times. He was a pioneering thinker of great stature, and with justification his contemporary Christoph Martin Wieland could characterize the years 1755–68 as "Winckelmann's epoch."

JOHN ROGER PAAS

Biography

Born in Stendal, near Berlin, 9 December 1717. Studied classical literature, theology, medicine, and mathematics at Halle and Jena; taught classics at Seehausen, 1743–48; librarian at Nöthnitz near Dresden; studied drawing with Adam Friedrich Oeser, 1753; converted to Catholicism and moved to Dresden, 1754; traveled to Rome 1755; entered the service of Cardinal Albani; in close contact with the German Painter Anton Raphael Mengs; visited Naples and Herculaneum, 1758 and 1762; appointed senior supervisor of classical antiquities in Rome by Pope Clement XIII, 1763; inducted into the Society of Antiquaries in London. Honored by Empress Maria Theresia in Vienna, 1768. Died (murdered in Trieste by Francesco Arcangeli for his gold medallion), 8 June 1768.

Selected Works

Collections

Sämtliche Werke, 12 vols., edited by J. Eiselein, 1825–39; reprint, 1965
Kleine Schriften, Vorreden, Entwürfe, edited by Walther Rehm, 1968

Treatises

Gedanken über die Nachahmung der griechischen Werke in der Malerei und Bildhauerkunst, 1755; edited by Ludwig Uhlig, 1995; as *Reflections on the Painting and Sculpture of the Greeks*, translated by Henry Fuseli, 1765; as *Reflections on the Imitation of Greek Works in Painting and Sculpture*, translated by Elfriede Heyer and Roger C. Norton, 1987
Description des pierres gravées du feu baron de Stosch, 1760
Anmerkungen über die Baukunst der Alten, 1762
Sendschreiben von den Herculanischen Entdeckungen, 1762
Abhandlung von der Fähigkeit der Empfindung des Schönen in der Kunst, 1763
Geschichte der Kunst des Alterthums, 1764–67; as *The History of Ancient Art*, translated by G. Henry Lodge, 1849–70
Nachrichten von den neuesten Herculanischen Entdeckungen, 1764
Versuch einer Allegorie, besonders für die Kunst, 1766
Monumenti antichi inediti, 1767–68

Further Reading

Butler, E.M., *The Tyranny of Greece over Germany: A Study of the Influence Exercised by Greek Art and Poetry over the Great German Writers of the Eighteenth, Nineteenth, and Twentieth Centuries*, Cambridge: Cambridge University Press, and New York: Macmillan, 1935

Hatfield, Henry Caraway, *Winckelmann and His German Critics 1755–1781: A Prelude to the Classical Age*, New York: King's Crown Press, 1943

Justi, Carl, *Winckelmann, sein Leben, seine Werke, und seine Zeitgenossen*, 2 vols., Leipzig: Vogel, 1866–72; 5th edition as *Winckelmann und seine Zeitgenossen*, 3 vols., Cologne: Phaidon, 1956

Leppmann, Wolfgang, *Winckelmann*, New York: Knopf, 1970; London: Gollancz, 1971

Morrison, Jeffrey, *Winckelmann and the Notion of Aesthetic Education*, New York: Oxford University Press, and Oxford: Clarendon Press, 1996

Potts, Alex, *Flesh and the Ideal: Winckelmann and the Origins of Art History*, New Haven, Connecticut: Yale University Press, 1994

Gedanken über die Nachahmung der griechischen Werke in der Malerei und Bildhauerkunst 1755

Art criticism by Johann Joachim Winckelmann

The *Reflections on the Imitation of Greek Works in Painting and Sculpture* already contain the central ideas that underlie Johann Joachim Winckelmann's subsequent writings on art. In the short term, they proved to be a major document in European neoclassicism, which prepared the ground for key texts such as Joshua Reynolds's *Discourses* (1778); in the medium term, they became a seminal source for the Weimar classicism of Goethe, Schiller, and Wilhelm von Humboldt; and in the long term, they served as a point of reference for almost all those other German writers, from Hölderlin and Hegel to Nietzsche, Thomas Mann, and Gerhart Hauptmann, whose writings testify to the fascination exercised by the culture of classical antiquity.

The turning point in Winckelmann's life came in 1748, when he was appointed librarian to Graf Bünau and began his career as an art historian with a description of the paintings in the

Dresden Gallery. More important was Winckelmann's encounter with copies of Greek works of sculpture in the Collection of Antiquities; for him, they were so superior to contemporary work that he was compelled to wonder why others had failed to see what he saw.

Unlike his younger admirer Herder and his willful translator Füßli, Winckelmann had a horror of all that was dark and disordered; modern observers have recognized in this horror a sublimation of problems associated with his homosexuality. Yet however much Winckelmann's view of ancient Greece sprang from a dubious source and was based on a questionable interpretation of the limited evidence available to him, it furnished an ideal of beauty that was to play a defining role in Western European culture for over a century.

The art of ancient Greece is presented by Winckelmann as the expression of an ideal conjunction of geographical, climatic, and political conditions; this ideal forms the basis of the poetic contemplations of Hölderlin in the novel *Hyperion* (1797–99) and poems such as "Der Archipelagus" (1800; The Archipelago). This allowed the development of a perfect nature, which Goethe felt he recognized in the bright light of Italy. Notwithstanding the desire to relate the perfection of Greek art directly to the conditions that nurtured it, Winckelmann also approvingly recognized a tendency in this art to go beyond the imitation of nature to produce an ideal image of Man.

This ideal is encapsulated in his celebrated definition of classical Greek beauty as "eine edle Einfalt und eine stille Größe" (a noble simplicity and serene grandeur). The work that Winckelmann chose as the most characteristic embodiment of these qualities was, however, not a classical Greek work, but a late Hellenistic work the Laocoön group, whose most striking qualities of "baroque" vigor and energy Winckelmann ignored in order to emphasize in highly evocative language the dignity and control, which are at best marginally present. The art of Winckelmann's golden age, described with an enthusiasm that would inspire the Romantics, is itself rational and elegant. There is no place for the archaic, or for Aeschylus or Heraclitus, who came to figure significantly in the German image of Greece only after Winckelmann's picture was challenged by Nietzsche in *Die Geburt der Tragödie* (1872; The Birth of Tragedy).

The immediacy with which Winckelmann's vision of the classical past appealed to his contemporaries is explained by the context of his early writings, the dispute known as the "querelle des anciens et des modernes." The hegemony of Poussin and the linearists having been broken, the world into which Winckelmann was born was that of the Baroque. While formally acknowledging the greatness of Rubens in painting and Bernini in sculpture, Winckelmann deprecates the privileging of dynamic and dramatic effects and the emphasis on color rather than line. But at least the great exponents of the high Baroque maintained a manifest seriousness of purpose; not so the rococo artists who succeeded them and whose work dominated the German courts of the time. These rococo artists had come to ignore laws of proportion and order, substituting an arbitrariness, even playfulness, which for Winckelmann represented the opposite of classical form; and so he criticizes the preference of contemporary artists for unusual poses and actions, and, anticipating an idea of Hölderlin's, he objects that they require their figures to possess a soul that resembles a comet in orbit. Appended to the second edition of the *Reflections* (1756) were two further essays, *Sendschreiben über die Gedanken von der Nachahmung der*

griechischen Werke in der Malerei und Bildhauerkunst (Letter on the Reflections on the Imitation of Greek Works in Painting and Sculpture) and *Erläuterung der Gedanken von der Nachahmung der griechischen Werke in der Malerei und Bildhauerkunst* (Commentary on the Reflections on the Imitation of Greek Works in Painting and Sculpture), in which Winckelmann defends his own arguments against both real and anticipated criticisms of contemporary scholarship. Against this background, the call for form and proportion appeared as something fresh, original, and radical.

Winckelmann's ideal, the simple majesty of classical perfection, is to be found in the naked male figure. Similar to the Kant of the *Kritik der Urteilskraft* (1790; *Critique of Judgment*) and to neoclassical artists such as Carstens and Flaxman, Winckelmann is a linearist, but his attention is focused on the durable art of carving in stone; in sculpture, the figure is cleansed of the dross of humanity. Winckelmann is philosophically an idealist, but unlike his aestheticist followers, he did not set up a purely formal ideal of beauty; he was simultaneously elaborating a moral and educational ideal: the *exemplum virtutis* of 18th-century neoclassicism. This ideal would bear fruit on the one hand in the revolutionary paintings of Jacques-Louis David and in the freedom aspired to by the heroes and heroines of Schiller's late dramas, and on the other hand in the exemplary humanity of Goethe's *Iphigenie auf Tauris*. Winckelmann's main work, *Geschichte der Kunst des Alterthums* (1764–67; *The History of Ancient Art*), dates from his later Roman period; like his seminal formal and thematic principles, however, this historical account of the evolution of Greek art from primitive beginnings to classical perfection is also anticipated in the *Reflections*, in a brief comparison between the stages in the development of art and of human life in general. This idea proved to be an equally productive strand, which was to be woven into the work of major German historians of art from Herder to Hegel.

JOHN OSBORNE

See also Lessing, Laokoon

Editions

First edition: *Gedanken über die Nachahmung der griechischen Werke in der Malerei und Bildhauerkunst*, Dresden: Walther, 1755
Critical edition: edited by Ludwig Uhlig, Stuttgart: Reclam, 1995
Translation: *Reflections on the Imitation of Greek Works in Painting and Sculpture*, translated by Elfriede Heyer and Roger C. Norton, La Salle, Illinois: Open Court, 1987

Further Reading
Baumecker, Gottfried, *Winckelmann in seinen Dresdner Schriften: Die Entstehung von Winckelmanns Kunstanschauung und ihr Verhältnis zur vorhergehenden Kunsttheoretik, mit Benutzung der Pariser Manuskripte Winckelmanns dargestellt*, Berlin: Juncker und Dünnhaupt, 1933
Butler, E.M., *The Tyranny of Greece over Germany: A Study of the Influence Exercised by Greek Art and Poetry over the Great German Writers of the Eighteenth, Nineteenth, and Twentieth Centuries*, Cambridge: Cambridge University Press, and New York: Macmillan, 1935
Hatfield, Henry Caraway, *Winckelmann and His German Critics 1755–1781: A Prelude to the Classical Age*, New York: King's Crown Press, 1943
Honour, Hugh, *Neo-Classicism*, Harmondsworth: Penguin, 1968
Justi, Carl, *Winckelmann, sein Leben, seine Werke, und seine Zeitgenossen*, 2 vols., Leipzig: Vogel, 1866–72; 5th edition as

Winckelmann und seine Zeitgenossen, 3 vols., Cologne: Phaidon, 1956

Mason, Eudo C., "Heinrich Füßli und Winckelmann," in *Unterscheidung und Bewahrung: Festschrift für Hermann Kunisch zum 60. Geburtstag,* Berlin: de Gruyter, 1961

Potts, Alex, *Flesh and the Ideal: Winckelmann and the Origins of Art History,* New Haven, Connecticut, and London: Yale University Press, 1994

Rosenblum, Robert, *Transformations in Late-Eighteenth-Century Painting,* Princeton, New Jersey: Princeton University Press, 1967

Sweet, Denis Marshall, "An Introduction to Classicist Aesthetics in 18th-Century Germany: Winckelmann's Writings on Art," Ph.D. diss., Stanford University, 1978

Uhlig, Ludwig, editor, *Griechenland als Ideal: Winckelmann und seine Rezeption in Deutschland,* Tübingen: Narr, 1988

Ludwig Wittgenstein 1889–1951

Ludwig Wittgenstein, one of the most influential philosophers of the 20th century, represents the last of a long line of intellectual giants whose cultural and scientific development emerged in the fertile landscape of the Viennese fin de siècle milieu.

By the time of Ludwig Wittgenstein's birth in 1889, the Wittgensteins had already established themselves as one of Vienna's most wealthy and prominent families. Both his paternal and maternal grandparents had by the 1850s disassociated themselves from their Jewish faith and heritage, and they were well on their way in laying the foundation for the prominence for their 11 children. Among these children was Karl Wittgenstein, Ludwig's father, a skillful engineer with a strong entrepreneurial will, who amassed an incredible fortune as a steel industrialist in the 1880s. The Wittgenstein household became the center of Vienna's cultural life. Young Ludwig was surrounded from a very early age by extravagance, as well as being brought up in the rich context of Vienna's world of music, art, and literature. The Wittgenstein Palais in the Alleegasse (now the Argentinergasse) was often the place where Vienna's most accomplished and innovative artists, musicians, and intellectuals converged in an atmosphere of lavish entertaining. Johannes Brahms, Gustav Klimt, and others from the Secessionist Movement were regular guests at the Wittgenstein residence. The family cultivated and encouraged their eight children actively to pursue musical as well as intellectual training. Karl Wittgenstein himself was a devout patron of the modernist movement and even funded a large part of the construction of the House of the Secession in Vienna.

A year prior to his graduation from the Realschule in Linz, Upper Austria, young Wittgenstein had decided to study physics with Ludwig Boltzmann at the university in Vienna. It was during his school years in Linz that Wittgenstein was first introduced to philosophical readings. His sister Gretl, with whom he shared a close relationship, directed him to Schopenhauer's classic, *Die Welt als Wille und Vorstellung* (1819; The World as Will and Representation), which formed the basis of Wittgenstein's early metaphysical understanding of the world. His plan to attend the university in Vienna, however, quickly changed in 1906, due in large part to Boltzmann's death. Wittgenstein saw as his only alternative (at the strong urging of his father) the Technische Hochschule in Berlin-Charlottenburg, where he matriculated in the fall of 1906. While in Berlin, Wittgenstein, out of duty to his father, committed himself to engineering studies and particularly to the new field of aeronautics but increasingly found his attention dominated by philosophical questions. In his attempt to overcome his growing philosophical preoccupations, Wittgenstein moved in 1908 to Manchester, England, to further his work in aeronautics. While at the University of Manchester, Wittgenstein was introduced to Bertrand Russell's book *The Principles of Mathematics* (1903), which would play the decisive role in his embarking upon a life of philosophical inquiry.

Wittgenstein's interest in logic and the philosophy of mathematics occupied his attention for the next two years. Delving ever deeper into the principles of mathematics and logic, Wittgenstein quickly learned of the pioneering work of the mathematics professor at the University of Jena, Gottlob Frege. Frege's two-volume work *Grundgesetze der Arithmetik* (1893; The Fundamental Laws of Arithmetic) attempts to formulate a logical definition of numbers by structuring them into classes and types. It was Frege's conceptual realism in this work that influenced Wittgenstein's abandonment of his earlier metaphysical concerns and, ultimately, his studies in engineering. Upon visiting Frege in Jena, the young Wittgenstein was advised to go to Cambridge to study with Bertrand Russell. With his arrival at Trinity College in 1911, Wittgenstein would establish a four-decade-long rich and fertile intellectual relationship with Cambridge.

Wittgenstein inspired two important schools of philosophical thought. The first is a logical positivism or logical empiricism, which Wittgenstein developed in the decade just prior to World War I, and which is often looked upon as his "early" phase. During this period emerged the philosophical study for which Wittgenstein is best remembered, the *Logisch-philosophische Abhandlung,* better known in the English-speaking world by the name G.E. Moore proposed: *Tractatus Logico-Philosophicus* (1922). Wittgenstein's *Tractatus* is best explained as a synthesis of the theory of truth-functions and the notion that language is a picture of reality. As a result of this synthesis arises a third important concept, namely, the doctrine of that which cannot be said, but only shown.

The second period (and often seen as the "later" phase) in the development of Wittgenstein's philosophical thought is best described as a more heterogeneous period in which he produced two large typescripts: *Philosophische Bemerkungen* (1965; *Philosophical Remarks*), and the other, for which he contemplated the two following titles, *Philosophische Betrachtungen* (Philosophical Reflections) and *Philosophische Grammatik* (published as *Philosophische Grammatik,* 1969; translated as *Philosophical Grammar*). These works evolved out of notes on philosophical thoughts that developed between 1929 and 1932 and are often referred to as the Cambridge School of Analysis. By the end of World War II, however, this linguistic philosophy found more fertile ground at Oxford University and quickly became known as the Oxford School. These works, although complete, were only published posthumously. During the decade of the 1930s, Wittgenstein produced a series of philosophical notebooks that were compiled into what later became known as the *Brown Book* and the *Blue Book*. The *Blue Book* of 1933–34 can best be described as a rough outline of a radically new philosophy. Some scholars regard it as an early version of the philosophical thoughts that lead up to his *Philosophical Investigations*. It was the thorough revision of this book, begun in 1936, that became known as the *Philosophische Untersuchungen* (1951; *Philosophical Investigations*). The *Tractatus* and the *Philosophical Investigations* are the two treatises for which Wittgenstein is best known today.

An important aspect of Wittgenstein, the man and thinker, is his understanding of the concept of knowledge. For him, knowledge was interconnected with the idea of doing. It is little wonder that his first important studies were all connected with technical sciences. He had a thorough knowledge of mathematics and physics not so much from any theoretical training but rather from his experimental work with aeronautics. Wittgenstein the philosopher was also unique in that he was not known to have had any formal training in classical philosophy but found great insights and inspiration in readings of literature and religion. Among some of his favorites were the works of Tolstoy, Dostoyevsky, Kierkegaard, and St. Augustine. His *Tractatus* and *Philosophical Investigations* also reveal a language and style that is free, simple, and rhythmic. His writings are not laden with technical terminology or ornamentation but instead show a careful choice of words that are rich in imagination and thought. Indeed, Wittgenstein represents the last of a generation that nourished itself on the modernist genius of Vienna's fin de siècle culture.

ISTVAN VARKONYI

Biography

Born in Vienna, Austria, 26 April 1889. Engineering student at the Technische Universität Berlin-Charlottenburg, 1908–11; enrolled at the University of Manchester, 1912, and Trinity College, University of Cambridge, 1913; moved to a farm in Skjolden, in Sogn, Norway, 1913; volunteer in the Austro-Hungarian army, 1916; trained as an officer in the army; captured in Italy and held as a war prisoner until the end of the war; completed work on his *Tractatus,* 1918; attended a college for teachers of elementary education, 1919–20; taught in various remote villages in the district of Schneeberg and Semmering, 1920–26; returned to Cambridge as a research student, 1929; received his doctorate for his *Tractatus,* 1929; fellow of Trinity College, 1930–36; returned to Norway, 1936–37; adopted British citizenship after the Anschluss, 1938; elected to the chairmanship of the philosophy department at Trinity College, 1939; last lecture as a

professor at Cambridge, 1947; settled on a farm in the Irish countryside near Galway, 1948; diagnosed with cancer, 1949; travel to the United States, 1949; travel to Vienna and Norway, 1950. Died in Cambridge, England, 29 April 1951.

Selected Works

Philosophy

Tractatus Logico-Philosophicus (German and English texts), 1922
Philosophische Untersuchungen, 1951; as *Philosophical Investigations* (German and English texts), edited by G.E.M. Anscombe, 1953
Remarks on the Foundations of Mathematics (German and English texts), edited by G.H. von Wright, Rush Rhees, and G.E.M. Anscombe, 1956
Preliminary Studies for the "Philosophical Investigations," Generally Known as the Blue and Brown Books, 1958
Notebooks 1914–1916 (German and English texts), edited by G.E.M. Anscombe and G.H. von Wright, 1961
Philosophische Bermerkungen, edited by Rush Rhees, 1965; as *Philosophical Remarks*, translated by Raymond Hargreares and Roger White, 1968
On Certainty (German and English texts), edited by G.E.M. Anscombe and G.H. von Wright, 1969
Philosophische Grammatik, edited by Rush Rhees, 1969; as *Philosophical Grammar*, translated by Anthony Kenny, 1974
Philosophical Remarks, edited by Rush Rhees, 1975
Wittgenstein's Lectures on the Foundations of Mathematics, Cambridge, 1939, edited by Cora Diamond, 1976
Vermischte Bemerkungen, edited by G.H. von Wright, 1977; as *Culture and Value*, 1980
Remarks on Colour, edited by G.E.M. Anscombe, 1977
Remarks on the Philosophy of Psychology, edited by G.E.M. Anscombe and G.H. von Wright, 1980
Letzte Schriften über die Philosophie der Psychologie—Last Writings on the Philosophy of Psychology, edited by G.H. von Wright and Heikki Nyman, 1982

Further Reading

Bearn, Gordon C., *Waking to Wonder: Wittgenstein's Existential Investigations*, Albany: State University of New York Press, 1997
Bloor, David, *Wittgenstein, Rules and Institutions*, London and New York: Routledge, 1997
Bradley, Raymond, *The Nature of All Being: A Study of Wittgenstein's Modal Atomism*, Oxford and New York: Oxford University Press, 1992
Cook, John W., *Wittgenstein's Metaphysics*, Cambridge and New York: Cambridge University Press, 1994
Diamond, Cora, *The Realistic Spirit: Wittgenstein, Philosophy, and the Mind*, Cambridge: MIT Press, 1991
Hagberg, Garry, *Art as Language: Wittgenstein, Meaning, and Aesthetic Theory*, Ithaca, New York: Cornell University Press, 1995
Monk, Ray, *Ludwig Wittgenstein: The Duty of Genius*, New York: Macmillian Press, and London: Vintage, 1990
Schulte, Joachim, *Wittgenstein: An Introduction*, translated by William H. Brenner and John F. Holley, Albany: State University of New York Press, 1992

Christa Wolf 1929–

Christa Wolf is an East German author who has contributed substantially to modern literature since the end of World War II. In 1990, however, after the fall of the Berlin Wall, she was made to answer for her political attitude and moral stance over 40 years as an author and citizen of the German Democratic Republic (GDR). Indeed, Wolf has twice undergone the traumatic experience of having to deny her ideological beliefs: first, during adolescence, through the abrupt change from National Socialism to communism; and second, at the age of 60, through the no-less-abrupt replacement of socialism with Western democracy.

In spite of the pressures of recriminations and censorship from the mid-1960s onward, Wolf refused to leave the GDR, strongly basing her reasons on her desire to uphold humanist values and to make a contribution to preserve world peace from within the GDR system. Her idealism and moral stance were based in her belief in the antifascist roots and utopian goals of socialism. Yet, after 1989, in a bitter ironic twist, critics in the West accused her of supporting the GDR state and upholding a system whose demise was inevitable; those critics had, while the GDR lasted, hailed the moral values for which she stood—values that had put her increasingly at odds with the state.

An author with a moral conscience who searched for truth and intellectual individuality, not conformity, Wolf became a prime target for secret investigation by the Stasi (Staatssicherheitsdienst—State Security Service), which, up to the early 1980s, gathered 42 secret files of material on her and her husband. Wolf's public admission, after reading her own files in 1992, that she herself had been persuaded to report to the Secret Services from 1959 to 1961, in her position as a member of the Schriftstellerverband (Writers' Union) and editor of the literary periodical *Neue Deutsche Literatur*, were blown out of proportion by the media. This led to further recriminations, especially after the publication of her narrative prose work *Was bleibt* (1990; *What Remains*) had sparked off an acrimonious debate among intellectuals from East and West about the role of literature under the GDR regime and, in particular, Wolf's part in it. She was accused of suppressing the truth when it was most needed, in 1979, when she first drafted the story, which is a first-person account of a day in the life of the author under close Stasi supervision.

Indeed, Wolf's probing attempt to gauge her reactions as an author and human being to a situation that threatened her very existence is entirely in character with her approach in her major fictional works: *Nachdenken über Christa T.* (1968; *The Quest for Christa T.*), *Kindheitsmuster* (1976; *A Model Childhood*, revised in later editions as *Patterns of Childhood*), *Kein Ort, Nirgends* (1979; *No Place on Earth*), and *Kassandra* (1983; *Cassandra: A Novel and Four Essays*). Her latest prose fiction, *Medea: Stimmen* (1996; *Medea: A Modern Retelling*), must be read with the traumatic experiences of recent years in mind, which led her, more fundamentally than ever, to question her position as a writer and to cast doubt over her future. Through the refracted perspective of several different voices, the book tells of Medea's ostracization by two states and their people; Medea's powers of healing and her knowledge of uncomfortable truths make her the target of false accusation and abuse. Rewriting Euripides, Wolf exonerates Medea as the murderess of her children, putting the responsibility for the murders on the enraged people of Corinth.

Wolf's works up to 1989 trace the biography of the author, whose development is bound up with the rise and fall of the GDR. As a young student whose imagination was fired by reading Marx, Engels, and Lenin, which filled the vacuum left by the collapse of the ideological indoctrination of National Socialism of her childhood and early youth, she joined the leading state party, the Socialist Unity Party (SED), in 1949 and remained a member until the summer of 1989. This does not so much contradict Wolf's moral integrity as it reflects her idealistic belief in a utopian vision, which is present in all her works. This integrity is not only richly documented in the numerous frank interviews she has given over four decades but also in her recent retrospective attempt to evaluate her development as an author in the collection of prose texts *Auf dem Weg nach Tabou: Texte 1990–1994* (1994; *Parting from Phantoms: Selected Writings, 1990–1994*). The texts include three diary essays in which she addresses problems of the writer, dated 27 September 1991, 1992, and 1993, and letters she exchanged with leading intellectuals who continue to support her, notably her West German contemporary Günter Grass.

The widening gulf between her utopian vision and the reality of GDR socialist practice became painfully apparent to Wolf from the mid-1960s onward. Her early phase as writer and critic in sympathy with the state's cultural policies was reflected in her first narrative fiction, *Moskauer Novelle* (1961; *Moscow Novella*) and, already to a lesser extent, in *Der geteilte Himmel* (1963; *Divided Heaven*). A subsequent phase of the writer out of step with the state manifested itself in the theme and structure of the fictionalized biography of a young contemporary, Christa T., whose sufferings and premature death bear witness to the conflict of the individual in a society that does not fulfill her vision and that denies her self-fulfillment. Wolf defended the right of the author to be truthful to her own experience in her speech at the Eleventh Plenum of the SED in 1965, and she resisted threats over the publication of *The Quest for Christa T.* at the equally infamous Writers' Congress of 1969. Her defiant stance lost Wolf her credibility in the party and undermined her candidateship for the Central Committee of the SED (1964–67).

From the 1960s until the 1980s, Wolf was effectively disenfranchised in the literary establishment of the GDR, despite the fact that, during the 1970s and 1980s, her works continued to be published and firmly established her reputation among a steadily growing readership, not only in East and West Germany, but more widely in the West. This reputation was reflected in the invitations and honorary fellowships that she received internationally. She was a writer-in-residence at Oberlin College, Ohio (1973) and guest professor at Ohio State University (1983), where she received an honorary doctorate. In 1985, she was elected Honorary Fellow of the Modern Language Association of America. The increasing attention paid to her work among West German readers and critics, from the publication of the critically acclaimed *Divided Heaven* onward, was also reflected in numerous honors, among them the guest lectureship at the Chair of Poetics of the University of Frankfurt/Main. This put her on a par with Ingeborg Bachmann, Paul Celan, and Günter Grass, who had all held this position at various stages. Wolf delivered four lectures on the theme of Cassandra, followed by the story *Cassandra* as the fifth lecture. (Lectures and story were first published in 1983: as two separate volumes in the West German edition and as one volume in a censored East German edition, which omitted references to unilateral disarmament.)

All Wolf's works from her story *Juninachmittag* (1967; *June Afternoon*) onward establish a special relationship between text and subtext. As fiction, they reflect her self-perception as a writer against social and political antagonisms. Eager to harmonize conflict, the author found herself, in her characters, attacked, suppressed, and misunderstood. All her creative energies were therefore spent on forging an active, positive role for herself in the increasingly insoluble conflict between writer and state, between *Geist* and *Macht* (intellect and power).

But it is in her essays, spread over three decades, that Wolf allowed herself free range in developing her ideas on writing, as a process of both finding herself and defining her role in society. In the collection *Lesen und Schreiben* (1972; *The Reader and the Writer*), Wolf shakes off the influence of Lukács and acknowledges her debt to the tradition of 19th-century realism, Georg Büchner, and such diverse influences as Thomas Mann and Brecht. Her concept of *epic prose* reinstates the author's subjective experience and memory as vital elements in creating prose that makes reality transparent to the truth rather than superimposing a truth onto reality. In this process, she follows the examples of her revered mentor Anna Seghers, the Swiss author Max Frisch, and the Austrian Ingeborg Bachmann, a contemporary female author to whom she felt a special affinity, which she acknowledges in the fourth of the *Cassandra* lectures.

During the 1970s, and particularly after her major contribution to the subject of *Vergangenheitsbewältigung* (working through the past), *Patterns of Childhood*, Wolf immersed herself in the themes of women and Romanticism. She resurrected the life and work of the all but forgotten figure of Karoline von Günderrode, contemporary of prominent authors of the early 19th century: Clemens Brentano, Achim von Arnim, and Heinrich von Kleist. In Wolf's interpretation, contained in the novella *No Place on Earth*, Kleist and Günderrode are drawn to each other as outsiders, as two human beings who defy gender boundaries and as two authors who feel excluded from the literary and political establishments, which tolerate them only as eccentrics. Simultaneously, Wolf reedited Günderrode's work in a volume of poetry, drama, and letters, *Der Schatten eines Traumes* (1979; The Shadow of a Dream). In two extensive essays on Günderrode and her friend and correspondent Bettine Brentano, Wolf re-created a spiritual relationship between two women who sustained each other under the alienating conditions of an age that did not tolerate individuality. The essays, "Der Schatten eines Traumes: *Karoline von Günderrode—Ein Entwurf*" (1979) and "'Nun ja! Das nächste Leben geht aber heute an': Ein Brief über die Bettine" (1981), together with the novella *No Place on Earth* (1979), were written when Christa Wolf felt deeply threatened both as a writer and as human being—in the aftermath of the protest against the expatriation of Wolf Biermann in 1976, in which she joined. Through the juxtaposition of the poetic dialogue of Bettine and Karoline, Wolf develops the beginnings of a female aesthetics against the prevailing canon of writing, thereby giving a voice to women such as the author manqué Christa T. Using the first person, the *Ich*, had been a mere *hope*, an essential part of her as-yet-unfulfilled vision of herself for *Christa T.* The conflict between the third- and first-person narrative became a major issue for Wolf when she wrote about her own past in *Patterns of Childhood*; she

found a compromise by using the familiar form of self-address, the second person singular, *Du.*

The power of a woman's voice was put to the test in the figure of Cassandra, the protagonist of her major fictional narrative of the 1980s. With *Cassandra,* justifiably regarded as her aesthetically most advanced narrative fiction, Wolf moved further into the ranks of feminist authors. Yet, in four essays in the form of diaries, letters, and a travelogue, Wolf separates her own authentic voice from the interior monologue of the Cassandra figure. In *Cassandra,* we witness Wolf's attempt to reassert herself as the writer who craves influence in the public sphere, whose concerns are no longer restricted to socialism but extend to the worldwide issues of ecology and the threat of nuclear extermination. The latter was felt to be imminent with the stationing of SS 20 and Pershing II missiles in East and West Germany in the early 1980s. Nuclear threat is the major issue of her next slim narrative prose work, *Störfall: Nachrichten eines Tages* (1987; *Accident: A Day's News*), also a would-be diary of a day in the life of the author, describing both her reactions to the nuclear accident at Chernobyl and her fears and hopes during a major operation on her brother to remove a brain tumor. Science, as both a life-threatening and life-saving force, puts the author/narrator in a dilemma, casting poetic language itself into doubt. *Accident* is of lesser quality than her other works, perhaps, but it is a step further toward a fundamental questioning of her identity as an author. Increasingly, Wolf moved toward a form of writing that allows immediate access to her own thoughts and feelings without recourse to the transformation into fictional narrative, a form that she perceived as self-alienating. In her last stories coming out of the era of the GDR, *Sommerstück* (1989; Summer Play) and *What Remains,* she once again breaks down the division between fiction and diary. With the publication of these texts that had both been drafted ten years earlier, Wolf found herself exposed to a mixture of personal, aesthetic, and political criticism.

Although strongly in sympathy with liberal democratic humanist values, Wolf had held on to her faith in a utopian socialist democracy, which, for a brief moment in the autumn of 1989, seemed to be within her grasp. Along with a number of leading GDR authors, she felt inspired to raise her voice in public speeches, in the misguided hope of being able to exert political influence directly—only to be faced with a political reality that left her on the sidelines, deprived of her previous role as the moral conscience of and lifeline to her readers.

What remains of the reputation of an author who was one of the leading literary voices of her generation arising out of the postwar era and whose prose created a major literary event with every new work? Will she, in the future, continue to be counted among those German-language authors who appear to have a place in world literature: Günter Grass, Ingeborg Bachmann, Max Frisch, and, in her best works, Anna Seghers?

Wolf's lasting reputation as an author of integrity, moral concerns, and narrative authenticity rests with those major works of fiction and fictionalized biography that have secured her a fellowship of readers beyond ideological boundaries: *The Quest for Christa T., Patterns of Childhood, No Place on Earth, Cassandra,* and, as time may prove, *Medea: A Modern Retelling.* To these, we have to add her highly accomplished shorter stories (in *What Remains and Other Stories*), as well as her essays, which mark her way toward becoming a major contributor to modern prose writing. Her philosophical roots are bound up with the traditions of classical German literature and the philosophy of Enlightenment, despite her attempts to engage in the discourses of Marxism, modernism, and feminism. The unmistakable tone of her prose, at times elevated, at times deceptively banal; her commitment to aiming at truthfulness; and her honesty in attempting to extend the boundaries of self-reflection (linguistically, emotionally, and psychologically)—all these give her work a special place in contemporary writing. Subjective authenticity, the underlying trend in all her prose, has come to mean for her speaking with her own voice, bridging the gap between "living" and "writing." "Life"—for Wolf her family, people, political issues, cultural influences, but most of all her personal hopes, fears, happiness, and despair—is the fiber of her works. Her reliance on women as narrators, protagonists, and protectors of human values makes "female" rather than "feminist" a fitting epithet to describe her writing.

KARIN M.D. McPHERSON

See also German Democratic Republic

Biography

Born in Landsberg an der Warthe (now Gorzow Wielkopolski, Poland), 18 March 1929. Refugee in Mecklenburg, 1945; secretary to the mayor of Gammelin, Mecklenburg, 1945–46; studied German and philosophy at the universities of Jena and Leipzig, 1949–53; married the author Gerhard Wolf, 1951; member of the Socialist Unity Party (SED, the merged KPD and SPD), 1949–89 (resigned); technical assistant, East German Writer's Union, 1953–55; reader for Verlag Neues Leben, Berlin, 1956, and Mitteldeutscher Verlag, Halle, 1959–62; executive member of the Writers' Union, 1955–77; editor of *Neue deutsche Literatur*, 1958–59; move to Halle/Saale, 1959; resident writer for a freight car manufacturing company, Halle, 1960–61; moved to Kleinmachnow, near Berlin, 1962; freelance writer, 1962–; candidate member of the Central Committee of Socialist Unity Party (SED), 1963–67; member of PEN (GDR), 1965; speech at the 11th plenary of the central committee of the SED, 1965; chair of poetics at the University of Frankfurt am Main, 1982; gave a speech at the demonstration on Berlin Alexanderplatz, 4 November 1989. Heinrich Mann Prize, 1963; Theodor Fontane Prize, 1972; Raabe Prize, 1972; City of Bremen Prize, 1977; Büchner Prize, 1980; Schiller Prize, 1983; Franz Nabl Prize, Graz, 1984; Austrian State Prize for European Literature, 1985; National Prize for Art and Literature (GDR), first class, 1987; Geschwister Scholl Prize, Munich, 1987; Medal of the "Officiers des arts et des lettres," Paris, 1990; member of the German Academy of Language and Poetry, Darmstadt, 1979; member of the Academy of Arts, West Berlin, 1981; member of the European Academy of Arts and Sciences, Paris, 1984; member of the Free Academy of Arts, Hamburg, 1986; honorary member of the American Academy and Institute of Arts and Letters, 1991; scholar of the Getty Center for the History of Art and the Humanities, Santa Monica, California, 1992–93; numerous honorary doctorates. Currently lives in Berlin.

Selected Works

Fiction

Moskauer Novelle, 1961
Der geteilte Himmel, 1963; as *Divided Heaven*, translated by Joan Becker, 1965
Nachdenken über Christa T., 1968; as *The Quest for Christa T.*, translated by Christopher Middleton, 1970
Till Eulenspiegel: Erzählung für den Film, 1972
Unter den Linden: Drei unwahrscheinliche Geschichten, 1974
Kindheitsmuster, 1976; as *A Model Childhood*, translated by Ursule

Molinaro and Hedwig Rappolt, 1980 (also published as *Patterns of Childhood*, 1984)
Kein Ort, Nirgends, 1979; as *No Place on Earth*, translated by Jan van Heurck, 1982
Gesammelte Erzählungen, 1980
Kassandra, 1983; as *Cassandra: A Novel and Four Essays*, translated by Jan Van Heurck, 1984
Störfall: Nachrichten eines Tages, 1987; as *Accident: A Day's News*, translated by Heike Schwarzbauer and Rick Takvorian, 1989
Sommerstück, 1989
Was bleibt: Erzählung, 1990
What Remains and Other Stories, translated by Heike Schwarzbauer and Rick Takvorian, 1993
Medea: Stimmen, 1996; as *Medea: A Modern Retelling*, 1998
Hierzulande Andernorts: Erzählungen und andere Texte 1994–1998, 1999

Poetry

Das Leben der Schildkröten in Frankfurt am Main: Ein Prosagedicht, 1989

Film Scripts

with Gerhard Wolf et al., *Der geteilte Himmel* (directed by Konrad Wolf), 1964
with Joachim Kunert et al., *Die Toten bleiben jung* (directed by Joachim Kunert), 1958
with Gerhard Wolf, *Till Eulenspiegel* (directed by Rainer Simon), 1972

Other

Lesen und Schreiben: Aufsätze und Prosastücke, 1972; revised edition, 1981; as *The Reader and the Writer*, translated by Joan Becker, 1977
Fortgesetzter Versuch: Aufsätze, Gespräche, Essays, 1979
Voraussetzungen einer Erzählung; Kassandra, 1983
Ins Ungebundene gehet eine Sehnsucht: Gesprächsraum Romantik, with Gerhard Wolf, 1985
Die Dimension des Autors: Essays und Aufsätze, Reden und Gespäche, 1959–1985, 2 vols., 1986; selection published as *The Fourth Dimension: Interviews with Christa Wolf*, 1988
Ansprachen, 1988
Reden im Herbst (also as *Christa Wolf im Dialog. Aktuelle Texte*), 1990
The Author's Dimension: Selected Essays, edited by Alexander Stephan, translated by Jan van Heurck, 1993
Auf dem Weg nach Tabou: Texte 1990–1994, 1994; as *Parting from Phantoms: Selected Writings, 1990–1994*, translated by Jan van Heurck, 1997
with Brigitte Reimann, *Sei gegrüßt und lebe: Eine Freundschaft in Briefen 1964–1973*, 1993
with Franz Fühmann, *Monsieur, wir finden uns wieder: Briefe, 1968–1984*, 1995

Edited Works

Wir, unsere Zeit: Gedichte aus zehn Jahren, edited with Gerhard Wolf, 1959
In diesen Jahren: Deutsche Erzähler der Gegenwart, 1959
Proben junger Erzähler: Ausgewählte deutsche Prosa, 1959
Anna Seghers, *Glauben an Irdisches*, 1969
Karoline von Günderrode, *Der Schatten eines Traumes*, 1979
Bettina von Arnim, *Die Günterrode*, 1981
Anna Seghers, *Ausgewählte Erzählungen*, 1983

Further Reading

Ankum, Katharina von, *Die Rezeption von Christa Wolf in Ost und West: Von Moskauer Novelle bis "Selbstversuch,"* Amsterdam and Atlanta, Georgia: Rodopi, 1992
Arnold, Heinz Ludwig, editor, *Christa Wolf*, Munich: Text und Kritik, 1975; 4th edition, 1994

Drescher, Angela, editor, *Christa Wolf, ein Arbeitsbuch: Studien, Dokumente, Bibliographie*, Berlin: Aufbau-Verlag, 1989

——, editor, *Dokumentation zu Christa Wolf: Nachdenken über Christa T.*, Hamburg and Zurich: Luchterhand, 1991

Fries, Marilyn Sibley, editor, *Responses to Christa Wolf: Critical Essays*, Detroit, Michigan: Wayne State University Press, 1989

Hilzinger, Sonja, *Christa Wolf*, Stuttgart: Metzler, 1986

Hörnigk, Therese, *Christa Wolf*, Göttingen: Steidl, and Berlin: Volk und Wissen, 1989

Kuhn, Anna K., *Christa Wolf's Utopian Vision: From Marxism to Feminism*, Cambridge and New York: Cambridge University Press, 1988

Sauer, Klaus, editor, *Christa Wolf, Materialienbuch*, Darmstadt and Neuwied: Luchterhand, 1979; revised edition, 1983

Stephan, Alexander, *Christa Wolf*, Munich: Beck and Edition Text und Kritik, 1976; 4th expanded edition, 1991

——, *Christa Wolf*, Forschungsberichte zur DDR-Literatur, vol. 1, Amsterdam: Rodopi, 1980

Vinke, Hermann, editor, *Akteneinsicht Christa Wolf: Zerrspiegel und Dialog: Eine Dokumentation*, Hamburg: Luchterhand, 1993

Wallace, Ian, editor, *Christa Wolf in Perspective*, Amsterdam and Atlanta, Georgia: Rodopi, 1994

Wolf, Christa, *The Fourth Dimension: Interviews with Christa Wolf*, translated by Hilary Pilkington, with an introduction by Karin McPherson, London and New York: Verso, 1988

Kindheitsmuster 1976
Novel by Christa Wolf

Christa Wolf's fictionalized autobiography *Kindheitsmuster* (*Patterns of Childhood*) represents both an aesthetic and a cultural-political threshold in her oeuvre. As a committed socialist writer in the (former) GDR, Wolf focuses on the relationship of her generation, who grew up during World War II, to its compromised past and its role in defining the present generation. In this work, the possibility of individual engagement, already marked by an economy of disillusion and utopian energy in *Nachdenken über Christa T.* (1971; *The Quest for Christa T.*), finds its limit not so much in the GDR *qua* socialist state, but in the unmasterable Nazi past and its "patterns" of socialization, which lasted long after 1945. Wolf thereby confronts the tendency to see the postwar era in Germany, and in East Germany in particular, as a radical break with the past and to accord to her generation, in Helmut Kohl's words, "the blessing of a late birth." The novel begins with a denial of historical distance from an epistemological standpoint: "the past is not dead; it is not even past." Such distance is ascribed instead to the (collective) subject, which separates itself from the past and feigns distance to it as something strange, as other. Approaching this question of "how did we become how we are today," however, involves confronting a personal and collective history that is highly cathected with anxiety and shame.

Wolf adopts a narrative strategy that attempts to do justice to this history, which surfaces in the intersections of the individual and the collective, and the past and the present. Rather than narrating her childhood in the first person, the autobiographical persona is split through a temporal and pronominal dialogue. During a trip to her former hometown in contemporary Poland, the narrator is forced to confront the otherness of her own past.

Patterns of Childhood dramatizes the subsequent attempt at writing this uncanny intersection of past and present as a "process [*Verfahren*]" to accord the tear that goes through time the respect it deserves." Concomitant with this temporal rift is the division of the autobiographical "Ich" into the second and third person. To seek a voice that can speak of this remembered past is thus to experience self-alienation. The narrator describes this process as a cross-examination of the self by the self, where the first-, second-, and third-person pronouns are estranged from one another. Indeed, the text is marked not so much by a dramatic as a juridical language that circles around questions of guilt and innocence, penance, and possible acquittal. In this respect, the greatest danger to an appropriate treatment of the past becomes self-censorship. The narrator acknowledges that bracketing the authority of so-called objective history and the sovereign self through the form of the text does not solve the problem that the writer can still manipulate the subject matter. She refers to the child Nelly as a puppet on a string who is made to take the fall for "you," the adult. Beyond temporal distance, the division of child and adult in the text thus indicates the author's profound ambivalence toward her past. Such ambivalence belongs to the "subjective authenticity" Wolf once identified as a principle of her writing. The emphasis on personal experience does not imply privileging subjectivism per se; rather, the task consists in illustrating how individuals experience history and the forces that shape the process of remembrance.

Viewed in this way, the child's socialization under the Nazis serves as a pattern that illuminates a collective history and its problematic legacy. Verifiable statements by historical figures such as Goebbels are juxtaposed with the child's sentiments, which the narrator deems authentic. Nelly's participation in the League of German Girls (Bund deutscher Mädchen) and her ideological education in school—as well as through radio and newspapers—demonstrate how a seemingly innocent childhood falls under the shadow of National Socialism. Motivated by desire and fear, the child learns to identify herself with the nation and its ultimate object of cathexis, the führer. The death of her Aunt Jetty, a victim of the Nazi's euthanasia program, further illuminates the connection between fear, complicity, and repression. Although the family is grief stricken and horrified, no one dares speak of this crime, even privately. Nelly learns this mode of not knowing, which will culminate in Germany's postwar amnesia. Only bodily signals such as fever and cramps testify to the fact that the child, indeed, knows what is at stake. Thus, the news of Hitler's death sends Nelly into illness and melancholy. Reminiscent of Alexander and Margarete Mitscherlichs's thesis of the German "inability to mourn," the belated homecoming and its literary assimilation both allow the author to "work through" her past. Yet the text betrays apologetic tendencies at crucial junctures, most notably in the chapter dealing with the Shoah.

By introducing the category of survivors (*Überlebende*), the narrator elides the distinction between victim and perpetrator and, more specifically, the differences between Germans who lived through the war and those the Nazis deemed unfit to live. Nelly's appropriation of the term *survivor* is related in the context of a discussion of "survivor syndrome," which is used to describe the condition of former concentration camp inmates after their release. Moreover, the author claims that suffering undermines the credibility of the witnesses, a point of view diametrically opposed to that of writers such as Paul Celan, Primo Levi, or Elie Wiesel, who emphasize the responsibility of the "saved" to tell their unique story. Despite the aesthetic merits and striking honesty of *Kindheitsmuster*, the text seems to fall prey to its own utopian energy.

While it is tempting to speak of a "victim myth" (Waldeck) underlying the text, one might also view *Patterns of Childhood* as performing the limits of engaged (socialist) writing. The narrator claims that "the deeper our memory, the freer the space for the goal of all our hopes: the future." The geological figure of deep structure evokes not only psychoanalytic models but also the utopianism Andreas Huyssen identifies with Ernst Bloch's philosophy in *The Quest for Christa T.* Since the past can never be entirely lost, engaging it opens a window of hope for the realization of *Heimat*. Therefore, the hope that sustains the project of *Patterns of Childhood* is not so much personal absolution as the realization of a model socialist society. If the child Nelly represents the compromised past, then the author's daughter Lenka is the carrier of this utopian future. To be sure, this utopian project involves incorporating the Nazi legacy into a teleological view of history and instrumentalizing the work of mourning. Nevertheless, the apparent resolution at the end of the text rings false, indicating a relativization, if not the failure, of such utopian projects. Despite the fact that the narrator assumes the position of "I" for the first time, she also promises to "not revolt against the limits of the expressible." Wolf had previously interpreted Ingeborg Bachmann's positing of such a limit as intrinsic to Western bourgeois society and as a challenge to socialist writers. The fact that the socialist narrator invokes the very limit for which she criticizes Bachmann earlier in the text suggests the crumbling of Wolf's faith in socialism as well as language, which is increasingly evident in her next work, *Kein Ort, Nirgends* (1979; *No Place on Earth*).

JEFFREY GOULD

Editions

First edition: *Kindheitsmuster*, Darmstadt: Luchterhand, 1976

Translation: *A Model Childhood*, translated by Ursule Molinaro and Hedwig Rappolt, New York: Farrar, Straus, and Giroux, 1980; London: Virago, 1983; this translation later published as *Patterns of Childhood*, New York: Farrar, Straus, and Giroux, 1984

Further Reading

Ginsburg, Ruth, "In Pursuit of the Self: Theme, Narration, and Focalization in Christa Wolf's *Patterns of Childhood*," *Style* 26, no. 3 (1992)

Kosta, Barbara, *Recasting Autobiography*, Ithaca, New York: Cornell University Press, 1994

Levine, Michael, "Writing Anxiety: Christa Wolf's *Kindheitsmuster*," *Diacritics* 27, no. 2 (1997)

Waldeck, Ruth, *"Heikel bis heute," Frauen und Nationalsozialismus: Der Opfermythos in Christa Wolfs Kindheitsmuster*, Frankfurt: Brandes und Apsel, 1992

Nachdenken über Christa T. 1968
Novel by Christa Wolf

Christa Wolf rose to prominence as one of the outstanding writers of the German Democratic Republic (GDR); today she is a world-renowned author who has exercised a strong critical voice about both Eastern communism and Western capitalism. Many of her works, including *Nachdenken über Christa T.* (*The Quest for Christa T.*), were originally criticized in East Germany for their demands for individual fulfillment. They seemed to run counter to the communist agenda. Ironically, however, Wolf was one of those writers who called for her countrymen not to abandon the communist experiment when the Berlin Wall fell and Germany was reunited in 1989. It is now clear that her works were an attempt to examine candidly the socialist experiment of East Germany and to point out those problems that needed to be remedied. *Christa T.* focuses on the problem of balancing a desire to serve society against the needs of the individual for personal fulfillment.

The Quest for Christa T., published in 1968, was Wolf's breakthrough as a major writer. In the novel, a first-person female narrator attempts to reconstruct the life of a friend who has recently died in her 30s of leukemia—and of an inability to fit into her society. In the process the narrator reflects on her own time and society. She ponders the process of writing and its ability to save or falsify people by seeing them through biased memories. The book investigates the struggle to define individual identity in a newly developing communist East Germany that sees conformity as necessary to its survival.

In a 1968 essay entitled "Selbstinterview" (Self-Interview), Wolf indicates that she wrote *Christa T.* from a subjective impulse, because someone very close to her had died, and she could not accept the death. Writing about it was a means of protecting herself. In the novel, Wolf delves into the early life of this friend and uses documentary material such as dairies, letters, and sketches of Christa T. Wolf also discovered, however, that in the process of writing about Christa T., she was forced to confront herself and the relationship between the first-person narrator and the character.

Christa T. is as much about relationships as it is about recovering Christa T. as an individual. A curious doubling of memory takes place as Christa T. herself attempts to come to terms with the painfully recurrent images of death and destruction that are grounded in her childhood memories. The repetition of the destruction of the vulnerably innocent—the baby birds crushed by malicious boys at play, the old cat flung against the wall by an angry farmer, and the child frozen to death just beyond the reach of help during World War II—becomes a recurrent sign both of the questioning of guilt and responsibility and of the implicit vulnerability of the character herself, who is in danger of being destroyed by those of lesser conscience.

A second type of doubling of memory complicates matters further, as the narrator seeks other characters' memories about Christa T. and, inevitably, about their own past lives in relationship to hers. The narrator must constantly question her feelings about Christa T. and her own motives in seeking to retrieve her. But all those who knew Christa T.—her former teachers, companions, and superiors—are forced to reassess their relationship to her and to her stubbornly humane view of humankind in a world of increasing dehumanization and bureaucracy.

In *Christa T.*, memory is also deconstructed. The narrator admits that she is working from scraps of Christa's writings, pieces of the narrator's own memories, and bits of the memories of others. The narrator is forced, therefore, in her re-membering into suppositions, guesses, and fictions. She describes in detail conversations that did not in fact happen but that "could or even must" have happened as she describes them. The narrator, then, is always conscious of the process of falsification through personal projection and selection. But any memory falls into a pattern and takes on structure when it is inscribed as literature. What keeps the remembering of Christa T. from becoming untrue is the multivoiced dimension of the text, the merging of many memories from Christa herself, the narrator, friends, and teachers. The communalization of memory allows at least for a complexity and diversity that resists the neat patterning of a *single* mind and that avoids turning the self into a finished object.

The constant interplay between reality and fiction, self and narrator breaks down the boundaries between the two. Just as the narrator of *Christa T.* is forced to invent certain scenes in order to produce a "true" text, Wolf mixes fiction and reality to produce a realism of "subjective authenticity." By "subjective authenticity," Wolf means writing in which the author is intimately involved with her material and comes to terms with the reality around her through the writing process. This method respects no traditional literary boundaries and does not artificially separate reality and fiction.

Christa T. challenged a number of tenets of East German society in the 1960s. It values individual difference and creativity over conformity. In this work, Wolf also acknowledges that the ideal utopian society that she and her contemporaries foresaw in the 1950s has not materialized in Eastern Europe. (The crushing of the Hungarian Revolt by Russian troops in 1956 and the disillusionment it caused is recorded in her text.) She depicts the failure of East German society to absorb its most idealistic individuals and to give someone like Christa T. a productive role. This alienation and lack of productive belonging contribute to Christa T.'s death. Wolf, however, is equally critical of West Germany's emphasis on money and the possession of luxury objects. This balanced critique of the abuses of both the communist and the capitalist systems marks Wolf's entire work.

Christa Wolf has always resisted labels. When asked in an interview if she was a feminist, she responded that she wasn't any "ist." Nevertheless, recent critical readings align *Christa T.* with a broader feminist attempt to define a viable female self. Christa T. tries out several traditionally "female" roles—teacher, wife, mother, lover, homemaker, and hostess—all of which produce some satisfaction but not fulfillment. She attempts (as do the narrator and Wolf herself) to explore her self through writing. She is constantly seeking her own identity and her place in society. Christa Wolf, her narrator, and her protagonist are thus all women searching for identity through writing. The search is not concluded in the text, however; rather, it is extended to the reader. Wolf remains true to her own ideals and social vision despite drastic and traumatic changes in the political structures around her. This attempt to find a self and remain true to it despite social pressures forms a central theme in several of her novels.

In *Christa T.*, Wolf also focuses on the difficulty of achieving an individual identity, what she calls "the difficulty of saying 'I'"—particularly for women. Christa T. grows up during World War II and later in a developing GDR that stressed conformity. Christa T., however, is an idealist who does not fit into this highly regimented society. In this novel, Wolf values both Christa T.'s individual struggling to realize herself and the idea that we must create a society that cares for all of its members. She realizes the shortcomings of the communist East as it developed in the 1950s and 1960s, but she believes in the possibility of a socialist society that cherishes both the group and the individual. A

supporter of the rights of the individual in a socialist context, Wolf also champions the needs of society as a whole (and particularly its most vulnerable members) in a capitalist context.

Wolf's various foci of interests—coming to grips with the past through painful memory, antiwar attitudes, the position of women, and the struggle of the individual to find a stable self despite social pressures—combine to define her overall literary themes. Her stylistic complexity and her political courage and conviction make Wolf's work a compelling record of the shifting historical context in the second half of the 20th century.

KATHLEEN L. KOMAR

See also Neue Subjektivität

Editions

First edition: *Nachdenken über Christa T.,* Halle: Mitteldeutscher Verlag, 1968

Critical edition: *Nachdenken über Christa T.,* Darmstadt und Neuwied: Hermann Luchterhand Verlag, 1969

Translation: *The Quest for Christa T.,* translated by Christopher Middleton, New York: Farrar, Straus, and Giroux, 1970; London: Virago, 1982

Further Reading

Fries, Marilyn Sibley, editor, *Responses to Christa Wolf: Critical Essays,* Detroit, Michigan: Wayne State University Press, 1989

Herrmann, Anne, *The Dialogic and Difference: "An/Other Woman" in Virginia Woolf and Christa Wolf,* New York: Columbia University Press, 1989

Hörnigk, Therese, *Christa Wolf,* Göttingen: Steidl, and Berlin: Volk und Wissen, 1989

Komar, Kathleen L., "The Difficulty of Saying 'I': Reassembling a Self in Christa Wolf's Autobiographical Fiction," in *Redefining Autobiography in Twentieth-Century Women's Fiction,* edited by Janice Morgan and Colette T. Hall, New York: Garland Press, 1991

Kuhn, Anna K., *Christa Wolf's Utopian Vision: From Marxism to Feminism,* Cambridge and New York: Cambridge University Press, 1988

Sauer, Klaus, editor, *Christa Wolf, Materialienbuch,* Darmstadt and Neuwied: Luchterhand, 1979; revised edition, 1983

Stephan, Alexander, *Christa Wolf,* Munich: Beck and Edition Text und Kritik, 1976; 4th expanded edition, 1991

Stephan, Alexander, editor, *Christa Wolf, the Author's Dimension: Selected Essays,* translated by Jan van Heurck, New York: Farrar, Straus, and Giroux, 1993

Wolf, Christa, *Lesen und Schreiben: Neue Sammlung,* Darmstadt and Neuwied: Luchterhand, 1980

Was bleibt: Debate 1990

In the middle of 1990, four months before unification, German intellectuals became engaged in a literary controversy of quite uncommon ferocity. The immediate catalyst was Christa Wolf's *Was bleibt* (1990; *What Remains*), a slim tale set in East Berlin in the late 1970s and recounting one day in the life of a GDR woman writer under observation by the Stasi. Although it was a fictional narrative, the autobiographical underlay was apparent, since Wolf had herself experienced such treatment at that time. The critical reaction to the work was immediate, launched in *Die Zeit* on 1 June. In the subsequent debate, which included charges of a "concerted campaign" against Wolf, it tended to be overlooked that two reviews were published face-to-face in that edition. One was a positive assessment by Volker Hage, but it was the excoriating piece by Ulrich Greiner, the paper's literary editor, that grabbed all of the attention. *What Remains*, as a note in the book explains, was originally written in 1979, but it was not reworked for publication until November 1989. For Greiner, this was evidence of opportunism and duplicity on Wolf's part: in no other work had she referred so directly to the GDR's oppressive structures, but instead of helping to overcome them by publishing at once, she had chosen instead to wait until there was no longer any risk to herself. Furthermore, Greiner suggested, she now had the gall to present herself as a victim of those very forces that, by her advocacy or her silence, she had helped to preserve.

The next day, Greiner's counterpart on the *Frankfurter Allgemeine Zeitung*, Frank Schirrmacher, published in that paper a long article on Wolf, equally hostile in tone but extending beyond a discussion of *What Remains* into a wholesale demolition of her entire work. The nub of Schirrmacher's charge was that, throughout her career, in her desire to preserve the GDR as an alleged antipode to the Nazi state of her youth, Wolf had blinded herself to its totalitarian character and viewed it as a kind of father figure to whom the population had a duty of loyalty. In this, Schirrmacher argued, she not only demonstrated an authoritarian cast of mind herself but illustrated, yet again, the failure of German intellectuals to respond adequately to the abuse of political power.

Until this point in time, Wolf had been almost universally respected in both Germanies for her personal and moral integrity. That such a figure should now be attacked so savagely in two of West Germany's leading publications produced howls of protest from her defenders in both East and West Germany, among the most prominent of whom were Günter Grass and Walter Jens, and the air was soon thick with cries of "witch-hunt," "conspiracy," "McCarthyism," "public execution," and the like. The intemperate language on both sides not only added to the rancor of the dispute but also indicated how sensitive were the issues that had been raised. It has since been suggested, notably by some U.S. Germanists, that the reason Wolf was singled out for this treatment was that she was a woman, that the whole *Literaturstreit* was in essence a battle of the sexes, but the charge is unsustainable. Wolf was not only the most representative figure of East German letters but was also the first after the GDR's collapse who was brave (or foolish) enough to put her head above the parapet. It was consequently she who drew the first fire, especially because she also chose specifically to highlight some of the contradictions of literary life in East Germany.

Significant in the early discussions, however, was the scant attention paid by Wolf's critics to the tone of the text supposedly at the heart of the argument. For although the narrator of *What Remains* is undoubtedly politically naive in her failure to consider that the system itself might be flawed, she also shows herself intensely aware of the tensions in her own position and deeply troubled by her inability to sustain them. This attitude indicates moral thoughtfulness rather than the perfidy or cynicism attributed to the book's author. But as Schirrmacher's article had already implied and the subsequent direction of the debate confirmed, Wolf's detractors were less interested in her as an individual than in the posture she was believed to exemplify. In essence, a younger generation of critics was using the collapse of the GDR to challenge not just the behavior of East German intellectuals but the whole postwar tradition, common to both Germanies, of a socially committed literature and the left-liberal consensus that had undergirded it. The point was made explicit in two further articles by the principal contenders, Frank Schirrmacher's "Abschied von der Literatur der Bundesrepublik" ("Farewell to the Literature of the Federal Republic") in the *FAZ* on 2 October, the eve of unification, and in *Die Zeit* on 2 November, Ulrich Greiner's "Die deutsche Gesinnungsästhetik." This last term (approximately an "aesthetic of moral conviction") derived from ideas already propagated in *Merkur* by that magazine's publisher, Karl Heinz Bohrer. It was coined in this form by Greiner, however, and came to denote what had been the principal target throughout: namely, a view of literature that assessed the value of a work primarily by the political and social attitudes that it conveyed rather than by its literary or artistic qualities. One of the effects of this, so it was argued, had been to grant a disproportionate "dissident bonus" to literature from the GDR that, from an aesthetic point of view, did not merit such esteem.

A call to reemphasize aesthetic criteria is not in itself reprehensible, although neither was it as devoid of its own political agenda as its advocates seemed to imply. By this stage in the *Literaturstreit*, however, Wolf herself had receded as a focus of the debate. By its unfortunate timing, her text had simply been the trigger for a controversy that, in the prevailing circumstances, was almost certainly inevitable, one that was marked by a wider clash of generations and beliefs rather than simply being a straightforward conflict between West and East. But its acrimony surprised participants and observers alike, and although it petered out inconclusively, it has left a legacy of bitterness in German literary life that has still not wholly dissipated.

PETER J. GRAVES

Further Reading

Anz, Thomas, editor, *"Es geht nicht um Christa Wolf": Der Literaturstreit im vereinten Deutschland*, Munich: Edition Spangenberg, 1991

Baumgart, Reinhard, "Der neudeutsche Literaturstreit," in *Vom gegenwärtigen Zustand der deutschen Literatur*, edited by H.L. Arnold, Munich: Edition Text und Kritik, 1992

Brockmann, Stephen, "The Politics of German Literature," *Monatshefte* 84 (1992)

Deiritz, Karl, and Hannes Krauss, editors, *Der deutsch-deutsche Literaturstreit*, Hamburg: Luchterhand, 1991

Kuhn, Anna, "Rewriting GDR history: The Christa Wolf Controversy," *GDR Bulletin* 17 (1991)

Rey, William H., "Christa Wolf im Schnittpunkt von Kritik und Gegenkritik: Gedanken zu dem Literaturstreit in der deutschen Presse," *Orbis Litterarum* 46 (1991)

Special Issue on German Unification, *New German Critique* 52 (1991)

Wolfram von Eschenbach fl. 1195–1220

With Hartmann von Aue, Gottfried von Straßburg, and the narrator of the *Nibelungenlied,* Wolfram von Eschenbach contributes to the remarkable narrative literature in German written around 1200. His few extant lyric poems derive from the traditions of the Minnesang but break new ground, in his dramatic and highly individualized dawn songs. Wolfram's reputation has grown steadily since the rediscovery of his works in the early 19th century, extending beyond the German-speaking world and the province of scholars. He is arguably the greatest German poet of the Middle Ages, whose appeal rests on his preoccupation with timeless human issues—man's spiritual journey, the conflict of faiths, the relationships between men and women, to name some of the most important—and his ability to treat them in an entertaining way. His style is challenging and sometimes eccentric, his syntax complex, and his vocabulary innovatory. His works, narrative and lyric, abound in color and visual effects, and he commands a wide range of mood.

It is difficult to distinguish the real Wolfram from his narrative persona, and there are few firm biographical details. A small town in Middle Franconia now bears the name Wolframs-Eschenbach. His status is unclear: he claims to be a poor man, and he may not even have been a *ministerialis,* despite his profound understanding of chivalry. He boasts that he is uneducated, even maintaining that he is illiterate, but he has abundant general knowledge, possibly gained from hearsay as much as from books, and he dispenses it freely. He probably traveled widely, depending on patrons for support, and he was certainly at the court of Hermann of Thuringia.

Wolfram's fame rests, now as in the Middle Ages, on *Parzival,* his first narrative work, although possibly it was preceded by some lyric poems. *Parzival* is an Arthurian romance, based on the unfinished *Perceval* or *Le Conte del Graal* of Chrétien de Troyes, and Wolfram has added material almost certainly his own, together with his own reinterpretation, resulting in a work of over 25,000 lines. He relates Parzival's failure to ask the question that would release the current king of the Grail from his suffering and ensure his own accession, his anguished efforts to make amends, his recognition that he cannot do this only by means of chivalrous achievements but must rely on God's help, and his second visit to the Grail Castle, which, with the right question asked at the right time, seals his destiny.

Juxtaposed with Parzival's spiritual struggle are the worldly adventures of Gawan, whose domain and goal are very different and whose exploits verge at times on comedy. The poem is set in a chronological and thematic framework, with Wolfram's emphasis on heredity in his story of Parzival's father and his account of the continuation of the Grail dynasty through Parzival's sons. The relationship between East and West is established in the love of Gahmuret for the heathen Belakane and taken up powerfully when their son is converted, so that he may marry the former bearer of the Grail and return to spread the gospel in his own kingdom. The nature of Parzival's search is emphasized: the Grail is a wondrous stone, entrusted to the elect family of Titurel and, above all, a spiritual objective, the goal of human striving. Wolfram's poem transcends the Arthurian romance and, particularly through his reconception of the Grail ceremony and Parzival's conversation with the hermit, attains a place in world literature on the quest.

The two fragments known as *Titurel* belong to the latter years of Wolfram's life, along with his uncompleted epic *Willehalm,* which can be fairly confidently dated between 1210 and 1220. For *Titurel* Wolfram appears to have invented a unique strophic form, while *Willehalm,* like *Parzival,* is composed in traditional rhymed couplets.

Titurel takes up a story partially told in *Parzival* of the relationship between Parzival's cousin Sigune and Schionatulander, the dead knight cradled in Sigune's arms when Parzival first meets her, and who is later assigned to a coffin in Sigune's anchorite's cell. The story of their early love is told in brilliant, impressionistic episodes, together with their separation when Schionatulander accompanies Gahmuret, soon to be the father of Parzival, on a campaign. In the second fragment, Schionatulander vows to retrieve for Sigune a hound's leash encrusted with gemstones and inscribed with a fascinating love story. The work breaks off without relating how Schionatulander died during this adventure, which was undertaken to prove his love for Sigune and in the hope that his love would be returned. These puzzling fragments present problems of interpretation and generic designation.

Willehalm is based on the Old French *Bataille d'Aliscans* and recounts the two battles between Christians and Saracens that result from the marriage of Willehalm to the daughter of the emperor Terramer. Arabel-Gyburg—the woman doubly named—has forsaken her husband, Tibalt, her children, and her heathen faith to lead the life of relative poverty she embraces out of love of God and of Willehalm. It is a powerful story, in which vivid depiction of fighting is interspersed with scenes of tenderness and introspection. The validity of baptism is not questioned, but Gyburg herself defends her faith and urges the Christian knights to display their love for God's creatures by the honorable treatment of their opponents. Willehalm's devastating defeat in the first battle is balanced by his victory in the second, yet there is no triumphalism as the work breaks off, and scholars debate the reason for the lack of a proper ending, asking whether Wolfram could not continue for practical reasons or whether the subject matter meant that the optimistic conclusion of his source was ultimately impossible for him.

Willehalm combines courtly and heroic qualities, differing in substance, ambience, and tone from the traditional medieval romance and corresponding to no established genre. In the Middle Ages, it was probably almost as popular as *Parzival,* and modern scholars value it highly within the work of a poet remarkable for his originality, humanity, and a myriad of moods in narrative and lyric.

MARION E. GIBBS

See also Arthurian Romance

Biography

Flourished 1195–1220. Born near Ansbach, Bavaria. Probably in the service of various courts.

Selected Works

Collections
[Complete Works], edited by Karl Lachmann, 1833; 6th edition by Eduard Hartl, 1926

Poetry

Parzival, revised and with commentary by Eberhard Nellmann,
    translated into German by Dieter Kühn, 2 vols., 1994; translated into
    English by Helen M. Mustard and Charles E. Passage, 1961;
    translated into English by A.T. Hatto, 1980

Die Lyrik, edited with commentary and translation into German by
    Peter Wapnewski, 1972; translated into English with commentary by
    Marion E. Gibbs and Sidney M. Johnson, 1988

Willehalm, edited by Werner Schröder, 1978; edited by Joachim Heinzle
    with translation into German and commentary, 1991; translated into
    English by Charles E. Passage, 1977; translated into English by
    Marion E. Gibbs and Sidney M. Johnson, 1984

Titurel, with detailed commentary by Joachim Heinzle, 1972; translated
    into English by Charles E. Passage, 1984; translated into English by
    Marion E. Gibbs and Sidney M. Johnson, 1988

Further Reading

Blamires, David, *Characterization and Individuality in Wolfram's
    "Parzival,"* Cambridge: Cambridge University Press, 1966

Bumke, Joachim, *Wolfram von Eschenbach*, Stuttgart: Metzler, 1964;
    6th edition, 1991; 7th edition, 1997

Green, Dennis Howard, *The Art of Recognition in Wolfram's
    "Parzival,"* Cambridge and New York: Cambridge University Press,
    1982

Green, Dennis Howard, and Leslie Peter Johnson, *Approaches to
    Wolfram von Eschenbach: Five Essays*, Bern and Las Vegas, Nevada:
    Lang, 1978

Greenfield, John R., *Vivianz: An Analysis of the Martyr Figure in
    Wolfram von Eschenbach's "Willehalm" and in His Old French
    Source Material*, Erlangen: Palm und Enke, 1991

Greenfield, John R., and Lydia Miklautsch, *Einführung zum
    "Willehalm,"* Berlin and New York: Niemeyer, 1998

Kiening, Christian, *Reflexion, Narration: Wege zum "Willehalm"
    Wolframs von Eschenbach*, Tübingen: Niemeyer, 1991

Kratz, Henry, *Wolfram von Eschenbach's "Parzival": An Attempt at a
    Total Evaluation*, Bern: Francke, 1973

Lofmark, Carl, *Rennewart in Wolfram's "Willehalm": A Study of
    Wolfram von Eschenbach and His Sources*, Cambridge and London:
    Cambridge University Press, 1972

Mertens, Volker, "Wolfram von Eschenbach: *Titurel*," in
    Mittelhochdeutsche Romane und Heldenepen, edited by Horst
    Brunner, Stuttgart: Reclam, 1993

Poag, James, *Wolfram von Eschenbach*, New York: Twayne, 1972

Richey, Margaret Fitzgerald, *Studies of Wolfram von Eschenbach*,
    Edinburgh: Oliver and Boyd, 1957

Ruh, Kurt, *Höfische Epik des deutschen Mittelalters*, Berlin: Erich
    Schmidt, 1980

Rupp, Heinz, editor, *Wolfram von Eschenbach*, Darmstadt:
    Wissenschaftliche Buchgesellschaft, 1966

Sacker, Hugh D., *An Introduction to Wolfram's "Parzival,"* Cambridge:
    Cambridge University Press, 1963

Schmid, Elisabeth, "Wolfram von Eschenbach: *Parzival*," in
    Mittelhochdeutsche Romane und Heldenepen, edited by Horst
    Brunner, Stuttgart: Reclam, 1993

Wynn, Marianne, *Wolfram's Parzival: On the Genesis of Its Poetry*,
    Frankfurt and New York: Lang, 1984

Wolkenstein, Oswald von, *see* Oswald von Wolkenstein

Women and Literature

Employing *women* as a grouping when we categorize literary
writing is both useful and obstructive: useful because it makes
explicit the gendered nature of a problem, namely, that it is not
mere coincidence when the authors we think of as "literary" are
overwhelmingly male; but also obstructive, because it lumps together many different approaches to writing under one heading.
Where men who write are classified as (for example) naturalists
or political poets, their female counterparts—whether naturalist,
political, feminist, or whatever—tend to be joined under the
heading "women writers." "Men writers" is not a category we
use, nor would we expect to find an encyclopedia entry on the
topic "men and literature." Such phrases have an odd ring to

them because, unconsciously, we all tend to the view that writers
are "normally" men. Until recently, literary history has tended to
confirm this view, not so much by deliberately excluding women
writers from its halls of fame, as simply by not seeing them, with
the blindness caused by unconscious assumptions.

   The absence of women as writers in German literature—
which, since "literature" needs a definition, we shall take (however unwillingly) to mean the body of German-language texts
now considered worthy of attention in schools and universities
across the world—is marked, particularly before the mid–20th
century. That body of texts, sometimes called the "canon," is of
course variable, and shifts as tastes change, but the canon has

traditionally centered on a core of works by writers who have "stood the test of time" and are now generally recognized as "great." Yet, where in English-language literature we would expect to find works by Jane Austen, Charlotte Brontë, Emily Brontë, Mary Shelley, George Eliot, and Emily Dickinson at that core, in German we are likely to find the work of just one woman: Annette von Droste-Hülshoff. An educated reader of German will probably have *heard* of Luise Gottsched, Bettina von Arnim, Sophie Mereau, Karoline von Günderrode, and Marie von Ebner-Eschenbach, but these authors have not been granted a place among the "greats," and most of their work is neither well known, nor widely available. The work of women writers who were massively popular in their day, such as Charlotte Birch-Pfeiffer (1800–1868), whose plays were performed more frequently than Schiller's or Goethe's in the 19th century, or the novelist Fanny Lewald (1811–89), had until very recently disappeared from view under the rubric *Trivialliteratur* (trivial literature); even those writers who were celebrated for their literary genius, including Sybilla Schwarz (1621–38), Sophie Mereau (1770–1806), and Ebner-Eschenbach (1830–1916), have not generally found their way on to modern syllabi and bookshelves. This does nothing to revise our perception that writing literature is, generally speaking, something that *men* do. Nor do common modes of referring to women writers in German, which mark them as exceptions rather than as the rule. Where we speak, in formal German, of "Goethe" or "Nietzsche," it is standard practice to refer to "*die* Droste" and "*die* Bachmann," and thus to emphasize the "unusual" gender of the female author. Relationships with famous men have often been seen as a good reason for remembering women writers (Charlotte von Stein is a prime example) and have also affected their naming: where Achim von Arnim is identified primarily by his surname, his wife is almost invariably referred to simply as "Bettina."

Women may tend toward invisibility as writers of German literature, but as its subject they are ubiquitous. In fictional, historical, mythological, and philosophical form, ideas about the female and the feminine abound in the best-known works of the best-known authors: Kant's "Beobachtungen über das Gefühl des Schönen und Erhabenen" (1764; Observations on the Feeling of the Beautiful and Sublime); Lessing's *Emilia Galotti* (1772); Goethe's *Iphigenie* (1788); Schiller's *Maria Stuart* (1801); Kleist's *Penthesilea* (1807); and works by Nietzsche and Freud. Whatever else we find in these writers' undoubtedly major contribution to world literature, we shall also find one implicit message: that women's experience and existence, in literary terms, is *not their own*—it has constantly been defined and interpreted by men. And the unspoken assumption that writing literature is something that men do is transmitted in the process of reading: both men and women readers have traditionally been used to seeing male experience reflected in the text and, therefore, to viewing women *through the eyes of men*. Until quite recently, we were all in some sense, then, "male" readers. It has taken the feminist discourse of the 1970s, 1980s, and 1990s to position the *woman* reader in relation to the text and to challenge both the perception of male experience as universal experience, and, in particular, the depictions of "female experience" offered by men of letters. An important scholarly project of the last quarter century has been the discovery and reappropriation of women's experience as it is mirrored in their *own* writing. Many literary works by German-speaking women are now back in print, and hundreds are at least on record as extant. The importance of this exercise cannot be overstated, as making such writing available is the first, essential step on the way to developing our perceptions of what literature is. As Sigrid Weigel pointed out in her influential essay "Der schielende Blick" (1983; "Double Focus"), however, such a project also necessitates historical and theoretical work. Literature is not written in a vacuum, and when women write, they do so within masculinist social and literary structures. This has had consequences for both the production and the reception of women's writing.

Women's production of literature in German or, indeed, in any other language is bound to be linked to the provision of education for women, which has generally been regulated by men. The educational ideals propagated by reformers such as Luther and humanists such as Melanchthon in the 16th century were directed primarily at boys; if girls were literate enough to read the Bible, that was generally thought to be sufficient. Some women in the early modern period did receive a proper education, privately, and did write—Anna Ovena Hoyers (1584–1655) and Catharina Regina von Greiffenberg (1633–94) are frequently cited examples—but these women were the exception, not the rule. Over the next century, there developed a philosophy of education and gender destiny (*Bestimmung*) that found what was perhaps its most influential expression in the writings of the Swiss/French novelist and philosopher Jean Jacques Rousseau (1712–78).

Rousseau was widely received in Germany, and his work inspired a spate of epigonic theories. According to these theories, which are grounded in both religious (divine will) and secular (the order of nature) arguments, men are to be educated for active, articulate participation in public life, and women for a strictly limited, supportive existence in the home. In these theories, moreover, both excessive reading and writing are detrimental to a woman's performance of her destined role. This is not to say that real women in this period did not write; but when they did, it was with an awareness of indulging in an illegitimate activity. Even the remarkable Dorothea Leporin, who was awarded a doctorate in medicine at Halle in 1754, felt obliged to preface her book on women's education, *Gründliche Untersuchung der Ursachen, die das Weibliche Geschlecht vom Studiren abhalten* (1742; *Thorough Examination of the Reasons Preventing Women from Study*), with an introduction by her father in which he emphasizes her domestic capabilities and her unwillingness to enter the public arena as an author. Both claims are clearly intended to prove that Leporin *is* suitably womanly, not an unfeminine monster.

From the 18th to the early 20th century, one of the most persistent modes of constructing German womanhood was as *nature* incarnate. Such an idea grew out of older notions of woman as earth mother, animalistic, and passionate rather than rational; but just as the idea of nature came to be idealized in the 18th century, so did that of woman, and both new ideas functioned as a flattering backdrop to the developing male-dominated bourgeois culture. This, again, has implications for women's literary production, especially in terms of its reception: for if woman is conceived of as nature, then writing by women must be seen either as a "natural" outpouring, and, hence, *not* as a proper part of cultural production, or else as artificial, "unnatural," and therefore illegitimate—at worst, monstrous. Women writers have been left with the sense that they are tasting forbidden fruit, which is not only a pleasurable experience: Marie von Ebner-Eschenbach, for example, experienced her literary talent both as an incurable addiction and as a kind of curse.

A semipublic space for women intellectuals, and one in which their literary interests and even literary activity were regarded as licit, emerged with the rise of salon culture in the later 18th century. The term *salon* was first used by Madame de Staël in 1807, and it derives from the drawing room in which a socially established woman would encourage her literary and intellectual circle to gather. The Parisian salons of the 17th and 18th centuries found their counterparts in the German salons of the late 18th and early 19th centuries, the most prominent of which were hosted in Berlin by Jewish-German women such as Henriette Herz and Rahel Varnhagen. These salons were a remarkable and emancipatory social institution in that intellectual capacity generally went before social rank; men mixed with women and Jews with Christians, for distinctions of gender and religion could be suspended in the special, almost extrasocietal, space the salons offered. At the same time, however, the salon—as opposed to the public arenas of the university or the court—connoted the domestic space to which women's intellectual endeavor was still confined.

The construction of woman as natural and domestic stood in a relation to the perception of literary genre. Diaries and letters, for example, which connote naïveté (outpourings of the heart) and a private ambiance, came to be regarded as feminine forms, as did the related epistolary novel. Short stories, too, were found acceptable, particularly as they were not likely to distract the writer from her household duties for too long. Sophie Mereau, dedicating her *Bunte Reihe kleiner Schriften* (1805; *A Bright Assortment of Little Writings*) to the novelist Sophie von la Roche, is able to maintain a calculatedly feminine stance. Brentano styles herself a hostess at a society party where she "presents" her work to a noble patron: "Placing my trust in your benevolence I permit myself the pleasure of introducing you to this company. . . . I have arranged it, as a clever housewife should, as a bright assortment." Thus, she wards off accusations of trespass on the masculine territory of literature: she is no bluestocking, she suggests, but a "clever housewife," who in her choice of adjectives—the infantile "bunt" (bright, colorful) and the diminutive "little"—deprecates her own achievement even in the title of her work.

Drama, by contrast, with the formality and high status it acquired from its classical origins, as well as its overtly public reception through performance, was viewed as archetypally masculine. One of the many critics to have put this viewpoint into words around the turn of the last century was Johannes Wiegand, author of *Die Frau in der modernen deutschen Literatur: Plaudereien* (1903; *Woman in Modern German Literature: A Cosy Chat*), who adjudges women writers capable of poetry and prose epic, but not of drama, whose logical form will defeat them. The force of this kind of essentialist thinking is such that we find it reproduced by women: Marieluise Fleisser, probably the only well-known woman dramatist writing in German before the mid–20th century, notes in her essay "Das dramatische Empfinden bei den Frauen" (1930; Women's Dramatic Sensibility) that women's plays "easily give an impression of being one-offs, of having been attempted with a great effort of nerves; usually only the one attempt is ever made, and the author turns back to epic, because that is more in her nature." Again, we

should not be misled by such theories of gender and writing into thinking that real women did not write drama: they did. But gendered assumptions about genre have rendered German women writers more invisible than usual in this area, assumptions that are only now coming under review.

One way of attempting to avoid exposure to gender prejudice or sometimes to spare the family the shame of being seen to harbor an "unnatural" woman has been the choice of anonymity or the use of a pseudonym. In German literary history, both men and women have availed themselves of these means of masking authorship; the difference, as Susanne Kord indicates in her study of literary anonymity, *Sich einen Namen machen* (1996; Making One's Name), is that men generally dispensed with their alias after publishing a successful first work, whereas women generally retained theirs. The necessity of going unrecognized remained, for them, unchanged. And there seems to have been a developing reluctance on the part of women writers to have their work gendered female: whereas in the 18th century, 80 percent of the women authors found by Kord identified themselves, albeit in pseudonyms, as women, by the later 19th century, 70 percent were hiding their sex behind initials or a male alias. Their unwillingness to write openly as women should be linked to the debate around gender and natural sexual predisposition that reached its zenith at the turn of the 20th century, inspiring such popular scientific works as Paul Julius Möbius's *Über den physiologischen Schwachsinn des Weibes* (*On the Physiological Weak-Mindedness of Woman*), which appeared in seven editions from 1900 to 1905 and which admonishes its male readers to engage in latter-day chivalric combat with the dragon of women's intellectual emancipation.

The effects of a perceived need to be masculine were not only superficial. Women writers' use of pseudonyms was one sign of their search for the legitimation to write within a literary critical economy that (reflecting, of course, a wider social situation) granted the right to public self-expression to a subject predefined as male. Their situation as women and authors was, in the terms of their society, paradoxical, and their awareness of this may also find expression in their writing, including the not uncommon scenario in which a heroine strives both to free herself from the confines of socially prescribed womanhood *and* to subjugate herself to a beloved man. From a traditional literary critical perspective, this exposes the writer to accusations of unevenness or even self-contradiction. To describe this mode of authorship more exactly, Weigel formulated the concept of "der schielende Blick" (double focus), by which the writer may both portray a world that approximates to the accepted patriarchal norms and yet simultaneously approaches that world from her position as a woman on the edges of those norms, practicing a kind of contrary reading.

One characteristic feature of critical responses to women's writing before the 20th century is the accusation of epigonism, what Otto Heller, writing for a Boston press in 1905, unsympathetically called "a startling absence of freshness and originality, counterbalanced in a measure by a great imitative faculty . . . that fatal want of outlook and that seeming incapacity for the fullest self-expression which exclude the greater part of feminine fiction from the legitimate domain of letters." The conception of the epigone is clearly problematic: all writing is in some sense a process of collation (sometimes called intertextuality) and imitation of forms, structures, or content. But even modern feminist critics such as Sandra M. Gilbert and Susan Gubar have identi-fied what they call "copy work": a mode of writing in which the female author strives to appropriate, by imitation, the represen-tative power of the masculinist "norm." This may be achieved perhaps by the use of a male first-person narrator—employed, for example, by Ricarda Huch in her first novel, *Erinnerungen von Ludolf Ursleu dem Jüngeren* (1893; *The Memoirs of Ludolf Ursleu the Younger*)—or simply by viewing events through a masculinist lens: that is, in the light of their effects on and ulti-mate usefulness to male rather than female characters. Reception history indicates that women writers have been rewarded for successful "copy work"; witness the case of Wilhelmine Karoline von Wobeser's anonymously published *Elisa; oder, Das Weib wie es seyn sollte* (1795; *Elisa; or, Woman as She Ought to Be*), assumed at the time to have been the work of a man. In this novel, an unremittingly virtuous heroine rejects a lover and her personal well-being for the sake of an adulterous husband, who needs her for his own moral improvement. The work so clearly reproduces the notion of "woman as she ought to be" that was propagated by Wobeser's male contemporaries that it can scarcely be read as female literary self-expression. But it was also successful enough to be reprinted in four editions, indicating that Wobeser's assessment of how she should best use her liter-ary talent was at some level correct. Nearer our own time, we might take the examples of Ernst Rosmer (Else Bernstein-Porges, 1866–1949) and Ilse Frapan-Akunian (Ilse Levien, 1849–1908). The former, whose rather sentimental plays present a broadly conservative view of gender relations, was quickly exposed by critics as a woman writer but nonetheless well received in her day: her style was praised as "beinah männlich" (almost mascu-line) by Theodor Lessing in 1898. The latter, Ilse Frapan, whose novel *Wir Frauen haben kein Vaterland: Monologe einer Fleder-maus* (1899; *We Women Have No Fatherland: Monologues of a Bat*) is a gritty account of the kinds of hardship and privation to which women's lack of rights and recognition in society can ex-pose them, was accused of hysteria, while her work was charac-terized as "Altjungfernliteratur" (the literature of old maids) by Theodor Ebner in 1899.

These are scattered examples, but taken in context they docu-ment a pattern in the production and reception of women's writ-ing, especially before the latter part of the 20th century. Similar to the women writers of the past, we as modern readers are faced with a double problem regarding women and literature. On the one hand, we will find that women such as Wilhelmine Karoline von Wobeser, and many before and after her, have been exposed to various notions of "woman as she should be" to the extent that their path to literary self-expression is strongly colored by masculinist ideology; in such cases, we may need to look a little harder for the "writing between the lines" that, more genuinely documents female experience. On the other hand, we are likely to discover that when women's experience *is* powerfully and readably written, as it is, for example, by Frapan-Akunian, this writing has still not tended to make the leap to the status of "lit-erature"; for the woman's lens is not what tradition has led us to *expect* to look through when we open a work of literature.

In the 20th century, and especially since 1945, the status of women's writing in German has undergone rapid development. Ingeborg Bachmann has incontestably been accepted into the ranks of the "great" writers of our century, as has Christa Wolf, who is probably East Germany's best-known literary representa-tive. Elfriede Jelinek, Austria's enfant terrible, is also one of her country's most acclaimed writers internationally and a recent re-cipient of the prestigious Büchner Prize for literature. On school and university syllabi, contemporary and "reclaimed" women writers of the past feature ever more prominently, not only on syllabi of courses devoted to women's studies. It has been noted on many occasions that the literary history of women is always also a social history: when women are tied to domestic duties, denied access to birth control and abortion, or expected to shoulder the double burden of wage earning and housekeeping, these factors are bound to impinge on their freedom of literary self-expression. As a consequence, it should come as no surprise that the rise of women as authors is closely linked to the emer-gence of the two women's movements: the earlier women's rights campaign at the end of the 19th and the beginning of the 20th centuries (whose achievements were systematically undermined by the fascist regime in Germany from 1933 to 1945) and the later emancipation movement that gathered momentum in the late 1960s and the 1970s.

Fascism features powerfully in writing by women. Anne Seghers and Ilse Aichinger were among the earliest authors to engage critically with National Socialism, and Ingeborg Drewitz was the first German playwright to deal with the concentration camps, in her drama *Alle Toren waren bewacht* (1951; *Every Gate Was Guarded*). While novelists such as Christa Wolf (*Kind-heitsmuster*, 1973; *Patterns of Childhood*), Anne Duden (*Das Ju-dasschaf*, 1985; *The Judas Sheep*), and Ruth Klüger (*Weiter Leben*, 1992; *Living On*) deal retrospectively with the effects of Nazism on individual women and men, Ingeborg Bachmann in her novel fragment *Der Fall Franza* (1979; The Case of Franza) puts forward a more radical and generalized notion: namely, that fascism is not dead but has survived in the German-speaking world of the 1960s in human relations and, particu-larly, in men's oppression of women.

It was in the 1970s that the already extant term *Frauenliter-atur* (women's literature) came to be used widely by feminists and women writers as a means of placing women within the cat-egory of "literature." At this time, writers and readers also grew conscious of the struggle to find an "authentic" female voice within the patriarchally structured systems of language and liter-ature. A "weibliche Sprachlosigkeit" (female speechlessness) was identified, signifying women's discomfort in using languages that operate in masculinist modes; the generic use of "he" rather than "she," and in German the generic male plural ("die Studenten") or the use of "man" to mean "one" are obvious examples of lin-guistic gender bias. All such biases have provided the basis for a feminist critique of language led by linguists such as Luise Pusch. Novels—most notably Verena Stefan's *Häutungen* (1975; *Shed-ding*)—began to assert an autobiographical literary style that is specifically woman centered and to investigate the very language of literature in the quest to give expression to specifically female experiences. Stefan also stakes out territory for lesbian writing, which was just beginning to establish itself, uncloseted, in the heterosexually oriented literary world. Her work was published by one of a new breed of publishing houses, the feminist press Frauenoffensive (Women's Offensive), which had been founded in 1974.

It is important to differentiate between the situation of women in postwar West and East Germany. The second women's move-ment, with its concentration on oppression within language and its uncloseting of lesbian self-expression, was not a feature of GDR society at the same time. This is not least because the political system in the German Democratic Republic gave a level of consideration to "women's issues" that was not nearly matched by its Western neighbor. Similar to men, women in the socialist state had a right to employment, and they were extremely well represented in the workforce. Child care was heavily subsidized, and one paid "housework day" per month was available to most working women. Whatever one thinks about the tendentious categorization of child care and housework as "women's issues," women's status as working members of GDR society, in every sphere from politics and law to the production line, also affected their status as writers of literature, which helped enable a woman, Christa Wolf, to become the best-known representative of GDR fiction, closely followed by Irmtraud Morgner, Helga Königsdorf, and Brigitte Reimann. Yet there are also similarities between East and West Germany in the field of women's writing. Wolf in particular has given literary and theoretical consideration to the problems of authenticity and the status of the subject in writing: what she describes as "die Schwierigkeit, 'ich' zu sagen" (the difficulty of saying "I"). The autobiographical, deliberately "subjective" approach that is also championed by Western women writers is an important aspect in Wolf's and other East German women's work. While Wolf's approach is not specifically feminist, many would regard the difficulty of saying "I" as one common to women in patriarchal society, across national boundaries.

These days we are more likely to find women's writing in German described more specifically as *Literatur von Frauen* (literature by women). This avoids the implication contained in *Frauenliteratur* that this writing is not only by, but primarily *for* women, and to some extent the term avoids the difficult question of whether *Frauenliteratur* is *essentially* different from writing by men. This issue has, of course, been raised. In France, Hélène Cixous and Luce Irigaray have led the discussion regarding "écriture féminine"—an essentially female/feminine mode of writing—and in Germany a related question has been formulated by Silvia Bovenschen and others: "gibt es eine weibliche Ästhetik?" (Is there such a thing as a female/feminine aesthetic?). Answers to this inquiry have revolved around issues including women's perception of the female body, which is both the traditional, passive object of "human" (that is, heterosexual male) desire and the active subject of a female worldview, and women's potential to find a liberating energy in their very absence from or marginalization in masculine culture.

In this context, the whole idea of status and the canonization of certain works as "literature" is problematic; one might argue that the rise of certain women authors in the 20th century is closer to assimilation into an oppressive system of categorization than to emancipation. But whatever direction literary studies takes during the 21st century, a level of assimilation between its traditional form and newer approaches, including the feminist approach, seems inevitable. The ghettoization of women's literature, as something written by women and read exclusively by women, would in the end only reproduce the old assumptions: namely, that women's experience, unlike men's, is not of universal interest.

SARAH COLVIN

Further Reading

Bovenschen, Silvia, "Über die Frage: Gibt es eine weibliche Ästhetik?" in *Die Überwindung der Sprachlosigkeit*, edited by Gabriele Dietze, Darmstadt and Neuwied: Luchterhand, 1979; 2nd edition, 1989

Brinker-Gabler, Gisela, editor, *Deutsche Literatur von Frauen*, 2 vols., Munich: Beck, 1988

Eigler, Friederike, and Susanne Kord, editors, *The Feminist Encyclopedia of German Literature*, Westport, Connecticut and London: Greenwood Press, 1997

Fleißer, Marieluise, "Das dramatische Empfinden bei den Frauen," in *Gesammelte Werke*, vol. 4, Frankfurt: Suhrkamp, 1994

Gilbert, Sandra M., and Susan Gubar, *The Madwoman in the Attic: The Woman Writer and the Nineteenth-Century Literary Imagination*, New Haven, Connecticut and London: Yale University Press, 1979

Kord, Susanne, *Ein Blick hinter die Kulissen: Deutschsprachige Dramatikerinnen im 18. und 19. Jahrhundert*, Stuttgart: Metzler, 1992

——, *Sich einen Namen machen: Anonymität und weibliche Autorschaft, 1700–1900*, Stuttgart: Metzler, 1996

Littler, Margaret, editor, *Gendering German Studies: New Perspectives on German Literature and Culture*, Oxford and Malden, Massachusetts: Blackwell, 1997

Lukens, Nancy, and Dorothy Rosenberg, *Daughters of Eve: Women's Writing from the German Democratic Republic*, Lincoln: University of Nebraska Press, 1993

Pusch, Luise F., *Das Deutsche als Männersprache: Aufsätze und Glossen zur feministischen Linguistik*, Frankfurt: Suhrkamp, 1984

Weigel, Sigrid, "Double Focus," translated by Hamet Anderson, in *Feminist Aesthetics*, edited by Gisela Ecker, London: Women's Press, 1985; as "Der schielende Blick: Thesen zur Geschichte weiblicher Schreibpraxis," in *Die verborgene Frau: Sechs Beiträge zu einer feministischen Literaturwissenschaft*, edited by Inge Stephan and Sigrid Weigel, Berlin: Argument, 1983

Z

Zauberstücke

Zauberstücke (magic drama), also known as *Zauberspiele,* constituted one of the principal dramatic genres in the Viennese *Volkstheater* (popular theater) in the 18th and early 19th centuries. These suburban theaters, which arose as alternatives to the court theater, appealed to the broad mass of the populace below the educated bourgeoisie, but they also attracted members of the nobility, the middle classes, and foreign tourists. The *Volkstheater,* whose productions were created through a close cooperation and interaction among theatrical producers, actors, authors, and the public, had its roots in a combination of elements from the Baroque tradition, which survived longer in Austria than in most other parts of Europe, and the comedy of traveling players in the manner of commedia dell'arte. Baroque theatrical productions included the didactic Jesuit plays, which attempted to show how metaphysical powers, represented by saints and allegorical figures as well as by ancient gods and magical figures, guide human life, and court operas, which provided music and elaborate visual spectacles. Plays evolving from these traditions received an indigenous quality through the introduction of the comic, especially through language and localized characters such as Hanswurst and Kasperle. These different influences resulted in a wide variety of overlapping genres in the offerings of the *Volkstheater* from its beginnings in 1712 through the period following the revolution of 1848. Such offerings included the extemporaneous *Stegreifkomödie* (improvisational comedy), whose spontaneous wit and sometimes coarse humor caused difficulties for the censors and the proponents of a more uplifting type of literature who wished to ban the Hanswurst from the stage; the *Singspiele,* or musicals, which provided entertainment through the addition of songs; various forms of *Parodie,* which made fun of existing models in literature and mythology; the *Posse,* or farce, often based on plots from French and other foreign sources; the *Besserungsstücke,* or plays of moral betterment, in which a character learns to overcome his flaws and reintegrate himself into society; the *Lokalstück,* or local-color play, which incorporated specifics from the immediate environment; and the *Zauberstücke,* which combined magic and mythological figures with the elaborate sets of the *Maschinenkomödie* (machine comedy). These genres did not have fixed limits and displayed constant development: moreover, there was much overlap within individual plays. In fact, the *Zauberstücke* combined elements from many or all of these genres.

There are a number of reasons for the popularity at this time of plays containing magical, fairy-tale, or mythological elements. Providing entertainment by catering to the public demand for spectacle was a primary factor, but using allegorical representatives from a higher world to present a theodicy that taught erring mortal characters the folly of their ways was also a motivation that drew on didactic elements within the Baroque tradition. This fit in with the wishes of the authorities that members of the populace integrate themselves into the existing order, but, ironically, the magic backdrop could also provide a means for criticism that would have failed to pass the censors if a more realistic setting had been used. In any case, the magic realm could serve as both an escape from the real world and a concrete expression of the frustrations that arose from it. Early examples include the burlesques of Joseph Felix von Kurz (1717–84), which combined the extemporaneous humor of his comic figure Bernardon with the magic of machine comedy. The subsequent triumph of the *Zauberstück* came with plays such as *Mägera, die förchterliche Hexe* (1764; Mägera, the Frightful Witch), in which Philipp Hafner found a place for magic, but within the context of rationalism. Hafner gave new form to the genre by seeking a middle ground between the older, unrestrained comedies and the newer, reformed dramas and by stressing the literary character of the text. Later in the century, authors such as Joachim Perinet and Karl Friedrich Hensler wrote *singspielhafte Zauberstücke* (musical magic plays); Mozart's score for Emanuel Schikaneder's *Die Zauberflöte* (1791; The Magic Flute) introduced this genre to a world audience. In its magic and allegory, its combination of the comic and the serious, its mixture of genres, its incorporation of comic figures from the *Volk* (the servant Papageno), and its theatrical spectacle, *The Magic Flute* provides a fitting example of the most important elements of the *Volkstheater* tradition. Written earlier the same year, Perinet's *Kaspar der Fagottist; oder, Die Zauberzither* (1791; Kaspar the Bassoon Player; or, the Magic Zither) contains spirits so diminished in stature that they need human helpers to survive.

By the early 19th century, the inhabitants of the spirit world were taken even less seriously in the popular magic parodies. In Karl Meisl's *Orpheus und Euridice; oder, So geht es im Olympus zu* (1813; Orpheus and Euridice; or, That's the Way They Carry On in Olympus), the mythical figures serve as vehicles to satirize Viennese reality. A short time later, the *Zauberstück* flourished anew by incorporating aspects of the dramas of moral betterment. In plays such as *Der Berggeist; oder, Die drei Wünsche* (1819; The Mountain Spirit; or, the Three Wishes), Joseph Alois Gleich combined the local with the magical by letting spirits intervene to effect an improvement in an imperfect mortal. Ferdinand Raimund continued this tradition, but, not content merely to provide a diversion through parody or visual spectacle, he allegorized his mythical figures to let them represent, in his view, a more serious, higher truth. To indicate his changes, he added the word "original" to the genre designation of *Der Bauer als Millionär; oder, Das Mädchen aus der Feenwelt* (1826; The Farmer as Millionaire; or, the Girl from the Fairy World). This play received great acclaim, but when Raimund stressed the message even more by setting his next plays almost entirely in the mythical world, audiences were less receptive. He regained success with *Der Alpenkönig und der Menschenfeind* (1828; The King of the Alps and the Misanthrope), in which human figures again occupy center stage and the spirit antagonist, rather than effecting change through magic alone, procures an inner development in the misanthrope by allowing him to learn through experience. The mythical is thus better integrated into the plot than if it had been used for its own sake.

Even though the *Zauberstück* remained popular through the 1840s, the plays of Raimund represent this genre's last great flowering and one of its best manifestations. The cost of producing the elaborate sets was no doubt one reason for its decline, but so was the fact that the public's beliefs no longer corresponded in the same way to the world of magic. Johann Nestroy's *Lumpazivagabundus* (1833) makes use of the spirit world as a dramatic vehicle that is itself parodied rather than used as a means for conveying a moral message through a metaphysical perspective. Nestroy's talent for verbal wit and satire, as well as theatrical constraints, led him to abandon the *Zauberstück* altogether in favor of the *Posse*. Later dramatists employing aspects of the *Zauberstück* tradition included Hugo von Hofmannsthal and Jura Soyfer. In works by other 20th-century authors such as Ödön von Horváth and Elfriede Jelinek, however, it appears mainly as allusion rather than as a genre to be employed.

CALVIN N. JONES

See also Johann Nepomuk Nestroy

Further Reading

Aust, Hugo, et al., *Volksstück: Vom Hanswurstspiel zum sozialen Drama der Gegenwart*, Munich: Beck, 1989

Branscombe, Peter, *W.A. Mozart: Die Zauberflöte*, Cambridge and New York: Cambridge University Press, 1991

Hein, Jürgen, *Ferdinand Raimund*, Stuttgart: Metzler, 1970

———, *Das Wiener Volkstheater*, Darmstadt: Wissenschaftliche Buchgesellschaft, 1978; 3rd edition, 1997

Hein, Jürgen, editor, *Theater und Gesellschaft: Das Volksstück im 19. und 20. Jahrhundert*, Düsseldorf: Bertelsmann-Universitätsverlag, 1973

Jones, Calvin N., *Negation and Utopia: The German Volksstück from Raimund to Kroetz*, New York: Lang, 1993

Klotz, Volker, *Dramaturgie des Publikums*, Munich: Hanser, 1976

May, Erich Joachim, *Wiener Volkskomödie und Vormärz*, Berlin: Henschel, 1975

Rommel, Otto, *Barocktradition im österreichischen-bayrischen Volkstheater*, 6 vols., Leipzig: Reclam, 1935–39

———, *Die Alt-Wiener Volkskomödie: Ihre Geschichte vom barocken Welt-Theater bis zum Tode Nestroys*, Vienna: Schroll, 1952

Schaumann, Frank, *Gestalt und Funktion des Mythos in Ferdinand Raimunds Bühnenwerken*, Vienna: Bergland, 1970

Schmidt-Dengler, Wendelin, "Der Alpenkönig und der Menschenfeind," in *Die deutsche Komödie: Vom Mittelalter bis zur Gegenwart*, edited by Walter Hinck, Düsseldorf: Bagel, 1977

Urbach, Reinhard, *Die Wiener Komödie und ihr Publikum: Stranitzky und die Folgen*, Vienna and Munich: Jugend und Volk, 1973

Yates, W.E., and John R.P. McKenzie, editors, *Viennese Popular Theatre: A Symposium*, Exeter: University of Exeter, 1985

Sidonia Hedwig Zäunemann 1714–1740

An independent streak characterized both the life and work of Sidonia Hedwig Zäunemann. One of three daughters of fairly ordinary Lutheran parents, the Erfurt lawyer Paul Nicolaus Zäunemann and his wife Hedwig Dorothea, she was essentially self-educated, reading and writing mostly at night (much to her mother's disapproval) after the day's chores were done. Sidonia soon revealed herself to be no friend of conventional domesticity by spurning marriage—in one of her poems she writes: "Ich will lieber Sauerkraut und die ungeschmelzten Rüben / In dem Kloster vor dem Fleisch in dem Ehstandshause lieben" (I will rather have sauerkraut and unbuttered turnips in the convent than the flesh in the matrimonial home). Yet she was not afraid to imagine the joys of the marriage bed, as her poem "Wie steht es, Fräulein Braut! um deinen Jungfer-Kranz?" (Bride, how is your virginal wreath?) reveals. Another sign of her rugged determination is that, at a time when young women scarcely dared to venture out unescorted, she frequently braved wind and rain, riding through the deep valleys and dark forests of Thuringia on horseback, dressed as a man, to Ilmenau, where one of her sisters was married to the local physician. It was on one of these trips that she met with a fatal accident, falling from her horse on a weakened bridge and drowning in the River Gera on 11 December 1740. She was buried at Plaue.

Her whole life and poetry show a determination to assert her own personality. Inspired not least by the example of Laura Bassi, who was awarded a doctorate at Bologna in 1732, and Christiana Mariane von Ziegler, who was crowned poet laureate at Wittenberg in 1733, she endeavored to make a mark as a woman in a man's world: "Ihr Vorbild hat mein Blut erhitzt" (Their example fired my blood). She had begun writing poetry already in the 1720s, but some of this work she later burned. Among her early work were deeply religious poems—versifications of passages from the Old Testament or from the *Buch vom Wahren Christentum* (1606–9; Book of True Christianity) of Johann

Arndt—and conventional occasional verse for weddings, baptisms, and funerals. She later extended her range to include poems on events and personalities of greater public interest, including the great fire of Erfurt (*Das am 21- und 22ten October 1736 unter Gluth und Flammen ächzende Erfurt*) and the death of the Elector Franz Ludwig and the accession of his successor. What made her famous were her manly poems in praise of heroism and the soldier's life, which contained sentiments such as "Die Wahlstatt ist das Ehrenbette, / Wer darauf stirbt, der stirbet schön" (The battlefield is a bed of honor; he who dies on it, dies a fine death). These works included a poem about the imperial hussars ("Ode auf die zum Dienst Sr. Römischen Kayserlichen Majestät Carl des VI. am Rhein stehende sämtliche Herren Hussaren"), which was famous for the lines "Soll Trau-Ring, Wiege, Leichenstein, / Nur bloss der Lieder würdig sein?" (Are wedding ring, cradle, and tombstone the only topics fit for song?). Other poems concerned the departure of the Erfurt garrison in 1733 and the capture of Kehl the same year. Her poem in praise of the great commander Prince Eugen of Savoy earned her a letter of approval from him, and she also received encouragement from the Duke of Saxe-Weimar in the welcome form of gifts of books. In her own opinion, her most important work was "Das Ilmenauische Bergwerk" (1737; The Mine at Ilmenau) which was dedicated to King August III of Poland, Elector of Saxony. Written with a sense of admiration of and gratitude to miners and displaying considerable skill and wit, the poem describes Zäunemann's two exhilarating visits underground on 23 and 30 January 1737. She was proud of being perhaps the first woman ever to undertake such an adventure (dressed in miners' garb). By overstepping the bounds of convention in this way, she reaped disapprobation in the petty bourgeois circles in Erfurt. When a clergyman upbraided her for venturing into the mine, for example, she stoutly defended herself by asking whether then women were not permitted to admire the wonders of God's creation. Defensiveness and self-justification permeate her work.

Polite conversation or gossip about fashion, marriage, children, or homemaking were not for her. Her own interests lay in the more public sphere, the world of men. She rejected men's claims to be the sole arbiters on books and art. In a letter to the *Hamburgische Berichte* in 1737, she wrote:

> Our horrid Germans are not yet accustomed to allowing women to engage in the liberal arts. Their public lecture theaters would be just as much desecrated by our sex as the mosques of the superstitious Moslems. A woman who strives for knowledge can expect to experience loathing worse than a Catholic Pretender would in England.

In a verse epistle to the Duke of Meiningen, she outlines the prevailing attitude: "Ein Weib, das an Kiel und Wissenschaft gedenkt / Und sie zu forschen sucht, das muss ein Monstrum heissen" (A woman who thinks about writing and learning and tries to find out more must be a monster). She attempted to cultivate scholars, admiring Johann Christoph Gottsched greatly, and, indeed, she was so successful in this effort that after she had composed a poem to celebrate the foundation of the University of Göttingen, she was awarded a signal honor: in January 1738, to her great delight, as is evident from her poem of thanks, the University conferred upon her the dignity of an Imperial Poet Laureate. The same year she dedicated to Empress Anna of Russia a comprehensive collection of her poems, *Poetische Rosen in Knospen* (1738; Poetic Roses in Buds)—the image of the rosebud was deliberately chosen as a promise of the future flowering of her poetic art. It comprises 638 pages of verse, divided into religious poems, funeral poems, wedding poems, other poems of celebration, and various miscellaneous pieces; there is also a substantial appendix of poems written in her honor and a reproduction of the diploma awarded her as poet laureate. The next year, 1739, she published *Die von denen Faunen gepeitschte Laster* (The Vices Chastised by the Fauns), a wide-ranging satire of almost 3,200 lines on the vices and virtues of men and women in contemporary German society. Although touched by the spirit of the Enlightenment, the poem surprisingly perpetuates many conventional views, for example: "Kurz, ein vernünftig Weib läst dieses von sich lesen, / Sie ist des Mannes Lust und süsser Trost gewesen" (A sensible wife will like to read of herself: she was joy and sweet consolation to her husband). Unless the whole poem is to be read as having ironic intent, such views contrast with the strident emancipatory tones of her earlier verse; perhaps, as Tragnitz has argued, she was attempting to advocate women artists' rights to artistic self-expression while simultaneously endorsing other conventional role conceptions. Her satire elicited a critical riposte from an anonymous woman writer (possibly Christiana Rosina Spitz from Augsburg), *Die von der Tugend gezüchtigte Faunen* (1740; The Fauns Disciplined by Virtue), in which Sidonia Zäunemann is taken to task for overstepping the boundaries as a woman in writing in a genre not considered acceptable for a respectable lady.

JOHN L. FLOOD

Biography

Born in Erfurt, 15 January 1714. Largely self-educated; crowned poet laureate by the University of Göttingen, January 1738. Died (drowned in an accident) near Plaue, 11 December 1740.

Selected Works

Das am 21- und 22ten October 1736 uner Gluth und Flammen ächzende Erfurt, n.d.
Das Ilmenauische Bergwerk, wie solches den 23sten und 30sten Jenner des 1737. Jahres befahren, und bey Gelegenheit des gewöhnlichen Berg-Festes mit poetischer Feder uf Bergmännisch entworfen wurde, 1737
Poetische Rosen in Knospen, 1738
Die von denen Faunen gepeitschte Laster, 1739

Further Reading

Brinker-Gabler, Gisela, "Das weibliche Ich: Überlegungen zur Analyse von Werken weiblicher Autoren mit einem Beispiel aus dem 18. Jahrhundert: Sidonia Hedwig Zäunemann," in *Die Frau als Heldin und Autorin,* edited by Wolfgang Paulsen, Bern: Francke, 1979
Brinker-Gabler, Gisela, editor, *Deutsche Dichterinnen vom 16. Jahrhundert bis zur Gegenwart,* Frankfurt: Fischer, 1978
Cassel, Paulus, "Erfurt und die Zäunemannin: Eine literarhistorische Skizze," *Weimarisches Jahrbuch für Deutsche Sprache, Literatur und Kunst* 3 (1855)
DeBerdt, August Josef Julien, "Sidonia H. Zäunemann: Poet Laureate and Emancipated Woman 1714–1740," Ph.D. diss., University of Tennessee, 1977
Gresky, Wolfgang, "Eine Göttinger Dichterkrönung von 1738: Sidonia H. Zäunemann (1714–1740)," *Göttinger Jahrbuch* 32 (1984)
Heuser, Magdalene, "'Soll Trau-Ring, Wiege, Leichenstein / Nur bloss der Lieder würdig seyn?' Sidonia Hedwig Zäunemann," in *Deutsche Literatur von Frauen,* vol. 1, edited by Gisela Brinker-Gabler, Munich: Beck, 1988

Lippert, W., "Zäunemann, Sidonia Hedwig," in *Allgemeine Deutsche Biographie*, vol. 44, Leipzig: Duncker und Humblot, 1898

Schuchardt, Hans, "Sidonia Hedwig Zäunemann, Erfurts 'gekrönte Poetin,'" *Erfurter Heimatbriefe* 8 (1964)

Tragnitz, Jutta, "Sidonia Hedwig Zäunemann: Feminist Poet Manqué? Discrepancies between Her Early Poetry and Her Last Work *Die von denen Faunen gepeitschte Laster*," *Lessing Yearbook* 24 (1992)

——, "Zäunemann, Sidonia Hedwig," in *The Feminist Encyclopedia of German Literature*, edited by Friedericke Eigler and Susanne Kord, Westport, Connecticut and London: Greenwood Press, 1997

Voss, Lieselotte, "Zäunemann, Sidonia Hedwig," in *Literatur-Lexikon: Autoren und Werke deutscher Sprache*, vol. 12, edited by Walther Killy, Gütersloh: Bertelsmann, 1992

Zero Hour *see* Stunde Null

Christiana Mariane von Ziegler 1695–1760

With her poetry, addresses, a translation, and letters, Christiana Mariane von Ziegler is one of the leading women writers of the early Enlightenment in 18th-century Germany. This was a movement that regarded the production of literature as amenable to rational analysis and prescriptive poetics and that worked to standardize literary diction and writing conventions for the German language (and correspondingly to suppress variations in dialect). Ziegler strove to conform aesthetically to the new expectations and was equally energetic in pursuing a controversial new discourse about gender relations. Her poetry ranges from religious to domestic, from witty to devout. Her literary work, published over 11 years in four substantial volumes ranging from 352 to 611 pages each, began with poetry; she later added prose to her repertoire.

In early 18th-century Germany with its many privileges reserved only for men, a woman did not simply begin to write because she had decided to. Ziegler's literary and cultural career occurred when she had returned as a young widow to her patrician family home in Leipzig, which was a prosperous Saxon business city and center of the book trade. Aided by her class status and her position as a woman who had been married but was no longer either a wife or a mother (both her children having also died), she was able to conduct a literary and musical salon—a rarity in Germany until almost the end of the 18th century—and to meet two key German cultural figures of the 1720s, Johann Christoph Gottsched and Johann Sebastian Bach. The newcomer Gottsched was soon to become a university professor and the zealous regulator and ambitious reformer of German literature in the 1730s. Bach, already an established composer, turned nine of Ziegler's religious poems into cantatas. For example, he set "Es ist ein trotzig und verzagt Ding" ("[The heart] is an obstinate and timid thing") to music as Cantata 176, written for Trinity Sunday and telling the story of Nicodemus, who feared to show his interest in Jesus and so met him only at night.

Ziegler's poetry, which she began publishing in 1728, deals frequently with issues associated with women: being a woman writer, rejecting a suitor (since she prizes the freedom of widowhood), demanding that men reflect on their interpretations of masculinity. She admonishes them:

> Vergebt, ich muß die Namen nennen,
> Wodurch man eure Sitten zeigt.
> Ihr mögt euch selber wohl nicht kennen,
> Weil man von euren Fehlern schweigt.

> Forgive—I must some bad names ink
> whereby your conduct is defamed.
> You hardly know yourselves, I think
> because your faults are never named.

In keeping with her interest in women's accomplishments, Ziegler translated a book of conduct by Madeleine de Scudéry. Of her speeches, the most cited is her treatise on whether women should be allowed to become scholarly. Remarkably, Ziegler dared to publish a collection of her own letters, about half of them addressed to (unnamed) women, revised and edited and explained as examples both of moral reflection and of prose style. Despite displays of solidarity with women, Ziegler does not seem to have been friendly with Leipzig's other famous woman writer, almost 20 years Ziegler's junior: Luise Adelgunde Gottsched, who came to the city when she married Johann Christoph in 1735.

Explaining that she wished to turn the task of writing over to other women and have more time for her musical interests, Ziegler announced the end of her poetry composition in 1729, but did not actually carry out the threat until after 1739. That year, when the reign of her mentor, Professor Gottsched, over German literature was deteriorating into factionalism as his phase of the Enlightenment made way for a less rigid and more creative mode of understanding and producing literature, she published her last book.

The reception of Ziegler in her own lifetime mixed two themes, German pride and women's situation. Many Germans boasted enthusiastically that Ziegler's success as a skilled woman writer demonstrated that German culture was keeping up with the French and Italians, an important goal of the educated middle class. Women's situation was not viewed with as much consensus. One group of Ziegler's male contemporaries disliked and belittled women as writers, while another, led by Gottsched, sought examples of women's intellectual ability, nurtured of course by egalitarian early Enlightenment principles. Ziegler was thus selected for two unprecedented honors: She was the first and only woman to join the Deutsche Gesellschaft (German Society) a prestigious organization promoting good literature under Gottsched's direction. And she was crowned imperial poet laureate by Wittenberg University (but not by the far more prestigious university in Leipzig).

After she stopped publishing in 1739, and well before her death, she began to be forgotten. By late in the 18th century she was often omitted from lists of women writers and has in general been completely neglected by literary history except for that focusing explicitly on women.

Since the late 1970s, feminist scholars have been rediscovering Ziegler, appreciating her achievements despite difficulties, her self-confidence, her many forthright and positive statements about women, and her critiques of men, but also noticing that even this relatively independent and privileged woman often needed to defend herself and probably to moderate her critique of the gender relations of her time.

RUTH P. DAWSON

Biography

Born Christiana Mariane Romanus in Leipzig, 1695. In 1701, while he was mayor of Leipzig, her father was accused of a crime, jailed in 1706, and spent the remaining decades of his life in prison awaiting trial; at age 27, the twice widowed Mariane Ziegler returned to her family home and began her musical and literary salon; beginning in 1728 and throughout the 1730s, very involved in writing for publication, becoming one of the more prolific women writers of the 18th century; in 1741, married Professor von Steinwehr and moved to Frankfurt an der Oder. Died 1760.

Selected Works

Poetry and Prose

Versuch in gebundener Schreib-Art, 2 vols., 1728–29
Der Saechsische Unterthanen Getreue Wuensche und frohe Hoffnung
bey dem gluecklichen Antritte des grossen Stuffenjahres Sr. Koeniglichen Maj. . . . in einem Gedichte vorgestellet, [1732]
Die Zufriedenheit eines Landes, das nach einem schweren Kriege durch den Frieden wieder erfreuet wird, 1734 [containing as foreword *Zwo Schriften welche in der Deutschen Gesellschaft zu Leipzig auf das Jahr 1734 die Preise der Poesie und Beredsamkeit erhalten haben*]
Vermischete Schriften in gebundener und ungebundener Rede, 1739

Letters

Moralische und vermischte Send-Schreiben an einige Ihrer vertrauten und guten Freunde gestellet, 1731

Translation

Madeleine de Scudéry, *Scharfsinnige Unterredungen von Dingen die zu einer wohlanständigen Aufführung gehören*, 1735 (translation of *Conversations Morales*, 1686, and *Nouvelles Conversations Morales*, 1688)

Further Reading

Bach, Johann Sebastian, *Es ist ein trotzig und verzagt Ding (Festo Trinitatis), Cantata no. 176*, edited by Arnold Schering, London: Eulenburg, and New York: Eulenberg Miniature Scores, 1934?
Becker-Cantarino, Barbara, *Der lange Weg zur Mündigkeit: Frau und Literatur (1500–1800)*, Stuttgart: Metzler, 1987
Bovenschen, Silvia, *Die imaginierte Weiblichkeit: Exemplarische Untersuchungen zu kulturgeschichtlichen und literarischen Präsentationsformen des Weiblichen*, Frankfurt: Suhrkamp, 1979
Brinker-Gabler, Gisela, editor, *Deutsche Dichterinnen vom 16. Jahrhundert bis zur Gegenwart*, Frankfurt am Main: Fischer Taschenbuch, 1978
Goodman, Katherine, *Amazons and Professionals: Women and the German Parnassus in the Early Enlightenment*, Rochester, New York: Camden House, 1999
Heuser, Magdalene, "Das Musenchor mit neuer Ehre zieren: Schriftstellerinnen zur Zeit der Frühaufklärung," in *Deutsche Literatur von Frauen*, edited by Gisela Brinker-Gabler, vol. 1, Munich: Beck, 1988
Lamprecht, Jacob Friedrich, *Sammlung der Schriften und Gedichte welche auf die poetische Krönung der hochwohlgebohrnen frauen, frauer Christianen Marianen von Ziegler gebohrnen Romanus, verfertiget worden*, Leipzig: Breitkopf, 1734

Zionism

In response to the anti-Semitism that he had witnessed in Paris as foreign correspondent for the *Neue Freie Presse* (the Dreyfus trial was held at this time, and racially anti-Semitic literature such as Drumont's *La France Juive* also had a widespread popularity), the massacre of Jews in Russian pogroms, and the growing anti-Semitism in Germany and Austria (which included the growth of *völkisch* nationalism in Germany, and the election of the virulent anti-Semite Viennese mayor Karl Lueger), Viennese author, feuilletonist, and journalist Theodor Herzl published the pamphlet *The Jewish State: An Attempt at a Modern Solution of the Jewish Question* (1896). In this pamphlet, he argued that Jewish emancipation and assimilation had failed because the majority would not allow Jews to integrate fully and that Jews could therefore achieve total equality only by becoming a "normal" nation with its own national territory. Although he was not the first to propose that the Jews were one people and that the "Jewish Question" was a "national question" that could be solved only by political means (several notable forerunners were Leon Pinsker, Moses Hess, Rabbi Zevi Hirsch Kalischer, and Nathan Birnbaum), Herzl is generally considered the founder of the modern Zionist movement. In 1897, Herzl succeeded in uniting disparate factions of Zionists worldwide in the World Zionist Congress, which was to serve not only as a forum for Jewish national self-definition but as a policy-making surrogate government until the establishment of a Jewish state with its own territory. The first Zionist Congress produced the movement's manifesto, the "Basel Program," which stated that "Zionism endeavors to create for the Jewish people a homeland in Palestine secured by public law," and which recommended the following means toward this end: "promoting the settlement of Jewish farmers, artisans and tradesmen in Palestine, organizing and uniting world Jewry, strengthening Jewish national feeling and national consciousness, and taking preparatory steps toward procuring the government approvals necessary to realizing the Zionist goal."

Until 1933, only a small minority of German Jews were members of the organized Zionist movement. Of the roughly 500,000 German Jews, the peak Zionist membership was about 9,000 before World War I and just over 33,000 between World War I and 1933 (Poppel, 1977). Zionist ideology went against the grain of the self-definition of the vast majority of German Jews, who considered themselves to be "German citizens of Jewish faith," a term coined by the assimilationist Centralverein deutscher Staatsbürger jüdischer Glaubens, which in 1924 claimed to represent up to 90 percent of German Jews. German-Jewish assimilationists accused Zionists of adding fuel to anti-Semitic slander by confirming the anti-Semitic notion that Jews were an "unassimilable and potentially disloyal foreign body" within the German nation (Poppel, 1977). The German Zionist Federation (founded in 1897 by Max Bodenheimer and ten others), however, argued in its "Theses" that Zionist convictions in no way detracted from "the patriotic consciousness and fulfillment of civil duties by the Jews, especially by the German Jews for their German fatherland." Even after the Posen Resolution of 1913 prescribed that all Zionists include *aliyah* (return to Israel) in their life programs, few German Zionists seriously contemplated emigrating to Palestine before Hitler's rise to power in 1933. Although German Jews actively promoted, especially through fundraising, the emigration to Palestine of their impoverished, persecuted, and uprooted Eastern Jewish brethren, they tended to view Palestine (for themselves) not as a physical destination but as a spiritual homeland, a spiritual center for a "Jewish Renaissance" in the Diaspora. Believing that anti-Semitism was exacerbated by Jews' apparent disdain for their own culture (as exhibited by wholesale assimilation), many Zionists claimed that the Zionist self-affirmation of Jewish national identity would win the respect of anti-Semites and thus secure Jews' existence in Germany.

Despite the relatively small percentage of German Zionists in the international movement, German culture and especially German language played important roles in shaping the movement during its early decades (see Berkowitz and Poppel for discussions of the "Germanic tenor" of early Zionist congresses and Zionist borrowings from both the form and content of German nationalism). Michael Berkowitz observes that, despite Zionists' success in propagating the myth that the Hebrew language was the most effective cohesive force in the Zionist movement, the German language predominated in early decades of the World Zionist Organization, serving as the language of the Zionist congresses and the official monthly, *Die Welt* (1897–1914). Although Hebrew was acknowledged in principle as the official language of the Zionist movement by 1913, it faced opposition from various camps (including orthodox Jewry and defenders of Yiddish culture). Because of the controversy surrounding the adoption of Hebrew (as well as many Zionists' inability to communicate in Hebrew), German, which was largely accessible not only to native German-speakers but also to Yiddish-speaking Eastern European Jews, remained the primary language of early Zionist discourse. German prevailed over Yiddish for several reasons. While German and Yiddish were for the most part mutually comprehensible, many assimilated Western European Jews harbored prejudice against Yiddish as a corrupt "jargon," the product of the ghetto and of Diaspora persecution, which they viewed as unsuitable for the Zionist project. In addition, the world press and established governments would have likely ignored a movement that conversed in Yiddish or Hebrew (Berkowitz 1993; Berkowitz 1997).

The first decades of the Zionist movement produced an extensive body of German-language Zionist writing. In hopes of promoting a secular, Jewish national culture, Martin Buber and several colleagues founded in 1902 the Jüdischer Verlag, which published literature with Zionist themes and German translations of Hebrew and Yiddish writers. The Schocken Verlag, founded in 1931, had a similar mission. Zionist writing in German included pamphlets and treatises, novels (Herzl's *Altneuland*, 1902; Jaffe's *Ahasver*, 1900; Gronemann's *Tohuwabohu*, 1900; Sommer's *Gideon's Auszug*, 1912; and Brod's *Zauberreich der Liebe*, 1928), adventure stories (Böhm, Gelbart, and Simon), novellas (Sturmann's *Abschied von Europa*, 1928), dramas, poetry, fairy tales (Strauß, Loewe, Abeles, and Neumann), fables, scholarly and scientific studies concerning Jewish life in the Diaspora or Palestine, and journalism. In addition to *Die Welt*, the most notable German language Zionist periodicals were the German Zionist Federation's weekly, the *Jüdische Rundschau* (1902–38); the Viennese daily *Wiener Morgenzeitung* (1918–27); the satirical magazine *Shlemiel*; Martin Buber's highly influential journal *Der Jude* (1916–24) and Leo Winz's *Ost und West* (1901–23), which, although they were not official Zionist organs, featured numerous Zionist contributors; and the bimonthly *Neue Jüdische Monatshefte* (1916–20), an unprecedented joint venture of Zionists and Liberal Jews. Conversely, the emergence of the Zionist movement prompted numerous anti-Zionist rebuttals from German Jews who likewise reexamined issues of Jewish-German identity in the German-Jewish press, scholarly writing, and literary works.

ELIZABETH LOENTZ

See also Theodor Herzl; Jewish Culture and Literature

Further Reading

Berkowitz, Michael, *Zionist Culture and West European Jewry before the First World War*, Cambridge and New York: Cambridge University Press, 1993
——, "Publication of Theodor Herzl's 'Der Judenstaat' Begins a Diverse Tradition in Central Europe of Zionist Writing in German," in *Yale Companion to Jewish Writing and Thought in German Culture, 1096–1996*, edited by Sander L. Gilman and Jack Zipes, New Haven, Connecticut, and London: Yale University Press, 1997
Brude-Firnau, Gisela, "The Author, Feuilletonist, and Renowned Foreign Correspondent Theodor Herzl Turns toward Zionism and

Writes the Manifesto 'The Jewish State,'" in *Yale Companion to Jewish Writing and Thought in German Culture, 1096–1996,* edited by Sander L. Gilman and Jack Zipes, New Haven, Connecticut, and London: Yale University Press, 1997

Hadomi, Leah, "Jüdische Identität und der zionistische Utopieroman," *Bulletin des Leo Baeck Instituts* 86 (1990)

Heuer, Renate, and Ralph-Rainer Wuthenow, editors, *Antisemitismus, Zionismus, Antizionismus, 1850–1940,* Frankfurt and New York: Campus, 1997

Laqueur, Walter, *A History of Zionism,* New York: Holt, Rinehart, and Winston, London: Weidenfeld and Nicolson, 1972; revised edition, New York: Schocken Books, 1989

Poppel, Stephen M., *Zionism in Germany, 1897–1933: The Shaping of a Jewish Identity,* Philadelphia, Pennsylvania: Jewish Publication Society of America, 1977

Reinharz, Jehuda, editor, *Dokumente zur Geschichte des deutschen Zionismus, 1882–1933,* Tübingen: Mohr, 1981

Robertson, Ritchie, "Nationalism and Modernity: German-Jewish Writers and the Zionist Movement," in *Visions and Blueprints: Avant-Garde Culture and Radical Politics in Early Twentieth-Century Europe,* edited by Edward Timms and Peter Collier, Manchester: Manchester University Press, and New York: St. Martin's Press, 1988

Shedletzky, Itta, "Im Spannungsfeld Heine-Kafka: Deutsch-jüdische Belletristik und Literaturdiskussion zwischen Emanzipation, Assimilation und Zonismus," *Bulletin des Leo Baeck Instituts* 75 (1986)

Vital, David, *The Origins of Zionism,* Oxford: Clarendon Press, 1975

———, *Zionism: The Formative Years,* New York: Oxford University Press, and Oxford: Clarendon Press, 1982

———, *Zionism: The Crucial Phase,* New York: Oxford University Press, and Oxford: Clarendon Press, 1987

Yehuda, Eloni, *Zionismus in Deutschland: Von den Anfängen bis 1914,* Gerlingen: Bleicher, 1987

Zurich

Ever since its founding in pre-Roman times, Zurich has been a center of trade and exchange, a marketplace of goods and ideas, and, later, a haven for political refugees and dissidents from all over Europe. The stronghold of Swiss-German Protestantism since the Reformation and, in the past two centuries, Switzerland's most important industrial city and its center of banking, Zurich has also played a significant role as a place of literary encounters and literary production; moreover, it has served as the home or workplace of some of the most prolific authors in German literature.

The 14th-century *Codex Manesse,* a magnificently illustrated collection of medieval poems by various German-speaking troubadours, marks the beginning of Zurich's role as a center of learning and literary ambition. The collection, named for its sponsors Johannes (d. 1296) and Rüdiger (d. 1304) Manesse, two Zurich noblemen, was rediscovered and published by Johann Jakob Bodmer (1698–1783), a Zurich professor who became the soul of literary Zurich during the rococo period.

Together with his colleague Johann Jakob Breitinger (1701–76), Bodmer published *Critische Dichtkunst* (1740; Critical Poetics), a book directed against Johann Christoph Gottsched of Leipzig, who represented a conservative and dogmatic school of poetics. As a consequence, Bodmer became the champion of the anti-Gottsched writers of Germany, among them Christoph Martin Wieland, Friedrich Gottlieb Klopstock, and the young Goethe, who visited him in Zurich. Goethe referred to Bodmer mockingly as a "mother hen for talents" and a "midwife of geniuses." He himself was less influenced by Bodmer than by Johann Caspar Lavater (1741–1801), a Zurich theologian whose *Physiognomische Fragmente zur Beförderung der Menschenkenntnis und Menschenliebe* (1775–78; Physiognomic Fragments for the Knowledge and the Love of Man) made him world famous. Johann Heinrich Pestalozzi (1746–1827), also a citizen of Zurich and the author of the best-selling novel *Lienhard und Gertrud* (1781), became, together with Jean-Jacques Rousseau,

one of the great educators of modern Europe. With so many illustrious writers about town, the German poet Ewald von Kleist gave the following assessment in 1752: "In the large city of Berlin you can barely meet 3 to 4 people of genius and taste. In small Zurich you will meet more than 20 to 40 of them."

During the 19th century, Zurich prospered and grew. Its solid republican reputation made it a favorite haven for many refugees of the failed German revolutions of 1830 and 1848. Among them was Gottfried Semper, who built the first federal Swiss university, the Federal Institute of Technology, in Zurich. The University of Zurich was founded in 1833, and many of its first generation of professors were German refugees, among them the eminent German playwright Georg Büchner, who died in Zurich in 1837. The University of Zurich was the first European university to admit women (1864).

Two of Switzerland's most important novelists, Gottfried Keller (1819–90) and Conrad Ferdinand Meyer (1825–98), lived in Zurich, as did Johanna Spyri (1827–1901), the world-renowned author of *Heidi* (1881). There was also a colorful Zurich circle of literati, refugees, artists, and musicians, among them Richard Wagner (1813–83), who wrote some of his most important operas in Swiss exile while unsuccessfully trying to raise funds for their production among the city's wealthy industrialists. This circle met regularly in the home of the industrialist Otto Wesendonck and added luster to Zurich's reputation as an open, liberal, and worldly city. When Bismarck prohibited socialism in Germany in 1878, a new wave of refugees, among them Gerhart Hauptmann and August Bebel, settled in Zurich. The city became known as "the secret capital of socialism."

This reputation continued until World War I, when Zurich, once again, attracted many German refugees. This time they were mostly pacifists, among them Hermann Hesse (1877–1962; 1946, Nobel Prize in literature), who eventually became a Swiss citizen and who used Zurich as a backdrop for his novel *Der Steppenwolf* (1927). Another refugee, Vladimir Ilich Ulyanov

(Lenin), started the Bolshevik Revolution by leaving for St. Petersburg in 1917. A few steps away from Lenin's apartment was the Cabaret Voltaire, where in 1916 German and Austrian refugee writers (including Hugo Ball, Tristan Tzara, Hans Arp, Richard Huelsenbeck, and Emmy Hennings) started the Dada movement, the first avant-garde experiment in 20th-century German literature.

Hitler's rise to power prompted another wave of immigration from Germany and Austria to Zurich. This time, however, the restrictive asylum policy of the Swiss government made it increasingly difficult for Jewish and leftist refugees to live and find work in Zurich. New immigrant writers realized that the political climate had changed. Those who had the means moved to the United States (including Thomas Mann, Bertolt Brecht, Carl Zuckmayer, and Franz Werfel), France (Ödön von Horváth), or Palestine (Else Lasker-Schüler). Others such as Robert Musil and Georg Kaiser spent the last years of their lives wandering about Switzerland. At about the same time, James Joyce, too, lived in Zurich, where he died in 1941. After the war, Thomas Mann chose to return to the region and made Kilchberg on Lake Zurich his last home. The Thomas Mann Archives are located in the Johann Jakob Bodmer House in Zurich.

As one of the last free German-speaking theaters in Europe, the Zurich Schuspielhaus became a place of hope and opportunity for exiled writers. Brecht, now in his Californian exile, honored the antifascist reputation of the Schauspielhaus by having several of his most important plays (*Mother Courage* [1941], *Galileo* [1943], and *The Good Woman of Sezuan* [1943]) premiered on that stage. It also produced the first postwar plays of the Swiss authors Max Frisch (1911–91) and Friedrich Dürrenmatt (1921–90). When, in 1966, Frisch attacked professor Emil Staiger for his invective against contemporary literature, Zurich was, as in Bodmer's days, once again the center of intellectual controversy.

While there are numerous writers in Zurich—either established or promising—none of them has, to this date, filled the vacuum created by Max Frisch's death in 1991.

ROLF KIESER

See also Switzerland

Further Reading

Bolliger, Hans, et al., editors, *Dada in Zürich,* Zurich: Kunsthaus Zurich, 1985

Craig, Gordon Alexander, *The Triumph of Liberalism: Zurich in the Golden Age, 1830–1869,* New York: Scribner, 1988; London: Collier Macmillan, 1990

Humm, Rudolf Jakob, *Bei uns im Rabenhaus: Literaten, Leute, und Literatur im Zürich der Dreissigerjahre,* Zurich: Fretz und Wasmuth, 1975

Huonker, Gustav, *Literaturszene Zürich: Menschen, Geschichten, und Bilder 1914 bis 1945,* Zurich: Unionsverlag, 1985

Kieser, Rolf, *Erzwungene Symbiose: Thomas Mann, Robert Musil, Georg Kaiser, und Bertolt Brecht im Schweizer Exil,* Bern: Haupt, 1984

Mittenzwei, Werner, *Das Zürcher Schauspielhaus: 1933–1945 oder Die letzte Chance,* Berlin: Henschelverlag, 1979

Pezold, Klaus, and Hannelore Prosche, editors, *Geschichte der deutschsprachigen Schweizer Literatur im 20. Jahrhundert,* Berlin: Volk und Wissen, 1991

Schumacher, Hans, editor, *Zürich: Eine Stadt im Spiegel der Literatur,* Zurich: Artemis, 1970

Wehrli, Max, editor, *Das geistige Zürich im achtzehnten Jahrhundert,* Zurich: Atlantis-Verlag, 1943

Widmer, Sigmund, and Fritz Hofer, *Zürich: Eine Kulturgeschichte,* 13 vols., Zurich and Munich: Artemis-Verlag, 1975–85

Arnold Zweig 1887–1968

Arguably among the most prolific German-Jewish writers of the 20th century, and one of the great historical novelists, Arnold Zweig achieved his first share of fame during the Weimar Republic. He had already begun publishing work as a young student, and in 1915, shortly before enlisting in the German army, he received the Kleist Prize for his tragic play *Ritualmord in Ungarn* (1914; Ritual Murder in Hungary), a critical treatment of a 19th-century Jewish blood libel case. His much-acclaimed *Der Streit um den Sergeanten Grischa* (1927; *The Case of Sergeant Grischa*), a gripping antiwar novel that presents a brutal case of exploitation and victimization at the hands of the war machinery, brought Zweig international recognition and established him as a leading figure in modern German letters.

It was in the interwar years that Zweig launched a full-time career as an author. As he enthusiastically announced to his friend Helene Weyl (née Joseph) in 1919, "I want to write! Novels and tragedies shall emerge!" Even though it would be several years before he fulfilled his wish, he spent the early part of the Weimar Republic actively engaged in literary and cultural debate. He contributed essays to the German and German-Jewish press, most notably to Siegfried Jacobson's *Die Weltbühne* and to Martin Buber's *Der Jude,* and in 1924, he became an editor at the *Jüdische Rundschau,* the Berlin-based Zionist newspaper.

His brand of Zionism, which he had initially developed under the tutelage of Buber, owed much to German utopian and socialist thought. In addition to his journalistic contributions, Zweig also published his views on Zionism in two monographs from the 1920s, both written in collaboration with Jewish artist Hermann Struck: *Das ostjüdische Antlitz* (1920; The Face of Eastern Jewry) and *Das neue Kanaan: Eine Untersuchung über Land und Geist* (1925; The New Canaan: An Investigation of Land and Spirit). Suggestive perhaps of Zweig's later *aliyah* (migration) to Palestine in 1933, these texts explore the social and cultural potential of self-contained Jewish life in the East European shtetl and the Holy Land, respectively.

Around the same time that Zweig was most intensely preoccupied with Jewish concerns, he also began to develop a sustained interest in the work of Sigmund Freud. In 1927 he published his *Caliban; oder, Politik und Leidenschaft* (Caliban; or, Politics and Emotion), in which he applies Freudian concepts to the study of anti-Semitism, and he also initiated a lively correspondence with the "father" of psychoanalysis—subsequently published in German and English—that would last over a decade. (Zweig visited Freud in London in 1939, on his return trip from the United States to Palestine.)

With the enormous success of his 1927 *Grischa* novel, the English translation of which made an enduring mark in the United States (25,000 copies were sold in the first print run alone), Zweig decided to produce a Grischa cycle. Initially dubbed the "Trilogie des Übergangs" (Transition Trilogy), the cycle was to be anchored by the *Grischa* novel at the center and surrounded two additional novels: *Erziehung vor Verdun* (1935; *Education before Verdun*), which deals with the tale's prehistory, and *Einsetzung eines Königs* (1937; *The Crowning of a King*), which proceeds with the story. Instead of adhering to his original outline, however, Zweig first wrote *Junge Frau von 1914* (1931; *Young Woman of 1914*), a novel that chronicles the early war years and the individual saga that leads up to the narrative in *Education before Verdun* and the other two novels. He then went on to complete his only novel set in Palestine, *De Vriendt kehrt heim* (1932; *De Vriendt Goes Home*), a work that he adapted from the controversial case of an orthodox and outspoken anti-Zionist Dutch Jew living in 1920s Palestine.

None of Zweig's later historical novels would enjoy the reception of *Grischa*. Although Zweig remained a prolific writer while living in Palestine, the fame he was granted in Weimar Germany continued to dwindle until his repatriation to the German Democratic Republic in 1948, just two months after the founding of the state of Israel. The auspicious circumstances under which he emigrated to East Berlin, as an official state author whose novels' moral and political didacticism might assist in rebuilding a socialist republic, revived the spirit of the formerly disillusioned émigré. He played a vital role in East German politics, first in the Kulturbund zur demokratischen Erneuerung Deutschlands (Cultural Alliance for the Democratic Renewal of Germany) and then, as representative of cultural affairs, in the Volkskammer (East German parliament); he was also named president of the (East) German Academy of Arts. Zweig's literary production, although less vigorous during the first years of his return, eventually came back to the familiar terrain of the war novel as he had conceived of it in his Grischa cycle. He published several works within this context, among them *Feuerpause* (1954; Cease-Fire) and *Die Zeit ist reif* (1957; The Time is Ripe), which, together with the previous four war novels, were supposed to form a multivolume cycle entitled "Der große Krieg der weißen Männer" (The Great War of the White Men).

During the final decade of his life in East Germany, Zweig witnessed the publication of his 16-volume collected works; throughout East Germany, his work was lauded with distinguished prizes and awards, and he was given honorary degrees and titles. The celebration, however, did not extend beyond the Berlin Wall, where Zweig's postwar reception was nominal at best. The same man whom Lion Feuchtwanger—an eminent novelist and a contemporary of Zweig's—had pronounced "one of the few great storytellers among the Germans" did not figure prominently in the literary pantheon of postwar West Germany.

In 1967, in the wake of the Six-Day War in Israel and just a year before his death, Zweig found himself the target of the conservative, Axel Springer–dominated West German press. In what came to be known as the "Springer affair," Zweig was accused of having written to friends in Israel of his growing antagonism toward the politics of the GDR. Zweig publicly renounced the West German slander, declaring his allegiance to the socialist state; at the same time, he refused to sign a statement issued by East German intellectuals condemning Israel's assault in the Arab-Israeli war. The central ideologies with which Zweig had grappled most of his adult life (i.e., Zionism, pacifism, and socialism), even if often at odds with each other, would remain with him until the end.

NOAH ISENBERG

See also War Novels

Biography

Born in Glogau, 10 November 1887. Studied German literature, modern languages, philosophy, history, psychology, art history, and economics in Breslau, Munich, Berlin, Göttingen, Rostock, and Tübingen; editor for the *Jüdische Rundschau;* emigrated to Palestine, 1933; contributor to numerous emigré magazines; co-editor of *Orient,* Haifa; returned to Berlin, 1948; president of the East-Berlin Academy of the Arts, 1950–53. Died in 1968.

Selected Works

Plays

Abigail und Nabal, 1912
Ritualmord in Ungarn, 1914
Die Umkehr der Abtrünnigen, 1925
Laubheu und keine Bleibe, 1930
Bonaparte in Jaffa, 1939

Novels

Der Streit um den Sergeanten Grischa, 1927; as *The Case of Sergeant Grischa,* translated by Eric Sutton, 1928
Junge Frau von 1914, 1931; as *Young Woman of 1914,* translated by Eric Sutton, 1932
De Vriendt kehrt heim, 1932
Erziehung vor Verdun, 1935; as *Education before Verdun,* translated by Eric Sutton, 1936
Einsetzung eines Königs, 1937; as *The Crowning of a King,* translated by Eric Sutton, 1938
Versunkene Tage, 1938
Das Beil von Wandsbeck, 1947
Die Feuerpause, 1954
Die Zeit ist reif, 1957

Novellas and Shorter Prose

Vorfrühling, 1909
Aufzeichnungen über eine Familie Klopfer, 1911
Geschichtenbuch, 1916
Die Bestie, 1919
Drei Erzählungen, 1920
Das zweite Geschichtenbuch, 1920
Söhne, 1923
Gerufene Schatten, 1923

Frühe Fährten, 1925
Regenbogen, 1925
Pont und Anna, 1928
Knaben und Männer, 1931
Mädchen und Frauen, 1931
Spielzeug der Zeit, 1933
Ein starker Esser, 1948
Allerleirauch, 1949
Stufen, 1949
Abschied vom Frieden, 1949
Über den Nebeln, 1950
Der Elfenbeinfächer, 1952

Essays
Das ostjüdische Antlitz, 1920
Lessing, Kleist, Büchner, 1925
Das neue Kanaan: Eine Untersuchung über Land und Geist, 1925
Brennendes Bilderbuch, 1926
Juden auf der deutschen Bühne, 1927
Caliban; oder, Politik und Leidenschaft, 1927
Herkunft und Zukunft, 1929
Bilanz der deutschen Judenheit, 1933
Die Aufgabe des deutschen Judentums (with Lion Feuchtwanger), 1933
Baruch Spinoza, 1961

Edited Works
Soldatenspiele, 1956
Essays, 1959
Novellen 1907–1955. 2 Bände, 1961
Ausgewählte Werke in Einzelausgaben, 1957

Further Reading

Cohen, Robert, "Arnold Zweig's War Novellas of 1914 and Their Versions: Literature, Modernity, and the Demands of the Day," in *War, Violence, and the Modern Condition*, edited by Bernd-Rüdiger Hüppauf, Berlin and New York: de Gruyter, 1997

Goldstein, Moritz, "Arnold Zweig," in *Juden in der deutschen Literatur*, edited by Gustav Krojanker, Berlin: Welt, 1922

Hermand, Jost, *Arnold Zweig: Mit Selbstzeugnissen und Bilddokumenten*, Reinbek bei Hamburg: Rowohlt, 1990

Hilscher, Eberhard, "Wiederentdeckung Arnold Zweigs? Zur Forschungssituation der achtziger Jahre," *Weimarer Beiträge* 36, no. 3 (1990)

Isenberg, Noah, *Between Redemption and Doom: The Strains of German-Jewish Modernism*, Lincoln: University of Nebraska Press, 1999

Midgley, David R., *Arnold Zweig: Zu Werk und Wandlung 1927–1948*, Konigstein: Athenäum, 1980

Midgley, David R., et al., editors, *Arnold Zweig: Poetik, Judentum, und Politik*, Bern and New York: Lang, 1989

Müller, Hans-Harald, "Arnold Zweig und der Zionismus," in *Text und Kritik* 104 (1989)

Salamon, George, *Arnold Zweig*, New York: Twayne, 1975

Weissberg, Liliane, "Arnold Zweig," in *German Fiction Writers, 1885–1913*, edited by James N. Hardin, Detroit, Michigan: Gale Research, 1988

Wenzel, Georg, editor, *Arnold Zweig 1887–1968: Werk und Leben in Dokumenten und Bildern*, Berlin: Aufbau-Verlag, 1978

White, Ray Lewis, *Arnold Zweig in the USA*, New York: Lang, 1986

Wiznitzer, Manuel, *Arnold Zweig: Das Leben eines deutsch-jüdischen Schriftstellers*, Königstein: Athenäum, 1983

Stefan Zweig 1881–1942

From the 1920s until the early 1930s, when the National Socialists banned his books, Stefan Zweig was not only one of the most popular authors in the German-speaking countries but also one of the most widely read and translated authors in the world. Today, Zweig's books are rarely read in schools or universities, and his works have attracted only scant attention by literary critics.

Born into an affluent and assimilated Jewish family in Vienna in 1881, Zweig's youth and early artistic influences were molded by the Young Vienna Group and fin de siècle literary circles. In his early poetry, collected in *Silberne Saiten* (1901; Strings of Silver) and *Die frühen Kränze* (1906; The Early Wreaths), Zweig combined Viennese poetic Impressionism with neo-Romanticism and French symbolism. The poetic style has been compared to that of Rainer Maria Rilke and Hugo von Hofmannsthal, both of whom Zweig admired greatly. After these early volumes of poetry, which he himself considered immature, Zweig primarily devoted himself to other literary genres—essays, short stories, legends, drama, and literary biographies.

Although Zweig's early works earned him a reputation as a young poetic talent, it was as the author of short fiction that he gained a wider readership. His collection of novellas, *Erstes Erlebnis: Vier Geschichten aus Kinderland* (1911; First Experience: Four Stories from the Land of Childhood), was inspired by dis-

cussions with the Swedish educator Ellen Key, to whom the collection is dedicated. These novellas explore the problems of adolescence, fear of sexuality, and adults' double standards. Using his knowledge of Freudian psychology, Zweig penetrated the unconscious and complex inner workings of his characters. In the collection *Amok* (1922), which contains two of his most famous novellas, *Der Amokläufer* (Amok) and *Brief einer Unbekannten* (Letter from an Unknown Woman), he investigates the minds of adults rather than children. Similarly, however, it is the conflict between inner psychological workings and societal norms that is at the center of these works.

Zweig's fascinating observations of the human psyche are perhaps best depicted in his last novella, the masterful *Schachnovelle* (1943; The Royal Game), written during the final four months of his life. The narrator of *The Royal Game* is sailing on a ship from New York to Buenos Aires. Also on the ship is the world chess champion, an unkempt, almost illiterate robot who has no talent other than a cool calculating mind. An additional passenger is Dr. B., a cultivated, well-educated Austrian émigré, who tells his story to the narrator. As a banker, he and his family had managed the riches of the Austrian elite, the royal family, and the Church. When Hitler took over Austria, Dr. B. was arrested by the gestapo and held prisoner in a hotel room. During his imprisonment, Dr. B. managed to steal a chess manual containing 150 tournament chess games. To combat the monotony, he learned how to play the games in his mind, and when he ran out of games, he invented new games by dividing his mind into two players trying to defeat each other. The resulting mental breakdown led to his release, and he was able to emigrate. Now on the ship, he agrees to play the chess champion and wins the first game. Breaking his own promise not to play more than one game, he then accepts the challenge of another game. During the second game, he approaches a new mental breakdown and decides to break off the game, never to touch a chess board again.

In this intriguing novella, Zweig depicts the confrontation between the fascist minds of the gestapo and the world chess master on the one hand and the humanist, old Austrian mind of Dr. B. on the other. In this battle of the minds, Dr. B. successfully defeats his tormentors at first, but he ultimately surrenders and withdraws. *The Royal Game* has been considered one of Zweig's most successful works. While strictly following the genre-specific structure of the classic novella, he reinvents the form by using the contemporary political situation as a backdrop and by depicting the intellectual battle that must be won in order to defeat fascism.

In the period leading up to World War I, Zweig not only dedicated himself to his own literary works but also translated and promoted foreign authors, above all, the Belgian poet Emile Verhaeren. Later, his translations of the French poet Romain Rolland became best-sellers in Germany. Zweig saw his furtherance of other European authors as fostering cross-cultural understanding, something that he hoped would in turn lead to the political unification of Europe. World War I crushed all such hopes and dreams. The division of Europe into a brutal battlefield deepened his pacifism, which would stay with him even in the face of Hitler's war preparation. Even then, he never let his pacifism develop into political agitation or activism. As a humanist, he had a deep love for and belief in human reason. Only through his literary work did he think he could influence the historical situation. This is illustrated by his drama *Jeremias* (1917; *Jeremiah*). Conceived during a journey he made as a war correspondent for the Austrian war archives, it was the first drama in Germany or Austria that had an openly antiwar message. Censored in Germany and Austria, it was first performed in Zurich in 1918 and was an immediate success.

Apart from *Jeremiah* and the comedy *Volpone* (1926), Zweig's most well-known dramatic work is the libretto for Richard Strauss' opera *Die schweigsame Frau* (1935; *The Silent Woman*). The libretto is less known for its content than for the controversy it stirred in Nazi Germany. Strauss was one of the few leading musicians to work closely with the Hitler regime, but, at the same time, he withstood pressure to remove Zweig's text. Hitler himself had to make the decision to allow the premiere to take place.

Zweig's popularity rested above all on his historical biographies. In the 1920s and 1930s, the historical biography was an immensely popular genre. Zweig's biographies include works on historical and literary figures ranging from Magellan, Mary Stuart, and Calvin to Freud and Dostoevsky. The biographies are all written from a humanist perspective. Defying all notions of determinism, they portray individuals who have the freedom to choose, and it is because of the choices they make that historical development takes place. In their structure, the biographies combine the storytelling of a novella and the dramatic action of a play. Even though Zweig spent considerable time researching different historical circumstances, it is not the objective reality that takes center stage; it is the subjective decisions of the actors.

Zweig's most popular work in this genre was *Sternstunden der Menschheit* (*The Tide of Fortune*). The 1927 edition contained five historical miniatures and the 1943 edition an additional seven. For Zweig, history itself is the greatest poet and storyteller of all, and in the miniatures he attempts to portray short but decisive moments in human history, including Scott's race to be the first to reach the South Pole, Lenin's return to Russia, and the battle of Waterloo. In the miniatures, the reader follows the thought processes of the leading character as he approaches the formidable task in front of him. It is the protagonist's ability to live up to the challenge, or his failure to do so, that becomes the deciding moment of human history. In this sense, the biographies are didactic. They contain the message that individuals, even insignificant individuals, can make a mark in history. In other miniatures, Zweig expands on his investigations of the human mind, exploring the creative moments of great geniuses as they conceive masterpieces of creative works, such as Goethe's writing of *Die Marienbader Elegie* or Handel's composing of the *Messiah*.

In his historical biography of Erasmus of Rotterdam, Zweig's didactic approach goes a step further, as he metaphorically brings in the contemporary political situation. Written in 1934, the story of Erasmus has also been considered a veiled self-portrait. In several letters, Zweig describes himself as being in the same predicament as Erasmus. Both are trying to cling to a humanist ideal in a world of increasing fanaticism and hate. In the face of overwhelming opposition, Erasmus suffers temporary defeat, but in the long course of history, according to Zweig, his humanist approach gains sympathy. Agitation and political propaganda, however, were not methods that suited Zweig's cultured, intellectual approach. The only means that he used to work against Hitlerism was to educate the reading public. In his own mind, his Erasmus biography was such an attempt.

As Hitler extended his control over Germany and Europe, Zweig developed a deep sense of pessimism, since he believed that human reason would be destroyed for the foreseeable future. Not only had his dreams of a unified Europe based on tolerance and humanism been defeated, but even the possibility of reaching his readers in the German-speaking world had been ended. Zweig loved and cherished the German language, and the loss of his German-language readers was for him as difficult as losing his homeland, Austria. In 1942, this pessimism led to his suicide, while he was in exile in Brazil.

Since the 1981 centennial of Zweig's birth, there has been a modest increase in Zweig scholarship, primarily by U.S. Germanists. Recent research has focused on his novellas, in particular *The Royal Game*. At the same time, his role as a Jewish writer has come into focus. In this context, a reassessment of Zweig as a writer and historical personality is taking place, and in this reassessment his autobiography, *Die Welt von Gestern* (1942; *The World of Yesterday*), is taking on new significance. It is not only a document of an historical era but also of a lost central European Jewish culture.

KERSTIN GADDY

Biography

Born in Vienna, Austria, 28 November 1881. Studied philosophy and literature at the universities of Vienna and Berlin, 1900–1904; Ph.D. in philosophy, 1904; prior to 1914, extensive travel to Germany, Paris,

London, Belgium, India, the United States, Canada, and Central America; worked for the Austrian War Archives, 1914–17; antiwar efforts in Zurich, Switzerland, 1917–18; lived in Salzburg, 1919–34; traveled to Russia, 1928, Italy, 1930, 1932, France, 1932; lived in London, 1934; British citizen, 1938; left England, 1940; traveled to New York and New Haven, United States; settled in Petropolis, Brazil, 1941. Died (suicide) 22 February 1942.

Selected Works

Collections
Gesammelte Werke in Einzelbänden, edited by Knut Beck, 10 vols., 1982
Zeit und Welt: Gesammelte Aufsätze und Vorträge 1904–1940, 1946

Short Fiction
Die Liebe der Erika Ewald: Vier Novellen, 1904
Erstes Erlebnis: Vier Geschichten aus Kinderland, 1911
Brennendes Geheimnis: Novellen, 1914; as *The Burning Secret*, translated by C. and E. Paul, in *Kaleidoscope*, 1934; translated by Jill Sutcliff, in *The Royal Game and Other Stories*, 1981
Angst, 1920; as *Fear*, translated by C. and E. Paul, in *Kaleidoscope*, 1934; translated by Jill Sutcliff, in *The Royal Game and Other Stories*, 1981
Amok: Novellen einer Leidenschaft, 1922; *Die Amokläufer* translated as *Amok* by C. and E. Paul, in *Kaleidoscope*, 1934; translated by Jill Sutcliff, in *The Royal Game and Other Stories*, 1981
Der Flüchting: Episode vom Genfer Zee, 1927; as *The Runaway*, translated by C. and E. Paul, in *Kaleidoscope*, 1934
Verwirrung der Gefühle: Novellen, 1927; as *Conflicts*, translated by C. and E. Paul, 1928
Sternstunden der Menschheit, 1927; expanded edition, 1943; as *The Tide of Fortune*, translated by C. and E. Paul, 1940
Schachnovelle, 1943; as *The Royal Game*, translated by B.W. Huebsch, 1944; translated by Jill Sutcliff, in *The Royal Game and Other Stories*, 1981

Essays and Biographies
Paul Verlaine: Monographie, 1905; translated by O.F. Theis, 1913
Emile Verhaeren: Monographie, 1910; translated by Jethro Bithell, 1914
Drei Meister: Balzac, Dickens, Dostojewski, 1920; as *Three Masters*, translated by C. and E. Paul, 1930
Romain Rolland: Der Mann und das Werk, 1921; translated by C. and E. Paul, 1921
Frans Masereel: Der Mann und Bildner, 1923
Der Kampf mit dem Dämon: Hölderlin, Kleist, Nietzsche, 1925; as *The Struggle with the Daimon*, translated by C. and E. Paul, 1939
Drei Dichter ihres Lebens: Casanova, Stendahl, Tolstoi, 1928; as *Adepts in Selfportraiture*, translated by C. and E. Paul, 1928
Joseph Fouché: Bildnis eines politischen Menschen, 1929; as *Joseph Fouché: The Portrait of a Politician*, translated by C. and E. Paul, 1930
Die Heilung durch den Geist: Franz Anton Mesmer, Mary Baker-Eddy, Sigmund Freud, 1931; as *Mental Healers*, translated by C. and E. Paul, 1932
Marie Antoinette: Bildnis eines mittleren Charakters, 1932; as *Marie Antoinette, the Portrait of an Average Woman*, translated by C. and E. Paul, 1933
Triumph und Tragik des Erasmus von Rotterdam, 1934; as *Erasmus of Rotterdam*, translated by C. and E. Paul, 1934
Castellio gegen Calvin; oder, Ein Gewissen gegen die Gewalt, 1936; as *The Right to Heresy: Castellio against Calvin*, translated by C. and E. Paul, 1936
Die Welt von Gestern: Erinnerungen eines Europäers (autobiography), 1941; as *The World of Yesterday*, anonymous translation, 1943

Amerigo: Die Geschichte eines historischen Irrtums, 1944; as *Amerigo: A Comedy of Errors in History*, translated by Andrew St. James, 1942
Balzac: Der Roman seines Leben, 1946; translated by W. and D. Rose, 1946

Legends
Die Augen des ewigen Bruders, 1922; as *The Eyes of the Undying Brother*, translated by C. and E. Paul, 1934
Buchmendel, 1929; translated by C. and E. Paul, 1934
Rachel rechtet mit Gott, 1930; as *Rachel Arraigns with God*, translated by C. and E. Paul, 1934
Der begrabene Leuchter, 1936; as *The Buried Candelabrum*, translated by C. and E. Paul, 1937
Die Legende der dritten Taube, 1945; as *The Legend of the Third Dove*, translated by C. Fitzgibbon, 1955

Plays and Librettos
Tersites: Trauerspiel in drei Aufzügen (produced 1908), 1907
Das Haus am Meer: Schauspiel (produced 1912), 1912
Der verwandelte Komödiant (produced 1912), 1913
Jeremias: Eine dramatische Dichtung in 9 Bildern (produced 1918), 1917; as *Jeremiah*, translated by C. and E. Paul, 1929
Legende eines Lebens: Ein Kammarspiel in drei Aufzügen (produced 1918), 1919
Volpone: Eine komödie nach Ben Jonson (produced 1926), 1926; translated by Ruth Lagner, 1928
Qui pro quo: Komödie in drei Akten (with Alexander Lernet-Holenia under the pseudonym Clemens Neydisser) (produced 1928), 1928
Das Haus des Armen (produced 1930), 1929
Die schweigsame Frau (libretto), music by Richard Strauss (produced 1935), 1935; as *The Silent Woman*, translated by Arthur Jacobs

Poetry
Silberne Saiten, 1901
Die frühen Kränze, 1906
Die gesammelten Gedichte, 1924

Novels
Ungeduld des Herzens, 1939; as *Beware of Pity*, translated by P. and T. Blewitt, 1939

Other
Abschied von Rilke, 1927
Worte am Grabe Sigmund Freuds, 1939
Brasilien: Ein Land der Zukunft, 1941; as *Brazil: Land of the Future*, translated by Andrew St. James, 1942

Translations
Charles Baudelaire, *Gedichte in Vers und Prose*, 1902 (with Camill Hoffmann)
Paul Verlaine, *Eine Anthologie der besten Übertragungen*, 1902
Emile Verhaeren, *Ausgewählte Gedichte*, 1904
——, *Rembrandt*, 1912
Romain Rolland, *Den hingeschlachteten Völkern*, 1918
——, *Die Zeit wird kommen*, 1919

Further Reading
Gelber, Mark H., editor, *Stefan Zweig heute*, New York: Lang, 1987
Gelber, Mark, and Klaus Zelewitz, editors, *Exil und Suche nach dem Weltfrieden*, Riverside, California: Ariadne, 1995
Klawiter, Randolph J., *Stefan Zweig: A Bibliography*, Chapel Hill: University of North Carolina Press, 1965
Müller, Hartmut, *Stefan Zweig: Mit Selbstzeugnissen und Bilddokumenten*, Reinbek bei Hamburg: Rowohlt, 1988

Prater, Donald A., *European of Yesterday: A Biography of Stefan Zweig*, Oxford: Clarendon Press, 1972

Prater, Donald A., and Volker Michels, editors, *Stefan Zweig: Leben und Werk im Bild*, Frankfurt: Insel, 1981

Sonnenfeld, Marion, editor, *Stefan Zweig: The World of Yesterday's Humanist Today*, Albany: State University of New York Press, 1983

Strelka, Joseph, *Stefan Zweig: Freier Geist der Menschlichkeit*, Vienna: Österreichischer Bundesverlag, 1981

Turner, David, *Moral Values and the Human Zoo: The Novellen of Stefan Zweig*, Hull: Hull University Press, 1988

Zweig, Friderike, *Stefan Zweig*, New York: Crowell, and London: Allen, 1946

Die Welt von Gestern: Erinnerungen eines Europäers 1941

Memoirs by Stefan Zweig

Die Welt von Gestern (*The World of Yesterday*), Stefan Zweig's memoir of the period from his youth in Vienna through World War I and up to the early phase of World War II, is less of an autobiography in the traditional sense than a document of a historical period. The book lacks personal information of a more private character. His two wives are never mentioned by name, nor are his stepchildren. His relationships with other family members play no role in the book, and friends are mentioned only if they are well-known personalities. Indeed, Zweig frequently uses the plural "we" or even the impersonal "one" rather than the first person singular "I," especially in the first part of the memoir.

Despite the lack of private personal information, the reader becomes familiar with Zweig and his relationship to historical events and personalities. Zweig had originally intended to describe only the period up to 1918, but during the course of writing he changed his mind to let the memoir cover his whole life. The focus is still the early 20th century. More than half the book is dedicated to the pre-1918 period. But the world Zweig presents is not the whole world: it is one defined from his own particular perspective. Geographically, it is limited to Central Europe, especially the French- and German-speaking parts. Although he mentions his travels to India and the Americas, these continents are only of peripheral interest insofar as they relate to Zweig's own development. Only in the end of the book, when the "old" world has been destroyed by Hitlerism, does the non-European world take on significance. Zweig then pins his hopes on Latin America. Sociologically, Zweig's world is confined to the educated upper middle class, in particular the artistic and cultural elite. And the world of Stefan Zweig is limited in yet another way, for it is primarily a male society. Even though his first wife was an active feminist, Zweig never explores feminist concerns or his relationship to the feminist movement.

With these limitations in mind, the memoir is a fascinating portrait of a historical period and some of its leading actors. Zweig counted some of Europe's most famous names among his personal friends and correspondents, including Thomas Mann, Arthur Schnitzler, Sigmund Freud, Walther Rathenau, James Joyce, Maurice Ravel, Richard Strauss, Rainer Maria Rilke, Theodor Herzl, and many, many others. The remarkable ability to portray different personalities, which Zweig had demonstrated in his popular biographies, is also prominent in *The World of Yesterday*, with the only difference that here he portrays famous people who at the same time were his personal friends and acquaintances.

In the memoir, two related themes run parallel. The first concerns Zweig's relationship to his national and Jewish identities. In his ideal or idealized world, the world before 1914, neither his Austrianness nor his Jewishness meant much in themselves. For Zweig, both contributed to his Pan-European identity, an identity that transcended both nationality and religion. Austria-Hungary as a multinational, almost federal state fostered a supranational identity. Similarly, the very fact that the Jews did not have a homeland made them, in Zweig's opinion, the ideal world citizens. Wherever they were, because they had an identity that transcended borders and languages, the Jews were able to contribute on a higher level. Before Hitler and Nazism, Zweig could not sympathize with the Zionist movement even though the founder of modern Zionism and editor of the literary section of the *Neue Freie Presse,* Theodor Herzl, was the first to publish Zweig's early works. But despite Zweig's gratitude to and admiration for Herzl, he did not join the Zionist movement. Not until both his nationality and his Jewishness were threatened did he begin to understand the importance of both. When he was stripped of his Austrian nationality, he felt as if he were a nonperson. Similarly, when the Jews were being persecuted, his identification with his Jewish heritage grew stronger, and he came to accept the necessity of a Jewish state.

The other theme in his autobiography concerns Zweig's relationship to politics. This relationship appears as quite paradoxical. On the one hand, Zweig never openly engaged in political activities nor even exercised his right to vote. He took pride in the fact that he never openly agitated against Germany, even after Germany's occupation of Austria. On the other hand, he firmly believed that the individual not only can but must make an impact on historical events. For him, however, this impact could not be by traditional political methods but rather through his work as an author and private person. During World War I, he and Romain Rolland attempted to organize a European-wide movement of authors and artists for peace. Having unsuccessfully tried to win Gerhart Hauptmann, Thomas Mann, Rilke, and others for the idea, Zweig gave up the ideas of organized activities. All that remained for him was to use his pen, to express his ideas in writings that he hoped would educate his readers. During the Nazi period, he did everything in his power to help authors, artists, and other refugees from continental Europe to settle in England, the United States, Latin America, and other countries.

Zweig's paradoxical relationship to politics can also be seen in his perceptions of Hitler. In the chapter "Incipit Hitler," Zweig admits that he underestimated Hitler's importance in the beginning, thinking the Nazi storm troopers were merely rabble-rousers. At the same time, having seen up close from his home in Salzburg how the Nazis operated in Munich and Berchtesgaden, he realized that they were very well organized and backed by considerable amounts of money. Nevertheless, he was not overtly worried, somehow hoping the evil would go away. As Hitler consolidated his power in Germany, Zweig realized that Austria was going to be his next goal. If Austria fell, he predicted, all of Europe would fall into Hitler's hands. Personally, he drew his own conclusions from this insight and started to plan his exile already in the fall of 1933, when his books had been burned by the Nazis. Spending more and more time abroad, he finally left Salzburg in 1937.

Zweig's opposition to Hitler and Nazism was not only a result of Hitler's anti-Semitism and his threats against Austria. More fundamentally, the Nazi ideology of "Blut und Boden" ran counter to every tenet of Zweig's personal philosophy. Nazism was based on German nationalism and a belief in racial superiority; Zweig cherished multiculturalism and internationalism. Nazism promoted war and violence; Zweig was a pacifist. Nazism was based on fanaticism; Zweig believed in tolerance. Nazism was founded on mass psychosis; Zweig advocated human reason and individual responsibility.

Zweig never attempted a psychological portrait of Hitler, as he did with so many other personalities. Nor does he try to explain how Hitler could control the German people. But he does offer two suggestions. On the one hand, he points to the inflation of the 1920s as making the German people ripe for order and a strong leadership. On the other hand, he points to Hitler's method of behavior modification of the German masses. He explains how Hitler introduced his program in small doses to let the people get used to it little by little.

Today, *The World of Yesterday* is still available in German and English editions and is considered one of the richest books of memoirs of the period. Nevertheless, as with Zweig's other works, it has received little attention from literary critics. So far, the research has focused on Zweig's relationship to Austria and his Jewishness, but a critical evaluation of the whole work is still missing.

KERSTIN GADDY

See also Austria: Late Habsburg Literature in Vienna

Editions

First edition: *Die Welt von Gestern: Erinnerungen eines Europäers,* London: Hamilton, 1941

Critical edition: in *Gesammelte Werke in Einzelbänden,* edited by Knut Beck, Frankfurt: Fischer, 1982

Translation: *The World of Yesterday,* anonymous translation, New York: Viking Press, 1943

Further Reading

Arendt, Hannah, "Juden in der *Welt von Gestern,*" in *Sechs Essays,* Heidelberg: Schneider, 1948

Gelber, Mark H., "*Die Welt von Gestern* als Exilliteratur," in *Exil und Suche nach dem Weltfrieden,* edited by Mark Gelber and Klaus Zelewitz, Riverside, California: Ariadne, 1995

Iggers, George, "Some Introductory Observations on Stefan Zweig's *World of Yesterday,*" in *Stefan Zweig: The World of Yesterday's Humanist Today,* edited by Marion Sonnenfeld, Albany: State University of New York Press, 1983

Iggers, Wilma, "The World of Yesterday in the View of an Intellectual Historian," in *Stefan Zweig: The World of Yesterday's Humanist Today,* edited by Marion Sonnenfeld, Albany: State University of New York Press, 1983

Sommer, Fred, "Nostalgia, Francophilia, and the Agony of Hitlerism: The Autobiographies of Heinrich Mann and Stefan Zweig," *New German Studies* 16, no. 2 (1990–91)

Wiedel, Birgit, "Stefan Zweigs *Die Welt von Gestern: Erinnerungen eines Europäers,*" in *Politische Betrachtungen einer "Welt von Gestern": Öffentliche Sprache in der Zwischenkriegszeit,* edited by Helmut Bartenstein, Stuttgart: Heinz, 1995

Zweig, Friderike, *Stefan Zweig wie ich ihn erlebte,* Stockholm and New York: Neuer Verlag, 1947

INDEXES

TITLE INDEX

The names in parentheses given after the titles listed below will direct readers to the entry in which additional publication information is given. The dates given are those of first publication. Revised titles and English-language translations, if different from the original, are listed with their appropriate dates. Titles that appear in **bold** are the subjects of individual essays.

In Goethes Hand (M. Walser), 1982
In Kupfer, auf Stein (Grass), 1986
In laudem gloriose virginis Mariae
    multorumque sanctorum varii generis
    carmina (Brant), 1494
In Phanta's Schloß (Morgenstern), 1895
In Probepackung (Kästner), 1957
In Sachen de Sade (Drach), 1974
In Search of Wagner (Adorno), 1981
In Sight of Chaos (Hesse), 1923
In St. Jürgen (Storm), 1867
In Stahlgewittern (Jünger), 1920
In the Cold (Bernhard), 1985
In the Desert (May), 1955
In the Egg and Other Poems (Grass), 1977
In the Jungle of Cities (Brecht), 1957
In the Land of Cockaigne (H. Mann), 1929
In the Penal Settlement (Kafka), 1949
In the Play of Summer Breezes (Schnitzler),
    1996
In These Great Times (Kraus), 1976
Inaugural Dissertation of 1770 (Kant), 1894
Incident at Twilight (Dürrematt), 1968
Inclusion of the Other (Habermas), 1998
Incognito (Einstein), 1901
Inconnue de la Seine. Le Diner de 500 Francs
    (C. Goll), 1944
Incredible Borgia (Klabund), 1929
Indian Summer (Stifter), 1985
Indication of the Cause (Bernhard), 1985
Indipohdi (Hauptmann), 1920
Indizienbeweise (Fried), 1966
Industrialisierung des Bewußtseins (Kluge),
    1985
Infantile Cerebral Paralysis (Freud), 1968
Infantile Cerebrallähmung (Freud), 1897
Ingrid Babendererde (Johnson), 1985
Inhibition, Symptom, and Anxiety (Freud),
    1927
Inklusive (Kroetz), 1972
Inmarypraise (Grass), 1974
Innenwelt der Aussenwelt der Innenwelt
    (Handke), 1969
Inner Man (M. Walser), 1984
Innerworld of the Outerworld of the
    Innerworld (Handke), 1974
Ins Leere gesprochen (Loos), 1921
Ins Ungebundene gehet eine Sehnsucht (Wolf),
    1985
Insel der grossen Mutter (Hauptmann), 1924
Inselfrühling (Jünger), 1948
Interpretation of Dreams (Freud), 1913
Intrigue and Love (Schiller), 1971
Introduction to Metaphysics (Heidegger),
    1959
Introduction to the Human Sciences (Dilthey),
    1988
Introduction to the Sociology of Music
    (Adorno), 1976
Introductory Lectures on Psycho-Analysis
    (Freud), 1922
Invertar (Ausländer), 1972
Investigation (Weiss), 1966
Invisible Lodge (Jean Paul), 1883
Ion (A.W. Schlegel), 1803
Iphigenia in Tauris (Goethe), 1793

Iphigenie (Goethe), 1787
Iphigenie in Freiheit (Braun), 1992
Irene (Klabund), 1918
Irenomachia (Rist), 1630
Iris (Mörike), 1839
Irisches Tagebuch, 1957
Irish Journal (Böll), 1967
Irmenstrasse und Irmensäule (J. Grimm), 1815
Ironhand (Goethe), 1965
Ironie vom Glück (Drach), 1994
Irreführung der Behörden (Becker), 1973
Irrstern (Kirsch), 1986
Irrtum und Leidenschaft (Hasenclever), 1969
Irrungen, Wirrungen (Fontane), 1888
Isabella von Ägypten (Arnim), 1812
Island of the Great Mother (Hauptmann),
    1925
Ist kein Papagei (Schami), 1994
Italian Journey (Goethe), 1962
Italian Travel Sketches (Heine), 1892
Italians at Home (Lewald), 1848
Italiener (Bernhard), 1971
Italienische Nacht (Horváth), 1930
Italienische Reise (Goethe), 1816–17
Italienische Reise 1897 (Hauptmann), 1976
Italienisches Bilderbuch (Lewald), 1847
Ithaka (Benn), 1914
Ithaka (Strauß), 1996
Iwein (Hartmann von Aue), 1827
Izanagi und Izanami (Fried), 1960

Ja (Bernhard), 1978
Jaákobs Traum (Beer-Hoffmann), 1918
Jacob the Liar (Becker), 1975
Jacob's Dream (Beer-Hoffmann), 1946
Jacobowsky und der Oberst (Werfel), 1944
Jacques Offenbach und das Paris seiner Zeit
    (Kracauer), 1937
J'adore ce qui me brûle (Frisch), 1943
Jagd (M. Walser), 1988
Jagd auf Außenseiter. Jagdszenen aus
    Niederbayern (Sperr), 1971
Jagd nach Liebe (H. Mann), 1903
Jagdgesellschaft (Bernhard), 1974
Jäger am Rand der Nacht (Reinshagen), 1993
Jäger des Spott (S. Lenz), 1958
Jahr der Kirche (Hahn-Hahn), 1854
Jahr der Seele (George), 1897
Jahre der Okkupation (Jünger), 1958
Jahrestage (Johnson), 1970–83
Jahrmarktsfest zu Plundersweilern (Goethe),
    1790
Jakob der Lügner (Becker), 1969
Jakob Littners Aufzeichnungen aus einem
    Erdloch (Koeppen), 1992
Jakob the Liar (Becker), 1990
Jakob und Joseph (Bodmer), 1751
Jakob und Rachel (Bodmer), 1752
Jakob von Gunten (R. Walser), 1909
Jakobs, des Handwerksgesellen, Wanderungen
    durch die Schweiz (Gotthelf), 1846–48
Jakobsleiter (Schoenberg), 1917
Jakub Brandl (Moníková), 1997
Jargon der Eigentlichkeit (Adorno), 1965
Jargon of Authenticity (Adorno), 1973

Jasager/Der Neinsager (Brecht), 1931
Jean Pauls biographische Belustigungen unter
    der Gehirnschale einer Riesin (Jean Paul),
    1796
Jean Pauls Briefe und bevorstehender
    Lebenslauf (Jean Paul), 1799
Jean sans terre (Y. Goll), 1958
Jeanne d'Arc deux fois brulée (C. Goll), 1961
Jeder stirbt für sich allein (Fallada), 1947
Jedermann (Hofmannsthal), 1911
Jedermanns Geschichten (Graf), 1988
Jedes Opfer tötet seinen Mörder (C. Goll),
    1977
Jeffers-Akt I and II (Strauß), 1998
Jefta und seine Tochter (Feuchtwanger), 1957
Jenatsch (Meyer), 1876
Jenny (Lewald), 1843
Jenny Treibel (Fontane), 1976
Jenseit des Tweed (Fontane), 1860
Jenseits (Hasenclever), 1920
Jenseits der Berge (Hahn-Hahn), 1840
Jenseits der Liebe (M. Walser), 1976
Jenseits der Nation (Heiner Müller), 1991
Jenseits des Lustprinzips (Freud), 1920
Jenseits von Gut und Böse (Nietzsche), 1885
Jephta and His Daughter (Feuchtwanger),
    1958
Jeremias (S. Zweig), 1917
Jeremias (Werfel), 1956
Jerusalem (Mendelssohn), 1783
Jery und Bätely (Goethe), 1790
Jest, Satire, Irony, and Deeper Significance
    (Grabbe), 1966
Jesu Christo S. Natalitium (Fleming), 1631
Jew as Pariah (Arendt), 1978
Jew of Rome (Feuchtwanger), 1936
Jewess of Toledo (Grillparzer), 1914
Jewish Mother from Berlin (Kolmar), 1997
Jewish State (Herzl), 1896
Jewish Stories and Hebrew Melodies (Heine),
    1987
Jewishness of Mr. Bloom (Hildesheimer),
    1984
Jew's Beech Tree (Droste-Hülshoff), 1975
Jews of Barnow (Franzos), 1882
Jews of Zirndorf (Wasserman), 1933
Jew's Tree (Droste-Hülshoff), 1958
Joan of Arc (Schiller), 1987
Job (J. Roth), 1931
Job (Kokoschka), 1963
John Pierpont Morgan (Sternheim), 1930
Jokes and Their Relation to the Unconscious
    (Freud), 1960
Jonas und sein Veteran (Frisch), 1989
Joseph and His Brothers (T. Mann), 1934–44
Joseph, der Ernährer (T. Mann), 1943
Joseph Fouché (S. Zweig), 1929
Joseph in Ägypten (T. Mann), 1936
Joseph Kerkhovens dritte Existenz
    (Wasserman), 1934
Joseph the Provider (T. Mann), 1944
Joseph und seine Brüder (T. Mann), 1933–43
Joseph Wassermanns Heimkehr (Hilsenrath),
    1993
Josephslegende (Hofmannsthal), 1914
Josephus (Feuchtwanger), 1932

GENERAL INDEX

Page numbers in **bold** indicate subjects with their own entries.

NOTES ON ADVISERS
AND CONTRIBUTORS

Abbott, Scott. Associate Professor, Department of Germanic and Slavic Languages and Literatures, Brigham Young University, Provo, Utah. Author of *Fictions of Freemasonry* (1991) and *Ponavljanje* (with arko Radakovic, 1994). Translator of *A Journey to the Rivers* by Peter Handke (1997). Editor of *Various Atmospheres* (1998). Contributor to many publications including *German Quarterly, Critical Essays on Günter Grass,* and *Goethe Yearbook.* **Essays:** Peter Handke; *Wunschloses Unglück* (Handke).

Adams, Jeffrey. Associate Professor of German, University of North Carolina, Greensboro. Author of *Eduard Mörike's "Orpeid"* (1984). Editor of *Mörike's Muses* (1990). Co-editor of *Mimetic Desire: Essays on Narcissism in German Literature* (1995). Contributor to *Deutsche Vierteljarsschrift, German Quarterly, Carleton Germanic Papers,* and *Dictionary of Literary Biography.* **Essays:** Eduard Mörike; Patrick Süskind.

Adelson, Leslie. (Adviser). Professor of German Studies, Cornell University, Ithaca, New York. Author of *Making Bodies, Making History: Feminism and German Identity* (1993) and *Crisis of Subjectivity: Botho Strauß' Challenge to West German Prose in the 70s* (1984). Editor/editorial board member for many scholarly journals. Contributor to numerous journals and collections.

Adler, Hans. Professor, Department of German, University of Wisconsin, Madison. Author of *Soziale Romane im Vormänz* (1980) and *Die Prägmanz des Dunklen* (1990). Editor of *Herder Yearbook* (1994–), *On World History* by Johann Gottfried Herder (1997), and other publications. Contributor to numerous books and journals including *Studies in Eighteenth-Century Culture,* and *Das achtzehnte Jahrhundert.* **Essays:** Johann Gottfried Herder; *Ideen zur Philosophie der Geschichte der Menschheit* (Herder).

Adler, Jeremy D. Professor, Department of German, Kings College, London. **Essay:** Concrete Poetry.

Aikin, Judith P. Professor, Department of German, University of Iowa, Iowa City. Author of *German Baroque Drama* (1982), *Scaramutza in Germany: The Dramatic Works of Caspar Stieler* (1989), and other books. Contributor to many anthologies and journals. **Essay:** Johann Rist.

Ammerlahn, Hellmut. Associate Professor, Department of Germanics and Comparative Literature, University of Washington, Seattle. Author of *Aufbau und Krise der Sinn-Gestalt: Tasso und die Prinzessin im Kontext der Goetheschen Werke* (1990). Contributor to *German Quarterly, Colloquia Germanica,* and other publications. **Essay:** *Wilhelm Meisters Lehrjahre* (Goethe).

Andersen, Elizabeth A. Senior Lecturer, Department of German Studies, School of Modern Languages, University of Newcastle upon Tyne. Author of *The Voice of Mechthild von Magdeburg* (forthcoming). Co-editor of *Autor und Autorschaft im Mittelalter* (1998). Contributor to *Women, the Book, and the Godly* (1995), *Spannungen und Konflikte Menschlichen Zusammenlebens in der Deutschen Literatur des Mittelalters* (1995), and other publications. **Essays:** Arthurian Romance; Mechthild von Magdeburg.

Anderson, Mark. (Adviser). Associate Professor, Department of Germanic Languages and Literatures, Columbia University, New York, New York. Author of *Kafka's Clothes: Ornament and Aestheticism in the Habsburg fin de siècle* (1992). Editor of numerous works by Bachmann and Kafka as well as collections of scholarly essays.

Archibald, Linda. Professor and Director, School of Modern Languages, Liverpool John Moores University. Translator of *Yiddish Literature: A Franconian Genizah* (1988) and *The Damned and the Elect* (1992). Editor of *Proceedings of the Third National IWLP Conference* (1994). Contributor to many books and journals. **Essays:** *Tonio Kröger* (T. Mann); Old High German; Otfrid von Weißenburg; Religion and Literature.

Ashcroft, Jeffrey. Senior Lecturer, Department of German, University of St. Andrews. Editor of *Liebe in der Deutschen Literatur des Mittelalters* (1989) and *Forum for Modern Language Studies* (1984–). Contributor to anthologies and journals including *Leid im Mittelalter* (1996) and *Zeitschrift für Literaturwissenschaft und Linguistik.* **Essay:** Court Culture.

Bachem, Michael. Professor of German, Miami University, Oxford, Ohio. Author of *Heimito von Doderer* (1981). Contributor to *Doderer Jahrbuch* (1998), *Colloquia Germanica, Modern Language Studies,* and *Modern International Drama.* **Essays:** Heimito von Doderer; *Die Strudlhofstiege* (Doderer); Jacob Grimm and Wilhelm Grimm; Napoleonic Era.

Baer, Ulrich. Assistant Professor, Department of German, New York University. Contributor to *Yale Journal of Criticism, Semiotics,* and *South Atlantic Quarterly.* **Essay:** *Todesfuge* (Celan).

Baginski, Thomas. Associate Professor, Department of Classics and German, University of Charleston, Charleston, South Carolina. Author of *Psychologie und Zeitkritik in Oskar Loerkes Traumgedichten* (1990) and *Gesichtspunkte* (1994). Contributor to *Dimension '95: The Future Is Now* (1995), *Literatur in Wissenschaft und Unterricht,* and *German Studies Review.* **Essay:** Gino Chiellino.

Bagley, Petra M. Senior Lecturer, Department of Languages, University of Central Lancashire. Author of *Somebody's Daughter* (1996). Contributor to *Frauen: Mitsprechen Mitschreiben* (1997), *Babel Guide to German Fiction in English Translation* (1997), and *New German Studies.* **Essay:** *Die Klavierspielerin* (Jelinek).

Bahti, Timothy. Professor, Department of German, University of Michigan, Ann Arbor. Author of *Allegories of History: Literary Historiography after Hegel* (1992) and *Ends of the Lyric: Direction and Consequence in Western Poetry* (1996). Editor of *Jewish Writers, German Literature: The Uneasy Examples of Nelly Sachs and Walter Benjamin* (1995). Editorial board member of *Comparative Literature Studies* (1987–). Contributor to *Logomachia: The Conflict of the Faculties Today* (1992), *Paul Celan: Translator and Translated* (1998), *MLN,* and *Diacritics.* **Essays:** *Das Kunstwerk im Zeitalter seiner technischen Reproduzierbarkeit* (Benjamin); Johann Christian Friedrich Hölderlin.

Baldwin, Claire. Assistant Professor, Department of Germanic Languages and Literatures, Washington University, St. Louis, Missouri. Contributor to *Bettina Brentano-von Arnim: Gender and Politics* (1995), *Wendezeiten/Zeitenwenden* (1997), and *Colloquia Germanica*. **Essays:** Barbara Honigmann; Sophie von La Roche.

Barker, Andrew. (Adviser). Professor of Austrian Studies, School of European Languages and Cultures, University of Edinburgh. Author of *Peter Altenberg: "Rezept die Welt zu sehen"*. *Krittishe Essays, Briefe an Karl Kraus, Dokumente zur Rezeption, Titelregister der Bücher* (with Leo A. Lensing, 1995), *Telegrams from the Soul: Peter Altenberg and the Culture of the Viennese fin-de-siècle* (1996), *Telegrammstil der Seele: Peter Altenber—Eine Biographie* (1998). Editorial board member of *Austrian Studies* (1989–98). Contributor to *The Frontiers of Europe* (1998), *Austrian Studies, Modern Language Review,* and numerous other publications. **Essays:** Austria: Late Habsburg Literature in Vienna; Hermann Bahr.

Batley, Edward M. Director, Institute of Germanic Studies, University of London. Author of *A Preface to the Magic Flute* (1969) and *Catalyst of Enlightenment—Gotthold Ephraim Lessing* (1990). Editor of *Modern Languages* (1970–79) and *Dem Frieden entgegen—Hundert Texte zum Thema* (1989). Contributor to collections and journals including *Karl Philipp Moritz* (1995) and *Modern Language Review*. **Essay:** Gotthold Ephraim Lessing.

Behler, Diana Ipsen. Professor of Germanics and Comparative Studies, University of Washington, Seattle. Author of *The Theory of the Novel in Early German Romanticism* (1978). Editorial board member of *German Quarterly* (1988–96). Contributor to *Heinrich Heine und die Romantik/Heinrich Heine and Romanticism* (1997), *Athenäum,* and other collections and journals. **Essay:** *Kristische Fragmente* (F. Schlegel).

Belgardt, Raimund. Professor, Department of Linguistics and Languages, German Section, Michigan State University, East Lansing. Author of *Romantische Poesie: Begriff und Bedeutung bei Friedrich Schlegel* (1969). Contributor to many anthologies and journals including *Friedrich Schlegel und die Kunsttheorie seiner Zeit* (1985), *Germanic Review,* and *Neophilologus*. **Essays:** Klassik; *Penthesilea* (Kleist).

Berger, Stefan. Senior Lecturer, School of European Studies, University of Wales, Cardiff. Author of *The British Labour Party and the German Social Democrats 1900–31: A Comparison* (1994), *Ungleiche Schwestern? Die britische labour Party und die deutsche Social demokratie 1900–31* (1997), and *The Search for Normality: National Identity and Historical Consciousness in Germany since 1800* (1997). Editor of *The Force of Labour: The West European Labour Movement and the Working Class in the Twentieth Century* (1995), *Writing the Nation: Historiography and Nation-Building in Western Europe since 1800* (1998), and *Nationalism, Labour and Ethnicity in the Age of Imperialism* (1999). Contributor to many journals and books. **Essays:** Historians' Debate; Historiography.

Berghahn, Klaus. (Adviser). Professor of German, University of Wisconsin, Madison. Author of *Formen der Dialogführung in Schillers klassischen Dramen* (1970) and *Am Beispiel Wilhelm Meisters: Einführung in die Wissenschaftsgeschichte der Germanstik* (1980). Contributor to numerous journals. Editor of many scholary texts and collections.

Berka, Sigrid. MIT-Germany Program, Massachusetts Institute of Technology, Cambridge. Author of *Mythos-Theory und Allegorik bei Botho Strauß* (1991). Editor of *Weimarer Beiträge* (1994). Contributor to *Romantik—eine lebenskräftige Krankheit* (1991), *Goethes Mignon und ihre Schwestern* (1993), *Poetry, Poetics, Translation* (1994), *Elfriede Jelinek: Framed by Language* (1994), and many journals. **Essays:** Botho Strauß; *Anschwellender Bockgesang* (Strauß); Marlene Streeruwitz.

Betz, Frederick. Professor of German, Department of Foreign Languages and Literatures, Southern Illinois University, Carbondale. Editor of *Erläuterungen und Dokumente zu Theodor Fontanes "Grete Minde"* (1986), *Erläuterungen und Dokumente zu Heinrich Manns "Der Untertan"* (1993), and many other works. Contributor to several publications including *Orbis Litterarum* and *Fontane Blätter*. **Essay:** *Der Untertan* (H. Mann).

Bishop, Paul. Senior Lecturer, Department of German, University of Glasgow. Author of *The Dionysian Self* (1995). Contributor to several publications including *Journal of European Studies, Goethe Yearbook,* and *Jahrbook der Deutschen Schillergesellschaft*. **Essays:** Sigmund Freud; Immanuel Kant; *Kritik der Urteilskraft* (Kant); Friedrich Wilhelm Joseph von Schelling.

Boerner, Peter. Professor Emeritus, Department of Germanic Studies, Indiana University, Bloomington. Author of *Johann Wolfgang von Goethe. Rowohlts Monographien* (1964), and *Tagebuch* (1969). Editor of many works including *Faust through Four Centuries* (1989). Contributor to *Amerikastudien, Il Confronto Letterario, Jahrbuch des Freien Deutschen Hochstifts,* and other publications. **Essays:** Johann Wolfgang von Goethe; *Die Leiden des jungen Werther* (Goethe).

Bond, Greg. Coordinator for English, Language Center, Technische Fachhormschule Wildau. Author of *German History and German Identity: Uwe Johnson's "Jahrestage"* (1993). Contributor to several publications including *The Individual, Identity and Innovation: Signals from Contemporary Literature and the New Germany* (1994), *Contemporary German Writers: Their Aesthetics and Their Language* (1996), and *German Quarterly*. **Essay:** *Jahrestage: Aus dem Leben von Gesine Cresspahl* (Johnson).

Bottigheimer, Ruth B. Adjunct Professor, Department of Comparative Studies, State University of New York, Stony Brook. Author of *Grimm's Bad Girls and Bold Boys* (1987), and *The Bible for Children from the Age of Gutenberg to the Present* (1996). Editor of *Fairy Tales and Society: Illusion, Allusion, and Paradigm* (1986), *Estudios de Literatura Oral* (1995–), *Children's Literature* (1997–), and *Marvels and Tales* (1997–). Contributor to many books and journals. **Essay:** Fairy Tales.

Bourke, Eoin. Professor, Department of German, National University of Ireland, Galway. Author of *Stilbruch als Stilmittel* (1980), and *Das Irlandbild der Deutschen* (1991). Editor of many publications including *German Political Poetry* (1988), *Women's Image of Women/Men's Image of Women in German Literature* (1991), and *Schein und Wilderschein—Festschrift für T.J. Casey* (1997). Contributor to several books including *Text into Image, Image into Text* (1996). **Essay:** Erich Kästner.

Braunbeck, Helga G. Associate Professor, Foreign Languages and Literatures, North Carolina State University. Author of *Autorschaft und Subjektgenese: Christa Wolfs Kein Ort Nirgends* (1992). Contributor to *Frauen—Literatur—Revolution* (1992), *The Significance of Sibling Relationships in Literature* (1993), and *Monatshefte*. **Essays:** Libuše Moníková; Prague.

Breithaupt, Fritz. Assistant Professor, Germanic Studies, Indiana University. Author of *Eidolatrie: Goethes Politik des Bildlichen* (1998). Contributor to many publications including *Benjamin's Ghosts* (1998), *Kleist-Lektüren* (1998), *Modern Language Notes*, and *Amsterdamer Beiträge zur Germanistik*. **Essays:** *Die Wahlverwandtschaften* (Goethe); *Der blonde Eckbert* (Tieck).

Bridgham, Fred. Senior Lecturer, German Department, University of Leeds. Author of *Rainer Maria Rilke, Urbild und Verzicht* (1975), *Germany from Unification to Reunification* (1993), and *The Friendly German-English Dictionary* (1996). Contributor to several books including *Schein und Widerschein, Festschrift for T.J. Casey* (1996), and *Feste Freundschaft, Festschrift for Peter Johnson* (1997). **Essays:** Gottfried Benn; Gesamtkunstwerk; Michael Kohlhaas.

Brown, Jane K. Professor of Germanics and Comparative Literature, University of Washington. Author of several works on Goethe including *Ironic und Objectivität: Aufsätze über Goethe* (1998). Editor of *Interpreting Goethe's Faust Today* (with Meredith Lee and Thomas P. Saine, 1994), *Essays on Goethe* by Stuart Atkins (with Thomas P. Saine, 1995), and *ELN* (1981–95). Editorial board member of *Goethe Yearbook* (1986–). Contributor to several publications. **Essays:** Empfindsamkeit; *Faust: Part I, Part II* (Goethe).

Browning, Barton W. Associate Professor, Department of German, Pennsylvania State University, University Park. Editorial board member of *Colloquia Germanica* (1980–). Contributor to many journals including *Modern Austrian Studies, Modern Language Notes*, and *Wolfenbüttler Barock-Nachrichten*. **Essay:** Daniel Casper von Lohenstein.

Bullock, Marcus. Professor, Comparative Literature, University of Wisconsin, Milwaukee. Author of *Romanticism and Marxism* (1997) and *The Violent Eye* (1992). Editor of *Discourse* (1995–) and *Walter Benjamin: Selected Writings* (1997). Contributor to many publications including *The Yale Companion to Jewish Writing and Thought in German Culture 1096–1996* (1997) and *New German Critique*. **Essays:** Walter Benjamin; Ernst Jünger; Jakob Wassermann.

Burns, Barbara. Department of Modern Languages, University of Strathclyde, Glasgow. Author of *Theory and Patterns of Tragedy in the Later Novellas of Theodor Storm* (1996). Contributor to *Reference Guide to World Literature* (1995) and *German Life and Letters*. **Essays:** Louise von François; *Die Weber* (Hauptmann).

Bushell, Anthony. Head of German, School of Modern Languages, University of Wales, Bangor. Author of *The Emergence of West German Poetry from the Second World War to the Early Post-War Period* (1989). Contributing editor of *Essays in Germanic Studies* (1993) and *Austria 1945–55* (1996). Contributor to many books and journals. **Essays:** *Heldenplatz* (Bernhard); *Professor Berhardi* (Schnitzler).

Cafferty, Helen. Professor of German, Bowdoin College, Brunswick, Maine. Editor of *Women in German Yearbook* (1987–90). Editorial board member of *Women in German Yearbook* (1992–). Contributor to several publications including *Feminist Encyclopedia of German Literature* (1997), *Common Ground: Feminist Collaboration in the Academy* (1997), and *West Virginia Philological Papers*. **Essay:** Berlin.

Calomino, Salvatore. Associate Professor, Department of German, University of Wisconsin, Madison. Author of *From Verse to Prose: The Barlaam and Josaphat Legend in Fifteenth-Century Germany* (1990). Editor of *Monatschefte* (1991–98). Contributor to many books and journals including *Enzyklopädie des Märchens* (1989) and *Utopian Vision* (1990). **Essays:** König Rother; Konrad von Regensburg.

Chinca, Mark. Lecturer, Department of German, University of Cambridge. Author of *History, Fiction, Verisimilitude: Studies in the Poetics of Gottfried's Tristan* (1993) and *Gottfried um Strassburg: Tristan* (1997). Editor of *Displacement and Recognition* (1990), *The Practice of Medieval Literature* (1997), and *Arthurian Literature* (1995–98). Contributor to many publications including *Roland and Charlemagne in Europe* (1996). **Essays:** Biblical Drama; Minnesang.

Classen, Albrecht. Professor, Department of German Studies, University of Arizona. Author of several books including *The German Volksbuch* (1995) and *Die Klage* (1997). Editor of numerous collections including *Eroticism and Love in the Middle Ages* (1994–95). Contributor to many books and journals. **Essays:** Christine Ebner; Gustav Freytag; Hildegard von Bingen; Journals; Liselotte von der Pfalz; Mysticism.

Colvin, Sarah. Lecturer in German, University of Edinburgh. Author of *The Rhetorical Feminine: Gender and Orient on the German Stage* (1999). Contributor to several journals and collections including *Pedagogy and Power* (1998) and *German Life and Letters*. **Essay:** Women and Literature.

Conacher, Jean E. Senior Lecturer in German, Department of Languages and Cultural Studies, University of Limerick. Contributor to *Women and the Wende* (1994) and *Translation Ireland*. **Essay:** Helga Königsdorf.

Conard, Robert. Professor, Department of Languages, University of Dayton, Dayton, Ohio. Author of *Heinrich Böll* (1981) and *Understanding Heinrich Böll* (1992). Editor of several journals and collections including *University of Dayton Review* (1979–98). Contributor to numerous books and journals. **Essay:** *Ansichten eines Clowns* (Böll).

Cook, Roger F. Professor, Department of German and Russian Studies, University of Missouri, Columbia. Author of *The Demise of the Author* (1993) and *By the Rivers of Babylon: Heinrich Heine's Late Songs and Reflections* (1998). Editor of *The Cinema of Wim Wenders* (1997). Contributor to many books and journals. **Essay:** Alexander Kluge.

Costabile-Heming, Carol Anne. Associate Professor, Department of Modern and Classical Languages, Southwest Missouri State University, Springfield. Author of *Intertextual Exile: Volker Braun's Dramatic Re-Vision of GDR Society*. Contributor to numerous books and journals including *The Berlin Wall* (1996) and *The Feminist Encyclopedia of German Literature* (1997). **Essay:** Peter Huchel.

Coulson, Anthony. School of Applied Language and Intercultural Studies, Dublin City University. Editor of *Exiles and Migrants: Crossing Thresholds in European Culture and Society* (1997). Contributor to *Text into Image: Image into Text* (1997), *DEFA: East German Cinema* (1998), and other publications. **Essays:** *Geschichten aus dem Wiener Wald* (Horváth); Johann Nepomuk Nestroy.

Coupe, W.A. Professor Emeritus, Department of German, University of Reading. Author of several books including *German Political Satires from the Reformation to the Second World War* (1985–93) and *Germany through the Looking Glass* (1986). Editor of many collections and journals including *New German Studies* (1973–). Contributor to numerous books and journals. **Essays:** *Romeo und Julia auf dem Dorfe* (Keller); Angelus Silesius.

Coury, David N. Assistant Professor, German and Humanistic Studies, University of Wisconsin, Green Bay. Co-editor of *Focus on Literature* (1994–95). Contributor to many books and journals including *Annual of Film and Literature* (1996) and *Encyclopedia of Novels into Film* (1998). **Essay:** Sten Nadolny.

Coxon, Sebastian. Wolfson College, University of Oxford. Contributor to several books and journals including *Autor und Autorbewußtsein in der mittelhochdeutschen Literatur* (1998), *Natur und Kultur im deutschen Mittelalter* (1999), and *Medium Aevum*. **Essay:** Rudolf von Ems.

Craig, Charlotte M. Professor of German, Department of Foreign Languages, Kutztown University, Kutztown, Pennsylvania. Author of *Christoph Martin Wieland as the Originator of the Modern Travesty in German Literature* (1970). Editor of numerous books and journals including *Blendung and Wandlung. Lessings Dramen in Psychologischer Sicht* (1993) and *Lichtenbergs Gedankensystem* (1995). Contributor to many publications. **Essay:** August Wilhelm Schlegel.

Dawson, Ruth P. Associate Professor, Women's Studies, University of Hawaii. Contributor to numerous journals and collections including *In the Shadow of Olympus: German Women Writers around 1800* (1992), *Anthropology and the German Enlightenment* (1995), and *Thalia's Daughters* (1996). **Essay:** Christiana Mariane Ziegler.

Dickson, Sheila Janet. Lecturer in German, Department of Modern Languages, University of Strathclyde. Author of *The Narrator, Narrative Perspective, and Narrative Form in the Short Prose Works of the German Romantics* (1994). Co-editor of *Encounters with Modern German Texts* (1992) and *German Life and Letters* (special issue, 1994). Contributor to numerous journals and collections. **Essay:** Ludwig Tieck.

Diethe, Carol. Research Fellow, School of Philosophy, Middlesex University. Author of *Towards Emancipation: German Women Writers in the Nineteenth Century* (1998), *Historical Dictionary of Nietzcheanism* (1998), and other works. Editor of several journals including *German Life and Letters* (1995). Contributor to many books and journals. **Essay:** *Also sprach Zarathustra* (Nietzsche).

Di Maio, Irene Stocksieker. Associate Professor of German, Department of Foreign Languages and Literatures, Louisiana State University. Author of *The Multiple Perspective: Wilhelm Raabe's Third-Person Narratives of the Braunschweig Period* (1981). Contributor to many books and journals including *Autoren damals und heute* (1990–91) and *Yearbook of German-American Studies*. **Essays:** *Altneuland* (Herzl); Fanny Lewald.

Dollenmayer, David. Associate Professor of German, Department of Humanities and Arts, Worcester Polytechnic Institute. Author of *The Berlin Novels of Alfred Döblin* (1988) and *Neue Horizonte* (fourth edition, 1996). Contributor to many journals including *Modern Austrian Literature*. **Essay:** *Berlin Alexanderplatz* (Döblin).

Donahue, William Collins. Assistant Professor, Department of German, Rutgers University, New Brunswick, New Jersey. Guest co-editor of *German Politics and Society* (1992, 1995). Contributor to *Die Unterrichtspraxis, German Quarterly*, and other journals. **Essays:** *Die Blendung* (E. Canetti); *Masse und Macht* (E. Canetti).

Duncan, Bruce. Professor, Department of German Studies, Dartmouth College, Hanover, New Hampshire. Author of *"Lovers, Patricides, and Raging Fools": Aspects of Sturm und Drang Drama* (1999). Contributor to many journals and book collections including *Momentum Dramaticum. Aufsätze zu Ehren von Eckehard Catholy* (1990) and *Bitter Healing: German Women Authors, 1700–1830* (1990). **Essays:** Achim von Arnim; Johann Christoph Gottsched.

Dunphy, Graeme. Lecturer, Department of English and German, University of Regensburg. Author of *Daz waz ein Michel Wunder: The Presentation of Old Testament Material in Jans Enikel's Weltchronik* (1998). Contributor to several journals including *Neuphilologische Mitteilung* and *Zeitschrift fuer Deutsches Altertum*. **Essays:** Annolied; Rafik Schami.

Dürr, Volker. Associate Professor of German and Comparative Literary Studies, Northwestern University, Evanston, Illinois. Editor of *Versuche an Goethe* (1976), *Imperial Germany* (1985), and *Nietzsche: Literature and Values* (1988). Contributor to numerous anthologies and journals. **Essays:** Theodor Fontane; *Der Stechlin* (Fontane).

Ehrstine, Glenn. Assistant Professor, Department of German, University of Iowa. Contributor to several books and journals including *Dictionary of Literary Biography* (1997), *Künste und Natur in Diskursen der Frühen Neuzeit* (forthcoming), and *Daphnis* (forthcoming). **Essays:** Neidhart (von Reuental); Hans Sachs.

Eigler, Friederike. Associate Professor, Department of German, Georgetown University, Washington, D.C. Author of *Das autobiographische Werk von Elias Canetti* (1988). Editor of *Cultural Transformations in the New Germany: American and German Perspectives* (with Peter Pfeiffer, 1993) and *The Feminist Encyclopedia of German Literature* (with Susanne Kord, 1997). Contributor to many books and journals. **Essays:** Lou Andreas-Salomé; Elias Canetti; Uwe Johnson.

Elliott, Rosemarie. University of Glasgow. Author of *Wilhelm Heinse in Relation to Wieland, Winckelmann, and Goethe* (1996). Contributor to *Wilhelm Heinse—"eines beßern Schiksals Werth": Weltbürger—Textwelten* (1995), *Goethe and the Image of Wilhelm Heinse: Mitteilungen der Winckelmann Gesellschaft* (1996), and other works. **Essay:** Johann Jakob Wilhelm Heinse.

Erb, Peter C. Professor, Department of Religion, Wilfrid Laurier University, Waterloo, Ontario. Author of several books including *A Question of Sovereignty: The Politics of Meaning's Conversion* (1995) and *Newman on the Idea of a Catholic University* (1997). Editor of *An Annotated Hutterite Bibliography* (1998) and other books. Contributor to many anthologies and journals. **Essays:** Jakob Böhme; Elisabeth Langgässer.

Erlin, Matthew. Department of German, University of California, Berkley. **Essay:** Friedrich Nicolai.

Evans, Tamara S. Professor, Program in German, Graduate School and University Center, City University of New York. Author of *Formen der Ironie in Conrad Ferdinand Meyers Novellen* (1980) and *Robert Walsers Moderne* (1989). Editor of *Pro Helvetia Swiss Lectureship Series* (1982–). Contributor to many journals and book collections. **Essays:** Conrad Ferdinand Meyer; *Die Hochzeit des Mönchs* (Meyer); Robert Walser.

Fehervary, Helen. Associate Professor, Department of Germanic Languages and Literatures, Ohio State University. Author of several books including *Mit den Toten Reden: Fragen on Heiner Müller* (with Josh Hermand, 1999) and *Anna Seghers: The Mythic Dimension* (forthcoming). Editor of *New German Critique* (1973–92) and other journals. Contributor to numerous journals and books. **Essays:** Anna Seghers; *Das siebte Kruez* (Seghers).

Fenves, Peter. (Adviser). Associate Professor, Department of German, Northwestern University, Evanston, Illinois. Author of

"Chatter": Language and History in Kierkegaard (1993) and *A Peculiar Fate: Metaphysics and World History in Kant* (1991).

Fetz, Bernhard. Archivist, Austrian Literary Archive, Austrian National Library. Author of *Vertauschte Köpfe. Studien zu Wolfgang Koeppens erzählender Prosa* (1994). Editor of several books and journals including *In Sachen Albert Drach* (1995) and *Der Literarische Einfall. über das Entstehen von Terten* (1998). Contributor to numerous journals and anthologies. **Essay:** Albert Drach.

Fischer, Barbara. Department of WLAC, Samford University, Birmingham, Alabama. Contributor to several collections including *Insiders and Outsiders: Jewish Gentile Culture in Germany and Austria* (1994), *Patterns of Prejudice* (1994), and *Verkörperte Geschichtsentwürfe: George Tabori's Theaterarbeit* (1998). **Essay:** George Tabori.

Fischer, Bernd. Department of Germanic Languages and Literatures, Ohio State University, Columbus. Author of several books including *Christoph Hein* (1990) and *Das Eigene und das Eigentliche* (1995). Editor of *Neue Tendenzen der Arnimforschung* (with Roswitha Burwick, 1990) and other works. Contributor to numerous anthologies and journals. **Essays:** Aufklärung; *Uber die ästhetische Erziehung des Menschen in einer Reihe von Briefen* (Schiller); Charles Sealsfield.

Fischer, Sabine. Tutor, Department of Germanic Studies, University of Sheffield. Editor of *Denn du tanzt auf einem Seil: Positionen der deutschsprachigen MigantInnenliteratur* (with Moray McGowan 1997). Contributor to several collections including *Turkish Culture in German Society Today* (1996) and *Materialien Deutsch als Fremdsprache* (1997). **Essays:** Franco Biondi; Aysel Özakin; Emine Sevgi Özdamar; Yoko Tawada.

Fisher, Rod. Associate Professor, Department of German, University of Canterbury. Author of several books including *The Narrative Works of Hartmann von Aue* (1983), *Heinrich von Veldeke: Eneas* (1992), and *The Minnesinger Heinrich von Morungen* (1996). Contributor to many journals and anthologies. **Essays:** Heinrich von Veldeke; Walther von der Vogelweide.

Fleming, Heather. Lecturer, Department of Germanic Languages and Literatures, University of Pennsylvania, Philadelphia. **Essays:** Der Bitterfelder Weg; Anna Luise Karsch.

Flood, John L. Professor of German, University of London, Institute of Germanic Studies. Author of several books including *Die Historie von Herzog ernst; Die Frankfurter prosafassung des 16. Jahrhunderts* (1991) and *Johannes Sinapius (1505–1560), Hellenist and Physician in Germany and Italy* (with David J. Shaw, 1997). Editor of numerous collections including *The German Book 1450–1750* (1995). Contributor to many journals and books. **Essays:** Mastersingers; Sidonia Hedwig Zäunemann.

Fox, Thomas C. Associate Professor, Department of German and Russian, University of Alabama. Author of *Border Crossings: An Introduction to East German Prose* (1993), *Stated Memory: East Germany and the Holocaust* (1999), and other books. Editor of several journals and anthologies including

GDR Bulletin (1984–92). Contributor to many journals and anthologies. **Essay:** Jurek Becker.

Frisch, Shelley. German Department, Rutgers University, New Brunswick, New Jersey. Executive editor of *Germanic Review* (1984–92). Contributor to journals and anthologies including *The Scope of the Fantastic* (1985) and *Exile across Cultures* (1986). **Essays:** *Die Physiker* (Dürrenmatt); Klaus Mann.

Gaddy, Kerstin. Visiting Assistant Professor, Department of Foreign Languages, Catholic University of America, Washington, D.C. Contributor to several journals including *Modern Drama, Seminar,* and *Colloquia Germanica.* **Essays:** Stefan Zweig; *Die Welt von Gestern: Erinnerungen eines Europäers* (S. Zweig).

Gaskill, Howard. Reader in German, University of Edinburgh. Author of *Hölderin's Hyperion* (1984). Editor of several journals and collections including *New Comparison* (1995–) and *From Gaelic to Romantic: Ossianic Translations* (1998). Contributor to many books and journals. **Essay:** *Hyperion; oder, Der Eremit in Griechenland* (Hölderlin).

Gentry, Francis G. Professor, German and Slavic Languages, Pennsylvania State University, University Park. Author of *Triuwe und Vriont in the Nibelungenleid* (1975) and *Bibliographie zur Fröhmittelhochdeutschen Dichten* (1992). Editor of many journals and collections including *German Quarterly* (1991–94). Contributor to numerous publications. **Essays:** Hartmann von Aue; Kaiserchronik.

Gibbs, Marion E. Reader, Department of German, Royal Holloway, University of London. Author of several books including *Wolfram von Eschenbach "Titurec" and the Songs* (1988), *Kudrun* (1992), and *Medieval German Literature: A Companion* (1997). Contributor to many anthologies and journals. **Essay:** Wolfram von Eschenbach.

Gillespie, Jill. Doctoral candidate, Department of German, Cornell University, Ithaca, New York. **Essay:** Marieluise Fleißer.

Gillett, Robert. Lecturer, Department of German, Queen Mary and Westfield College, University of London. Contributor to many collections and journals including *Medium und Maske: Die Literatur Hubert Fichtes zwischen den Kulturen* (1995), *The Individual Identity and Innovation* (1996), and *New German Studies.* **Essays:** Johann Peter Hebel; Homosexuality and Literature; Oskar Loerke.

Glier, Ingeborg. (Adviser). Professor of German, Yale University, New Haven, Connecticut. Author of *Die deutsche Literatur im spaten Mittelalter* (1987), *Deutsche Metrik* (with Otto Paul) (1974), *Artes amandi: Untersuchung zu Geschichte, Überlieferung, und Typologie der deutschen Minnereden* (1971), and *Struktur und Gestaltungsprinzipien in den Dramen John Websters* (1958). Contributor to numerous scholarly journals and collections.

Gould, Jeffrey. Graduate student, Yale University, New Haven, Connecticut. **Essay:** *Kindheitsmuster* (Wolf).

Graves, Peter J. Senior Lecturer in German, University of Leicester. Editor of *Three Contemporary German Poets: Wolf Biermann, Sarah Kirsch, Reiner Kunze* (1985). Contributor to many books and journals including *Retrospect and Review: Aspects of the Literature of the GDR, 1976–1990* (1997) and *German Life and Letters.* **Essays:** *Die Ermittlung* (Weiss); *Was bleibt: Debate* (Wolf).

Gross, Sabine. Associate Professor, Department of German, University of Wisconsin, Madison. Author of *Lese-Zeichen* (1994). Editor of *Monatshefte* (1993–), *Time and Society* (1996–), and other journals. Contributor to many journals and anthologies. **Essays:** *Publikumsbeschimpfung* (Handke); Herta Müller.

Gundermann, Christian. Graduate student, Department of German Studies, Cornell University, Ithaca, New York. Contributor to *Legacies of Freud* (forthcoming), *Vagabondage: The Poetics and Politics of Movement* (forthcoming), and *Diacritics.* **Essay:** Hubert Fichte.

Gustafson, Susan E. Associate Professor, Department of Modern Cultures, University of Rochester, Rochester, New York. Author of *Absent Mothers and Orphaned Fathers: Narcissism and Abjection in Lessing's Dramatic Production* (1995). Contributor to many books and journals including *Outing Goethe and His Age* (1997) and *PMLA.* **Essays:** *Emilia Galotti* (Lessing); *Nathan der Weise* (Lessing).

Hahn, Barbara. Professor, German Department, Princeton University, Princeton, New Jersey. Author of *Antworten sie mir: Rahel Levin Varnhagens Brief Wechsel* (1990) and *Unter falschem Namen* (1991). Editor of numerous collections and journals including *Pauline Wiesels liebes Geschichten* (1998). **Essays:** Salons; Rahel Levin Varnhagen.

Ham, Jennifer. Associate Professor, Department of Modern Languages, University of Wisconsin, Green Bay. Author of *Urban Amusements: Wedekind, Physicality, and Popular Entertainment at the Turn of the Century* (forthcoming). Editor of *Animal Acts: Configuring the Human in Western History* (1997). Contributor to many books and journals including *Encyclopedia of Contemporary German Culture* (1998). **Essay:** Wilhelm von Humboldt.

Harper, Anthony J. Glasgow. Author of several books including *Schriften zur Lyrik Leipzigs 1620–1670* (1985) and *The Song-Books of Gottfried Finckelthaus* (1988). Editor of many volumes including *The Emblem in Renaissance and Baroque Europe* (1992). Contributor to numerous books and journals. **Essays:** Paul Fleming; Sophie Mereau.

Harris, Nigel. Senior Lecturer, Department of German Studies, University of Birmingham. Author of *The Latin and German "Etymachia"* (1994). Editor of *"Etymachia," Version C* (1995). Contributor to several books and journals including *The Narrative Fiction of Heinrich Böll* (1995). **Essays:** Sebastian Brant; Oswald von Wolkenstein.

Helbling, Robert E. Professor, Department of Languages and Literature, University of Utah. Author of *The Major Works of*

Heinfich von Kleist (1975). Editor of several collections including *The Intellectual Tradition of the West* (1967, 1968) and *Heinrich von Kleist. Erzählungen* (1983). Contributor to many books and journals. **Essay:** Friedrich Dürrenmatt.

Heller, Reinhold. Professor, Department of Art History and Germanic Studies, University of Chicago. Author of several books including *Wilhelm Lehmbruck* (1973) and *Gabriele Münter: The Years of Expressionism 1903–1920* (1998). **Essay:** Der Blaue Reiter.

Helmetag, Charles H. Professor, Department of Modern Languages and Literatures, Villanova University, Villanova, Pennsylvania. Contributor to *Deutsche Exilliteratur seit 1933,* (volume 4, 1994), *German Quarterly, Monatshefte,* and other publications. **Essay:** Walter Hasenclever.

Hempel, Wolfgang. Professor, Department of Germanic Languages and Literatures, University of Toronto. Author of *Superbia* (1970) and *An Introduction to German-English Etymology* (1996). Contributor to many books and journals including *Medieval Germany: An Encyclopedia* (1997). **Essay:** Heliand.

Herhoffer, Astrid. Senior Lecturer, School of Humanities and Social Sciences, Staffordshire University. Contributor to numerous journals and anthologies including *Journal of Area Studies, Journal of Area Studies,* and *German Life and Letters.* **Essay:** Irmtraud Morgner.

Herzog, Hillary Hope. Ph.D. candidate, Department of Germanic Studies, University of Chicago. **Essay:** Irmgard Keun.

Hill, David. Senior Lecturer, Department of German Studies, University of Birmingham. Author of *Klinger's Novels: The Structure of the Cycle* (1982). Editor of *Nathan der Weise* by G.E. Lessing (1988), *Prince Tandi of Cumba or the New Menoza* by Jakob Michael Reinhold Lenz (1995), and other works. Contributor to numerous collections and journals. **Essay:** Gottfried August Bürger.

Hill, Murray. Senior Lecturer, Center for Modern Languages, Robert Gordon University. Contributor to several journals including *NGS, FMLS,* and *Scotsman.* **Essay:** Karl Valentin

Hillen, Gerd. Professor Emeritus, German Department, University of California, Berkley. Author of several books including *Gotthold Ephraim Lessing Chronik. Daten zu Leben und Werk* (1979) and *Gotthold Ephraim Lessing. Das dichterische Werk* (1979). Editor of *Andreas Gryphius: Papinian* (1984) and other books and journals. Contributor to numerous journals and collections. **Essay:** Martin Luther.

Hoesterey, Ingeborg. (Adviser). Professor, Departments of Germanic Studies and Comparative Literature, Indiana University. Author of *Verschlungene Schriftzeichen: Intertextualität von Literatur und Kunst in der Moderne/Postmoderne* (1988) and *Pastiche: Cultural Memory in Art, Film, Literature* (forthcoming). Editor of several anthologies including *Zeitgeist in Babel: The Postmodernist Controversy* (1991). Contributor to numerous books and journals. **Essays:** Aldolf Loos; Postmodernism.

Humble, Malcolm. Lecturer, Department of German, University of St. Andrews. Author of *A Companion to Twentieth Century German Literature* (with Raymond Furness, 1991, 1997) and *Introduction to German Literature 1871–1990* (with Raymond Furness, 1994). Editor of *Forum for Modern Language Studies* (1989). Contributor to many books and journals. **Essays:** Antifascist Literature; Nationalism and Nationhood.

Hunt, Irmgard. Professor of German, Colorado State University. Author of many books including *Pazifische Elegie—Ein Poem* (1993) and *Urs Jaeggi: Ein Werkbiographie* (1993). Editor of several journals and collections including *Paul Gurk: Gedichte 1939–45* (1987). Contributor to numerous publications. **Essays:** Ingeborg Bachmann; Urs Jaeggi.

Hüppauf, Bernd. Professor, Department of German, New York University. Author of *Von Sozialer Utopie zur Mystik* (1972) and *Methodendiskussion* (6th edition, 1994). Editor of several collections including *War, Violence, and the Modern Condition* (1996). Contributor to many anthologies. **Essays:** *Frost* (Bernhard); Robert Musil; Stunde Null.

Hutchinson, Peter. (Adviser). Vice Master, Trinity Hall, University of Cambridge. Author of many books including *Stefan Heym: The Perpetual Dissident* (1992) and *Stefan Heym: Dissident and Lebenezeit* (1999). Editor of *Rilke's "Duino Elegies"* (1996) and several other works. Contributor to numerous books and journals. **Essays:** Bertolt Brecht; *Die Dreigroschenoper* (Brecht); Stefan Heym.

Hylenski, Kristen. Graduate student, Department of Germanic Languages and Literatures, Yale University, New Haven, Connecticut. **Essay:** Maxim Biller.

Isenberg, Noah. Assistant Professor, Department of German Studies, Wesleyan University, Middletown, Connecticut. Author of *Between Redemption and Doom: The Strains of German-Jewish Modernism* (1999). Contributor to several collections and journals including *Yale Companion to Jewish Writing and Thought in German Culture 1096–1996* (1997) and *The Nation.* **Essay:** Arnold Zweig.

Jones, Calvin N. Professor, Department of Foreign Languages and Literatures, University of South Alabama, Mobile. Author of *Negation and Utopia: The German Volksstück from Raimund to Kroetz* (1993) and *The Literary Reputation of Else Lasker-Schüler 1901–1993* (1994). Contributor to several journals including *Germanic Review.* **Essays:** Else Lasker-Schüler; Zauberstücke.

Jones, David H.R. Lecturer, Department of Modern Languages: German, Keele University. **Essay:** Ernst Theodor Amadeus Hoffmann.

Jones, Michael T. Associate Professor, Department of German, University of Kentucky. Editor of *German Quarterly* (1984–88) and *Colloquia Germanica* (1991–95). Contributor to several books and journals including *New German Critique.* **Essays:** Athenäum; Friedrich Schlegel.

Kagel, Martin. Assistant Professor, Department of Germanic and Slavic Languages, University of Georgia. Author of *Straigericht und Kriegstheater: Studien zur Ästhetik von Jakob Michael Reinhold Lenz* (1997). Contributor to several books and journals including *Brecht Jahrbuch* and *Colloquia Germanica*. **Essay:** Jakob Michael Reinhold Lenz.

Kane, Martin. Reader in Modern German Studies, University of Kent, Canterbury. Author of *Weimar Germany and the Limits of Political Art* (1987). Editor of *Socialism and Literary Imagination* (1991) and *Retrospective and Review* (1976–90). Contributor to many publications. **Essays:** Sarah Kirsch; Ernst Toller.

Keith-Smith, Brian. Senior Research Professor, Mellen University, Iowa. Author of *Johannes Bobrowski* (1970) and *Lothar Schreyer* (1990). Editor of many books and journals including *Lothar Schreyers Werke* (1992–) and *New German Studies* (1973–96). Contributor to numerous anthologies and journals. **Essays:** Ilse Aichinger; Rose Ausländer; Expressionism; Clare Goll; Yvan Goll; Georg Kaiser; Poetry, (Bachmann).

Kelling, Hans-Wilhelm. Professor, Department of Germanic and Slavic Languages, Brigham Young University, Provo, Utah. Author of several books including *Wiemar's sagt und schreibt* (1972) and *Deutsche Kulturgeschichte* (1974, 1978, 1998). Editor of *From Virgil to Akhmatova* (1983) and other works. Contributor to many books and journals. **Essays:** Joseph Freiherr von Eichendorff; *Der Schimmelreiter* (Storm).

Kieser, Rolf. Professor, European Languages and Literatures, City University of New York Graduate School and Queens College. Author of several books including *Erzwungene Symbiose* (1985) and *Benjamin Franklin Wedekind: Biographie Einer Jugend* (1990). Editor of *The New Switzerland: Problems and Politics* (1996) and other publications. Contributor to numerous anthologies. **Essay:** Zurich.

King, Ian. Reader in German Studies, Division of Languages, South Bank University, London. Author of *Kurt Tucholsky als Politischer Publizist* (1983). Co-editor of *Journal of the Association for the Study of German Politics* (1982–84). Contributor to several books and journals including *German Life and Letters*. **Essay:** Kurt Tucholsky.

Kirkbright, Suzanne. Department of German, School of Languages and European Studies, Aston University, Birmingham. Author of *Border and Border Experience* (1997). Contributor to *Nachdenken über Grenzen* (1998). **Essays:** Hannah Arendt; Bettina von Arnim; Martin Heidegger.

Kniesche, Thomas W. Associate Professor, Department of German Studies, Brown University, Providence, Rhode Island. Author of *Die Genealogie der Post-Apokalypse* (1991). Editor of *Dancing on the Volcano: Essays on the Culture of the Weimar Republic* (1994) and *Körper/Kultur: Kaliformische Studien zur Deutsche Moderne* (1995). Contributor to many books and journals. **Essay:** Günter Grass.

Koelb, Clayton. Guy B. Johnson Professor and Chair, Department of Germanic Languages, University of North Carolina,

Chapel Hill. Author of several books including *Kafka's Rhetoric: The Passion of Reading* (1989) and *Legendary Figures: Ancient History in Modern Novels* (1998). Editor of many works including *Thomas Mann, Death in Venice: A New Translation, Backgrounds and Contexts, Criticism* (1994). Contributor to numerous journals and collections. **Essays:** Aesthetics; Franz Kafka.

Koepke, Wulf. Distinguished Professor of German, Emeritus, Texas A&M University, College Station. Author of several books including *Johann Gottfried Herder* (1987) and *Understanding Max Frisch* (1990). Editor of *J. G. Herder's Academic Disciplines and the Pursuit of Knowledge* (1996) and other works. Contributor to many books and journals. **Essays:** Alfred Döblin; Jean Paul (Johann Paul Friedrich Richter); *Vorschule der Ästhetik* (Jean Paul).

Kohl, Katrin. Fellow and Tutor in German, Jesus College, and Faculty Lecturer in German, University of Oxford. Author of *Rhetoric, the Bible, and the Origins of Free Verse: The Early "Hymns" of Friedrich Gottlieb Klopstock* (1990) and *A Dictionary of Contemporary Germany* (with Tristam Carrington-Windo)(1996). Editor of several publications including *Oxford Studies in Modern European Literature, Film, and Culture* (series editor with E. Fallaize and R. Fiddian). Contributor to numerous journals and anthologies. **Essays:** Friedrich Gottlieb Klopstock; *Die deutsche Gelehrtenrepublik* (Klopstock).

Komar, Kathleen L. Professor of German and Comparative Literature, University of California, Los Angeles. Author of *Pattern and Chaos: Multilinear Novels by Dos Passos, Faulkner, Döblin, and Koeppen* (1983) and *Transcending Angels: Rainer Maria Rilke's "Duino Elegies"* (1987). Co-editor of *Lyrical Symbols and Narrative Transformations* (with Ross Schideler, 1998). Contributor to many books and journals. **Essays:** *Die Aufzeichnungen des Malte Laurids Brigge* (Rilke); *Duineser Elegien* (Rilke); *Nachdenken über Christa T.* (Wolf).

Kontje, Todd. Assistant Professor of German, Literature Department, University of California, San Diego. Author of *Constructing Reality: Schiller* (1987), *Private Lives in the Public Sphere* (1992), *The German Bildungsroman* (1993), and *Women, The Novel, and the German Nation* (1998). **Essay:** Bildungsroman.

Konzett, Delia Caparoso. Ph.D. English, University of Chicago, 1997. Contributor to *Journal of Film and Video* (1999), *American Literature* (1997), and *Encyclopedia of the Novel* (1998). **Essay:** *Eichmann in Jerusalem* (Arendt).

Konzett, Matthias. Assistant Professor of German, Yale University, New Haven, Connecticut. Author of *The Rhetoric of National Dissent in Peter Handke, Thomas Bernhard, and Elfriede Jelinek* (forthcoming). Editor of *A Companion to Thomas Bernhard* (forthcoming). Contributor to many books and journals. **Essays:** Austria: Post 1945; Thomas Bernhard; *Wittgensteins Neffe* (Bernhard); *Totenauberg* (Jelinek); Robert Schindel; Zafer Şenocak.

Kosta, Barbara. Associate Professor, Department of German Studies, University of Arizona. Author of *Auf deutsch: First Year*

German Textbook (1990) and *Recasting Autobiography: Women's Counterfictions in Contemporary German Literature and Film* (1994). Contributor to many books and journals including *Beyond 1989* (1997). **Essays:** Autobiography; Elfriede Jelinek.

Kraft, Helga W. Professor and Head, Department of German, University of Illinois, Chicago. Author of several books including *Auf Deutsch: Kompetenz durch kommunikatives Lernen* (1991) and *Ein Haus aus Sprache: Dramatikerinnen und das andere Theater* (1996). Editor of *Mütter—Töchter—Frauen. Weiblichkeitsbilder im der Literatur* (1993). Contributor to many books and journals. **Essays:** Hrotsvit von Gandersheim; Gerlind Reinshagen.

Krajewski, Bruce. Professor and Chair, Department of Literature, Georgia Southern University. Author of *Travelling with Hermes: Hermeneutics and Rhetoric* (1992). Editor of several books and journals including *Gadamer on Celan* (with Richard Heinemann, 1997) and *Arachne* (1993–98). Contributor to many journals. **Essay:** Hans-Georg Gadamer.

Krauss, Hannes. Akademischer Rat, Universität Essen. Editor of *Der deutsch-deutsche Literaturstreit* (1991), *Verat an der Kunst? Rückblicke auf die DDR-Literatur* (1993), and *Der Deutschunterricht* (1996, 1998). Contributor to many books and journals. **Essays:** German Democratic Republic; Christoph Hein.

Lamb-Faffelberger, Margarete. Associate Professor, Department of Foreign Languages and Literatures, Lafayette College, Easton, Pennsylvania. Author of *Valie Export und Elfriede Jelinek im Spiegel der Presse* (1992). Editor of *Out from the Shadows: Essays on Contemporary Women Writers and Filmmakers* (1997). Contributor to *Modern Austrian Literature* and other publications. **Essay:** Christoph Ransmayr.

Lareau, Alan. Associate Professor, Department of Foreign Languages and Literatures, University of Wisconsin, Oshkosh. Author of *The Wild Stage: Literary Cabarets of the Weimar Republic* (1995) and *Kurt Tucholsky-Discographie* (1997). Contributor to many journals and collections including *Friedrich Hollaender: Wenn ich mir was wünschen dürfte* (1996). **Essay:** Cabaret.

Large, Duncan. Lecturer, Department of German, University of Wales, Swansea. Editor of *Journal of Nietzsche Studies* (1998), *New Comparison* (1998–), Nietzsche's *Twilight of the Idols* (also translator, 1998), and other publications. Contributor to numerous journals and anthologies. **Essays:** Friedrich Wilhelm Nietzsche; Parsifal: Wagner/Nietzsche Debate (Wagner).

Larkin, Edward T. Associate Professor, Department of Languages, Literatures, and Cultures, University of New Hampshire. Author of *War in Goethe's Writings: Representation and Assessment* (1992). Contributor to many collections and journals including *Encyclopedia of the Essay* (1997) and *Carleton Germanic Papers*. **Essays:** Johann Gottlieb Fichte; Friedrich Daniel Ernst Schleiermacher; Weimar.

Latimer, Dan. Professor of English and Comparative Literature, Department of English, Auburn University, Auburn, Alabama. Author of *The Elegiac Mode in Milton and Rilke* (1977). Editor of *Contemporary Critical Theory* (1989). Contributor to several journals and collections including *Reference Guide to World Literature* (1995) and *Comparatist*. **Essays:** *Aus dem Leben eines Taugenichts* (Eichendorff); *Die Räuber* (Schiller).

Lawrie, Steven W. Lecturer, Department of German, University of Aberdeen. Author of *Erich Fried: A Writer without a Country* (1996). Editor of *Research in German Studies* (with G. Burgess and G. Sharman) and *Institute of Germanic Studies/University of Aberdeen* (1996–98). Contributor to numerous journals and collections. **Essays:** Berliner Ensemble; Erich Fried; *Mutter Courage* (Brecht).

Lea, Henry A. Professor Emeritus, Department of Germanic Languages and Literature, University of Massachusetts, Amherst. Author of *Gustav Mahler: Man on the Margin* (1985) and *Wolfgang Hildesheimers Weg als Jude und Deutscher* (1997). Contributor to many books and journals including *Wolfgang Hildesheimer* (1989). **Essay:** Wolfgang Hildesheimer.

Lensing, Leo A. Professor of German Studies, Wesleyan University, Middletown, Connecticut. Author of *Peter Altenberg* (with Andrew Barker, 1995). Editor of *Rainer Werner Fassbinder: The Anarchy of the Imagination* (with Michael Töteberg, 1992). Contributor to *Die Fackel von Karl Kraus* (1999). **Essay:** Oskar Kokoschka.

Lewis, Ward B. Associate Professor, Department of Germanic and Slavic Languages, University of Georgia. Author of several books including *Eugene O'Neill: The German Reception of America's First Dramatist* (1984) and *The Ironic Dissident: Frank Wedekind in the View of His Critics* (1997). Editor of *The Birds in Langfoot's Belfry* by Paul Zech (1993). Contributor to many anthologies and journals. **Essays:** Egon Erwin Kisch; *Frühlings Erwachen* (Wedekind).

Leydecker, Karl. Lecturer, Department of German, University of Stirling. Author of *Marriage and Divorce in the Plays of Hermann Sudermann* (1996). Contributor to several books and journals including *Mutual Exchanges* (1998) and *Modern Language Review*. **Essay:** Frank Wedekind.

Littlejohns, Richard. Professor of Modern Languages, University of Leicester. Author of *Wackenroder-Studien* (1987) and *A German Text and Its European Context* (1993). Editor of Wilhelm Heinrich Wackenroder's *Sämtliche Werke und Briefe*, volume 2 (1991). Contributor to many books and journals. **Essays:** Die Horen; Novalis; Romanticism; *Lucinde* (F. Schlegel).

Löb, Ladislaus. Professor of German, School of European Studies, University of Sussex. Author of many books including *Grabbe über seine Werke. Christian Dietrich Grabbes Selbstzeugnisse zu seinen Dramen, Aufsätzen, und Plänen* (1991) and *Christian Dietrich Grabbe* (1996). Co-editor of *Forms of Identity: Definitions and Changes* (with István Petrovics and György E. Szönyi, 1994). Contributor to numerous journals and anthologies. **Essays:** *Woyzeck* (Büchner); Christian Dietrich

Grabbe; Friedrich Hebbel; Heinrich von Kleist; *Der Zebrochne Krug* (Kleist); *Masse-Mensch* (Toller).

Loentz, Elizabeth. Graduate associate, Department of Germanic Languages and Literatures, Ohio State University. **Essays:** *Jud Süß* (Feuchtwanger); Theodor Herzl; Zionism.

Lorenz, Dagmar C.G. (Adviser). Professor, Department of German, University of Illinois, Chicago. Author of *Keepers of the Motherland: German Text by Jewish Women Writers* (1997), *Verfolgung bis zum Massenmord* (1992), *Franz Grillparzer* (1986), and *Ilse Aichinger* (1982). Editor of numerous books and *German Quarterly* (1997–present). Contributor to many books and journals. **Essays:** Austria: Interwar; *Die Fackel im Ohr* (E. Canetti); Franz Grillparzer; *Die Jüdin von Toledo* (Grillparzer); Edgar Hilsenrath; Gertrud Kolmar; Friedrich Torberg.

Lorey, Christoph. Associate Professor, Department of Culture and Language Studies, University of New Brunswick, Fredericton. Author of *Lessings Familienbild* (1992) and *Die Ehe im Klassischen Werk Goethes* (1995). Editor of *International Fiction Review* (1995–) and several other publications. Contributor to many books and journals. **Essay:** Luise Adelgunde Victorie Gottsched.

Lubich, Frederick A. Professor, Department of Foreign Languages and Literatures, Old Dominion University, Norfolk, Virginia. Author of *Die Dialektik von Logos und Eros im Werk von Thomas Mann* (1986) and *Max Frischs "Stiller," "Homofaber," und "Mein Name sei Gantenbein"* (1990). Editor of *Thomas Mann, Tonio Krüger, Death in Venice, and Other Writings* (1999). Contributor to numerous books and journals. **Essays:** Thomas Mann; *Der Zauberberg* (T. Mann).

Madland, Helga Stipa. Professor of German, Department of Modern Languages, Literatures, and Linguistics, University of Oklahoma, Norman. Author of several books including *Image and Text: J. M. R. Lenz* (1994) and *Marianne Ehrmann: Reason and Emotion in Her Life and Works* (1998). Co-editor of *Space to Act: The Theater of J. M. R. Lenz* (with Alan Leidner, 1993). Contributor to many publications. **Essays:** Bourgeois Tragedy; Marianne Ehrmann; Sturm und Drang.

Marshall, Donald. (Adviser). Professor and Head, Department of English, University of Illinois, Chicago. Editor of numerous books and editor/editorial board member of many journals, including *Partisan Review* (1978–94), *Arachne* (1992–present), and *Symploke* (1995–present). Contributor to many books and journals. **Essay:** Arnold Franz Walter Schoenberg.

Martin, Bernhard R. Department of German, Russian, and Asian Languages and Literature, Tufts University, Boston. Author of *Dichtung und Ideologie: Völkisch-nationales Denken im Werk Rudolf Georg Bindings* (1986) and *Niebelungen-Metamorphosen: Die Geschichte eines Mythos* (1992). Contributor to many journals and anthologies including *Medieval Studies as Paradigm for German Studies* (1999). **Essays:** Criticism; Wilhelm Dilthey; *Versuch einer critischen Dichtkunst vor die Deutschen* (Gottsched).

Mason, Eve. Affiliated Lecturer, Department of German, University of Cambridge, and Official Fellow, Newnham College, University of Cambridge (retired). Author of *Prolog, Epilog und Zwischenrede im deutschen Schanspiel des Mittelalters* (1949), *Switzerland* (1951), and *Adalbert Stifter, Bunte Steine* (1986). Contributor to numerous journals and collections. **Essays:** Gottfried Keller; *Der Grüne Heinrich* (Keller).

Maurer, Warren R. Professor, Department of Germanic Languages and Literatures, University of Kansas. Author of *Gerhart Hauptmann* (1982), *Understanding Gerhart Hauptmann* (1992), and other books. Editor of *Rilke: The Alchemy of Alienation* (1980). Contributor to several books and journals. **Essays:** Gerhart Hauptmann; Naturalism.

McConnell, Winder. Professor, Department of German, University of California, Davis. Author of many books including *The Nibelungenlied* (1984) and *The Epic of Kudrun* (1992). Editor of *Romanticism and Beyond: A Festschrift for John F. Fetzer* (with Clifford A. Bernd and Ingeborg Henderson, 1996), and *Companion to the Nibelungenlied* (1998). Contributor to many journals and collections. **Essays:** Gottfried von Straßburg; Das Nibelungenlied.

McCumber, John. Professor, Department of German, Northwestern University, Evanston, Illinois. Author of several books including *The Company of Words* (1993) and *Metaphysics and Oppression* (1999). Co-editor of *Endings* (1999). Contributor to several journals. **Essays:** Jürgen Habermas; Georg Wilhelm Friedrich Hegel; *Der Ursprung des Kunstwerks* (Heidegger).

McGowan, Moray. (Adviser). Professor of German, University of Sheffield. Author of *Marieluise Fleißer* (1987). Co-editor of *From High Priests to Desecrators: Contemporary Austrian Writers* (with Ricarda Schmidt, 1993) and *Denn du tanzt auf einem Positionen Deutschsprachiger Migrantinnenliteratur* (with Sabine Fischer, 1997). Contributor to *Cambridge History of German Literature* (1997). **Essay:** Aras Ören.

McLeish, Alastair. Lecturer in Communication, School of Information and Media, Robert Gordon University, Aberdeen. Contributor to *Studies in Marxism* (1994, 1995, 1997). **Essay:** Marx and Marxism.

McPherson, Karin M.D. Lecturer, Honorary Fellow, Department of German, University of Edinburgh. Author of *Christa Wolf: Der Geteilte Himmel* (1996). Co-editor of *Neue Ansichten: The Reception of Romanticism in the Literature of the GDR* (1990) and *In the Party Spirit—Socialist Realism and Literary Practice in the Soviet Union, East Germany, and China* (1996). Contributor to many books and journals. **Essay:** Christa Wolf.

Melin, Charlotte. Associate Professor, University of Minnesota. Author of *English Grammar for Students of German* (1990, 1994) and *German Poetry in Translation 1945–90* (forthcoming). Contributor to several journals including *Studies in Twentieth Century Literature* (1997). **Essay:** Hans Magnus Enzensberger.

Menhennet, Alan. Emeritus Professor of German, University of New Castle upon Tyne. Author of several books including *The Romantic Movement* (1981) and *Grimmelshausen the Storyteller* (1997). Editor of *Seventeenth Century* and *Quinquereme.* Contributor to many journals. **Essays:** Christian Fürchtegott Gellert; Hans Jakob Christoffel von Grimmelshausen; *Der Abenteuerliche Simplicissimus* (Grimmelshausen); *Der Fräulein von Scuderi* (Hoffmann).

Metzger, Erika A. Professor of German, Department of Modern Languages and Literatures, University of Buffalo, Buffalo, New York. Author of *Im bezirk des schnees* (1986), *Reading Andreas Grypius: Critical Trends 1664–1993* (with M.M. Metzger, 1994), and other books. Editor of many journals and anthologies including *Sprachgesellschaften-Poetinnen* (with R.E. Schade, 1989). Contributor to numerous collections and journals. **Essays:** Andreas Gryphius; Karoline Frederike Louise Maximiliane von Günderrode; Georg Trakl.

Metzger, Michael M. Professor of German, Department of Modern Languages and Literatures, University of Buffalo, Buffalo, New York. Author of several books including *Stefan George* (with E.A. Metzger, 1972) and *Reading Andreas Grypius: Critical Trends 1664–1993* (with E.A. Metzger, 1994). Editor of many books and journals including *NDL.* Contributor to numerous journal and anthologies. **Essays:** Blätter für die Kunst; Stefan George; *Des Teppich des Lebens und die Lieder von Traum* (George).

Meyer, Franziska. Lecturer, School of European Studies, University of Wales, Cardiff. Author of *Avantgarde im Hinterland: Caroline Schlegel-Schelling in der DDR-Literatur* (1998). Contributor to many collections including *Post-War Women's Writing in German: Feminist Critical Approaches* (1997) and *German Writers and the Cold War 1945–61* (1992). **Essays:** Caroline Schlegel; Dorothea Schlegel.

Midgley, David. (Adviser). University Lecturer in German, University of Cambridge. Author of *Arnold Zweig: Zu Werk un Wandlung* (1980) and *Writing Weimar* (forthcoming). Editor of *Arnold Zweig-Poetik, Judentum und Politik* (1989) and *The German Novel in the 20th Century* (1993). Contributor to several journals and anthologies. **Essays:** Episches Theater; Ödön von Horváth; Neue Sachlichkeit; Joseph Roth; *Radetzkymarsch* (J. Roth).

Mitchell, Michael. Senior Lecturer, German Department, Stirling University. Author of *Harrap's German Grammar* (1988) and *Peter Hacks: Drama for a Socialist Society* (1990). Editor of *The Dedalus/Ariadne Book of Austrian Fantasy* (1992) and *The Babel Guide to German Fiction in English Translation* (1997). Contributor to many books and journals. **Essay:** Gustav Meyrink.

Morgan, Ben. Affiliated Lecturer, Department of German, University of Cambridge. **Essay:** Meister Eckhart.

Mueller, Agnes C. Visiting Assistant Professor, University of South Carolina, Columbia. Author of *Lyrik "Made in USA":* *Vermittlung und Rezeption in der Bundesrepublik* (1999). Contributor to *Encyclopedia of the Essay* (1997). **Essay:** Helmut Heißenbüttel.

Munn, Kenneth E. Doctoral candidate, Department of Linguistics and Germanic, Slavic, Asian, and African Languages, Michigan State University, East Lansing. **Essays:** Johann Jakob Bodmer; Johann Jakob Breitinger.

Murdoch, Brian. (Adviser). Professor of German, University of Stirling. Author of several books including *Cornish Literature* (1993) and *The Germanic Hero* (1996). Editor of many collections including *Remarque against War* (1998). Contributor to numerous anthologies and journals. **Essays:** Carolingian Period; Heimatroman; Ludwigsleid; Merseburger Zaubersprüche; Erich Maria Remarque; War Novels.

Murti, Kamakshi P. Associate Professor, Department of German Studies, University of Arizona. Author of *Die Reinkarnation des Lesers als Autor* (1990) and *India the Seductive and Seduced "Other" of German Orientalism* (1999). Contributor to *The Feminist Encyclopedia of German Literature* (1997) and other publications. **Essays:** May Ayim; Marie Luise Kaschnitz; Minority Literature.

Nehring, Wolfgang. Professor of German, Department of Germanic Languages, University of California, Los Angeles. Author of *Die Tat bei Hofmannsthal* (1967) and *Spätromantiker* (1997). Editor of many works including *Florentin* by Dorothea Schlegel (1993). Contributor to numerous journals and anthologies. **Essay:** Hugo von Hofmannsthal.

Nelson, Don. Associate Professor, Department of German, Bowling Green State University, Bowling Green, Ohio. Author of *Portrait of Artist as Hermes* (1971). Contributor to several journals including *Psychohistory Review* and *Word.* **Essays:** Decadence; Hermann Hesse; *Der Steppenwolf* (Hesse); Philosophy and Literature.

Oergel, Maike. Lecturer in German, Department of German, University of Nottingham. Author of *The Return of King Arthur and the Nibelungen: National Myth in 19th Century England and Germany* (1998). Contributor to publications including *Imagining Nations* (1998) and *Myth and the Making of Modernity* (1998). **Essays:** Irony, Romantic; Mythology.

O'Flaherty, James C. Professor Emeritus of German, Wake Forrest University, Winston Salem, North Carolina. Author of several books including *Johann Georg Hamann* (1979) and *The Quarrel of Reason with Itself* (1988). Editor of books and journals including *Studies in Nietzsche and the Judeo-Christian Tradition* (1985). Contributor to numerous journals and collections. **Essay:** Johann Georg Hamann.

Ohnesorg, Stefanie. Assistant Professor, Department of Modern Foreign Languages and Literatures, University of Tennessee, Knoxville. Author of *Mit Kompaß, Kutsche, und Kamel* (1996). Editor of *Die von denen faunen gepeitschte Laster* by Sidonia Zaünemann (forthcoming). Contributor to several volumes including *Wahnsinnsfrauen* (1999). **Essays:** Louise Aston; Ida von Hahn-Hahn; Satire; Travel Literature.

Osborne, John. Professor of German, University of Warwick. Author of many books including *Vom Nutzen der Geschichte; Studien zum Werk Conrad Ferdinand Meyers* (1994) and *Gerhart Hauptmann and the Naturalist Drama* (1998). Editor of *Die Meininger: Texte zur Rezeption* (1980). Contributor to many books and journals. **Essays:** Bismarck Era; Arno Holz and Johannes Schlaf; *Gedanken über die Nachahmung der griechischen Werke in der Malerei und Bilderhauerkunst* (Winckelmann).

Paas, John Roger. Professor, German Department, Carleton College, Northfield, Minnesota. Editor of *Unbekannte Gedichte und Lieder des Sigmund von Birken* (1990), *Hollstein's German Engravings, Etchings, and Woodcuts 1400–1700* (volumes 38–41, 1994–95), *"Der Franken Rom: Nürnbergs Blütezeit* (1995), and other works. *Turkish Culture in German Society Today* (1996). Contributor to numerous books and journals. **Essays:** Martin Opitz; Johann Joachim Winckelmann.

Parkes, Stuart. Reader in German Literature and Society, University of Sunderland. Author of *Writers and Politics in West Germany* (1986) and *Understanding Contemporary Germany* (1997). Editor of numerous books including *Contemporary German Writers, Their Aesthetics, and Their Language* (1996). Contributor to many books and journals. **Essays:** Federal Republic of Germany; Gruppe 47; Neue Subjektivität; Universities; Martin Walser.

Pausch, Holger A. Professor, Department of Modern Languages and Cultural Studies, University of Alberta, Edmonton. Author of *Sprachmodelle* (1988), *Arno Schmidt* (1992), and other books. Editor of several works including *George Kaiser* (1981). Contributor to many books and journals. **Essays:** *Das Passagen Werk* (Benjamin); Günter Eich.

Pender, Malcolm. Reader in German Studies, Department of Modern Languages, University of Stramclyde. Author of books including *Max Frisch: Biedermann und die Brandstuftes* (1988) and *Contemporary Images of Death and Sickness: A Theme in German-Swiss Literature* (1998). Editor of *25 Years of Emancipation? Women in Switzerland 1971–1996* (with J. Charneley and A. Wilkin, 1998) and other works. Contributor to numerous books and journals. **Essay:** Max Frisch.

Peucker, Brigitte. (Adviser). Professor of German, Yale University, New Haven, Connecticut. Author of *Incorporating Images: Film and the Rival Arts* (1995), *Lyric Descent in the German Romantic Tradition* (1987), and *Arcadia to Elysium: Preromantic Modes in 18th Century Germany* (1980). Contributor to many scholarly journals.

Pfanner, Helmut F. Professor of German, Vanderbilt University, Nashville, Tennessee. Author of several books including *Oskar Maria Graf: Eine Kritische Bibliographie* (1976) and *Exile in New York: German and Austrian Writers after 1933* (1983). Editor of many books and journals including *Der Zweite Weltkrieg und die Exilanten/World War II and the Exiles* (1991). Contrib-

utor to numerous collections and journals. **Essays:** Oskar Maria Graf; *Der Prozeß* (Kafka); *Die Verwandlung* (Kafka).

Phelan, Anthony. Fellow in German, Keble College, Oxford. Author of *Rilke: Neue Gedichte: A Critical Guide* (1992). Editor of *The Weimar Dilemma* (1984). Contributor to several books and journals including *German Cultural Studies: An Introduction* (1995). **Essays:** Heinrich Heine; *Deutschland: Ein Wintermärchen* (Heine); *Gespräch über die Poesie* (F. Schlegel).

Pickar, Gertud Bauer. Emeritus Professor, Department of German, University of Houston, Houston, Texas. Author of several books including *The Dramatic Works of Max Frisch* (1976) and *Ambivalence Transcended: A Study of the Writings of Annette von Droste-Hülshoff* (1997). Editor of *Leseerfahrungen mit Martin Walser* (with Heike Doane, 1993) and other publications. Contributor to many books and journals. **Essay:** Annette von Droste-Hülshoff.

Pike, Burton. Professor of Comparative Literature and German, Graduate School, City University of New York. Author of *Robert Musil: An Introduction to His Work* (1961) and *The Image of the City in Modern Literature* (1981). Editor of many books and journals including *Thomas Mann: Six Early Stories* (1997). Contributor to numerous collections and journals. **Essays:** *Der Mann ohne Eigenschaften* (Musil); *Die Verwirrungen des Zögling Törleß* (Musil).

Preece, Julian. Lecturer in German, University of Kent at Canterbury. Editor of *Contemporary German Writers: Their Aesthetics and Their Language* (1996) and *"Whose Story?": Continuities in Contemporary German-Language Literature* (1998). Contributor to publications including *Modern Language Review* and *Modern Austrian Literature*. **Essays:** Veza Canetti; *Effi Briest* (Fontaine); Peter Schneider.

Prochnik, Peter. Lecturer, Department of German, Royal Holloway, University of London (retired). Editor of *Berlin '87* (1988) and *Das Dritte Reich im Spiegel der Literatur* (1991). Contributor to several books and journals including *Günter Grass's "der Butt": Sexual Politics and the Male Myth of History* (1990). **Essay:** Der Ruf.

Purver, Judith. Senior Lecturer, Department of German, University of Manchester. Author of *Hindeutung auf das Höhere: A Structural Study of the Novels of Joseph von Eichendorff* (1989). Co-editor of *German Romantics in Context. Selected Essays 1971–86* by Elisabeth Stopp (1992). Contributor to numerous books and journals including *Publications of the English Goethe Society* (1996). **Essay:** Caroline Auguste Fischer.

Ragg-Kirkby, Helena. Independent Scholar. Contributor to *German Life and Letters* and *Jahrbuch des Adalbert-Stifter-Institutes des Landes Oberösterreich*. **Essay:** Adalbert Stifter.

Rasche, Hermann. Lecturer, Department of German, National University of Ireland, Galway. Editor of *Eiswasser* (1996). Contributor to many books and journals including *Exiles and Migrants* (1997) and *Irish Studies* (1998). **Essay:** Paul Heyse.

Read, Malcolm. Senior Lecturer, German Department, Stirling University. Co-author of *Siegfried Lenz* (with B.O. Murdoch, 1978). Contributor to several journals including *Modern Languages* and *New German Studies*. **Essays:** Ernst Jandl; Klabund (Alfred Henschke); Martin Sperr.

Redmann, Jennifer. Assistant Professor, Department of German, Ripon College, Ripon, Wisconsin. Contributor to *Postmodern Pluralisms and Concepts of Totality* (1995). **Essay:** *Die Wupper* (Lasker-Schüler).

Reershemius, Gertrud. Lecturer, Department of German, Aston University, Birmingham. Author of *Biographisches Erzählen auf Jiddisch* (1997). Contributor to *Arbeiten zur Mehdspachigkeit* (1996), *Osnabrücker Beiträge zur Spachtheorie* (1997), and *Info-Daf* (1998). **Essays:** Jewish Culture and Literature; Moses Mendelssohn.

Reid, J.H. Professor Emeritus, Department of German, University of Nottingham. Author of several books including *Heinrich Böll* (1988) and *Writing without Taboos* (1990). Editor of *Reassessing the GDR* (1994) and other publications. Contributor to many anthologies and journals. **Essay:** *Die Ästhetik des Widerstands* (Weiss).

Reinhart, Max. Associate Professor, Department of Germanic and Slavic Languages, University of Georgia. Author of several books including *Johann Hellwig's "Die Nymphe Noris" (1650): A Critical Edition* (1994) and *Georg Philipp Harsdörffer: "Lamentation for France" and Other Polemics on War and Peace (The Latin Pamphlets of 1641–42)* (1998). Editor of *Early Modern German Studies* series (1998–), *Cultural Spaces: Utopia, Society, and Communication from Dante to Goethe* by Klaus Garber (1999), and other works. Contributor to many journals and anthologies. **Essays:** Baroque; Humanism; Utopianism.

Reitter, Paul B. Graduate Student, Department of German, University of California, Berkley. Editorial board member of *Qui parle* (1997–). Contributor to *Heinrich Heine's Contested Identities* and *Judaism*. **Essays:** Karl Kraus; *Die Fackel* (Kraus); *Die letzten Tage der Menschheit* (Kraus).

Rennie, Nicholas. Assistant Professor, Department of Germanic Languages and Literatures, Rutgers University, New Brunswick. Contributor to *Goethe Yearbook* and *Comparative Literature Studies*. **Essay:** *Laokoon; oder, Über die Grenzender Malerei und Poesie* (Lessing).

Rickels, Laurence A. Professor, Department of Germanic, Slavic, and Semitic Studies, University of California, Santa Barbara. Author of several books including *Der Unbetrauerbare Tod* (1990) and *The Case of California* (1991). Editor of several journals and collections including *Substance* (special issue, 1990). Contributor to numerous works. **Essays:** Theodor W. Adorno; Aestheticization of Politics; Frankfurt School; Otto Weininger.

Ridley, Hugh. Department of German, University College, Dublin. Author of several books including *Gottfried Benn* (1990) and *The Problematic Bourgeois* (1995). Editor of a num-

ber of publications including *Rilke und der Wandel in der Sensibilitat*. **Essays:** Alfred Andersch; Restoration; Vormärz.

Ritchie, J.M. Emeritus Professor and Chairman, Research Centre for German and Austrian Exile Studies, Institute of German Studies, University of London. Author of *German Literature under National Socialism* (1983), *German Exiles: British Perspectives* (1998), and other books. Editor of many collections and journals including *German Life and Letters* (1980–98). Contributor to numerous publications. **Essays:** Exile Literature; Fascism and Literature; National Socialism.

Rizza, Steve. Lektor für englishe Sprache, Institut für Anglistik/Amerikanistik, Pädagogische Hochschule Erfurt. Author of *Hugo von Hofmannsthal and Rudolf Kassner: Criticism as Art* (1997). Contributor to *Ossian Revisited* (1991). **Essays:** *Eine Brief* (Hofmannsthal); Alfred Kubin.

Robb, David. School of Modern Languages, Queen's University of Belfast. Author of *Zwei Clowns im Lande des verlorener Lachens: Das Lieder theater Wenzel and Mensching* (1998). Contributor to *Literatur für Leser* (1996). **Essay:** Liedermacher.

Roe, Ian F. Senior Lecturer, Department of German Studies, University of Reading. Author of *An Introduction to the Major Works of Franz Grillparzer* (1991) and *Franz Grillparzer: A Century of Criticism* (1995). Editor of *The Biedermeier and Beyond* (1998). Contributor to several books and journals. **Essays:** *Der arme Spielmann* (Grillparzer); Biedermeier Period.

Rogowski, Christian. Associate Professor, Department of German, Amherst College, Amherst, Massachusetts. Author of *Implied Dramaturgy* (1993) and *Distinguished Outsider* (1995). Contributor to many publications including *A User's Guide to German Cultural Studies* (1997). **Essays:** Heiner Müller; *Die Hamletmaschine* (Müller).

Rorrison, Hugh. Senior Lecturer, Department of Linguistics and Phonetics, University of Leeds. **Essay:** *Germania Tod in Berlin* (Müller).

Rowland, Herbert. Professor of German, Department of Foreign Languages and Literatures, Purdue University, Lafayette, Indiana. Author of several books including *Matthias Claudius: Language as "Infamous Funnel" and Its Imperatives* (1997). Editor of *The Eighteenth-Century German Book Review* (1995). Contributor to numerous journals and anthologies. **Essays:** Anacreontic Poetry; Matthias Claudius.

Rumold, Inca. Associate Professor, Department of Modern Languages, DePaul University, Chicago, Illinois. Author of *Die Verwandlung des Ekels: Zur Funktion der Kunst in Rilkes Malte Laurids Brigge und Sartres La Nauseé* (1979). Contributor to several books and journals including *Monatshefte* and *Women in German Yearbook* (1999). **Essay:** Nelly Sachs.

Ryan, Judith. Robert K. and Dale J. Weary Professor of German and Comparative Literature and Harvard College Professor, Harvard University, Cambridge, Massachusetts. **Essays:** Paul Celan; *Das Schloß* (Kafka); *Die Sonette an Orpheus* (Rilke).

Sagarra, Eda. Professor, Department of Germanic Studies, Trinity College, Dublin. Author of several books including *Germany and the Nineteenth Century* (1990) and *Theodor Fontane: Der Stechlin* (1986). Editor of *Anthropologie und Literatur um 1800* (1992) and other works. Contributor to numerous books and journals. **Essays:** Karl Gutzkow; Johann Heinrich Voß.

Sammons, Jeffrey L. (Adviser). Leavenworth Professor of German, Yale University, New Haven, Connecticut. Author of several books including *Heinrich Heine* (1991) and *Ideology, Mimesis, Fantasy: Charles Sealsfield, Friedrich Gerstäcker, Karl May, and Other German Novelists of America* (1998). Detour of many collections and journals including *Die Protokolle der Weisen von Zion* (1998). Contributor to numerous publications. **Essays:** Ludwig Börne; Karl Emil Franzos; Das Junge Deutschland; Karl May; Wilhelm Raabe; Friedrich von Schiller.

Schindler, Stephan K. Associate Professor, German Department, Washington University, St. Louis, Missouri. Author of *Das Subjekt als Kind: Die Erfindung der Kindheit im Roman des 18 Jahrhunderts* (1994) and *Eingebildete Körper: Phantasierte Sexualität in der Goethezeit* (1998). Editor of journals and books including *Knowledge, Science, and Literature in Early Modern Germany* (1996). Contributor to numerous journals and collections. **Essays:** Film and Literature; Hermeneutics; Holocaust (Shoah) Literature; *Der Sandmann* (Hoffmann).

Schneider, Gerd K. Professor of German, Department of Languages, Literatures, and Linguistics, Syracuse University, Syracuse, New York. Author of *Topical Bibliography in Theoretical and Applied German Linguistics* (1972) and *Die Rezeption von Arthur Schnitzlers Reigen 1897–1994* (1997). Editorial board member of *Symposium*. Contributor to numerous books and journals. **Essays:** Tankred Dorst; Arthur Schnitzler; *Fräulein Else* (Schnitzler).

Schwab, Eric J. Assistant Professor of Germanic Languages and Literatures, Yale University, New Haven, Connecticut. Contributor to *Lessing Yearbook* and *Encyclopedia of the Essay*. **Essay:** Das Genie.

Schweitzer, Christoph E. Professor Emeritus, Department of Germanic Languages, University of North Carolina, Chapel Hill. Author of *Men Viewing Women as Art Objects* (1998). Editor of many books and journals including *Dictionary of Literary Biography* (1988, 1990) and Carové's *Kinderleben* (1995). Contributor to numerous anthologies and journals. **Essays:** Wilhelm Hauff; Wilhelm Heinrich Wackenroder.

Scott Linton, Marilyn. Associate Professor, Department of Germanic Languages, University of North Carolina, Chapel Hill. Co-author of *Deutsche Sprache und Landeskunde* (4th edition, 1993) and *Testing Program to Accompany Deutsche Sprache und Landeskunde* (4th edition, 1993). Contributor to many publications including *Modern Austrian Literature*. **Essay:** Catharina Regina von Greiffenberg.

Sharpe, Lesley. Professor, Department of German, University of Exeter. Author of *Friedrich Schiller: Drama, Thought, and Politics* (1991) and *Schiller's Aesthetic Essays: Two Centuries of Criticism* (1995). Editor of several journals and anthologies including *Modern Language Review* (Germanic editor, 1994–). Contributor to numerous books and journals. **Essays:** *Kabale und Liebe* (Schiller); *Über naïve und sentimentalische Dichtung* (Schiller).

Shipe, Timothy. Curator, International Dada Archive, University Libraries, University of Iowa. Contributor to many books and journals including *The Complete Works of Marcel Duchamp* (3rd edition, 1997), *Women in Dada* (1998), and *Art Documentation*. **Essays:** Hugo Ball; Dadaism; Richard Huelsenbeck; Kurt Schwitters.

Shirer, Robert K. Associate Professor, Department of Modern Languages and Literatures, University of Nebraska, Lincoln. Author of *Difficulties of Saying "I"* (1989). Editorial board member of *Studies in Twentieth Century Literature* (1986–). Contributor to several books and journals including *Monatshefte*. **Essay:** Johannes R. Becher.

Shookman, Ellis. Associate Professor, Department of German Studies, Dartmouth College, Hanover, New Hampshire. Author of *Noble Lies, Slant Truths, Necessary Angels: Aspects of Fictionality in the Novels of Christoph Martin Wieland* (1997). Editor of *Eighteenth Century German Prose* (1992) and *The Faces of Physiognomy: Interdisciplinary Approaches to Johann Caspar Lavater* (1993). Contributor to many books and journals. **Essays:** Johann Caspar Lavater; *Der Tod in Venedig* (T. Mann); Christoph Martin Wieland; *Geschichte des Agathon* (Wieland).

Siefken, Hinrich. Emeritus Professor, Department of German, University of Nottingham. Author of several books including *Thomas Mann: Goethe—Ideal der Deutschheit* (1981) and *Theodor Haecker* (1989). Editor of *Die Flugblätter der Weissen Rose* (1994) and a number of other works. Contributor to many journals and anthologies. **Essays:** Heinrich Böll; *Wo warst du, Adam?* (Böll); *Doktor Faustus* (T. Mann).

Silverman, Lisa. Ph.D. candidate, German Studies, Yale University, New Haven, Connecticut. **Essay:** Doron Rabinovici.

Simon, Sunka. Assistant Professor, Department of Modern Languages and Literatures, German Section, Swarthmore College, Swarthmore, Pennsylvania. Contributor to *Inner Space—Outer Space: Humanities, Technology, and the Postmodern World* (1993) and *Queering the Canon: Defying Sights in German Literatures and Culture* (1998). **Essays:** Epistolary Novel; Popular Literature.

Skrine, Peter. Professor of German, Department of German, University of Bristol. Author of several books including *Hauptmann, Wedekind, and Schnitzler* (1989) and *A Companion to German Literature* (with Eda Sagarra, 1997). Editor of several collections including *Hans Sachs and Folk Theatre in the Late Middle Ages* (1995). Contributor to numerous journals and anthologies. **Essays:** Jeremias Gotthelf; Albrecht von Haller; Jesuit Drama; Switzerland.

Smith, Duncan. Professor, Department of German Studies, Brown University, Providence, Rhode Island. Author of *Kon-*

frontation (1972) and *Walls and Mirrors* (1988). Editor of *Proceedings of GDR Conference, Remembering Rostock* (volumes 1 and 2, 1991). Contributor to numerous books and journals. **Essays:** Rainer Werner Fassbinder; *Der Tod des Empedokles* (Hölderlin); Realism; W.G. Sebald; *Der Nachsommer* (Stifter).

Springman, Luke. Associate Professor, Department of Languages and Cultures, Bloomsburg University, Bloomsburg, Pennsylvania. Author of *Comrades, Friends, and Companions* (1989). Contributor to several books and journals including *Carver.* **Essay:** Children's Literature.

Stanley, Patricia H. Professor, Department of Modern Languages and Linguistics, Florida State University, Tallahassee. Author of several books including *Wolfgang Hildesheimer and His Critics* (1993) and *A Thousand Thanks: Dr. Albert Schweitzer's Correspondence with Dr. Antonia Brico* (1999). Contributor to *The European Legacy: Toward New Paradigms* (1996) and other publications. **Essay:** Novella.

Stern, H. Senior Lecturer, Department of Germanic Languages and Literatures, Yale University, New Haven, Connecticut. Author of *Gegenbild, Reihenfolge, Sprung: An Essay on Related Figures of Argument in Walter Benjamin* (1982). Contributor to several books and journals including *Mörike's Muses* (1990) and *Journal of Music Theory.* **Essay:** Christian Morgenstern.

Stewart, Mary E. Robinson College, Cambridge. Contributor to numerous collections including *Rejection and Emancipation: Writing in German-Speaking Switzerland 1945–91* (1991), *The German Novel in the Twentieth Century* (1993), and *Deutsche Biographische Enzyklopädie* (1996). **Essays:** Helene Böhlau; *Mutmaßungen über Jakob* (Johnson).

Stillmark, Alexander. Reader in German, University of London. Editor of several books including *Erbe und Umbruch in der neueren deutschsprachigen Komödie* (1990), *Lenau zwischen Ost und West* (1992), and *Joseph Roth. Der Sieg über die Zeit* (1996). Contributor to numerous journals and collections. **Essay:** *Buch der Lieder* (Heine).

Stott, Michelle. Associate Professor, Department of Germanic and Slavic Languages, Brigham Young University, Provo, Utah. Author of *Behind the Mask: Kierkegaard's Pseudonymic Treatment of Lessing in the "Concluding Unscientific Postscript"* (1993). Co-editor of *Im Nonnengarten: An Anthology of German Women's Writing 1850–1907* (with Joseph O. Baker, 1997). Contributor to *Family Perspective* (1992). **Essay:** Marie von Ebner-Eschenbach.

Subiotto, Arrigo V. Professor and Fellow, Institute for Advanced Research in the Arts and Social Sciences, University of Birmingham. Author of *Bertolt Brecht's Adaptations for the Berliner Ensemble* (1975) and *Hans Magnus Enzensberger: Poems* (1985). Editor of *Year's Work in Modern Language Studies* (1961–63). Contributor to numerous books and journals. **Essays:** Hans Fallada; Siegfried Kracauer; Socialist Realism; Peter Weiss.

Tailby, John E. Senior Lecturer, Department of German, University of Leeds. Editor of *Der Reimpaardichter Peter Schmieher*

(1978) and *The Staging of Religious Drama in Europe in the Later Middle Ages* (1983). Contributor to several books and journals including *Hans Sachs and Folk Theatre in the Later Middle Ages* (1995). **Essay:** Mystery Plays.

Taylor, Rodney. Associate Professor of German, Division of Languages and Literature, Truman State University. Author of *History and the Paradoxes of Metaphysics in Danton's Tod* (1990) and *Perspectives on Spinoza in Works by Schiller, Büchner, and C.F. Meyer: Five Essays* (1995). Contributor to *Encyclopedia of the Essay* (1997) and other publications. **Essays:** Georg Büchner; *Dantons Tod* (Büchner).

Thomaneck, J.K.A. Professor of German, German Department, University of Aberdeen. Author of many books including *Ulrich Plenzdorf's Die neuen Leiden des jungen W.* (1989, 1992) and *The German Democratic Republic: Politics, Government, and Society* (1989). Editor of *German Life and Letters* (special issue, 1992). Contributor to numerous books and journals. **Essays:** Johannes Bobrowski; Theodor Storm.

Varkonyi, Istvan. Assistant Professor of German, Department of Modern Languages, Temple University, Philadelphia, Pennsylvania. Author of *Florenc Molnar and the Austro-Hungarian Fin de Siecle* (1992). Contributor to *Young Lukács, the Sunday Circle, and Their Critique of Aestheticism* (1995) and *Mit meinem Leibe wider den Krieg, mit meinem Leben für den Frieden* (1995). **Essays:** Peter Altenberg (Richard Engländer); Richard Beer-Hoffmann; Jung Wien; Ludwig Wittgenstein.

Vazsonyi, Nicholas. Assistant Professor of German, Department of Germanic, Slavic and Oriental Languages, University of South Carolina. Author of *Lukács Reads Goethe: From Aestheticism to Stalinism* (1997). Contributor to several books and journals including *Journal of the American Liszt Society* and *Studies in 20th Century Literature.* **Essays:** Georg Lukács; Richard Wagner.

Vilain, Robert. Lecturer in German, Royal Holloway University of London. Author of *Hugo von Hofmannsthal: Tradition and Inhibition* (forthcoming). Editor of *Yvan Goll—Clair Goll: Texts and Contexts* (with Eric Robertson, 1997). Contributor to numerous book and journals. **Essay:** Jugendstil.

Wagener, Hans. Professor of German, Department of Germanic Languages, University of California, Los Angeles. Author of several books including *Understanding Franz Werfel* (1993) and *Carl Zuckmayer Criticism: Tracing Endangered Fame* (1995). Editor of numerous collections including *Von Böll bis Buchheim: Deutsche Kriegsprosa nach 1945* (1997). Contributor to several books and journals. **Essays:** Lion Feuchtwanger; Siegfried Lenz; Franz Werfel.

Walker, Richard Ernest. Associate Professor, Department of Germanic Studies, University of Maryland, College Park. Author of *Peter von Staufenberg: Its Origins, Development, and Later Adaptation* (1980), *The Corpus Christi Sermons of Johannes: An Edition with Commentary* (1988), and *The Uses of Polemic: The Centuriae of Johannes Nas* (1998–99). Contributor to *Encyclopedia of the Reformation* (1997). **Essays:** Das Ezzolied; Das Hildebrandslied; Georg (Jörg) Wickram.

Wallace, Ian. Professor of German, Department of European Studies and Modern Languages, University of Bath. Author of *Volker Braun* (1986) and *Berlin* (1993). Editor of numerous books and journals including *Forum Deutsch* (1995–). Contributor to many journals and anthologies. **Essay:** Volker Braun.

Walther, Ingeborg. Assistant Professor, Department of Germanic Languages and Literatures, Duke University, Durham, North Carolina. Author of *The Theater of Franz Xaver Kroetz* (1990). Contributor to several journals including *Modern Drama* and *Unterrichtspraxis*. **Essay:** Franz Xaver Kroetz.

Weninger, Robert. Professor of German and Comparative Literature, Washington University, St. Louis, Missouri. Author of several books including *Arno Schmidt Bibliographie* (1995) and *Framing a Novelist: Arno Schmidt Criticism 1970–1994* (1995). Editor of *Wendezeiten/Zeitenwenden. Positionsbestimmungen zur Deutschsprachigen Literatur 1945–1995* (1997). Contributor to many books and journals. **Essay:** Arno Schmidt.

Werres, Peter. Professorial Lecturer, Department of German and Slavic Languages and Literatures, George Washington University, Washington, D.C. Author of *Die Liedermacher Biermann und Degenhardt* (1990). Co-author of *Faust as Archetypal Subtext at the Millennium* (1998). Editorial board member of *Philological Papers* (1997–). Contributor to numerous journals and collections. **Essay:** Wolf Biermann.

West, Jonathan. Senior Lecturer, Department of German, University of Newcastle upon Tyne. Author of many books including *Categories and their Exponents* (1993) and *Particles and Their Use* (1993). Editor of *The Web Journal of Modern Language Linguistics* (1995–). Contributor to several books and journals. **Essay:** German Language.

Wheeler, Brett R. School of Foreign Service, Georgetown University, Washington, D.C. Contributor to numerous books and journals including *European Legacy, CGES Forum,* and *German Quarterly*. **Essays:** Bildung; *Strukturwander der Öffentlichkeit* (Habermas).

White, Alfred D. School of European Studies, Cardiff University. Author of many books including *Theodor Storm: Der Schimmelreiter* (1988), *Brecht: Der gute Mensch von Sezuan* (1990), and *Max Frisch, the Reluctant Modernist* (1996). Contributor to numerous books and journals. **Essays:** Documentary Literature; *Die Blechtrommel* (Grass); Heinrich Mann; Die Moderne; 1950s; Ranier Maria Rilke; Weimar Republic.

White, I.A. Senior Lecturer, Department of German, Royal Holloway, University of London. Author of *Names and Nomenclature in Goethe's "Faust"* (1980). Co-editor of *Thomas Mann: "Tonio Kröger"* (with J.J. White, 1996). Contributor to *Lessing Yearbook* and other publications. **Essay:** Karl Philipp Moritz.

White, J.J. Professor of German and Comparative Literature, King's College, University of London. Author of several books including *Literary Futurism: Aspects of the First Avant-Garde* (1990) and *Brecht's "Leben des Galilei": A Critical Study* (1996). Editor of many works including *The Gruppe 47* (1998). Contributor to numerous books and journals. **Essays:** Avant-Garde; Hermann Broch; *Die Schlafwandler* (Broch).

Whobrey, William. Assistant Professor, Germanic Languages and Literatures and Medieval Studies, Yale University, New Haven, Connecticut. Contributor to *The Year's Work in Medievalism* (1998), *Manuscripta,* and *JEGP*. **Essays:** Middle High German; Manuscripts (Medieval).

Wickham, Christopher J. Associate Professor, Division of Foreign Languages, University of Texas, San Antonio. Author of *Longing and Belonging: Constructing Heimat in Postwar Germany* (1998). Co-editor of *Was in den alten Bücher Steht* (with Karl-Heinz Schoeps, 1991) and *Framing the Past* (with Bruce A. Murray, 1992). Contributor to numerous publications. **Essays:** Adelbert von Chamisso; Munich.

Wigmore, Juliet. Lecturer in German, Department of Modern Languages, University of Salford. Editor of *Peter Handke, Wunschloses Unglück* (1993). Contributor to many books and journals including *German Life and Letters* and *From High Priests to Desecrators: Contemporary Austrian Writing* (1993). **Essays:** *Malina* (Bachmann); *Simultan* (Bachmann); Verena Stefan.

Williams, Rhys W. Professor of German, University of Wales, Swansea. Author of *Carl Sternheim: A Critical Study* (1982). Co-editor of several anthologies including *Berlin seit dem Kriegsende* (with H. Peitsch, 1989) and *German Writers and the Cold War* (with C.D. Riordan and S. Parker, 1992). Contributor to numerous collections and journals. **Essays:** Carl Einstein; Wolfgang Koeppen; Carl Sternheim.

Winkler, Michael. Professor of German Studies, Rice University, Houston, Texas. Author of *Stefan George* (1970) and *George-Kreis* (1972). Editor of several works including *Der große Kreuzzug/Tagebuch 1937: Aus dem Spanischen Bürgerkrieg* by Gustav Regler (1996). Contributor to many books and journals. **Essays:** Gerhard Roth; Vienna.

Winthrop-Young, Geoffrey. Assistant Professor, Department of Germanic Studies, University of British Columbia. Contributor to many books and journals including *Literature and Science* (1994), *Reading Matters: Narrative in the New Media Ecology* (1997), and *Mosaic*. **Essay:** Georg Christoph Lichtenberg.

Wolf, Gregory H. Visiting Assistant Professor, Department of Linguistics and Languages, Michigan State University, East Lansing. Contributor to *Michigan Germanic Studies, Seminar, Medieval Germany: An Encyclopedia,* and *Austrian Writers of the 19th Century*. **Essays:** Clemens Brentano; Drama (Strauß).

Zohn, Harry. Professor Emeritus of German, Brandeis University, Waltham, Massachusetts. Author of several books including *Austriaca and Judaica* (1995) and *Karl Kraus and the Critics* (1997). Editor of many books including *Die Stimme des Wortes* (1998). Contributor to numerous books and journals. **Essays:** *Deutschland, Deutschland über alles* (Tucholsky).